Artificial Life VIII

Complex Adaptive Systems
John H. Holland, Christopher G. Langton, and Stewart W. Wilson, advisors

Adaptation in Natural and Artificial Systems: An Introductory Analysis with Applications to Biology, Control, and Artificial Intelligence, John H. Holland

Genetic Programming: On the Programming of Computers by Means of Natural Selection , John R. Koza

Intelligent Behavior in Animals and Robots, David McFarland and Thomas Bösser

Genetic Programming II: Automatic Discovery of Reusable Programs, John R. Koza

Turtles, Termites, and Traffic Jams: Explorations in Massively Parallel Microworlds, Mitchel Resnick

Comparative Approaches to Cognitive Science, edited by Herbert L. Roitblat and Jean-Arcady Meyer

Artificial Life: An Overview, edited by Christopher G. Langton

An Introduction to Genetic Algorithms, Melanie Mitchell

Catching Ourselves in the Act: Situated Activity, Interactive Emergence, and Human Thought, Horst Hendriks-Jansen

Elements of Artificial Neural Networks, Kishan Mehrotra, Chilukuri K. Mohan, and Sanjay Ranka

Growing Artificial Societies: Social Science from the Bottom Up, Joshua M. Epstein and Robert Axtell

An Introduction to Natural Computation, Dana H. Ballard

An Introduction to Fuzzy Sets: Analysis and Design, Witold Pedrycz and Fernando Gomide

From Animals to Animats 5: Proceedings of the Fifth International Conference on Simulation of Adaptive Behavior, edited by Rolf Pfeifer, Bruce Blumberg, Jean-Arcady Meyer, and Stewart W. Wilson

Artificial Life VI: Proceedings of the Sixth International Conference, edited by Christoph Adami, Richard K. Belew, Hiroaki Kitano, and Charles E. Taylor

The Simple Genetic Algorithm: Foundations and Theory, Michael D. Vose

Advances in Genetic Programming: Volume 3, edited by Lee Spector, William B. Langdon, Una-May O'Reilly, and Peter J. Angeline

Toward a Science of Consciousness III: The Third Tucson Discussions and Debates, edited by Stuart R. Hameroff, Alfred W. Kasniak, and David J. Chalmers

Truth from Trash: How Learning Makes Sense, Chris Thornton

From Animals to Animats 6: Proceedings of the Sixth International Conference on Simulation of Adaptive Behavior, edited by Jean-Arcady Meyer, Alain Berthoz, Dario Floreano, Herbert Roitblat, and Stewart W. Wilson

Artificial Life VII: Proceedings of the Seventh International Conference, edited by Mark A. Bedau, Norman Packard, and Steen Rasmussen

Learning and Soft Computing: With Support Vector Machines, Neural Networks, and Fuzzy Logic Models, Vojislav Kecman

From Animals to Animats 7: Proceedings of the Seventh International Conference on Simulation of Adaptive Behavior, edited by Bridget Hallam, Dario Floreano, Gillian Hayes, Jean-Arcady Meyer, and John Hallam

Artificial Life VIII: Proceedings of the Eighth International Conference on Artificial Life, edited by Russell K. Standish, Mark A. Bedau, and Hussein A. Abbass

Artificial Life VIII:
Proceedings of the Eighth International Conference on Artificial Life

Edited by Russell K. Standish, Mark A. Bedau, and Hussein A. Abbass

A Bradford Book

The MIT Press
Cambridge, Massachusetts
London, England

Library of Congress Control Number: 2002112965
ISBN: 978-0-262-69281-6

Complex Adaptive Systems Series

Contents

Development and Differentiation

Evolutionary and Adaptive Dynamics

Robots and Autonomous Agents

Communication, Cooperation and Collective Behaviour

The Broader Context

Preface

This conference continues a series of successful conferences started with the first "Artificial Life" workshop organised by Chris Langton in 1987. It is the second time this conference series has been held outside of the United States (the first being ALife V, held at Nara in 1996), indicating the international nature of the field. This conference presents a great opportunity for those Australian researchers and postgraduate students who might otherwise be unable to justify the travel costs to the Northern Hemisphere. I hope it also proves just as good an opportunity for our overseas delegates to sample a little of Australia's hospitality and lifestyle.

At ALife VII, Mark Bedau organised a workshop involving all the conference delegates to take stock of the achievements in the field, and also to reflect on what might be the most important open questions to be tackled. This led to the paper in Artificial Life **6**, p.636–376. We asked contributers to ALife VIII to relate their results to these identified open problems, where possible. Not only did this make the afore-mentioned paper the most cited publication in this proceedings, it gives the opportunity to measure advances in the field. Whilst I have yet to have the opportunity of reading all the papers in detail, I have read perhaps a quarter, and I think it is fair to say that none of the open problems has yet been convincingly resolved, but that substantial progress is being made in a lot of areas.

Out of the 89 papers submitted to the conference, 32 were accepted as oral presentations, and a further 35 as shorter poster presentations. Each paper was independently reviewed by at least 3 reviewers, and acceptance or rejection based entirely on the reviewers decisions. Poster presentations are important to our field — they are often interesting new ideas that haven't had the opportunity of being fully developed. As delegates, you should take the time to look at the posters and critically discuss the work with the presenters, as this is an important source of future ideas for the field.

Of the 67 accepted papers, 9 are from the host country Australia. In ALife VII, Australians accounted for just 3 out of the 67 papers. Clearly, ALife VIII has proved a boon for Artificial Life in Australia.

The format for this proceedings has not changed much from the previous one. The same 7 topic areas were chosen for dividing the proceedings, except that there are no papers of applied technological character (except for the robotics field, which gets its own topic area of course).

The *Australian Partnership for Adavanced Computing* (APAC) generoursly sponsored this conference. I have a great number of people to thank: my co-editors, Mark Bedau, who energetically rallied the Artificial Life community to act as reviewers for the conference, and also encouraged a number of submissions to the conference itself; Hussein Abbass, who has acted as my 2nd in charge on a number of occasions when I was away, and is also responsible for organising the Workshop and Tutorial programme; my conference organisers: Christine Dorner, Nadine Giatras, Leanne Constantino and Nicole Rayner of ICE Australia; the Programme Committee, listed below; Titus Brown for the development of the online submissions and reviewing system, Collar[1]; and finally my family, Kim Crichton and Hal Crichton-Standish for their forebearance during the gruelling couple of months that this proceedings took to put together.

Russell K. Standish
Conference Chair, Artificial Life VIII
Sydney, August 2002

Programme Committee

Hussein Abbass	David Green	John McCaskill	Moshe Sipper
Wolfgang Banzhaf	Takashi Ikegami	Barry McMullin	Andre Skusa
Mark Bedau	Inman Harvey	J.J. Merelo	Russell Standish
Eric Bonabeau	Paulien Hogeweg	Jean-Arcady Meyer	Chuck Taylor
Seth Bullock	Phil Husbands	Melanie Mitchell	Tim Taylor
Raffaele Calabretta	Norman Johnson	Alvaro Moreno	Guy Theraulaz
Angelo Cangelosi	Kristian Lindgren	Chrystopher Nehaniv	Adrian Thompson
Alistair Channon	Kunihiko Kaneko	Jason Noble	Peter Todd
Sung-Bae Cho	Brian Keeley	Charles Ofria	Mike Wheeler
John Collier	Graham Kendall	Norman Packard	Ian Wilkinson
Ezequiel Di Paolo	Simon Kirby	Steen Rasmussen	Andy Wuensche
Dario Floreano	Hod Lipson	Tom Ray	

[1]Collar is an open-source project, available soon for use by other conferences

Classification of Random Boolean Networks

Carlos Gershenson †,‡
†School of Cognitive and Computer Sciences
University of Sussex
Brighton, BN1 9QN, U. K.
C.Gershenson@sussex.ac.uk
http://www.cogs.sussex.ac.uk/users/carlos
‡Center Leo Apostel, Vrije Universiteit Brussel
Krijgskundestraat 33, B-1160 Brussels, Belgium

Abstract

We provide the first classification of different types of Random Boolean Networks (RBNs). We study the differences of RBNs depending on the degree of synchronicity and determinism of their updating scheme. For doing so, we first define three new types of RBNs. We note some similarities and differences between different types of RBNs with the aid of a public software laboratory we developed. Particularly, we find that the point attractors are independent of the updating scheme, and that RBNs are more different depending on their determinism or non-determinism rather than depending on their synchronicity or asynchronicity. We also show a way of mapping non-synchronous deterministic RBNs into synchronous RBNs. Our results are important for justifying the use of specific types of RBNs for modelling natural phenomena.

Introduction

Random Boolean Networks (RBNs) have been used in diverse areas to model complex systems. There has been a debate on how suitable models they are depending on their properties, mainly on their updating scheme (Harvey & Bossomaier 1997; Di Paolo 2001). Here we make a classification of different types of RBNs, depending on their updating scheme (synchronous, asynchronous, deterministic, non-deterministic), in order to study the properties, differences, and similarities of each one of them. The aim of this study is to increase the criteria for judging which types of RBNs are suitable for modelling particular complex systems.

In the next section we present our classification of RBNs, first mentioning the previously defined types of RBNs, and then defining three new types of RBNs. In Section 3 we present the results of a series of experiments carried out in a software laboratory, developed by us specially for this purpose, and available to the public. Particularly, we present our studies on point attractors, statistics of attractor density in different types of network, and the homogeneity of RBNs (which validates our statistical analyses). In Section 4 we propose a (non-optimal but general) method for mapping deterministic RBNs into synchronous RBNs. In Section 5 we identify further directions for studying and understanding different types of RBNs. We conclude estimating the value of our work, and we use our results to clarify a controversy on the proper use of RBNs as models of genetic regulatory networks (Kauffman 1993; Harvey & Bossomaier 1997).

Random Boolean Networks

There has been no previous classification of different types of RBNs, perhaps because of the novelty of the concept, but there has been enough research to allow us to make a classification of RBNs according to their updating schemes.

Classical Random Boolean Networks (CRBNs) were proposed by Stuart Kauffman (1969) to model genetic regulation in cells. They can be seen as a generalization of (binary) cellular automata (CA). These were first developed in the late 1940's by John von Neumann (1966), for studying self-replicating mechanisms.

A RBN has n nodes, which have connections (k) between them ($n, k \in \mathbb{N}, k \leq n$). The state (zero or one) of a node at time $t+1$ depends on the states at time t of the nodes which are connected to the node. Here we will limit our study only to homogeneous RBNs, where k is the same for all nodes. Logic rules ($n2^k$ values in lookup tables) are generated randomly, and they determine how the nodes will affect each other.

In CRBNs, the updating of the nodes is synchronous, in the sense that all the nodes in the network are updated at $t+1$ depending their states at t. Boolean random maps are equivalent to CRBNs with $n = k$. The dynamics arising from CRBNs are very interesting, since depending on the values of n and k, they can be ordered, complex, or chaotic (Kauffman 1993; Wuensche 1998). Therefore, they have been also used to study these types of dynamics in deterministic systems. Diverse properties of CA and CRBNs have been studied, among others, by Wuensche (1997; 1998) and by Aldana, Coppersmith and Kadanoff (2002). They have been used to model phenomena in physics, biology, cognition, economy, sociology, computation, artificial life, and complex systems in general (Wuensche 1998).

CRBNs have attractors, which consist of a state ("point attractor") or a group of states ("cycle attractor") which "capture" the dynamics of the network. Since CRBNs are deterministic, once the state of a network reaches an attractor, it will never have states different from the ones in the attractor. And since the number of states of a CRBN is also finite, in theory, an attractor will always be reached.

Harvey and Bossomaier (1997) studied Asynchronous Random Boolean Networks (ARBNs) They have the characteristics of CRBNs, but their updating is asynchronous. Well, in ARBNs, the updating is not only asynchronous, but also random. Each time step a single node is selected at random in order to be updated. Because of this, in ARBNs there are no cycle attractors (although there are point attractors). The system cannot escape from a point attractor, because no matter which node is selected, the state of the network will not change. ARBNs also have "loose attractors" (Harvey & Bossomaier 1997), which are parts of the state space which also capture the dynamics, but since the updating order of the nodes is random, the order of the states will not be repeated deterministically. Although, Di Paolo (2001) evolved successfully ARBNs for finding rhythmic and non- rhythmic attractors, but ARBNs with these attractors seem to be a very small subset of all possible ARBNs.

In order to have a more complete taxonomy of RBNs, we define three types of RBNs, setting all of them and the previously exposed under Discrete Dynamic Networks (DDNs), a term introduced by Wuensche[1] (1997), since we can say that DDNs have all the properties common in all types of RBNs: they have discrete time, space, and values. DDNs outside of our scope would be multivalued networks, but they would be DDNs also. Real-valued networks would not be DDNs, since their values are not discrete, but continuous. Dynamical Systems Theory studies such systems.

We define Deterministic Asynchronous Random Boolean Networks (DARBNs) as ARBNs which do not select at random which node to update. Each node has associated two parameters: p and q ($p, q \in \mathbb{N}, q < p$), which determine the period of the update (how many time steps the node will wait in order to be updated), and the translation of the update, respectively. A node will be updated when the modulus of time t over p is equal to q. If two or more nodes will be updated at a specific time, the first node is updated, and then the second is updated taking into account the new state of the network. This order is arbitrary, but since there is no restriction in the connection of the nodes by their locality (as with CA), we can have any kind of possible DARBNs with this updating scheme. The advantage is that with DARBNs we can model asynchronous phenomena which are not random, a thing which is quite difficult with ARBNs. Therefore, DARBNs have cycle (and point) attractors.

ARBNs have another limitation: they only update one node at a time. We define Generalized Asynchronous Random Boolean Networks (GARBNs) as ARBNs which can update any number of nodes, picked at random, at each time step. This means that GARBNs can go from not updating any node at a time step, passing to updating only one (as ARBNs), updating some nodes synchronously, to updating all the nodes synchronously (as CRBNs). As ARBNs, they are non-deterministic, so again there are no cycle attractors, only point and loose attractors.

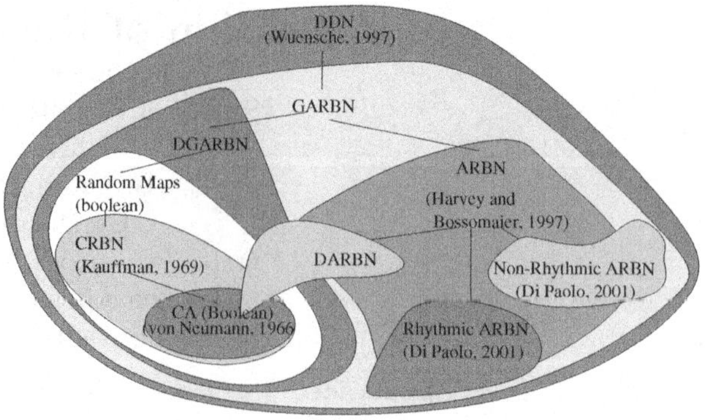

Figure 1: Classification of Random Boolean Networks

As we did with DARBNs, we introduce the parameters p and q associated to each node to define Deterministic Generalized Asynchronous Random Boolean Networks (DGARBNs). They do not have the arbitrary restriction of DARBNs, so if two or more nodes are determined by their p's to be updated at the same time step, they will be updated synchronously, *i.e.* they will all be updated at time $t+1$ taking into account the state of the network at time t. Note that DGARBNs and DARBNs overlap in the specific cases when p and q are such that one and only one node is updated each time step (for example, a network of two nodes ($n = 2$), one being updated at even time steps ($p = 2, q = 0$), and another being updated at uneven time steps ($p = 2, q = 1$)).

Also other specific configurations produce the same behaviour for all the types of network independently of their updating schemes (e.g. when $k = 0$, or when all states are point attractors).

Figure 1 shows a graphic representation of the classification just described above.

As we stated, we classify all RBNs under DDNs. The most general are GARBNs, since all the others are particular cases of them. If on one hand, we make them deterministic with parameters p and q, we will have DGARBNs. Random maps are emerging when $n = k$, and for all nodes $p = 1$ and $q = 0$. These ones can simulate with redundancy any CRBN, but not otherwise. Therefore, CRBNs can be seen as a subset of random maps. Boolean CA are specific cases of CRBNs, where the connectivity is limited by the spatial organization of the nodes. On the other hand, if we limit GARBNs for updating only one node at a time, we will have ARBNs. If we make them deterministic, we will have DARBNs. There are also special cases of ARBNs

[1]Although he studied only synchronic DDNs in (1997), the terminology is appropriate.

RBN	updating scheme
CRBNs	synchronous, deterministic
ARBNs	asynchronous, non-deterministic
DARBNs	asynchronous, deterministic
GARBNs	semi-synchronous, non-deterministic
DGARBNs	semi-synchronous, deterministic

Table 1: Updating schemes of RBNs

net(t)	net($t+1$)
11	11
10	01
01	00
00	10

Table 2: Transition table for a RBN $n = 2, k = 2$.

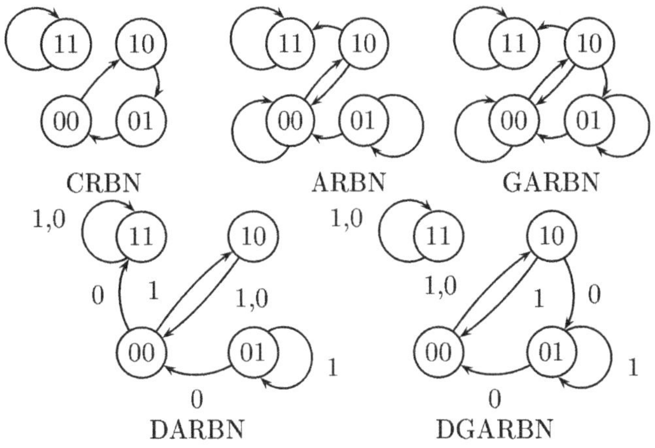

Figure 2: Graphs of RBNs with different updating schemes. The arrows with numbers indicate which transition will take place depending on the modulus of time over two.

with rhythmic and non-rhythmic attractors. Very probably GARBNs with rhythmic and non-rhythmic attractors can be found. Most types of RBNs can behave in the same way in limit cases (e.g. when k equals zero, or when the number of attractors equals n).

Here we will study the properties of CRBNs, ARBNs, DARBNs, GARBNs, and DGARBNs. Table 1 shows the characteristics of the updating schemes for each one of these RBNs. Note that there are no synchronous, non-deterministic RBNs. We say that GARBNs and DGARBNs have semi-synchronous updating because in some cases they can behave synchronously (all nodes updated at once), and in some cases as asynchronously (only one node is updated at once), but mainly in all the possibilities in between, *i.e.* when *some* nodes are updated synchronously.

As a simple example, in Table 2 we show the transition table of a RBN of $n = 2, k = 2$, p's=$\{1, 2\}$, and q's=$\{0, 0\}$. Figure 2 shows the different trajectories that the RBN will have, depending on its updating scheme.

We can see that all types of updating schemes produce different behaviours of the RBN. Some of them are more similar than others, though. In the next section we explore the properties of different types of RBNs.

Experiments and Analysis

We developed a software laboratory for studying the properties of different types of RBNs. It is available online to the public (Java source code included) at http://www.cogs.sussex.ac.uk/users/carlos/rbn. It can be used through a web browser, providing a friendly interface for generating, editing, displaying, saving, and loading RBNs, and analysing their properties. The results presented in this section are product of experiments carried out in our laboratory.

Point Attractors

Our first finding is that the point attractors are the same for any type of RBN. In other words, if we find a point attractor in an ARBN, if we change the updating scheme to CRBN (or any other), the point attractor will be the same. This is because a point attractor is given when for all the nodes, their rules determine that when they will be updated, they will have the same value. Therefore, it is not important in which order or how many nodes are updated, since none will produce a change in the state of the network.

We should note that the basins of the point attractors in most cases are very different for different types of RBNs. The cycle and loose attractors and their basins also change (tough not always) depending on the updating scheme. But for a determined network connectivity and rules, the point attractors will be the same.

Attractor density

For this section, we obtained with our laboratory statistics from 1000 networks of each of the presented values of n and k. First we generated randomly a RBN with the specified n, k, p, and q, and then we tested the RBN with the different updating schemes. For each type of network we tested all possible initial states, running them for 10000 time steps, expecting to reach an attractor. Then we searched for attractors of period smaller than 50 for CRBNs and 200 for the other deterministic cases (checking that the state and periods would be the same as the ones as $t = 10000$), and point attractors for the random cases (if state(10000)=state(10001)=... =state(10050)). For all our experiments the p's for all the nodes were generated randomly, taking values between 1 and 4, and all q's=0.

Figure 3 shows the average number of deterministic attractors for networks of n's between 1 and 5, with all their possible k's (from 0 to n). Figure 4 shows the same information for networks of $k = 3$ and n between 3 and 8. Remember that RBNs which are updated with random schemes (ARBNs and GARBNs) can only have deterministic attractors of period one (point attractors), and if one network has a point attractor, the other types of network will have the same point attractor. We can see from Figure 3 that the average of point attractors in ARBNs is roughly lower for $k = 3$, consistent with results of Harvey and Bossomaier (1997)[2]. From both figures we can see that DARBNs, and DGARBNs even more, are very close to the number of attractors found in CRBNs. We can see here that there is a very big difference due to the randomness of the updating, and not so much due to the degree of synchronicity.

We can also see that, for deterministic RBNs, the growth of the average number of attractors as we increase n, with constant k, seems to be linear, consistent with the results of Bilke and Sjunnesson (2002) for CRBNs.

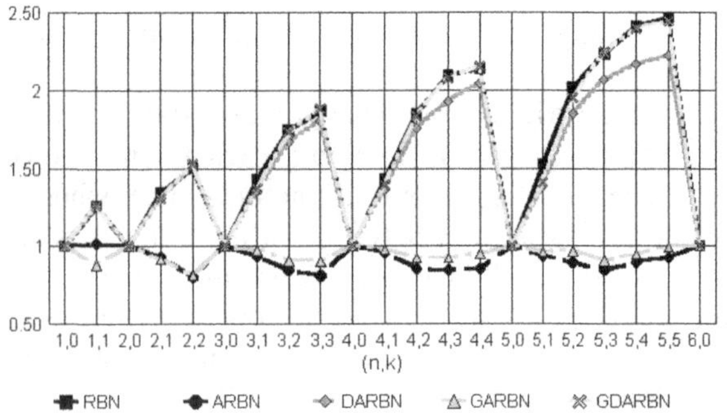

Figure 3: Average number of deterministic attractors.

Note that when there is no connectivity ($k = 0$), there is no interesting updating, since the networks, independently of their initial state or updating scheme, will reach a final state. It is because of this that all RBNs have one and only one point attractor for any value of n when $k = 0$. We can appreciate the percentage of states which belong to an attractor for the same networks in Figure 5 and Figure 6. Here we can see that RBNs have more states in attractors than DGARBNs and DARBNs. This suggests that the average period of the cycle attractors

[2]Even when the *expected* number of points attractors is one. This is, mathematically we can find that if we consider all possible ARBNs, their number is equal to the possible point attractors (Harvey & Bossomaier 1997). Of course some networks will have no point attractors, or more than one, but if our search would be exhaustive, the average would be one. Since out search is not exhaustive, what we can see is that for $k = 3$, the point attractors "hide themselves" more than for other values of k (there are few networks with several point attractors and many networks with none).

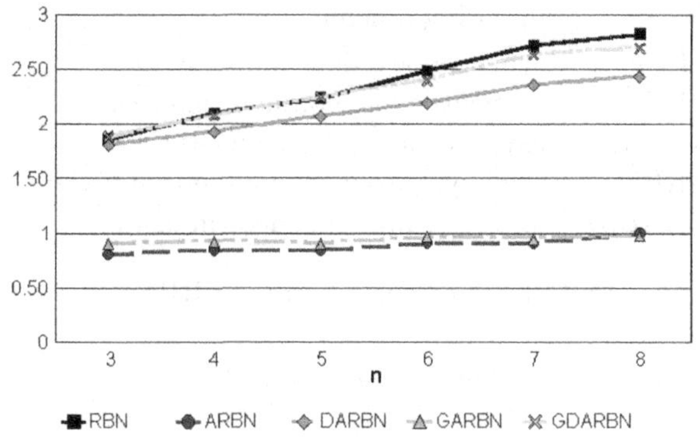

Figure 4: Average number of deterministic attractors, $k = 3$.

is higher for RBNs.

We can also see in Figure 5 that for deterministic RBNs, the number of states in an attractor increases with k. But the percentage of the states in attractors seems to decrease exponentially as n increases for all types of RBN.

We would also like to know exactly how many states there are in each attractor, not only their percentage. But we should note that, even when CRBNs, ARBNs, and GARBNs have 2^n possible states, this is increased in DARBNs and DGARBNs, because of the introduction of the updating periods. This is, a network with the same state, may be updated in a different way depending on the time it reaches that state. Therefore, in DARBNs and DGARBNs we need to take into account the least common multiple of all p's, and we will have $LCM(p_i)* 2^n$ possible states. As we can see, the periods of the attractors in DARBNs and DGARBNs grow in comparison to CRBNs, but since there are also more states, the ratio between states in attractors and total states is equivalent. But for calculating the number of states, we normalized the number of states dividing them by their total number of states divided by 2^n. Note that this produces a change only in DARBNs and DGARBNs (since all other RBNs have 2^n states), setting them in values comparable to the ones in the other RBNs. These results can be seen in Figure 7 and Figure 8.

The values of ARBNs and GARBNs are the same as the ones in Figure 3 and Figure 4, since the states in attractors are point attractors. Again we can see that the period of the cycle attractors are higher for RBNs than for DGARBNs, and these are a bit higher than the ones of DARBNs. In deterministic RBNs we can see that the number of states increases with k. They also seem to increase with n, but CRBNs increase this number much faster than the normalized DGARBNs and DARBNs. This increment for the deterministic networks (as we increase n) appears to be linear. The steepness of this increment seems to be increased with k. But as we have seen, the percentage of states in deterministic attractors decreases with n, since the number of states of the network is doubled for each node we add to the network.

Finally, we obtained the percentage of the initial states which did not reach an attractor (after more than 10000 time steps). The results can be appreciated in Figure 9 and Figure 10. All CRBNs reached an attractor, and very few DARBNs and DGARBNs had attractors of period larger than 200 (less than 0.1%, only in large networks), so the interesting results are only for ARBNs and GARBNs. This percentage reflects the size of the basins of attraction of their point attractors (that is, the states which do reach an attractor), and of course the size of the basins of attraction of the loose attractors. It seems, but is not clear, that the percentage of states which do not reach point attractors increases as n does. On the other hand, it is obvious that there is a lower probability to reach a point attractor when point attractors are harder to find ($k = 3$).

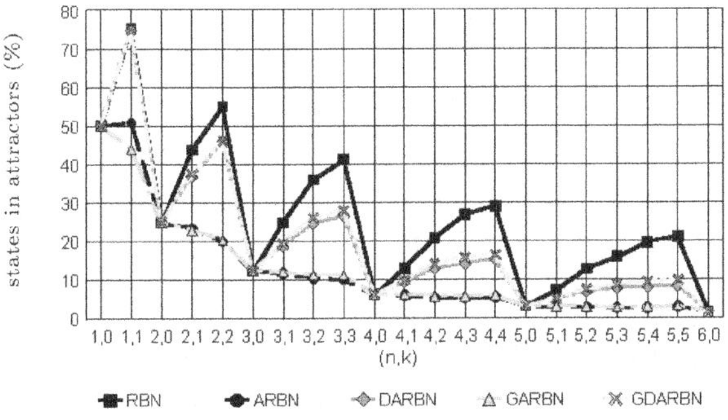

Figure 5: Percentage of states in attractors.

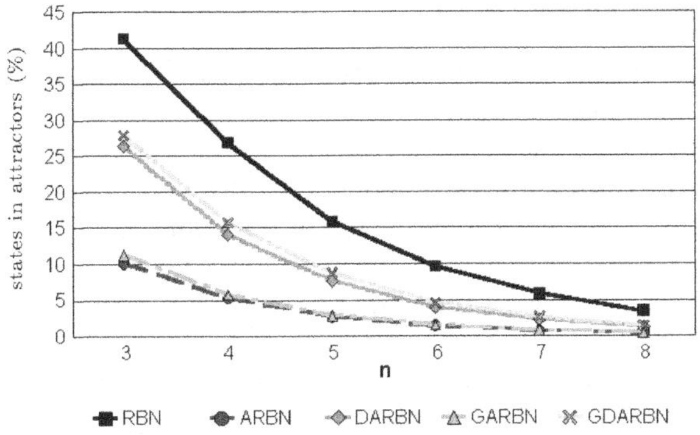

Figure 6: Percentage of states in attractors.

From the information gathered in all these charts, we can see that there is a regular order (with very few exceptions) on the number of attractors, and states in attractors for the different types of RBNs. CRBNs are on top, having the highest number of attractors and states in attractors. On the bottom, there are ARBNs, which have the lowest values. In the middle of the rest, there are DARBNs, and the generalized versions are in the spaces left in between, but very close and above DGARBNs of

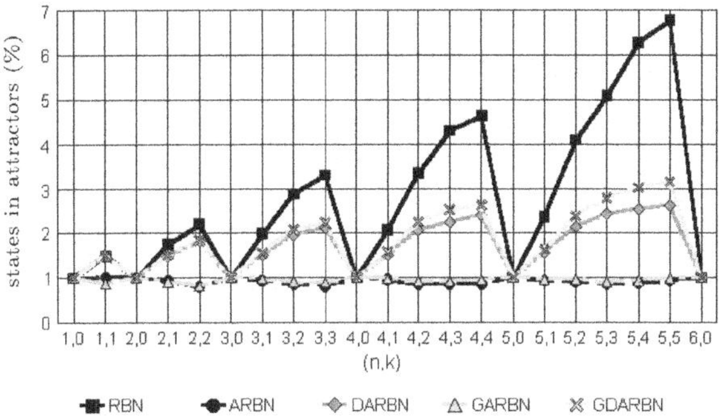

Figure 7: States in attractors (relative).

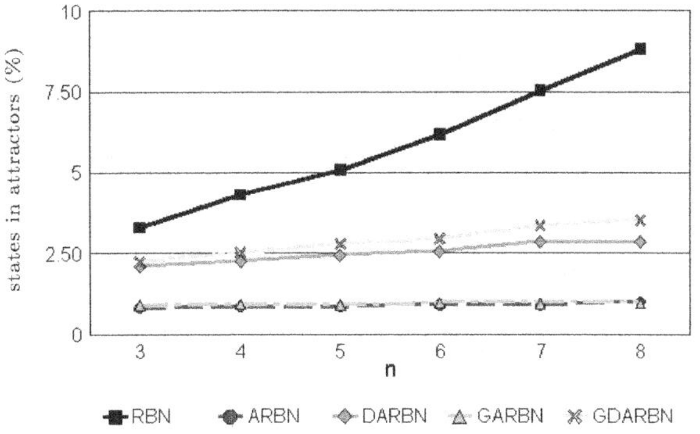

Figure 8: States in attractors (relative).

DARBNs and GARBNs of ARBNs.

The reason of this can be explained with the different updating schemes. RBNs with non-deterministic updating will have less deterministic attractors because they can only have point attractors. Anyway, GARBNs have a slightly higher probability than ARBNs to reach one faster since their updating is semi-synchronous, and this should enlarge their basins of attraction. Since RBNs with deterministic updating have cycle attractors, this explains why they have more attractors and states in attractors than non-deterministic ones. But we can see that these numbers increase from asynchronous to semi-synchronous to synchronous. The lack of synchronicity increases the complexity of the RBN, because we need parameters p and q to make the updating, enhancing the number of possible states and interactions. And this

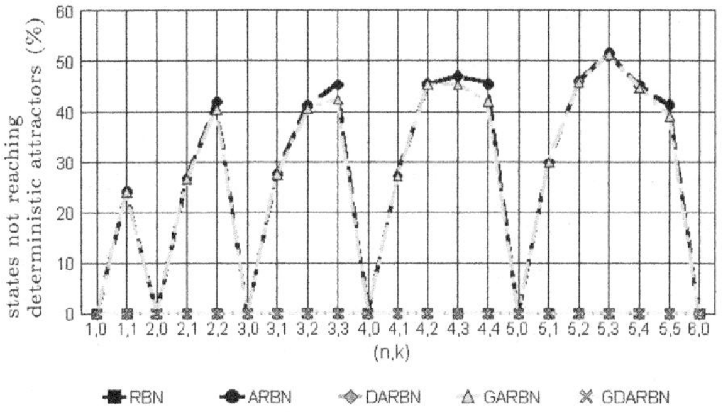

Figure 9: Percentage of initial states not reaching a deterministic attractor.

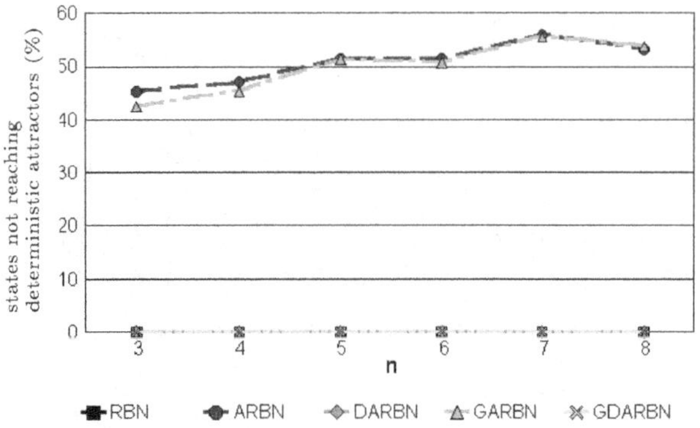

Figure 10: Percentage of initial states not reaching a deterministic attractor.

complexity changes the attractor basins, transforming and enlarging them. This reduces the number of attractors and states in attractors.

Possible Networks and Statistics

We saw that for a specific network with homogeneous connectivity, there are $n2^k$ (binary) values in the rules of the network. Therefore, there are 2^{n2^k} possible networks.

For any fixed n and k, if we change the connectivity, we will have networks redundant with these 2^{n2^k} (in the number of attractors, attractor basins, etc.). Thus, if we are not interested in the particular connectivity, but on the general properties of RBNs, we will find "only" 2^{n2^k} equivalent networks. To get a broad picture of how fast the number of possible networks grow, Table 3 shows the number of possible networks for small n's and k's.

As we can see, the number of possible networks grows tremendously fast. So, if we managed a statistical space of only 1000 sample networks, how representative will it be for $n = 8, k = 3$, if our sample is roughly 1.84×10^{-16} of the possible networks?

For testing how diverse our different samples were, we compared several samples of the same values of n and k, in order to see how much do they diverge. Particularly, we made five samples of 1000 networks with $n = 4, k = 4$, where the number of possible networks is 1.84×10^{19}. For the average number of attractors, we calculated the percentage of the differences between the maximum and minimum values, and the maximum and the average values, obtained in the samples. The results can be appreciated in Figure 11. Note that the difference between the average and the minimum is the difference between the two calculated differences. Therefore, the sample space is a bit skewed. Anyway, we could see (at least for this case) that the farthest we can get from an average value is less than 5%, even when our samples are taking 1.84×10^{-16} of the possible networks. This means that the global properties of RBNs are very uniform. This is, it is not that there are no networks with n attractors, but there is only one. There are also very few networks with all their states in an attractor, and there are many networks with the characteristics we extracted in our experiments. All the values that we extracted in different trials in our experiments also were very close to each other.

Also, since the plots we obtained for attractor density (Figures 3–8) fit very well with linear or exponential curves, it appears that our statistics match the actual attractor density without much error. This is not the case for Figures 9–10.

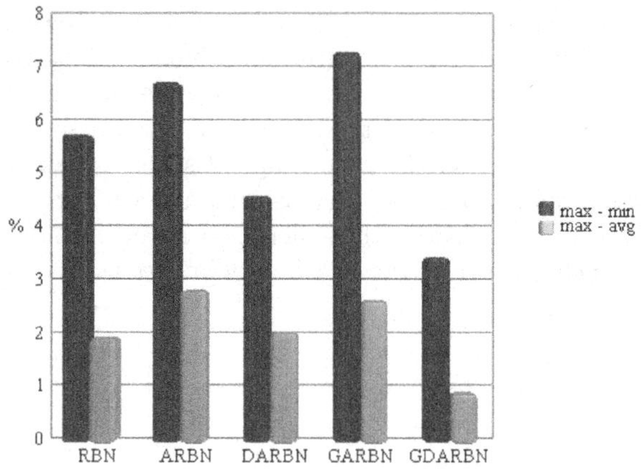

Figure 11: Percentages of differences between five samples of 1000 networks (number of attractors).

Mapping Deterministic RBNs to CRBNs

If a RBN is deterministic, we can map it to a CRBN. Of course, this is interesting only if the RBN is a DARBN or a DGARBN.

Perhaps this is not optimal, but a way of obtaining the same behaviour of a DARBN or DGARBN of specific n, k, p's, and q's is to create a CRBN of $n+m$ nodes and $k+m$ connectivity, where $2^m \geq \text{LCM}(p_i)$. We use the least common multiple of all p's in order to contemplate all the possible combinations of different nodes being updated, but in specific networks this might be redundant. The m nodes to be added should encode in binary base the time modulus $\text{LCM}(p_i)$. What was a function of time in the DARBN or DGARBN, now is a function in the network. Of course there is a redundancy at least when in the m nodes encoding time there is a binary value greater than $\text{LCM}(p_i)$.

In Table 4 we can appreciate the mapping to a CRBN of the DARBN with transitions shown in Table 2 and graph in Figure 2. Table 5 shows the mapping for the case of the respective DGARBN. The node m ($2^m \leq \text{LCM}(p_i), \text{LCM}(p_i) = 2, m = 1$) which is added is shown in grey. These CRBNs have the same behaviour than the deterministic non-synchronous networks from Figure 2, but the network itself is more complex ($n = 3, k = 3$).

It would be too rushed to say that therefore all deterministic non-synchronous RBNs can be seen as CRBNs,

net(t)	net($t+1$)
111	110
101	000
011	010
001	100
110	111
100	001
010	001
000	111

Table 4: Map of DARBN to CRBN

net(t)	net($t+1$)
111	110
101	000
011	010
001	100
110	111
100	011
010	001
000	101

Table 5: Map of DGARBN to CRBN

since we do not know how redundant the proposed mapping is, and therefore the complexity of the network might be increased too much. It should still be studied how similar are the properties of CRBNs and deterministic RBNs mapped to CRBNs.

We can see that the fact that CRBNs have a higher attractor density is related to the fact that DARBNs and DGARBNs are more complex than a CRBN of the same n and k (because of the p's and q's). As we have seen in our experiments, the attractor density of RBNs decreases exponentially as we increase n. If we want to map the behaviour of a deterministic non-synchronous RBN to a CRBN, we need to add m nodes ($2^m \geq \text{LCM}(p_i)$), and such CRBN would see its attractor density reduced, just as DARBNs and DGARBNs have a lower attractor density.

Unattended Issues

In order to understand better the differences of the different types of RBNs, we should also study how similar or different are the attractor basins of the RBNs as we change the updating schemes. From our experience, we have seen that sometimes they can be very similar, and sometimes very different, but we do not have yet any clear criteria for determining when each of these takes place. Also, for non- deterministic RBNs, different attractor basins might overlap (but not the attractors!). Tools such as DDLab (Wuensche 1997; 1998) have proven to be very useful for studying attractor basins and many other properties of CRBNs and CA. Similar tools should be developed for studying further properties of different types of RBNs, such as Garden-of-Eden densities. Also, to our knowledge, the basins of loose attractors are an area virgin for formal study. The study of order-complexity-chaos in the types of RBNs defined here also needs to be addressed. The study of non-homogeneous RBNs and hybrid RBNs should also increase our understanding of these models. Finally, since cellular automata could be seen as special cases of RBNs, the results presented here can be applied for understanding the differences caused by the updating schemes of cellular automata.

Because of the computational complexity of RBNs, it is difficult to study their mathematical properties straightaway. We believe this is a challenge for mathematicians, which could be addressed with the aid of our software laboratory. For example, it would be very useful to find formulae for determining the information we obtained statistically for any given n and k, especially for non-deterministic RBNs, where statistics seem to be more evasive. This would also validate or nullify the results presented here.

All these issues should be addressed if we desire to increase our understanding of RBNs.

Conclusions

In this work we presented the first proposed classification of different types of random boolean networks, depending on the synchronicity and determinism of their updating schemes. While doing so, we defined three new types of RBNs: DARBNs, GARBNs, and DGARBNs. Using a software laboratory we developed (source code available), we obtained some of the general properties of the different RBNs through statistical analysis, noticing when they have similarities and differences, but further study is required to fully understand all the properties of different RBNs.

CRBNs and ARBNs are different mostly because the first ones are deterministic and the second are not, but CRBNs are not that different to non-synchronous deterministic RBNs. DARBNs are much more similar to CRBNs than to ARBNs. We agree to the critics to synchronous CRBNs in the sense that when they are used to model any phenomena, their synchronicity needs to be justified somehow. But as we have seen, asynchronous DARBNs are similar to CRBNs, because both are deterministic, as opposed to ARBNs. Of course, while modelling, the choice for deterministic or non- deterministic RBNs should be also justified.

Particularly, Stuart Kauffman's work (1993) was criticized (Harvey & Bossomaier 1997) because it assumed that genetic regulatory networks were synchronic. We agree with the critic that the synchronicity was an assumption without a base, but we do not believe that genetic regulatory networks are random. They should be most probably modelled better with DARBNs, if we can model the updating periods for each gene. But one of the main results of Kauffman was that the number of attractors on CRBNs could explain why there are very few cell types in comparison with all the possible initial states of their genes. Since the number of attractors in DARBNs is very close to the ones in CRBNs (and the number in DGARBNs is much closer, since they are semi- synchronic), we can say that this particular result, still holds (perhaps with minor adjustments), since the number of attractors does not depend too much in the synchronicity of the updates, as they depend on their

$n\backslash k$	0	1	2	3	4	5	6
1	2	4					
2	4	16	256				
3	8	64	4096	1.68×10^{07}			
4	16	256	65536	4.29×10^{09}	1.84×10^{19}		
5	32	1024	1048576	1.10×10^{12}	1.21×10^{24}	1.46×10^{48}	
6	64	4096	16777216	2.81×10^{14}	7.92×10^{28}	6.28×10^{57}	3.94×10^{115}
7	128	16384	2.68×10^{08}	7.21×10^{16}	5.19×10^{33}	2.70×10^{67}	7.27×10^{134}
8	256	65536	4.29×10^{09}	1.84×10^{19}	3.40×10^{38}	1.16×10^{77}	1.34×10^{154}
9	512	262144	6.87×10^{10}	4.72×10^{21}	2.23×10^{43}	4.97×10^{86}	2.47×10^{173}
10	1024	1048576	1.10×10^{12}	1.21×10^{24}	1.46×10^{48}	2.14×10^{96}	4.56×10^{192}

Table 3: Possible equivalent networks for n nodes and k connections (2^{n2^k}).

determinism.

Acknowledgements

I appreciate the valuable comments and suggestions received from Inman Harvey, Ezequiel Di Paolo, Andrew Wuensche, and two anonymous referees. This work was supported in part by the Consejo Nacional de Ciencia y Tecnología (CONACYT) of México and by the School of Cognitive and Computer Sciences of the University of Sussex.

References

Aldana, M.; Coppersmith, S.; and Kadanoff, L. P. 2002. *Boolean Dynamics with Random Couplings.*

Bilke, S., and Sjunnesson, F. 2002. Stability of the Kauffman model. *Physical Review E* 65:016129.

Di Paolo, E. A. 2001. Rhythmic and non-rhythmic attractors in asynchronous random boolean networks. *Biosystems* 59(3):185–195.

Harvey, I., and Bossomaier, T. 1997. Time out of joint: Attractors in asynchronous random boolean networks. In Husbands, P., and Harvey, I., eds., *Proceedings of the Fourth European Conference on Artificial Life (ECAL97)*, 67–75. MIT Press.

Kauffman, S. A. 1969. Metabolic stability and epigenesis in randomly constructed genetic nets. *Journal of Theoretical Biology* 22:437–467.

Kauffman, S. A. 1993. *The Origins of Order.* xford University Press.

von Neumann, J. 1966. *The Theory of Self-Reproducing Automata.* University of Illinois Press.

Wuensche, A. 1997. *Attractor Basins of Discrete Networks.* Ph.D. Dissertation, University of Sussex. CSRP 461.

Wuensche, A. 1998. Discrete dynamical networks and their attractor basins. *Complexity International* 6.

Complexity Classes in Three-dimensional Gravitational Agents

Jean-Claude Heudin
International Institute of Multimedia
Pôle Universitaire Léonard de Vinci
92916 La Défense Cedex - France
Jean-Claude.Heudin@devinci.fr

Abstract

Three-dimensional Gravitational Agents are presented as discrete dynamical systems with simple construction but showing ordered, chaotic and complex behaviors. This paper explores these systems searching for complexity classes and emerging patterns. It shows the existence of a phase transition in the space of their transition functions and it argues that the most complex pattern dynamics is located in the vicinity of this phase transition.

Introduction

In this paper we introduce and explore a class of discrete dynamical systems named three-dimensional (3D) Gravitational Agents (GA) based on a multi-agent model. The aim of this study is to show that this class of dynamical system exhibit a large spectrum of behaviors including ordered and chaotic dynamics, and that the most complex emerging patterns can be found in the vicinity of a phase transition between the ordered and chaotic phases. Such a study has already been performed on other classes of dynamical systems such as one- and two-dimensional Cellular Automata (Wolfram 1984; Langton 1991; Heudin 1996; Magnier & Heudin 1997). This research is part of a project addressing the "evolution of complexity" in various classes of dynamical systems (Heudin 1998).

First, we introduce the 3DGA model more formally. Then, we turn to a qualitative overview of its dynamics given a parameterization of the 3DGA space. Evidence is presented that these dynamics fall into a small set of distinct classes. We show the existence of a phase transition in the space of 3DGA rules and we argue that we can locate the most complex pattern dynamics in the vicinity of this phase transition. Finally we discuss these results and their possible relationships with cosmological simulations and observations, and biological evolution.

Three-dimensional Gravitational Agents

The 3DGA model Gravitational

Agents are defined as a model for a class of complex systems containing large numbers of identical or heterogeneous agents in which each agent interacts with all other agents in a 3D space. The state S_i of an agent i is completely specified by a floating point variable and two floating point vectors:

Let m_i be the "mass" of the agent specified as a double floating point value,

Let x_i be the 3D coordinates of the agent in the 3D space as double floating point values,

Let vx_i be the 3D velocities of the agent in the 3D space as double floating point values.

The state of an agent i evolves by iteration of the mapping:

$$S_i^{(t)} = F[S_0^{(t-1)}, S_1^{(t-1)}, \ldots, S_{i-1}^{(t-1)}, S_{i+1}^{(t-1)}, \ldots, S_N^{(t-1)}] \quad (1)$$

where N specifies the number of agents in the 3D space. F is the function specifying the transition rule which is described by the equation:

$$\frac{d_i^x}{dt^2} = G \sum_{j,j \neq i} \frac{m_j(x_j - x_i)}{(r_{ij}^2)^{\frac{3}{2}}} \quad (2)$$

where G is the gravitational constant and r_{ij} the distance between the agent i and the agent j in the 3D space. Note that this equation reflects the computer implementation of the transition rule.

The resulting transition function F constitutes a physics for a simple and discrete space-time universe. We theoretically consider an infinite 3D space even if we are interested in a small region of this space. The rationale is that this is the most realistic way to simulate the evolution of an agent distribution, since an artificial periodicity would lead to undesirable results due to boundary conditions.

Integration scheme

As agents approach each other, the forces get much bigger and the integration errors can get unacceptably large. To avoid this, we used a 4th-order Runge-Kutta integration scheme for computing both x_i and vx_i when considering a small number of agents (Garcia 1994). In addition we used a variable *dt* that cut the time step down when agents are near each other and increase it when agents are far away. For experiments with a large number of agents, we used a simple time-centered leap-frog integration scheme (Garcia 1994). The main reason is the high computational cost of a more complete Taylor series when considering large sets. The consequence is that we have reduced the rate at which the error accumulates by choosing small step size. Thus, for each experiment, *dt* was chosen in order to keep the global energy near constant, that is conserved to $\approx 1\%$.

Parameterizing the space of 3DGA rules

3DGA are characterized by two sets of parameters which influence the behavior of the resulting dynamical system. The first set concerns by the transition rule itself, while the second concerns initial conditions.

There are two parameters for the transition rule: G is the gravitational constant and dt defines the time step used by the integration. These two parameters define the set D of possible transition functions.

For the second set, we consider the initial conditions characterized by a configuration of N agents which are distributed in a cubic area of the infinite 3D space. When considering a random distribution, the initial density is given by the size D_{scale} of this cube and the number N of agents. The V_{scale} parameter determines the range of the initial velocity vectors, which are then set randomly using a Gaussian random process. In the case of homogeneous masses, all values are set to the M_{scale} parameter. In the case of heterogeneous masses, each agent gets a randomized mass value using M_{scale} as a range.

Imposing a parameterization scheme on the space of GA rules is quite straightforward and allows us to define a natural ordering of the rules. In this paper, we address the subspace of Δ characterized by a progression of the G parameter.

Implementation issues

The main problem with 3DGA is that it is highly computationally intensive due to the nature of the transition function. A simple experiment with only 10^3 agents requires up to 10^6 calls to a procedure for one update phase. Let assumes that this procedure includes 10 floating point operations and that we want to simulate 10^3 steps of interactions, this results in 10^{10} floating point operations. To reduce the amount of computation, many methods have been considered (Bertschinger & Gelb 1991). All the experiments reported in this paper were conducted using the direct summation approach because of its accuracy and flexibility.

The probability of a configuration leading to collisions is small in our experiments. However, in order to avoid divergence of the system at $r_{ij} = 0$, we implemented a "catching exception" approach. This solution was chosen rather than the classical ε softening parameter that adds an epsilon value to the distance between agents (Bertschinger & Gelb 1991). Thus the implementation is more accurate and is well suited for processing agents collisions in future works.

Qualitative Overview of 3D GA dynamics

Experiments with a small number of agents

In this section, we describe experiments using 3 or 5 agents with increasing G values. The initial conditions are inspired from (Diacu & Holmes 1996). We use the

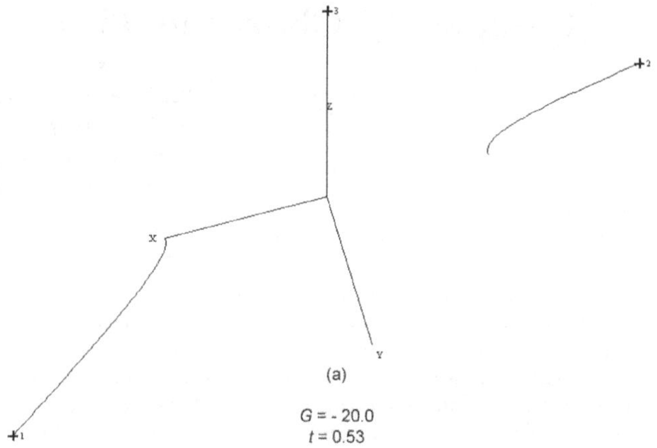

Figure 1: 3-agent example with $G < 0$

4th-order Runge-Kutta integration scheme with a maximum dt of 0.01. In most of these experiments, agents are initialized with the following states:

1. $m_1 = 1.0, x_1 = \{1, 0, 0\}, vx_1 = \{0, 1, 0\}$,
2. $m_2 = 1.0, x_2 = \{-1, 0, 0\}, vx_2 = \{0, -1, 0\}$,
3. $m_3 = 1.0, x_3 = \{0, 0, 1\}, vx_3 = \{0, 0, 0\}$.

With a negative gravitational constant (cf. figure 1), the distance between each agent increases regularly with time. The negative gravitation modifies the initial velocity conditions and results in an endless expanding dynamical behavior. Since this behavior is fully predictible with no change in time, it is interpreted as an ordered behavior.

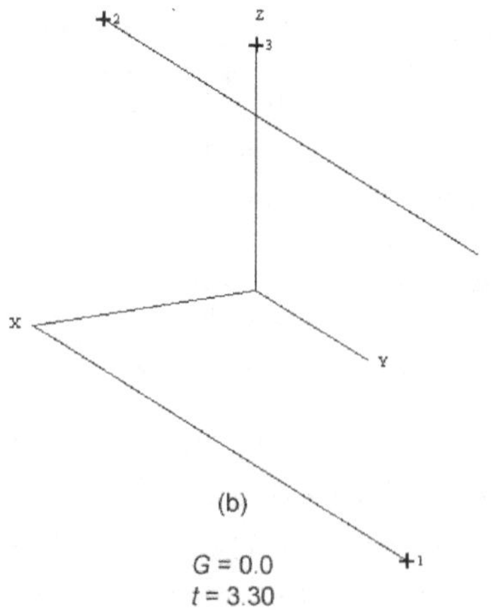

Figure 2: 3-agent example with $G = 0$

With no gravitation ($G = 0.0$), each agent follows its initial velocity conditions. Figure 2 shows that agents 1 and 2 are moving straightforward in opposite directions while agent 3 remains in its initial position. This dynamical behavior is interpreted as a steady state since the system keeps its initial velocity conditions without any change.

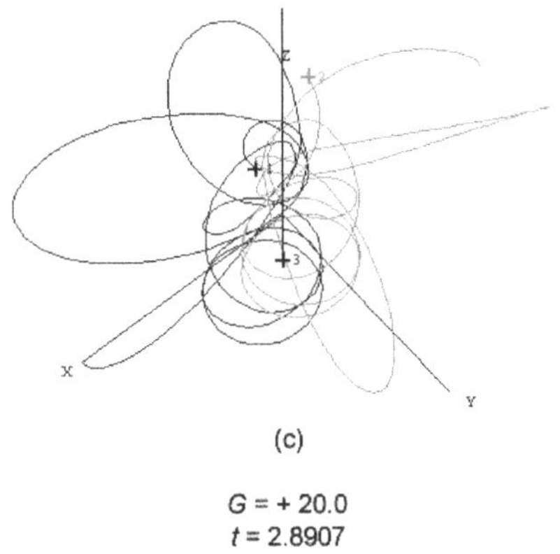

Figure 3: 3-agent example with $G > 0$

A positive gravitation induces a collapsing dynamical behavior which is combined with initial velocities of the three agents (cf. figure 3). Agent 1 and 2 show complex orbits. Agent 3 bounces up and down along the z axis in a chaotic way, as it picks up energy from the two other masses. This collapsing motion is interpreted as a chaotic dynamical behavior.

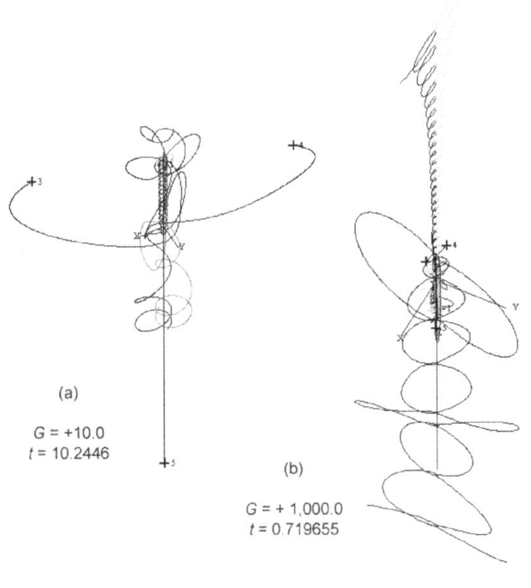

Figure 4: 5-agent experiment with $G = +10$ (a) and $G = +10^3$ (b)

Figure 4 shows collapsing behaviors with 5 agents instead of 3. This experiment creates a system of two pairs of orbiting agents, with the fifth agent located on the z axis. When run, the two agent pairs orbit each other

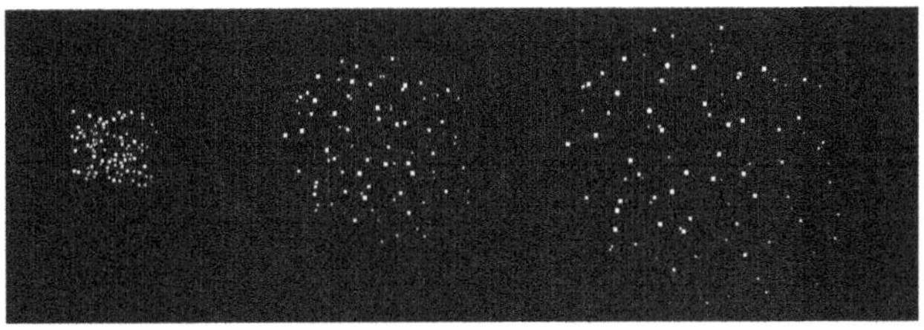

Figure 5: Expanding behavior with $G = -100$ for 100 heterogeneous agents ($t = 0, 10$ and 20)

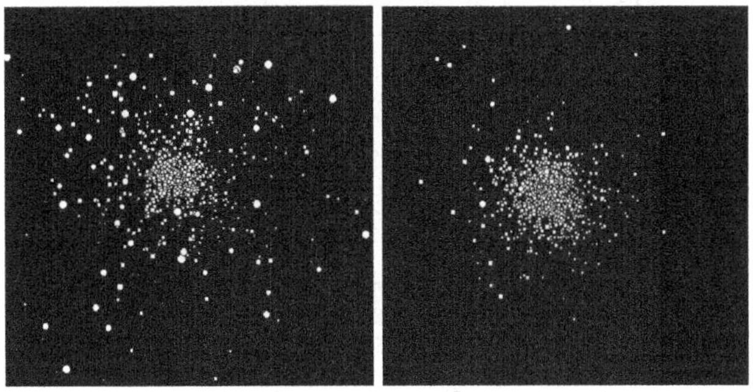

Figure 6: Collapsing behavior for 10^3 agents at $G = +10, t = 30,000$ (left) and $G = +0.1, t = 32,313$ (right)

with unstable ellipses, while agent 5 is bounced back and forth between them chaotically.

When considering increasing values of the gravitational constant, the collapsing behavior becomes more violent. Note that an excessive increase in G generally results in an unstable system where the error accumulates in the first steps of the run, thus making agents shoot out very fast.

Experiments with a large number of agents

The same kinds of experiments have been conducted with $N = 100$, 10^3, 10^4 and 10^5 agents with increasing G values. Even with this greater number of agents, the resulting rules are seen to generate the same qualitative behaviors. Patterns obtained with different randomized initial states differ in details, but exhibit the same global qualitative features.

Figure 5 shows an experiment involving 100 heterogeneous agents ($M_{\text{scale}} = 10^4$) with a negative gravitational constant. The agents cloud seems to explode with an overall speed which is proportional to the G value. This expanding behavior continues forming a quasi-sphere of agents with a decreasing density as the simulation goes on.

Figure 6 shows two typical patterns for small positive values of the gravitational constant. After a transient of several hundred time steps, a majority of agents forms a high density core with local chaotic dynamics, while some agents continue to move away from it. This agent cloud keeps its integrity and exhibits a chaotic regime around its gravity center which remains close to its initial position. Sometimes, in the case of a relatively low positive gravity, one can observe ephemeral collective behaviors like some agents orbiting around the center of gravity of the cloud in the same direction. These dynamical patterns disappear when a fluctuation of the agents' cloud is sufficient for breaking the movement.

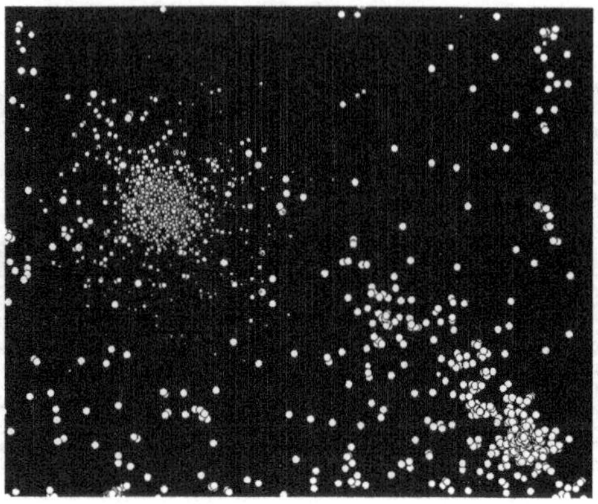

Figure 7: Collapsing behavior for 10^4 agents at $t = 200$

We report some experiments with $N = 10^4$ and 10^5. Again, we observe the same kinds of dynamical behaviors. Figures 7–8 shows two examples for $G = +10$. Figure 7 shows 10^4 agents grouped in one main core and a small set of aggregates, each of them composed of nearly 100 agents.

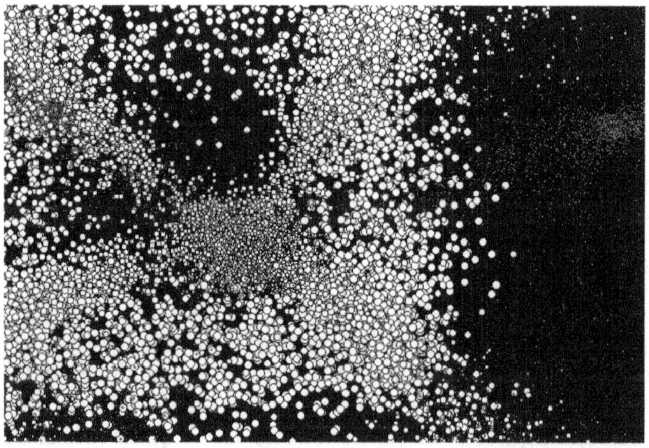

Figure 8: Collapsing behavior for 10^5 agents at $t = 81$

Figure 8 shows 10^5 agents distributed in four clusters and a main chaotic aggregate of agents in the center of the system. Note that in this case, we have relaxed the energy conservation constraint.

Ordering complexity classes and phase transition

In the framework of Cellular Automata (CA), Wolfram has shown that CA exhibit the full spectrum of dynamical behaviors (Wolfram 1983) and proposed a qualitative classification of their dynamics in four classes (Wolfram 1984):

Class I is associated to limit points in the phase space.

Class II is associated to limit cycles.

Class III is associated to chaotic behaviors.

Class IV is associated to complex behaviors ; also some Class IV CA are suspected to support universal computation.

In 1991, Langton has proposed the "edge of chaos" hypothesis which claims the existence of a phase transition between ordered and chaotic behaviors for one-dimensional CA and locates complex dynamics in the vicinity of this transition (Langton 1991). Therefore, CAs with computational capabilities are likely to be found in the vicinity of the phase transition between ordered (Class I & II) and chaotic behaviors (Class III). More recently, evidence of this location have also been given in (Gutowitz & Langton 1995; Magnier & Heudin 1997; Packard 1998).

The experiments related in the previous sections of this paper give empirical evidence for the existence of three basic qualitative classes of dynamical behaviors for 3DGA:

- for $G < 0.0$, evolution leads to the "explosion" of the agents cloud,
- for $G = 0.0$, evolution follows the initial velocity conditions of the agents,
- for $G > 0.0$, evolution leads to the formation of a chaotic aggregation of agents.

There is a strong evidence that the value $G = 0.0$ forms a phase transition between ordered (expanding) behaviors and chaotic (collapsing) behaviors. We argue that complex patterns are located in the chaotic side near this transition. This hypothesis is based on the fact that low values of the gravitational constant create long transients and enable the formation of more structured patterns while high values create violent behaviors which are not compatible with the emergence of these patterns.

While this classification cannot be strictly compared to the one proposed by Wolfram, we argue that 3DGA also exhibit the full spectrum of dynamical behaviors. As for CA, 3DGA configurations show limit points, limit cycles like orbiting agents and chaotic regimes. Also,

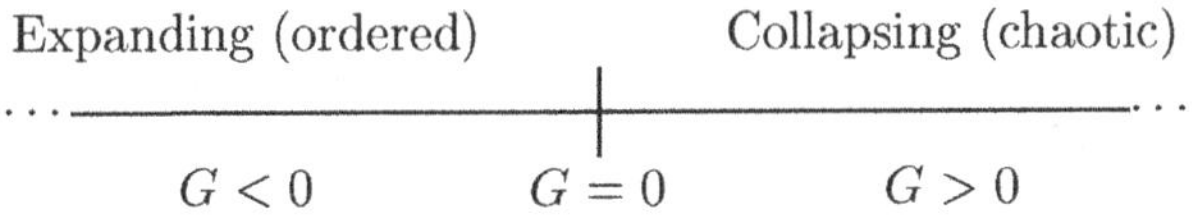

Figure 9: Ordering of the dynamical behavior classes as G increases

emerging complex patterns in the form of agents aggregates can be located near the phase transition on its chaotic side. We suspect that the 3DGA model is able to support computation. A proof of this hypothesis remains to be done, for example by constructing "logical gates" using dedicated configurations of agents. However, it seems that the 3DGA model proposed in this paper cannot support universal computation since one cannot implement a structure which create an infinite and regular stream of agents, like the so-called "glider gun" of Conway's Life CA (Berlekamp, Conway, & Guy 1982).

Discussion

Relationships with cosmological simulations and observations The formation of galactic structures has traditionally been the domain of cosmological studies using Newtonian dynamics. Many simulations have been performed based on the so-called gravitational many-body problem — also called the N-body problem (Bertschinger & Gelb 1991). However, the focus has been on the simulation of observed features of our universe, such as interacting galaxies or large-scale patterns, using accurate models reflecting the reality "as-we-know-it". In this paper, we have rather studied the 3DGA model as an abstract class of dynamical system. It must be pointed out that one must add more features to get an accurate simulation of cosmological phenomena, like the expansion effect for example. However, the precision of our model is sufficient to compare our results to observations if we look for global patterns rather than detailed phenomena.

We can only compare results obtained with a positive G close to 0.0 since the value of the real gravitational constant is of $6.67259 \times 10^{-8} \text{cm}^3\text{g}^{-1}\text{s}^{-2}$. As expected, observed globular clusters and 3DGA patterns are characterized by surprising similarities, as shown by the two following examples.

Figure 10 shows a real globular cluster NGC1904 (M79) on the left part, while the right part present a 3DGA composed of 10^3 agents with $G = +10.0$. This image is the same as in figure 6 (left), except that we have applied a simple rendering for adding light. Figure 11 shows a similar example with the NGC5897 globular cluster and a 3DGA composed of 10^3 heterogeneous agent with $G = +1.0$.

Figure 10: Globular cluster NGC1904 also called M79 (left), 3DGA with 10^3 agents (right)

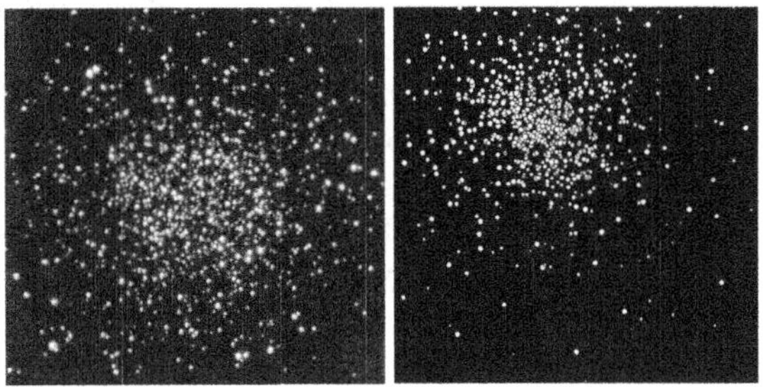

Figure 11: Globular cluster NGC5897 (left), 3DGA with 10^3 agents with $G = +1.0$ at $t = 32,500$ (right)

The fact is that some emerging structures obtained by 3DGA close to the phase transition are similar to observed patterns of our universe. This partially confirms our hypothesis about the location of complex patterns in the vicinity of the transition between the ordered and chaotic phases.

Relationships with biological evolution

One of the main speculative questions in Biology is the origin of life. Interestingly, many cosmologists are also speculating on the origin of the universe. This leads to the idea that, in both cases, the same principles of evolving complexity might be at work. While we are convinced that life is self-organized, might evolution and natural selection has some relationships with the creation of our universe?

This is not a new point of view. The theoretical physicist Lee Smolin was certainly the first to propose that natural selection might operate on the cosmic scale (Smolin 1997). Smolin's speculations were supported by many scientists from various fields, including Stuart Kauffman (1996). Smolin's theory is based on the idea that space and time can be modelized by a lattice structure on a tiny scale. In contrast, the 3DGA model attempts to study the evolution of complexity on a larger scale using Newtonian dynamics and an agent-based implementation. These two approaches are complementary by addressing a new research path to the study of life and complexity on the cosmic scale.

However, a lot of works remain to be done. Our first

results are encouraging but some points need to be thoroughly addressed. First, an important difference compared to previous works on CA complexity classes (Langton 1991; Heudin 1996; Magnier & Heudin 1997) is that the phase transition is smooth rather than critical. This must be studied with both quantitative and qualitative experiments.

Secondly, the presented 3DGA model seems unable to support universal computation. This problem leads us to the idea that this model is too simple for showing emerging complex dynamics other than globular clusters (such as black holes, pulsar, etc). Thus, we plan to modify the model by including agents with matter aggregation and emission capabilities. We must also investigate other transition functions based on gravitational relativity and quantum theory. It is also probable that we need to run simulations with many more agents ($> 10^6$). However, these new features will not so difficult to integrate thanks to the flexibility and scalability of the agent-based approach.

Conclusion

In this paper, we have first introduced the three-dimensional (3D) Gravitational Agents (GA) model as a class of discrete dynamical systems using an agent-based approach. Then, we have presented a qualitative overview of 3DGA dynamics given a progression of the gravitational parameter. Evidence have been presented that these dynamics fall into three qualitative classes: steady, expanding, and collapsing, with a phase transition between ordered and chaotic behaviors. Then, we have argued that we can locate complex patterns in the vicinity of this phase transition. Future works include the study of the computational capabilities of the 3DGA model with more sophisticated agents, and the implementation of a fast hierarchical transition function based on the Barnes-Hut algorithm (Barnes & Hut 1996) in order to address simulations with more than 10^6 agents.

References

Barnes, J., and Hut, P. 1996. A hierarchical $o(n \log n)$ force-calculation algorithm. *Nature* 324:446–449.

Berlekamp, E.; Conway, J.; and Guy, R. 1982. *Winning Ways for your Mathematical Plays.* Academic Press.

Bertschinger, E., and Gelb, J. 1991. Cosmological n-body simulations. *Computers in Physics* 164–179.

Diacu, F., and Holmes, P. 1996. *Celestrial Encounters: the Origins of Chaos and Stability 76.* Princeton.

Garcia, A. 1994. *Numerical Methods for Physics.* Prentice-Hall.

Gutowitz, H., and Langton, C. 1995. Mean field theory and the edge of chaos. volume 929 of *Lecture Notes in Computer Science.* Springer. 52.

Heudin, J. 1996. A new candidate rule for the game of two-dimensional life. *Complex systems* 10:367–381.

Heudin, J. 1998. *L'évolution au bord du chaos.* Paris: Hermès Science.

Kauffman, S. 1996. Investigations: The nature of autonomous agents and the worlds they mutually create. In http://www.santafe.edu/sfi/People/kauffman/Investigations

Langton, C. 1991. Life at the edge of chaos. In Langton, C.; Taylor, C.; Farmer, J.; and Rasmussen, S., eds., *Proceedings Artificial Life II*, 41–91. Addison-Wesley.

Magnier, M.; Lattaud, C., and Heudin, J. 1997. Complexity classes in the two-dimensional life cellular automata subspace. *Complex Systems* 11:419–436.

Packard, N. 1998. Adaptation at the edge of the chaos. In Kelso, S., and Shlesinger, M., eds., *Complexity in Biological Modeling.*

Smolin, L. 1997. *The Life of the Cosmos.* Oxford University Press.

Wolfram, S. 1983. Statistical mechanics of cellular automata. *Reviews of Modern Physics* 55:601–644.

Wolfram, S. 1984. Universality and complexity in cellular automata. *Physica D* 10:1–35.

Formal Description of Autopoiesis for Analytic Models of Life and Social Systems

Tatsuya Nomura

Faculty of Management Information, Hannan University,
5–4–33, Amamihigashi, Matsubara, Osaka 580–8502, Japan

Abstract

Since the concept of autopoiesis was proposed as a model of minimal living systems by Maturana and Varela, and applied to social systems by Luhmann, there has been still few mathematically strict models to represent the characteristics of it because of its difficulty for interpretation. In order to verify the validity of this concept, this paper proposes a formal description of autopoiesis based on the theory of category and Rosen's perspective of "closure under efficient cause", provides analytic models of life and social systems, and discusses the effectiveness of autopoiesis in systems sciences through implication from the model.

Introduction

In order to consider possibility of realization of artificial life, we should discuss whether life systems themselves and societies as collective phenomena of life systems are able to be formalized within the conventional formal theories. Autopoiesis (Maturana & Varela 1980; Kneer & Nassehi 1993) is one of the most important meterials for this discussion.

Autopoiesis gives a framework in which a system exists as an organism through physical and chemical processes, based on the assumption that organisms are machinery (Maturana & Varela 1980). According to the original definition of it by Maturana and Varela, an autopoietic system is one that continuously produces the components that specify it, while at the same time realizing itself to be a concrete unity in space and time; this makes the network of production of components possible. An autopoietic system is organized as a network of processes of production of components, where these components (1) continuously regenerate and realize the network that produces them, and (2) constitute the system as a distinguishable unity in the domain in which they exist. However, there has been still few mathematically strict models that represent autopoiesis. In Nomura (1997; 2000), we discussed the difficulty of interpreting autopoiesis within system theories using state spaces and problems of some models proposed for representing autopoiesis.

The aim in this paper is to discuss possibility of formal description of life and social systems by clarifying whether autopoiesis can really be represented within more abstract mathematical frameworks. For this aim, we use the theory of category (Takeuchi 1978), one of the most abstract algebraic structure representing relations between components. In this paper, we propose another closed systems by extending Rosen's (M,R) systems (Rosen 1972), and coupling of these closed systems for a possibility to formally represent Luhmann's social system (Kneer & Nassehi 1993).

Closure under Entailment

Rosen compared machine systems with living systems to clarify the difference between them, based on the relationship among components through entailment (Rosen 1991). In other words, he focused his attention on where the function of each component results from in the sense of Aristotle's four causal categories, that is, material cause, efficient cause, formal cause, and final cause. As a result, Rosen claimed that a material system is an organism if and only if it is closed to efficient causation.

For example, (M,R) systems (Rosen 1972) satisfy closure under efficient cause. This system model maintains its metabolic activity through inputs from environments and repair activity.

$$A \xrightarrow{f} B \xrightarrow{\phi_f} H(A,B) \xrightarrow{\Phi_f} H(B,H(A,B)) \qquad (1)$$

Here, A is a set of inputs from an environment to the system, B is a set of outputs from the system to the environment, f is a component of the system represented as a map from A to B, and ϕ_f is the repair component of f as a map from B to $H(A,B)$ ($H(X,Y)$ is the set of all maps from a set X to a set Y). In biological cells, f corresponds to the metabolism, and ϕ_f to the repair. If $\phi_f(b) = f$ ($b = f(a)$) is satisfied for the input $a \in A$, we can say that the system self–maintains itself. In addition, Φ_f can be constructed by the preceding (M, R) system in the following way: For a and b such that $b = f(a)$ and $\phi_f(b) = f$, if $\hat{b} : H(B,H(A,B)) \to H(A,B)$ ($\hat{b}(\phi)(a') = \phi(b)(a')$ ($\phi \in H(B,H(A,B)), a' \in A$)) has the inverse map $\hat{b}^{-1}$, it is easily proved that $\hat{b}^{-1}(f) = \phi_f$. Thus, we can set $\Phi_f = \hat{b}^{-1}$. The right half in figure 1 shows the aspect that the components except for a are closed under entailment, by a hyperdigraph (Higuchi et al. 1997).

It is considered that closure under entailment or production is a necessary condition for a system to be autopoietic because the components reproduce themselves in the system.

Some Systems Closed under Entailment

In order to clarify what system is closed under entailment in more general framework than the naive set theory, we

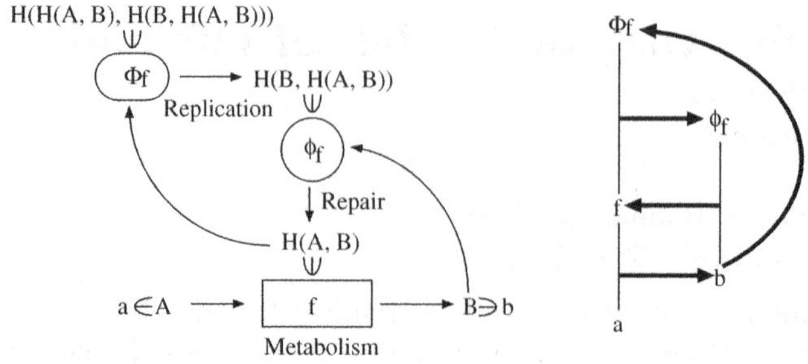

Figure 1: A (M,R) System and Its Hyperdigraph of Entailment

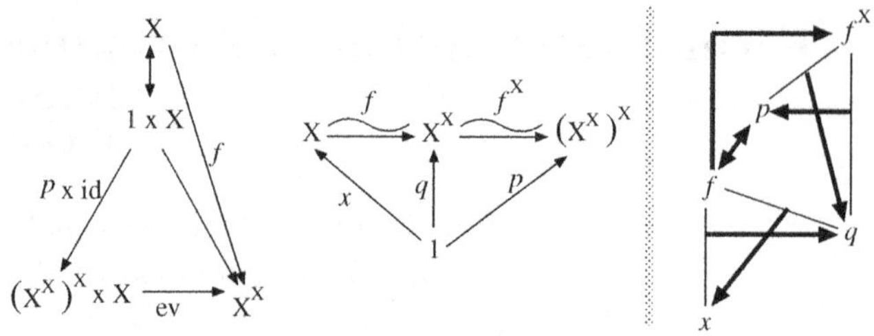

Figure 2: The Diagrams of a Completely Closed System and Its Hyperdigraph on Entailment

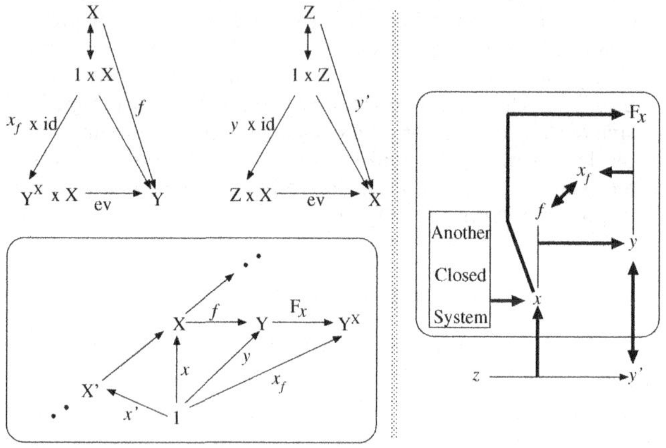

Figure 3: The Diagrams of a Generalized (M,R) System and Its Hyperdigraph on Entailment

use the theory of category. We assume that a category $\mathcal{C}$ has a final object 1 and product object $A \times B$ for any pair of objects A and B. The category of all sets is an example of this category. Moreover, we describe the set of morphisms from A to B as $H_{\mathcal{C}}(A, B)$ for any pair of objects A and B. A element of $H_{\mathcal{C}}(1, X)$ is called a morphic point on X. For a morphism $f \in H_{\mathcal{C}}(X, X)$ and a morphic point x on X, x is called a fixed point of f iff $f \circ x = x$ ($\circ$ means composition of morphisms)(Soto-Andrade & Varela 1984). Morphic points and fixed points are respectively abstraction of elements of a set and fixed points of maps in the category of sets.

Based on the above framework, we proposed "completely closed systems" under entailment (Nomura 2001). When components in a system are not only operands but also operators, the easiest method for representing this aspect is the assumption of existence of a isomorphism from the space of operands to the space of operators (Kampis 1991). Now, we assume an object X with powers and an isomorphism $f : X \simeq X^X$ in $\mathcal{C}$. Then, there uniquely exists a morphic point p on $(X^X)^X$ naturally corresponding to f induced in the theory of category (Takeuchi 1978). Since the morphism from X^X to $(X^X)^X$ entailed by the functor $\cdot^X$, f^X, is also isomorphic, there uniquely exists a morphic point q on X^X such that $f^X \circ q = p$. We can consider that p and q entail each other by f^X. Furthermore, there uniquely exists a morphic point x on X such that $f \circ x = q$ because f is isomorphic. Since we can consider that x and q entail each other by f, and f and p entail each other by the natural correspondence induced in the theory of category, the system consisting of x, q, p, f, and f^X is completely closed under entailment.

Generalized (M,R) Systems

We can generalize the closed part of (M,R) systems mentioned in section as follows.

For objects X and Y in $\mathcal{C}$, we assume that X has powers. When a morphism $f : X \to Y$ and a morphic point x on X are given, we assume that x satisfies the following conditions:

$$\begin{aligned} &\exists\, G_x \in H_{\mathcal{C}}(Y^X, Y) \qquad (2)\\ &s.t.,\ G_x \circ z = z' \circ x \text{ for any } z \in H_{\mathcal{C}}(1, Y^X)\\ &\text{and } G_x \text{ has its inverse morphism } F_x \in H_{\mathcal{C}}(Y, Y^X) \end{aligned}$$

Here, z' is the morphism from X to Y naturally corresponding to the morphic point z on Y^X. When $y = f \circ x$ and x_f is the morphic point on Y^X naturally corresponding to f, we obtain $F_x \circ y = F_x \circ f \circ x = F_x \circ G_x \circ x_f = x_f$. Thus, x_f is entailed by y and F_x. If we regard F_x as entailed by x, then f, y, F_x, and x_f are entailed by themselves and x. Although x is not entailed by x, f, y, x_f, or F_x, we can consider a larger system closed under entailment if x is one of morphic points of another closed system (for example, a completely closed system).

Infinite Regressive Systems

In this section, we consider a system like (M,R) systems including a kind of infinite regress. Now, we assume objects $X_i := {X_{i-1}}^{X_{i-2}}$, morphisms $f_i \in H_{\mathcal{C}}(X_i, X_{i+1})$, and morphic points x_i on X_i narurally corresponding to f_{i-2} and $f_i \circ x_i = x_{i+1}$ ($i = 0, \pm 1, \pm 2, \ldots$). Although any morphic point and morphism are closely entailed each other in this system, its entailment cannot be reduced to any finite subset of components and represents a kind of infinite regress. Moreover, we assume that there exist the limit X^∞ and colimit X_∞ of (X_i, f_i), and X^∞ coincides with X_∞. Furthermore, when we put $X = X^\infty = X_\infty$, and p_i and q_i are the projection from X^∞ to X_i and injection from X_i to X_∞ respectively, we assume $p_i \circ q_i = \mathrm{id}_{X_i}$ $(i = 0, \pm 1, \pm 2, \ldots)$.

Then, there uniquely exists a morphic point x on X such that $p_i \circ x = x_i$ for any i since X is the limit. On the other hand, the morphic point $y = q_i \circ x_i$ (determined independent on i because of $q_i = q_{i+1} \circ f_i$) satisfies $p_i \circ y = p_i \circ q_i \circ x_i = x_i$. Thus, we obtain $x = y$ from the uniqueness of x. Moreover, when $\pi_2^{(i)}$ is the projection of $X_i \times X$ to X, the morphism g_i naturally corresponding to $\pi_2^{(i)}$ satisfies $g_i = g_{i+1} \circ f_i$. Thus, there uniquely exists a morphism $f : X \to X^X$ such that $f \circ q_i = g_i$ since X is the colimit. Figure 4 shows the diagrams of this system and its hyperdigraph on entailment.

If the above f is isomorphic, we can construct a completely closed system including f as one of its components. Then, if x is a component in this closed system, x is entailed in the system independent of $\{x_i, f_i\}$. Moreover, x_i is entailed by x and p_i, and p_i is entailed by p_{i-1} and f_{i-1}. This represents a possibility that a system consisting of infinite regress constructs a finite closed system and entailment from it by the system itself, that is, a kind of projection from the finite system to the infinite system.

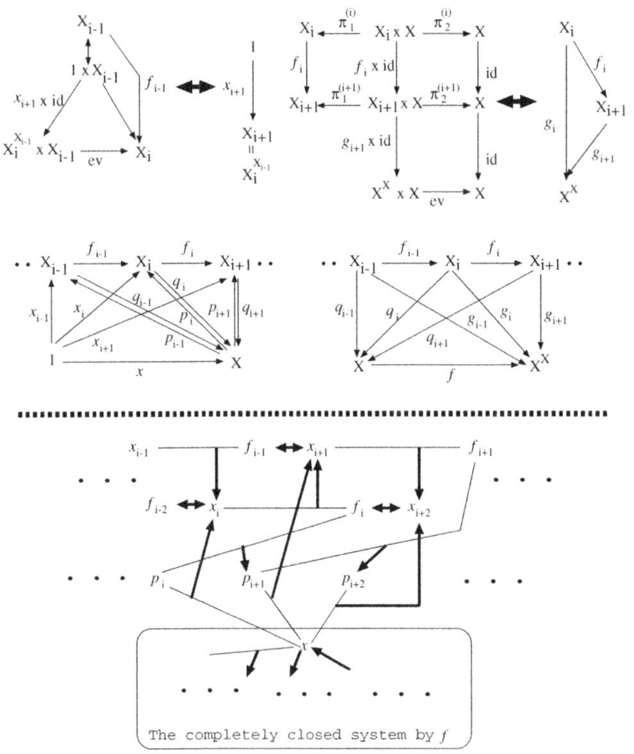

Figure 4: The Diagrams of an Infinite Regressive System and Its Hyperdigraph on Entailment

Coupling of Closed Systems

Coupling is a situation that two systems are dependent each other while each system maintains its independence. In this section, we provide some forms that two systems closed under entailment in the previous section are coupling by regarding this situation as that two systems affect each other while each system maintains its closure under entailment.

First, we can consider a form of coupling of systems in the same category $\mathcal{C}$. In this case, if one of components is shared by two closed systems, it is considered that two systems affect each other while maintaining their closure. Figure 5 shows this type of coupling and the hyperdigraphs on entailment. Given a completely closed system with { x, q, p, f, f^X }, and another completely closed system with { y, a, b, g, g^Y }, for example, if $X^X = Y$ and $q = y$, or $(X^X)^X = Y$ and $p = y$, these two systems affect each other while maintaining their closure.

Next, we consider a form of coupling of systems in the different categories $\mathcal{C}$ and $\mathcal{D}$. This case can represent an aspect in Luhmann's system theory, that is, the aspect that two mental systems that are independent autopoietic systems are coupled with communication system that is an autopoietic system in another level (Kneer & Nasschi 1993). Figure 6 shows this type of coupling and the hyperdigraphs on entailment. In this case, we assume a completely closed system in $\mathcal{C}$ with { x, q, p, f, f^X }, and another completely closed system in $\mathcal{D}$ with { y, a, b, g, g^Y }. Then, we assume a functor $\mathcal{F}$ from $\mathcal{C}$ to $\mathcal{D}$ such that $\mathcal{F}(1) = 1$, $\mathcal{F}(X) = Y$, $\mathcal{F}(X^X) = Y^Y$, $\mathcal{F}((X^X)^X) = (Y^Y)^Y$, $\mathcal{F}(f) = g$, $\mathcal{F}(f^X) = g^Y$, $\mathcal{F}(x) = y$, $\mathcal{F}(q) = a$, and $\mathcal{F}(p) = b$. In other words, the former system in $\mathcal{C}$ is mapped to the latter in $\mathcal{D}$ by $\mathcal{F}$. This functor exists in the level different from those where these closed systems exist, and no components in $\mathcal{C}$ and $\mathcal{D}$ entail $\mathcal{F}$. However, if there exists a subcategory of the category consisting of all the categories and functors such that it has a final object and a closed system having $\mathcal{F}$ as one of its components, $\mathcal{F}$ is entailed independent of the systems in $\mathcal{C}$ and $\mathcal{D}$.

Discussion

Although in this paper we required that operands coincide with operators ($X \simeq X^X$ or $Y \simeq Y^X$), this condition is difficult to be satisfied in the naive set theory. Although Soto–Andrade and Varela provided a category satisfying this condition (the category of partially ordered sets and continuous monotone maps with special conditions)(Soto–Andrade & Varela 1984), this category is very special. Furthermore, Rosen showed that systems closed under efficient cause cannot be described

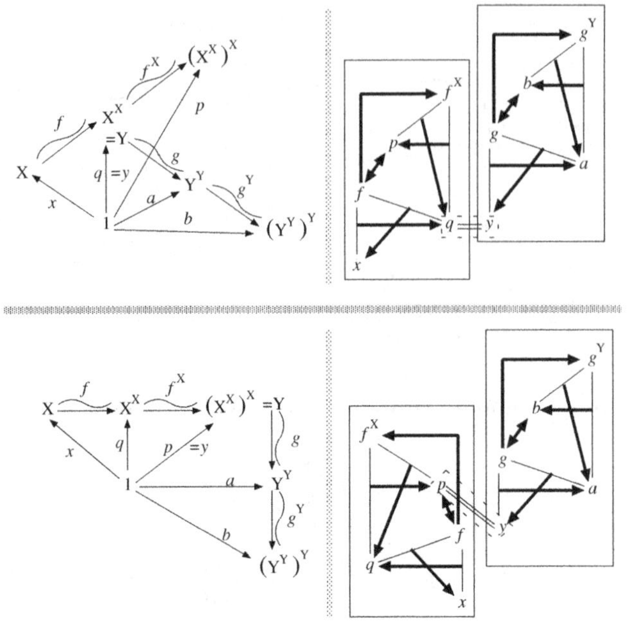

Figure 5: Coupling of Two Completely Closed Systems in the Same Category and the Hyperdigraphs on Entailment

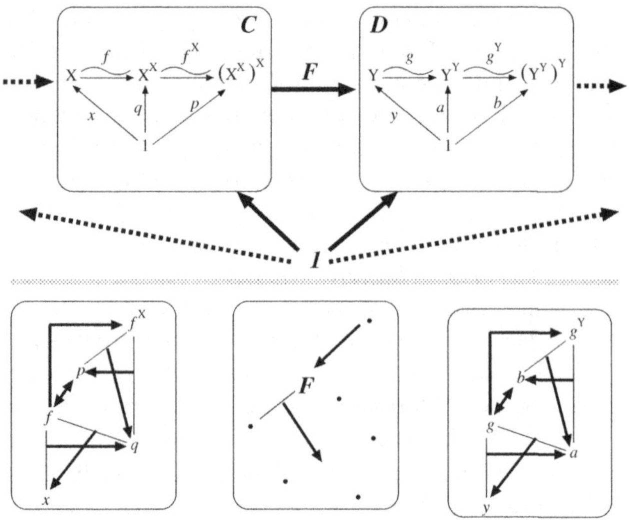

Figure 6: Coupling of Completely Closed Systems in the Different Categories and the Hyperdigraphs

with their states because they lead to infinite regress (Rosen 1991). In addition, we needed to introduce a functor in order to connect a closed system with another system between the different categories, and needed to introduce a special category in order to entail this functor in a closed system. If these closed systems can exist only in special categories not observable in the conventional sense, autopoiesis may be hard to be a general theory of a variety of systems.

References

Higuchi, A., Matsuno, K., and Tsujishita, T. 1997. Deductive Hyperdigraphs, A Method of Describing Diversity of Coherence. preprint.

Kampis, G. 1991. *Self-Modifying Systems in Biology and Cognitive Science: A New Framework for Synamics, Information, and Complexity.* Pergamon Press.

Kneer, G. and Nassehi, A. 1993. *Niklas Luhmanns Theorie Sozialer Systeme.* Wilhelm Fink Verlag. (Japanese Edition: T. Tateno, et. al. Shinsensha (1995).)

Maturana, H. R., and Varela, F. J. 1980. *Autopoiesis and Cognition: The Realization of the Living.* D. Reidel Publishing. (Japanese Edition: Kawamoto, H. Kokubun–sha Publishers. (1991).)

Nomura, T. 1997. An Attempt for Description of Quasi–Autopoietic Systems Using Metabolism–Repair Systems. in *Proc. the Fourth European Conference on Artificial Life*, 48–56.

Nomura, T. 2000. A Computational Aspect of Autopoiesis. in *Proc. the Fourth Asian Fuzzy Systems Symposium*, 1–6.

Nomura, T. 2001. Formal Description of Autopoiesis Based on the Theory of Category. in *Advances in Artificial Life: 6th European Conference, ECAL 2001, Proceedings*, 700–703.

Rosen, R. 1991. *LIFE ITSELF.* Columbia University Press.

Rosen, R. 1972;. Some Relational Cell Models: The Metabolism–Repair Systems. In *FOUNDATIONS OF MATHEMATICAL BIOLOGY*, 217–253, Academic Press.

Soto–Andrade, J., and Varela, F. J. 1984. Self–Reference and Fixed Points: A Discussion and an Extension of Lawvere's Theorem. Acta Applicandae Mathematicae, 2:1–19.

Takeuchi, G. *Sheaf, Category, and Topos.* Nihon Hyoron–sha. (in Japanese).

The Birth and Death Process of Hypercycle Spirals

Kazumasa Oida
ATR Adaptive Communications Research Laboratories
2-2-2 Hikaridai Seika-cho Soraku-gun Kyoto 619-0288 Japan
oida@atr.co.jp

Abstract

The behavior of hypercycle spirals in a two-dimensional cellular automaton model is analyzed. Each of these spirals can be approximated by an Archimedean spiral and the center, width, and phase of the hypercycle spiral change according to Brownian motion. A barrier exists between two spirals if the phase synchronization hypothesis is taken into account, and the occurrence rate of pair decay (the simultaneous disappearance of two spirals) can be explained by the random walk simulation with the barrier. Adjacent species violation is shown to be a necessary condition for creating new spirals. A hypercycle system can live long if the spirals in the system are somewhat unstable, since new spirals cannot emerge when existing spirals are too stable.

Introduction

A hypercycle, as introduced by Eigen (Eigen 1971) in 1971, is a system that consists of a number of self-replicative molecular species that are linked cyclically by catalysis (Fig. 1). The idea of the hypercycle is important in the study of pre-biotic evolution because it may explain how molecular species having a small number of molecules can evolve into an entity with a great amount of genetic information. Since Eigen's initial work, hypercycles have been experimentally and theoretically verified (Gebinoga 1995). In particular, the stability of hypercycles has been extensively studied in terms of non-linear ordinary differential equations (ODE) (Eigen & Schuster 1979; Hofbauer & Sigmund 1988). The results from ODEs have indicated that hypercycles are not always stable systems; they tend to be vulnerable to parasites. ODEs, however, do not take into account any spatial effects among molecules.

In 1991, Boerlijst and Hogeweg (Boerlijst & Hogeweg 1991; 1992) were the first to show the spatial dynamics caused by hypercyclic interactions; "spiral waves" emerged in their cellular automaton (CA) model and, interestingly, the spirals made the hypercycles resistant to parasites. In 1995, Cronhjort and Blomberg (Cronhjort & Blomberg 1996) considered a more realistic case, i.e., the maximum concentration (c_0) of all molecules is limited (growth limitation), and reported that hypercycles with a few components, which do not exhibit spiral waves but homogeneous clusters, are also resistant to parasites. In 1995, Vespalcova et al. (Vespalcova, Holden, & Brindley 1995) introduced inhibitory connections into the hypercycle structure and found that, under some circumstances, these connections enhance the resistance to parasites. In 1998, Altmeyer et al. (Altmeyer, Wilke, & Martinetz 1998) reported that hypercycle interactions generate rotating screws and corn-like structures in their three-dimensional CA model.

As mentioned above, previous works have mainly focused on how hypercycle systems can coexist with parasites. In contrast, this paper focuses on a more basic question: how do spirals in a two-dimensional CA model appear and disappear? The birth and death mechanism of hypercycle spirals, which should provide important information on the stability of hypercycles, is currently unclear. Our model is similar to the Cronhjort model (a two-dimensional CA model under growth limitation). However, it has six species, so that spirals emerge.

To understand the mechanism, we follow the behavior of spirals in an analytic way. We show quantitatively that the shape of a spiral can be approximated by an Archimedean spiral and that its center, width, and phase change according to Brownian motion. Then, we show the impact of c_0 and the decay probability of a molecular species (P_{decay}) on the birth and death process of hypercycle spirals. Parameter space (c_0, P_{decay}) can be divided into three regions: systematic (S), quasi-systematic (Q), and chaotic (C) regions. In the S region, the number of spirals monotonically decreases with time due to pair decay (the simultaneous disappearance of two spirals), which was first mentioned by Boerlijst and Hogeweg (Boerlijst & Hogeweg 1991). In the Q region, not only is there pair decay, but also independent decay. New spirals may emerge after the occurrence of an independent decay. In the C region, spirals do not form.

Next, we explain how two spirals interact based on the phase synchronization hypothesis, which states that two spirals are in contact with each other such that molecules of the same species meet at the boundary between these spirals. This hypothesis yields a barrier between spirals. The shape of the barrier depends on the spirals' rotation directions and affects the occurrence rate of pair decay. We then introduce the term "adjacent species violation (ASV)," which represents a phenomenon in which a belt of species i touches a belt made up of species other than $i-1$, i, and $i+1$, where a spiral is composed of six belts and each belt is made up of molecules of the same species. We show from computational experiments that ASV is a necessary condition for creating new spirals. Lastly, we show that in order for a hypercycle system to live long, spirals in the system must be somewhat unstable, since new spirals cannot emerge when existing spirals are too stable.

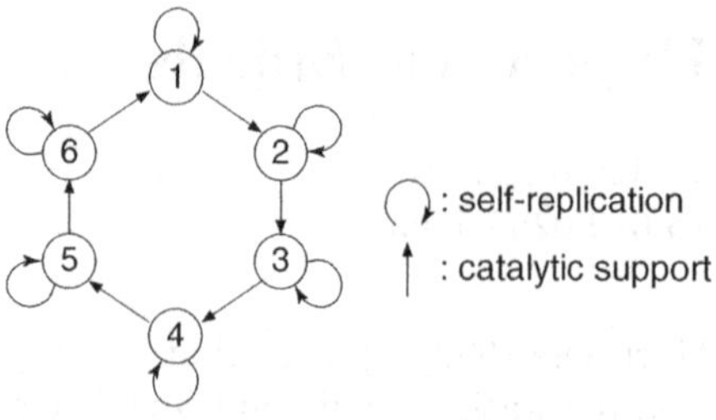

Figure 1: A hypercycle consisting of six species.

The CA Model

In order to model a reaction-diffusion system of six molecular species in a hypercycle organization (in Fig. 1) in a two-dimensional medium, we consider a two-dimensional cellular automaton (CA) model, which is on a 200×200 lattice of square cells with periodic boundaries. Let s_k be the state of a cell k. Cell k is either occupied by a molecule of species i (i.e., $s_k = i$) or empty (i.e., $s_k = 0$). Hereafter, we call the states of all cells on the lattice an image. The CA starts at $t = 0$ with an image consisting of $200^2 c_0$ molecules, whose species and positions are randomly selected according to a uniform distribution. c_0 is a parameter indicating the maximum total concentration ($0 < c_0 \leq 1$).

We explain our model concisely since it is mostly derived from the Boerlijst and Cronhjort models (Boerlijst & Hogeweg 1991; 1992; Cronhjort & Blomberg 1996). At each time step, for all cells k (200^2 in total), s_k is updated in random order as follows:

if $(s_k = 0)$
  for each $i \in S_i$ **do**
    $P_i := (1 - \frac{c_{\text{tot}}}{c_0}) \frac{\text{support}(i)}{\max(\sum_{i \in S_i} \text{support}(i), \alpha)}$;
  if $(\sum_{j=1}^{i-1} P_j < X_1 \leq \sum_{j=1}^{i} P_j)$
    $s_k := i$;
    $c_{\text{tot}} := c_{\text{tot}} + \frac{1}{200^2}$;
else
  if $(X_2 \leq P_{\text{decay}})$
    $s_k := 0$;
    $c_{\text{tot}} := c_{\text{tot}} - \frac{1}{200^2}$;
  else $(X_3 \leq P_{\text{diff}})$
    diffuse(k);

In the above algorithm, S_i $(= \{1,2,3,4,5,6\})$ is the set of species in the hypercycle (Fig. 1). X_1, X_2, and X_3 represent random numbers generated according to the uniform distribution in range [0,1]. Function diffuse(k) interchanges s_k with s_j, where j is a randomly selected neighboring cell of k. Throughout this paper, a neighboring cell of cell k is one of eight cells surrounding cell k (Moore neighborhood).

P_i in the algorithm denotes the probability that a molecule of species i is replicated into cell k. To obtain probability P_i, we first calculate the amount of replication support for species i at cell k such that

$$\text{support}(i) = N_i \text{self}(i) + N_{i,i-1} \text{cat}(i, i-1),$$

Table 1: Parameter values used to obtain all results in this paper, unless stated otherwise.

self(i)	0.01 for all $i \in S_i$
cat$(i, i-1)$	1 for all $i \in S_i$
α	1
P_{diff}	0.5

where N_i is the number of k's neighboring cells that are occupied by species i. $N_{i,j}$ is the number of pairs of cells ℓ and m that satisfies three conditions: $\ell, m \in$ {neighboring cells of cell k}, $(s_\ell, s_m) = (i,j)$ or (j,i), and ℓ is a neighbor of m. Functions self(i) and cat(i,j) represent relative replication rates of species i by self-replication and by replication with catalytic support from j, respectively.

In the same way as in the Cronhjort model (Cronhjort & Blomberg 1996), we introduce the growth limiting factor $\gamma = 1 - c_{\text{tot}}/c_0$, where c_{tot} is the fraction of cells occupied by any molecule. We introduce the growth limitation to observe the effect of the amount of components used for building up molecules. When $\gamma \approx 0$ (i.e., $c_0 \approx c_{\text{tot}}$), all replication probabilities are almost zero; therefore, the growth stops under such a condition. Parameter α controls the probability that one molecule of any species is replicated into an empty cell. If α increases, the probability decreases, so that replications occur only at empty cells having large R values, where $R = \sum_{i \in S_i} \text{support}(i)$. Therefore, c_{tot} decreases as α increases. A molecule decays with probability P_{decay}. All parameter values in this model except for c_0 and P_{decay} are shown in Table 1.

The following summarizes the characteristics of our model. (1) The states of all cells are asynchronously updated at each time step. (2) The replication probability of species i is larger than that of species j if support(i) > support(j). (3) Growth limitation is taken into account. (4) Parameter α controls the replication probability at all empty cells.

Dynamics of Hypercycle Spirals

In this section, we first explain analytically the shape and movement of an individual spiral, and then describe the effects of c_0 and P_{decay} on the dynamics of spirals, especially on their birth and death process.

Archimedean Spiral

A spiral consists of six belts, each of which is made up of molecules of the same species. Although the boundary between two belts is not smooth, it can be approximated by an Archimedean spiral (see Fig. 12(a)) with our spiral identification method. This result is the starting point of our work. Based on this result, the boundary between belts of species i and $i-1$ can be written with orthogonal

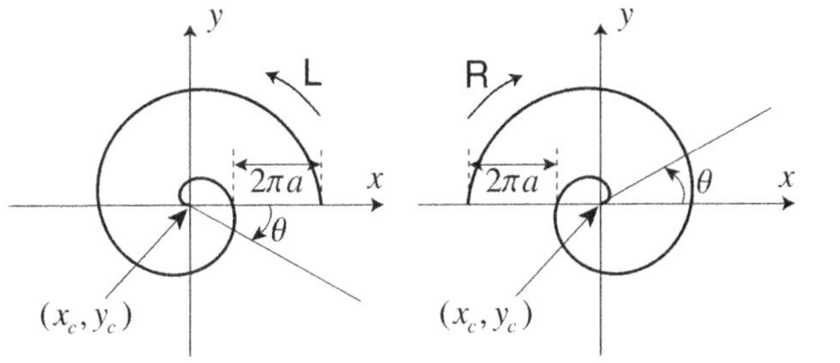

Figure 2: θ advancing in the opposite direction against the rotation direction of a spiral.

coordinates (x, y) as

$$x = x_c + a\theta \cos(\theta - \frac{2\pi}{6} i + \varphi), \quad (1)$$

$$y = y_c \pm a\theta \sin(\theta - \frac{2\pi}{6} i + \varphi), \quad (2)$$

where (x_c, y_c), φ, and a are, respectively, the center, phase, and width of the spiral, and $0 \le \theta \le 2n\pi$ when the number of turns is n. Each spiral has its own rotation direction, which is either clockwise (R) or counterclockwise (L). As shown in Fig. 2, θ advances in the opposite direction against the rotation direction. Therefore, the second term on the right-hand side of Eq. (2) takes the positive (negative) sign if the rotation direction is R (L).

We obtained time series of center $(x_c(t), y_c(t))$, phase $\varphi(t)$, and width $a(t)$ of a spiral from about 6000 images. Figure 3 shows the case of $(c_0, P_{\text{decay}}) = (0.2, 0.04)$; the case of $(c_0, P_{\text{decay}}) = (0.7, 0.06)$ is almost the same. Let

$$\dot{x}_c(k) = x_c(t+k) - x_c(t), \quad \dot{\varphi}(k) = \varphi(t+k) - \varphi(t),$$
$$\dot{y}_c(k) = y_c(t+k) - y_c(t), \quad \dot{a}(k) = a(t+k) - a(t).$$

We can see that histograms of the four increments $(\dot{x}_c(k), \dot{y}_c(k), \dot{\varphi}(k), \dot{a}(k))$ approximate normal distributions. Figure 3(b) shows the histogram of $\dot{\varphi}(k)$. In the figure, $N(\mu, \sigma^2)$ indicates a normal distribution with mean μ and variance σ^2. Furthermore, as shown in Fig. 3(c), the sample standard deviations of the four increments linearly increase with $\sqrt{k}$ for large k's; therefore, their behavior can be regarded approximately as Brownian motion. (However, we show exceptions later.) The absolute value of the correlation coefficient between any two increments is almost zero (less than 1.5×10^{-3} when $(c_0, P_{\text{decay}}) = (0.2, 0.04)$) except for that between $\dot{\varphi}(t)$ and $\dot{a}(t)$ (its maximum is 0.0216 when $(c_0, P_{\text{decay}}) = (0.2, 0.04)$).

Figure 3(a) shows a random walk of a spiral's center $(x_c(t), y_c(t))$. Its movement is perceptible to the naked eye. The angular frequency $\omega (= \dot{\varphi}(1))$ of a spiral is almost constant, since its variance is very small. The rotation time $T_r = 2\pi/\bar{\omega}$ agrees with that computed by Boerlijst's method (Boerlijst & Hogeweg 1992), where $\bar{\omega}$ is the sample mean of ω. T_r decreases with an increase

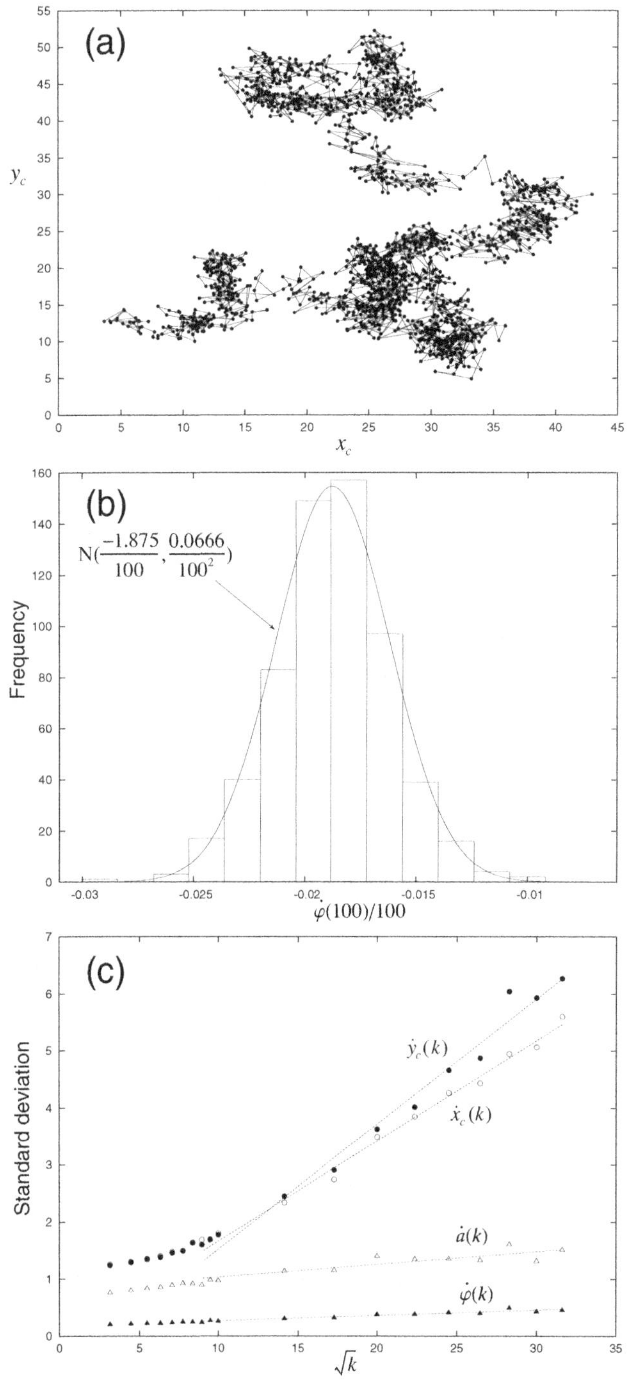

Figure 3: Behavior of a spiral derived from 6116 images when $(c_0, P_{\text{decay}}) = (0.2, 0.04)$. (a) Random walk of center $(x_c(t), y_c(t))$. (b) A histogram of $\dot{\varphi}(100)/100$ (radian/time-step), where the cell size is 1.6×10^{-3} radians. (c) Standard deviations increasing linearly with $\sqrt{k}$.

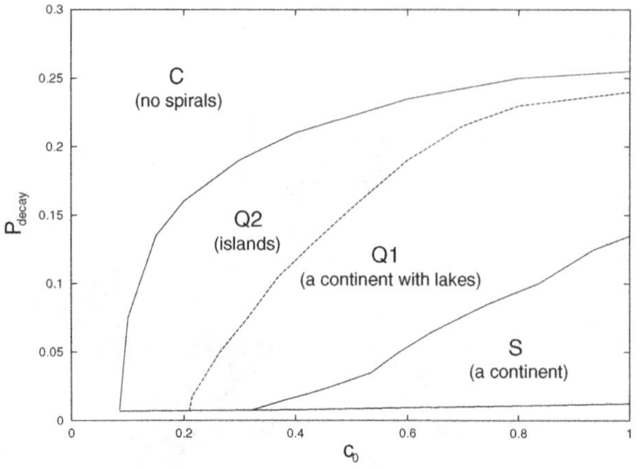

Figure 4: Regions in parameter space (c_0, P_{decay}).

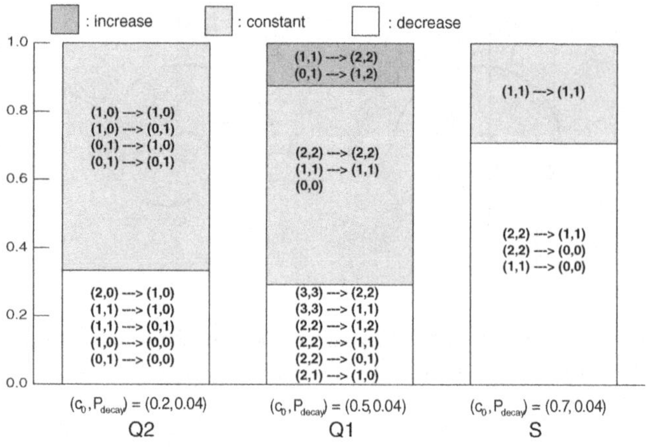

Figure 5: Probabilities that the number of spirals increases, decreases, and remains unchanged between $t = 10^4$ and $t = 10^5$ in three regions (Q1, Q2, S). The number of trials is 24. The patterns of changes are described as "(L_1, R_1)—> (L_2, R_2)," where L_1 (R_1) and L_2 (R_2) are numbers of spirals rotating clockwise (counterclockwise) observed at $t = 10^4$ and $t = 10^5$, respectively.

in P_{decay}. For many c_0 and P_{decay} pairs, their relation is roughly $T_r P_{\text{decay}} \approx 130$. The sample mean of width a also decreases with an increase in P_{decay}.

Parameter Space

Based on the behavior of spirals, parameter space (c_0, P_{decay}) is divided into three regions: systematic (S), quasi-systematic (Q), and chaotic (C) regions (Fig. 4). The Q region is made up of Q1 and Q2 sub-regions. In the S region, all spirals die out due to pair decay (see Figs. 12(d)-(f)). A pair decay is the simultaneous disappearance of two spirals and occurs when the distance between their centers becomes very short. A pair decay occurs only if the rotation directions of two spirals are different. As shown in Fig. 5, the number of spirals in this region is always an even number and the number gradually decreases two by two with time, until it eventually becomes zero.

In the Q region, not only pair decay, but also independent decay can be observed. An independent decay is the collapse of a spiral caused by the intensive decay of molecules in the spiral. If such intensive decay occurs at the center of a spiral, before long the spiral disappears (this type of independent decay is called a complete decay); otherwise it survives (this is called a partial decay). New spirals are often born just after a partial decay. Accordingly, the number of spirals decreases after a pair or a complete decay, but it may increase after a partial decay (Fig. 5).

In the S region, spirals cover the whole square lattice. In the Q1 region, on the other hand, a few masses of empty cells exist between spirals (they look like lakes on a continent, as shown in Fig. 12(b)), while in the Q2 region, a few spirals are surrounded by empty cells (they look like islands, as shown in Fig. 12(c)).

In the C region, molecules cannot form spirals, so all molecules die out shortly after the model starts. There are some reasons why they cannot form spirals. For example, if P_{decay} is very large, the life spans of the molecules become too short to form spirals, while if P_{decay} is very small, the width a of a spiral becomes too large to form spirals on the 200×200 lattice.

Phase Synchronization

Hypothesis

The CA lattice can be divided into n areas when there are n spirals in an image. One Archimedean spiral exists in each area and the shape of each area gradually changes with time. Two belts belonging to different spirals meet at a boundary of two areas (for example, see Fig. 7). At each point on the boundary, six belts composed of different species cyclically arrive from both areas. We have noticed that two belts meeting on the boundary are always made up of the same species. We call such a state of two spirals "phase synchronization" and establish the following hypothesis.

Phase synchronization hypothesis: All spirals that are in contact with one another are in the phase synchronization state if no partial decays are in progress.

If the hypothesis is true, a belt of species i is always enclosed only by belts of species $i-1$, i, and $i+1$. This hypothesis is very natural since species i is created at an empty cell next to species $i-1$ (with the catalytic support of $i-1$) or next to species i (by self-replication). Note that this hypothesis states that the phase synchronization holds even though complete or pair decays are in progress. The progress of these decays is such that a mass of empty cells expands outward from the center until it reaches area boundaries (see Fig. 12(f)); therefore, the hypothesis holds even during these decays.

We use the hypothesis as a basis to explain the following facts:

- A pair decay occurs only if the rotation directions of two spirals are different.
- If the distance between the centers of two spirals rotating in the same direction becomes very short, they repel each other.

Barrier between Spirals

We first show how close two spirals can come to each other while maintaining the phase synchronization state. Here, we express the four parameters (x_c, y_c, φ, a) of Archimedean spiral i as $(x_i, y_i, \varphi_i, a_i)$. Let d be the distance between the centers of two spirals and let S_d denote the range of distances d that do not allow two spirals to be in the phase synchronization state. Figure 6 shows range S_d as a function of phase difference $(\Delta\varphi = \varphi_2 - \varphi_1)$ obtained with Eqs. (1) and (2) under the condition that $y_1 = y_2 = 0$ and $a_1 = a_2 = a$. We computed the boundary between two spirals since if their complete boundary can be obtained, they are in the synchronization state. As shown in the figure, spirals with different directions can come closer to each other than spirals with the same direction. Let d_s be the greatest lower bound in the complementary range of S_d $(\bar{S}_d)$. When the directions are different, there are no S_d barriers $(d_s = 0)$ between them if $\Delta\varphi \approx \pi$; however, since the gap in the barrier is extremely narrow (less than 10^{-5} radians) when $d < 1.97a$, it may be difficult to enter the gap. Meanwhile, if the rotation directions are the same, $d_s \approx 3.107a$ when $\Delta\varphi = \pi$.

We next show the reason why the pair decay occurs. The direct cause of pair or complete decay is that at least one of the six belts disappears from the center of the spiral. Figure 7 shows two spirals with different rotation directions, which are depicted according to Eqs. (1) and (2). As shown in the figure, if distance d is very small, a belt with a small area appears (belt 1 in Fig. 7). Since two spirals with different rotation directions can come very close to each other, the chance of a belt disappearing (due to an intensive decay of molecules in the belt) is large. Figure 12(e) shows two spirals in our CA model whose shapes are similar to those in Fig. 7. Contrarily, if their directions are the same, such a small area does not appear even if $d = d_s$.

Phase Difference

The phase difference between two spirals is a relative quantity; therefore, it should be an invariant with respect to the translation and rotation of the coordinate axes. In the previous section, we dealt with the case $y_1 = y_2$, and expressed the phase difference as $\Delta\varphi = \varphi_2 - \varphi_1$. In this section, we assume that $y_1 \neq y_2$.

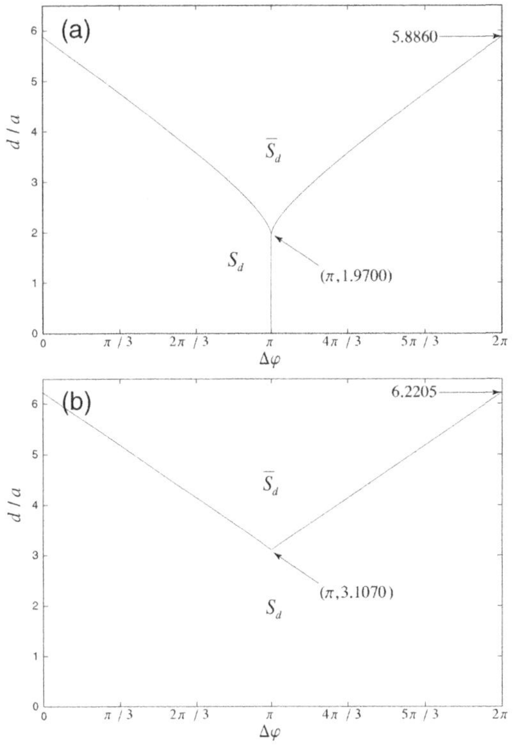

Figure 6: Range S_d of distances that do not allow two spirals to be in the phase synchronization state when rotation directions are (a) different and (b) the same.

We first consider the case where the rotation directions of two spirals are different. Suppose the center of spiral 2 in Fig. 8 moves from (x_2, y_1) to (x_2, y_2) while its phase φ_2 remains unchanged. After the movement, by observing spiral 1 from spiral 2 (in other words, by regarding the line that passes points (x_1, y_1) and (x_2, y_2) as the X-axis), the phase of spiral 1 (φ_1) decreases by $\phi = \tan^{-1}\frac{y_2 - y_1}{x_2 - x_1}$ $(-\pi \leq \phi \leq \pi)$, where

$$\begin{cases} 0 \leq \phi \leq \frac{\pi}{2}, & \text{if } x_2 - x_1 \geq 0 \text{ and } y_2 - y_1 \geq 0, \\ \frac{\pi}{2} < \phi \leq \pi, & \text{if } x_2 - x_1 < 0 \text{ and } y_2 - y_1 \geq 0, \\ -\frac{\pi}{2} \leq \phi < 0, & \text{if } x_2 - x_1 \geq 0 \text{ and } y_2 - y_1 < 0, \\ -\pi < \phi < -\frac{\pi}{2}, & \text{if } x_2 - x_1 < 0 \text{ and } y_2 - y_1 < 0. \end{cases}$$

By observing spiral 2 from spiral 1, on the other hand, the phase of spiral 2 (φ_2) advances by ϕ. Therefore, phase difference $\Delta\varphi$ after the movement can be written as

$$\Delta\varphi = (\varphi_2 + \phi) - (\varphi_1 - \phi) = \varphi_2 - \varphi_1 + 2\phi. \quad (3)$$

If the rotation directions of spirals 1 and 2 are, respectively, R and L, $\Delta\varphi = \varphi_2 - \varphi_1 - 2\phi$.

We next consider the case where the rotation directions are the same. Suppose that spiral 2 in Fig. 8 rotates counterclockwise (L). Then, φ_2 decreases by ϕ by observing spiral 2 from spiral 1 after the movement;

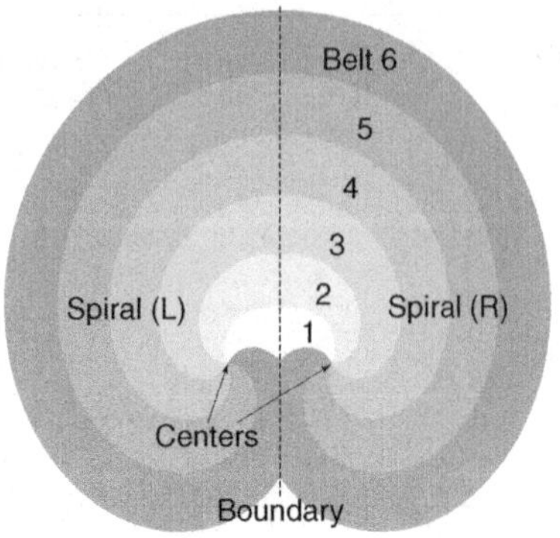

Figure 7: Two Archimedean spirals in the phase synchronization state when $d = 2a$ and $\Delta\varphi = \pi$.

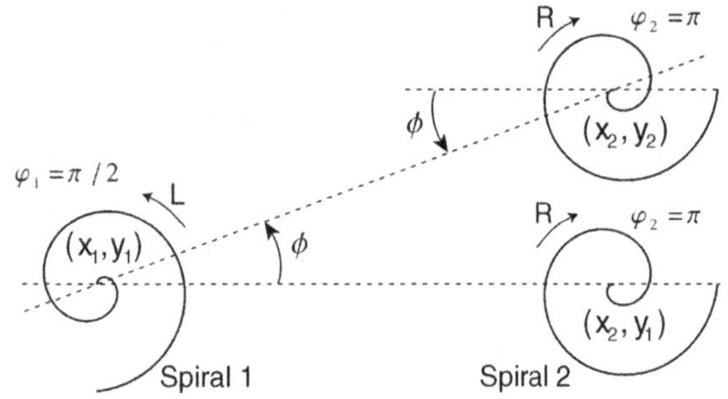

Figure 8: Phase difference depending on the relative positions of two centers.

therefore, the phase difference does not change in this case. To sum up, the phase difference depends on the relative positions of two spirals only if their rotation directions are different.

Based on the above-mentioned dependence, we show how large the barrier is when the rotation directions of spirals 1 and 2 are L and R, respectively. Figure 9 shows the area of center (x_2, y_2) that satisfies $d \in S_d$ (S_d is given in Fig. 6(a)) when $\varphi_2 - \varphi_1 = \pi$ and $(x_1, y_1) = (0, 0)$. Note that in this case, distance d and phase difference $\Delta\varphi$ are written as $d = \sqrt{x_2^2 + y_2^2}$ and $\Delta\varphi = \pi + 2\tan^{-1}\frac{y_2}{x_2}$, respectively. From the figure, the barrier is deeply dented when $y = 0$. This unique shape affects the pair decay rate, as discussed in the subsequent section.

Behavior after First Touch

Adjacent Species Violation

The adjacent species violation (ASV) indicates that a belt of species i touches a belt that is made up of species other than $i-1$, i, and $i+1$. If the phase synchronization hypothesis is true, ASV occurs only in two cases. (1) At the beginning of the CA model when newborn spirals touch one another for the first time. (2) When some spiral belts encounter one another after they invade an

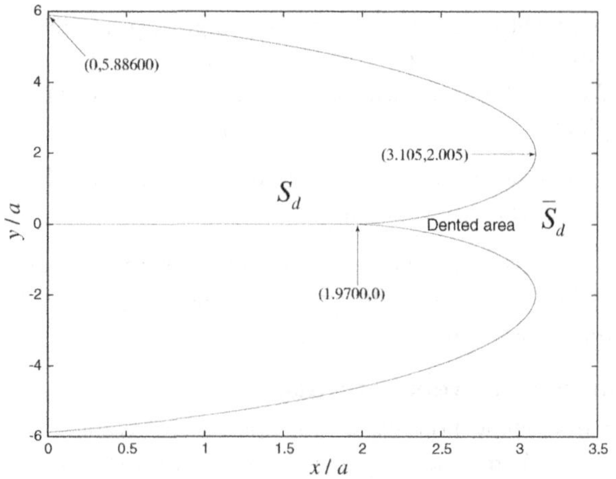

Figure 9: Barrier between two spirals when $\varphi_2 - \varphi_1 = \pi$ and center $(x_1, y_1) = (0, 0)$. The widths of the two spirals are a.

empty area created by a partial decay.

In the above-mentioned two cases, new spirals often appear. The following experiment clarifies the relationship between the appearance of new spirals and ASV. Two circles are used as the initial state of the CA model (see Fig. 10). Each circle is equally divided into six parts and each part is filled with molecules of the same species. The two circles become two spirals soon after the beginning of the CA model, they grow larger (i.e., their numbers of turns increase), and then they touch each other. The rotation directions of the two spirals and the phase difference between them can be determined *a priori* depending on how the six species are arranged on the 12 parts in the two circles. Figure 10 shows the initial state (the arrangement of species in the two circles and distance d_0 between their centers) and what happens after their first touch until $t = 3000$.

The following summarizes the experimental results shown in Fig. 10.

1. Without ASV ($\Delta\varphi = \pi$), no new spirals appear.

2. When ASV occurs ($\Delta\varphi = 0$) and two spirals are both L, one spiral deterministically appears with the R direction. When $\Delta\varphi = 0$ and one spiral is L and the other is R, one of the following four cases happens: two new spirals with different directions, one new spiral with the L direction, one new spiral with the R direction, or no new spirals. Which of these cases occurs is random, even if the experiments are made under the same conditions excluding random numbers.

3. When the centers are inside the barrier ($d_0 \in S_d$), pair decay occurs with a high probability. If the directions are both L, the distance between the centers deterministically increases. Figures 12(j)–(l) illustrate the

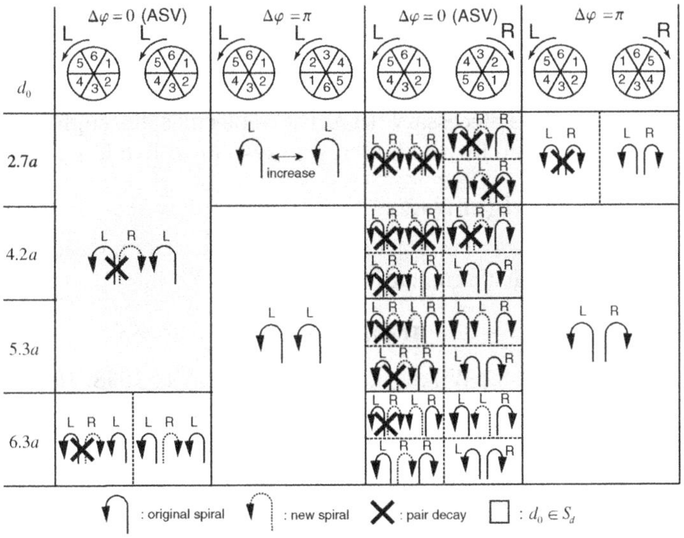

Figure 10: Relationship between ASV and the birth of new spirals. For clarity, we set $\gamma = 1$. The sample mean of width $a = 10.47$. ASV occurs when $\Delta\varphi = 0$.

increase of the distance. In this case, the movement of the centers is not according to Brownian motion, but they repel each other perhaps to enter the phase synchronization state.

Emergence of New Spirals

We learned from the above experiments that ASV is a necessary condition for creating new spirals. Then, how does a new spiral emerge after ASV? From our observations, after belts of species i and j ($\neq i-1, i, i+1$) commit ASV, the molecules of species $i+1$ ($j+1$) in the belt of species j (i) begin to actively reproduce after touching the belt of species i (j), so that they form a small cluster of species $i+1$ ($j+1$) between the belts. (Note that a belt of species i includes a small number of molecules of species $i-1, i-2, \ldots$) The number of clusters increases as the two spirals rotate, and eventually the clusters form a spiral. Figures 12(g)-(i) show the generation process of a new spiral when $(\gamma, P_{\text{decay}}) = (1, 0.1)$. It takes about 100 time steps to create a new spiral.

Effect of Barrier on Pair Decay

Table 2 shows the occurrence rate (r_p) of pair decay, which is obtained by carrying out the same experiment as shown in Fig. 10 when $\Delta\varphi = \pi$ and the directions are L and R. From the table, the following two results are obtained. (1) A pair decay occurs almost deterministically when $d_0 = 2a$. (2) Rate r_p largely changes when d_0 is between $2.4a$ and $3.0a$. The above two results can be expressed in different words with the random walk of a center and the S_d barrier: a pair decay occurs at the inner part of the dented area in Fig. 9, and the probability that a center enters the inner part is sensitive to d_0 if

Table 2: Pair decay rate r_p and probability $p_c(2.4a)$. r_p is measured over 200 experiments for $(c_0, P_{\text{decay}}) = (0.7, 0.06)$. $a = 11.69$

d_0	$2.0a$	$2.4a$	$2.7a$	$3.0a$	$3.4a$	$3.8a$
r_p	0.995	0.90	0.71	0.42	0.21	0.11
$p_c(2.4a)$	1.0	0.973	0.643	0.439	0271	0.169

d_0 is near the entrance of the dented area. By means of the random walk simulation, we obtain probability $p_c(\ell)$ that the shortest distance between two centers during a random walk is less than ℓ. Table 2 demonstrates that p_c(2.4a) approximates r_p.

Survivability Evaluation

In this section, we evaluate how long the hypercycle system can live depending on c_0 and P_{decay}. Here, the death of the system means that the concentration of at least one species is zero. Figure 11 shows average life spans for various c_0 and P_{decay} pairs. From the figure, we can see that a system can live long if P_{decay} is a little larger than that on the boundary between the S and Q regions in parameter space (c_0, P_{decay}), where we assume that the S region in Fig. 4 still exists even under the Q2 region as a long and very narrow region.

We explain this result as follows. In order for the system to live long, forming a spiral is definitely required. Experiments verify that hypercycle systems cannot live long if spiral structures are completely broken at each time step without changing the concentrations of each species. Namely, the system's death comes soon after the number of spirals becomes zero. As shown in Fig. 5, compared with the S region, the Q region has an advantage since the number of spirals in the region may increase (due to ASV after a partial decay). A large P_{decay} value increases not only the frequency of partial decays, but also the frequency of complete decays; therefore, there is an optimal P_{decay} value for each c_0, which is a little larger than P_{decay} on the boundary.

Discussion

A hypercycle system consists of two levels of dynamical systems: species (low-level systems) and spirals (high-level systems). One significant result of our study is that although the stability of low-level systems has an effect on the behavior of high-level systems (Fig. 4), the survivability of the hypercycle system (Fig. 11) can be explained only by interactions among high-level systems. The stability analysis of a hypercycle system based only on the dynamics of the concentrations (or numbers) of low-level systems, which does not take into account the high-level system, may lead to different conclusions from those in this paper.

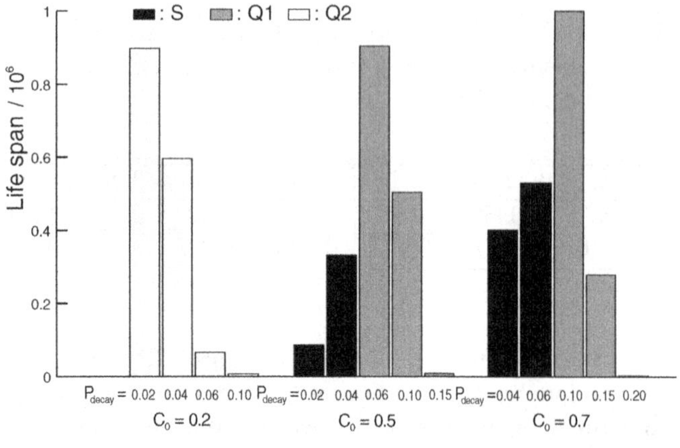

Figure 11: The life span of a hypercycle system averaged over ten trials. For all trials, the execution of CA stops at $t = 10^6$ time steps.

Our results also suggest that the fitness of a species in a hypercyclic organization depends not only on its stability and its efficiency of reproduction, but also on the interactions of high-level systems; furthermore, an increase in the stability of high-level systems does not always result in an increase in the fitness. Although all of our results are experimental, some of them may be theoretically derived, for example, by solving the Ginzburg-Landau equation (Gabbay, Ott, & Guzdar 1998).

Conclusions

We have analytically and experimentally described the behavior of hypercycle spirals in the two-dimensional CA model. The following summarizes our main results:

- A spiral can be approximated by an Archimedean spiral and the center, width, and phase of the spiral change according to Brownian motion.
- From the phase synchronization hypothesis, there is a barrier that does not allow two spirals to come close to each other. Pair decay occurs at the inner part of a dented area of the barrier with a high probability.
- Computational experiments indicate that adjacent species violation (ASV) is a necessary condition for creating new spirals.
- Parameter space (c_0, P_{decay}) consists of three regions. A hypercycle system can live long if P_{decay} is a little larger than that on the boundary between the S and Q regions.

From the above results, the survivability of a hypercycle system can be explained based on the birth and death process of spirals. In order for the system to live long, the spirals in the system should be somewhat unstable, since new spirals cannot emerge when existing spirals are too stable. The stability of spirals can be controlled by the stability (P_{decay}) of molecular species. If the amount of components used for building up molecules (c_0) increases, it is necessary that the molecules be slightly more unstable for the hypercycle system to live long.

Acknowledgements

This work was supported by the Telecommunications Advancement Organization of Japan.

References

Altmeyer, S.; Wilke, C.; and Martinetz, T. 1998. How fast do structures emerge in hypercycle-systems? In *GWAL*.

Boerlijst, M. C., and Hogeweg, P. 1991. Spiral wave structure in pre-biotic evolution: Hypercycles stable against parasites. *Physica D* 48:17–28.

Boerlijst, M. C., and Hogeweg, P. 1992. Self-structuring and selection: Spiral waves as a substrate for prebiotic evolution. In *Artificial Life II*, 255–276.

Cronhjort, M., and Blomberg, C. 1996. Chasing: A mechanism for resistance against parasites in self-replicating systems. In *Artificial Life IV*, 413–417.

Eigen, M., and Schuster, P. 1979. *The Hypercycle, A Principle of Natural Selforganization.* Berlin: Springer-Verlag.

Eigen, M. 1971. Self-organization of matter and the evolution of biological macro-molecules. *Naturwissenschaften* 58:465–523.

Gabbay, M.; Ott, E.; and Guzdar, P. N. 1998. Reconnection of vortex filaments in the complex Ginzburg-Landau equation. *Physical Review E* 58:2576–2579.

Gebinoga, M. 1995. Hypercycles in biological systems. In *Endocytobiology VI*, 263–276.

Hofbauer, J., and Sigmund, K. 1988. *The Theory of Evolution and Dynamical Systems.* Cambridge Univ. Press.

Vespalcova, Z.; Holden, A. V.; and Brindley, J. 1995. The effect of inhibitory connection in a hypercycle: a study of the spatio-temporal evolution. *Physics Letters A* 197:147–156.

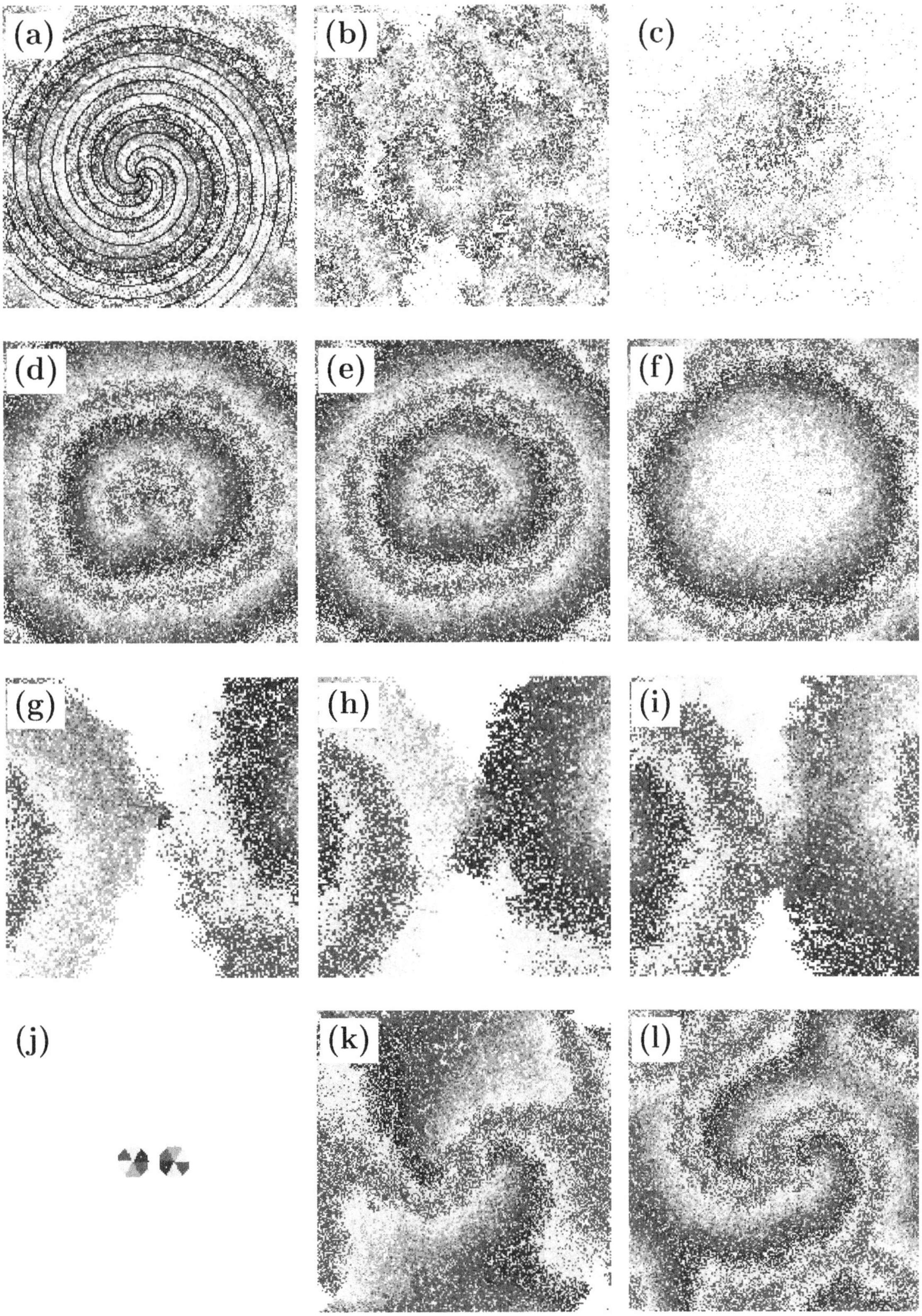

Figure 12: Spiral patterns on a 200 × 200 CA lattice. (a) Identification by an Archimedean spiral. $(c_0, P_{\text{decay}}) = (1, 0.12)$. (b) Empty areas existing between spirals in the Q1 region. $(c_0, P_{\text{decay}}) = (0.7, 0.1)$. (c) Spirals in the Q2 region surrounded by empty cells. $(c_0, P_{\text{decay}}) = (0.2, 0.04)$. (d)–(f) Pair decays in progress. $t = 2070, 2450, 2650$. (g)–(i) Emergence of new spirals between two spirals. $t = 390, 420, 450$. (j)–(l) Two spirals repelling each other. $t = 0, 450, 850$.

Do Artificial Ants March in Step? Ordered Asynchronous Processes and Modularity in Biological Systems

David Cornforth, **David G. Green**, **David Newth** & **Michael Kirley**
School of Environmental and Information Sciences
Charles Sturt University, Albury, Australia
Email: {dcornforth|dgreen|dnewth|mkirley}@csu.edu.au

Abstract

Processes that occur in many biological systems are not synchronous, but are governed by asynchronous updating. Although some previous models of multi agent systems have incorporated asynchronous updating in an informal or implicit way, the importance of asynchronous behaviour has been largely overlooked. However, the update scheme chosen is very important in determining the overall system behaviour. We illustrate this point using several updating schemes in simple models. The implication is that care should be given to selecting an update scheme that is appropriate for the modelling application. We also observe that certain ordered asynchronous processes play a role in emergent modularity, an important process in the evolution of complexity in living systems.

Introduction

Most biological systems are composed of many interacting elements. The way in which elements update their internal states plays an important role in many processes. Most published models of such systems update internal states in parallel and synchronously. However, we show that state updating is asynchronous in biological systems, and may be described as either Random Asynchronous (RAS) or Ordered Asynchronous (OAS). The recognition of such processes has far reaching implications for the way in which we model biological systems. We also show that OAS processes have a role in emergent modularity. This in turn may contribute to the formation of dynamical hierarchies in biological systems. Understanding such mechanisms is an open problem in Artificial Life (Bedau *et al.* 2000).

Models of multi agent systems have rarely focused on the temporal pattern of interactions within the system. In particular, updating is usually assumed to occur synchronously and in parallel. That is, all agents in the system are assumed to update their state in a single pass, and before any of the new states are allowed to influence other agents. This assumes the existence of a "global clock" that dictates the pace of all local processes in the system. However, several authors (Thomas 1979; Kanada 1994; Di Paolo 2000) (amongst others) have pointed out that a global clock is not indicative of any observed natural phenomenon. This raises the question of how state updating should be handled in models.

We examine some different updating schemes in simple models, and shows that the scheme chosen has a very strong effect on the type of global behaviour observed. We conclude that the choice of updating scheme is an important part of the specification of the model, and should reflect the purpose to which the model will be used.

Finally, we observe that models using OAS updating can be used to demonstrate the emergence of modularity. Modularity is of increasing interest, since it is becoming apparent that biological systems employ modularity to cope with the exponential increase in complexity as these systems grow in size (Green *et al.* 2001).

Asynchronous Processes in Biological Systems

In many living systems, there is abundant evidence that agents update their state asynchronously. The examples below also show that these processes are ordered, and demonstrate self-synchronisation as a mechanism that forms and perpetuates modules.

Ants participating in a colony exhibit complex collective activity. Ants do not work constantly, but spend between 55% and 72% of their time resting, depending on species (Cole 1991; Delgardo & Sole 1999; Franks *et al.* 1990). Individual ants separated from the colony display active and resting periods with an aperiodic pattern. However, a whole colony displays a synchronised periodic pattern of active and resting behaviour, with period of between 15 and 30 minutes.

Individual ants update their activity state autonomously, but are able to adjust the update frequency in response to interactions with other ants. Ants living in a colony were observed to wake each other (Franks *et al.* 1990). From these observations, it appears that global synchronous behaviour in the colony arises from local asynchronous behaviour. This behaviour has been recognised in models, for example, Goss and Deneubourg (1988).

The behaviour of interconnected neurons in the brain leads to global patterns of behaviour across the whole brain. This activity does not exhibit stationary patterns, but periodic, quasi-periodic and chaotic patterns (Freeman 1992). There is no known mechanism such as a global clock in the brain, yet neurons exhibit synchronised behaviour for a time, suggesting a mechanism of asynchronous updating as in the previous example.

Bushfires are propagated when fuel is heated until it ignites. The rate of heating depends on the fire intensity, the distance from the flames, the fuel moisture, and so on. When a plant ignites, its neighbours ignite asynchronously, with the order determined by heat accumulation.

The competition of different species within a forest system, coupled with catastrophe such a forest fire, leads to a complex system of interactions that have been studied as a means of developing better management strategies, among other reasons. Transitions between different community classes (e.g. rainforest, open sclerophyll woodland) require vastly different times to complete (Noble & Slatyer 1980), so are examples of asynchronous updating.

Asynchronous Processes in Models

The examples in the previous section suggest that asynchronous updating is the default, rather than the exception, in natural multi agent systems. This raises the question of what update method should be chosen in models of such systems. This will depend on the purpose of the model. Asynchronous models may provide more realistic representations of natural systems than synchronous models, and may provide a deeper understanding of system behaviour.

The majority of published models use synchronous updating. This may be because little is known about asynchronous updating, and how it may change the behaviour of the model. Asynchronous updating has been incorporated in cellular models of bushfire, for example, by using a list of cells due to ignite (Kourtz & O'Regan 1971), or by adding extra states (Green 1983). The asynchronous nature of forest succession has led to the adoption of the semi-Markov model, (Howard 1971). There have also been attempts to investigate the effects of random asynchronous (RAS) processes in more abstract models. Not surprisingly, RAS updating changes the characteristics of a system. For example, Harvey and Bossomaier (1997) have pointed out that stochastic updating in RBNs results in the expression of point attractors, but no cyclic attractors, although they introduce the notion of loose cyclic attractors. Kanada (1994) has shown that some one-dimensional CA models, that generate non-chaotic patterns when updated synchronously, generate edge of chaos patterns when randomised. Other researchers have claimed that RAS models can exhibit all the behaviour normally associated with synchronous models. For example, Orponen (1997) has demonstrated that any synchronously updated network of threshold logic units can be simulated by a network that has no constraints on the order of updates. However, this work depends on a carefully crafted network connectivity that is unlikely to be observed in natural systems.

Cellular Automata Models of Asynchronous Processes

The relative merits of different updating schemes are not well understood. An important research question is to determine their characteristics and their suitability for representing various kinds of multi agent systems. As an initial survey, we have implemented CA models using five distinct updating schemes. Source code is available from http://life.csu.edu.au/~dcornfor/masys.html.

The *Clock* scheme (Thomas 1979; Low & Lapsley 1999) assigns a timer to each cell. The period of each timer is set at random, as is the initial phase of the timer. The model is evolved by incrementing the values of all timers at each time step, then checking the values. Those timers that have exceeded the value of their period variable are updated in order, with new states being implemented immediately. After a cell has been updated, its timer is set to zero.

In the *Cyclic* scheme, a node is chosen at each time step according to a fixed update order. This order is decided at random during initialisation of the model. This follows Kanada (1994).

In the *Random Independent* scheme (Harvey & Bossomaier 1997), one cell is randomly selected for update at each time step. Subsequent selections are independent of each other.

The *Random Order* scheme (Harvey & Bossomaier 1997), makes a list of all cells at each time step, and sorts them into a random order. It then uses this list to decide which cell to update. In this variant, each cell is updated once only for every time step, but the order of updating is random.

The *Synchronous* scheme is included for comparison. It has been described in many papers, and its properties are well-known (Wolfram 1984). At each time step, the state of each cell is calculated, but held in a temporary store until all states have been calculated. Then the cells are all updated to their new state synchronously.

These five schemes were implemented as a one dimensional CA having 250 cells and 2 states, with each cell connected to its two neighbours and itself. Further details are provided in Cornforth *et al.*, (2001). For each rule, the five models were initialised to random states. Time space diagrams were obtained, each one representing the evolution of the model from initialisation for the first 500 time steps.

A few of the more interesting results from our preliminary studies are shown below. Figs. 1 and 2 show the evolution of the CA models for rule 38 and 146. These rules were chosen for their examples of the possible divergence between the behaviour of different schemes.

For both rules, the random independent scheme and the random order scheme show similar behaviour, which appears to be complex. However, after multiple tests using many rules, both of these schemes always converged to a point attractor. This is to be expected from the results of Harvey and Bossomaier (1997). However, the results shown here suggest that the transients can be very long.

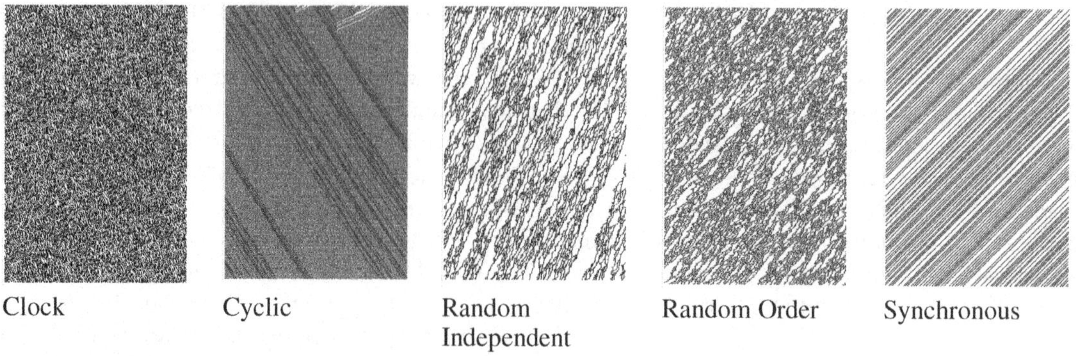

Figure 1: Time state diagrams for Cellular Automata models of different update processes for rule 38.

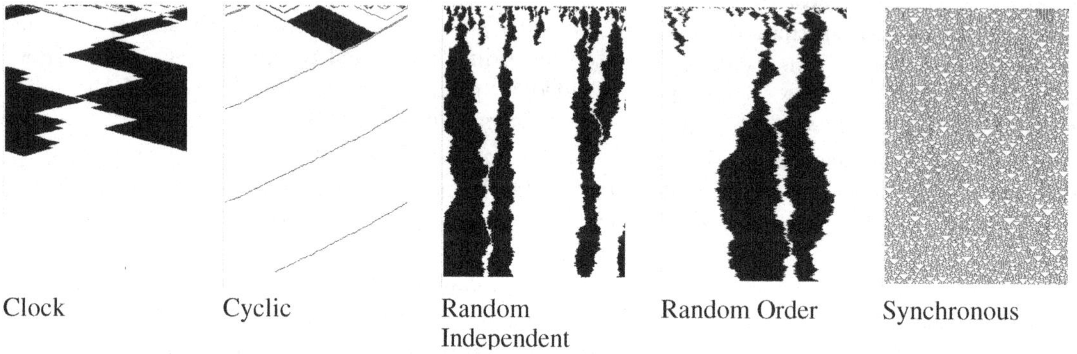

Figure 2: Time state diagrams for Cellular Automata models of different update processes for rule 146.

The *synchronous* scheme shows cyclic behaviour for rule 38, and chaotic behaviour for rule 146. This is to be expected, as its properties are already well known.

The cyclic scheme converges to a cyclic attractor. After multiple tests using different rules, the cyclic scheme always evolved to a cyclic or point attractor. This scheme never showed any evidence of chaotic behaviour.

The *clock* scheme seems to show the widest range of behaviour. For example, in Fig. 1, it shows evidence of chaotic behaviour when the synchronous scheme shows cyclic behaviour. In Fig. 2, it shows complex behaviour converging to a point attractor (all cells white), while the synchronous scheme shows complex behaviour.

These preliminary results suggest that the properties of such models are changed by the particular update scheme chosen. Any researcher attempting to build a model of a multi agent system should question the type of updating used, and ensure that an appropriate scheme is chosen for the system being studied and the uses to which the model will be put.

A Cellular Automata Model of Self Synchrony

We now extend the *clocked* update scheme to show how self-synchrony, observed in ant colonies and neural tissue, may be easily modeled. Our model is similar to the Kuramotos model of self-synchronising oscillators (Strogatz 2000), but each cell is connected only to its two adjacent neighbours.

All experiments were performed with a one dimensional CA having 250 cells and 2 states. The model was run using a variety of rules, and the network was completely homogenous. States, clock periods and phases were all initialised by drawing from a uniform distribution. At each time step, the frequency ω of each oscillator is updated according to the phase θ of its neighbours, using a gain term β:

$$\omega_{i(t+1)} = \omega_{i(t)} + \beta(\theta_{i+1(t)} - \theta_{i(t)}) + \beta(\theta_{i-1(t)} - \theta_{i(t)}) \quad (1)$$

Results are shown in Fig. 3. In the early stages of the evolution of the model (a), cells states are randomly distributed, and state transitions occur independently of each other. However, further evolution of the model (b to d) reveals the formation of clusters or modules of cells that update their states together. Modules appear as vertical sections of cells displaying a similar pattern. The cells in a module have achieved synchronisations within the module. This synchronisation persists for some time, and then the modules break apart and re-form. This may be helpful in explaining the presence of patches of burning forest during bushfires, synchronous behaviour

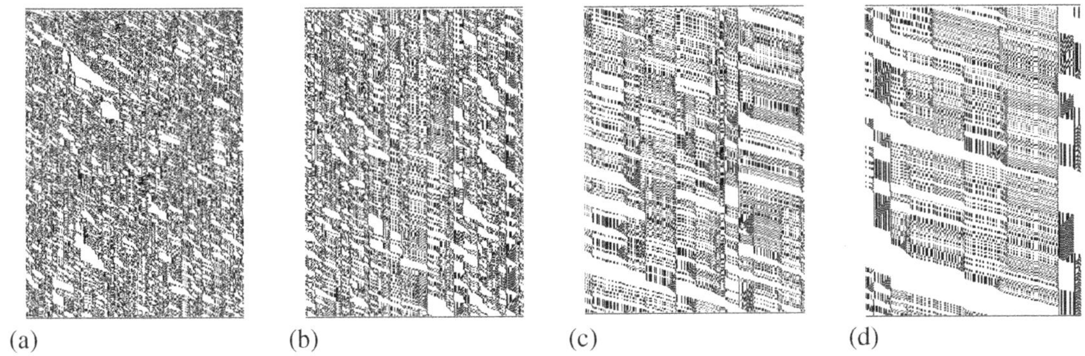

Figure 3: Time space diagrams showing four stages of the self-syncronising model. Initialisation is shown in (a), the next stage is shown in (b) and so on. Modules appear a vertical regions separated by vertical lines.

in ant colonies, and the ability of neural tissue to form transient resonant modules.

Discussion

A consideration of some biological systems reveals that state updating in such systems is usually asynchronous. This implies that anyone building models of such systems should at least consider using asynchronous updating.

A review of the literature reveals that different updating schemes do exist, including random and ordered asynchronous updating.

Implementing these schemes in a simple Cellular Automata model show that different schemes produce different global behaviour. This implies that anyone building models should be aware of these differences, and choose an updating scheme that is appropriate to the model being constructed, and its purpose.

A modification of one of these schemes shows how easy it is to model self-synchronisation once asynchronous updating is used.

This model demonstrates a possible mechanism for the emergence of modularity in complex systems. The implications of this include a possible explanation of the origin of some types of modularity in living systems.

References

Bedau, M. A.; McCaskill, J. S.; Packard, N. H.; Rasmussen, S.; Adami, C.; Green, D. G.; Ikegami, T.; Kaneko, K.; and Ray, T. S. 2000. Open problems in artificial life. *Artificial Life* 6:363–376.

Cole, B. 1991. Short-term activity cycles in ants: Generation of periodicity by worker interaction. *American Naturalist* 137:244–259.

Cornforth, D.; Green, D.; Newth, D.; and Kirley, M. 2001. Ordered asynchronous processes in natural and artificial systems. In *Proceeding of the Fifth Australia-Japan Joint Workshop on Intelligent and Evolutionary Systems*, 105–112. Dunedin, New Zealand: The University of Otago.

Delgardo, J., and Sole, R. 1999. Self-synchronisation and task fulfillment in ant colonies. Forthcoming.

Di Paolo, E. A. 2000. Searching for rhythms in asynchronous random boolean networks. In Bedau, M. A.; McCaskill, J. S.; Packard, N. H.; and Rasmussen, S., eds., *Alife VII: Proceedings of the Seventh International Conference*. Cambridge, Mass.: MIT Press.

Franks; Bryant; Griffiths; and Hemerik. 1990. ynchronisation of the behaviour within nests of the ant *Leptothorax Acervorum (Fabricus)* — I. discovering the phenomenon and its relation to the level of starvation. *Bulletin of Mathematical Biology* 52(5):597–612.

Freeman, W. 1992. Tutorial on neurobiology: from single neurons to brain chaos. *International Journal of Bifurcation and Chaos* 2(3):451–482.

Goss, S., and Deneubourg, J. 1988. Autocatalysis as a source of synchronized rhythmical activity in social insects. *Insectes Soc.* 35:310–315.

Green, D.; Newth, D.; Cornforth, D.; and Kirley, M. 2001. On evolutionary processes in natural and artificial systems. In *Proceeding of the Fifth Australia-Japan Joint Workshop on Intelligent and Evolutionary Systems*, 1–10. Dunedin, New Zealand: The University of Otago.

Green, D. 1983. Simulated fire spread in discrete fuels. *Ecological Modelling* 20:21–32.

Harvey, I., and Bossomaier, T. 1997. Time out of joint: Attractors in asynchronous random boolean networks. In Husbands, P., and Harvey, I., eds., *Proceedings of the Fourth European Conference on Artificial Life (ECAL97)*, 67–75. MIT Press.

Howard, A. 1971. *Dynamic Probabilistic Systems, Volume II: Semi-Markov and Decision Processes.* John Wiley and Sons.

Kanada, Y. 1994. The effects of randomness in asynchronous 1D cellular automata. In *proceedings of ALIFE IV.*

Kourtz, P., and O'Regan, W. 1971. A model for a small forest fire to simulate burned and burning areas for use in a detection model. *Forest Science* 17(2).

Low, S., and Lapsley, D. 1999. Optimization flow control, i: Basic algorithm and convergence. *IEEE/ACM Transactions on Networking.*

Noble, I. R., and Slatyer, R. O. 1980. The use of vital attributes to predict successional changes in plant communities subject to recurrent disturbances. *Vegetatio* 43:5–21.

Orponen, P. 1997. Computing with truly asynchronous threshold logic networks. *Theoretical Computer Science* 174(1-2):123–136.

Strogatz, S. 2000. From Kuramoto to Crawford: exploring the onset of synchronization in populations of coupled oscillators. *Physica D* 143(1-4):1–20.

Thomas, R., ed. 1979. *Kinetic Logic: A Boolean Approach to the Analysis of Complex Regulatory Systems,* volume 29 of *Lecture Notes in Biomathematics.* Springer Verlag.

Wolfram, S. 1984. Cellular automata as models of complexity. *Nature* 311:419.

Importance of Evolved Structure for Emerging Self-organization in a Complex Competitive Situation

Satoshi Kurihara, **Kensuke Fukuda**, **Toshio Hirotsu**, **Osamu Akashi**,
Shinya Sato, and **Toshiharu Sugawara**
NTT Network Innovation Labs.
3-9-11, Midori-cho, Musashino-shi, Tokyo 180-8585 JAPAN
kurihara@t.onlab.ntt.co.jp

Abstract

In this paper, we analyze a simple adaptive model of competition called the "Minority Game" that is used in analyzing the competition phenomena in markets. The Minority Game consists of many simple autonomous agents, and self-organization occurs as a result of simple behavioral rules. Up to now, the dynamics of this game has been studied from various angles, but so far the focus has been on the macroscopic behavior of all the agents as a whole. We are interested in the mechanisms involved in collaborative behavior among multi-agents, so we focused our attention on the behavior of individual agents. In this paper, we suggest that core elements responsible for self-organization to occur are:

1. rules of the game that potentially include a mechanism for a form of self-organization,
2. rules that place a good constraint on each agent's behavior, and
3. the existence of some rule that lead to indirect interaction; a process called "stigmergy".

Introduction

The Minority Game, which is a simulation program for analyzing models of adaptive competition that consist of many autonomous elements like those in the market (Cavagna 1998; Challet & Zhang 1997; Zhang 1998; Challet *et al.* 2001). First, we summarize the rules of the Minority Game. There are N agents, each of which independently chooses between two alternatives ("*group 0*" or "*group 1*".) In one step of the game, all of the agents choose one alternative or the other, and the agents that, as a result, belong to the minority group are awarded a point as a winner (the best case is a split of 100:101, and the worst case is a split of 1:200). The selections by each agent are based on the strategy tables that the agent holds. A strategy table consists of a set of histories that records the past m winning group choices, and a corresponding set of choices which indicates which decision to make for each history (see table 1). The strategy table contains 2^m entries, each of which consists of a {history, next decision} pair. Each agent can randomly select s strategy tables from a pool of strategy tables at the beginning of the game (all agents have the same number of strategy tables.) Each agent uses the s strategy tables in the following way. For the first step, a strategy table is randomly selected, and 1 point is given as a profit to the strategy table if one time step of the game is won or 1 point is deducted if the game is lost. In the second and subsequent time steps, the strategy table that has the highest number of points is always selected. Fig. 1 shows the standard deviation for the number of agents that chose group 0, reported in the previous studies. The game was played for the number of time steps described below for the various numbers of strategy tables possessed by the agents, $s = 2 \dots 64$ and various history depths in the strategy table, $m = 1 \dots 16$. For each parameter pair, $\{s, m\}$, the game was played for 10,000 time steps in one trial, and each trial was done in sets of 10. In this graph, the horizontal line represents the standard deviations when all the agents made their choices randomly, and the actual standard deviations were lower than for the random cases, mainly when m was 3, 4 or 5. This means that a winning group ratio that was intentionally near 100:101 arose. However, their only information is the history of past winning groups. What is characteristic is that actually a history depth of 3 cases produced good behavior, whereas a history depth of 10 rounds produces results that were the same as random behavior.

← m →			Next decision ↓
0	0	0	0
0	0	1	1
0	1	0	1
0	1	1	0
1	0	0	0
1	0	1	1
1	1	0	0
1	1	1	1

Table 1: Strategy table

Potential advantage among agents

We investigated how many times each agent could win in several situations, and Fig. 2 shows the rankings of the 201 agents based on their average scores.

Where each agent could randomly select "*group 0*" or "*group 1*", all of the agents were only able to get approximately 4750 points. In contrast, when the standard deviation was small ($m = 3, 4, 5$), the mean score was high and, although some differences can be seen in the scores, all the agents were able to achieve stable scores. As m increased, either a large number of wins or a large number of losses occurred for a very small number of agents, but

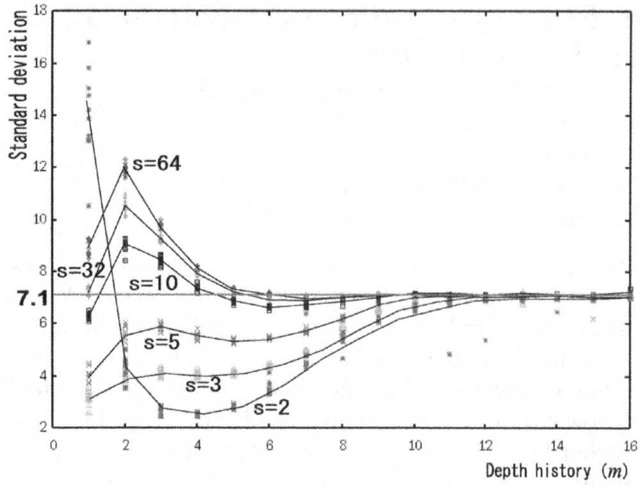

Figure 1: Standard deviation for the number of agents that selected "*group 0*"

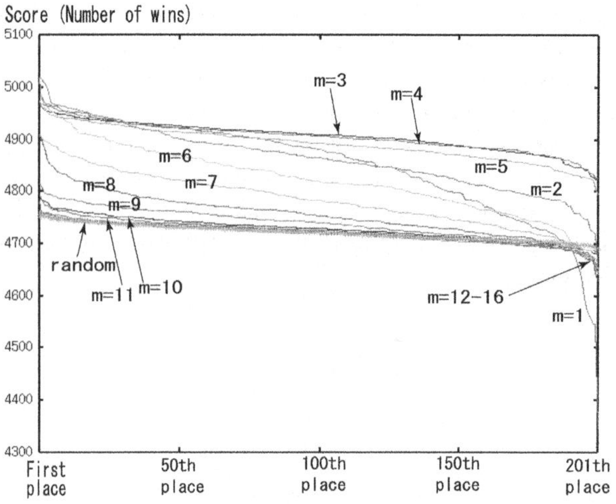

Figure 2: Agent Advantages and Disadvantages ($s = 2$)

at the same time the mean score decreased, and when m was greater than 12, the trend was toward the same level as seen in the random selection case. Why, in a situation like $m = 3, 4$, or 5, could almost all agents get higher points than for $m = 12$ or higher and the random selection case? In an attempt to explain this, we set up the following hypothesis:

[Assumption] Situations like $m = 3, 4$, or 5 can initially produce good strategy tables, where self-organization can easily occur.

[Reason] Now, let's think about the Minority Game using five agents ($m = 3$) where each agent has two strategy tables ($s = 2$), as shown in table 2

Then, for example, if the winning group history is "010", each agent must select one of two strategy tables based on their obtained points, where the strategy of each table of entry "010" is shown as Entries-A in table 3. If the winner group history is "110", the above selected strategies will change as shown in Entries-B.

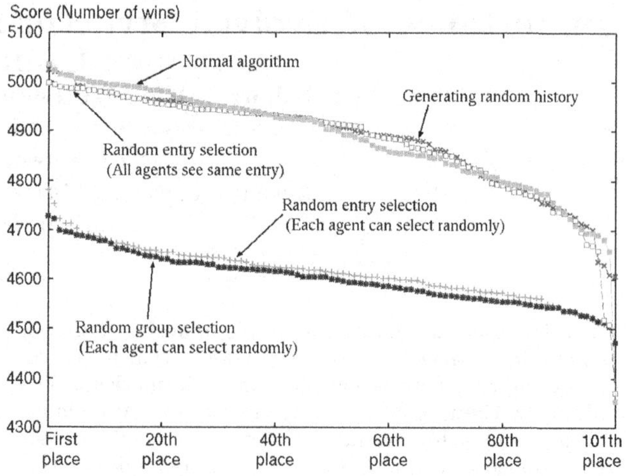

Figure 3: Is memory necessary?

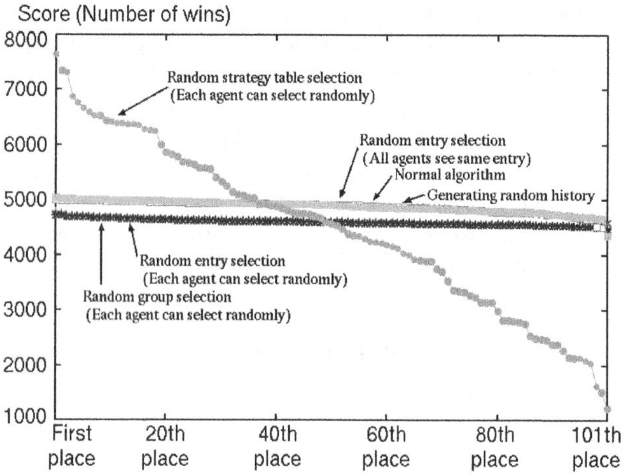

Figure 4: How to select the strategy tables

An important point is that, in this situation, even if each agent selects table 1 or table 2, four agents (Agent 1, Agent 2, Agent 3, and Agent 4) select "group 0", and only one agent (Agent 5) selects "group 1". Therefore, the ratio of minority to majority becomes "group 0" : "group 1"=4:1. Also, in the situation where the winning group history is "111", two agents (Agent 1 and Agent 3) can always win (marked Entries-C).

Although the above two cases are examples of radical combinations, in a situation like $m = 3$ or 4, the possibility of including Entries-B will be low, whereas in a situation like $m = 12$ or higher, this possibility will be very high.

The reason for this is as follows. There are only five possible combinations type of Entries-B but ten of Entries-C. Further, when $m = 3$, there are only eight en-

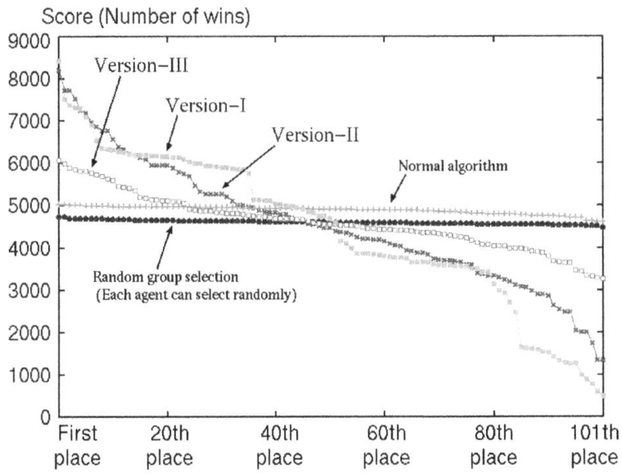

Figure 5: Existence of Stigmergy

tries in each strategy table, but when $m = 12$, there are 4096, so, when $m = 3$, the probability of a situation like Entries-B being included is low, but when $m = 12$, a situation like Entries-B will certainly be included. Therefore, considering all the combinations of the strategy table, the combination of "group 0" : "group 1" = 2:3 or 3:2 is larger than that of "group 0" : "group 1" = 0:5 or 5:0 or "group 0":"group 1" = 1:4 or 4:1, therefore, when $m = 3$ or 4, the probability of situations like Situation-B being included is quite low and in each game, the ratio of "group 0":"group 1" is nearly always 2:3 or 3:2. Consequently, all agents can get high points.

Testing

If self-organization occurs by initial combinations of the strategy tables, the winner group history may not be an important element of the Minority Game. In other words, self-organization may be able to occur without each agent deciding its selection using the winning group history.

To test this hypothesis, we examined the following situations: In the normal algorithm, if the current winner group history is "010", each agent sees the entries of "010" of their holding strategy tables, and selects one of these depending on their points.

At this stage, we raise the following questions:

1. If each agent is allowed to select the entry of strategy tables randomly, can self-organization occur?

2. If only one agent-A is allowed to select the entry using its own rules based on the winning group history and the other agents use the same entry as agent-A, can self-organization occur? The game's rules are where agents can decide which entry to use on their own, not by the winning group history.

Agent 1			
Strat. 1		Strat. 2	
Hist		Hist	
000	1	000	0
001	0	001	1
010	1	010	0
011	1	011	1
100	1	100	1
101	0	101	0
110	0	110	0
111	1	111	1

Agent 2			
Strat. 1		Strat. 2	
Hist		Hist	
000	1	000	0
001	0	001	0
010	1	010	1
011	0	011	1
100	1	100	1
101	1	101	1
110	0	110	0
111	0	111	0

Agent 3			
Strat. 1		Strat. 2	
Hist		Hist	
000	1	000	0
001	1	001	0
010	0	010	1
011	1	011	1
100	0	100	1
101	1	101	0
110	0	110	0
111	1	111	1

Agent 4			
Strat. 1		Strat. 2	
Hist		Hist	
000	1	000	1
001	0	001	0
010	0	010	1
011	1	011	0
100	1	100	0
101	0	101	0
110	0	110	0
111	0	111	0

Agent 5			
Strat. 1		Strat. 2	
Hist		Hist	
000	0	000	1
001	0	001	0
010	1	010	1
011	0	011	1
100	1	100	0
101	0	101	0
110	0	110	0
111	0	111	0

Table 2: Strategy tables for example $m = 5, s = 2$ game

3. If we intentionally generate a random winner group history, can self-organization occur?

If self-organization can be formed in the above situations, our hypothesis that the memory of the winner group history is ineffective may be correct.

Fig. 3 has the memory results: the same self-organization as in the normal algorithm could occur in situations (2) and (3). Even when we established a random winner group history, and none of the agents used the entry of the strategy tables that depended on the memory of history, they could organize themselves well. This means that the memory of the winner group history may not be important in self-organization. However, when each agent could select the entry of strategy tables randomly, their behaviors were the same as for the random selection version. Therefore, an important point concerning the strategy tables is that, in the normal algorithm, the winner group history applies a constraint

Entries-A			Entries-B			Entries-C		
Agt	S1	S2	Agt	S1	S2	Agt	S1	S2
1	1	0	1	0	0	1	1	1
2	1	1	2	0	0	2	0	0
3	0	1	3	0	0	3	1	1
4	0	1	4	0	0	4	0	0
5	1	1	5	1	1	5	0	0

Table 3: Strategy outcomes for various winning histories: Entries-A="010", Entries-B="110" and Entries-C="111".

that has evolved from the agents' using the strategy tables. In other words, we can use any kind of rule that enables us to apply a constraint on using strategy tables like situation (2). Applying a good constraint on the agents means the same as decreasing their freedom, and through this constraint, organization must occur. In a previous work (Kurihara, Onai, & Sugawara 1998), we also discussed how to achieve self-organization by using other frameworks, and came to the same conclusion we have in this study.

Indirect interaction

If self-organization is formed only by the mechanism based on our hypothesis, then it raises the following question: Even if each agent can select the strategy tables randomly, will the game results be the same as with the normal algorithm? Fig. 4 has the results for how the strategy tables are selected. If each agent could select the strategy tables randomly, there would be a very big gap between the winner and loser and self-organization would not occur. This means that, in the Minority Game, indirect interaction between agents is also an important element of organization forming. The reason is as follows. The process whereby each agent selects strategy tables by points means that they decide their behavior based on the results of each step, and their decision changes in the next step.

At this point, if we change the rules for selecting the strategy tables, will self-organization still occur? Fig. 5 plots the results of doing this. We implemented the following rules.

(Version-I) Each agent selects one of two strategy tables in turn. The interval of the exchange is randomly set up.

(Version-II) If it wins, 1 point is add to the selected strategy table, but if it loses, 2 points are subtracted.

(Version-III) If the agent loses one game, the strategy table is changed even if the table produced several wins.

Unfortunately, self-organization did not occur using any of these versions. The way the strategy table is selected must bear a close relationship with the initial combinations of the strategy tables of each agent, so a detail investigation will be necessary to determine what is an essential mechanism responsible for selecting strategy tables, and this is for future work.

Can we easily control agents?

In terms of the strategy tables, if we assume that the variance in the correlations within agents and the correlations between agents has a major effect on good scores, then we can expect that a change in the behavior of the agents will result from intentionally increasing the variance. Therefore, we selected one appropriate agent from among the 201 agents, and 19 agents were made to positively (100%) correlate with that agent. This means that they possessed exactly the same set of strategy tables. In addition, 20 agents were made to have reverse (−100%) correlation with that agent. This means that their behavior was always the opposite, and the game was played with $m = 3$, for which good scores were obtained, and with $m = 12$, for which the results were the same as for random choices. The results for these two cases are compared in Figs. 6 and 7.

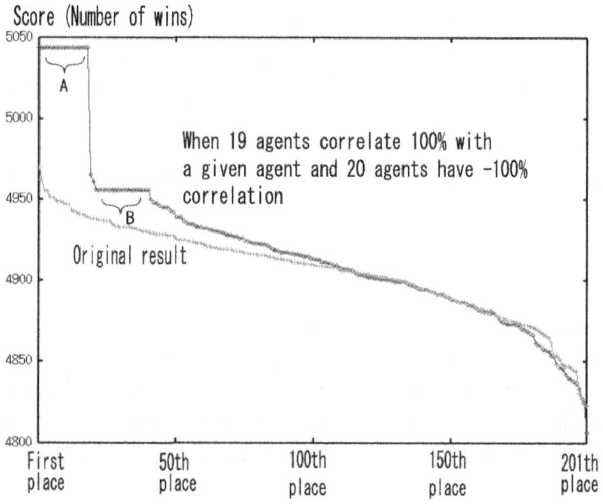

Figure 6: For $m = 3$

This comparison yields profoundly interesting results. Initially, we expected that one of the two groups of 20 agents (either the 100% group or the −100% correlation group) would get the highest scores and the other group would get the lowest scores. Contrary to our expectations, both groups were able to attain high scores. Moreover, the overall average scores for the agents as a whole improved considerably, for both cases ($m = 3$ and $m = 12$), as a result of intentionally setting the behavior of the 40 agents, and the scores of the other agents that were not modified also improved above the agent ranked in 100th place. In addition, the scores of the agents in the vicinity of the lowest score also increased.

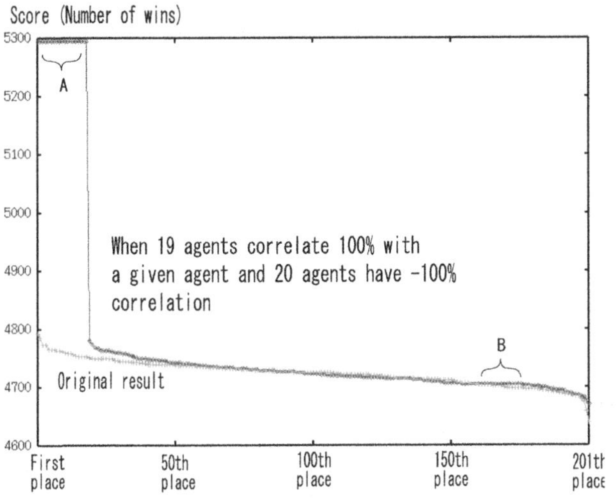

Figure 7: For $m = 12$

These results strongly suggest that agents that possess strategy tables that have extremes of positive and reverse correlations are a major factor in improving the efficiency of the collective behavior of the agents as a whole, and we are currently in the midst of evaluating various changes in the settings.

Conclusion

In this paper, we analyzed a simple adaptive competition model called "the Minority Game," which is used in the analysis of competition phenomena in markets. The Minority Game consists of many simple autonomous agents, and self-organization occurs through simple behavioral rules.

As we were interested in the mechanisms for collaborative behavior in multi-agent systems, we focused our attention on the behavior of individual agents. We suggest that core elements for self-organization to occur are:

1. rules of this game that potentially include a mechanism for a form of self-organization,

2. rules that place a good constraint on each agent's behavior, and

3. the existence of some rule that lead to indirect interaction; a process called "stigmergy".

In terms of the rules for good constraint (2), A. Cavagna (1998) suggested basically the same as us. He said that, in the Minority Game, the memory of the winning group is irrelevant, and the important point is sharing data among agents. However, we think that it is more important to place a good constraint on agents' behaviors, and to constrain them to share some data. In the normal algorithm, this data is designed for use by the winning group history. Finally, in terms of stigmergy (3), a detailed investigation will be necessary to clarify the essential mechanism responsible for selecting strategy tables. Of course, we will continue with further analysis aimed at establishing a general algorithm that can be applied to other competition problems.

Acknowledgements

We are grateful to Keiichi Koyanagi, director of the Network Intelligence Research Laboratory, for his support during the course of this research, and to all members of the Network Information Processing Research Group for their fruitful discussions related to this work.

References

Cavagna, A. 1998. Irrelevance of memory in the minority game. *Phys. Rev. E* 59(4):R3783.

Challet, D., and Zhang, Y. 1997. Emergence of cooperation and organization in an evolutionary game. *Physica A* 246:407.

Challet, D.; Chessa, A.; Marsili, M.; and Zhang, Y. 2001. From minority games to real markets. *Quantitative Finance.*

Kurihara, S.; Onai, R.; and Sugawara, T. 1998. Self-organization based on nonlinear nonequilibrium dynamics of autonomous agents. *Artificial Life and Robotics* 2(3).

Zhang, Y. 1998. Modeling market mechanism with evolutionary games. *Europhys. News* 29–51.

Is Self-replication an Embedded Characteristic of Artificial/Living Matter?

Eleonora Bilotta, **Antonio Lafusa** and **Pietro Pantano**

Centro Interdipartimentale della Comunicazione, Universitá della Calabria
Cubo 17, 87036 Arcavacata di Rende (CS) Italy
bilotta@unical.it, alafusa@tiscalinet.it, piepa@unical.it

Abstract

This paper introduces a method through which, using genetic algorithms on two dimensional cellular automata, we obtain emergent phenomena of self-replication. Three indices of complexity, based on input entropy have been developed and used as fitness functions in the evolutionary experiments. The genetic algorithm, realized by a special design of the genome, is efficient and the research in the CA rules space has given appreciable results, both for the quantity and for the quality of the emergent phenomena. We found that each of these indices is strictly connected to the complexity of the rules and to the self-reproducers behavior contained in them. We noticed that self-reproduction is a widespread process also in artificial life simulations. Almost all the evolved rules manifest self-reproducers, as if this process were an embedded characteristic of artificial/living matter. The self-reproducers, different in shape, function and behavior, reveal an algorithmic logic in self-replication, which follows different but synchronized rhythms, evidencing variation, increasing structural complexity and some of them general constructive capacity.

Introduction

One of the most important properties of living beings is reproduction that is the capacity of organisms to create copies of themselves, through highly specialized processes of duplication or multiplication. In the biological domain, different reproduction mechanisms exist. Reproduction allows the multiplication of the number of individuals of one species, starting from examples of the same species. The reproduction of a living organism, however small or simple, involves a programme able to build a new entity, which itself contains the same programme and transmits it in its turn (Maynard Smith and Szathmáry 1995). The problem of reproduction of life-like forms into other digital media is one of the main goals and challenges of contemporary research (Bedau et al. 2000). Almost all the applications that deal with the simulation and synthesis of living systems are linked to the seminal work of John von Neumann (1966), who proposed a machine able to reproduce itself. Since then, systems in which space, time and states are discrete, called Cellular Automata (CA), have been mainly used to study self-reproduction in the realm of artificial life. The research of self-reproducing structures can be divided into four categories. The first deals with the implementation of universal constructors, based on the approach of von Neumann's self-reproducing automaton, traceable to a series of studies made in the 50's and 60's (von Neumann 1966; Codd 1968; Vitányi, 1973). Subsequently, research into a minimum system capable of non-trivial reproduction took place, thanks to a series of studies started by Langton (1984), which stimulated other similar works (Byl 1989; Sipper 1994 and 1998; Morita and Imai 1996). During the 90's, many studies provided other computing capabilities of the self-reproducers, (Perrier, Sipper and Zahnd 1996; Chou and Reggia 1998). From the 90's to today, many researchers have been investigating the self-reproducers' emergence and evolution (Lohn and Reggia 1995; Chou and Reggia 1997; Sayama 1998).

In von Neumann's endeavor, the basic idea of such works is that a self-reproduction machine could have the characteristic of computational universality, that is the ability to operate as a universal Turing machine and the ability to construct any kind of configuration in the cellular space, starting from a given description. In particular, self reproduction is a special case of universal construction. (Langton 1984). But von Neumann's analysis also shows a series of different problems involved in the self-reproduction process: the method through which self-reproduction is obtained, the reproducer's strength to mutation, the possibility of variation, heredity, the notion of complication of the system, the increasing in complexity of the system, and the essence of the concept of self-reproduction, related to the general constructive capacity of the automaton. Only recent studies have focused on understanding the complexity of the process of self-reproduction in this direction (McMullin 2000). Moreover, almost all self-reproduction systems based on CA are hand-designed, not changeable, subject to environmental perturbations and only some of them consider evolution (for example, Sayama 2000).

This paper deals with the development of a new method for obtaining self-reproduction in the artificial domain, trying to individuate some of the basic mechanisms of self-reproducer systems. We began by considering a set of fundamental questions: Is it possible that the logic of computing that von Neumann looked for, is the essence of life and that these very informational and computing capacities originate life also in the artificial domain? Is self-reproduction an innate characteristic of living matter, which can also be re-proposed in the process of artificial synthesis? To what extent does synthetic life have to be complex to show itself? A second group of problems concerns such questions as: Which are the mechanisms that lead to self-reproduction? Is it possible to identify some of the basic mechanisms of self-reproducer systems? Is it possible to think that gliders, in evolving, lead to self-reproduction? Is it possible to structure a fitness function that in some way evolves self-reproducers? Is there a relationship between complexity or levels of complexity and self-reproduction?

We used Genetic Algorithms to evolve two-dimensional CA in order to obtain self-reproducing systems. We had to limit our attention to a subset of the CA rules space, which we defined as k-totalistic rules. We assumed that self-reproducers can be found inside the complex rules of class IV (Wolfram, 1984). Within such rules, we found different types of self-reproducers. Moreover, we developed three fitness functions that roughly correspond to the three complexity indices functions, which we have used to perform different evolutionary runs. In our opinion, each of these indices is strictly connected to the complexity of the rules and to the self-reproducer's behavior contained in them. We believe that different types of self-reproducers exist that show a great variety of shapes, functions and behavior.

This work has a second paragraph that deals with a CA and GA overview. In particular, the design of the k-totalistic rule, used for representing the genome and to start the evolutionary process for two-dimensional CA, is described. The indices of complexity are given in the third paragraph. Three experiments, each one with a different fitness function and thus with a different index of complexity, are reported in the fourth paragraph, together with the results and some examples of the self-reproducers obtained. In the fifth paragraph, some self-reproducers are described, according to the shape, function and behavior which characterize them. The conclusions try to extrapolate a coherent view of these complex problems.

Cellular Automata and Genetic Algorithms overview

The environment considered is a two-dimensional CA. A CA can be thought as a tuple:

$$A = (d, S, N, f) \tag{1}$$

where d is a positive integer that indicates the CA dimension (one, two, three-dimensional or more), S a set of finite states, $k = |S|$, $N = (x_1, ..., x_n)$ a neighborhood vector of n different elements of Z^d, f a transition rule defined as:

$$f : S^n \longrightarrow S. \tag{2}$$

In our case $d = 2$, and the neighborhood identifies the cells with a local interaction radius r. So (2) to the $n = (2r+1)^2$ elements of S associates another element of S, i.e.

$$\begin{pmatrix} \cdots & \cdots & \cdots \\ \cdots & s_{ij} & \cdots \\ \cdots & \cdots & \cdots \end{pmatrix} \longrightarrow s_{ij}, \tag{3}$$

with $s_{ij} \in S \ \forall i, j$.

An exhaustive rule considers all $k^{(2r+1)^2}$ possible cases. In a previous work (Bilotta, Lafusa and Pantano, submitted), we used a GA based on input-entropy to find the complex rules of class IV (Wolfram, 1984) for one-dimensional CA. With the increase of k and r, the exhaustive rule becomes non-treatable and it is necessary to use a new simple form to be used as the genome, to start the evolutionary process. Here we define a rule (called hereafter the k-totalistic rule), considering rules that don't distinguish the position of neighbors in the surrounding area, but just consider how many cells are in a given state. Let $h_s(t)$ be the number of cells of the neighborhood that are in the state s at time t. We denote with V the set of all possible configurations of the neighborhood, whose elements can be represented by a numerical string $(h_0 h_1 ... h_{k-1})$. h_i values are not arbitrary, but they must satisfy the following constraints:

$$\begin{array}{l} h_0 + h_1 + ... + h_{k-1} = (2r+1)^2 \\ \text{and} \\ h_i \geq 0, \ for\ i = 0, 1, ..., k-1. \end{array} \tag{4}$$

By definition a totalistic rule T is an application that associates with any configuration $v \in V$ an S element:

$$T : V \longrightarrow S \tag{5}$$

In particular, the application (5) can be represented explicitly as a table that associates with the first $k-1$ totals (for the constraints (4), the last of which depends on the others) a number included between 0 and $k-1$. For example, according to (4), the string (240), for a CA $k = 4$ and $r = 1$, indicates that 2 elements of the neighborhood, composed of 9 cells, are in the state 0; 4 elements are in the state 1; 0 in the state 2, and 3 in the state 3. To the string (240) will correspond one element $q \in S$. In this example, 220 local rules of this kind will exist. In this way, the constraints (4) allow a substantial lowering of the number of possible configurations. To estimate this value, we consider the problem as being the same as that of placing $(2r+1)^2$ undistinguishable objects in k containers. From the elements of combinatorial analysis, such a number is given by:

$$N_T = \begin{pmatrix} k + (2r+1)^2 - 1 \\ (2r+1)^2 \end{pmatrix} = \frac{(k + (2r+1)^2 - 1)!}{(2r+1)^2!(k-1)!} \tag{6}$$

The table of rules, that allows the association of an element of S with any configuration of the neighborhood, can be represented as a numerical sequence, of

N_T length:

$$l = (s_1, s_2, ..., s_{N_T}) \quad (7)$$

with $s_i \in S$. To make a configuration $(h_0 h_1 ... h_{k-1}) \in V$ correspond to an s_i value of the string (7) and vice versa, we fix the convention that s_i corresponds to the ith configuration in lexicographical order. To deal with the rule algorithmically, it is convenient to characterize it as a decisional tree (Knuth 1997), whose intermediate knots are represented by the values of h_j, whose arcs stand for the alternatives and whose leaves are the s_i of the string (7). In this case, a configuration $(h_0 h_1 ... h_{k-1}) \in V$ is a path along the oriented tree. For $k = 2$, the k-totalistic rules become the well-known totalistic rules for binary CA. Using the k-totalistic rule, given by (5), the rule becomes treatable even for higher values of k and r. With the k-totalistic rules used as a genome, we adapted a relatively standard method for designing the GA (Holland 1975; Mitchell 1996). The important design parameters were: initial generation of rules casually chosen, crossover and mutation operators, generational replacement with elitism, updating of the fitness scores. We used the variance of the input-entropy as fitness function. Such a function is an index of the degree of order-chaos that we applied to the k-totalistic rules, following the method devised by Wuensche (Wuensche 1999) for exhaustive rules. For a step of simulation, the input-entropy ε^t is defined as:

$$\varepsilon^t = -\sum_{i=1}^{N_T} \left(\frac{Q_i^t}{n} \log \left(\frac{Q_i^t}{n} \right) \right) \quad (8)$$

where n is the number of cells in the grid of the CA, and Q_i is the frequency of consultation of the i^{th}local rule. From our experiments, we verified that the input-entropy on k-totalistic rules works in a similar way as it does for exhaustive rules in one-dimensional CA. In ordered systems, it goes immediately to a minimum constant value; in chaotic systems, it stays constantly on high values, with very little variations. On the contrary, in complex systems, (8) varies remarkably over time. The initial population of rules in the GA are generated using the string (7). Crossover and mutation operators generate the rules of the next generations, between the rules of the elite and successive mutations. The GA parameters will be given later.

Indices of complexity which indicate the presence of self-reproducers

We started up many evolutionary runs using as a fitness function the variance of input-entropy, given in (8. Results were, at first, not very satisfactory. In fact, designing a fitness function to evaluate self-replication is a very difficult task, since this is a highly dynamic complex process. Is it possible to evaluate complexity by means of some indices, which indicate the presence of self-reproducers? In evaluating the fitness of each rule, we observed two classes of curves for the rules, which scored high fitness values:

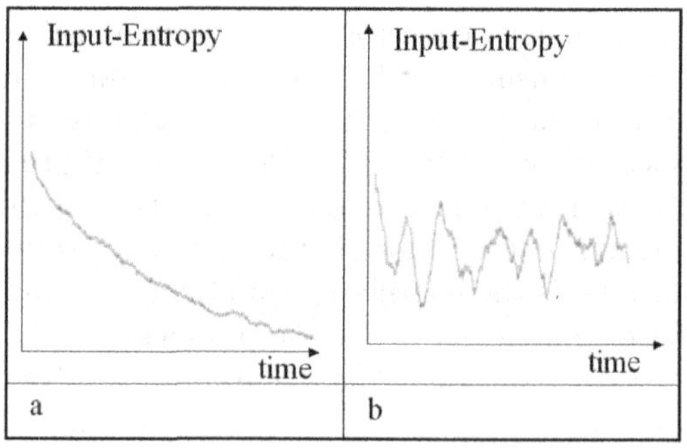

Figure 1: Input-entropy curves. 1a shows the tendency of the curve after 350 steps of simulation, for an ordered rule; 1b, another tendency of the curve after 350 steps of simulation for a rule that presents oscillatory phases.

a) an input-entropy tendency, slowly decreasing, from an initial chaotic phase to an ordered phase (see figure 1a). These systems show a transitory that extinguishes after a very long time.

b) an oscillatory tendency, which continuously alternates different phases (figure 1b).

Furthermore, we observed that for systems in which self-reproducing structures emerge, the tendency of the input-entropy is of the type 1b. To select just the systems of the type given in figure 1b, we used the strategy of directly detecting an oscillatory tendency, defining a second index of complexity to be used as a fitness function. For the values of ε^t we calculate:

I) the absolute minimum $\varepsilon_{\min}$:

$$\varepsilon_{\min} = \min \ \varepsilon^t$$

II) the absolute maximum $\varepsilon_{\max}$, calculated starting from the minimum point $t_{\min}$:

$$\varepsilon_{\max} = \max \ \varepsilon^t; \ t > t_{\min}$$

III) the absolute minimum $\varepsilon'_{\min}$, calculated starting from $t_{\max}$:

$$\varepsilon'_{\min} = \min \ \varepsilon^t; \ t > t_{\max}$$

We define the index I_1 as the sum of the width of the two peaks between the minimum and the maximum of the curves, from $t_{\min}$ to $t_{\max}$ and from $t_{\max}$ to $t'_{\min}$

$$I_1 = (\varepsilon_{\max} - \varepsilon_{\min}) + (\varepsilon_{\max} - \varepsilon'_{\min}) \quad (9)$$

The higher the input-entropy peaks are, the greater I_1 will be. We moreover observed that some rules, which present self-reproducers, obtain medium fitness values.

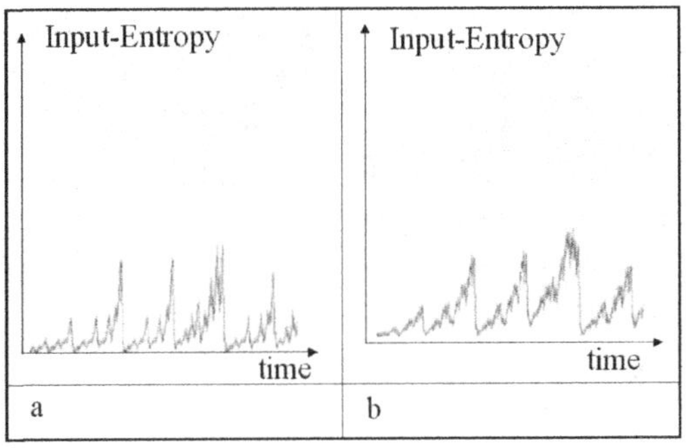

Figure 2: Different input-entropy curves. 2a shows the tendency of the input-entropy curve for a rule with high fitness after 350 steps of simulation; 2b, the tendency of the input-entropy curve for a rule with high fitness after 350 steps.

More precisely, these systems are characterized by an oscillatory tendency of the input-entropy, but with a moderate width. To modify the I_1 index, so that the oscillations around values lower than ε^t would be detected, we divided the I_1 by the values of the ε^t mean, obtaining a measure independent of the scale of the peaks. So, we define I_2 as:

$$I_2 = I_1/M \tag{10}$$

where M is the mean of ε^t values, calculated during a simulation. Figure 2 shows the typical tendency of the input-entropy, for rules with a high value of the index I_2. In the rule which produces the curve in Figure 2a, one or two self-reproducers are present. In the rule which produces the curve in Figure 2b, we found many self-reproducers.

Experiments

Three experiments, each with a different index of complexity, as above mentioned, were performed. Given a k and r, the genetic parameters that might be chosen are listed in Table 1. Crossover works on a point of the genome, randomly chosen.

P	number of rules for each generation
G	Number of generations
E	Elite
M	Mutation
w	Time window
F	Initial steps
n	Number of CA sites
T	Steps of the simulation

Table 1: Parameters of the genetic algorithm.

In calculating the fitness function, in order to eliminate the high frequencies of entropies, we do not estimate the entropy of every time step, but we take a mean of the entropies on a time window of w steps, on which we evaluate the variance. Furthermore, we determine the fitness, starting from F time steps, to allow the CA to adhere to its typical behavior (Wuensche 1999), allowing the system to exit from the initial chaotic configuration. To avoid rules with good fitness in one generation being discarded in the next, we update the fitness of a rule only if that of the next generation is higher; otherwise, we maintain the previous value.

We have also used the lambda parameter, as devised by Langton (Langton 1990), in order to ascertain if there is a relation between the lambda values and the emergence of self-reproducers in the evolved CA.

Experiment 1. Complexity index: input entropy

The parameters we chose for the CA are listed in Table 2. The experimental results for such an evolutionary run are given in Figure 3. In Figure 3a, it is possible to note the curves of the best, the mean and the elite fitness for each generation. The best fitness is low for nearly 10 generations, and then goes up suddenly.

States number	$k = 4$
Neighborhood radius	$r = 1$
Generations	$G = 20$
Populations	$P = 40$
Ignored initial steps	$F = 50$
Steps of simulation	$T = 350$
Elite (%)	$E = 50.0$
Mutation (%)	$M = 2.0$
CA sites	size $x = 40$; size $y = 40$ ($n = 160$)

Table 2: Parameters for experiment 1.

Figure 3b shows how the rules of the last generation are distributed in the lambda parameter.

In order to ascertain the differences among the evolved rule of the last generation, we determined the Hamming distance, calculated with regard to the rule which obtained the best fitness in the last generation, for this evolutionary run. This distance evaluates the differences in the genome of each rule. The maximum value which resulted is 177, realized by the 34th rule. The minimum value obtained is 4, achieved by the 2nd and 17th rules. This evolutionary run produced a number of complex rules, many of which have self-reproducers. The rule with the best fitness has many self-reproducers (see Figure 4) and clearly belongs to Wolfram's fourth class. For

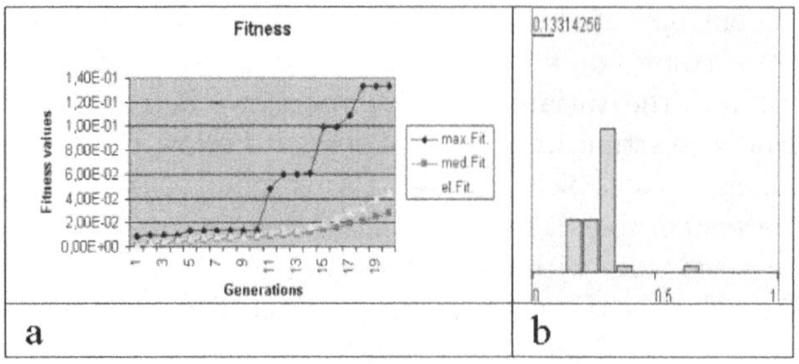

Figure 3: This figure illustrates, in a, the curves of the best, the mean and the elite fitness for each generation. b shows how the rules of the last generation are distributed in the lambda parameter in experiment 1.

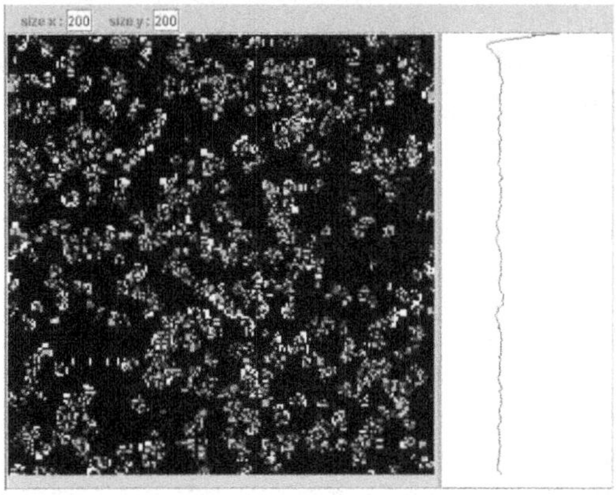

Figure 4: A pattern generated with the best fitness rule of the last generation after 200 time steps, starting from an initial casual configuration. On the right is the curve of the input-entropy. Starting from an initial very high value, it rapidly goes down, to stop, successively, on a stationary value regarding which it will have weak oscillations. Many self-reproducers can be observed.

example, the structure given in Figure 5,

$$\begin{pmatrix} 0 & 0 & 2 & 0 & 0 \\ 0 & 0 & 0 & 0 & 0 \\ 2 & 0 & 0 & 0 & 2 \\ 0 & 0 & 0 & 0 & 0 \\ 0 & 0 & 2 & 0 & 0 \end{pmatrix}$$

evolves in two copies of itself, after two time steps. It evolves further into more complex patterns, which show scaling invariance. Concisely, we can say that this run has produced a lot of complex CA rules, which are clustered in the lambda parameter with values which go from 0.15 to 0.43.

Experiment 2. Complexity index: I_1

The parameters used for the CA are the same as those of experiment 1, varying only the fitness function. The

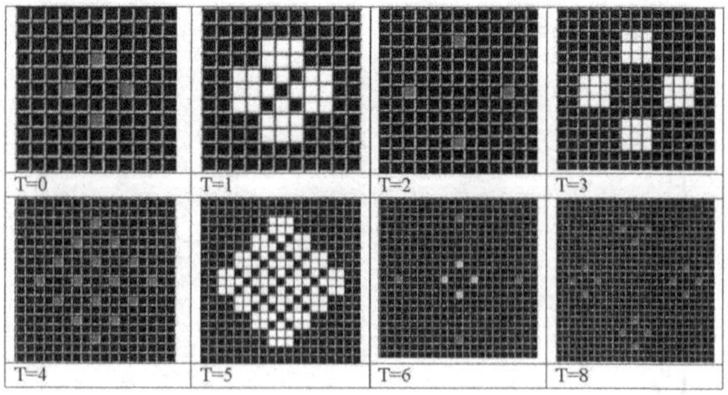

Figure 5: Process of self-reproduction which manifests scaling invariance.

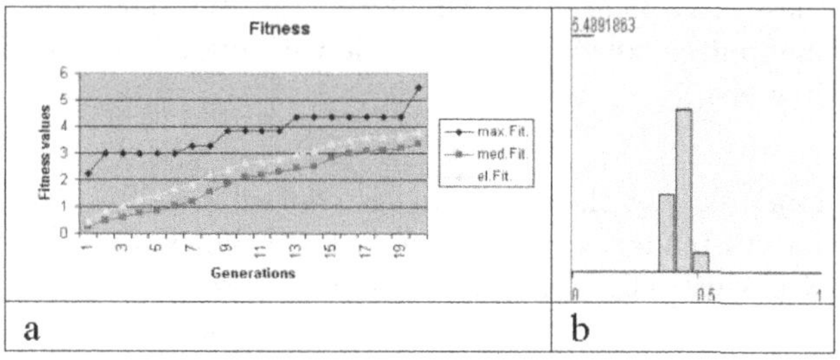

Figure 6: This figure illustrates, in a, the curves of the best, the mean and the elite fitness for each generation. b shows how the rules of the last generation are distributed in the lambda parameter for experiment 2.

experimental results for this evolutionary run are given in Figure 6. In this experiment, the curves for the maximum, mean and elite fitness for each generation have grown remarkably, with a quantitative increase in their values. Figure 6b shows how the rules of the last generation are distributed in the lambda parameter. The Hamming distance presents a greater dispersion with regard to the previous run, with a maximum value of 122 for the 20th rule, and a minimum value of 31 for the 18th rule. In this run, the rules of the last generation are clustered in the values of the lambda parameter nearer to 0.5, going from 0.36 to 0.57. Using I_1 as a fitness function, it is possible to see that the rules with higher fitness have an input-entropy curve tendency of the type highlighted in figure 1b. Moreover, the percentage of systems in which there are self-reproducing structures increases remarkably with regard to those obtained using the variance of input-entropy. Those CA with self-reproducing structures constitute the greater part of the rules of the last generation. The best fitness rule of the last generation presents many gliders, as shown in Figure 7. It is worth noting that the glider in Figure 7a becomes a complex self-reproducer if we use this structure as input data in other rules of this evolutive run. This could mean that evolution links together glider, reproduction and complexity by means of a specialized function which evolved

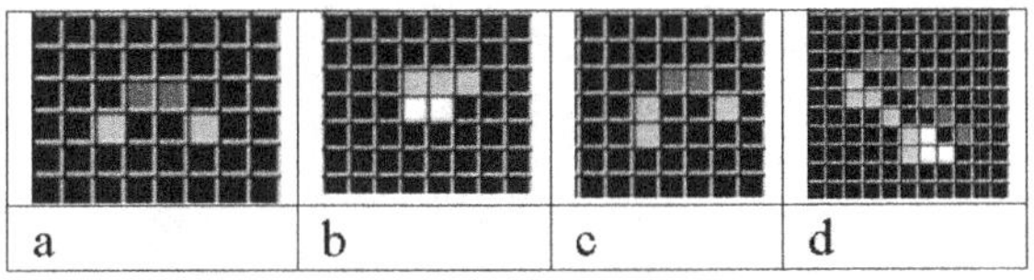

Figure 7: Examples of gliders from the best fitness rule of the last generation of experiment 2

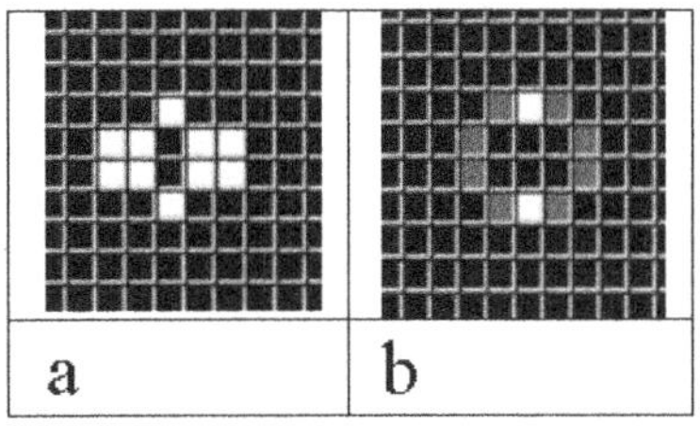

Figure 9: Two examples of self-reproducing structures found in the rules of the last generation of experiment 3

from a simple carrying on behavior to self-reproducing behavior or viceversa, and that reproduction is a way to carry on information in the environment.

Experiment 3. Complexity index: I_2

For this evolutionary run too, we varied only the fitness function. The experimental results for such an evolutionary run (8) show how the curves for the maximum,

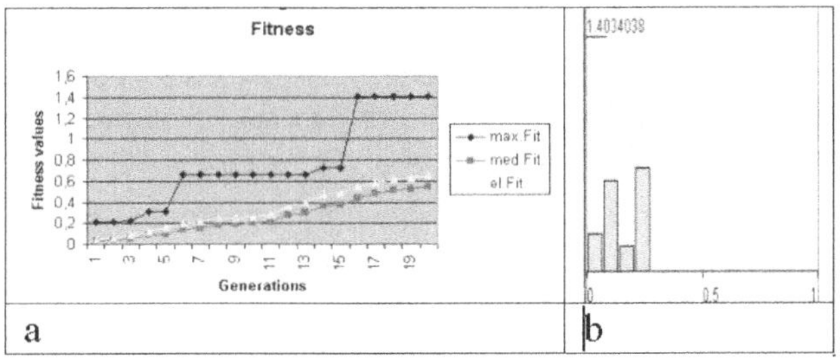

Figure 8: This figure illustrates, in a, the curves of the best, the mean and the elite fitness for each generation. In b, the rules of the last generation are distributed in the lambda parameter for experiment 3.

mean and elite fitness for each generation have grown. Figure 8b shows how the rules of the last generation are distributed in the lambda parameter. The Hamming distance presents a different organization with regard to the previous run, with a maximum value of 67 for the 16th rule, and a minimum value of 4 for the 12th rule. In this run, the distribution of the last generation rules in the lambda parameter highlights a different clustering, going from 0.05 to 0.30. Even having a fitness value inferior both to the first and to the second experiment, the rules of the last generation of this experiment present a large number of self-reproducers. In some rules, particularly those in which I_2 is high, larger structures emerge after a certain time, formed by self-reproducers, which, in their turn, are self-reproducing structures. Also for this evolutionary run, the rules of the last generation present a lot of replicators, from which we choose those presented in Figure 9.

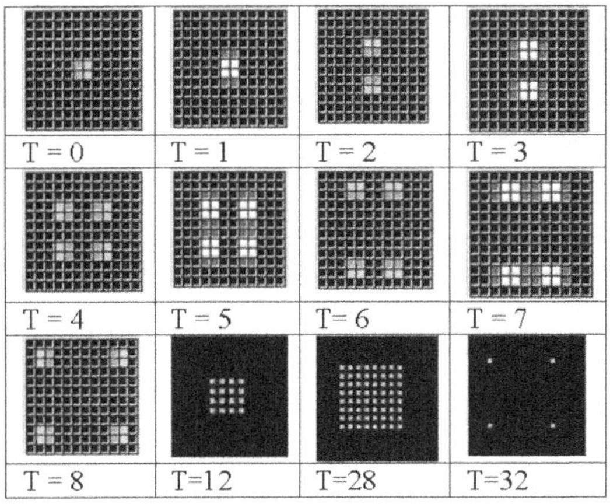

Figure 10: Evolution of a simple self-reproduction structure in different time steps.

Self-reproducers shapes, functions and behavior

If after a short transient period, we start simulation of an evolved rule, self-replicating patterns emerge. The behavior of the self-reproducer takes place at micro and macro-levels of the simulation time steps. The typical outline of the micro-level deals with self-replication. Self-reproducers grow over time, showing scaling invariance, change their position in the CA space, rotate and change their orientation, and change their spatial coordinates, undergoing annihilation when replication is no longer possible. But they never disappear, instead beginning a new loop of replication. We call this kind of behavior simple self-replication, especially when it happens in the cellular automata space in isolation. Many of the structures we found exhibit this kind of simple self-replication. In Figure 10, we illustrate an example of how, starting from self-reproducer data, this process occurs. At time $T = 0$ (initial state) there is a single structure formed by states (44, 66). At step $T = 1$ the structure is transformed and a new structure, formed by the states (22, 00, 00, 22), appears, which will follow its own path with its own behavior law. At step $T = 2$, the initial self-reproducer repeats itself, generating two copies in different positions. At step $T = 3$,

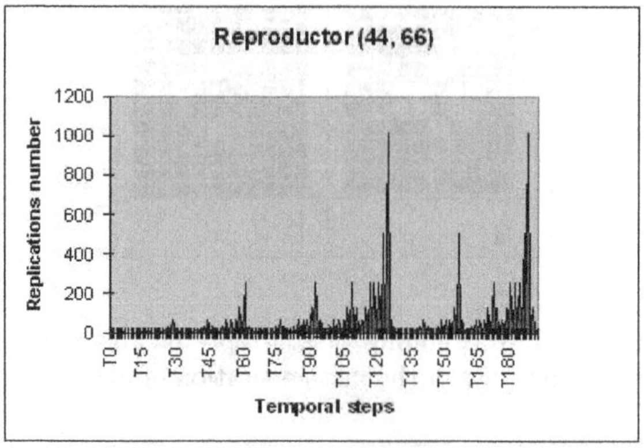

Figure 11: Graphic of the self-reproduction process of the structure formed by the states (44, 66)

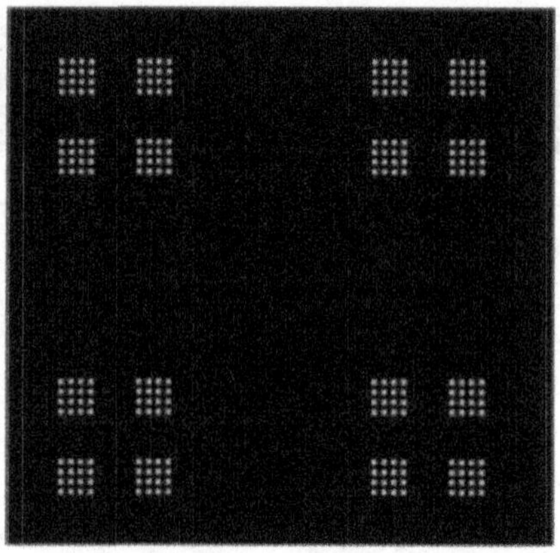

Figure 12: Patterns which represent scaling invariance in the reproduction process of the structure (44, 66).

two copies of the configuration of step $T = 1$ are generated, in different positions. At step $T = 4$, four copies of the self-reproducer (44,66) are obtained. At step $T = 5$, four copies of the self-reproducer (22, 00, 00, 22) are obtained. And so on. Let us now consider the self-reproducer (44, 66). If we make such a reproducer evolve for a relevant number of steps (190), we can see that it describes in time the curve shown in Figure 11. As the graphic shows, the increasing of the self-reproducer follows a constant and repeated tendency over time, with changes in the replication scale. Such a replication occurs at different time scales (different time steps of the simulation) and with different size scales (number of different replications). This curve led us to understand that the process of replication follows a specific law, since it is possible to note how some recurring patterns behave as if they were musical rhythms which repeat themselves as refrains, along a growing and changing scale. To explain this analogy, we can say that the curve seems to be a musical canon which recurs on different scales, with groups of 8, slightly different notes, as are listed in Table 3. The curve presented in Figure 11 subsumes a

2	4	4	4	8	16	8	4
8	16	16	16	32	64	16	4
8	16	16	16	32	64	32	16
32	64	64	64	128	256	32	4
8	16	16	16	32	64	32	16
32	64	64	64	128	256	64	16
32	64	64	64	128	256	128	64
128	256	256	256	512	1024	64	4

Table 3: Numerical representation of the self- reproduction process.

specific reproduction algorithm, that is the number of copies which the structure is able to reproduce, at any time step, for a given time. Such an algorithm could be the logical part of reproduction as von Neumann and Langton meant it. The self-reproducers move, occupying ever-increasing portions of space to allow other copies of themselves to appear. Such a portion of space seems to be proportional to the number of copies that appear in a given time. The reproducer also presents two basic movements in the CA space, one in the cardinal directions N-S, E-W, and the other in a rotatory sense.

Moreover, the copying progression presents the interesting characteristic of scaling invariance, as can be observed in Figure 12. Each new configuration, emerging by replication, maintains the shape of the reproducer, with a different size. These geometric figures are similar, since they have the same shape, or new emerging shape, given by the sum of the parts which compose the new structure. Together with the reproducer (44, 66) another self-reproducer exists, (with the following data 22, 00, 00, 22) which seems to be connected to the reproducer by which it is in some way manifested. The datum, if given on its own as input, is able to self-reproduce, manifesting also the reproducer (44, 66). It looks as if the two reproducers are in some way related, even though they have a different structure, both sharing a reproductive processes in which they are involved. In the graphics of Figures 13 and 14 respectively, the time development of the reproducer (22, 00, 00, 22) and the process of the two reproducers represented together, are shown. From the graphic in Figure 13, it can be seen how the reproduction rhythm for (22, 00, 00, 22) is slower, it is therefore more scattered in the time flow and less dense in the number of reproductions (we have excluded, for the time being, in order to better understand the phenomenon, the steps of simulation in which the copies interact through some functional junctions amongst themselves, that surely highlight other processes usually explained as overpopulation, from which other phases of annihilation follow).

Instead, the copies reproduced by the structure (44, 66) never come into contact with one another. The same categories as have been noticed for the reproducing structure (44, 66) are valid for (22, 00, 00, 22). There are changes in scale and invariance of shape while the progression follows a rhythm of evolution with increasing-decreasing phases. The rhythm of this reproducer, formed only by two beats or notes, is the following: 1-2; 4-8; 4-8; 4-8; 16-32; 4-8; 16-32; 16-32; 64-128; 4-8; 16-32; 16-32, and so on. From the graphic in Figure 14,

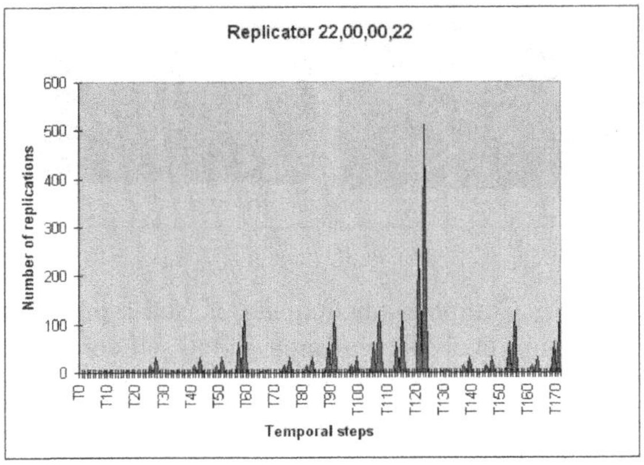

Figure 13: Graphic of the self-reproduction process of the structure formed by the states (22, 00, 00, 22).

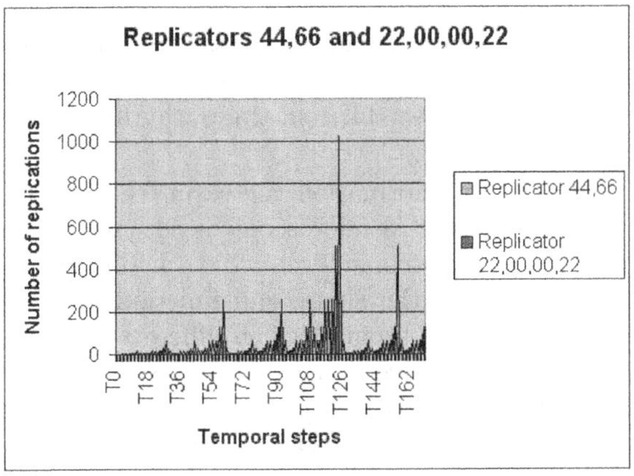

Figure 14: Process of reproduction of the two reproducers considered to be unitary.

it can be seen how the reproducer (44, 66) is quantitatively preponderant and seems to be in the foreground with regard to the other reproducer, that seems to be in the background.

The most interesting phenomenon, (which could be von Neumann 's idea about the general constructive capacity of the automaton) for the reproducer (44, 66) is the possibility of reproducing structures realized ad hoc. Any macro-structure, generated in this way, and formed by the arbitrary combination of simple structures made by the reproducer (44, 66), is, in its turn, a self-reproducing structure (see Figure 15). This property was noticed for different self-reproducers. In order

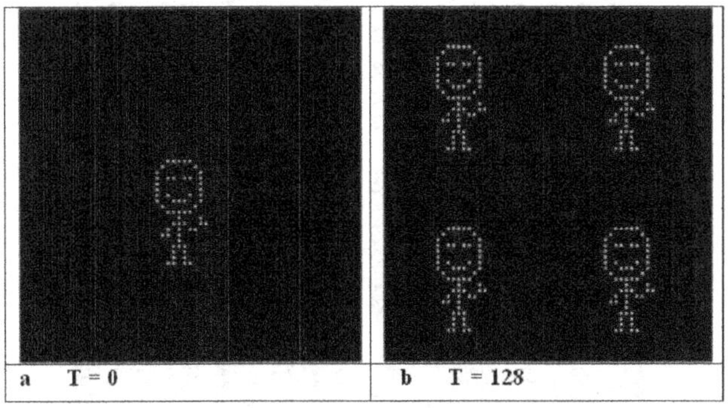

Figure 15: Self-reproduction of an arbitrary configuration (14a). After 128 steps, four copies of the homunculus are obtained (14b).

that any component of whatever structure we want to replicate can interact correctly, it is necessary that each element have the same orientation, or that the elements are turned around by 180° with respect to each other and that each element is at a distance of 2 cells, or at a distance of 2 cells plus a multiple of four. The mechanism of reproduction of these components put together is similar to a simple reproducer's behavior.

The structure (22) is one of the many replicators contained in the best fitness rule of the last generation, evolved by the experiment 3. (22) is the simplest one. As can be seen in Figure 16, the structure replicates itself at $T = 4$ and $T = 8$, and produces in $T = 1$, $T = 2$ and $T = 3$ other structures which, in turn, reproduce themselves in $T = 5$, $T = 6$ and $T = 7$. In the same rule, as shown in Figure 17, using as initial data (22, 22, 55, 55), it is possible to obtain a reproduction process which occurs in almost every reproducer which this rule contains, like a Sierpinski Triangle, with the typical geometrical features that this phenomenon manifests in one dimensional CA.

Other kinds of reproducer are different as regards structure and behavior. We realized different evolutionary runs for different values of k and r, and we found that self-replication does not depend on k and r values. In all evolved rules, self-reproducers are always present, and they seem to stand for the basic but widespread potential of artificial matter to reproduce and to evolve. In the following, we present a complex phenomenon of reproduction for a $k = 4$, $r = 2$ CA rule. The simulation begins with an initial casual state, and, after many time steps, the self-replicating structure shown in Figure 18 can be observed. The self-replicating structure creates four different directions of the replication process,

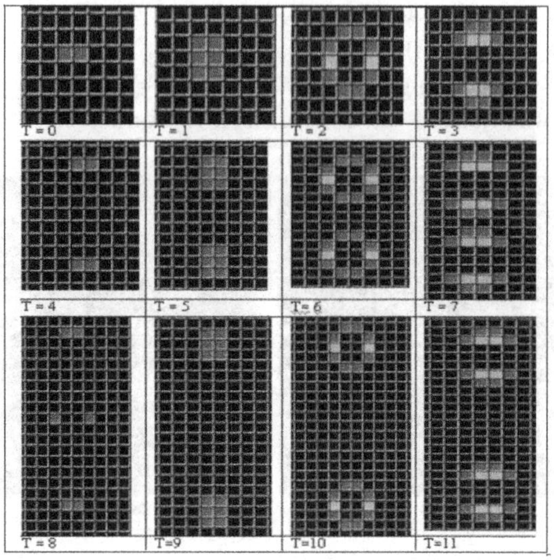

Figure 16: Self-reproduction with a simple behavior.

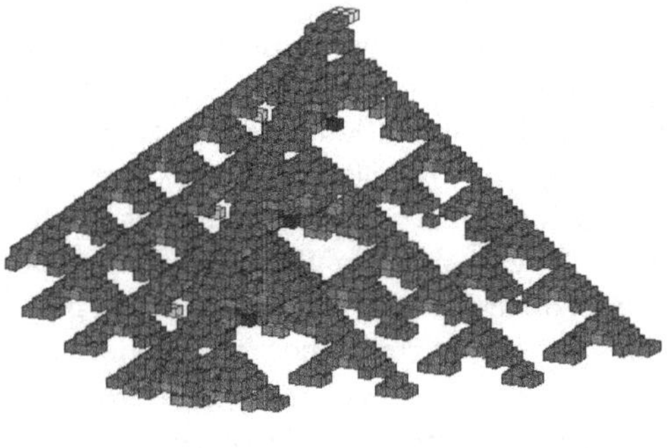

Figure 17: 3d spatial-temporal pattern from the data (22, 22, 55, 55) which has a Sierpinski Triangle configuration.

each generating many copies and giving life to a population of other entities, which in their turn begin to reproduce. Moreover, during the explosion of the population, many gliders are produced, so it seems that, globally, the macro-structure behaves as a glider gun.

Conclusions

Making use of two-dimensional Cellular Automata and Genetic Algorithms, it is possible to evolve complex rules that contain self-reproducers, which emerge spontaneously during the evolutionary process. The GA realized is efficient and research in the space of k-totalistic rules has given appreciable results, both for the quantity and for the quality of the phenomena which have emerged. The three types of fitness functions, related to the three indices of complexity that were developed, manifest types of reproducers which are different in shape, function and behavior. The self-reproducers

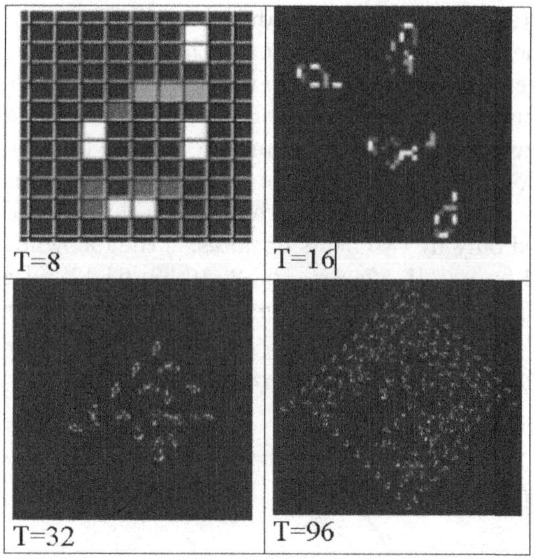

Figure 18: Complex phenomena of self-reproduction. The structure evolves creating a global self-constructing macro-structure. The last configuration seems similar to the initial structure, but, in the middle of the pattern, many other processes take place.

emerge from the primeval soup, are very stable, emerge again after collisions, and are able to self-inspect and reconstruct the information so that they can reproduce again. They are dominant over a long time period and exhibit changes in scale and invariance in shape. These kinds of structure reveal an algorithmic logic in reproduction, which follows different times, rhythms and phenomenology.

The duplicated information, increasing the total quantity of the system at a microscopic level, creates global changes at a macroscopic level, which modify the quality of the system: the shape and function of the self-reproducer organize themselves on different time, quantitative and qualitative scales. An increase of quantity will occur that will certainly be functional with regard to a change of quality or function, as occurs in the biological world where an additional production of DNA will be the basis for further programs that will concern it. Duplication in itself does not produce significant novelties, nor does it cause any increase in complexity, but it does provide the primary matter which allows the occurrence of such an event.

We have noticed that, as opposed to what is commonly believed, self-reproduction is a widespread process: almost all the evolved rules, even of the first generations, manifest self-reproducers, as if this process were an embedded characteristic of living matter, which can also be re-proposed in the artificial synthesis processes. The phenomenon of a structures replication can be seen as the creation of a redundancy of the system; that is the possibility of spreading some characteristics that they posses within more complicated systems, manifesting equally complicated behavior and so creating new organizations of living/artificial matter. We think that replication is the combination of many phenomena put together. Because we are operating in a context which is dynamic, and interactions with other data, information tends to multiply until a single structure has different dynamics and goes beyond what, at a first glance, it might seen to be. Replication phenomena may be similar, slightly different, different, and so on, in various degrees of quantitative and qualitative differences, but in some way harmonized or synchronized, and included in more general phenomena or on different scales. The mathematical language through which these phenomena are described is given by the specific algorithm of replication. These embedded characteristics can be considered as an evolved modality that living matter uses in order to reproduce itself. We have rediscovered it in artificial systems.

References

Bedau M. A., McCaskill J. S., Packard N. H., Rasmussen S., Adami C., Green D. G., Harvey I., Ikegami T., Kaneko K., and Ray T. S. 2000. Open problems in artificial life. Artificial Life 6: 363-376.

Bilotta E., and Pantano P. 2001. Observations on Complex Multi-state CAs. In J. Kelemen and P. Sosik eds. Advances in Artificial Life: Proceedings of the 6th European Conference on Artificial Life, 226-235. Springer-Verlag, Berlin.

Bilotta E., Lafusa A., and Pantano P. Searching for complex CA rules with GAs. submitted.

Byl J. 1989. Self-Reproduction in small cellular automata. Physica D 34: 295-299

Chou H. H., and Reggia J. A 1997. Emergence of self-replicating structures in a cellular automata space. Physica D 110(3-4): 252-276.

Chou H. H., and Reggia J. A 1998. Problem solving during artificial selection of self-replicating loops Physica D 115:293-312.

Codd E. F 1968. Cellular Automata. Academic Press, New York.

J. Holland. 1975 Adaptation In Natural and Artificial Systems. The University of Michigan Press, Ann Arbour.

Knuth D.E. 1997. The Art of Computer Programming, Vol. I. Addison-Wesley, New York.

Morita, K., and Imai K. 1996 Self-reproduction in a reversible cellular space. Theoretical Computer Science, 168:337-366.

Morita, K., and Imai K. 1997 Simple self-reproducing cellular automaton with shape-encoding mechanism. In Langton C.G., and Shimohara K., eds, Artificial Life V: Proceedings of the Fifth International Workshop on the Synthesis and Simulation of Living Systems, 450-457 Cambridge, MA,. MIT Press.

Langton C. G. 1984 Self-reproduction in cellular automata. Physica D 10:.135-144.

Langton C. G. 1990 Computation at the edge of chaos. Physica 42D 12-37.

Lohn J. D., and Reggia J. A. 1995 Discovery of self-replicating structures using a genetic algorithm, Proceedings of IEEE International Conference on Evolutionary Computation, 678-683.

Maynard Smith J., and Szathmáry E. 1995 The Major Transitions in Evolution. W.H. Freeman, Oxford.

McMullin B. 2000 John von Neumann and the Evolutionary Growth of Complexity: Looking Backwards, Looking Forwards. In Bedau M. A.,McCaskill J. S., Packard N. H., and Rasmussen S. eds. Artificial Life VII: Proceedings of the Seventh International Conference, 467-476. MIT Press.

Mitchell M. 1996 An introduction to Genetic Algorithms MIT Press. Cambridge, Massachusetts. London, England.

Perrier J. Y., Sipper M., and Zahnd J 1996 Toward a viable, self-reproducing universal computer. Physica D, 97:335-352

Sayama H. 1998 Introduction of Structural Dissolution into Langton's Self-reproducing Loop. In Adami C., Belew R. K., Kitano H., and Taylor C.E. eds. Artificial Life VI: Proceedings of the Sixth International Conference on Artificial Life, 114-122 Los Angeles, California, MIT Press.

Sayama H. 2000 Self-Replicating Worms that Increase Structural Complexity through Gene Transmission. In Bedau M. A., McCaskill J. S., Packard N. H., and Rasmussen S. eds. Artificial Life VII: Proceedings of the Seventh International Conference, 467-476. MIT Press.

Sipper M. 1994 Non-Uniform Cellular Automata: Evolution in Rule Space and Formation of Complex Structures Artificial Life IV, In R. A. Brooks and P. Maes eds. Proceedings of the 4th International Workshop on the Synthesis and Simulation of Living Systems, 394-399.

Sipper M. 1998 Fifty years of research on self-replication: An overview. Artificial Life, 4(3): 237-257.

Vitányi P. M. B. 1973 Sexually reproducing cellular automata Mathematical Biosciences 18: 23-54.

von Neumann J. 1966 Theory of Self-Reproducing Automata. University of Illinois Press, Illinois. Edited and completed by A.W.Burks.

Wolfram S. 1984 Universality and Complexity in Cellular Automata Physica 10D, 1-35.

Wuensche A. 1999 Classifying cellular automata automatically; finding gliders, filtering, and relating space-time patterns, attractor basins, and the Z parameter. Complexity, 4(3): 47-66.

Von Neumann's Machine in the Shell: Enhancing the Robustness of Self-Replication Processes

Hiroki Sayama
Department of Human Communication, University of Electro-Communications
1-5-1 Chofugaoka, Chofu, Tokyo 182-8585, Japan
sayama@hc.uec.ac.jp

Abstract

One of the grand challenges in artificial life is to create an artificial system that demonstrates self-replication and evolution in the real physical world (Bedau *et al.* 2000). This question was obviously initiated by von Neumann's seminal work on the self-replicating and evolving automaton that was presented more than five decades ago (von Neumann 1951; 1966). Unlike his well known idea of universal computer, however, von Neumann's universal constructor has never been subject to physical implementation (Friedman 1996). This is mainly due to the fragility of its mechanisms against perturbations that are unavoidable in more realistic kinematic settings. In this brief concept paper, I present a simple, but substantial, I believe, idea of enhancing the robustness of the self-replication processes, by introducing an additional subsystem that constructs a "workplace" prior to automaton construction. Workplaces are assumed to be solid structures that can be easily assembled under perturbations and can rigidly hold other components during the automaton construction processes. Similar kind of strategies are found to be prevalent in biological organisms, suggesting the effectiveness of the presented idea for the realization of kinematic models of self-replication and evolution.

Introduction

It is well acknowledged that von Neumann, a great mathematician/physicist who may be best known as a father of the programmable architecture adopted in today's computers, is also one of the pioneers of artificial life for his seminal work on the self-replicating and evolving automaton (von Neumann 1951; 1966). In his latest years, von Neumann challenged an empirical rule that was believed in engineering disciplines that the complexity of products is always smaller than that of the manufacturing machines that produce them. To grapple with this problem, he developed a theoretical discussion and concluded that a counterexample to this rule could exist if a system is made of the following (von Neumann 1951):

A: a universal constructor that creates any arbitrary structure by referring to a static "description tape".

B: a tape duplicator that makes a copy of the description tape.

C: a controller that reads the description tape and passes the written information to the above A and B and appropriately coordinates their behaviors.

I_{A+B+C}: a description tape that specifies how to construct the entire system itself.

These are symbolically written as

$$A + I_X \rightarrow A + I_X + X, \quad (1)$$

$$B + I_X \rightarrow B + I_X + I_X, \quad (2)$$

$$(A + B + C) + I_X \rightarrow (A + B + C) + I_X + X + I_X, \quad (3)$$

$$(A + B + C) + I_{A+B+C} \rightarrow (A + B + C) + I_{A+B+C} + (A + B + C) + I_{A+B+C}, \quad (4)$$

where the last form represents a self-replicating process. More importantly, this model also captures the capability of the evolutionary growth of complexity (McMullin 2000): If the description tape happens to contain an additional content that does not interfere the corrent functioning of $A + B + C$, the system produces a mutated system, possibly of higher complexity than its parent, i.e.,

$$(A + B + C) + I_{A+B+C+F} \rightarrow (A + B + C) + I_{A+B+C+F} + (A + B + C + F) + I_{A+B+C+F}, \quad (5)$$

where F is an additional component that happened to emerge in the tape by mutation. The existence of and the relationship between phenotypes ($A+B+C$, $A+B+C+F$) and genotypes (I_{A+B+C}, $I_{A+B+C+F}$) illustrated in this formulation hold a close resemblance with those found in reproduction and variation of real (asexually reproducing) organisms.

Later, von Neumann tried to show that such a counterexample *does* exist, at least theoretically, by implementing his very complex universal constructor in cellular automata—an artificial but totally mechanistic universe. Although he passed away before the completion of this work, it was posthumously completed and published by Burks in 1966 (von Neumann 1966).

Almost needless to say, von Neumann's idea of self-replicating automata was so profound that it was followed by a number of succeeding studies that ranges from cellular automata based self-replicating systems to core memory based evolutionary systems, which now forms one of the central parts of artificial life (Sipper 1998).

Universal Computation vs. Universal Construction

Many think of von Neumann's work on self-replicating machines as something different, and even weird, compared to his other (probably more famous) achievements in computer science, game theory, quantum physics, nuclear physics, and so on. However, it is worth pointing out that his idea of universal construction with instruction tapes has a fundamental correspondence with his another idea of universal computation with program codes stored in memory. These two are actually the same in that a system contains an arbitrary sequense of information inside itself, and provided it has a universal capability, it can immitate the behavior of any arbitrary system described in the sequence. Presumably von Neumann had no substantial distinction between these two in his mind when he considered these ideas.

There is a practical difference, however, between the universal computer and the universal constructor in terms of the requirement for the robustness of the systems to perturbations. The universal computer does not have to be robust by itself, because the computation theory assumes discrete mathematical entities and their state transition in a noiseless world. The responsibility of realizing such a noiseless condition is primarily on the device manufacturing side and not on the system itself. On the other hand, the universal constructor should be robust *per se*, because its construction capability best makes sense in our real, three-dimensional kinematic universe. Thus the system should be able to deal with more or less continuous physical entities that inevitably involve fructuations and uncertainty. In such settings, the system itself *is* responsible for the robustness of its workings.

The robust universal construction is apparently a very difficult problem to attain. Von Neumann himself tried to consider a kinematic model at first, but later he abandoned it and switched to cellular automata, following Ulam's suggestions, to avoid this difficulty. Although his work was still monumental and stimulative enough even on cellular automata, the lack of robustness was crucial when considered as a model of real biological and/or engineering systems. Therefore, in spite that his universal computer has been implemented hundreds of millions of times (i.e., computers we use nowadays), there has been *no* physical implementation of his universal constructor (Friedman 1996). This fact is now recognized as one of the grand challenges in artificial life (Bedau *et al.* 2000). So the relevant question to ask here is: *How can we enhance the robustness of self-replication processes?*

Workplace Construction

In this section I present a simple extension of von Neumann's theoretical model, which I tentatively call a *workplace construction model*, to illustrate a possible solution for the question mentioned above. The key idea is the introduction of an additional subsystem that constructs a "workplace" prior to automaton construction. This model can be described within von Neumann's framework by putting the added subsystem as a variant of automaton F in his formulation, except for three additional assumptions I am going to make in what follows.

The first assumption is a reasonable statement that we all know empirically:

> **Assumption 1:** The construction and duplication processes that are originally sensitive to perturbations can be substantially stabilized by putting them on some solid supporting structure, or *workplace.*

For example, drawing a straight line is rather difficult by a free hand but is quite easy and precise by using a ruler. Using this assumption, I symbolically represent such stabilized processes by

$$A + I_X + S_X^A \;\; \boldsymbol{\Rightarrow} \;\; A + I_X + S_X^A + X, \qquad (6)$$

$$B + I_X + S_X^B \;\; \boldsymbol{\Rightarrow} \;\; B + I_X + S_X^B + I_X, \qquad (7)$$

$$(A + B + C) + I_X + S_X^A + S_X^B$$
$$\boldsymbol{\Rightarrow} (A + B + C) + I_X + S_X^A + S_X^B + X + I_X, \quad (8)$$

where S_X^A and S_X^B represent the workplaces that support automaton construction and tape duplication, respectively. Subscript X means that the size and/or shape of the workplaces may depend on the product, if not always. The bold right arrow "$\boldsymbol{\Rightarrow}$" denotes that the process is significantly robust to perturbations, i.e., the outcome is not affected virtually by small but positive amount of perturbations. Here let us keep ourselves quite loose in evaluating the robustness; I just classify processes as either "robust" or "sensitive" to perturbations. Such a simplification enables us to think about the problem more clearly and concisely. Detailed quantitative analysis of the robustness is far beyond the range of this brief paper.

The above forms (6)–(8) look quite similar to the original ones (1)–(3), except for the addition of the two workplaces, so one may want to simply apply $X = (A + B + C) + S_X^A + S_X^B$ to the last form to obtain a robust self-replication process. However, this would result in a non-trivial problem: By definition, workplaces are assumed to hold and support the construction process of the product, so its size in general should be equal to or greater than that of the product. Therefore, if one lets $X = (A + B + C) + S_X^A + S_X^B$, then, for example, S_X^A must be large enough to hold the entire product X that includes S_X^A, resulting in a vicious circle that never closes.

Note that this problem is deeply related to the complexity decreasing rule empirically seen in engineering:

To obtain a highly organized product, one needs a stabilized and well controlled manufacturing process, which requires a machine that can control the local environment that should be equal to or larger than the product. Part of the reason why von Neumann's machine can seemingly construct a product more complex (larger) than itself is, in this context, because his machine is implicitly supported by an infinite array of cellular automata that virtually works as a solid workplace. In other words, he intended to overcome this empirical rule, but what he actually chose was avoiding it by putting away the crux of the issue out of consideration.

In order to resolve the above problem, here I make the second assumption:

> **Assumption 2:** Workplaces are generally made of a simple but extensive repetition of the same kind of components, so they can be generated with enough preciseness by itself (without another workplace) even under perturbations.

Readers may wonder if making this assumption might be just another way of avoiding the problem. Since the main aim of this paper is to show the argument and promote discussions on it, I do not mean this is the one and only right solution. Nonetheless, many empirical observations seem to support this assumption. For example, one can create a straight line in a robust fashion by combining tiny rods into triangular meshes or trusses. As long as the tiny rods are at the same length, the outcome can be precise enough. This is intuitively because the product of this process is not complex; it can be produced by a repetition of the same simple tasks, which is not the case for more sophisticated processes like automaton construction.

With this second assumption, I introduce a set of new robust construction processes, i.e.,

$$R^A + I_X \;\Rightarrow\; R^A + I_X + S^A_X, \qquad (9)$$
$$R^B + I_X \;\Rightarrow\; R^B + I_X + S^B_X, \qquad (10)$$

where R^A and R^B are subsystems that estimate the size of needed workplaces for A and B from the description tape and construct them in a robust fashion. Note that the exact estimation of the size of needed workplaces might be another complex task that needs another workplace to carry it on. We thus need the third assumption:

> **Assumption 3:** The size (or the upper bound of the size) of workplaces for construction and duplication processes can be estimated from the instruction tape in a simple operation, even under perturbations.

This assumption is much less obvious than the previous two, and should be subject to discussion and verification. If it would not be the case in some condition, the arguments developed below would lose its universality, but I believe it would still have sufficient implications for how to create robust systems.

Provided the third assumption applies, the previous form of stabilized automaton construction (8) can be rewritten as

$$\begin{aligned}&(A+B+R^A+R^B+C)+I_X\\&\Rightarrow (A+B+R^A+R^B+C)+I_X+S^A_X+S^B_X \qquad (11)\\&\Rightarrow (A+B+R^A+R^B+C)+I_X+S^A_X+S^B_X+X+I_X,\end{aligned}$$

where the entire system $(A+B+R^A+R^B+C)$, which we call G hereafter, is now capable of both constructing X and duplicating I_X in a robust manner, while keeping its own size finite and independent of what is written in I_X. Note that the function of controller C is more complex than before; it now has to coordinate the behaviors of four other subsystems, A, B, R^A, and R^B.

Then, finally, we put the system G itself into X in the above form, to obtain

$$\begin{aligned}G+I_G \;&\Rightarrow\; G+I_G+S^A_G+S^B_G\\&\Rightarrow\; G+I_G+S^A_G+S^B_G+G+I_G. \qquad (12)\end{aligned}$$

This represents a robust self-replication process of G, which also produces some byproducts (S^A_G and S^B_G).

Discussion

The workplace construction model presented above is by no means theoretically proven. It uses three assumptions, each of which must be carefully checked about its validity. Whether such a robust automaton can be actually implemented is another key issue to be investigated, probably with a lot of efforts, just like what von Neumann did with cellular automata to show a concrete example of his self-replicating machine.

Despite these problems all, one can obtain a supportive implication for the model from a variety of phenomena observed in real biological systems at various scales. They imply the applicability and effectiveness of the central idea of the presented model. For example, at the smallest level, the formation of cell membranes is probably the most fundamental instance of workplace construction; it isolates the metabolic process of the cell from environmental perturbations and keeps all the sensitive parts at the same place without diffusion. At a much higher level, niche construction seen in ecology (Laland, Odling-Smee & Feldman 2000) is another clear instance of workplace construction, such as dam building of beavers.

More directly relevant cases can be found in animals that are about to produce their next generation. For example, firm eggshells of birds and reptiles are probably the most direct example of workplace construction. Although the automaton constructors are embedded in the fetuses in these cases, the purpose of eggshells are exactly the same as is discussed in this paper, i.e., to stabilize the process of offspring construction by isolating it from the outside and holding it on a solid structure. More sophisticated instance is the uterus of mammals, where the workplace is included in the parent's body, but can be refurbished and extended as needed to hold its offspring under construction. It is also interesting that the production of S_G^A and S_G^B in (12) correctly captures the nature of the process that these workplaces constructed in real organisms (eggshells, endometriums, placentas, etc.) are all just for temporary use and they will eventually become garbages after birth of the offspring.

To conclude, the only goal of this short paper is to shed light on this trivial fact: the more complex a system becomes, the better controlled local environment the system needs in order to construct its replica under perturbations. Biological organisms seem to evolve such sophisticated "workplaces" for their survival and prosperity. However, this point has been long missing in the earlier studies of artificial self-replicating systems, and it must be taken into account to proceed toward the next step of artificial life.

References

Bedau, M. A., McCaskill, J. S., Packard, N. H., Rasmussen, S., Adami, C., Green, D. G., Ikegami, T., Kaneko, K., and Ray, T. S. 2000. Open Problems in Artificial Life. *Artificial Life* 6:363–376.

Friedman, G. 1996. The Space Studies Institute View on Self-Replication. *The Assembler: Newsletter of the Molecular Manufacturing Shortcut Group of the National Space Society* 4:4 (http://www.islandone.org/MMSG/9612.html).

Laland, K. N., Odling-Smee, J., and Feldman, M. W. 2000. Niche Construction, Biological Evolution, and Cultural Change. *Behav. Brain Sci.* 23:131–175.

McMullin, B. 2000. John von Neumann and the Evolutionary Growth of Complexity: Looking Backwards, Looking Forwards... In Bedau, M. A., McCaskill, J. S., Packard, N. H., and Rasmussen, S., eds., *Artificial Life VII: Proceedings of the Seventh International Conference on Artificial Life*, 467–476. Cambridge, MA: MIT Press.

Sipper, M. 1998. Fifty Years of Research on Self-Replication: An Overview. *Artificial Life* 4:237–257.

von Neumann, J. 1951. The General and Logical Theory of Automata. In Jeffress, L. A., ed., *Cerebral Mechanisms in Behavior—The Hixon Symposium*, 1–41. New York: John Wiley. Originally presented in September, 1948. Also collected in Aspray, W., and Burks, A. W., eds., *Papers of John von Neumann on Computing and Computer Theory*, 391–431. 1987. Cambridge, MA: MIT Press.

von Neumann, J. 1966. *Theory of Self-Reproducing Automata*. Urbana, IL: University of Illinois Press. Edited and completed by A. W. Burks.

Interactive Self-Replicating, Self-Incrementing and Self-Decrementing Loops

André Stauffer[1] and **Moshe Sipper**[2]

[1]Swiss Federal Institute of Technology in Lausanne, CH-1015 Lausanne, Switzerland
andre.stauffer@epfl.ch
[2]Department of Computer Science, Ben-Gurion University, Beer-Sheva 84105, Israel
sipper@cs.bgu.ac.il

Abstract

Self-replicating loops presented to date are usually worlds unto themselves, inaccessible to observer once the replication process is launched. In this paper we present a self-replicating loop which allows for user interaction. Specifically, the user can control the loop's replication as well as the size of the replica. After presenting the design of this novel loop, we delineate its physical implementation in our electronic wall for bio-inspired applications, the *BioWall*.

Introduction: Interactive Self-Replication

All self-replicating loops presented to date (Langton 1984; Byl 1989; Reggia 1993) are usually worlds unto themselves: once the initial loop configuration is embedded within the cellular automaton (CA) universe (at time-step 0), no further user interaction occurs, and the CA chugs along in total oblivion of the observing user.

In previous works we have described the design of self-replicating loops which could be activated by the user (Stauffer 2001; 2002). The user was able to control the loop's replication and induce its destruction. In this paper we present another interactive self-replicating loop which give birth to a daughter loop whose size is identical, incremented by one or decremented by one. The next section explains the corresponding self-replication, self-incrementation and self-decrementation processes. Section III discusses the hardware implementation of the loop in our electronic wall for bio-inspired applications, the *BioWall*. Finally, we present concluding remarks in Section IV.

Loop Design and Operation

Contrary to previous loops, which self-replicate continually, the novel one presented below is idle *unless externally activated.* This $n \times n$ loop, with $n \geq 3$, is therefore an interactive self-replicator.

Defined in a two-dimensional, five-neighbor cellular space, with seven basic states per cell (Figure 1), our minimal 3×3 loop is made up of eight cells. As long as no external input is provided, the loop is inert, continually undergoing an eight-time-step cycle (Figure 2).

In order to launch the self-replication process, the self-incrementation process or the self-decrementation process, the user activates the idle loop by providing an external input on one of its eight cells (in Section activation occurs by physically touching the BioWall). This external input presets respectively one out of three control variables: the replication-activate variable A, the data-increment variable I or the data-decrement variable D of the cell.

```
 0: empty component
 1: building component
 2: east-moving growth signal
 3: north-moving growth signal
 4: west-moving growth signal
 5: south-moving growth signal
 6: left-turn signal
 7: east-branching signal (rep),
    east data-decrement and cut-off signal (inc)
 8: east-branching and cut-off signal (rep),
    east data-increment and cut-off signal (dec)
 9: north-branching signal  (rep),
    north data-decrement and cut-off signal (inc)
10: north-branching and cut-off signal (rep),
    north data-increment and cut-off signal (dec)
11: west-branching signal (rep),
    west data-decrement and cut-off signal (inc)
12: west-branching and cut-off signal (rep),
    west data-increment and cut-off signal (dec)
13: south-branching signal (rep),
    south data-decrement and cut-off signal (inc)
14: south-branching and cut-off signal (rep),
    south data-increment and cut-off signal (dec)
15: cut-off signal (rep),
 A: replication-activate variable (rep,inc,dec)
 I: data-increment variable (inc)
 D: data-decrement variable (dec)
```

Figure 1: The seven basic cellular states 0 to 6 used for the idle loop and the nine additional states 8 to 15 involved in the self-replication (rep), self-incrementation (inc) or self-decrementation (dec) processes when the control variables A, I or D are activated.

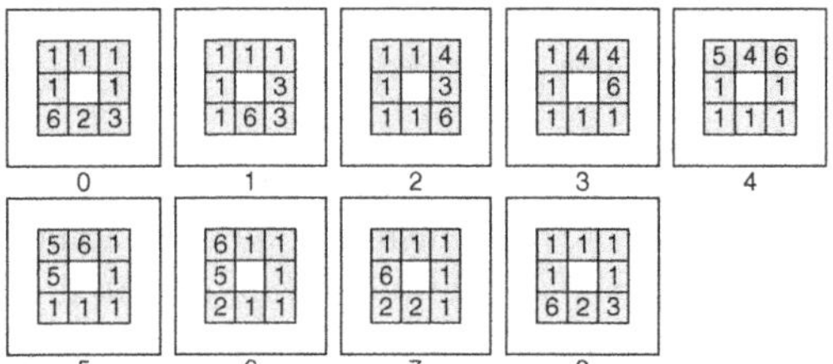

Figure 2: The eight-time-step idle cycle of the inactive loop.

Presetting the replication-activate variable ($A = 1$) leads to the appearance of a shadowed state 6 which corresponds to an activated left-turn signal at time-step 0 (Figure 3). The activated loop is then ready to self-replicate and the process is performed in 48 time-steps. In addition to the seven basic cellular states and to the replication-activate variable, the self-replication process requires the nine extra cellular states defined in Figure 1. The control part of each cell involves the three variables A, I and D as well as the state C of the cell itself. When the left-turn signal $C = 6$ is activated ($A, I, D = 100$), the replication-activate variable A is reset and the self-replication process is launched (see Appendix).

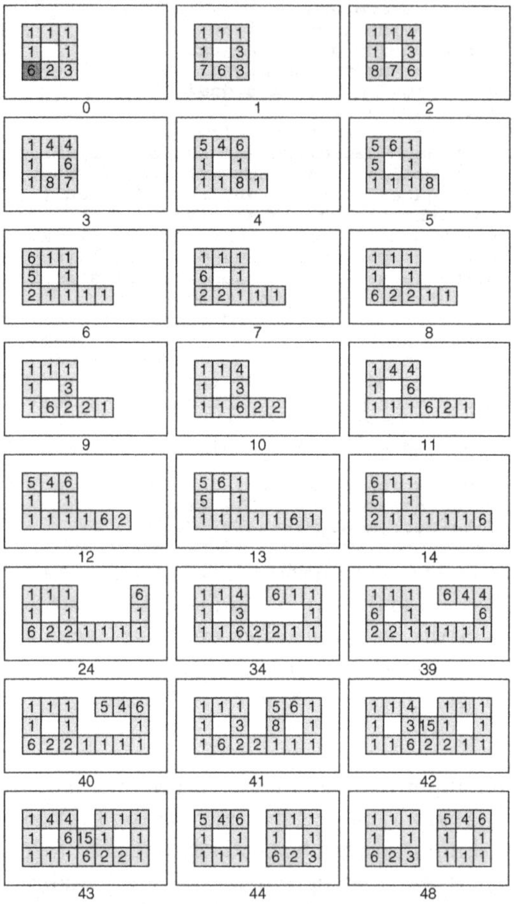

Figure 3: When the lower-left cell is activated after presetting control variable A, the loop self-replicates eastward within 48 time-steps (1 to 7 are the branching steps, 41 to 44 are the cut-off steps).

Presetting the data-increment variable ($I = 1$) results in the extension of the sequence of moving signals in the idle loop and in the appearance of an activated left-turn signal at time-step 2 (Figure 4). The activated loop is then ready to self-increment and the process is performed in 57 time-steps. The self-incrementation process introduces thus the data-increment variable and the five cellular states 7, 9, 11, 13, 15 (Figure 1). These states permit to reduce afterwards the sequence of moving signals in the mother loop at time-step 50 and to detach the daughter loop from the mother loop at time-step 53. At the control variable level, when $A, I, D = 010$, a data-increment signal $C = 15$ is first introduced instead of the usual left-turn signal $C = 6$ (time-step 1). It is then replaced by an activated left-turn signal $C = 6$ when the control variables A, I, D become 100 (time-step 2). During this prodedure, the size of the sequence of moving signals is effectively increased by one and the idle loop activated in order to perform the self-incrementation process.

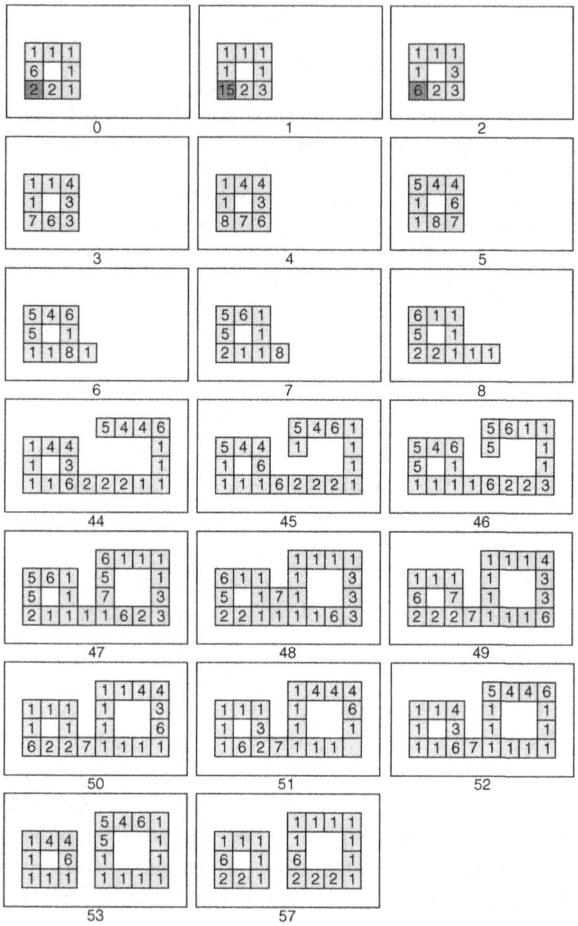

Figure 4: When the lower-left cell is activated after presetting control variable I, the loop self-increments eastward within 57 time-steps (1 to 8 are the sequence extension and branching steps, 44 to 53 are the sequence reduction and cut-off steps).

Presetting the data-decrement variable ($D = 1$) results in the reduction of the sequence of moving signals in the idle loop and in the appearance of an activated left-turn signal at time-step 4 (Figure 5). The activated loop is then ready to self-decrement and the process is performed in 73 time-steps. Figure 1 represents the data-decrement variable and the four cellular states (8, 10, 12, 14) involved in the self-decrementation process. Towards the end of the process, these states allow the extension of the sequence of moving signals in the mother loop at time-step 68 and the separation of the daughter loop at time-step 69. At the control variable level, when $A, I, D = 001$, the first moving signal of the sequence is suppressed (time-step 1). The control variables A, I, D become then 100 and the remaining signals of the sequence are maintained. In the procedure, the size of the sequence of moving signals is decreased by one and the idle loop activated in order to perform the self-decrementation process.

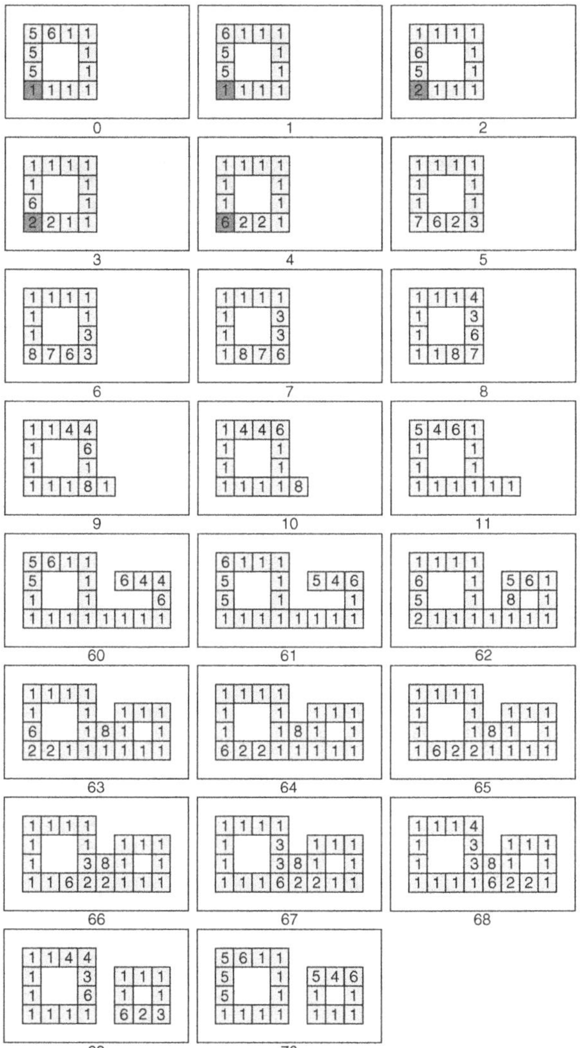

Figure 5: When the lower-left cell is activated after presetting control variable D, the loop self-decrements eastward within 73 time-steps (1 to 11 are the sequence reduction steps and branching steps, 62 to 69 are the sequence extension and cut-off steps).

The BioWall Implementation

We have physically implemented the five-neighbor CA described above in a two-dimensional electronic wall for bio-inspired applications, the *BioWall*, which is an undergoing project in our lab (Figure 6). The BioWall is ultimately intended as a self-repairing display medium, capable of interacting "intelligently" with the user and recovering from faults. In our implementation, each CA cell is made up of one unit in the wall. The physical realization of this unit includes: (1) an input device, (2) a digital circuit, and (3) an output display.

Figure 6: The BioWall used to physically implement our loop (Photograph by A. Badertscher).

The unit's outer surface consists of a touch-sensitive panel which acts like a digital switch, enabling the user to activate the randomly self-replication, the self-incrementation or the self-decrementation process (Figure 7).

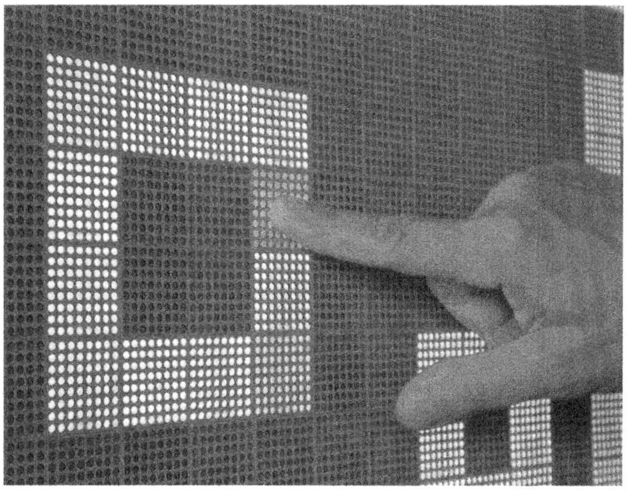

Figure 7: Touching a unit in order to activate the loop (Photograph by A. Badertscher).

The unit's internal digital circuit is a field-programmable gate array (FPGA), configured so as to implement: (1) external (touch) input, (2) execution of the CA state-transition and variable-transition rules necessary for the three loop processes, and (3) control of the output display. This latter is a two color light-emitting diode (LED) display, made up of 128 diodes arranged as an 8×8 dot-matrix, each dot containing a green and a red LED. The display allows the user to view a CA cell's current state (of the sixteen possible) and whether this cell is in activated or deactivated mode.

Concluding Remarks

We presented an interactive self-replicating loop wherein the user can control the size of the daughter loop. In addition to the usual self-replication process, the user can therefore induce a self-incrementation process and a self-decrementation process. We then described the loop's physical implementation within our electronic wall for bio-inspired applications, the BioWall.

The ability to interact with a CA universe—a little-studied issue—is of fundamental import where cellular devices are concerned: one must be able to enter input and to view the output if any practical application is envisaged (Sipper 1998). Our work herein is but a first step in the domain of interactive cellular replicators, an issue which we believe will play an important role in the future of such devices.

Acknowledgments

This work was supported in part by the Swiss National Science Foundation under grant 20-63711.00, by the Leenaards Foundation, Lausanne, Switzerland, and by the Villa Reuge, Ste-Croix, Switzerland.

References

Langton, C. 1984. Self-reproduction in cellular automata. *Physica D*, 10:135–144.

Byl, J. 1989. Self-reproduction in small cellular automata. *Physica D*, 34:295–299.

Reggia, J. A., Armentrout, S. L., Chou, H. H., and Peng, Y. 1993. Simple systems that exhibit self-directed replication. *Science*, 259:1282–1287.

Stauffer, A., and Sipper, M. 2001. Externally controllable and destructible self-replicating loops. In Kelemen, J., and Sosik, P. eds., *Advances in Artificial Life: Proceedings of the 6th European Conference on Artificial Life (ECAL 2001). Lecture Notes in Artificial Intelligence*, 2159:282–291. Heidelberg: Springer-Verlag.

Stauffer, A., and Sipper, M. 2002. An interactive self-replicator implemented in hardware. *Artificial Life*, 8:175–183.

Sipper, M. 1998. Fifty years of research on self-replication: An overview. *Artificial Life*, 4:237–257.

Appendix: Specification of the CA Variable-Transition Rules

The variable-transition rules of the CA appears in Figure 8. In this figure, C, N, E, S, and W correspond to the current states of the cell and of its neighbors to the north, east, south, and west, respectively. A, I, D are the current states of the control variables. Knowing the current state of the cell, of its neighbors and of the control variables, the set of rules defines the state $A+$, $I+$, $D+$ of the control variables at the next time-step.

C,N,E,S,W	A,I,D	->	A+,I+,D+
6,X,X,X,X	1,0,0	->	0,0,0
15,X,X,X,X	0,1,0	->	1,0,0
1,X,X,X,2	0,0,1	->	1,0,0
1,X,X,3,X	0,0,1	->	1,0,0
1,X,4,X,X	0,0,1	->	1,0,0
1,5,X,X,X	0,0,1	->	1,0,0

Figure 8: CA variable-transition rules.

Selection of Catalysts through Cellular Reproduction

Naoaki Ono[1] and **Takashi Ikegami**[2]

[1]ATR, Human Information Science Laboratories, 2-2-2Hikaridai,
"Keihanna Science City" (Seika-cho, Soraku-gun), Kyoto 619-0288, Japan
[2]Institute of Physics, Graduate School of Arts and Sciences,
University of Tokyo, 3-8-1 Komaba Tokyo 153-8902, Japan

Abstract

A series of simulation studies (Ono & Ikegami 1999; 2001) show that a proto cell spontaneously emerges from a chemical soup by acquiring membrane structures. In 2-dimensional space, the emergence of proto cells is followed by the reproduction of cells. A major unsolved problem is the evolution of proto cells; how the proto cells evolve into modern cells with higher functionalities. Here we examine, as the first step, the evolution of catalysts within the proto-cells. Catalytic chemicals have different catalytic activity in generating membrane chemicals. We show that cells with higher activity of membrane production evolve through cellular selection.

Introduction

It is widely accepted that the origin of life was a set of molecules that catalyzed the reproduction of each other. However, when we consider the evolution of such primitive chemical systems, the compartmentalization of molecules is indispensable for establishing the co-evolution of cooperative catalytic reactions and protecting them from parasites that would spoil the evolution (Szathmáry & Maynard Smith 1997). Though it is difficult to know about the structure of primitive cells because there remain few physical records of the earliest living cells, there have been various theoretical approaches to understanding the emergence and evolution of proto-cell systems.

Gánti proposed a minimal model of primitive self-maintaining cells named "chemoton" (Gánti 1975; 1997). It is composed of (1) a metabolic system of autocatalytic molecules, (2) self-replicating molecules that inherit genetic information and (3) a self-organizing membrane molecule to enclose the whole system. This system maintains itself by consuming resources and discharging waste into the environment. It can be easily imagined that if the reproduction of the cell is appended to this system, it would be a primitive unit of Darwinian selection and evolve into more stable structures.

It should be stressed that a cell defines itself as an individual by producing a membrane that distinguishes itself from the outside. Maturana and Varela pointed out that this is a unique feature of living organisms, and named it "autopoiesis" (Maturana & Varela 1980). To demonstrate the self-maintenance of an autopoietic structure, abstract computational models of an autopoietic cell based on a Cellular Automaton were proposed (originally by Varela (Varela, Maturana, & Uribe 1974), and re-implemented by Zeleny (Zeleny 1977) and by McMullin (McMullin & Varela 1997)). Breyer and McCaskill introduced the metabolism of a catalyst into this model (Breyer, Ackermann, & McCaskill 1998). It was also shown that an autopoietic proto-cell can reproduce itself automatically (Ono & Ikegami 1999; 2001). Speroni di Fenizio and Dittrich proposed another approach to represent proto-cells that are embedded in a triangular planar graph (Speroni di Fenizio, Dittrich, & Banzhaf 2001).

The remaining question is "How was the *first* cell organized?" Answering this question will give us the first step in understanding the emergence of higher order structures in life's evolution. This paper consists of two parts. The computational algorithm of the model is explained in detail in the first part. We introduce a Lattice Artificial Chemistry (LAC) model that simulates the chemical reactions and spatial interactions of abstract chemicals. In the second part, an emergence of a proto-cell from a non-organized initial state, its reproduction and the selection of inside catalysts through the cell reproduction are reported in order.

Lattice Artificial Chemistry

Our model is based on discrete and stochastic dynamics, which is extended from a lattice-gas model. Chemicals are represented by particles on reaction sites that are arranged as a two-dimensional triangular lattice. Note that any number of particles can be placed on a single site. The vector $\mathbf{n}(\mathbf{x}) = (n_1(\mathbf{x}), n_2(\mathbf{x}), \ldots, n_m(\mathbf{x}))$ gives the number of each type of particles on the site $\mathbf{x}$. N_i gives the total amount of i-th particles in the system.

Chemical reactions are expressed by the probabilistic transition of particle types. The diffusion of chemicals is expressed by random walks of particles on the sites. These transition probabilities are given as the products of the associated rate coefficients and the following function of the potential change ΔE,

$$f(\Delta E) = \frac{\Delta E}{e^{\beta \Delta E} - 1}. \quad (1)$$

where β represents the inverse of the product of the Boltzmann constant and temperature (note that, $f(\Delta E)/f(-\Delta E) = e^{-\beta \Delta E}$). In the simulations reported hereafter, the value of β is normalized and fixed to 1.

Hydrophobic Interaction

The probabilities of random walks of particles are biased according to the gradient of the potential $\Psi(\mathbf{x})$ which is given by summing up the interaction from all particles in the same and adjacent sites. The probability p with which a particle i moves from a site $\mathbf{x}$ to $\mathbf{x}'$ is calculated as follows,

$$\Psi_i(\mathbf{x}) = \sum_{|\mathbf{x}'-\mathbf{x}|\leq 1} \sum_j \psi_{ij}(\mathbf{x}'-\mathbf{x})n_i(\mathbf{x}) \quad (2)$$

$$p_i(\mathbf{x} \to \mathbf{x}') = Dif_i \, f(\Psi_i(\mathbf{x}') - \Psi_i(\mathbf{x})) \quad (3)$$

where $\Psi_i(\mathbf{x})$ denotes the potential of particle i in the site $\mathbf{x}$, Dif_i denotes the diffusion coefficient of particle i, and $\psi_{ij}(d\mathbf{x})$ denotes the interaction on particle i from particle j. Diffusion coefficients depend on the species of the particles. Autocatalytic and membrane particles are assumed to be larger molecules so that their diffusion coefficients are smaller than those of other particles ($Dif_{A_i} = Dif_M = 0.003$, $Dif_{\text{others}} = 0.01$).

To simulate the formation of membranes, we introduce hydrophobic interactions between particles. First, the particles are grouped into three classes: hydrophilic, hydrophobic and neutral. In general, all particles repel each other, but repulsion between hydrophilic and hydrophobic particles is much stronger than that between other particles so that phase separation between different classes of particles takes place. On the other hand, neutral particles do not repel other particles very strongly so that they can diffuse more freely.

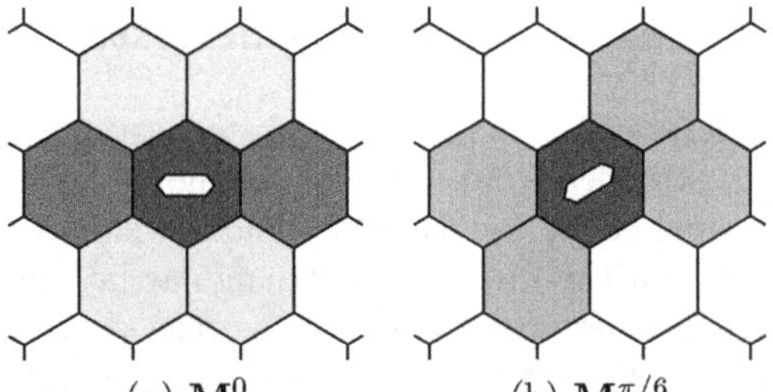

(a) $\mathbf{M}^0$ (b) $\mathbf{M}^{\pi/6}$

Figure 1: Illustration of repulsion around a particle **M**. The honeycomb cells represent the lattice sites. The depth of gray shade corresponds to the magnitude of repulsion against a hydrophilic particle on the site from the particle **M** on the center site. The repulsion becomes stronger on the dark gray sites than on the light gray sites.

Next, we assume that hydrophobic particles **M** are anisotropic. Namely, the repulsion around a particle **M** depends on its orientation and the configuration of the particles as illustrated in Fig. 1. There are specific directions in which the repulsion becomes strong, while the repulsion becomes weak in the other directions Taking its symmetry into account, a particle **M** can rotate to six different orientations ($\mathbf{M}^0$, $\mathbf{M}^{\pm\pi/6}$, $\mathbf{M}^{\pm\pi/3}$, $\mathbf{M}^{\pi/2}$) stochastically according to the gradient of the potential as follows,

$$p_{\mathbf{M}^{k\to k'}}(\mathbf{x}) = Rot \, f(\Psi_{\mathbf{M}^{k'}}(\mathbf{x}) - \Psi_{\mathbf{M}^k}(\mathbf{x})) \quad (4)$$

where $Rot = 0.01$ denotes the rotation coefficient. The repulsion between two particles **M** becomes strong when their orientations are different, so that they tend to align in the same orientation. According to these interactions, particles **M** gather together to form stretched clusters. We call these stretched structures of particle **M** "membrane". Though the characters of membranes, such as flexibility, depends on these values, the formation of membranes can be observed in a wide range of parameters. The detail values of repulsion $\psi_{ij}(d\mathbf{x})$ which are arbitrary chosen for the following experiments are listed in Tables 1a and 1b.

Table 1: a. Repulsion between isotropic particles.

particles		position	
		$dr = 0$	$dr = 1$
hydrophilic	hydrophilic	0.0100	0.0033
	neutral	0.0010	0.0003
neutral	neutral	0.0010	0.0003

Chemical Reaction

We introduce a simple metabolic system of autocatalytic particles. Consider that there are various species of self-replicating particles, and some of them have the ability to catalyze the production of membrane particles. Resources of these particles are supplied from some external source homogeneously.

Figure 2 illustrates the reaction paths. The probabilities of chemical reactions depend on the enthalpy change along with the transition, as follows,

$$\Delta H_{ij} = \Delta H_j - \Delta H_i \quad (5)$$

$$p_{i\to j}(\mathbf{x}) = k_{ij}(\mathbf{x}) \, f(\Delta H_{ij} + \Psi_j(\mathbf{x}) - \Psi_i(\mathbf{x})) \quad (6)$$

where ΔH_{ij} denotes the enthalpy change that is given by the difference in the formation enthalpy listed in Table 2.

Table 1.b Repulsion between hydrophobic and other particles

particles		position			
		$dr = 0$	$dr = 1$		
			$\theta = 0, \pi$	$\theta = \pi/3, -2\pi/3$	$\theta = 2\pi/3, -\pi/3$
$\mathbf{M}^0$	hydrophilic	0.2000	0.1600	0.0200	0.0200
	neutral	0.0010	0.0008	0.0001	0.0001
	$\mathbf{M}^0$	0.0100	0.0033	0.0033	0.0033
	$\mathbf{M}^{\pi/6}$	0.0777	0.0259	0.0259	0.0259
	$\mathbf{M}^{\pi/3}$	0.1433	0.0477	0.0477	0.0477
	$\mathbf{M}^{\pi/2}$	0.2100	0.0700	0.0700	0.0700
$\mathbf{M}^{\pi/6}$	hydrophilic	0.2000	0.1000	0.1000	0.0000
	neutral	0.0010	0.0005	0.0005	0.0000
	$\mathbf{M}^{\pi/6}$	0.0100	0.0033	0.0033	0.0033
	$\mathbf{M}^{-\pi/3}$	0.2100	0.0700	0.0700	0.0700

$k_{ij}(\mathbf{x})$ denotes the coefficient of reaction $i \leftrightarrow j$ that may depend on the number of catalysts on the site. Note that the effects of the interactive potential, namely, the effects of hydrophilic/hydrophobic environments are also taken into account here, therefore, for example, it becomes more difficult to synthesize a hydrophilic particle in a hydrophobic environment.

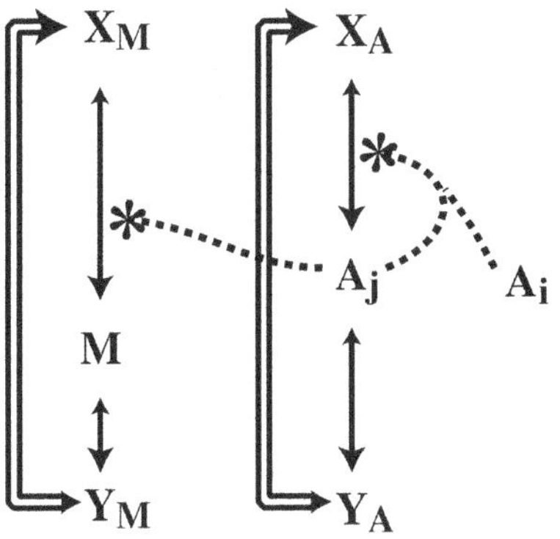

Figure 2: Schematic drawings of reaction paths. An autocatalyst ($\mathbf{A_i}$) catalyzes the reproduction of another particle $\mathbf{A_j}$ from a resource particle ($\mathbf{X_A}$) that has a higher chemical energy. It also catalyzes the production of a membrane particle ($\mathbf{M}$) from another resource particle ($\mathbf{X_M}$). All particles decay into waste particles ($\mathbf{Y_A}$ and $\mathbf{Y_M}$, respectively), spontaneously, however, an external energy supply recycles $\mathbf{Y_A}$ and $\mathbf{Y_M}$ into $\mathbf{X_A}$ and $\mathbf{X_M}$, respectively. The number of total particles is preserved.

Table 2: Formation enthalpy

particle	$\mathbf{X_A}, \mathbf{X_M}$	$\mathbf{A_i}$	$\mathbf{M}$	$\mathbf{Y_A}, \mathbf{Y_M}$
ΔH_i	12.0	6.0	4.0	0.0

There are ten species of autocatalytic particles ($\mathbf{A_0} \ldots \mathbf{A_9}$). An autocatalytic particle $\mathbf{A_i}$ catalyzes the replication of another particle $\mathbf{A_j}$ using it as a template and consuming a resource particle ($\mathbf{X_A}$).

$$\mathbf{A_i} + \mathbf{A_j} \longleftrightarrow \mathbf{A_i A_j} \quad (7)$$

$$\mathbf{A_i A_j} + \mathbf{X_A} \longleftrightarrow \mathbf{A_i A_j} + \mathbf{A_j} \quad (8)$$

There is a probability of mutation μ with which a particle $\mathbf{A_i}$ mutates to $\mathbf{A_{i\pm 1}}$ when it is reproduced. Assuming that the rate of the first reaction is much faster than that of the second one, the rate coefficients between $\mathbf{X_A}$ and $\mathbf{A_j}$ can be given as follows,

$$n'_{A_i}(\mathbf{x}) = \mu n_{A_{j-1}}(\mathbf{x}) + (1 - 2\mu) n_{A_j}(\mathbf{x}) + \mu n_{A_{j+1}}(\mathbf{x}) \quad (9)$$

$$k_{X_A \leftrightarrow A_j}(\mathbf{x}) = k_A + C_A n'_{A_i}(\mathbf{x}) \sum_i n_{A_i}(\mathbf{x}) \quad (10)$$

where $n_{A_i}(\mathbf{x})$ denotes the number of particles $\mathbf{A_i}$ on the site $\mathbf{x}$, and k_A denotes the rate of spontaneous reaction. Note that all autocatalysts share a common catalytic activity C_A and catalyze the replication of each other equally.

An autocatalytic particle also catalyzes the production of a membrane particle ($\mathbf{M}$) from a resource ($\mathbf{X_M}$). The activity (C_{M_i}) depends on the species. The catalytic activity of each species $\mathbf{A_i}$ is given by the following equation, namely, the activity of particle $\mathbf{A_i}$ is i-th times larger than that of particle $\mathbf{A_1}$, so that the rate coefficients between $\mathbf{X_M}$ and $\mathbf{M}$ are given as follows,

$$C_{M_i} = C_M \times i \quad (11)$$

$$k_{X_M \leftrightarrow M}(\mathbf{x}) = k_M + \sum_i C_{M_i} n_{A_i}(\mathbf{x}), \quad (12)$$

where C_M is a given constant, and k_M denotes the rate of spontaneous reaction.

These particles naturally decay into waste particles ($\mathbf{Y_A}$ and $\mathbf{Y_M}$, respectively) at a constant rate k_Y. However, we introduce an external source that supplies resources. To preserve the total number of particles, the resource supply is expressed by the exchange from waste to resource particles.Thus the transition coefficients are given as follows,

$$k_{A_j \leftrightarrow Y_A} = k_{M \leftrightarrow Y_M} \equiv k_Y \quad (13)$$

$$k_{X_A \to Y_A} = k_{X_M \to Y_M} \equiv k_Y \quad (14)$$

$$k_{Y_A \to X_A} = k_{Y_M \to X_M} \equiv k_Y + S_X. \quad (15)$$

Due to the term S_X, the whole system is kept in a non-equilibrium state. The last particle (**W**) represents water that does not change into other particles. We assume that water and autocatalytic particles are hydrophilic particles that are repelled by membranes, and resource and waste particles are neutral particles which can diffuse through membranes.

The rate coefficients of spontaneous reactions are $k_A = k_M = 1.0 \times 10^{-8}$, $k_Y = 1.0 \times 10^{-4}$. The coefficients of catalytic activity are $C_A = 1.0 \times 10^{-5}$ and $C_M = 1.0 \times 10^{-5}$. The mutation rate is $\mu = 1.0 \times 10^{-12}$. The rate of resource supply is given a constant $S_X = 16$.

The simulation is based on a Metropolis method. At each iteration, the following steps are repeated,

1. Calculate the potential of each particle.
2. Calculate the probabilities of diffusion, rotation and chemical transition according to the potential difference.
3. Change the state of particles according to the probabilities synchronously.

In the initial state, the particles are placed randomly. There are 30 particles on a site on average, and the mean numbers of particles on a site are listed in Table 3. There is a sufficient number of resource particles and supplies to sustain metabolism. The average production rate of membranes is set very low at first. Catalysts with higher activity only emerge through random mutations. The reaction sites are arranged as a 64×64 triangular lattice whose boundaries are periodic.

Table 3: Mean numbers on a site in the initial state

particle	$\mathbf{A_0}$	$\mathbf{A_1}$	$\mathbf{A_2}$	$\mathbf{A_3}$	$\mathbf{A_4 \ldots A_9}$	
$\overline{n}_i$	1.6	1.2	0.8	0.4	0.0	
particle	$\mathbf{X_A}$	$\mathbf{Y_A}$	$\mathbf{M}$	$\mathbf{X_M}$	$\mathbf{Y_M}$	$\mathbf{W}$
$\overline{n}_i$	2.0	2.0	0.0	5.0	5.0	10.0

Simulation Results

The evolution of this system is roughly divided into three characteristic stages: (1) Chemical evolution, (2) Emergence of proto-cells, and (3) Cellular evolution.

Chemical Evolution

Fig. 3(1) shows the initial configuration. Before cellular selection starts, the chemical evolution simply depends on the reproduction rate of each species. In this model, because they share the same reproduction rate, the evolution is mostly driven by mutations and random fluctuation. At first, the largest part of the autocatalytic particles is $\mathbf{A_0}$ which does not produce membrane particles. Table 4 shows a profile of the population after 30,000 iterations for a single run. However, as the populations of other species increase, small pieces of membranes are gradually formed. (Fig. 3(2)).

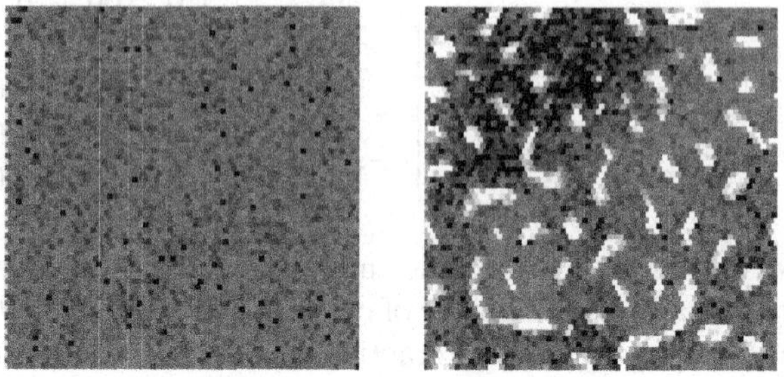

(1) Initial state (2) After 30,000 iterations

Figure 3: Chemical evolution. The white regions are dominated by particle **M**. The depth of gray shade represents the total population of the autocatalysts ($\sum \mathbf{A_i}$). The black regions are dominated by particle **W**. Resource and waste particles are not displayed in the figures. Pieces of membranes are produced by the catalysts which emerged through mutations.

Table 4: A profile of the population of particles after 30,000 iterations.

particle	$\mathbf{A_0}$	$\mathbf{A_1}$	$\mathbf{A_2}$	$\mathbf{A_3}$	$\mathbf{A_4}$
$\overline{n}_i$	1.00	0.60	0.42	0.20	0.05
particle	$\mathbf{A_5}$	$\mathbf{A_6}$	$\mathbf{A_7}$	$\mathbf{A_8}$	$\mathbf{A_9}$
$\overline{n}_i$	0.07	0.08	0.05	0.04	0.06
particle	$\mathbf{X_A}$	$\mathbf{Y_A}$	$\mathbf{M}$	$\mathbf{X_M}$	$\mathbf{Y_M}$
$\overline{n}_i$	3.00	4.43	1.57	3.68	4.77

Emergence of Proto-cells

Once membranes are formed, they begin to restrict the diffusion of catalysts. Thus, membranes can keep the local population and also their reaction rate high. As resource particles are consumed faster in such regions, resource particles diffuse into these regions according to the gradient of the population. It increases their reaction rate more. Due to this osmotic competition for resources, a small difference in the population of autocatalysts between the two sides of the membrane becomes larger.

When the density of resources becomes too low in some regions, autocatalysts are no longer able to sustain their replication. Autocatalysts and membrane particles in these regions decay. At last, most regions become in-

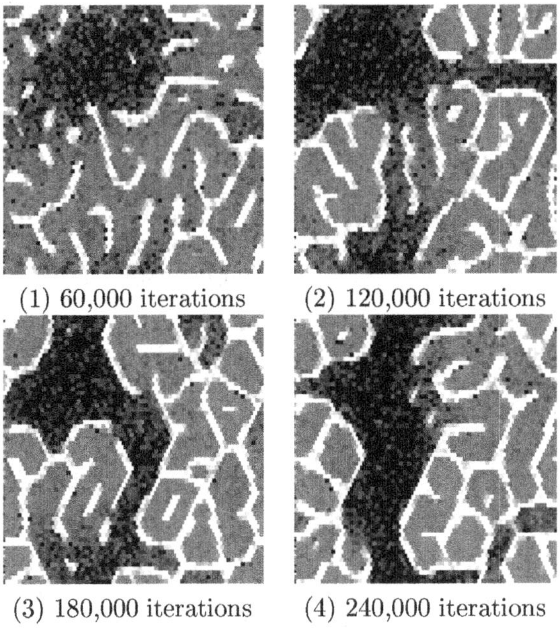

(1) 60,000 iterations (2) 120,000 iterations (3) 180,000 iterations (4) 240,000 iterations

Figure 4: Emergence of Proto-cell structures. As the membranes grow, competition for resources between regions separated by membranes takes place. The regions differentiate into two states. In some regions that are enclosed by membranes, the density of autocatalysts stays high. In the other regions, their density becomes almost zero.

active, namely, filled with only resource and waste particles (and water), while there remain some active regions in which autocatalysts keep reproducing. These structures maintain themselves autopoietically, namely, the autocatalysts inside them reproduce themselves and metabolize the membrane particles to maintain their membranes. We call this structure a "proto-cell" hereafter.

Cellular Reproduction

A proto-cell can not only maintain itself but can reproduce itself. Figure 5 shows snapshots of the reproduction process. A proto-cell structure grows in size by assimilating resource particles from neighboring regions. As it grows, it comes to produce more membrane particles than it needs to maintain its membrane. When it reaches a certain size, surplus membrane particles begin to form another membrane inside the cell. This divides the mother cell into a few daughter cells. The daughter cells can continue to grow and reproduce recursively.

On the other hand, if a cell fails to maintain its membrane, the density of catalysts lowers quickly due to diffusion through the defect of membrane. When the density becomes too low, the catalysts can not sustain the metabolism any longer, and the whole structure finally disappears. This mutual dependency between membrane and metabolic system is essential to the evolution of proto-cells.

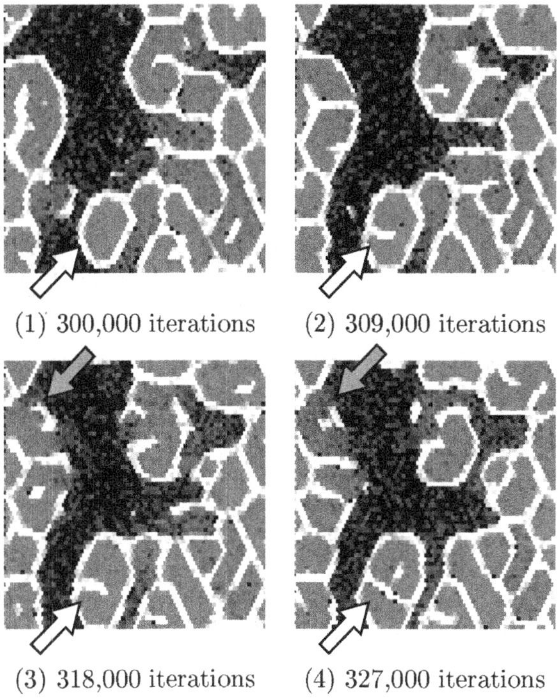

(1) 300,000 iterations (2) 309,000 iterations (3) 318,000 iterations (4) 327,000 iterations

Figure 5: Reproduction of proto-cell. Snapshots from 300,000 iterations to 327,000 iterations. The proto-cell indicated by the white arrow grows gradually in size. When it becomes too large, another membrane appears inside it. At last, it divides the cell into daughter cells. On the other hand, the cell indicated by the gray arrows could not produce enough membrane particles to keep its membrane. Catalysts in the cell diffuse away through the defect of the membrane.

Selection of Catalysts Through Cellular Reproduction

Figure 6 shows the evolution of the population of catalysts. If there is no spatial structure, the populations of catalysts just randomly drift around the equilibrium where all populations are equal. However, once the differentiation into active and inactive regions has advanced, it becomes difficult to sustain metabolism without membranes, because the density of autocatalysts lowers fast.

Note that when a proto-cell divides itself, the composition of the population of replicators contained in the cell is roughly inherited by the daughter cells. This implies that catalysts that can sustain a proto-cell more stably are selected regarding a proto-cell as a new unit of Darwinian evolution. Therefore, due to cellular selection, the populations of catalysts are biased toward higher membrane production activity against the random drift. The populations of catalysts and their relative amount ($\rho_i = \overline{n_i}/\sum \overline{n_j} \times 100$) after 600,000 iterations for the same run as the previous one are listed in Table 5.

To make the effects of the cellular selection more clear,

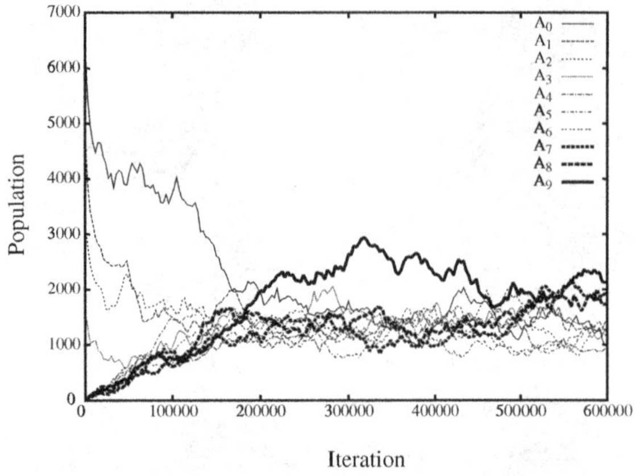

Figure 6: Evolution of the population of autocatalysts. At first, the population of $\mathbf{A_0}$, which does not produce membrane particles, is the largest. However, other species arise through mutation, and after the formation of proto-cells, species which can produce membranes have an advantage over $\mathbf{A_0}$ (see the thick lines which denote species $\mathbf{A_7}$ – $\mathbf{A_9}$).

Table 5: A profile of the populations of catalysts after 600,000 iterations.

particle	$\mathbf{A_0}$	$\mathbf{A_1}$	$\mathbf{A_2}$	$\mathbf{A_3}$	$\mathbf{A_4}$
$\overline{n}_i$	0.24	0.36	0.28	0.30	0.23
$\rho_i(\%)$	7.0	10.5	8.1	8.7	6.7
particle	$\mathbf{A_5}$	$\mathbf{A_6}$	$\mathbf{A_7}$	$\mathbf{A_8}$	$\mathbf{A_9}$
$\overline{n}_i$	0.31	0.31	0.46	0.43	0.52
$\rho_i(\%)$	9.0	9.0	13.4	12.5	15.1

we investigated evolution under a lower resource supply. The initial configuration and the parameters are the same as those of the previous run. After the formation of the proto-cell structures (after 300,000 iterations), the rate of resource supply S_X was decreased to $S_X \times 0.75$. Because the density of resource particles decreases, catalysts have to keep their density high to maintain a sufficient reproduction rate more tightly, and a cell that fails to maintain its membrane disappears faster. The pressure to acquire higher membrane production activity becomes stronger. Table 6 shows the populations after 900,000 iterations for another run. The dominance of catalysts with higher activity is clearer.

To see the detailed process of cellular selection, the evolution of the mean activity ($\overline{C_{M_i}} = \sum C_{M_i} N_{A_i} / \sum N_{A_i}$) of membrane production is shown in Fig. 7. Within a cell, because competition among the autocatalysts is neutral, the mean activity of each cell fluctuates randomly. But among the cellular assembly, a proto-cell in which membrane production activity is low becomes extinct more often. As a result, cells with higher catalytic activity outperform the lower ones and

Table 6: A profile of populations after 900,000 iterations under the lower resource supply.

particle	$\mathbf{A_0}$	$\mathbf{A_1}$	$\mathbf{A_2}$	$\mathbf{A_3}$	$\mathbf{A_4}$
$\overline{n}_i$	0.19	0.10	0.11	0.16	0.13
$\rho_i(\%)$	8.6	4.5	5.0	7.3	5.9
particle	$\mathbf{A_5}$	$\mathbf{A_6}$	$\mathbf{A_7}$	$\mathbf{A_8}$	$\mathbf{A_9}$
$\overline{n}_i$	0.18	0.25	0.20	0.42	0.46
$\rho_i(\%)$	8.2	11.4	9.1	19.1	20.9

the total average of $\overline{C_{M_i}}$ gradually increases.

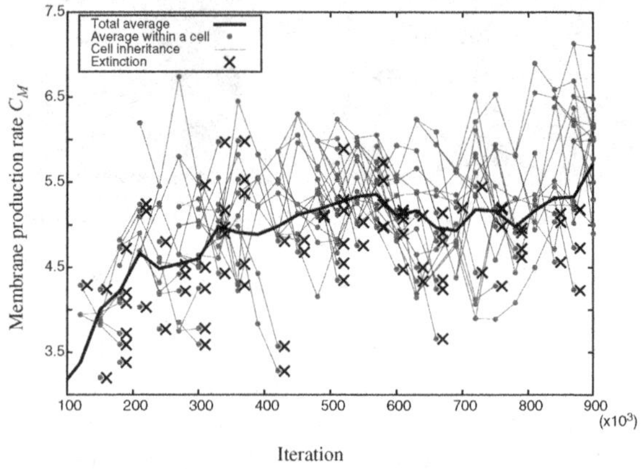

Figure 7: Evolution of the mean activity of membrane production ($\overline{C_{M_i}}$). A cell with lower membrane production breaks more often because its membrane is weaker.

Though there often appear cells with very high activity of membrane production, the $\overline{C_{M_i}}$ of these cells soon drops again. These drops are caused by the invasion of "parasitic" catalysts. Namely, the evolved cells are dominated by catalysts that have higher activity and produce enough membrane particles, however, the catalysts with lower activity, e.g., $\mathbf{A_0}$, can always emerge through mutation and increase through the random fluctuation within these cells. Snapshots of the process of cellular selection are shown in Fig. 8. At 780,000 iterations, the cells indicated by the white arrows are deeply infected by parasites. It becomes difficult for these cells to maintain their membranes and they disappear before 900,000 iterations. The cells at 900,000 iterations are produced from survived cells that have higher catalytic activity, but, there are cells that are newly invaded by parasites (indicated by the gray arrow). This result indicates that these proto-cells have limited "life spans". A proto-cell has to keep dividing itself to escape from parasites, otherwise, the parasitic catalysts increase in it before long.

As the cellular evolution proceeds, it is observed that the size of the cells becomes smaller. Figure 9 shows a histogram of cell sizes (namely, the number of sites within the membranes) for the same run, after 300,000,

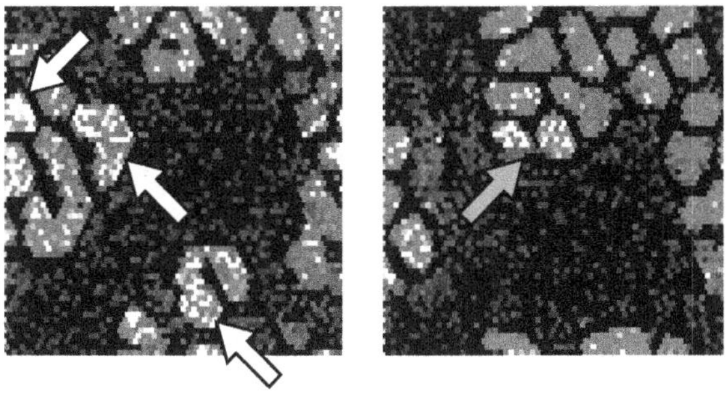

(1) 780,000 iterations (2) 900,000 iterations

Figure 8: Invasion of parasitic catalysts. The white sites are where the mean catalytic activity is low.

600,000 and 900,000 iterations. The mean sizes of cells at each iteration are 103.8, 82.7, and 66.2, respectively. When the mean activity of the membrane production of a cell increases, it can maintain its membrane with fewer catalysts, and it can divide itself faster. However, it is sometimes observed that a cell whose size is too small fails to maintain itself. When a cell produces too many membrane particles or the size of cell become too small, the rate of replication of the autocatalysts decreases, because the hydrophobic environment suppress the synthesis of hydrophilic particles. A certain optimum size of the cell will be achieved through the selection of catalysts. This expectation is supported by the result that, in the evolved state, the dispersion of cell sizes becomes smaller.

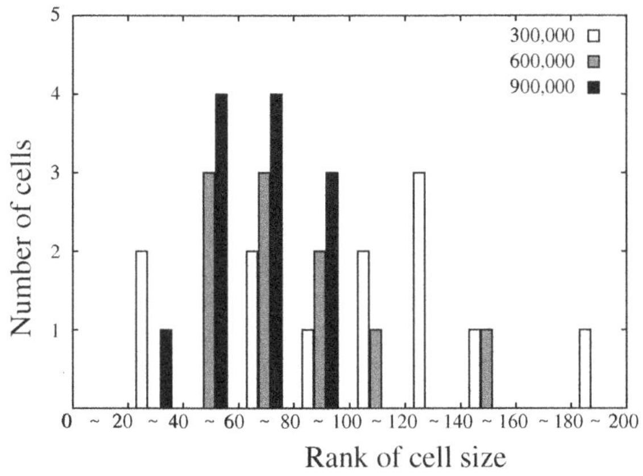

Figure 9: The distribution of cell sizes after 300,000, 600,000 and 900,000 iterations. The standard deviations of the sizes are 47.52, 26.58,and 24.26, respectively.

Conclusion and Discussion

In this article, we have presented a model for the evolution from molecular to cellular reproduction. Starting from a homogeneous, random initial state, we demonstrated the emergence of proto-cells. This goes through three stages: (1) Metabolic cycles that produce membrane molecules can arise through pre-cellular chemical evolution. (2) Proto-cell structures, i.e., self-maintaining structures that maintain their own membranes by themselves emerge spontaneously. (3) A proto-cell structure reproduces itself. Because the molecules contained inside a proto-cell can pass genetic information into daughter cells, it can be regarded as a unit of Darwinian evolution. Cells that can maintain themselves more stably evolve through cellular selection.

Excess production of membrane particles generates a hydrophobic environment, which is less optimal for the self-reproduction of the particles. Nevertheless, particles with higher catalytic ability replicate more via cellular level selection. As a result, the average value of catalyzation with membrane formation becomes higher than that without membrane formation. We insist here that the emergence of cellular structures produces a new rugged evolutionary landscape on the particle level.

The entire behavior is insensitive to parameter values whenever we have the conditions of, 1) a membrane formation and 2) transportation of resource particles through membranes. This robust behavior gives an advantage to our model over other cellular formation systems such as Grey-Scott, whose spatio-temporal pattern is sensitive to reaction and diffusion rates. In our model, the size of cells and replication rates change but their qualitative behaviors never change. Instead, our model behavior is sensitive to the form of repulsion potential of the membrane particles. In this study, we chose a set of values which provide flexible membranes to make the organization of proto-cells easier. We take the advantage of this sensitivity to the potential form in order to study the evolutionary dynamics of these characteristics of membranes of proto-cells.

In the simulations reported here, the resources supply was homogeneous. And the pressure to evolve membrane production became clear when the resource supply rate was lowered. These results suggest that, if the supply of resource is not homogeneous, namely, if there is a small region where the resource supply is plenty enough to sustain metabolism, but the supply is rather poor in the other regions, pre-cellular evolution will take place where the resource supply is high enough, and once the proto-cell structures are acquired, they can migrate where the resource supply is lower, which will promote the further evolution of cellular structures.

Though the model introduced in this article is simple and abstract, we are now extending our model to implement more complex metabolic reactions that can produce more diverse membrane particles and various cell types. Our next objective is to investigate the co-evolution of metabolic systems and cellular structures. Because in our model, the birth and death of cells are all actualized through the elemental interactions of particles, without any ad-hoc rules, the way in which the proto-cell is organized itself can evolve. In this sense, it can be regarded as a basic model for the organization of a dynamical hierarchy. We expect that higher order structures (e.g., cell differentiation and cooperative interaction between cells) are yielded.

Furthermore, the dynamics of our model is based on a local equilibrium system. A quantitative analysis of this model may bring insight to the evolution of primitive cells as a non-equilibrium system from a thermodynamical aspect. Along these lines, computational models of artificial chemistry will provide useful tools for understanding the earliest evolution of life.

Acknowledgments

This work was partially supported by the COE project ("complex systems theory of life"), a Grant-in-aid (No. 11837003) from the Ministry of Education, Science, Sports and Culture and afiis project (Academic Frontier, Intelligent Information Science 2000 - 2004 Doshisha University).

References

Breyer, J.; Ackermann, J.; and McCaskill, J. 1998. Evolving reaction-diffusion ecosystems with self-assembling structures in thin films. *Artificial Life* 4:25–40.

Gánti, T. 1975. Organization of chemical reactions into dividing and metabolizing units: The chemotons. *BioSystems* 7:15–21.

Gánti, T. 1997. Biogenesis itself. *J. theol. Biol.* 187:583–593.

Maturana, H. R., and Varela, F. J. 1980. *Autopoiesis and Cognition: the Realization of the Living.* D. Reidel Publishing.

McMullin, B., and Varela, F. J. 1997. Rediscovering computational autopoiesis. In Husbands, P., and Harvey, I., eds., *4th European Conference on Artificial Life*, 38–47. Brighton, UK: MIT press.

Ono, N., and Ikegami, T. 1999. Model of self-replicating cell capable of self-maintenance. In Floreano, D.; Nicoud, J. D.; and Mondada, F., eds., *Proceedings of the 5th European Conference on Artificial Life (ECAL'99)*, 399–406. Lausanne, Switzerland: Springer.

Ono, N., and Ikegami, T. 2001. Artificial chemistry: Computational studies on the emergence of self-reproducing units. In Kelemen, J., and Sosik, S., eds., *Proceedings of the 6th European Conference on Artificial Life (ECAL'01)*, 186–195. Prague, Czech Republic: Springer.

Speroni di Fenizio, P.; Dittrich, P.; and Banzhaf, W. 2001. Spontaneous formation of proto-cells in a universal artificial chemistry of a planar graph. In Kelemen, J., and Sosik, S., eds., *Proceedings of the 6th European Conference on Artificial Life (ECAL'01)*, 206–215. Prague, Czech Republic: Springer.

Szathmáry, E., and Maynard Smith, J. 1997. From replicators to reproducers: the first major transitions leading to life. *J. theor. Biol* 187:555–571.

Varela, F. J.; Maturana, H. R.; and Uribe, R. 1974. Autopoiesis: The organization of living systems, its characterization and a model. *BioSystems* 5:187–196.

Zeleny, M. 1977. Self-organization of living systems: A formal model of autopoiesis. *International Journal of General Science* 4:13–28.

Evolution in Asynchronous Cellular Automata

Chrystopher L. Nehaniv

Adaptive Systems Research Group
Faculty of Engineering & Information Sciences
University of Hertfordshire
Hatfield Herts AL10 9AB
United Kingdom

Abstract

Building on the work of Von Neumann, Langton, and Sayama among others, we introduce the first examples of evolution in populations of self-reproducing configurations in *asynchronous* cellular automata. Reliance on a global synchronous update signal has been a limitation of all solutions since the problem of achieving self-production in cellular automata was first attacked by Von Neumann half a century ago. Results of the author obviate the need for this restriction.

We review our simple constructive mechanism to transform any cellular automata network with synchronous update into one with essentially the same behavior but whose cells may be updated randomly and asynchronously. The generality of this mechanism is guaranteed by a general mathematical theorem that any synchronous cellular automata configuration and rule can be realized asynchronously in such a way that the behavior of the original synchronous cellular automata can be completely recovered from that of the corresponding asynchronous cellular automaton, in which temporal synchronization locally stays within small tolerances.

It follows that most results on self-reproduction, universal computation and construction, and evolution in populations of self-reproducing configurations in cellular automata that have been obtained in the past carry over to the asynchronous domain using the method described here.

Here we discuss requirements for evolutionary systems in cellular automata and describe implemented examples of our procedure applied to a variety of self-reproducing systems (Byl, Reggia et al., Langton, Sayama).

In particular, we have implemented Sayama's evo-loop system asynchronously, giving the first example of evolution in asynchronous cellular automata.

Introduction

From the beginnings of the study of self-reproduction in artificial systems initiated by John Von Neumann in 1948, the primary formal model has been synchronous cellular automata in which configurations develop that eventually may include an unbounded number of copies of the original. The models constructed by Von Neumman and his successors have amply demonstrated that self-reproduction is indeed possible in artificial systems. Furthermore, Von Neumann's work on his automata models even anticipated the important transcription ("blind copying") and translation ("executability") properties of genetic material later found for DNA.

Naturally, the different possible mechanisms for achieving self-reproduction have implications for our understanding of the origin of life, the nature of organic life and evolution, and for the possibilities of life as it may exist elsewhere in the universe. Szathmáry (1999) has proposed a classification of replicators that is applicable to natural and artificial systems, but this has by no means settled the controversies and questions regarding what types of self-replication are, in principle, possible, or regarding what modes of self-replication are necessary or minimal for evolvability. Thus, further study of replication and possible bases for heritability are called for, as self-reproduction is an indispensible prerequisite for any independent evolutionary process. Moreover, self-reproduction and self-repair (or self-maintenance) are often closely related in biology, and an understanding of self-reproduction can thus contribute to our ability to create self-repairing, self-maintaining hardware and software. Sending information, instructions on how to build copies of desired structures using local materials, into an environment rather than sending all necessary materials into that environment represents more economical methods of space exploration and colonization. A NASA report edited by Freitas and Gilbreath (1980) discusses further potential examples and applications of self-reproduction to space science, e.g. proposed self-replicating and self-maintaining lunar factories.

Cellular automata models of self-reproduction have always relied on global synchronous updates. However, the need for an assumption of synchronous update in these spaces may be questioned. In building an artificial self-reproducing entity is it really necessary to have a single global synchronization signal that reaches all parts of the entity simultaneously (or at least within a well-defined tolerance)? If local parts of the configuration are ready to change their state, is it realistic and practical to assume that they must wait until all other parts of the cellular space are also ready to update their states? Will our assumption of synchronous update unnecessarily constrain and limit the types of self-reproducing systems we are able to build?

In (Nehaniv, 2002), we presented a method to free all cellular automata models of self-reproduction (as well as all cellular automata models of evolution, universal computation, and universal construction) from the need for synchronous update. This is accomplished by an elegant simple mechanism that allows one to construct an asynchronous cellular automaton that is capable of emulating the behavior of a given synchronous cellular automaton. State updates in the asynchronous model may be produced by any asynchronous update mechanism whatsoever (e.g. updates may be random, sequential, locally Poisson-distributed, partially simultaneous, etc., or even synchronous). This result for cellular automata is a special case of a more general mathematical theorem, due to the author (Nehaniv, 2002 (accepted)), for automata networks with inputs. Nehaniv (2002) also gave the first implemented examples of self-reproduction in asynchronous cellular automata by applying this method to Langton's example of synchronous self-reproduction in cellular automata (Langton 1984).

In this paper, we first review the concepts of cellular automata and our construction for making any cellular automata computation asynchronously realizable. In the companion paper (Nehaniv 2002) appear illustrations of implementations of this method to (1) Conway's Game of Life (which entail that, in principle, universal computation can be achieved by an asynchronous version of Life) and to (2) the first examples of self-reproduction in cellular automata. Going beyond these results, in this paper we describe additional, implemented models of self-reproduction in asynchronous cellular automata. Moreover, we exhibit the first implemented example of evolution occurring in asynchronous cellular automata.

Preliminaries on Cellular Automata

In this section we review the necessary background on synchronous and asynchronous cellular automata.

Cellular Automata: Definitions

Cellular automata were introduced by J. Von Neumman and S. Ulam to model natural physical and biological phenomena, in particular, for Von Neumann's pioneering studies of self-reproduction.

A *graph* Γ is a set of *nodes* V and a set of *edges* E. An edge $e \in E$ is an unordered pair of nodes $\{v, v'\} \subseteq V$. The *neighborhood* of a node is the set of nodes directly connected to it in the graph by an edge. That is, node v is a neighbor of v' if $\{v, v'\}$ is an edge in the graph. We shall write $v' \in nbhd(v)$ if node v' is a neighbor of node v.

A deterministic *finite state automaton* $\mathcal{A}$ is finite set of states Q, a finite set of inputs X and a transition function $\delta : Q \times X \to Q$.

A *cellular automaton* is a finite or infinite network of identical deterministic finite state automata and a graph structure such that:
(1) each node has the same (finite) number of neighbors,
(2) at each node we have a fixed ordering on the neighbor nodes (e.g. north, south, east, and west if there are exactly four neighbors to every node), and
(3) the next state of an automaton at node v is always the same function δ of its current state and the current states of its neighbors. (Thus the ordered list of states at neighbor nodes is the input to the automaton at node v.)
We shall denote the ordered list of the states of the neighbors of node v by $(q_w)_{w \in nbhd(v)}$.

Although cellular automata are more general, for our purposes, we may assume that the graph can be realized in some N-dimensional Euclidean space, for example as the set of points with integer coordinates, with edges connecting points that differ by at most exactly 1 in exactly one position ("the Von Neumman neighborhood") or, alternatively by at most 1 in each coordinate ("the Moore neighborhood"). For example, in a two-dimensional case the point (2,3) has neighbors (1,3), (3,3), (2,4), and (3,3) if our cellular automaton uses a Von Neumann neighborhood, and has additional neighbors (1,2), (1,4), (3,2), (3,4) if we instead have a cellular automaton with Moore neighborhoods. We may allow "wrap around" or a "toroidal topology" by identifying nodes which differ by a fixed vector. For example, in a 25 $\times$ 50 node toroidal topology with Von Neumann neighborhood, node (1,1) has neighbors (1,2), (2,1), (25,1) and (1,50) since (25,1) is identified with node (0,1) and (1,50) is identified with (1,0).[1]

Such cellular automata network topologies are specific examples, but the methods presented here and the supporting mathematical results apply to all cellular automata networks regardless of the details of their particular topologies.

In addition there is usually assumed to be a *quiescent state* $q_0 \in Q$ in the local finite state automata such that if the automaton at node v is in state q_0 and all of its neighbors are in state q_0, then in the next time step the automaton at node v will still be in state q_0. (We will not have a strictly quiescent state in our asynchronous cellular automata.)

A *configuration* is any assignment of local state values to the set of automata at nodes in a finite subgraph of Γ.

[1]We remark that these definitions of Von Neumann and Moore neighborhoods, and that of toroidal topology, are applicable to any dimension N.

Synchronous vs. Asynchronous Update Rules

Usually a cellular automaton $\mathcal{A}$ is required to update the state of the finite automata at all of its nodes simultaneously and in discrete steps. Thus, for all discrete times $t \geq 0$, if at discrete time step t each node v is in some state $q_v(t)$ then at the next discrete time step $t+1$ node v is in its next state $q_v(t+1)$. In the notation introduced above,

$$q_v(t+1) = \delta(q_v(t), (q_w(t))_{w \in nbhd(v)}).$$

Thus the new state $q_v(t+1)$ at node v is given by the local update rule as a function of $q_v(t)$, the current state of v, and the (finite) list $(q_w(t))_{w \in nbhd(v)}$ of all current states $q_w(t)$ of all nodes w in the neigborhood of v. In this case of globally simultaneous update, we say that the cellular automaton is *synchronous*. The *global state* of the cellular automaton $\mathcal{A}$ at time t is comprised of the states $q_v(t)$ of all its nodes at time t and can be regarded as a function from nodes V to local states Q.

If the updates of the local component automata are not required to take place synchronously, but each one will be updated to its next state an unbounded number of times as (locally discrete) time goes on, then we speak of an *asynchronous* automata network. The updates are otherwise unconstrained, e.g. they may be deterministic, non-deterministic, random, sequential, etc., or even synchronous. For further discussion of the relevance of synchronous and asynchronous cellular automata to the modelling of biological systems see for example (Schönfisch and de Roos, 1999). Prior to this paper and (Nehaniv, 2002), all published models of self-reproduction and evolution in cellular automata have used only synchronous cellular automata update rules.

Following the general method and theorem of (Nehaniv, 2002 (accepted)), which also applies to more general types of automata networks than cellular automata, for each synchronous cellular automaton $\mathcal{A}$ on graph Γ, we construct another particular cellular automaton $\mathcal{A}'$ on the same graph. Moreover, if the local finite automata in $\mathcal{A}$ have n states then component automaton in $\mathcal{A}'$ at each node v will have $3n^2$ states. The author's theorem guarantees that if $\mathcal{A}'$ is updated by any asynchronous method whatsoever, for each time t in the computation of $\mathcal{A}$, the global state of $\mathcal{A}$ at t is completely determined by a "continuous spatio-temporal section" of the behavior of $\mathcal{A}'$ (see below).

This mathematical theorem implies that all computations that can be carried out on any synchronous automata network can be recovered from the computation of an asynchronous automata network with no constraints on how the updates actually occur in the latter.

Construction of Equivalent Asynchronous Models

The construction of the local automata of the asynchronous cellular automaton $\mathcal{A}'$ from local automata of the synchronous cellular automaton $\mathcal{A}$ is extremely straightforward: Suppose the local automaton of $\mathcal{A}$ has states $Q = \{q_0, \ldots, q_{n-1}\}$ with q_0 quiescent and update function $\delta : Q \times X \to Q$.

The states of the local automaton in $\mathcal{A}'$ are the $3n^2$ states $Q \times Q \times \{0,1,2\}$.

For $r \in \{0,1,2\}$, we say the neighborhood of a node v in the asynchronous cellular automaton $\mathcal{A}'$ is *ready*(r) if none of v's neighbors is in a state with third component equal to $r+2 \pmod 3$.[2] Recall that we write $w \in nbhd(v)$ if w is a node in the neighborhood of v.

The update rule of this local automaton is given as follows: suppose node v is in state (q, q', r) with q and q' in Q, and $r \in \{0,1,2\}$, and has neighborhood with list of states $(q_w, q'_w, r_w)_{w \in nbhd(v)}$, then, if $r = 0$, the next state of node v is

$$\delta'((q,q',0),(q_w,q'_w,r_w)_{w \in nbhd(v)})$$

$$= \begin{cases} (\delta(q,(q''_w)_{w \in nbhd(v)}), q, 1) & \text{if the neighborhood of } v \text{ is } ready(0) \\ (q,q',0) & \text{otherwise,} \end{cases}$$

$$\text{where } q''_w = \begin{cases} q_w & \text{if node } w \text{ is in a state of the form } (q_w, q'_w, 0) \\ q'_w & \text{if node } w \text{ is in a state of the form } (q_w, q'_w, 1). \end{cases}$$

(Since the neighborhood is *ready*(0), these are the only possibilities. Note the use of the original local transition function δ of the synchronous cellular automaton $\mathcal{A}$ in this case of the definition of δ'.)
For the remaining cases with $r \in \{1,2\}$, the next state is

$$\delta'((q,q',r),(q_w,q'_w,r_w)_{w \in nbhd(v)})$$

$$= \begin{cases} (q,q',r+1 \pmod 3) & \text{if the neighborhood of } v \text{ is } ready(r) \\ (q,q',r) & \text{otherwise.} \end{cases}$$

The state (q, q', r) can be thought of as encoding the following information: The first coordinate q shows the "visible" state of the corresponding network $\mathcal{A}$ at this node. The second coordinate q' is "hidden" and is used to remember the most recent old state of this node, in case any neighbor needs to refer to it. The third coordinate is used to locally synchronize updates of the visible and hidden nodes.

[2]For any integer n, "$n \pmod 3$" denotes the least nonnegative integer k such that $n - k$ is divisible by 3. Of course k must then be one of $\{0,1,2\}$.

The above rule δ' only allows a local state of $\mathcal{A}'$ to change if no node in the neighborhood will get more than one step behind if the update were to be made, otherwise it allows no change at all to the current state. The important $ready(0)$ and $r = 0$ case occurs exactly when the asynchronous cellular automaton is locally ready to emulate the transition of the synchronous cellular automata at this local node using the local transition function of $\mathcal{A}$. Intuitively, the third component of a node v's state can locally distinguish 'present', 'future', and 'past' for neighboring nodes, respectively, by whether they have modulo 3 value equal to, one more than, or one less than the value of the third component of v's state.

Properties of the Emulation

The asynchronous cellular automaton has two important properties established with detailed mathematical proofs in the main theorem of (Nehaniv, 2002 (accepted)):

Suppose the synchronous cellular automaton $\mathcal{A}$ is started in configuration C with node v in state $C(v)$ and all other cells quiescent. Also suppose that asynchronous cellular automaton $\mathcal{A}'$ is started with each node v of the configuration active in state $(C(v), C(v), 0)$ and all other nodes in state $(q_0, q_0, 0)$.

Freedom from Deadlocks. At each node v of the asynchronous network, if the state of v has third component $r \in \{0, 1, 2\}$ eventually the neighborhood of v will be $ready(r)$, and the third component will change value to $r + 1 \pmod 3$.

Existence of Continuous Spatio-Temporal Sections. The state $q_v(0)$ at time 0 of node v of $\mathcal{A}$ is equal to the first component of the state of node v of $\mathcal{A}'$ in its initial configuration. By mathematical induction, one shows that the state $q_v(t)$ of node v in $\mathcal{A}$ at time t is equal to the first component of the state of node v in $\mathcal{A}'$ on the tth time that the third component of node v becomes 1.

The latter property implies that it is possible to completely recover the behavior of $\mathcal{A}$ from the behavior of $\mathcal{A}'$ by simply recording the first components in the initial configuration of $\mathcal{A}'$ and recording the first component of each node v whenever its local automaton makes a transition so that the third component changes from 0 to 1.[3]

[3]The author discovered this construction of asynchronous cellular automata emulating any synchronous cellular automaton on 4 August 1998. An anonymous referee has kindly pointed out that independently Tommaso Toffoli (1978) described a closely related construction, using a modulo 4 counter for local synchronization. (See also Toffoli and Margolus (1987, pp. 90–94)). However complete proofs of the above properties appear not to have been published. Even earlier and also independently, Katsuo Nakamura (1974) discovered the same construction as the author (thanks to Ferdinand Peper for this observation). The multiple independent discoveries of this and related methods is clear evidence of their naturality and importance. See (Nehaniv (2002), accepted) for complete, detailed proofs of the above mentioned properties, also in the more general setting of automata networks (i.e., inhomogeneous cellular automata with inputs, and with topologies given by general directed graphs of finitely bounded degree).

Temporal Waves

To an observer, time as it occurs in the synchronous cellular automata may seem to pass at different rates in different parts of the asynchronous cellular space. In fact, locally all neighboring cells are guaranteed to show a visible state (first component) that occurs at most one unit of time in the past or future relative to the corresponding state in the synchronous automaton. Thus, time of the synchronous cellular automaton is emulated in a manner such that it can never get very far out of sync locally in the emulating asynchronous cellular automaton.

This results in waves of temporal update in the cellular space with continuous wavefronts all in the same state of temporal synchronization (i.e., all with the same third component) representing the same moment in the synchronous cellular automaton.

In many of the figures below the relative temporal synchronization of each cell is indicated by differences in shading. Another example is illustration of temporal waves occurs in (Nehaniv 2002) for the example of an asynchronous version of John Conway's famous "Game of Life". Note that the possibility of implementation of Conway's Game of Life in an asynchronous cellular automaton entails that universal computation is possible in a two-dimensional asynchronous cellular automata running the modified rules (Nehaniv 2002).

Self-Reproduction in Asynchronous Cellular Automata

Detailed background on self-reproduction in cellular automata, including a survey of proposed definitions and problems with these can be found in (Nehaniv 2002), so we give only a brief overview before illustrating our various implementations of self-reproduction in asynchronous cellular automata. Discussions of the relationship of self-reproduction to individuality and the heritability of fitness can also be found there.

Some Synchronous Implementations

Langton (1984) implemented and studied the first example of feasible self-reproduction in cellular automata, using an 8-state cellular automaton with an initial configuration of 86 cells, that produces a first offspring after 151 time steps and then proceeds to fill up available space with copies. To avoid trivialities while avoiding the complexity of Von Neumann's model, *Langton's criterion* (1984, 1986) was proposed as a necessary condition on self-reproduction and requires that information is treated in two ways: as instructions that are *executed* ('translation') and as data which are blindly *copied* ('transcription'). These properties are also present in and abstracted from the general constructive and general copying capacities of Von Neumann's and later Codd's (1968) examples, and by that time also known to be characteristic of biological self-reproduction. Subsequent examples of Byl (1989) and Reggia et al. (e.g., Reggia, Armentrout, Chou, and Peng (1993), Lohn and Reggia (1997)) simplified the self-replicating loop of Langton with fewer states or less cells in the initial configuration. Subsequently, various researchers kept Langton's requirement for self-reproduction, but have added more and more computational power to the relatively small self-reproducing cellular automata configurations (in comparison to Von Neumann's solution). These trends are surveyed by Lohn (1999), who also describes the evolution of cellular automata rules that support self-reproduction (see also Lohn and Reggia (1997)). A fairly complete and up to date annotated bibliography with links to various relevant on-line resources can be found at Moshe Sipper's Artificial Self-Replication page. H. Sayama (1998b, 1999) has constructed variants of the self-reproducing Langton loop which exhibit self-dissolution once they can no longer reproduce, thus freeing up space for reuse by progeny, and most interestingly, another similar variant called "evo-loop" which exhibits heritable variability in loop size and is subject to evolution via interaction among descendants of a common ancestor acting as a selective force (Sayama 1998a, 1999). Heritability, variability, and differential survival in an environment with limited resources are present in his evo-loop when run in finite spaces. Thus evo-loop appears to be the first convincing example of an evolutionary process occurring in synchronous cellular automata. An asynchronous version is given below.

Asynchronous Langton, Byl, Reggia et al. Self-Reproducing Loops

Using the method above it is now straightforward to construct asynchronous cellular automata that exhibit self-reproduction. Taking any of the models of Von Neumann (1966), Codd (1968), Langton (1984, 1986), Byl (1989), Reggia et al. (1993), Sayama (1998a, 1998b, 1999), etc., we merely apply the construction above. The first implemented example of self-reproduction in asynchronous cellular automata was given by applying our construction to Langton's self-reproducing loop (Nehaniv 2002); see Figure 1. In this paper, we give another asynchronous implementation of Langton's example together with asynchronous adaptations of Byl's, Reggia and Chou's, and Sayama's examples.

Using the rule of Langton (1984) for a synchronous cellular automaton exhibiting self-reproduction, we derive by the method above an asynchronous cellular automaton with $192 (= 3 \times 8^2)$ states possible in the local automata at each node. Using random asynchronous update of the nodes we achieved an implementation of self-reproduction in an asynchronous cellular automaton. Figure 1 shows the state of the cellular automaton near the end of the first reproduction cycle: a sheath of cells encloses an asynchronously counterclockwise circulating stream of instructions to extend a construction arm and turn left. The instructions are copied as they flow through a fork in the sheath. After this stream has been executed four times, an offspring asynchronous loop is present in the cellular space (right in Figure 1).

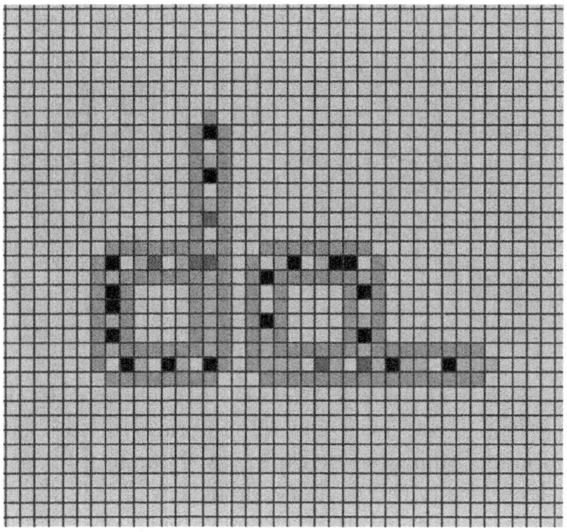

Figure 1: Asynchronously Self-Replicating Loop after First Reproduction (from (Nehaniv 2002)).

Figure 2 shows another implementation of the asynchronous Langton loop with temporal synchronization information indicated by shading.

Simplifications of Langton's loop by Byl (1989) and Reggia et al. (1993) reduced the size of the self-reproducing loop and are illustrated with asynchronous implementations in Figure 3.

Evolution in Asynchronous Cellular Automata

In this section we review some obstructions to evolution in cellular automata models such as Langton's self-reproducing loop, and Sayama's introductions of (1) self-dissolution (apoptosis: "programmed cell death" or "suicide" by individual loops that cannot replicate anymore) and of (2) variability into cellular automata replicators. We discuss how these properties relate to evolvability and give illustrations of the first asynchronous implementations of these as we proceed.

Finite Resources and an Obstruction to Turn-over of Generations

In Langton's original example (1984) a finite space is filled with loops which then become inert, and the space

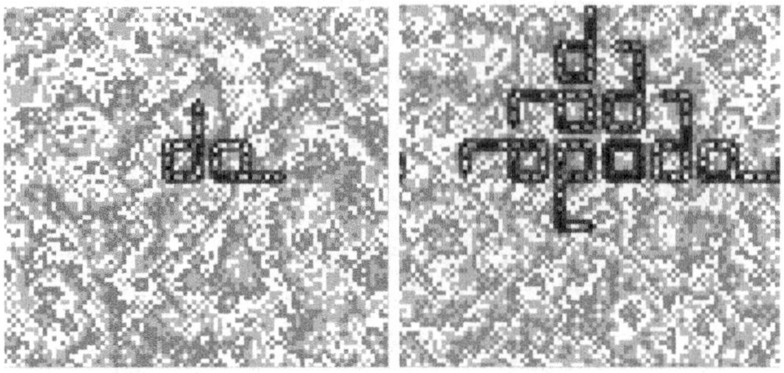

Figure 2: Temporal Waves: Asynchronously Self-Replicating Loop with Local Temporal Synchronization Component Indicated by Darkness of Shading. Contiguous locations with the same shade have local states of cells that correspond to the same moment of time in the emulated synchronous cellular automaton. There are 3 levels of darkness to indicate the modulo 3 value in the synchronization counter component of state in the asynchronous cellular automaton. The author has proved that any two cells at distance d in the asynchronous automaton have states corresponding to moments in time at most $\lfloor \frac{d}{3} \rfloor$ time units apart in the synchronous cellular automata (Nehaniv, 2002 (accepted)).

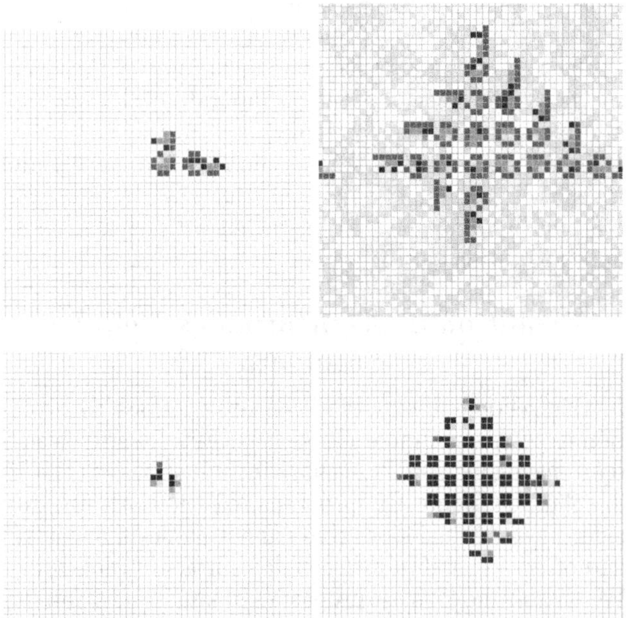

Figure 3: Asynchronous Versions of Byl's (top panels) and Reggia et al.'s (lower panels) Small Self-Replicating Loops after One (left) and Several Reproductive Cycles (right).

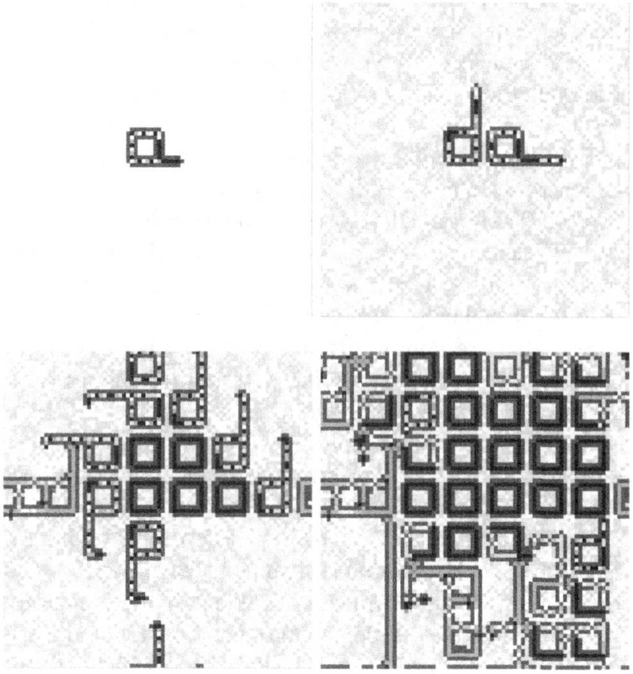

Figure 4: Asynchronously Self-Replicating Loop Population Nearly Exhausting Available Space Resources. (Langton Loop, 4 snapshots from a single run; toroidal topology). Replicants with monochromatic 'cores' have ceased to reproduce due to lack of available space, but persist and thus obstruct their descendants from reproducing.

cannot be reused by descendants of the original ancestral loop.

Figure 4 shows a space in which self-reproduction is about to halt, since all available space will soon be filled with the inert husks of replicators, that are no longer active. The structure is reminiscent of a coral reef, and could have continued to expand indefinitely in an unbounded space. However, if as in this case, the world is finite, all available space is filled and cannot be reclaimed for further replication to occur. This occurs for the asynchronous implementation of Langton's loop illustrated here.

Programmed Cell Death

Sayama (1998) introduced self-dissolution into the study of self-reproduction in cellular automata by modifying Langton's construction. This allows a loop to dissolve – i.e. its cells return to a quiescent state – if the available surrounding space is already occupied so that no more offspring can be produced near the loop. A new "dissolution" state is added to the local finite automata states which the local automaton moves into if reproduction is no longer possible and triggers cell-death in neighoring cells as it moves around within the sheath, yielding

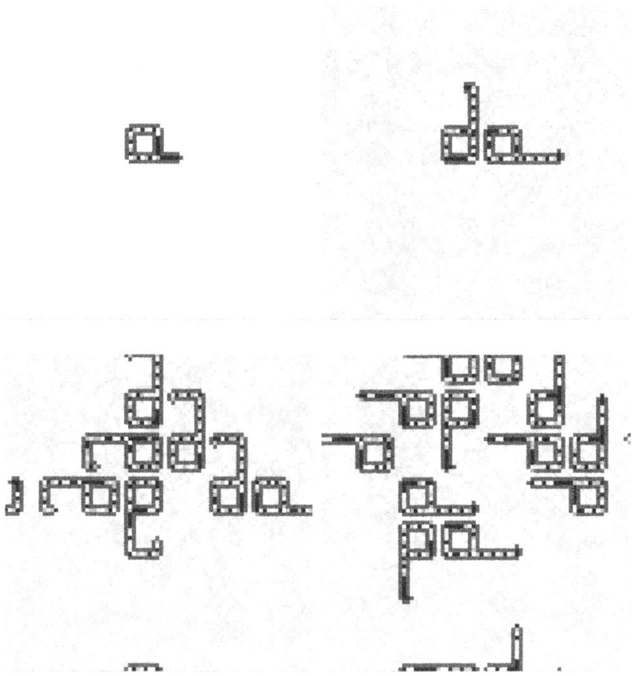

Figure 5: Asynchronous Version of Sayama's Structurally Dissolvable Self-Reproducing Loop. Space is liberated by "programmed cell death" and can be reused by descendents of the original loop (4 snapshots of a single run; toroidal topology). Differences in shading correspondent to differences in the synchronization component of local state. (See text.)

structural dissolution of the entire loop. Thus space can be freed up and later reused by descendants of the ancestral (or potentially other) self-reproducing loops. This occurs for the asynchronous implementation of Sayama's structurally dissolvable loop (see Figure 5).

Any evolutionary process without such turn-over of generations in a finite space would necessary halt. Sayama's introduction of self-dissolution eliminates this obstruction to evolution in cellular automta.

Evolvability, Robustness, and Heritable Variability

Conrad (1980) discussed the importance of genetypic robustness for evolvability in relation to mutational buffering and extra-dimensional by-passes. Kirschner and Gerhart (1998) have discussed the importance for biological evolvability of robustness to environmental and phenotypic variation.

Sayama also extended Langton's cellular automata rules and his own structural dissolution rule to allow replication and survival of the self-reproducing loops to occur in many more possible situations than was possible for Langton's case. At the same time, he introduced simple variability in size and contents. Combined with the self-dissolution mechanism, the added robustness transformed Langton's recipe for self-replication into an system that was evolution ready, "Evo-loop" (Sayama 1999). This result depends on the freeing up of finite resources (space) to permit a turn-over of generations and on the introduced robustness of replicators to environmental, phenotypic, and heritable variation. Our asynchronous version is shown in Figure 6.

In a finite cellular space, this provides all the requirements, identified by Darwin, for a rudimentary evolutionary process: populations of self-replicators with heredity, variability, turn-over of generations with bounded resources (Sayama 1999). Since replicated offspring resemble their parent and the environment has the same cellular automata "physics" as the environment of the parent, reproductive success tends to be heritable as well in the evo-loop model. However, due to the changing state of the cellular space, with loops of various sizes reproducing and colliding within it, the "biotic" enviroment of offspring may differ from that experienced by a parent. Thus, as for organic evolution, reproductive success in evo-loop is generally but not completely heritable. In Sayama's evo-loop model, heritable variation may arise when collisions occur between loops giving rise to new self-reproducing loops which may differ in size from the 'parents' involved in the collision. That is, direct interaction of the phenotypes produces heritable variability. Interestingly, given the cellular update rule and initial configuration in a cellular array, this example of evolution is completely deterministic, although Sayama has also experimented with stochastic variants. [4]

The implementation described here and illustrated in Figure 6 thus comprises the first example of evolution occurring in an asynchronous cellular automata space.

Summary and Conclusions

Previous results (Nehaniv 2002) exhibited the first implemented example of self-reproduction in asynchronous cellular automata, and demonstrated that, in principle, other cellular models of self-reproduction, universal computation and universal construction can be implemented in asynchronous cellular automata by applying our construction to Von Neumann's self-reproducing configuration. Moreover, universal computation can also be realized by our method as we have implemented Conway's Game of Life using asynchronous cellular automata.

Here, we have demonstrated the systematic implementation of asynchronous cellular automata that fully emulate the behavior of any synchronous cellular automata. This was used to give numerous examples

[4] On-line illustrations and movies of implementations of Langton's and Sayama's synchronous can be accessed at Sayama's webpage:
http://necsi.org/postdocs/sayama/sdsr/.

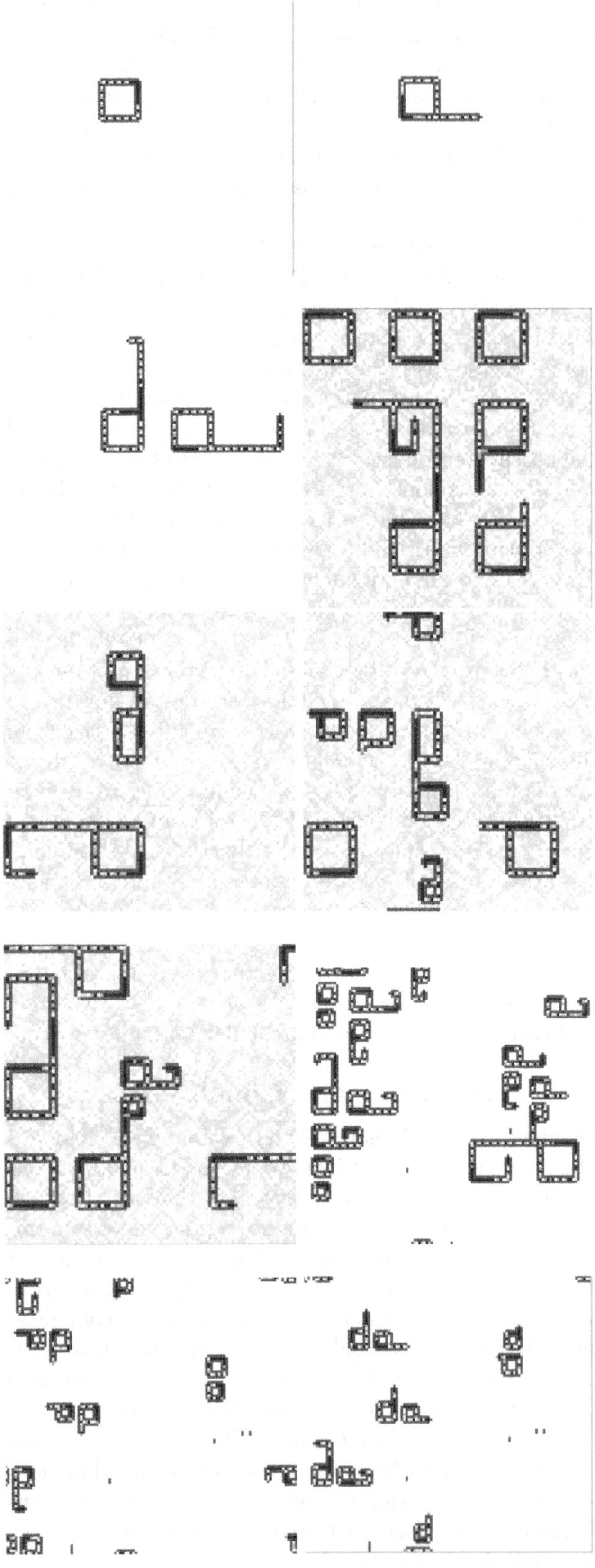

Figure 6: Evolution in Asynchronous Cellular Automata: Asynchronous Version of Self-Reproducing Evo-loop. (10 snapshots (not all from the same run); toroidal topologies). Heritable variability of characteristics of individuals (e.g. loop size) entails that this is an evolutionary system.

of self-reproduction in asynchronous cellular automata. Similarly, implementing the asynchronous version of Sayama's evo-loop we also have created the first instance of evolution in a population of self-replicators in an asynchronous cellular automaton.

In general, most results about synchronous cellular automata carry over automatically now to the asynchronous realm. Thus these methods free those using cellular automata models of computation, self-reproduction, and evolution from the restriction of synchronous global update. With asynchronous (e.g. random) update, the same results are attained as guaranteed by the theorem of (Nehaniv, 2002 (accepted)), as described above.

The type of evolution achieved here is still very rudimentary. The range of variability possible using Sayama's construction seems largely limited to variability in size of the replicators and to the particularities of inherited genetic information. Unlike most currently studied models of self-reproduction in cellular automata, Von Neumann's "general constructive automata" held more promise for achieving open-ended evolvability with potential for increasing complexity. For instance, the genotype-phenotype map was largely under control of Von Neumann's self-replicating configuration itself, and thus heritable mutations (if somehow introduced in a robust way) might potentially affect this mapping, and might in principle lead to an open-ended evolutionary process (see Von Neumman's discussions related to such "inheritable mutations" (1966, pp. 64-87) and the useful illumination of this issue by McMullin (2000)). Exhibition in cellular automata (whether synchronous or not) of an open-ended evolutionary process still remains an unachieved goal for Artificial Life.

Fault-tolerance and self-repair (and their connections to evolvability) in the asynchronous cellular automata are natural next directions to explore. A generalization of the methods presented here to cellular automata networks of variable size and shape, i.e. allowing dynamic growth or changing topology of the cellular space, would also be a desirable development as it would help us study whether it is possible for an asynchronous cellular automata space to expand under the activity of, for example, evolving self-reproducers. This may provide the basis for physical realizations of asynchronous self-replication, and related scientific and technological applications.

Acknowledgements

The author is grateful to three anonymous reviewers for helpful comments, especially to the reviewer who pointed out Toffoli's (1978) related independent construction and to Ferdinand Peper for the reference to Katsuo Nakamura's (1974) discovery of the same asynchronous construction as found by the author independently.

The implementations here were carried out by author applying the method explained here for constructing corresponding asynchronous cellular automata to a (synchronous) java applet written by Eli Bachmutsky (Batchmutsky 1999), which gives a classical synchronous implementation of the rules designed by Byl, Reggia et al., Langton, and Sayama.

The earlier asynchronous implementations of the Langton loop and Conway's Game of Life mentioned here and in (Nehaniv 2002) were obtained by the author using the same method as described in the text applied to adapting synchronous java applet code for Conway's Life by Andreas Ehrencrona and incorporating the synchronous Langton's rules as given in David I. Bell's `xca.c` implementation of Langton's loop.

The source and compiled code of the author's derived asynchronous implementations is available on-line at http://homepages.feis.herts.ac.uk/~nehaniv/async/

References

Bachmutsky, E. Self-replicating Loops and Ant Java Applet, applet and source code available on-line at: `http://necsi.org/postdocs/sayama/sdsr/java/`, 1999.

Byl, J. "Self-Reproduction in Small Cellular Automata", *Physica D*, Vol. 34, pp. 295–299, 1989.

Burks, A. W. (ed.), *Essays on Cellular Automata*, University of Illinois Press, Urbana, Illinois, 1970.

Codd, E. F. *Cellular Automata.* Academic Press, New York, 1968.

Conrad, M. "The Geometry of Evolution", *BioSystems*, Vol. 24, 61–81, 1990.

Freitas, R. A., Jr., and Gilbreath, W. P. (eds.) *Advanced Automation for Space Missions, Proceedings of the 1980 NASA/ASEE Summer Study; sponsored by the National Aeronautics and Space Administration and the American Society for Engineering Education.* NASA Conference Publication 2255. On-line extracts at http://www.zyvex.com/nanotech/selfRepNASA.html and http://www.islandone.org/MMSG/aasm/ .

Kirschner, M. and Gerhart, J. "Evolvability", *Proc. National Academy of Sciences*, Vol. 95, pp. 8420–8427, July 1998.

Langton, C. G. "Self-reproduction in Cellular Automata", *Physica D*, Vol. 10, pp. 135–144, 1984.

Langton, C. G. "Studying Artificial Life with Cellular Automata", *Physica D*, Vol. 22, pp. 120–149, 1986.

Lohn, J. D. "Self-replicating Systems in Cellular Space Models". In C. L. Nehaniv (ed.), *Mathematical and Computational Biology: Computational Morphogenesis, Hierarchical Complexity, and Digital Evolution.* Vol. 26 in Lectures on Mathematics in the Life Sciences, Providence, Rhode Island, American Mathematical Society, pp. 11–30, 1999.

Lohn, J. D. and Reggia, J. A. "Automatic Discovery of Self Replicating Structures in Cellular Automata", *IEEE Transactions on Evolutionary Computation*, Vol. 1 No. 3, pp. 165–178, 1997.

McMullin, B. "John von Neumann and the Evolutionary Growth of Complexity: Looking Backwards, Looking Forwards...". In M. A. Bedau, J. S. McCaskill, N. H. Packard, and S. Rasmussen (eds.), *Artificial Life VII*, MIT Press, 467–476, 2000.

Nakamura, K. "Asynchronous Cellular Automata and their Computational Ability", *Systems, Computers, Controls*, Vol. 5, No. 5, 1974, pp. 58–66, translated from *Denshi Tsushin Gakkai Ronbunshi*, Vol. 57–D, No. 10, Oct 1974, pp. 573–580.

Nehaniv, C. L. "Self-Reproduction in Asynchronous Cellular Automata", Proc. 2002 NASA/DoD Conference on Evolvable Hardware (15-18 July 2002, Alexandria, Virginia, USA), IEEE Computer Society Press, pp. 201–209, 2002.

Nehaniv, C. L. "Asynchronous Automata Networks Can Emulate Any Synchronous Automata Network", *International Workshop on Semigroups, Automata, and Formal Languages (June 2002 – Crema, Italy)*, 2002 (accepted). *journal version in preparation.*

Reggia, J. A., Armentrout, S., Chou, H. H., Peng, Y., "Simple Systems that Exhibit Self-Directed Replication", *Science*, Vol. 259, pp. 1282–1288, 1993.

Sayama, H. *Constructing Evolutionary Systems on a Simple Deterministic Cellular Automata Space*, Ph.D. Dissertation, Department of Information Science, Graduate School of Science, University of Tokyo, December 1998.

Sayama, H., "Introduction of Structural Dissolution into Langton's Self-Reproducing Loop", *Artificial Life VI: Proceedings of the Sixth International Conference on Artificial Life*, C. Adami, R. K. Belew, H. Kitano, and C. E. Taylor, eds., pp. 114–122, 1998, MIT Press. On-line material at: http://necsi.org/postdocs/sayama/sdsr/

Sayama, H. "A New Structurally Dissolvable Self-Reproducing Loop Evolving in a Simple Cellular Automata Space", *Artificial Life*, Vol. 5, no. 4, pp. 343–365, 1999.

Schönfisch, B. and de Roos, A. "Synchronous and Asynchronous Updating in Cellular Automata", *BioSystems*, Vol. 51, 123–143, 1999.

Sipper, M. The Artificial Self-Replication Page http://www.cs.bgu.ac.il/~sipper/selfrep/

Szathmáry, E . "Chemes, Genes, Memes: A Classification of Replicators". In C. L. Nehaniv (ed.), *Mathematical and Computational Biology: Computational Morphogenesis, Hierarchical Complexity, and Digital Evolution.* Vol. 26 in Lectures on Mathematics in the Life Sciences, Providence, Rhode Island, American Mathematical Society, pp. 1–10, 1999.

Toffoli, T. "Integration of the Phase-Difference Relations in Asynchronous Sequential Networks", in *Automata, Languages and Programming (Fifth Colloquium, Udine, July 1978)*, G. Ausiello and C. Bohm (eds.), LNCS 62, Springer Verlag, pp. 457–463, 1978.

Toffoli, T. and Margolus, N. *Cellular Automata Machines*, MIT Press, 1987.

Von Neumann, J. *Theory of Self-Reproducing Automata.* Edited and completed by A. W. Burks, University of Illinois Press, Illinois, 1966.

An Abstraction of Intercellular Communication

Thomas E. Portegys
Illinois State University
Campus Box 5150
Normal, Illinois, USA 61790-5150
portegys@ilstu.edu

Abstract

Multi-cellular organisms exhibit many mechanisms of intercellular communication for control and developmental purposes. Neurotransmitters, hormones, and signals mediating such processes as apoptosis and angio-genesis are but a few of these mechanisms. An abstraction of intercellular communication is presented here to provide a basis for constructing artificial life forms and self-organizing systems. Although the investigational vehicle is a cellular automaton, a cell in this context can be viewed in a broader sense. An intercellular signal is defined as a parameterized entity, a powerful paradigm that expresses not only lateral but also hierarchical and even recursive control structures. "Game of Life", Turing machine and other examples are included.

Introduction

A few years ago I found myself in the familiar surroundings of a coffee house, reading about a tragic disease in which the internal organs of the body fail to form proper left-right asymmetry (Belmonte 1999). The cause of this disease was discovered to be an abnormal distribution of a chemical signal during early development resulting from defective cilia, the hair-like projections that cells use to produce mechanical motion in their environment.

It is commonplace knowledge that cells communicate and collaborate in myriad ways, yet for some reason this article particularly inspired me. Hence the paper you are reading. And of course, since for a computer scientist nature's creations are but suggestions and not mandates for artificial systems, the resulting work represents what nature would have designed, had she only the proper education.

This work was done using a two-dimensional cellular automaton, although, as will become apparent, the abstraction does not pertain only to this model. Cellular automata (von Neumann 1966) are inherently parallel computers (Talia 2000), and are popular in artificial life research projects such as *Avida* (Adami & Brown 1994) and *Amoeba* (Pargellis 1996). Extensively analyzed (Langton 1991; Wolfram 1984), cellular automata exhibit fascinating self-organizing behavior with the simplest of rules, such as those in Conway's classic *Game of Life* (Berlekamp, Conway, & Guy 1982).

In a conventional cellular automaton, the state of a cell at time t is typically determined by the states of a neighborhood of nearby cells at time $t-1$. An inherent assumption is that a cell must be "aware" of its neighbors. A cell may affect a distant (not in its neighborhood) cell only by, at least temporarily, changing the states of intervening cells. The drawback of this method is that it requires additional states and carefully orchestrated rules, especially if the intervening cells are to return to their former states.

The abstraction proposed here is that a cell's state is determined by the ***signals*** it receives, regardless of their origin. The naturally reasonable notion of locality is preserved, as signals are in fact transferred from cell to cell. However, a signal can be constructed analogously to a nerve impulse, so as to use intervening cells as transport vehicles, arriving and taking effect only in an intended destination cell. In addition, interacting signals from different sources can be "focused" on an intended cell or group of cells. But it is not just the concept of a signal that enables this and, as will be demonstrated, other complex intercellular communication mechanisms, but also that a signal is defined as a parameterized entity, expressing not only lateral but also hierarchical and even recursive control structures.

The following examples are presented to illustrate the abstraction:

- Fractal Spiral.
- Spiraling "Game of Life" glider guns.
- Turing machine.
- Bug.

Description

The cellular automaton consists of a two-dimensional array in which each cell can exchange signals directly with itself and the eight adjacent cells (Moore neighborhood). A cell state represents a set of properties, such as color, orientation, etc. It is produced by *morphogenic* functions over the set of input signals from the environment:

$$\text{state}_i(t+1) = \text{morphogenic}_j(\text{Input-signals}(t))$$

A cell may also produce directional output signals that are a function of the input signals:

$$\text{output-signal}_i(t+1) = \text{morphogenic}_j(\text{Input-signals}(t))$$

A signal is a parameterized entity that may recursively contain other signals to be subsequently unloaded and issued:

```
<signal> := <signal type>[<parameter>0...]
<parameter> := <signal>|<number>|<other>
```

A morphogenic function is an arbitrary, unconstrained function that uses combinations of signal types and parameters as input. A set of related functions and signals are called a *morphogen*.

Examples

The following examples are presented to demonstrate the capabilities of the abstraction. All cells initially reside in a quiescent state, producing no signals. The center cell is stimulated by an INITIAL signal to begin, causing the automaton to exhibit patterns determined by its morphogen.

The programs are written in the Java programming language as web-publishable applets. All morphogen objects are derived from a base object, and may be used as building blocks to construct new morphogens. The cell object contains state information, currently consisting of cell color, shape, and orientation. Cell orientation provides for relative directionality, including mirroring. Signal types are uniquely scoped to morphogens, and by convention each morphogen contains an INITIAL signal type for initialization purposes.

Fractal Spiral

The cellular automaton in this example produces the fractal pattern of square-cornered spirals shown in Figure 1, demonstrating the use of parameters to achieve this effect. There are three levels of scale to this fractal, the black lines representing the largest scale, proceeding to lighter shades of gray lines for the smaller scales. The fractal is constructed by planting a smaller scale spiral at each turn of a larger spiral.

The INITIAL signal initiates the process by creating a SPIRAL signal oriented northward. The SPIRAL signal contains the following parameters: initial length, length increment, length count, number of turns, turn count, turn angle, orientation, and color.

The length parameters serve to draw the straight sides of a spiral. The turn, angle, and orientation parameters count turns and specify side directions. When a cell receives a SPIRAL signal, its morphogen performs as follows:

```
cell.color = signal.color;
if (signal.lengthCount > 1)
{
  // Continue building side.
  signal.lengthCount = signal.lengthCount-1;
  output signal in received direction;
} else {
  // Turn spiral and lengthen next side.
  signal.turnCount = signal.turnCount+1;
  if (signal.turnCount > signal.numberTurns)
    return;
  signal.rotate(signal.turnAngle);
  signal.length = signal.length +
    signal.lengthIncrement;
  output signal in computed direction;
  // Create smaller scale spiral.
  fractalSignal = new signal object;
  fractalSignal.color =
    lighter(signal.color);
  fractalSignal.initialLength =
    signal.initialLength-fixed amount;
  if (fractalSignal.initialLength > 0)
  {
    output fractalSignal;
  }
}
```

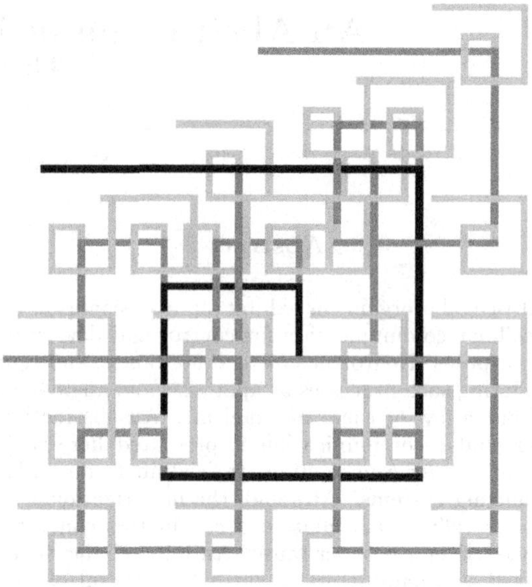

Figure 1: Fractal Spiral

Spiraling Glider Guns

This example repeats the spiral pattern of the previous example for the purpose of demonstrating orientation as a state variable. In this case, the spiral deposits "Game of Life" *glider guns* at each turn juncture. A glider gun is an oscillating pattern that producing moving patterns called *gliders*. Figure 2 shows four glider guns oriented in the four cardinal directions, each emitting a stream of gliders.

At each turn, the Spiral morphogen changes the cell orientation to match that of the incoming signal. This will cause any subsequent signals output from the cell to be relatively oriented. A simple modulo addition of the signal orientation and the cell orientation, starting with a value of 0 for the north direction and incrementing clockwise, does this. So for example, if the cell is oriented

The source code is available at http://www.acs.ilstu.edu/faculty/portegys/research/morphone.zip.
The examples described here are viewable as applets at
http://www.acs.ilstu.edu/faculty/portegys/programs/morphone/fractalspiral.html, gliderguns.html, turing.html and bug.html respectively.

Figure 2: Spiraling Glider Guns

east, a northeast signal will proceed in the southeast direction. The Spiral morphogen then issues a GliderGun INITIAL signal to create the glider gun.

The Game of Life rules demand that the glider gun configuration must start synchronously. To accomplish this, the GliderGun morphogen utilizes two service morphogens: Transporter and Timer. The TRANSPORTER signal for the Transporter morphogen carries a destination cell "address" in the form of x and y displacements, and a payload signal as parameters. The TIMER signal for the Timer morphogen carries a countdown timer and a payload signal as parameters. The GliderGun morphogen nests its START signals within TIMER signals, which are in turn nested within TRANSPORTER signals, bound for the cells that form the glider gun configuration.

The GliderGun morphogen consists of several signals and associated functions. In the Game of Life, each cell must know how many neighbor cells are "alive" in order to determine whether it is alive or dead. This is accomplished by cycling an ALIVE signal in a live cell. The ALIVE signal causes the morphogen to issue NEIGHBOR signals to neighboring cells. Counting the NEIGHBOR signals allows the morphogen to decide whether the cell is alive or dead.

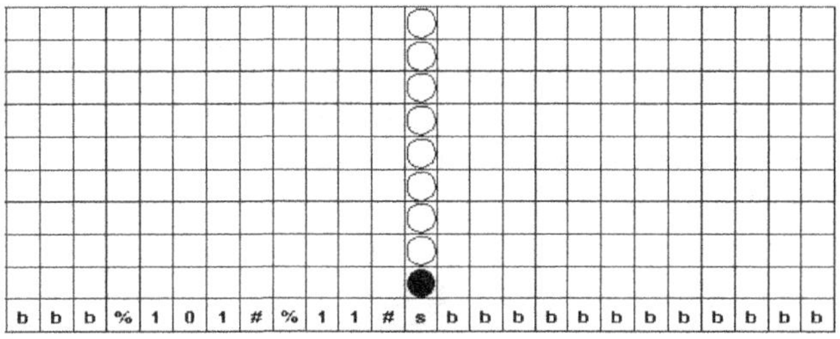

Figure 3: Turing Machine Binary Adder

INITIAL	Initial external stimulus.
EGG	Lays out tape and states using transporter and timer morphogens.
VALUE	Tape value.
MOVE	Move tape command sent from state cell to tape; contains LEFT or RIGHT signal.
LEFT	Move tape left.
RIGHT	Move tape right.
SENSE	Command to sense value on tape.
READ	Response to sense command; contains value read.
WRITE	Command to write tape; contains value to write.
STATE	State information: read, write, move, and next state.
CURRENT	Current state.

Table 1: Turing Morphogen Signals

Turing Machine

A Turing machine is a well-known, fundamental computer (Turing 1936) often used as a benchmark of computing capability. In this example, a binary adder is implemented, shown in Figure 3 in its starting configuration. The cells in the bottom row comprise the tape, containing the binary numbers to be added, 101 and 11. Other symbols are: 's' for start, 'b' for blank, '%' and '#' for separators. The answer will be written to the left of the leftmost '%'. The column of circles comprises the states of the machine; the filled circle representing the current state. The tape "read/write head" is over the cell beneath the column.

The Turing morphogen signals are shown in table 1. The machine works as follows: The cell containing the CURRENT (state) signal issues a SENSE command to the tape, which responds with a READ signal containing its value. If the current state calls for a write command, the WRITE signal is issued. Similarly, if the tape is to be moved, the MOVE signal is issued containing either a LEFT or RIGHT signal. Lastly, the current state sends the CURRENT signal to the cell containing the next state.

Bug

The somewhat whimsical "bug" example shown in Figure 4 is intended to suggest the possibilities of the abstraction for artificial life research.

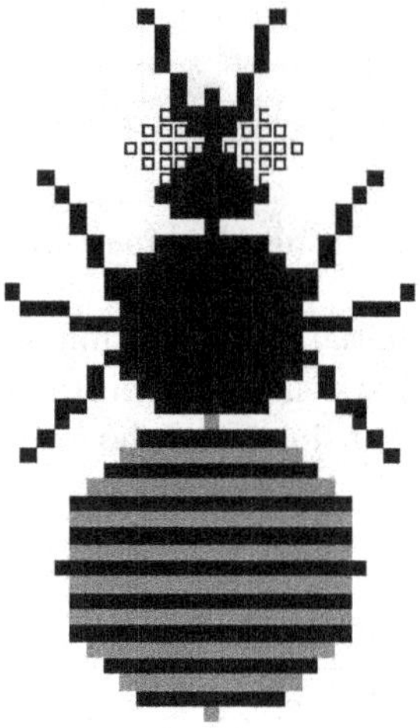

Figure 4: Bug

Conclusion

The use of signals allows a cell's state transition processing to occur independently of the source of the signals, effectively making a cell's neighborhood a variable, dynamic entity. This feature also makes programming a cellular automaton significantly easier, as the examples should illustrate. In addition, cellular systems not based on the grid-like cellular automata motif may benefit from this abstraction; for example, a cluster of embryonic cells moving and replicating in a three-dimensional space.

References

Adami, C., and Brown, C. 1994. Evolutionary learning in the 2D artificial life system "Avida". In Brooks, R., and Maes, P., eds., *Artificial Life IV*, 337. Cambridge, Mass.: MIT Press.

Belmonte, J. 1999. How the body tells left from right. *Scientific American.*

Berlekamp, E.; Conway, J.; and Guy, R. 1982. *Winning Ways for your Mathematical Plays.* New York: Academic Press.

Langton, C. 1991. Life at the edge of chaos. In Langton, C. G.; Taylor, C.; Farmer, J. D.; and Rasmussen, S., eds., *Artificial Life II.* Reading, Mass.: Addison-Wesley.

Pargellis, A. 1996. The spontaneous generation of digital life. *Physica, D* 91:86.

Talia, D. 2000. Cellular processing tools for high-performance. *Computer* 33(9):44–52.

Turing, A. 1936. On computable numbers, with an application to the entscheidungsproblem. *Proceedings of the London Mathematical Society,ser. 2.* 42:230–265.

von Neumann, J. 1966. *Theory of Self Reproducing Automata.* Champaign, Ill.: University of Illinois Press.

Wolfram, S. 1984. Universality and complexity in cellular automata. *Physica D* 10:1.

Dynamic Relationship between Diversity and Plasticity of Cell types in Multi-cellular State

Hiroaki Takagi and **Kunihiko Kaneko**
Department of Pure and Applied Sciences
University of Tokyo, Komaba, Meguro-ku, Tokyo 153, JAPAN

Abstract

Dynamics maintaining diversity of cell types in a multi-cellular system are studied in relationship with the plasticity of cellular states. First, we introduce a new theoretical framework, reaction-diffusion system on 'chemical species space' to model intra-cellular chemical reaction dynamics. Then, by considering the cell division and death of such cells, developmental process from a single cell is studied. Cell differentiation process is found to occur through instability in transient dynamics and cell-cell interaction. In a long time behavior, extinction of multiple cells is repeated, which leads to itinerancy over successive quasi-stable multi-cellular states consisting of different types of cells. By defining the plasticity of a cellular state, it is shown that the plasticity of cells decreases before the large extinction, from which diversity and plasticity are recovered. After this switching, decrease of plasticity again occurs, leading to the next extinction of multiple cells. This cycle of diversification and extinction is repeated. Relevance of our results to the development and evolution is briefly discussed.

Introduction

In multi-cellular organisms, developmental process from a single cell or few homogeneous cells with multi-potency leads to an organism that consists of various cell types. Furthermore, in some multi-cellular organisms such as insects, the developmental process is generally accompanied by metamorphosis. There, several multi-cellular states are realized, which form quasi-stable distribution of cell types. In the event of metamorphosis, both the number of cells and the number of cell types decrease drastically, and then a different multi-cellular state is realized. In general, to consider the diversity of tissues in a multi-cellular organism, it is important to study how several stable distributions of different cell types are formed, sustained, or collapsed. What mechanism causes the transition between different quasi-stable states with several cell types? How is it related with the plasticity of cellular states?

As a theoretical framework for developmental process of multi-cellular organisms, "isologous diversification theory" is proposed by Kaneko, Yomo, and Furusawa (Kaneko & Yomo 1997; 1999; Furusawa & Kaneko 1998a; 1998b). In these studies, dynamical systems approach is adopted, to show that robust developmental process with various cell types emerges based on the interplay between intra-cellular dynamics and inter-cellular interactions without finely tuned mechanisms. On the other hand, there are diversity at a tissue level, i.e., different stable distributions consisting of different cell types, in a usual multi-cellular organism. Switches among such quasi-stable multi-cellular states are also important. So far spontaneous formation of switches between several quasi-stable states is not much studied [1]. In this paper, we study the dynamics to maintain the diversity of cell types and the emergence of switches among several quasi-stable multi-cellular states. Here all the cells change their states drastically in each switching accompanied by deaths of multiple cells. To quantify the switching mechanism, we define plasticity of a cellular state, as changeability of the state against external environmental change. As will be shown, the switching accompanied by multiple cell deaths is tightly related with the loss of plasticity.

As the development progresses, several cell types with low plasticity increase their number, which leads to extinction of multiple cell types, following the lack of chemical resources. Then a drastic change in environment is caused by the extinction, which leads to a large change of internal states of all the surviving cells. Then, different cell types with high plasticity are generated. From this 'undifferentiated state' as in the initial state, a new cell society with a different set of differentiated cell types is formed. This cycle is repeated.

For the purpose of the present study, we introduce a new modeling framework for internal chemical reaction dynamics, that is reaction-diffusion system on "chemical species space". It can be regarded as an extended version of Boolean network model (Kauffman 1969), so that each variable takes a continuous value. By adopting this modeling, one can correspond the dynamics of chemical concentrations with the fixed expression of genes, which is a common representation for each differentiated cell type. In this sense, the symbolic representation of cell types and differentiation rules are discussed from the dynamics, as is cast as the 5th problem in open problems of Artificial Life (Bedau et al. 2000). We then discuss both the stability of realized cell states and their diversity. We show that the above cycle of increasing and decreasing diversity and plasticity generally appears in our dynamical systems model.

In the next section, we describe the details of our model. After presenting the behavior of a single cell state in terms of the number of attractors in section III, developmental process is introduced in section IV. The condition for the present interacting cell system to exhibit

[1] In ref (Furusawa & Kaneko 1998b), a proto-type of the life cycle of multi-cellular organisms is shown. However, the results are still preliminary.

cell differentiation and to show switching over several quasi-stable cell societies is presented. In section V, we reveal a feedback process leading to this switching, and confirm the relationship between the switching and the plasticity of total cells. Finally, in section VI, we briefly mention the generality of the present phenomenon and discuss the relevance to the development and evolution.

model

The basic strategy of the modeling follows the previous works (Kaneko & Yomo 1997; 1999; Furusawa & Kaneko 1998a; 1998b). Our model consists of the following three parts:

- intra-cellular chemical reaction network
- cell-cell interaction
- cell division and cell death

Now we describe each process. In Fig.1, we show the schematic representation of our model.

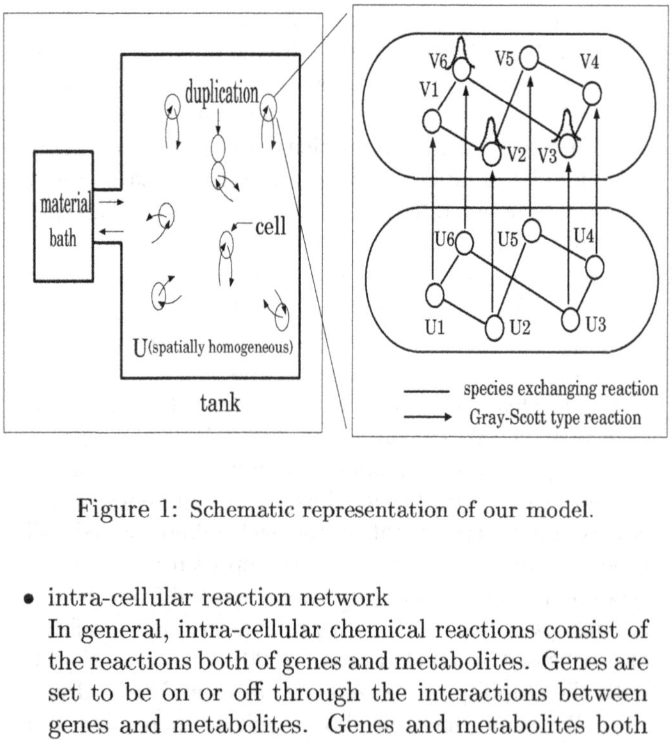

Figure 1: Schematic representation of our model.

- intra-cellular reaction network
  In general, intra-cellular chemical reactions consist of the reactions both of genes and metabolites. Genes are set to be on or off through the interactions between genes and metabolites. Genes and metabolites both compose reaction networks, while the time scale of reactions among genes are relatively slower than those of metabolites. Here, simple intra-cellular chemical reaction dynamics is chosen as an abstract model, so that it satisfies basic features described above.

  First, we assume a reaction network consisting of many product and resource chemicals similarly as that by genes and metabolites. The concentration of the j-th resources in i-th cell is denoted by $u_i^j(t)$, while that of products denoted by $v_i^j(t)$. Here, product chemicals are synthesized autocatalytically by consuming corresponding resource chemicals. We adopt a variant of Gray-Scott model (Gray & Scott 1984; Pearson 1993) as this autocatalytic reaction scheme[2]. In this paper, we mainly present the results of the case where the number of chemical species is commonly set to $P = 30$.

  In the model the product $v_i^j(t)$ is assumed to correspond to the degree of expressions of a gene (or RNA), and $u_i^j(t)$ to concentration of metabolite. Besides the reaction dynamics between them, there are dynamic change of chemical concentrations within a gene network and metabolic network. To take into account of such dynamics, we assume species-exchanging reactions in each of product and resource chemicals, which form two random reaction networks. Each chemical is converted to other chemicals specified in reaction networks in proportion to the concentration difference between them. Here we adopt the same network for products and resources for simplicity, though it is plausible that these two networks are different from each other. It is noticed, however, that we also investigated models with different networks and obtained qualitatively the same results. The reaction network is represented by a reaction matrix $W(i,j)$, which is 1 if there is a reaction from chemical i to chemical j, and 0 otherwise. Here the reaction network is assumed to be symmetrical by considering reversible reaction, that is, if $W(i,j) = 1$, then $W(j,i) = 1$. This network matrix is chosen randomly under the constraint of this symmetry while the number of reaction paths per chemical is kept constant. The rate constant of species-exchanging reaction is set to C in common with all resources, and D in common with all products. Here we assume that C is larger than D, by considering the difference in the time scales between genes and metabolites. These values are fixed throughout the simulation. Then, it is necessary to note that the system of random reaction network of species-exchanging reactions mentioned above is regarded as "diffusion" on random 'chemical species space', and with the reaction between products and resources, the intra-cellular reaction is regarded as a reaction-diffusion system. In that representation, each cell state corresponds to a discrete genetic expression pattern. We can realize multi-attractor states through bifurcations caused by the change of parameter C or D.

  Since this model consists of the interacting gene network where all the gene expressions take continuous values, it includes both the concepts of Boolean network model (Kauffman 1969) and reaction-diffusion

[2]Gray-Scott model is a reaction-diffusion system composed of two chemicals, resource and product. It is a simplified version of autocatalytic Selkov model that explains self-sustained oscillation of glycolysis.

system (Turing 1952). Thus, we can discuss both stability of each cell state and diversity of cell states.

- cell-cell interaction
  Assuming that environmental medium is completely stirred, we can neglect spatial variation of chemical concentrations in it, so that all the cells share the spatially homogeneous environment. Here we consider only the diffusion of some chemicals through the medium as a minimal form of interaction. In this model, we assume that only resource chemicals are transported through the membrane, in proportion to the concentration difference between the inside and the outside of a cell. All the resource chemicals have the same diffusion coefficient D_u. Each cell grows by taking resource chemicals from the medium and transforms them to product chemicals. U^j is the concentration of j-th resources in the medium. Resource chemicals in the medium are consumed by cells, while we assume material bath outside of the medium and impose a flow of resource chemicals to the medium in proportion to the difference between the concentration in the bath and the medium. Again, all the resource chemicals have the same diffusion coefficient D_U in the medium. The concentrations of all resources in the material bath, U are set to be 1. The parameter Vol is the volume ratio of a medium to a cell, and N is the number of cells.

- cell division and cell death
  Each cell gets resource chemicals from the medium and grows by changing them to the product chemicals. When the total amount of product chemicals in a cell becomes twice the original, then the cell is assumed to divide, while if it is less than half the original, then the cell is put to death. In real biological system, cell division occurs after replication of DNA (which has smaller diffusion coefficient and cannot penetrate through the membrane). Hence these assumptions are rather natural. After cell division, each cell volume is set to be half, and each cell is divided into two almost equal cells, with some fluctuations. To be concrete, chemical concentration a (a is representation of u, v) is divided into $(1+\eta)a_i^{(j)}$ and $(1-\eta)a_i^{(j)}$ respectively, where η is uniform random number over $[-10^{-3}, 10^{-3}]$. These fluctuations can give rise to a small variation among cell states, which eventually reaches to cell differentiation.

Accordingly, the concentration change of each chemical species is given by

$$du_i^j(t)/dt = D_u(U^j(t) - u_i^j(t)) - u_i^j(t)v_i^j(t)^2 + C\sum_{k=1}^{P} W(j,k)(u_i^k(t) - u_i^j(t))$$

$$dv_i^j(t)/dt = u_i^j(t)v_i^j(t)^2 - Bv_i^j(t) + D\sum_{k=1}^{P} W(j,k)(v_i^k(t) - v_i^j(t))$$

$$dU^j(t)/dt = \frac{D_u}{\mathrm{Vol}}\{\sum_{i=1}^{N}(u_i^j(t) - U^j(t))\} + D_U(U - U^j(t))$$

In the model introduced above, a single cell has many fixed-point attractors, in contrast to the previous studies (Kaneko & Yomo 1997; 1999; Furusawa & Kaneko 1998a; 1998b), where a single cell can take one or a few attractors. The reasons why we adopt the present modeling are as follows. First, many stable cellular states are realized in our model that allow for differentiations to many cell types. Second, as will be shown, by the instability through the interplay between transient states of cells and cell-cell interaction, cells are differentiated, although a single cell state eventually reaches fixed-point attractors after the transient time. Third, it is easy to classify cell types as different fixed point states, and is natural to relate them with different cellular states represented by different gene expressions.

Behavior of a single cell state

Initial conditions and methods

First we investigate the behavior of a single cell state without cell division and cell death. In all the simulations, we set the parameters $C = 2.0$, $D = 0.020$, $D_u = 0.50$, $D_U = 1.0$, Vol=3.0, $A = 0.020$, $B = 0.060$. These values of A$\sim$D correspond to typical values at which the original Gray-Scott model forms a self-replicating spot pattern in a one dimensional system. For numerical integrations, we used $\Delta t = 0.010$, while we have confirmed that the numerical results are qualitatively unchanged by using smaller values for Δt. We choose such initial condition that all the resource chemicals are 0.5 and all the product chemicals are randomly distributed in a cell. With this parameter setting, we get fixed point attractor for all cases.

Multiple attractors

Now we investigate how the number of attractors depends on the number of reaction paths per chemical and the number of chemical species. The path number is varied from 1 to 6, and the number of chemical species P is varied from 6 to 121. Examples of fixed point attractors for the cases with the path number 1(a), 2(b), 4(c), 6(d) with the number of chemicals $P = 30$ are shown in Fig.2 using a gray scale for the concentration of product chemicals. All the attractors are fixed points, and can be distinguished easily. For each number of chemical species, we take one reaction network chosen arbitrarily, and take 500 different initial conditions to count the number of attractors. Although we study only one reaction network for each, we can get the number dependence rather well, by carrying out simulations taking various values of P. The dependence of attractor number on P is given in Fig.3.

As the number of species P is increased, the number of attractors also increases, while as the number of reaction paths per chemical increases, the number of attractors decreases. In case of one reaction path per chemical, the reaction network is decomposed into $P/2$ pairs consisting of 2 chemicals, and each pair can take 2 states, so that the the number of attractors increases as $2^{P/2}$. In case of more reaction paths per chemical, the the number of attractors increases with some power of P, that is larger than 1.

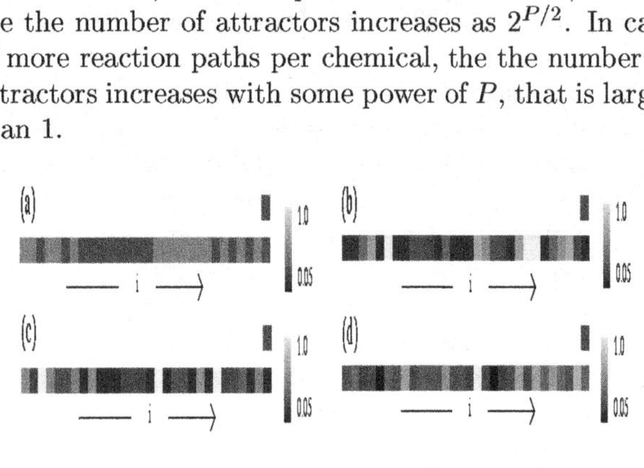

Figure 2: Examples of fixed point attractors. The concentrations of all the product chemicals for $i = 1, 2, \cdots, P = 30$ are plotted with a gray scale. The unit size of the figure is also putted. As the fixed point attractors, we adopt the state at $t = 10000$. Four cases are studied, namely, one reaction path (a), two reaction paths (b), four reaction paths (c), and six reaction paths (d) per chemical. Only one example is shown per each case.

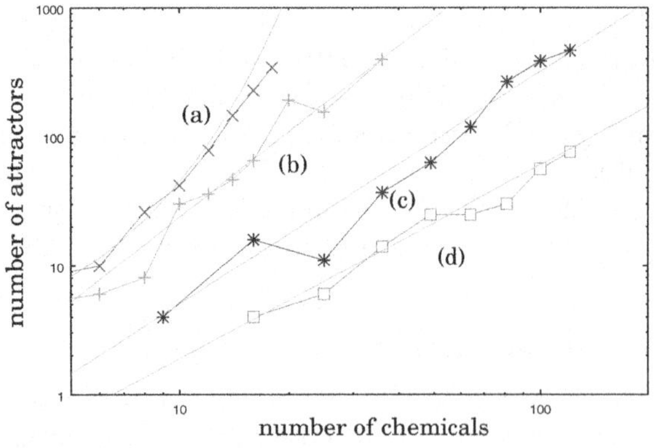

Figure 3: Dependence of the number of attractors on the number of chemicals P. Four cases are studied, namely, one reaction path (a), two reaction paths (b), four reaction paths (c), and six reaction paths (d) per chemical. For each point of the figure, we take 500 different initial conditions with the use of only one reaction network. Numerically we check the state at $t = 10000$ and classify the fixed-point attractors with the precision of 10^{-4}.

In a Boolean network model, the number of attractors also increases with some power when the number of paths per gene is 2 or 3, where the exponent of the power is less than 1. Kauffman suggested that this relatively small number of attractors against the number of all genes brings about the stability of cell types in living systems (Kauffman 1969). We must point out, however, that all the states realized in the Boolean network model are attractors of a single cell state. In fact, in real multi-cellular systems, cell states are not necessarily determined as attractors only of a single cell. Rather, it is often the case that cells take different states realized through cell-cell interaction (Gurdon, Lemaire, & Kato 1993). It is plausible that such cellular states are selected that are stabilized through mutual relationship between intra-cellular dynamics and inter-cellular interaction. Hence we study multi-cellular states in the next section.

Developmental process with cell division and cell death

Now we discuss the change of cellular states under the process of cell division and cell death. Here the intracellular state and the inter-cellular interaction are mutually influenced. By cell-cell interaction, a homogeneous cell society of a single cell attractor may be destabilized, so that novel states may appear. We study such cell differentiation processes here.

Initial conditions and methods

First, we set an initial cellular state not exactly at an attractor of a single cell. If we start precisely from an attractor of a single cell state, then the cells cannot differentiate by divisions any more. Once the state is on an attractor, the cell division gives two identical cells, as long as the fluctuation in cell division is not large to make a jump to different attractor. With the increase of cell numbers, all the cells compete for taking the same resources, and eventually they go to extinction for lack of them. Here we simply adopt the initial condition of a single cell with $u_i^j(0) = 0.50$ and $v_i^j(0) = 0.250 + 0.01 \times rand(j)$, where $j = 1, 2, ..., P$ and $rand(j)$ is a uniform random variable over [-1,1].

Now we adopt two coarse-grained representations to analyze the cell differentiation events. The first one is introduced in order to distinguish cell types. We define a vector representation of each cell state denoted by $\vec{X}$, where each element takes 0 or 1. This value is determined by the function given below and the concentration of each product chemical. All the cells that have the same $\vec{X}$ are regarded to belong to the same cell type.

$$\vec{X} = F(\vec{V}), \vec{V} = (v^1, v^2, ..., v^{(P)}),$$

$$F(Y) = \begin{cases} 1 & (Y \geq 0.5) \\ 0 & (Y < 0.5) \end{cases}$$

Second, we define recursiveness of each cellular state through the reproduction, as similarity between a mother and its daughter cell. To quantitatively characterize the recursiveness, we compare the average concentrations of product chemicals in each cell between two successive division processes. Let $\overrightarrow{V_i(n)}$ denote the vector representation of the average concentration of all product chemicals in i^{th} cell between $(n-1)^{th}$ and n^{th} cell division, that are denoted by $\overline{v_i^j}$ for $j = 1, 2..., P$, and $\overrightarrow{X_i(n)}$ denotes a digital representation of $\overrightarrow{V_i(n)}$, using the above threshold function $F(Y)$. As an index for the recursiveness of cellular state, we introduce an inner product denoted by $\theta_i(n)$ between $\overrightarrow{X_i(n)}$ and $\overrightarrow{X_i(n-1)}$. If $\theta_i(n) = 1$, the cell is regarded to keep the same type between successive cell divisions, that is, recursive reproduction.

$$\theta_i(n) = \frac{\overrightarrow{X_i(n)} \cdot \overrightarrow{X_i(n-1)}}{|\overrightarrow{X_i(n)}||\overrightarrow{X_i(n-1)}|}, \overrightarrow{X_i(n)} = F(\overrightarrow{V_i(n)}),$$

$$\overrightarrow{V_i(n)} = (\overline{v_i^1}, \overline{v_i^2}, ..., \overline{v_i^{(P)}}), F(Y) = \begin{cases} 1 & (Y \geq 0.5) \\ 0 & (Y < 0.5) \end{cases}$$

In the present model, each differentiated cell type is represented as distinctly separated chemical states of cells where each cell type can produce its own type recursively. We study the cell differentiation events with these two representations, by which we can distinguish a variety of cell states correctly.

The condition for cell differentiation

Here we study the frequency dependence of differentiation event on the structure of reaction network. As an index of network structure, we adopt the number of reaction paths per chemical. We investigate four cases where the number of reaction paths per chemical is 1, 2, 3, 4 respectively. In each case, we take 100 different reaction networks, each having the same initial condition. We carry out a simulation up to $t = 20000$, to check the number of cells that exist at the moment, and the number of cell types. Here we note that if cell differentiation does not occur at all, all the cells go to extinction by the lack of resource chemicals. The other parameters and an initial condition are kept at the same values as previous section. The frequency of differentiation event for each case thus obtained is given in Fig.4.

Differentiation events occur with highest probability when the number of reaction paths is 2. This is explained as follows:
In the case with a single reaction path, there are $2^{P/2}$ attractors consisting of disjointed pairs of chemicals. The transient time before falling onto each attractor is shorter than the case with more reaction paths, in general. Since pairs of chemical species (connected by the species-exchange reaction) are mutually independent, no relationships among chemicals exists. Then even though

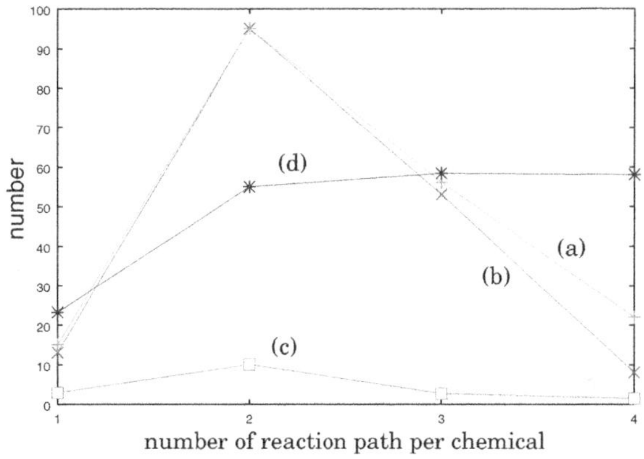

Figure 4: The frequency of cell differentiation plotted as a function of the number of the reaction paths per chemical. We study the cases where the number of reaction paths per chemical ranges from 1 to 4. For each point of the figure, we take 100 different reaction networks and carry out a simulation up to $t = 20000$ with the same initial condition and parameters mentioned in the text (without reaction network). Accordingly we plot the number of events where cells exist without complete extinction (a), the number of events where cell differentiation occurs (b), the average number of cell types in the case with cell differentiation (c), and the average number of total cells in the cases where total extinction hasn't occurred (d).

cell types may be different, they cannot make any relations to get resources effectively at a level of cell ensemble. Then with the increase of cell numbers, they soon come to a stage with lack of resources. As a result, the probability of extinction of all cells is high. On the other hand, in the case with 3 or 4 reaction paths, transient time is shorter and the number of attractors is smaller than the case with 2 reaction paths. In each cell, all the changes of chemical concentration within each cell are highly correlated due to more connections among them. Hence it is difficult to amplify the small difference to reach cell differentiation, so that cooperative relations among cells to get resources cannot be well organized. As a result, the probability of extinction of all cells is again rather high. In the case of 5 or more reaction paths per chemical, this tendency is observed more clearly. In the case with 2 reaction paths, however, transient time is longest and the number of attractors is the second largest. In each cell, all the chemicals can have global correlation among them, and also can form cooperative relations among cells to get resources, so that cells can exist with maintaining cell differentiation for the longest period. Thus, differentiation events occur most probably at this intermediate number of paths.

Switching between quasi-stable ensembles consisting of several cell types

Next we investigate the long time behavior of cell differentiation process. We set the number of reaction paths per chemical at 2, where the differentiation event is realized most clearly. We show an example of temporal evolution that is typically observed. Existing cell types and their population at every $t = 1000$ are plotted in Fig.5. A multi-cellular cooperative state consisting of several cell types is formed at a very early stage, and is maintained over a long period, which is much longer than typical transient time of a single cell state. Then a sudden crisis occurs, and after some generations, a new multi-cellular cooperative state with different cell types is recovered. This crisis is accompanied by the decrease of the cell number and diversity of cell types. This switching between diversification and extinction occurs generally independent of the choice of specific reaction networks.

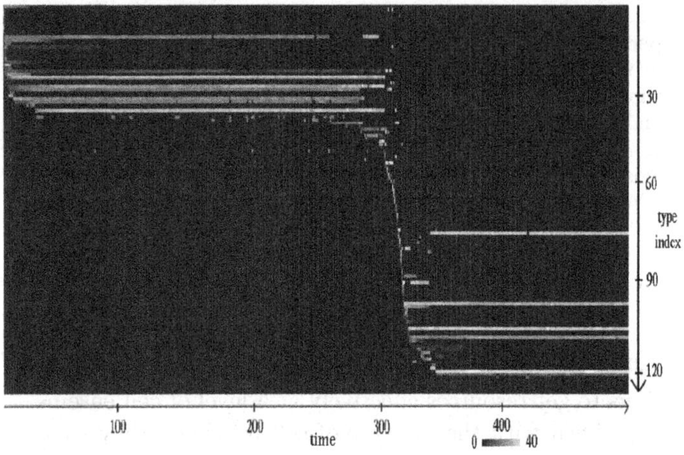

Figure 5: An example of the long time behavior of cell differentiation process. Simulation is carried out up to $t = 5 \times 10^5$ starting from a single cell, while the data for the total cells are sampled by every $t = 1000$, to classify all cell types and to get the temporal change of population of each cell type. The initial condition and method for the classification of cell types are mentioned in the text. All cell types are shown in order of their appearance; a cell type that appears earlier in the simulation has a smaller index for the cell type. The population of each cell type is represented with a gray scale. Here the unit time of the figures is 1000.

Further Analysis of the switching process

Quantitative characterizations of the plasticity of cell types

Now we investigate the switching among several quasi-stable multi-cellular states in more detail. Since the overall cell states are changed drastically in each switching, it is an effective way of studying the process in terms of the temporal change of plasticity of cell types. Here we define the plasticity of each cell type as changeability of the cell state against environmental fluctuations, which are the change of concentrations of resource chemicals in the environment caused by cell divisions and deaths. To characterize the plasticity of cell state, we introduce the following quantity:

First we take $v(o)_i^j$, the concentration of j-th product chemical of the type i cell, while we define $v(f)_i^j$ as the concentration of j-th product chemical of the attractor of the cell type i when the assumptions of cell division and cell death are eliminated, to check the attractor state at the fixed environment. Then we define the "attractor distance" Dist_i of the type i cell, as the Euclid distance between $v(o)_i^j$ and $v(f)_i^j$, namely, $\text{Dist}_i = \sqrt{\sum_{j=1}^{P}(v(f)_i^j - v(o)_i^j)^2}$.

As the distance is smaller, the cell type is closer to a specific attractor. Since the plasticity of a cell type means the changeability of the state by the environmental change, the plasticity should be smaller as the state is close to a given attractor. We conjecture that the cell plasticity (changeability) is characterized by the attractor distance in this model (or in a model with coupled dynamical system) and that the differentiation ability decreases as this attractor distance is smaller.

To confirm these two conjectures, we have checked the following two relationships. The first one is the relation between the distance and the degree of temporal fluctuations of each cell state when several cell types coexist stably for a long term. The second one is the relation between the distance and the frequency of the occurrence of re-differentiation event when a cell group that consist only of the single cell type is chosen and is put to a new environment. If there are positive correlations in both cases, then the above conjecture is confirmed. These two relations are given in Fig.6 and Fig.7, for the data shown in the temporal evolution in Fig.5.

In Fig.6, we computed the temporal fluctuation of each cell type for two ranges in the temporal evolution, namely, $t = 150000 \sim 250000$ and $t = 380000 \sim 480000$, where several cell types coexist stably. We measured the temporal fluctuation of each cell type as the average of all the Euclid distances of chemical concentrations between at the starting time and at some time span later. Here we take the time span as $t = 1000$, so that in both cases, temporal fluctuations are calculated from 100 data samples. The result shows that the temporal fluctuations of the chemical concentrations of a cell type are smaller as the attractor distance gets smaller.

In Fig.7, we computed the attractor distances of all cell types that appeared in the temporal evolution, and divide the whole range of these attractor distances by 0.1 bin size, and measured the ratio of the occurrence of re-differentiation event for all the cell types belonging to each bin (Here the population of each cell type is set to be 80. If the number is much larger, the homogeneous cell ensemble grown from the group goes to extinction by the lack of the resources. On the contrary, if the number is much smaller, then the effect to internal cell states caused by the change of the environment is so large that

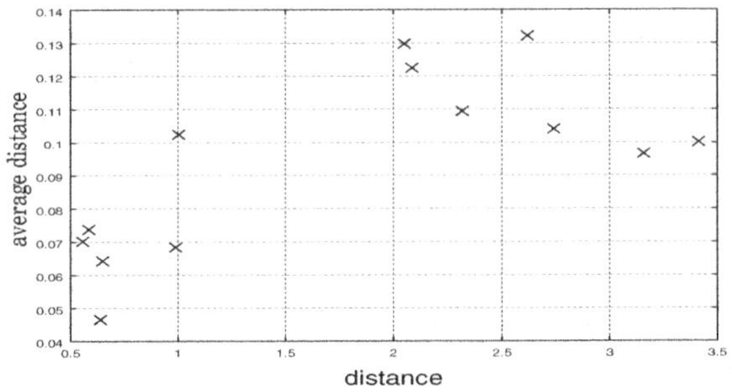

Figure 6: Relation between the attractor distance and degree of temporal fluctuations of cell states. We calculate a temporal fluctuation of each cell type in two ranges in the temporal evolution shown in Fig.5, namely, $t = 150000 \sim 250000$ and $t = 380000 \sim 480000$, where several cell types coexist stably. Temporal fluctuation of each cell type is computed as the average of all the Euclid distances between the starting state and the others. Here we take the data per $t = 1000$.

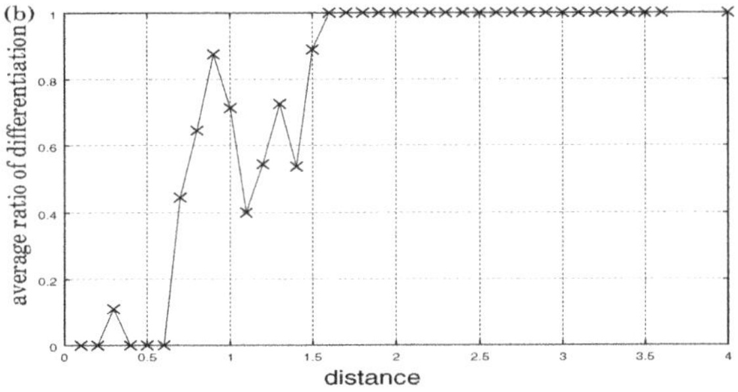

Figure 7: The relation between the attractor distance and the possibility of the re-differentiation. We compute attractor distance of all the cell types appeared in the temporal evolution shown in Fig.5. We take an ensemble of cells whose members have the same initial condition, and each cell is put it to a new environment and see whether cell differentiation occurs or not. By sampling the data for the attractor distance by 0.1 bin size, we compute the average ratio of the occurrence of re-differentiation event for each bin, to get the relationship between the differentiation ratio and the attractor distance.

the difference of cell types cannot be well distinguished. Hence we choose this medium number for cell population.). The result roughly shows sigmoidal function dependence, that is, there is a threshold for the attractor distance below which the corresponding cell type loses the ability of re-differentiation drastically. This result also supports the initial condition dependence of cell differentiation event mentioned previously.

Summarizing these two sets of data shown in Fig.6 and 7, it is confirmed that the attractor distance introduced above is valid as a measure of plasticity of cell type.

Mechanism for switching through extinction of many cells

Now we discuss the switching with multiple cell deaths in relationship with the loss of plasticity. Our results are summarized by the following scenario: At each stage of given quasi-stable multicellular states, cell types with different degrees of plasticity coexist. Then at each stage, cell types with relatively high plasticity (i.e., larger attractor distance) differentiate to other cell types with lower plasticity, so that the ratio of cell types with lower plasticity increase gradually. Then the sustained relation among cell types to cooperatively use resource chemicals is destroyed, and extinction of many cell types is resulted. With these multiple deaths, drastic change of the composition of environmental resource chemicals is brought about, which is large enough to make re-differentiation of some of surviving cells from the low plasticity state to a new state with high plasticity. Then, including with novel cell types with high plasticity, a novel multi-cellular state is brought about, allowing for cooperative use of resources. With this drastic change, spontaneous switch to a novel multi-cellular state is generated.

To verify this scenario, we computed the temporal change of the following four quantities in the temporal evolution of Fig.5: the average attractor distance for total cells (a), the total diversity of cell types (b), the average recursiveness of cell types over all cells (c), and total number of cell (d). Here, the average attractor distance is obtained by averaging the attractor distance of each existing cell type with the weight of the population ratio. The average recursiveness is also computed as the average over cells whose division event occurs in each $t = 1000$ period. They are plotted in Fig.8, while the population size for each cell type with given attractor distance is plotted in Fig.9, around the switching regime.

In Fig.8, first the average attractor distance (a) starts to decrease, the diversity of cell types is decreased. With these decreases, the recursiveness is increased with large fluctuations. Then, the attractor distance and diversity take plateau with low values, when almost complete recursive production is sustained. After slight decrease of the the attractor distance and diversity, then, they go up to large values, accompanied by multiple cell deaths and switching of cell types. Now, high plasticity and diversity are recovered. After this recovery, the values again decrease gradually, until the next multiple cell deaths occur. This switching process through the decrease of diversity, extinction, and recovery is repeated. The data of Fig.9 also show the accumulation of population to cell types with low plasticity before the extinction, and recovery of the types with high plasticity after it.

Although we show only one example here, qualitatively the same behavior is generally observed at each switching in our system. Hence, the scenario mentioned above is quantitatively demonstrated.

Summary and discussion

In this paper, we have studied a dynamical systems model of developmental process, by introducing a new framework, namely, reaction-diffusion system on 'chemical species space' for modeling internal chemical reaction networks. This modeling bridges between the two approaches: One is reaction-diffusion system proposed by Turing (Turing 1952) and the other is Boolean network model proposed by Kauffman (Kauffman 1969). By further including the developmental process, states with many differentiated cell types are obtained, where the differentiation process to increase diversity is observed. The condition to realize cell differentiation by cell-cell interaction is obtained. When the number of reaction paths per chemical species is larger than 2, the dynamics of all the chemical concentrations are highly correlated strongly and the probability of realizing cell differentiation is lower. On the contrary, when the number of reaction paths per chemical, changes of each pair of 'connected' chemicals are independent and the probability of realizing cell differentiation is again lower. Cell differentiation occurs most probably when the number of reaction paths per chemical is 2, that is, in the intermediate region above two cases. These results may be related with those obtained in the NKCS model by Kauffman (Kauffman & Johnsen 1991).

In the long time behavior, we have found the switching over multi-cellular states that maintain diverse cell types. In each multi-cellular state, diverse cell types coexist to use chemical resources cooperatively, while the switching is characterized by multiple cell deaths arising from the loss of diversity of cell types, and the destruction of the cooperative use of the resources. This switching behavior is first observed in our model.

Then we propose that this switching behavior is characterized by the loss of plasticity of total cells, that is a general consequence of our dynamical systems theory. In each developmental stage, the irreversible loss of plasticity is a general course of the development, i.e., differentiation from a cell type with relatively high plasticity to that with lower plasticity, so that the ratio of cell types with lower plasticity increases gradually. Then the sustained relationship among cell types for cooperative use of resource chemicals is destroyed, which can cause multiple cell deaths. Then, drastic change of the composition of environmental resource chemicals is resulted. Cells with low plasticity died out, and replaced by those with high plasticity. As a result, a new multi-cellular state with novel cell types is generated. This process is repeated.

This give a feedback process in a system with many degrees of freedom to maintain the diversity of cell types, as has also been discussed as homeochaos (Ikegami & Kaneko 1992; Kaneko & Ikegami 1992). The plasticity of each cell type in our study corresponds to the mutation rate of each species in the study of homeochaos.

The existence of several quasi-stable multi-cellular states is important to consider the origin of tissues in multi-cellular organisms. In multi-cellular organisms, several tissues coexist that are represented as a different distribution of different cell types, consisting of cells with the same gene set. The switching of the states will be important to study how the life cycle of a multi-cellular organism is formed. In future, the search for a rule of transitions between successive multi-cellular states will be important. The dynamics of metamorphosis will be discussed along the line.

In this paper, we discussed spontaneous cell differentiation and switching processes in a well-stirred medium, i.e., in a spatially homogeneous medium. To discuss morphogenesis with spatial pattern formation, it will also be interesting to include spatial inhomogeneity in the medium.

The present results also have some implications to the evolution. Punctuated equilibria (Eldredge & Gould 1972) in the evolutionary process are proposed, where extinction events after long quasi-stationary states are discussed. By regarding each cell as an organism, successive extinction events of many cells can be regarded to large extinction through evolution. Then the present results provide an example of punctuated equlibiria. Here it is interesting to note that the distribution of the lifetime of quasi-stable multi-cellular states in our model follows the power law distribution.

By including genetic mutations, the differentiation in our model can be extended to speciation process to multiple species. Indeed, a theory of sympatric speciation with using phenotypic plasticity is recently proposed (Kaneko & Yomo 2000; Takagi, Kaneko, & Yomo 2000). In the preliminary studies of our model including genetic mutation process, we have observed sympatric speciation process to form several species, while with this process, the plasticity of each species defined in this paper decreases. Here, the recovery of plasticity of species after extinction of many cells is important to study open-ended evolution.

We would like to thank T.Yomo and C.Furusawa for stimulating discussions. This work is supported by Grants-in-Aid for Scientific Research from the Ministry of Education, Science and Culture of Japan (11CE2006, Komaba Complex Systems Life Project, and 11837004).

References

Bedau, M. A.; McCaskill, J. S.; Packard, N. H.; Rasmussen, S.; Adami, C.; Green, D. G.; Ikegami, T.; Kaneko, K.; and Ray, T. S. 2000. Open Problems in Artificial Life. *Artificial Life* 6:363.

Eldredge, N., and Gould, S. J. 1972. Punctuated equilibria: The tempo and mode of evolution reconsidered. in *Modells in Paleobiology*(ed. Schopf, T. J. M.), Freeman.

Furusawa, C., and Kaneko, K. 1998a. Emergence

of rules in cell society: Differentiation, hierarchy, and stability. *Bull. Math. Biol.* 60:659.

Furusawa, C., and Kaneko, K. 1998b. Emergence of multicellular organisms with dynamic differentiation and spatial pattern. *Artificial Life* 4:79.

Gray, P., and Scott, S. K. 1984. Autocatalytic reactions in isothermal, continuous stirred tank reactor: oscillations and instabilities in the system A+2B→3B,B→C. *Chem. Eng. Sci.* 39:1087.

Gurdon, J. B.; Lemaire, P.; and Kato, K. 1993. Community effects and related phenomena in development. *Cell* 75:831.

Ikegami, T., and Kaneko, K. 1992. Evolution of host-parasitoid network through homeochaotic dynamics. *Chaos* 2:397.

Kaneko, K., and Ikegami, T. 1992. Homeochaos: Dynamical stability of symbiotic network with population dynamics and evolving mutation rates. *Physica D* 56:406.

Kaneko, K., and Yomo, T. 1997. Isologous diversification: A theory of cell differentiation. *Bull. Math. Biol.* 59:139.

Kaneko, K., and Yomo, T. 1999. Isologous diversification for robust development of cell society. *J. Theor. Biol.* 199:243.

Kaneko, K., and Yomo, T. 2000. Sympatric speciation: Compliance with phenotype diversification from a single genotype. *Proc. Roy. Soc. B* 267:2367.

Kauffman, S. A. 1969. Metabolic stability and epigenesis in randomly constructed genetic nets. *J. Theor. Biol.* 22:437.

Kauffman, S. A., and Johnsen, S. 1991. Coevolution to the edge of chaos: Coupled fitness landscapes, poised states, and coevolutionary avalanches. *J. Theor. Biol.* 22:467.

Pearson, J. E. 1993. Complex patterns in a simple System. *Science* 261:189.

Takagi, H.; Kaneko, K.; and Yomo, T. 2000. Evolution of genetic code through isologous diversification of cellular states. *Artificial Life* 6:283;

Turing, A. M. 1952. The chemical basis of morphogenesis. *Phil. Trans. Roy. Soc. B* 237:37.

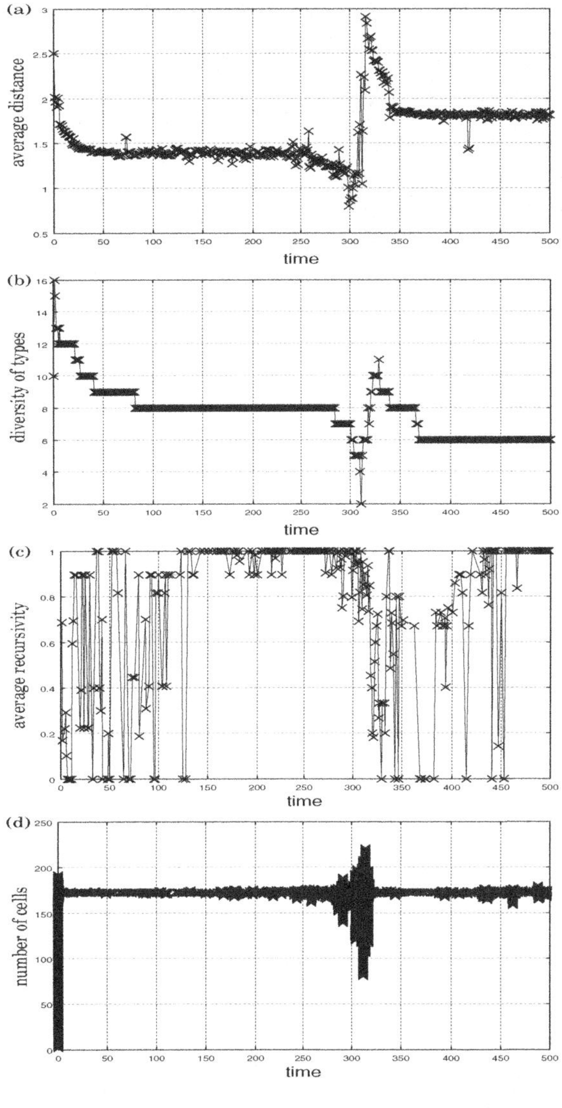

Figure 8: (a): The temporal change of the average attractor distance. (b): The temporal change of the average diversity over all cells. (c): The temporal change of the average recursiveness over cell types. (d): The temporal change of the total cell number. We computed all the quantities for the data given in the temporal evolution of Fig.5. Here the unit time of the figures is 1000.

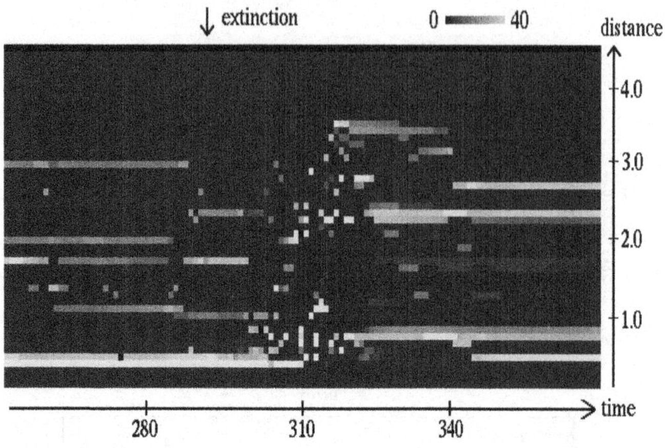

Figure 9: The temporal change of the population of existing cell types around the switching shown in Fig.5. The attractor distances of the cell types are plotted with their population. The time when the first extinction of many cells occurs is shown by the arrow. Here the unit time of the figures is 1000.

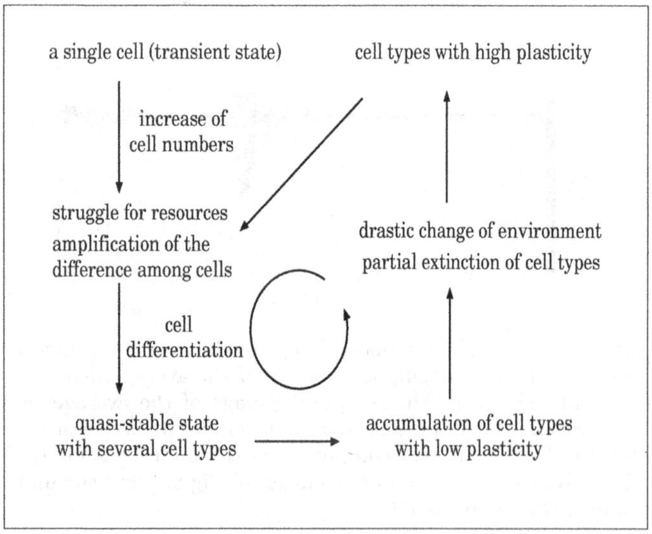

Figure 10: Schematic representation of our scenario for the mechanism to keep the diversity of cell types.

Generating Biomorphs with an Aesthetic Immune System

Dennis L. Chao and **Stephanie Forrest**
Department of Computer Science
University of New Mexico
Albuquerque, NM 87131 USA
{dlchao,forrest}@cs.unm.edu

Abstract

We describe an interactive search algorithm inspired by the immune system. The algorithm learns what parts of the search space are *not* useful to help a user explore large parameter spaces efficiently. The algorithm is capable of finding consensus solutions for parties with different selection criteria. A simple implementation of the algorithm applied to selecting Biomorphs (Dawkins 1986) is presented.

Introduction

In this paper we illustrate how an immune system-inspired filtering algorithm described in (Chao & Forrest 2002) can be applied to the filtering and generation of art. When the immune system is exposed to a novel pathogen, it learns to recognize it in what is called the *primary response*, and it remembers the pattern so that subsequent infections can be eliminated more efficiently in the *secondary response*. Analogously, an artificial immune system can be viewed as "protecting" users from undesirable data. We propose constructing an artificial immune system that learns what kinds of data patterns are unacceptable and then prevents exposure to similar data in the future. This approach scales to multiple users by using the superset of the undesirable data of many users to filter data. The data that survive this censoring is the set that could satisfy everyone. These solutions are useful for situations in which one solution must satisfy several people at once, such as music that is broadcast to an audience or artwork that is displayed in public spaces.

We demonstrate the principles of this idea by applying it to the generation of simple figures known as Biomorphs (Dawkins 1986). The system is capable of learning which regions of Biomorph parameter space produce images that are displeasing to a particular user and can generate diverse candidate solutions of high quality. Furthermore, the solutions produced by combining the profiles of a small group of users are likely to be pleasing to all of the group members.

An Aesthetic Immune System

An aesthetic immune system is a filter between users and a "stream" of art and eliminates undesired art before it can reach the user. Like the adaptive immune system, it "learns" from experience. If a user labels a work of art as "bad," the system will remember this and prevent this work from being shown to the user in the future. It would not be practical for the user to evaluate every item manually, so the algorithm must generalize. If the user dislikes a certain item, it is likely that the user will dislike similar items as well.

Aesthetic space is a framework for grouping "similar" works of art. In this space, the distance between the locations of two works of art is proportional to their similarity. Thus, similar works are close to each other while dissimilar works are far apart. For example, oil paintings of the Renaissance could occupy points in one part of the space, the paintings of the Enlightenment era might not be too far away, while the work of Abstract Expressionists would be quite distant from both of these. Clearly this space is impossible to construct accurately due to the subjective nature of similarity in the realm of aesthetics. However, when generating art algorithmically, we will assume that for many systems similar parameters produce aesthetically similar images.

If a user rejects one work, he or she will probably dislike most of its neighbors in aesthetic space. Therefore the system creates a *negative detector* that covers a small portion of space surrounding each rejected work. The detectors will behave like lymphocytes in the immune system, recognizing anything that is too similar to their pre-programmed targets. If a work is not rejected by any of the detectors, it is allowed to "survive." Therefore, the user should never be presented a new work that is similar to one explicitly rejected in the past.

The works of art that can pass through the system are not similar to previously rejected ones, but they are not guaranteed to be "good." If the user rejects one of these, the system will form a new detector for it, which will prevent similar "bad" works from being seen in the future. The untrained system with no detectors gradually constructs a profile of the user's tastes as it sees examples of art that the user rejects. Eventually, the accumulated detectors will form a model of the user's preferences and shield the user from a broad range of undesirable art.

To use an aesthetic immune system to help a user explore a wide variety of potentially good solutions, a random number generator can supply a stream of random candidate solutions to it. The system would filter out candidates that are likely to be bad, and when fully trained (if this is possible), it is a perpetual generator of novel but satisfactory art. Note that it does not attempt to find optimal solutions, so other techniques may be used to refine solutions presented to the user.

An important consequence of negative detection is

that detectors can be independently generated by users with different judgment criteria. The areas that are not excluded by the superset of their negative detectors can define the regions of "consensus" solutions, or solutions that are satisfactory to everyone. Many users can generate "bad art" detectors independently, and when the detector sets of many users are combined, the system will generate works that none of the users will dislike. One can think of each user's detector set acting as a sieve, blocking the passage of art that is disagreeable to that user. The solutions that pass through all the sieves are the consensus solutions. This method could potentially satisfy the aesthetic demands of multiple users efficiently and accurately, even if the users are specifying their preferences asynchronously and incrementally. The quality of the consensus solutions depends on the domain and the heterogeneity of the users. If the users have conflicting interests, consensus solutions might not exist.

Related work

Evolutionary art (evoart) usually relies on humans to provide the feedback needed by the computer to guide the "evolution" of a work of computer generated art. Typically, the user iteratively refines a work by selecting a subset of favorite works out of a small set, which are variants or combinations of the user's favorites from the previous time step. After many iterations, the quality of the works can improve. This process of "evolving" art is sometimes called *aesthetic selection.* Dawkins was the first to implement evolutionary art on a computer (Dawkins 1986). In his system, the user explores the space of images called "Biomorphs" in the iterative manner described above.

The aesthetic immune system approach has several advantages over the evolutionary approach. First, evoart systems usually require a user to compare many members of a population at once to pick a favorite, while an immunologically-based system does not. For some systems, such as the generation of musical phrases, it is difficult to evaluate many individuals at once (Nelson 1993). Second, the evolutionary process converges to single works of art, while the immunological approach evaluates the whole of parameter space and can be a source of perpetual novelty. Third, in order to produce innovative works, evolutionary systems often combine works of art (Sims 1991). The programmer is faced with the difficult task of defining operators to mix the "genotypes" of works in a manner such that the offspring's "phenotype" exhibits desirable traits of its parents. In some cases, the results are unpredictable and displeasing, suggesting that more complex combination rules are required. A trained aesthetic immune system can generate a very large range of aesthetically pleasing art without the use of a difficult-to-define art combination operator. This may be crucial in collaborative evoart, in which many users cooperate to generate works of art. Simply combining the favorite works of different users might yield unsatisfactory results. If a fan of Salvador Dalí's surrealist canvases were to meet a fan of Norman Rockwell's sentimental and more realistic style, a painting that combined the two painters' tendencies would probably be unsatisfying to both. A better solution might be to introduce both to something completely different, like the paintings of Paul Klee. This is the sort of solution an aesthetic immune system would be capable of proposing.

Application to Biomorphs

We applied the immunological framework to the exploration of Dawkins' Biomorphs (Dawkins 1986). A Biomorph is a recursively drawn figure defined by a nine-digit "genotype." The digits, all but one of which are allowed to take the values between -9 and 9 inclusively, are parameters that affect the appearance of the final image, or "phenotype." The final digit of the genotype, which defines the level of recursion used in drawing the Biomorph, is restricted to values between 2 and 9. The following sections describe how to implement an aesthetic immune system to help users find aesthetically pleasing regions of the Biomorph genotype space.

Defining the aesthetic distance

The first step is to define the distance between any two solutions. Fortunately, small changes in Biomorph parameters (the genotype) usually result in small phenotypic changes, so we were able to use genotype space as a proxy for the true aesthetic space. That is, Biomorphs with similar genotypes are assumed to look similar, while the appearance of Biomorphs with very different genotypes is assumed uncorrelated. For convenience, we define the distance in genotype space to be the maximum arithmetic difference between any two corresponding digits of the two genotypes, which is the Minkowski metric $L_\infty(a,b) = [\sum_i (|a_i - b_i|^\infty)]^{1/\infty}$, where a and b are the strings being compared and a_i and b_i are the ith element of a and b. For example, the distance between the two genotypes (0,0,0,0,1,8,1,1,2) and (7,3,6,2,1,1,3,3,2) is 7 because that is the maximum difference between the corresponding digits of the two strings (at both positions 1 and 6). Other distance measures are possible, such as the sum of the differences between corresponding positions in the genotype.

For some domains, one would not want to generate new works, such as with a collection of already existing work. In such cases, the immunological approach could be used to prevent the retrieval of entries that are too similar to previously rejected works. There is a large body of research on the problem of quantifying similarity between data, including content-based classification, metadata-based classification, and collaborative filtering techniques.

Defining the detectors

A detector should be large enough so that the user does not need to define "too many" of them but not so large that they eliminate as many good solutions as bad ones. We will define a detector of radius r to cover all genotypes within distance r from the center of the detector. The neighborhood size of a detector is the number of distinct locations in space that it covers. The detector neighborhood should cover a "large enough" portion of the total parameter space such that a reasonable number of detectors could cover a large portion of the total genotype space. It may be fruitful to augment the immunological approach with pattern classification techniques to more efficiently cover parameter space.

For the Biomorph user experiment, described below, we used large detectors in order to minimize the amount of time it took the subjects to cover a significant portion of space. We chose a detector size such that the average user could create enough detectors to fill about half of Biomorph parameter space in under ten minutes. The large detector size affects the results quantitatively, but hopefully not qualitatively. It is probably impossible to guarantee that no good genotype will be censored by a detector, but we would like to minimize this possibility. If the transition between high and low quality solutions is not too abrupt, there could be regions of expendable intermediate-quality solutions between them in parameter space. If the user is instructed to not reject solutions of low but acceptable quality, the detectors are less likely to interfere with good solutions.

We set the detector radius to be 6 for all parameters except for the last one, which we set to 2. Small changes in the last parameter greatly affect the appearance of Biomorphs, so a smaller radius is appropriate. Figure 1 shows a random Biomorph and various others that fall within its detector radius. Based on this and several other examples, we concluded that Biomorphs that are within the range of a single detector are qualitatively similar and assume that if a genotype yields an undesirable phenotype, then most genotypes within its detector are likely to be undesirable as well.

Experiment

Seven volunteers participated in a user study to determine the feasibility of the aesthetic immune system. All used a program to create their own Biomorph detector sets and were retested several days later to determine the effectiveness of system's detectors. To create a Biomorph detector set, a computer program displayed a series of randomly generated Biomorphs. For each Biomorph shown, the subject was given the option to reject it, creating a detector based on its genotype, or to accept it, which does not change the state of the detector set. The detectors were put to use as they were created to filter out new Biomorphs similar to the rejected ones.

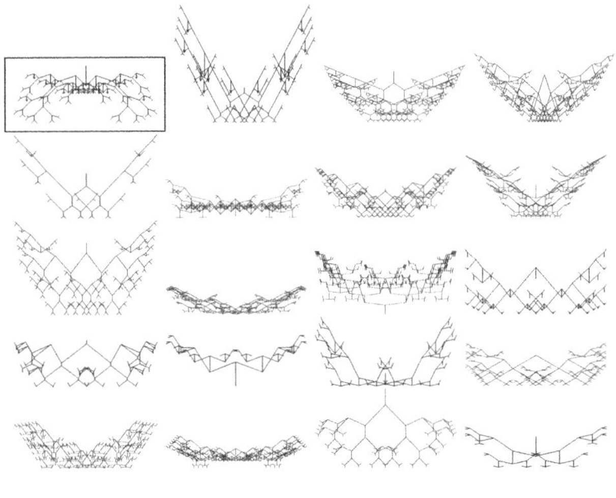

Figure 1: A sample from the range of Biomorphs covered by a single detector. The boxed figure in the upper-left is the detector's center, which is (3,6,6,-5,3,-2,-6,-5,8).

Thus, the aesthetic quality of images was expected to improve during a session because the increasing number of detectors could prevent more regions of "bad" genotypes from being displayed. The subjects were asked to rate Biomorphs until about 50% of the parameter space was covered by detectors. To test the effectiveness of the detectors, the subjects were asked to evaluate a series of 150 Biomorphs from three sets: random Biomorphs, Biomorphs that survived censoring by the subject's own detectors, and Biomorphs that survived the censoring by the superset of many subjects' detectors. The number of rejected Biomorphs from each set was recorded, and we assume user satisfaction to be inversely correlated with the number of rejections.

This test was performed using all seven subjects and the superset of all subjects' detectors to determine the efficacy of the consensus solutions. It was repeated using only three of the subjects and their detectors to determine the effects of group size on the quality of consensus solutions. The consensus solutions shown in the latter test were thus censored using only three sets of detectors instead of seven.

Results

The results of the experiments are summarized in Table 1. The system appeared to learn the Biomorph preferences of individual users to a statistically significant degree. For the testing involving all seven users, the rejection rate for the random Biomorphs was higher than that for Biomorphs that were filtered using a subject's own detectors ($>$ 95% significance using the Wilcoxon signed-rank test). For single users, the system clearly reduced the number of unacceptable solutions, thus improving the average quality of solutions presented to an individual. We believe that the system's performance could be improved dramatically for motivated users who a)

	1	2	3	4	5	6	7
none	52%	72%	50%	30%	58%	36%	54%
self	38%	48%	44%	32%	66%	30%	44%
all	46%	62%	38%	48%	64%	38%	60%

b)

	1	2	3
none	62%	52%	50%
self	56%	48%	28%
all	44%	42%	30%

Table 1: The user study results. The entries represent the percentage of Biomorph images rejected by a user for a particular detector set. Each column represents the data from one subject. The detector sets, indicated by the labels "none", "self" and "all", are no detectors, the subject's own detectors, and the superset of all subjects' detectors respectively. The results from testing all seven users are summarized in a), and the the results from the subset of three are shown in b).

are willing to invest more time to build their personal detector sets (e.g. for music, movies, or books that they like.) Using smaller detectors and covering a larger portion of the parameter space would likely increase the accuracy of user preferences. More importantly, a more accurate aesthetic distance measure needs to be defined.

Combining user preferences worked well for the set of three users but not for all seven. For the testing involving the seven users, the difference between rejection rates of random Biomorphs and those censored by the superset of all seven subjects' detectors is not statistically significant. For the testing involving only three of the seven subjects, the rejection rates for the group-selected Biomorphs were approximately the same or lower than the ones selected using their own detectors. The consensus solutions for three users appeared to be of equal or greater quality than the solutions generated for the individuals alone, while the solutions for all seven users appeared to be of low quality. The results suggest that it is hard to satisfy a large number of users and that consensus solutions may not even exist for groups with members with different preferences. The number of users that an aesthetic immune system can accommodate is likely dependent on the particular problem domain and the similarity of the users. If the users have conflicting preferences or if the problem domain is highly subjective, then consensus solutions would be hard to find. However, if user preferences are orthogonal to one another, then a large range of good consensus solutions could be discovered using this method. Inaccuracies in the user profiles can also lower the average quality of solutions found. If the profiles for all users were perfect and complete, solutions that are not censored by any profile would satisfy everyone. However, the Biomorph profiles were approximate and incomplete, so combining profiles did not always work.

Conclusions

We have presented an algorithm for identifying regions of interest in a parameter space using the subjective judgments of multiple individuals. It remains to be seen if the consensus solutions are more likely to be novel and innovative or bland and inoffensive. It would be easy to retrofit many existing evoart algorithms to use the immunological approach. We believe that this will reveal interesting parts of the parameter spaces that were not seen before due to the inefficiency of mutational search and the local aesthetic fitness optima that can stall evolution. The search for these regions could be accelerated by having multiple users create a common pool of detectors. If the set of cooperating users is large and representative of the tastes of the general public, the final result might be a system that generates art that many can appreciate.

Acknowledgments

We thank the participants in the user study. The authors gratefully acknowledge the support of the NSF (grants CDA-9503064 and ANIR-9986555), the ONR (grant N00014-99-1-0417), DARPA (grant AGR F30602-00-2-0584), the Intel Corporation, and the Santa Fe Institute.

References

Chao, D. L., and Forrest, S. 2002. Information immune systems. In *Proceedings of the First International Conference on Artificial Immune Systems.* (in press).

Dawkins, R. 1986. *The Blind Watchmaker.* Harlow, UK: Longman Scientific and Technical.

Nelson, G. L. 1993. Sonomorphs: An application of genetic algorithms to the growth and development of musical organisms. In *Proceedings of the Fourth Biennial Art & Technology Symposium*, 155–169.

Sims, K. 1991. Artificial evolution for computer graphics. *Computer Graphics* 25(4):319–328.

A Model of Biological Differentiation in Adaptiogenesis to the Environment

Takamasa Sawada, **Atsuko Mutoh**, **Shohei Kato** and **Hidenori Itoh**

Department of Intelligence and Computer Science,
Nagoya Institute of Technology
Gokiso-cho, Showa-ku, Nagoya 466-8555, Japan.
{sawada, atsuko, shohey, itoh}@ics.nitech.ac.jp

Abstract

In this paper, we propose a model of biological differentiation based on physical features and behavioral strategies in order to probe the mysteries of biological differentiation. We, then, implement the model, and perform the Alife simulations of birds' evolution in an artificial ecology. The ecology consists of two islands, and the atmospheric temperature in each of the islands fluctuates periodically. As a result of the simulations, we have observed that birds, adapting themselves to a change of temperature in their habitat, branch off in two types of biology: migratory bird and resident bird.

Introduction

This paper proposes a computationary evolution model for biological differentiation. A number of evolutionary models for an ecosystem has been proposed during past decade or so (e.g., (Takashina & Watanabe 1994),(Eiben & van Hemert 1999),(Downing 1998)). In the models, some species acquire behavioral and physical features suitable for a certain environment to which the species is exposed. The ecosystem of a few different species is well simulated by the evolutionary computation based on the models (e.g., (Michalewicz 1996),(Miychell 1996),(Kaneko & Yomo 2000)). Our research group (Moriwaki *et al.* 1996) has presented a computationary evolution model for a pseudo ecosystem including three types of artificial living things: herbivores, carnivores and plants. The model has well simulated food-chain. In the model, an ecological niche of the living things is given as fixed element. On the other hand, natural living things acquire an ecological niche, such as carnivore and herbivore, with the macro-evolution. It is obvious that the emergence of the variation in ecological niche is necessary for the development of an ecosystem. A long-range target of this research is to propose an evolution model for emergence of ecological niche.

In this paper, as a first step of this research, we propose a computationary evolution model of the biological differentiation. Our model is based on the interrelation between physical feature and behavioral strategy. This paper, then, presents a simulated ecology by our model, in which birds are taken. The ecology has two islands where atmospheric temperature fluctuates antithetically. The simulation shows that birds' behavior evolves so as to adapt themselves to the ecology, and then that the biology of the birds becomes to differentiate into two types: a migratory bird and a resident bird. As an interpretation on the results of the simulation experiment, we then discuss the generated differentiation from two points: physical feature and behavioral strategy. Moreover in respect of the two typical behavioral strategies which the migratory and resident birds have acquired, we also discuss their structure.

A Model of Biological Differentiation

Biological differentiation has been generally observed in the nature. It is said that the evolution of physical feature and behavioral strategy, as the one of many factors, causes the biological differentiation. In this paper, we propose a computationary evolution model of the biological differentiation. The following section gives a description of the definitions of an artificial living thing (called *autonomous agent*, or simply *agent*) and its reproductive activity, and also gives a brief description of the common property of reproductive isolation that the living things have.

Agent in the model

At an unit time, an agent chooses one from finite actions, and then, does it. The sensory information which an agent can perceive consists of a self state (internal state) and an environmental situation (external stimuli). An agent has a behavioral strategy for determining an action by the sensory information. Moreover, the relative merit of a behavioral strategy for an agent depends on the agent's body, and we call the body element *physical feature*. Let a_i be an agent (i is identifier), and let b_i and st_i be the physical feature and the behavioral strategy of a_i, respectively. a_i is, then, characterized as follows.

$$a_i(b_i, st_i). \tag{1}$$

The behavioral strategy st_i is represented as a function which determines action. Let ACT be a set of finite actions, and act_i^t be an action in ACT, which is selected by a_i at time t. act_i^t is determined by the value of the function for st_i, as follows.

$$act_i^t = st_i(in_i(t), ex_i(t)), \tag{2}$$

where in_i(t) and ex_i(t) are internal state and external stimuli of a_i at time t, respectively. This equation means that a behavioral strategy of the agent determines an action by agent's sensory information. After the action, the internal state of the agent is updated.

$$\begin{cases} in_i(t) = in_i(t-1) + d_{act_i^{t-1}}(b_i, e_i), \\ in_i(0) = C_0, \end{cases} \tag{3}$$

where $d_{act_i^t}(b_i, e_i)$ is the amount of change of the internal state at t, and C_0 is the initial amount of the internal state. It should be noticed that $d_{act_i^t}(b_i, e_i)$ depends on the action by agent $a_i(b_i, \_)$ under the external stimuli e_i at that time. It should be also noticed that time t means the elapsed time from birth. Agent a_i becomes extinct when fulfilling any of the following conditions

$$in_i(t) \leq C_1, \tag{4}$$
$$t \geq C_2, \tag{5}$$

where C_1 means the lower bound of the internal state to survive, and C_2 means the generation time.

Agent's reproductive activity

The generation of an agent is performed by only crossing. Let a_i and a_j be agents (i, j are identifiers). A child agent a_k is generated from a_i and a_j as its parents by the following crossover function.

$$a_k(b_k, st_k) = cr(a_i(b_i, st_i), a_j(b_j, st_j)). \tag{6}$$

Crossover function cr outputs a new agent as follows.

$$cr(a_i(b_i, st_i), a_j(b_j, st_j)) = a(mb(cb(b_i, b_j)), ms(cs(st_i, st_j))), \tag{7}$$

where cb and cs mean the crossover which crosses two physical features and two behavioral strategies, respectively, and mb and ms mean mutation which mutates a physical feature and a behavioral strategy, respectively.

Behavioral strategy and the evaluation

As our general idea in respect to an evaluation of the behavioral strategy, we are taking our stand on that there is some correlation between the relative merit of a behavioral strategy which an agent has and the physical feature of the agent.

Let st_i be a behavioral strategy (i is an identifier), and let $E(st_i(b))$ be the expectation of gain made by behaviors, based on st_i, of agents whose physical feature is b. For two different behavioral strategies st_l and st_m , we, then, consider the variation of $E(st_l(b))$ and $E(st_m(b))$ when b is changed. As the case may be, we observe a certain amount B of physical feature satisfying the following conditions.

$$E(st_l(B)) = E(st_m(B)), \tag{8}$$
$$E'(st_l(B)) \cdot E'(st_m(B)) < 0. \tag{9}$$

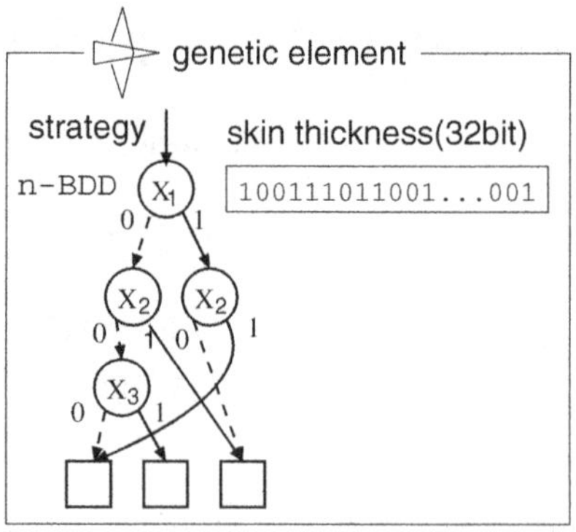

Figure 1: The structure of a bird agent.

We call such as the amount B *turning point* to the biological differentiation. Generally, living things evolve so as to heighten the expectation of gain made by their behaviors. We, thus, think that the behavioral strategy of agents differentiates into plural strategies, such as st_l and st_m, and physical feature, such as B, gives that occasion.

Reproductive isolation

Reproductive isolation may be one of the important factors for the biological differentiation. It acts as a trigger for biological differentiation, by making a gap in the amount of the physical features. It is said that the limitation of the reproductive range stimulates differentiation. By reproductive isolation, agents a_i and a_j can cross only when satisfying the following condition.

$$gd(a_i(b_i, st_i), a_j(b_j, st_j)) < K, \tag{10}$$

where gd is the function which returns the genetic distance between agents, and K is a constant.

Artificial Ecology

In this paper, we consider two islands where temperature fluctuates in antiphase.

Agent

Two kinds of agent: plants and birds, exist in the islands. Plant agents are living matter without evolution. Plant agents live their simple life cycle depending on the climate in the island. Bird agent a_i is defined as follows by concretization of the agent which defined in Section *"Agent in the model"*:

$$a_i(sk_i, bdd_i), \tag{11}$$

where sk_i and bdd_i are the thickness of the skin and n-BDD, respectively, which work as physical feature and behavioral strategy. Figure 1 shows the structure of a bird agent. The gene of sk_i is expressed by the 32 bit string, and the value of sk_i is from 0 to 1 by proportion of 1 in the bit string. On the other hand, the gene of bdd_i is expressed by n-BDD (n=5) with seven variables. n-BDD is an extension of BDD (Akers 1978), by assigning

Table 1: Sensory information.

X_1	Is it a full stomach?
X_2	Is it hungry?
X_3	Does a plant exist around there?
X_4	Does a friend exist around there?
X_5	Is it cold?
X_6	Is the temperature up?
X_7	Is the temperature down?

Table 2: Behavior of a bird agent.

do-nothing	(N)	Do not move
eat	(E)	Move toward a plant and eat
approach	(A)	Approach a friend
crossover	(C)	Approach a friend and cross with it
migrate	(M)	Migrate to another island

Table 3: Parameters setting in the proposed model.

an internal state of an agent

C_0	C_1	C_2
400	0	750

a reproductive isolation

$gd(a_i, a_j)$	$\lvert sk_i - sk_j \rvert$	K	$\frac{5}{32}$

genetic operation of an agent: mutation rate

n-BDD	addition	deletion	alteration
	$\frac{1}{5}$	$\frac{1}{20}$	$\frac{1}{20}$
physical feature	invert with the probability of $\frac{1}{16}$ for each bit		

a cycle of temperature change

steps	250

more than two values to the terminal nodes. We adopt one-point crossover and APPLY crossover (Mutoh *et al.* 1999) for crossover function *cb* and *cs*, respectively (see Equation (6) in Section *"Agent's reproductive activity"*).

Internal state consists of energy. A bird agent gains energy by eating a plant agent, and consumes energy by acting. A bird agent can move to one of eight neighborhood cells by an action at one step, and can perceive external stimuli from the circumference.

Sense, behavior, and consumption

Sensory information of bird agent a_i is expressed by the bit string. It is inputted to behavior strategy bdd_i. The output value of bdd_i determines the behavior of a_i. Table 1 shows what each bit of the string means.

The behavior of a bird agent consists of five actions shown in Table 2. A bird agent is going to take the behavior chosen as an output value of n-BDD, and consumes its energy in accordance with the behavior it acts. Energy consumption of the agent also depends on its physical feature and climate in the island it lives.

Experiments and Consideration

In this experiment, we consider two islands which consist of 50×50 cells, and take 120 bird agents in each island. At initial state, for all bird agents, $sk_i(i = 1, \ldots, 240) = 0.5$, and $bdd_i(i = 1, \ldots, 240)$ are composed in random, that is, all bird agent have the same physical feature and their behavioral strategy are blind. Table 3 shows a parameter setup for this experiment.

As a experimental results on the above conditions,

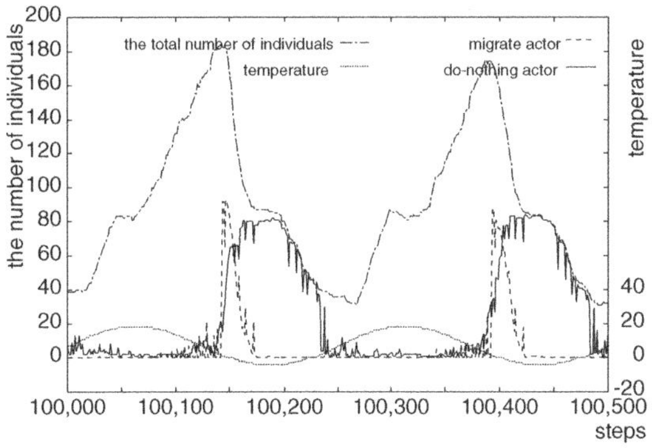

Figure 2: Transition of the number of individuals in an island.

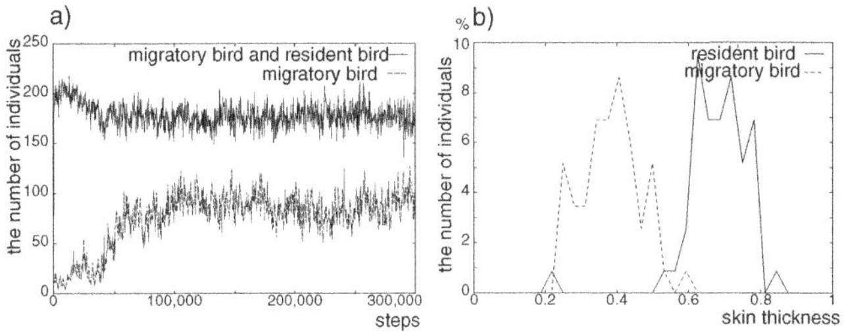

Figure 3: a) the transition of the number of individuals, b) the distribution of skin thickness in the ecology.

we observed two characteristic behavioral patterns when simulation was increasing in steps. One is the behavior which migrates periodically between the islands, and another is the behavior which continues remaining in the island. We have investigated the transition of the number of individuals which choose *migrate* or *do-nothing* in an island from 100,000 steps to 100,500 steps. Figure 2 shows the results. The results indicate that both *migrate* and *do-nothing* appear periodically in winter season, especially at the beginning of winter for *migrate*. In the season, the results also indicate that most of individuals select either of the two actions. We have, thus, classified individuals in two groups: *migratory birds* and *resident birds*, according to the behavior they select: *migrate* or *do-nothing*. Figure 3 a) shows transition of the total number of individuals and the number of individuals of migratory birds from an initial state to 300,000 steps (corresponding to 1,200 cycles of seasons). The figure shows that the balance of the number of migratory birds and resident birds becomes about even stably. Figure 3 b) shows the distribution of the skin thickness of a migratory bird and a resident bird at 300,000 steps. We suppose that the agent whose skin becomes thicker can bear colder climate in winter. Such the agent is considered to specialize in a resident bird. On the other hand, we also suppose that the agent whose skin becomes thinner can migrate at lower cost. Such the agent is considered to specialize in a migratory bird.

Finally, we have investigated the behavioral strategy,

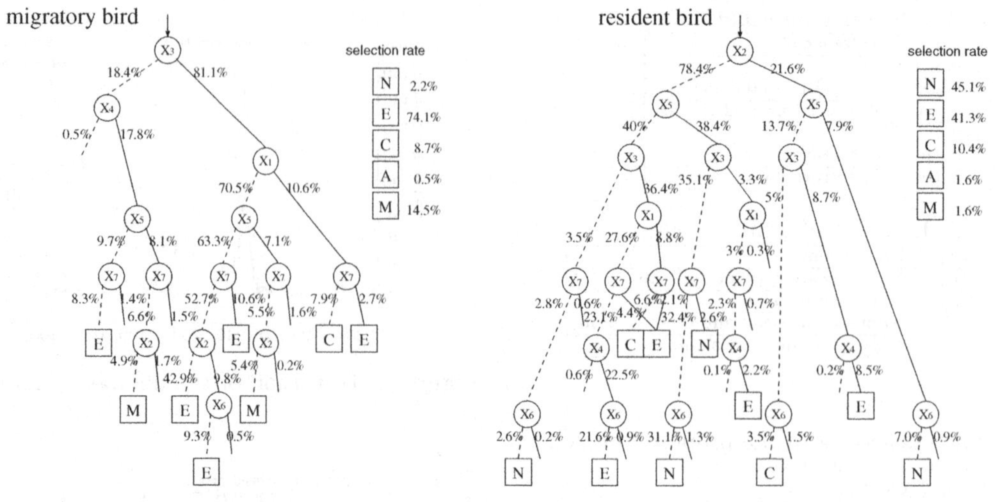

The path is omitted if its probability is less than 2 (%).

Figure 4: Typical behavioral strategies of bird agents.

which bird agents had acquired by evolution. Figure 4 shows typical n-BDD which migratory bird and resident bird acquired, respectively. This figure shows the common composition of n-BDD which birds had at 300,000 steps. In the figures, the value labeled with an edge in the n-BDD means the probability (%) that the edge was chosen. The strategy of migratory bird is characterized by *migrate*, and the selection rate in all behaviors is also high. On the other hand, resident bird does not migrate, and it seldom or never move while it is cold.

Conclusion

This paper proposed a computationary evolution model of biological differentiation. The model is based on the interrelation between physical feature and behavioral strategy. We, then, implemented our model in a simulated ecology of birds. The ecology has two islands where atmospheric temperature fluctuates in antiphase. Birds was differentiated into a migratory bird or a resident bird.

A living things' behavioral strategy consists of congenital element and acquired element. In this paper, behavioral strategy is decided only by gene, in other words, it decided by instinct. Learning, an acquired element, will affect acquiring ecological niche, too (e.g., (French & Messinger 1994)). As the future work, we will dedicate to introducing the learning mechanism, such as reinforcement learning, into our evolutionary behavioral model.

References

Akers, S. B. 1978. Binary decision diagrams. *IEEE Trans. Comput.* 509–516.

Downing, K. 1998. Combining genetic programming and genetic algorithms for ecological simulation. *Genetic Programming* 48–53.

Eiben, A., and van Hemert, D. E. J. 1999. Polulation dynamics and emerging mental features in aegis. *Proceedings of the Genetic and Evolutionary Computation Conference* 1257–1264.

French, R. M., and Messinger, A. 1994. Genes, phenes and the baldwin effect: Learning and evolution in a simulated population. *Artificial Life IV* 277–282.

Kaneko, K., and Yomo, T. 2000. Sympatric speciation from interaction-induced phenotype differentiation. *Artificial Life VII* 113–121.

Michalewicz, Z. 1996. Genetic algorithms + data structures = evolution programs. *Springer-Verlag.*

Miychell, M. 1996. An introduction to genetic algorithm. *MIT Press.*

Moriwaki, K.; Inuzuka, N.; Yamada, M.; Seki, H.; and Itoh, H. 1996. Self adaptation of agent's behavior using ga with n-bdd. *5th IEEE International Workshop on Robot and Human Communication* 96–101.

Mutoh, A.; Oono, S.; Moriwaki, K.; Nakamura, T.; Inuzuka, N.; and Itoh, H. 1999. An evolutionary method using crossover in a food chain simulation. *Proceedings of 5th European Conference on Artificial Life* 89–93.

Takashina, T., and Watanabe, S. 1994. Study of self adaptive behavior in quasi-ecosystem. *Proceedings of the Third Parallel Computing Workshop.*

Cellulat

Jaime Lagunez-Otero , Pedro Pablo González Pérez , Maura Cárdenas-García , Octavio Rosas , & Armando Franyuti
Instituto de Química, Universidad Nacional Autónoma de México
Ciudad Universitaria, 04510, MÉXICO, D.F.
ppgp@servidor.unam.mx, lagunez@servidor.unam.mx http://132.248.11.4

Abstract

In order to model the cell it is essential to understand the communication system that governs its behaviour. Though it is true that determining the kinetic equations of the biochemistry involved in vital functions is very useful, the management of the information in order for the cell to make the correct physiological decisions is even more so. This can be appreciated in the determinacy of the correct function of oncogenes coding for signal transduction components. We emulate a signal transduction network using behaviour-based systems and the blackboard architecture. Our construct, named Cellulat, allows one to observe two essential aspects of the intracellular signalling networks: (1) the apparent behavioural capabilities and (2) a spatial organization. The first user interfaces for creating a model cell are presented, the ontology used, as well as a simple example for the analysis of a kinase pathway.

Introduction

Most artificial life models have centred on the ability of describing external properties such as reproduction, competition, and selection in the better cases using biochemical considerations. This has done without seriously taking into account the internal communication mechanisms required to observe the phenomena. Our thesis focuses on the idea that in order to comprehend vital properties one must understand the cellular information processing system. Our construct is composed of autonomous agents representing elements involved in signal transduction. We present here the ontology used, the behaviour based architecture, the agent design and the interfaces which permit the creation of the model.

The effect of signals received by a cell can be the alteration of the cell metabolism, its differentiation, mitosis, or apoptosis, among other biological functions. Each cell in an organism receives specific combinations of chemical signals generated by other cells. Once the signals bind to the receptors, different processes are activated generating complex networks. Paradigms that have been used to model cellular signalling networks are artificial neural networks (Bray & Lay 1994; Pritchard & Dufton 2000), Boolean networks (Edwards 1995), petri nets (Fuss 1987), rule-based systems (Cárdenas 2000), cellular automata (Edwards 1995), and multi-agent systems (Fisher, Malcom, & Paton 2000; Paton, Staniford, & Kendall 1995; Schwab & Pienta 1997).

Because we are interested in the behavioural repertoire of the cell, the theory of behaviour based systems (Brooks 1986) is proposed to constitute a better approach for its simulation. Furthermore, the communication between agents in our model takes place through a blackboard architecture (Nii 1989) in which cellular elements related to signalling pathways can be explicitly represented.

In this paper, we postulate that an effective and robust model of intracellular signalling can be obtained when the main structural and functional characteristics of behaviour-based systems and the blackboard architecture are joined.

Signalling intracellular networks and Behaviour based systems

The transfer of the external milieu signal to the nucleus can come from the binding of the given signal by the receptor. This frequently generates a diffusible intracellular second messenger by way of a series of phosphorylations and multimerization of cytoplasmic and membrane bound enzymes. Many different receptors generate the same second messenger such as cAMP, cGMP, The convergence and divergence of the independent signals makes the system very interesting from the point of view of the studies of information transfer. When the delicate balance of transduction is affected there is a risk of damaging the cellular growth control by activating the replication machinery out of time and eventually inducing a pathologic state such as a neoplasia in the neighboring cells and tissue. Considering the relevance of the phenomena and the complexity of the network, it becomes essential to use computational techniques to deal with the system.

In computer science, an autonomous agent interacts directly with its problem domain; it perceives its environment through its sensors and acts on it through its actuators. The autonomous agent tries to satisfy a set of goals or motivations in an environment that can be dynamic and complex. It decides how to relate its external and internal inputs with its actions (Maes 1994). Adaptation is one of the desirable characteristics in autonomous agents. An autonomous agent is adaptive if it has abilities that allow him to improve its performance in time. The theory of behaviour-based systems (Brooks 1986) provides a new strategy for the construction of autonomous agents, inspired by etology. The aim of behaviour-based systems (BBS) is to provide control to autonomous agents which will eventually contribute to its capacity to adapt.

A cell signalling network can be seen as an adaptive autonomous agent or as a society of adaptive autonomous agents, where each agent can exhibit a particular behaviour depending on its "cognitive" capabilities. As an autonomous agent, the network perceives its external environment through its surface receptors and acts on it by means of the generation of new signals, which will be able to affect the behaviour of other cells. The cell's external environment is also dynamic and complex, in which an extensive range of signals and combinations of these can exist. Furthermore, as in an autonomous agent, the network and in consequence the cell itself decides how to relate the received external signals (signalling molecules) to its internal signals (secondary messengers), so that their goals (differentiation, proliferation, survival, among others) can be satisfied. The cell is now able also to adapt to its environment by constantly modifying its behaviour in order to respond to the changes that take place in the environment and to the pattern of signals received.

Cellulat: a signalling network based construct

The model presented constitutes a refinement and adaptation of an action selection mechanism structured on a blackboard architecture, termed, Internal Behaviours Network (IBeNet) (Gershenson, González, & Negrete 2000; Gershenson & Negrete 2000; González 2000; González *et al.* 2000). The IBeNet was initially built to study action selection in autonomous agents such as physical robots and animats, it constitutes a working environment for the bottom-up modelling of information processing systems characterized by:

1. coordination and opportunistic integration of several tasks in real time,
2. use of several abstraction or context levels for the different types of information that participate in the processing network,
3. decision making,
4. action selection and
5. adaptation.

Although, the intracellular signalling model proposed can be seen as the assignation of a new semantic to the components of the IBeNet, we assume here that this is equivalent to the creation of correspondence of these same semantics to the components of the blackboard architecture, when the two following considerations are done:

1. knowledge sources are seen as either internal autonomous agents or interface autonomous agents and
2. the blackboard architecture control is distributed now between these two types of autonomous agents.

The blackboard architecture described in section 3 takes into account the considerations (1) and (2). In this way, it is not necessary to explain the structural and functional details of IBeNet here to understand the intracellular signalling model proposed.

Three main components define the Cellulat structure: the blackboard, the internal autonomous agents and interface autonomous agents. The blackboard represents the cell's internal medium.

The blackboard levels correspond to different cellular structures through which the signal transduction occurs. In this way, the cellular membrane, the cytosol and the nucleus are different blackboard levels. The solution elements recorded on the blackboard represent two main types of intracellular signals: secondary messenger molecules and activation/inactivation signals. Both types are synthesized or created by internal autonomous agents and these, either directly or indirectly, promote the activation/inactivation of other internal autonomous agents. The internal autonomous agents model the components of the intracellular signalling network such as proteins, enzymes and other mechanisms necessary to carry out the signal transduction. On the other hand, the interface autonomous agents model the cell surface receptors and the mechanisms for the secretion of signalling molecules. Each agent, independently of its type, has a condition part and an action part; the way in which both parts are linked depends on the complexity of the intracellular component modelled by agent. The work of both types of agents is event-directed. This is, each intracellular signal registered on the blackboard or each extracellular signal perceived constitutes an event, which could activate or inactivate one or more autonomous agents. When an internal autonomous agent is activated then this one executes consists in the synthesis or modification of a signal on the blackboard.

Modelling spatial organization

An important aspect to consider in the modelling of intracellular signalling networks is their spatial organization. Experimental data recently obtained suggest clearly that many intracellular signalling networks exhibit a high level of spatial organization. Intracellular signalling models developed recently approach to this question (Fisher, Malcom, & Paton 2000). Cellulat allows modelling the spatial organization taking account two organizational criteria of the blackboard architecture. One is the horizontal organization, given by the different abstraction levels of the blackboard, which allow an intralevel signal processing. The other is the vertical organization, given by columns that cross different blackboard levels. These columns arise as result of the adjoining work of several internal autonomous agents

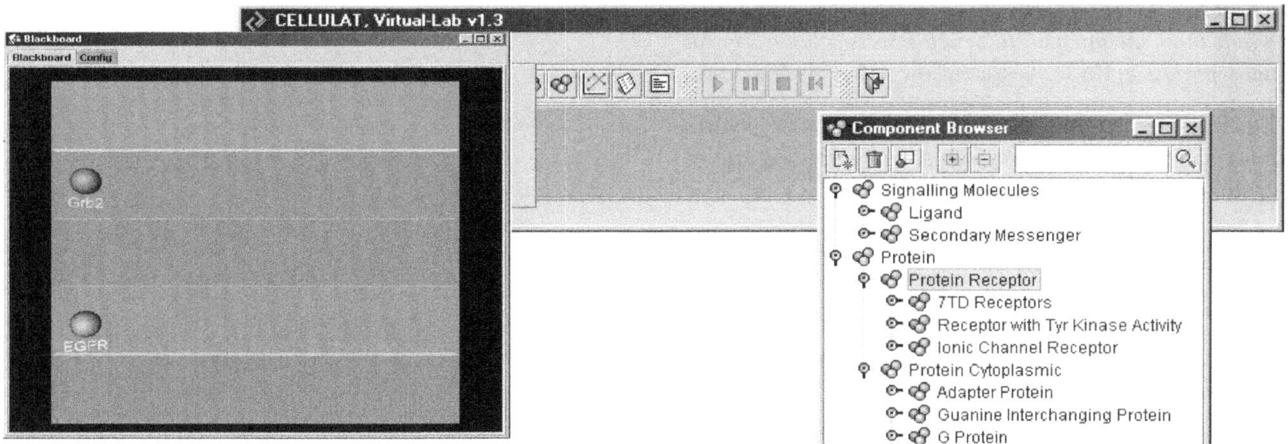

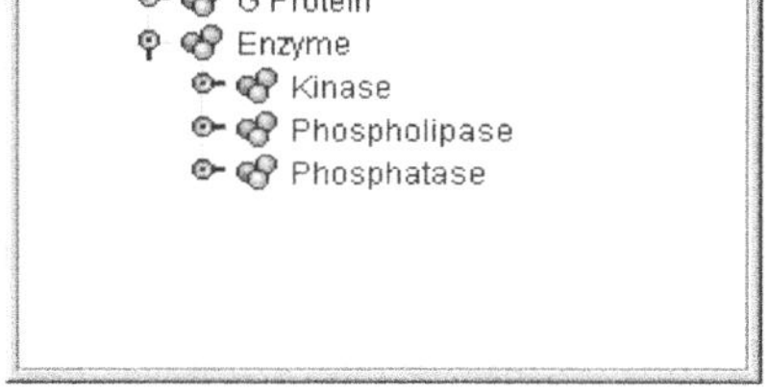

Figure 1: Main menu, component browser and blackboard in the Cellulat interface. All functionality of Cellulat is executed through the main menu. Among other tasks, the main menu permits the creation of data base and space works, the run of a simulation, the visualization of the signalling element state and the selection of 2D or 3D graphics showing the results of interaction between signalling elements. The function of the component browser is the creation, modification and visualization of the different signalling elements. The blackboard shows the characteristics of the intracellular milieu. In this case, on the compartment corresponding to the membrane a population of EGF receptors has been created, whereas on the compartment cytosol a population of adapter proteins Grb2.

that operate at a same section of blackboard. We have named these columns "agency columns". Convergence and divergence of agency columns can occur (González 2000).

The process of creation, modification and visualization of the signalling elements just as the process related with the activation of the pathway and visualization of the resultant interactions are all executed through the Cellulat interface. The figure shows three screens from the Cellulat graphic interface: the main menu and the component browser and the blackboard. Through the main menu the data base and work spaces are created, the simulation of the intracellular signalling is initiated or stopped and the results of the interactions between signalling elements are showed through 2D and 3D graphics. Through component browser the different signalling elements can be created, modified and visualised

Once concluded the creation of the two signalling elements, these are placed on their corresponding cellular compartments in the blackboard. The Components are incorporated into the blackboard as colour-coded rotating spheres (see Figure 1) The type of behaviour (phosphorylated, non phophorylated, activated, non activated) of these signalling elements is represented by the intensity of their colour and rotation rate during the simulation.

Conclusions

An artificial life model which takes into account the internal communication in the cell and its structure should provide a basis for a new generation of constructs which emulate biological behaviours with a mechanistically deeper basis.

In this paper we have discussed how the fusion of the behaviour-based systems theory and the blackboard architecture constitutes a suitable approach for the modelling of intracellular signalling networks. Two basic aspects of the cellular signalling networks are of interest in Cellulat: (1) the cognitive capabilities of the signalling components, and (2) the spatial organization in the cell. This is done when considering the functional components as adaptive autonomous agents. The second aspect is targeted by the shared blackboard data structure, which allows for the modelling of spatial parameters.

In the future the present infrastructure is to permit the visualization of emergent cognitive properties of the information processing network.

References

Bray, D., and Lay, S. 1994. Computer simulated evolution of a network of cell signalling molecules. *Biophysical Journal* 66(4):972–977.

Brooks, R. A. 1986. A robust layered control system for a mobile robot. *IEEE Journal of Robotics and Automation* RA-2:14–23.

Cairo, O.; Sucar, L.; and Cantu, F., eds. 2000. *MICAI 2000*, volume 1793 of *LNAI*. Berlin: Springer Verlag.

Cárdenas, M. 2000. *Búsqueda de blancos terapéuticos empleando un modelo de señales intracelulares mediadas por Ras.* Ph.D. Dissertation, UNAM, Mxico.

Edwards, C. 1995. Computational models for cellular information processing systems. unpublished undergraduate thesis, University of Liverpool.

Fisher, M.; Malcom, G.; and Paton, R. 2000. Spatiological processes in intracellular signalling. *BioSystems* 55:83–92.

Fuss, H. 1987. Simulation of biological systems with petri nets — introduction to modelling of distributed systems. In Moller, D., ed., *Advances in System Analysis.* Braunschweig, Wiesbaden: Vieweg. 1–12.

Gershenson, C. NS González, P. P., and Negrete, J. 2000. Thinking adaptive: Towards a behaviours virtual laboratory. In *Proceedings SAB'2000.*

Gershenson, C.; González, P.; and Negrete, J. 2000. Action selection properties in a software simulated agent. In Cairo et al. (2000). 634–648.

González, P.; Negrete, J.; Barreiro, A.; and Gershenson, C. 2000. A model for combination of external and internal stimuli in the action selection of an autonomous agent. In Cairo et al. (2000). 621–633.

González, P. 2000. *Redes de Conductas Internas como Nodos-Pizarrón: Selección de Acciones y Aprendizaje en un Robot Reactivo.* Ph.D. Dissertation, Instituto de Investigaciones Biomédicas/UNAM, México.

Maes, P. 1994. Adaptive autonomous agents. *Artificial Life* 1:135–162.

Nii, H. P. 1989. Blackboard systems. In Barr, A.; Cohen, P. R.; and Feigenbaum, E. A., eds., *The Handbook of Artificial Intelligence*, volume IV. Addison-Wesley.

Paton, R.; Staniford, G.; and Kendall, G. 1995. Specifying logical agents in cellular hierarchies. In Paton, R.; Holcombe, M.; and Staniford, G., eds., *Proceedings of IPCAT (Information Processing in Cells and Tissues)*, 302–317.

Pritchard, L., and Dufton, M. 2000. Do proteins learn to evolve? the hopfield network as a basis for the understanding of protein evolution. *Journal of Theoretical Biology* 202:77–86.

Schwab, E., and Pienta, K. 1997. Modeling signal transduction in normal and cancer cells using complex adaptive systems. *Medical Hypotheses* 48:111–123.

Embryonics: Electronic Stem Cells

Lucian Prodan[1], **Gianluca Tempesti**[2], **Daniel Mange**[2], and **André Stauffer**[2]
[1] "Politehnica" University (UPT), Timisoara, Romania
E-mail: lprodan@cs.utt.ro, WWW: http://www.cs.utt.ro
[2] Swiss Federal Institute of Technology (EPFL), Lausanne, Switzerland
E-mail: name.surname@epfl.ch, WWW: http://lslwww.epfl.ch

Abstract

Embryonics is a long-term research project attempting to draw inspiration from the biological process of ontogeny, to implement novel digital computing machines endowed with better fault-tolerant capabilities. This article discusses the degree of bio-inspiration attained while also attempting to start a similarity debate on various implementation decisions, on why and how nature developed its subtle, intricated means of growing, healing and reproducing.

Motto: "What makes stem cells special is that they're immortal, and they can become anything they want to be." — Dr. James Thomson, University of Wisconsin.

Introduction

The incredibly huge number of some 60 trillion (60×10^{12}) cells make up a human being, with as many as 10 billion (10^{10}) cells with 100 trillion (10^{14}) interconnections concentrated in each of our brains (Mange & Tomassini 1998). Intelligence, creativity, the capacity of abstractization and ultimately conscience are all possible thanks to this marvelously complex human machine. Yet its entire structure emerges from a single cell, the zygote, giving birth to a completely functional organism that will continue to develop and enhance its features throught its entire life.

However, there is a key question that arises, driving biologists and not only: how can all this be possible? How can this be, that a single cell would divide for such a large number of times even us humans find difficult to imagine? And what mechanisms direct the division process so perfectly that when it ends the result is a healthy organism? Would it be possible to exploit these mechanisms to inspire engineers, perhaps including novel computational implementations? It seems that nature has created a remarkable circle: we became complex enough to develop sciences and now scientists have reached the point that enables them to study how nature can reach such complexity.

A special type of cell appears to answer some of the previous questions, a cell that can give birth to other identical cells, and all being able to become specialized cells themselves, such as muscular or nerve cells. But it is not all that easy to discover nature, let alone to penetrate its mysteries. After nearly 20 years of hard work, two teams of scientists have succeeded in growing and replicating these mother cells (Thomson & others 1998). Called "stem cells", these basic units ultimately mature and differentiate to become the building material of all types of body tissue (May 2000).

The fact that scientists are all driven by common questions is remarkably demonstrated by recent history, the research on novel bio-inspired computing systems having roughly the same age as modern biology. In the late 1940's von Neumann began to develop a theory of automata in order to contribute to a better understanding of both natural automata (living beings) and of artificial automata (computational systems) (Sipper *et al.* 1998). In more recent years there has been significant research carried out in a new project, aiming at creating bio-inspired computer hardware, called Embryonics (Tempesti 1998; Tempesti, Mange, & Stauffer 1998).

The purpose of this article is not to delve into the ethical issues' debate — related to cloning or using the DNA molecule as a threat (Alexander 2000) — but to take a comparative look to the recent findings in the field of cellular biology and their virtual mirror, the world of Embryonics. Intriguingly, there are many more similarities and common ideas than it is possible to explain by a mere coincidence. Section 2 briefly describes the discovery of a new kind of cell. Section 3 presents the path to a new kind of bio-inspired computer hardware within the Embryonics research environment, together with a deeper look inside the characteristics of the newly discovered cell and how the two relate to each other. Finally, Section 4 presents the conclusions and some general guidelines for the future of the Embryonics.

Nature Reveals Its Ways

Each and every living multi-cellular organism consists of groups of specialized cells that make up tissues and organs. Throughout its entire life, the perfect operation of this magnificent massively parallel biological system is ensured by a ceaseless process of cellular division, activated in order to overcome wounds and illnesses. A great majority of such cases are successfully repaired, with the exception of extreme situations such as the complete destruction of a vital organ or tissue. When this occurs, there are no possibilities of healing, which leads to the death of the entire organism.

At its very beginning, each organism originates from a single cell, the zygote. Its development process takes place through successive cellular divisions and differentiations, proof for the existence of a very special cell, capable of differentiating into any kind of needed, specialized

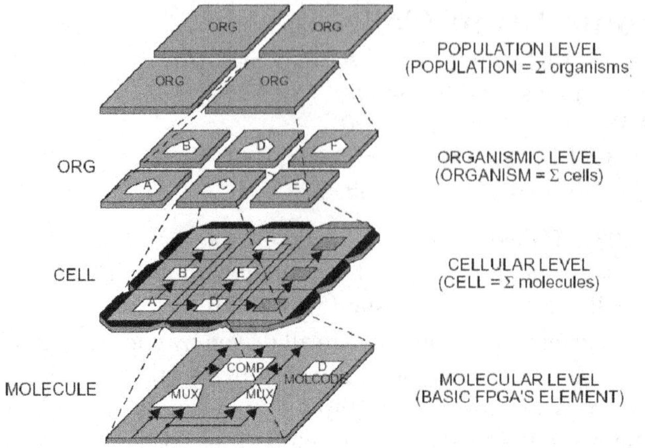

Figure 1: The 4 levels of organization of Embryonics.

cell. Christened *stem cell*, its unique transforming capacity could provide a solution for an organism's survival to extreme stress such as loss of a vital organ, giving it a huge potential in biology and medicine. Because this cell is the precursor to all other cell types in the human body, this accomplishment has set the stage for a revolution in medicine and basic biology (Thomson & others 1998; Anonymous 2001).

The zygote has the potential to form an entire organism as it has the remarkable feature of being *totipotent*, meaning that its potential is total (Anonymous 2000). Immediately following the fertilization, it starts to divide into identical totipotent cells that begin to specialize after several cycles of cell division, forming a hollow sphere of cells, called a blastocyst (May 2000).

But mastering the conditions necessary to witness the delicate phenomenon of cellular division is no simple matter. Yet the experiments made at Johns Hopkins University successfully verified that stem cells have the true potential of developing into basic cells found in all mammalian embryos (Shamblott & others 1998). However, directing the specialization process of the stem cells is another problem. We do know now that stem cells can in fact become any type of cell, either resulting new stem cells or specialized cells. What we are uncertain of is what exactly *instructs* a stem cell to specialize into a specific type of cell. Research conducted at Stanford reveals that in fact there are some stem cell "guardians", surrounding areas composed of stem cells, that determine which type of ordinary cell they will specialize in (Vaughan 2000).

As far as we know, the most interesting characteristics of the stem cells are the following:

- they can give rise to specialized cells;
- undifferentiated, they seem to have the ability to divide for apparently indefinite periods in culture;
- any of these cells can potentially develop into a fetus.

These are sufficient arguments to consider the fantastic potential of stem cells that lies in their ability to be ultimately directed to become specific types of cells or tissue. If, on one hand, this feature could be used to treat a host of cell-based diseases, on the other hand it might have a significant impact on the world of computer engineering.

The Embryonics Project — Biological Connections

As a long term research project, Embryonics has been developing for some years now becoming a consistent repository of bio-inspired solutions in computer engineering. Along with the proposed POE model (Sipper *et al.* 1997, also this volume, p111), the Embryonics project aims at developing ontogenetic hardware, i.e. hardware capable of self-replicating, self-repairing and evolving from its very own genetic material.

Fault tolerance has become a major requirement in modern computing. A great deal of research effort has been spent to achieve this feature and considerable boost comes from technological advancements, enabling system designers to consider new reconfiguration techniques applied to an entire computing universe made by connecting many identical entities (Mange *et al.* 1998; Negrini, Sami, & Stefanelli 1989; Shibayama *et al.* 1997). While the struggle for performance is still present, the term's definition has become somewhat loose due to a sufficient level of brute computing force available from nearly any digital machine. Today we witness the shift toward the first priority of the quest for ***distributed, highly redundant and massively reconfigurable systems*** and the Embryonics project makes no exception. Recent reliability analysis also show that embryonic structures open a new direction for building highly capable fault tolerant systems (Ortega & Tyrrell 1999).

Characteristics such as replication (self-replication), which can be seen as a special case of growth, and regeneration (self-repair), or recovery after wounds or illnesses, are part of the ontogeny process and are extremely attractive for many applications. The Embryonics project presents a consistent view of ontogenetic hardware and beyond (Gilbert 1991; Wolpert 1991; Prodan *et al.* 2001).

Embryonics quasi-biological artificial organisms are made up of a finite number of functionally identical cells (Mange & Tomassini 1998; Mange *et al.* 1998; Prodan *et al.* 2000; 2001), each of which is in turn made up of a finite number of functionally identical molecules (Figure 1). Each cell is a simple processor (a binary decision machine) realizing a unique function within the organism, defined by a set of instructions (program), which we call the *gene* of the cell. The functionality of the organism is therefore obtained by the parallel operation of all the cells while all the genes make up the genetic program or the *operative genome*. Cells are delimited by the existence of a rectangular cellular *membrane*, specified by a special part of the genome, called the *polymerase genome*. Each cell determines which gene is to be executed based on its coordinates inside the organism and stores a complete copy of the operative genome, thus making possible any task transfer. This feature makes the cells capable of *virtually replacing each other* (in the event of a detected malfunction) just like in real biological organisms.

The process of a cell deciding which gene to execute based on the coordinates from within its local environment, i.e. the surrounding cells, determines its functionality, not unlike cellular specialization in biological organisms. Furthermore, the access to the whole genetic program provides our electronic cell with *universality*, much as biological stem cells have the potential of becoming *any* type of specialized cell.

There are no limits on how large Embryonics cells can be. Then, the universality of the cell becomes actually the capacity of executing variable tasks — the more computationally complex the task, the more molecules required for the cell structure. Furthermore, by carefully selecting which portion of the code is to be executed by molecules, their universality is also assured — a molecule can effectively replace any other one by simply adapting its internal code.

Every living cell's innermass is delimited from the surrounding environment by the cellular membrane, which also acts as an *interface* with the exterior, allowing a limited exchange of substances. If the biological world allows and depends on exchanging substances, the world of silicon has more restrictive rules: the material replacing substances, but nonetheless allowed and dependent on its exchange, is *information*. Much as in nature, where substances entertain life by carrying energy and information, in the world of silicon electronic signals carry in a similar way the same ingredients, entertaining artificial life.

The artificial membrane (also called the space divider) has a triple role (Figure 2). Firstly, it acts like a spatial barrier, logically separating resources (molecules) belonging to different cells and ensuring an individual identity in the surrounding environment. Secondly, it acts as a guide for the entering configuration, which contains the operative part of the genome (genes from A to D for the left cell and from G to L for the right cell, Figure 2). All molecules pertaining to a cell are configured with the corresponding gene in a chain-like process, which does not allow information to get outside the cell and be wasted; in a similar manner, the existence of the cellular membrane in biological cells restricts the access of the environment to their inner part both ways, thus preventing any unwanted loss of substances or possible intrusions to or from the environment. Thirdly, its

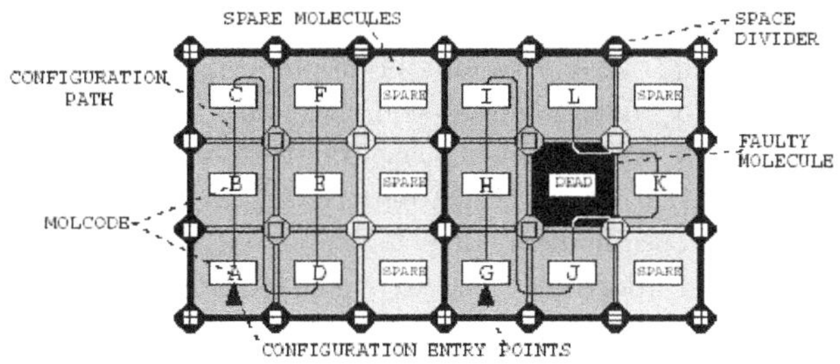

Figure 2: Self-repair at the molecular level

presence triggers a mechanism determining which gene is to be executed by each molecule. This can be seen as a specialization at the molecular level, the surrounding membrane directing the whole process in a similar way the stem cells' "guardians" (Vaughan 2000) control cell specialization in biology.

What makes living beings so complex is the subtle cooperation between various mechanisms helping to preserve the innate features of an organism and continuously adapting them to a quite considerable extent to environmental challenges. Life is a quite dramatic and long testing process, so it is perhaps best for biological entities to employ self-developed procedures in order to check for abnormalities and trigger the repair processes.

As in nature, where multiple self-testing happens in each and every living being, Embryonics also relies on more than one such mechanisms (Mange *et al.* 1998; Tempesti 1998; Tempesti, Mange, & Stauffer 1998). The very first self-testing procedure employs test-vectors and applies to the core of the molecule. An off-line testing procedure was considered to be sufficient, and takes place before any critical data is loaded. Nature does a similar process at the lowest level possible, contained by the very intimate structure of the DNA itself. The two strands that make up the DNA continuously test each other by subtle chemical bonds, preventing and detecting a majority of possible errors. During operation, the molecular core can act as an active memory, much as the DNA does. The self-testing is ensured by "breaking" its internal register into two halves storing complementary data and acting in a similar way the two DNA strands do (Prodan *et al.* 2001).

Another part of the molecule, the functional unit, is implemented as an on-line self-testing device, using the voting majority technique. Once the testing features in place, any detected error should allow the recovery, or healing of the organism. Due to the vast complexity of biological organisms, healing (self-repairing) mechanisms can only be effective if the task is hierarchically decomposed and dealt with accordingly.

Embryonics uses a hierarchy composed of two self-repairing mechanisms. The cellular structure is built of active and spare molecules. In the event of functional failure of an active molecule, all its functions are taken by the nearest spare molecule by means of shifting part of the cellular active resources one position. This is the self-repairing mechanism at the molecular level (Figure 2). A similar process takes place in nature, where the cell is capable of fabricating the resources needed. This is obviously impossible with current technology, the only way of providing additional resources at the molecular level being as spares. During its artificial life, the electronic organism may experience the situation when inside a cell a new fault is detected, but no more spares are available. This is the moment the second self-repair mechanism enters the stage, at the cellular level: the faulty cell "dies", then it is isolated, and all active cells are shifted a position by rerouting all the interconnections (Mange *et al.* 1998; Negrini, Sami, & Stefanelli 1989). This is again inspired by nature, where foreign bodies (objects or mutating cells) are isolated and eventually eliminated. Self-replication can be seen as a special case of growth; after configuring an initial cellular structure, the self-replication process considers this as a pattern and colonizes the whole environment (Sipper 1998; Tempesti 1998).

Conclusions

This article presented the essential bio-inspired features of the Embryonics project. It all started as a long-term research project, and, while it still remains largely so, the bio-inspired hardware developed allows us to build computing machines endowed with improved robustness, copied and adapted from biology to electronics. The technological advancements also give us now the opportunity to implement digital systems based on novel, complex operating principles but also put a higher pressure onto the design process and necessary trade-offs. Successful bio-inpired hardware may emerge only together with successful theory on nature's ways and the ways of implementing them in silicon.

All discussed issues lead us to believe that real bio-inspired hardware systems might just be closer than we think, thus narrowing the gap between biology and biologically inspired digital systems.

References

Alexander, D. 2000. The human genome project. *Science & Christian Belief* 12(2):98.

Anonymous. 2000. Stem cells: A primer. Technical report, National Institutes of Health. http://www.nih.gov/news/stemcell/primer.htm.

Anonymous. 2001. Opportunities and challenges: A focus on future stem cell applications. In *Stem Cells: Scientific Progress and Future Research Directions.* National Institutes of Health, Department of Health and Human Services.

Gilbert, S. F. 1991. *Developmental Biology.* MA: Sinauer Associates Inc., 3rd edition.

Mange, D., and Tomassini, M., eds. 1998. *Bio-inspired Computing Machines: Towards Novel Computational Architectures.* Lausanne, Switzerland: Presses Polytechniques et Universitaires Romandes.

Mange, D.; Sanchez, E.; Stauffer, A.; Tempesti, G.; Marchal, P.; and Piguet, C. 1998. Embryonics: A new methodology for designing field-programmable gate arrays with self-repair and self-replicating properties. *IEEE Transactions on VLSI Systems* 6(3):387–399.

May, M. 2000. Mother nature's menders. the battle against aging. *Scientific American.* Special Issue "The Quest to Beat Aging".

Negrini, R.; Sami, M. G.; and Stefanelli, R. 1989. *Fault Tolerance Through Reconfiguration in VLSI and WSI Arrays.* Cambridge, MA: MIT Press.

Ortega, C., and Tyrrell, A. 1999. Reliability analysis in self-repairing embryonic systems. In *Proc. 1st NASA/DoD Workshop on Evolvable Hardware*, 120–128.

Prodan, L.; Tempesti, G.; Mange, D.; and Stauffer, A. 2000. Biology meets electronics: The path to a bio-inpired FPGA. In *Proc. 3rd International Conference on Evolvable Systems: From Biology to Hardware*, 187–196.

Prodan, L.; Tempesti, G.; Mange, D.; and Stauffer, A. 2001. Embryonics: Artificial cells driven by artificial DNA. In *Proc. 4th International Conference on Evolvable Systems: From Biology to Hardware*, 100–111.

Shamblott, M., et al. 1998. Derivation of pluripotent stem cells from cultured human primordial germ cells. *Proc. Natl. Acad. Sci. USA* 95:13726–13731.

Shibayama, A.; Igura, H.; Mizuno, M.; and Yamashina, M. 1997. An autonomous reconfigurable cell array for fault-tolerant LSIs. In *Proc. 44th IEEE International Solid-State Circuits Conference*, 230–231.

Sipper, M.; Sanchez, E.; Mange, D.; Tomassini, M.; Perez-Uribe, A.; and Stauffer, A. 1997. A phylogenetic, ontogenetic, and epigenetic view of bio-inspired hardware systems. *IEEE Transactions on Evolutionary Computation* 1(1):83–97.

Sipper, M.; Tempesti, G.; Mange, D.; and Sanchez, E. 1998. Von Neumann's legacy: Special issue on self-replication. *Artificial Life* 4(3).

Sipper, M. 1998. Fifty years of research on self-replication: an overview. *Artificial Life* 4(3):237–257.

Tempesti, G.; Mange, D.; and Stauffer, A. 1998. Self-replicating and self-repairing multicellular automata. *Artificial Life* 4(3):259–282.

Tempesti, G. 1998. *A Self-Repairing Multiplexer-Based FPGA Inspired by Biological Processes.* Ph.D. Dissertation, EPFL, Lausanne. No. 1827.

Thomson, J., et al. 1998. Embryonic stem cell lines derived from human blastocysts. *Science* 282:1145–1147.

Vaughan, C. 2000. Stem cells' "guardians" found to control cell specialization. *Stanford Report.*

Wolpert, L. 1991. *The Triumph of the Embryo.* New York: Oxford University Press.

Tautomerism as a Constraint on the Composition of Alternative Nucleotide Alphabets

D. A. Mac Dónaill
Department of Chemistry, Trinity College, Dublin 2, Republic of Ireland. E-mail: dmcdonll@tcd.ie

Abstract

The factors determining the composition of the nucleotide alphabet are not self-evident. While, straightforward extensions to the alphabet such as iC:iG have received some theoretical attention, more exotic nucleotide pairs, such as α:Γ, β:δ, and κ:X, have been ignored. At the current state of knowledge the possibility of viable alternative nucleotide alphabets remains an intriguing possibility. In this paper the broader space of potential letters is considered in terms of hydrogen donor-acceptor patterns. Quantum chemical simulations at the PM3 semi-empirical level of approximation are employed to examine the stability of different tautomeric forms of candidate letters. The results suggest that tautomeric instability favoring hydroxyl elements over keto groups is one of the critical constraints on viable alternative alphabets. Rotation of a hydroxyl group changes the expressed hydrogen donor/acceptor pattern, destroying the integrity of the principal recognition feature. Two distinct alphabets appear viable, one containing the familiar aA:T/U and C:G, and a second containing just κ:X. Thus tautomerism offers an explanation for the composition of the natural alphabet, while posing challenges for the engineering of alternative alphabets.

Introduction

The replication of nucleotide texts is based on molecular recognition through the association of complementary hydrogen donor/acceptor (D/A) patterns and pyrimidine/purine motifs. Three positions with the capacity for H-bonding give a potential alphabet of 16 informationally distinct nucleotides, of which the natural nucleotide alphabet of A, C, G and T/U is a subset. This subset however is not self-evidently optimal; the successful incorporation by polymerase of the additional base pairs, iC:iG (Switzer, Moroney, & Benner 1989) and $\kappa : \pi$ (Picirilli *et al.* 1990) has been demonstrated, and thus viable alternative nucleotide alphabets seem possible.

Nature's failure to avail of a larger alphabet has prompted some discussion of the features shaping the natural alphabet (Szathmáry 1991; 1992). An alphabet of n letters, all equally employed, contains $\log_2 n$ bits of information per letter, and thus an alphabet of eight nucleotides would contain three bits of information per letter, compared to just two bits in the natural alphabet. A larger alphabet would appear to confer an advantage on a replicating system, allowing complex functionality to be specified in a shorter polymer than would the natural nucleotide alphabet.

The composition of an emergent alphabet is likely to be shaped by two parallel considerations, the prebiotic

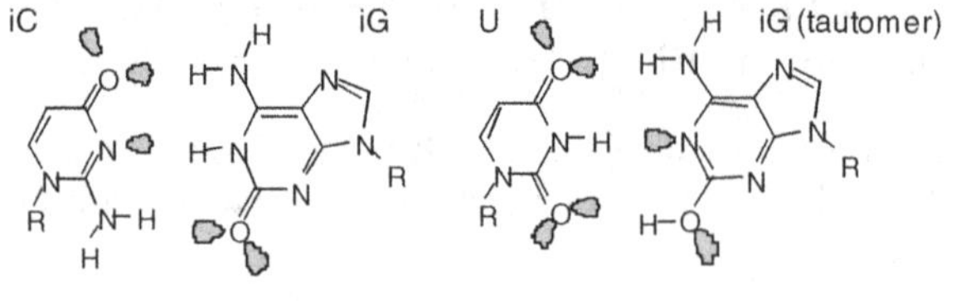

Figure 1: Tautomerism in iG gives it the capacity to bond with different pyrimidines, lowering fidelity.

availability of potential letters, and the suitability of candidate letters as information carriers. Orgel (1990) suggested that perhaps nature had simply failed to discover additional letters. However, this cannot be assumed, and it seems reasonable to explore any factors which might afford advantage, with regard to both the evolutionary emergence of the natural alphabet, and the engineering of alternative alphabets.

Information integrity is the most fundamental requirement of a molecular alphabet. As information in nucleotides is partly expressed in hydrogen D/A patterns, the phenomenon of tautomerism, whereby the position of hydrogen may be exchanged between different positions, is of critical importance. Tautomerism may affect information integrity in two ways; firstly, the simple existence of two or more thermally accessible forms destroys the integrity of information expressed in D/A patterns. Secondly, in the case of oxygen, whenever the enol form is favoured over the keto form, the expressed D/A pattern can be changed simply by the rotation of the hydroxyl group. The role of tautomerism in the iC:iG base pair was considered by Switzer group (Roberts, Bandaru, & Switzer 1997). Their results concurred with experimental observation of the existence of stable tautomeric forms for iG, one of which had a pattern analogous to aA (amino-adenine) and therefore complementary to U/T. Thus an instance of iG written, by polymerase or its equivalent, as the complement of iC, might in turn express a U, giving an iC → U transition (Fig. 1). The D/A pattern of iG may therefore be regarded as volatile, lowering the replication fidelity of any alphabet to which it belongs, so that the iC:iG base pair is likely to be excluded by selection pressure.

Curiously, other potential nucleotides have not figured significantly in the debate, and it is the purpose of this study to consider the broader family of nucleotides, beyond the natural four, which together with iC:iG, have been the most widely studied.

We preface our consideration of other nucleotides by a few observations which it is hoped will facilitate later

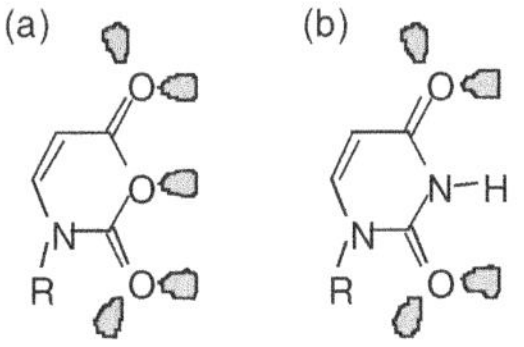

Figure 2: (a) The triple acceptor motif expressed on a 'pyrimidine', (b) a nitrogen in the central position must express a hydrogen.

discussion. With three H-bonding positions there are eight possible hydrogen D/A patterns, which in turn may be expressed as either 'purines' or 'pyrimidines', giving a total of 16 possible letters. Of these, four correspond to hypothetical nucleotides expressing patterns of three donors (hydrogens), and three acceptors (lone pairs). Simple chemical considerations show that the chemical expression of three acceptors requires an O in the central H-bonding position giving an acid anhydride, readily subject to hydrolysis (Fig. 2), since a N atom in the central position, as in U, must express a hydrogen. Because of its ease of hydrolysis nucleotides expressing the triple-acceptor or complementary triple donor motifs are not considered; for all other potential nucleotide letters however, the issue of prebiotic availability is set aside, the study focusing instead on the issue of tautomeric stability.

The reduced potential alphabet, now consisting of 12 letters, is usefully divided into two sets. Set I (Fig. 3a) consists of pyrimidines expressing two hydrogen acceptors and a single hydrogen donor, together with their complementary purines. This set consists of the natural alphabet, where A is represented by the 'ideal' form amino-adenine (aA), as well as iC and iG. Set II (Fig. 3b) consists of potential alphabet nucleotides in which the 'pyrimidines' now express two hydrogens, and their 'purine' complements. Set II is a digital mirror image of set I, the essential difference between the two sets being that the D/A patterns expressed on pyrimidines in set I are expressed on purines is set II, and vice versa. Labels for set II nucleotides are taken from Szathmáry (1991).

Viable alphabets may in principle arise within one or other of the sets, but are unlikely to contain pairs from both sets. Inspection will show that attempted purine-pyrimidine associations between non-complementary nucleotides within the same set may be opposed by mismatches in two positions, for example U:G or κ:δ. However, potential alphabets drawing on pairs from both sets I and II are opposed by mismatches in just a single position, facilitating replication errors. For example, an alphabet containing the pairs C:G and κ:X, admits the possibility of a mismatch between C and X, notwithstanding the opposed lone pairs (Fig. 4). Using PM3 calculations we estimate a binding energy of 4.9 kJ mol^{-1}.

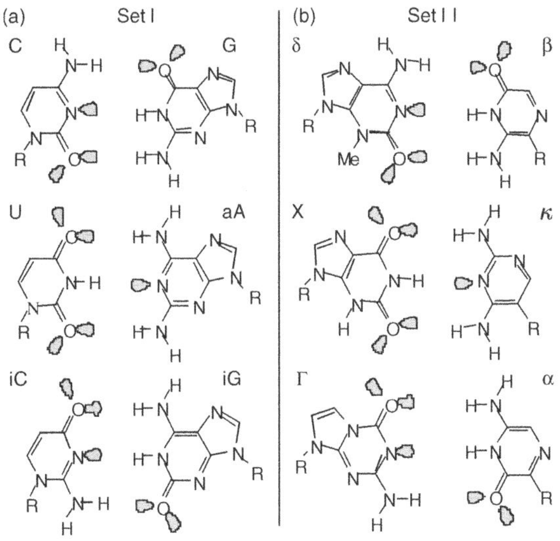

Figure 3: (a) Nucleotide set I, consisting of the natural alphabet and iC and iG. Purines express two hydrogens and a single lone pair, while pyrimidines express a single hydrogen; (b) Set II. Purines express a single hydrogen and two lone pairs. 'Pyrimidines' express two hydrogens.

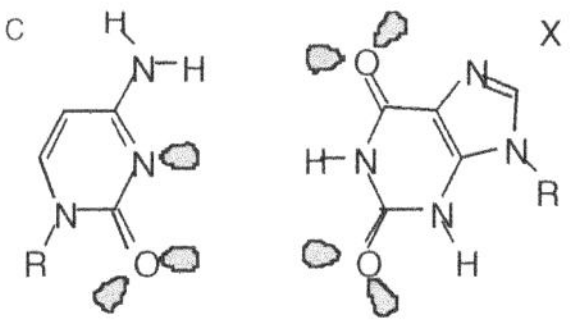

Figure 4: Possible mismatch in a hypothetical alphabet containing C:G from set I and κ:X from set II.

Net binding energies between non-complementary nucleotides is clearly quite untenable. Hypothetical alphabets drawing from both sets I and II would have little fidelity, and sets I and II may therefore be regarded as orthogonal. See Mac Dónaill (2002) for a discussion in terms of error-coding theory.

The alphabet of our own biological world is a subset of set I. Arguments based on tautomeric stability alone account for the deselection if iC and iG. Set II offers an alternative menu of potential nucleotides from which an alphabet might be constructed, and offers the possibility of an alternative replicating molecular alphabet. This paper examines the potential of set II nucleotides as viable information carriers, focusing on the integrity of the D/A patterns, as reflected in the relative stability of tautomeric forms.

Calculations

Many different hypothetical nucleotides could in principle express the D/A patterns required in set II. Those chosen for consideration in this preliminary study, and depicted in Fig. 3, are those already considered in the lit-

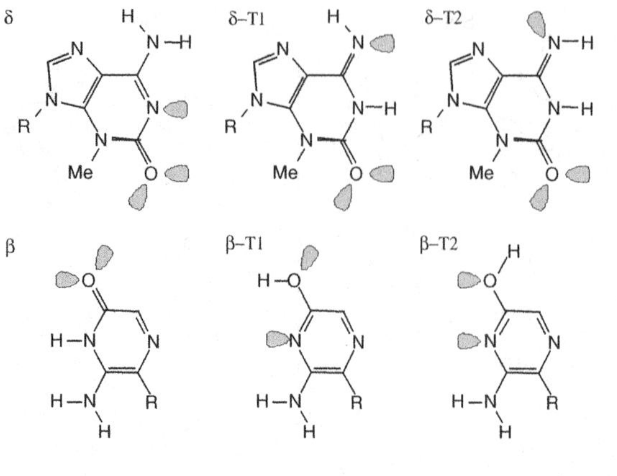

Figure 5: Tautomeric forms of Set II nucleotides δ and β.

Nucleotide	Heat of Formation	Relative Energy
δ	44.92	0.00
δ-T1	50.60	5.69
δ-T2	73.01	28.09
β	−22.31	0.00
β-T1	−42.84	−20.53
β-T2	−35.41	−13.10

Table 1: Heats of Formation and Relative Energies of the tautomeric forms of δ and β in kJ/mol.

erature (Picirilli *et al.* 1990; Szathmáry 1991). Quantum chemical calculations are performed at the PM3 level of approximation, one of the more reliable semi-empirical quantum computational methods. The backbone, represented in figures by R, is represented in calculations by H.

The δ:β Nucleotide Pair

We begin by considering the δ:β complementary pair (Fig. 5). The energies from PM3 calculations for nucleotides δ and β are given in table 1. The conventional form of δ is the most stable, tautomeric forms being less stable, although δ-T1 is thermally accessible. However, in the case of nucleotide β, hydroxyl forms exhibit greater stability than the conventional keto form.

The D/A pattern encoded by a hydroxyl group is not

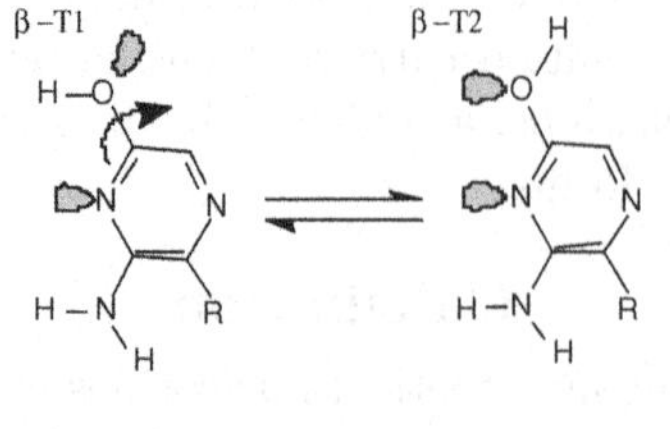

Figure 6: Rotation about the OH group changes the D/A pattern.

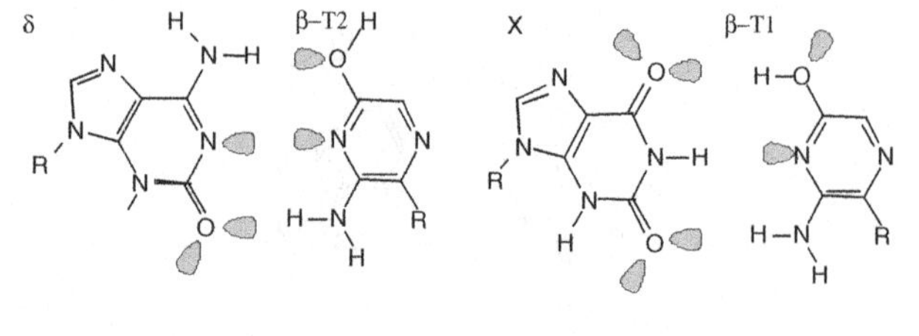

Figure 7: Tautomeric forms of β binding with both δ and X.

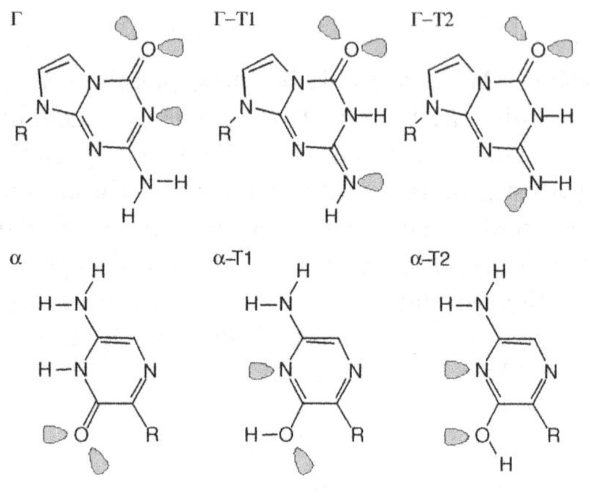

Figure 8: Tautomeric forms of Set II nucleotides Γ and α.

stable, and a simple, thermally accessible, rotation about the C–O bond of the hydroxyl group, exchanges tautomers β-T1 and β-T2 (Fig. 6). Tautomer β-T1 can bind with δ, with a binding energy of 33.4 kJ mol^{-1}, whereas tautomer β-T2 can bind to X with a binding energy of 4.0 kJ mol^{-1}, subject only to a relatively weak repulsion between two lone pairs (Fig. 7). The capacity of β in its hydroxyl manifestations to bind with two different purines renders β unsuitable as an information carrier. We conclude that δ:β cannot participate in a nucleotide alphabet

The Γ:α Nucleotide Pair

Tautomeric forms of Γ and α are depicted in Fig. 8. PM3 calculations on Γ indicate that the tautomeric forms of Γ are inaccessible, and that Γ is therefore a potentially viable letter. α however is essentially similar to β, differing only in its point of attachment to the backbone. Calculations, using both –H and –Me to represent the backbone confirm similarly stable tautomeric forms for α and β; α-T1 can bind to X, while α-T2 can bind to Γ (Fig. 9). Thus, as with δ:β, the nucleotide pair α:Γ may not participate in a molecular alphabet.

The κ:X Nucleotide Pair

Some simple tautomeric forms of nucleotides κ and X are depicted in Fig. 10. Calculations suggest that all tautomeric forms other than the conventional representation

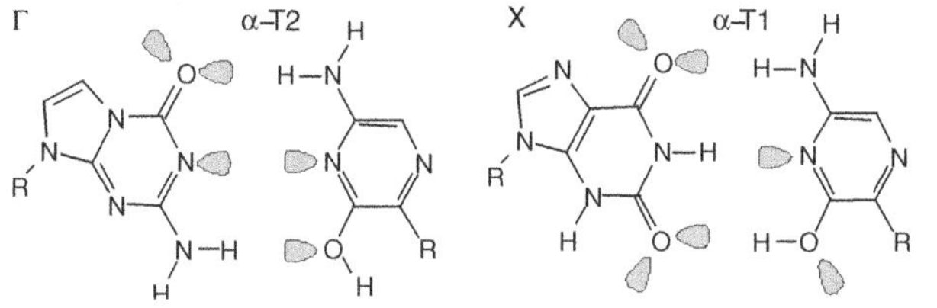

Figure 9: α-T2 can bind to Γ, while α-T1 can bind to X.

Nucleotide	Heat of Formation	Relative Stability
Γ	49.40	0.00
Γ-T1	98.33	48.93
Γ-T2	73.25	23.86
α	−22.31	0.00
α-T1	−42.84	−20.53
α-T2	−35.41	−13.10

Table 2: Heats of Formation and relative energies of nucleotides Γ and α in kJ mol^{-1}.

are thermally inaccessible. The D/A patterns encoded in κ and X are therefore stable, and κ:X are therefore a viable nucleotide pair.

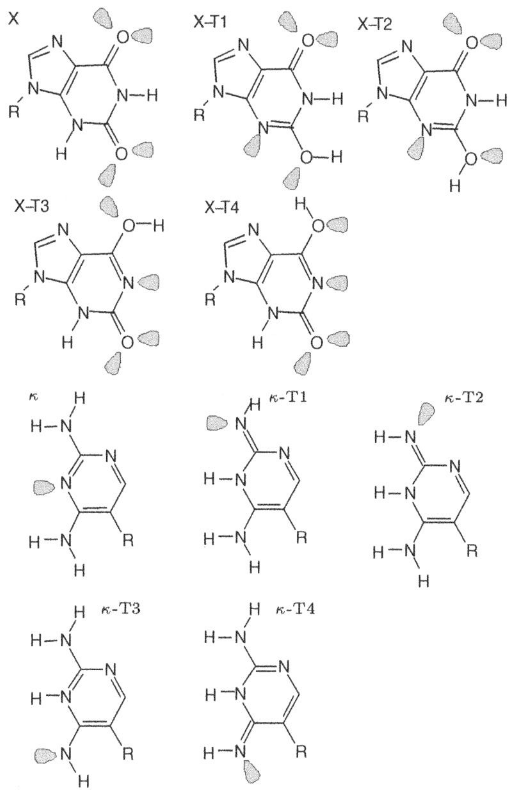

Figure 10: Some tautomeric forms of nucleotides κ and X.

Discussion

The stability of D/A patterns depends largely on the equilibrium between the keto and enol manifestations of oxygens. Carbonyl oxygens unambiguously express an acceptor, whereas hydroxyl groups ambiguously express an acceptor or donor, allowing binding with multiple pseudo-complements. Of the two sets of potential nucleotides, set I has four viable members, essentially the set we find in terrestrial biology today. Set II by contrast contains just two viable letters. In information terms set I alphabets have 2 bits/letter, whereas set II has just 1 bit/letter. The information necessary to express some biological functionality can be more succinctly expressed in set I, yielding superior fidelity, perhaps a partial explanation of why the natural alphabet derives from set I nucleotides.

If artificial alphabets are to be developed, by extension of set I or by exploitation of set II, problems associated with tautomerism must be overcome. This is quite a subtle problem; it is not self-evident for example, why κ is tautomerically stable whereas β is not. Moreover, the members of set II chosen for study are not definitive and it is quite possible that analogues with stable and desirable tautomeric properties might be forthcoming. Additionally, the difficult problem of the role of solvation must be considered. These and related problems are the focus of ongoing high level *ab initio* calculations.

References

Mac Dónaill, D. A. 2002. A parity code interpretation of nucleotide alphabet composition. *Chem. Comm.* in press.

Orgel, L. 1990. Adding to the genetic alphabet. *Nature* 343:18–20.

Picirilli, J. A.; Krauch, T.; Moroney, S. E.; and Benner, S. A. 1990. Enzymatic incorporation of a new base pair into DNA and RNA extends the genetic alphabet. *Nature* 343:33–37.

Roberts, C.; Bandaru, R.; and Switzer, C. 1997. Theoretical and experimental study of iso-C and iso-G: Base-pairing in an expanded genetic system. *J. Am. Chem. Soc.* 119:4640–4649.

Switzer, C. Y.; Moroney, S. E.; and Benner, S. E. 1989. Enzymatic incorporation of a new base pair into DNA and RNA. *J. Am. Chem. Soc.* 111:8322–8323.

Szathmáry, E. 1991. *Proc. Roy. Soc. London Ser. B* 245:91–99.

Szathmáry, E. 1992. What is the optimum size for the genetic alphabet? *Proc. Natl. Acad. Sci. USA* 89:2614–2618.

Nucleotide	Heat of Formation	Relative Stability
X	94.43	0.00
κ-T1	154.52	60.09
κ-T2	177.48	83.05
κ-T3	166.88	72.45
κ-T4	196.99	102.56
X	−187.25	0.00
X-T1	−146.04	41.21
X-T2	−169.22	18.03
X-T3	−145.48	41.77
X-T4	−142.06	45.19

Table 3: Heats of Formation for tautomers of X and κ in kJ mol^{-1}.

A POEtic Architecture for Bio-Inspired Hardware

Gianluca Tempesti*, **Daniel Roggen** , **Eduardo Sanchez** , **Yann Thoma**
Swiss Federal Institute of Technology at Lausanne (EPFL), Lausanne, Switzerland
*Corresponding author. Email: Gianluca.Tempesti@epfl.ch
Richard Canham , **Andy Tyrrell**
University of York, York, England
Juan-Manuel Moreno
Technical University of Catalunya (UPC), Barcelona, Spain

Abstract

The implementation of bio-inspired systems in hardware has traditionally been more a matter of artistry than of method. The reasons are multiple, but one of the main problems has always been the lack of a universal platform, of a standardized architecture, and of a proper methodology for the implementation of such systems.

The ideas presented in this article are the first results of a new research project, "Reconfigurable POEtic Tissue". The goal of the project is the development of a hardware platform capable of implementing systems inspired by all the three major axes (phylogenesis, ontogenesis, and epigenesis) of bio-inspiration in digital hardware.

A novel cellular architecture, capable of exploiting the main features of the future POEtic tissue and compatible with a relatively automatic design methodology, is then presented.

Introduction

The implementation of bio-inspired systems in silicon is quite difficult, due to the sheer number and complexity of interesting biological mechanisms. Most approaches exploit a very limited set of biologically-plausible mechanisms to solve a given problem, but often cannot be generalized due to the lack of a *methodology* in the design of bio-inspired machines and of *architectures* capable of implementing a wide range of bio-inspired mechanisms.

The aim of this work is to present some of the preliminary ideas developed in the framework of a new three-year research project, called "Reconfigurable POEtic Tissue" (or "POEtic" for short)[1], recently started under the aegis of the Information Society Technologies (IST) program of the European Community, involving the Swiss Federal Institute of Technology in Lausanne, Switzerland, the University of York, England, the Technical University of Catalunya (UPC), Spain, the University of Glasgow, Scotland, and the University of Lausanne, Switzerland.

The goal of the project is to address, at least partially, the above issues through the development of digital hardware, and more precisely of a *computational substrate*, specifically designed for the implementation of multiple bio-inspired approaches on a single platform.

[1]http://www.poetictissue.org

The POE Model

Biological inspiration in the design of computing machines finds its source in essentially three biological models (Sanchez *et al.* 1997): *phylogenesis* (P), the history of the evolution of the species, *ontogenesis* (O), the development of an individual as directed by his genetic code, and *epigenesis* (E), the development of an individual through learning processes influenced by the environment.

On the *phylogenetic axis* we find systems inspired by the processes involved in the evolution of a species through time. The process of evolution is based on alterations to the genetic information, occurring through two basic mechanisms: *crossover* and *mutation*. Both these mechanisms are, by nature, non-deterministic, which represents both their strength and their weakness.

Evolutionary algorithms are usually applied to problems which are either too ill-defined or intractable by deterministic approaches. Not guaranteed to find the best solution to a problem, they can often find an "acceptable" solution more efficiently than deterministic approaches, and have proven their use in hardware design (Floreano & Urzelai , for instance).

The *ontogenetic axis* concerns the development of a single multi-cellular organism. This process exploits very specific mechanisms to direct the *growth* of the organism. Cells divide, each offspring containing a copy of the genome (*cellular division*) and acquiring a functionality (e.g., liver cell) depending on its position (*cellular differentiation*). Every cell contains the blueprint for the entire organism (the genome), and thus can potentially replace any other cell (Pearson 2001), providing the possibility of *healing* (self-repair).

The Embryonics project (Mange *et al.* 2000; Ortega & Tyrrell 1998, also this volume, p101) is one of the few research efforts in this area. A part of ontogenesis, *morphogenesis*, has been the subject of research (Lindenmayer 1968), and the concept of *development* is also attracting growing attention (Kitano 1998).

The *epigenetic axis* concerns those processes and structures of an organism, such as the nervous or the immune systems, that are directly affected by the environment. The size of the genome does not allow it to completely describe the structure of an adult organism, and the only possible source of additional information for the development of an organism is the environment.

Epigenetic mechanisms have already had considerable impact on hardware design in the form of *artificial neural networks* (ANNs), two-dimensional arrays of massively-interconnected processing elements (the neural cells). ANNs cannot be expected to perform correctly for all input patterns, but have proved their worth in applications such as voice or character recognition, where a limited margin of error is acceptable.

The POEtic Project

The aim of the POEtic project is the development of a computational substrate optimized for the implementation of digital systems inspired by all of the three above-mentioned models. The POEtic tissue is a self-contained, flexible, and physical substrate designed to interact with the environment through spatially-distributed sensors and actuators, to develop and adapt its functionality through a process of evolution, growth, and learning to a dynamic and partially unpredictable environment, and to self-repair parts damaged by ageing or environmental factors in order to remain viable and perform the same functionality.

Following the three models of bio-inspiration, the POEtic tissue will be designed as a three-layer structure (Figure 1):

- The phylogenetic model acts on the genetic material of a cell. Typically, it could be used to find and select the genes of the cells for the *genotype layer*.
- Ontogenesis concerns the development of the individual, and thus the *mapping or configuration layer* of the cell, implementing cellular differentiation and growth. In addition, it has an impact on the system for self-repair.
- The epigenetic model modifies the behavior of the organism during its operation, and is therefore best applied to the *phenotype layer*.

Defining separate layers for each model allows the user to decide whether to implement any or all models for a given problem, and lets the structure of each layer be adapted to the model. This is achieved by implementing the cells on a *molecular substrate*, a surface of programmable logic. In fact, each of the corresponding algorithms is well suited for a particular class of problems. For example, artificial evolution is known to be competitive for non-linear and discontinuous problem domains; learning processes can adapt on a much faster time scale, while ontogenetic processes offer the possibility of fault-tolerance under changing and critical circumstances.

Finally, our tissue presents two innovative hardware-oriented aspects: a *cellular structure* with a full genome for every cell, and a *layered hardware* organization that matches the three axes of bio-inspiration.

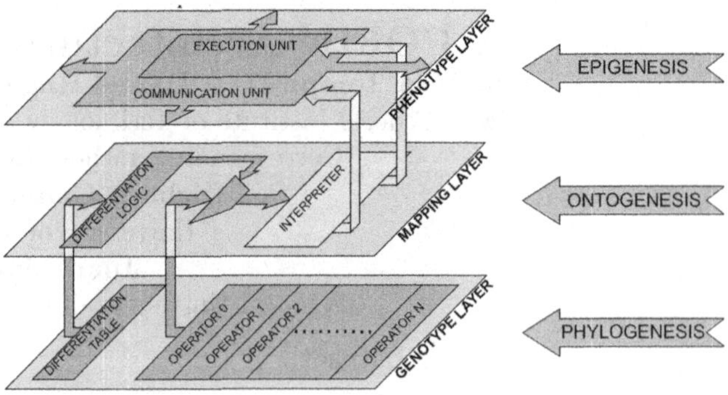

Figure 1: The three organizational layers of the POEtic project.

Cellular structure

Each cell in the POEtic tissue contains the entire "genome" for the whole tissue. This solution increases the robustness of the system by making it completely local and allowing individual cells to reconfigure their function for growth, self-replication, and self-repair (ontogenesis).

The ontogenetic concept of growth has been largely ignored in the past, for obvious reasons: growth implies the "creation" of new material during the lifetime of an organism, a feature that remains impossible to this day in the world of electronics. However, while the silicon substrate of an electronic circuit cannot grow, a reconfigurable circuit like our POEtic tissue allows its function to be modified at runtime, and thus a growth process based on information rather than matter.

The process of growth is based on cellular division and on cellular differentiation. From the standpoint of both biological organisms and electronic circuits, these two processes are made possible by the existence of the complete plan of the organism (the genome) in each cell. Each cell can specialize to perform a unique function by "executing" only a part of the genetic program depending on its position This differentiation allows multicellular organisms, and the POEtic tissue, to display behaviors of a greater complexity than those of single-cell organisms.

Finally, biological multi-cellular organisms can tolerate significant damage. Their "fault-tolerance" is based on a set of complex systems, from the organism-wide immune system to single-cell error correction. The POEtic tissue will include a hierarchy of fault-tolerance mechanisms, acting automatically with little or no user intervention.

Layered organization

As mentioned, the POEtic tissue is organized in three hardware layers that match the three main axes of biological organization (Figure 1). The hardware structure of each layer is specific to its role (e.g., the genotype layer will be mainly storage). The explicit distinction in three layers will allow the study and implementation of complex genotype-to-phenotype mappings that can exploit the growth and reconfiguration properties of the tissue.

The mapping between genotypes and phenotypes in evolutionary systems is usually a one-to-one function that does not capture the complex, but highly regulated, mechanisms of gene expression that characterize the development of biological organisms, barely supports the creation of genetic building blocks that could be exploited by crossover operators, and is not scalable to large structures, as the length of the genotype is proportional to the complexity of the phenotype. Our tissue, will provide a substrate that naturally supports the implementation in the configuration layer of smarter and more biologically inspired mechanisms of gene expression.

Finally, the three distinct hardware layers allows the implementation of different bio-inspired mechanisms of self-organization, allowing, for example, to implement neuronal structures without growth or evolution, or conventional fault-tolerant systems deprived of adaptation.

A Bio-Inspired Architecture

Nature is *change*. Adaptation and specialization are key features of all biological organisms. As a consequence, no bio-inspired architecture can be rigid, but must rather be able to adapt and specialize depending on the desired application. This requirement can be satisfied by exploiting *reconfigurable logic* (e.g., FPGAs) POEtic architectures will then consist of two-dimensional arrays of *cells*, where each cell is a small, fully reconfigurable processing element, specialized for the application and for the bio-inspired mechanisms to be implemented.

The role of the tissue, then, is to provide a *molecular substrate* for the implementation of the cells: as organic cells are constituted by molecules, so our artificial cells will be constituted by the programmable logic elements of our POEtic circuit. All three layers of the POEtic systems will all be implemented on this substrate.

The *genotype layer* is conceptually the simplest of the three layers of the tissue. It contains the genetic information of the organism (Figure 2):

- A *set of operators*, which define the set of all possible functions for the cell. The operators depend on the application (e.g., initial neuron parameters and weights).
- A *differentiation table*, used to determine which operators will be implemented in which cell. The table contains a compact, possibly redundant, representation of the operators to be implemented by the cells, to which evolutionary mechanisms will be applied.

The key feature of the genotype layer lies in the presence of a set of *dedicated connections*, used to provide access to the differentiation tables of all the cells in the system via an *external microcontroller*, whose function is to apply user-defined evolutionary mechanisms to the tables' contents.

The *configuration layer* of the POEtic systems is designed to implement the processes of cellular differentiation and cellular division (growth), the bases of the ontogenetic model (the fault-tolerance aspect of the model is in general distributed throughout the layers of the array)

In its simplest conception (Figure 3), the configuration layer selects which operator will be implemented depending on a set of coordinates, incremented in each cell and transmitted along both axes. However, this approach is only a very basic solution to achieve cellular differentiation, and does not exploit many of the most interesting features of the development process. More complex differentiation mechanisms, based for example on L-systems (Lindenmayer 1968). and on protein gradients, are under study.

The *phenotype layer* is probably the most application-dependent layer. If the final application is a neural network, the phenotype layer of the cell will consist of an artificial neuron. In particular, the POEtic project will concentrate on *spiking neurons*[2], but this choice does not imply that the tissue will be limited to such a model.

To be universal, however, the POEtic tissue will not be limited to neural-like cells, and a more general-purpose phenotype architecture is being researched. For example, a candidate architecture is outlined in Figure 4. It consists of:

- An execution unit, consisting of a set of application-dependent *resources* (e.g., adders, counters), defined by the user and accessed through a set of I/O ports.
- A communication unit that, in view of the massive connectivity of bio-inspired systems, will probably have to rely on *serial communication*.

This kind of architecture has two main advantages, in the context of the POEtic project: it can support specialization through the adaptation of the resources to the application and it can be integrated in a design environment.

A typical application-driven design flow for a bio-inspired system in such an environment could then be:

- Based on the application, the user defines the models to be implemented in the system. The user then accesses a *library of operators* and selects those that will be required by the application(e.g., a family of neurons).
- The environment will then (if desired) automatically integrate the desired operators into a *totipotent cell*, that is, a processing element capable of realizing any

[2]http://www.poetictissue.org

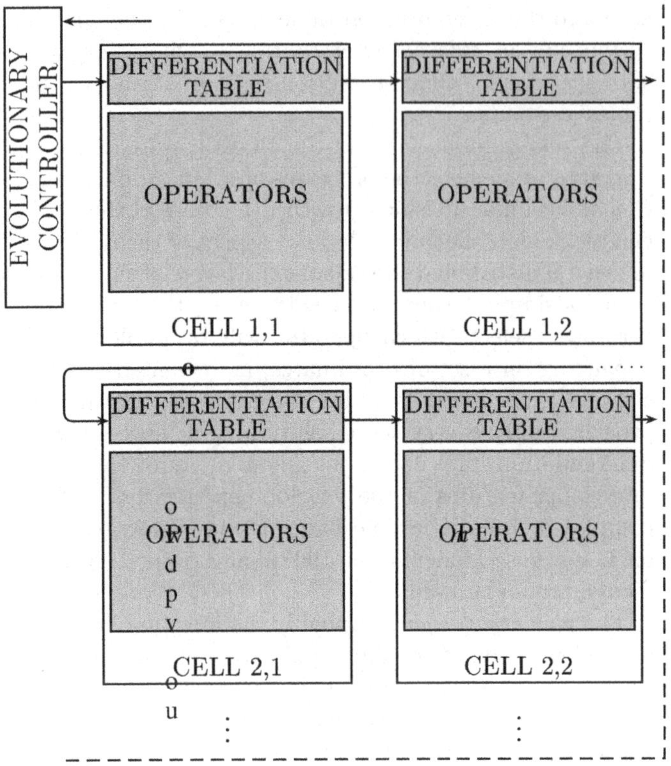

Figure 2: The genotype layer in an array of cells and the evolutionary controller

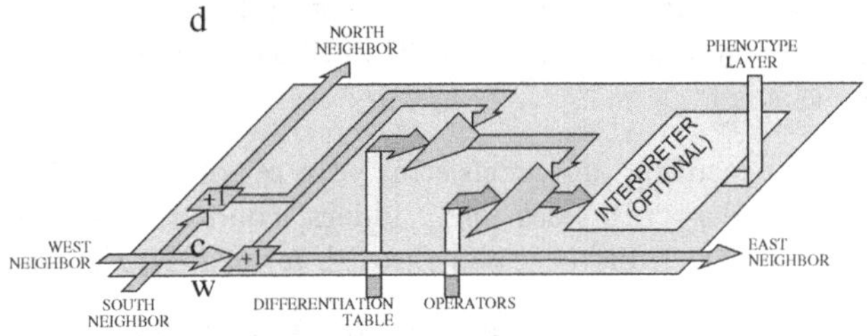

Figure 3: A possible structure for the configuration or mapping layer

of the functions. Other optional ontogenetic features, such as growth and self-repair, can be automatically added.

- Finally, the design environment assembles the cells into a two-dimensional array, integrates the I/O modules, and generates a configuration for the programmable logic.

The key feature of such an environment is the *automatization* of a large part of the design flow. The user need only decide which bio-inspired models and operators are required by the application.

Conclusions

The POEtic project proposes an hardware substrate capable of implementing bio-inspired systems. In other

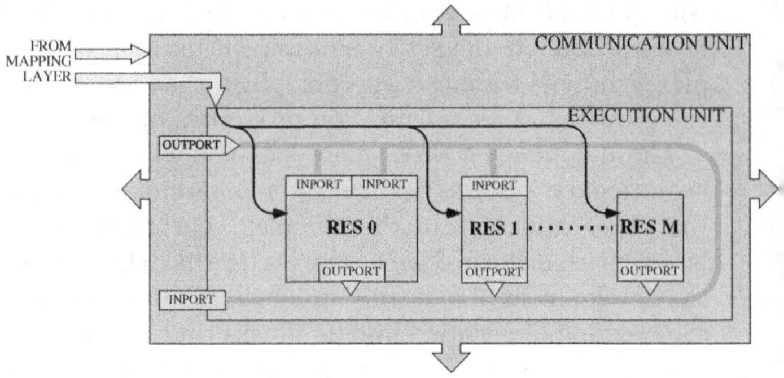

Figure 4: Outline of a possible architecture for the phenotype layer

words, it wants to develop the *molecules* necessary for the development of cellular systems. The usefulness and the practicality of the molecular surface will obviously be validated on a number of bio-inspired applications, ranging from neural networks to music synthesis. And beyond, it is our hope that the circuits created in this project will find users well beyond our group.

This article by no means presents the final version of the POEtic system: the project has started only recently, and the ideas presented here are simply the *first* results of our research. We invite all readers to access our website http://www.poetictissue.org, where we regularly post the progress reports and deliverables of the project.

Acknowledgements

First of all, the authors would like to acknowledge the contribution of all the other members of the POEtic project, who all contributed to the material presented herein.

This project is funded by the Future and Emerging Technologies programme (IST-FET) fo the European Community, under grant IST-2000-28027 (POETIC). The information provided is the sole responsibility of the authors and does not reflect the Community's opinion. The Community is not responsible for any use that might be made of data appearing in this publication. The Swiss participants to this project are supported under grant 00.0529-1 by the Swiss government.

References

Floreano, D., and Urzelai, J. Evolutionary robots with on-line self-organization and behavioral fitness. *Neural Networks* 13:431–443.

Kitano, H. 1998. Building complex systems using developmental process: An engineering approach. In Sipper and Mange (1998).

Lindenmayer, A. 1968. Mathematical models for cellular interaction in development, parts i and ii. *Journal of Theoretical Biology* 18:280–315.

Mange, D.; Sipper, M.; Stauffer, A.; and Tempesti, G. 2000. Towards robust integrated circuits: The Embryonics approach. *Proceedings of the IEEE* 88(4):516–541.

Ortega, C., and Tyrrell, A. 1998. MUXTREE revisited: Embryonics as a reconfiguration strategy in fault-tolerant processor arrays. In Sipper and Mange (1998).

Pearson, H. 2001. The regeneration gap. *Nature* 414:388–390.

Sanchez, E.; Mange, D.; Sipper, M.; Tomassini, M.; Perez-Uribe, A.; and Stauffer., A. 1997. Phylogeny, ontogeny, and epigenesis: Three sources of biological inspiration for softening hardware. In *Proc. 1st Int. Conf. on Evolvable Systems (ICES'96)*, volume 1259 of *LNCS*. Berlin: Springer-Verlag.

Sipper, M., and Mange, D. an Perez-Uribe, A., eds. 1998. *Proc. 2nd Int. Conf. on Evolvable Systems (ICES'98)*, volume 1478 of *LNCS*. Berlin: Springer-Verlag.

Digital Hormone Models for Self-Organization

Wei-Min Shen, **Cheng-Ming Chuong**, and **Peter Will**
University of Southern California, 4676 Admiralty Way, Marina del Rey, CA 90292, USA
shen@isi.edu, chuong@pathfinder.usc.edu, will@isi.edu

Abstract

How do multiple elements/agents self-organize into global patterns based on local communications and interactions? This paper describes a theoretical and simulation model called "Digital Hormone Model" (DHM) for such a self-organization task. The model is inspired by two facts: complex biological patterns are results of self-organization of homogenous cells regulated by hormone-like chemical signals (Jiang *et al.* 1999), and distributed controls can enable self-reconfigurable agents to performance locomotion and reconfiguration (Shen, Salemi, & Will 2000; Shen, Lu, & Will 2000; Salemi, Shen, & Will 2001). The DHM is an integration and generalization of reaction-diffusion model (Turing 1952) and stochastic cellular automata (Lee *et al.* 1991). The movements of agents (or cells) in DHM are computed not by the Turing's differential equations, nor the Metropolis rule (Kirkpatrick & Sorkin 1995), but by stochastic rules that are based on the concentration of hormones in the neighboring space. Experimental results have shown that this model can produce results that match and predict the actual findings in the biological experiments of feather bud formation among uniform skin cells (Jiang *et al.* 1999). Furthermore, an extension of this model may be directly applicable to self-organization in multi-agent systems using simulated hormone-like signals.

Introduction

This paper is to develop a general computational model for self-organization in multi-agent systems. In particular, we describe the Digital Hormone Model (DHM) that is generalized from an existing distributed control system for self-reconfigurable agents (Shen, Salemi, & Will 2000; Shen, Lu, & Will 2000; Salemi, Shen, & Will 2001). The model is inspired by the fact that many complex patterns in biological systems appear to be the results of self-organization among homogenous cells regulated by hormones, and self-organization is based on local interactions among cells rather than super-imposed and pre-determined global structures (Jiang *et al.* 1999; Chuong *et al.* 2000). The paper describes the model in detail, reports the experimental results in simulating feather buds formation among homogeneous skin cells, and finds a number of correlations between individual hormone diffusion profiles and the features of final patterns. These results match the findings in the actual biological experiments and predict cases that have yet been observed in biological experiments but consist with the expected behaviors of hormone-regulated self-organization.

Computational Models for Self-Organization

Throughout the history of science, there have been many computational models for self-organization. Perhaps one of the earliest is Turing's reaction-diffusion model (Turing 1952), in which he analyzed the interplay between the diffusions of reacting species and concluded that their nonlinear interactions could lead to the formation of spatial patterns in their concentrations. Turing's model uses a set of differential equations to model the periodic pattern formation in a ring of discrete cells or continuous tissues that interact with each other through a set of chemicals he called "morphogens". Assuming that there are $r = (1, \ldots N)$ cells in the ring, and two morphogens X and Y among these cells, and letting the concentration of X and Y in cell r be X_r and Y_r, the cell-to-cell diffusion rate of X and Y be u and v, and the increasing rate of X and Y caused by chemical reactions be $f(X, Y)$ and $g(X, Y)$, respectively, Turing modeled the dynamics of this ring as the following set of $2N$ differential equations:

$$\begin{aligned} dX_r/dt &= f(X_r, Y_r) + u(X_{r+1} - 2X_r + X_{r-1}), \\ dY_r/dt &= g(X_r, Y_r) + v(Y_{r+1} - 2Y_r + Y_{r-1}). \end{aligned}$$

By analyzing the solutions of these equations, Turing illustrated that a given ring of cells, which initially has the uniform concentration of Y and X, can self-organize through random fluctuations, chemical reactions, and diffusion, into a ring of periodic patterns in the concentration of Y. Two important conditions for Turing stability are: (1) between X and Y, one must be the inhibitor and the other activator, and (2) the inhibitor must have a greater diffusion rate than the actuator.

Turing's reaction-diffusion model was startlingly novel, and it has been supported both mathematically (Murray 1989) and experimentally (Ouyang & Swinney 1991), and many applications are described in (Meinhardt 1982). Interestingly, Witkin and Kass (1991) extended the traditional reaction-diffusion systems by allowing anisotropic and spatially non-uniform diffusion, as well as multiple competing directions of diffusion. They use these models to synthesize textures with different patterns.

Cellular Automata (CA) (Gutowitz 1991; Toffoli 2000), especially those that have stochastic characteristics (Lee *et al.* 1991), are another important modeling technique for self-organization. Perhaps the most famous illustration of self-organization using CA is the Game of Life, where randomly distributed cells on a space of grids will live or die based on a set of very simple and deterministic rules. Life is a deterministic CA, but when rules of a CA have stochastic characteristics, then they could also be capable of modeling random fluctuations in the environment, and that may be a critical element in simulating interactions among many autonomous elements that perceive and react to local information in the environment. In fact, the Digital Hormone Model to be proposed here is essentially an integration of stochastic CA, reaction-diffusion models, and network-like diffusion space with dynamic topology.

The Digital Hormone Model

The Digital Hormone Model (DHM) is designed for simulating, understanding, and controlling self-organization in large-scale multi-agent systems. In this model, agents are simulated as cells that secrete hormones, and hormones diffuse and influence the behaviors of other cells. The Digital Hormone Model consists of a space (we use grids in this paper) and a set of moving cells. The term "cell" here can stand for any type of autonomous and intelligent elements, such as agents, agents, unmanned vehicles, mobile sensors, network nodes, or weapons. Among the grids, cells can live, evolve, migrate, or die as time passes. Each living cell occupies one grid at a time and a cell can secrete chemical hormones (or communication signals in general), which diffuse into its neighboring grids to influence other cells' behaviors. Hormones may have different types and diffusion functions. Two types of hormones are most common: an *activator* hormone that will encourage certain cell actions, while an *inhibitor* hormone will prohibit certain cell actions. We assume that hormones may react to each other (summation, subtraction, or modification), and may diffuse to the neighboring grids according to certain functions. Similar to the extensions used in Witkin and Kass (1991), we allow anisotropic and spatially non-uniform diffusion. Cells are autonomous and intelligent agents that can react to hormones and perform actions such as *migration, secretion, differentiation, proliferation, death,* or *adhesion.*

At any given time, a cell selects and executes one or more actions according to a set of internal behavior rules. These rules can be deterministic or probabilistic. We assume that the rules are given and will not cause a cell to select conflicting actions. Given the grids, cells, hormones, actions, and rules, the DHM works as follows:

1. All cells select actions by their behavior rules;

2. All cells execute their selected actions;

3. All grids update the concentration of hormones;

4. Go to Step 1.

To illustrate the above definitions, let us consider a simple DHM_0 in Figure 1, where cells (shown as black dots in the grids) migrate on a space of N^2 grids. The

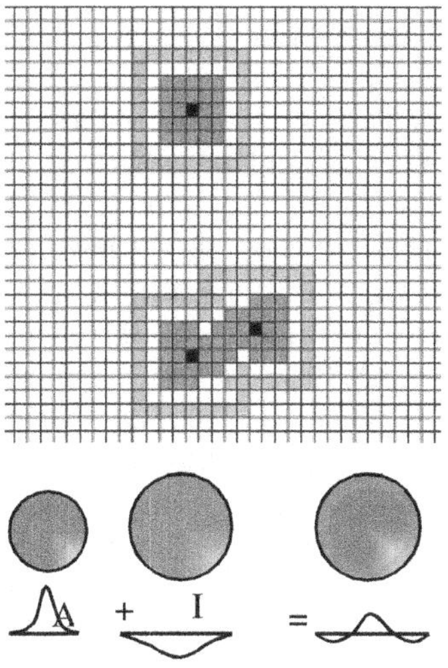

Figure 1: The simple DHM_0

space is a torus in the sense that the leftmost and rightmost columns are neighbors, and the topmost and bottommost rows are neighbors. Cells in DHM_0 have only two actions: secretion and migration, and the former is a constant action that always produces two hormones: the activator A and the inhibitor I. The diffusion rates for A and I secreted from a cell at the grid (a, b) to its surrounding grids are characterized by Guassian distributions:

$$f_A(x,y) = (2\pi\sigma^2)^{-1} exp\{[(x-a)^2 + (y-b)^2]/2\sigma^2\}$$
$$f_I(x,y) = -(2\pi\rho^2)^{-1} exp\{[(x-a)^2 + (y-b)^2]/2\rho^2\},$$

where $\sigma < \rho$ in order to satisfy Turing's stability condition. Notice that the activator A has the positive value and the inhibitor I has the negative value. Because $\sigma < \rho$, A has a sharper and narrower distribution then I. We assume that the two hormones react to each other so that the concentration of hormones in any given grid can be computed by summing up all present "A"s and "I"s in the grid. In Figure 1, we have illustrated in the grids the combined hormones around a single cell and around two nearby cells. Since the grids are discrete, the rings around the cells are shown as squares instead of circles.

In this simple model DHM_0, two simple rules govern the cell's actions. One rule states that "secrete A and I for every step", and this means that each cell secretes these hormones at every step. The second rule states that "migrate to an immediate neighbor grid based on the hormone distribution in these neighbors". More specifically, the probability for a cell to migrate to a particular neighboring grid (including the grid it is currently occupying) is proportional to the concentration of A and inversely proportional to the concentration of I in that grid. This rule is fundamentally stochastic, so that the selection of migrating grid is non-deterministic. To implement this rule, let the hormone value in the occupying grid be h_0 and let the values in the eight immediate neighbors be h_1, h_2, h_3, h_4, h_5, h_6, h_7, and h_8, respectively. Based on their signs, these values are grouped into three groups: $G1$, $G2$, and $G3$, where the members in $G1$ all have positive values (say sum to P_{G1}), those in $G2$ have zero values, and those in $G3$ have negative values. To decide which group to migrate to, a random number x is generated in the range of $(0, 100P_{G1}+10|G2|+|G3|]$. If $0 < x <= 100P_{G1}$, then the cell will migrate to $G1$. If $100P_{G1} < x <= 100P_{G1} + 10|G2|$, then the cell will migrate to $G2$. Otherwise, the cell will migrate to $G3$. The decision ensures that a cell will migrate to $G1$ with the highest probability, to $G2$ with lower probability, and to $G3$ with the lowest probability. After a group is selected, we then select a grid from the group with a similar procedure. For example, to select a grid from $G1$, a random number will be generated in the range of $(0, h_{i1} + h_{i2} + h_{i3} + \ldots + h_{i|G1|}]$, where h_{ij} are individual values in $G1$ ($h_{ij} > 0$), and a grid will be selected depending on where the number falls in the range. This ensures that grids with higher concentrations of the activator hormone will be selected with higher probabilities. To select a grid from $G2$, we order the grids in the group $g_1, g_2, \ldots, g_{|G2|}$ (note that all these grids have zero hormone values), and a random number y is generated in the range of $(0, |G2|]$, and the grid of g_y is selected. To select a grid from $G3$, a random number will be generated in the range of $(0, (-h_{j1})^{-1} + (-h_{j2})^{-1} + (-h_{j3})^{-1} + \ldots + (-h_{j|G3|})^{-1}]$, where h_{ij} are individual values in $G3$ ($h_{ij} < 0$), and a grid will be selected depending on where the number falls in this range. This ensures that grids with lower concentrations of the inhibitor hormone will be selected with higher probabilities.

Notice that the above rule for selecting migration direction is different from the Metropolis rules used in simulated annealing (Kirkpatrick & Sorkin 1995), which first randomly selects a neighbor without considering the concentration of hormones, and then makes a go or no-go decision based on the energy difference and the current temperature. In the Digital Hormone Model, the notion of temperature is embedded in the decision rules described above. Interestingly, our experiments show that the Metropolis rule does not allow cells to converge into patterns in this model no matter what temperature is set.

Since all movements are local and synchronized, there may be a chance where multiple cells "collide" in the same grid. The collision of cells is solved in a simple manner. All cells first "virtually" move to the grids they selected. If there are multiple cells in the same grid, then the extra cells will be randomly distributed to those immediate neighboring grids that are empty. This is an environmental function, not a cellular action. But this action will ensure that no grid is hosting more than one cell at any time.

The Experimental Results of the DHM

Using the digital hormone models, we hope to learn valuable detailed computational knowledge about how hormones and receptors affect the result of self-organization in a large system with many autonomous elements. In particular, the initial research issues we would like to investigate are as follows: Will the proposed Digital Hormone Model enable cells to self-organize into patterns at all? Will the size of final patterns be invariant to the cell population density? Will the hormone diffusion profiles affect the size and shape of the final patterns? Will an arbitrary hormone diffusion profile enable self-organization and pattern formation?

To find solutions for these questions, we ran two sets of experiments using the simplified digital hormone model DHM_0 described above. In the first set of experiments, we set the hormone diffusion profile to approximate the standard distributions. For any single isolated cell, let the cell's n^{th} ring of neighbors be the neighboring cells at a distance of n cells away from the cell. Using this definition, we define the concentration level of the activator hormone at the cell's surrounding grids as follows: 0.16 for the 0th ring (i.e., the occupying grid), 0.08 the 1st ring, 0.04 the 2nd ring, 0.02 the 3rd ring, and 0 the 4th and beyond. For the inhibitor hormone, the concentration levels for the 0th through the 4th rings of neighbors are: −0.05, −0.04, −0.03, −0.02, and −0.01, respectively, and 0.0 for the 5th ring and beyond. Thus the combined concentration levels of hormones at the 0th through 4th rings are: 0.11, 0.04, 0.01, 0, and −0.01, respectively, and 0.0 for the 5th ring and beyond. We assume that the concentrations of hormones secreted by a cell at grids beyond the 4th ring are so insignificant that they can be practically ignored.

Given this fixed hormone diffusion profile, we have run a set of simulations on a space of 100×100 grids with different cell population densities ranging from 10% through 50%. Starting with cells randomly distributed on the grids, each simulation runs up to 1,000 action steps, and records the configuration snapshots at steps of 0, 50, 500, and 1,000. As we can see from the results in the upper part of Figure 2, cells in all simulations indeed form clusters with approximately the same size. These results demonstrate that the digital hormone model indeed enables cells to form patterns. Furthermore, the results match the observations made in the biological experiments. The size of the final clusters does not change with cell population density, but the number of clusters does. Lower cell densities result in fewer final clusters, while higher densities form more clusters.

In the second set of experiments, we started with the same cell population density, but varied the hormone diffusion profiles. We wanted to observe the effects of different hormone profiles on the results of pattern formation. As we can see from the results shown in the lower part of Figure 2, when a balanced profile of activator and inhibitor is given (see the second row), the cells will form final patterns as in the first set of experiments. As the ratio of activator over inhibitor increases (see the third row), the size of final clusters also increases. These results are an exact match with the findings in the reported biological experiments (Jiang *et al.* 1999).

When the ratio of A/I becomes so high that there are only activators and no inhibitors (see the fourth row), then the cells will form larger and larger clusters, and eventually become a single connected cluster. On the other hand, when the ratio is so low that there is only inhibitor and no activator, then the cells will never form any patterns (see the first row), regardless of how long the simulation runs. This shows that not all hormone profiles enable self-organization. These results are yet to be seen in biological experiments, but they are consistent with the principles of hormone-regulated self-organization and thus qualified as meaningful predictions of cell self-organization by hormones.

The results presented in Figure 2 not only demonstrate that the proposed digital hormone model is indeed an effective tool for simulating and analyzing self-organization phenomena, but that it is also capable of producing results that match the actual findings in the biological experiments and can predict the possible outcomes for new biological experiments. The results show that hormones play a critical role in self-organization, and they enable many autonomous elements to form globally interesting patterns based on only their local information and interactions. This provides a departure point for new hypotheses, theories, and experiments for self-organization. Since the model is mathematically adjustable, it is much more economic and efficient for scientists, including biologists, to design new experiments and to hypothesize new theories.

In addition to changing the ratio of activator and inhibitor hormones, we also have also varied the shape of hormone diffusion profiles and observe their effects on the features of the final patterns. For example, we have observed that if the profile is a narrow and long sandwich with the same orientation (the activator is in the middle and the inhibitors are on the outside), then cells will form striped patterns. This shows that given the proper hormone diffusion profiles, the DHM will allow cells to form patterns with different shapes.

Furthermore, we have also experimented with different mechanisms for decision making when selecting the migration direction, including the random procedure and the Metropolis rule. Experimental results have shown that Metropolis rule does not enable cells to aggregate into groups no matter what temperature setting is used. This is a bit unexpected, but one possible reason is that Metropolis rule first randomly selects a neighbor without considering the concentration of hormones, and then makes a go or no-go decision based on probability. This does not reflect the true distribution of hormone concentration in the neighboring grids. Similarly, and as expected, the random procedure for selecting migrating directions does not produce any interesting results either.

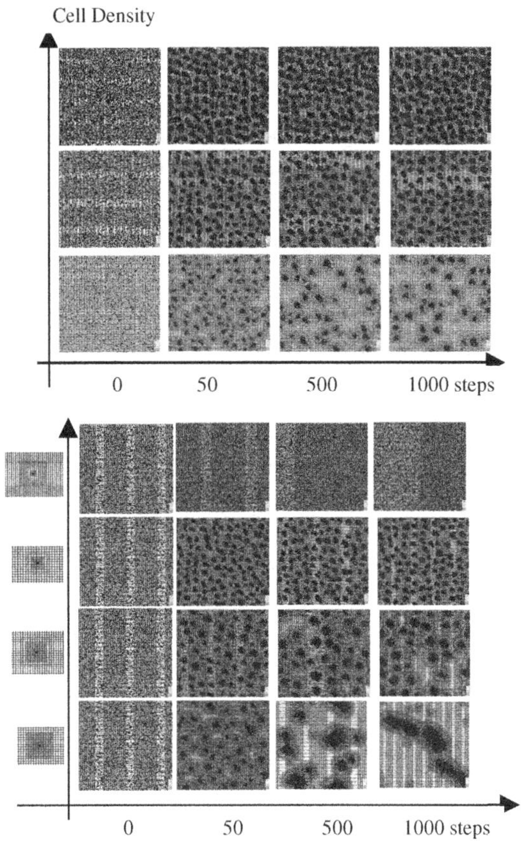

Figure 2: Two sets of experimental results on DMH_0

Acknowledgments

We are grateful that this reserach is in part supported by the AFOSR contract F49620-01-1-0020 and the DARPA contract DAAN02-98-C-4032. The second author is supported by NSF IBN 9808874 and NIH AR 42177.

References

Chuong, C.-M.; Chodankar, R.; Widelitz, R.; and Jiang, T. X. 2000. Evo-devo of feathers and scales: Building complex epithelial appendages. *Current Opinion in Development and Genetics* 10:449–456.

Gutowitz, H., ed. 1991. *Cellular Automata — Theory and Experiment.* Cambridge, MA: MIT Press.

Jiang, T.-X.; Jung, H. S.; Widelitz, R. B.; and Chuong, C.-M. 1999. Self organization of periodic patterns by dissociated feather mesenchymal cells and the regulation of size, number and spacing of primordia. *Development* 126:4997–5009.

Kirkpatrick, S., and Sorkin, G. 1995. Simulated annealing. In Arbib, M., ed., *The Handbook of Brain and Neural Networks.* Cambridge, MA: MIT Press.

Lee, Y.; Qian, S.; Jones, R.; Barnes, C.; Flake, G.; O'Rouke, M.; Lee, K.; Chen, H.; Sun, G.; Zhang, Y.; Chen, D.; and Giles, G. 1991. Adaptive stochastic cellular automata: theory and experiment. In Gutowitz, H., ed., *Cellular Automata.* Cambridge, MA: MIT Press. 159–188.

Meinhardt, H. 1982. *Models of Biological Pattern Formation.* London: Academic Press.

Murray, J. 1989. *Mathematical Biology.* New York: Springer-Verlag.

Ouyang, Q., and Swinney, H. 1991. Transition from a uniform state to hexagonal and striped Turing patterns. *Nature* 352:610–612.

Salemi, B.; Shen, W.-M.; and Will, P. 2001. Hormone-controlled metamorphic agents. In *Proc. International Conference on Agentics and Automation.*

Shen, W.; Lu, Y.; and Will, P. 2000. Hormone-based control for self-reconfigurable agents. In *Proc. International Conference on Autonomous Agents.*

Shen, W.; Salemi, B.; and Will, P. 2000. Hormones for self-reconfigurable agents. In *Proc. 6th International Conference on Intelligent Autonomous Systems.*

Toffoli. 2000. Cellular automata. In Arbib, M., ed., *The Handbook of Brain Science.* Cambridge, MA: MIT Press.

Turing, A. 1952. The chemical basis of morphogenesis. *Philos. Trans. R. Soc. London B* 237:37–72.

Witkin, A., and Kass, M. 1991. Reaction-diffusion textures. *Computer Graphics* 25(3). also Proc. Siggraph 91.

A Stress-based Speciation Model in LifeDrop

Marc Métivier *, **Claude Lattaud** *, **Jean-Claude Heudin** **
* Laboratoire d'Intelligence Artificielle de Paris 5
UFR de Mathématiques et d'Informatique, Centre Universitaire des Saints Pères
45, rue des Saints Pères 75006 Paris - France
{metivier, lattaud}@math-info.univ-paris5.fr
** International Institute of Multimedia, Pôle Universitaire Léonard de Vinci
92916 La Défense Cedex — France
Jean-Claude.Heudin@devinci.fr

Abstract

This paper presents a stress-based speciation model implemented within LifeDrop, a virtual world with bio-inspired agents. In this model, individuals are distributed among species separated by a "barrier" mechanism preventing the reproduction between individuals of different species. An analysis of species dynamics in relation to stress is presented. Results show diversity maintenance and a reactive capacity during crisis situations favoring the emergence of new species.

Introduction

Over the last decades, several studies of artificial ecosystems have been published in the field of Artificial Life. Typically, such a system includes a population of bio-inspired autonomous agents which compete to survive in a simulated environment. Each agent is described using a genotype which, associated to a speciation mechanism, provides an evolutionary process permitting the emergence of more adapted agents in the environment. Among them, LifeDrop is a virtual ecosystem consisting of creatures evolving in a virtual drop of water. One of the objectives is to provide a model for studying the complexity of species dynamics in the framework of a larger project addressing the "evolution of complexity" in various classes of dynamical systems (Heudin 1998).

An original feature of LifeDrop relies in its model and implementation of the species concept. In most previous artificial ecosystem experiments, individuals are generally spread over different groups that are considered as species, but the underlying models usually do not provide a well defined speciation mechanism. Rather, a separation between agents using a phenotypic observation is often used. Several works in molecular biology have proposed an explanation of speciation related to stress (Matic, Rayssiguier, & Radman 1995; Taddey, Matic, & Radman 1996). Based on these studies, this paper present a stress-based speciation model and its implementation within LifeDrop.

Related works

Several Artificial Life ecosystems have been designed during the last fifteen years. Among them, Tierra (Ray 1991) and Avida (Adami & Brown 1994) are based on populations of self-reproducing strings with a Turing-complete genetic basis subjected to Poisson-random mutations. PolyWorld (Yaeger 1994) and Gaïa(Gracias *et al.* 1996) are two-dimensional ecology simulators studying evolution of competing agents controlled with neural networks. Darwin Pond (Ventrella 1998) and Gene Pool[1] are two-dimensional virtual worlds where physics-based organisms, respectively called "swimbots" and "swimmers", evolve over time. Framsticks (Komosinski 2000) is a three-dimensional life simulation project where both the physical structure of creatures and their control systems are evolved.

All these systems implement populations of autonomous entities, sometimes spread over different species, but none of them proposes a well defined speciation model. In Framsticks, individuals are spread over species defined as sets of individuals having similar genotypes. The speciation is not managed by any mechanism, but is favored by lowering the fitness of new agents having similar genotype to existing ones. PolyWorld and Gaïa propose simulations where new species emerge. However, they use a qualitative determination based on observed behaviors. In Gaïa, a competition between two species in which individuals can mate only with individuals from the same species has been studied but no speciation mechanism has been proposed.

Fundamental principles of evolution dynamics have been explored in systems built by Conrad (1987) and Packard (1989). Wagner and Altenberg (1995) reports a study about the "evolvability" in evolutionary processes. Population dynamics as result of interactions between individuals have been studied, among others, in Taylor *et al.* (1989). Bedau has presented a comparison and a classification of evolvable capacities obtained in artificial ecosystems and from Biosphere examples (Bedau *et al.* 1998; Bedau, Snyder, & Packard 1998).

LifeDrop Overview

The environment

LifeDrop[2] is a java-based virtual ecosystem inhabited by bio-inspired creatures. The environment consist of a "virtual water drop" with boundaries acting as "walls" for creatures. It integrates a physical engine manag-

[1] http://www.ventrella.com

[2] LifeDrop can be experimented on-line on the following web site at http://www.virtual-worlds.net/lifedrop.

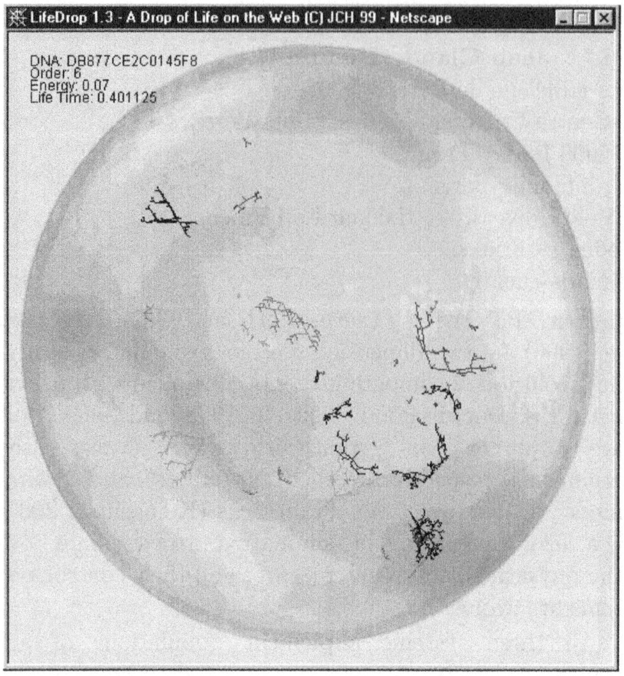

Figure 1: A screenshot of the first version of LifeDrop showing a small set of creatures moving in the 3D environment.

ing forces using the "steering behaviors" model for autonomous characters (Reynolds 1999).

The environment includes several parameters such as water fluidity, acidity, etc. The *pH* parameter ranges from 0.0 (no creature can live) to 1.0 (no impact). It simulates the chemical impact of the number of living creature in a closed environment.

The creatures

Each creature is an autonomous agent that can be described by a layered hierarchical model (Heudin 1998) inspired from the subsumption architecture (Brooks 1991). In this model, a given level relies on the existence of its sub-levels and all levels are intrinsically parallel. During a cycle, each layer receives information from the environment and selects an action to be executed. The current model implements five layers:

Genotype: the "digital DNA" of the creature. Metabolism: manages the essential cycles like lifetime, development and growth, mating, etc.

Dynamics: manages the creature's "incarnation" simulating the impact of the "physical conditions" such as water fluidity, *pH*, etc.

Reactive behaviors: manages basic reactive behaviors, such as obstacle avoidance, fleeing, etc.

Cognitive behaviors: manages behaviors such as the selection of a mating partner.

Creature genotype

Each creature is characterized by a genotype that determines most of its morphological and behavioral parameters. It is composed of 4 "chromosomes", each of them containing 8 "genes". Figure 2 gives the mapping of these encoded parameters.

Chromosome #0 — Meta genes	
Gene #0:	Number of chromosomes in the genotype.
Gene #1:	Matching level with another genotype.
Gene #2:	Mutation level.
Gene #3:	Internal clock: lifetime in cycles.
Gene #4:	Internal clock: cycle time.
Gene #5:	Maximum energy level.
Gene #6:	Maximum number of children per reproduction.
Gene #7:	Unused.
Chromosome #1 — Structural genes	
Gene #0:	Recursion order for development.
Gene #1:	Segmented or not (Dawkins 1988).
Gene #2:	Number of segments if segmented (Dawkins 1988).
Gene #3:	Delta parameter for segmentation (Dawkins 1988).
Gene #4:	Gradient parameter for segmentation (Dawkins 1988).
Gene #5:	Jaws force level.
Gene #6:	Color.
Gene #7:	Unused.
Chromosome #2 — Morphological genes	
Gene #0:	dx #3 parameter (Dawkins 1988).
Gene #1:	dx #4 parameter (Dawkins 1988).
Gene #2:	dx #5 parameter (Dawkins 1988).
Gene #3:	dy #2 parameter (Dawkins 1988).
Gene #4:	dy #3 parameter (Dawkins 1988).
Gene #5:	dy #4 parameter (Dawkins 1988).
Gene #6:	dy #5 parameter (Dawkins 1988).
Gene #7:	dy #6 parameter (Dawkins 1988).
Chromosome #3 — Behavioral genes	
Gene #0:	Number of creatures which can be perceived.
Gene #1:	Maximum radius for perception.
Gene #2:	Recognition rate.
Gene #3:	Mating behavior weight.
Gene #4:	Eating behavior weight.
Gene #5:	Fleeing behavior weight.
Gene #6:	Flocking behavior weight.
Gene #7:	Render behavior weight.

Figure 2: The encoded parameters in the genotype.

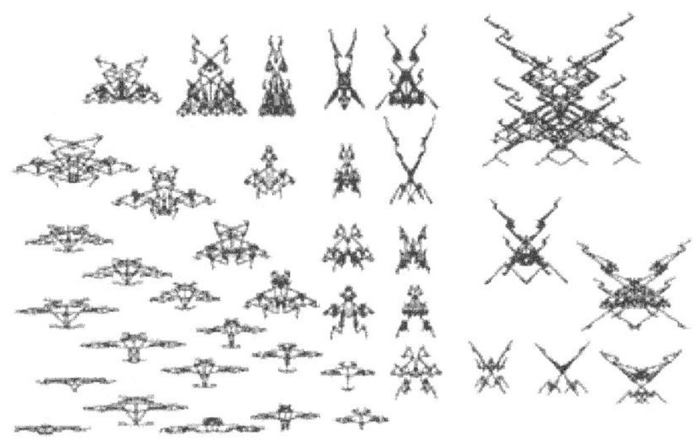

Figure 3: Examples of biomorphs' shapes (after Dawkins).

In addition to these parameters, each creature gets an additional set of parameters after its development process. These include, among others, the "alive", "hungry", "fecund" and "stressed" states. As we will see later, the "stressed" state has a direct impact on the creature's behaviors and also on the speciation mechanism.

Creature morphology and behaviors

The morphology of LifeDrop's creatures was inspired by the works done by Richard Dawkins with the *Blind Watchmaker* (Dawkins 1986; 1989). Within LifeDrop, these 2D shapes called "Biomorphs", have been extended to autonomous agents characterized by 3D shapes and showing a variety of behaviors.

Each agent has its own elementary perception system. It perceives all other creatures close enough in a "perception sphere" which main parameters are encoded in the fourth chromosome. Depending on these sensory information and its internal state, an agent selects an action in the set of possible behaviors at each simulation cycle. Examples of possible behaviors are the following: looking for mate, looking for food, fleeing a danger, moving randomly, flocking, etc.

All agents interact in the same virtual drop of water resulting in a complex (eco-)system. There is no explicit fitness function or any global selection procedure. The success of some phenotypes emerges from the interactions between agents in the environment. Some agents show a good adaptation while some others die quite rapidly (killed by others for example). Thus, any individual born inherits genes that have succeeded in building a series of successful phenotypes. In this sense, we can state that LifeDrop implements the principle of natural selection.

The Stress-based Speciation Model

Biological inspiration

The most widely accepted definition of a species is the one proposed by Ernst Mayr (1982). He defines a species as a set of individuals that "can mate and be fecund between them, and only between them". Such a definition implicitly involves a "species barrier" principle, which prevents reproduction between two individuals from different species.

Recently, Matic and his colleagues have proposed an explanation of the species formation at molecular scale for bacteria (Matic, Rayssiguier, & Radman 1995). This study shows that the species barrier is maintained by genes controlling a mismatch repairing system (MRS) of DNA. In addition to its repairing property, this system warrants that two genotypes with too high differences cannot recombine between them. Thus, when the MRS is active, only individuals having similar genotypes are fecund between them and will be able to mate successfully. However, if the MRS genes are inactivated, the species barrier becomes weak and individuals do not need anymore to have much genetic proximity to be fecund between them. Moreover, in such a case, the observed mutational rate becomes very high.

A key feature of this study is that inhibition occurs for individuals stressed by their environment. When individuals are stressed by difficult environmental conditions, they can reproduce with individuals that, in a non-stressed situation, would be considered from another species. Adding the fact that the mutational rate is then higher, stressed species go through diversification. When the stress decreases, the species barrier is restored.

Model implementation

Each LifeDrop agent is characterized by a parameter named *matching level* which is encoded in its first chromosome (cf. figure 2). This parameter represents the minimum "genetic proximity" value this individual must have with another to be able to reproduce. It simulates the structural compatibility between two different genotypes. As a consequence, the definition of a species is: ***Two individuals are considered of the same species if their genotypic proximity is greater than each of their respective matching level values.***

The genotypic proximity P_{g1g2} is given by the expression:

$$P_{g1g2} = k\left(1 - \frac{D_{g1g2}}{D_{\max}}\right) \quad (1)$$

where D_{g1g2} is the distance between genotype $g1$ and genotype $g2$, $D_{\max}$ the maximum possible distance between two genotypes, and k an implementation constant with a value of 100.

We have used the Euclidean distance for computing D_{g1g2}, each genotype being considered as a vector. Such a choice has been made in order to consider all genes from a neutral point of view. This means that the phenotypic impacts of genes are not taken into account. This constitutes a major difference with previous artificial life studies. Note that other distance expressions could be

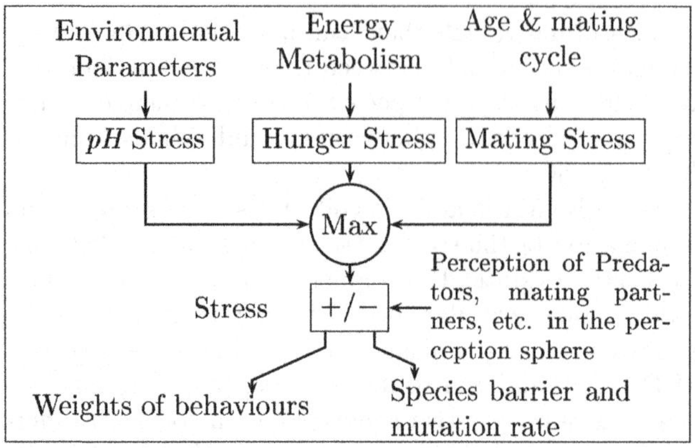

Figure 4: Stress computation of a creature during a cycle.

used in other experiments but they will not be addressed in this paper.

The stress plays an important role for each creature. It is implemented as a floating point value ranged from 0.0 (not stressed) to 1.0 (extremely stressed). The computation of this value, called S_i, takes further steps as shown in figure 4. It involves many parameters related to the environment, the energy metabolism, the reproduction metabolism, and the perception system.

Besides its impact on the behavior selection, it also acts on the species barrier. During important stress situations, the *matching level* M_i of an agent is lowered and its *mutational rate* Π_i is increased. These reproduction parameters are functions of the stress and two base values, M_{gi} and Π_{gi}, given by the first chromosome:

$$M_i = M_{gi} - \alpha S_i \quad (2)$$

$$\Pi_i = \Pi_{gi} + (\beta^{-1} S_i)^2 \quad (3)$$

where α and β are implementation dependant constants with a value of 20 and 2 respectively.

Experimental results

General observation

We have conducted three different types of experiments with varying initial conditions and parameters. The first type includes runs with a set of randomized genotypes and the observer does not act in any sort during the simulation. The second type includes also simulations with randomized initial genotypes but the user sets the *pH* value to 0.5 at a particular instant and during a certain time. This means that the environment suddenly becomes unfavorable for survival. These "crisis periods" allow one to study the impact of a difficult environment on species dynamics. In the third set of simulations, all initial creatures have the same genotype (randomly chosen) and the user can force crisis periods.

All experiments show a fast population decrease during the first 20,000 simulation cycles. In some rare cases, this decrease leads to a population extinction. However,

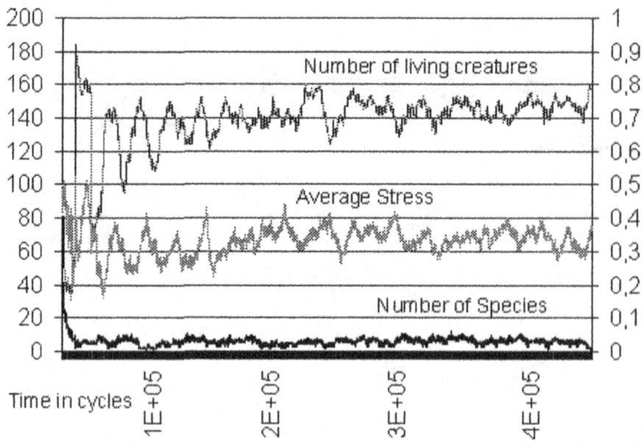

Figure 5: Time series of population, number of species (both on the left axis) and average stress (right axis).

in most cases the decrease is followed by an important increase. When some creatures are still living after 20,000 cycles, then no population extinction has ever been observed.

The number of species vary a lot during an experiment. This means that species frequently appear or disappear over the time. It is important not to simply relate this it with births or deaths. As a matter of fact, the species definition is based on the species barrier which itself depends on the stress of creatures. Thus, the species delimitation between individuals is in constant evolution.

Experiments without crisis

In these experiments, the species number decreases during a first phase and then stays relatively constant. The average stress of the creatures varies a lot during the first steps of simulation and then tends to stabilize itself as for the population. In all experiments of this type, the stable state corresponds to low number of species, usually ranged between 5 and 10. In any cases, the species number stay strictly greater than one, which means that different species co-evolve permanently in the environment. Figure 5 shows the time series for a typical experiment with an initial set of 100 creatures.

Experiments with crisis

All experiments of the second type show the same dynamics as in the first type with the exception of crisis periods. During these periods, the *pH* is forced to 0.5. This has the effect to reduce by half the lifetime of the creatures and to force their stress rate up to 0.5, which rarely appears in normal simulations.

As a result, the number of species decreases when the crisis begins. This is a consequence of two facts. First, a high number of individuals die, which may cause the disappearance of a number of species. Then the species barriers become low due to the high value of stress. Thus,

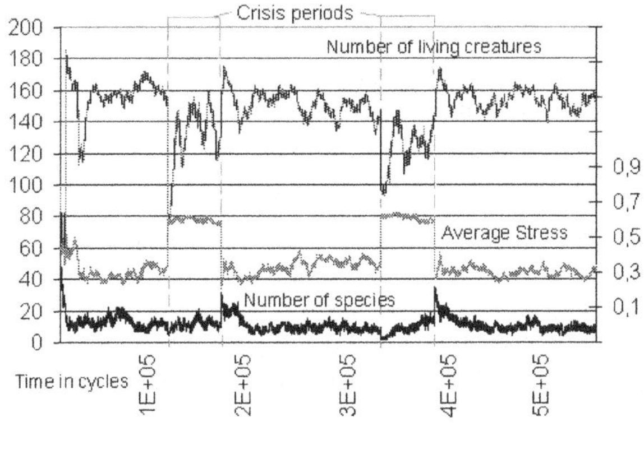

Figure 6: Time series of population, number of species (both on the left axis) and average stress (right axis).

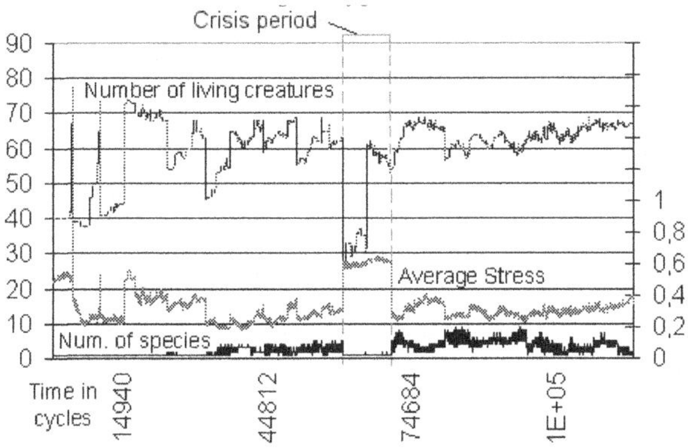

Figure 7: Time series of population, number of species (both on the left axis) and average stress (right axis).

surviving agents are distributed among few species. Despite the lowness of the barriers, the number of species increases slowly during the crisis. The stress rates having quite no variation, this means that newborn creatures present a high variability, enough to be considered as belonging to different species than the already present one. It is well showed at the end of the crisis. When the pH returns to a "normal" value, the species number strongly increases, showing that the diversity between individuals issued from the crisis is very high. Figure 6 shows results for a typical experiment of this kind with 100 initial randomized genotypes.

The third type of experiments shows this behaviors still better (cf. figure 7). When a simulation begins with a set of creatures having the same genotype, the number of species increases slowly even before a crisis period is forced by the user. The stress is rather high during a long period at the beginning of the simulation, around 0.4, which may be understood as the initial creatures were not well adapted to their environment. As a reaction, population goes through diversification and new species appear. This is followed by a decrease of the average stress. Later, after a crisis period, the diversity has become even more important and the system stabilizes, as seen in first type simulation. Note that the beginning of these experiments is rather different than previous ones. As a matter of fact, all creatures having the same genotype, population extinction is more frequent. The "success" of an experiment is thus highly dependent on the chosen genotype.

Discussion

Results showed that in "normal" situations the population, the species number and the mean stress tend to stabilize over the time. The evolution leads to a population composed of individuals well adapted to their environment spread over a few number of species. When environmental difficulties appear, results show a decrease of species and barriers become lower. This leads to new recombination between individuals and favors new species formation. At the end of a crisis, the barriers are restored and a high number of species emerge. The behavior of the system is thus to favor emergence of new species in response to the population lack of adaptation. As pointed out by Matic *et al.* (1995), this might be a possible explanation (at molecular scale) for the species dynamics observed in fossil record. These patterns, named "punctuated equilibria", reveal most species in stasis followed by abrupt appearance of newly derived species (Eldredge & Gould 1972). Of course, this hypothesis must be confirmed by further studies showing that this model could be also applied to the evolution of multicellular organisms.

In our experiments, the final species number has been always greater than one (with exception of some complete population extinctions). This property appears to be significant in comparison to previous artificial ecosystem studies. In Gaïa, Gracias (Gracias *et al.* 1996) observed that cohabitation between two species never occurs, even when beginning with two highly adapted species. The explanation of this phenomenon is that, in a system where individuals have to find a mating partner, the probability of achieving reproduction is highly dependant on the number of individuals of the same species. When two species cohabit, an implicit competition takes place, favoring the most numerous species. All Gaïa simulations ended with only one species. In contrast, LifeDrop allows cohabitation between different species. After a first chaotic phase, the number of species tends to stabilize around a global value proper to each simulation. Even after an increase at the end of a crisis period, the number of species decreases returning to a value near to the one observed before the crisis.

The stress is generally considered as a disagreement for an individual. It is an indicator of some difficulties to live in an environment and it impacts on behaviors. In our model, the stress has another property. It helps evolution, acting as a kind of dynamic fitness function for exploring the genotype space, favoring diversity by decreasing the species barrier between individuals and increasing the mutation rate during reproduction.

Conclusion

This paper has presented a genetically-based species definition involving a barrier mechanism and a stress-based speciation model. Results show a clear convergence with those obtained by biological experiments with bacteria (Taddey, Matic, Radman 1996), thus validating this approach. Future works include the study of species dynamics as complexity classes (Wolfram 1984) and their corresponding attractor structures. This will be then compared to observed species dynamics (phyletic gradualism, punctuated equilibria, etc) in nature.

References

Adami, C., and Brown, C. 1994. Evolutionary learning in the 2D artificial life system "Avida". In Brooks, R. A., and Maes, P., eds., *Artificial Life IV, Proceedings of the Fourth International Workshop on the Synthesis and Simulation of Living Systems*, 377. MIT Press.

Bedau, M. A.; Snyder, E.; Brown, T.; and Packard, N. H. 1998. A comparison of evolutionary activity in artificial evolving systems and in the biosphere. Technical Report WP 98-03-024, Santa Fe Institute.

Bedau, M. A.; Snyder, E.; and Packard, N. 1998. A classification of long-term evolutionary dynamics. In Adami, C.; Belew, R.; Kitano, H.; and Taylor, C., eds., *proceedings of the Artificial Life VI Conference*, 228–237. MIT Press.

Brooks, R. 1991. How to build complete creatures rather than isolated cognitive simulators. In VanLehn, K., ed., *Architectures for Intelligence.* Hillsdale: Lawrence Erlbaum Assosiates. 225–239.

Conrad, M. 1987. Computer test beds for evolutionary theory. Oral presentation at Artificial Life I Conference.

Dawkins, R. 1986. *The Blind Watchmaker.* Penguin Books.

Dawkins, R. 1989. The evolution of evolvability. In *Artificial Life* (1989), 201.

Eldredge, N., and Gould, S. 1972. Punctuated equilibria: an alternative to phyletic gradualism. In Schopf, T., ed., *Models in Paleobiology.* San Francisco: Freeman, Cooper.

Gracias, N.; Pereira, H.; Lima, J.; and Rosa, A. 1996. An artificial life environment for ecological systems simulation. In Langton, C., and Shimohara, K., eds., *Artificial Life V*, 124–133. MIT Press.

Heudin, J. 1998. Virtual worlds. In Heudin, J., ed., *Virtual Worlds: Synthetic Universes, Digital Life and Complexity.* Perseus Books. 1–28.

Komosinski, M. 2000. The world of Framsticks: Simulation, evolution, interaction. In Heudin, J.-C., ed., *Proceedings of the Second International Conference on Virtual Worlds*, volume 1834 of *Lecture Notes in Computer Science*, 214–224. Springer-Verlag.

Langton, C. G. 1989. *Artificial Life*, volume 6 of *Santa Fe Institute Studies in the Sciences of Complexity.* Addison-Wesley.

Matic; Rayssiguier, C.; and Radman, M. 1995. Interspecies gene exchange in bacteria: the role of sos and mismatch repair systems in evolution of species. *Cell* 80:507.

Mayr, E. 1982. *The Growth of Biological Thought : Diversity, Evolution and Inheritance.* Harvard University Press.

Packard, N. 1989. Intrinsic adaptation in a simple model evolution. In *Artificial Life* (1989), 141.

Ray, T. 1991. An approach to the synthesis of life. In Langton, C. G.; Taylor, C.; Farmer, J. D.; and Rasmussen, S., eds., *Artificial Life II.* New York: Addison-Wesley. 371.

Reynolds, C. 1999. Steering behaviors for autonomous characters. Presented at the 1999 Game Developer Conference.

Taddey; Matic; and Radman. 1996. Du nouveau sur l'origine des espèces. *La Recherche* 291:52–59.

Taylor, C.; Jefferson, D.; Turner, S.; and Goldman, S. 1989. RAM : Artificial life for the exploration of complex biological systems. In *Artificial Life* (1989), 275.

Ventrella, J. 1998. Designing emergence in animated artificial life worlds. In Heudin, J., ed., *Proceedings of the First International Conference on Virtual Worlds*, volume 1434 of *Lecture Notes in Computer Science*, 143. Springer-Verlag.

Wagner, G., and Altenberg, L. 1995. Complex adaptations and the evolution of evolvability. *Evolution* 50:967–976.

Yaeger, L. 1994. Computational genetics, physiology, metabolism, neural systems, learning, vision, and behavior or PolyWorld: Life in a new context. In Langton, C. G., ed., *Artificial Life III*, 263. Reading, Mass.: Addison-Wesley.

On Attaining Maximal Fitness or How to Evolve Virtual Redwoods

Gary R. Greenfield

Mathematics & Computer Science
University of Richmond, Richmond, VA 23173
ggreenfi@richmond.edu

Abstract

An understanding of the evolutionary mechanisms that lead to increased genome capabilities is essential for determining the potentials and limits of living systems. We evolve abstract aesthetic imagery on the basis of an image connectivity trait that has a theoretically determined maximum value. This trait can be influenced by "development" genes. We investigate simulated evolution when the development genes are not present, when they are fused with the existing genotype, and when they function semi-autonomously by residing in symbionts. Genome fusing initially impedes evolution while symbiosis initially accelerates evolution. Our findings suggest that symbiosis events play a more important role than genome fusion events for sustaining open-ended evolution.

Keywords: Evolving expressions, computational aesthetics, simulated evolution.

Introduction

We present evidence favoring genome "cooperation" over genome "fusion" as a mechanism for enhancing the survival of a species. Our results are based on simulated evolution experiments using a species that possesses a trait that is easy to formulate, has a theoretically determined maximum fitness value, and can be suitably influenced by genes. The genotypes for our species are postfix expressions and the phenotypes are abstract images. Image phenotypes undergo a development phase, after which they are evaluated for a "connectivity" trait. The development phase can be partially regulated by coefficient genome vectors. Our design allows these vectors either to be suppressed, to be fused with image genotype expressions, or to function semi-autonomously, as primitive, rapidly evolving symbionts.

If coefficient genome vectors are suppressed, then a randomly generated population of image genotypes will settle upon a genome "template" from which it will either successfully attain the maximum value of the trait within 250 of the 500 allotted generations or become trapped in an evolutionary cul-de-sac. If coefficient genome vectors are fused with image genotypes, then randomly generated populations support a wider range of genome templates to start with and provide a larger fitness landscape to explore, whence image populations maintain better *average* fitness and evolution proceeds slowly and inexorably along an evolutionary trajectory towards the maximum value of the trait. If a hill-climbing algorithm allowing coefficient genome vectors to function as independent, fast evolving subspecies of symbionts is used, then randomly generated image populations can either accelerate rapidly to the maximum value of the trait or evolve steadily towards the maximum value. These results support the claim that symbiosis events are more important than genome-fusion events for sustaining open-ended evolution. Moreover, they suggest that genome fusion is an evolutionary neutral event, contra-indicated when the traits affected by the fused genes are under immediate evolutionary pressure.

Background and Motivation

"User-guided evolution" requires a user to assign fitness rankings to the phenotypes in each generation in order to determine the breeding population for the next generation. This paradigm is cental to the genre of computer generated art referred to as evolutionary art or generative art. Difficulties arise when phenotype rendering times, the number of phenotypes to examine, or the number of generations needed to evolve acceptable aesthetics become too large. In such circumstances it becomes desirable to automate the phenotype acceptance/rejection process. When this is done, we say evolution is driven by *computational* aesthetics. Absolute measures of aesthetic fitness are usually a deterrent to open-ended evolution (Baluja et al 1994), therefore coevolutionary methods based on competition between two species (Greenfield 2000b)) or cooperation between two species (Greenfield 2002)) have been considered. In the latter study, aesthetic fitness based on geometric data obtained by color segmenting aesthetic image phenotypes was investigated. Color segmenting decomposed each image into simply-connected regions whose areas, boundary lengths, and number of region adjacencies could be calculated. In one experiment, the total number of region adjacencies was used as the fitness criterion to try and evolve images whose "compositions" exhibited multiple thread-like shapes. Surprisingly, compact, minimalist compositions were obtained (see Fig. 1.) The explanation is that the *graph* obtained by interpreting regions as vertices and adjacencies as edges is always a simple, connected, planar graph and there is a theoretical limit to the number of edges in a planar graph on n vertices, namely $3n-6$ (Behzad et al 1979), which is significantly smaller than the upper bound of $n(n-1)/2$ one might expect. The most fit images produced using these methods are long-lived organisms belonging to a species with few surviving specimens, capable of producing few, if any, breeding offspring. We are reminded of species such as

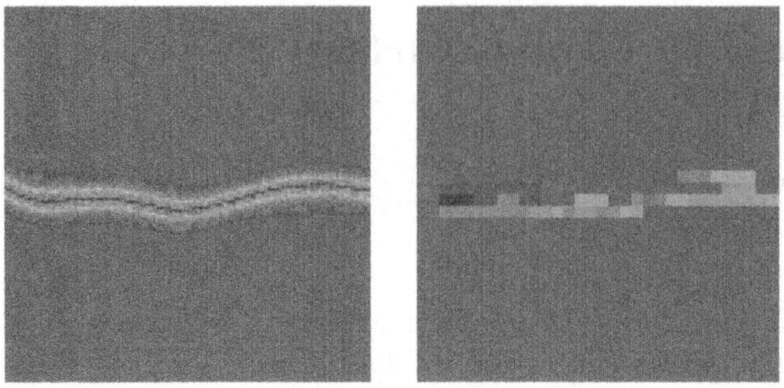

Figure 1: Left: Full resolution 128 × 128 color image evolved using computational aesthetics. Right: Color segmented 32 × 32 image used to determine aesthetic fitness.

the giant redwood (*Sequoia gigantea*) or bristlecone pine (*Pinus longaeva*).

The process of organizing a digital image into a prescribed number of simply-connected regions is the *development* phase a newly bred image phenotype undergoes before reaching maturity. Parameters, or genes, for controlling this development can be used to help formulate three types of simulated evolution: (1) evolution using fixed values for these genes so that development is determined by an environmental litmus test, (2) evolution where genes for regulating the environment are acquired by the species in a genome fusion event, and (3) evolution where genes for regulating the environment reside in a cooperating (i.e., symbiotic) species.

Color Images from Evolving Expressions

Let $\{c_1, \ldots, c_L\}$ be a set of colors. We let $L = 450$. Each color $c_k = (h_k, s_k, v_k)$ has hue $h_k \in [0,6]$, saturation $s_k \in [0,1]$, and value $v_k \in [0,1]$. A function $F : [0,1] \times [0,1] \longrightarrow [0,1)$ generates an $m \times m$ color image by assigning pixel $p_{i,j}$, where $0 \leq i, j < m$, color c_k if and only if $F(i/m, j/m) \in [(k-1)/L, k/L)$. The method of evolving expressions constructs an evolvable class of such functions from a set of *primitives* (Sims 1991). Image genotypes are postfix expressions built from such primitives. The primitives we use (Greenfield 2000a) include variables V_0 and V_1; constants $C_0, C_1, \ldots, C_{999}$; unary functions $U_0, U_1, \ldots, U_4$; and binary functions $B_0, B_1, \ldots, B_{14}$. An example postfix expression is:

```
V1 V1 V0 B6 V1 B4 V1 V1 V0 B6 B0 V0 V1 B9 V0
B1 B13 V0 V1 B1 V1 B14 V1 B4 V0 B5 V0 B11 V0
B1 B1 V1 V0 B11 V0 B3 V1 V0 B4 V0 B1 B2 B1
B14 B9
```

Image phenotypes are generated by setting $V_0 = i/m$, $V_1 = j/m$, and performing a postfix evaluation. The recombination operator is subtree crossover. The mutation operator is "bit-flipping" which replaces, with probability p_{mut}, each primitive by a new one of the same arity.

Segmentation of Color Images

To color segment, we render image phenotypes at a resolution of 32 × 32 and use each pixel to initialize a region of area one whose averaged color matches the pixel's color. Using a two-stage process, we perform a sequence of merges of adjacent regions until only 25 regions remain. The first stage, priority-merging, iteratively selects and merges the two adjacent regions whose average color is "closest" until the number of regions is reduced to 50. The second stage, absorption-merging, iteratively selects and merges the smallest remaining region with its largest adjacent neighbor until the number of regions is reduced to 25. Color "closeness" loses its meaning in darker areas so excessive priority-merging can "corrupt" an image. Moreover, since region adjacencies are determined from pixel *edges*, diagonal cascades of regions can disrupt the formation of adjacencies. Absorption-merging helps removes diagonal cascades (see Fig. 2.)

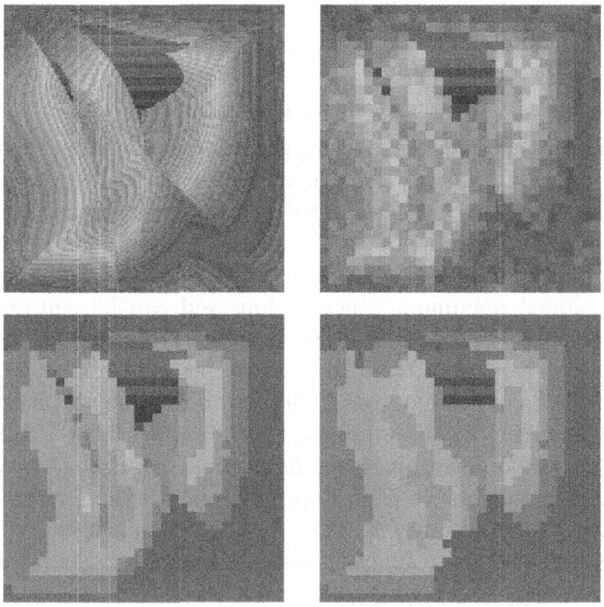

Figure 2: Top Left: High resolution 128 × 128 image. Top Right: Low resolution 32 × 32 image. Bottom Left: Low resolution image color segmented to 50 regions by priority-merging. Bottom right: Low resolution image further color segmented to 25 regions by absorption-merging.

To find the adjacent regions whose averaged colors are "closest" we must determine the boundary edge of minimal priority. Let (h_1, v_1, s_1) and (h_2, v_2, s_2) be the averaged colors of regions R_1 and R_2 bounded by edge e. Set $\Delta_h = \min(|h_1 - h_2|, 6 - |h_1 - h_2|)$, $\Delta_s = |s_1 - s_2|$, and $\Delta_v = |v_1 - v_2|$. Define the edge priority $p(e)$ to be

$$\begin{aligned} p(e) &= (1 + k_{h,s}\Delta_s + k_{h,v}\Delta_v + k_{h,v,v}\Delta_v^2 \\ &\quad + k_{h,v,s}\Delta_v\Delta_s + k_{h,s,s}\Delta_s^2)\Delta_h \\ &\quad + k_s\Delta_s + k_v\Delta_v. \end{aligned}$$

The coefficient genome vector is the 7-tuple

$$(k_{h,v}, k_{h,v,s}, k_{h,s}, k_v, k_s, k_{h,v,v}, k_{h,s,s}),$$

where each coefficient lies in the interval $[0, 3]$. Assuming $h_1 \geq h_2$, the merged region is assigned averaged color $(\bar{h}, \bar{s}, \bar{v})$ where $\bar{s}$ and $\bar{v}$ are the usual area weighted averages, but due to the circular nature of the hue scale its area weighted average is given by $\bar{h} = (a_1 h_1 + a_2(b + h_2))/(a_1 + a_2) \pmod 6$, with $b = 0$ if $h_1 - h_2 \leq 3$ and $b = 6$ otherwise. The recombination operator is one-point crossover and the mutation operator is coefficient perturbation. The coefficient genome used to color segment the image phenotype in Figure 2 was $(3.0, 0.0, 0.0982277, 1.22504, 0.0592963, 1.32771, 2.37181)$.

Planar Graphs and Image Fitness

To construct a graph from a color segmented image, first label the pixels within each color segmented region using unique vertex labels to obtain a 32×32 connectivity *tableau*, then use the tableau to construct a 25×25 adjacency matrix. Fig. 3 shows the top portion of the tableau produced from the example in Fig. 2 by using vertex labels a through y, while Fig. 4 shows the first few rows of the adjacency matrix obtained from this tableau. Image fitness is the sum of the vertex adjacencies divided by two. For our example, this fitness is $136/2 = 68$, one shy of the maximum.

```
yyyyyyyyyyyyyyyyyyyyyyyyyyyyyyyy
yyyyyyyyyyyyyyyyyyyyyyyyyyyyyyyy
yyyyyyyyyyyypppppppppppyyyyyyyyy
yylyyykkkkccccccccmmmmmpppppyyyy
lllrykkkkkgoooooooooooommmmpppyyyy
lllrykkkkgghooooooottmmmmppyyyy
lllrrrkkgghheeeeeeeettttttmppyyyy
lllrrwwgghhvvddddddttttmppyyyy
llrrrwwwghhvvxbbbbbbtnnttmppyyyy
llrrrwwwuhhvvxaaaaaatnnttmppyyyy
```

Figure 3: The top ten rows of the 32×32 connectivity tableau constructed from the example image phenotype following the development phase.

Experimental Design

Image population size is set to 30. After each image generation, the 12 most fit individuals provide replacements for the 18 least fit individuals by breeding 9 randomly selected pairs (with replacement). Since there is no "reaper" in the sense of (Ray 1992), and no provision for marginally fit images to survive to breed, with probability p_{sev}, a member of a breeding pair can be replaced with a randomly generated image genotype. The three types of simulated evolution we implemented were:

```
  abcdefghijklmnopqrstuvwxy
a 0100000001000000000110001 0   5
b 1001000000000000000100010     4
c 0000001000101011000000001     6
d 0100100000000000000101010     5
e 0001000100000001000010100 0   5
f 0000000001000100001000001     4
g 0010000100100010000010100     6
h 0000101000000001000001100 0   5
```

Figure 4: The first eight rows of the 25×25 adjacency matrix constructed from the connectivity tableau of our example. Vertex adjacency counts are shown on the right.

N-GENES. An organism genotype consists of an image genotype. The coefficients of the edge priority function are all set to zero, except for k_s and k_v which are set to one.

F-GENES. An organism genotype consists of an image genotype *fused* with a coefficient genotype. When images are bred, 75% of the time a newborn inherits its coefficient genotype from one of its parents, and 25% of the time it inherits a coefficient genotype resulting from the crossover of the coefficient genotypes of its parents.

S-GENES. An organism genotype consists of an image genome *partnered* with a coefficient genome. In between each *image* generation, for 20 *coefficient* generations, coefficient genomes are evolved asexually, and the coefficient genotype for the organism is replaced if and only if the fitness of its image phenotype will be improved. (This hill-climbing algorithm is an evolutionary algorithm that applies a separate local search process to refine individuals. It provides the illusion that each coefficient genotype is a canonical representative for a *population* of symbionts.) When images are bred, the 75:25 scheme for coefficient genotypes remains in effect.

Simulation Results

When genes for regulating development were suppressed, the average fitness, taken over 20 trials, of the most fit individual in the initial randomly generated population was 52.650. When such genes were present, the average fitness, taken over 40 trials, of the most fit individual in the initial population was 53.625. This shows there was no evolutionary bias due to randomization. After 100 image generations, the average fitness of the most fit individual, taken over 20 trials, was 65.75 for F-Genes organisms, 66.35 for N-Genes organisms, and 67.5 for S-Genes organisms. This shows that fitness transients had died out by this time, and helps support the argument that genome fusion events initially *slow* the rate of fitness improvement. However, after 500 image generations the average fitness for the most fit individual in the F-Genes case was 68.4, overtaking the average fitness in the N-Genes genes case which was 68.1.

S-Genes trials were only run for 100 generations, so in order to compare evolution rates, we considered only those trials where the most fit individual had obtained a fitness of at least 65 by that point. Table 1 dramatically reveals that genome fusion slowed evolution while symbiont genomes accelerated evolution. N-Genes and F-Genes trials were run for 500 generations. For 20 trials of each type, it took an average of 67.75 generations for the top individual to reach fitness 65 for N-Genes trials, and 76.25 generations for F-Genes trials.

Type	Trials	Ave. No. Gens.
N-Genes	17	52.35
F-Genes	15	61.53
S-Genes	18	37.22

Table 1: The average number of generations that it took for the most fit individual to reach fitness 65. The time limit was 100 image generations.

Our objective was to evolve individuals that attained the maximum fitness value of 69. Fig. 5 shows an example of a "perfect" specimen, our virtual redwood tree. Table 2 shows how successful we were in achieving our objective within the first 100 generations. It reveals the clear advantage symbionts provided. In 20 trials of the N-Genes simulation the fitness maximum was achieved 10 times within 500 generations, and in 20 trials of the F-Genes simulation the fitness maximum was achieved 11 times within 500 generations. Even though the probability for success was virtually identical, the average number of generations required to attain this limit soared from 167.3 in the N-Genes case to 288.4 in the F-Genes case. More striking is the fact that only twice during N-Genes trials was evolution able to attain the maximum after 250 generations, while it was attained seven times after 250 generations during F-Genes trials. Thus, when no genes for regulating development were present, either maximal fitness was reached very quickly or evolution got stuck.

This work conducted while on sabbatical at the Visualization Laboratory at Texas A&M University.

Type	Trials	Successes	Ave. No. Gens.
N-Genes	20	3	85.0
F-Genes	20	2	74.5
S-Genes	20	6	46.8

Table 2: The number of trials which successfully attained the fitness limit within 100 generations together with the average number of generations it took when this occurred.

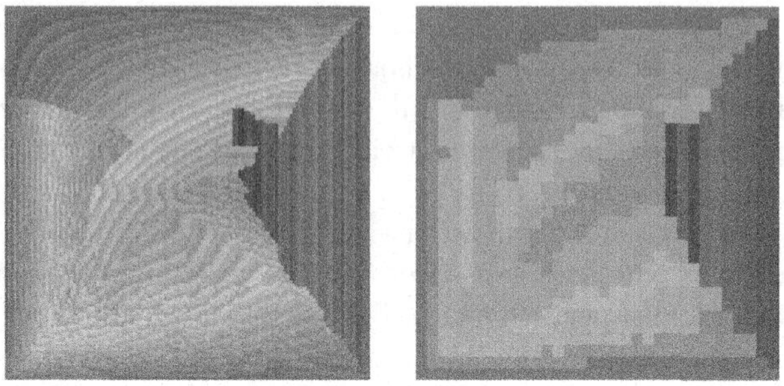

Figure 5: An maximally fit S-Genes example. Left: 128 × 128 resolution. Right: Color segmented image.

References

Baluja, S.; Pommerleau, D.; and Jochem, T. 1994. Towards automated artificial evolution for computer-generated images. *Connection Science* 6:325–354.

Behzad, M.; Chartrans, G.; and Lesniak-Foster L. 1979. *Graphs & Digraphs*. Belmont, CA: Wadsworth.

Greenfield, G. 2000a. Mathematical building blocks for evolving expressions. In Sarhangi, R., ed., *2000 Bridges Conference Proceedings*, 61–70. Winfield, KS: Central Plain Book Manufacturing.

Greenfield, G. 2000b. Art and artificial life — a coevolutionary approach. In Bedau, M. et al, eds., *Artificial Live VII Conference Proceedings*, 529–536. Cambridge, MA: MIT Press.

Greenfield, G. 2002. Color dependent computational aesthetics for evolving expressions. *2002 Bridges Conference Proceedings*, to appear.

Ray, T. 1992. An approach to the synthesis of life. In Langton, C., et al, eds., *Artificial Life II, SFI Studies in the Science of Complexity*, 372–405. Reading, MA: Addison-Wesley.

Sims, K. 1991. Artificial evolution for computer graphics. *Computer Graphics*, 25:319–332.

Diversity Evolution

Russell K. Standish
School of Mathematics, University of New South Wales
2052, Sydney, Australia
R.Standish@unsw,.edu.au
http://parallel.hpc.unsw.edu.au/rks

Abstract

Bedau has developed a general set of evolutionary statistics that quantify the adaptive component of evolutionary processes. On the basis of these measures, he has proposed a set of 4 classes of evolutionary system. All artificial life sytems so far looked at fall into the first 3 classes, whereas the biosphere, and possibly the human economy belongs to the 4th class. The challenge to the artificial life community is to identify exactly what is difference between these natural evolutionary systems, and existing artificial life systems.

At ALife VII, I presented a study using an artificial evolutionary ecology called *EcoLab*. Bedau's statistics captured the qualitative behaviour of the model. *EcoLab* exhibited behaviour from the first 3 classes, but not class 4, which is characterised by unbounded growth in diversity. *EcoLab* exhibits a critical surface given by an inverse relationship between connectivity and diversity, above which the model cannot tarry long. Thus in order to get unbounded diversity increase, there needs to be a corresponding connectivity reducing (or food web pruning) process. This paper reexamines this question in light of two possible processes that reduce ecosystem connectivity: a tendency for specialisation and increase in biogeographic zones through continental drift.

Introduction

During the Phanerozoic (540Mya–present), the diversity of the biosphere (total number of species, also known as biodiversity) has increased dramatically. The trend is most clear for intermediate taxonomic levels (families and orders), as fossil species data is too incomplete and higher taxonomic levels (phylum and class diversity) have been fairly constant since the Paleozoic. A recent review is given by Benton(2001). The most completely documented diversity trend is amongst marine animals, which exhibits a plateau during the Paleozoic (540-300Mya), followed by an accelerating diversity curve since the end of the Permian. The corresponding trend amongst continental, or land animals is characterised by a clear exponential growth since the first species colonised dry land during the Ordovician. Benton argues that the terrestrial trend is more characteristic than the marine trend, owing to the far greater diversity shown amongst land animals, even though the marine fossil record is more complete. Similar trends have been reported for plants(Tiffney & Niklas 1990).

Bedau *et al.*(1998) introduced a couple of measures to capture the amount of adaptation happening in a general evolutionary system. The basic idea is to compare the dynamics of the system with a neutral shadow system in which adaptation is destroyed by randomly mixing adaptive benefits amongst the components of the system (think of the effects ultra-Marxism might have on an economy!). The amount of adaptive activity (numbers of each component in excess of the shadow model integrated over time) and adaptive creativity (numbers of speciations per unit time exceeding a threshold of activity) is measured. Bedau has also introduced a general neutral shadow model that obviates the need to generate one on a case by case basis(Rechtsteiner & Bedau 1999).

Using these measures, it is possible to distinguish 3 classes of activity:

1. unadaptive evolution, when the mutation rate is so high that organisms have insufficient time to have their adaption tested before being killed off by another mutation
2. adapted but uncreative evolution, when species are highly adapted, but mutation is so low that ecosystems remain in perpetual equilibrium
3. creative, adaptive evolution, when new species continuously enter the system, and undergo natural selection

The Biosphere appears to be generating open ended novelty — not only is it creative, but it is *unboundedly* creative. Evidence for this exists in the form of the intricate variety of mechanisms with which different organisms interact with each other and the environment, and also in the sheer diversity of species on the planet. Whilst there is no clear trend to increasing organismal complexity(McShea 1996), there is the clear trend to increasing diversity mentioned above, which is likely to be correlated with ecosystem complexity. Bedau takes diversity as a third evolutionary measure, and distinguishes between *bounded* and *unbounded creative* evolution, according to whether diversity is bounded or not. All artificial evolutionary systems examined to date have, when creative, exhibited bounded behaviour[1]. This was also the case of the *EcoLab* model (Standish 2000). Bedau has laid down a challenge to the artificial life community to create an unbounded, creative evolutionary system.

Ecosystem Complexity

The heart of the idea of unbounded creative evolutionary activity is the creation and storage of information.

[1]Channon(2001) claims his Geb artificial life system exhibits unbounded creative behaviour

The natural measure of this process is *information based complexity*, which is defined in the most general form in(Standish 2001). The notion, drawing upon Shannon entropy and Kolmogorov complexity(Li & Vitányi 1997) is as follows:

A language $\mathcal{L}_1 = (S, \mu)$, is a countable set of possible descriptions S, and a map $\mu : S \to \{0,1\}$. We say that $s, s' \in S$ have the same meaning iff $\mu(s,s') = 1$. Denote the length of s as $\ell(s)$ and $S_n = \{s \in S : \ell(s) = n\}$. The information content (or *complexity*) of a description s is given by:

$$\mathcal{C}(s) = -\lim_{n\to\infty} \log_2 \frac{\mathrm{card}(\{s' \in S_n : \mu(s,s') = 1\})}{\mathrm{card}(S_n)} \quad (1)$$

In the usual case where the interpreter (which defines μ) only examines a finite number of symbols to determine a string's meaning, $\mathcal{C}(s)$ is bounded above by $\ell(s)\log_2 B$ where B is the size of the alphabet. This is equivalent to the notion of *prefix codes* in algorithmic information theory.

Now consider how one might measure the complexity of an ecosystem. Diversity is like a count of the number of parts of a system — it is similar to measuring the complexity of a motor car by counting the number of parts that make it up. But then a junkyard of car parts has the same complexity as the car that might be built from the parts. In the case of ecosystems, we expect the interactions between species to be essential information that should be recorded in the complexity measure. But a simple naive counting of food web connections is also problematic, since how do we know which connections are significant to a functioning ecology?

To put the matter on a more systematic footing, consider a tolerance ε such that $x, y \in \mathbb{R}$ are considered identical if $|x - y| < \varepsilon$. Now two different population dynamics $\dot{x} = f(x)$ and $\dot{x} = f'(x)$, where

$$x \in \mathbb{R}^{n+} \equiv \{x \in \mathbb{R}^n : x_i \geq 0\},$$

can be considered identical (i.e. $\mu(f, f') = 1$ iff[2]

$$|f(x) - f'(x)|_\infty < \varepsilon, \forall x \in \mathbb{R}^{n+}. \quad (2)$$

At this point for the sake of concreteness, let us consider Lotka-Volterra dynamics:

$$\dot{\mathbf{x}} = \mathbf{r} * \mathbf{x} + \mathbf{x} * \beta\mathbf{x} \quad (3)$$

where $*$ refers to elementwise multiplication, $\mathbf{r}$ is the net population growth rate and β is the matrix of interspecific interaction terms.

Over evolutionary time, the growth coefficients r_i, the self-interaction coefficients β_{ii} and the interspecific interaction coefficients $\beta_{ij}, i \neq j$ form particular statistical distributions $p_r(r_i), p_d(\beta_{ii})$ and $p_o(\beta_{ij})$ repectively.

Since inequality (2) must hold over all of the positive cone $\mathbb{R}^{n+}$, it must hold for population density vectors $|x| \ll 1$ and $|x| \gg 1$. In which case eq. (2) can be broken into independent component conditions on $\mathbf{r}$ and β can be written:

$$|r_i - r_i'| \leq \varepsilon, \forall i \quad (4)$$
$$||\beta - \beta'||_\infty \leq \varepsilon. \quad (5)$$

Since these conditions are independent, they contribute additively to the overall complexity (1). The term for the growth coefficients is given by:

$$\mathcal{C}_r = -\log_2 \prod_i \int_{|r_i - r_i'| \leq \varepsilon} p_r(r_i')dr_i' \approx -\sum \log_2 p_r(r_i) - D\log_2 2\varepsilon \quad (6)$$

where $\varepsilon \ll 1$, and D is the ecosystem diversity.

The complexity term for the interaction terms is given by

$$\mathcal{C}_\beta = -\log_2 \int_{\sum_j |\beta_{ij} - \beta_{ij}'| < \varepsilon} \prod_{i\neq j} p_o(\beta_{ij}') \prod_i p_d(\beta_{ij}') \prod_{i,j} d\beta_{ij}'$$
$$\approx \sum_{i\neq j} \log_2 p_o(\beta_{ij}) + \sum_i \log_2 p_d(\beta_{ii}) + D^2 \log_2 2\varepsilon - 1 \quad (7)$$

If ε is chosen very small, the total ecosystem complexity is proportional to D^2. This is because the zeros of the interaction matrix are encoding information. However, if $\varepsilon = \frac{1}{2p_o(0)}$, then (7) becomes:

$$\mathcal{C}_\beta = D^2 C \langle \log_2 p_o(\beta_{ij})\rangle + D\langle \log_2 p_d(\beta_{ii})\rangle + o(D) \quad (8)$$

This gives flesh to our intuitive notion that complexity should somehow be proportional to the number of connections making up the food web.

Empirically, Lotka-Volterra dynamics has been shown to exhibit an inverse relationship between connectivity and diversity $D \propto C^{-1}$(Standish 1998). May(1972) demonstrated this relationship in connection with dynamical stability. However, it seems unlikely that an ecology undergoing evolution is often stable. If this result holds more generally, it implies that complexity is directly proportional to diversity, so that diversity indeed is a good proxy for ecosystem complexity. Although earlier foodweb studies demonstrated this hyperbolic diversity-connectivity relationship, more recently collected data suggests a relationship of the form $D \propto C^{-1+\epsilon}$, with $\epsilon \approx$0.3–0.4 (Drossel & McKane 2002). If complexity indeeds scales superlinearly with diversity

[2] As an anonymous referee pointed out, trajectories described by f and f' may diverge exponentially in time, and that a better definition of equivalence would also require similarity of the attractor sets as well. The results derived here would only be a lower bound of the ecosystem complexity under this more refined definition of equivalence.

as suggested by latter data, then a system displaying open-ended diversity growth is indeed growing in complexity, however a system displaying bounded diversity growth may still be growing in complexity.

EcoLab

EcoLab is an evolutionary ecology, and is to my knowledge the first published account of population dynamics being linked to an evolutionary algorithm(Standish 1994). The next model to be developed in this genre is Webworld(Drossel, Higgs, & McKane 2001), which features a more realistic ecological dynamics, and handles resource flow issues better. Other models in this genre have appeared recently (Christensen *et al.* 2002; Anastasoff 2000).

EcoLab is also the name of a software package used for implementing this model, as well as other models. The software is available from http://parallel.hpc.unsw.edu.au/rks/ecolab.

The model consists of Lotka-Volterra ecology:

$$\dot{\boldsymbol{n}} = \boldsymbol{r} * \boldsymbol{n} + \boldsymbol{n} * \boldsymbol{\beta n} + \texttt{mutate}(\boldsymbol{\mu}, \boldsymbol{r}, \boldsymbol{n}) + \boldsymbol{\gamma} * \nabla^2 \boldsymbol{n}. \quad (9)$$

$\boldsymbol{n}$ is the population density vector, $\boldsymbol{r}$ the growth rates (net births-deaths in absence of competition), $\boldsymbol{\beta}$ the interaction matrix, $\boldsymbol{\mu}$ the (species specific) mutation rates and $\boldsymbol{\gamma}$ the migration rate. In the panmictic case, the $\boldsymbol{\gamma}$ term is left out, and $\boldsymbol{n}$ refers to total populations, rather than population densities.

The mutation operator randomly adds new species i into the system with phenotypic parameters (r_i, β_{ij}, μ_i and γ_i) varied randomly from their parent species. A precise documentation of the mutation operator can be found in the *EcoLab* Technical Report(Standish).

The $\boldsymbol{n}$ vector has integral valued components — in assigning a real valued vector to it, the values are rounded up *randomly* with probability equal to the fractional part. For instance, the value 2.3 has a 30% probability of being rounded up to 3, and a 70% probability of being rounded down. Negative values are converted to zero. If a species population falls to zero, it is considered extinct, and is removed from the system. It should be pointed out that this is a distinctly different mechanism than the threshold method usually employed to determine extinction, but is believed to be largely equivalent.

Diversity D is then simply the number of species with $n_i > 0$, and connectivity is the proportion of interspecific connections out of all possible connections:

$$C = \frac{1}{D^2} \sum_{i,j|\beta_{ij}\neq 0,\, n_i>0,\, \&n_j>0}$$

Spatial *EcoLab* is implemented as a spatial grid, with the ∇^2 term being replaced by the usual 5-point stencil.

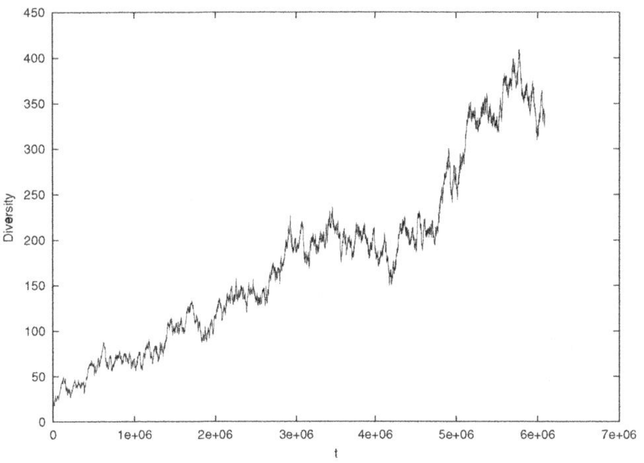

Figure 1: Diversity growth for a typical run with $g = -0.9$

Specialisation

A *specialist* is a species that only depends on a restricted range of food sources, as opposed to a *generalist* which might depend on many food sources. A specialist has fewer incoming predator-prey links in the food web than does a generalist. Much evolutionary variety is expressed in sophisticated defence mechanisms that serve to suppress outgoing predator-prey links. In this context, I will use the term *specialist* in a more general sense to refer to species with a small number of food web links. In order for the panmictic EcoLab model to generate an increasing diversity trend, a corresponding specialisation trend must also be present (which it isn't in the case of the usual mutation operator). Interestingly, specialisation is usually considered to be the default mode of evolution(Vermeij 1987). Generalists only exist because they happen to be more robust against environmental perturbation.

This experiment involves modifying the mutation operator to bias it towards removing interaction terms. The usual *EcoLab* mutation operator operator adds or removes connections according to $\lfloor 1/r \rfloor$, where $r \in (-1,1)$ is a uniform random variate(*EcoLab* Technical Report). In this experiment, a new experimental parameter $g \in (-1,1)$ (`gen_bias`) is introduced such that $r \in (-1+g, 1+g)$ and the number of connections added or deleted is given by $\lfloor (1+\mathrm{sgn}(r)g)/r \rfloor$. By specifying a very negative value of g, the mutation operator will tend to produce specialists more often than generalists. The code for this experiment is released as *EcoLab* 4.2.

A typical run with $g = -0.9$ is shown in Figs. 1–4. As described in (Standish 2000), activity is weighted by the population density, not just presence of a particular species. The results show unbounded creative evolutionary activity (Class 4 behaviour). As can be seen from Fig. 4, the system remains close to the hyperbolic critical surface, yet the dynamic balance has been re-

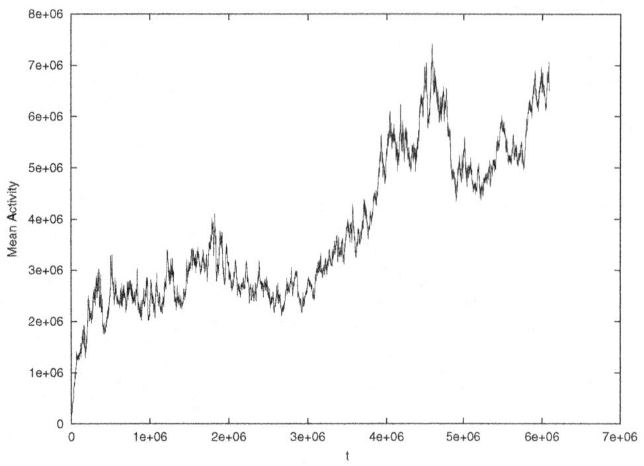

Figure 2: Mean cumulative activity $\bar{A}_{\text{cum}}(t)$

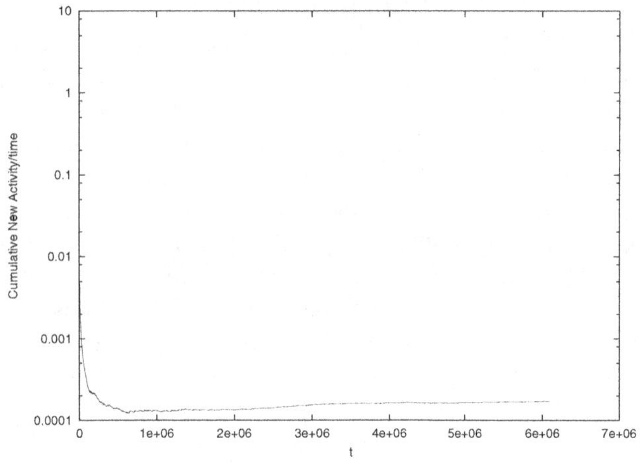

Figure 3: Cumulative New Activity over time $\frac{1}{t}\int_0^t A_{\text{new}}(t)dt$

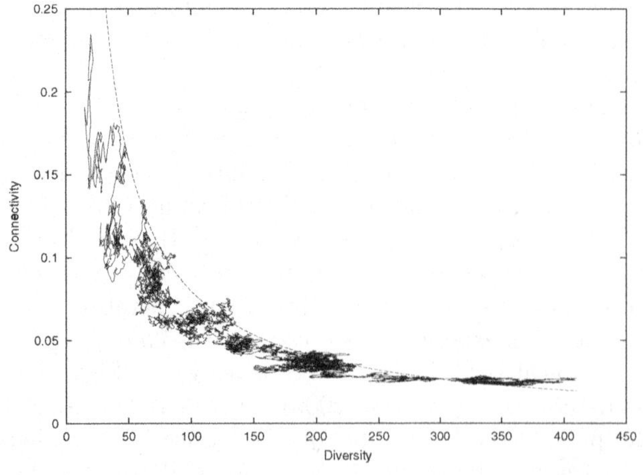

Figure 4: Connectivity vs Diversity for the same run depicted in Figs. 1–3. The dashed curve is $8/D$.

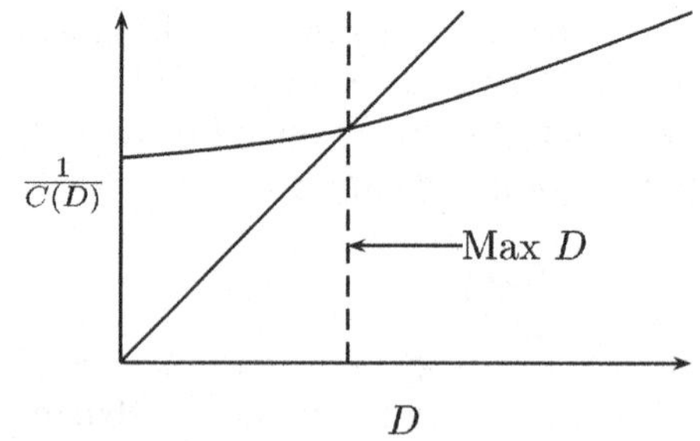

Figure 5: Diversity is constrained to lie under the curve $1/C(D)$. The intersection of this curve with line $y = D$ gives the maximum possible diversity in the ecosystem. If $C(D) \leq o(D^{-1})$, then diversity is unbounded.

moved by the specialisation trend. If we assume that $D \leq C_0/C(D)$, then unbounded diversity growth can only happen if C vanishes at least as fast as $1/D$ (see Fig. 5). An ecosystem consisting entirely of specialists has a constant number of foodweb links per species, or $C \propto 1/D$. The presence of generalists in the ecosystem damps the growth in diversity, and unbounded growth is only possible if the proportion of generalists continually diminishes over time.

Continental Drift

In (Standish 2000), I suggested that one possible explanation for the diversity growth since the end of the Permian was the breakup of the supercontinent Pangaea. A simple estimate given in that paper indicated that the effect might account for a diversity growth of about 3.5 times that existing during the Permian. This was remarkably similar to the growth reported by(Benton 1995), however it is worth noting that Benton's data referred to families, not species. It is expected that the numbers of species *per family* also increased during that time(Benton 2001). Furthermore, when continental organism are included, familial diversity today is more like 5 times the diversity during the Permian.

Unbeknownst to me at the time, Vallentine(1973) had proposed essentially the same theory, called *biogeographic provincialism* (the notion that the number of biological provinces is increased through rearrangement of the continents). The idea received some serious support by Signor(1990), although in a later review he was less enthusiastic(Signor 1994). Tiffney and Niklas(1990) examined plant diversity in the northern hemisphere and concluded that plant diversity correlated more with the land area of lowlands and uplands, rather than continental breakup. Benton(1990) is characteristically sceptical of biogeographic provicialism as an explanation of the diversity trend through the Phanerozoic. Biogeography theory depends on an assumed dynamic balance between speciation and extinction[3], which appears to be contradicted by the fossil data for continental animals(Benton

[3]Benton calls this a *dynamic equilibrium*, although it is

2001), which shows a strong exponential increase in diversity through the Phanerozoic.

Since the EcoLab model has this dynamic balance between speciation and extinction when the dynamics self-organise to the critical surface $D \approx (Cs^2)^{-1}$, I experimented with the spatial version of EcoLab reported in (Standish 1998). The maximum migration rate $|\gamma|_\infty$ was swept up and down exponentially in time according to $0.9^{t/1000}$, *i.e.* with a time constant of about 9500 timesteps, by scaling γ by 0.9 every 1000 timesteps (and then inverting the scaling factor every 174,000 timesteps). It is a little hard to relate EcoLab figures to biological evolution. The maximum growth rate in EcoLab is 0.01, so the doubling time for the fastest organism in the ecosystem is around 100 timesteps. This might correspond to a year or so of real time. So migration rates are being forced much faster than is typical in the real world. However, in EcoLab we also tend run the mutation rate quite high, with adaptive speciations happening every 1000 timesteps or so. If the mutation rate is too high, natural selection has no chance to weed out non-adaptive species, if too low, too much computing resource is need to obtain interesting dynamics. In practice, the mutation rate is set about 2 orders of magnitude less than the critical amount needed for adaptation. In terms of speciation rates, the migration rate time constant might correspond to something of the order of 10^4 years, instead of the 10 years or so one gets from considerations of doubling times.

This code is released as EcoLab 3.5. Due to a design flaw, performance of this code scales poorly with diversity, unless the code is run in parallel with one cell per execution thread. For this experiment, the runs took place on a 2×2 spatial grid, on a four processor parallel computer supplied by the Australian Centre for Advanced Computing and Communications, apart from one run of a 3×3 grid on a 9 processor system. Work is currently underway to implement a spatial version of the EcoLab 4.x code, which does not suffer from this performance problem.

The results of a typical run is shown in figure 6. The run started with a maximum migration rate of 0.01 at the bottom right hand corner of the figure and swept down to 10^{-10} before increasing. The migration rate was swept back and forwards 5 times over the 18 million time steps in the run.

The first thing to note was that the expected response of diversity to migration rate was not there. We would expect a response of the form $D \propto A^c$, with $A = 4$ in the 2×2 case, and c varying smoothly between 1 for the infinite migration (panmictic) case and 2 for zero migration. These results tentatively indicate that possibly

nothing like what the term equilibrium denotes in dynamical system theory, and characterises biogeograhic theories as *equilibrial*

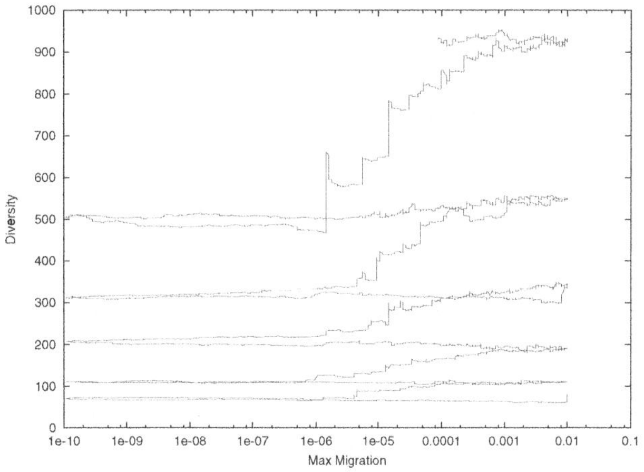

Figure 6: Typical run sweeping the maximum migration rate $|\gamma|_\infty$. The migration operator was applied every 100 time steps, so the units of the x-axis are 0.01 cells per timestep

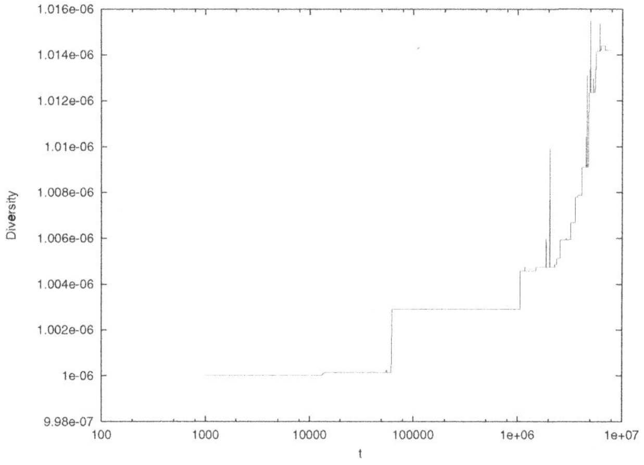

Figure 7: Diversity growth on a 2×2 grid, with $|\gamma|_\infty = 1 \times 10^{-6}$.

c does not vary smoothly at all, but is nearly constant for most values of $|\gamma|_\infty$. This needs to be resolved with further study.

The second thing to note is the completely unexpected "resonance" at about 1×10^{-5}. It is not peculiar statistical aberration, since the same result was obtained with completely different random number seeds, and fixing the migration rate at the resonance value produces an exponential growth in diversity (Figure 7).

3 more tests were performed to determine if this result is an artifact of discretisation, or a feature of the dynamics. The first involved changing the grid to a 3×3 grid, which did not affect the location of the resonance. The second involved scaling all parameters in the model $(\boldsymbol{r}, \boldsymbol{\beta}, \boldsymbol{\mu})$ by 0.1, which is equivalent to changing the timescale. If the effect was purely due to dynamics, one would expect the resonance to shift one order of magni-

tude higher on the scale, however little qualitative different was observed. The third test involved performing the migration operator every 1000 timesteps, instead of 100. This did change the resonance value by 1 order of magnitude, ruling out certain classes of software faults.

Conclusion

The choice of diversity as a proxy measure for ecosystem complexity is a good choice. Complexity is obviously constrained by diversity, so that bounded diversity dynamics also implies bounded complexity dynamics. However, in the case of evolutionary Lotka-Volterra dynamics, the system will tend to self-organise to a critical surface where speciation is balanced by extinction. This surface defines the maximum allowed complexity for a given diversity value, which turns out to be proportional to the diversity. The analysis presented in this paper could be extended to other evolutionary ecologies as well.

Whilst there is still debate about whether the biosphere is exhibiting unbounded complexity growth, I am persuaded by Benton's(2001) argument that the growth is nothing short of spectacular. In this paper I examined two possible mechanisms for diversity growth — *specialisation* which proves capable of delivering unbounded creative evolution in EcoLab, and *biogeographic provincialism*. Whilst I was only expecting biogeographic changes to deliver a modest impact on diversity, EcoLab delivered a unexpected result of a "resonance", where if the migration rate was tuned to this value, diversity grew exponentially.

Acknowledgements

I would like to thank the *Australian Centre for Adavanced Computing and Communications* for the computing resources needed to carry out this project.

References

Anastasoff, S. J. 2000. Ecology and extinction — macroevolutionary extinction dynamics in a simulated ecosystem. In Bedau et al. (2000).

Bedau, M. A.; McCaskill, J. S.; Packard, N. H.; and Rasmussen, S., eds. 2000. *Alife VII: Proceedings of the Seventh International Conference*. Cambridge, Mass.: MIT Press.

Bedau, M. A.; Snyder, E.; and Packard, N. H. 1998. A classification of long-term evolutionary dynamics. In Adami, C.; Belew, R.; Kitano, H.; and Taylor, C., eds., *Artificial Life VI*, 228–237. Cambridge, Mass.: MIT Press.

Benton, M. J. 1990. The causes of the diversity of life. In Taylor, P. D., and Larwood, G. P., eds., *Major Evolutionary Radiations*. Oxford: Clarendon. 409–430.

Benton, M. J. 1995. Diversification and extinction in the history of life. *Science* 268:52–58.

Benton, M. J. 2001. Biodiversity on land and in the sea. *Geological Journal* 36:211–230.

Channon, A. 2001. Passing the alife test: Activity statistics classify evolution in geb as unbounded. In Kelemen, J., and Sosík, P., eds., *Advances in Artificial Life*, volume 2159 of *Lecture Notes in Computer Science*, 417. Berlin: Springer.

Christensen, K.; di Collobiano, S.; Hall, M.; and Jensen, H. 2002. Tangled nature: A model of evolutionary ecology,. *J. Theor. Biol.* 216:73–84.

Drossel, B., and McKane, A. J. 2002. Modelling food webs. In Bornholdt, S., and Schuster, H. G., eds., *Handbook of Graphs and Networks*. Berlin: Wiley-VCH. arXiv:nlin.AO/0202034.

Drossel, B.; Higgs, P. G.; and McKane, A. J. 2001. The influence of predator-prey population dynamics on the long-term evolution of food web structure. *J. Theor. Biol.* 208:91–107.

Li, M., and Vitányi, P. 1997. *An Introduction to Kolmogorov Complexity and its Applications*. New York: Springer, 2nd edition.

May, R. M. 1972. Will a large complex system be stable. *Nature* 238:413–414.

McShea, D. W. 1996. Metazoan complexity and evolution: Is there a trend? *Evolution* 50:477–492.

Rechtsteiner, A., and Bedau, M. A. 1999. A genetic neutral model for quantitative comparison of genotypic evolutionary activity. In Floreano, D.; Nicoud, J.-D.; and Mondada, F., eds., *Advances in Artificial Life*, volume 1674 of *Lecture Notes in Computer Science*, 109. Berlin: Springer.

Signor, P. W. 1990. The geologic history of diversity. *Annual Reviews of Ecology and Systematics* 21:509–39.

Signor, P. W. 1994. Biodiversity in geological time. *American Zoologist* 34:23–32.

Standish, R. K. Ecolab documentation. Available at http://parallel.acsu.unsw.edu.au/rks/ecolab.

Standish, R. K. 1994. Population models with random embryologies as a paradigm for evolution. In *Complex Systems: Mechanism of Adaption*. Amsterdam: IOS Press. also *Complexity International*, **2**.

Standish, R. 1998. Cellular Ecolab. In Standish, R.; Henry, B.; Watt, S.; Marks, R.; Stocker, R.; Green, D.; Keen, S.; and Bossomaier, T., eds., *Complex Systems '98 — Complexity Between the Ecos: From Ecology to Economics.* http://life.csu.edu.au/complex: Complexity Online. 80. also in *Complexity International*, **6**.

Standish, R. K. 2000. An Ecolab perspective on the Bedau evolutionary statistics. In Bedau et al. (2000), 238–242.

Standish, R. K. 2001. On complexity and emergence. *Complexity International* 9.

Tiffney, B. H., and Niklas, K. J. 1990. Continental area, dispersion, latitudinal distribution and topographic variety: A test of correlation with terrestrial plant diversity. In Allmon, W., and Norris, R. D., eds., *Biotic and Abiotic Factors in Evolution.* Chicago: Univ. Chicago Press. 76–102.

Vallentine, J. W. 1973. *Evolutionary Paleoecology of the Marine Biosphere.* Englewood Cliffs, NJ: Prentice-Hall.

Vermeij, G. J. 1987. *Evolution and Escalation.* Princeton, NJ: Princeton UP.

Characterization of Multispecies Living Ecosystems With Cellular Automata

Xin-She Yang
Faculty of Engineering, University of Wales Swansea, Singleton Park, Swansea SA2 8PP, UK
(email: x.s.yang@swansea.ac.uk)

Abstract

A multispecies artificial ecosystem is formulated using cellular automata with species interactions and food chain hierarchy. The constructed finite state automaton can simulate the complexity and self-organized characteristics of the evolving multispecies living ecosystems. Simulations show that a small perturbation or extinction event may affect many other species in the ecosystem in an avalanche manner. Both the avalanches and the extinction arising from these changes follow a power law, reflecting that the multispecies living ecosytems have the characteristics of self-organized criticality.

Introduction

The modelling of artificial life is very important to the understanding of the origin of life and its evolution, thus the studies using computer simulations are very important. Since Langton (1986) relaunched the field of artificial life, the possibly universal aspects of living systems have been investigated by exploring artificial chemistries acting on artificial molecules in terms of rule-based cellular automata (CA). Langton (1986) carried out numerous CA simulations with a parameterization scheme allowing the relationship of Wolfram's classes cataloged the rules that generates different classes of dynamics. Since then there have been many extensive studies about artificial life. Artificial life simulations using cellular automata have received much of interests in the community of artificial life and evolutionary computing. Wolfram (1983, 1984, 1994) pioneered the classification and systematic studies of the complexity of cellular automata. Conway's Game of Life has popularized this area of research. However, most of the existing simulations of CA is about the evolutionary and classification of one single species, and this has demonstrated the complexity and richness of simple rule-based systems. Interestingly, multispecies models have begun to attract much attention (Sole and Manrubia, 1996; Amaral and Meyer,1999). In order to study the ecological effect and the interaction among different species, a multispecies system of artificial life should be explored in detail. It can be expected that the behavior and characteristics of multispecies living system could be very different from that of a single species cellular automaton. Several simulation platforms for artificial life have been developed such as `Avida` and `Tierra`. These powerful platforms can simulate an artificial environment on a two-dimensional grid with rule-based interactions. However, the understanding and studies of artificial life is still at a very early stage.

Since the pioneer work by Bak (1995) and Adami (1995) on self-organized criticality, there have been several studies on the criticality in living systems and other physical systems (Adami, 1995; Abramson and Zanette, 1998; Kauffman, 1995; Gil and Sornette, 1995; Sole and Manrubia, 1996). However, Newman et al (1997) argued that it may not be so. Thus, it still remains as an open issue and the studies of self-organized criticality in different systems require more work. In addition, more studies on the complexity of a multispecies artificial ecosystem and how the local rule-based interactions affect the behavior of the development of the ecosytem are highly needed.

The aim of this paper is to present some new results using a multspecies system of artificial life with cellular automata. By numerical experiments, we will find how the interactions among different species affect the evolutionary behavior and self-organization as well as species extinction events. This paper is orgainised as follows. In the next sections, we describe how to construct the cellular automaton for a multispecies living system, we then implement the system and give some simulations. Based on the simulations, the complexity and entropy of the evolving living system are measured, and the self-organized criticality is tested. The possible reason of extinction behavior of the living system is also explored. The implications of the multispecies interactions will be also discussed.

Rule-Based Cellular Automata for Multi-Species Living Systems

Cellular Automaton (CA) is a finite-state machine on a regular lattice. The input to the machine is the states of all cells in its neighborhood, the change of its state is based on the rules or transition functions. The states of all cells in the lattice are updated synchronously in discrete time steps. Each cell evolves according to the same rules which depend only on the state of the cell and a finite number of neighboring cells, and the neighborhood relation is local and uniform. One classic example is Conway's game of life where one takes a neighborhood consisting of the nearest 8 cells to a cell on a 2-D cellular automaton. Its transition function for the local automaton for two states (1 and 0, or alive and not alive) is as follows: If 2 or 3 neighbors of a cell are alive (or 1) and it is alive at present, then it is alive at next state; If 3 neighbors of a cell are alive and it is currently not alive, its next state is alive; the next state is not alive for all the other cases. Even with these simple rules, a universal computational machine can be constructed on an infinite 2-D grid, which is capable of emulating the computing power of any Turing machine or digital computer.

The present model is an extension of the combined version of the Solé-Manrubia model (1996) and Amaral-Meyer food chain model (1999). The next state C_i for a cell i is determined by the transition function in the general form

$$C_i(t+1) = H[\sum_j G_{ij} C_i(t) - \theta], \tag{1}$$

where H is the Heaviside step function, and θ is the threshold. G_{ij} of the influence of cell j on cell i, $G_{ij} > 0$ or < 0 if j is the food or predator for cell i. The summation is over the nearest neighborhood. The multispecies cellular automaton works in the following way:

1. The CA consists of M interacting species, when $M = 1$ it degenerates into the classic Conway's game of life and obeys the same simple rules.
2. Different sepcies interacts with each other in a way of food chain hierarchy. Each species is label as a hierarchy level and for simplicity, we use the level i for species i with species $i-1$ as the pray or food for species i and species $i+1$ as its predator.
3. In the nearest 8 cells of to a cell of species i, if the number of predators is greater than the number of preys, and the cell is currently alive, then its next state is not alive; If the number of the preys is more than the number of predators, then its next state is alive whether its present state is alive or not; If the predators are in the same number as the prey, the present state does not change.
4. If there is no predator or pray in the 8 neighborhood cells, then the transition function is the same as the single species Conway's cellular automaton.

In the numerical simulations, the 2-D lattice is randomly initialized with the highest population of the lowest level of species $i = 1$. Updating is synchronous. For a regular 100×100 lattice with $N = 256$ species initialized this way, we can investigate the complexity, self-organization, species interaction and avalanche events.

To simulate the effect of species interaction and extinction, a small probability of extinction rate is also introduced into some species, the influence of the extinction of one species on the other species in the food chain model can be studied in some detail. In addition, by introducing some extra population in one species, one can control some other species in the food chain model and give important implications on the ecological effect in reality such as the control of growth rates. A number of numerical experiments have also been investigated. Some trend and self-organized criticality is analyzed from the simulated results.

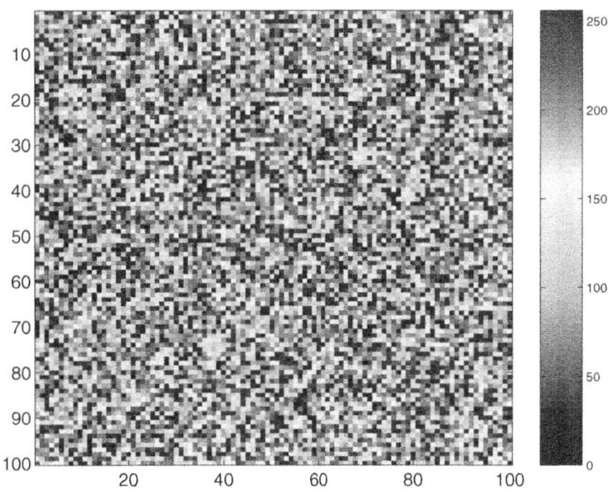

Figure 1: A random configuration of a multispecies cellular automaton with a lattice size of 100×100 and 256 species represented by different colors.

Computer Simulations

By using the cellular automaton described in the above section, we can simulate the behavior of a multspecies living system with multispecies interactions in a food chain hierarchy. In the rest of this paper, we present some results from a huge number of the simulations and parametric studies. A typical initial configuration is shown in Figure 1.

Variation in Complexity and Entropy

For a population size of $N = 100 \times 100$ with $M = 256$, the complexity of the cellular automaton can be measured by its entropy S

$$S = -\sum_i p_i \log p_i, \tag{2}$$

where p_j is the probability of find the species i in the total population (Adami,1998). For a finite population size, p_i can be approximated by the fraction of samples n_i or the number of ith species in the N-species,

$$p_i = \frac{n_i}{N}. \tag{3}$$

The variation of complexity of the 256-species cellular automaton is shown in Figure 2.

It is clearly seen that the complexity varies significantly at the early stage of the development process, then it gradually relaxes to the equilibrium at long time, indicating that the living system is in a quasi-steady state among different species. The relaxation time is typically about 10,000 from an initial configuration to a relative stable pattern or a dynamic equilibrium.

Self-Organized Criticality

Based on the pioneering work by Adami (1995) on the self-organized criticality in living systems using the

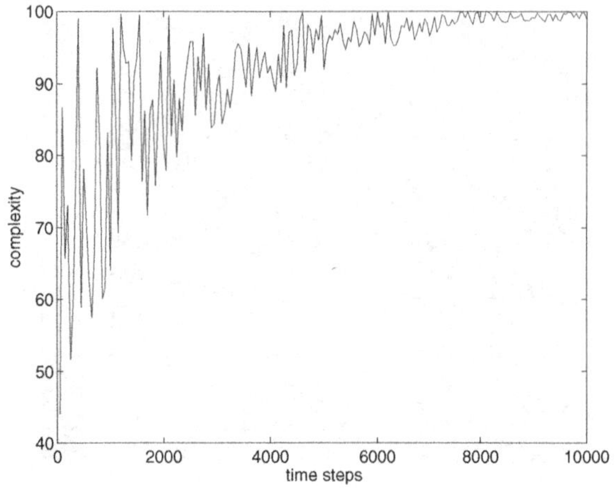

Figure 2: Variations of complexity versus time steps

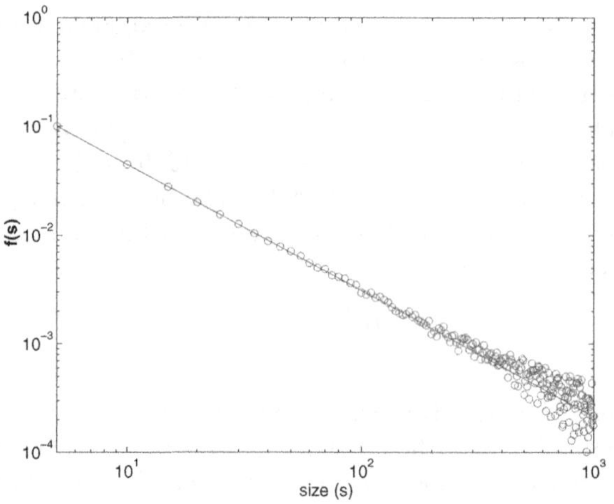

Figure 3: Self-organized criticality in a multispecies living system. The number of avalanches $f(s)$ is a function of avalanche size s. The exponent of the related power-law is $\gamma = 2.26 \pm 0.04$.

`Tierra` experiments, there is a good reason to believe that self-organized criticality exists in the artificial living system. However, the view of self-organized criticality has been challenged by Newman et al (1997) on the ground that the criticality is usually associated with second-order, not first order, critical phenomena. Gil and Sornette (1996) argued that self-organized criticality can be described in terms of first-order transitions.

In order to test whether the self-organized criticality exists in the multispecies living ecosystem, we introduce a small perturbation to ecosystem and measure the population changes affected by the perturbation or avalanche in population and species, this is because the ecosystem can form between all the competing and yet interconnected species. The change in response to any perturbation will enable this living to relax to a new equilibrium or the self-organized state. By tracing the 15000 avalanches obtained from simulations on 100×100 lattice grid, the results are shown in the log-log plot in Figure 3.

This figure clearly show that the avalanches size distribution follows a power-law with the exponent $\gamma = 2.26 \pm 0.04$. This implies that the multispecies living ecosystem has the characteristics of self-organized criticality. This is consistent with the earlier work by Adami (1995). Our present work implies that the self-organized criticality could be universal in living systems.

Extinction

In the above computer simulations, the changes or redistribution of populations of different species have been studied. There may not necessarily involve the extinction of some species. In some case, for example, when the initial population size for some species is very small and its predators are strong, the whole species could become extinct, and the extinction of one species may influence other species in the food chain. To simulate this effect, we introduce an extinction probability $p_e = 0.01$ for a species at some level, say $i = 16$, in the food chain hierarchy. The extinction obtained from the simulations is shown in Figure 4.

The extinction intensities at different time stages (100 time steps as a stage) follow a power-law with an exponent $\gamma = 2.05 \pm 0.1$, which implies that extinction is a self-organized phenomenon. This is consistent with the fitting data $\gamma = 1.7 \pm 0.3$ from the fossil record (Newman and Eble, 1999), and the extinction is a result of external change and species competition.

Discussion

The multispecies ecosystem of artificial life have been formulated in terms of 2-D cellular automata of the combined Sole-Manrubia type together with the Amaral-Meyer food chain model. By using the proper interactions between different species in the food chain hierarchy and the transition function, the finite state automaton can simulate the complexity of the evolving multispecies living ecosystem. Numerical experiments show that the complexity measured by the system entropy fluctuates at early stage of development, then it evolves to the self-organized or dynamic equilibrium sate under certain conditions. By introducing the extra fraction of population or a small perturbation, the species population may be affected at different scales. The avalanches arising from these changes obey a power-law with the exponent $\gamma = 2.26$, reflecting that the multispecies living ecosystem has the characteristics of self-organized criticality. This implies that the self-organized criticality arises naturally in the mulitspecies artificial ecosystem.

One the other hand, in the case of one species in the margin of extinction, it can affect many species in the

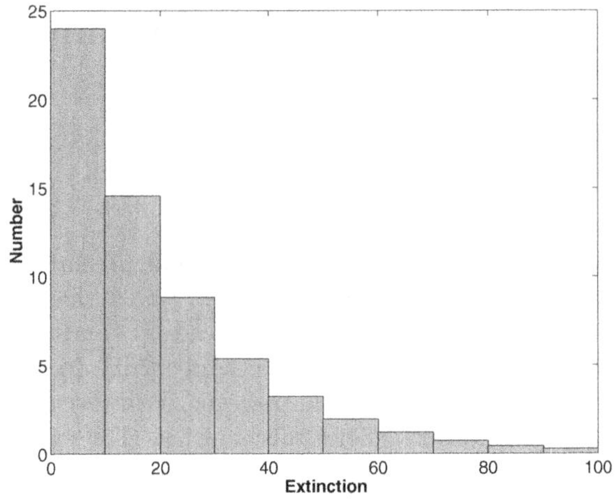

Figure 4: Extinction intensities or number of extinct species at different time stage. The fitting of a power law gives the exponent $\gamma = 2.05 \pm 0.1$.

multispecies living system and can lead some kinds of mass extinction. Simulations also show that the extinction intensities follow a power-law form with the exponent $\gamma = 2.05$, thus indicating the species interaction and competition is the mechanism for the extinction under the action of external changes. Although the present modelling provides a lot of features about the complexity of the artificial living system, much more work is clearly needed to investigate the system behavior such as how different extinction mechanisms and transition rules affect the development of a multispecies living ecosystem.

Acknowledgement: The author thanks the three referees for their very helpful comments.

Reference

Abramson, G and D H Zanette, (1998). Statistics of extinction and survival in Lotka-Volterra systems, *Phys. Rev. E*, 57: 4572.

Adami, C (1995). Self-organized criticality in living systems, *Phys. Lett. A*, 203:23.

Adami, C (1998). Introduction to artificial life, Springer-Verlag, New York.

Adami, C and C T Brown (1994). Evolutionary learning in the 2D artificial life system "Avida", *Proc. of Artificial Life IV*, R Brooks and P Maes, Eds, MIT Press, Cambridge MA, p.377

Amaral, L. A. N. and Meyer, M. (1999). Environmental changes, coextinction, and patterns in the fossil record. *Phys. Rev. Lett.* 82:652.

Bak, P. (1996). *How nature works: The science of self-organized criticality*, Springer-Verlag, New York.

Flake, G A (1998). The computational beauty of nature, MIT press.

Gil L and D Sornette (1996). Landau-Ginburg theory of self-organized criticality, *Phys. Rev. Lett.*, 76:3991.

Kauffman S (1995). *At home in the universe: The search for laws of self-organization and complexity*, Oxford University Press.

Langton (1986). Studying artificial life with cellular automata, *Physica D*, 22:120.

Newman, M. E. J. and Eble, G. J. (1999). Power spectra of extinction in the fossil record. *Proc. R. Soc. London*, B266:1267.

Newman, M E J, S M Fraser, K Sheppen and W A Tozier, (1997). Comment on "Self-organized criticality in living systems" by C Adami, *Phys. Lett. A*, 228:201.

Sole, R. V. and Manrubia, S. C. (1996). Extinction and self-organized criticality in a model of large-scale evolution *Phys. Rev. E*, 54:R42.

Wolfram S (1983). Statistical mechanics of cellular automata, *Rev. Mod. Phys.*, 55:601

Wolfram S (1984). Universility and complexity in cellular automata, *Physica D*, 10:1

Wolfram S (1994). *Cellular automata and complexity*, Reading, Mass.:Addison-Wesley.

Adaptive Populations of Endogenously Diversifying *Pushpop* Organisms are Reliably Diverse

Lee Spector
Hampshire College
Amherst, MA 01002
lspector@hampshire.edu

Abstract

This paper discusses the evolution of diversifying reproduction. We measured the average difference between mothers and their children, the number of species, and the degree of adaptation in evolving populations of endogenously diversifying digital organisms using the *Pushpop* system. The data show that the number of species in adaptive populations is higher than in non-adaptive populations, while the variance in the differences between mothers and their children is less for adaptive populations than for non-adaptive populations. In other words, in adaptive populations the species were more numerous and the diversification processes were more reliable.

Evolution of diversifying reproduction

Questions about the evolution of diversity have a long history, with many proposals having been made to account for the observed diversity of the biosphere (Gould 2002). For example, several authors have discussed how environmental variation and geographical separation can promote diversity, either under the influence of natural selection or without it (genetic drift). These discussions generally build on a foundational assumption that reproductive systems naturally and necessarily produce diversity upon which selection or drift can act. Questions about the evolution of diversity therefore depend on a more fundamental set of questions about the evolution of diversifying reproductive systems.

How do diversifying reproductive systems themselves evolve? Prior work on the origins of life has considered how quasi-reproductive processes in a primeval soup could become sufficiently *non*-diversifying to jump-start a truly reproducing lineage (Maynard Smith & Szathmáry 1999). A common assumption for the aftermath of such an event is that natural selection will act to refine the reproduction process to improve replication accuracy within limits imposed by the reliability of the underlying chemistry. George C. Williams made the case as follows:

> The fittest possible degree of stability is absolute stability. In other words, natural selection of mutation rates has only one possible direction, that of reducing the frequency of mutation to zero.
>
> That mutations should continue to occur after billions of years of adverse selection requires no special explanation. It is merely a reflection of the unquestionable principle that natural selection can often produce mechanisms of extreme precision, but never of perfection. (Williams 1966, pp. 138–9).

Perfectly accurate reproduction would preclude evolution; Williams understood this and wrote that "evolution takes place, not so much because of natural selection, but to a large degree in spite of it" (p. 139). Williams's view is in tension, however, with recent work on the evolution of genetic mechanisms. For example, the diversifying function of recombination is central to most theories of the evolution of sex, and Maynard Smith and Szathmáry note that "every sexual population that has been carefully studied has been found to have genetic variability in the rate of recombination" (Maynard Smith & Szathmáry 1999, p. 90). Recent work on microbiological mechanisms of diversification (e.g. gene duplication, shuffling, and horizontal gene transfer) reinforces the view that methods and degrees of diversification are themselves products of complex evolutionary histories and that an understanding of the origins and evolution of life will require an understanding of these histories.

Diversification of digital organisms

Populations of digital organisms (computer programs that run and reproduce in a simulated environment) can be used to study general features of evolutionary systems. For example, Ray's Tierra system (Ray 1991) has been used to study the evolution of parasitism, and Adami's Avida system has been used to study the "survival of the flattest" (that is, the survival of otherwise mediocre but reproductively robust replicators) in environments with high mutation rates (Wilke *et al.* 2001).

In most work on digital organisms diversification is exogenously controlled. In Tierra and Avida certain operations (for example code-copying) are automatically subject to random errors (mutations) that occur with a probability set by the experimenter. This provides a ready-made (and in fact unavoidable) diversification mechanism: exact cloning is usually a simple procedure in these systems, and any organism that attempts to clone itself will automatically produce diverse offspring. It is possible for programs in these systems to diversify in other ways as well, but the external control of diversification limits the questions that one can ask about the evolution of the diversification mechanisms themselves. Most prior work also requires seeding with a hand-crafted "ancestor" replicator, further pre-determining the resulting reproduction and diversification mechanisms. An exception is Amoeba (Pargellis 2001), in which replicators are produced by spontaneous generation in a process that is nonetheless driven by exogenously controlled mutation.

The biological phenomena at issue in the present study can best be studied in systems within which replication and diversification strategies must emerge *ex nihilo*, and within which the degrees and types of diversification are endogenously controlled and thereby subject to selection and evolution. Such systems can be used to explore questions about how the nature of the emergent diversification mechanisms relates to other features of an evolving population, for example adaptation.

A large body of previous work has explored "self-adaptive" evolutionary computation in problem-solving contexts (see, e.g., (Stephens *et al.* 1998)). In most of these studies the algorithms for reproduction and diversification are fixed in advance although numerical parameters (such as mutation rates) are subject to variation and selection. Systems capable of more completely endogenous diversification include Edmonds's tree-based "Meta-Genetic Programming" system (Edmonds 1998), Teller's graph-based PADO system (Teller 1996), and the stack-based Pushpop system described below.

Methods

The experiments were conducted using the *Pushpop* system that evolves digital organisms expressed in the Push programming language (Spector 2001; Spector & Robinson 2002). Push is a high-level, stack-based language that supports flexible manipulation of multiple types of data including Push code. Pushpop is an *autoconstructive evolution system*, which is defined in (Spector & Robinson 2002) to be "any evolutionary computation system that adaptively constructs its own mechanisms of reproduction and diversification as it runs." A more conventional genetic programming system that evolves Push programs (PushGP) has also been developed.

The Pushpop algorithm is best understood as a variant of a traditional genetic programming algorithm (Koza 1992). Evaluation of an organism's fitness in Pushpop produces a numerical measure of the organism's problem-solving ability and also a collection of potential children (Push programs). "Fitness" here, as in most genetic programming work, denotes the performance of an individual on a computational problem that is used to determine survival; fitness causes reproductive success here, in contrast to conventional biological usage. Children are added to the following generation on the basis of fitness tournaments between their mothers — they themselves have not yet been tested for fitness, so their own fitness values cannot be used for this purpose. If there are insufficient children to populate the next generation (in which case the population is not yet "reproductively competent") then randomly generated organisms are used. Most runs become permanently reproductively competent after at most a few hundred generations. We generally continue running Pushpop even after a solution has been found, in order to observe the changes in evolutionary dynamics that follow such an event. More information on Push, PushGP, and Pushpop, including source code for Push and PushGP, can be found at `http://hampshire.edu/lspector/push.html`.

In this study we enforced a "no cloning" policy: children were never added to a population if they were identical (genotypically) to their mothers or to other children already in the population. Without such a policy, and without imposed mutations, perfect replicators quickly overwhelm the population, precluding future evolution. It is critical to note that the no cloning policy forces mothers to diversify their children but it does *not* constrain, to any significant degree, the manner or amount of diversification. In particular, minimal diversification strategies (e.g. those that change only a single, unused symbol from mother to child) are possible and do in fact emerge (as shown in the data below). The no cloning policy mandates that *some* diversification occur, but neither the methods nor the degree of diversification are pre-determined by the no cloning policy.

The Push language includes a rich library of code-manipulation instructions that can be used by organisms to construct their offspring. These instructions *allow* for the use of copy-error-based reproduction strategies of the sort used in Tierra and Avida, but their availability does not mandate the use of such strategies, pre-determine parameters for such strategies, or limit the ways in which such strategies can be combined with different reproductive methods.

Pushpop is capable of solving relatively difficult computational problems in comparison to other digital organism systems. Avida is usually assessed on simple 2-input Boolean problems, which is reasonable considering the low-level assembly language in which Avida programs are expressed. Tierra and Amoeba were not designed to be used in problem-solving contexts, so problem-based measures of the adaptation of a population are not available. With Pushpop we generally use standard test problems from the genetic programming literature, often involving numbers or other data types.

Parameters were chosen to produce roughly the same number of adaptive and non-adaptive populations. The population size was 1024, the number of generations was 2048, the tournament size was 4, the fitness-conferring problem was integer symbolic regression (Koza 1992) of $y = 5x^2 + x - 2$ with 16 fitness cases($x = 0$ to $x = 15$), the instruction execution limit was 64, the maximum number of points (symbols and pairs of parentheses) in a program was 64, and the full standard Push instruction set was available. In half of the runs we included instructions (`NEIGHBOR`, `ELDER`, and `OTHER`) that support sexual recombination of evolving organisms by allowing an executing organism to access the code of other organisms; see (Spector & Robinson 2002) for details.

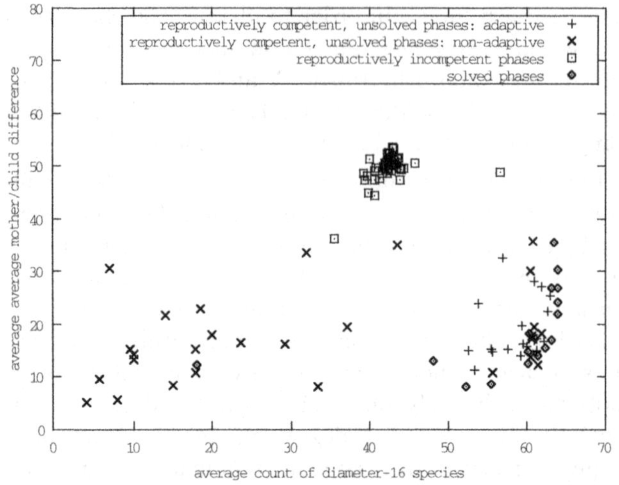

Figure 1: Data from runs that included sexual operators.

We measured the average difference between mothers and their children, the number of species, and the degree of adaptation of each population each generation. The difference between two organisms was calculated as the sum, over all unique expressions in either of their programs, of the difference between the numbers of occurrences of the expression in the two programs. The number of species in a population was estimated from a sample of 64 organisms, using a "greedy" algorithm that attempts to merge the organisms into a minimum number of groups while ensuring that the maximum difference between organisms in a group does not exceed a specified species diameter (16 here, though we obtained similar results using other diameters). The degree of adaptation of a population was assessed from the fitness of the best organism in the population each generation.[1] We report the sum of the errors that the best organism produces over a set of inputs for the fitness-conferring problem ("fitness cases"); the lower this number is, the better the organism is adapted to its environment. We classified an entire run as "adaptive" if the average best fitness over the last 20 generations of the run was less than 200 (significantly better than is normally achieved by random individuals), and "non-adaptive" otherwise. We conducted 48 independent runs that included the sexual instructions and 48 independent runs without the sexual instructions.

Results and Analysis

Figure 1 shows the results of the 48 independent runs that included the sexual instructions. The graph plots *phases* of runs on axes of number of species (averaged over the phase) and average mother/child difference (also averaged over the phase). Each run begins with a reproductively incompetent phase; these phases are represented with square points. All of the runs in the study eventually achieved reproductive competence, and their reproductively competent phases (minus any generations at which there was a perfect solution to the fitness-conferring problem) are plotted using + for adaptive runs or × for non-adaptive runs. For runs that eventually produced perfect solutions to the fitness-conferring problem the phases during which they did so are plotted with diamond-shaped points.

The most obvious effect visible in the data is the clustering of most adaptive runs (in their reproductively competent, non-solution phases) between 50 and 64 (which is the maximum) diameter-16 species, a pattern clearly different from the results for non-adaptive runs, which span a range from about 5 to 64. Another notable effect is the clustering of the adaptive runs (in their reproductively competent, non-solution phases) between approximately 10 and 30 on the measure of mother/child differences. Non-adaptive runs exhibit a wider variance, ranging from less than 5 to approximately 35. This difference is significant with $p < 0.001$ using an F test.

Data from sexual vs. asexual runs appeared to differ only with respect to their reproductively incompetent phases, during which the asexual runs (not shown here) exhibited lower average mother/child differences and much lower numbers of diameter-16 species. This reflects the combinatorics of the available instruction set rather than any feature of an evolving population, as most organisms are random and there is no selection pressure during these phases. It is interesting that after reproductive competence the sexual and asexual runs are nearly indistinguishable. The data show that the sexual instructions are in fact used throughout the runs in which they are available, but their use does not seem to have an impact on mother/child differences or numbers of species.

A final set of observations concerns the effects of finding a perfect solution to the fitness-conferring problem. One might expect that the production (and maintenance) of a perfect solution would decrease the selective advantage to species that diversify their children; when one is already doing as well as possible there would seem to be little advantage to be gained from further diversification. Indeed, in many runs the mother/child differences did decrease after a solution was found. But the effect seems to be more complex than this simple analysis would suggest. In some instances the mother/child differences *increased* after a solution was found and there appear to be effects on numbers of species as well. Figure 1 reveals an interesting pattern here; the diamonds (representing the solved phases) form a semicircle around the cluster of plusses (representing the unsolved phases of the adaptive runs). It appears that the production of a

[1]We did not use average fitness because large fitness penalties for arithmetic errors and nontermination, inspired by standard practice in GP, make such averages erratic.

perfect solution is generally followed by movement away from the center of the cluster of points characterizing adaptive phases (and generally, but not always, in the direction of more species and/or smaller mother/child differences).

In summary the data show that the number of species in adaptive populations falls within a narrow, high range relative to non-adaptive populations. The data also show that the variance in the differences between mothers and their children is less for adaptive populations than for non-adaptive populations. In other words, in adaptive populations the species were more numerous and the diversification processes were more reliable. If the populations studied here were sub-populations within a larger environment then population-level selection effects (such as those called for in hierarchical theories of selection (Gould 2002)) would indirectly favor species-rich sub-populations with reliable diversification mechanisms. This provides one possible explanation for the evolution of diversifying reproductive systems.

Conclusions and Future Work

The reported data show patterns in the reproductive strategies of evolving populations of digital organisms. In the context of the studied parameters, adaptive populations were reliably diverse. In particular, the number of species in adaptive populations fell within a narrow, high range relative to non-adaptive populations, and the variance in the differences between mothers and their children was less for adaptive populations than for non-adaptive populations. These results are relevant to several open problems in artificial life, including challenges to achieve the transition to life in silico and to determine what is inevitable in the open-ended evolution of life.

The system used for the experiments, an "autoconstructive evolution" system called Pushpop, allows the reproductive and diversification mechanisms of the evolving organisms to evolve, thereby providing data not readily available from other digital organism systems. Pushpop runs produce large volumes of data and there are many other phenomena of biological interest that might be studied in this data. One avenue of research that we are currently pursuing derives from the observation that Pushpop organisms can exhibit ontogenetic development (through the use of self-modifying code) and that this development, along with other aspects of their behavior, may vary depending on input and environment. This opens the possibility that Pushpop runs could be used to study relations between adaptation and developmental and behavioral plasticity, an issue of considerable current interest in evolutionary biology.

Acknowledgments Thanks are due to Rebecca S. Neimark, Mark Feinstein, Alan Robinson, Ray Coppinger, and the Defense Advanced Research Projects Agency and Air Force Research Laboratory (agreement number F30502-00-2-0611).

References

Edmonds, B. 1998. Meta-genetic programming: Co-evolving the operators of variation. CPM Report 98-32, Centre for Policy Modelling, Manchester Metropolitan University, UK, Aytoun St., Manchester, M1 3GH. UK.

Gould, S. J. 2002. *The Structure of Evolutionary Theory.* Cambridge, MA: Harvard University Press.

Koza, J. R. 1992. *Genetic Programming: On the Programming of Computers by Means of Natural Selection.* Cambridge, MA: MIT Press.

Maynard Smith, J., and Szathmáry, E. 1999. *The Origins of Life.* Oxford University Press.

Pargellis, A. N. 2001. Digital life behavior in the amoeba world. *Artificial Life* 7:63–75.

Ray, T. S. 1991. Is it alive or is it GA. In Belew, R. K., and Booker, L. B., eds., *Proceedings of the Fourth International Conference on Genetic Algorithms*, 527–534. University of California - San Diego, La Jolla, CA, USA: Morgan Kaufmann.

Spector, L., and Robinson, A. 2002. Genetic programming and autoconstructive evolution with the push programming language. *Genetic Programming and Evolvable Machines* 3(1):7–40.

Spector, L. 2001. Autoconstructive evolution: Push, pushgp, and pushpop. In Spector, L.; Goodman, E.; Wu, A.; Langdon, W. B.; Voigt, H.-M.; Gen, M.; Sen, S.; Dorigo, M.; Pezeshk, S.; Garzon, M.; and Burke, E., eds., *Proceedings of the Genetic and Evolutionary Computation Conference, GECCO-2001*, 137–146. Morgan Kaufmann Publishers.

Stephens, C. R.; Olmedo, I. G.; Vargas, J. M.; and Waelbroeck, H. 1998. Self-adaptation in evolving systems. *Artificial Life* 4:183–201.

Teller, A. 1996. Evolving programmers: The co-evolution of intelligent recombination operators. In Angeline, P. J., and Kinnear, Jr., K. E., eds., *Advances in Genetic Programming 2.* Cambridge, MA, USA: MIT Press. chapter 3, 45–68.

Wilke, C. O.; Wang, J. L.; Ofria, C.; Lenski, R. E.; and Adami, C. 2001. Evolution of digital organisms at high mutation rates leads to survival of the flattest. *Nature* 412:331–333.

Williams, G. C. 1966. *Adaptation and Natural Selection.* Princeton, NJ: Princeton University Press.

Multilevel Selection and the Evolution of Predatory Restraint

Joshua Mitteldorf[1], **David H. Croll**[2] and **S. Chandu Ravela**[3]
[1]University of Pennsylvania, Philadelphia, PA 19104, josh@mathforum.org
[2]Regis College, Weston, MA 02493 david.croll@regiscollege.edu
[3]University of Massachusetts, Amhest, MA 01003, ravela@cs.umass.edu

Abstract

Individual selection favors that predator which can most efficiently turn its prey into increased reproductive capacity. But any species that becomes too successful in this game sows the seed of its own demise; for its progeny may be delivered into an environment where prey populations are depleted, and starvation a danger. From this danger derives a compensatory evolutionary pull toward moderation. The latter effect derives from a cost that is shared generally by the community that claims a common prey population. A widely accepted argument from classical evolutionary theory holds that the selective force of such group effects is likely to be weak and slow-acting compared to the efficiency of individual selection. We offer a numerical simulation in defiance of this wisdom, demonstrating how under general assumptions and a wide range of parameter values, predatory restraint may evolve as a group adaptation.

Introduction

Do animal populations self-regulate for the sake of demographic stability? Over-exploitation of food resources may threaten the viability of the species on which a predator depends, leading to extinction of both predator and prey. But maintaining consumption within sustainable limits requires cooperation, explicit or implicit, as individual fitness may be diminished by any moderation of consumption. Classical population genetics, based on the maximization of individual reproductive potential, supports the conclusion that the evolution of population limits as an adaptation is improbable. Field studies and the experience of wildlife managers suggest that population regulation may be a reality, though clean tests of group adaptation are rare. We report the results of simulation studies, indicating one mechanism by which predator restraint and population regulation may evolve.

Historic context

Population control is a stark example of strong conflicting interests, pitting the individual against the group. It is not surprising that this issue has played a key role in a historical debate concerning the viability of group selection as an evolutionary force. Evidence for the thesis was first described comprehensively by Wynne-Edwards (1962), but a new breed of quantitative evolutionary theorists met his claims with skepticism bordering on derision (Williams 1966). Williams argued persuasively that populations with large numbers of altruistic individuals would be susceptible to invasion by selfish individuals. Maynard Smith (1964, 1976) noted that the high extinction rate required for limiting the spread of selfish individuals from invaded populations would be unlikely to attain in nature.

But even as the concept of group selection lost currency in circles of theoretical evolution, minority theorists were already suggesting ways that nature might find paths to those adaptations that would succeed at higher levels of organization, over longer periods of time. Multilevel selection theory, developed by Wilson (1975, 1983, 1997) on the foundation of the Price (1970) Equation, seeks to predict the outcome when selection at the individual and the group level are at odds. But a key parameter in this calculation is the relatedness (or genetic covariance) within groups (Hamilton 1964), which is difficult to measure or to predict. Numerical simulations provided a complementary way to explore a variety of assumptions about population dynamics within and among groups. An early simulation by Gilpin (1975) made the most of limited computer resources, to demonstrate ways that predatory restraint might evolve, and predator-prey population dynamics might be damped.

Gilpin's model used difference equations to track the frequencies of two genes, for restrained and unrestrained predation, across an ensemble of patches, linked by random migration. He found that this system was robust in its ability to evolve prudent predation, and argued in his monograph that his assumptions were conservative and generally applicable, his results realistic. Nevertheless, few evolutionary theorists of the era were ready to accept his conclusions.

Field evidence

There is abundant suggestive evidence from field and experimental studies indicating the reality of population self-regulation. Fruitflies and nematodes appear to suppress their fertility in response to crowding, even with abundant nutrition (Guarente & Kenyon 2000). Observations in the wild suggest that rabbits exhibit the same response (Bittner & Chapman 1981). Arctic caribou in a fragile tundra environment breed less frequently than animals of the same species further south (Wynne-Edwards 1962). When deer are plentiful, wolves kill more deer and consume less of each (Kolenosky 1972). And the accumulated anecdotal experience of wildlife managers has created in that culture a belief that predator populations self-regulate (Nudds 1987). For each of these examples, evidence is not clean enough to rule out explanations from individual self-interest, which are deemed theoretically more conservative.

Recent models of predator restraint

Recent computer simulations suggest a renewed examination of the theoretical issue. Pepper and Smutts (2001) have modeled competing populations of restrained and unrestrained foragers, interacting in an environment where the only group structure is imposed by isolated patches of available food. Like Gilpin, they report a range of parameter values under which the restrained foragers can prevail. Rand et al (1995) have modeled a generic host-pathogen system using a simple CA model. They evolve a gene for pathogen transmissibility, and find that above a critical value, the pathogen experiences local extinctions, creating a void that is refilled from the boundary by pathogens with lower transmissibility. Haraguchi and Sasaki (2000), and Rauch and Bar-Yam (2002) each report similar results, with enriched detail. These models are conceptual kin to our own, but with simpler rules and a map that allows a maximum of one predator per grid site. Most recently, models by Pels *et al.* (2002) have sought to characterize environments under which predator evolution does not lead to global extinction.

Description of Our Model

We have implemented an individual-based model that features competition among predators within each site on an $n \times n$ viscous grid. Within each site, predators reproduce in proportion to the prey that they capture. Their rate of prey capture is controlled by a single gene (*appetite*). Adjacent grid sites are connected by slow, random migration of both predators and prey, allowing for between-group competition in exportation of migrants.

Prey and predator behaviors

Prey are programmed individually so as to conform collectively to a logistic population dynamic. In each time step, they acquire *maturity* points, with probability inverse proportion to the current prey population at the site. When a fixed number of points is accumulated, the prey reproduces, simply turning into two prey, each with zero points. Except for point count, prey are indistinguishable. Prey interact in each time step with each predator at the same grid site, and the interaction carries a risk of death for the prey in proportion to the predator's *appetite*. This is the only manner in which prey may die.

Predator behaviors

Predators are characterized by a single gene, an integer variable controlling their *appetite*. Predators are programmed to keep track internally of an *energy reserve*. A fixed quantity of *energy (cost-of-living)* is lost in each time step. If *energy* falls to zero, the predator dies; if *energy* reaches a *threshold* value, the predator reproduces, passing half its *energy* to an offspring. The *appetite* gene is inherited, with a small *mutation* probability that it will be increased or decreased by one unit. There is also a fixed probability per time step that each predator might experience *accidental-death*.

Global aspects of the ensemble

Sites are statistically identical, and are arrayed on a cartesian grid, typically 16×16 or 32×32. *Migration* rates (the same for predators and prey) control the probability that each individual would migrate to a von Neumann neighbor in a given time step.

Heuristic dynamics of the model

Within each grid site, predators with higher *appetite* reproduce at a faster rate. But as *appetite* evolves to values that are unsustainably high, the prey population is depleted and the predators starve. The site may have a small residual population of prey, or it may have to await prey migration from a neighboring site. Once a prey population is established, the site can again support predators that migrate in from a neighboring site. The migrants are likely to come from a site which has not yet reached unsustainable levels of *appetite*, so local extinction and migration serves as a tempering influence on the individual selection pressure for unbounded *appetite*.

Relationship to Lotka-Volterra Equations

The Lotka-Voltera equations can be written

$$\begin{aligned}\frac{d\ln(x)}{dt} &= r(1 - x/K) - cy \\ \frac{d\ln(y)}{dt} &= bcx - d \qquad (1)\end{aligned}$$

The three dynamic variables are:

x, the prey population

y, the predator population

t, time

and the five parameters are:

r, the exponential growth rate of the prey population, capped by a logistic population ceiling, K

K, the population scale of prey species. Though it was not originally part of Lotka or Voltera's formulation, it has become accepted as a common modification, because it is a realistic generalization that allows for solutions that oscillate less wildly.

c, the capture rate per individual predator-prey encounter

b, the predator population growth associated with each capture event

d, the predator death rate, conventionally taken as constant and independent of other conditions

Relationship of individual behaviors to population behaviors in Lotka-Voltera

The present model is individual-based, so our parameters relate to individual behaviors; nevertheless, a correspondence can be seen between the model parameters and the L-V parameters. Our parameters are:

maturity, the quantity of points accumulated by a prey that triggers reproduction

threshold, the quantity of energy accumulated by a predator to trigger reproduction

accidental-death, the probability per time step of a predator dying when he is not starving

cost-of-living, an amount of energy lost by each predator in each time step, meal, the quantity of predator energy credited to each successful act of predation

K, crowding factor, inhibiting prey reproduction

Some of the connections between our individual-based parameters and the population dynamic parameters of L-V are clear; others are less obvious. The crowding factor K that inhibits prey reproduction in our model corresponds closely to the logistic K, which is also the K of the L-V equation. *Maturity* is the doubling time for prey population, and should relate to r of L-V simply by

$$r = \ln(2)/maturity$$

The *appetite* variable which is the target of evolution in our model corresponds closely to the capture rate c of L-V.

The other correspondences are more subtle. The L-V variables are numbers of organisms; our model also tracks internal energy of the predators. How much energy is equivalent to one animal? An accumulation of *threshold/2*, is sufficient to create a new predator, so we take this as an equivalent. Then the L-V parameter b, which controls what fraction of a predator is created each time a prey is consumed, may be related to our parameters by

$$b = 2 \times meal/threshold$$

Corresponding to the L-V death rate, the parameter d, we have two ways in which a predator may die; *accidental-death* kills one predator at a time, but also takes with him the energy he may have accumulated toward creating another. A reasonable estimate is to call this a loss of 3/2 predators. In addition, cost-of-living is the energy that is subtracted from each predator in each time step, so the fraction of a predator lost is

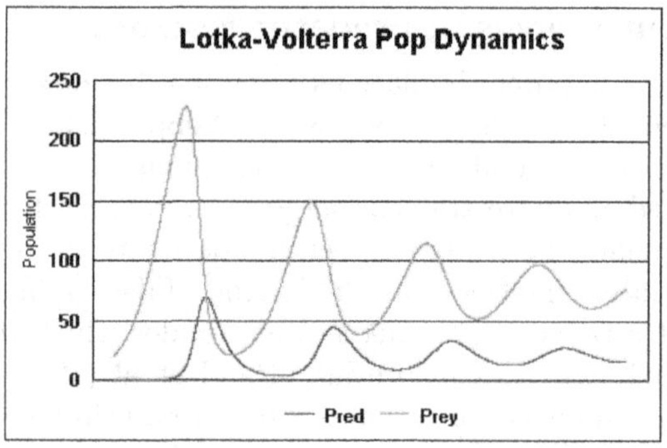

Figure 1: Lotka-Voltera population dynamics, showing the familiar predator and prey cycles, with damping due to the logistic limit K to prey population growth. Both predator and prey populations tend to steady-state values over time.

$2 \times cost - of - living/threshold$. Putting these together, we have

$$d = 3/2 \times accidental - death + 2 \times cost - of - living/threshold$$

Lotka-Voltera dynamics

With the added parameter K, the L-V dynamic variables follow a damped version of the familiar periodic curves, relaxing exponentially toward their steady state values x_o and y_o with a decay time of Q cycles (Figure 1).

The values x_o and y_o can be found algebraically by setting both logarithmic derivatives of Eqn 1 to zero:

$$\begin{aligned} x_o &= d/(bc) \\ y_o &= (r/c)(1 - d/(bcK)) \end{aligned}$$

The damping parameter Q is given by

$$Q = K/x_o = bcK/2d$$

This analysis has informed our exploration of parameter space for the model. x_o and y_o should simply scale the predator and prey population sizes, while Q should control the dynamic stability; large Q (high K) leads to an unstable dynamic, in which predators must be more conservative to avoid extinction. We have also explored the response to r and d, the dynamic time scales associated with prey and predator populations, respectively; the ratio of these two time scales is a dimensionless parameter that also has an interesting effect. (The other variable which we have explored in our analysis is migration rate, which is a property of the ensemble rather than the site dynamics, and hence has no analog within L-V.)

Results

Confirming the viability of group selection

Gilpin's major result was that "over a wide range of parameter values and initializations, group selection can

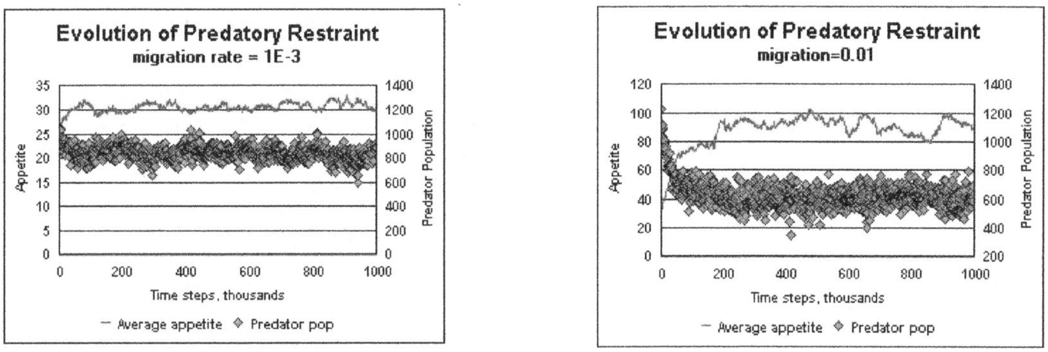

Figure 2: For intermediate values of the migration parameter, the appetite gene is found to stabilize at a moderate value, and populations fluctuate within limits.

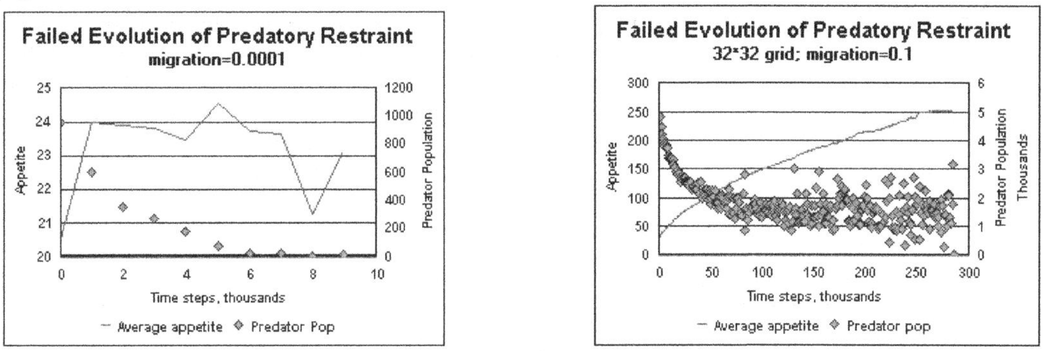

Figure 3: For values of the migration parameter that are too low, the population quickly drives itself to extinction; for values that are too high, the appetite gene increases without bound, in a grid that is dense with prey but mostly empty of predators.

prevail against individual selection and send gene a, the less efficient exploitation gene, to fixation throughout an ensemble of predator populations". In the present model, selection is not restricted to an either-or choice, but is permitted a range of the *appetite* gene corresponding to exploitation efficiency. We find that over a wide range of parameter values, group selection can compete effectively with individual selection to temper the pressure toward an unsustainable level of exploitation, and establish a steady state with bounded appetite that is (globally) stable over many generations and many site extinction times.

Effect of varying migration rate

Interaction among groups is mediated by the migration rate. For values of the migration parameter that are too high, the entire ensemble behaves as a single population. Inter-site differences are washed out, so there can be no effective competition between groups. The result is that *appetite* increases without bound, and the entire predator population is driven to extinction. Typically, a few prey survive to regenerate full population of the grid. In our model, *migration* levels higher than ≈ 0.03 led to this scenario. (This represents the probability of a given predator emigrating from the site in a given time step.)

If the migration parameter is too low, the sites are effectively isolated. One site may evolve an unsustainably high level of *appetite*, and disappear; before it can be reseeded, its neighbor sites may also evolve to extinction. Again, in our model a few prey escape and survive to repopulate the grid. This scenario prevailed for migration values less than ≈ 0.0002.

In a few runs, we allowed the two species to have separate *migration* rates. High prey migration rates posed a substantial danger to stability, and selection for a moderate *appetite*; predator *migration* rates were associated with runaway *appetite* only at levels an order of magnitude higher.

Some results for a range of migration rates are plotted in Figures 2 – 3.

Thus we find *appetite* remains stably enough within bounds over two orders of magnitude in the *migration* parameter. More complex and realistic scenarios in which migration rates are sometimes within and sometimes outside this range are explored below.

Effect of varying per-site carrying capacity

The parameter K controls the maximum number of prey that can be supported at a site in the absence of predation. Both total predator and prey populations increase

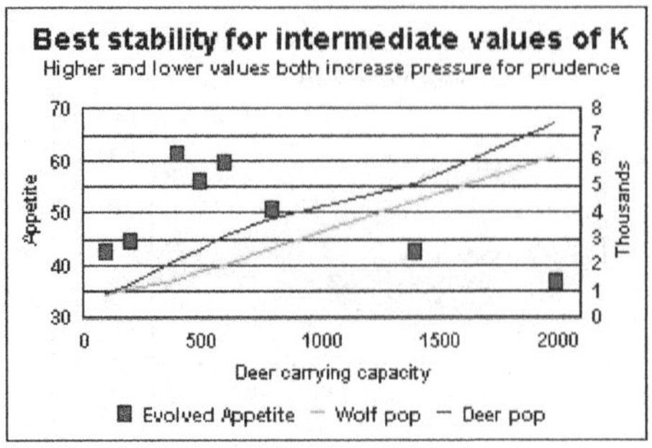

Figure 4: The carrying capacity per site, K, controls steady-state prey population linearly, as we would expect. But evolved appetite exhibits a surprising response, declining for values that are either too high or too low. Low K is inherently unstable because small numbers may fluctuate to zero; high K implies high Q, which decreases the stability of L-V population dynamics.

quasi-linearly with K. (Figure 4) Selection pressure for moderating appetite is lowest for intermediate values of K. When K is low, the prey population is vulnerable to extinction via random fluctuations; but large values of K correspond to insufficient damping of the wide population swings characteristic of Lotka-Voltera dynamics. Predator population maxima increase linearly with K, but population minima actually decrease exponentially for large values of K. Hence group selection pressure for moderating appetite increases for larger sites. The case of mixed high- and low-K ensembles is explored below.

Relative time scales of pred and prey life histories

There are two parameters of the L-V equations that scale time evolution: r is the time scale for exponential increase of the prey population in the absence of predation, and d is the time scale for exponential extinction of the predator population in the absence of food. Together, these two rates determine the time scale on which L-V dynamics unfolds. The ratio of r/d is also important. The dynamic is stabilized by a large ratio corresponding to a prey life cycle that is shorter than the predator; as the ratio decreases, evolved appetite becomes smaller and smaller to compensate; for ratios $r/d \lesssim 1$, the dynamic is unstable, and will not support a steady-state at all.

Territoriality

Territoriality is one mechanism by which predators in nature limit their numbers. To the extent that the owner of a site successfully keeps his competitors at bay, the mechanism is adequately explained by individual selection; but to the extent that the disenfranchised passively accept the system, it can only be supported by group selection.

We modified the model to include the rule that predator migration would proceed only into sites that had no existing predator population. The result was that appetite stabilized at a value about half of that which evolved when territoriality was not included. Total predator and prey populations were both increased by territoriality.

Variable mutation rate

Mutation rate itself may be an object of evolution. With a high mutation rate, *appetite* values can only be stabilized by an ongoing tension between within-group selection and between-group selection, a conflict which exacts a cost in over-predation and local extinctions. We added a second predator gene that controls the rate of mutation in the *appetite* gene. (The mutation rate gene itself is inherited with a fixed mutation rate.) After a stable *appetite* value was established, the mutation rate controlled by this gene evolved to much lower values, with concomitant benefits for the predator population: *appetite* stabilized at a slightly lower value, leading to higher prey populations, which supported higher predator populations; *appetite* values and population levels were both more stable; there were fewer local extinctions.

Letting parameters vary randomly across the grid

In seeking to apply model results in the real biosphere, the question arises whether qualitative results depend critically on parameters choices, or whether the results are more robust and likely to apply more generally. To aid in addressing this question, we have run the model with random values of two key parameters, assigned site-by-site across the grid. First, carrying capacity K was assigned random values at different sites, following a logarithmic distribution from a minimum of 10 to a maximum of 1000, on a 32×32 site grid. *Appetite* was found to evolve to a sustainable value and fluctuate within limits about that value. In another series of experiments, the *migration* connections between adjacent sites were programmed to random values, varying (log distribution) from a minimum of 10^{-5} to a maximum of 10^{-1} per time step. *Appetite* values fluctuated more widely than in the previous experiment, varying K, but population fluctuations were a little less wide. A broader range of random values, 10^{-6} to 1, produced runs in which K climbed out of control, then a population crash brought K values back to begin another climb. We also ran cases in which both K and *migration* varied randomly across the grid, and results were comparable to those just described (Figure 5).

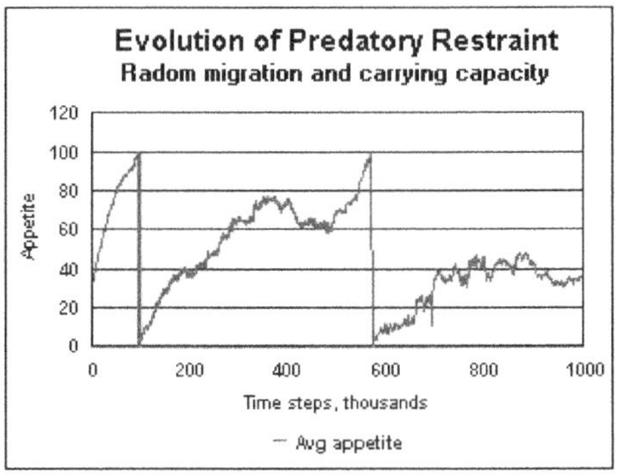

Figure 5: With randomly varying values of both carrying capacity K and migration rate in the ensemble, we find that appetite can evolve dangerously high, causing population crashes that allow appetite to climb once more from low values.

Summary and conclusions

Our model is considerably more general and more explicit than that of Gilpin (1975), but our conclusions are similar. We simulate situations in which group selection is able to temper individual selection, keeping individual reproductive potential from rising so far as to threaten demographic stability. Evidence concerning the extent to which this happens in nature is both equivocal and controversial. To a field biologist, it may seem obvious that populations are regulating themselves in the interest of long-term stability; however mechanisms that involve individual self-interest in an indirect way are difficult to exclude. Most field biologists have heard that group selection is out of favor among evolutionary theorists; but few have a basic appreciation for the way in which the short-term interest of the individual can be deeply at odds with the long-term survival of the species (Nudds 1987, for instance).

We also have uncovered hints of two intriguing connections between model results and field studies: First, in our simulations, it appears that population dynamics are stabilized when the fundamental time scale of the prey species is shorter than that of the predator. This suggests a connection to the observation that predator life spans are typically somewhat longer than those of their prey. Second, it is intuitively expected that small population numbers can lead to fluctuations that cause statistical extinctions; our results indicate that large, unstructured populations may also lead to unstable population dynamics. The mechanism for this unexpected phenomenon is best understood in terms of the parameter we have called Q which plays the role of a damping constant for the amplitude of L-V population cycles. Roughly speaking, the dynamic is driven by too large a difference between the steady-state prey population levels in the presence and in the absence of predators.

Results from the experiment with variable mutation rate illustrate the principle that any allele established via group selection faces constant challenge from individual selection, and this process carries a cost which is borne by the population. There will generally be a selective advantage (again, requiring group selection) in preventing reverse mutations toward alleles that are advantageous to the individual at the expense of the group. In real biological systems, there is evidence that chromosomes are structured so as to suppress certain mutations and enhance the frequency of others, and evidence that mutation rate may be subject to stabilizing selection (Sniegowski, Gerrish, & Lenski 1997).

Generality and scope of application

Abrams (2000) emphasizes that most animals are predators in that they depend for nourishment on the culling of animal or plant populations. Every living thing is part of a local ecosystem, and its short-term interest in maximally exploiting that ecosystem is balanced by the long-term interest of its relatives and its progeny in maintaining the productivity of that ecosystem. Thus it is possible that the results of our model could find application that is nearly universal in scope.

Acknowledgements

This paper grew out of a collaborative project during a one-week course taught by Yaneer Bar-Yam in January, 2002 at MIT. Others who contributed ideas to the project's development were Robert Bell, Dominic Boccelli, and Deva Seetharam.

References

Abrams, P. 2000. The evolution of predator-prey interactions: Theory and evidence. *Annual Review of Ecology and Systematics* 31:79–105.

Bittner, S., and Chapman, J. A. 1981. Reproductive ad physiological cycles in an island population of *Sylvilagus floridanus*. In Myers, K., and MacInnes, C. D., eds., *Proc World Lagomorph Conf.*, 182–203.

Gilpin, M. 1975. *Group Selection in Predator-Prey Communities.* Princeton, NJ: Princeton University Press.

Guarente, L., and Kenyon, C. 2000. Genetic pathways that regulate ageing in model organisms. *Nature* 408:255–262.

Hamilton, W. 1964. The genetical evolution of social behavior, I and II. *Journal of Theoretical Biology* 7:1–52.

Haraguchi, Y., and Sasaki, A. 2000. The evolution of parasite virulence and transmission rate in a spatially structured population. *Journal of Theoretical Biology* 203:85–96.

Kolenosky, G. B. 1972. Wolf predation on wintering deer in east-central Ontario. *J. Wildl. Manage.* 36:357–368.

Maynard Smith, J. 1964. Group selection and kin selection. *Nature* 20:1145–1147.

Maynard Smith, J. 1976. Group selection. *Quarterly Review of Biology* 51:277–283.

Nudds, T. 1987. The prudent predator. In Novak, M.; Baker, J.; Obbard, M.; and Mallock, B., eds., *Wild furbearer management and conservation in North America.*

Pels, B.; deRoos, A.; and Sabelis, M. 2002. Evolutionary dynamics of prey exploitation in a metapopulation of predators. *American Naturalist* 159:172–189.

Pepper, J., and Smutts, B. 2001. Agent-based modeling of multilevel selection of feeding restraint as a case study. In Pitt, W., ed., *Swarmfest 2000, Proceedings of the 4th Annual Swarm User Group Conference,* volume XIII of *Natural Resources and Environmental Issues*, 57–68.

Price, G. R. 1970. Selection and covariance. *Nature* 227:520–521.

Rand, D.; Keeling, M.; and Wilson, H. 1995. Invasion, stability and evolution to criticality in spatially extended, artificial host-pathogen ecologies. *Proceedings of the Royal Society of London B* 259:55–63.

Rauch, E. M. Sayama, H., and Bar-Yam, Y. 2002. Dynamics and genealogy of strains in spatially extended host-pathogen models. Forthcoming.

Sniegowski, P. D.; Gerrish, P. J.; and Lenski, R. E. 1997. Evolution of high mutation rates in experimental populations of *E. coli. Nature* 387:703–705.

Williams, G. 1966. *Adaptation and Natural Selection: A Critique of Some Current Evolutionary Thought.* Princeton, NJ: Princeton University Press.

Wilson, D. 1975. A theory of group selection. *Proceedings of the National Academy of Science* 72:143–146.

Wilson, D. 1983. The group selection controversy. *Annual Review of Ecology and Systematics* 14:159–187.

Wilson, D. 1997. Altruism and organism: Disentangling the themes of multilevel selection theory. *American Naturalist* 150:S122–S134.

Wynne-Edwards, V. 1962. *Animal Dispersion in Relation to Social Behaviour.* Edinburgh, UK: Oliver and Boyd.

Stability and Task Complexity: A Neural Network Model of Evolution and Learning

James R. Watson[1], **Nicholas Geard**[1] and **Janet Wiles**[1,2]

[1]School of Information Technology and Electrical Engineering
[2]School of Psychology
The University of Queensland, Australia

Abstract

Since Hinton and Nowlan introduced the Baldwin effect to the evolutionary computation community, agent-based studies of genetic assimilation have uncovered many details of the dynamic processes involved. In a previous paper, we demonstrated genetic assimilation with a simple food/toxin discrimination task using neural network agents that could evolve their learning rate. The study reported in this paper investigated the genetic assimilation of more complex learning tasks.

Kauffman's NK landscape model, which can generate landscapes with a variable degree of correlation, was used to define learning tasks of varying levels of complexity. Simulations indicate an increased tendency of genetic assimilation to occur as the complexity of the learning task decreases and the environmental stability increases. These results are explained in terms of the shifting balance between the evolutionary costs and benefits of learning.

Introduction

The interaction between evolution and learning has been an area of continual interest to the field of artificial life ever since Hinton and Nowlan's first computer simulation of the Baldwin effect (Hinton & Nowlan 1987). What initially appeared to be a relatively simple process has been found to be a complex phenomena with many interacting components.

The Baldwin effect was first described independently by Morgan (1896), Baldwin (1896) and Osborn (1896), and accounts for the tendency of learned behaviours to become genetically specified without resorting to a Lamarckian justification. Hinton and Nowlan's introduction of this biological concept into the evolutionary computation and artificial life communities marked the beginning of a growing body of research.

In Hinton and Nowlan's original simulation, the benefit of being able to learn was that it enabled an individual to solve a 'needle in a haystack' task within their lifetime. However, the advantage of learning was balanced by a fitness function that favoured individuals who were genetically closer to the solution. This cost of learning was sufficient to encourage the population to move, over time, towards a genetically specified solution.

The reason that genetic assimilation occurs at all, given the constraints of Darwinian selection, relies on the balance between the relative benefits and costs associated with the ability to learn (Mayley 1996). The Baldwin effect can be conceptualized in two distinct phases:

(i) initially, the ability to learn a task gives some subset of the population a selective advantage, resulting in subsequent generations becoming increasingly dominated by individuals with the ability to learn;

(ii) once the majority of individuals are able to learn, the costs of learning (e.g., resulting from increased intra-population competition between capable learners) cause selection to favour those individuals who, due to mutation and/or recombination, are more genetically predisposed towards the desired behaviour and therefore don't have as much to learn.

Genetic assimilation occurs when the balance between the benefits and costs of learning shifts so that selective pressures drive the ability to learn out of the population. Empirical demonstrations have shown that genetic assimilation is not always a straightforward process. Hinton and Nowlan's original simulation framework rarely, if ever, results in the complete genetic specification of the solution (see Harvey (1993) for a discussion). Other factors, such as the mutation rate (Fontanari & Meir 1990), selection algorithm (Wiles *et al.* 2001), the cost of learning (Mayley 1996), the amount of phenotypic plasticity (French & Messinger 1994) and population size have been shown to have an effect on the occurrence of genetic assimilation.

In a previous paper, Watson and Wiles (2002) demonstrated an equivalent result to that of Hinton and Nowlan (1987) using a population of evolving neural networks as agents. The task was to learn to discriminate between distinct sets of bit-string representations corresponding to food and toxin. The task was difficult enough that agents who were able to learn initially had a significant advantage. The learning rate was allowed to evolve, providing an indication of the level of phenotypic plasticity in the population. The practical effect of the learning rate is to amplify an agent's corrective action to a given situation, therefore the cost of learning arose from the noisy responses that resulted from a high learning rate. The magnitude of this cost of learning could be altered by varying the stability of the environment, implemented as a change in the number of consecutive presentations of each representation.

The relationship between landscape complexity and the Baldwin effect has been investigated previously. Bull (1999) found that a high rate of learning was more beneficial as landscapes became less correlated. However, he compared the effect of using different fixed learning rates, rather than learning rates that were able to evolve over time. Bull's study therefore illustrated the benefits of learning in terms of finding a solution more rapidly, but not the relationship between the benefits and costs of learning that drive the occurrence of genetic assimilation.

What remains to be investigated is the relationship between the tendency for genetic assimilation to occur and the complexity of the learning task. To address this question, we extended Watson and Wiles methodology by using multi-layer feed-forward neural networks as agents, with a tunably complex food/toxin discrimination task based on the NK landscape model (Kauffman 1993) as the learning task.

The NK landscape model was originally developed to model the fitness landscapes that result from systems with varying degrees of epistatic interaction between their components. By altering the level of interaction (the parameter K), the resulting landscape can be varied from smooth and unimodal ($K = 0$) to rugged and highly multimodal ($K = N - 1$). In the simulations reported in this paper, the landscape was comprised of length N bit strings corresponding to food or toxin representations.

Each bit of a representation contributes to the total fitness in a manner dependent on its setting and on the settings of the other K bits to which it is linked. It is assigned a fitness table mapping each of the 2^{K+1} possible combinations to a random fitness value — in this case, a real number in the range [0, 1]. The fitness of the entire representation is given by the average of the N fitness contributions and also falls in the range [0, 1] (see Kauffman (1993) for further details). In this study the epistatic linkages were specified to be to the K nearest elements.

The complexity of the learning task was therefore derived from the correlation of the underlying NK landscape. If the landscape was highly correlated, the food and toxin representations would form easily separable subsets of the problem space (Figure 1a). As the landscape became less correlated, the partitioning of the problem space became more complicated (Figure 1b). A major advantage of this approach was that it resulted in a decoupling of the genotype space (defined by the agent's neural network weights – see next section) and the phenotype space (defined by the NK landscape).

Methodology

The simulation consisted of a population of agents, represented by fully-connected, multi-layer feed-forward neural networks. Each network had N input units (corresponding to the N elements of a representation), $N/2$ hidden units and a single output unit (whose output values were determined by a sigmoidal activation function). The (real-valued) connection weights between the input units and the hidden units, between the hidden units and the output unit, the unit biases, and the value of the learning rate, formed each agent's genotype.

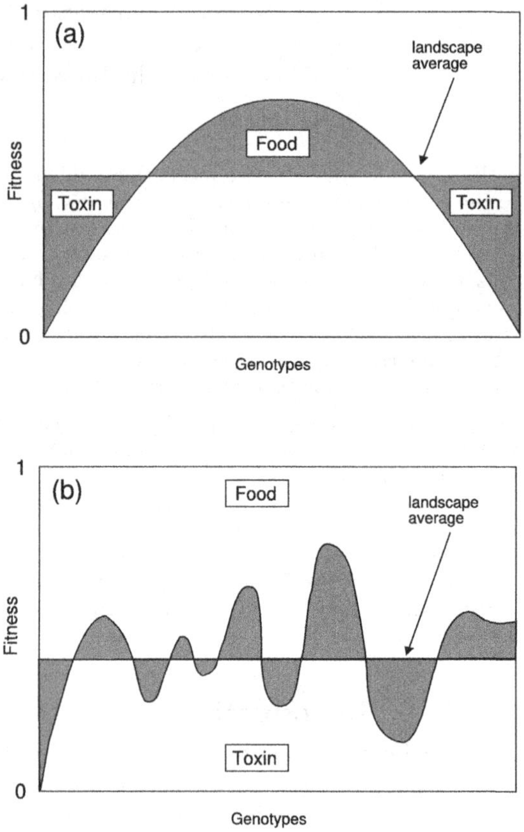

Figure 1: Problem spaces for (a) a simple ($K = 0$) learning task and (b) a more complex ($K > 0$) learning task.

Each agent lived for a fixed number of 'days'. For each day, an agent's task was to differentiate between two strings; one representing food and the other toxin (see below). The food/toxin representations were length N bit-strings chosen randomly from the set of 2^N possible representations of the pre-generated NK landscape. If an agent's response to an input string was higher than a fixed threshold, the agent was deemed to have 'eaten' the representation.

If a representation was eaten, the agent's score was adjusted according to the fitness of the corresponding point on the associated NK landscape, normalized by the landscape average. That is, representations above the landscape average were considered to be food and made a positive contribution to an agent's score, while representations below the landscape average were toxins and made a negative contribution to an agent's score. The magnitude of the contribution was based on the difference between the value and the landscape average.

Thus, each day consisted of: (i) evaluating each

agent's output given the current (length N bit-string) representation of food; (ii) updating the agent's score accordingly; (iii) using the backpropagation learning algorithm, updating agent weights to bring the next output closer to what was expected for the current representation (i.e. above or below the threshold); and then repeating (i), (ii) and (iii) for the current toxin representation.

The level of environmental stability (i.e., the length of time between changes to the current food and toxin representations) was varied according to parameter C. For example, if $C = 1$, a new food and toxin representation were chosen each day; if $C = 10$, the same representations were presented for 10 days before being changed. This allowed the benefits and costs of learning to be altered independently of the complexity of the learning task.

The simulations were run with $N = 12$ and a range of values for K and C. Each simulation was run for 5,000 generations, with each generation consisting of 100 neural-network agents (as described above) with a lifespan of 50 days. The score for each individual was given by the cumulative score over these 50 days. Tournament selection (see Mitchell (1996)) was used to create each successive generation. Neural network populations were asexual, and selected agents reproduced by passing on their inherited connection weights (*not* the learned weights) to the next generation. The network connections, the biases and learning rate were mutated by adding uniform random noise with a probability of 0.1.

Results and Discussion

After an initial period of low performance, the agents acquired the ability to discriminate between food and toxin via learning. Marked increases in the evolved learning rate corresponded to significant improvement in population performance (with the exception of maximally complex learning tasks with highly unstable landscapes).

Subsequent genetic assimilation (i.e. the learning rate falling to zero after the task was learned) occurred most frequently when the learning task was simple and the level of environmental stability was low. For learning tasks based on maximally correlated ($K = 0$) landscapes, complete genetic assimilation occurred when the environment was highly unstable ($C = 1$ and $C = 2$, see Figure 2). When the environment was more stable ($C = 10$), the learning rate began to fall, but was still quite high after 5,000 generations (more extensive simulations are required to investigate whether the learning rate does eventually fall to zero or if this residual learning remains).

These results can be explained in terms of the balance between the benefits and costs of learning. At a low level of environmental stability, each agent saw a

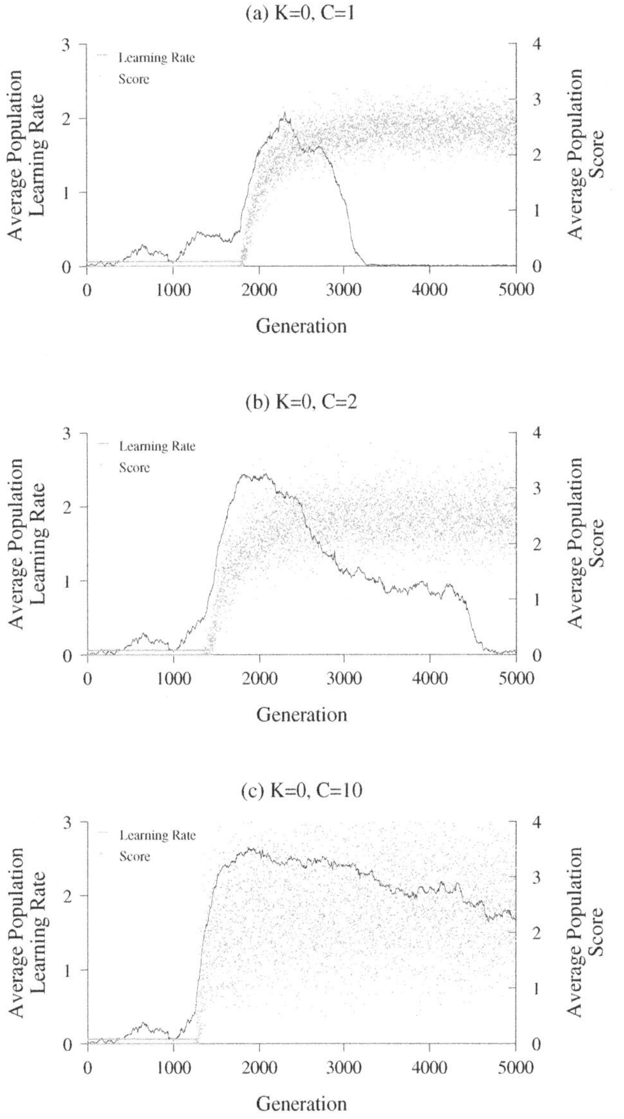

Figure 2: Performance and evolved learning rate over a simple landscape ($K = 0$) with increasing environmental stability. (a) maximally unstable conditions ($C = 1$): the rise and fall of the learning rate demonstrates the 2 stages of the Baldwin effect; initial acquisition via learning followed by genetic assimilation of the food/toxin discrimination task. Note that the average population score rises with the steep increase in learning rate and remains high even when the learning rate returns to 0. (b) and (c) display similar initial behaviour (acquiring the task through learning) as conditions became more stable. However, the rate of genetic assimilation was markedly slower for $C = 2$ and incomplete for $C = 10$.

constantly changing sequence of representations. In this situation, having an instinctive (i.e., genetically specified) response was more important than being able to learn the appropriate response during the agent's lifetime – the benefits of learning were low relative to the costs, and genetic assimilation occurred. As the level of environmental stability increased, the same representation was seen repeatedly during the agent's lifetime. The resulting increase in the benefits of learning, relative to the costs, was such that selective pressure was insufficient to drive the learning rate to zero. Consequently, genetic assimilation did not occur.

As the learning task became more complex (i.e., as K approached $N-1$) and environmental stability was low, the task could not be achieved. As environmental stability was increased, learning became more beneficial and agents were able to discriminate between food and toxin via learning. The low costs of learning in this situation prevented genetic assimilation from occurring.

A further observed trend was an increase in the variance of the average population score as the representation change rate decreased (with increasing C). This trend was due to the fact that, as the change rate decreased but the agent's lifespan remained constant, a smaller sample of the total problem space was seen by each generation.

Conclusions

The acquisition and subsequent genetic assimilation of phenotypic traits occur when the relative costs and benefits of learning are balanced so that selective pressures first favour plasticity, then shift over evolutionary time to favour innate specification of what has been learned. The results from this study demonstrate how this balance is affected by the complexity of the learning task and level of environmental stability.

The primary benefit of learning, performing correctly in the absence of innately correct network weights, far outweighs the costs while the task is initially being acquired. Once the majority of a population can learn the task, the costs begin to outweigh the benefits and genetic assimilation can occur. The likelihood of such assimilation occurring has been found to depend on task complexity and environmental stability.

When task complexity is low and the representation change rate is high, learning is selected against and genetic assimilation occurs. As task complexity increases and the change rate decreases, the benefit of learning increases and genetic assimilation does not occur.

References

Baldwin, J. M. 1896. A new factor in evolution. *American Naturalist* 30:441–451 536–553.

Bull, L. 1999. On the Baldwin effect. *Artificial Life* 5:241–246.

Fontanari, J. F., and Meir, R. 1990. The effect of learning on the evolution of asexual populations. *Complex Systems* 4:401–414.

French, R., and Messinger, A. 1994. Genes, phenes and the Baldwin effect: Learning and evolution in a simulated population. In Brooks, R. A., and Maes, P., eds., *Artificial Life IV*, 277–282.

Harvey, I. 1993. The puzzle of the persistent question marks: A case study of genetic drift. In Forrest, S., ed., *Proceedings of the Fifth International Conference on Genetic Algorithms*, 15–22. San Mateo, CA: Morgan Kaufmann.

Hinton, G., and Nowlan, S. 1987. How learning can guide evolution. *Complex Systems* 1:495–502.

Kauffman, S. A. 1993. *The Origins of Order - Organization and Selection in Evolution.* New York: Oxford University Press.

Mayley, G. 1996. The evolutionary cost of learning. In Maes, P.; Mataric, M. J.; Meyer, J.-A.; Pollack, J.; and Wilson, S. W., eds., *From Animals to Animats 4: Proceedings of the Fourth International Conference on Simulation of Adaptive Behavior*, 458–467. MIT Press.

Mitchell, M. 1996. *An Introduction to Genetic Algorithms.* Cambridge, MA: MIT Press.

Morgan, C. L. 1896. On modification and variation. *Science* 4:733–740.

Osborn, H. F. 1896. Ontogenic and phylogenic variation. *Science* 4:786–789.

Watson, J., and Wiles, J. 2002. The rise and fall of learning: A neural network model of the genetic assimilation of acquired traits. In *Proceedings of the 2002 Congress on Evolutionary Computation (CEC 2002)*, 600–605.

Wiles, J.; Schulz, R.; Bolland, S.; Tonkes, B.; and Hallinan, J. 2001. Selection procedures for module discovery: Exploring evolutionary algorithms for cognitive science. In Moore, J. D., and Stenning, K., eds., *Proceedings of the 23rd Annual Conference of the Cognitive Science Society (CogSci 2001)*, 1124–1129. Lawrence Erlbaum Associates.

Aesthetic Selection of Developmental Art Forms

Dale Thomas
Artificial Intelligence Laboratory
Department of Information Technology
University of Zürich
Winterthurerstrasse 190
CH-8057, Zürich, Switzerland
thomas@ifi.unizh.ch

Abstract

Aesthetic selection has been employed in a system such that users can guide the evolution of art forms. The attributes of these forms are defined implicitly by an artificial genome, requiring a growth period to generate the final structure. During this growth phase, artificial chemicals react and diffuse across the surface of the developing structure, causing growth and other structural changes. The forms are part of a small evolving population in which fitness of each individual is entirely defined by the user. Throughout evolution user can design objects interactively or simply to explore the range of possible forms of the system.

Introduction

Genetic Algorithms (GA) were originally designed as a search technique, inspired by evolution using natural selection (NS) to 'breed' good solutions (Holland 1992). The concept is quite simple: from a population of information strings (genotypes) which define solutions (phenotypes) to a problem, a new population is created by breeding the solutions with a probability proportional to their fitness. This can lead to fitter populations, optimising solutions to the problem. Two elements of this method are very important in determining how well a GA performs: the mapping from genotype to phenotype and the fitness function. The fitness function defines the shape of the fitness landscape and the phenotype defines the position of an individual on it. In order for GAs to work, it is essential for the child solutions to be relatively similar to their parents. This requires that the fitness function should lead to a relatively smooth shape of landscape and that the mapping from genotype to phenotype must be such that a small change in genotype should generally lead to a small movement on the fitness landscape. Otherwise, evolution has nothing to work with because the fitness of the 'child' solutions, which are genetically similar to their parents, may be almost random, leading to an inefficient parallel random search. The advantages of GAs over other search techniques are that they are inherently parallel, simple to implement, do not require explicit knowledge of the problem, they can often find a good solution quickly and can search high-dimensional parameter space very well. The disadvantages are that they do not guarantee the optimal solution and that the performance very much depends on the shape of the 'fitness landscape', which is greatly influenced not only by the fitness function but also genetic encoding. In addition, the fitness landscapes of agent-based systems are further affected by co-evolution, changing environment/resources and sensory-motor interactions with the environment. These other factors can provide very strong evolutionary forces affecting the fitness of individuals in the system (Mitchell, Forrest, & Holland 1991). Also, the fitness will be greatly influenced by certain assumptions implicit in the implementation. Implicit information is a big problem when designing fitness functions and can lead to fragile solutions. For example, the AE system in (Bongard & Pfeifer 2001) had a simple fitness function in which the creatures were evolved to move toward a block in a simulated physical environment. The simulation was run for eight seconds and the fitness defined by the reciprocal of the final distance to the block. The distance measure was explicit in the fitness function but the timing was implicit. Evolution found it easier to make creatures move at a particular speed so as to be near the block at the end of the eight seconds evaluation period, rather than complex 'block-following' neural architecture. The fitness function should have been 'go toward the block' but the actual function was 'be here in eight seconds'. This simple example shows that even automated fitness functions can be highly biased due to implicit designing.

A central problem with GAs is that due to the algorithmic nature of fitness functions, they cannot be applied to problems with a subjective or qualitative aspect. Fitness functions such as size of a structure, speed of an agent, strength of a bridge, etc, are relatively easy to calculate but some things like 'looks like?' and 'appeals to me' are subjective choices and therefore impossible to encode. To overcome this limitation, another evolutionary selection method called Aesthetic (or Artificial) Selection (AS) is sometimes used. Many animal and plant species or have been subjected to this selection method since humans started to domesticate them. The fitness of individuals is based on human needs or desires. Some examples include dogs bred for 'beauty', hunting ability and affection, horses for speed and stamina and cows for milk yield. Also plants are selectively bred for yield and beauty. AS is a much simplified selection pressure since it concerns only very few aspects, whereas NS has to balance many aspects in order to keep the species alive. For this reason AS is faster at evolving specific traits. Also, NS has no goal and so just meanders whereas AS has a goal albeit biased and subjective. In Artificial Evolution (AE) systems this could potentially be a useful design tool for somewhat subjective problems.

In addition, since a human observer is controlling the selection, the fitness function can be flexible, have global information, and be adaptive and subjective which can sometimes lead to 'one step back for many steps forward'. For example, if the problem is to evolve agents for locomotion, a naive fitness function may be simply based on distance or speed of an individual. However, a human observer may see an individual that moves less far, but has an extra pair of legs or a particularly promising gait. An automated fitness function may not be able to detect this unless it was very complex (computationally intensive) but a human could easily see potential, even if the distance travelled was less.

Artificial Life (AL) systems have been used many times to produce interesting shapes and structures employing various methods including GAs. Usually GA methods include an explicit mapping from genotype to phenotype. This has the advantage of being intuitive and readable by the researchers but the main drawback is that the complexity of the phenotype is proportional to the length of the genotype. This is no real problem for small, manageable problems but as the size and complexity of artificial agents and structures increase, the disadvantage of this approach comes to bear with increasing force. Nature uses a different approach in which the complexity is not directly correlated to genome size. DNA does not directly encode the size, shape or function of the organism; rather it defines proteins and the organism's structure emerges through the interaction of these proteins and also the interaction with the environment.

The way that an organism grows is certainly one of the greatest mysteries of modern science. A seminal paper by Alan Turing (Turing 1952) described reaction-diffusion (RD) systems as a possible mechanism to explain some areas of morphogenesis. The information storage capacity of a system can be substantially less if there is a growth period exploiting self-organisation principles.

The work presented here combines the elements of artificial growth and artificial evolution using aesthetic selection into an education system for public use.

In the next section there is a discussion of related work and then the system is described starting with the interface, then a description of the physics and the chemistry and genetics are given in the subsequent two sections. Following that is a section on the graphics and then a general discussion on AS. Conclusions and future work are given in the final section.

Science et Cité

The system detailed here was exhibited in Zürich at the 'Science et Cité', a science fair held throughout Switzerland every year to promote public awareness of science. Many people tried out the system and were able to evolve something unique to their own aesthetic taste. Each user could save a picture of their form, which was later e-mailed to them in return for answering a few questions.

More information about this project can be found at: http://www.ifi.unizh.ch/ailab/people/thomas/

Related Work

There have been many interesting interactive art systems using artificial life. The first such system was Biomorphs (Dawkins 1986). This allowed the user to evolve binary trees where the genome consisted of nine integer values. To produce the phenotype, a recursive binary tree was rendered directly taking into account the genome which encoded things like recursion depth, branching angle, segment length, etc.

The user of the program was presented with a single biomorph surrounded by eight children with slightly mutated copies of the genotype. Once selected, a particular child would become the parent surrounded by eight of its children and the selection continued. This was simple asexual reproduction and even though it was simple, the author was able to direct the evolution to produce many desired shapes including the letters of his name.

Another similar system was an AS program for producing two-dimensional pictures from equations (Sims 1991). The equations were encoded as Lisp expressions and evolved using Genetic Programming (GP) (Koza 1992).

Sometimes some components of the fitness function are somewhat subjective while others may be quantifiable. Ventrella (1995) created a system that mixed automatic and aesthetic selection to evolve stylistic locomotion behaviour in simulated three-dimensional animats for computer animation. Some aspects of walking are objective, e.g. speed, distance/path travelled and efficiency whereas style is totally subjective. The fastest or most efficient method of moving may not necessarily be interesting from a subjective observer's point of view, which is of course very important in entertainment. In the system, the animator could breed a population for locomotion using standard AE techniques but also guide the evolution based on his or her whims. This was accomplished by being able to view a population and tweak the fitness after it had been calculated. This mixed the creative aspects of designers and animators with the automatic optimisation of evolution. Another advantage of this is that the user could help the system escape local minima if detected.

RD systems were originally designed to explain some areas of morphogenesis (Turing 1952). In these systems, there are interactions between diffusing chemicals, which are capable of a wide range of pattern formation. These systems can show stable spots, stripes, travelling waves, spirals, splitting structures and spatiotemporal chaos, and the patterns are very robust. Many such systems have been designed to model real chemical interactions or theoretical systems for use in biology, physics or mathematics. A lot of these systems have been used to explain some areas of biology including models of animal skin textures (Murray & Myerscough 1991), seashell patterning (Meinhardt 1994), nerve conduction (Fitzhugh 1962; Nagumo, Arimoto, & Yoshizawa 1962) and cellular aggregation (Vasiev, Hogeweg, & Panfilov 1994). In addition, RD systems have been used in computer graphics to model natural looking textures on an arbitrary, though static mesh (Turk 1991). Evolution has been used together with RD systems (Takai, Takai, & Nakamori 1998) but only in the optimisation of parameters for a specified system. The actual equations and parameters of RD systems have never been explored in an evolutionary context, mainly due to the requirement of positive and negative feedback in just the right amount.

The Interface

The interface to the system is similar to most other AS systems (Dawkins 1986; Sims 1991; Todd & Latham 1992; Ventrella 1994). It involves having a number of individuals on screen together (sixteen in this work) of which the user can select one to mutate, or two to breed. This then creates a new generation composed of individuals similar to the ones selected and the process repeats. This allows the user to have direct control over the evolution by exercising his or her own fitness value. Since this system was designed for public use using a touch screen, the interface needed to be as user-friendly and intuitive as possible. There are two views of the forms available to the user, one view showing all sixteen individuals and the other showing a close-up of just one. Other actions possible are to regrow an individual or to save its image. Regrowing an individual is included because the way it grows is an important part of the aesthetic appeal and since the system is completely deterministic the final form would be exactly the same.

Physics

A very important aspect of development is the action of physical forces from the environment, (such as a womb or egg shell) and from the material properties of the internal structure. For example, when a sheet of cells invaginates, it does so also because of physical buckling, not just as a result of chemical properties. Chemical and physical processes are two highly important and interdependent aspects of morphogenesis.

The forms in this work are defined in a simulated three-dimensional environment as a surface mesh structure consisting of springs. These springs are generally passive and exert a force on the two connected vertices proportional to the deviation from the spring's rest length. Some springs can be active: this simply means that their rest length varies in proportion to a sine wave. The frequency and amplitude of this change is constant and equal for all active springs but the phase is determined by the time of creation for each spring. This allows for a 'rippling' effect over the form; for example, a bulge would travel down a long 'tail' structure since the time of creation increases toward the tip. This results in a very organic looking motion.

Chemical Number	Function	Affects
1	Growth Factor	Springs
2	Active Springs	Springs
3	Hair	Faces
4	Horns	Faces
5	Lights	Faces
6	Colour Component (red)	Vertices
7	Colour Component (green)	Vertices
8	Colour Component (blue)	Vertices

Table 1: The effect of the structural chemicals

Initially, all forms begin as a standard, well-defined 'egg'. This is just a small cube with a chemical gradient across the eight verticies. As they grow, if a face or edge becomes too large the surface can split and increase its complexity in that area. Figure 1 shows a form growing from an initial egg. The normal of the surface at each vertex is important for two of reasons. Firstly, it helps to define the surface, which will also be discussed further in the discussion section, and secondly, all vertices are subjected to a small force along their normal which acts as a kind of internal pressure, keeping the structure from folding in on itself. Another force exists to keep the faces somewhat rectangular. This is just a small force on each corner of a face across the diagonal with the magnitude proportional to the difference of the diagonal lengths. These forces also help to keep the structure solid and inflated. All masses are defined as 1 and so the acceleration on a vertex is equal to the sum of the forces and the system was solved using simple Euler integration. A lot of damping was included for two reasons: to avoid instabilities when a vertex was connected to many springs, and also to give the motion a viscous liquid look for aesthetic appeal.

Chemistry and Genetics

During development, the effect of physical forces is only one side of the story. The other side is the interactions between proteins and the differentiation of cells. Just as in biology, the genotype in this work does not explicitly encode for structure and detail; rather it encodes a description of the interactions between a number of abstract chemicals, N. Every vertex in the growing forms contains an N-dimensional vector of chemical concentra-

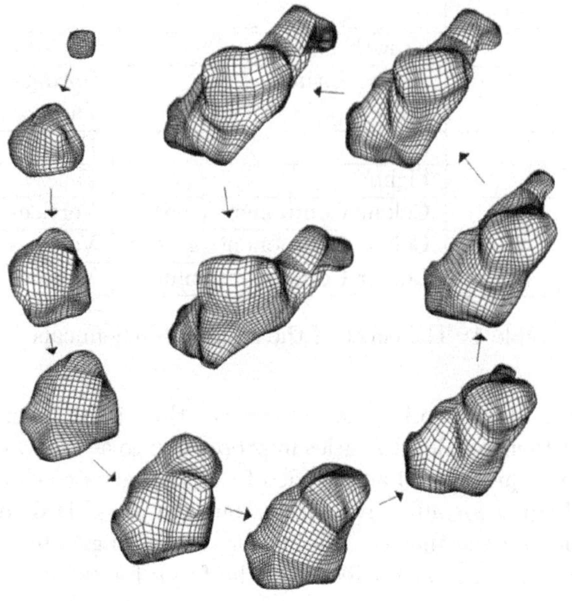

Figure 1: The growth of an individual.

tions and as the growth progresses the chemicals react locally with one another and diffuse through the springs with rates also defined by the genotype. The structure of the genotype is divided into two parts: the first N values are the diffusion rates of the respective chemicals and the rest is divided up into a number of genes, each consisting of five values. Each gene represents an interaction and these five numbers correspond to the FROM chemical, the TO chemical, the interaction weight and the upper and lower thresholds of the interaction. Each part of the genotype is represented as a real value in the range $[0,1]$. These values are mapped onto the diffusion rates in the range $[0,0.1]$ and the weights in the range of $[-0.1,0.1]$. This creates an interaction network for the chemicals and as growth occurs, the reaction diffusion system affects the characteristics of the form. The interaction proceeds as follows: if the FROM chemical is between the limits of the interaction, the TO chemical is modified by the concentration of the FROM chemical multiplied by the weight. One main problem with evolving RD systems is that the systems need both positive and negative feedback in just the right amounts, otherwise the chemicals just decay to zero or saturate. This is very difficult to achieve and so the fitness landscape would be almost random. To solve this, each chemical was normalised over all vertices at every time-step. This is not biologically plausible but it did make the system stable. Also, this method is a very abstract model of transcriptional regulation in that one chemical can promote or inhibit the production of another. There are no

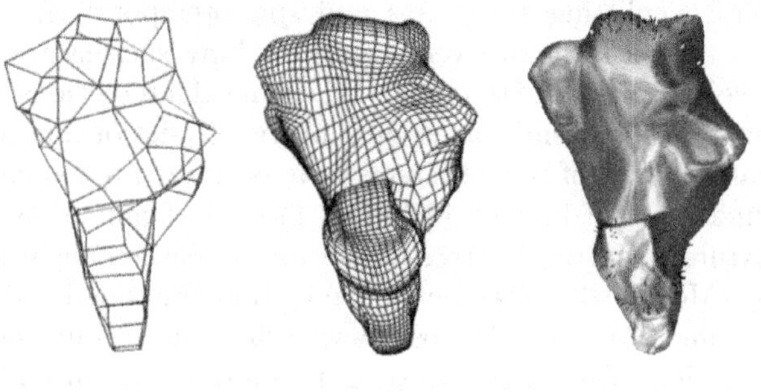

Figure 2: The three stages of object construction. On the left, the geometric wire frame spring structure is 'grown' from an initial cube. In the centre, the wire frame structure is used to generate a curved surface defined by the positions and normals of the vertices and finally this is rendered to the screen with many graphical effects.

other types of interactions such as enzymatic regulation.

Usually there are fifteen chemicals ($N = 15$), and the first seven are both structural and regulatory which means that they affect the physical form and also other chemicals while the rest are just regulatory. The functions of the structural chemicals are given in Table 1.

Since each form is uniquely defined by a string of numbers (artificial DNA), the standard genetic operators can be applied, i.e. mutation and crossover. In this work a simple one-point crossover was used and a variable mutation rate was used from 0.001 for the first child to 0.015 the fifteenth.

Graphics

The individuals in this work were evolved using AS so their appearance is obviously very important. Also, the motion and growth are aspects of the aesthetic appeal, which helps a user to decide which individual to choose and since the system is an entertainment package for public use the graphics were a major part. The graphics were implemented with OpenGL, a cross-platform graphics library with hardware support for fast 3D rendering.

In order to make interesting and unusual 'art' shapes, the overall look of the system was given an organic feel. The wire-frame mesh of the individuals was rendered with curved surfaces. Every face of the object was defined by four vertices and displayed as a curved surface by taking the positions of the vertices and their normals and calculating the positions of intermediate, internal vertices lying on the curved surface, which could then be rendered as much smaller quadrangles. These quadrangles were then rendered to the screen with appropriate lighting and texturing. Each vertex had a particular colour defined by the concentrations of three chemicals representing the red, green and blue components.

A copy of the rotating background clouds was environment mapped onto the surface and the colours interpolated across it (environment mapping means displaying an object as though it was reflective). This gave the objects a slightly coloured chrome look. The resolution of this face division was dynamic and was controlled by the frame-rate of the system. If the objects became very complex then the system would begin to slow down and lower the resolution of the surfaces to keep the frame-rate relatively constant. Figure 2 shows the three stages of object construction. Beginning with the wire-frame spring structure, a curved surface mesh is generated and then rendered with texture and environment mapping, lighting and surface elements.

In order to increase the organic look of the system, natural looking elements like hair and horns were included to give subjective appearances of cute, disgusting, etc. These surface elements had no function other than aesthetic appeal and particular chemicals controlled the number of each element per face.

The hairs (or bristles) were rendered as simple black lines attached to the face and extending in the direction of the normal. The horns were similarly attached but rendered as a texture mapped pyramid. Also, orbiting lights were included and rendered as two quadrangle glare textures on billboards (i.e. they always faced the camera), rotating at different speeds and blended together. Each light was anchored to a fixed point on the surface as well but the distance varied along the normal as a sine wave with random phase. This gave a shimmering point cloud around the forms (depending on the chemical concentrations). As the form moved, (wobbling, rippling, growing, splitting), the normals were recalculated and so the elements move and wave with the form's motion. This gave a very unique look and helped with the aesthetics of the system.

If a face or edge became too long, it would split to extend the surface. Figure 3 shows the two splitting methods used. Since all faces are rendered as curved surfaces, the resulting faces after the splitting needed to have exactly four edges.

The forms here can have active springs spanning across the interior of an individual. When they are created, they are created independent of the structural springs. Then if the structural spring in the same place splits due to growth, the active spring spans across the inside of the form.

Some sound was included for a more complete system. This just consisted of background noises: wind, bubbling, bird chirping and also a Taiko (Japanese drumming) song. The sounds did not relate to the forms in any way, except for an organic bubbling/crunching sound for when the user interacted with the forms.

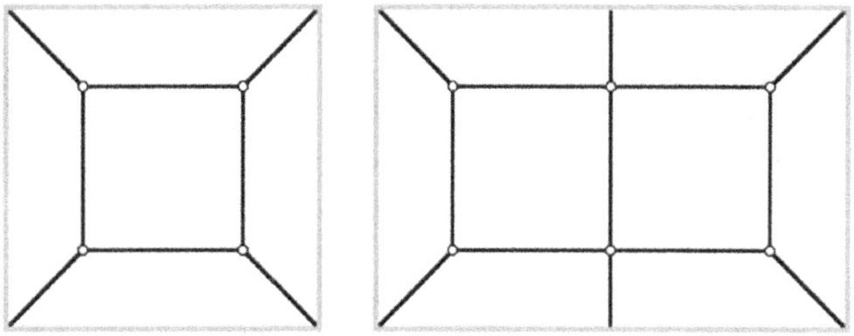

Figure 3: If a face becomes too large it will split into five new faces (left). If an edge becomes too long it will split into three new edges and also split the connected faces (right). All faces must be quadrangles. The grey lines are the original faces, the black lines show the new springs and the small circles show the newly created vertices.

Discussion

The main advantages of using a developmental mapping from genotype to phenotype is that the solution can adapt to environment during growth, and that the complexity of phenotype is not constrained to the length of genotype. Unfortunately, in artificial algorithms without the complex growth feedback checking available to biological systems, small changes in genotype can sometimes lead to large movements across the fitness landscape. However, by using an AS method this problem can be reduced due to a subjective, adaptive and sympathetic fitness function. Another advantage of this type of design method is that any fitness function can be implemented at any time. Here is a system where the fitness is based on the user's whims, it is unquantifiable and highly subjective but this can be a good thing in many ways. Also, since this is 'Art by Criticism' the user (or designer) does not need to have great artistic ability; he or she just needs some aesthetic sense. This may be useful for some areas of engineering or design where the computer could reduce the amount of technical ability needed by the user.

By 'playing around' with the system one can get a good intuition of the shape of phenotypic space, to see what is possible and what is easy to produce. The motivation can be to 'break' the system or just to explore it. The user can try to find the weak points, limitations and range of the system. For example, the work here uses an implicit mapping and so the phenotypic space is not at all intuitive.

AS is needed in some situations so that a simple, artificial system can find solutions that not only optimise their fitness criteria but also have aesthetic or natural appeal. Biological structures and behaviours evolved as a response to many different interactions with the environment and other agents. The world is a rich tapestry of dynamically changing variables due to physical forces and other organisms competing for resources and coevolving. In an artificial system it is either impossible, inefficient or undesirable to include such complexity just to be able to evolve natural-looking structures or behaviours. However, without such complexity it may be too much to ask that the resulting solution looks natural.

A general problem with developmental algorithms is that of growth termination. In biology there are many ways for an organism to stop growing after reaching maturity. For example, terminal differentiation of cells, which disables their ability to divide, the activity range of chemicals, environmental constraints, etc. In this work this issue was not addressed; rather the growth will terminate after a particular time. After this growth phase, the chemicals can still react and diffuse but only affecting the colours, so no more growth can occur. This would be a good area of future work, as it seems to be a very important aspect of development but as yet not included in artificial growth algorithms.

There are two potential problems with automated fitness functions, which can hinder the performance of a GA. Firstly, implicit information can lead to solutions which are not what the designer wanted, simply because the fitness function was not specific enough, due to the designer, expecting evolution to design as he does, and secondly, the designer can over-specify the function, restricting evolution to the his way of thinking and inhibiting evolutions inherent innovation. These are both problems of bias and as a result, many fitness functions are not truly objective. AS is subjective but it is also adaptive, so that sometimes, implicit information can be recognised and dealt with. Presumably, a mixture of AS and NS such as described by (Ventrella 1994) can overcome many problems with both approaches.

An additional feature of the program was the ability to 'touch' an individual. Touching the screen applied some perturbation forces to the vertices, which would initiate a few seconds of damped rippling. The main reason for this was to better connect the user to the forms. The idea of the system was to create 'art forms' but the use of evolution meant that the user is not in contact with the individual forms, rather just the whole population. The result of this is that the process of design has moved away from hands-on sculpting. However, most people like to be able to interact with the forms directly.

Conclusions and Future Work

Since this project was primarily designed as an interactive art project, the results are the images created by the users activities.

There are many possible directions for future research. One possible direction is the inclusion of an automatic selection system for a particular problem like locomotion (Sims 1994; Ventrella 1994; Bongard & Pfeifer 2001). Implementing gravity and collisions with the environment/self/other agents could enhance the physical environment. In all of these systems so far, the agents under evolution have been rigid body hierarchies. However, the material properties of an agent play an important role in its behaviour (Hara & Pfeifer 2000), and this system could be used to study this aspect in an evolutionary context. One point which would need to be addressed, is the need for some internal structure. In this work, the forms can have internal active springs but this is not enough to evolve interesting locomotive behaviour. What is needed is a rigid body skeleton covered with a soft 'skin'. Then for these agents the control, morphology and material parameters could be evolved in synchrony.

Acknowledgements

I would like to thank Rolf Pfeifer and Josh Bongard for interesting discussions on various topics pertaining to this work. Also thank you to Daniel Bisig for very helpful suggestions and advice, and also for providing the sounds used in the system.

References

Bongard, J. C., and Pfeifer, R. 2001. Repeated structure and dissociation of genotypic and phenotypic complexity in artificial ontogeny. In *Proceedings of The Genetic and Evolutionary Computation Conference, GECCO-2001*, 829–836. San Francisco, CA: Morgan Kaufmann.

Brooks, R., and Maes, P., eds. 1994. *Artificial Life IV: Proceedings of the Fourth International Workshop on the Synthesis and Simulation of Living Systems.* Cambridge, Mass.: MIT Press.

Dawkins, R. 1986. *The Blind Watchmaker.* Harlow, UK: Longman Scientific and Technical.

Fitzhugh, R. 1962. Impulse and physiological states in models of nerve membrane. *Biophysics J.* 1:445–466.

Hara, F., and Pfeifer, R. 2000. On the relation among morphology, material, and control in morpho-functonal machines. In *From animals to animats 6. Proceedings of the 6th Int. Conf. on Simulation of Adaptive Behavior*, 33–42. Cambridge, Mass.: MIT Press.

Holland, J. 1992. *Adaptation in Natural and Artificial Systems.* Cambridge, MA: MIT Press, 2nd edition.

Koza, J. R. 1992. *Genetic Programming - on the programming of computers by means of natural selection.* MIT Press.

Meinhardt, H. 1994. Biological pattern-formation — new observations provide support for theoretical predictions. *Bioessays* 627–632.

Mitchell, M.; Forrest, S.; and Holland, J. 1991. The royal road for genetic algorithms: Fitness landscapes and GA performance. In *Proceedings of the First European Conference on Artificial Life*, 245–254. Cambridge, MA: MIT Press.

Murray, J. D., and Myerscough, M. R. 1991. Pigmentation pattern formation on snakes. *J. Theor. Biol.* 149:339–360.

Nagumo, J. S.; Arimoto, S.; and Yoshizawa, S. 1962. An active pulse transmission line simulating nerve axon. *Proc. IRE* 50:2061–2071.

Sims, K. 1991. Artificial evolution for computer graphics. In *Computer Graphics (Siggraph '91 proceedings)*, 319–328.

Sims, K. 1994. Evolving 3D morphology and behavior by competition. In Brooks and Maes (1994), 28–39.

Takai, Y.; Takai, N. K.; and Nakamori, K. J. 1998. Exploration of the reaction-diffusion textures. In *Proc. Int. Conf. on Modelling and Simulation.*

Todd, S., and Latham, W. 1992. *Evolutionary Art and Computers.* London, San Diego CA: Academic Press.

Turing, A. 1952. The chemical basis of morphogenesis. *Phil Trans R Soc B* 237:37–72.

Turk, G. 1991. Generating textures on arbitrary surfaces using reaction-diffusion. *Computer Graphics* 25(4):289–298.

Vasiev, B.; Hogeweg, P.; and Panfilov, A. 1994. Simulation of dictyostelium discoideum aggregation via reaction-diffusion model. *Physical Review Letters* 73:31733176.

Ventrella, J. 1994. Disney meets Darwin. In Brooks and Maes (1994), 436–441.

Chemical Genetic Algorithms — Coevolution between Codes and Code Translation

Hideaki Suzuki[1] **Hidefumi Sawai**[2]

[1]ATR, Human Information Science Laboratories, Kyoto 619-0288 Japan
[2]Communications Research Laboratory, Kyoto 619-0289 Japan

Abstract

A chemical genetic algorithm (CGA) in which several types of molecules (information units) react with each other in a cell is proposed. Translation from codons (short substrings of bits) in DNA to amino acids (real value units) is specified by a particular set of translation molecules created by the reaction between tRNA units and amino acid units. This adaptively changes and optimizes the fundamental genotype-phenotype mapping during evolution. Through the struggle between cells containing a DNA unit and small molecular units, the codes in DNA and the translation table described by the small molecular units coevolve, and a specific output function (protein), which is used to evaluate a cell's fitness, is optimized. To demonstrate the effectiveness of the CGA, the algorithm is applied to a set of deceptive problems, and the results by using the CGA are compared to those by using a simple GA. It is shown that the CGA has far better performance for the tested functions than the conventional simple GA.

Introduction

An evolutionary system's ability to evolve a variety of adaptive functions or solutions (evolvability) is specified by a set of fundamental functional units. In a real biological system, the set comprises twenty amino acids, and genetic information written in DNA is translated into these units by using a set of translation molecules known as *aminoacyl-tRNAs* (Alberts *et al.* 1994). The aminoacyl-tRNAs define the fundamental mapping from genotype to phenotype, a fitness landscape on the DNA genotype space, and are one of the key molecules determining a biological system's ability. At an early stage of biological evolution, life succeeded in choosing an appropriate set of aminoacyl-tRNAs (translation relation from codes to amino acids) (Bedian 2001; Wills 2001), which enabled life to evolve a variety of adaptive functions or higher organisms like dinosaurs or mammals. This poses a fundamental question: how was the appropriate set of translation molecules chosen during biological evolution?

A recent study by one of the authors (Suzuki 2000a; 2000b; 2001) attempted to answer the above question. His basic idea is that an artificial system's evolvability is enhanced by an objective measure. He proposed a measure for evolvability as well as the approach of numerically optimizing fundamental functional units prior to an experimental evolution run. In biological systems, however, the fundamental functional units (amino acids) and the fundamental code translation (aminoacyl-tRNAs) did not evolve prior to the evolution of codes (RNA or DNA). It is natural to assume that a number of different translation relations had been variously chosen and tested while assessing and evolving DNA codes, and in this sense the codes and the code translation simultaneously evolved (coevolved). When we design an artificial evolutionary system, the introduction of *coevolution* between codes and code-translation might help explore a better translation relation than a man-made relation and improve the evolutionary performance.

Based on the above notion, this paper introduces the coevolution between genetic codes and the translation table into genetic algorithms (GAs). Though GAs were originally invented through an inspiration to mimic the evolutionary strategies of living things (Holland 1992), since Goldberg (Goldberg 1989a) established a simple form of GA (simple GA, or SGA) and proved that it could be successfully applied to a real engineering problem, many GA studies have followed this line: a population of chromosomes (DNA strings) are prepared and subjected to genetic operations such as selection, mutation, and crossover. However, a selection unit in biological evolution is basically not a chromosome but a cell. A cell not only includes DNA strands for genetic codes but also functional units (amino acids) and translation molecules (aminoacyl-tRNAs). Genetic information on DNA has no meaning without the construction of these smaller components in a cell (Bedian 2001; Wills 2001). Imitating this biological structure, we prepare an artificial cell that includes a DNA string, a set of aminoacyl-tRNAs, a set of tRNAs, and a set of indexed amino acids. The tRNAs and amino acids are respectively created by the transcription and translation of the DNA, and the aminoacyl-tRNAs are created by the chemical reaction between tRNAs and indexed amino acids. A population of cells having this structure is evolved by using operations for selection, DNA mutation, DNA crossover, molecular exchange, and chemical reaction. The cell's fitness is evaluated from the target function, which is calculated from the specific output amino acid values. To assess the validity of the proposed algorithm (which we refer to as the *chemical genetic algorithm* or CGA), we apply it to a few functional optimization problems that are hard to solve by SGA. Numerical experiments show great advantage of CGA vs. SGA for the tested optimization problems.

The organization of the paper is as follows. After explaining biochemical reactions for the translation of DNA information in a living cell in Section 2, Section 3 presents a proposed model for the CGA in detail. Section 4 introduces three types of deceptive functions and describes experimental conditions. The results are given in Section 5. Some discussions on the meaning of the model and future problems are given in Section 6, and concluding remarks are presented in Section 7.

Lesson from a Biological Cell

The translation of genetic information in a biological cell is achieved by a set of metabolic reactions catalyzed by several enzymes as shown in Fig. 1 (Alberts *et al.* 1994). First of all, a cell must prepare a necessary set of amino acids by the assimilation of smaller inorganic compounds (mostly in plants) or by the digestion of food (mostly in animals). Specifically, photosynthesis by plants plays a key role in creating larger organic molecules from smaller inorganic compounds. The amino acids are produced as products or by-products of a sequence of metabolic reactions starting from sugars produced by the photosynthesis. The created amino acids constitute a fundamental set of functional units in a cell.

On the other hand, a set of elementary units of genetic information in a cell is made up of RNA units that are created by the transcription of DNA. Specifically, a tRNA (transfer RNA), which is a sequence of about 80 nucleotides, is folded into a particular clover-shaped (or L-shaped) structure in a cell and works as an adapter of the codon. It has both an anti-codon (which complementarily matches a codon in mRNA, messenger RNA) and an identifier of an amino acid and thus specifies a correspondence of codon to amino acid.

Then, these two molecules, an informational unit (tRNA) and a functional unit (amino acid), are combined into an aminoacyl-tRNA catalyzed by the enzyme named aminoacyl-tRNA systhetase (ATS). An ATS recognizes an identification sequence included in the clover structure of tRNA, selects an appropriate amino acid that matches the identification sequence, and combines them. It is known that for each amino acid, one specific ATS is prepared. Therefore, there are twenty different ATS enzymes in a living cell.

The final process of the translation is accomplished by a large complex of proteins and RNA units, which is a ribosome. A ribosome reads an mRNA, compares a codon on the mRNA to the codon on an aminoacyl-tRNA, and, if they match, joins the amino acid on the aminoacyl-tRNA to a polypeptide (protein).

A major lesson from this biological translation system is the changeability of the mapping between a genotype and a phenotype. In life, the basic mapping from a codon (genotype unit) to an amino acid (phenotype unit) is specified by a set of translation molecules, aminoacyl-tRNAs. The aminoacyl-tRNAs are created in reference to the information on tRNA derived from DNA; consequently, the translation table can be changed by modifying the genetic information in the DNA.

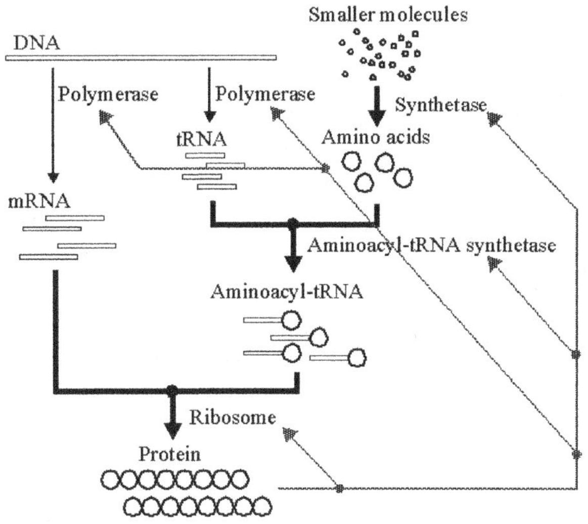

Figure 1: Biochemical reactions for the translation of genetic information in a living cell. The rectangles represent informational molecules such as DNA and RNA, and the large circles represent functional molecules (amino acids).

Another important point in life is the interdependence between molecules. The information for the production of all molecules in a cell comes from the DNA strands, and at the same time, the evolution of the information on DNA is influenced by the smaller molecules because the selective advantage of the DNA is determined by proteins created by the translation. In this sense, the codes (DNA information) and the code translation (repertory of aminoacyl-tRNAs) coevolve, which optimizes the system evolvability during evolution.

The Model

In our model that imitates the translation scheme of a biological system, we prepared four different types of molecular units in a cell for CGA: a DNA string, aminoacyl-tRNA units (aa-tRNAs), tRNA strings, and indexed amino acid units (iAminos) (Fig. 2). A DNA unit and the tRNAs are represented by binary strings, and the aa-tRNAs and iAminos are represented by combinations of a binary string and a real value. All of the proteins catalyzing the reactions are omitted. The parameters used in the model are summarized below.

- J_1 : Number of bits in a codon,
- J_2 : Number of bits in an index,
- K : Number of output amino acids for the target protein, or the number of dimensions for the target function F,
- L : Number of tRNA units in the DNA,
- M : Number of codons for iAminos in the DNA,

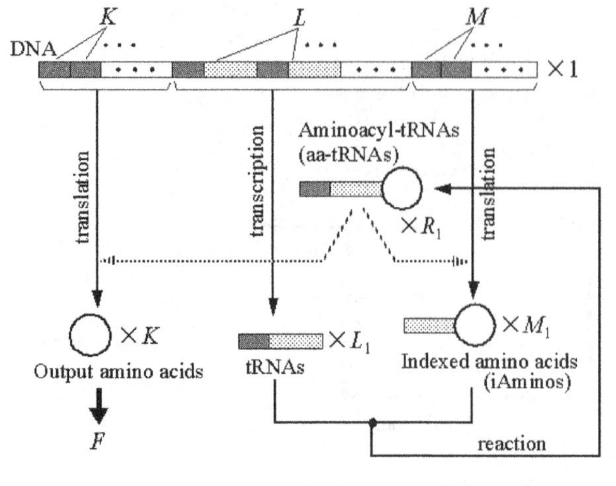

Figure 2: A cell structure used in the CGA. Dark hatched rectangles are codons described with J_1-bit strings, bright hatched rectangles are indexes described with J_2-bit strings, and circles are amino acids described with real numbers.

- I : Total length of (number of bits in) the DNA $= KJ_1 + L(J_1 + J_2) + MJ_2$,
- L_1 : Maximum number of tRNAs in a cell,
- M_1 : Maximum number of iAminos in a cell,
- R_1 : Initial/maximum number of aa-tRNAs in a cell,
- R_2 : Number of new aa-tRNAs created by the reaction between tRNAs and iAminos per cell per generation,
- p_m : Mutation rate (probability of flipping of DNA bits) per bit per generation,
- p_c : Crossover rate (occurrence probability of one-point crossover between a DNA pair) per cell pair per generation,
- N : Population size (the number of cells in the population),
- β : Exponent for the target function F,
- a,b : Fitness coefficient for linear scaling,
- c : Fitness coefficient for exponential scaling.

The reactions in Fig. 2 proceed as follows. Every generation, L tRNAs are created by the transcription of a DNA string, and M iAminos are created by the translation of DNA. The *indices* for the iAminos are the implementation of the amino acid identifiers on the real tRNA units in a biological cell. Though there is no 'index' data for a biological amino acid, we explicitly attach an index string to every iAmino to enable matching between a tRNA and an amino acid. The newly created tRNAs and iAminos are mixed with older tRNAs and iAminos, and if the total molecule numbers exceed L_1 and M_1, respectively, some of the molecules are randomly chosen and eliminated. Then, the reaction between tRNAs and iAminos is put into action. A pair of randomly chosen tRNA and iAmino is compared and, if their indices are the same, a new aa-tRNA is created. The aa-tRNA's *codon* is copied from the tRNA's codon, its index is copied from the tRNA's or the iAmino's index, and its amino acid is copied from the iAmino. This process is repeated until R_2 aa-tRNAs are created, and then some of the aa-tRNAs are randomly chosen from the new or older aa-tRNAs and eliminated so that the total number of aa-tRNAs does not exceed R_1.

A set of aa-tRNAs created in this way is used for the codon-amino acid translation. To translate a codon (J_1-bit string) in the DNA string, an aa-tRNA is randomly chosen from the aa-tRNA set, and if its codon is the same as the codon on the DNA, its index and amino acid value are copied to create a new iAmino or a new output amino acid. Every generation, K output amino acids are calculated in this way and used to evaluate the fitness value of the cell. In the selection operation (see below), every cell is assessed with the fitness value of the K-amino protein. This model can be regarded as a simplification of the selective environment wherein every cell is evaluated in terms of the efficiency of a single protein.

The entire procedure of the CGA is described as follows:

1. **[Initialization]** Prepare a population of N cells with the archtecture shown in Fig. 2. In the initial state, no cell has an aa-tRNA, a tRNA, or an output amino acid; each cell only includes a DNA string and M_1 iAminos. The sequence of bits in the DNA string is randomly chosen for each strand. The iAminos (pairs of index and amino value) are also randomly chosen for each iAmino, but they are assumed to be common for all cells of the initial population.

2. **[Chemical Reaction]** Conduct the transciption, translation, and reaction described above for each cell.

3. **[Selection]** Calculate the fitness value from the output amino acids for each cell and conduct roulette-wheel selection using the fitness values. When a cell is reproduced, the entire information (all four kinds of molecules) is copied from the mother cell to the daughter cell.

4. **[DNA Mutation]** Conduct the conventional mutation (bit flipping) operation on the DNA strings of the cells.

5. **[DNA Crossover & Molecular Exchange]** Mate all cells to make $N/2$ pairs. For each pair, conduct the conventional crossover (exchange of DNA substrings) operation and a molecular exchange operation. In the latter operation, half of the aa-tRNAs, tRNA, and iAminos are randomly chosen for each parent cell and they are exchanged.

6. Examine the population, and terminate if a particular condition is satisfied. Otherwise, go to Step 2.

At the outset, every cell has M_1 different (but common for all cells) iAminos, so if M_1 is large enough, the amino acid diversity stored in the iAminos is sufficiently large. As evolution goes on, this diversity gradually decreases, and at the same time, the amino acid diversity in the aa-tRNAs increases. If by chance an appropriate aa-tRNAs is created by the reaction in a cell, the cell gets a higher fitness value than the others and its genetic information on the DNA strand and smaller molecules begins to spread not just through reproduction in the selection operation but also through the molecular exchange operations. An appropriate set of amino values is chosen in this way from a large initial amino acid repertory.

Experiments

To verify the effectiveness of the CGA, we solve a functional optimization problem using the CGA. The problem includes three types of deceptive functions, types I to III, and is difficult to solve by conventional GAs such as a simple GA.

The fitness function is defined as fitness $= a + bF(x)$ for linear scaling or fitness $= \exp(cF(x))$ for exponential scaling where a, b and c are constant values. $F(x)$ is defined as:

$$F(x) = \left(\frac{1}{K}\sum_{k=0}^{K-1} f_k(x)\right)^{\beta},$$

where β is a non-linearity factor. The deceptive function $F(x)$ is classified into the following three types, depending on the location of a global optimum in K-dimensional space.

Type I is a simple deceptive problem:

$$f_k(x) = \begin{cases} \alpha - x & \text{if } 0 \le x \le 0.8 \\ \frac{x-\alpha}{1-\alpha} & \text{if } 0.8 < x \le 1 \end{cases}$$

where $\alpha = 0.8$.

Type II is a medium-complex deceptive problem:

$$f_k(x) = \begin{cases} \alpha - x & \text{if } 0 \le x \le 0.8 \\ \frac{x-\alpha}{1-\alpha} & \text{if } 0.8 < x \le 1 \end{cases}$$

or

$$f_k(x) = \begin{cases} \frac{1-\alpha-x}{1-\alpha} & \text{if } 0 \le x < 0.2 \\ x - 1 + \alpha & \text{if } 0.2 \le x \le 1 \end{cases}$$

is randomly chosen according to each dimension k ($k = 0, 1, \cdots, K-1$), where $\alpha = 0.8$.

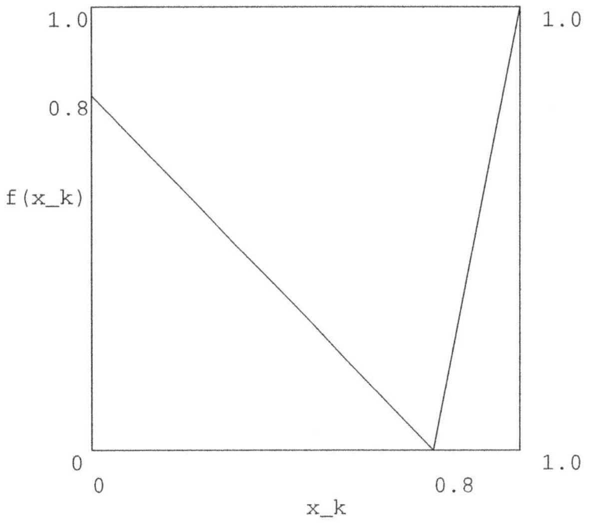

Figure 3: Type I: simple deceptive problem

Type III is a complex deceptive problem:

$$f_k(x) = \begin{cases} -\frac{x}{\alpha_k} + \frac{4}{5} & \text{if } 0 \le x < \frac{4}{5}\alpha_k \\ \frac{5x}{\alpha_k} - 4 & \text{if } \frac{4}{5}\alpha_k \le x \le \alpha_k \\ \frac{5(x-\alpha_k)}{\alpha_k - 1} + 1 & \text{if } \alpha_k \le x \le \frac{1+4\alpha_k}{5} \\ \frac{x-1}{1-\alpha_k} + \frac{4}{5} & \text{if } \frac{1+4\alpha_k}{5} < x \le 1, \end{cases}$$

where α_k is a different random number between 0 and 1 depending on each dimension k ($k = 0, 1, \cdots, K-1$).

Type I is a simple deceptive problem where the global optimum is located at $x_k = 1.0$ ($k = 0, ..., K-1$). The $2^K - 1$ local optima exist at locations with either $x_k = 0$ ($k = 0, \cdots, K-1$). Type II is a medium-complex deceptive problem where the global optimum is located at either $x_k = 0$ or 1 ($k = 0, \cdots, K-1$) and is randomly chosen according to each dimension. Similar to Type I, the number of local optima is $2^K - 1$. Type III is a complex deceptive problem where the location of the global optimum is randomly set in K-dimensional space; however, unlike types I and II, the number of local optima is $3^K - 1$ because the locations at both $x_k = 0$ and 1 are local optima in each dimension.

The attractor with a global optimum only has a length of 0.2, whereas the attractors with local optima have much more and wider regions in K-dimensional space. The region with local optima is $5^K - 1$ times wider than the region with a global optimum for all types of deceptive problems.

Experiments were performed for the three types of deceptive problems in five- and ten- dimensional cases. According to some preliminary experiments, we set the following experiment conditions: J_1 is set as 4 and 6 for the CGA in five and ten dimensions, respectively. Fitness as exponential scaling for the SGA was not adequate

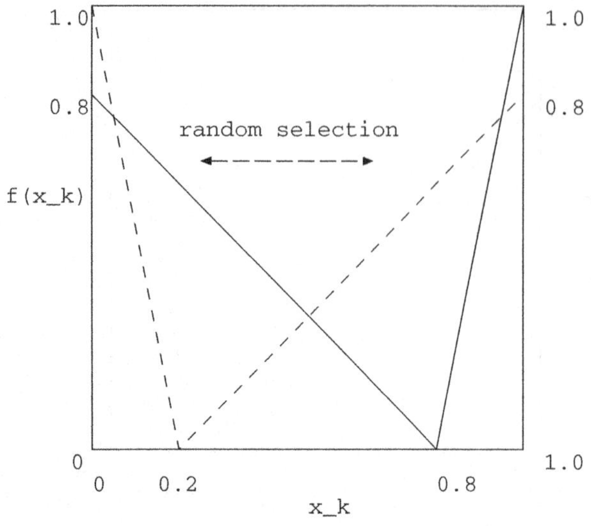

Figure 4: Type II: medium-complex deceptive problem

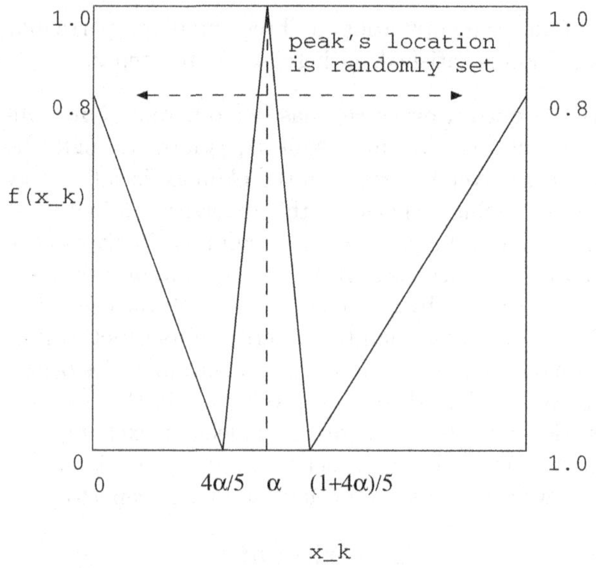

Figure 5: Type III: complex deceptive problem

because none of the ten runs was successful because exponential scaling was too strong for the SGA to succeed in finding a global optimum for all types of deceptive problems. On the other hand, linear scaling was also not adequate for the CGA because none of the runs was successful to find a global optimum for the complex deceptive problem. Therefore, linear scaling and exponential scaling of the fitness function was adopted for the SGA and the CGA, respectively. A DNA string in the SGA is the left part of the CGA string. Its length is $J_1 \times K$ bits, and the codons in the SGA are interpreted as real values by using the binary coding method. p_m and p_c were respectively set to 0.005 and 0.7 in common for both GAs, the number of cells (i.e., population size) N was set to 256, and the roulette-wheel selection with an elite selection of one individual was adopted for the selection operation. The non-lineality factor β in $F(x)$ was set to 5. Ten different runs with different random seeds were conducted for the SGA and CGA in both five- and ten-dimensional cases. Table 1 shows the set of parameters used for the CGA.

Table 1: Parameter set for CGA

K	J_1	J_2	L	M	L_1	M_1	R_1	R_2	I
5	4	8	16	32	80	1280	80	16	340
10	6	8	64	128	320	1280	320	64	1724

Results

Table 2 compares results between the SGA and CGA for five and ten dimensions. The case of $J_1 = 10$ in the SGA approximately corresponds to the case of the CGA with an initially different amino-value of $M_1 = 1280$. Fitness was defined as linear scaling with $a = 0$, $b = 1$ for the SGA and as exponential scaling with $c = 20.79$ for the CGA. Computational cost for the SGA and CGA to run 1000 generations is respectively a few minutes and 20-30 minutes using a general-purpose SUN workstation. Therefore, the computational cost of the CGA is about ten times larger than that of the SGA. Comparing the results between the SGA and CGA, almost all runs of the CGA were successful for the three types of deceptive problems, except for type III in ten dimensions, whereas the SGA never succeeded aside from one run for the complex deceptive problem.

Figure 6 shows the function values $F(x)$ of the CGA. Ten different runs are superimposed. Diversity during evolution of the CGA is well maintained because the best and average values are different from each other. Although the function values of the CGA rose up slowly, both the best and average values became better and better and finally reached a global optimum.

For comparison to the CGA, Fig. 7 shows the evolution of the SGA's function values for the complex deceptive problem in five dimensions. Almost all runs converged to local optima without converging to a global optimum because diversity in the function values was small due to the fact that the average and best values were approximately the same.

To further investigate the reason why the SGA shows such poor performance, we again performed the SGA with different bits of DNA strings. Table 3 shows comparative results with different parameters of the codon's bit J_1 and dimension K in the SGA. J_1 varies from 4 to 10, and K is 5 and 10. According to the results in Table 3, the appropriate value for J_1 cannot be determined for

Table 2: Success ratio in SGA and CGA

GA	SGA	CGA	SGA	CGA
K	5	5	10	10
J_1	10	4	10	6
scaling	linear	exp.	linear	exp.
Type I	0/10 (0%)	10/10 (100%)	0/10 (0%)	10/10 (100%)
Type II	0/10 (0%)	10/10 (100%)	0/10 (0%)	10/10 (100%)
Type III	1/10 (10%)	10/10 (100%)	0/10 (0%)	5/10 (50%)

For each condition, the number of successful runs out of ten different trials is shown with the success ratio in parentheses. For example, 1/10 (10%) means that one run out of ten runs succeeded in finding the global optimum, so the success ratio is 10%. Almost all runs of the CGA were successful for the three types of deceptive problems except for type III in ten dimensions, whereas the SGA never succeeded aside from one run for the complex deceptive problem.

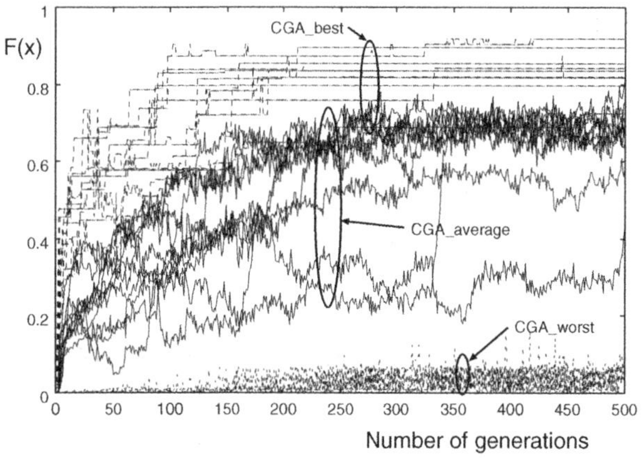

Figure 6: Evolution of chemical GA for type III deceptive problem in five dimensions. $J_1 = 4$. The solid fluctuating lines represent the average values, the dotted lines represent the best values, and the lower fluctuating dashed lines represent the worst values. Ten different runs are superimposed.

all types of deceptive problems in the SGA. More runs are necessary to identify the appropriate setting for each parameter.

Figures 8 and 9 are amino value histograms representing the number of cells with each dimensional amino value x_k $(k = 0, 1, \cdots, K-1)$ classified into 16 classes. Figure 8 shows the case of the CGA taking a global optimum, while Fig. 9 shows the case of the SGA taking a local optimum with x_4. Note that the diversity of the CGA is larger than that of the SGA because the values are maintained at a magnitude in the region that is even irrelevant to the global optimum, i.e., $0.3 < x_k < 0.6$.

Figure 10 shows the number of different amino values in aminoacyl-tRNAs and that in indexed amino acids (iAminos) as a function of generations. The number of different values in the iAminos was initialized as 1,280 and gradually decreased during evolution. On the other hand, the number of different values in the aa-tRNA was initialized as zero, suddenly increased at an early stage of generations, and then decreased as generations proceeded. Two kinds of numbers nearly converged to a final constant value, 22, at the 300th generation.

Discussion

Comparing results of the CGA to those of the SGA: To verify the performance of the CGA compared to that of the SGA, three kinds of deceptive problems were introduced and tested. According to the main results shown in Table 2, we can say that for the three tested deceptive functions, the CGA can find a global optimum solution far more often than can the SGA. This great advantage of the CGA over the SGA comes from the appropriate control of diversity in the population. As shown in Figs. 6 and 8, the CGA can recurrently generate a variety of amino acid values even after a population is stuck around the vicinity of a local optimum. Since the output amino values are affected by both the DNA sequence and the smaller molecules, the CGA can explore the search space more extensively than the SGA, which enables the CGA to escape from local optimums. This is especially the case for an early stage of evolution. For later stages of evolution, on the other hand, the CGA exhibits another behavior, the convergence to the optimum repertory of amino acids. As shown in Figs. 8 and 10, as evolution goes on, the diversity in amino values gradually decreases. The coevolution between DNA and smaller molecules controls this convergence in an appropriate manner, so that the CGA can finally obtain the optimum translation relation. For the SGA, on the other hand, once a population is stuck at a local optimum, evolution enters a long period of stasis due to the lack of cell diversity as shown in Figs. 7 and 9. Because the translation relation from DNA to real output values is fixed through a run, it is very hard for the SGA to escape from a local optimum wherein a population of DNA strands loses the diversity at some loci. The SGA offers far smaller possibility of exploration than the CGA does. Although the computational cost of the CGA is about ten times larger than that of the SGA, the excellent property of the CGA in controlling diversity makes the CGA a profitable algorithm for difficult problems such as deceptive problems.

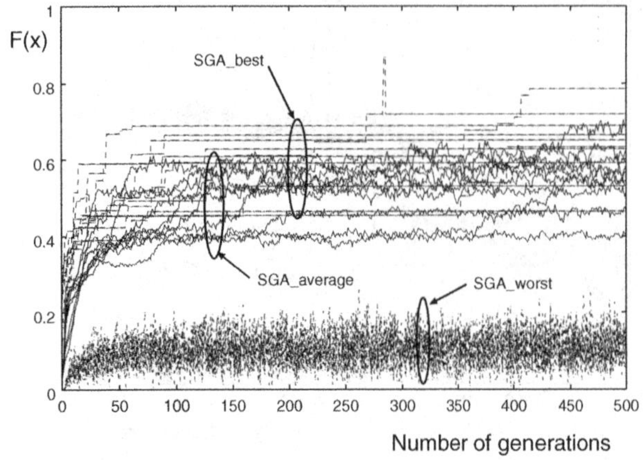

Figure 7: Evolution of the simple GA for type III deceptive problem in five dimensions. $J_1 = 10$. See the Fig. 6 caption for the description of lines.

Table 3: Success ratio in SGA with different parameters

K	5	5	5	5
J_1	4	5	6	10
Type I	7/10 (70%)	0/10 (0%)	0/10 (0%)	0/10 (0%)
Type II	1/10 (10%)	5/10 (50%)	1/10 (10%)	0/10 (0%)
Type III	0/10 (0%)	5/10 (50%)	1/10 (10%)	1/10 (10%)
K	10	10	10	10
J_1	4	5	6	10
Type I	2/10 (20%)	0/10 (0%)	0/10 (0%)	0/10 (0%)
Type II	3/10 (30%)	0/10 (0%)	0/10 (0%)	0/10 (0%)
Type III	0/10 (0%)	3/10 (30%)	3/10 (30%)	0/10 (0%)

For each condition, the number of successful runs out of ten different trials is shown with the success ratio in parentheses. There is no optimum value of J_1 that makes the success ratio maximum for all types of deceptive functions.

Coding in GAs: Since their proposal, GAs have been studied from a variety of viewpoints: a number of different versions of genetic operations have been tested (Goldberg 1989a), an island model and other population models have been proposed for maintaining genetic diversity in a population (Tanese 1989; Mühlenbein 1989), and various coding methods have been devised to solve engineering problems using binary string chromosomes (Caruana & Schaffer 1988; Goldberg, Korb, & Deb 1989b). Among them, the coding is one of the most important factors in GAs because it determines the fitness landscape on the genotype space affecting the GA performance. Man-made codings such as binary, Gray (Caruana & Schaffer 1988; Goldberg 1989a), and other methods (Goldberg, Korb, & Deb 1989b; Wright 1991) have been proposed to project a fitness function on the genotype space so that the GA operations might search for solutions more stably and more effectively. However, as discussed in Section 2, life did not determine the coding before its evolution. The coding, or in other words, the genotype-to-phenotype association, was coded in the DNA/RNA units and was changed and optimized together with the codes in DNA/RNA during evolution. The CGA introduced this mechanism to conventional GAs and achieved far better performance than the simple GA for a deceptive problem. This result suggests that further work is worthwhile for the evaluations and refinements of the CGA.

Future problems: The present version of CGA is just a simple actualization of molecular reactions in a cell. The moleculer types prepared in Fig. 2 is a minimal set for the translation of DNA information, and some other important molecules such as enzymes (proteins catalyzing reactions or synthesizing amino acids) are omitted. We consider introducing these molecules to CGA as an important problem for the future. Also, in the present model, the amino values are not synthesized but are initially created on indexed amino acids. Making amino values newly synthesized during evolution is also a future problem to be tackled. For the evaluation of the CGA, the test function $F(x)$ used in this paper is insufficient. $F(x)$'s value is determined from the sum of independent functions for x_ks, so $F(x)$ is basically a function with separable variables. Applying the CGA to functions with inseparable variables or real engineering problems and comparing its performance with more effective evolutionary algorithms other than the SGA are to be solved in the future.

Conclusions

We have developed a new bio-molecular algorithm, a chemical genetic algorithm (CGA), in which several types of molecules react with each other in a cell. Translation from codons in DNA to amino acids is specified by a particular set of translation molecules (aminoacyl-tRNAs), which are created by the reaction between tRNAs and amino acids. Those smaller molecules are created from DNA, so the codes in DNA and the code translation in smaller molecules coevolve in the model. During evolution, the fundamental genotype-phenotype mapping is adaptively changed and converges to the optimum one. Through the struggle between cells with a DNA strand and smaller molecules, a specific output

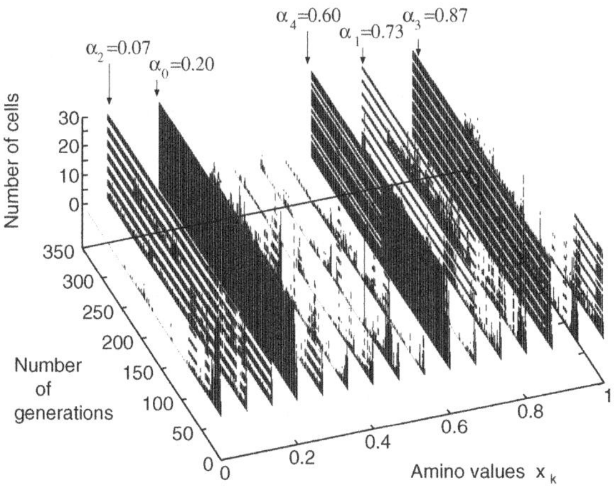

Figure 8: Time series of amino value histograms during a typical run of chemical GA for the five-dimensional type III deceptive problem. Numbers of cells, which are truncated at 30, represent the numbers of amino values x_0 to x_4 outputted by the cells, and they are shown using different pulse line patterns for x_0 to x_4. The global optimum solution of this problem is given by $(x_0, x_1, x_2, x_3, x_4) = (\alpha_0, \alpha_1, \alpha_2, \alpha_3, \alpha_4) = (0.20, 0.73, 0.07, 0.87, 0.60)$. The CGA succeeded in finding this solution because the coevolution of DNA and aa-tRNA provided sufficient diversity in output amino acid values at early stages of evolution, and also allowed the convergence of those values at later stages of evolution.

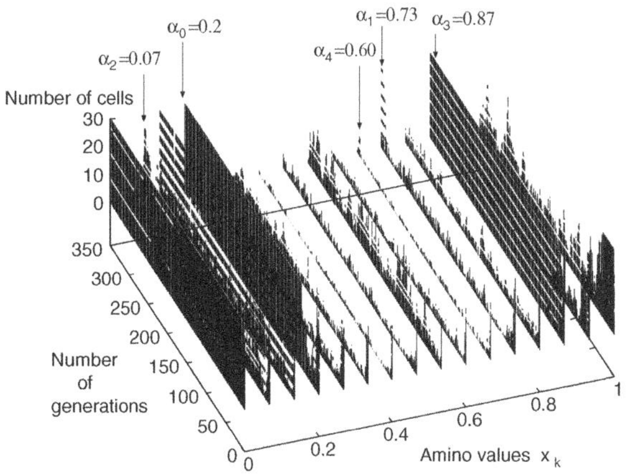

Figure 9: Time series of amino value histograms during a typical run of simple GA for the same deceptive problem as was used in Fig. 8. The SGA fails to find the global optimum because the amino values are not diversified enough to find the global optimum at early stages of evolution. Instead, quite a lot of cells converge to local optimal values of amino acids.

function (protein), which is used to evaluate a cell's fitness, is optimized. To demonstrate the effectiveness of the CGA, the presented algorithm was applied to a set of deceptive problems in five and ten dimensions, and the results by using the CGA were compared to those by using a simple GA as a conventional GA. As a result, it was shown that in the constructed chemical reaction model, the coevolution between codes and code translation appropriately controls the diversity of population and makes the population to converge to the global optimum with far higher probability than the conventional SGA.

Thanks are due to Dr. Ono of ATR labs for daily discussions with the first author. Dr. K. Shimohara of ATR labs also actively encouraged the study. The first author's research work was supported in part by the Telecommunicatios Advancement Organization of Japan and Doshisha University's Research Promotion Funds.

References

Alberts, B., Bray, D., Lewis, J., Raff, M., Roberts, K., Watson, J.D. 1994. *Molecular Biology of the Cell, The Third Edition.* New York: Garland Publishing.

Bedian, V. 2001. Self-description and the origin of the genetic code. *BioSystems* **60** 39–47

Caruana, R.A., Schaffer, J.D. 1988. Representation and hidden bias: Gray versus binary coding in genetic algorithms. In: Laird, J. (ed.): *Proceedings of 5th International Conference on Machine Learning.* San Mateo, CA: Morgan Kaufmann 153-161

Goldberg, D.E. 1989. *Genetic Algorithms in Search, Optimization and Machine Learning.* New York: Addison-Wesley

Goldberg, D.E., Korb, B., Deb, K. 1989. Messy genetic algorithms: Motivation, analysis, and first results. *Complex Systems* **3** 493-530

Holland, J.H. 1992. *Adaptation in Natural and Artificial Systems.* Boston: MIT Press

Mühlenbein, H. 1989. Parallel genetic algorithms, population genetics and combinatorial optimization. In: Schaffer, J.D. (ed.): *Proceedings of the 3rd International Conference on Genetic Algorithms.* San Mateo, CA: Morgan Kaufmann Publishers 416-421

Suzuki, H. 2000a. Minimum Density of Functional Proteins to Make a System Evolvable. In: Sugisaka, M., Tanaka, H. (eds.): *Proceedings of The Fifth International Symposium on Artificial Life and Robotics (AROB 5th '00).* Vol. 1, 30-33

Suzuki, H. 2000b. Evolvability Analysis: Distribution of Hyperblobs in a Variable-Length Protein Genotype

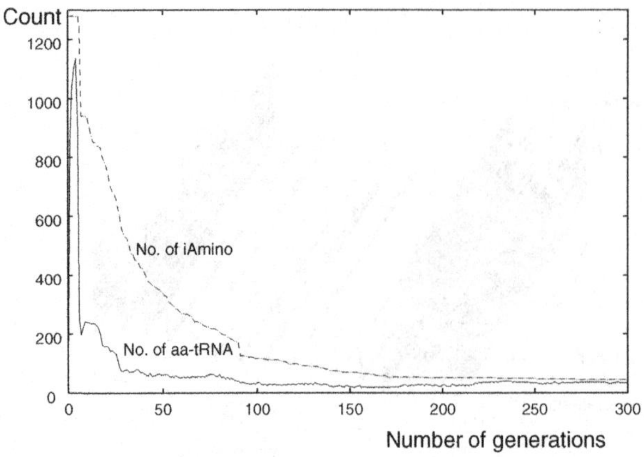

Figure 10: Number of different amino values in aa-tRNAs (a solid line) and iAminos (a doted line) in evolution of chemical GA

Space. In: Bedau, M.A. et al. (eds.): *Artificial Life VII: Proceedings of the Seventh International Conference on Artificial Life.* Cambridge: MIT Press, 206–215

Suzuki, H. 2001. String Rewriting Grammar Optimized Using an Evolvability Measure. In: Kelemen, J., Sosik, P. (eds.): *Advances in Artificial Life (6th European Conference on Artificial Life Proceedings).* Berlin: Springer-Verlag, 458-468

Tanese, R. 1989. Distributed genetic algorithms. In: Schaffer, J.D. (ed.): *Proceedings of the 3rd International Conference on Genetic Algorithms.* San Mateo, CA: Morgan Kaufmann Publishers 434-439

Wills, P.R. 2001. Autocatalysis, information, and coding. *BioSystems* **60** 49–57

Wright, A.H. 1991. Genetic algorithms for real parameter optimization. In: Rawlins, G.J.E. (ed.): *Foundations of Genetic Algorithms (FOGA-1).* San Mateo, CA: Morgan Kaufmann Publishers 205-218

Improving and Still Passing the ALife Test: Component-Normalised Activity Statistics Classify Evolution in Geb as Unbounded

Alastair Channon
Department of Electronic and Computer Engineering
Anglesea Road, University of Portsmouth, PO1 3DJ. UK
alastair@channon.net http://www.channon.net/alastair[1]

Abstract

Bedau's (1998a) classification system for long-term evolutionary dynamics provides a test for open-ended evolution. Making this ALife test more rigorous, and passing it, are two of the most important open problems in the field. Previously (Channon 2001) I presented the result that 'Geb', a system designed to verify and extend theories behind the generation of evolutionary emergent systems (Channon & Damper 2000), has passed this test. However I also criticised the test, most significantly with regard to its normalisation method for artificial systems. This paper details a modified normalisation method, based on component activity normalisation, that overcomes these criticisms. It then presents the results of the revised test when applied to Geb, which indicate that this system does indeed exhibit open-ended evolution.

Introduction

As the discipline of Artificial Life has developed, so has the need for quantifiable measures of success. This is especially true with regard to evolvability and open-ended evolution. Bedau et al. (1991,1997b,1998a,1999a) have developed not only elegantly simple statistical measures for long-term evolution, but also a test for unbounded evolution. The test is so adaptable that it can be applied to any evolving system with an available record of its components' existence times, such as the biosphere's fossil record. Any artificial system can be tested, and those that have been include Tierra-like systems (Adami & Brown 1994; Taylor & Hallam 1998), Echo (Holland 1975), Bugs (Packard 1989), Lindgren's (1991) model of evolving strategies in the iterated prisoner's dilemma, Arthur's (1994) "Bar Problem" and *EcoLab* (Standish 2000). Previously only taxonomic families in the fossil record have passed the test.

Bedau et al.'s test is based on the following statistics (from (Bedau *et al.* 1997; Bedau, Snyder & Packard 1998)) which are calculated from the record of components' existence times.

Activity increment (by presence).

$$\Delta_i(t) = \begin{cases} 1 & \text{if component } i \text{ exists at } t \\ 0 & \text{otherwise} \end{cases} \quad (1)$$

This is not the only activity increment that they have used, but it is the best for comparison across systems because it can be calculated for any system with a record of components' existence times.

Evolutionary Activity of a component.

$$a_i(t) = \begin{cases} \sum_{\tau=0}^{t} \Delta_i(\tau) & \text{if component } i \text{ exists at } t \\ 0 & \text{otherwise} \end{cases} \quad (2)$$

Diversity (number of components present).

$$D(t) = \#\{i : a_i(t) > 0\} \quad (3)$$

Total cumulative evolutionary activity (or just 'total activity').

$$\bar{A}_{\text{cum}}(t) = \sum_i a_i(t) \quad (4)$$

Mean cumulative evolutionary activity (or just 'mean activity').

$$\bar{A}_{\text{cum}}(t) = \frac{\bar{A}_{\text{cum}}(t)}{D(t)} \quad (5)$$

New evolutionary activity per component (or just 'new activity').

$$A_{\text{new}}(t) = \frac{1}{D(t)} \sum_{i:a_i(t)\in[a_0,a_1]} a_i(t) \quad (6)$$

For A_{new} to be a good measure of new activity, the range $[a_0, a_1]$ should be chosen such that component activities within it can be considered both adaptively significant and not amongst the highest. For artificial systems, a 'shadow' is run, mirroring the real run in every detail except that whenever selection (artificial or natural) operates in the real system, random selection is employed in the shadow. The statistics from this shadow can then be used to determine a_0 and levels of total and mean activity that can be considered adaptively significant.

After determining long-term trends in these statistics, the system being examined can be classified according to table 1. The hallmark of class 3 (unbounded evolutionary dynamics) is unbounded total cumulative evolutionary activity in combination with positive new evolutionary activity per component. Other possibilities exist with zero A_{new}, but these belong in class 1 (no evolutionary activity) because such cases have no significant new components. Table 1 in (Bedau, Snyder & Packard 1998) only shows the first row (3a) for class 3, but footnote 1 in that paper acknowledges the other rows (3b and 3c).

[1] Source code and instructions for replicating the runs discussed in this paper are available from the author's home page.

[2] Note that Bedau has since altered his class numbering scheme.

CLASS	EVOLUTIONARY DYNAMICS	STATISTICAL SIGNATURE D	A_{new}	$\bar{A}_{\text{cum}}$
1	none	bounded	zero	zero
2	bounded	bounded	positive	bounded
3a	unbounded (D)	unbounded	positive	bounded
3b	unbounded ($\bar{A}_{\text{cum}}$)	bounded	positive	unbounded
3c	unbounded (D & $\bar{A}_{\text{cum}}$)	unbounded	positive	unbounded

Table 1: Classes of evolutionary dynamics and their statistical signatures, based on table 1 from (Bedau, Snyder & Packard 1998)[2]. Rows 3b and 3c have been added to class 3 (see text).

Note that table 1 includes all possibilities for positive A_{new}, because zero $\bar{A}_{\text{cum}}$ implies zero A_{new}. So any system with unbounded evolutionary dynamics will belong to class 3 (one of 3a, 3b and 3c).

Previously (Channon 2001) I presented the result that the artificial system 'Geb' (Channon & Damper 1998a; 1998b; 2000) has passed this test. However I also criticised the test, most significantly with regard to its normalisation method for artificial systems. The test relies on normalisation (or validation) from a shadow that can drift away from core aspects of the real run that it is intended to shadow. For example, the components that exist in the real population at any one time (well into evolution) are almost certainly more densely clustered than those in the shadow. So the mutation of a real component is more likely to produce another high-activity component than the mutation of a shadow component. Once the real and shadow populations have been allowed to evolve, we are no longer comparing the real run with a true shadow. The longer the period since the shadow was initialised to match the real run, the less relevant the shadow is to the real run.

My other criticism of the test was in its use of mean activity when looking for unbounded activity growth, especially when classifying a system as belonging to class 3b. When diversity is bounded, retention (forever) of a single component results in unbounded mean activity. The test should not be so influenced by such components, and should rather look for trends in typical components. So it is median activity, not mean activity, that should be measured, and required to be unbounded for a system to be classified as within class 3b.

Before progressing to the two main contributions of this paper (the new normalisation method and its results when applied to Geb) it is first necessary to outline how the statistics have been implemented in Geb. These details apply equally to both the original and modified tests, which use the same statistics for the real run and only differ in their shadow and its use in normalising the real run's statistics.

Implementing the statistics in Geb

Geb is a virtual world containing autonomous organisms, each controlled by a neural network. Each neuron has a bit-string label, or 'character', which is used during development and for matching the neural outputs of one organism with basic behaviours (turning, killing, etc.) and with inputs of other organisms. An organism is born with a simple axiom network that results in reproduction. This develops through the application of a genetically determined Lindenmayer system (L-system) (Lindenmayer 1968). Each L-system production rule has the following form:

$$\mathcal{P} \rightarrow \mathcal{S}_r, \mathcal{S}_n \ ; \ b_1, b_2, b_3, b_4, b_5, b_6$$

$\mathcal{P}$	Predecessor (first bits of node's character)
$\mathcal{S}_r$	Successor 1: *replacement* node's character
$\mathcal{S}_n$	Successor 2: *new* node's character
bits:	$b_1, b_2, b_3, b_4, b_5, b_6$ specify linkage details

The *successors* (1 and 2) are characters for the node(s) that replace the old node. If a successor has zero length then that node is not created.

An evolved genotype contains a large number of production rules (once decoded), but only the rules found to match neuron's characters most closely are used during development. In this way, increasingly specific production rules can evolve, with regressive rules existing as fall-back options should a rule be damaged by crossover or mutation, and as material for further evolutionary exploration.

When a new organism is 'born', all possible production rules are decoded from its genotype. Then the developmental process is part-simulated in advance of it truly taking place, as a means of filtering out all the production rules that would never be used, either because they would never match any possible node's character, or because more specific rules exist for each node that could develop. All rules that remain will be used if the organism lives long enough.

This makes the choice 'production rules that survive the filtering process at birth' a good choice for the component class. It turns out that there is a high degree of neutrality in successors, making them difficult to track.

So a better choice for the component class, and the one I have used, is 'predecessor plus link details' from production rules that survive the filtering process. See (Channon 2001) for details. Having chosen this component class, there is a clear consequence for the possible classifications of evolutionary dynamics. Because the number of neurons that an organism can have is limited (for practical reasons), the number of production rules that can survive filtering is limited. And because the population size is small (a maximum of four hundred organisms), there is little room for more than a couple of species at a time. So diversity of these components will certainly be bounded, and we can rule out class 3a and 3c dynamics.

Geb's shadow mirrors the real run in every detail except that selection is random. Whenever a real organism is killed, a randomly chosen shadow organism is also killed. Whenever a real organism is born (as the product of two real organisms), a new shadow organism is born as the product of two randomly chosen shadow organisms, using the same reproduction procedure with the same rates of crossover and mutation. For each initial real organism born with single-bit genotype '0', an initial shadow organism is also born with single-bit genotype '0'.

Component snapshots were taken every one thousand timesteps. To put this in context, the example run reported lasted six million timesteps, during which time there were over five hundred and eighty million organism reproductions. In each timestep, every organism is updated. Because activity is intended as a measure of how much a component both is used (already covered above) and *persists*, I screen out (in each of the real and shadow populations) isolated occurrences: when a component occurs in the current snapshot but not the previous one.

In previously published work on Geb (before the implementation of evolutionary statistics), total extinction (population size dropping to one individual) was not mentioned because it had not been encountered. However, there was no mechanism in place to prevent it and, during the long trial runs undertaken when experimenting with evolutionary statistics, I encountered occasional runs in which total extinction occurred. So for the set of runs from which the example reported here is taken, I set a minimum number of organisms to twenty. The fact that total extinction is so rare despite the population size being so small (a maximum of four hundred organisms at any one time) indicates that there is no serious problem here. Once population sizes can feasibly be increased, the problem should in practice disappear rapidly.

The shadow-resetting method

Because there is reason to doubt a method of normalising (or validating) evolutionary statistics that relies on a shadow that can drift away from core aspects of its real

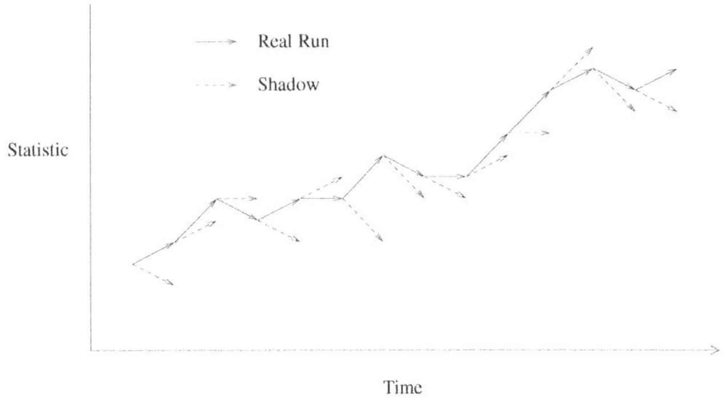

Figure 1: Illustration of the shadow-resetting method.

run, a new method needed to be developed that regularly resets the shadow (both components and activity history) to be identical to the real run. The rest of this paper details the development of such a method and reports on its results when applied to Geb.

The basic idea is that immediately after each snapshot (when an entry is made in the component existence record), the shadow run has its components reset to those of the real run. This allows us to compare inter-snapshot changes in activity in the real run with the changes we would expect from random selection, the result being an improved generic shadowing mechanism. When calculating evolutionary statistics (and indeed when recording component numbers), the shadow's history is taken to be that of the real run - see figure 1.

Most of the results below are from a typical run, drawn from a set of twenty carried out using this procedure. Atypical variations found within this set are also reported and discussed. Figure 2 shows the raw real and shadow activity wave diagrams from the typical run. One obvious feature is that many of the waves keep increasing. As discussed in (Channon 2001), this would also be true in a similar analysis of the biosphere's evolution. Genes that are beneficial to life tend to become basic for many species: humans have a significant proportion of genes in common with mice, flies and even plants.

Shadow waves follow the real waves, because the shadow is reset after each snapshot. The shadow loses components between snapshots far more frequently than the real run does. This is especially true of the lower-activity components, as we should expect. Adaptively significant production rules have many redundant copies on a typical genome such that should mutation break the rule at one point, it will still be decoded from elsewhere on the genome. Such components can survive even sustained periods of random selection. Yet even the highest activity components are frequently lost in the shadow and this provides verification that the snapshot interval (one thousand timesteps) is sufficient for comparing activity by presence. Employing a much higher reset

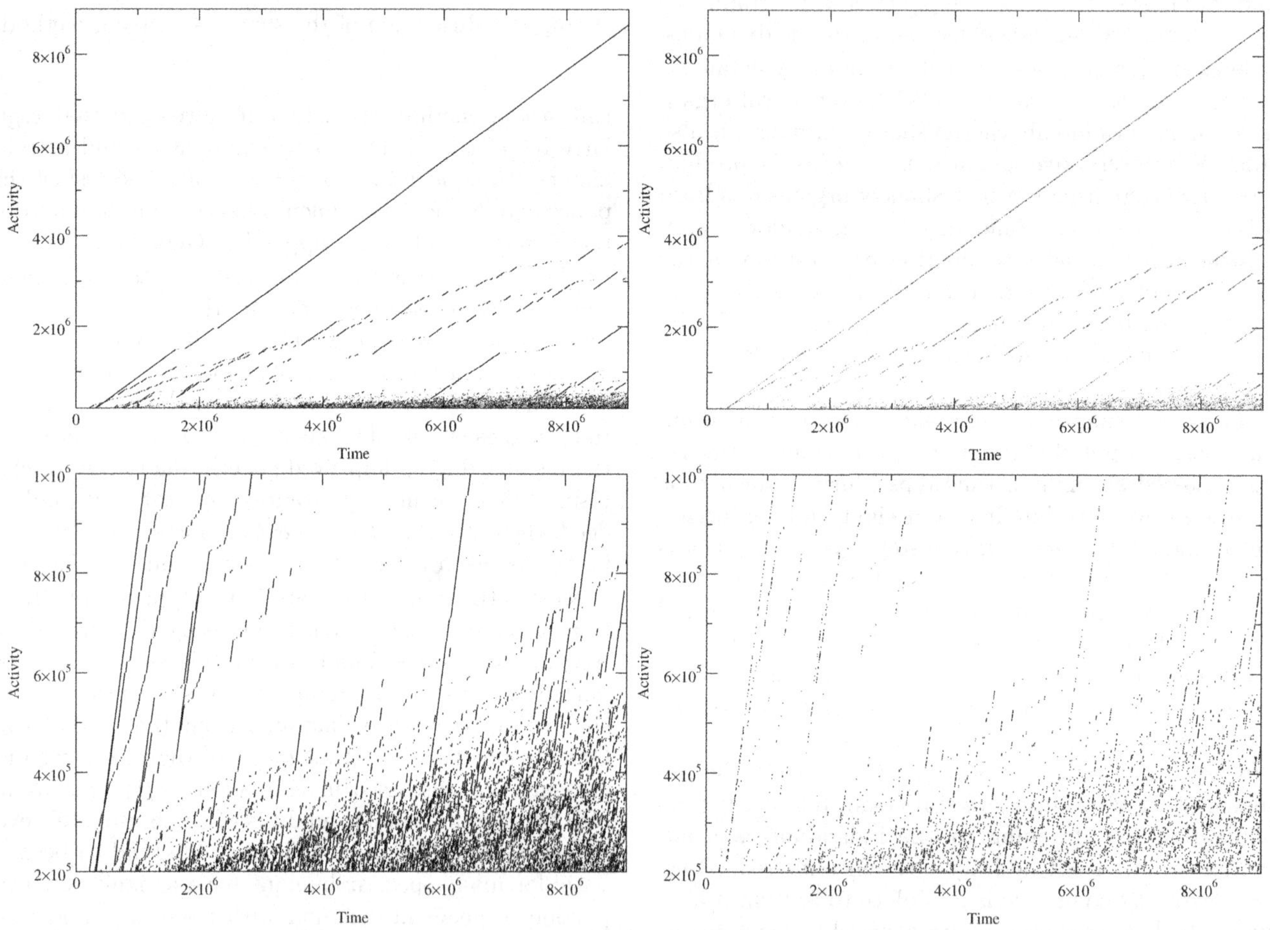

Figure 2: Activity wave diagrams for the real (left) and shadow (right) runs, with all horizontal (no-increase) lines removed. The lower diagrams show a magnified view of the activity range below 1 million.

frequency would require the use of an activity increment function which is sensitive to the number of occurrences of a component at any one time[3], for example $\Delta_i(t) =$ fraction of organisms that have the ith component at time t. However, because significantly more frequent snapshots are not feasible with the computational resources currently available, comparing activity by presence is still the best option.

Of course it would not make sense to calculate activity statistics based solely on the shadow's component existence record. Perhaps the most obvious course of action (and the one I took at first) is to calculate activity statistics for the shadow on the basis that at each timestep t we use the real run's component record for timesteps before t, and the shadow's component record at t. Figure 3 shows the resulting statistics from the shadow, alongside the real run's statistics. Activity (total, mean and median) is unbounded in the shadow only because the shadow has its components reset to those of the real run after each snapshot. On average both total activity and diversity drop sharply in the shadow over each short (1000 timesteps) interval after it has been reset to the real run's state. The shadow's mean and median activity statistics show that (on average) it is the higher activity components that remain in the shadow, in agreement with the discussion (above) of the activity wave diagrams. Do not be confused by the fact that mean and median activity increase in the shadow over each inter-snapshot interval. This is due to the loss of lower activity components, not the result of any increase in component activity.

These results are encouraging, but they provide no route to normalising the real run's statistics in order to demonstrate a presence or lack of unbounded growth in, say, median activity. The method so far also provides no sound way of measuring new activity. So naively calculating the shadow's activity statistics leads us to a dead-end. The idea of resetting the shadow run's state to match the real run's state just after each snapshot is a good one, but how can it be used to normalise the real run's statistics?

Component activity normalisation

The solution is to normalise at the lower level of individual components' activities, rather than at the component-population level. This is done by subtracting the shadow's component activity increment from the real run's component activity increment, for each component. So when calculating activity by presence, a component's normalised activity is incremented if and only if it persists (and is used) in the real run but not in the shadow, and is decremented if and only if it persists (and is used) in the shadow but not in the real run (although activity will still be read as zero for that timestep). Here are the revised statistics:

[3]Thanks to Mark Bedau for bringing this to my attention.

Real run's component activity increment.

$$\Delta_i^{\mathrm{R}}(t) = \begin{cases} 1 & \text{if component } i \text{ exists in the real run at } t \\ 0 & \text{otherwise} \end{cases} \tag{7}$$

Shadow's component activity increment.

$$\Delta_i^{\mathrm{S}}(t) = \begin{cases} 1 & \text{if component } i \text{ exists in the shadow at } t \\ 0 & \text{otherwise} \end{cases} \tag{8}$$

Normalised component activity increment.

$$\Delta_i^{\mathrm{N}}(t) = \Delta_i^{\mathrm{R}}(t) - \Delta_i^{\mathrm{S}}(t) \tag{9}$$

Normalised component activity.

$$a_i^{\mathrm{N}}(t) = \begin{cases} \sum_{\tau=0}^{t} \Delta_i^{\mathrm{N}}(\tau) & \text{if component } i \text{ exists in the real run at } t \\ 0 & \text{otherwise} \end{cases} \tag{10}$$

Normalised diversity.

$$D^{\mathrm{N}}(t) = \#\{i : a_i^{\mathrm{N}}(t) > a_0^{\mathrm{N}}\} \tag{11}$$

Note that this formula for D^{N} is only a suggestion for how diversity could be normalised when investigating systems with unbounded diversity: by counting the number of components whose normalised activity has passed the threshold at which we consider them to be adaptively significant (see below). This method of normalising diversity is debatable. However, because Geb does not exhibit unbounded diversity I safely ignore that debate here, and do not calculate D^{N} for Geb. This is valid because no claim of unbounded diversity is being made, and because D^{R} (not D^{N}) is the relevant value to use when calculating $\bar{A}_{\mathrm{cum}}^{\mathrm{N}}$, $\tilde{A}_{\mathrm{cum}}^{\mathrm{N}}$ and $A_{\mathrm{new}}^{\mathrm{N}}$, because D^{R} is the number of components that contribute to those statistics. Normalised total cumulative evolutionary activity.

$$A_{\mathrm{cum}}^{\mathrm{N}}(t) = \sum_{i:\ \substack{\text{component i exists} \\ \text{in the real run at t}}} a_i^{\mathrm{N}}(t) \tag{12}$$

Normalised mean cumulative evolutionary activity.

$$\bar{A}_{\mathrm{cum}}^{\mathrm{N}}(t) = \frac{A_{\mathrm{cum}}^{\mathrm{N}}(t)}{D^{\mathrm{R}}(t)} \tag{13}$$

Normalised median cumulative evolutionary activity.

$$\tilde{A}_{\mathrm{cum}}^{\mathrm{N}}(t) = \operatorname*{Median}_{i:\ \substack{\text{component i exists} \\ \text{in the real run at t}}} a_i^{\mathrm{N}}(t) \tag{14}$$

Normalised new activity per component.

$$A_{\mathrm{new}}^{\mathrm{N}}(t) = \frac{1}{D^{\mathrm{R}}(t)} \sum_{i:\text{component i `new'}} a_i^{\mathrm{N}}(t) \tag{15}$$

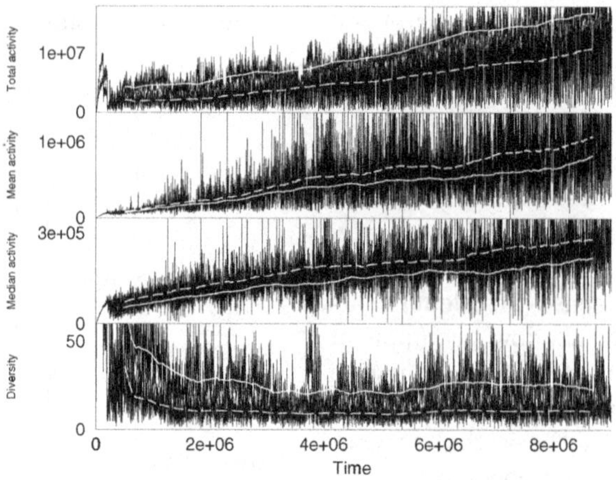

Figure 3: Total activity, mean activity, new activity and diversity from a typical Geb run and its regularly-reset shadow. Running averages are shown in white: solid for the real run, dashed for its shadow.

See below for the details of calculating normalised new activity per component.

This is clearly the better approach, for it produces normalised component activities that measure how much each component's activity has increased above the increase that would have occurred had selection been random. So a component's normalised activity is a direct measure of the degree to which adaptive selection in the real run is causing the component to persist (and be used).

Determining the normalised new-activity criteria

The final requirement, before these statistics can be used to classify evolutionary dynamics, is a method of determining when a component is newly adaptively significant: Clearly the method from (Bedau, Snyder & Packard 1998) cannot be used with the revised shadowing mechanism. The method must provide a (normalised) activity level $a_0^{\rm N}$ at which a component can be considered adaptively significant, and a procedure for dropping a component from the list of new components. For the second of these concerns, a simple upper bound cannot be used, because normalised activity can both increase and decrease, so a component could potentially be considered 'new' forever. The simplest (and adequate) solution is to consider a component to be 'new' (newly adaptively significant) in the snapshot at which its activity reaches $a_0^{\rm N}$, and never after that. So each component is considered new at most once. This leaves the issue of determining $a_0^{\rm N}$.

If the presence or absence of a component confers no adaptive advantage or disadvantage, then the real and shadow systems are equivalent for this component. Further, which is used as the reset-to system (after each snapshot) makes no difference to the component's activity. So the (normalised) activity distribution for this class of components will be symmetric about the origin. Therefore, provided we can make the assumption that the most negative normalised activity encountered during a run is from such a component, we can negate this value to find a level at which normalised activity can be considered adaptively significant. Even if this assumption does not hold, negating the most negative activity encountered provides a value above which activity can be considered adaptively significant, even if this bound is higher than necessary.

This method can be expected to work well when activity is calculated by presence (as it is in Bedau and Packard's test and so also here), where changes in component activity (Δ_i) are small when compared with the activities of non-adaptive components. However, we should not expect it to provide a good bound when calculating activity by, for example, usage ($\Delta_i =$ #components i at t), where the most negative activities arise from neutral mutations of high usage components, some of which a shadow will encounter before its real run does.

Results and Discussion

Figure 4 shows the normalised activity waves from the typical run, already discussed above, drawn from the full set of twenty runs. Notice that the activity values are significantly lower than before normalisation - see figure 2.

In each of the twenty runs, the lowest normalised activity encountered was greater than -30, with -10 being a more typical value. For simplicity I used a new-activity threshold ($a_0^{\rm N}$) of 30 on all runs. Figure 5 shows the resulting statistics for the typical run. Normalised median activity is unbounded (as are normalised total activity and normalised mean activity) and normalised new activity is positive. These results clearly fall into class 3b (according to this classification system): unbounded

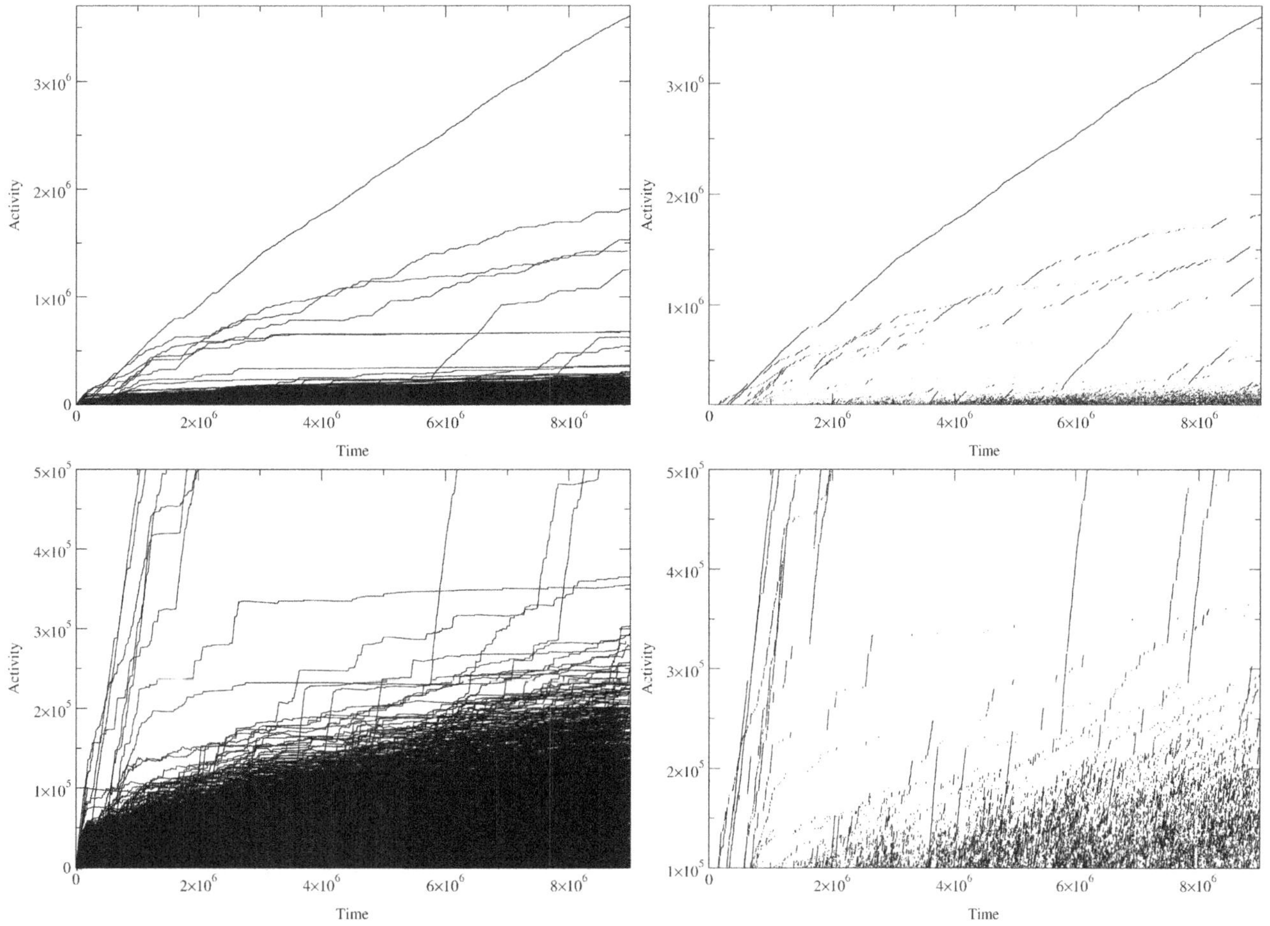

Figure 4: Normalised activity wave diagrams. Those on the right have had all horizontal (no-increase) lines removed. The lower diagrams show a magnified view of the activity range below 0.5 million.

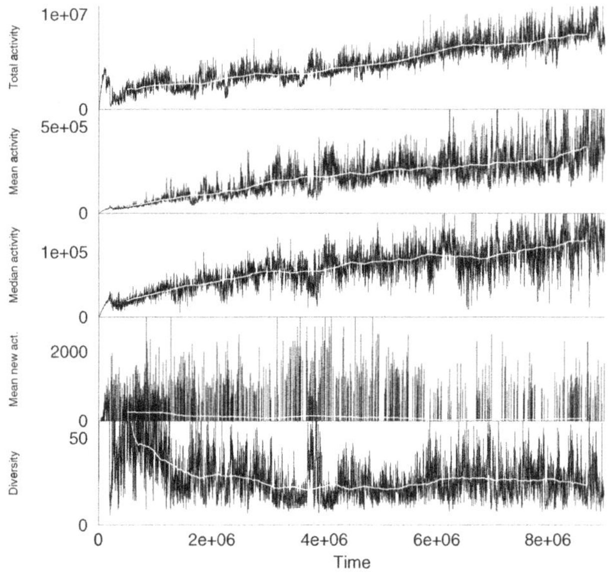

Figure 5: Normalised total activity, normalised mean activity, normalised median activity, normalised new activity, and real diversity. Running averages are shown in white.

evolutionary activity.

These results are typical of the twenty runs carried out for this set of experiments. However, five of the runs encountered problems, causing their results to be atypical. Three of these effectively met total extinction. In the implementation section I noted that I imposed a minimum limit on the number of organisms, in an attempt to avoid total extinction. However, if population size hits this limit and does not increase rapidly, then many reproductions may occur with selection effectively random. This causes evolutionary activity to plummet as adaptive traits are lost. Once lost, this activity cannot be regained, except by the evolution of new adaptive components. These results are not a cause for concern, for the same reasons mentioned above: once population sizes can feasibly be increased, the problem should in practice disappear rapidly.

Each of the other two atypical runs stagnated when the only existing species stopped reproducing. Of course this would ordinarily be a very poor strategy. It is easy to imagine how the bad gene (production rule) could have spread through a population of just one species as fit individuals reproduced with the new unfit ones, causing their children to pick up the dominant bad gene. However, one would not expect this to pose a threat to a different species. This is easily verified: introducing just a few organisms from any of the other evolved populations (from the other runs), causes the old organisms to be rapidly displaced by the newcomers. So this result is also not a cause for concern, for the same reason: it is due to the small population size, which cannot support more than one or two species at a time. Note also that both types of atypical run were also seen in (Channon 2001).

It is easy to demonstrate that unbounded growth (or more accurately unbounded non-monotonic but *directed* increase) in activity, with positive new activity, is not a trivial consequence of unbounded genotype length. Consider the analogous system Geb^R, in which selection is random but all other details are as in Geb. Whenever a (randomly chosen) real organism is killed in Geb^R, a randomly chosen organism is also killed in its shadow. Whenever a real organism is born in Geb^R (as the product of two randomly chosen real organisms), a new shadow organism is born as the product of two randomly chosen shadow organisms. Of course running either real or shadow system from the same snapshot more than once would produce different results on each run, because of the stochastic nature of the systems. So normalised activity would unfold as a random walk, with 'step' probability distribution changing at each snapshot but always symmetric about zero.

Could unbounded growth in activity, with positive new activity, be a trivial consequence of unbounded genotype length in a biotic selection system? Certainly not, for new activity drops to zero in systems such as Tierra. Could unbounded growth in activity be a trivial consequence of unbounded genotype length in a biotic selection system that exhibits unending positive new activity? No, because the requirement remains that activity be retained, so that it can accumulate. For example, a (diversity-bounded) biotic selection system that continually generates new components only by mutation along (phenotypically) neutral networks would only be able to *use* a finite number of neutral variants at any one time. It would lose activity whenever a component is lost from (ceases being used in) the system.

Conclusions

Both of my criticisms of the original test have been addressed. The revised shadowing method used here ensures that the normalisation of statistics is through a shadow that remains true to its real run, and median rather than (or rather as well as) mean activity has been used in the classification.

Geb has demonstrated class 3 behaviour: unbounded evolutionary activity. And this time we can have a greater degree of confidence in the results. However, this is a new variant of a previous test, and it is not beyond possibility that it could be improved upon. Certainty in these results can only come about through the application of the test to a range of evolutionary systems. That may take some time, since there are no other known artificial systems that even pass the original test. So for now we must be content with the conclusion that there is reason to believe that this system exhibits unbounded evolution.

While the caution of the previous paragraph is warranted, it is at least possible to say with certainty that these results qualitatively surpass those from previous artificial evolutionary systems. No previous biotic selection artificial evolutionary system has demonstrated unbounded evolutionary activity with positive new activity. As such these results provide validation of the theory behind Geb's design: a design constructed to satisfy the set of requirements for an evolutionary system within which increasingly complex advantageous behaviours can emerge, as uncovered by evaluating previous artificial systems.

Acknowledgements

Thanks to Mark Bedau for discussion and many helpful comments on this work. Thanks also to the anonymous reviewers for constructive criticism.

References

Adami, C., and Brown, C. T. 1994. Evolutionary learning in the 2D artificial life system 'Avida'. In Brooks, R. A., and Maes, P., eds., *Proceedings of Artificial Life IV*, 377–381. Cambridge, MA: MIT Press.

Arthur, W. B. 1994. Inductive reasoning and bounded rationality. *American Economic Review (Papers and Proceedings)* 84:406–411.

Bedau, M. A., and Brown, C. T. 1999. Visualizing evolutionary activity of genotypes. *Artificial Life* 5(1):17–35.

Bedau, M. A., and Packard, N. H. 1991. Measurement of evolutionary activity, teleology, and life. In Langton, C. G.; Taylor, C.; Farmer, J. D.; and Rasmussen, S., eds., *Proceedings of Artificial Life II*, 431–461. Redwood City, CA: Addison-Wesley.

Bedau, M. A.; Snyder, E.; Brown, C. T.; and Packard, N. H. 1997. A comparison of evolutionary activity in artificial evolving systems and the biosphere. In Husbands, P., and Harvey, I., eds., *Proceedings of the Fourth European Conference on Artificial Life (ECAL97), Brighton*, 125–134. Cambridge, MA: MIT Press.

Bedau, M. A.; Snyder, E.; and Packard, N. H. 1998. A classification of long-term evolutionary dynamics. In Adami, C.; Belew, R.; Kitano, H.; and Taylor, C., eds., *Proceedings of Artificial Life VI, Los Angeles*, 228–237. Cambridge, MA: MIT Press.

Channon, A. D., and Damper, R. I. 1998a. Evolving novel behaviors via natural selection. In Adami, C.; Belew, R.; Kitano, H.; and Taylor, C., eds., *Proceedings of Artificial Life VI, Los Angeles*, 384–388. Cambridge, MA: MIT Press.

Channon, A. D., and Damper, R. I. 1998b. Perpetuating evolutionary emergence. In Pfeifer, R.; Blumberg, B.; Meyer, J.-A.; and Wilson, S., eds., *From Animals to Animats 5: Proceedings of the Fifth International Conference on Simulation of Adaptive Behavior (SAB98), Zurich*, 534–539. Cambridge, MA: MIT Press.

Channon, A. D., and Damper, R. I. 2000. Towards the evolutionary emergence of increasingly complex advantageous behaviours. *International Journal of Systems Science* 31(7):843–860.

Channon, A. D. 2001. Passing the ALife test: Activity statistics classify evolution in Geb as unbounded. In Kelemen, J., and Sosik, P., eds., *Advances in Artificial Life: Proceedings of the Sixth European Conference on Artificial Life (ECAL2001), Prague*, 417–426. Heidelberg: Springer-Verlag.

Holland, J. H. 1975. *Adaptation in Natural and Artificial Systems.* Ann Arbor, MI: University of Michigan Press. 2nd edition: MIT Press, 1992.

Lindenmayer, A. 1968. Mathematical models for cellular interaction in development. *Journal of Theoretical Biology* 18:280–315. Parts I and II.

Lindgren, K. 1991. Evolutionary phenomena in simple dynamics. In Langton, C. G.; Taylor, C.; Farmer, J. D.; and Rasmussen, S., eds., *Proceedings of Artificial Life II*, 295–312. Redwood City, CA: Addison-Wesley.

Packard, N. H. 1989. Intrinsic adaptation in a simple model for evolution. In Langton, C. G., ed., *Santa Fe Institute Studies in the Sciences of Complexity, Vol VI: Proceedings of the Interdisciplinary Workshop on the Synthesis and Simulation of Living Systems (Artificial Life I)*, 141–155. Redwood City, CA: Addison-Wesley.

Standish, R. K. 2000. An ecolab perspective on the Bedau evolutionary statistics. In Bedau, M. A.; McCaskill, J. S.; Packard, N. H.; and Rasmussen, S., eds., *Proceedings of Artificial Life VII*, 238–242. Cambridge, MA: MIT Press.

Taylor, T., and Hallam, J. 1998. Replaying the tape: An investigation into the role of contingency in evolution. In Adami, C.; Belew, R.; Kitano, H.; and Taylor, C., eds., *Proceedings of Artificial Life VI, Los Angeles*, 256–265. Cambridge, MA: MIT Press.

Adaptive Crossover in Genetic Algorithms Using Statistics Mechanism

Shengxiang Yang

Department of Mathematics and Computer Science, University of Leicester
University Road, Leicester LE1 7RH, UK. Email: s.yang@mcs.le.ac.uk

Abstract

Genetic Algorithms (GAs) emulate the natural evolution process and maintain a population of potential solutions to a given problem. Through the population, GAs implicitly maintain the statistics about the search space. This implicit statistics can be used explicitly to enhance GA's performance. Inspired by this idea, a statistics-based adaptive non-uniform crossover (SANUX) has been proposed. SANUX uses the statistics information of the alleles in each locus to adaptively calculate the swapping probability of that locus for crossover operation. A simple triangular function has been used to calculate the swapping probability. In this paper two new functions, the trapezoid and exponential functions, are proposed for SANUX instead of the triangular function. Experiment results show that both functions further improve the performance of SANUX.

Introduction

Genetic Algorithms (GAs) emulate the natural evolution process and maintain a population of potential solutions to a given problem, which are evaluated by a problem-specific fitness function. This population is evolved by randomly selecting relatively fit members and performing genetic operations, especially recombination and mutation, on them to generate a new population (Goldberg 1989). With the progress of the GA, the average fitness of the population increases, hopefully leading to the optimal solution(s) to the problem. Through the population GAs implicitly maintain statistics about the search space. That is, useful materials or building blocks permeate in the population. GAs use the selection, crossover and mutation operators to explicitly extract the implicit statistics from the population to reach the next set of points in the search space.

In fact, this implicit statistics in the population can be used explicitly to enhance GA's performance. Inspired by this idea, a statistics-based adaptive non-uniform crossover, called SANUX, has been proposed by Yang (2002). SANUX explicitly uses the statistics information of the alleles (values of a gene) in each locus to adaptively calculate the swapping probability of that locus for crossover operation. In Yang (2002) a simple triangular function has been used to calculate the swapping probability from the statistics of allele distribution. In this paper, two new functions, a trapezoid function and an exponential function, are proposed for SANUX instead of the simple triangular function. These two functions are proposed with the aim of using the statistics more efficiently with respect to construction and protection of useful building blocks with the progress of the GA.

Related Work on Crossover Operators

Traditionally, GAs have used one-point or two-point crossover (De Jong 1975; Holland 1975). Researchers have also carried out experiments with multi-point crossover: n-point crossover (Eshelman, Caruana, & Schaffer 1989) and uniform crossover (Syswerda 1989). With the n-point crossover, n cut points are randomly chosen within the strings and the $n-1$ segments between the n cut points of the two parents are exchanged. Uniform crossover is the generalization of n-point crossover. It creates offsprings by swapping each bit of two parents with a probability p_s of 0.5. Spears and De Jong (1991) proposed the parameterized uniform crossover where the decision of whether to swap for each locus is made by a biased coin flipping, i.e., the swapping probability p_s could be other than 0.5.

Traditional crossover operators are inherently all based on uniformly randomization mechanism, i.e., generating cut points (n-point crossover) or swapping points (uniform crossover) uniformly randomly across the chromosome. This situation is not very true with natural evolution because it is intrinsically dynamic and adaptive. Recently, researchers have applied adaptation techniques to crossover to enhance GA's capabilities (Eiben, Hinterding, & Michalewicz 1999). According to Yang (2002), adaptation in crossover happens in three levels from top to bottom. In the top level, crossover operators are themself adapted during a run of the GA. In the medium level, the rate or probability of crossover is altered during a run of the GA. In the bottom level, the position of crossing or swapping probability in each locus is adapted during a run of the GA.

Statistics-based Adaptive Non-Uniform Crossover

Description of SANUX

For the convenience of description and analysis, Yang (2002) has introduced the concepts of intrinsic attribute and extrinsic tendency of allele valuing for a gene locus. In the optimal binary-encoded solution(s) of a given problem, a gene locus is called *1-intrinsic* if its allele is 1, *0-intrinsic* if its allele is 0, or *neutral* if its allele can be either 0 or 1. During the running of a GA, for a gene locus, if the frequency of 1's in its alleles over the population tends to increase (to the limit of 1.0) with time, it is called *1-inclined*; if the frequency of 1's tends to decrease (to the limit of 0.0), it is called *0-inclined*; otherwise, if there is no tendency of increasing or decreasing, it is called *non-inclined.*

Usually and hopefully as the GA progresses, those gene loci that are 1-intrinsic (or 0-intrinsic) will appear to be 1-inclined (or 0-inclined), i.e., the frequency of 1's in the alleles of these loci will eventually converge to 1 (or 0). This convergent information is implicit in the population. Traditional crossover operators make no use of this implicit information and consistently generate cut points or swapping points randomly but uniformly across the chromosome. Obviously it will be beneficial to link these partially or fully converged genes into groups or building blocks and co-evolve them during crossover operations. This is realized in SANUX. SANUX explicitly uses the convergence information as feedback to adaptively adjust the swapping probability for each locus based on the statistics of alleles in that locus.

We use the frequency of 1's in the alleles in a locus over the population (equivalently we can also use the frequency of 0's as the argument) to calculate corresponding swapping probability of that locus. The frequency of 1's in the alleles of a locus can be looked as the degree of convergence to "1" for that locus. Let L be the length of binary strings, $f_1(i,t)$ $(i = 1, \ldots, L)$ denote the frequency of 1's in the alleles in locus i over the population at time (generation) t and $p_s(i,t)$ $(i = 1, \ldots, L)$ denote the swapping probability of locus i at time t. In Yang (2002), a simple triangular function is used to calculate $p_s(i,t)$ from $f_1(i,t)$, defined as follows:

$$p_s(i,t) = P_{\max} - 2|f_1(i,t) - 0.5|(P_{\max} - P_{\min}) \quad (1)$$

where $|.|$ is an absolute function, $P_{\max}$ and $P_{\min}$ are the maximum and minimum allowable swapping probabilities for a locus respectively.

Now during the evolution of the GA, after a new population has been created, we first calculate $f_1(i,t)$ for each locus i over population t and from this obtain $p_s(i,t)$ of locus i. Then we can perform SANUX operations similarly as traditional parameterized uniform crossover, as illustrated in Figure 1.

1's Freq. in loci:	0.9	0.2	0.6	0.9	0.4	0.2
Calculating:	⇓	⇓	⇓	⇓	⇓	⇓
Swapping Prob.:	0.1	0.2	0.4	0.1	0.4	0.2
Biased Flipping:	⇓	⇓	⇓	⇓	⇓	⇓
Created Mask:	0	0	1	0	1	0
Applying Mask:			⇓		⇓	
Parent P_1:	1	1	0	1	0	1
Parent P_2:	1	1	1	1	1	0
Swapping:			⇓		⇓	
Child C_1:	1	1	1	1	1	1
Child C_2:	1	1	0	1	0	0

Figure 1: An example operation of SANUX with triangular calculation function where $P_{\max} = 0.5$ and $P_{\min} = 0$.

From above descriptions, it can be seen that SANUX is very simple. With SANUX, what we add to traditional uniform crossover are spatially only one real vector that records the swapping probability for each locus, and computationally only one statistics per generation that calculates the frequency of ones (hence the swapping probability) for each locus. Another more important point of SANUX is its property of implicit *gene linkage*. Gene linkage is the property of grouping interactive genes to evolve them together. For example, in Figure 1 loci 1 and 4 are more convergent and implicitly linked though they are not adjacent because the probability for them to co-evolve via crossover is $0.1 * 0.1 + 0.9 * 0.9 = 0.82$, which is very high.

New Calculating Functions

From above discussions, we can see that there is a close loop control in SANUX in the sense of constructing and preserving building blocks. The GA is first used to construct useful building blocks. Then after some time when some useful building blocks have been built up the statistics information is used to protect these building blocks from being destroyed by the crossover and hence divert the crossover to search unconverged loci for more unknown useful building blocks because they have relatively higher swapping probabilities. With this understanding, we can further enhance this close loop by introducing new functions instead of the triangular function to calculate the swapping probability of each locus from its allele distribution statistics.

The first function is a trapezoid function, as shown in Figure 2, defined by the following equation.

$$p_s(i,t) = \begin{cases} P_{\max}, & \text{if } |f_1(i,t) - 0.5| \le a \\ \frac{b - |f_1(i,t) - 0.5|}{b-a} * (P_{\max} - P_{\min}) + P_{\min}, & \\ & \text{if } a < |f_1(i,t) - 0.5| < b \\ P_{\min}, & \text{if } |f_1(i,t) - 0.5| \ge b \end{cases} \quad (2)$$

where a and b are parameters that satisfy the relation of $0 \le a \le b \le 0.5$. As shown in Figure 2, the parameters a and b split the whole range of $f_1(i,t)$ into three zones: I) $|f_1(i,t) - 0.5| \le a$; II) $a < |f_1(i,t) - 0.5| < b$; III) $|f_1(i,t) - 0.5| \ge b$. Zone I is called *constructive zone* where useful building blocks are mainly constructed by SANUX. Zone II is called *transient zone* where building blocks are constructed as well as destroyed. And Zone III is called *protective zone* where building blocks found so far are protected from being destroyed by SANUX while exploring unknown useful building blocks is still carried out by SANUX on unconverged loci. From Figure 2 it can be seen that the larger the value of a, the wider the region that allows the GA to construct building blocks, and that the smaller the value of b, the stronger the protection to converged genes or found building blocks from being destroyed by SANUX.

The second function we introduce here is an exponen-

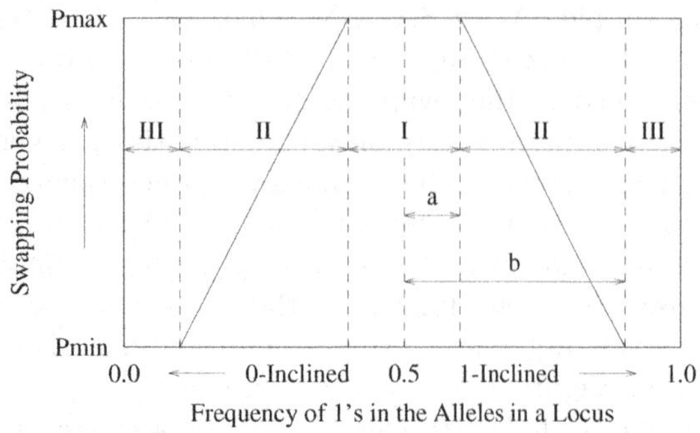

Figure 2: Trapezoid function for calculating the swapping probability of a locus.

tial function, as shown in Figure 3, defined as follows:

$$p_s(i,t) = \alpha * \exp(-(f_1(i,t) - 0.5)^2/\beta) \quad (3)$$

where α is the parameter with the same functionality as $P_{\max}$ in Equations (1) and (2), and β is the parameter that combines the functionalities of parameters $P_{\min}$, a and b in Equation (2) and controls the falling speed of $p_s(i,t)$ when $f_1(i,t)$ diverts away from 0.5. The smaller the value of β, the faster the falling speed of $p_s(i,t)$, and the stronger the protection to converged genes or building blocks found so far. As shown in Figure 3, the solid curve shows the function with $(\alpha, \beta) = (0.5, 0.04)$ while the dashed curve is when $(\alpha, \beta) = (0.5, 0.02)$.

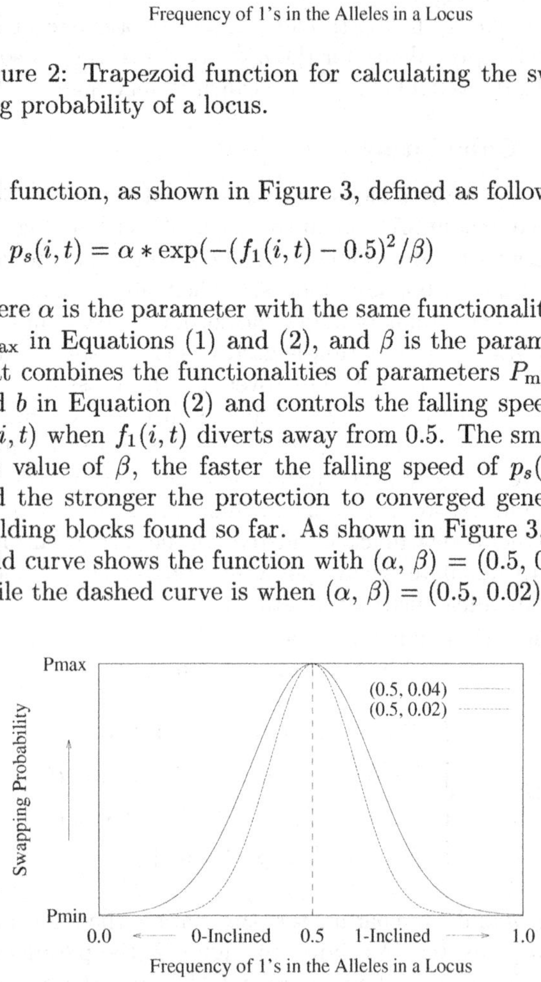

Figure 3: Exponential function for calculating the swapping probability of a locus.

Both the two functions enlarge the region for the GA to construct building blocks and enhance the protection to found building blocks at the same time. Both sides are expected to be beneficial for SANUX's performance.

Experimental Study

The Test Problems

The Max Ones Problem The Max Ones problem is simply to maximize 1's in a binary string. The fitness of a string is the number of 1's it contains. A string length of 100 bits is used for this study.

Royal Road Functions The Royal Road functions R_1 and R_2 are devised by Forrest and Mitchell (1993) to investigate GA's performance with respect to schema processing and recombination in an idealized form. The optimal fitness for R_1 and R_2 is 64 and 192 respectively.

Experiment Results

To test the performance of proposed two calculating functions for SANUX, in our experiment study we compared the SANUX with the trapezoid and exponential functions over SANUX with the triangular function and traditional 2-point, 0.5 uniform and 0.2 uniform crossover on the test problems. The parameters for different functions of SANUX were set as follows: $P_{\max} = 0.5$ and $P_{\min} = 0.0$ for triangular and trapezoid functions, $(a, b) = (0.1, 0.4)$ for trapezoid function, and $(\alpha, \beta) = (0.5, 0.04)$ for exponential function.

For each experiment of combining different crossover and test problems, 100 independent runs were executed under the same 100 different random seeds. In all the experiments, the GA used the fitness proportionate selection with the stochastic universal sampling (SUS) and elitist model, and bit flip mutation. And typically the probabilities of crossover and mutation were fixed to 0.6 and 0.001 respectively and the population size was set to 100 for each run. For each run, we recorded the best-so-far fitness every 100 evaluations. Here, only those chromosomes changed by crossover and mutation operations were evaluated and counted into the number of evaluations. Each experiment result was averaged over the 100 independent runs. The experiment results are shown in Figure 4 and Figure 5 respectively.

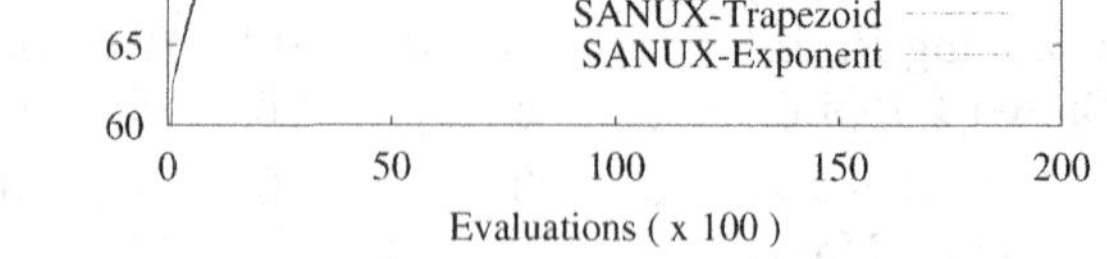

Figure 4: Average best-so-far curves for GAs with different crossover operators on Max Ones problem.

From Figure 4 and Figure 5 it can be seen that SANUX with different calculating functions has outperformed traditional crossover operators on the test problems. On the test problems lowering the swapping probability p_s from 0.5 to 0.2 improves the performance of uniform crossover (0.2 uniform crossover outperforms 2-point and 0.5 uniform crossover), however 0.2 uniform

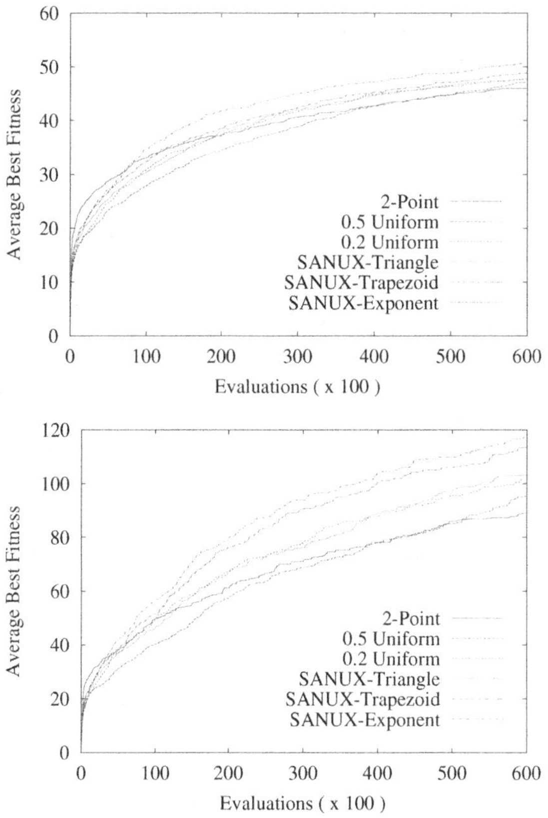

Figure 5: Average best-so-far curves for GAs with different crossover operators on (Top) R_1 and (Bottom) R_2.

crossover is beaten by SANUX. The relative performance of different crossover seems quite consistent on the test problems, approximately from best to worst in the following order: SANUX-Exponent ⇒ SANUX-Trapezoid ⇒ SANUX-Triangle ⇒ 0.2 uniform ⇒ 0.5 uniform ⇒ 2-point crossover. Within SANUX both the trapezoid and exponential functions have outperformed the triangular function. This confirms our prediction.

Conclusions

In this paper, we propose two new functions, the trapezoid and exponential functions, that can be used within SANUX instead of the triangular function (Yang 2002) to calculate the swapping probability for a locus from its allele distribution statistics. Both these two functions widen the region for the GA to construct building blocks and enhance the protection to searched building blocks at the same time, hence are expected to be beneficial for the performance of GAs.

The experiment results show that SANUX with the trapezoid and exponential functions performs better than SANUX with the triangular function and traditional two-point and uniform crossover (parameterized or not) on the test problems. Our experiment results indicate that the exponential function is a good choice to be used in SANUX for its performance and simplicity, and that SANUX with the exponential calculating function is a good candidate crossover operator for GAs.

References

De Jong, K. A. 1975. *An Analysis of the Behavior of a Class of Genetic Adaptive Systems.* PhD Thesis, University of Michigan, Ann Abor.

Eiben, A. E.; Hinterding, R.; and Michalewicz, Z. 1999. Parameter control in evolutionary algorithms. *IEEE Trans. on Evolutionary Computation* 3(2):124-141.

Eshelman, L. J.; Caruana, R. A.; and Schaffer J. D. 1989. Biases in the crossover landscape. In Schaffer, D., ed., *Proc. of the 3rd Int. Conf. on Genetic Algorithms*, 10-19. Morgan Kaufmann.

Forrest, S., and Mitchell, M. 1993. Relative building-block fitness and the building-block hypothesis. In Whitley, D., ed., *Foundations of Genetic Algorithms 2.* Morgan Kaufmann.

Goldberg, D. E. 1989. *Genetic Algorithms in Search, Optimization, and Machine Learning.* Reading, MA: Addison-Wesley,

Holland, J. H. 1975. *Adaptation in Natural and Artificial Systems.* Ann Arbor, MI: University of Michigan Press.

Spears, W. M., and De Jong, K. A. 1991. On the virtues of parameterized uniform crossover. In Belew, R. K., and Booker, L. B., eds., *Proc. 4th Int. Conf. on Genetic Algorithms*, 230-236. Morgan Kaufmann.

Syswerda, G. 1989. Uniform crossover in genetic algorithms. In Schaffer, J. D., ed., *Proc. of the 3rd Int. Conf. on Genetic Algorithms*, 2-9. Morgan Kaufmann.

Yang, S. 2002. Adaptive non-uniform crossover based on statistics for genetic algorithms. In Langdon, W. B., *et al*, eds., *Proc. of the Genetic and Evolutionary Computation Conference, GECCO 2002*, 650-657. Morgan Kaufmann.

The Origins of Mimicry Rings

Daniel W. Franks and **Jason Noble**
School of Computing, University of Leeds
Email: [dwfranks|jasonn]@comp.leeds.ac.uk

Abstract

Mutualistic Müllerian mimicry and parasitic Batesian mimicry can co-exist in *mimicry rings*, i.e., mimetic relationships between multiple species. Theory suggests that all Müllerian mimics in an ecosystem should converge into one large ring. Potentially, the presence of Batesian mimics will encourage convergence. It has been suggested that rare species should seek out common species as models. Mimicry rings have not previously been modelled; we present an evolutionary simulation to investigate the above questions. Complete convergence is not observed although Batesian mimicry is shown to be important factor in the origin of mimicry rings.

Bees and wasps both possess yellow and black striped warning colourations, making an obvious display of their unpleasantness. But why do they display the same pattern? Imagine a situation where they both have different patterns. A predator, such as a bird, would have to sample many of *each* species in order to learn to avoid them both. However, when sharing the same pattern, the predator will see them both as the same type of prey and so will eat fewer individuals before developing an aversion to them. Thus, each individual has less chance of being eaten as it is protected by numbers. It therefore makes sense that two unpalatable (bad-tasting) species would become co-mimics by converging upon the same colour pattern. This is assuming that the predator must learn which prey types to avoid, rather than having innate aversions — an assumption in line with past mimicry research. This type of relationship, in which both species benefit, is known as Müllerian mimicry (Müller 1879).

The honest displays of unpalatability given by species such as bees and wasps are ready targets for free-riders. A good example is the harmless hoverfly, which has black and yellow stripes. It is easy to imagine the benefit gained by a tasty species in being confused for an unpalatable one. So, gaining protection without evolving a costly toxin or sting, the species evolves the same warning colour as an unpalatable species. The species that is being mimicked is termed "the model". This type of mimicry was the first to be described in the literature and is known as Batesian mimicry (Bates 1862). Although beneficial to the mimic, Batesian mimicry is detrimental to the survival of the model, as the presence of tasty individuals dilutes the honesty of the warning coloration. This means that Batesian mimicry is a parasitic relationship between mimic and model (see e.g., Wickler, 1968) .

Predators have fallible sensory systems and they generalize from their predation experiences. Thus, although they are much more likely to mistake a perfect mimic for its model, they can still mistake approximate resemblances for the real thing. This gives a greater level of protection to a mimic the more accurate its mimicry becomes. However, if the appearances of two prey species are sufficiently distinct, the predator will never mistake one for the other. Therefore, before mimics can undergo a process of pattern refinement, an initial resemblance in the eyes of the predator is needed at first so that it may occasionally confuse the two. An approximate resemblance can be arrived at due to random drift, or fairly large major mutations (Turner 1988).

Population sizes have a considerable effect on mimicry. When two unpalatable species converge as Müllerian mimics, they are doing so in order to increase the population size of individuals with their type of warning coloration. It follows, then, that unpalatable species with higher population sizes are better defended against predators than those with lower population sizes (positive frequency dependence). Conversely, Batesian mimics are better protected by lower population sizes. This is because higher populations would dilute the model's protection so much as to make predators more willing to risk eating a prey of that colour pattern (negative frequency dependence) (Pilecki & O'Donald 1971).

The coevolutionary dynamics involved in the two separate cases of mimicry differ considerably (Turner 1987; 1995). Müllerian mimics *converge* upon the same colour pattern. That is, they 'move' together serving both as co-mimics and models. Batesian mimicry is a different matter. A Batesian mimic's colour pattern 'moves' toward that of the model's in order to gain protection. The model then attempts to escape the parasitic mimic by evolving its pattern 'away' from the invading mimic, as individuals that are slightly less parasitized (due to minor pattern differences) are more likely to survive. The Batesian mimic is, however, expected to usually keep up in the resulting coevolutionary arms race (Nur 1970). This is because the selection pressure on a tasty species to gain protection is generally greater than the selection pressure on a model to reduce the dilution of predator aversions. This type of mimetic arms race has been termed *advergence* (Brower, Brower, & Collins 1972).

Mimicry rings are Müllerian mimetic relationships between two or more species, and are common among butterflies and bumblebees. It is called a "ring" because each species in the relationship has an effect on each of the others. Plowright (1980) showed that there are five different patterns of bumblebee in north-west Europe, each constituting a mimicry ring of several species. A good example of a mimicry ring is the 'tiger' pattern

Figure 1: Mimicry ring example. Three separate species of butterfly that all share the same pattern in a 'yellow' ring in Sirena. Note the subtle differences in the patterns.

shared by different species of *Heliconius* butterflies in Sirena (Mallet & Gilbert 1995), alongside other ring patterns (see, e.g., Figure 1). It would be highly profitable for a palatable species to invade these rings as a Batesian mimic, as it would have less of a dilution affect on the palatibility associated with the colour pattern.

The co-existence of mimicry rings in nature has prompted the question: why do the co-mimics (in the same geographical region) not all converge into one large ring (Mallet & Gilbert 1995)? This question is posed because all of the mimics would mutually, and optimally, benefit from evolving into one large ring. The authors have previously shown (Franks & Noble 2002) in a simple, one-dimensional, three-species case that Batesian mimics can 'chase' unpalatable species to within convergence range of each other, provoking a Müllerian relationship. This suggests a potential for Batesian mimics to influence the dynamics of mimicry rings.

The above points suggest two working hypotheses:

1. All of the Müllerian mimics in a given ecosystem should eventually converge into one large ring in order to gain maximum protection;

2. If the Müllerian mimics do not converge into one large ring, then the presence of Batesian mimics could entice them to do so, by adverging upon the rings;

Although there are many mathematical and stochastic models of mimicry in the biological literature, this topic has not yet received any attention in the artificial life literature, apart from the authors' own previous work (Franks & Noble 2002). Mimicry *rings* have hardly been explored at all in any literature, mainly due to the difficulty that a mathematical or stochastic model would have in modeling the large and complex ecosystem that would be required. This is where evolving artificial life models become the most practical and promising approach. To that end, we present a simulation model that explores the evolution of mimicry rings under varying conditions.

The Simulation Model

To model prey we needed to create populations of 'agents' which each have an appearance and palatibility level. Multiple populations of prey species were used in each experiment. Different species of prey were each assigned a fixed palatibility level on a scale between zero and one (least to most palatable), where 0.5 is neutrally palatable. Each individual had two genes with values compositely representing their external appearance (e.g., a colour pattern) or phenotype.[1] Both genes were constrained to values from 1–200. The Euclidean distance of one phenotype from another represented their level of similarity. Palatable species have values greater than 0.5, and unpalatable species have values lower than 0.5.

A population of abstract predators was modelled with a Monte Carlo reinforcement learning system, as used in a stochastic model by Turner *et. al.* (1984). The predator's experience of each phenotype was represented by a score of attack probability, which was initialized to ambivalence at 0.5. After eating prey of a particular phenotype, the predator would make a post-attack update of the relevant probability according to the palatibility of the individual consumed. The predator would use its experience of different prey appearances to help it decide on whether or not to attack them at the next opportunity. Unlike the stochastic model, the predator generalized on the basis of experience and thus would also, to a lesser extent, update its scores for the closest neighbouring phenotypes accordingly. The formula used for generalizing and updating the probabilities after eating a prey was:

$$P_1 = (P_0 + \alpha(\lambda - P_0)) \times W \tag{1}$$

This produces an updated palatability score P_1, based on the previous score P_0, for phenotypes at a given distance from the consumed prey whose palatability was λ. α is a variable learning rate and is calculated using:

$$\alpha = 0.5 + |\lambda - 0.5| \tag{2}$$

W is a weighting (for generalization) which is calculated according to the distance of the phenotype from the consumed prey's phenotype, and is calculated with:

$$W = \frac{G - D}{G} \tag{3}$$

Where G is the predator's generalization rate and D is the Euclidean distance between the phenotype and the consumed prey's phenotype.

[1] Clearly a two-dimensional representation of possible phenotypes is a simplification. We have also looked at the evolution of mimicry rings in higher dimensional spaces; similar conclusions are reached but there are significant difficulties in visualizing and conveying the results.

The above equations have the effect of updating a predator's opinion of a particular phenotype. The rate of learning is dependent on how far the predator's current opinion is from the palatibility of the consumed prey (equations 1 and 2). The predator's memory is updated by generalizing over similar phenotypes within the predator's generalization range from the consumed prey's phenotype (equation 3). This update can be imagined as a cone shape, where the tip of the cone is the update for the consumed phenotype. The further away from the consumed phenotype the pattern is, the less it is updated.

Before being used to express the probability of consuming a prey item, scores were transformed with the logistic function, which meant that predators were more decisive about prey for which they had a relatively strong opinion. Predators made decisions about whether or not to eat a prey by comparing the transformed score to a random number in the range of zero to one. This meant that a predator could become averse to eating some or even all of the prey species — note that we must assume that an alternative food source is available as predators in the model will not starve even if they refuse all prey. To implement predator memory degradation over time, each predator's memory gradually reverted back toward ambivalence (0.5) at a constant rate of two percent per prey offering.

The predator population size was kept constant throughout the experiments at 160. Each predator was presented with 10 potential prey items per prey generation. Prey individuals were randomly selected in proportion to their relative population numbers from across all prey populations. The predator would then make a probabilistic choice of whether or not to eat the prey based on its experience of the phenotype. After being offered a prey item the predator's memory would degrade, regardless of its decision. Random asexual reproduction then took place amongst the surviving prey. Every generation the oldest predator would die, and be replaced with a new predator with its memory initialized to the naive attack level of 0.5 representing ambivalence. All of the experiments were run over 200,000 generations and prey populations were kept constant after reproduction.

Mutation was implemented as follows:

1. A random direction in the multidimensional space is chosen by selecting a random number from a normal distribution (0 mean, unit variance) for each gene.[2]

2. The distance is then selected over a normal distribution (0 mean, unit variance) to allow for varying mutation sizes, with a bias towards smaller ones.

3. The offspring then mutates in the selected direction at the selected distance.

[2]If a uniform distribution was used here, it would give a bias to diagonal directions.

Note that the operator is performed on *every* offspring. The result is that most offspring are slight variants or replicas of their parent. This method was used in order to avoid the orthogonal bias present with stepwise mutation operators. Also, the issue of mutation bias due to unnatural boundaries (Bullock 1999) was handled using a wrap-around function (making alleles 1 and 200 neighbours) on prey mutations and predator generalization. These mutation issues are important to any simulation model as they can help to avoid artefactual results. They are, however, of particular significance to mimicry models as random-drift and mutation are vital to the initiation of mimicry.

Results

For our purposes, a mimicry ring is defined as a mimetic relationship between two or more unpalatable species. A mimetic relationship is defined as a Euclidean distance of less than fifteen between the modes of the two species. The distance of fifteen was calculated by multiplying the generalization rate by two and deducting one (which gives the minimum distance of overlapping generalization), and then multiplying that by 1.5 (to allow for spread of individuals within a species and generalization over each of them), which gave clusters that matched that of manual observations for the experiments.

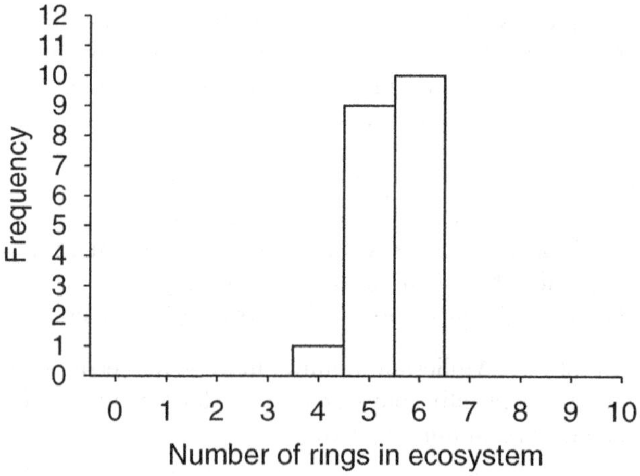

Figure 2: Frequency of mimicry rings after 200,000 generations, with 20 unpalatable species with equal populations of 300 and palatibility levels of 0.1. Results were recorded over 20 runs.

Experiment 1 was conducted with 20 unpalatable prey species. Each had a palatibility of 0.1 and population size of 300. After 200,000 generations of evolution, the number of co-existing mimicry rings formed were tallied. Figure 2 shows that five or six mimicry rings usually evolve, and no run resulted in less than four rings. Figure 3 shows the position of the initial modal phenotypes as well as the final coevolved modal phenotypes.

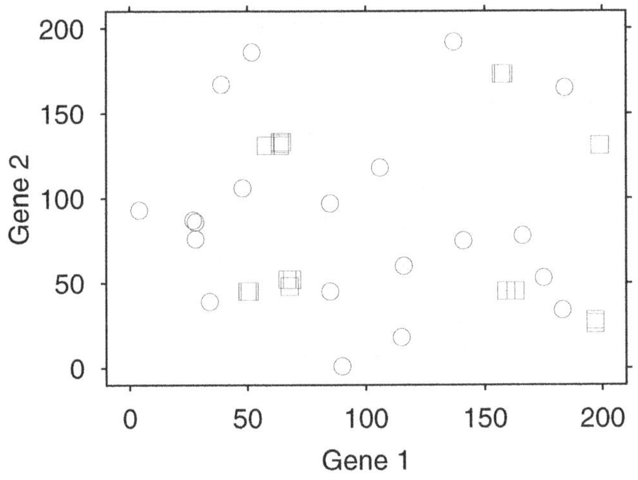

Figure 3: Initial random and final evolved position of each prey species' modal phenotype for a typical run with equal population numbers. Circles represent starting phenotypes and squares represent end phenotypes. Note the formation of six mimicry rings and one solitary species.

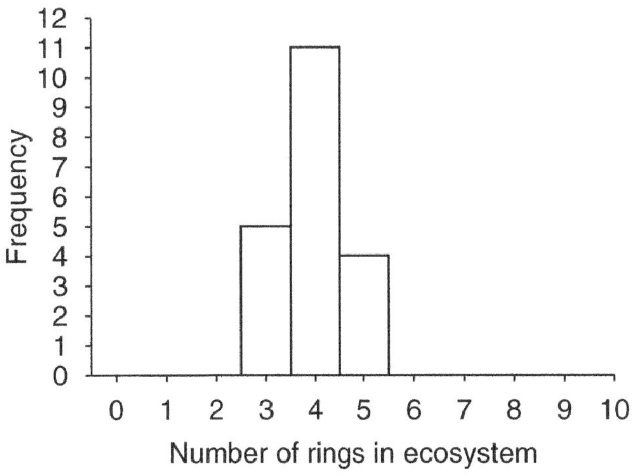

Figure 4: Frequency of mimicry rings after 200,000 generations, with 20 unpalatable species and four palatable species of palatibility 0.9 and population size 300 added. Results were recorded over 20 runs. Notice how there are fewer rings when palatable species are present.

Experiment 2 was conducted with the same conditions as experiment 1 except that four palatable species, of population size 300 and palatibility 0.9, were also included to allow for Batesian mimetic relationships. Figure 4 shows strong shift toward a lower number of mimicry rings, with four rings being the most common. Figure 5 shows the position of the initial modal phenotypes as well as the final modal phenotypes. Different population sizes were tried for the two experiments, and gave similar results.

A statistical comparison of the number of mimicry rings found in each of the two experiments indicated a significant difference ($t = 7.333, p < 0.001$) with more rings being found in experiment 1 than in experiment 2.

Discussion

Experiment 1 shows that, under conditions in which all species are (equally) unpalatable, hypothesis 1 was not borne out and thus, at least with the population sizes used, a single large mimicry ring should perhaps not be *expected* in nature. This shows that current mimicry theory explains the co-existence of multiple mimicry rings without the need to bring in other selective forces such as sexual selection. Results show that mimics cluster in rings in different areas of phenotypic space, sometimes far enough apart so that it would be rare for a large enough mutation to bridge the gap. Thus, the phenotypes of the rings are sufficiently different so that the predator would not mistake a member of one for a member of another. Of course, on freak occasions it would be possible for an individual to mutate across the gap. However, it is very unlikely and not guaranteed to be in the right 'direction' or beneficial to the individual. Such a state would be well suited to further examination with evolutionary simulation models, as they do not rely finding an equilibrium. A further examination of the results showed that in all runs there is very little (if any) change from generation 150,000 to 200,000, suggesting that the ecosystem has reached a steady state and the various rings are not about to collapse into one large ring given more time. Such an explanation for the diversity of mimicry rings in nature has been suggested in previous mimicry literature (see e.g., Turner , 1977; Sheppard et. al., 1985). However, observations of the individual simulation runs shows that the coexisting rings are not *always* far apart. The diversity could perhaps also be explained by the fact that a mutation is unlikely to take an individual from being a perfect mimic of its species' current ring to being a perfect mimic of another ring; being an imperfect mimic of another ring is not as selectively advantageous as being a perfect mimic of the original ring. Most of the time a mutation will result in an individual no longer being protected by numbers. The simulation shows that current mimicry theory alone does explain the coexistence of multiple mimicry rings.

The results of experiment 2 show that the introduction of palatable species induced a smaller number of mimicry rings, supporting hypothesis 2. This is because, due to pressure to evolve a different phenotype from the modal phenotype of the species (because of negative frequency dependence), the palatable species would inevitably become Batesian mimics. The presence of Batesian mimics would provide positive selection pressure on mutants and would, therefore, increase the probability that they would evolve an initial resemblance to another unpalat-

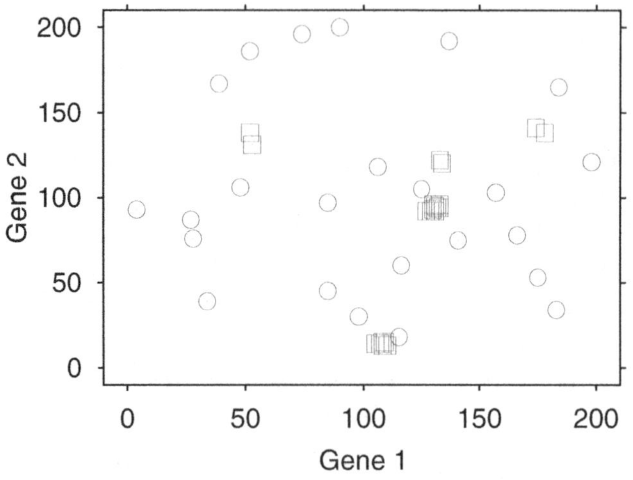

Figure 5: Initial random and final evolved position of each prey's modal phenotype for a typical run with four palatable species added. Circles represent starting phenotypes and squares represent final phenotypes. Palatable species are not shown; unpalatable species form two large rings and three small rings. Notice how there are fewer rings when palatable species are present.

able species. Also, Batesian pressure on mimicry rings has the potential to push one ring into the range of another, helping to bridge a large phenotypic difference between them. Once mimicry rings have enough members they can 'tolerate' the presence of a Batesian mimic. It appears that situation will persist, unless additional Batesian mimics invade in sufficient numbers to destabilize the ring. As a result, Batesian mimics can induce the convergence of nearby mimicry rings.

Although prey in the model presented had only two genes, work in progress shows that the same conclusions seem to hold for a four-gene case. However, as noted earlier, the two-gene case is easier for display purposes. Future work will endeavour to co-evolve the population of predators with the prey, and to move away from the standard assumption in the mimicry literature that predators learn from a blank slate. This should help to settle any misgivings about the arbitrariness of predator attributes such as generalization distance, learning rate and forgetting rate. Co-evolving predators with prey may also influence the emergence of mimicry rings.

Acknowledgments

Thanks to John Turner for his expert advice on theories of mimicry; any misrepresentation of his ideas is our responsibility. Thanks also to Seth Bullock for help with the mutation operator and to Dave Harris for useful comments on the draft.

References

Bates, H. W. 1862. Contributions to an insect fauna of the Amazon valley. *Lepidoptera: Heliconidae. Transactions of the Linnean Society* London 23:495–566.

Brower, L. P.; Brower, J. V. Z.; and Collins, C. T. 1972. Parallelism, convergence, divergence, and the new concept of advergence in the evolution of mimicry. In Deevey, E., ed., *Ecological essays in honour of G. Evelyn Hutchinson.* Connecticut Academy of Arts and Science. 57–67.

Bullock, S. 1999. Are artificial mutation biases unnatural? In Floreano, D.; Nicoud, J.-D.; and Mondada, F., eds., *Fifth European Conference on Artificial Life (ECAL99)*, 64–73. Springer, Heidelberg.

Franks, D. W., and Noble, J. 2002. Conditions for the evolution of mimicry. In *Proceedings of the Seventh International Conference on Simulation of Adaptive Behavior.* MIT Press, Cambridge, MA.

Mallet, J., and Gilbert, L. E. 1995. Why are there so many mimicry rings? Correlations between habitat, behaviour and mimicry in *Heliconius* butterflies. *Biological Journal of the Linnean Society* 55:159–180.

Müller, F. 1879. *Ituna* and *Thyridia*; a remarkable case of mimicry in butterflies. *Trans. Entomol. Soc. Lond.* May 1879:xx–xxix.

Nur, U. 1970. Evolutionary rates of models and mimics in Batesian mimicry. *American Naturalist* 104:477–486.

Pilecki, C., and O'Donald, P. 1971. The effects of predation on artificial mimetic polymorphisms with perfect and imperfect mimics at varying frequencies. *Evolution* 55:365–370.

Plowright, R. C., and Owen, R. E. 1980. The evolutionary significance of bumblebee color patterns: A mimetic interpretation. *Evolution* 34:622–637.

Sheppard, P. M.; Turner, J. R. G.; Brown, K. S.; Benson, W. W.; and Singer, M. C. 1985. Genetics and the evolution of Muellerian mimicry in *Heliconius* butterflies. *Philosophical Transactions of the Royal Society of London: Biological Sciences* 308:433–607.

Turner, J. R. G.; Kearney, E. P.; and Exton, L. S. 1984. Mimicry and the Monte Carlo predator: The palatability spectrum and the origins of mimicry. *Biological Journal of the Linnean Society* 23:247–268.

Turner, J. R. G. 1977. Butterfly mimicry: The genetical evolution of an adaptation. *Evolutionary Biology* 10:163–206.

Turner, J. R. G. 1987. The evolutionary dynamics of Batesian and Mullerian mimicry: Similarities and differences. *Ecological Entomology* 12:81–95.

Turner, J. R. G. 1988. The evolution of mimicry: A solution to the problem of punctuated equilibrium. *American Naturalist* 131:S42–S66.

Turner, J. R. G. 1995. Mimicry as a model for co-evolution. In Arai, R.; Kato, M.; and Doi, Y., eds., *Biodiversity and Evolution.* Tokyo: National Science Museum Foundation. 131–150.

Wickler, W. 1968. *Mimicry in Plants and Animals.* London: Wiedenfeld and Nicholson.

Will Selection for Mutational Robustness Significantly Retard Evolutionary Innovation on Neutral Networks?

Seth Bullock

Informatics Research Institute, School of Computing, University of Leeds, Leeds, LS2 9JT, UK

seth@comp.leeds.ac.uk

Abstract

As a population evolves, its members are under selection both for rate of reproduction (fitness) and mutational robustness. For those using evolutionary algorithms as optimisation techniques, this second selection pressure can sometimes be beneficial, but it can also bias evolution in unwelcome and unexpected ways. Here, the role of selection for mutational robustness in driving adaptation on neutral networks is explored. The behaviour of a standard genetic algorithm is compared with that of a search algorithm designed to be immune to selection for mutational robustness. Performance on an RNA folding landscape suggests that selection for mutational robustness, at least sometimes, will not unduly retard the rate of evolutionary innovation enjoyed by a genetic algorithm. Two classes of random landscape are used to explore the reasons for this result.

Introduction

It is well known that evolution will select for solutions with both high fitness and high robustness. That is, evolution favours *volumes* of search space associated with fit phenotypes, rather than single points of high fitness. The robustness of a solution is here defined in terms of its insensitivity to the action of the genetic operators at work during its evolution. By definition, then, perturbing a robust solution's genotype through mutation (or perhaps crossover) will not tend to perturb its fitness.

It is easy to see why this type of robustness (hereafter termed mutational robustness) is implicated in evolutionary adaptation. An individual's biological fitness is often equated with the number of progeny it leaves, but it might be more accurate to use the propensity to leave *viable* offspring as an indicator of fitness (Mills & Beatty 1994). This move encourages us to view fitness as the property of a *lineage* rather than a single genotype. Two genotypes that give rise to equivalent phenotypes (and thus have an equivalent propensity to leave offspring) may nevertheless differ in fitness under this interpretation. If the mutant offspring of one tend to be non-viable whereas those of the other tend to be viable, lineages stemming from the latter will be more successful than those stemming from the former (see Figure 1). For the remainder of the paper, I will reserve the term fitness to refer to the proximal propensity to leave offspring in the next generation and *effective fitness* to refer to the tendency for lineages stemming from a genotype to be successful over generational time. A more detailed treatment of this type of issue is presented in association with

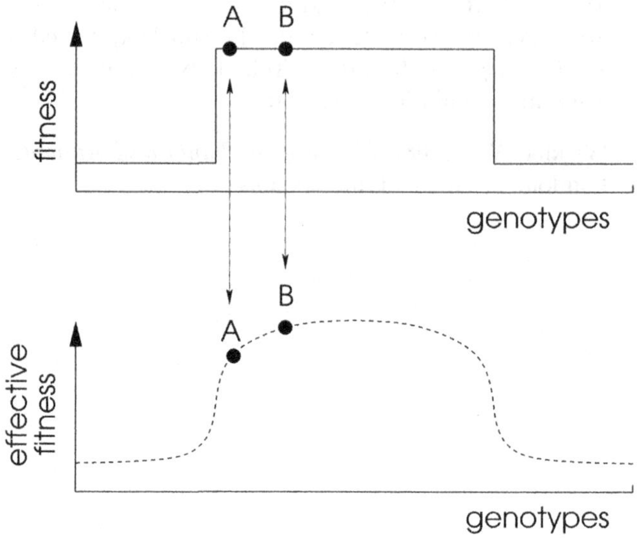

Figure 1: Two genotypes, A and B, achieve equivalent fitness scores (top). However, A's relative proximity to a fitness cliff ensures that it is less mutationally robust than B, and that, as a result, its effective fitness is somewhat reduced, while B's is increased (bottom).

the concept of the quasi-species (Eigen & Schuster 1979; Eigen, McCaskill, & Schuster 1988; 1989; Nowak 1992).

For certain optimisation problems, the tendency for a genetic algorithm (GA) to favour mutationally robust solutions can be very useful. Consider a parametric design problem in which we assess the performance of each solution in simulation, but can only realise a solution in the real world subject to certain manufacturing tolerances. If the genetic operators at work during evolution mirror the nature of the real-world manufacturing errors, it is possible that a standard GA will discover not only a good solution, but one that is robust to manufacturing errors. By exploiting the genetic algorithm's natural tendency to discover a fit volume of the search space, we can automatically steer the search towards realisable solutions.

Of course, if one wishes to discover the best *point* in a search space, a GA's tendency to be distracted by genotypes that are not as fit but are more mutationally robust can be frustrating (Schuster & Swetina 1998). In contrast, the behaviour of a hill-climbing algorithm (where a single solution is repeatedly mutated until an improvement is discovered at which point the improved mutant is repeatedly mutated, and so on) will not be affected by mutational robustness. Such a search process is able to scale ridges of increasing fitness that would be difficult or impossible for a genetic algorithm to climb due to their low mutational robustness. However, rather than infer that one class of algorithm is better or worse than another on the basis of these considerations, these different algorithmic biases should be understood to ensure that different algorithms are suited to different optimisation problems (Mitchell, Holland, & Forrest 1994; Wolpert & Macready 1997). Characterising which algorithms suit which problem types is the challenge that arises from this perspective.

Furthermore, comparing the behaviour of search algorithms as they traverse *flat* fitness landscapes may also reveal the presence of inherent biases. For example, the manner in which a search algorithm's mutation operators deal with illegal mutants may influence its search behaviour (Bullock 1999; 2001). Biases such as these can also be interpreted in terms of selection for mutational robustness. For instance, consider a real-valued, n-dimensional genotype where the value at each of the loci must lie in the range $[0, 1]$, and a mutation operator that perturbs the value at each of the loci by a small value drawn from a random distribution. Occasionally, the mutation operator will generate a genotype featuring one or more illegal values. Dealing with these illegal mutants may introduce a mutation bias.

For example, replacing any illegal mutant offspring with the nearest legal genotype increases the mutational robustness of solutions at the edges of the search space by lowering their effective mutation rate. In contrast, ignoring an illegal mutant offspring and replacing it with the offspring of a newly chosen parent will tend to reduce the mutational robustness of solutions close to the edges of the search space. The former approach will tend to bias evolutionary search in favour of extreme-valued genotypes, the latter away from these genotypes. Although the landscape appears to be flat, it is effectively warped by the mutation operator, which imposes a gradient in effective fitness where none was intended. The arbitrariness of these edge effects may retard evolutionary optimisation or introduce artefacts into an evolutionary simulation model (Bullock 1999; 2001).

Here this approach is extended to explore the impact of selection for mutational robustness on the behaviour of search algorithms trapped on neutral networks. First, the notion of neutrality and its relation to mutational robustness will be introduced.

Neutrality and Mutational Robustness

In the context of a search space, neutrality is the property of adjacent genotypes enjoying equivalent fitness scores. A neutral network consists of a set of genotypes with equal fitness, where each member of the set neighbours at least one other member. Again, these notions of adjacency and neighbourhood must be cashed out in terms of an algorithm's genetic operators.

For specific real-world search spaces, such as the RNA folding map, it has been demonstrated that the neutrality present is of a useful kind (Huynen 1996; Huynen, Stadler, & Fontana 1996; Fontana & Schuster 1998a; 1998b). Neutral networks *percolate* the search space, neighbouring a large proportion of possible alternative phenotypes. In addition, these neutral networks enjoy a property of *constant innovation* in that, over many generations, a neutral walk across these neutral networks tends to encounter novel phenotypes at a constant rate comparable to that which would be achieved by a random walk in the search space.

As such, a landscape exhibiting the right kind of neutrality will be much easier to search than the canonical rugged landscapes typically associated with complex search problems (Kauffman 1993). Rather than conceive a population to be hill-climbing in a rugged landscape, the picture painted by recent studies of neutrality is one of a population enduring periods of neutral drift punctuated by brief transitions to higher-fitness neutral networks (Barnett 1998; 2001).

Within the field of evolutionary computation, researchers have discovered that some difficult evolutionary optimisation problems already exhibit potentially useful neutral networks (Harvey & Thompson 1996). Others have attempted to encourage neutral networks where there are none by introducing redundancy into the genetic encoding, in the hope that this will improve the ability of evolutionary algorithms to find optimal solutions in general (Shipman *et al.* 2000). This research has prompted analysis of both naturally occurring neutral networks (Smith *et al.* 2002) and artificially crafted ones (Bullock 2001).

Implicit in the description so far has been the assumption that as genotypes on a neutral network code for equivalent phenotypes, they are selectively neutral with respect to one another. However, if a search algorithm has a tendency to favour mutationally robust genotypes this assumption does not hold. Rather than drift at random across a neutral network, a genetic algorithm will tend to favour those parts of the network that have a higher degree of neutrality, since these parts are more mutationally robust (van Nimwegen, Crutchfield, & Huynen 1999; Wilke *et al.* 2001; Wilke 2001a; 2001b).

From the perspective of evolutionary optimisation, this tendency raises a concern. If we are interested in maintaining a high rate of constant innovation, we might not want our drifting population to concentrate on the most mutationally robust areas of the network, since these are precisely the areas in which the rate of innovation is at its lowest.

Here we will explore this issue by comparing the performance of a GA, in terms of the rate at which it discovers novel network neighbours, with that of a similar algorithm, termed a plateau crawler (PC), that has been designed to be immune to selection for mutational robustness.

A Simple Search Problem

In order to demonstrate the effects of selection for mutational robustness on evolutionary dynamics, and to specify the two search algorithms we will concentrate on in this paper, a very simple toy search problem will be introduced. The *thresholded counting ones problem* is intended to be a trivial example of a problem featuring neutrality and neutral networks with which to introduce the effects of selection for mutational robustness. **It is by no means intended to reflect the character of neutrality as it occurs in typical real-world problems.**

Each genotype is a binary string of length L with an associated phenotype dependent on the number of genotypic bits that are set to one. Genotypes with more than t bits set to one enjoy maximum fitness. All other genotypes have zero fitness. (All problems explored in this paper share the property that genotypes are assigned a fitness of zero if they lie off the neutral network being considered, and maximal fitness otherwise.)

As a result, the search space can be divided into two neutral sets of genotypes. One sub-threshold set with fitness zero, and one super-threshold set with maximum fitness. We will consider the case in which $L = 100$ and $t = 50$. For this problem, the search space comprises a single neutral network associated with fitness zero and a second neutral network associated with maximum fitness.

We can expect a search algorithm that commences searching somewhere on the upper network to drift across this network in some manner. Periodically, the algorithm may generate sub-threshold mutants that lie off the upper network. Given that we are interested in the rate at which algorithms discover novel genotypes that neighbour a neutral network, i.e., the rate at which they generate potentially useful innovations, we will record the rate at which novel sub-threshold genotypes are generated as a measure of performance.[1]

The Algorithms

We will contrast the behaviour of two simple search algorithms, a standard genetic algorithm and a plateau crawler. The motivation for the design of the latter was to create an algorithm that is identical to the genetic algorithm in all respects save that it is provably immune from selection for mutational robustness. The resulting algorithm shares similarities with both the *random mutation hill-climber* (Forrest & Mitchell 1993) and the Barnett's (2001) *net-crawler.*

Genetic Algorithm

1. Initialise a population of S clones of a random chosen genotype, G, with the phenotype P
2. Pick parents at random from the current generation until one is found with phenotype P
3. With probability $1 - M$: Copy the chosen parent unchanged to the next generation

   With probability M:

   (a) Mutate the parental genotype, forming a mutant genotype, G_m, by replacing the value at a randomly chosen loci with a randomly chosen legal alternative

   (b) Determine the phenotype, P_m, of the resulting mutant

   (c) If $P_m \not\equiv P$ and G_m has not been encountered before, increment C, a cumulative tally of the number of novel off-network genotypes discovered by the algorithm so far

   (d) Add the resulting offspring to the next generation
4. Repeat steps 2 and 3 until a complete new generation has been produced
5. Record the value of C for this generation, C_n
6. Repeat steps 2 thru 5 until N generations of search have been completed

Plateau Crawler

In order to implement a plateau crawler (PC), we need only add the following step between 3(c) and 3(d):

- If $P_m \not\equiv P$ replace the mutant with an exact copy of its parent.

Notice that, for each algorithm, population size is fixed, parents are chosen in a standard roulette-wheel fashion, and reproduction involves only single point mutations and no crossover. Mutation rate, M, was set to 0.5 for all runs reported in this paper - i.e., 50% of offspring were identical to their parents, while 50% differed by exactly one allele.

This mutation rate is relatively low compared to rates typically used in evolutionary computation. To the extent that error-free reproduction can occur, pressure for mutational robustness will decrease. If every offspring were a perfect copy of its parent there would be no pressure to avoid genotypes that neighboured non-viable mutants. However, such a situation would lack the heritable variation that drives mutation – there would be no selection at all. As mutation rate is increased, we would

[1] In reality, we are interested in the discovery of fit phenotypes, but in the absence of any information concerning how phenotypes are distributed in the space, the discovery of novel genotypes is a good proxy.

expect selection for mutational robustness to become a more significant driver of evolutionary change. In the case where every offspring is a mutant, selection for mutational robustness will be critical. Fit points in genotype space will not be represented in a population unless they are surrounded by similarly fit mutant genotypes.

Although the plateau crawler algorithm is practically identical to the genetic algorithm, in operation it more closely resembles a population of S hill-climbers. It differs from the genetic algorithm in that every parent chosen to reproduce is guaranteed to either leave a copy of itself or a mutated offspring that shares its phenotype and fitness. As such the plateau crawler ensures that all offspring, and grandchildren, etc., have an equal chance of being chosen as parents themselves. This implies that the plateau crawler should be unaffected by mutational robustness, spending on average an equal amount of time at each point on a neutral network (Hughes 1996).

By contrast, the fact that the genetic algorithm allows parents to leave mutant offspring that are not viable ensures that lineages featuring genotypes with many non-neutral neighbours will not leave as many descendants as lineages featuring genotypes that are mutationally robust. This implies that, on average, the genetic algorithm should spend more time in the parts of the neutral network that enjoy a high degree of neutrality (van Nimwegen, Crutchfield, & Huynen 1999; Wilke 2001a).

Notice also that the plateau crawler *differs* slightly from a population of S independent hill-climbers in that rather than ensuring that each of the S members of the population generate exactly one offspring, the algorithm (like a GA) samples S parents at random from the population with replacement. As a result of the sampling error that this method entails, we can expect that a plateau crawler population, like a GA population, will tend to remain clustered rather than simply diffuse across the network as a population of independent hill-climbers would (Derrida & Peliti 1991; Barnett 2001).

Results

For our purposes, an algorithm should be rewarded for discovering novel non-neutral genotypes quickly and often. As such, each algorithm's performance is equated with the cumulative frequency which it discovers unique off-network genotypes (hereafter termed an algorithm's *discovery rate*). This value can be calculated as the area under a cumulative plot of unique off-network genotypes discovered over generational time,

$$D_{\text{alg}} = \sum_{n=1}^{N} C_n$$

The discovery rate of each algorithm for the thresholded counting ones game with $L = 100$ and $t = 50$, averaged over 500 runs of 100 generations each, is depicted in Figure 2. As might be expected given the above discussion, the genetic algorithm is outperformed by the plateau crawler. We can see why when we consider the manner in which the 500 populations were distributed over the phenotype space at the end of the runs (Figure 3). The plateau crawler has, on average, distributed the evolving population across the entire neutral network, closely approximating a random sampling of the high-fitness plateau. By contrast, the genetic algorithm has tended to avoid genotypes associated with phenotypes close to 50. For the genetic algorithm, this volume of the search space suffers from poor mutational robustness, and as a result is not successful.

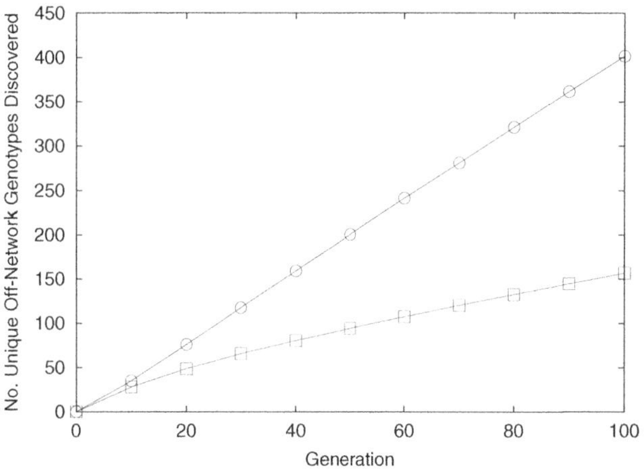

Figure 2: Mean (n=500) discovery rate of a plateau crawler (circles) and a genetic algorithm (squares) solving the thresholded counting-ones problem with genotype length 100 and threshold 50 for 100 generations of search.

These results, although drawn from a trivial search problem, raise some interesting possibilities. Could the difference between the performance of the two algorithm's somehow be used as an on-line metric with which to dynamically measure the strength of selection for mutational robustness? With this type of information at our disposal, could we dynamically alter a search algorithm to control for this search bias? Perhaps increasing or decreasing the mutation rate might allow us to counter an algorithm's tendency to concentrate on unproductive volumes of search space (Barnett 1998)? Alternatively, perhaps this information might be used by a hybrid algorithm to appropriately swapped from GA-style search to PC-style search. Before we can assess these possibilities, let us explore the performance of the same algorithms on a more realistic search problem.

RNA Folding Landscape

The manner in which different RNA sequences fold into their associated secondary structures has been a useful test case for assessing the role of neutrality and neutral

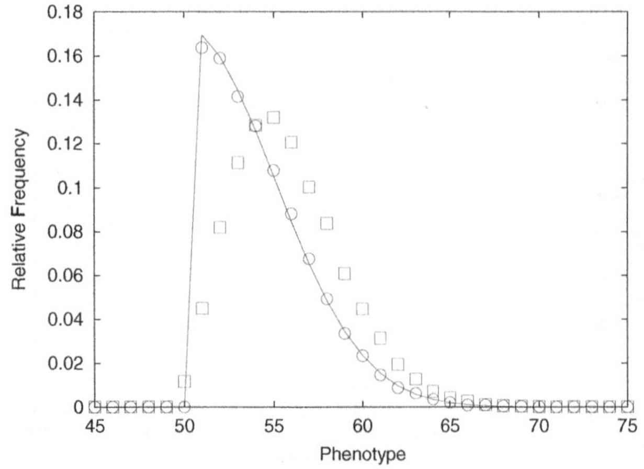

Figure 3: Three phenotypic frequency distributions for the counting-ones problem with genotype length 100 and threshold 50. The solid line represents the frequency distribution that would result from a population of randomly drawn super-threshold genotypes. Circles denote the aggregate phenotypic frequency distribution, after 100 generations of search, achieved by 500 runs of a plateau crawler. Squares denote the equivalent aggregate distribution achieved by 500 runs of a genetic algorithm. See text for details.

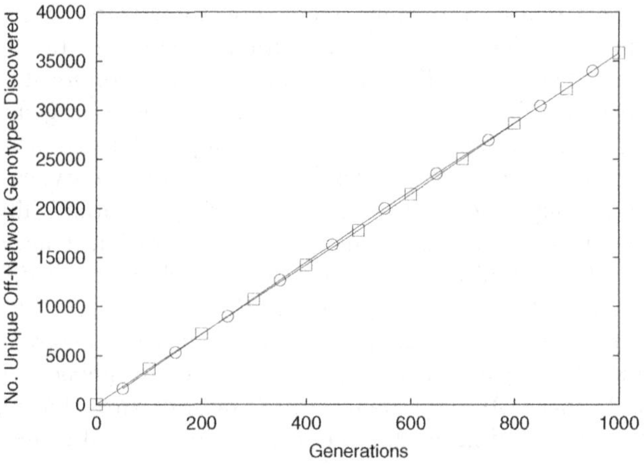

Figure 4: Discovery rate for a plateau crawler (circles) and a genetic algorithm (squares) searching an RNA folding landscape. Each algorithm was initialised with a population of 100 clones of the same randomly chosen RNA sequence of length 100.

networks in adaptive evolution (Schuster *et al.* 1994; Huynen, Stadler, & Fontana 1996; Schuster & Fontana 1999; Wilke 2001a). These studies have revealed that many RNA sequences fold into equivalent secondary structures and that the frequency distribution over these secondary structures exhibits a Zipf-like power law, with only a few very frequent secondary structures and very many rare secondary structures. In addition, it is common that a phenotype is easily accessible from an arbitrary point in sequence space, with randomly chosen phenotypes being separated by only a small number of point mutations. Recent studies have begun to explore the role of mutational robustness in influencing adaptation on these landscapes (van Nimwegen, Crutchfield, & Huynen 1999; Wilke 2001b; Wilke *et al.* 2001), concluding that selection for mutational robustness is an important driver at high mutation rates.

Here we compare the performance of the GA and PC algorithms on neutral networks chosen at random from a space of RNA sequences of length 100. Secondary structures were computed using version 1.4 of the Vienna RNA Package (Hofacker *et al.* 1994) which uses the free energies described in (Mathews *et al.* 1999) and is freely available from `http://www.tbi.univie.ac.at/~ivo/RNA/`. Folding was calculated at 30°C, and secondary structures were considered equivalent if the edit distance separating their tree representations was zero.

Since we expect that, in practice, search algorithms traversing a neutral network will not need to explore a large proportion of the network before encountering a transition to a higher-fitness phenotype, we will focus on the relatively short- or medium-term behaviour of search algorithms on neutral networks. In particular, we will not be particularly interested in the behaviour of these algorithms in the limit of infinite time.

Figure 4 shows the performance of the two algorithms run from the same initial RNA sequence for 1000 generations of search. In marked contrast to the results from the thresholded counting ones problem, both algorithms perform comparably. Does this result hold in general for neutral networks drawn at random from this search space? Figure 5 shows the results obtained by running each algorithm for 100 generations from the same 100 randomly chosen RNA sequences. The two algorithms continue to perform comparably, with, on average, the GA slightly outperforming the PC, discovering novel network neighbours at a slightly higher rate.

Given that we expect the PC algorithm to sample the neutral network evenly, spending the same amount of time at each point on the network, whereas the GA is expected to favour the less productive parts of the network, how can we account for this result?

Figure 6 demonstrates that during the same runs depicted in Figure 5 the GA consistently visited a greater number of unique genotypes on the neutral network. The plateau crawler may, in the limit, visit the entire network, but the genetic algorithm, in the short-term is doing a better job of sampling the network. In addition, Figure 7 shows that the during the same runs, the plateau crawler revisited already explored network neighbours more frequently than the genetic algorithm.

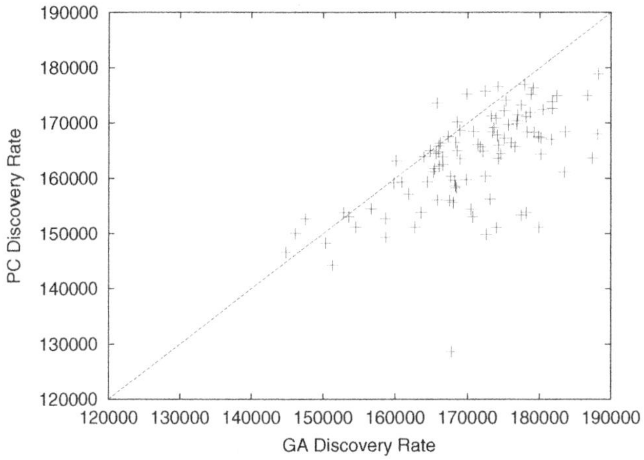

Figure 5: Scatterplot comparing the discovery rate of a genetic algorithm with that of a plateau crawler. Each of the 100 points represents a pair of 100-generation runs from a randomly chosen ancestral RNA sequence of length 100. The line $y = x$ separates the graph into a lower area in which the genetic algorithm outperforms the plateau crawler and an upper area in which the converse is true. On average, the genetic algorithm outperforms the plateau crawler across the sample.

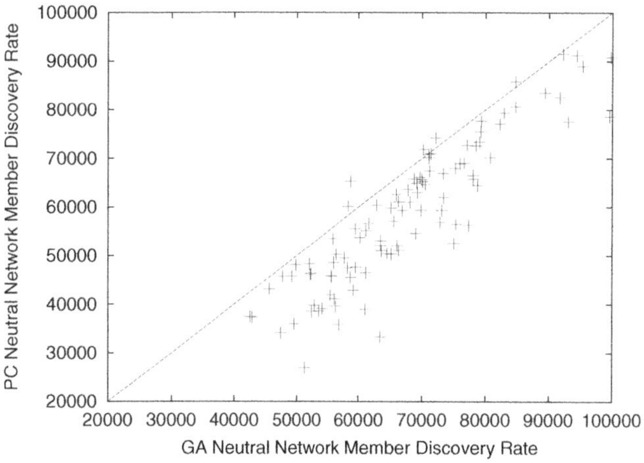

Figure 6: Scatterplot comparing the rate at which a genetic algorithm discovers novel members of a neutral network with the rate achieved by a plateau crawler. Points represent the same runs depicted in Figure 5.

While the plateau crawler is not confined to mutationally robust volumes of the search space, it has a tendency to repeatedly sample the same neighbours, and in doing so wastes time that the genetic algorithm spends in novel parts of the neutral network.

How generic are the results we have obtained for first the thresholded counting ones problem and now the RNA landscape? What are the properties of each that are responsible for the performance of the two algorithms that we have tested? Clearly, there exist landscapes for which genetic algorithms are significantly retarded by selection for mutational robustness. Equally clearly there exist different landscapes for which this is not the case. Before addressing these questions, a class of random landscapes with which to explore these phenomena further will be introduced.

Random Landscapes

A useful class of fitness landscape has been proposed by Barnett (1998) in order to study the role of neutrality in adaptive evolution. Dubbed *NKp landscapes* they extend Kauffman's (1993) NK landscape formalism to include a tunable degree of neutrality. Future work will explore replicating the results presented here on NKp landscapes, but for the moment we will focus on a simpler, and perhaps as a result less interesting, scheme.

Search commences at an arbitrary genotype which is assigned a fitness of 1. Whenever, through mutation, a search algorithm generates a novel genotype, we determine its fitness by reference to the landscape's degree of neutrality, p. With probability p, the mutant enjoys fitness 1, otherwise it is assigned fitness zero. In this manner, the fitness landscape is generated at random as the population traverses it. In this simple random landscape, each point has, on average, an equivalent degree of neutrality (although, of course, each offspring genotype may be adjacent to genotypes that have already been encountered and thus have already had their fitness specified). By varying p, we can specify landscapes in which neutrality is rare or commonplace.

Figure 8 depicts how the two search algorithms perform across a range of landscapes, as we vary p. At extreme values of p both algorithms perform comparably since there are either very few off-network genotypes to discover ($p \approx 1$) or very few neutral neighbours to discover ($p \approx 0$). At intermediate values of p, both algorithms improve, with the GA outperforming the PC over the entire range. The genetic algorithm appears more able to take advantage of the tendency for intermediate degrees of neutrality to increase the number of network neighbours available for discovery.

Figure 9 suggests that again an explanation for this disparity is to be found in the PCs tendency to resample network neighbours at a higher rate than the GA. Even though, on average, no point on the neutral network is more mutationally robust than any other, and hence no more productive, there still appears to be a significant difference between the ability of each algorithm to traverse the network.

In fact, the PC suffers a tendency to linger at each point in the neutral network that is inversely proportional to the degree of neutrality at that point. This tendency is necessary if the algorithm is to sample the

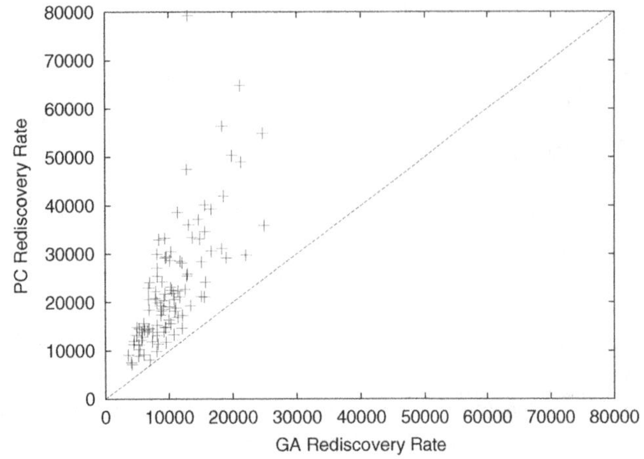

Figure 7: Scatterplot comparing the rate at which a genetic algorithm *rediscovers* genotypes that neighbour a neutral network with the rate achieved by a plateau crawler. Points represent the same runs depicted in Figures 5 and 6.

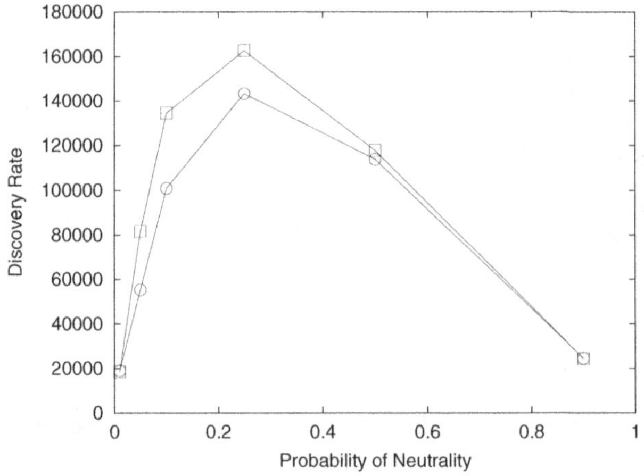

Figure 8: Variation in mean (n=50) discovery rate of a genetic algorithm (squares) and a plateau crawler (circles) after 100 generations of search on random graphs as the degree of neutrality, p, is varied from low ($p \approx 0$) to high ($p \approx 1$).

entire network equally. Since, by definition, there are fewer neutral transitions to genotypes with a low degree of neutrality, they are hard to find. As a result, an algorithm that must spend equal amounts of time at each point on a neutral network must linger at these points when they are discovered. Unfortunately, during these periods there is a tendency to repeatedly generate the same mutant offspring.

In contrast, the GA has a tendency to desert points in the network that suffer a low degree of neutrality, exposing it to the complementary risk of repeatedly generating the same *neutral* mutants in an area of mutational robustness. However, it appears that these complementary risks do not negate one another in these landscapes—eschewing the most peripheral parts of a neutral network does not prohibit the GA encountering novel network neighbours at a higher rate than the PC.

Introducing Local Structure

By slightly altering the manner in which a random landscape is generated, we can introduce some of the local structure that is absent from the random landscapes explored above, but is presumably present in real search spaces such as that of the RNA folding problem. In this way, rather than tending to distribute neutrality evenly across the landscape, we can ensure that different parts of the network exhibit different degrees of neutrality, and can alter the degree to which genotypes with a high degree of neutrality tend to cluster together.

When a novel genotype is generated by a search algorithm, we assign it a fitness value as before, but assign that point in the search space a unique p value as follows:

$$p_{\text{offspring}} = \begin{cases} \Phi^{\kappa} & (p_{\text{parent}} < 0.5) \\ 1 - (\Phi^{\kappa}) & (p_{\text{parent}} \geq 0.5) \end{cases}$$

Where Φ is a uniformly distributed random variate in the range $[0, 1]$, and κ is a clustering parameter used to control the extent to which genotypes with a high degree of neutrality tend to neighbour genotypes with a similar high degree of neutrality. For $\kappa = 1$ the degree of neutrality associated with each point in the space is chosen at random from the range $[0, 1]$, and as such is independent of its neighbours. As κ increases, a genotype's degree of neutrality becomes increasingly determined by that of its "parent".

Figure 10 depicts the manner in which the performance of each algorithm varies with the clustering parameter, κ. For $\kappa = 1$ the GA outperforms the PC. As κ increases, the performance of each algorithm falls to an equivalent asymptotic level. However, PC performance declines at a slower rate than GA performance, ensuring that the PC enjoys an advantage for the majority of the range explored. Here we begin to see the deleterious effects of selection for mutational robustness that were expected given the results from the thresholded counting ones problem.

Where there is a degree of local structure to the search space, the tendency for a genetic algorithm to concentrate on mutationally robust genotypes tends to retard the rate at which it discovers off-network novelty, at least by comparison with a plateau crawler.

It is likely that the locally structured random landscapes characterised by intermediate values of κ resemble that of the thresholded counting ones problem with which this study opened. Such landscapes will feature

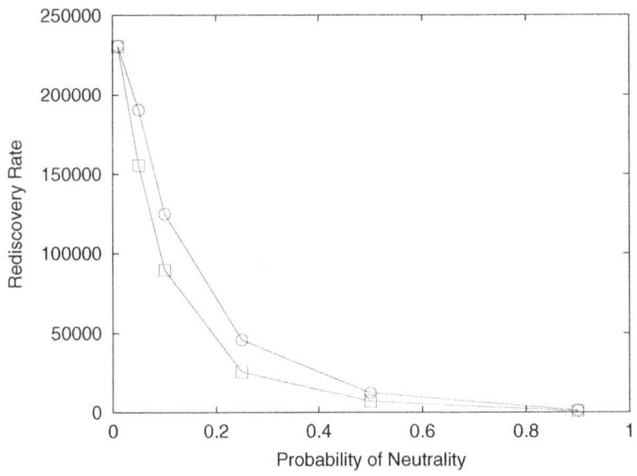

Figure 9: Variation in the mean (n=50) rate at which previously discovered off-network genotypes are revisited by a genetic algorithm (squares) and a plateau crawler (circles) after 100 generations of search on random graphs as the degree of neutrality, p, is varied from low ($p \approx 0$) to high ($p \approx 1$).

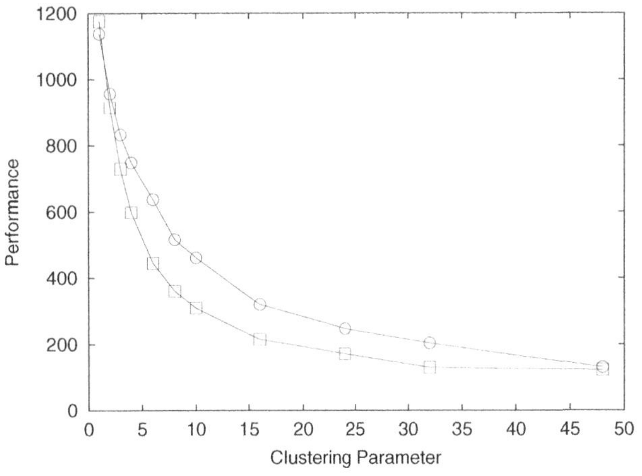

Figure 10: Variation in mean (n=50) discovery rate of a genetic algorithm (squares) and a plateau crawler (circles) after 100 generations of search on random graphs as a clustering parameter, κ, is varied from no clustering ($\kappa = 1$) to highly clustered ($\kappa \approx 50$).

densely interconnected neutral networks separated by relatively sharp boundaries.

Discussion

The results presented here are preliminary in the sense that they should be regarded as the precursor to analytical work. Currently it is unclear what definitive answers can be given to the question raised in the title of this paper. Nevertheless, these simulations serve to demonstrate that different search algorithms cope with different types of neutrality in different ways. As such they suggest the potential for algorithms to be tailored to suit particular classes of neutrality, or to dynamically reconfigure themselves to cope with changes in the character of the landscape they find themselves searching.

Moreover, these results show that although selection for mutational robustness will impede evolutionary innovation on a neutral network, that this is a significant problem for evolutionary optimisation is by no means a foregone conclusion. It may well be that significant numbers of real-world search problem share the structural properties of the RNA landscape such that standard evolutionary algorithms will remain largely untroubled by selection for mutational robustness.

The extent to which the topology of a neutral network is a critical determiner of the dynamics of evolution adaptation is beginning to be appreciated (van Nimwegen, Crutchfield, & Huynen 1999). Here, we identify the character of a network's local structure as critical in determining the impact of selection for mutational robustness on the performance of a search algorithm.

We have also highlighted the difference between an algorithm's search properties in the limit and its short-term behaviour on a neutral network. While a plateau crawler is guaranteed to be immune to selection for mutational robustness and to sample an entire neutral network in an unbiased manner, this guarantee does not prevent its short-term behaviour from being inefficient. For certain landscapes, including the RNA folding map, this inefficiency is such that a search algorithm impeded by selection for mutational robustness is nevertheless able to outperform it.

Conclusion

Selection for mutational robustness (alongside selection for rate of reproduction) drives the evolutionary adaptation of natural and artificial populations. While this selection pressure may sometimes appear serendipitous, it is capable of frustrating evolutionary progress towards fit solutions (Schuster & Swetina 1998) or biasing simulation results (Bullock 1999). Here, numerical simulations were used to demonstrate the role of selection for mutational robustness in the dynamics of two classes of population-based search algorithm. Rather than suffer from selection for mutational robustness, the genetic algorithm achieved a level of performance comparable to or exceeding that of a plateau crawler designed to be immune to selection for mutational robustness.

A formal analysis of the manner in which selection for mutational robustness influences the dynamics of real search algorithms on neutral networks is still required, but the current study suggests that in comparison to an unbiased search algorithm and for real-world problems with fitness landscapes that resemble that of the RNA folding problem, the ability of a standard genetic algorithm to generate potentially useful innovations will not be significantly retarded by selection for mutational robustness.

Acknowledgements

The paper benefited from reviewers comments, discussion with Lionel Barnett, Matt Glickman, Inman Harvey, and Tom Smith and conversation with the University of Leeds biosytems reading group.

References

Barnett, L. 1998. Ruggedness and neutrality—the NKp family of fitness landscapes. In Adami, C.; Belew, R.; Kitano, H.; and Taylor, C., eds., *Artificial Life VI*, 18–27. MIT Press, Cambridge, MA.

Barnett, L. 2001. Netcrawling: Optimal evolutionary search with neutral networks. In *Proceedings of the Congress on Evolutionary Computation*, 3037. IEEE Press.

Bullock, S. 1999. Are artificial mutation biases unnatural? In Floreano, D.; Nicoud, J.-D.; and Mondada, F., eds., *Fifth European Conference on Artificial Life*, 64–73. Springer, Berlin.

Bullock, S. 2001. Smooth operator? Understanding and visualising mutation bias. In Kelemen, J., and Sosik, P., eds., *Sixth European Conference on Artificial Life*, 602–612. Springer, Heidelberg.

Derrida, B., and Peliti, L. 1991. Evolution in a flat fitness landscape. *Bulletin of Mathematical Biology* 53:355–382.

Eigen, M., and Schuster, P. 1979. *The Hypercycle—A Principle of Natural Self-Organization.* Berlin: Springer-Verlag.

Eigen, M.; McCaskill, J.; and Schuster, P. 1988. Molecular quasi-species. *Journal of Physical Chemistry* 92:6881–6891.

Eigen, M.; McCaskill, J.; and Schuster, P. 1989. The molecular quasi-species. *Advances in Chemical Physics* 75:149–263.

Fontana, W., and Schuster, P. 1998a. Continuity in evolution: On the nature of transitions. *Science* 280:1451–1455.

Fontana, W., and Schuster, P. 1998b. Shaping space: The possible and the attainable in rna genotype-phenotype mapping. *Journal of Theoretical Biology* 194:491–515.

Forrest, S., and Mitchell, M. 1993. Relative building block fitness and the building block hypothesis. In Whitely, D., ed., *Foundations of Genetic Algorithms 2.* Morgan Kaufmann, San Mateo, CA.

Harvey, I., and Thompson, A. 1996. Through the labyrinth evolution finds a way: A silicon ridge. In Higuchi, T.; Iwata, M.; and Weixin, L., eds., *First Internatonal Conference on Evolvable Systems*, 406–422. Springer-Verlag.

Hofacker, I. L.; Fontana, W.; Stadler, P. F.; Bonhoeffer, L. S.; Tacker, M.; and Schuster, P. 1994. Fast folding and comparison of RNA secondary structures. *Monatshefte Für Chemie* 125(2):167–188.

Hughes, B. D. 1996. *Random Walks and Random Environments*, volume 2. Oxford: Clarendon.

Huynen, M.; Stadler, P.; and Fontana, W. 1996. Smoothness within ruggedness: The role of neutrality in adaption. *Proceedings of the National Academy of Science USA* 93(1):397–401.

Huynen, M. 1996. Exploring phenotype space through neutral evolution. *Journal of Molecular Evolution* 43:165–169.

Kauffman, S. A. 1993. *The Origins of Order: Self-organisation and Selection in Evolution.* New York: Oxford University Press.

Mathews, D. H.; Sabina, J.; Zuker, M.; and Turner, D. H. 1999. Expanded sequence dependence of thermodynamic parameters improves prediction of RNA secondary structure. *Journal of Molecular Biology* 288(5):911–940.

Mills, S. K., and Beatty, J. H. 1994. The propensity interpretation of fitness. In Sober, E., ed., *Conceptual Issues in Evolutionary Biology.* Cambridge, MA: MIT Press. 3–23.

Mitchell, M.; Holland, J. H.; and Forrest, S. 1994. When will a genetic algorithm outperform hill climbing? In Cowan, J. D.; Tesauro, G.; and Alspector, J., eds., *Advances in Neural Information Processing Systems*, volume 6, 51–58. Morgan Kaufmann Publishers, Inc.

Nowak, M. 1992. What is a quasispecies? *Trends in Ecology and Evolution* 7:118–121.

Schuster, P., and Fontana, W. 1999. Chance and necessity in evolution: Lessons from RNA. *Physica D* 133:427–452.

Schuster, P., and Swetina, J. 1998. Stationary mutation distributions and evolutionary optimization. *Bulletin of Mathematical Biology* 50:635–660.

Schuster, P.; Fontana, W.; Stadler, P. F.; and Hofacker, I. L. 1994. From sequences to shapes and back: A case study in RNA secondary structures. *Proceedings of the Royal Society of London, Series B* 255:279–284.

Shipman, R.; Shackleton, M.; Ebner, M.; and Watson, R. 2000. Neutral search spaces for artificial evolution: A lesson from life. In Bedau, M. A.; McCaskill, J. S.; Packard, N. H.; and Rasmussen, S., eds., *Artificial Life VII*, 162–169. MIT Press, Cambridge, MA.

Smith, T. M. C.; Husbands, P.; Layzell, P.; and O'Shea, M. 2002. Fitness landscapes and evolvability. *Evolutionary Computation* 10(1):1–34.

van Nimwegen, E.; Crutchfield, J. P.; and Huynen, M. 1999. Neutral evolution of mutational robustness. *Proceedings of the National Academy of Science USA* 96(17):9716–9720.

Wilke, C. O.; Wang, J. L.; Ofria, C.; Lenski, R. E.; and Adami, C. 2001. Evolution of digital organisms at high mutation rates leads to survival of the flattest. *Nature* 412:331–3.

Wilke, C. O. 2001a. Adaptive evolution on neutral networks. *Bulletin of Mathematical Biology* 63(4):715–730.

Wilke, C. O. 2001b. Selection for fitness versus selection for robustness in RNA secondary structure folding. *Evolution* 55(12):2412–2420.

Wolpert, D. H., and Macready, W. G. 1997. No free lunch theorems for optimization. *IEEE Transactions on Evolutionary Computation* 1(1):67–82.

Multiobjective Evolutionary Search for One-Dimensional Cellular Automata in the Density Classification Task

Gina M. B. Oliveira, **José C. Bortot** and **Pedro P. B. de Oliveira**
Universidade Presbiteriana Mackenzie
Rua da Consolação 896, 6° andar — Consolação
01302-907 São Paulo — Brazil
{gina, jbortot, pedrob}@mackenzie.br

Abstract

A key concern in artificial-life-oriented research in complex systems has been the relationship between the dynamical behaviour of cellular automata (CA) and their computational ability. Along this line, evolutionary methods have been used to look for CA with predefined computational behaviours, the most widely studied task having been the Density Classification Task (DCT). It has recently been showed that the use of an heuristic guided by parameters that estimate the dynamical behaviour of CA, can improve evolutionary search. On the other hand, an approach that has been successfully applied to several kinds of problems is the Evolutionary Multiobjective Optimization (EMOO). Here, the EMOO technique called Non-Dominated Sorting Genetic Algorithm is combined with the parameter-based heuristic, and successfullly applied to the DCT, suggesting a positive synergy out of using the two techniques in the search for CA.

Introduction

One of the greatest motivations for studying cellular automata (CA) is their ability to perform computations (Mitchell 1996). However, the comprehension about how these computations are carried out is still extremely vague, what has entailed various studies on methods to make CA programming possible. One of these possibilities is the use of evolutionary techniques to design CA that perform a predefined computation. The most widely studied CA task is the Density Classification Task (DCT) (Andre, Bennett, & Koza 1997; Mitchell, Hraber, & Crutchfield 1993; Juillé & Pollack 1998; Oliveira, de Oliveira, & Omar 2000). Even with evolutionary techniques, the high cardinality of CA rule spaces may become a serious obstacle to be skipped over in order to find CA that perform the desired computational task. This aspect turns the search slow and sometimes unproductive.

In (Oliveira, de Oliveira, & Omar 2000) a set of static parameters (i.e., directly derived from the CA rule table) was proposed, aiming at the reduction of the latter problem, as they are used as an auxiliary metric to guide the processes underlying the genetic search. Based on this set, it was possible to build a guide to a standard genetic algorithm (GA) to find CA rules for DCT. The parameter-based heuristic was incorporated into the GA in two aspects: in the fitness function, and in the genetic operators (of crossover and mutation). The fitness function of a cellular automaton rule was made by the weighed sum between a fitness component due to its efficacy in a sample of initial configurations (ICs), with a second fitness component that represents the bias due to the parameter-based heuristic (Oliveira, de Oliveira, & Omar 2000). Although this solution yielded an improvement on the genetic search in all the tasks studied, the weight of the heuristic in the rule evaluation interferes on this performance.

Instead of using any weighted sum to evaluate the rule, new experiments are reported here, where an evolutionary multiobjective approach is used. Accordingly, the heuristic and the efficacy in the IC sample are kept separate, as independent objectives to be followed by the genetic search.

This work is totally related to the idea of understanding the impact of the inherently local information processing of CA on their ability to perform a coordinated computation at the global level, as mediated by an evolutionary process. It is very much in tune with one of the alife open problems in (Bedau *et al.* 2000), namely, that we should be able to "*develop a theory of information processing, information flow and information generation for evolving systems*".

Evolutionary Multiobjective Methods

Several real-world problems involve simultaneous optimization of multiple objectives, so that it is not always possible to achieve an optimum solution in respect to all objectives, individually considered. In this kind of problem, there is a set of solutions better than all the other solutions in the search space (Srinivas & Deb 1994). This solution set is called the *Pareto optimum* or non-dominated solutions. Multiobjective evolutionary methods try to find this solution set by using each objective separately, without aggregating them as an unique objective (Coello 1999).

The Nondominated Sorting Genetic Algorithms (NSGA) method was proposed by Srinivas and Deb (1994) and is based on the concept of non-domination. Suppose that there are N objectives $f_1, f_2, \ldots f_N$ to be simultaneously optimised. A solution A is said to be dominated by another solution B, if B is better than A in relation to at least one of the objectives f_i, and is better or equal to A in relation to the other objectives. Two solutions A and B are non-dominated in relation to each other if A does not dominate B and B does not dominate A. The Pareto optimum is the set of non-dominated solutions considering the entire search space.

The basic difference of NSGA in relation to a simple GA is the way in which the individuals are evaluated: in order to obtain the fitness value of an individual, the fitness components associated with each objective involved in the problem are used to rank the individuals according to their degree of domination over the others in the population. A classification is performed based on several layers of non-domination. Initially, all individuals in the population that are non-dominated are separated as the first, outer layer, and a (dummy) fitness value is assigned to them whose role is simply to characterise their degree of domination over the others in the population, as mentioned above; for the outer layer, the highest fitness value is assigned as the individuals in it exhibit the highest degree domination (the actual value assigned is proportional to the population size, but other details do exist which are being omitted here). Then, the remaining individuals are classified again, also based on the non-domination criterion, and the second layer is formed with a (dummy) fitness lower than the first one. This process continues until all individuals are classified in their respective layers. A stochastic remainder proportional selection is used so that the outer the layer an individual is in, the likelier its chance to reproduce. The other steps of the NSGA are very similar to the simple GA.

CA Dynamics and Parameterisation

Through the analysis of the dynamic behaviour exhibited by CA, Wolfram (1984) proposed a qualitative behaviour classification. Later on, Li and Packard (1990) proposed a refinement in the original Wolfram classification that divides the rule space into six classes: Null, Fixed Point, Two-Cycle, Periodic, Complex and Chaotic.

The dynamics of a cellular automaton is associated with its transition rule. In order to help forecast the dynamic behaviour of CA, several parameters have been proposed, directly calculated from their transition table (Langton 1990; Li & Packard 1990; Binder 1993; Oliveira, de Oliveira, & Omar 2001). A set of five parameters was used in (Oliveira, de Oliveira, & Omar 2001): two of them were chosen from among those already published, and three new ones. In the experiments involving the DCT task described in the next section, four parameters from that set were used: Sensitivity (Binder 1993), Absolute Activity, Neighborhood Dominance and Activity Propagation (Oliveira, de Oliveira, & Omar 2001). All of them have been normalized between 0 and 1, for one-dimensional CA with any radius.

Computational Tasks and CA Evolving

CA have the potential of executing computations in a non-standard fashion. Various investigations have been carried out on the their computational power, with concentrated efforts in the study of 1D CA capable of performing computational tasks. The most widely studied CA task is the Density Classification Task (DCT) (Packard 1988). In this task the objective is to find a binary 1D CA that can classify the density of 1s in the Initial Configuration: if the initial lattice has more 1s than 0s, the automaton should converge to a null configuration of 1s; otherwise, it should converge to a null configuration of 0s. Once a computational task is defined, manual programming is difficult and costly, and exhaustive search of the rule space becomes impossible, due to its high cardinality. A solution is the use of search methods, particularly evolutionary methods (Mitchell, Hraber, & Crutchfield 1993; Oliveira, de Oliveira, & Omar 2000). Packard (1988) was the first to publish results using a GA as a tool to find CA rules. Other evolutionary techniques were used to find such kind of rules (Juillé & Pollack 1998; Andre, Bennett, & Koza 1997). In a recent work (Oliveira, de Oliveira, & Omar 2000), a simple GA environment was modified so as to incorporate an heuristic based on the forecast parameters selected and then used to find DCT rules. First, parameter value regions where good rules should be more likely to occur were obtained by calculating the parameter values for some published CA rules. This information was used as an auxiliary metric to guide the processes underlying the GA search. A simple GA was adapted so as to incorporate the parameter-based heuristic in two aspects. First, the fitness function F of a rule was defined as a weighed composition between the heuristic-based component (Hp) and the fitness component derived from the actual performance of the rule (F_{IC}) in the attempt to solve the DCT as in Equation (1).

$$F = F_{IC} + \rho \times Hp \tag{1}$$

The parameter-based heuristic is coded as a function that returns a value between 0 and 100 for each rule, depending on the values of the its parameters: Hp returns 100 if all parameter values match the ranges of the published rules; otherwise, the value returned decreases linearly as the parameter values became increasingly away from those ranges. All parameters contribute equally in the calculation of Hp. The function F_{IC} also returns a value between 0 and 100, acccording to the rule efficacy in solving 100 different initial configurations. Finally — and crucially, to the point being made in this paper — ρ is the weight that establishes the influence of the heuristic component in the overall rule fitness. The second aspect in which the heuristic information was used was in that it allowed the definition of biased genetic operators of reproduction and mutation: in order to select the crossover point and the rule table bits to be mutated, N_{CM} attempts were made; among them, those that generated rules with high Hp value were selected. In (Oliveira, de Oliveira, & Omar 2000), it was used $\rho = 40\%$, $N_{CM} = 10$ and the insertion of the parameter information managed to improve the performance of the

Number of individuals	100
Number of generations	100
Number of ICs per generation	100
Number of ICs at the final evaluation of the run	10,000
Number of GA runs	500
Elitism rate	20%
Crossover selection	Random selection out of the elite
Mutation rate	1% per bit
CA radius	3
Number of CA cells	149
Number of CA steps	300

Table 1: Specification of the simple GA experiments.

rules found for the DCT.

DCT Experiments

Simple GA experiments: ρ influence

Since an analysis of the effect of weight ρ has not been done in (Oliveira et al., 2000), this is what we go about now, in the context of DCT. For this matter, a series of experiments were performed, with varying values of ρ from 0% (corresponding to Mitchell *et al.*, (1993)), up to 100%. The specification of the GA and CA environment is presented in Table 1, and the results of the experiments are shown in Table 2, where each row corresponds to one experiment. The efficacy of the GA run was measured by testing the performance of the best rule found, at the end of the run, in the classification of 10^4 random initial configurations. The columns 2 through 7 in Table 2 display the percentage of runs in which the efficacy of the best rule found was within the corresponding interval. The last column shows the average efficacy of the ten best rules found in each experiment. One can also observe that all experiments with the parameter-based heuristic yielded superior results in comparison with the experiment without the heuristic; however, it is clear that an adequate value of ρ is necessary to improve the search. Within the values tested, the best experiment relied on ρ = 40%, as used in (Oliveira, de Oliveira, & Omar 2000). Nevertheless, a question remains of whether there may be another ρ value, which might yield better results and whether that value would be adequate for other parameter ranges and other computational tasks.

Multiobjective experiments

In a second stage, instead of using the weighed sum of Equation (1), a multiobjective approach was used; the parameter-based heuristic is still introduced in crossover and mutation in the same way as in (Oliveira, de Oliveira, & Omar 2000). However, the fitness is no longer given by the composition of the two separated objectives F_{IC} and Hp from Equation (1): instead of establishing any *a priori* heuristic weight, the multiobjective dynamics is expected to define the relative importance of the objectives during the search.

A multiobjective environment was implemented after the NSGA method, with a major modification referring to the selection method: instead of the stochastic remainder proportional selection, elitism of 20% was used, as in Mitchell *et al.*, (1993), with the crossover pairs being randomly selected directly from the elite. The elite classification was based on the dummy fitness of each individual, after the non-domination classification. The results of the multiobjective experiment are presented in Table 3, referred to as MO, also obtained out of 500 runs. It replicates some results from Table 2: the GA experiment without the heuristic, called WH, as well as the experiment with ρ = 40%, called ρ40. The efficacy of the best rule found in all the runs is presented for each experiment. Figure 1 shows the ten best rules efficacies. It should be observed that the MO experiment behaved in a similar way to the ρ40, which was the best experiment with the simple GA. In fact, MO is only slightly better than ρ40.

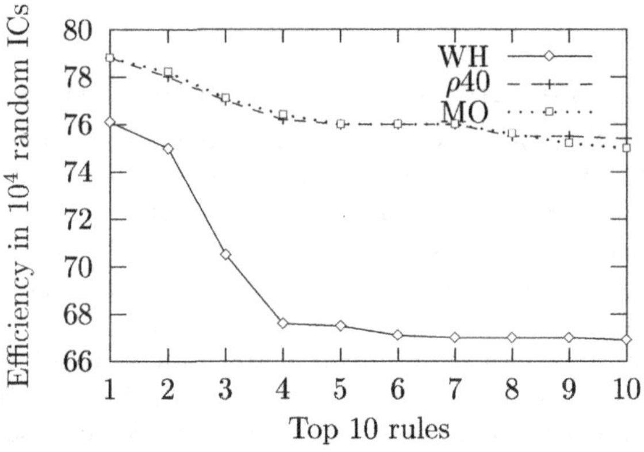

Figure 1: Efficacy of the top 10 rules in simple GA and NSGA experiments, with population of 100 individuals.

Subsequently, additional experiments were performed, so that the search could run freer, the idea being to check whether the NSGA could better explore the search space in less stricter conditions. The following parameters of the GA were used: 200 individuals in the populations, 200 initial configurations for testing the rules at each generation, and 1000 generations per run. One experiment was performed with the GA without the parameter-based heuristic, named WH_2. A GA was also used but with the parameter-based heuristic incorporated as in Equation (1) with ρ = 40%; this was called ρ40_2. Finally, the experiment MO_2 was performed with the NSGA adapted with the heuristic information. All experiments were composed of 200 GA runs. Table 4 and Figure 2 show the results. Comparing with

ρ(%)	(0,55)	(55,60)	(60,65)	(65,70)	(70,75)	(75,80)	Top10
0	8.2	0.2	49.8	41.2	0.4	0.2	69.26
10	0.0	0.0	18.0	79.6	2.2	0.2	74.12
20	0.0	0.2	16.4	81.4	1.4	0.6	73.94
30	0.0	0.0	12.6	86.4	0.8	0.2	71.27
40	0.0	0.2	12.8	83.8	0.8	2.4	76.49
50	0.0	0.0	10.4	88.2	0.8	0.6	73.02
60	0.0	0.2	17.0	81.4	0.8	0.6	72.96
70	0.0	0.4	17.8	79.4	1.2	1.2	75.49
80	0.0	0.2	16.2	80.6	1.4	1.6	76.26
90	0.0	0.2	13.4	83.4	1.6	1.4	76.20
100	0.0	0.0	13.2	85.0	0.8	1.0	74.42

Table 2: Experiments with the simple GA.

	Best Rule	(0,60)	(60,65)	(65,70)	(70,75)	(75,80)	Top10
WH	75.98	8.4	49.8	41.2	0.4	0.2	69.26
ρ40	78.65	0.2	12.8	83.8	0.8	2.4	76.49
MO	78.94	0.4	17.8	79.2	1.0	1.6	76.57

Table 3: Results obtained with the simple GA and NSGA experiments, with 100 individuals in the population

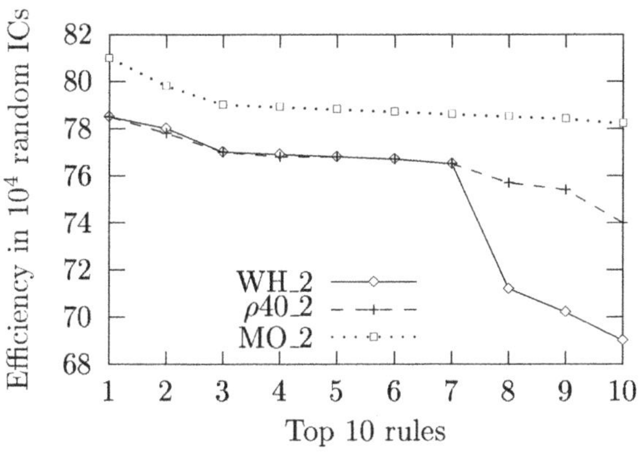

Figure 2: Efficacy of the top 10 rules in simple GA and NSGA experiments, with population of 200 individuals.

the corresponding experiments with 100 individuals in Table 3, all experiments improved with the more flexible parameter settings. The multiobjective experiment is also better than the others. But notice that now, it is more evident that the multiobjective experiment performed much better in relation to the non-multiobjective approach with $\rho = 40\%$.

Final Remarks

The experiments have shown that the multiobjective solution is a good approach for the incorporation of the parameter-based heuristic we have used in previous works, as way to help automatic CA programming. The results obtained with the multiobjective approach are clearly at least as good as the one derived from the adequate choice of a weight to balance the role of heuristic, with the advantage that no actual choice has to be made.

The lesson the experiments discussed here are bringing forth is that the notion of Pareto dominance seems to be prevailing also in the context of the parameter-based heuristic in CA search. However, it is still premature to draw a final conlusion on this issue. In fact, although the heuristic information was considered as an independent objective, it is composed of four different parameters, each of them contributing equally for the fitness component *Hp* (through a simple average). However, it is possible that in other tasks the individual guidance role of each parameter may have distinct effectiveness over the search. The next step in our investigation is to break the heuristic in different objectives, associated with each individual parameter, thus allowing the evolutionary multiobjective algorithm to directly handle the resulting multi-directed search.

Acknowledgments

G.M.B.O. and P.P.B.O. are grateful to Univ. Mackenzie for their support, and CAPES, FAPESP and MACK-PESQUISA for funding.

References

Andre, D.; Bennett, F.; and Koza, J. 1997. Evolution of intricate long-distance communication signals in cellular automata using programming. In Langton, C., and Shimohara, K., eds., *Artificial Life V*. Cambridge, Mass.: MIT Press.

Bedau, M.; McCaskill, J.; Packard, N.H. Rasmussen, S.; Adami, C.; Green, D.; Ikegami, T.; Kaneko, K.;

	Best Rule	(0,60)	(60,65)	(65,70)	(70,75)	(75,80)	Top10
WH_2	78.73	17.6	77.8	0.9	2.8	0.0	71.76
ρ40_2	78.86	10.5	83.0	2.0	4.5	0.0	76.62
MO_2	81.16	4.0	83.8	5.2	6.4	0.6	78.76

Table 4: Results obtained with the simple GA and NSGA experiments, with 200 individuals in the population

and S., R. T. 2000. Open problems in artificial life. *Artificial Life* 6:363–376.

Binder, P. 1993. A phase diagram for elementary cellular automata. *Complex Systems* 7:241–247.

Coello, C. 1999. A comprehensive survey of evolutionary-based multiobjective optimization techniques. *Knowledge and Information Systems* 1(3):269–308.

Juillé, H., and Pollack, J. 1998. Coevolving the "ideal" trainer: Application to the discovery of cellular automata rules. In *Proceedings of Genetic Programming Conference 3*.

Langton, C. 1990. Computation at the edge of chaos: Phase transitions and emergent computation. *Physica D* 42:12–37.

Li, W., and Packard, N. 1990. The structure of elementary cellular automata rule space. *Complex Systems* 4:281–297.

Mitchell, M.; Hraber, P.; and Crutchfield, J. 1993. Evolving cellular automata to perform computations. *Physica D* 75:361–391.

Mitchell, M. 1996. Computation cellular automata: a selected review. In Gramss, T., ed., *Nonstandard Computation*. Weinheim: VCH Verlagsgesellschaft.

Oliveira, G.; de Oliveira, P.; and Omar, N. 2000. volving solutions of the density classification task in 1D cellular automata, guided by parameters that estimate their dynamic behavior. In Bedau, M. A.; McCaskill, J. S.; Packard, N. H.; and Rasmussen, S., eds., *Alife VII*, 428–436. Cambridge, Mass.: MIT Press.

Oliveira, G.; de Oliveira, P.; and Omar, N. 2001. Definition and applications of a five-parameter characterization of one-dimensional cellular automata rule space. *Artificial Life* 7(3):277–301.

Packard, N. 1988. Adaptation towards the edge of the chaos. In Kelso, J.; Mandell, A.; and Shlesinger, M., eds., *Dynamic Patterns in Complex Systems*. World Scientific. 293–301.

Srinivas, N., and Deb, K. 1994. Multiojective optimization using nondominated sorting in genetic algorithms. *Evolutionary Computation* 221–248.

Wolfram, S. 1984. Universality and complexity in cellular automata. *Physica D* 10:1–35.

Evolutionary Dynamics of a Food Web with Recursive Branching and Extinction

Hiroshi Ito[1] and **Takashi Ikegami**[2]

Department of General Systems Sciences, The Graduate School of Arts and Sciences,
University of Tokyo, 3-8-1 Komaba, Meguro-ku, Tokyo 153-8902 Japan
[1]itoh9@dolphin.c.u-tokyo.ac.jp
[2]ikeg@sacral.c.u-tokyo.ac.jp

Abstract

A dynamic systems approach to evolutionary branching and its development in an artificial food web is presented. Predator-prey interaction among trophic species with two traits generates a variety of evolutionary branching patterns, depending on interaction strengths and mutation rates. Studying branching patterns in a phenotypic space reveals three branching patterns: prey-bifurcation, predator-bifurcation, and net-bifurcation. In particular, a complex food web network emerges through net-bifurcation. A relationship between biomass and the number of species is analysed by changing the interaction strength. We report that the branching and extinction rates of trophic species reaches a maximum when the number of species, but not the entire biomass, reaches a maximum.

Introduction

The origin and evolution of species have been tested by many mathematical models. Recent advances in models for sympatric speciation (Dieckmann & Doebeli 1999; Higashi, Takimoto, & Yamamura 1999; Doebeli & Dieckmann 2000; Kaneko & Yomo 2000) have shown that various intra- and inter-species interactions split a single founding population into two different populations, called "evolutionary branching". Doebli and Dieckmann have demonstrated that various ecological interactions (resource competition, mutualism and host-parasite relationships) can cause branching with the evolution of assortative mating. Highashi's sexual selection model has shown evolutionary branching only through evolutionary divergence of sexual preferences, while Kaneko and Yomo have shown that dynamic clustering caused by the internal degrees of freedom in each reproductive unit drives the branching.

The main concern of these models is evolutionary branching at each trophic level. Here we are more concerned with higher-order branchings, which generate populations at new trophic levels. In particular, we investigate how the complexity of the ecosystem may be built up from a bottom trophic species (e.g. plants) only by predator-prey interaction.

Mathematical studies on the evolution of a food web have been mainly based on the replicator or Lotka-Volterra models. Yasutomi and Tokita (Tokita & Yasutomi 2002) have studied the evolution of replicator dynamics by adding new columns and rows to the original interaction matrix. Jain and Krishna (Jain & Krishna 2002) have shown the role of innovation and of keystone species in large extinctions using an evolutionary replicator model. The other approach can be found in Lindgren and Mats Nordal's (Lindgren & Nordahl 1993) study on the evolution of a food web, using the model of the iterated prisoner's dilemma game. In this model, a basic strategy (Tit for Tat) is used and new strategies are constantly introduced through genetic algorithms. They analysed what kind of food web emerges.

These previous approaches for evolutionary dynamics of a food web invite new species from outside. Namely, these models cannot deal with the mechanism of creating new species from the intrinsic ecological dynamics that maintain the food web. In this paper, we investigate how patterns of autonomous development and collapse of a food web with recursive branching and extinction may be classified and we show how ecological diversity and evolution are interrelated.

Modelling phenotype space and dynamics

In nature, individuals use inorganic resources and other individuals as foods. Individuals are also used by other individuals as resources. Quantifying those characteristics of individuals as a resource by a simple measure, we represent individuals as a resource distribution on the measured space. Suppose that a single variable z for the measure and each individual is characterized by two traits, which are measured by the factor z and interpreted as a resource trait (prey) and a utilizer trait (predator). Formally, they are labelled as $\mathbf{r}$ and $\mathbf{u}$, respectively. With these labels, we define a phenotypic space (Fig.1). A phenotype distribution function $p(u, r)$ is defined on this space. A resource distribution $R(z)$ and a resource utilization distribution $U(z)$ are computed as follows:

$$R(z) = \int_u p(u, z)du + L(z), \quad (1)$$

$$U(z) = \int_r p(z, r)dr, \quad (2)$$

where $L(z)$ is a constant inward resource distribution given from without. Species at the lowest trophic level in the focussed range of the food web use this resource. Thus, the type of the inward resource (organic/inorganic, plants/animals) depends on what range

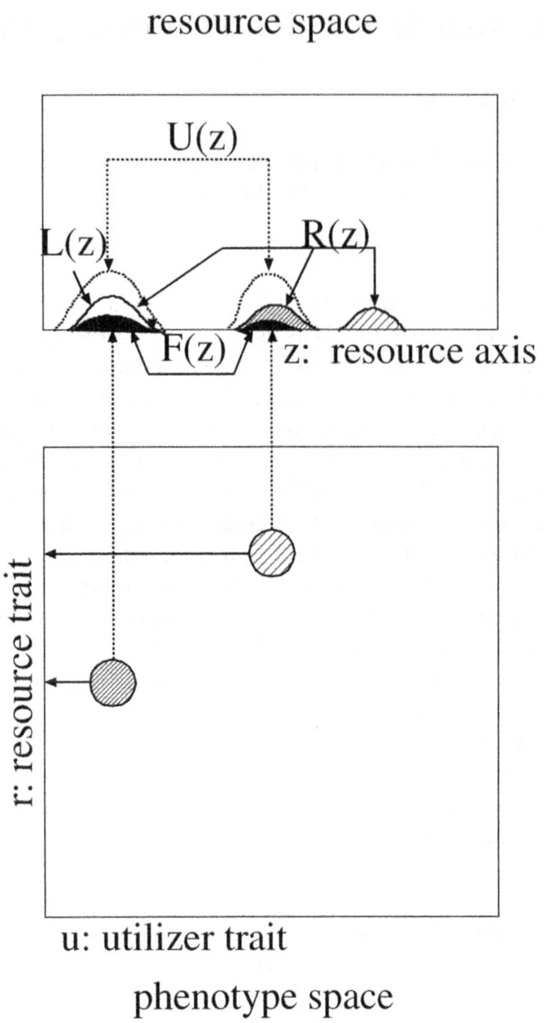

Figure 1: A phenotype space (u, r) and a resource space. Light grey and dark grey circles denote phenotypic clusters in the phenotype space (below rectangle) with axes of utilizer trait u and resource trait r. In this case, the dark phenotype uses the light source (L(z)) and is eaten by the light grey phenotype. On the resource space (above), we express the situation in terms of the distributions of $U(z)$ and $R(z)$.

of food web we consider. Because we are concerned with the total biological community here, the inward resource L(z) corresponds to sunlight. We define L(z) as the Gaussian distribution function:

$$L(z) = L_0 \cdot \frac{1}{\sqrt{2\pi\sigma_L}} \exp[\frac{-(z-\mu_L)^2}{2{\sigma_L}^2}], \quad (3)$$

where L_0 is the total resource amount. μ_L and σ_L denote the position and the width of the resource, respectively.

An assumption here is that phenotypes whose r are equal to u of phenotypes will be eaten by those phenotypes. In other words, the phenotypes that have the trait u utilize the phenotypes whose r is equal to u. We now define a "resource flow" at each point in the resource space (Fig. 1) as follows:

$$F(z) = \Omega \cdot \frac{U(z)R(z)}{1 + \frac{R(z)}{M}} \quad (4)$$

where Ω determines the strength of predator-prey interaction, and M gives a maximum predation constant per individual when there are infinite amounts of food. This formula is a type II function response, which is known to be a characteristic response of actual predator populations to prey density.

It should be noted that, when $R(z)$ is relatively much smaller than $U(z)$, the resource flow is proportional to the cross term $U(z) \cdot R(z)$. However, when $R(z)$ becomes larger, F(z) becomes proportional to $M \cdot U(z)$, because the maximum predation amount per individual is saturated to M. To keep the amount of the maximum resource flow into the system constant irrespective of changes to the interaction strength Ω, we assume that the amount of the inward resource L_0 is given by L_a/Ω, where L_a is a constant positive value.

Each individual of phenotype (u, r) acquires a $1/U(u)$ rate of resource flow, assuming that it is equally distributed. Similarly, each phenotype (u, r) is used by the others at the rate $1/R(r)$. Concerning this point, we compute the gain $(g(u))$ and loss $(l(r))$ per individual of each phenotype as,

$$g(u) = F(u)/U(u) \quad (5)$$
$$l(r) = F(r)/R(r) \quad (6)$$

We finally obtain the following equation for the time of evolution of the density function $p(u, r)$ as,

$$\frac{\partial p(u,r)}{\partial t} = p(u,r) \cdot (c \cdot g(u) - l(r) - d) \cdot (1 - \frac{p(u,r)}{K}) + D_u \cdot \frac{\partial^2 p(u,r)}{\partial u^2} + D_r \cdot \frac{\partial^2 p(u,r)}{\partial r^2} \quad (7)$$

where c denotes the efficiency of resource use, which in practice is estimated at 0.1 in empirical studies (Pauly & Christensen 1995). and K denotes the physical carrying-capacity of the habitat. The natural death rate is given by the parameter d. The last two terms correspond to the mutation flow in the phenotype space. The mutations generate new phenotypes in parents' neighbours in the phenotype space. In practice, we run the above equation by discretizing the explicit Euler method. To avoid unnecessary numerical underflow, we remove the phenotype whose population density is below a given threshold ε that is significantly small. We also assume that the phenotype space has absorbing boundaries to avoid numerical divergences.

Practically, when the number of predators is much larger than that of prey, the consumption rate may be proportional to the number of prey irrespective of the number of predators. In order to compensate for this fact, we can also use a modified version for the resource flow as,

$$\tilde{F}(z) = \Omega \cdot \frac{U(z)R(z)}{U(z) + \frac{R(z)}{M}} \quad (8)$$

With this formulation, $\tilde{F}(z)$ approaches to $MU(z)$ for $R(z)/U(z) \to \infty$ and to $R(z)$ for $R(z)/U(z) \to 0$. We mainly report below the simulation results of the first model. However, we also argue for a difference between the first and second model by comparing the main result with preliminary results of the second model. Instead of parameter value c (i.e. an efficiency of resource utility), we chose other parameters arbitrarily. However, the basic scenario presented below (three type of branching patterns, etc.) is not sensitive to the parameter values.

Simulation Results

An initial food web is prepared with a single phenotype utilizing an inward resource ($L(z)$), that corresponds to, for example, plants (Fig.2 (a)). Within the wide range of parameter values, several isolated phenotype clusters are generated.

These clusters correspond to "trophic species" which are functional groups of taxa consisting of species sharing the same predators and prey in a food web. Here, we call these phenotypic clusters "trophic species." To count these species, we define a base line level for the density function $\epsilon(> \varepsilon)$ to identify each connected cluster in the phenotype space. The number of species does not change significantly unless we take base line values that are too low or too high. Below, we report the details of this branching phenomenon and analyse it with regard to the interaction strengths and biomass.

Branching pattern

We observe evolutionary branching of trophic species in a wide range of parameter values. These bifurcation patterns are classified into three types in terms of biological functions, by referring to Figure 2 (a–i).

- Type u: predator-branching

  In Figure 2(a) → (d), the initial trophic species branches to produce new trophic species. The r-trait of the initial trophic species, expressed as a distribution function (with a broken line) on the u-axis, provides another potential resource to the initial trophic species. Thus, a part of the trophic species evolves to exploit the new resource by branching its u-trait.

  This predation forces "prey" species to evolve an r-trait to avoid being predated and "predator" species also evolve a u-trait to pursue the "prey" species, which gives rise to a evolutionary "arms race" (Fig. 2 (c) → (d)). Whenever we start from a single trophic species, the primary branching is always this type.

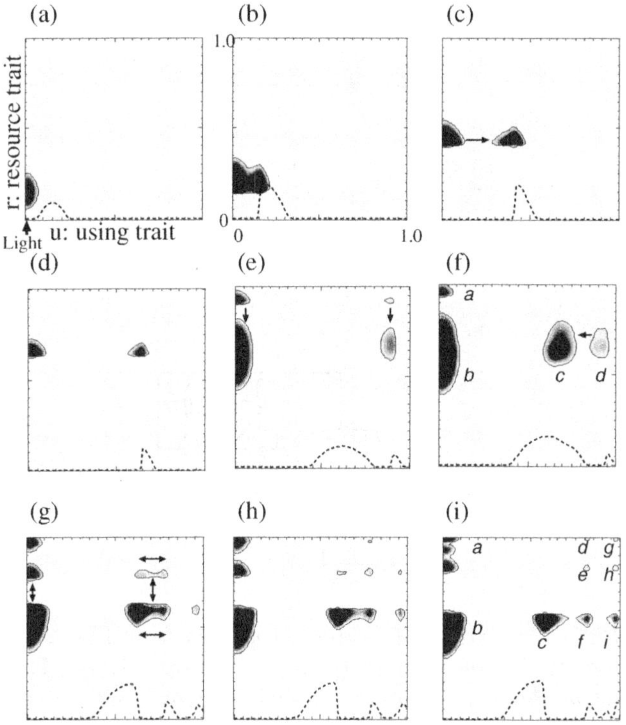

Figure 2: Evolutionary branching of trophic species is simulated. Darker colours indicate higher densities of the phenotype. Contours with solid lines correspond to the base line abundance truncated by ϵ. Dashed lines on the u axis indicate the organic resource distributions (R(z)-L(z)). Model parameters: $M = 10.0, \Omega = 13.0, D_u = 1.2 \cdot 10^{-7}, D_r = 0.6 \cdot 10^{-7}, c = 0.1, d = 1.0, K = 1.0 \cdot 10^4, \varepsilon = 1.0 \cdot 10^{-9}, \epsilon = 5.0 \cdot 10^{-2}, L_0 = 15/\Omega, \mu_L = 0, \sigma_L = 0.08, \Delta t = 5.0 \cdot 10^{-4}$

- Type r: prey-branching

  Instead of escaping from predators, a trophic species as prey sometimes branches its r-trait. In Figure 2(e), the two phenotypes simultaneously branch their r-characteristics, developing four new phenotypes.

- Type n: net-branching

  Simultaneous branching of both r- and u-traits. A clear example can be found in Figure 2(g). Some other cases are found when two predators exploit a single prey from both sides or when two predator-prey systems collide with each other. By this branching, the structure of the entire food web diverges abruptly and becomes complicated. The complexity of the network

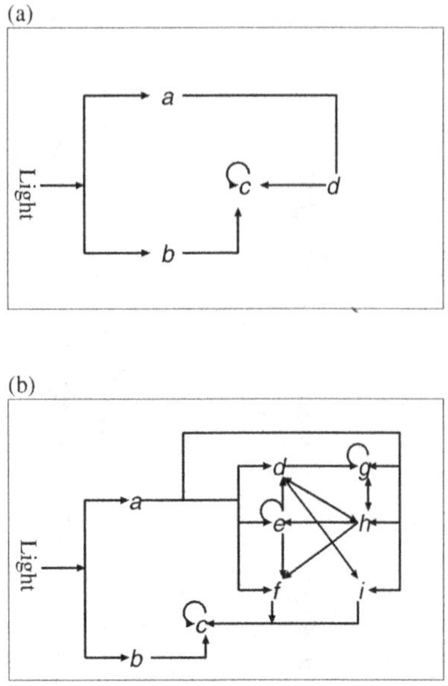

Figure 3: Extracted food-web topology from Fig. 2. (a) and (b) correspond to (g) and (i), respectively. Each letter denotes a trophic species. Arrows indicate the resource flows among the trophic species.

is well observed by abstracting the relational network topology as in Figure 3. A topology associated with Figure 2(f) is depicted in Figure 3(a). This will evolve into the network-Figure 3(b)-of Figure 2(i).

Because each trophic species acts both as prey and predator for other trophic species at the same time, the generic mechanism of the evolutionary branching is complicated. The network evolves from a directed graph (Fig. 3 (a)) to a rhizome structure (Fig. 3 (b)). To see this whole process, the total branching tree is depicted in three-dimensional space (Fig. 4). Successive branchings occur along the time axis. A type-n branching only occurs at the later stages.

The degree of complexity a network can attain depends on, for example, the interaction strength. The evolution is not a homogeneous process, but accompanies various dynamics, We study these features below.

Dynamics of evolutionary branching

This evolutionary branching is associated with various temporal dynamics related to the numbers of trophic species and the total biomass. The critical control parameter is the strength of interaction in the equation (7). The dynamic changes from periodic to chaotic by increasing its strength. In the strong interaction region, the large number of species is sustained via intermittent chaotic dynamics.

In the relatively lower strength regions of Figures 5 (a) and (b), divergences and extinctions of biomass occur repeatedly. In these regions, the system repeats type-r

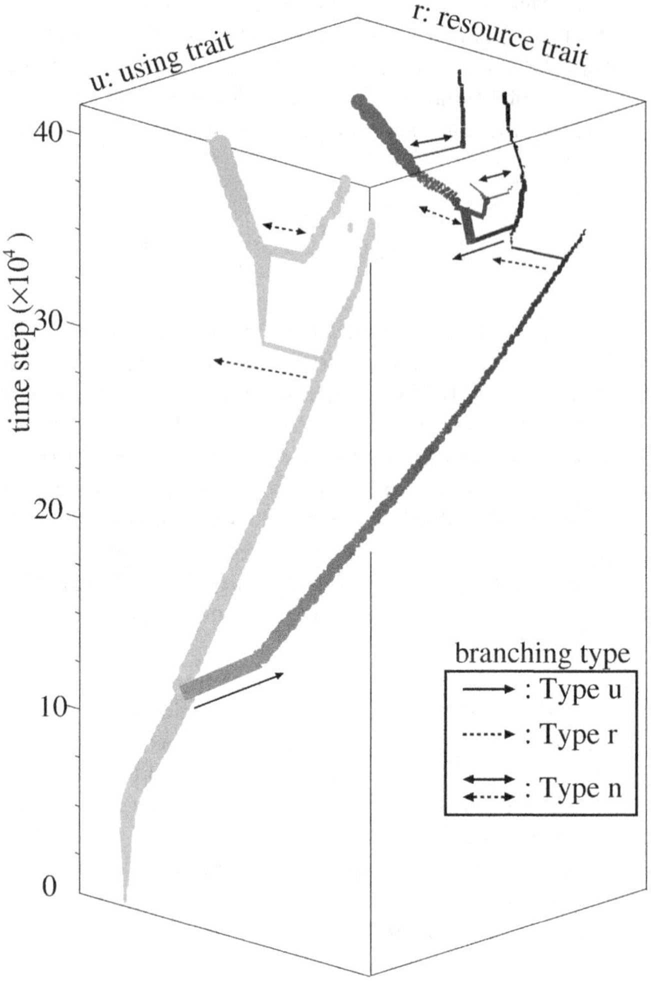

Figure 4: Phylogenetic tree extracted from the simulation with the same conditions as in Figure 2. Each line indicates an historical trace of each trophic species, where the line width expresses the population size of the trophic species at that time. The time slice of this phylogenetic tree gives a phenotype distribution on a phenotype space (u, r). Each branching type is denoted by a different line style.

and -u branchings, but seldom shows type-n branching. Finally, several large clusters of phenotype spread the region, arriving at massive extinction. As a result, the entire food web resets and it starts again from the bottom trophic species that use the inward resource $(L(z))$. The same scenario; an excess reproduction of a particular trophic species, triggers excess reproduction and its distribution is repeated. The associated two-dimensional phenotype space is depicted in Figure 5(e), where four trophic species are expanding without branching. Thus, no food web increases in complexity.

On the other hand, the larger interaction strength evolves into a regular lattice on the two-dimensional phenotype space (Figure 5(f)). The excess reproduction

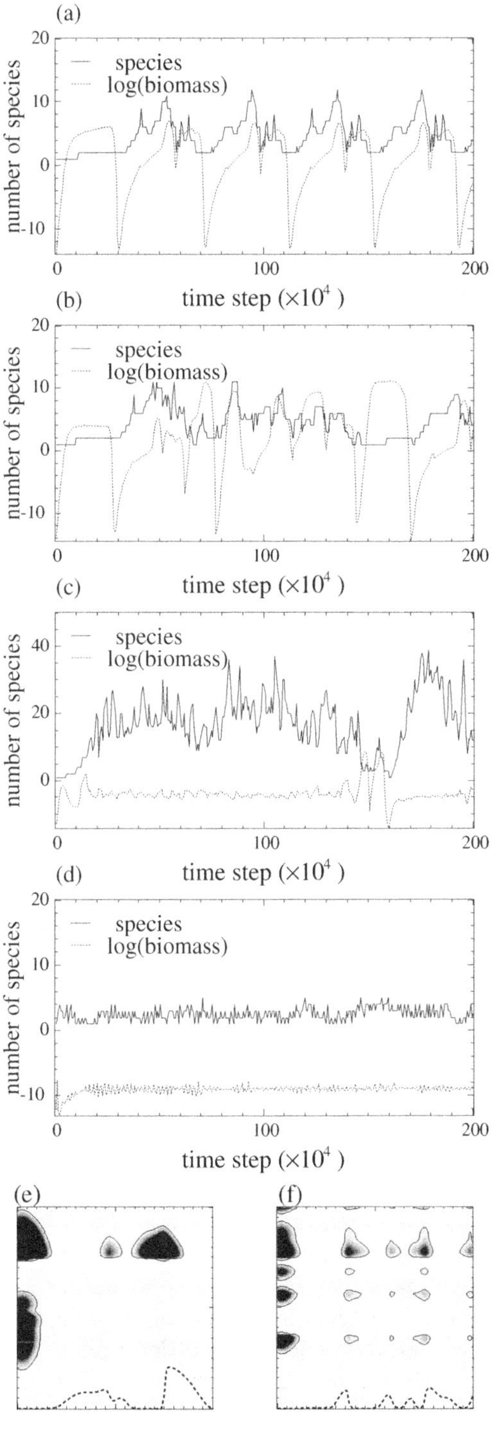

Figure 5: Time evolution of the number of trophic species and the biomass at different strengths of interaction (Ω). (a):$\Omega = 10$,(b):$\Omega = 11$,(c):$\Omega = 20$,(d):$\Omega = 100$. Other parameters used have the same values as in Figure 2 except that $L_0 = 22/\Omega$. (e) is a typical phenotype distribution of (a) and (b), and (f) is a typical phenotype distribution of (c).

of trophic species is suppressed by forming a laterally-inhibiting network. The organized food web continues expanding outwards. At the outside of the food web, sub-networks based on the bottom trophic species become extinct. At the same time, new networks based on the new bottom trophic species are created in the inside of the food web. Because the speed of this extinction and expansion of the network is stabilized, the total biomass and the numbers of all trophic species are maintained dynamically. This picture is well demonstrated in Figure 5(c). It is interesting to note that the system has a much larger number of species in Figure 5(c) rather than in (a) and (b): even the entire biomass is suppressed in the case of (c). However, a big extinction is aperiodically induced in Figure 5(c). When the interaction strength is much larger, the amplitude of biomass changes is suppressed and shows more stable oscillations. Instead, the food web at this stage cannot sustain a large number of species because of the shortage of biomass.

Whether a system shows periodic, chaotic or other dynamics is mostly determined by the parameters. Practically, the interaction strength Ω determines the kinds of branchings. The maximum predation level M has asimilar effect to Ω.

In the next section, we study how the entire dynamics depend on interaction strengths and other ecological parameters.

Interaction Strengths and Mutation Rates

By changing parameter values, we measured the long time averages of the number of species, and the speciation and extinction rates.

1)Interaction Strength (Ω): (Fig. 6)

A larger strength of interaction leads to a smaller biomass without temporal oscillation. Because it is difficult to sustain species, the number of species becomes smaller. On the other hand, the smaller interaction strength delays the increase in the number of predators. Therefore, this can produce a large biomass but with an unstable temporal oscillation that easily leads to extinction. The number of species is suppressed.

With a middle strength (around 20), the average number of species attains a maximum value having the same temporal variation as the biomass. When the number of species attains a maximum value, the extinction and speciation rates also become maximum, as is seen in Figure 6. Note that those two rates have almost equal average values. This reflects that the food web temporally collapses to the initial state so that it reorganizes the entire network, or the food web with balanced speciation and extinction.

2) Mutation rates (Fig.7)

When the mutation rates of two traits (D_u, D_r) are set at the same, the number of species gets larger. In general, when D_r is less than D_u, a system holds more species than in the opposite situation. A similar ar-

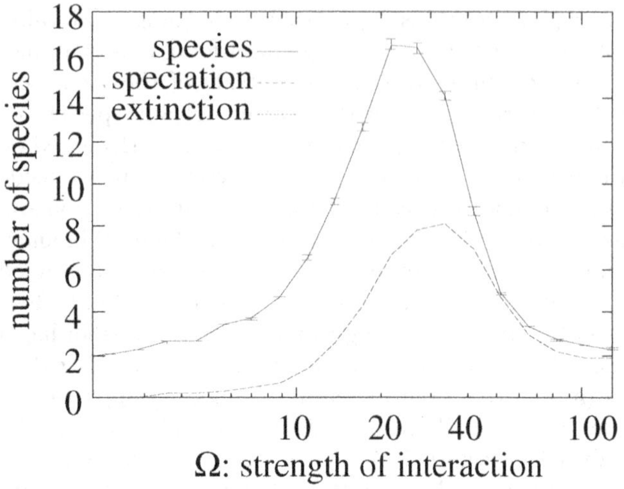

Figure 6: A relation between the strength of interaction (Ω) and the numbers of trophic species. An average number of species, extinction and evolutionary branching through a long time-step ($6 \cdot 10^5$) is computed. The relative amounts of extinction and branching almost coincide over this wide range. Model parameters: $L_0 = 22/\Omega$, and the others are used with the same values as in Figure 2.

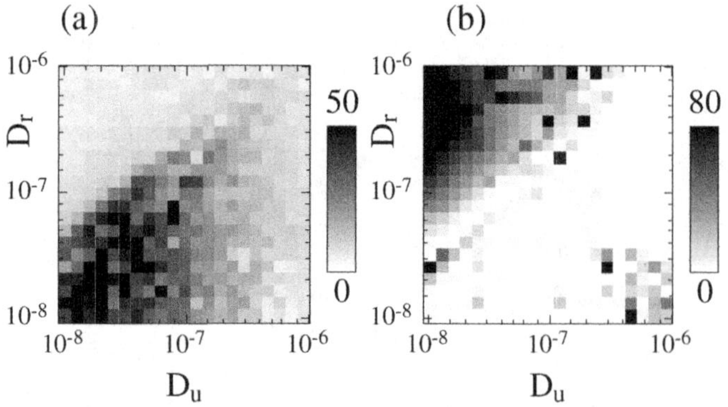

Figure 7: The effect of mutation rates on the numbers of trophic species (a) and of biomass (b). Horizontal and vertical axes are mutation rates of the utilizer trait u and resource trait r, respectively. Model parameters: $\Omega = 13.0, L_0 = 20/\Omega$, and the others are used at the same values as in Figure 2.

gument can be found given by Ikegami and Kaneko (T.Ikegami & K.Kaneko 1990). The entire biomass (Fig. 7(b)) becomes larger when the absolute values of D_u and D_r are smaller and the asymmetry is larger.

A relation between biomass and species diversity

A large biomass does not necessarily imply a maximal number of species. In Figure 8, the relationship between the number of species and the biomass is depicted. The number of species forms a convex function of the biomass. This convex form is observed over a wide range of parameter values (e.g. mutation rates and the interaction strength). Figure 8(a) is computed from Figure 5(d), which shows a sharp peak around 0.1. Here the biomass is well distributed over the trophic species and the hole in the network caused by sub-extinction will soon be compensated for by the new network.

This convex shape is also observed in different parameter changes such as mutation rate (Fig. 8(a)) and interaction strength.

A case of $\tilde{F} = UR/(U + R/M)$

Instead of using F, we analysed a model equation with $\tilde{F}$. In this case too, type-r, -u and -n were observed. By these branchings, development and sudden extinctions of trophic species occur (Fig.9 (a)). As a result, the mutation rate produces the same effect on the average number of trophic species and biomass.

However, we could not observe a dynamic stable state as in Figure 5(c). Instead, a nearly fixed phenotype distribution lasts for a long time in the region of $D_u > D_r$ (Fig.9 (b)). It seems that many different organizations can be possible in this stable phase.

Some oscillating phases that hold stable phenotypic distribution also appear in Figures 9(c) and (d). These phases tend to collapse by oscillationary divergence. After the extinction, a new food web structure becomes reorganized.

Discussions

In this model, we have studied the evolution of "trophic species", which are functional groups of taxa consisting of species sharing the same predators and prey in a food web. The concept of trophic species is sometimes criticized but is widely accepted, and structural food web studies can reduce biases in the data by using it (Williams & Martinez 2000).

We distinguish two different time scales in the present simulations. A longer time scale corresponds to an evolutionary food web scale, which is determined by successive large extinctions. A shorter time scale corresponds to a within-food web developmental time scale, where new trophic species are synthesized on the local portions of the phenotypic space. The term *evolvability* usually implies inheritance of genetic potential to produce new characteristics over a longer time scale. The term ecological diversity means to develop a food web network in a shorter time scale. An advantage of our model is that evolvability and ecological diversity are studied in the same model. Both evolvability and diversity require a certain degree of instability in the system. Evolvability needs to destabilize the established food web to introduce new trophic species and thus introduce a new form

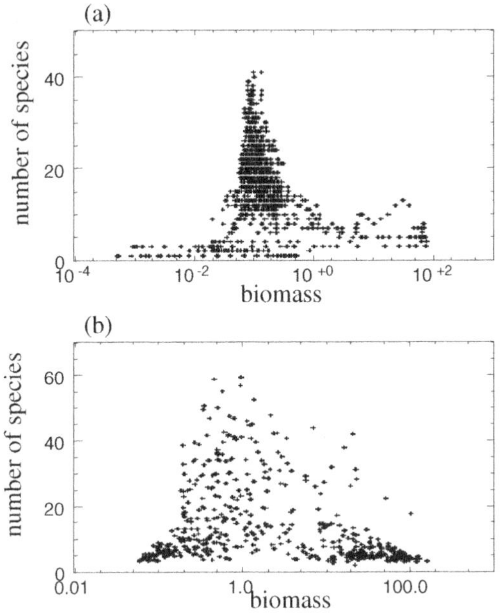

Figure 8: A relationship between biomass and the number of trophic species. (a) generated from Fig. 5(d), and (b) from Fig. 6.

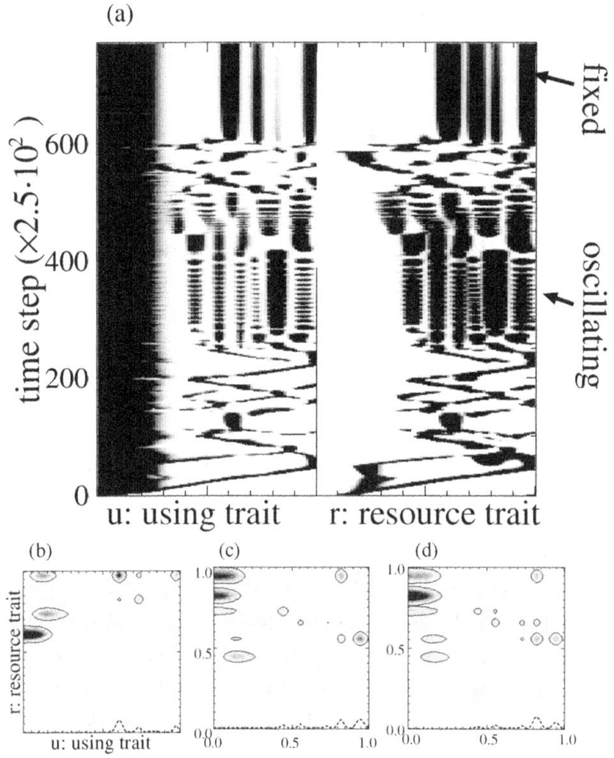

Figure 9: Evolutionary dynamics with $\tilde{F}$. (a) Time evolution of distributions of traits u(left) and r(right). A phenotype distribution in a stable phase (b), and in that of the oscillating phase ((c) & (d)). Model parameters: $M = 10.0, \Omega = 10.0, D_u = 8.45 \cdot 10^{-8}, D_r = 9.0 \cdot 10^{-8}, c = 0.1, d = 1.0, K = 1.0 \cdot 10^4, \varepsilon = 1.0 \cdot 10^{-9}, \epsilon = 1.0 \cdot 10^{-2}, L_0 = 300/\Omega, \mu_L = 0, \sigma_L = 0.08, \Delta t = 4.0 \cdot 10^{-3}$

of a food web into the system. Under a certain range of interaction strengths with the condition of mutation rates, $\mu_u < \mu_r$, large diversity is developed. Thus, predators should have larger mutation rates than prey to produce diversity. A similar condition has been reported for host-parasitoid systems (T.Ikegami & K.Kaneko 1990). In the wide parameter range of our model, a system autonomously breaks down its own food web structure to synthesize a new food web. In other words, instability that generates a local species branching event will finally lead to a large scale instability that resets the entire food web.

Evolutionary branching of the trophic species in the present model is categorized into three types. Type-u is branching as a competitor (or predator), which corresponds to previous models for evolutionary branching through niche-shift for new resources by intra-species competition (Doebeli 1996; M. Kawata 2002). On the other hand, type-r and type-n are branchings produced by predator-prey interaction, that is inter-species competition. Previous models for evolutionary branching by predator-prey interaction have shown that, at one time, a single pair of predator-prey systems splits into two pairs (four populations) or a single prey splits into two preys exploited by the same predator (three populations) (Savill & Hogeweg 1998; Doebeli & Dieckmann 2000). Type-n can generate more than two species at a time, because a single pair of predator-prey system splits effectively into six trophic species (two preys and four predators) at one time. This type of speciation might be possible in real populations, which have both resource competition and intra-guild predation.

Based on our model simulations, we suggest the following insights into the relationships between 1) interaction strength and stability, and 2) biomass and species-diversity.

1) Interaction Strength vs. Stability

Evolution of trophic species in our model may correspond to a travelling wave phenomenon in the phenotype space. The stability of the trophic species is sustained when there exists a time lag between the growth of prey and that of predators, as it generates a traveling waves of prey chased by predators. Thus, each species maintains its population evolving directionally. This time lag increases when the interaction strength is weak (a small Ω).

However, a weak interaction rate tends to destabilize the whole food web and results in relatively small diversity. By contrast, there are studies reporting that weak interaction has a stabilizing effect to maintain high diversity by dumping the population dynamics of the food web (McCann 2000; Neutel, Heesterbeek, & de Ruiter 2002). This paradox may arise because we are concerned with dynamic stability through the directional evolution of each trophic species. On the other hand, these empirical studies do not concern evolutionary dynamics, but population dynamics.

2) Biomass vs. Species-Diversity

Another important result is that the number of trophic species becomes maximum at a medium biomass. We argue that this dependency on the biomass can be explained as follows. When the amount of biomass is low, the system simply cannot afford to have any higher order niches, and the number of species may be suppressed. On the other hand, the system may develop a large biomass only when plant species are prospering in the absence of predators. Thus, the number of trophic species is kept lower. Only the mid range of biomass corresponds to a rich and complex food web network. There are many empirical studies investigating the relationships between biomass or productivity and species diversity. Most of them (Abramsky & Z 1984; Tilman & Pacala 1993; Leibold 1999; Ritchie & Olff 1999; Waide *et al.* 1999; Dodson, Arnott, & Cottingham 2000; Gaston 2000) report the same tendency as our results here: that diversity peaks at intermediate productivity or biomass. However these empirical researches were focused on a restricted range of trophic levels in the whole food web; on the other hand, we investigated the relationship at a higher level between the whole biomass of a food web and the numbers of trophic groups, each of which may contain several species. This interesting concordance beyond scale difference in a food web might imply a universal restriction on the relationship between biomass and diversity.

A criticism of the present model is that to represent a resource by a single dimension is an extreme simplification. Indeed, our simplification from actual multidimensional niche-space should be reducing some aspects of real evolutionary dynamics. For example, in our model, when two pairs of arms-racing predators and preys are approaching each other in the phenotype space they always collide. On the other hand, they may not collide if there is enough distance between the pairs in the direction of another niche-axis. Thus, an extension of the present model to take multidimensional traits into account may be necessary. However, as food webs are assembled in the same way in our model, assigning each species on one dimensional niche-axis helps explain many characteristics of real complex food webs (Williams & Martinez 2000) and may provide a certain assurance that the evolutionary dynamics of food webs are also described sufficiently in our simple rule.

To make the present model closer to real food webs, the introduction of mating mechanisms is important. This provides a certain viscosity with populations by gene-flow between phenotypes, which will converge each mating group as a "species" under ecological definition and will provide more realistic evolutionary dynamics of a food web consisting of those species. Another extension will be to improve a new form of resource flow $F(z)$. As we have described, the new form of $\tilde{F}(z)$ certainly provides more rich evolutionary pathways. It is also interesting to note a connection between the present model and the approaches based on the replicator equations (K.Hashimoto & T.Ikegami 2001; T.Ikegami & K.Hashimoto 2002). For example, the notion of keystone species should also be examined in the present model.

References

Abramsky, Z., and Z, M. L. R. A. 1984. Tilman predicted productivity diversity relationship shown by desert rodents. *Nature* 309:150–151.

Dieckmann, U., and Doebeli, M. 1999. On the origine of species. *Nature* 400:354–357.

Dodson, S. I.; Arnott, S. E.; and Cottingham, K. L. 2000. The relationship in lake communities between primary productivity and species richness. *Ecology* 81:2662–2679.

Doebeli, M., and Dieckmann, U. 2000. Evolutionary branching and sympatric speciation caused by different types of ecological interactions. *American Naturalist* 156:s77–s101.

Doebeli, M. 1996. A quantitative genetic competition model for sympatric speciation. *Journal of Evolutionary Biology* 9:893–909.

Gaston, K. J. 2000. Global patterns in biodiversity. *Nature* 405:220–227.

Higashi, M.; Takimoto, G.; and Yamamura, N. 1999. Sympatric speciation by sexual selection. *Nature* 402:523–526.

Jain, S., and Krishna, S. 2002. Large extinctions in an evolutionary model: The role of innovation and keystone species. *Proc. Natl. Acad. Sci. USA* 99:2055–2060.

Kaneko, K., and Yomo, T. 2000. Sympatric speciation: compliance with phenotype diversification from a single genotype. *Proc. Roy. Soc. B* 267:2367–2373.

K.Hashimoto, and T.Ikegami. 2001. Emergence of a new attracting set by a mixed strategy in game dynamics. *j. Phys. Soc. Japan* 70:3221–3224.

Leibold, M. A. 1999. Biodiversity and nutrient enrichment in pond plankton communities. *Evol. Ecol. Res.* 1:73–95.

Lindgren, K., and Nordahl, M. G. 1993. Artificial foodwebs. *Artificial Life III, C. Langton (ed.).*

M. Kawata, J. Y. 2002. Invasion of vacant niches and subsequent sympatric speciation. *Proc. Roy. Soc. B* 269:55–63.

McCann, K. S. 2000. The diversity-stability debate. *Nature* 405:228–233.

Neutel, A. M.; Heesterbeek, J. A. P.; and de Ruiter, P. C. 2002. Stability in real food webs: Weak links in long loops. *Science* 296:1120–1123.

Pauly, D., and Christensen, V. 1995. Primary production required to sustain global fisheries. *Nature* 374:255–257.

Ritchie, M. E., and Olff, H. 1999. Spatial scaling laws yield a synthetic theory of biodiversity. *Nature* 400:557–560.

Savill, N. J., and Hogeweg, P. 1998. Spatially induced speciation prevents extinction: the evolution of dispersal distance in oscillatory predator-prey models. *Proc. Roy. Sic. B* 265:25–32.

T.Ikegami, and K.Hashimoto. 2002. Dynamical systems approach to higher-level heritability. *J. Biol. Phys. (in press).*

T.Ikegami, and K.Kaneko. 1990. Computer symbiosis— emergence of symbiotic behavior through evolution. *Physica D* 42:235–243.

Tilman, D., and Pacala, S. 1993. *Species Diversity in Ecological Communities : Historical and Geographical Perspectives.* Univ. Chicago Press. 12–25.

Tokita, K., and Yasutomi, A. 2002. Emergence of a complex and stable network in a model ecosystem with extinction and mutation. *submitted to Journal of Theoretical Biology.*

Waide, R. B.; Willig, M. R.; Steiner, C. F.; Mittelbach, G.; Gough, L.; Dodson, S. I.; Juday, G. P.; and Parmenter, R. 1999. The relationship between productivity and species richnes. *Annu. Rev. Ecol. Syst.* 30:257–300.

Williams, R. J., and Martinez, N. D. 2000. Simple rules yield complex food webs. *Nature* 404:180–183.

A Network of Dynamic Keystone Species

Takashi Ikegami [1], **Tomoharu Iwata** [1] and **Koh Hashimoto** [2]
Department of General Systems Sciences[1],
The Graduate School of Arts and Sciences,
University of Tokyo, 3-8-1 Komaba, Meguro-ku, Tokyo 153-8902 Japan
Department of Applied Physics[2],
The Graduate School of Engineering,
University of Tokyo, 7-3-1 Hongo, Bunkyo-ku, Tokyo 113-8656 Japan

Abstract

A concept of dynamic keystone species is proposed based on simulation studies of replicator equations. We report that the variables of this equation can be categorized into three groups based on their individual dynamic behaviour. They are dominant, neutral and recessive phenotypes. Because the growth rates are small in average, they are termed neutral phenotypes.

Especially with a chaotic attractor, neutral phenotypes work as keystone species to control the stability of the system. The removal of neutral phenotypes may be a subtle perturbation, but it can have a large effect compared with its relative abundance, as it triggers an attractor switch. We also report that these neutral phenotypes form a network that can provide combinatorial effects on the attractor switch. A mere topological structure of the interacting matrix is not sufficient for determining which may be a keystone species; instead, it is determined by the kind of the attractors they organize.

Introduction

Even without a genetic basis, experimental studies have reported that there are quasi-heritable properties in ecosystems (Goodnight 2000). In particular, Swenson's group has reported that small soil and aquatic ecosystems can show significant responses against certain artificial selection pressures (Swenson, Wilson, & Elias 2000). In their experiments, successive selections of system units were conducted with respect to pH (aquatic systems) or surface biomass (soil systems). Then, new units were reproduced by taking the selected units as parents, in which sexual recombination effects can also be taken into account. In contrast to individual selection mechanisms, an ecosystem has no genetic base. Therefore, heritability at the ecosystem level is not very reliable, as was observed in Swenson's experiments. This unreliable but still heritable nature of information in Swenson's system is well known in agriculture. For example, if one continually plants the same crops in the same area, the quality of the soil will decay. Moreover, it is known that soil-borne diseases are exacerbated by repetitive monoculture. We attribute those qualitative and heritable features of ecosystems to underlying networks of microbes. Indeed Yokoyama argues that topological changes in a microbe network may explain the existence of soil-borne diseases (Yokoyama 2000).

In this paper, we simulate the dynamics of the underlying microbe network (preliminary results have been published in Ikegami and Hashimoto (2002). However, we do not pay attention here to the topological nature of the network. Rather, we focus on the dynamic nature of the microbes that constitute the network. In other words, we study the hierarchical nature of the (chemical) species constituting the network with respect to its contribution to the system's stability. We first propose a dynamic definition of a keystone species. Such species are usually noticed when they are removed from an ecosystem or when their disappearance from an ecosystem causes a significant change to it. Second, we demonstrate some combinatorial effects of those keystone species. We show that the keystone species actually consists of a subnetwork, providing a combinatorial effect on a system when it is removed. We show that partial removal of any keystone species releases the other keystone species, resulting in a drastic change to the entire system.

Replicator dynamics

We simulated the time-based evolution of phenotypes of (chemical) species by the replicator equation. The reproduction rate of each phenotype was assumed to be proportional to the difference between the individual gain and the average gain of the whole system. The replicator equation is equivalent to the Lotka-Volterra equation with some variable transformations. This equation was initially proposed by Maynard Smith (1982) and was developed thereafter to describe generic evolutionary dynamics (for example see Hofbauer (1981)).

Some new observations have been reported recently (Chawanya 1995; 1996), where unexpectedly rich behaviour of this equation has been revealed. For example, we note a strange hierarchy of attractors even within a system of only a few degrees of freedom. The mechanism is attributed to the heteroclinic cycle underlying the equation. However, this cycle also brings dysfunctional biological behaviour into the system. For example, the relative abundance of phenotype falling down to the order of e^{-100} is thought unrealistic. A remedy is to introduce a removal threshold into the system; a phenotype whose population size is lower than the given threshold must be removed from the system. As the result, the model avoids the heteroclinic instability inherent in the original system (Tokita & Yasutomi 1999). The system presents some universal phenomena, however by compensation it loses aspects of rich dynamics.

We studied the effect of mutation processes in the original replicator system. The mutation process naturally gives a lower boundary to each amount of phenotype, so that it can also avoid dysfunctional behaviour (Ikegami & Yoshikawa 1995; Hashimoto & Ikegami 2001). A mutation process from one phenotype to another was introduced in the original replicator model as follows:

$$\frac{dx_i}{dt} = x_i(\sum_j a_{ij}x_j - \sum_k \sum_j x_k a_{kj} x_j) - \mu x_i + \frac{\mu}{N-1}\sum_{j \neq i} x_j. \tag{1}$$

where $\sum x_i = 1$ and the total number of variables is given by N. Throughout this paper, we take $N = 100$.

The first two terms express the idea that the growth rate of any phenotype is proportional to the difference between its fitness and the average fitness. The remaining terms can be recognized as mutations among phenotypes. We assume that every phenotype is produced with the same rate. This second term is then rewritten as $\frac{\mu N}{N-1}(\frac{1}{N} - x_i)$, that is, a source term of the first order (x_i).

The controlling parameters of this system are the structure of the interaction matrix $\{a_{ij}\}$ and the mutation coefficient μ. Therefore, we basically have $N^2 + 1$ independent parameters. The initial distribution of phenotypes also determines the reachable attractors.

Kinds of Attractors and Hierarchy of Species

The equation can have more than one attractor when the number of possible phenotypes is sufficiently large or when the interaction matrix is carefully selected. We paid attention to the hierarchical organization of phenotypes that constitute each attractor.

The results show that, for most attractors the relative frequency of each phenotype changes from the lowest order (limited by the mutation effect) to the order of unity except for fixed-point states. Generally no single phenotype dominates the population eventually, as it is immediately out-competed by the others, except for the trivial fixed-point cases. However, we found that several phenotypes can also dominate the population in a chaotic attractor. Such an attractor can be observed by carefully tuning the interaction matrix with a mutation rate and an initial state. (see the upper figure of Fig. 1). This matrix also enables several quasi-periodic/periodic attractors and fixed-point ones. The interaction matrix was searched under the condition where $\mu = 0.0125$ and each matrix element was assigned a random number from $(-2.5$ to $+2.5)$. It is difficult to find a matrix structure that has attractors with clear separation between dominant and recessive phenotypes. Note that dominant phenotypes have relatively larger abundances compared with the other phenotypes.

Let us suppose that we try to select for and replicate attractors as in the case of Swenson's experiment.

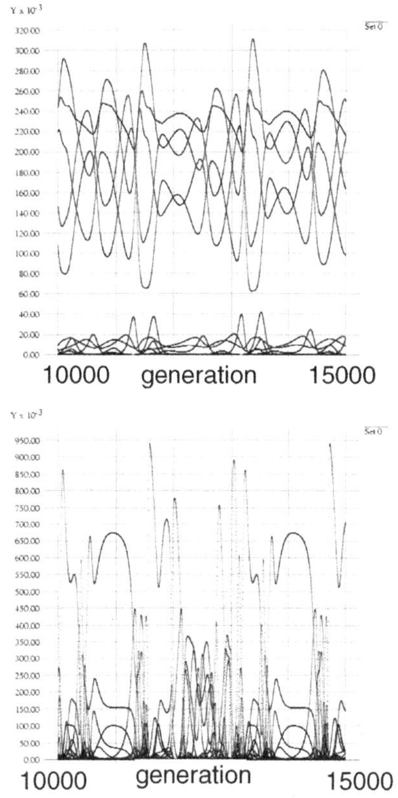

Figure 1: Temporal evolution of phenotype frequencies in chaotic (above) and quasi-periodic attractors (below). $\mu = 0.0125$ and a_{ij} has been assigned a random number from $(-2.5to+2.5)$. We only studied these values in this paper.

We assume that replication of attractors has to sacrifice infrequent phenotypes below some given threshold. Because replication at an ecological level is assumed to be a macro-operational process, we cannot select for rare communities whose abundance is below the threshold.

In Fig. 2, the switching probabilities among attractors are computed against the removal threshold. The phenotypes whose abundance below the given threshold will be removed at a given time step. Below, a kind of attractor has been automatically detected by computing the first Lyapunov exponent and the time-averaged momentum $(\sum_i x_i^2)$.

An attractor is called a stable replicator if it can recover after the removal of infrequent phenotypes. In particular, a fixed point attractor can rebuild a whole structure from dominant phenotypes. However, this is not true for the other attractors. For the quasi-periodic attractors, we have a non-negligible probability of switching to the other attractors, even for small thresholds. However, for the chaotic attractor, there exists a clear threshold around 0.005. Below this threshold, replication seems to be perfect, while above it there are dominant phenotypes and it is getting difficult to reorganize

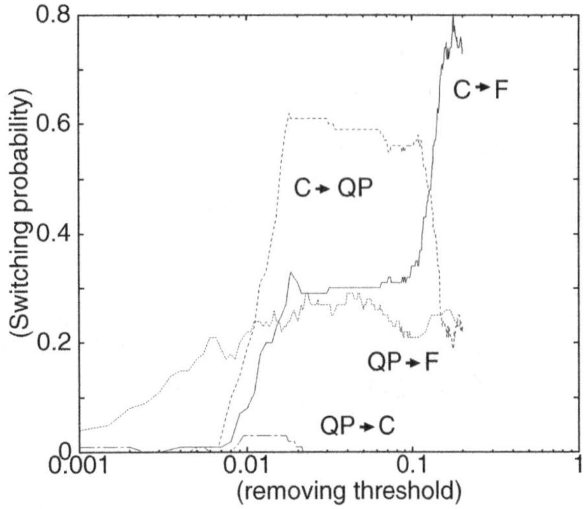

Figure 2: Switching probabilities among chaotic(C), quasi periodic (QP) and fixed point (F) attractors. After a system attains an attractor, phenotypes whose frequency are lower than a given threshold (X-axis) are removed. Renormalizing the rest of the phenotypes, we restart the system to see which attractor it attains. Each switching probability (Y-axis) is computed by averaging over 100 different states for each threshold value. When it attains a fixed point attractor, it never switches to other attractors.

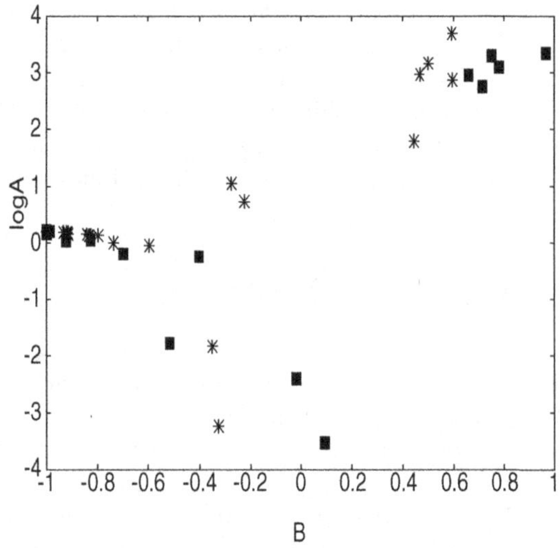

Figure 3: A characteristic measure of $(B_i, \ln(A_i)$ averaged over 10000 time generations has been computed for each phenotype. The square symbols correspond to the chaotic attractor and the other symbol to a quasi-periodic one.

the entire state from them. However, this threshold is much smaller than the average abundance of the dominant phenotypes.

Our conclusion from this observation is that the relative abundance of any given phenotypes does not simply correspond to its significance for the stability of the attractor. This means that we have to pay attention to the roles of these minor phenotypes, which cannot dominate the system but nevertheless control its entire stability. For the chaotic attractor, the effective removal threshold emerges around a value of 0.005, which is much smaller than the order of the dominant phenotypes (about 0.2). Therefore, between the lowest threshold and the average amount of the dominant phenotypes, we have a certain class of phenotype that can control the system's stability. In the (quasi) periodic attractors, it is difficult to label such phenotypes as we have no everlasting dominant forms. However, the significance of phenotypes varies from one to the other with reference to the removal event. To characterize these better, we have introduced some macro quantities to classify the phenotypes that constitute attractors.

Classification of phenotypes

The dynamics of each phenotype are governed by equation (1). We first decompose the right-hand side of the equation into two parts, the reproduction term (the first and second term) and the mutation term (the last two terms). By computing the time-based average of the reproduction term, we obtain a net reproduction rate as;

$$r_i(T) = \int_{\tau}^{\tau+T} dt(x_i(\sum_j a_{ij}x_j - \sum_{lm} x_l a_{lm} x_m)), \quad (2)$$

$$R_i(T) = \lim_{T\to\infty} \frac{1}{T} r_i(T) \quad (3)$$

that characterizes the frequency- dependent selection in this system. The time average of the mutation term

$$m_i(T) = \int_{\tau}^{\tau+T} dt \frac{\mu N}{N-1}(\frac{1}{N} - x_i), \quad (4)$$

$$M_i = \lim_{T\to\infty} m_i(T)/T \quad (5)$$

$$= \frac{\mu N}{N-1}(\frac{1}{N} - < x_i >)$$

gives a genetic flow from the other phenotypes. In particular, the last form of M_i denotes that the quantifier is almost proportional to the time average of the abundance $< x_i >$. On the long time average, R_i becomes equal to $-M_i$, if the average is taken within an attractor. That is because the time average of each dx_i/dt converges to a zero value by definition.

Using these quantifiers (R_i, M_i), we can classify phenotypes into dominant $(+,-)$, recessive $(-,+)$ and neutral groups (ϵ,ϵ), where $\epsilon \ll 1$ is a small value. The dominant group exploits others and produces variants. In addition, the recessive ones are only exploited by the dominants. Therefore, we see that this classification, due to the quantifiers, makes sense.

This classification is sufficient for classifying the attractors with the dominant phenotypes. However, those without everlasting dominant phenotypes require another quantifier. Actually, when the time oscillation shows rugged peaks, those quantifiers may lose too much information for the attractor state.

The other quantifier, for example, is the alternating rate between positive and negative values of the derivatives, $\dot{r}_i$ or $\dot{m}_i$. We use the $\Theta(x)$ function, where $\Theta(x) = 1(x > 0)$ and 0 (otherwise), to define the second quantifier. Practically, we define the number of sign alternation (B_i) as,

$$B_i = \lim_{T\to\infty} \frac{1}{T} \int_{\tau}^{\tau+T} dt\Theta(\dot{r}_i(t)) - \Theta(\dot{m}_i(t)) \quad (6)$$

This is also given as a time-averaged quantity. Dominant phenotypes tend to have large B_i values, and in particular completely dominating phenotypes have $B_i = 1$. On the other hand, recessive phenotypes have negative B_i values. Completely dominated phenotypes have $B_i = -1$. Neutral phenotypes should have a value of B_i that is not equal to 1 or -1. The ideal neutral case might be $B_i = 0$. Since $R_i + M_i = 0$ should hold, we define the absolute value of R_i as A_i. It is true that A_i and B_i basically provide similar information, so that either is sufficient in general. However, as we have described, it is very rare to have such attractors that have everlasting phenotypes. Most attractors are (quasi) periodic without having dominant phenotypes. We cannot always distinguish dominant phenotypes from others in terms of population size, however, they may be defined as dominant phenotypes by the quantity B_i. Thus, the measure (A_i, B_i) may work in such generic cases.

Using A_i and B_i, we plot the characteristics of each phenotypes on the A-B plane in Fig.3. In the chaotic attractor, dominant phenotypes exist close to $B_I = 1$ and larger A_i values. Recessive phenotypes are found at $B = -1$ with smaller A_i values. The neutral phenotypes are found around $B_I = 0$ with much smaller A_i values. A set of phenotypes that constitutes a quasi-periodic attractor also shows a similar classification as depicted in Fig.3.

What is important here is that the removal of some neutral phenotypes disintegrates the whole system. In particular, neutral phenotypes in the chaotic attractor can produce significant impacts on the stability of the attractor, and even their relative frequencies are small. This aspect fits the definition of a **keystone species** by Power et al. (1996) In the following sections, we study the effects of neutral phenotypes on the whole system. We will show that neutral phenotypes, as keystone species, have dynamic natures and so the neutral phenotypes themselves form a sub-network.

Keystone species as a network of neutral phenotypes

Following Paine's definition (1966), a keystone species provides a larger impact on its ecological system than would be expected from its relative abundance. A good example of keystone species is the sea otter found widely in the Northern Pacific ocean. Since Paine's paper was published, many studies have been performed on the effects of keystone species (see for example (Power & others 1996; Carpenter 1985)). Keystone phenotypes are usually made apparent when their removal or disappearance from a particular ecosystem causes a significant change to it. Thus the notion of keystone species is important in conservation biology.

As we noted in the preceding section, attractor switching occurs by removing less-abundant phenotypes. Here we concentrate more on individual phenotypes to see their impact on the whole system. To do this, we specifically selected and removed phenotypes from the population. The results show that removing dominant phenotypes produces a large effect on the system and that removing recessive phenotypes does not have any effect. The impact of each phenotype on attractor switching is, interestingly, correlated with its neutrality (i.e., the smallness of A_i). Those phenotypes are recovered immediately through mutation, however the attractor itself may change after some transient periods. The relative abundance of the neutral phenotypes is the lowest, specially for the chaotic attractor, but the impact is far larger than expected (Fig.4). In this example, a neutral phenotype with the second smallest R_i value (phenotype 19) is removed from the system.

While Paine's original and other keystone concepts are still limited to a single phenotypes, we have studied the combined effects of keystone species, i.e. of neutral phenotypes with small A_i values. Simultaneous removal of several neutral phenotypes combine to cause an attractor-switching event as in Figure5. We selected phenotypes with the seven lowest A_i values and tested all 127 patterns of combinatorial removal of those phenotypes. By putting the seven neutral phenotypes in order, we produced a binary representation of the removed set of phenotype. This was done by setting

$$\begin{aligned} y_a(t) &= (\Theta(x_{13}(t)), \Theta(x_{15}(t)), \Theta(x_{16}(t)), \Theta(x_{19}(t)), \\ &\quad \Theta(x_{64}(t)), \Theta(x_{76}(t)), \Theta(x_{87}(t))), \quad (7) \end{aligned}$$

where the subscript a runs from 0 to 127 and the string, $y_{42}(t) = [0101010]$ is read as a removal of the phenotypes 13,16,64 and 87, for example. Fig.5 shows that the phenotypes 19 and 76 are the two most salient ones that constitute keystones in the attractor with the two smallest A_i values. However, the removal of a single phenotype 76 does not cause any destruction; only when this is coupled with phenotype 19 does it cause a drastic change. Thus it appears that the simultaneous removal of other phenotypes often weakens the cooperative actions of phenotypes 19 and 76.

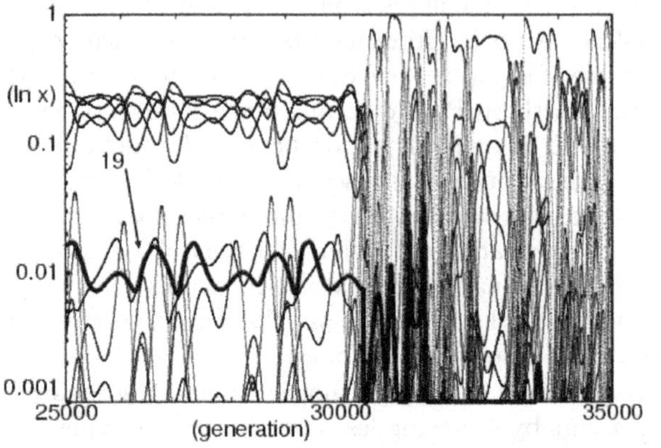

Figure 4: A time-based evolution of population in a log scale, plotted against generation steps. Every phenotype is superimposed. When phenotype #19 (with a wider line) is removed at generation 30000, the entire structure abruptly collapses and switches to a quasi-periodic attractor.

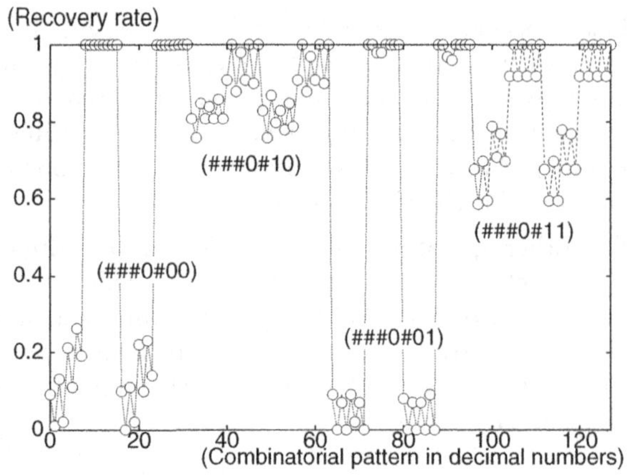

Figure 5: The combinatorial pattern is decimally encoded on the horizontal line. We have examined 100 events for each combination and the recovery rate has been averaged. The recovery rate becomes zero when the chaotic attractor is never recovered. In the figure, the four most unstable regions are labelled with the associated binary string, (###0#00), (###0#10), (###0#01) and (###0#11), where # denotes either 0 or 1. Here the salient neutral phenotypes are #19, #76 and #87.

This kind of combinatorial effect implies the existence of a network of neutral phenotypes. Because dominant phenotypes are mostly mutually cooperative, having large A values, they are insensitive to small population changes. On the other hand, if the recessive phenotypes have negative R values, they are also insensitive to small population changes. However, a subtle dynamic balance exists in networks of neutral phenotypes. Therefore, the removal of a neutral phenotype does not release either dominant or recessive ones but only other neutral phenotypes. In Figure6, we show how a single neutral phenotype causes a cascading impact on the whole system after a certain time lag.

Keystone phenotypes in a mutation-free system

To compare the result of the preceding sections with the original replicator dynamics, we briefly describe here a specific version of an original replicator equation without mutation terms. Putting $\mu = 0$ in the equation (1) but taking $a_{ii} = -1$ for all i in the interaction matrix, we study the fate of the system. By randomly generating the off-diagonal elements of the interaction matrix, we find a system with a keystone species in the above sense. Unlike the previous system, a fixed-point attractor is studied here. Other dynamics are not often observed, due to the structure of the diagonal elements of the interaction matrix.

The relaxation time to the attractor is so long that a removal experiment was conducted during the transient time of the attractor. Since this equation has no mutation term and the attractor is a fixed point, every $A_i(= R_i)$ and B_i value of phenotypes becomes zero. Thus, every visible phenotype is neutral in this sense. As is expected from the basic nature of the replicator equation, removal of a single phenotype cannot produce a large impact on the other phenotypes, given the relatively larger population, and it can only affect the lower population value phenotypes. Removal of a single phenotype releases two far lower population value phenotypes (see Fig.7). When the population becomes comparable in size to other phenotypes, the system shows a drastic change. The same scenario holds true here, but we have not checked the combinatorial effect in this case.

The keystone species in the replicator equation with mutation terms have more dynamic natures than those in this section. As a result, the neutral phenotypes constitute a complex basin boundary for the attractor. It can be shown that the basin boundary becomes glassy-like for neutral phenotypes. On the other hand, of particular interest here — lacking a mutation term — is the release of significantly small phenotypes compared with the former model.

Discussion

To conclude, we have shown that the removal of neutral phenotypes may produce a subtle perturbation to the system, but the results can be large compared with its relative abundance. In this sense, the attractor switch by neutral types produces a non-trivial mechanism, re-

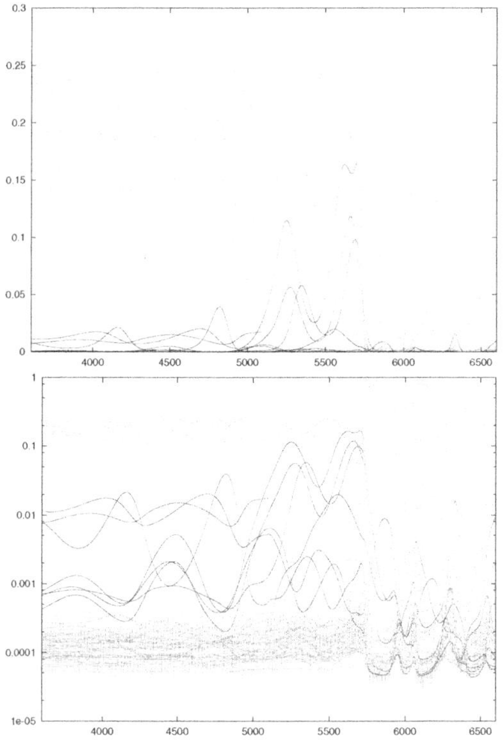

Figure 6: Relative abundance is plotted against time steps in a bar (above) and in a log scale (below). Neutral phenotypes are denoted with darker lines in the middle area (x_i is in the range of $0.01 - 0.001$). After the neutral phenotype 19 is removed at time step 5200, other neutral phenotypes increase their abundance and reach the order of the dominant phenotypes at around step 5700. Then a drastic change occurs, and the attractor switches.

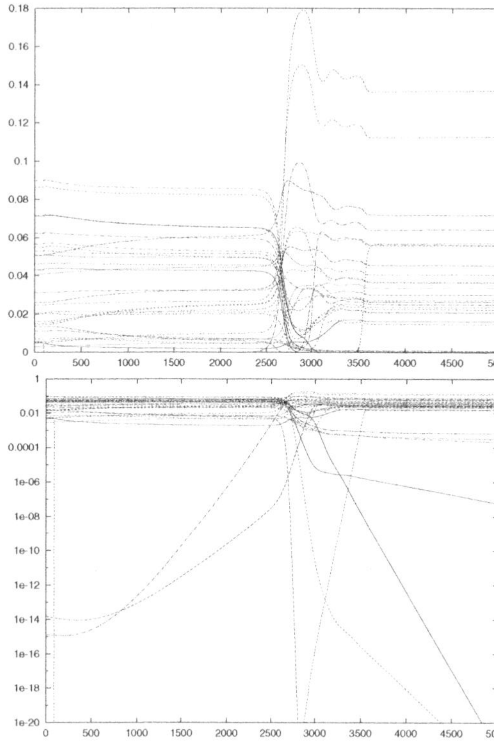

Figure 7: The removal of a single phenotype (of abundance = 0.00527) at time =100 will release a pair of far less abundant phenotypes. They increase in size exponentially and, when they reach a certain level, a drastic change occurs. Because any given population size is not bounded by the mutation flow, this demonstrates effectively how removal affects the system. Normal scale a) and logarithmic scale b).

lated to the notion of keystone species. Further, we have shown a combinatorial effect of such neutral phenotypes on the system's stability.

The existence of such a combinatorial effect implies that neutral phenotypes form a sub-network in which neutral phenotypes mutually suppress each other. The keystone species acts as a gene or a system's parameter in this higher level ecosystem. That a neutral, and thereby minor phenotype, can control the entire system has also been reported in different systems (see for example (Kaneko & Yomo 2002; Hogeweg 1998)).

The relationship between a keystone species and the concept of evolvability (Ikegami 1999) is worth discussing here. If some neutral phenotypes acting as keystone species can work as genes or parameters, this should be evolutionary favourable, as to evolve an ecosystem as a selective unit, some mechanisms are needed to reset the whole system. If this requires the removal of dominant phenotypes, the re-setting of the system requires major changes and it cannot occur spontaneously. However, if the resetting only requires the removal of phenotypes with small population sizes, it may occur spontaneously. In this sense, those keystone species may have developed as an evolutionary switch for higher order ecosystems to produce internal evolvability. A point here is that the switch is not a static notion with one degree of freedom, but it has a dynamic nature made possible by many degrees of freedom, i.e. there must be a network of neutral phenotypes.

Acknowledgments One of the authors (T.I.) would like to thank Kunihiko Kaneko and Pauline Hogeweg for their useful comments and discussions. This work is partially supported by the COE project ("Complex Systems Theory of Life") and the grant-in-aid (No. 13831003) from the Ministry of Education, Science, Sports and Culture.

References

Carpenter, S. 1985. Cascade trophic interactionss and lake diversity. *BioSci* 35:634–639.

Chawanya, T. 1995. A new type of irregular motion

in a class of game dynamics systems. *Progress of Theoretical Physics* 94:163–179.

Chawanya, T. 1996. Infinitely many attractors in game dynamics system. *Progress of Theoretical Physics* 95:679–684.

Goodnight, C. 2000. "heritability at the ecosystem level" commentary. *PNAS* 97(17):9365–9366.

Hashimoto, K., and Ikegami, T. 2001. Heteroclinic chaos, chaotic itinerancy and neutral attractors in symmetrical replicator equations with mutations. *J. Phys. Soc. Japan* 70:349–352.

Hofbauer, J. 1981. On the occurrence of limit cycles in the Volterra-Lotka equation. *Nonlinear Analysis* 5:1003–1007.

Hogeweg, P. 1998. On searching generic properties in non-generic phenomena: an approach to bioinformatic theory formation. In Adami, C.; Belew, R.; Kitano, H.; and Taylor, C., eds., *Artificial Life VI*, 285–294. Cambridge, Mass.: MIT Press.

Ikegami, T., and Hashimoto, K. 2002. Dynamical systems approach to higher-level heritability. *J. Biol. Phys.* in press.

Ikegami, T., and Yoshikawa, E. 1995. Chaos and evolution of cooperative behavior in a host-parasite game. In Yamaguchi, M., ed., *Towards the Harnessing of Chaos*. Tokyo: Springer-Verlag. 63–72.

Ikegami, T. 1999. Evolvability of machines and tapes. *J. Artificial Life and Robotics* 3(4):242–245.

Kaneko, K., and Yomo, T. 2002. On a kinetic origin of heredity: Minority control in a replicating system with mutually catalytic molecules. *J. Theor. Biol.* 214:563–576.

Maynard Smith, J. 1982. *Evolution and the Theory of Games*. Cambridge University Press.

Paine, R. 1966. Food web complexity and species diversity. *The Amer. Natur.* 100:65–75.

Power, M., et al. 1996. Challenges in quest for the keystone species. *BioSci.* 46:609–620.

Swenson, W.; Wilson, D.; and Elias, R. 2000. Artificial ecosystem selection. *PNAS* 97(16):9110–9114.

Tokita, K., and Yasutomi, A. 1999. Mass extinction in a dynamical system of evolution with variable dimension. *Physical Review E* 60:682–687.

Yokoyama, K. 2000. presented at the Mathematical Biology Meeting (Hamamatsu, October).

Multi-level Selection and Immune Networks: Preliminary Discussion of an Abstract Model

Tom Lenaerts, **Anne Defaweux**, **Piet van Remortel**, **Joke Reumers** and **Bernard Manderick**
Computational Modeling Lab, Computer Science Department, Vrije Universiteit Brussel,Belgium

Abstract

An important gap in the relation between artificial evolutionary systems and their biological counterpart is the inability of artificial models to construct functional hierarchical structures in an emergent way. For composite structures to emerge and prosper in a biological hierarchical system, some form of selection is required at each level . In this paper we examine an abstract model of immune networks in terms of the selection dynamics present at the individual level and at the network level. In this context, a property of the individuals is examined in relation to its impact on the reproductive succes on the individual and network level.

Introduction

In Biology, more and more evidence is discovered that selection operates on different levels and produces individuals whose properties (or traits) cause them to survive successfully at their focal level in a hierarchically organised environment. Moreover, these studies also show, that there is often conflict between these forces at the different levels, i.e. what is adaptive at one level can be maladaptive at another.

Multi-level Selection (MLS) and Evolutionary Transition (ET) theory are two relatively new theories which offer an explanation of why these individuals were able to evolve group-beneficial traits in a selfish environment. In order to discuss selection at multiple hierarchical levels, some prerequisites need to be in place in the system.

First, for Darwinian selection to occur at any level, certain properties need to be present at that level of selection in the biological hierarchy. These properties are 1) phenotypic variation, 2) heritability of phenotypic traits and 3) differential survival based on this phenotypic variation. Second, the selective forces at the different levels need to be linked in such a way that they can balance or counter each other. The combination of these two prerequisites results in a dynamical interplay where the quantitative ratio of group-beneficial traits versus individual traits changes over time. More info on MLS and ET and their products in Biology can be found in (Hogeweg 1994; Smith & Szathmáry 1995; Sober & Wilson 1998; Frank 1995; Keller 1999; Michod 2000).

In this paper we start with an examination of the relevance of MLS in the context of artificial evolutionary system using a simple problem of recognisers and target patterns based on an simplified abstract immune model. The goal of this paper is to get a better understanding of the forces which can be in place and not to deduce any conclusions about immune systems in general.

The Metaphor

The model used in this paper is a simplification in a number of ways of the immune network theory proposed by N.K. Jerne (Jerne 1973) and a model discussed by J.D. Farmer in the context of different connectionism examples (Farmer 1990). Our simplified model consists of a population of individuals which correspond to all the antibodies (free and surface antibodies) in the immune system and does not take into account the constant production of new B-cells by the bone-marrow as is the case in the immune system.

An individual in the population is represented by a couple (e, p) and e of one individual can interact with p of another. Each individual (e, p) consists of two strings of length l, where the string $p \in \{0,1\}^l$and the string $e \in \{0,1,*\}^l$ ($*$ is the don't care symbol). Two individuals match when they are complementary and the specificity of the match is defined as the proportion of non-$*$ values in the e-part of the individual. Hence if $e = 001101$ and it matches with some p then the specificity is equal to 1. Otherwise if $e = ******$ then the specificity is 0. Note that the e-part will detemine the type of the individual.

Hence it is assumed that there exist general locks (general e_j) which can be opened by many keys and specialised locks (specialised e_j) which can be opened by a unique key. This assumption can be made since match specificity (and in the case of the immune system, the binding specificity) does not determine the source of the matching value.

For more details on the immunological metaphor we refer to (Jerne 1973; Richter 1975; Hoffmann 1975; Hiernaux 1977; Farmer 1990)

Of Specialists and Generalists

An important property of the immune system is the ability of the B-cells and free antibodies to recognise foreign elements. In other words, it is an example of an abstract pattern matching algorithm.

Here, the example was selected to examine the impact of the selection scheme on the resulting individuals in the population. What kind of individuals (in terms of their properties) will evolve when using 1) a standard selection strategy or 2) a MLS strategy.

The general idea is that, on the one hand, in the standard strategy individuals will evolve which possess properties beneficial for the individuals themselves and not for the network (group) of interacting antibodies. On the other hand, in the MLS approach, it is expected that other properties which are beneficial for the group will emerge.

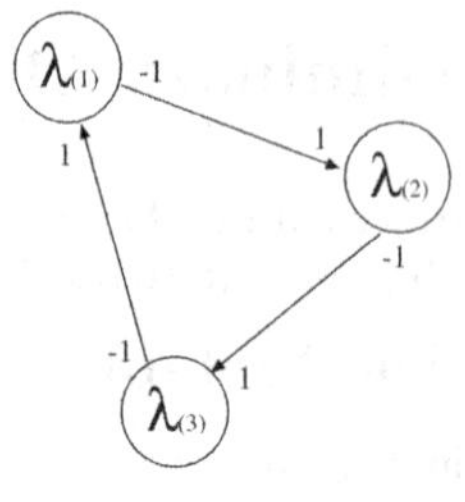

Figure 1: Three interacting individuals λ_1,λ_2 and λ_3 which maximally stimulate each other.

To summarise, it is assumed that an individual which has a specialised e has a cooperative behaviour. Alternatively, an individual which has general e is selfish in the sense that it tries to get as much stimulation as possible without reinforcing the rest of the individuals.

The Example Model

The dynamics of our simplified system can be summarised by:

$$\frac{db_i}{dt} = (c_1 f(s_i) - c_2 h_i - c_3)b_i \quad (1)$$

with

$$s_i = \sum_{j\in\{1...N\}} m_{ij}\ (b_j/b) \quad (2)$$

$$h_i = \sum_{j\in\{1...N\}} m_{ji}\ (b_j/b) \quad (3)$$

b_i represents the absolute number of an individual type (determined by e). The change in density of this particular type depends of the stimulation (s_i), the inhibition h_i) and a damping effect (c_i). The values s_i and h_i are calculated in terms of the matching operation between the e_j-part and the p_i-part of the interacting individuals (given by the coefficient m_{ij} in equations 2 and 3). The function f describes the degree of stimulation and is expressed as a bell-shaped curve.

Hence, b_j benefits the production of b_i with an amount equal to m_{ij}, at a personal cost, m_{ji}. Furthermore this benefit and cost are frequency dependent since they are proportional to the frequency of other types in the population.

Selection Dynamics in a Population of Types

In order to understand the selection dynamics of the model, the replicator dynamics can be derived. Generally, the replicator dynamics is a mathematical description for the selection mechanism which specifies which individual will be favoured over others. In other words it highlights the role of selection.

$$\dot{\lambda_i} = [\pi_i - \overline{\pi}]\,\lambda_i \quad (4)$$

Equation (4) is the replicator dynamics for our model described in equation (1) where $\pi_i = c_1 f(s_i) - c_2 h_i$ is the type's current fitness and $\overline{\pi} = c_1 f(s) - c_2 h$ is the current average success of the entire population The entire state of the population is represented by the vector $\lambda = (\lambda_1, \lambda_2, ..., \lambda_N)$.

For example, assume a population with N types and assume that the strength of stimulation (m_{ij}) and inhibition (m_{ji}) values are the same for all three types (Figure 1), then the dynamics of this system produces an asymptotically stable rest point with the same value for every λ_i.

The Dynamics of Individual Properties

The selection mechanism will promote individuals whose properties are beneficial for their reproductive success. Properties which give these individuals above average fitness compared to other members of the population. This fact can be expressed through an equation similar to the Price covariance equation (Price 1970; 1972; Frank 1995).

The same equation as presented by Price can easily be derived from starting from a discrete version of the replicator dynamic. The resulting equation will show how to determine if there exists a relation between the reproductive success of an individual and the fact that the individual possess the property z.

The average change of the property z in the population written into a covariance equation is:

$$\overline{\pi}\Delta\overline{z} = \mathrm{COV}(\pi, z) + \mathrm{E}[\pi\Delta z] \quad (5)$$

If the covariance is positive then the property z is beneficial for the reproductive success of the population. If it is negative, the property z makes the individuals bearing it less fit and if it is close to zero there is no relation between the property and the reproductive success of the individual. The second term is negative if the property under investigation renders the individuals bearing it less fit.

Equation (5) can be simplified further to:

$$\overline{\pi}\Delta\overline{z} = \mathrm{COV}(\pi, z) \quad (6)$$

This simplification holds as a very good approximation of equation (5) under certain circumstances which are fulfilled in the present case (for details see: (Price 1972))

In the example under investigation, we assume that the property z is the frequency of a certain type of individuals in the population. Thus for instance $\Delta\overline{z}$ can express the average change in the frequency of antibodies with very general e-parts. This would allow us to analyse whether the trait is beneficial under particular selection schemes.

Levels of Selection and the Price Covariance Equation

Equation (6) is a general selection mechanism which can be extended to model selection on different selection levels. This equation can be recursively expanded towards populations and groups of individuals. A derivation similar to the one by Price was performed here (Price 1972; Frank 1995; Gintis 2000).

A group G_j is defined, here, as a collection of types λ_i where all the λ_i in this collection form a network in which each member is stimulated and inhibited in some degree. The group G_j corresponds to the population state λ we defined in the previous section with the only difference that λ can consist of a collection of interacting networks and G_j does not contain any individuals which do not match with one of the individuals in the group. As a result, a group is defined as a collection of individuals which influence each other's fitness.

Assume a population P divided into M groups G_j. Λ_j is the frequency of individuals from P that are contained in G_j. Each group contains a distribution of the different individual types $G_j = (\lambda_{j1}, \dots, \lambda_{jN})$. In a MLS model, each group evolves in isolation and after one selection step, these groups are merged proportionally into a new population P'. Hence after one generation P' observes the new frequencies Λ'_j.

To make a distinction between the group and individual notation,the average fitness of one group is $\Pi_j = (\overline{\pi})_j$ and the frequency of individual that possess property z within the group $Z_j = (\overline{z})_j$. Hence, $\overline{\Pi}$ and $\overline{Z}$ are respectively the average fitness of the total population ($\overline{\Pi} = \sum_j \Lambda_j \Pi_j$) and the average property value in the entire population ($\overline{Z} = \sum_j \Lambda_j Z_j$).

In the same way the covariance equation at individual level was derived, (5), the expression for the groups behaviour can be derived. In the following equation the subscript g identifies that the covariance and the expected value are taken relatively to the groups.

$$\overline{\Pi}\Delta\overline{Z} = \mathrm{COV}_g(\Pi, Z) + \mathrm{E}_g[\mathrm{COV}(\pi, z)] \tag{7}$$

The first term of this equation represents selection between groups (intergroup selection). It shows the relation between the presence of a property in the groups and the fitness of the population. The second term on the right side of the equation expresses intra-group selection which is shown as the difference among the individuals within the group averaged over the different groups.

Discussion

In order to validate the model and to examine whether selection occurs at the higher-level, the three necessary properties for Darwinian selection need to be present at that higher level.

In order for selection to take place at the group level, groups have to differ in content. Sober and Wilson, in (Sober & Wilson 1998), describe clearly that, on the one hand, if there is much variation within the groups the chances are high that there will be little variation between the groups since each group will more or less contain similar elements. On the other hand, if there is little variation within each group, groups will differ more and as a result there will be more variation between the groups. For selection to occur at the group level, the latter case is required. In the first case, no variation means similar reproductive success and hence no observable selection at that level.

In the immune network example presented here, each group was defined as a collection of individual types which influence each others fitness and no individuals outside this group. It was concluded that each group contains a network of individuals which stimulate and inhibit each other with varying strengths. When comparing the different groups there should be variation since the members of the different groups respond to different (e,p) individuals. This indicates that under the assumptions of the previous sections, selection at a higher level can occur in this simple example. Based on this variation, groups which contain more individuals with above average fitness, will produce larger offspring groups and hence will contribute more to the population in next generation.

The phenotypic property (z) under investigation was the defining length of the e-part of the different individuals. At the individual level it was explained that for an individual it is better to possess an e-part with low defining length (general) since this results in a maximal stimulus and as a consequence in maximum fitness. At the level of the group or network the opposite is true. The network as a whole obtains its 'maximum' when all the members collaborate in an optimal manner. As a result it is better for the group's average phenotypic property Z to have individuals with high defining length since these groups will contribute more to the next generation.

Inheritance is defined as the tendency of the offspring to resemble their parents. To know whether properties of the group are heritable, there has to be a relation between the properties of the group in this generation and the next.

In terms of the property z or Z this means that there has to be a relation between the average specificity of the individual/group in the current and next generation. In the model we investigate here, there were no mutation or any other reproduction operators. Only a cloning mechanism which produces a number of offspring based on the difference between stimulation and inhibition. Hence, the offspring of individuals always resemble their parents since no property change occurs. A similar argumentation holds for the groups. The only change that can occur is a shift in the number of individuals for a specific type in the group. Hence, the property z and

Z are inheritable.

As a result of both previous properties and that the resources are finite, although the population can be large, differential survival and the clonal selection of these units will cause evolutionary change, leading to properties which are 'fit' for the environment. As discussed in the first paragraph, there is a conflict between the property which is considered to be fit for the individual and the network of individuals (the group). Hence, what will evolve will depend on the relative strengths between the two selective forces at the different levels.

Assume that selection at the higher level is the only force then those groups which possess collaborative individuals will perform better (in terms of reproductive success) than others. This occurs when there is strong difference between the different groups in their Z value.

Alternatively, assume that selection at the lower level is the only force, then all groups will contain on average the same kind of individuals in terms of the property and hence no clear variation exists and selection can not take place.

Conclusion

In this paper, a model of an abstract immune system was constructed to examine the difference between standard individuals selection and multi-level selection. The first step in building this model was to derive the selection dynamics which take place in an abstract immune network. As a second step, this selection dynamic was translated to a different selection model which expresses the relation between the properties of the individuals and the evolutionary success of these individuals. This second model has the property of being scalable to different levels. Hence as a third step this model was scaled to the level of a population of groups. To verify this model an argumentation in terms of the properties which allow selection to occur was performed for both levels. From this argumentation it can be concluded that, in the model presented here, selection can occur at different levels and that both levels produce individual types which have different conflicting properties.

Further work on the computational model is currently conducted in order to verify the remaining arguments of this paper.

References

Farmer, J. 1990. A rosetta stone for connectionism. *Physica D* 42:153–187.

Frank, S. 1995. George price's contributions to evolutionary genetics. *Journal of Theoretical Biology* 175:373–388.

Gintis, H. 2000. *Game Theory Evolving; A problem-centered introduction to modeling strategic interaction.* Princeton, New Jersey: Princeton University Press.

Hiernaux, J. 1977. Some remarks on the stability of the idiotypic network. *Immunochemistry* 14:733–739.

Hoffmann, G. 1975. A theory of regulation and self-nonself discrimination in an immune network. *European Journal of Immunology* 5:638–647.

Hogeweg, P. 1994. Multilevel evolution: replicators and the evolution of diversity. *Physica D* 75:275–291.

Jerne, N. 1973. The immune system. *Scientific American* 229(1):52–64.

Keller, L., ed. 1999. *Levels of Selection in Evolution.* Monographs in Behaviour and Ecology, Princeton University Press.

Michod, R. 2000. *Darwinian Dynamics; evolutionary transitions in fitness and individuality.* New Jersey: Princeton Paperbacks.

Price, G. 1970. Selection and covariance. *Nature* 227:520–521.

Price, G. 1972. Extension of covariance selection mathematics. *Annals of Human Genetics, London* 35:485–490.

Richter, P. 1975. A network theory of the immune system. *European Journal of Immunology* 5:350–354.

Smith, J. M., and Szathmáry, E. 1995. *The major transitions in evolution.* Oxford University Press.

Sober, E., and Wilson, D. 1998. *Unto Others, the Evolution and Psychology of Unselfish Behaviour.* Cambridge, MA:Harvard University Press.

Evolution of Stable Ecosystems in Populations of Digital Organisms

Tim F. Cooper and **Charles Ofria**

Center for Microbial Ecology
Michigan State University, East Lansing, MI 48824

Abstract

Competition for resources has long been believed to be fundamental to the evolution of diversity. However, the difficulty of working with natural ecosystems has meant that this theory has rarely been tested. Here, we use the Avida experimental platform to demonstrate the evolution of ecosystems composed of digital organisms. We show that stable ecosystems are formed during evolution in an environment where organisms must compete for limiting resources. Stable coexistence was not observed in environments where resource levels were not limiting, suggesting that competition for resources was responsible for coexistence. To test this, we restarted populations evolved in the resource-limited environment but increased resource levels to be non-limiting. In this environment, ecosystems previously supporting multiple genotypes could maintain only a single genotype. These results demonstrate the utility of the Avida platform for addressing ecological questions and demonstrate its potential in addressing questions involving ecosystem-level processes.

Introduction

One of the most striking features of life is its diversity. However, the selective pressures which have led to this diversity have not yet been comprehensively identified (Morin 2000; Schluter 2000; Tilman 2000). In part, the lack of progress has been due to the inherent difficulty of performing precise, replicated and controlled experiments on whole ecosystems (Morin 2000). In an effort to ameliorate these limitations, some researchers have turned to laboratory microcosms (reviewed in Travisano & Rainey 2000). However, even in these model systems, ecosystems can evolve to be much more complex than is experimentally tractable and identification of the causes of diversity can still be difficult (Notley-McRobb & Ferenci 1999; 1999; Rainey & Travisano 1998).

Competition between organisms for limited resources has long been suspected to play a key role in the structuring of communities (Tilman 2000; Schluter 1996; Tilman 1982). Though proof of this idea has been deceptively difficult to come by (Schluter 1996; 2000), the reason for its enduring appeal is obvious: if organisms deplete resources as they use them, the benefit for their continued use will diminish and organisms able to use underutilized resources will be favored. Over time density-dependent selection created by this process can lead to adaptive radiation and even speciation as organisms diverge to into distinct lineages (Schluter 2001).

In this study, we use digital organisms (self-replicating and evolving computer programs) to examine the diversity arising in populations during adaptation to an environment containing nine distinct resources. (We use the term population to refer collectively to all organisms in the environment.) We compare the result of adaptation when resources are in infinite supply to when resources can be depleted. Because there are no limiting resources in the former environment, only one niche is present; the organism most efficiently using the most valuable resource combination will always have a selective advantage and be able to outcompete all other organisms (Kassen, *et. al.* 2000; Hardin 1960; Tilman 1982). In contrast, in the depletable resource environment, all resources can be limiting, potentially creating as many niches as resources and thus allowing as many species as resources to coexist (Bell 1997; Huisman 1999).

We show that stable ecosystems evolved in populations grown in environments where organisms competed for depletable resources. Diversity was maintained for many thousands of generations when the mutation rate was set to zero but rapidly disappeared when we changed the environment to make resource levels infinite.

The Experimental System

The Avida platform is a computer software system in which digital organisms evolve by means of random mutation and natural selection (as opposed to artificial selection, as in genetic algorithms) (Ofria, Brown, & Adami 1998)[1]. The genetic code of the digital organisms in Avida is a Turing complete programming language. To replicate, a digital organism performs a self-analysis that determines information about its genome, it then allocates enough extra memory to hold its offspring, and copies its genome line by line into that extra space before finally dividing off the offspring as an independent organism. This replication process is subject to two types of errors: copy mutations, where a random instruction is written in place of the ancestral one and insertion/deletion mutations, where a random instruction is added or removed from the genome.

In Avida, the success of an organism depends upon its growth rate. This is determined by an organism's replication efficiency and by its interactions with the environment. An Avida environment determines the mutation rates the organisms are subjected to, as well as the collection of resources that they can use to increase the rate at which they execute the instructions contained in their genomes. To "metabolize" a resource and garner a benefit from it, an organism must perform a mathematical

[1]The Avida software is available from http://nemus.dllab.caltech.edu/avida/

computation specified by the experimenter. Resources are globally available to all organisms. In previous versions of Avida, resource levels were infinite, such that the number of organisms using that resource did not affect its level or the benefit gained for its use. In this study, we add the capability of feedback between the use of a resource and its level, such that the use of a resource by one organism lowers the availability of that resource to all others. A low concentration of a resource will reduce the benefit that can be gained by performing its associated computation. This model of resource competition is analogous to that occurring during competition in bacterial chemostats.

In Avida the experimenter determines the environment that populations will evolve in, but does not specify which organisms are favored. Instead, the outcome of the evolutionary process is determined by population genetic processes, that is, natural selection and genetic drift. For this reason, Avida populations are genuinely evolving systems, rather than being "simulations" of evolution. Avida allows perfect knowledge of the genetic, phenotypic and ecological state of the system at all times and ensures that no measurement influences the course of evolution. These attributes have enabled Avida to be used to address fundamental evolutionary questions in ways not possible with traditional systems (Lenski, *et. al.* 1999; Adami, *et. al.* 2000; Wilke, *et. al.* 2001).

Materials and Methods

The experiments reported here were performed using version 2.0beta of the Avida software. Unless otherwise noted, each replicate evolving population was started with identical initial conditions but with a different random number seed. This seed causes runs to differ at points where a random choice is made, such as the occurrence of mutations or the location of an offspring in the population.

The genome of the ancestral organism in each run was 100 instructions in length. This organism could self-replicate but could not perform any logical computations. The descendants of this organism rapidly filled up each population (to its maximum capacity of 2500). During the first 100,000 updates[2] of evolution the copy mutation rate was set to 0.0075 per instruction and the insertion/deletion rate was set to 0.05 per genome. After the first 100,000 updates we turned off all mutations and let the population replicate for an additional 50,000 updates. This latter phase allowed us to identify genotypes able to stably coexist as a result of ecological interactions without the complications of new genotypes being introduced through mutation. Hereafter, we call the 100,000 updates of evolution with mutation turned on the "evolution phase" and the subsequent 50,000 updates with mutation turned off the "ecology phase".

We evolved a total of 69 populations; 30 in a limited resource chemostat environment, and 39 in an environment where all resources were infinitely abundant. In both environments 9 resources were present. These could be "metabolized" by performing logical computations. The full set of computations rewarded were: Not, Nand, And, OrNot, Or, AndNot, Nor, Xor, and Equals. To complete one of these computations, the organisms must input one or two 32-bit numbers, perform the logic operation in a bitwise fashion on them, and output the correct 32-bit result. The ability to perform one of these computations (and therefore use the associated resource) increases the speed at which an organism executes its instructions, allowing it to replicate more often. The output of a computation must be exact–a single bit in error disallows the organism to use the resource in question.

To determine the genotypic diversity present in populations we used the Shannon-Weaver index, calculated as $-\sum p_i \ln(p_i)$, where p_i is the frequency of the ith genotype in the population. The same formula was used to measure phenotypic diversity except substituting the frequency of phenotypes (based on the logic tasks each organism could perform) in a population for the frequency of genotypes. Mann-Whitney rank sum tests were used to compare measures of diversity between the two treatments because diversity values were non-normally distributed.

Results: Ecosystem Evolution

We measured the effect of competition for resources on genotypic and phenotypic diversity present in the evolving populations. If competition for limited resources creates multiple niches, we expect diversity to be higher in resource-limited populations. We found that both phenotypic and genotypic diversities were significantly higher in populations evolved in the environment where there was competition for resources (Mann-Whitney test: genotypic diversity, $U = 1586$, $n_1 = 39$, $n_2 = 30$, $P \ll 0.0001$; phenotypic diversity, $U = 1635$, $n1 = 39$, $n2 = 30$, $P \ll 0.0001$). A comparison of the average diversity present after 100,000 updates of evolution in the two environment types is shown in Figure 1.

The high mutation rate used in the evolution of these populations causes the continual production of mutant genotypes. Although many of these mutants are destined to become extinct, they nevertheless increase the number of coexisting genotypes and thus the basal level of diversity within populations. The effect of high basal diversity is to reduce the fraction of total diversity caused by truly coexisting genotypes. For this reason, all populations were extended for a further 50,000 updates in an environment identical to the one they had experienced

[2] An update is a unit of "real time" for the organisms during which 30 × population size instructions are executed globally. The number of instructions executed by a particular organism depends on its use of resources.

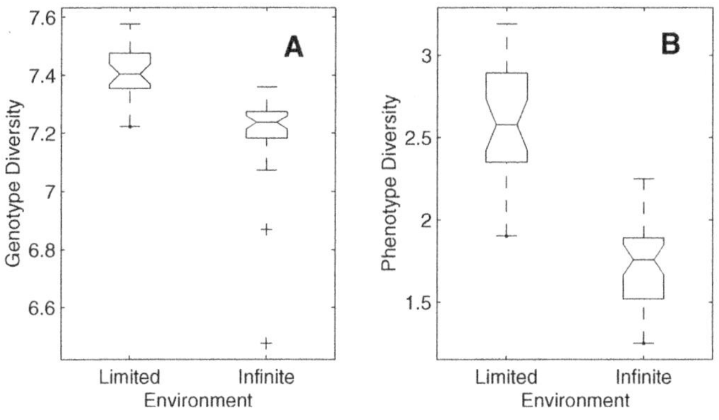

Figure 1: Diversity present in limited-resource and infinite-resource populations after 100,000 updates of evolution. (A) Genotype diversity. (B) Phenotype diversity. Whiskers and box edges represent 95% confidence intervals and quartiles, respectively. The mean is indicared by a line inside the box. Outliers are indicated by a '+' .

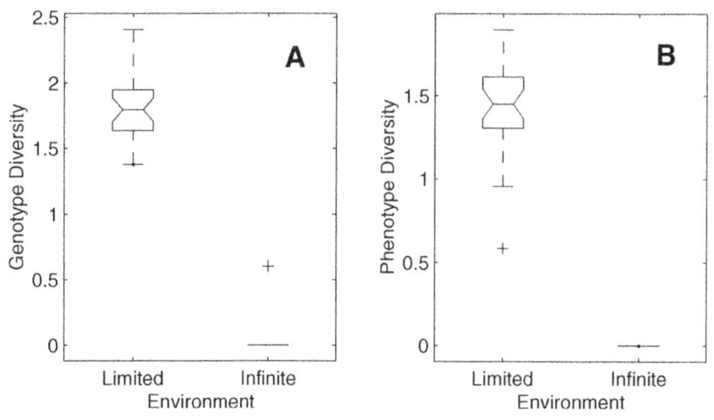

Figure 2: Diversity present in limited-resource and infinite-resource populations after 50,000 additional updates with mutations off (ecology phase). (A) Genotype diversity. (B) Phenotype diversity. Whiskers and box edges represent 95% confidence intervals and quartiles, respectively. The mean is indicared by a line inside the box. Outliers are indicated by a '+' .

before, but with the mutation rate set to zero (the ecology phase). In this environment, ecological processes determine the dynamics of diversity without the complication of the continual production of new genotypes. Unfit mutant genotypes already present will be removed by population genetic processes. If the higher diversity in the resource-limited populations was caused by stabilizing pressures allowing organisms to coexist, then we expected diversity to be maintained in these populations. In the infinite resource populations we expected only the single fittest organism to be retained, decreasing diversity to zero. Consistent with these expectations, in figure 2 we show that whereas genotypic and phenotypic diversity was maintained in populations where organisms competed for resources, it dropped to near-zero in populations grown in the infinite resource environment (Mann-Whitney tests: genotypic diversity, $U = 1635$, $n1 = 39$, $n2 = 30$, $P \ll 0.0001$; phenotypic diversity, $U = 1635$, $n1 = 39$, $n2 = 30$, $P \ll 0.0001$).

Evolution of Specialists and Generalists

To examine the nature of the ecological mechanisms allowing coexistence in the resource limited populations we chose two case-study populations, one consisting of generalist organisms and one of specialist organisms, to study further. Figure 3 shows which resources were used by each genotype remaining after the ecology phase described above. In the population consisting of specialist organisms, the use of each resource was heavily dominated by only one genotype (Figure 3a). In the population consisting of generalist organisms, eight genotypes were present. These genotypes could be grouped into three distinct resource utilization groups based on the logic computations they could perform: group 1- Xor, AndNot and OrNot; group 2- Equ, And and Nand; group 3- Nor, Or and Not (Figure 3b). Two explanations could account for the continued coexistence of genotypes that shared the same phenotype. (1) Coexistence might reflect organisms that had very similar fitnesses, such that very long periods of selection would be required to separate them. (2) Subtle differences in the number of times an organism with a particular genotype performed a computation might cause oscillations in resource concentrations, allowing coexistence of organisms specialized to different levels of resource.

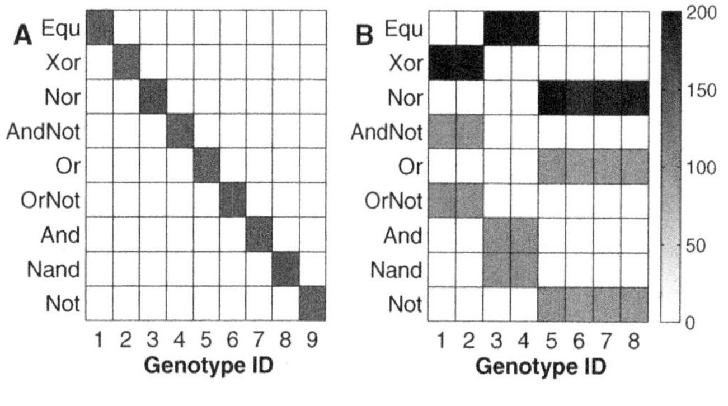

Figure 3: Map defining the phenotypes of each genotype present at the end of two runs. (A) Population consisting of specialist genotypes; (B) Population consisting of generalist genotypes. The colorbar indicates the number of times a given logical computation is performed during one generation. The more often a computation is done the more the cognate resource is used.

To distinguish between these possibilities, the generalist population collected after the ecology phase was restarted with five-fold replication in an identical environment. If coexistence was due to the presence of genotypes of quasi-equivalent fitness, we expected the number of coexisting genotypes to decrease over time. We found that the number of coexisting genotypes had declined to three in all replicate populations by 300,000 updates. These three genotypes were then stably maintained up to the end of the experiment at 500,000 updates (Figure 4a). In all cases, only one member of each resource utilization type was maintained. Genotypes 1 and 5 from groups 1 and 3, respectively, were maintained in all of the runs. From group 2, genotype 3 was maintained in two runs and genotype 4 in three runs. In five control runs restarted from the specialist population, all nine genotypes were maintained for 100,000 updates (Figure 4b). These results suggest that the nine genotypes of the specialist population represent a stable ecosystem, whereas the eight genotypes of the generalist population can be grouped into three types by their resource use profile. A stable ecosystem is formed when only one genotype from each of these types remains.

The most likely explanation for the continuing coexistence of genotypes in the specialist and generalist populations described above is that density-dependent selection acts to favor rare phenotypes. This selection is caused by the reciprocal relationship between the benefit for using a resource and the number of organisms using it. To test this hypothesis, we took the five specialist and five generalist populations saved from the extended ecology runs described above, and restarted them in the same environment, except that resource levels were set to be infinite. In this environment there is no inherent advantage in using an underutilized resource so that the genotype most efficiently doing the most valuable task(s) is expected to exclude all other genotypes. As shown in figure 5, all populations quickly became dominated by a single genotype. This genotype was always the one calculated as having the highest absolute fitness based on the rewards given for the tasks it was able to perform. These results indicate that density-dependent selection was responsible for the stable coexistence of genotypes during the ecology runs.

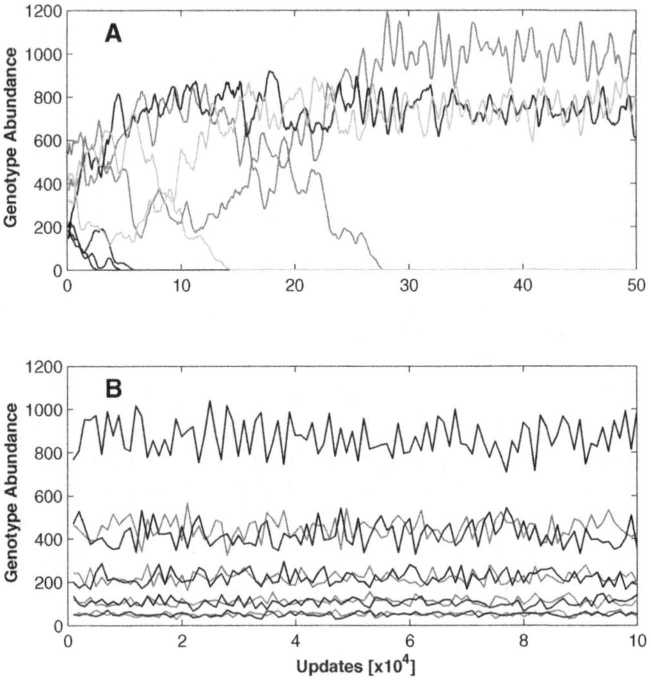

Figure 4: Coexistence of genotypes during the continued ecology phase with limited-resources. Genotypes are numbered as in Figure 3. (A) Genotype dynamics throughout this phase in a representative generalist population. Dark-gray, genotypes 1/2; light-gray, genotypes 3/4; black, genotypes 5/6/7/8. Genotypes 1,3 and 5 coexist at the end of the run. (B) Genotype dynamics throughout this phase in a representative specialist population. In decreasing order of abundance genotypes are: 1, 2/3, 4/5, 6/7 and 8/9. Differences in equilibrium genotype abundances result from the different rewards gained for using each resource.

Discussion

Despite decades of study, the role of resource-based competition in promoting diversity remains unresolved (Schluter 1996). In this study, we demonstrate the evolution of high diversity in environments in which organisms were forced to compete with one another for resources. This diversity was caused by the stable coexistence of genotypes in these populations and continued to be stable for many generations. In contrast, when resources were not limiting, only one genotype was ever maintained. Coexistence did not depend on any spatial or temporal heterogeneity in the environment.

The most likely explanation for the maintenance of multiple genotypes in a resource-limited environment is that density-dependent selection acts to create multiple niches. This selection is generated because the level of a particular resource depends on the number of organisms using it, and the benefit for being able to use a resource depends on its level. This reciprocal relationship creates selection for the use of underutilized resources. Two broad outcomes of density-dependent selection can be imagined. At one extreme, organisms could specialize, adapting to one resource at the expense of their competitiveness for others. The effect of this is to partition the environment such that as many species as there are resources are potentially able to coexist. At the other extreme, generalist organisms, able to use underutilized resources while retaining the ability to use those used by their progenitor, may result. To test whether density-dependent selection was responsible for the coexistence of genotypes in the resource-limited populations

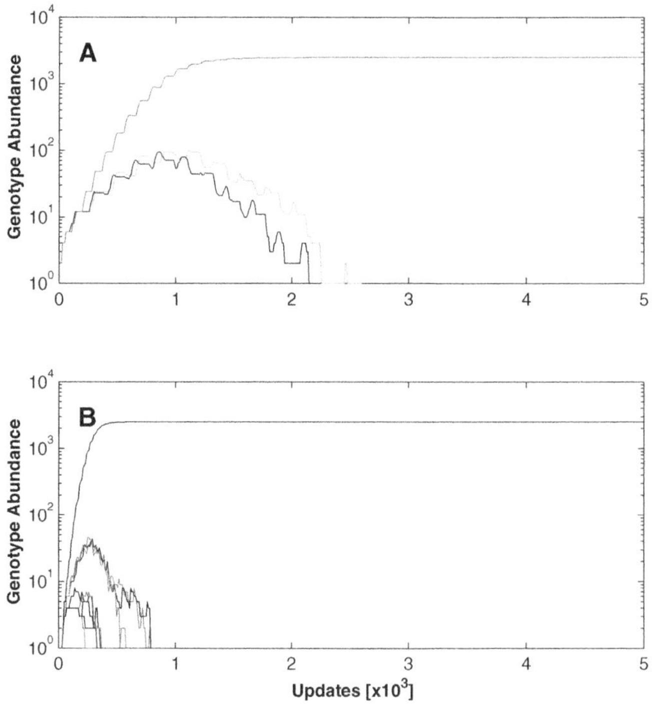

Figure 5: Coexistence of genotypes during the continued ecology phase with infinite-resources. Genotypes are numbered as in Figure 3. Note that a log scale was used for the y-axis. (A) Genotype dynamics throughout this phase in a representative generalist population. Dark-gray, genotype 1; light-gray, genotype 3; black, genotype 5. Genotype 1 remains at the end of the run. (B) Genotype dynamics throughout this phase in a representative specialist population. Genotype 1 remains at the end of the run.

we evolved, we increased the level of resources in the environment so that they were not limiting. This disrupts density-dependent selection by removing the penalty for using the same resource as other organisms and by no longer providing an advantage for being one of a few organisms using a resource. Effectively a single niche is created wherein only the fittest genotype is expected to survive (Kassen, *et. al.* 2000). When we did this, as expected, only one genotype was maintained.

The theory of competitive exclusion predicts that each environmental niche can support only one species, thus putting an upper bound on the number of species able to coexist in an environment (Hardin 1960). However, the number of species actually coexisting depends also on the genetics and physiology of the organisms. Whilst there is a general expectation that selection will tend to favor organisms which specialize on few resources (i.e. adaptive radiation), this expectation assumes that there are inherent trade-offs of adaptation such that for a given resource a specialist will be more competitive than a generalist (Futuyma & Moreno 1988). Whilst trade-offs have been observed in some studies (for example (Dykhuizen & Davies 1980; Cooper & Lenski 2000)), in others they have not (Reboud & Bell 1997; Bennett, *et. al.* 1992). Further underlining the uncertainty involved in making this assumption, in this study we observe the evolution of both specialists and generalists starting from the same ancestral genotype and evolving in the same environment (compare Figure 3 panels A and B). This finding may reflect either evolutionary contingencies in the physiology of the organisms or that evolution of one or other of the populations was stopped before a final strategy had been reached. Future work will address this issue.

As the ability of humankind to influence ecosystems increases, the search for mechanisms that underlie the diversity observed in nature has come to be of pragmatic as well as scientific interest (Tilman 2000). The Avida platform represents a uniquely tractable and powerful experimental model that has previously been used to answer evolutionary questions on a scale not possible with traditional systems (Lenski, *et. al.* 1999; Wilke, *et. al.* 2001). The extension that we introduce here will allow this system to be used to address ecological questions requiring the generation of resource dependent interactions between organisms within Avida populations. These studies may be valuable in giving heuristic insight into the workings of natural ecosystems.

Acknowledgements

We thank C. Adami, R. Lenski and C. Wilke for helpful discussion. We are grateful for comments from R. Lenski and C. Adami on an earlier version of this manuscript. This work was supported by a grant from the National Science Foundation.

References

Adami, C. 1998. *Introduction to Artificial Life.* Santa Clara: TELOS Springer-Verlag.

Adami C, Ofria C, and Collier TC 2000. Evolution of Biological Complexity. *Proc. Natl. Acad. Sci. USA* **97**:4463-4468.

Bell GAC 1997. Experimental evolution in *Chlamydomonas.* I. Short-term selection in uniform and diverse habitats. *Heredity* **78**:490-497.

Bell GAC 1999. Biodiversity of plankton by species oscillations and chaos. *Nature* **402**:407-410.

Bennett AF, Lenski RE, and Mittler JE 1992. Evolutionary adaptation to temperature. I. Fitness responses of *Escherichia coli* to changes in its thermal environment. *Evolution* **46**:16-30.

Cooper VS, and Lenski RE 2000. The population genetics of ecological specialization in evolving *Escherichia coli* populations.

Nature **407**:736-739.

Dykhuizen D, and Davies M 1980. An experimental model: Bacterial specialists and generalists competing in chemostats. *Ecology* **61**:1213-1227.

Futuyma D, and Moreno G 1988. The evolution of ecological specialization. *Ann. Rev. Ecol. Syst.* **19**:207-233.

Hardin G 1960. The competitive exclusion principal. *Science* **131**:1292-1297.

Kassen R, Buckling A, Bell G, and Rainey PB 2000. Diversity peaks at intermediate productivity in a laboratory microcosm.

Nature **406**:508-512.

Lenski RE, Ofria C, Collier TC, and Adami C 1999. Genome complexity, robustness and genetic interactions in digital organisms. *Nature* **400**:661-664.

Morin PJ 2000. Biodiversity's ups and downs. *Nature* **406**:463-464.

Notley-McRobb L, and Ferenci T 1999. Adaptive *mgl*-regulatory mutations and genetic diversity evolving in glucose-limited *Escherichia coli* populations. *Env. Microbiol.* **1**:33-43.

Notley-McRobb L, and Ferenci T 1999b. The generation of multiple co-existing mal-regulatory mutations through polygenic evolution in glucose-limited populations of *Escherichia coli*. *Env. Microbiol.* **1**:45-52.

Ofria C, Brown, CT, and Adami, C. 1998. The avida user's manual. In *Introduction to Artificial Life* (1998).

Rainey PB, and Travisano M 1998. Adaptive radiation in an heterogeneous environment.

Nature **394**:69-72.

Reboud X, and Bell G 1997. Experimental evolution of *Chlamydomonas*. III. Evolution of specialist and generalist types in environments that vary in space and time. *Heredity* **78**:507-514.

Schluter D 1996. Ecological causes of adaptive radiation. *Am. Nat.* **148**:s40-s64.

Schluter D 2000. Ecological character displacement in adaptive radiation. *Am. Nat.* **156**:s4-s16.

Schluter D 2001. Ecology and the origin of species. *Trends Ecol. Evol.* **16**:372-379.

Tilman, D.. 1982. *Resource Competition and Community Structure*. Princeton: Pirnceton University Press.

Tilman D 2000. Causes, consequences and ethics of biodiversity. *Nature* **405**:208-211.

Travisano M, and Rainey PB 2000. Studies of adaptive radiation using model microbial systems.

Am. Nat. **156**:s35-s44.

Wilke CO, Wang JL, Ofria C, Lenski RE, and Adami C 2001. Evolution of digital organisms at high mutation rate leads to survival of the flattest. *Nature* **412**:331-333.

Towards a Comparison of Evolutionary Creativity in Biological and Cultural Evolution

Andre Skusa and **Mark A. Bedau** *

Reed College, 3203 SE Woodstock Blvd.,Portland OR 97202
andre.skusa@reed.edu, mab@reed.edu

*To whom correspondence should be addressed.

Abstract

Bedau and Packard have defined evolutionary activity statistics that illuminate the adaptive evolutionary creativity of biological evolution. The statistics enable us to visualize adaptive evolutionary dynamics and to measure the intensity and extent of adaptive evolution, and can be used to define qualitatively different kinds of evolving systems. Here we describe how to apply evolutionary activity statistics to systems undergoing *cultural* rather than biological evolution, and we report preliminary results of implementing this method in technological evolution as reflected in patent record data. Measuring evolutionary activity in patent records provides a clear picture of the major adaptive phenomena at work in the evolution of technology. It also enables the quantitative and empirical comparison of the adaptive evolutionary dynamics of biological and cultural evolution.

Evolution of life and culture

A key question about evolving systems is to explain the source of their adaptive creativity. This question has broad applicability, concerning both artificial and natural evolving systems, and it applies to systems exhibiting either biological or cultural evolution. In a series of papers Bedau and Packard have shown how evolutionary activity statistics can be used to visualize and measure the creation of adaptations in many evolutionary systems (Bedau & Packard 1992; Bedau *et al.* 1997; Bedau, Snyder, & Packard 1998; Bedau & Brown 1999; Rechtsteiner & Bedau 1999) . These statistics are quite general and apply to data generated by both artificial and natural systems, and they apply at different levels of analysis. The study of evolutionary activity in natural and artificial biological evolution has yielded an intriguing picture of qualitatively different kinds of evolving systems (Bedau, Snyder, & Packard 1998). The biosphere as reflected in the fossil record shows an especially interesting and explosive kind of evolutionary creativity (Bedau *et al.* 1997; Bedau, Snyder, & Packard 1998), and it has been conjectured that the same kind of explosive adaptive creativity would be seen in certain kinds of cultural evolution (Bedau, Snyder, & Packard 1998). This paper takes the first step toward assessing that conjecture. We show how to apply evolutionary activity statistics to cultural evolution as reflected in patent records. This is a pilot project applied to patent data covering the past five and a half years. Our aim is to show how to create an empirical picture of the adaptive evolutionary dynamics in the evolution of patented inventions. Such pictures will enable us to compare the dynamics of patented technology with those exhibited in biological evolution. It is especially interesting whether this kind of cultural evolution is qualitatively like that exhibited in the fossil record.

The ultimate aims of this work is to illuminate the relationship between life and culture. One relationship is trivial: cultural phenomena involve the behavior or psychology of living creatures, especially humans. A much more interesting and controversial question is whether living and cultural phenomena and the mechanisms shaping them are in some way essentially the same. This is closely connected to question thirteen in the list of grand challenges in artificial life produced at Artificial Life VII (Bedau *et al.* 2000), and it is our focus here.[1] We approach this issue by showing how to compare the statistical signature of biological and cultural evolution in empirical evolutionary activity data.

There is plenty of previous work on cultural evolution and on patents, but none quite like ours. For many years cultural change has been treated as a process of the diffusion of ideas (Rogers 1995), and the scientometrics community has been investigating scientific and technological change by analysis of patent records and the like for decades (Pavitt 1985; Garfield & Welljams-Dorof 1992; Narin 1994; Albert 1998). But these approaches understand "evolution" in the sense of physics rather than biology, that is, simply as any change in time rather than just change resulting from differential imperfect replication and selection.

Sociobiology (Wilson 1978; Lumsden & Wilson 1981) and its contemporary sibling evolutionary psychology (Barkow, Cosmides, & Tooby 1992) explore one kind of connection between biological and cultural evolution, specifically, the extent to which certain psychological and cultural phenomena (e.g., homosexuality and altruism) can be explained by appeal to the operation of biological evolution itself. This reduction of social science to biology is contrasted with the approach to culture illustrated by memetics (Lynch 1996; Blackmore 1999; Aunger 2000), which considers the evolution of cultural phenomena in its own right, independent from and even

[1] The work reported in this paper is related to at least two further grand challenges in artificial life: question six about the nature of open-ended evolution and question eleven about the emergence of intelligence and mind in artificial living systems.

competing with biological evolution. The two classic quantitative treatments of cultural evolution (Cavalli-Sforza & Feldman 1981; Boyd & Richerson 1985) tend toward different answers to the question whether cultural evolution is ultimately explainable in terms of biological evolution, with Cavalli-Sforza and Feldman leaning toward explanatory dependence and Boyd and Richerson leaning toward a limited autonomy for culture. Our approach is neutral on this issue. We study cultural evolution as an evolutionary process in its own right, ignoring whether and how it might depend on biological evolution. Our goal is to provide an empirical and quantitative picture of the evolution of culture, one which allows us to compare its evolutionary dynamics with those of biological evolution. Both reductionists and antireductionists could profit from objective empirical measurement of cultural dynamics.

Although cultural evolution is not a common subject in artificial life, work on topics like the evolution of language and the evolution of economic phenomena does appear from time to time in artificial life journals and conferences; see, e.g., two recent reviews (Kirby 2002; Tesfatsian 2002). However, cultural evolution is typically construed as tangential to artificial life's central questions, connected mainly because of a similar methodology deploying evolutionary and agent-based models. Artificial life's marginalization of cultural evolution probably largely reflects the uncertainty about how life and culture are related. We aim to reduce this uncertainty and place the study of cultural evolution at the heart of artificial life.

Evolutionary activity in life

Bedau and Packard developed evolutionary activity statistics in order to visualize and measure the dynamics of the process by which evolution creates significant adaptations. Detailed definitions and illustrations of the evolutionary activity method have been presented in earlier publications (Bedau & Packard 1992; Bedau *et al.* 1997; Bedau, Snyder, & Packard 1998; Bedau & Brown 1999; Rechtsteiner & Bedau 1999). This section reviews the method and summarizes results relevant to the present paper. Precise definitions of evolutionary activity statistics as we apply them to patented innovations appear in a later section.

Adaptations are components of an evolving system with properties that allow them to preferentially survive, replicate, and in general play an active role in the system's behavior. Evolutionary activity statistics are derived from bookkeeping about things like the survival, replication, and activity or use of system components. The details of this bookkeeping can vary from case to case, depending on what properties of the system in question reflect the adaptive success of components of interest. For example, if the issue is the adaptive success of genotypes in a system in which a genotype's concentration reflects its adaptive success, then the bookkeeping simply integrates a genotype's concentration over its lifetime in the system (Bedau & Brown 1999). If the issue is the adaptive success of alleles in a system in which the continual expression or use of an allele reflects its adaptive success, then the bookkeeping simply sums an allele's use over its lifetime in the lineage (Bedau & Packard 1992).

Evolutionary activity data can be processed to yield various statistics that summarize the dynamics of adaptive evolution. Two statistics are especially relevant here. One is the *intensity* of evolutionary activity, which measures the rate at which new activity is being created by the system. The other is the *extent* of evolutionary activity, which measures the total amount of activity present in the system at a given time. These notions have been defined in a variety of ways in previous publications, but the underlying inspiration behind them has remained constant.

It is sometimes ambiguous whether activity data provide evidence of adaptations, because non-adaptive (or even maladaptive) components can generate a certain amount of activity before natural selection weeds them from the system. One can filter such non-adaptive "noise" from the activity data with a *neutral* model of the system under investigation (the "target" system). A neutral model is designed to be like the target system in all relevant respects except that by construction there is no natural selection; instead, all selection is random. Thus the neutral model is a no-adaptation null hypothesis that can be used to normalize the activity data observed in the target system. The *excess* activity that remains after normalization with a neutral model can be confidently interpreted as a reflection of significant evolutionary adaptations. With appropriate scaling of the data, neutral normalization allows quantitative comparison of evolutionary activity statistics across different evolving systems (Rechtsteiner & Bedau 1999).

The experience of measuring evolutionary activity in various artificial and natural evolving systems has supported two conclusions relevant here. The first is that evolutionary activity statistics, especially when normalized with a neutral model, do highlight the significant adaptive innovations created in the process of evolution, and their broad applicability enables adaptive evolutionary dynamics in different systems to be compared. Second, comparing data from a variety of different systems suggests that evolutionary activity statistics can be used to partition evolutionary dynamics into four qualitatively different classes. Table 1 summarizes these four classes and their statistical signatures. Class 1 consists of systems in which evolution creates no adaptations at all (e.g., all neutral models, systems in which the mutation rate is too high, and systems in which the selection pressure is too low). Systems in which evolution has created adaptations but in which no new adaptations are

CLASS	DESCRIPTION	EVOLUTIONARY ACTIVITY SIGNATURE excess intensity	excess extent	PARADIGM EXAMPLES
1	no activity	zero	zero	neutral model
2	uncreative activity	zero	unbounded	stable ecosystem
3	bounded activity	positive	bounded	continual adaptive succession
4	unbounded activity	positive	unbounded	Phanerozoic biosphere

Table 1: Empirical classification of evolutionary dynamics, their statistical signatures, and paradigm examples of systems in each class. This classification modifies and augments the classification presented at Artificial Life VI (Bedau, Snyder, & Packard 1998).

being created fall into class 2 (e.g., stable ecosystems). Class 3 consists of systems that continually create new adaptations but are bounded in the amount of adaptive structure they contain (e.g., if new adaptations always supplant old adaptations). If new adaptations are continually created and the total amount of adaptive structure continues to grow, then the system falls into class 4. The biosphere as reflected in the fossil record exhibits class 4 dynamics. It would be interesting to be able to ask where cultural evolution falls in this classification.

Cultural evolution in patents

Those who seek to measure cultural evolution face formidable challenges in finding appropriate empirical data. A threshold issue is forming a clear and operational idea of the units of evolution. It is especially difficult to distinguish new innovations from copies of old innovations when the subject is ideas or other mental aspects of culture. Another difficulty is finding a complete time series of rich assays of some aspect of culture in which genealogical relationships can be precisely ascertained.

One can finesse these difficulties if one studies the evolution of patented inventions. Although the evolution of inventions involves the diffusion and selection of ideas, one can operationally identify individual inventions with individual patents. To be patentable an invention must meet three criteria: novelty, usefulness, and non-obviousness. So patented inventions are certified to be new and functional. A patent's novelty is documented by citing the previous patents (and sometimes published papers) that involve related ideas; these are called the patent's "prior art." The citations should identify all the important prior art on which the invention improves and, as Perko and Narin emphasize, patent examiners are charged with ensuring that no relevant prior art is missed (Perko & Narin 1997):

> These references are chosen and screened by patent examiners, who are "not called upon to cite all references that are available, but only the best." (*Manual of Patent Examining Procedures*, Section 904.02)

Such citations to prior art provide a record of a patent's evolutionary genealogy; in the aggregate the references

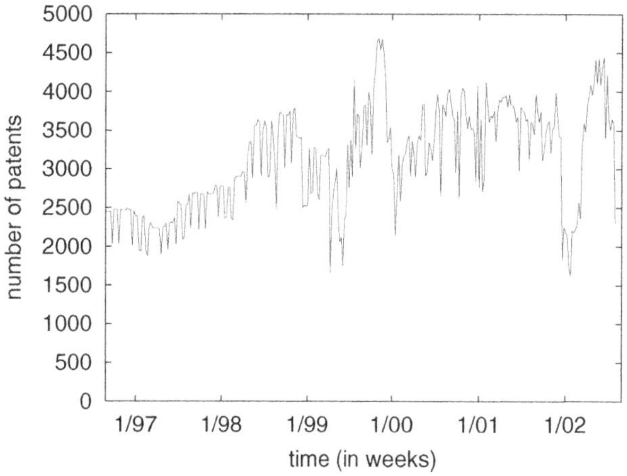

Figure 1: The number of patents issued each week. This number seems to be rising and getting more volatile.

imply a precise and complete phylogeny of all patents.[2]

We studied the evolution of culture in the complete set of utility patents granted by the United States Patent and Trademark Office (USPTO) during the period 9/96–7/02. (The complete record of all patent applications granted over this period is available for download at http://www.uspto.gov/web/menu/patdata.html.) Our data set contains 868,535 patents. Figure 1 shows the number of patents issued each week during this period. The USPTO classifies patents according to the category of the invention, and US patents are currently placed in one of 419 main classifications. The USPTO occasionally revises its classification scheme, dropping outmoded classes, splitting overburdened classes, and adding new classes, so the class numbering sequence has gaps. Although there are only 419 classes, some classes are now

[2]Caveat: patent applications must cite important prior art whether or not it plays a *causal* role in an invention's origin. So the evolutionary lineages derived from patent citation data can connect inventions with independent etiologies. This is a limitation of our method, for we would like to interpret evolutionary activity etiologically. We expect that most prior art cited in patents does play some causal role in the generation of those patents, but we have no strong evidence for this in hand.

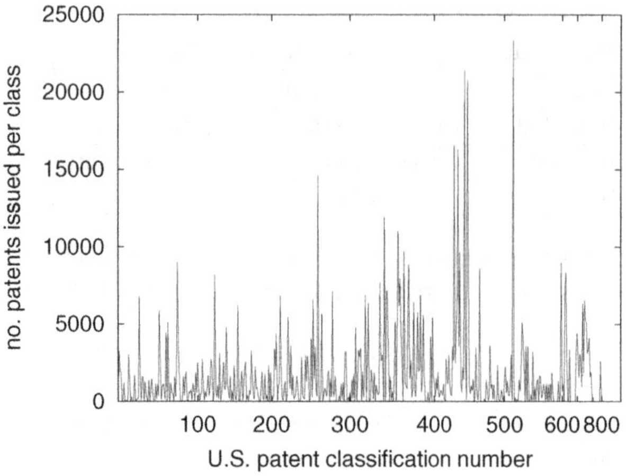

Figure 2: Number of patents issued in each class during 9/96–7/02. The number of patents in various patent classes can differ by an order of magnitude.

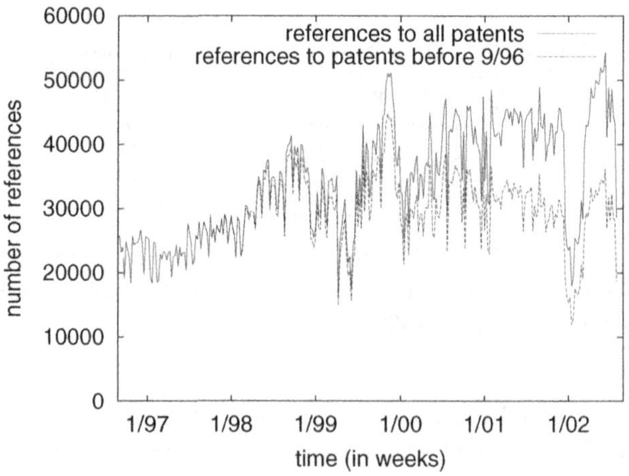

Figure 3: Time series of the number of references in the patents issued each week. The dashed line shows the references to patents issued prior to the time period shown. The gap between the solid and dashed lines shows the growing number of references to patents issued during 9/96–7/02. Note that two to three year time lag before patents issued after 9/96 start to be cited (i.e., before there is an appreciable gap between the two lines).

numbered over 800. Figure 2 shows the wide variability in the number of patents issued in different classes in our data.

The analogies and disanalogies between biological and cultural evolution are a matter of controversy (Hull 1988), but it is relatively straightforward to extract evolutionary activity data from patent records. The units of evolution with which we are concerned (at least in the first instance) are individual patents; these are analogous to genes (or, as memeticists might suggest, "memes"). A gene could vanish forever from an evolutionary system. By contrast, a patented invention never goes fully extinct because the invention exists forever in the patent records. We consider that a patent "reproduces" when it leads to the production of *other* patents; that is, in contrast with most biological evolution, patent reproduction necessarily involves innovation—the creation of new inventions.

Typically two or more years elapse between when a patent application is filed and the USPTO issues a patent. Thus our method of using citations to reflect when a patent reproduces introduces a time lag.[3] Figure 3 shows the total number of references contained in the patents issued each week in our data. (The shapes of Figures 1 and 3 are similar because the average number of references per patent is roughly constant.) Since a patent can cite only patents that have been issued earlier, the two or more year delay while the USPTO examines patent applications means that patents issued at a given time are typically never cited until they are two or more years old. This is evident in Figure 3 as the two to three year lag before patents in our data (i.e., those issued after 9/96) start to be cited.

[3]We could remove this time lag by dating a citation back to when a patent is filed rather than issued.

Figure 4 shows that the average number of citations to patents varies from class to class. Especially successful or valuable patents tend to be those that are especially heavily cited. A raft of work in scientometrics has repeatedly confirmed that number of citations is a good reflection of the technological significance and economic value of a patented invention (Pavitt 1985; Albert 1991; Narin 1994; Perko & Narin 1997; Albert 1998). This parallels the extensive evidence validating the usefulness of science citation data for measuring the importance of scientific publications (Garfield & Welljams-Dorof 1992). Once a patent has received more than ten citations, the economic value reflected by each additional citation has been estimated to be more than one million US dollars (Harhoff *et al.* 1999). For these reasons our bookkeeping of an individual patent's evolutionary activity is based on summing the citations the patent has received. ¿From this perspective, the adaptive success of a patented innovation is measured by the extent to which it spawns subsequent patented innovations.

Definitions of patent activity

Applying evolutionary activity statistics in a given context requires settling two issues: (1) choosing which components of the evolving system will have their activity measured, and (2) choosing how to increment their activity. Our response to (1) is to examine the activity of individual patents; this allows us subsequently to examine the activity of patent classes by aggregating the activity of the patents in those classes. Our response to (2) is to increment a patent's activity at a

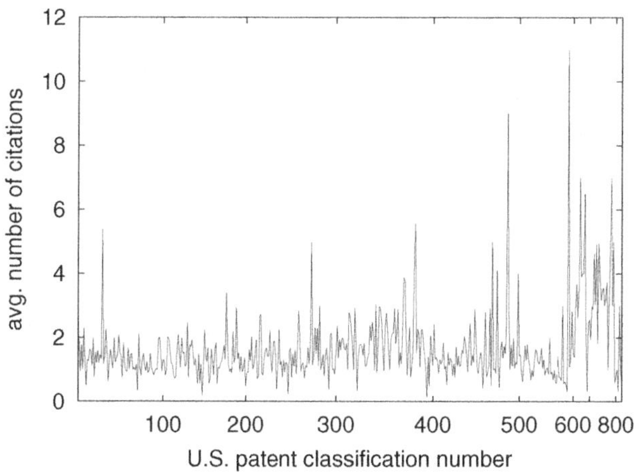

Figure 4: Average number of citations per patent in each class during 9/96–7/02. Note the wide variability between patent classes.

given time by the number of citations it receives from patents issued at that time. More specifically, we let Ξ_i^t be the set of patents issued at t that cite patent i, i.e., $\Xi_i^t = \{j : j \in \Upsilon_t \wedge j \text{ cites } i\}$, where Υ_t is the set of patents issued at t. We let $\Delta_i(t)$ be the amount that i's activity increases at t and we define this as the number of new citations i receives at t, i.e., $\Delta_i(t) = \#(\Xi_i^t)$. Then, we let the counter $a_i(t)$ reflect the activity of patent i at time t and define this as the number of citations it has received up to t:

$$a_i(t) = \sum_{u=t_i}^{t} \Delta_i(u), \qquad (1)$$

where t_i is the time when patent i is issued. The activity $a_c(t)$ of a patent class c at time t is then defined as the sum of the activity of the patents in it, i.e., $a_c(t) = \sum_{i \in c} a_i(t)$.

Patent neutral shadows

The mere fact that a patent has received a few citations does not prove that the invention significantly shapes the evolution of subsequent inventions. A patent might be cited by one or two subsequent patents even if patents to cite were chosen entirely at random. As with evolutionary activity measurements in other contexts, we can evaluate a patent's adaptive significance by comparing its activity with the activity observed in a neutral model of patent evolution.

Our patent neutral model mirrors a few key aspects of the real patent data. In both the same number of patents are issued each week, and they exhibit the same distribution into the various patent classes. Patent citations refer to the same number of pre-9/96 and post-9/96 patents, so real and neutral model patents both exhibit time lags before collecting many citations. Furthermore, the references to post-9/96 patents fall into the various patent classes according to the same distribution. The key distinguishing feature of the neutral model is that the patents to be cited are always chosen randomly.

More precisely, here is how the neutral model works. When a real patent is issued in a given class in a given week, a shadow patent is issued in the same class in the same week. Furthermore, when the real patent cites a post-9/96 patent, its corresponding shadow patent cites a previously issued shadow patent. Since patents in different patent classes have different expected likelihoods of being cited (recall Figure 4), we have the shadow patents mirror this bias. This gives the shadow neutral model and the real patents the same number of patents per class and the same number of citations per class. The crucial difference between the real patent system and its neutral shadow concerns the process for randomly choosing which patents to cite. Specifically, when it is time for a shadow patent to cite a previously issued shadow patent, we first randomly choose the patent class in which we will choose the patent to cite, but our random choice of patent class is *not* made with equal probability. Rather, we weight the random choice of patent class by the frequency with which real patents cite patents in different classes. This guarantees that real and shadow patent classes will have the same distribution of citations. After a patent class is randomly chosen, we randomly choose with equal probability which prior patent in that class to cite.[4]

Excess activity, its intensity and extent

Once we have a neutral model for the patents, normalizing by the neutral model yields a measure of the excess activity in the patents—that is, the amount of activity that is unambiguously attributable to the patent's adaptive significance. To achieve this effect, we define the excess activity $a_{i \in c}^{\text{excess}}$ of an individual patent i in class c at time t as the amount by which i's activity exceeds the maximum activity of *any* shadow patent in class c. More specifically, we let $a_{i \in c}^{\text{shadow}}$ be the activity of shadow patent i in class c after the neutral shadow has run its course (i.e., after it has shadowed the real patents for the entire period over which the patents are under investigation). Then $\Psi_c = \{a_{i \in c}^{\text{shadow}} : i \in c\}$ is the set of activity values of all the shadow patents in class c.

[4]An anonymous reviewer called our attention to a disanalogy in the time lags exhibited by our neutral model and the real patents. Although there are some exceptions, a real patent usually cites only patents that were issued before the application patent was filed. The time lag before patents start to accrue citations largely reflects the gap between filing and issuing dates. But a shadow patent issued in one week is just as likely to cite a shadow patent issued in the previous week as any other patent in the same class. This disanalogy could be corrected by having the neutral model mirror the distribution of the dates of cited patents. We suspect that this correction would not substantially alter our results.

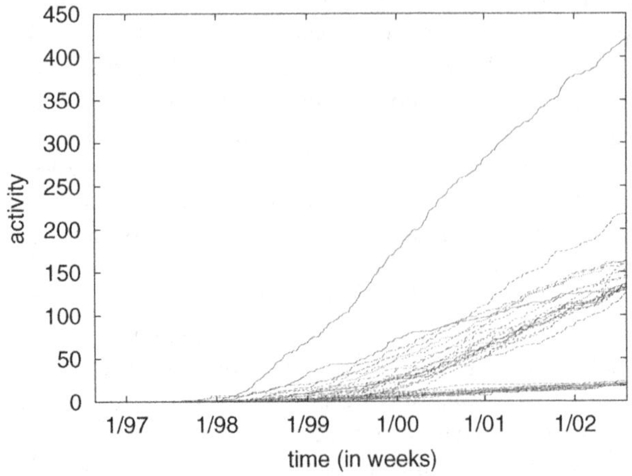

Figure 5: Comparison of the activity of real patents and shadow patents, showing the twenty most heavily cited real patents and the twenty most heavily cited shadow patents. The activity waves of the real patents all rise above 100 while those of the shadow patents remain below 25. Note that the activity accrued by significant real patents can vastly exceed that accrued by any shadow patent.

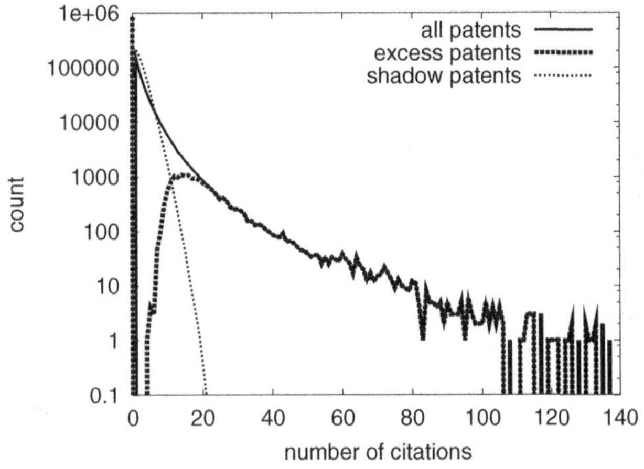

Figure 6: Log-normal plot of the distribution of final activity for all patents at 7/02, shadow patents, and just those patents with positive excess activity. Note that shadow patent activity never approaches the activity of the most heavily cited patents.

Finally, we define the excess activity of patent i in class c at t as follows:

$$a_{i \in c}^{\text{excess}}(t) = \begin{cases} a_i(t) - \max(\Psi_c) & \text{if } a_i(t) > \max(\Psi_c) \\ 0 & \text{otherwise} \end{cases} \tag{2}$$

So, patents in a given class with positive excess activity have acquired more citations than those acquired by any shadow patent in the same class. The excess activity of a patent class c at time t is defined as the sum of the excess activity at t of all the patents in class c: $a_c^{\text{excess}}(t) = \sum_{i \in c} a_{i \in c}^{\text{excess}}(t)$.

Figure 5 shows the dramatic difference between the activity accrued by shadow patents and real patents with excess activity. Another picture of this difference comes from comparing the distribution of the patents' final activity values (Figure 6). Overall, the citation levels of shadow patents are much lower than the citation levels of patents with excess activity.

Only 17,783 of the patents issued during 9/96–7/02 have positive excess activity; this represents about 2% of the patents issued during this period. Thus our neutral model is a very liberal no-adaptation null hypothesis. It might well screen out some significant innovations, i.e., it might yield some false negatives, but it should allow no false positives. This liberality is no problem in the present context for our primary concern is to focus on those patents that unequivocally play a significant role in the evolution of inventions.

In order to classify the kind of evolutionary dynamics evident in the patent record, we must define two global activity statistics—excess intensity and excess extent of activity—in a way that can be usefully applied to the evolution of patented inventions. Excess intensity of activity is intended to reflect the rate at which new significant innovations are being created. We define the excess intensity of evolutionary activity of the patented inventions at time t as the number of patents issued at t that have positive excess activity at the time when excess intensity is measured. More precisely, we define the excess intensity of activity of the patents at time t, as measured at time τ, as:

$$\text{intensity}_{\tau}^{\text{excess}}(t) = \#\{i : i \in \Upsilon_t \wedge a_{i \in c}^{\text{excess}}(\tau) > 0\}, \tag{3}$$

where c is ranges over all classes and where Υ_t is the set of patents issued at t, as before. That is, excess intensity at t as measuered at τ is the number of patents issued at t that will have positive excess activity at τ. When we report excess intensity below, our observations are made at the end of the data we examine; i.e., we set $\tau = 7/02$.

The excess intensity at t is not absolute; rather, it depends on the time τ when it is measured. Thus, the value of the excess intensity at t can increase as later and later measurements are made, i.e., $\tau - t$ increases. No moment in the evolution of patented technology can be seen to have positive excess activity contemporaneously, i.e., if $t \approx \tau$. Positive excess intensity can be observed only years later, after the patents have accumulated a sufficient number of citations.[5] A true reckoning of the

[5]It is possible to define excess intensity at t in a way that is not relative to time of observation, perhaps most naturally as the number of patents whose excess activity first become positive at t. This kind of definition has the drawback that its value at one time reflects the patents that were issued years previously. We employ a future-dependent definition to avoid precisely this problem.

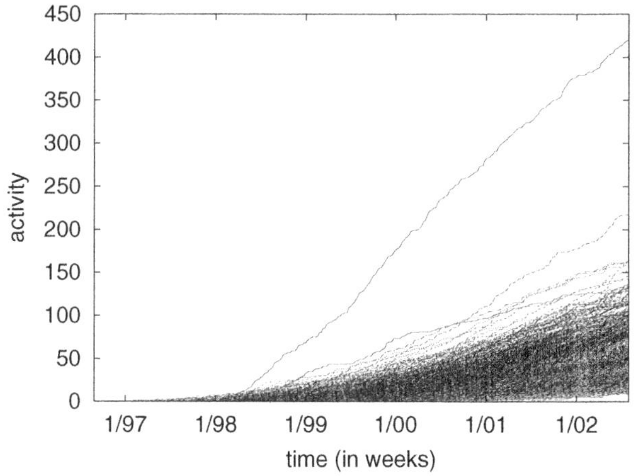

Figure 7: The activity waves of patents with positive excess activity. We graph the top two hundred excess waves and then omit redundant information by sampling the remaining excess activity waves.

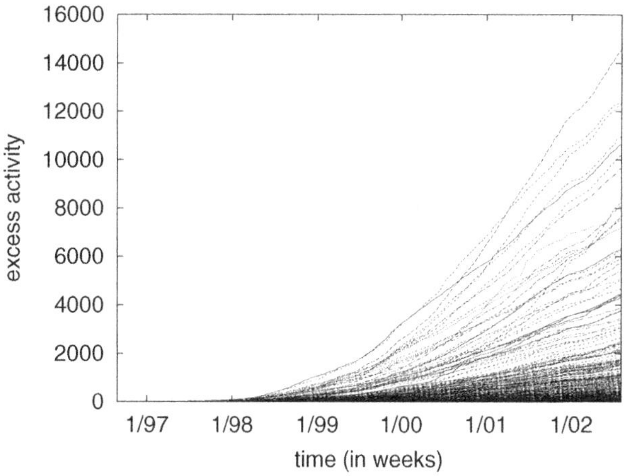

Figure 8: The excess activity of all patent classes. Note that very many patent classes show significant positive excess activity.

eventual excess intensity can be settled only when those patents are no longer cited—a time measured in generations.

Excess extent of evolutionary activity is intended to reflect the mass of excess evolutionary activity at a given time. We define the excess extent of activity of patented inventions as the sum of the activity of those patents that have positive excess activity:

$$\text{extent}^{\text{excess}}(t) = \sum_{i,c} a_{i\in c}^{\text{excess}}(t). \qquad (4)$$

Unlike the definition of excess intensity of activity, the definition of excess extent of activity is not relative to a time of observation. The value of excess intensity at t cannot change if it is measured at different times, and the excess extent of activity of the present moment can be determined at the present. Nevertheless, excess extent is an "historical" statistic, so the value of excess extent at t depends on the amount of data collected before t. Including earlier patents in our data would enable more patents to have a chance at positive excess activity.

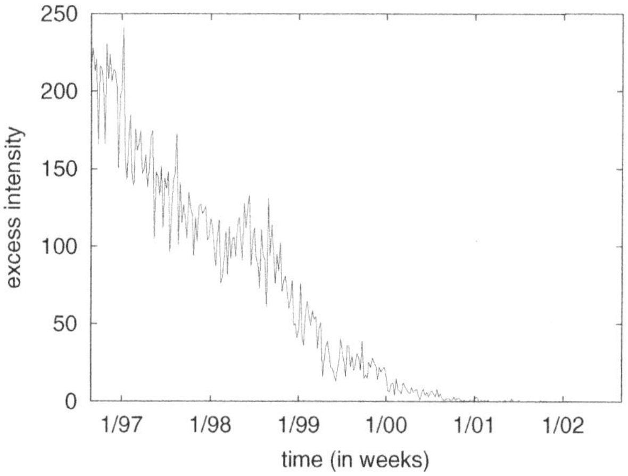

Figure 9: Time series of the excess intensity of activity of patents. The drop in excess intensity to zero is a finite-size effect. See text.

Observations of excess activity

Figure 7 shows the activity accrued by patents with positive excess activity. Note that one patent stands far above the rest; it accrues almost twice as many citations as any other patent. This patent covers the technology that allows web browsers to display information such as advertisements while a page is being loaded a link is clicked. The second most heavily cited patent covers the technology that allows cell phones to receive email and faxes, and the third most heavily cited patent allows remote control of the receipt and delivery of wireless and wireline voice and text messages. All of the ten most heavily cited patents fall into the information technology sector (see Table 2).

Figure 8 shows the excess activity of all patent classes. Information technology covers ninety percent of these classes. The most-heavily cited patent falls in class number 709. This class has the third highest excess activity, and it has the highest average excess activity per patent. The ten patent classes with the most excess activity are listed in Table 3. Most of these concern information technology, and the second largest group concerns health. When these patent classes are ranked according to average excess activity per patent, the top three information technology patent classes have a 15–30% lead over all other patent classes.

To place the cultural evolution exhibited by patents into the classification of Table 1 we need to measure the

Rank	Excess Activity	Patent Number	Patent Title	Class Numb.
1	420	5572643	Web browser with dynamic display of information objects during linking	709
2	218	5608786	Unified messaging system and method	379
3	163	5742905	Personal communications internetworking	455
4	162	5708780	Internet server access control and monitoring systems	709
4	162	5557518	Trusted agents for open electronic commerce	705
6	159	5632021	Computer system with cascaded peripheral component interconnect (PCI) buses	710
7	152	5774660	World-wide-web server with delayed resource-binding for resource-based load balancing on a distributed resource multi-node network	709
8	147	5655081	System for monitoring and managing computer resources and applications across a distributed computing environment using an intelligent autonomous agent architecture	709
9	142	5623601	Apparatus and method for providing a secure gateway for communication and data exchanges between networks	713
10	137	5610910	Access to telecommunications networks in multi-service environment	370

Table 2: The ten patents with the highest excess activity. Note the total dominance by information technology.

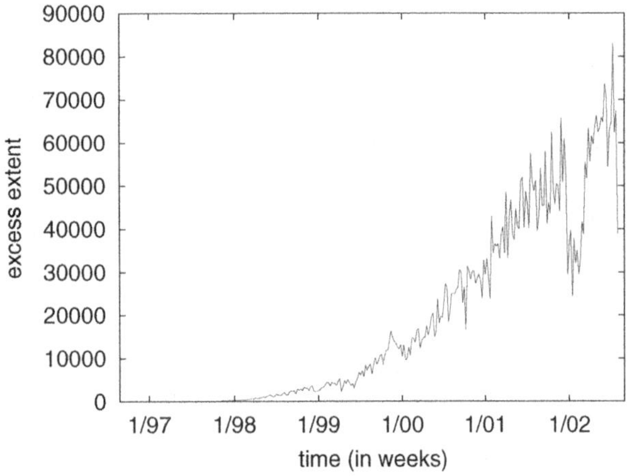

Figure 10: Time series of the excess extent of activity of patents. The initial period of zero or very low excess extent is a finite-size effect. See text.

excess intensity and extent of evolutionary activity in the patent data. Figure 9 shows the excess intensity of activity. The dramatic fall to zero over this graph is an artifact of the finite size of the data. We saw above that it takes two or more years for the USPTO to process a patent application. This means that it takes two or more years before a patent can receive many citations. Hence a patent's status of receiving excess citations can become recognized only two or more years after it has been issued. So, we would expect to continually learn that additional patents have excess activity—and hence learn that excess intensity is higher than we previous thought—two or more years after patents have been issued. (Recall that excess intensity depends on the time τ of observation.) So as we collect additional patent record data for the months and years following 7/02, the calculated excess intensity over the time period shown in Figure 9 will continue to increase. This increase will not continue forever, though, since sufficiently old patents are no longer cited. Thus, as long as some patents achieve positive excess activity, the excess intensity of the patents will be positive over data with a sufficiently long time course (on the order of decades). So, even though our excess activity data suffers a finite size effect, we can still tell that the cultural evolution of patented inventions shows the positive excess intensity signature of classes 3 and 4.

So whether the cultural evolution of patented inventions falls into class 3 or 4 turns on whether its excess extent of activity is bounded or unbounded. Figure 10 shows excess extent over 9/96–7/02. The first thing to notice about this graph is that it also shows a finite size effect. Our data starts with the patents issued in 9/96, and no patent issued at that time will have positive excess activity in 9/96. It's excess activity can become positive only some months or (more likely) years in the future, when it has accumulated more citations than shadow patents. We could remove this finite size effect at 9/96 by collecting information about patents issued earlier. If this were done, the excess extent of activity in the the first fifth of the period shown in Figure 10 would start to rise. But this will not *remove* the finite-size effect; it will just shift it back in time. There will be an initial period of zero excess extent of activity no matter when we start collecting data.

What is more intriguing—and ambiguous—is the pattern in excess extent toward the *end* of the period shown in Figure 10. Excess activity is clearly positive; the question is whether it is bounded, that is, whether it will continue to show an overall rising trend into the future or whether it will top out. The excess extent of activ-

Rank	Total Excess Activity	Average Excess Activity	Class Number	Class Title
1	14553	30.38	438	Semiconductor device manufacturing: process
2	12483	35.36	370	Multiplex communications
3	12343	40.74	709	Electrical computers and digital processing systems: multiple computer or process coordinating
4	10973	29.11	606	Surgery
5	10640	35.12	707	Data processing: database and file management, data structures, or document processing
6	10198	26.91	257	Active solid-state devices (e.g., transistors, solid-state diodes)
7	9649	27.49	345	Computer graphics processing, operator interface processing, and selective visual display systems
8	8258	19.52	435	Chemistry: molecular biology and microbiology
9	8105	30.13	600	Surgery
10	7646	16.48	514	Drug, bio-affecting and body treating compositions

Table 3: The ten patent classes that collect the most excess activity during 9/96–7/02, with the total excess activity class and the average excess activity per patent. Note that most of the most activity classes fall into the information technology sector, including the four classes with the highest average excess activity. The USPTO descriptions of all patent classes are available at http://www.uspto.gov/web/patents/classification.

ity shown in Figure 10 is consistent with the hypothesis of unbounded growth, but it is also consistent with a finite bound. Extrapolating long-term trends is always somewhat uncertain, and the volatility in the number of patents issued during the first half of 2002 (the tail end of our data) makes it especially risky. However, analyzing patent records for the preceding decade or two should go a long way toward revealing whether the extent of excess activity for the patents is unbounded. So, although our pilot data cannot resolve whether the evolutionary dynamics of patented inventions is in class 3 or 4, the question is now precisely formulated and quite amenable to empirical investigation.

Conclusions

Our pilot project has proved the feasibility of visualizing and quantitatively assessing the adaptive evolutionary dynamics exhibited in cultural evolution. We have applied the method to technological evolution as reflected in patent record data, but it can be applied at a variety of levels of analysis in a variety of cultural systems. The main problem is getting enough appropriate data. This problem should be easily solvable for cultural evolution reflected in such things as scientific citation data, financial data about economic markets, databases of newspaper articles, and data about the evolution of the world wide web.

Our preliminary analysis of technological evolution underscores the vast importance of information technology, and especially the Internet, over the past five years. This conclusion is not news, of course; it just corroborates what we already know. But it does confirm the aptness and probity of evolutionary activity analysis of cultural evolution, and it opens the door to myriad subsequent empirical investigations of cultural evolution.

The most intriguing issue highlighted by our pilot results is the question whether the technological evolution exhibits class 3 or 4 dynamics. This question can be answered once we have data with a significantly long time horizon. Whatever the answer, cultural evolution will be shown to have a precise quantitative similarity with one or another kind of biological evolution. Resolving this issue will shed new light on the nature and scope of class 3 or 4 evolutionary dynamics, and it might help us to formulate deeper and more refined classifications of evolutionary creativity. So, evolutionary activity analysis of patented technology opens a constructive path toward understanding whether life and culture are two manifestations of one fundamental kind of process.

Acknowledgments

Thanks to Norman Packard for helpful discussion and extensive collaboration on evolutionary activity statistics. For constructive suggestions, thanks to Steen Rasmussen, Mike Raven, the Artificial Life VIII reviewers, and the audiences at Lake Arrowhead, California (May 2002), and at the Fraunhofer Gesellschaft in Sankt Augustin, Germany (July 2002), where MAB presented these results. Thanks to Howard Gutowitz for the suggestion at Artificial Life VI of applying evolutionary activity statistics to patent record data. AS thanks the Studienstiftung des deutschen Volkes (German National Merit Foundation), Bonn, Germany, for financial support.

References

Albert, M. B. 1998. *The new innovators: Global patenting trends in five sectors.* Washington D.C.: U.S. Department of Commerce.

Albert, M.; Avery, D; Narin, F.; and McAllister, P. 1991. Direct validation of citation counts as indicators of industrially important patents. *Research Policy* 20: 251–259.

Aunger, R., ed. 2000. *Darwinizing culture: The status of memetics as a science.* New York: Oxford University Press.

Barkow, J. H.; Cosmides, L.; and Tooby, J., eds. 1992. *The adapted mind: Evolutionary psychology and the generation of culture.* New York: Oxford University Press.

Bedau, M. A.; and Brown, C. T. 1999. Visualizing evolutionary activity of genotypes. *Artificial Life* 5: 17-35.

Bedau, M. A.; McCaskill, J. S.; Packard, N. H.; Rasmussen, S.; Adami, C.; Green, D. G.; Ikegami, T.; Kaneko, K.; Ray, T. S. 2000. Open problems in artificial life. *Artificial Life* 6: 363-376.

Bedau, M. A.; Snyder, E.; Brown, C. T.; and Packard, N. H. 1997. A comparison of evolutionary activity in artificial evolving systems and in the biosphere. In *Proceedings of the Fourth European Conference on Artificial Life*, P. Husbands and I. Harvey, eds., pp. 125-134. Cambridge: MIT Press.

Bedau, M. A.; Snyder, E.; and Packard, N. H. 1998. A classification of long-term evolutionary dynamics. In *Artificial Life VI*, C. Adami, R. Belew, H. Kitano, and C. Taylor, eds., pp. 228-237. Cambridge: MIT Press.

Bedau, M. A.; and Packard, N. H. 1992. Measurement of evolutionary activity, teleology, and life. In *Artificial Life II*, C. Langton, C. Taylor, D. Farmer, S. Rasmussen, eds., pp. 431-461. Redwood City, CA: Addison-Wesley.

Blackmore, S. 1999. *The meme machine.* New York: Oxford University Press.

Boyd, R; and Richerson, P. J. 1985. *Culture and the evolutionary process.* Chicago: University of Chicago Press.

Cavalli-Sforza, L. L.; and Feldman, M. W. 1981. *Cultural transmission and evolution: A quantitative approach.* Princeton: Princeton University Press.

Garfield, E.; and Welljams-Dorof, A. 1992. Citation data: Their use as quantitative indicators for science and technology evaluation and policy making. *Science and Public Policy* 19: 321–327.

Harhoff, D.; Narin, F.; Scherer, F. M.; and Vopel, K. 1999. Citation frequency and the value of patented innovation. *Research Policy* 81: 511–515.

Hull, D. L. 1988. *Science as process: An evolutionary account of the social and conceptual development of science.* Chicago, London: The University of Chicago Press.

Kirby, S. 2002. The evolution of language. *Artificial Life* 8: 185–215.

Lumsden, C. J.; and Wilson, E. O. 1981. *Genes, mind, and culture.* Cambridge: Harvard University Press.

Lynch, A. 1996. *Thought contagion: How belief spreads through society.* New York: Basic Books.

Narin, F. 1994. Patent bibliometrics. *Scientometrics* 30: 147–155.

Pavitt, K. 1985. Patent statistics as indicators of innovative activities: Possibilities and problems. *Scientometrics* 7: 77–99.

Perko, J. S.; and Narin, F. 1997. The transfer of public science to patented technology: A case study in agricultural science. *Journal of Technology Transfer* 22: 65–72.

Rechtsteiner, A.; and Bedau, M. A. 1999. A generic model for quantitative comparison of genotypic evolutionary activity. In *Advances in Artificial Life*, D. Floreano, J.-D. Nicoud, F. Mondada, eds., pp. 109-118. Heidelberg: Springer-Verlag.

Rogers, E. M. 1995. *Diffusion of innovations.* Fourth edition. New York: Free Press.

Tesfatsian, L. 2002. Agent-based computational economics: growing economies from the bottom up. *Artificial Life* 8: 55-82.

Wilson, E. O. 1978. *On human nature.* Cambridge: Harvard University Press.

Evolving the Morphology of a Neural Network for Controlling a Foveating Retina — and its Test on a Real Robot

Peter Eggenberger Hotz[1,2], **Gabriel Gómez**[1] and **Rolf Pfeifer**[1]

[1]Artificial Intelligence Laboratory
Department of Information Technology, University of Zurich
Winterthurerstrasse 190, CH-8057 Zuerich, Switzerland
eggen@ifi.unizh.ch

[2]Emergent Communication Mechanisms Project
ATR Human Information Science Laboratories
2-2 Hikaridai, Seika-cho, Soraku-gun
Kyoto 619-0288
Japan

Abstract

The standard approach in evolutionary robotics is to evolve neural networks for control by encoding the parameters of the network in the genome. By contrast, we have evolved a neural controller based on biological principles from molecular and developmental biology. The key principles employed in our algorithms model the specific ligand-receptor interactions and gene regulation. These mechanisms were used to control the growth of the axons, the generation of synapses including the synaptic efficiencies (i.e. the synaptic weights in a neural network model). The evolved neural network was then transferred to a real robotic system with results comparable to the ones achieved the simulation. We hypothesize that the incorporation of mechanisms of gene regulation potentially leads to more adaptive neural networks, that can help bridging the "reality gap" between simulation and the real world.

Introduction

In order to create an artificial evolutionary system (AES) able to evolve complex neural networks for real robots, this paper proposes to combine artificial evolutionary techniques with biological principles. Although this approach is more complicated than a direct encoding scheme or predefined developmental rules, there are a number of advantages of an AES with developmental processes (especially continuous ligand-receptor interactions and genetic regulatory networks) that justify their implementation. In Nature the genome encodes a program of instructions for the development of an organism (Gerhart & Kirschner 1997), (Wolpert 1998). What is stored in the DNA is not so much a detailed description of the body and its parts, but how to build it. The advantage of such an approach is to reduce the amount of genetic information, the number of parameters required to specify the organism. A developmental program is in this sense similar to a data-compression algorithm program. Instead of storing information of each individual point of a picture, it stores instructions on how to re-create the picture with a reduction of information of at least an order of magnitude (Barnsley 1993). A reduction of the number of parameters in an AES for the same problem means higher evolvability and faster convergence towards a solution. In the literature other indirect encoding schemes for artificial evolution were proposed (Fleischer & Barr 1992; Belew 1993; Cangelosi, Parisi, & Nolfi 1994; Gruau & Whitley 1993; Kitano 1994; Michel & Bondi 1995; Sims 1995; Dellaert & Beer 1996; Vaario & Shimohara 1997; Kodjabachian & Meyer 1998). In contrast to these approaches in the proposed model the genes controlled by continuous-valued regulatory genes that control the structure of the neural network as well as the mechanisms for changing the synaptic weights. Different developmental mechanisms (cell division, axonal outgrowth, synaptogenesis, learning) were used to evolve a foveating retina. (By foveating we mean "image tracking"). The retina which is moved by two pairs of antagonistic motors has to learn to focus on an incoming stimulus. The simulations show that the AES with the proposed encoding scheme is able to find solutions for a non-trivial problem, the foveating task, that the genetic code is independent of the number of cells (the number of neurons and synapsis are much bigger than the number of genes) and that the different developmental mechanisms work effectively together. Furthermore we were able to transfer the evolved foveating mechanism on a robot arm guided by a CCD-camera.

The Model

Figure 1 gives an overview of the general levels of the AES. The genetic parameters are defined on the first level and they are directly changed by the evolutionary strategy. These parameters do not encode directly the properties of a neural network, but specify the properties of the cells (second level) by defining the characteristics of the genes and their regulators and they affect the response of the genes. The properties of the third (tissue) and possibly higher levels (organs, organisms) are, again, not directly specified, but have to be created by developmental processes. To do so the evolution strategy was used to explore the parameter space for those processes that are able to fulfil a designer specified fitness function. The use of processes to create structures instead of specifying the structure directly has the advantage that the encoding needs less genetic information and therefore decreases the search time in the parameter space. The obvious drawback of this approach is the increased computational load for the development. But as the number of parameters can be decreased drastically there is still an overall advantage, especially for large complex organisms.

Overview of the AES algorithm

Set population size
Set initial gene number

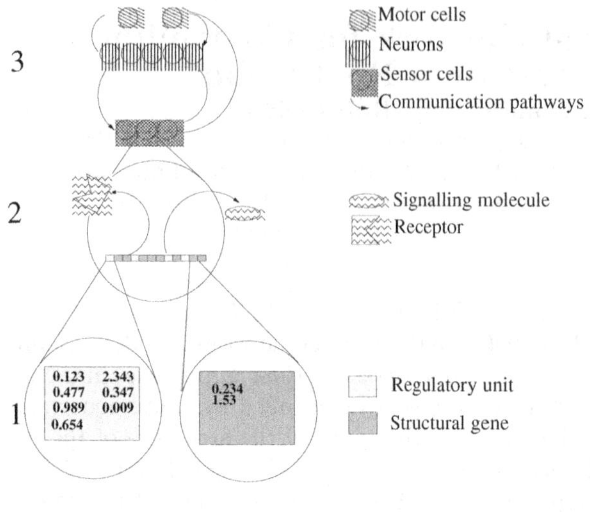

Figure 1: Schematic overview of the artificial evolutionary system (AES). The schema is divided in three levels of increasing complexity. The first level is the parametric level, the second is the cellular level and the third is the tissue level. **Level 1** The parameters of the evolution strategy are grouped in sets of two and seven parameters to define the properties of the regulatory units and the structural genes. **Level 2** The sum of all regulatory units and structural genes is the genome. Although all the cells of a tissue or an organism have the same genome, different sets of genes can be active in different cells and produce different cell types. **Level 3** On the third level the cells have to be able to create structures fulfilling the specified tasks encoded in the fitness function.

```
Create n x n x n grid
Repeat
    Initialize first cells
    Diffuse organizing gradients in the grid
    Repeat
      Do for every grid point
        Update cell
          Update gene activities
          Update gene products
          Call developmental processes
        Update environment
          Update diffusing signals
          Update synapses
          Update axons
      End Do
    Until designer set end is reached
  Calculate fitness
  Reproduce and select
    Put fitness in sorting table
    Sort table
    Reproduce the fittest individuals
Until stop criterium is fulfilled
```

The Structural Genes

Seven parameters (all real valued numbers) encode the properties of each structural gene.

- The first parameter determines what happens if a gene is activated. In the current implementation an active gene either produces a substance such as a signalling molecule or it can activate a predefined function such as cell division. The designer can choose how many of these functions he wants to investigate. Section " Classes of gene products" enumerates which substances and functions were used for the experiments described in this paper.

- The second parameter is used to calculate the probability of an interaction with a partner molecule. This affinity parameter *aff* determines which molecule (signalling molecule or axonal receptor) interacts with which partner (regulatory unit or receptor). To each molecule in the simulation a real valued number and a function is assigned, which calculates an artificial binding affinity between the molecules. This function is implemented as follows:

$$a_{12} = f_{aff}(aff_1, aff_2) = e^{-\alpha(aff_1 - aff_2)^2} \quad (1)$$

aff_1, aff_2 are the real valued numbers representing the geometric properties of the substances and are encoded in the parameter set of the evolutionary strategy. α is the affinity parameter with positive values. If α is high, the two substances have to be very similar (i.e.$aff_1 \sim aff_2$) to get a high functional f_{aff} value, if α is low, the substances can be more different to still get high f_{aff} values. Molecules compete for a docking site (cis-regulator, receptor) and their success of binding depends on the affinity between the molecule and the docking site and on the concentrations of the competitors.

- The third parameter determines the sign of the effect e_{ij}, i.e. inhibitory or excitatory.

- The fourth parameter specifies the threshold ϑ. This parameter determines how high the sum of the products of all the affinities a_{ij} between the signalling molecules and the regulators times their concentrations has to be in order to turn on or off the associated structural gene.

- The fifth parameter designates the decay d_i rate for the product.

- The sixth parameter is used to store the affinity parameter α

- The seventh parameter is used as the diffusion parameter D_1

The Regulatory Units

One or several regulatory units control a structural gene. Regulatory units are switches that control the activity of the structural gene. Active regulatory units influence the activity of the structural gene, but only an activated structural gene is able to generate a response such as cell migration or the production of a receptor. Two parameters are assigned to every regulatory unit:

- an affinity aff_{RU}. This parameter has the same use as the affinity parameter in a structural gene. A signalling molecule is defined by the parameters encoded in the structural gene. Both affinity parameters are used to calculate the probability for an interaction between a regulator and a signalling molecule. Both factors are variables of the affinity function $aff_{Tot} = f_{aff}(aff_T, aff_S)$ and its value will influence the probability of a gene's activation.

- threshold. In order to activate a gene, the product of the affinity aff_{Tot} and the concentration of the signalling molecule has to exceed this value.

Gene Regulation

Whether a given gene at position (i, j, k) in a cell on the grid will be activated depends on the affinity and concentration of all the signalling molecules at that position. All these influences are summed up and if this sum exceeds the gene's threshold the gene will be activated or inhibited according to the sign of the effect. All these parameters are varied by the evolutionary strategy and used to explore the interaction space for useful developmental processes able to solve the designer defined tasks. The gene activity of the i-th gene depends on parameters of the structural gene and its regulatory units. The genetic regulatory mechanism is implemented according to the following equations:

$$G_i(c_{sm_0}, \ldots, c_{sm_m}) = \frac{1}{2}(1.0 + \tanh(x)) \qquad (2)$$

$$x = \sum_{j=0} (\Theta(a_{ij} c_{sm_j} - \vartheta_j))$$

$$\Theta(x) = \begin{cases} 1.0 & : \text{ if } x > 0 \\ 0.0 & : \text{ otherwise} \end{cases}$$

Where:

- G_i is the activity of the i-th gene
- $\tanh(x)$ is the hyperbolic tangent.
- $a_i j$ affinity to encode the effect between the regulatory unit i and the signalling molecule j (also referred to as transcription factors if they regulate the gene activity).
- c_{SM_j} concentration of the signalling molecules j
- θ_j is a threshold value
- β is a parameter affecting the steepness of Θ

The regulatory units function as reading heads for the concentrations of signalling molecules (inside the cell they are also called transcription factors), which will then determine the state of a gene. The differential equations describing the whole system are:

$$\frac{dg_i(x, y, z, t)}{dt} =$$

$$G_i(c_{sm_0}, .., c_{sm_m}) + D_1 \nabla^2 g_i(x, y, z, t) \qquad (3)$$

where:

- $gi(x, y, z, t)$: concentration of substance i at grid point (x, y, z) at time t
- m: number of signalling molecules
- D_1: diffusion constant
- $G_i(c_{SM_0}, .., c_{SM_m})$: see formula (2)
- $D1 \; \nabla^2 gi(x, y, z, t)$: diffusion term

Classes of Gene products

The activation of a gene leads to two types of responses: Either a simulated molecule is produced or a function (implemented as a procedure) is executed. The link between the activation of a gene and its response depends on the first of the seven parameters of a structural gene. The following responses were implemented for the experiments in this paper:

1. Production of chemical substances
   (a) a signalling molecule is produced to communicate between the cells.
   (b) a cell adhesion molecule (CAM) is produced to connect the current cell to another one.
   (c) receptors are produced for signalling molecules, axons and synapses.
   (d) synapses bound receptor controlling the synaptic weight
2. The activation of a gene calls a predefined function of the following types:
   (a) cell division
   (b) axonal outgrowth
   (c) synaptogenesis

The number of different substance classes as well as the number of functions is designer specified and depends on the problem the designer wants to solve. The possible interactions of a chemical substance with a partner molecule depend on the affinity between them (see formula 1) and therefore it is possible that a signalling molecule can interact with different partners.

Inter-cellular communication and cell differentiation

By the gene regulatory mechanism described above the AES is able to simulate cell differentiation based on positional information of diffusible factors or uneven distribution of factors inside the cell. Cell differentiation is the process by which the cells become different because different subset of genes are active in them. Depending on the history of influences a cell has been exposed to, different subset of genes will be active and therefore different cell types will emerge. Note that no genetic information is needed to specify the cell type, because the latter is determined by the inter-cellular communication. (Remember all the cells contain the same genome!). Signalling molecules produced by a cell can diffuse to nearby cells, where they may induce a change of state of some genes, which are influenced differently by the different concentrations of the signalling molecules. Note that this communication mechanism depends on the concentration, the affinity of the signalling molecules as well as the regulatory units of the genes. The reading mechanisms (the regulatory units) vary in their affinity, which explains the different effects on the different cells. The possibility of a cell group to produce a signalling molecule to induce another cell type is an important exploratory mechanism of the AES. It allows exploring new possibilities of communication pathways or neural connections (see Figure 2).

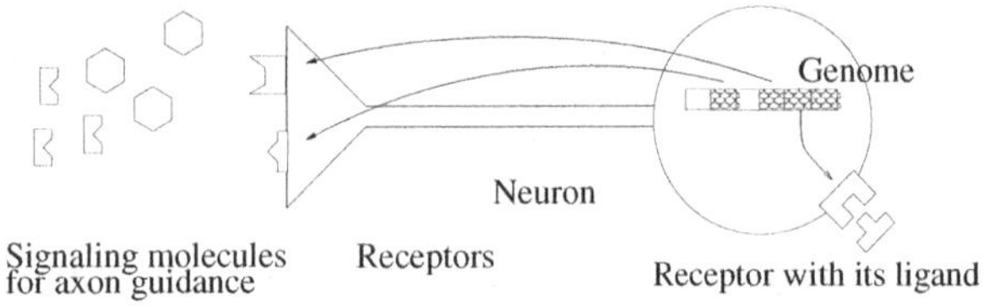

Figure 2: Gene activation. Every cell contains a genome with regulatory units and structural genes. The interactions between regulatory units and signalling molecules determine when a gene becomes active; an active structural gene will then produce a product such as a receptor or will call a function such as axonal outgrowth or cell division.

Neurons

In this section mechanisms pertinent to neural growth and change of synaptic weights are described.

Axonal Outgrowth The interactions between the axonal receptors and the signalling molecules and their respective concentrations determine the direction of the next move an axon will undertake. The effect of the interactions between receptors and signalling molecules at a position (x, y, z) is calculated as follows:

$$I_i = \frac{1}{1 + e^{-(\sum_{i=1}^{n} \omega_{i,j} r_i s_j - \theta_i)}} \tag{4}$$

$I_i = I_i(w, r, s, x, y, z, t)$ is the influence of signalling molecules on the i-th receptor at location (x, y, z) on the grid at time t. The influence is a function of the ligand-receptor interactions and their respective concentrations. r_i is the concentration of the i-th receptor at position (x, y, z) and time t, s_j the concentration of the j-th signalling molecule at position (x, y, z) and time t, $\omega_{i,j}$ the affinity between signalling molecule i and the receptor j and θ_i is a threshold. This formula is calculated in a user-specified range around the current location of the axons, and the next position of the axon on the grid will be in the direction of the biggest influence. The axons are able to read gradients of chemicals and avoid or approach them by reading the concentration differences locally. If an axons finds a cell with matching receptors a link is established.

Neuronal Activity Standard artificial neurons were used in the model and their activities were calculated according to the following formula:

$$S_i = \sigma(\sum_{i=1}^{n} \omega_{i,j} S_j - \Theta) + \text{noise} \tag{5}$$

S_i activity of the i-th neuron, $\omega_{i,j}$ synaptic weight between the i-th and the j-th neuron, Θ is the threshold and σ is the sigmoidal function $\sigma(x) = \frac{1}{1+e^{-x}}$.
The noise term is a randomly added value to allow for spontaneous neural activity.

Control of the Synaptic Weights The change of the synaptic weight depends on specific molecular interactions. The synapses can express receptors whose activity is proportional to the synaptic weight change. One or more receptors can control the weight change and therefore the AES is able to evolve sophisticated learning rules without pre-defining rules how to apply them.

$$\Delta\omega_{i,j} = (\eta \text{rec}_{N_i} \text{rec}_{\text{Syn}_i} \text{rec}_{A_j} - d)\omega_{i,j} \tag{6}$$

Where $\omega_{i,j}$ is the synaptic weight, η the rate of weight change, rec_{N_i} the receptor activity specific for a signalling molecule N_i, $\text{rec}_{\text{Syn}_i}$ the receptor activity for the synapse i, rec_{A_j} represents the activity of neuron j and d the decay rate of the synaptic weight.

Description of the robot arm

Our experiments are performed using a five degrees of freedom industrial robot manipulator (Mitsubishi MELFA RV-2AJ), equipped with a color CCD - camera that is mounted on the robot's end effector. This setup is often called an eye-in-hand configuration. Two Pentium(r) III 600 MHz computers, with 256MB are used, one for capturing the frames with a Hauppauge frame grabber, with a resolution of 256 × 256 pixels at a rate of 20Hz, and the other for controlling the robot itself. We

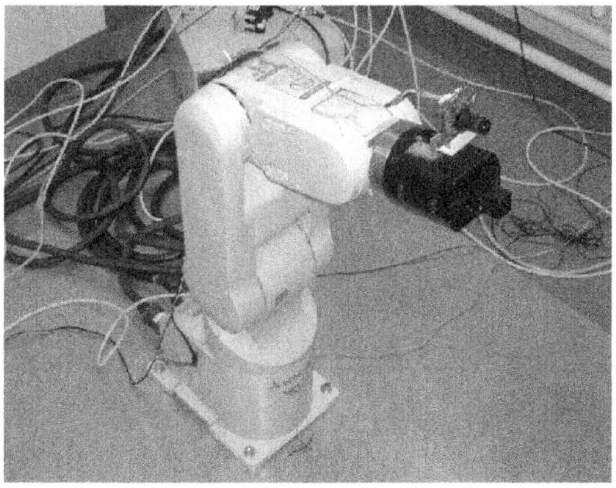

Figure 3: See also Figure 11 for the details of how the camera is mounted on the arm.

built a local area network (LAN) to allow the computers communicate with each other and with the robot, by a client server application made in C++ over the TCP/IP protocol.

Simulations

In order to evolve a foveating retina the following setting was used (see figure 4). Sensors in the receptor field can be activated by light. One or several neuronal fields of growing neurons and one motor field are prepared. All fields are arrays of cells and the designer fixes their maximal size (this maximal size was fixed to limit the computational load). The motor field is connected to two pairs of antagonistic motors, which turn the retina around two orthogonal axes to allow simulating foveating movements. To illustrate the proposed evolutionary approach a retinal structure was evolved. Figure 4 gives a schematic overview of the neural network. The task of the system is to evolve a neural network that can move the eye in such a way that an incoming peripheral sensory stimulus falls in the center of the "eye", in other words the eye has to learn to foveate on the stimulus. The fitness function depends on the number of cells, on the movements, and on the precision of the movements measured by the deviation of the position of a stimulus from the center of the eye after peripheral stimulation. The evolutionary results are illustrated in figure 5. The progress during the learning of the foveating task of a successful individual is illustrated in Figure 9 and the learning progress over several runs is shown in Figure 5. In the beginning the genome consisted of 18 genes, each controlled by maximally four regulatory genes. Three symmetry breaking sources were used for each run. To tune the genetic parameters for the developmental processes, a (μ, λ)-evolution strategy with a global step size σ (initial value 0.2) was used. The notation indicates that the procedure generates λ offsprings from μ parents and that it selects the parents only from the best offspring for the next generation. The step size is inherited from the parents to the offspring and is modified by log-normally-distributed random numbers. Every retinal sensor was activated independently of the others and the difference between the wished and the actual movement

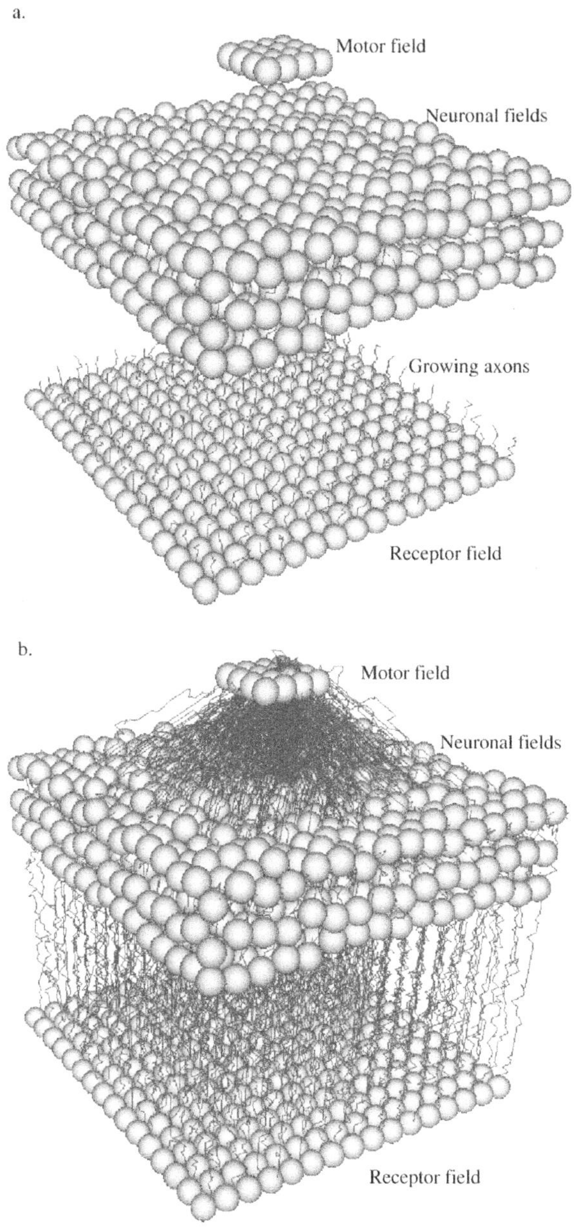

Figure 4: a. Growing neural network, b. The final neural network controlling a foveating retina. One single cell is placed in every field which have for computational reasons an upper limit of 20×20. The cells are allowed to grow inside the predefined fields. All connections and the cellular properties are under evolutionary control and are determined by genetic and developmental processes. The receptor field (bottom row of the cells which emit topological, parallel axons) captures the light stimulation. The activity of the cells in the motor layer causes the eyes to move in four directions (up, down, right and left).

vector was summed up and used as fitness value.

$$f = \sum_{i,j} a_{i,j} + (v_{a_{i,j}} - v_{r_{i,j}})^2 \quad (7)$$

- f fitness value
- i, j are indexes running over all retinal sensors
- $a_{i,j}$ activity of motor neurons after stimulation of retinal sensor (i, j)
- $v_{a_{i,j}}$ actual motor vector after activating the retinal sensor at the position (i, j).
- $v_{r_{i,j}}$ designer specified target value for the motor vector

Results

Simulation Results

Figure 5 shows a typical evolutionary run over time. Typically the task was solved after 300-500 generations using a (20,600)-evolution strategy. First the fitness in-

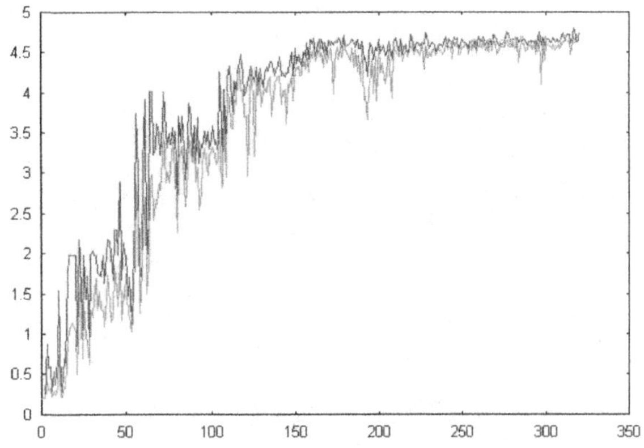

Figure 5: Fitness of a typical run of the evolution of the foveating retina plotted against number of generations.

creased because the sensory cells and the neurons learned to link each other to the motor cells. Over time more and more motor cells received input from the other layers and were able to move. A typical example is illustrated in figure 6a, which shows the movement patterns of evolved neural controllers after stimulating each single sensor and indicating the motor response to it. Over time the results became better and the system learned to foveate. A typical fitness curve is shown in Figure 5. Figure 6 shows some typical examples of individuals with increasingly higher fitness. Preliminary analysis of the cellular dynamics by blocking genes showed that the center of the retina contained special sensory cells, which diffused a signalling molecule whenever they become active. This molecule was able to increase the synaptic weight of the synapses between the neuronal fields and the motor field when the motor neurons were active (see Figure 7). The emitted substance had a receptor on the synapses connecting to the motor neurons. Active motor neurons in turn emitted a substance that could bind to another synaptic receptor. If both of the receptors were active, the synaptic weights were increased by producing a substance representing the synaptic weight. The effect of this mechanism was that sensory stimulation resulted in a direct jump into the rewarding center (see Figures 6b and 6h as such examples).

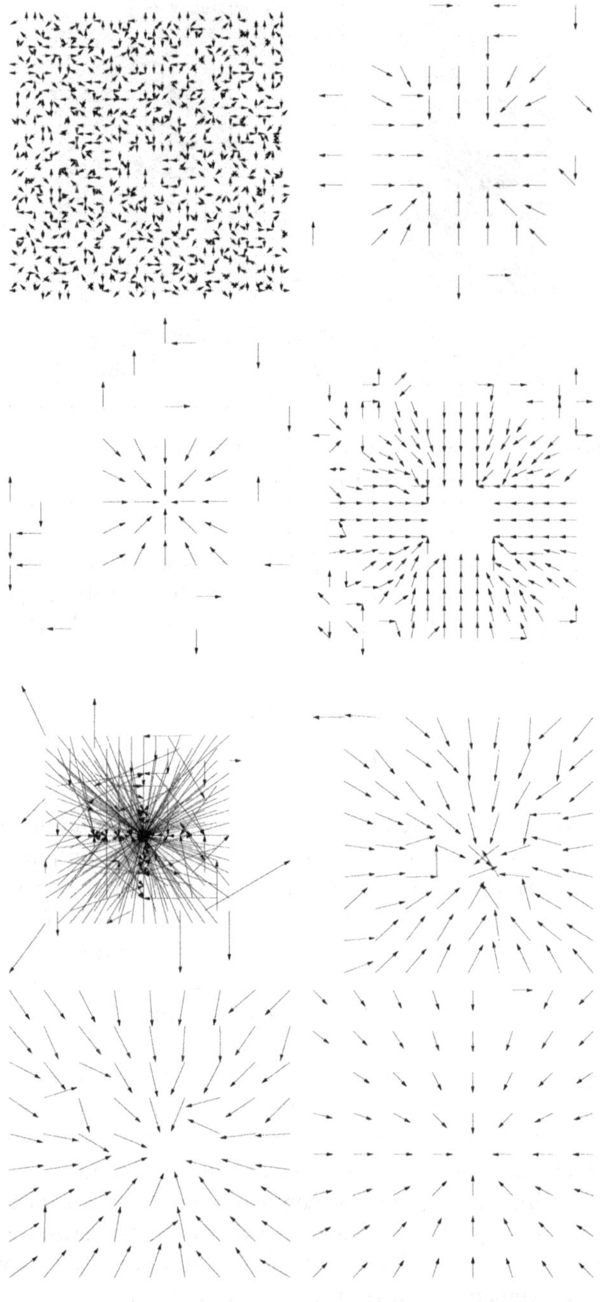

Figure 6: Examples of evolved behaviors. A vector representing the movement of the evolved retina after the stimulation of the corresponding sensor is plotted at every location of the sensor.

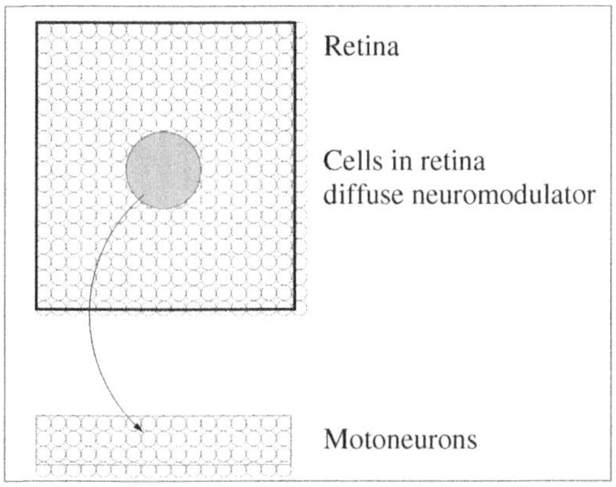

Figure 7: First example of two different evolved foveating systems. In the center of the retina specialized cells emerged, which emit a signalling molecule if the central cells are activated.

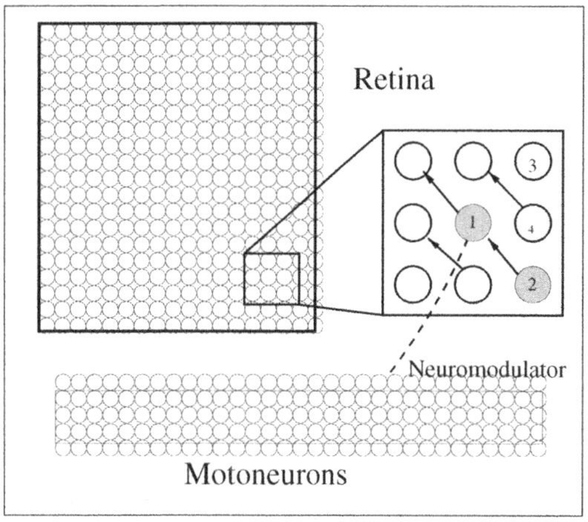

Figure 8: Second example of two different evolved foveating systems. The sensory neurons of the evolved neural network are connected in such a way that a peripheral sensory neuron is connected to neighbor cell closest to the center of the retina. If a sensory neuron is activated it will transmit a signalling molecule to its neighbor cell. In case that this cell will also be activated, a neuromodulator is diffused to the motor field and the weights of the active motor neurons are changed in order to increase the probability to repeat the same movement again.

By adding a new term to the fitness function, namely how long the network needed to learn the foveating tasks, a new mechanism was found. The diffusing cells were connected in a concentric manner (see Figure 8). A signalling molecule for the synapses was only emitted if the direction of the movement from one cell to the other was correct. This morphological change of the neural net allowed for a faster learning mechanism, because the chances to evoke a correct movement were higher in this scheme. Using this second scheme we succeeded in increasing the number of cells without a decrease of the fitness. This second mechanism was robust against an increase of the number of cells and the result is illustrated in Figure 9. Over time the movements get better and better. To check the performance of the learning mechanism we repeated the learning task seven times and the results are shown in Figure 10.

Transfer of the evolved results to a real robot arm

We used a Mitsubishi robot arm equipped with a CCD-camera to see if we were able to transfer the evolved solution to the real world. The arm with the camera is shown in Figure 11. In a first trial we just used the evolved synaptic weights and the structure of the evolved neural network to control the movements of the robot arm. First, the movements of the arm were gauged in order to get the same units for the movements. In other words we multiplied the motor values in such a way that the arm moved in the same direction and with the same amplitude as the same vector in the simulation. Secondly we had to make sure that the sensory input was similar to the evolved one as shown in Figure 12. For this we choose a monitor at a distance of 1.60 m from the camera as a sensory input, which gave us a small, rectangular input. After that we performed foveating experiments in order to test the controller. The sensory input was put on the periphery of the camera and the tracking paths to the center were stored on a computer. Although the tracks wiggle considerably the overall picture resembles quite nicely to the results shown in Figure 9. The wiggling is due to the fluctuations of the sensory input (see Figure 12), which caused small deviations from the evolved movements. Despite of this fact the arm was still able to foveate considerably well as Figure 13 illustrates.

Conclusions and Discussions

Though the use of models of developmental processes based on genetic regulatory networks, of patterning mechanisms and of mechanisms for synaptic weight change the information encoded in the genome required are significantly reduced. Although more complex than a direct encoding scheme the proposed AES shows good scaling behavior and is independent on the number of cells, neurons or synapses. Furthermore, the rules where and when to apply a developmental rule are all evolved and the designer restrictions are only on the level of the different structural genes (representing effectors, sensor types, pigments for wing patterns etc). Also the interplay between the patterning of a neural structure and the mechanisms changing the neural communication (synaptic as well as cellular) are now within the reach of the proposed AES as illustrated with the example of the evolved retina.

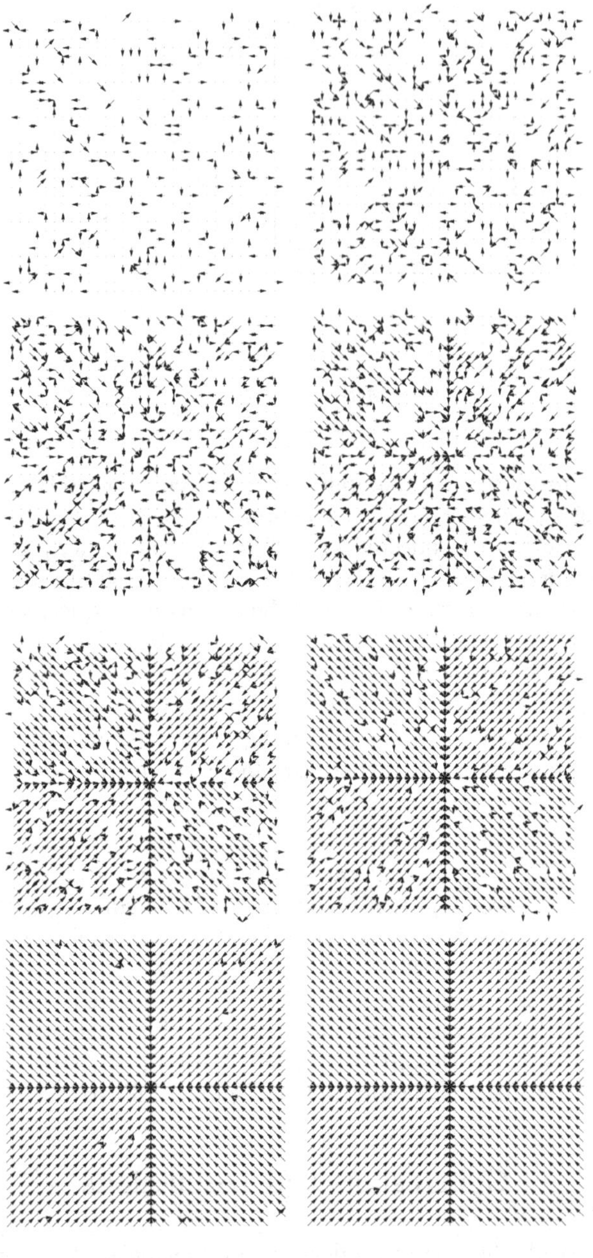

Figure 9: Change of the eye movements over ontogenetic time. At every location of a sensor a vector is plotted, which represents the movement of the retina. Guided by the evolved learning mechanisms the systems learns over time to foveate almost perfectly. The observed errors in the best plot are due to random movements due to noise.

Future Work

In a next step we will use not only the neural net, but also the learning mechanism to control the robot arm and investigate the robustness of the system against change of external conditions such as motor force and sensory input. Moreover we will extend the foveating mechanism to binocular vision and vergence control. At a later stage, the entire visuo-motor system will be evolved.

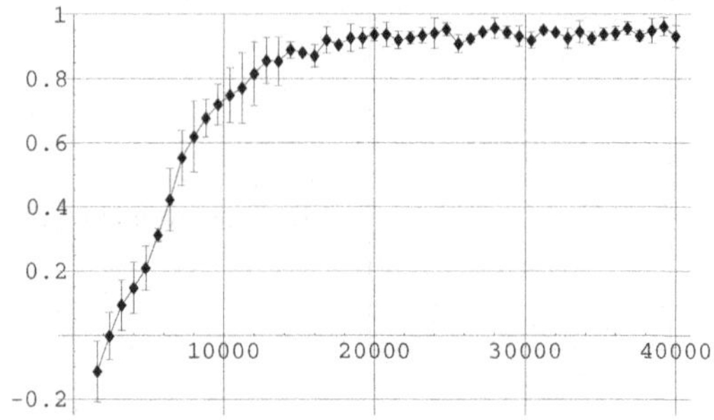

Figure 10: Learning curves for acquisition of foveation of the retina by actuating the four motors. The performance is illustrated as the mean and standard deviation over seven runs. The system was able to perform foveation after 30000 iterations with a retina of 32×32 sensory input cells.

Figure 11: Test of the evolved controller on a CCD camera mounted on a Mitsubishi robot arm.

Acknowledgments

Part of this work was supported by Dr. K. Shimohara of ATR. The other part was funded by HYDRA, an EU project.

References

Barnsley, M. 1993. *Fractals Everywhere.* Morgan Kaufmann Publishers.

Belew, R. K. 1993. Interposing an ontogenic model between genetic algorithms and neural networks. In *Advances in Neural Information Processing Systems (NIPS),S.J. Hanson and J.D. Cowan and C.L.Giles,Morgan Kauffman:San Mate,1993.*

Brooks, R., and Maes, P., eds. 1994. *Artificial Life IV: Proceedings of the Workshop on Artificial Life.* Cambridge, MA: MIT Press. Workshop held at the MIT.

Cangelosi, A.; Parisi, D.; and Nolfi, S. 1994. Cell divi-

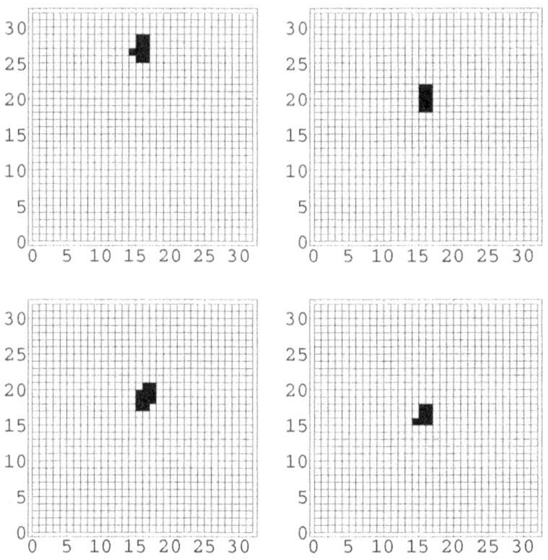

Figure 12: Typical retina activities during a foveation process. Note that always several light sensors of the retina are active and that the activity pattern is changing.

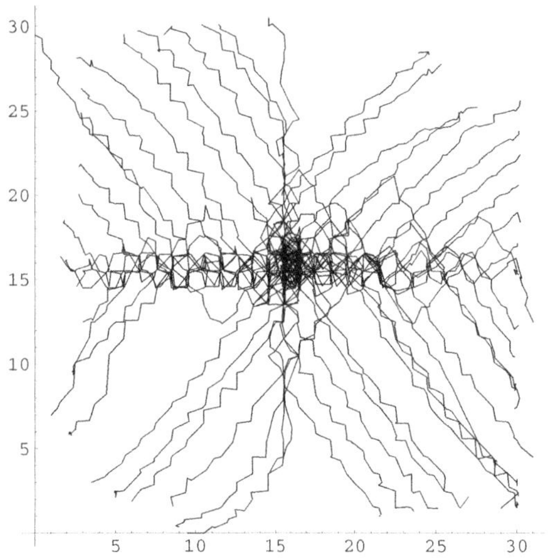

Figure 13: Trajectories from 57 trials of a light point recorded from the camera mounted on the robot arm. All the trajectories move from the periphery towards the center, thus modelling foveating behavior.

sion and migration in a 'genotype' for neural networks. *Network* 5:497–515.

Dellaert, F., and Beer, R. D. 1996. A developmental model for the evolution of complete autonomous agents. In (Maes *et al.* 1996), 393–401.

Fleischer, K., and Barr, A. H. 1992. A simulation testbed for the study of multicellular development: The multiple mechanisms of morphogenesis. In (Langton 1994), 389–416.

Gerhart, J., and Kirschner, M. 1997. *Cells, Embryos and Evolution: Toward a cellular and Developmental Understanding of Phenotypic Variation and Evolutionary Adaptability.* Oxford: Blackwell.

Gerstner, W.; Germond, A.; Hasler, M.; and (Eds.), J.-D. N., eds. 1997. *Seventh International Conference of Artificial Neural Networks (ICANN'97).* Cambridge, MA: Springer.

Gruau, F., and Whitley, D. 1993. The cellular developmental of neural networks: the interaction of learning and evolution. Technical Report 93-04, Laboratoire de l'Informatique du Parallélisme, Ecole Normale Supérieure de Lyon, France.

Kitano, H. 1994. Evolution of metabolism for morphogenesis. In Brooks, R. A., and Maes, P., eds., (Brooks & Maes 1994), 49–58.

Kodjabachian, J., and Meyer, J.-A. 1998. Evolution and development of neural controllers for locomotion, gradient-following, and obstacle-avoidance in artificial insects. *IEEE Transactions on Neural Networks* 9(5):796–812.

Langton, C. G., ed. 1994. *Artificial Life III: Proceedings of the Workshop on Artificial Life.* Reading, MA: Addison-Wesley. Workshop held June, 1992 in Santa Fe, New Mexico.

Maes, P.; Mataric, M. J.; Meyer, J.-A.; Pollack, J.; and Wilson, S. W., eds. 1996. *From animals to animats 4: Proceedings of the fourth international conference on simulation of adaptive behavior.* MIT Press.

Michel, O., and Bondi, J. 1995. From the chromosome to the neural network. In *Proceedings of the internatioal conference on artificial Neural Networks and Genetic Algorithms (ICANNA'95).*

Sims, K. 1995. Evolving 3D morphology and behavior by competition. *Artificial Life* 1:353–372.

Vaario, J., and Shimohara, K. 1997. Synthesis of developmental and evolutionary modeling of adaptive autonomous agents. In (Gerstner *et al.* 1997), 721–726.

Wolpert, L. 1998. *Principles of Development.* Oxford University Press.

A Stochastic Evolutionary Neuron Migration Process with Emerged Hebbian Dynamics

Janne Haverinen and **Juha Röning**
Infotech Oulu and Department of Electrical Engineering
P.O. Box 4500, FIN-90014 University Of Oulu
FINLAND
e-mail: janne.haverinen@oulu.fi

Abstract

In this paper, we propose a phenomenological developmental model based on a stochastic evolutionary neuron migration process (SENMP). Employing a spatial encoding scheme with lateral interaction of neurons for artificial neural networks representing candidate solutions within a neural network ensemble[1], neurons of the ensemble form problem-specific geometrical structures as they migrate under selective pressure. The SENMP is applied to evolve purposeful behaviors for autonomous robots and to gain new insights into the development, adaptation and plasticity in artificial neural networks. We demonstrate the feasibility and advantages of the approach by evolving a robust navigation behavior for a mobile robot. We also present some preliminary results regarding the behavior of the adapting neural network ensemble and, particularly, a phenomenon exhibiting Hebbian dynamics.

Introduction

Brain nerve cells are initially produced in the center of the developing brain. To function normally, neurons must migrate to the brain cortex and other structures. Migration is a process that relies on chemical communication between many different cells. The geometrical structure of the brain is a result of this complex process, following an inside-out sequence of development (Pinel 1997).

Recent discoveries in neuroscience confirm the relation between the shape of neural tissue and its function (Csernansky, Joshi, & Wang 1998). Using a technique called morphometrics, which is a mathematical way of studying shape, investigators have found that, in some brain disorders of developmental origin, a functional abnormality in the brain may be accompanied by a structural malformation. While differences in size seem less important, the deformities appear consistent.

Inspired by the recent findings regarding the development and function of the brain, we implemented a phenomenological developmental model based on the stochastic evolutionary neuron migration process, (SENMP)[2] to gain new insights into the development, adaptation, and plasticity in artificial neural networks.

Employing a spatial encoding scheme with lateral interaction of neurons for artificial neural networks representing candidate solutions within a neural network ensemble and applying an evolutionary algorithm to implement the stochastic motion of neurons through generations of ensembles, problem-specific neural structures emerge that are able to solve real problems in perception and robot control.

This study is part of a long-range goal to understand the universal mechanisms acting in a successfully adapting neural circuit of an artificial life form interacting with its environment. We underline the role of geometrical structures in the computational properties of artificial neural circuits, believing that they also have an essential role in living organisms, providing compact genetic representations and neural plasticity.

We demonstrate the feasibility of our approach by developing a robust navigation behavior for a mobile robot. We also show some preliminary results about the behavior of the adapting neural network ensemble, particularly a phenomenon exhibiting Hebbian dynamics.

The Model

The Encoding Scheme

From a neurobiological viewpoint, there is evidence of lateral interaction between neurons in the sense that a firing neuron tends to excite more the neurons in its immediate vicinity than the more distant neurons (Pinel 1997). Furthermore, the recent findings in neuroscience provide new evidence for the relation between the shape and function of neural tissue (Csernansky, Joshi, & Wang 1998), (Castellano Smith 1999). The above-mentioned evidence motivated us to employ a spatial encoding scheme for an artificial neural network that exhibits simple lateral interaction of neurons and promotes the role of morphology in the function of the neural circuit.

The idea of using 2-D geometry to evolve neural networks has been studied earlier by at least Nolfi (Nolfi & Parisi 1995), Cangelosi (Cangelosi, Nolfi, & Parisi 1994), Husbands (Husbands 1998), and Kodjabachian (Kodjabachian & Meyer 1998). With the exception of Husbands, the spatial encoding scheme has been mainly a tool for defining the topology of the artificial neural

[1] In this paper, the term 'neural network ensemble' is used to refer to the neural network population in order to emphasize the fact that the continuous behavior of the robot is a result of the evaluation sequence of the individual neural networks.

[2] In this paper, the term 'stochastic evolutionary neuron migration' is used to refer to the stochastic motion of the neurons of the neural network ensemble through generations of ensembles under selective pressure, not the real-time motion of neurons.

network, i.e. the number of neurons and their connectivity. In Husbands' GasNets, however, network geometry has a crucial role in describing the modulating effect of "diffusing gas" on neuron outputs. Although our approach is based on more connectionistic networks than Husbands', it shares the important role of spatial distribution of neurons to the function of the neural network.

The genotype G of the neural network is a set

$$G = \{g_k : k = 0, 1, \ldots, n-1\}$$

where n is the number of neurons and

$$g_k = (x_k, y_k, \theta_k, \phi_k)$$

where x_k, y_k, θ_k, and ϕ_k are the coordinates in 2-D space, the phase, and the feedback factor (explained in the next section) of neuron k, respectively. The index k specifies whether g_k represents an input neuron, a hidden neuron, or an output neuron. $k = [0, l-1]$ for input, $k = [l, l+m-1]$ for hidden, and $k = [l+m, n-1]$ for output neurons, respectively. l is the number of input neurons, and m is the number of hidden neurons. The number of output neurons is $n - (m+l) > 0$.

The connection weights are implicitly determined by the corresponding spatial distribution of neurons, i.e. the Euclidean distances of neurons and their phases as shown in Equation 1, which indicate the strength of the connection between neuron j and neuron i.

$$w_{ji} = \sin(\theta_j - \theta_i) e^{-d_{ji}^2/2\sigma^2} \quad (1)$$

where d_{ji} is the Euclidean distance between the neurons j and i in 2-D space normalized by the maximum distance between any two neurons in the network. More precisely, if $p_k = [x_k \; y_k]^T$ then

$$d_{ji} = \frac{\|p_j - p_i\|}{\max_{l \neq m}(\|p_l - p_m\|)} \quad (2)$$

The Gaussian neighborhood function in Equation 1 defines the physical constraints for the local interactions between neurons and, thus, for the information pathways present in the network. The neuron phase ϕ provides a mean for the evolutionary algorithm to modulate the neighborhood function and to define the signs of the connection weights between neurons.

The Neural Network Model

The neuron model used in our experiments is shown in Equation 3,

$$\frac{\partial a_i}{\partial t} = -\tau a_i + \sum_{j \neq i}^{n} \Theta(\phi_i) w_{ji} \Phi(a_j) + I_i \quad (3)$$

where a_i, Φ, ϕ_i, I_i are the activation potential, the activation function, the feedback factor, and the current sensory input of neuron i, respectively. w_{ji} is the connection weight between the neurons j and i. The definition of Θ, shown in Equation 4, depends on whether the connection from neuron j to neuron i is a feed-forward (i.e. a connection from the lower layer) or a feedback connection (i.e. a connection from the upper or the same layer).

$$\Theta(\phi) = \begin{cases} 1 & \text{, for feedforward conns.} \\ \tanh(\phi) & \text{, for feedback conns.} \end{cases} \quad (4)$$

The feedback factor ϕ is used to tune the effect of the local environment (i.e. the surrounding neurons) outside the initial topology to the state of the neuron. The activation function $\Phi(x) = \tanh(x)$.

The SENMP

We implemented the stochastic motion of neurons, establishing the geometrical structure of the neural network ensemble, using an evolutionary algorithm (EA). The fundamental reason to use the stochastic motion of neurons over developmental models (i.e. rules) ((Fleischer & Barr 1994), (Nolfi & Parisi 1995), (Astor & Adami 2000), (Cangelosi, Nolfi, & Parisi 1994), (Kodjabachian & Meyer 1998)) was to avoid heuristic constraints in pattern formation. Furthermore, we used the stochastic process to learn how the neurons within the neural network ensemble behave while the ensemble adapts to an environment.

The SENMP is started by creating a set P of random genotypes (i.e. neural networks)

$$P = \{G_n : n = 0, 1, \ldots, N-1\}$$

where N is the population size (i.e. the size of the neural network ensemble). For each neuron k, the phase θ_k gets a random value between $[-\pi, \pi]$ and the coordinates x_k and y_k get random values between $[-\lambda, \lambda]$, where λ is the amplitude of the random noise ν introduced by the mutation operator to the parameters g_k of the neuron k. The feedback factor ϕ is initialized to zero for all neurons, meaning no feedback prior the adaptation process (i.e. no connections outside the initial (feedforward) topology).

When the initial neural network ensemble is created, a fitness function $f(G)$ is used to assign a fitness value for each genotype G (i.e. a neural network within the ensemble). For each neural network k, there is a time window Δt_c for controlling the robot, after which fitness $f(G_k)$ is assigned for the neural network. The next neural network taking control over the robot inherits the neuronal (i.e. the action potentials, ϕ) and environmental state of the previous one. The behavior of the robot is a result of the evaluation sequence of the individual neural networks. State inheritance (both internal and external) is used to establish a state continuum providing information about the actions of the previous neural networks.

When all neural networks have been evaluated, a new neural network ensemble is created of the best m individuals (according to the assigned fitness value) of the previous ensemble. In our experiments, m is 40% of the original population size. The new generation is created out of these m individuals by using roulette wheel selection. Two different parents are selected for the new individual, which is built up by taking each of its g_k (i.e. neuron) from one of its two parents with equal probability and from the same genotype index k. After the recombination, a mutation operator is applied for each neuron of the new individual in such a way that

$$g_k = (x_k + \nu_x, y_k + \nu_y, \theta_k + \nu_\theta, \phi_k + \nu_\phi)$$

for all k. ν_x,ν_y, ν_θ, and ν_ϕ get random values from the interval $[-\lambda, \lambda]$. After the new generation has been created, the evaluation proceeds as explained above.

Figure 1 illustrates how neurons migrate through generations of neural network ensembles. At the beginning of the SENMP, all neurons locate within a circle whose radius is λ. As the SENMP proceeds, the neurons migrate through the 2-D space to their 'final' locations due to the selective pressure.

While the amplitude λ of the noise ν introduced by the mutation operator is constant, the effect of noise on the behavior of the robot (i.e. the connection weights of the neural networks) is most significant at the beginning of the adaptation due to the Equations 1 and 2 and the fact that the diameter of the neuron distribution is of the same order than λ. At this phase, the robot is in its most adaptive state, making most of the mistakes necessary for learning. As the SENMP proceeds and the neurons get farther away from each other, the effect of noise ν decreases and the behavior of the robot stabilizes.

The evolution of the diameter of the neuron distribution is analogous to the cooling schedule of the well known optimization method called simulated annealing (Kirkpatric, C.D. Gelatt, & Vecchi 1983) based on principles found from the statistical mechanics.

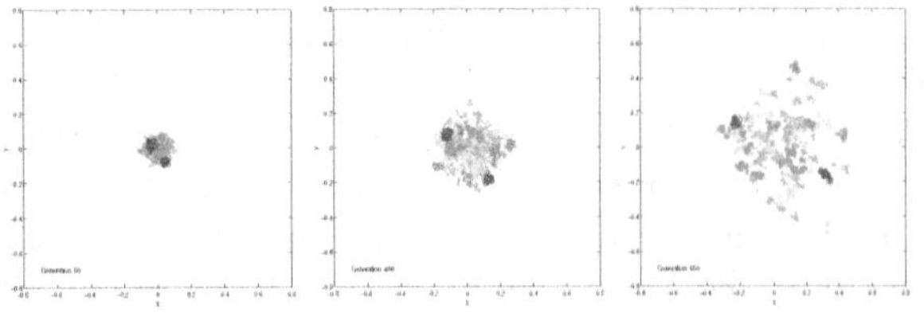

Figure 1: The distribution of neurons of the neural ensemble at generations 50, 400 and 950, respectively. Intermediate gray, light gray and dark gray are used to indicate input, hidden, and output neurons, respectively.

Experiment

The purpose of the experiment was to develop a neural network ensemble exhibiting a *working* navigation behavior for a real office environment and to collect data from the SENMP for subsequent analysis.

The learning phase was carried out in a simulator implemented for the Nomad Super Scout mobile robot[3].The robot has a differential driving system and 16 ultrasonic sensors. In our navigation experiments, we used only 9 of the sensors covering a sector of 180 degrees in front of the robot. The measuring range of the sensors was limited to 3.5 meters (11 ft).

The navigation experiment was successfully repeated several times. The SENMP parameters used were: $\lambda = 0.01$, $N = 48$ (i.e. population size), $\sigma^2 = 0.025$, and $\tau = 0.1$. The neural network were fully connected with two hidden layers. The numbers of neurons were 11-41-21-2 for the input layer, for the two hidden layers, and for the output layer, respectively. The input layer consists of 9 sonar sensor neurons and two collision detector (i.e. bumper) neurons. The sonar readings were normalized to the range $[0, 1]$ before feeding to the input neurons. If the robot collides with an obstacle, the two bumper readings get the value of 1, while otherwise they get the value 0. The output layer consists of two velocity control neurons, one for each wheel, having a value between $[-1, 1]$. The sign indicates the direction of rotation. The maximum speed of the real robot was limited to 0.3m/s (1 ft/s).

The fitness function used to assign a score for each individual neural network within the neural ensemble was

$$f(d) = d/(1 + pc_r) \qquad (5)$$

where d, p, and c_r are the radial distance traveled by the robot, the collision penalty rate, and the number of collisions, respectively. In our experiments $p = 0.1$.

Figure 2 illustrates how the robot adapts to the three different environments used in the navigation experiment. The results gained in the simulator were successfully verified with a real Nomad Super Scout mobile robot.

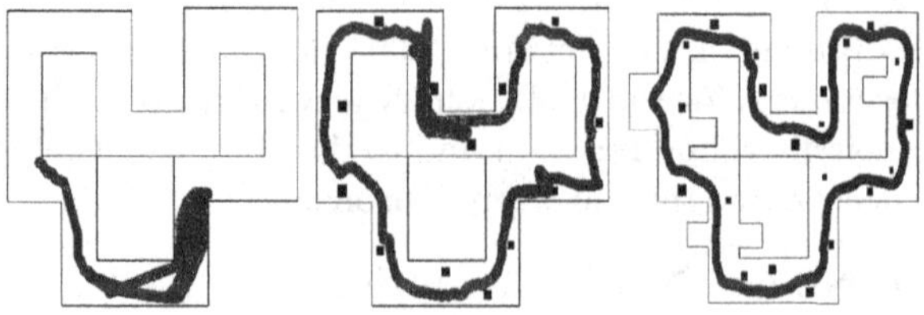

Figure 2: Learning to navigate. Three different environments were introduced to the robot, incrementally increasing the complexity of the world where the robot had to operate. The traces show how the robot gradually adapted to its environment and became able to smoothly navigate through the simulated corridor.

[3]By Nomadic Technologies, Inc.

Discussion

We have shown here that the SENMP can be applied to evolve and adapt neural control structures for mobile robots. The SENMP provides a tool for open-ended modification of geometrical neural structures under selective pressure. The spatial encoding scheme couples the geometry and the function of the neural structure enabling modification of the robot's behavior through migration of neurons, which implements the necessary neural plasticity to the neural network ensemble.

Clusters of neurons emerge over time, and the population of neural networks converges. The clusters provide an opportunity to statistically analyze the behavior of neurons in the adapting neural network ensemble. Although the behavior of neurons is not under local control, it seems that the selective pressure may create such an illusion to an external observer.

After an environmental shift, we collected 15000 activation samples (i.e. outputs of the activation function Φ) for each neuron for 25 generations of adaptation. From the samples we computed the mean correlation coefficients for each pair of neurons[4]. By analyzing the firing correlations, the corresponding connection weights, and the connection weight changes between the neurons, we found out that a significant change[5] in a connection weight was consistently[6] accompanied by a firing correlation with equal sign (See Figure 3). This suggests that Hebbian dynamics, in some form, is an emerged property of the SENMP.

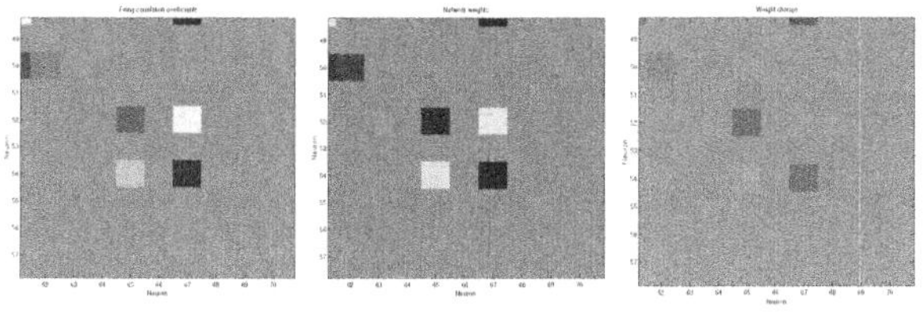

Figure 3: Hebbian dynamics. Closeups from the firing correlation, the connection weight, and the weight change matrices, respectively. The images illustrate the relation between the firing correlation and the evolution of the connection weights. The weight change matrix has been computed for 25 generations of adaptation. The connection weight matrix has been computed from the neural network ensemble at the generation 80. The bright and dark pixels represent positive and negative values, respectively.

[4]Each neuron represents a cluster in the neural network ensemble

[5]The weight change was greater than 75 percent of the maximum weight change

[6]In about 80 and 70 percent of cases with a positive, and a negative weight change, respectively

Acknowledgments

This work is supported by the Finnish Academy.

References

Astor, J., and Adami, C. 2000. A developmental model for the evolution of artificial neural networks. *Artificial Life* 6(3):189–218.

Cangelosi, A.; Nolfi, S.; and Parisi, D. 1994. Cell division and migration in a 'genotype' for neural networks. *Network: Computation in Neural Systems* 5:497–515.

Castellano Smith, A. D. 1999. *The Folding of the Human Brain: From Shape to Function.* Ph.D. Dissertation, University of London (Kings College London).

Csernansky, J.; Joshi, S.; and Wang, L. 1998. Hippocampal morphometry in schizophrenia by high dimensional brain mapping. *Proc Natl Acad Sci USA* 95:11406–11411.

Fleischer, K., and Barr, A. H. 1994. A simulation testbed for the study of multicellular development: The multiple mechanisms of morphogenesis. In Langton, C. G., ed., *Proceedings of the Workshop on Artificial Life (ALIFE '92)*, volume 17 of *Sante Fe Institute Studies in the Sciences of Complexity*, 389–416. Reading, MA, USA: Addison-Wesley.

Husbands, P. 1998. Evolving robot behaviours with diffusing gas networks. In Husbands, P., and Meyer, J., eds., *Proceedings of the First European Workshop on Evolutionary Robotics*, 123–136. Springer Verlag.

Kirkpatric, S.; C.D. Gelatt, J.; and Vecchi, M. 1983. Optimization by simulated annealing". *Science* 220:671–680.

Kodjabachian, J., and Meyer, J.-A. 1998. Evolution and development of neural controllers for locomotion, gradient-following, and obstacle-avoidance in artificial insects. *IEEE-NN* 9(5):796.

Nolfi, S., and Parisi, D. 1995. Evolving artificial neural networks that develop in time. In *European Conference on Artificial Life*, 353–367.

Pinel, J. 1997. *Biopsychology.* Allyn & Bacon Inc., 3rd edition.

Territory Formation in Mobile Robots

Amelie Schmolke and **Hanspeter A. Mallot**
Kognitive Neurowissenschaft
Universität Tübingen, Tübingen, Germany
http://www.uni-tuebingen.de/cog/

Abstract

Animals navigate through their environment using diverse strategies. These navigation strategies might be highly dependent on the animal's ecological niche. Though a lot of work is focused on biological navigation mechanisms, the cognitive ecology of spatial memory is poorly understood. The performances of different navigation mechanisms in the context of a biologically relevant behavior can be assessed by using mobile robots. For this task, territorial behavior was built on Khepera miniature robots. Territoriality is strongly dependent on spatial learning and thus provides a powerful context for testing of sensory and computational complexity needed by animals solving special tasks. Simultaneously, the principles underlying the establishment of territories in a previously uninhabited area and how it is dependent on environmental parameters can be investigated. In the present paper, territoriality in robots is introduced. The robots navigate by relying on poor sensor input and a representation of the environment of a low complexity. Qualitative results show that territories form. Subsequently, the consequences of the introduction of a newcomer in already established territories are presented.

Introduction

If animals navigate through their environment, they generally rely on various orientation mechanisms. By navigating they have to solve problems according to their ecological niche. It can be expected that the navigational mechanisms found in animals are strongly dependent on this niche or — the other way around — that a certain mechanism might be favorable for one species but useless for another. Hence, the performances of navigational strategies have to be determined dependent on their context.

Many attempts have been made to adapt biologically inspired navigation strategies in robotics (for review see Franz & Mallot 2000). In these applications the general functionality and use of certain mechanisms for navigation were shown. However, if the cognitive ecology of spatial memory should be assessed by using mobile robots, the navigational strategies have to be integrated in a behavior. The goal is to find out how valuable different mechanisms are for spatial behaviors since animals usually rely on combinations of multiple mechanisms. Thereby, the least sensory and computational complexity needed for the behavior can be investigated and the performance of individuals with different strategies can be compared.

Territoriality is a behavior which is based on a representation of the animal's environment and thus provides a biological relevant context for the use of navigational strategies. The territorial behavior of Khepera robots presented in this work is based on a model for territory establishment proposed by Stamps and Krishnan (1999). This model is based on spatial learning, but otherwise only uses few assumptions concerning the animals. Besides providing a context for the testing of mechanism of spatial memory, the robot implementation will also improve understanding of territorial behavior in animals.

The building of this model on autonomous robots combines the challenges of navigation with the establishment of a territory. The navigation is based on poor sensory input and a parsimonious memory. Territory formation is a consequence of attractiveness values assigned to each place. This value reflects the probability of return which is dependent on the previous encounters with competitors in that patch of the habitat. The implications of external constraints, like changing environments, on a special behavior can be tested and favorable sensory and cognitive equipment adapted to the ecological niche can be determined. This relates to the question of the evolutionary consequences of changing properties of organisms and ecosystems which is posed by Bedau et al.(2000) as an open problem in artificial life.

The present work addresses the question which mechanisms of spatial memory subserve territorial behavior in a real world environment. We will introduce territoriality in animals and the open problems in this field. A summary of the model of territory formation (Stamps & Krishnan 1999) will be provided afterwards and the territorial robots will be presented.

Territoriality in Animals

A lot of research has been conducted focusing on territorial behavior in different animals. A territory is defined as the part of an individual's (or group's) home range, i.e. the part of the space the animal uses regularly and which it defends against conspecific competitors (Maher & Lott 1995; Stamps & Krishnan 1999). The animal thereby endures the costs of the defense in order to monopolize the resources of the territorial area. Hence, territoriality can only occur if the defended resources are not strongly clustered since the intruder pressure would become too high (Adams 2001).

Territorial behavior appears in various forms in diverse animals. However, similar principles might underly many of the observed behavioral patterns. Such principles are sought to be pinpointed by using models. Many models consider the optimal behavior of a single individual in a habitat which is already divided in territories.

All other individuals are assumed to behave according to one fixed strategy (Adams 2001; Kokko & Lundberg 2001; Baird, Sloan, & Timanus 2001). Maynard Smith (1982) proposed a game-theoretical model in which two individuals "negotiate" the border between their territories. Depending on the costs of fights, an optimal strategy can be found which maximizes the territory size with minimal costs.

A Model of Territory Establishment

The mechanisms that lead to the division of a previously uninhabited area are not well understood. Stamps and Krishnan (1999) proposed a model for the establishment of territories in habitats with homogenous distribution of resources. The model is based on the animals' ability of spatial learning, i.e. the animals first explore their habitat starting from an arbitrary location and simultaneously gaining advantage over individuals that are not familiar with the same patch of the environment. However, the ability of spatial learning is only reflected in a value A_i associated to the patches; the representation of space by the individuals is assumed.

In the following, we summarize the model. It is assumed that the animal gains a better knowledge about an area, consisting of a small part of its habitat, each time it visits it. Since this knowledge is an advantage for the animal, it will return to this area with a higher probability as compared to areas which it visited less frequently. On the other hand, encounters with conspecifics always lead to fights and are thus considered as negative experiences. Hence, the probability of returning to an area where fights took place is reduced. These probabilities are reflected by "attractiveness values" A_i of each area i in the model. They are computed according to the following equation:

$$A_i = P_{\max}\left[1 - e^{-\frac{N_{pi}}{R_p}}\right] - F_{\max}\left[1 - e^{-\frac{N_{fi}}{R_f}}\right]$$

with

$P_{\max}$ = *maximal attractiveness of an area*
N_{pi} = *number of positive visits to area i (i.e. without encounter of a conspecific)*
R_p = *constant defining the attractiveness increase per positive visit*
$F_{\max}$ = *maximal attractiveness reduction of an area*
N_{fi} = *number of visits to area i with fights (i.e. with encounter of a conspecific)*
R_f = *constant defining the attractiveness decrease per fight*

The agent in the model as well as the robot constantly move around in the environment, computing the new attractiveness value of an area after each visit. The selection of the next area is accomplished stochastically from the nearest neighbors, whereby the areas with the highest attractiveness values are more likely to be visited.

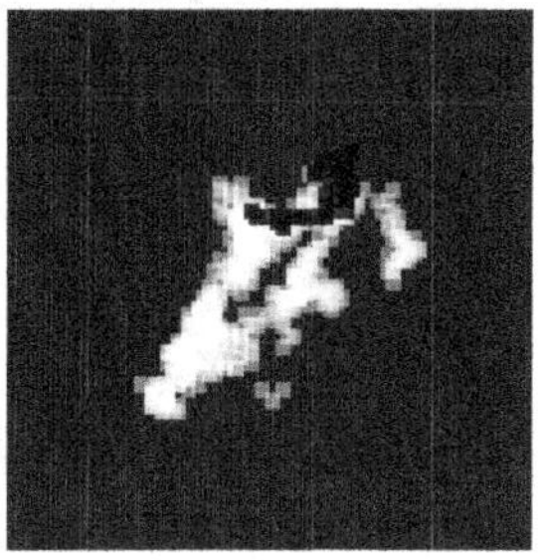

(a) Attractiveness values by robot 1 in robot coordinates.

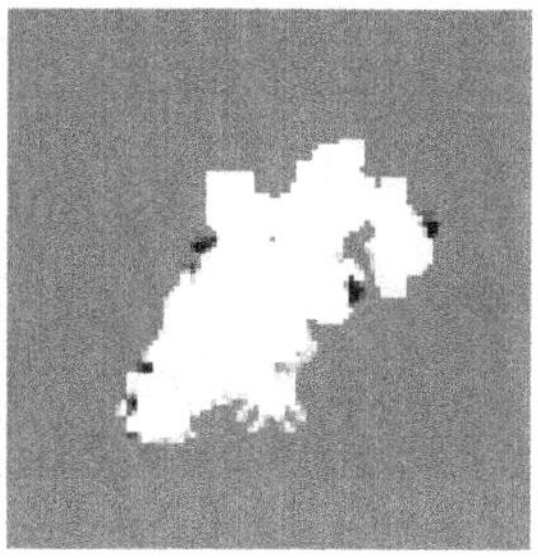

(b) Occupancy grid by robot 1 in robot coordinates.

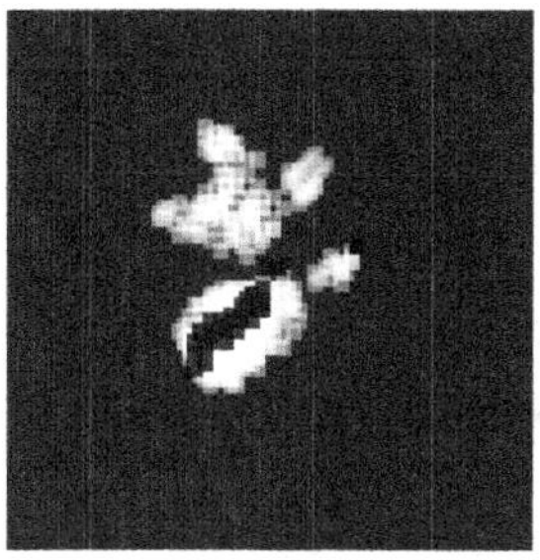

(c) Attractiveness values by robot 2 in robot coordinates.

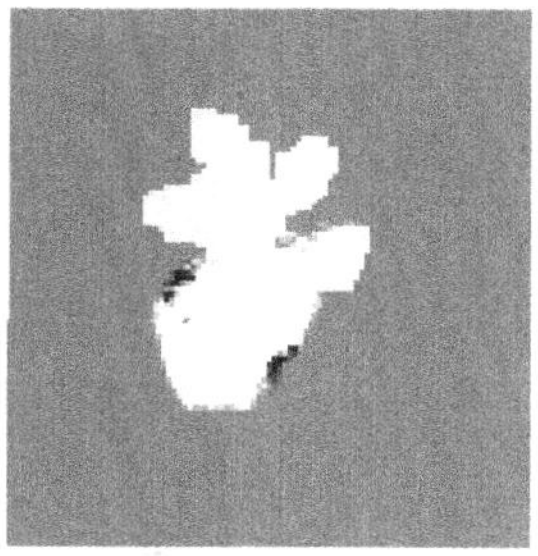

(d) Occupancy grid by robot 2 in robot coordinates.

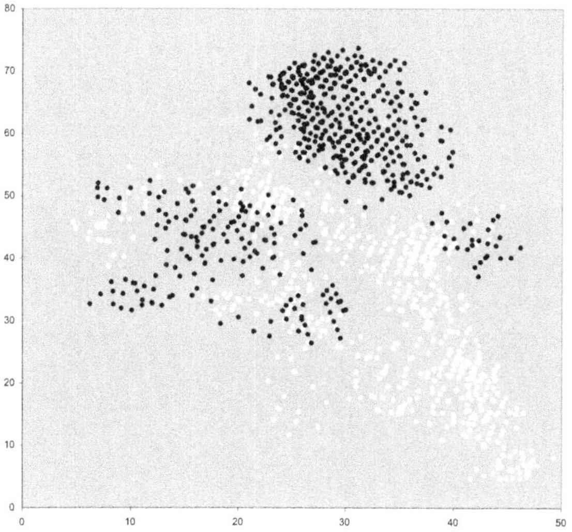

(e) Places visited by the robots in arena coordinates. Robot 1 is marked by black dots, the places visited by robot 2 are plotted in white.
Each robot made 700 steps.

Figure 1: Two robots establishing their territories.

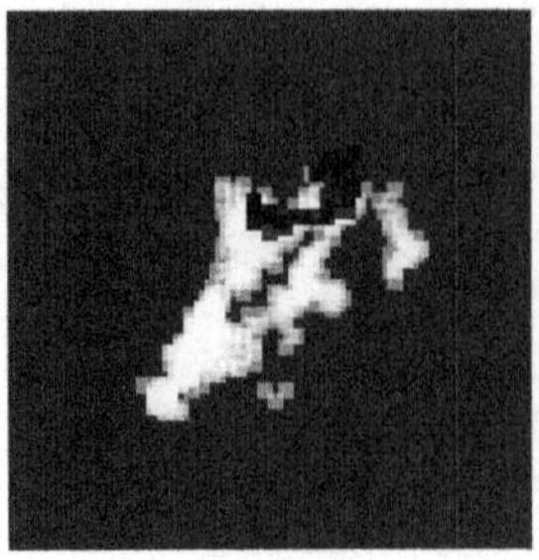

(a) Attractiveness values from robot 1 in its own coordinates after introduction of the newcomer.

(b) Attractiveness values from robot 2 in its own coordinates after introduction of the newcomer.

(c) Attractiveness values from the newcomer in its own coordinates.

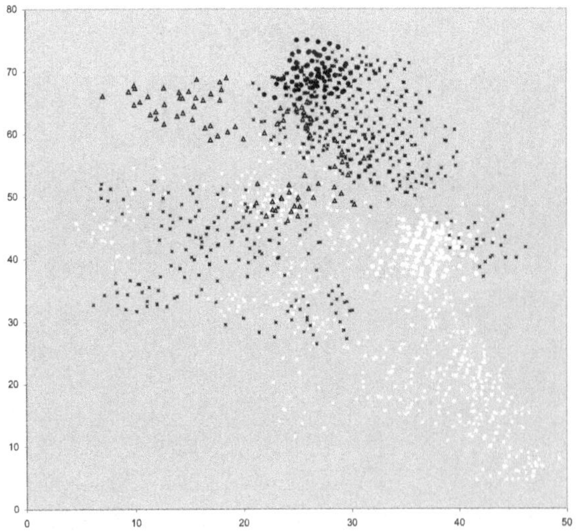

(d) Places visited by the three robots in arena coordinates. Robot 1 is marked with black, robot 2 white signs. The places which were visited before the introduction of the third robot are marked by small crosses (compare Fig.1e). The places visited by the newcomer are plotted as triangles. Each robot visited 80 places since the introduction of the newcomer.

Figure 2: Introduction of a newcomer in a system of two established territories.

Territoriality in Robots

The territorial behavior is built on Khepera miniature robots. They are placed in an environment with obstacles of random locations and controlled via a radio module. Using its short-range infrared sensors, each robot can detect obstacles while its position information is provided externally. As a representation of the environment an occupancy grid was chosen that divides the environment in discrete cells (Elfes 1987). To each cell a probability value is assigned reflecting the robot's belief of finding an obstacle in this cell. Each time the robot detects an object in the area of a cell, it elevates the probability value associated to this cells. The integration of the probabilities over time are computed according to the algorithm presented by Thrun (1998).

Parallel to the grid map, a second map of the same size is built up. In this map, the attractiveness values of the patches in the environment are stored. Each time the robot moves to a new area, the attractiveness value is changed according to the model of Stamps and Krishnan (1999) as described above. In each time step, a new area in the neighborhood is chosen with a probability which is proportional to the attractiveness value:

$$p_i = \frac{A_i}{\sum_j^k A_j}, \quad \forall\, j : occ_j \leq 0.5$$

with

p_i = *visit probability for area* i
A_i = *attractiveness value of area* i
k = *number of neighbors of the area* i
occ_j = *occupancy probability of area* j

The robot considers its occupancy grid map by rejecting the areas which are occupied by obstacles from its choice of a new area.

Results

It is shown that the simple model presented above leads to the formation of territories, even though parsimonious spatial representation and sensors are used. Each robot in the arena builds up a territory, i.e. it does not use all the accessible space, but stays restricted to a part located around its starting position. The territory is defined as the space that covers all the positions visited by the robot (Fig.1e). The shape of the territory is reflected in the known parts of the occupancy grid (Fig.1b/d) as well as in the areas of elevated attractiveness values (Fig.1a/c). Between the territories of the two robots exploring the environment simultaneously, a buffer zone visited by both robots can be observed. However, the buffer zone is visited less frequently by both individuals (Fig.1e).

In the attractiveness grids, gaps become obvious (Fig.1a/c). These arise if a robot meets an opponent in an area that it visited before. By decreasing the attractiveness value of this area, the areas lying behind it become separated from the main territory region.

After 700 time steps and the formation of two territories, a third robot was introduced (Fig.2). In order to observe the impact of a new individual on already established territories, the third robot was placed in between the two existing territories. While the effects on the existing territories is small, in 80 steps the new robot was not able to establish a stable territory which is reflected in the low number of areas with increased attractiveness values (Fig.2c).

Conclusions

In the present paper, territorial behavior was implemented on mobile Khepera miniature robots. This behavior will provide a platform for the investigation of navigational mechanisms in a biologically relevant context.

The establishment of a territories in two robots roaming around in the same environment was shown. The resulting territories are exemplary. The arena was chosen larger than the space which two territories would claim. However, the introduction of a third individual in the border zone between two established territories shows that limited space complicates the formation of a stable territory.

The relatively simple mechanisms that were used in our presented work suffice for the appearance of a complex behavior. In future work, individuals with different sensory and computational equipment will be run against each other. The performance of the navigation mechanisms can be determined directly by comparing the individuals. On the other hand, the influence of changing parameters of the environment will be tested.

Acknowledgments

This work is supported by the Deutsche Forschungsgemeinschaft within the Sonderforschungsbereich 550.

References

Adams, E. S. 2001. Approaches to the study of territory size and shape. *Ann. Rev. Ecol. Syst.* 32:277–303.

Baird, T. A.; Sloan, C. L.; and Timanus, D. K. 2001. Intra- and inter-seasonal variation in the socio-spatial behavior of adult male collard lizards, *Crotaphytus collaris* (Reptilia, Crotaphytidae). *Ethology* 107:15–32.

Bedau, M. A.; McCaskill, J. S.; Packard, N. H.; Rasmussen, S.; Adami, C.; Green, D. G.; Ikegami, T.; Kaneko, K.; and Ray, T. S. 2000. Open problems in artificial life. *Artificial Life* 6:363–376.

Elfes, A. 1987. Sonar-based real-world mapping and navigation. *IEEE Journal of Robotics and Automation* 3(3):249–265.

Franz, M. O., and Mallot, H. A. 2000. Biomimetic robot navigation. *Robotics and Autonomous Systems* 30:133–153.

Kokko, H., and Lundberg, P. 2001. Dispersal, migration, and offspring retention in saturated habitats. *Am. Nat.* 157(2):188–202.

Maher, C. R., and Lott, D. F. 1995. Definitions of territoriality used in the study of variation in vertebrate spacing systems. *Animal Behaviour* 49.

Maynard Smith, J. 1982. *Evolution and the Theory of Games.* Cambridge University Press.

Stamps, J. A., and Krishnan, V. V. 1999. A learning-based model of territory establishment. *Quart. Rev. Biol.* 74(3):291–318.

Thrun, S. 1998. Learning metric-topological maps for indoor mobile robot navigation. *Artificial Intelligence* 99(1):21–71.

Self-Organization in Ad Hoc Sensor Networks: An Empirical Study

Elaine Catterall, **Kristof Van Laerhoven** and **Martin Strohbach**
Computing Department
Lancaster University
Lancaster LA1 4YR, United Kingdom
{elaine,kristof,strohbach}@comp.lancs.ac.uk

Abstract

Research in classifying and recognizing complex concepts has been directing its focus increasingly on distributed sensing using a large amount of sensors. The colossal amount of sensor data often obstructs traditional algorithms in centralized approaches, where all sensor data is directed to one central location to be processed. Spreading the processing of sensor data over the network seems to be a promising option, but distributed algorithms are harder to inspect and evaluate. Using self-sufficient sensor boards with short-range wireless communication capabilities, we are exploring approaches to achieve an emerging distributed perception of the sensed environment in real-time through clustering. Experiments in both simulation and real-world platforms indicate that this is a valid methodology, being especially promising for computation on many units with limited resources.

Introduction

It is obvious that distributed sensing has been inspired to a great extent by biological systems, where highly redundant sensors appear in the form of *duplicate sensing* (e.g. having two eyes), *fusory sensing* (e.g. seeing and touching the same object), and *distributed sensing* (e.g. networks in the skin) (Brooks 1988). It is our aim to investigate what the impact of distributed algorithms, self-organization, and sheer number (scalability) of sensor modules will have on sensing and perception of the environment.

Moving sensing tasks to real-world applications often proves to be impractical, as the concepts that have to be learned and distinguished are too complex to be captured by just a few sensors. Instead of improving the quality of the used sensor(s), the quantity is increased in distributed sensing. Benefits of this approach have been mentioned early on in sensor fusion literature (Ayache 1990; Brooks & Iyengar 1998):

1. redundancy in sensors leads to a more robust system since faulty sensors have little effect on the output,

2. distributed sensors have a higher chance to capture relevant aspects because of their spatial spreading, and

3. the cost of producing many sensor modules that perform recognition concurrently is considered to be smaller, since sensors can be smaller and are not required to be as precise.

We will concentrate in this paper on clustering data originating from a numerically fixed set of sensors, concurrently operating in the same environment. A prime requirement is that the clustering should be done in a decentralized way, since it is being implemented on a hardware platform based on microcontrollers with limited memory. The output of this distributed sensor network is the distributed storage of typical representations of various states, or contexts, of the environment.

Research into new interaction techniques in ubiquitous computing is gradually moving towards 'smarter' objects that are able to monitor their environments with hardware sensors. This research is usually referred to as 'context awareness' (Abowd, Dey, & Brotherton 1997). The many sensors approach in context awareness has attracted attention from various research domains (Kahn, Katz, & Pister 1999; Lim 2001).

The Hardware Platform

The platform for the experiments in this paper is a collection of 'Smart-Its'[1]. In this section we describe some of the characteristics of the Smart-Its in order to provide insight into the experimental setup, and illustrate some of the limitations. One Smart-It unit embodies a *sensor module*, and a *communication module*, which are interconnected.

The core of sensor module is a PIC 16F877 microcontroller clocked at 20 MHz, which offers 384 bytes of data memory and 8K×14 bits of memory. See Figure 1 for the arrangement of the sensors. A library comes with the module that provides easy access to the sensor values. A serial line connector is available for connecting the sensor module to a PC. Of the two I^2C connectors, one is used to interface to the communication module.

The communication module is based on the PICF876. An RF stack provides wireless communication, at a maximum rate of 125 kbit/s. The current implementation of the RF stack only supports broadcast. Two of the I/O pins are used for communication with the sensor module over I^2C. The I^2C interface offers read and write access to field strength information, as well as access to the sender's IP and the application data packet.

The Kohonen Self-Organizing Map

Self-organization of neuronal functions seems to exist on very abstract levels in the brain. When a laboratory rat has learned its location in a labyrinth, certain brain cells

[1]Smart-Its Project Home Page. http://smart-its.teco.edu/

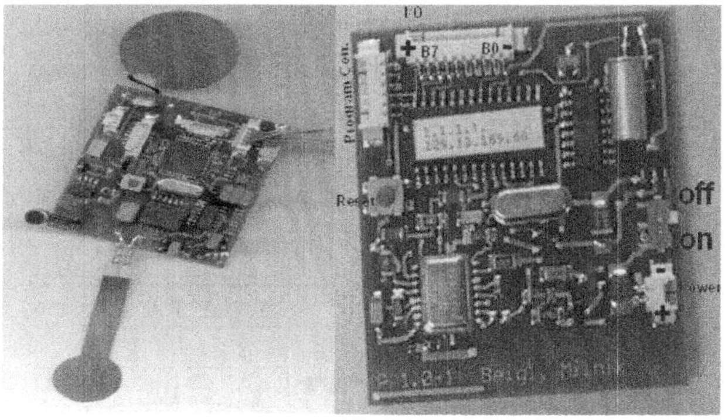

Figure 1: The two modules that combined make up the Smart-It unit: Left, the sensor module with light sensor, microphone, 2 accelerometers, thermometer, pressure sensor (bottom) and buzzer (top). Right, the wireless communication module. Both boards measure 43 × 50 mm.

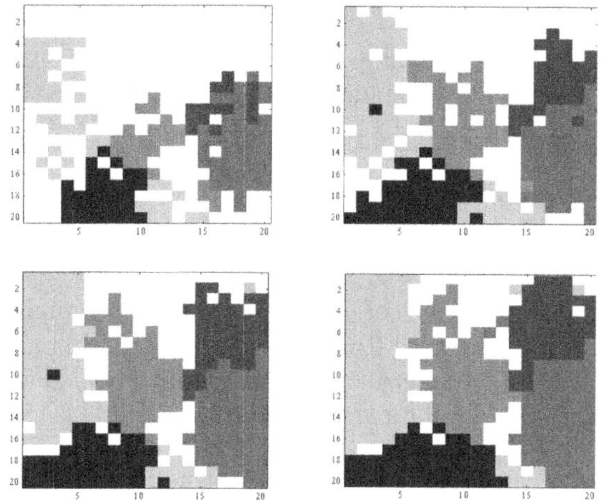

Figure 2: A 2D Self-Organizing Map showing different regions of winning units for different states of the environment.

on the hippocampal cortex respond only when it is in a particular location. The Kohonen Self-Organizing Map (SOM) (Kohonen 1997) has a similar principle: units (referred to as neurons) are recruited topologically for tasks depending on the sensory input. It is commonly classified as a neural network, and more specifically a winner-takes-all competitive algorithm, since the units *compete* with each other for specific tasks.

Each unit i has its own prototype vector w_i (also referred to as codebook vector or weight vector), being a local storage for one particular kind of input vector that has been introduced to the system. Initially these prototype vectors with a dimension n equal to the input space, start out as vectors with random small components and, as new input enters the SOM, are improved following this update rule:

$$w_i = w_i + \alpha \cdot \eta(\text{winner}) \cdot (x_i - w_i),\ \forall i \in \{1, \ldots, n\}$$

where α is called the learning rate and is situated between 0 and 1, and $\eta(\text{winner})$ is the neighbourhood function ranging from 0 to 1 as well, depending on the distance between the current SOM unit and the winner. The winner is the unit that has a prototype vector that is closest to the current input vector using the Euclidean distance:

$$\text{winner} = \arg\min_j \sqrt{\sum_{j=1}^{n}(x_j - w_j)^2}$$

The neighbourhood function is traditionally implemented as a Gaussian (bell-shaped) function:

$$\eta(\text{winner}) = \frac{1}{\sqrt{2\pi nb}} e^{-0.5\cdot(\text{winner}-\text{current})^2/nb^2}$$

with nb a parameter indicating the width of the function, and thus the radius in which the neighbours of the winning unit are allowed to update their prototype vectors significantly. The map of units is usually taken as a two-dimensional grid, although many other organisations have been applied (such as a map of hexagons).

After a sufficient amount of input data has been presented to the SOM, self-organization will result in a topographic map, where similar data is mapped onto units in a particular region of the map, and neighbouring units will be activated (i.e. become winners) for similar input data. Figure 2 shows how different units become recruited for different states of the environment by colouring the units according to the state in which they were declared as winners.

Implementation

The Kohonen SOM mainly has implementations based on a single-processor, centralized method. Therefore, it is necessary that we elaborate on the implementation for the smart-its platform and the simulation[2].

The distributed implementation of the Kohonen Self-Organizing Map (SOM) produces an algorithm that has several variations from the traditional centralized version:

- The units of the SOM are embodied by the Smart-Its: each Smart-It records a prototype vector that resembles one particular kind of input it has experienced. Note that this creates little stress on the resources, since one vector easily fits into the microcontroller's memory.

- The topology of the SOM, instead of being a fixed grid, has a loose topology, defined by the physical distances between the Smart-It units.

[2]The source code and data files are available for download from http://www.comp.lancs.ac.uk/~catterae/alife2002

1	Unit ID
2	Packet Timestamp
3	Error (Euclidean distance between prototype and input)

Table 1: Packet description for the Kohonen Self-Organizing Map implementation.

- The input for each of the units is different, though similar since it comes from readings from the same state of the environment. In a traditional SOM however, inputs for all units are exactly the same.
- Units can be moved, removed, or added, resulting in a truly ad-hoc network. This resembles research done on growing SOMs and SOMs where 'dead units' (i.e. units that never tend to win) perish (Fritzke 1997).

Communication between the units across the network consists of packets that encapsulate all the necessary information to complete both the find-winner and the update-prototype-vectors phases. After having read the sensor values, each unit compares those values with its internal values, stored in the randomly initialised prototype vectors and calculates the Euclidean distance between both vectors. A packet is then created and broadcast across the network with the elements as they are listed in Table 1. The timestamp is provided to eliminate outdated packages.

After receiving packets from the units in its neighbourhood, a Smart-It can identify the winner by searching for the minimum error. By then calculating how close it is to the winner (in physical distance), the prototype vector can be updated as shown in the update rule above.

The output of the network is the 'activation' of the winning unit, which will be consistent with a self-organized topology, provided enough iterations have been introduced to the network, or if the network does not change too rapidly.

Discussion

Experiments on both simulation and Smart-Its platform are discussed in this section. All results presented here were produced using datasets containing real-world data from the actual sensor modules, and executed on the simulation platform that was designed to be as close as possible to the hardware units. This was done to allow us to evaluate the impact of varying the learning rate and neighbourhood radius parameters, whilst using the same sets of sensor data.

The five datasets (one for each smart-it) are visualized by time series plots in Figures 3. Note that, although the sensor data is very similar (as the units are physically close to each other), it is not exactly the same. The intensity of the light for instance (marked in the legends by 'Light'), is higher for units 1 and 2 since they were

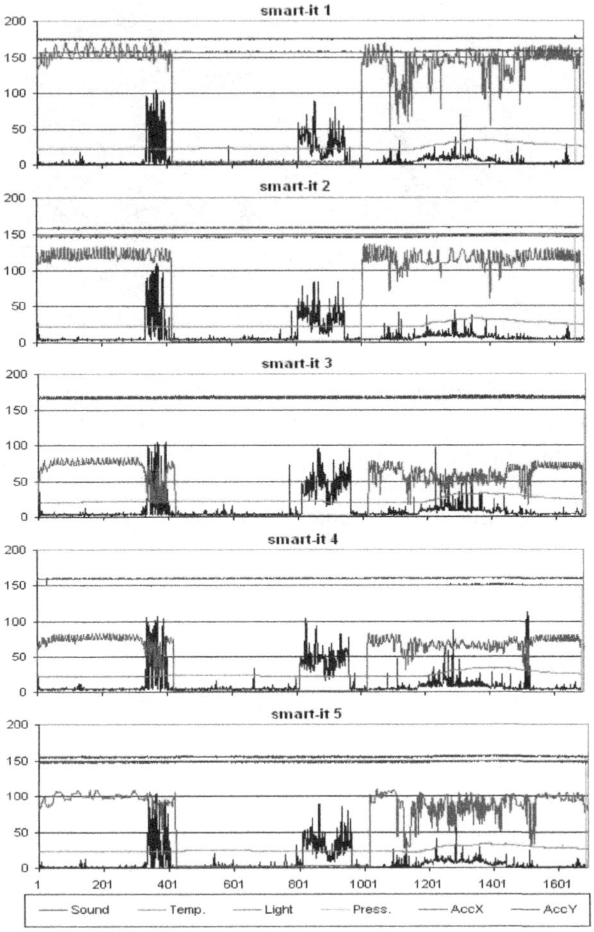

Figure 3: Datasets with sensor values from each of the smart-it units during several states of the environment ('contexts'): Lights on (1–330), talking people nearby while lights remain on (331–400), lights turned off (401–800), talking people nearby while light remain turned off (801–1000), and heating on (1090–1400).

positioned directly underneath the light source. The accelerometer data is also a bit different as not all boards were positioned in the same fashion (the readings from the accelerometers reflect position in the X-axis and Y-axis). Also notice how some sensors, such as the temperature sensor, change only slightly and gradually, while others such as the sound level, tend to vary a lot. The pressure sensor on each unit was used to synchronize the data amongst the smart-its, as can be observed around sample 1680 on the X-axis.

The success of our implementation of the Kohonen Map, as on any of its implementations, depends heavily on the choice for the learning rate and neighbourhood radius parameters. We will concentrate on the first, as it is the most important one and the number of smart-it units is not large enough to evaluate the impact of a changing neighbourhood radius.

Figures 4 and 5 show the behaviour of the SOM with a different learning rate. With a high learning rate, units

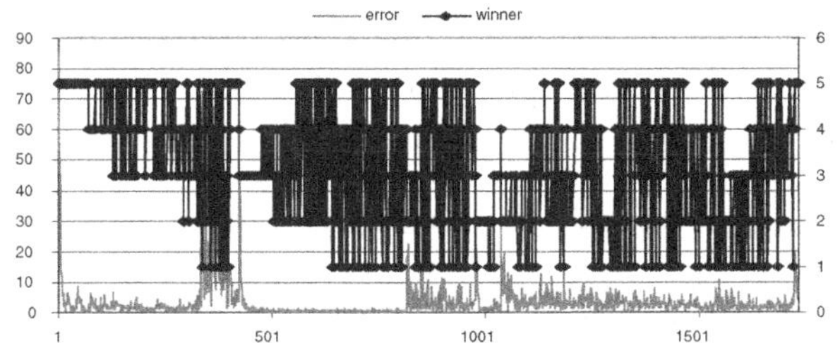

Figure 4: Error (left Y-axis) and winning unit IDs (right axis) over time with a high learning rate. Units 'forget' the stored prototype vector, which gets overwritten by the current input.

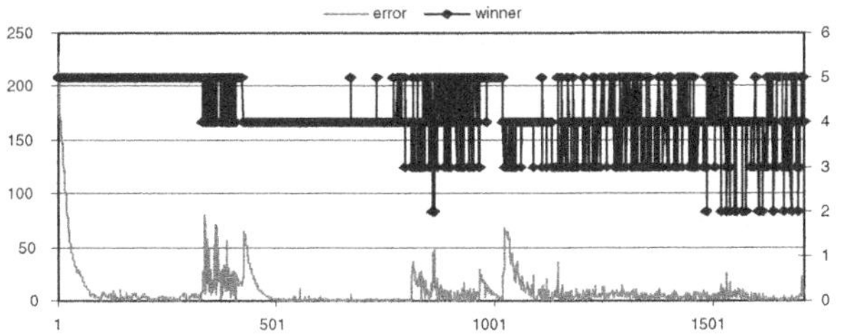

Figure 5: Error (left Y-axis) and winning unit IDs (right axis) over time with a normal learning rate. Unit 5 specializes for the first context, unit 4 specializes for the third context, while the other two contexts are not introduced long enough to be claimed by one unit.

easily overwrite their prototype vector with each new kind of input vector. This problem is known in machine learning as 'catastrophic forgetting' and relates to the 'plasticity-stability dilemma' (Grossberg 1976). Results with a smaller learning rate (Figure 5) do preserve their prototype vectors, although fluctuating sensor data causes the recruitment of several units for one context (331–400 and 801–1000 for instance, where the sound level varies heavily).

The results from our experiments show that self-organization does take place and that similar sensor data maps onto sensor units topographically. Similar data clusters in a particular region of the environment populated with sensor units.

Conclusions

Our aim in applying artificial life principles to the domain of context clustering and eventually context classification and discovery is to provide flexibility and robustness in a constantly changing environment. The sensor boards themselves are relatively simple. By harnessing their collective intelligence arising from their interactions, we aim to produce systems where individual sensor boards and/or sub networks of sensor boards in the collection, learn to specialize in recognizing a particular state of the environment or context.

Our experiments demonstrate that clustering of incoming sensor data through self-organization on many distributed sensor modules with limited processing capabilities is possible.

Acknowledgements

We would like to express our gratitude to our colleagues in the Smart-Its project, sponsored by the Information Systems and Technology framework of the European Commission.

References

Abowd, G.; Dey, A.; and Brotherton, J. 1997. Context awareness in wearable and ubiquitous computing. In *Proceedings of the First International Symposium on Wearable Computing (ISWC)*, 179–180. Boston, M: IEEE Press.

Ayache, N. 1990. *Stereovision and sensor fusion.* MIT Press.

Brooks, R. R., and Iyengar, S. S. 1998. *Multi-Sensor Fusion.* Prentice Hall.

Brooks, M. 1988. Highly redundant sensing in robotics — analogies from biology: Distributed sensing and learning. In *Proceedings of the NATO Advanced Research Workshop on Highly Redundant Sensing in Robotic Systems,.*

Fritzke, B. 1997. Some competitive learning methods. Technical report, Artificial Intelligence Institute, Dresden University of Technology.

Grossberg, S. 1976. Adaptive pattern classification and universal recoding, I: Parallel development and coding of neural feature detectors. *Biological Cybernetics* 23:121–134.

Kahn, J. M.; Katz, R. H.; and Pister, K. S. J. 1999. Mobile networking for smart dust. In *Proceedings of the ACM/IEEE International Conference on Mobile Computing and Networking (MobiCom 99).*

Kohonen, T. 1997. *Self-Organizing Maps.* Heidelberg: Springer-Verlag, 2nd edition.

Lim, A. 2001. Distributed services for information dissemination in self-organizing sensor networks for real-time systems with adaptive reconfiguration. *Journal of Franklin Institute* 338:707–727.

SOS++: Finding Smart Behaviors Using Learning and Evolution

Bertrand Mesot[1], **Eduardo Sanchez**[1], **Carlos-Andres Peña**[1] and **Andres Perez-Uribe**[2]

[1]Swiss Federal Institute of Technology, EPFL-LSL, Lausanne (Switzerland)
[2]Swiss Federal Institute of Technology, EPFL-LSA, Lausanne (Switzerland)

Abstract

We present SOS++, a bioinspired method combining evolution and learning, allowing the automatic design of the controller of autonomous agents, described as a finite-state machine. The application of this method to well-known problems, for example the follow-up of a trail or the resolution of a maze, led to the emergence of some behaviors we could qualify as intelligent. Moreover, it is possible to use the method in a hierarchical way in order to obtain complex behaviors starting from a set of basic actions. We have used an algorithm which is a variation of reinforcement learning with a reward adapted to the degree of uncertainty of the performed prediction.

Introduction

According to Brooks' work (Brooks 1999), the best way to program an autonomous robot is to provide it with a set of basic behaviors and to let more complex behaviors emerge by interactions between the robot and the environment.

The robot's creator must design the body, thus choosing a set of possible basic actions and perceptions: the actions are implemented by actuators (motors, for example), and the perceptions of the environment are acquired by sensors. The designer then implements some simple behaviors as a sequence of basic actions commanded by a controller, generally a neural network. More complex behaviors appear in an autonomous way, by learning and/or evolution of the controller while interacting with the environment. This same principle can be applied, in a more general way, to the design of autonomous agents.

In this paper we present another approach, using finite state machines (FSM) to implement the controller. As in the preceding case, the FSM controlling a complex behavior is the result of an autonomous process of interaction with the environment, using bioinspired methods of evolution and learning.

After a section explaining the bioinspired basis of our approach, we present a first method using a variation of reinforcement learning illustrated by a solution of the well-known Santa Fe trail problem (Koza 1992). Evolution is not always important for this first method (a solution for the Santa Fe trail is found during the first generation, for example) and, in fact, proves to be unable to provide solutions to more complex problems (the Los Altos Hills trail (Koza 1992), for example). In the next section, we present a second method, using two hierarchical levels of FSM: we added a set of FSM-implemented macroactions to the basic simple actions. This method finds a solution to the problem of Los Altos trail, but the designer has a more important contribution: the first hierarchical level of FSM, implementing the macroactions, is the result of her work and not the result of evolution or learning. We then present a third method, where evolution plays a greater role, that finds very interesting solutions for complex problems such as the Los Altos trail or the Wiering and Schmidhuber maze (Wiering & Schmidhuber 1997) using only the set of basic actions (e.g., our method is able to find sequences of actions that can be reused at different times, thus providing an automatic definition of macroactions and consequently of hierarchical behaviors). We finish with a concluding section and an outline of our future work, using real robots as examples.

Biological Inspiration

Evolution has provided each animal species with a set of basic actions which make it possible for its members to interact with their environment. From one species to another one can find similar actions but their implementation differs: evolution has found different solutions in each case. The execution of one of these actions, using several organs of the animal's body, is commanded by its nervous system (the brain for the more complex animals).

The realization of a given task implies the execution of several actions in a given sequence: it is a behavior. In this case, learning can play a greater role than evolution. The sequence of actions can be culturally transmitted to an individual during its life time, without need to wait several generations so that it gets genetically coded in its DNA (thus being transformed into an additional basic action).

This body-brain duality, (organs of the action)-(command of the action), exists also in digital systems, as the pair (data path unit)-(control unit). In these cases, the data path unit contains all the elements of storage and data processing, while the control unit is a FSM responsible for sequencing the operations carried out in the data path unit.

In the case of an autonomous robot, the duality is clearer: the various sensors and actuators play the body role and its controller plays the brain role. The design of the robot's body is not left to evolution, as this would take an unbearably long time. Therefore, in the large majority of cases it is the task of an engineer: the design of the robot always includes the choice of its sensors and actuators. Although this task is far from being easy, it is a problem within a good engineer's reach. On the other hand, the design of the brain (the robot's controller) is much more difficult, particularly when one wants to see it carrying out complex,"intelligent", behaviors. For a living being, intelligence is the capacity to individually find the behavior to respond to an excitation of its environment or to solve a complex problem.

As with our analogy of living beings, it is common to use neural networks to implement the controller of autonomous agents. For these kind of networks, there are several well-known and tested learning algorithms, thus making the design easier: the designer chooses the starting network structure and the task is executed by self-organization, following a given learning algorithm. A more recent variation of this methodology uses genetic algorithms to evolve the neural network structure or some learning parameters (Nolfi & Floreano 2000).

Our approach is quite different, oriented towards a hardware implementation of the controller: the body of the agent, an autonomous robot for example, is designed by traditional methods, while we consider the controller as a FSM, commanding the possible actions of the body. A FSM is fully described by two elements: the set of its states and the transitions between them. In a Moore FSM, an action is associated to each state (Sanchez 1998). We use a genetic algorithm to find the set of states-actions pairs used by the learning algorithm. A variation of the reinforcement learning, a learning algorithm well known in the field of neural networks, is used to dynamically build the interconnections between the states. Some of the learning parameters are also calculated by the genetic algorithm.

To design a controller starting from its FSM description is a classic problem for digital systems engineers. In addition to the ease of implementation, this representation gives a much higher level of interpretability when compared to neural networks. Indeed it is much easier to explain and interpret a behavior starting from its FSM representation than of that of the neural network. The possibility to understand the way the solution works can help us when designing new systems or optimizing existing solutions.

First Method: SOS, A Variation of Reinforcement Learning

Reinforcement learning (Sutton & Barto 1998) is an iterative mathematical method rendering an agent able to learn how to carry out a given task while interacting with its environment by the means of rewards.

At each instant t, the agent receives a representation of the state of its environment, s^t. According to this information, the agent carries out an action selected among those which it is able to realize (this selection can be seen as a prediction). At the next moment, it receives a reward of value r^t and the environment passes to a new state s^{t+1}. To correctly carry out a given task, i.e. to correctly learn it, the agent must seek to maximize the sum of the obtained rewards: in other words, it must minimize the *temporal-difference error*, calculated as the difference between two predictions at successive moments.

For the choice of the action, the agent uses a *value function*, generally implemented as a *lookup table*, where each line corresponds to a state of the environment and each column to a possible action of the agent. Each entry in the table contains an *action value*, $Q(s,a)$, giving the maximum reward that an agent can hope to receive when, being at state s, uses action a. Learning implies correctly updating the values of the lookup table, as a function of the rewards obtained. This update is calculated using the following equations:

$$\delta = r^t + \gamma\, Q(s^{t+1}, a^{t+1}) - Q(s^t, a^t)$$

$$Q(s^t, a^t) \leftarrow Q(s^t, a^t) + \alpha\,\delta$$

where δ is the temporal-difference error, r^t is the reward obtained at time t, and α and γ are learning parameters.

With this method, the agent is able to correctly learn a task only if the state of the environment gives sufficient information: the state coding thus has a great influence on the learning quality. Our approach is completely different: we do not code the state of the environment but, quite simply, we use values from some of its parameters (those which are accessible to the input organs or sensors of the agent). These inputs of the agent (perceptions) will allow it to change its internal state: we thus learn the states of the agent's controller and not those of the environment. In this way, we use raw data from the environment, without needing to interpret them and to code them as states.

The controller of the agent is seen now as a FSM, where each state summarizes all the knowledge an agent needs to plan the continuation of its behavior. In addition, the transition between two states is done according to the perceived input. In the case of a Moore FSM, an action is associated to each possible state. Consequently, the relationship (state of the environment)-(action of the agent) of the traditional reinforcement learning now becomes a relationship (current state of the agent, input)-(next state of the agent). In other words, to learn now means to find the appropriate transition between two states of the agent for a given input.

FSMs are generally represented as state diagrams or, in an equivalent way, as lookup tables called state tables. We use a table inspired by state tables to replace the table of state-action values $Q(s,a)$ in our method. Figure 1 shows the format of such a table: there is a line per given state S_k and m columns (next states S_i) per input O_j. To each one of these triplets (an entry of the table) is associated a value $T(S_k, O_j, S_i)$, giving the maximum reward that the agent can hope to receive when, being in the state S_k, and perceiving the input O_j, it chooses S_i as the next state of S_k. Like in traditional reinforcement learning, to learn means to update the table. Thus, the equations for learning become in our case:

	O_0				O_n		
	S_0	$\cdots$	S_m	$\cdots$	S_0	$\cdots$	S_m
S_0	0.5	0.3	0.6	$\cdots$	$T(S_0, O_n, S_i)$		
$\vdots$		$\vdots$		$\vdots$		$\vdots$	
S_m	$T(S_m, O_0, S_i)$			$\cdots$	$T(S_m, O_n, S_i)$		

Figure 1: Lookup table of estimations of the state values $T(S_m, O_n, S_i)$, where S_m is the current state of the environment, O_n is the current observation of the environment made by the agent, and S_i is the next state.

$$\delta = r + \gamma T(s', o', s'') - T(s, o, s')$$
$$T(s, o, s') \leftarrow T(s, o, s') + \alpha\,\delta \tag{1}$$

where r, α and γ hold the same meaning as previously

The preceding equations perform the adaptation of a state-value function implemented by the $T(S_m, O_n, S_i)$ table. There is no action selection mechanism in our system. Instead, there is a single action associated to each state, as this is the case for a Moore FSM. Therefore, we must suppose that the state-action associations are the right ones. Indeed, we achieve this by using a genetic algorithm, as we will soon explain.

An individual (agent) of the population used by the genetic algorithm (Michalewicz 1996; Vose 1996) is represented by a fixed-size genome, containing as many genes as S_k states (note that the genome encodes a fixed maximum number of states, it is learning which further reduces this number). The value of a gene is an integer indicating the action associated to the corresponding state. For example, the genome 212 indicates that we work with a FSM containing a maximum of three states, and that state S_0 is associated to action 2, S_1 to action 1, and S_2 to action 2. At each generation, the less adapted $\frac{2}{3}$ of the population is replaced by new individuals resulting from the crossover of the remaining third (the elite, the fittest). The parents of these new individuals are selected by *roulette wheel*, and the offsprings may be modified by mutation. The crossover operation is done by cutting the two genomes in a single point, and always at genes' border. The mutation, carried out with a probability PMUT, randomly gives a new valid value to a gene. It is significant to notice that not all the genes of an individual are necessarily used in the solution of a problem: the learning will be given the responsibility to interconnect needed states, leaving the other states without connection.

To solve a given problem, we start by creating a random population. Then, the *fitness* of each individual is calculated as a function of its learning capabilities. This value is then used to determine the individuals authorized to reproduce. During its life, each individual thus uses the reinforcement learning method described previously, formalized in the following way, under the name of SOS *(State-Observation-State)* algorithm (Sanchez & Perez-Uribe & Mesot 2001):

1. Initialize the table. $\forall s \forall o \forall s' : T(s, o, s') = c$ where c is a constant equal to the maximum possible reward (optimistic initialization).
2. Place the agent at the initial position: define $s = S_0$ and observe the input o corresponding to the position.
3. Choose s' such that $T(s, o, s') = \max_{i \in [0, |S|[} T(s, o, S_i)$, where S is the set of the states. If several future states are possible, take that with the smallest index i.
4. Go to the state s', carry out the action corresponding to this state (given by the genome) and recover the reward r.
5. Observe the input o' corresponding to the new position and choose s'' such that $T(s', o', s'') = \max_{i \in [0, |S|[} T(s', o', S_i)$. Again, if several cases are possible, choose the smallest index i.
6. Update the value $T(s, o, s')$, using the equation:
$$\delta = r + \gamma T(s', o', s'') - T(s, o, s')$$
$$T(s, o, s') \leftarrow T(s, o, s') + \alpha\,\delta$$
7. Let $s = s'$, $s' = s''$, $o = o'$ and go to 4 as long as the end condition is not reached.

The Santa Fe Trail

The first problem on which we tested our algorithm is the Santa Fe trail, proposed by Christopher Langton (Koza 1992). An artificial ant is placed on a grid of 32 × 32 cells, of which some contain food (black cells in figure 2). The goal is to collect, in a limited number of steps, the greatest quantity of food, starting from the top left position. The ant "sees" only one cell in front of it: at every step, it receives an input of value 1 if there is food in the cell and 0 if not. At each step of the course, the ant can perform one of four possible actions, corresponding to the following genes: 0 (NOP), 1 (turn left), 2 (turn right) and 3 (move ahead a step). With each unit of collected food, the agent receives a positive reward ($r = 1$); in all the other cases, the reward is null ($r = 0$). The problem is to find a strategy enabling the ant to follow the trail in the most direct possible way, in spite of the trail's discontinuities.

We used our algorithm with the parameters given in the following table:

POP	SMAX	STEPS	TRIALS	PMUT
100	10	500	400	5%

where POP is the size of the population used, SMAX is the maximum number of states (i.e. the size of the genomes), STEPS determines the maximum number of actions which the agent is authorized to make in order to achieve the task, and TRIALS specifies the number of learning iterations (i.e. the number of times that the agent is placed back at the starting point and that a new chance is given to it to find a good strategy). Finally, PMUT indicates the probability of genome mutation. In addition, the learning parameters use the following values: $\alpha = 0.6$ and $\gamma = 0.9$. For the evolution, the measurement of fitness more strongly supports the individuals who accumulate maximum units of food, rather than those which have a minimum of states, and, finally, those which use a minimum of actions. Therefore we compute the fitness according to the following equation:

$$f = w_1 a_{\text{rew}} + w_2(|S| - a_{\text{st}}) + w_3(STEPS - a_{\text{stp}}) \quad (2)$$

where a_{rew} is the sum of all rewards obtained by the agent, a_{st} is the number of used states and a_{stp} is the number of steps needed to go all over the trail. These values are those computed during the last trial of the agent on the trail. For this problem, the weights w_i are set as follows: $w_1 = 10^5$, $w_2 = 10^3$ and $w_3 = 1$. Thus individuals with good fitness will tend to collect as many foods pellets as possible, using the smallest number of states and steps.

In less than 10 generations, our algorithm is always able to find a solution requiring only 5 states, after about 30 learning iterations. One of the minimal solutions very often obtained is presented in figure 2. By taking a glance at this solution, some remarks can be made. Firstly, the evolution action can be regarded as unimportant: indeed, good solutions are always obtained after less than 10 generations and, in certain cases, even at generation 0. This implies that we are dealing with an easy problem since the learning can use virtually any genome in order to obtain a solution, provided that it contains at least two actions. Secondly, only two actions out of four are used: turn right (2) and move ahead of a step (3). Last but not least, the FSM representation renders the solutions highly understandable. Indeed, the analysis of the state diagram of figure 2 enables us to easily understand the behavior of the agent: each time the ant perceives an input of value 1, it passes to state 5, where it carries out the action 3 (move ahead of a step). Not perceiving food forces it into a cycle of exploration, turning each time to the right (action 2) to seek food. If food is not found after a full rotation, the ant moves straight ahead. In short, trail discontinuities are always in straight lines with food and their end can be determined by a simple rotation of the ant.

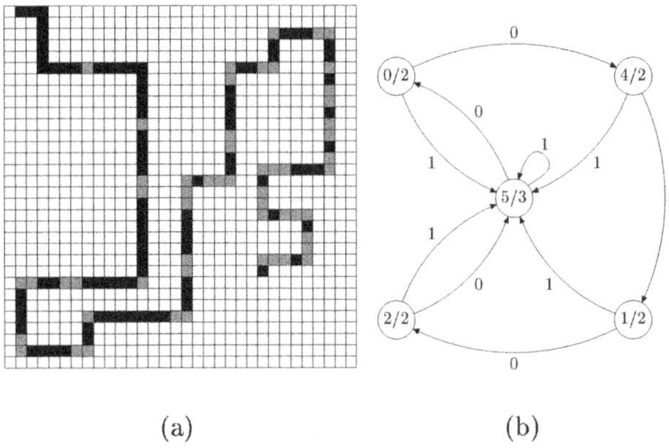

Figure 2: a) The Santa Fe trail and b) the best state diagram found by the SOS algorithm. The numbers on the arrows indicate the input value (0: no food, 1: food), the numbers on the circles indicate the state and the associated action respectively (0: NOP, 1: turn left, 2: turn right, 3: move ahead of a step).

Second Method: SOS+, Learning with Hierarchical Actions

The simplicity of the Santa Fe trail led us to test another problem: the Los Altos Hills trail, proposed by Koza (Koza 1992). This trail is in fact an extension of the Santa Fe trail, since eight deviations were added there in its final portion (see figure 3). Among these additions, four are deviations no longer presenting any direction guide (as in the Santa Fe case): inside a discontinuity, the agent cannot determine the direction to follow simply by turning on the spot.

Los Altos Hills

Initially, our SOS algorithm did not find a solution to the problem, even by using great values for parameters STEPS and TRIALS (2000 and 1000 respectively): no agent was able to collect the totality of the 157 units of food. This observation led us to suppose that this problem is too complex to be entirely solved with the basic actions NOP (0), turn left (1), turn right (2) and move ahead of a step (3). This is the reason for which we brought two new actions (in fact, Koza had also been obliged to add other actions for his solution). Our approach is hierarchical: the two new actions, called macroactions, are in fact other FSMs using the four basic actions. The two following paragraphs give a description of the behavior associated with each of the two macroactions we added.

Action 4 With this action, the agent is able to move ahead two steps, to turn on itself, then to return to its initial position but in the direction opposed to that which it had at its departure. If during this action a unit of

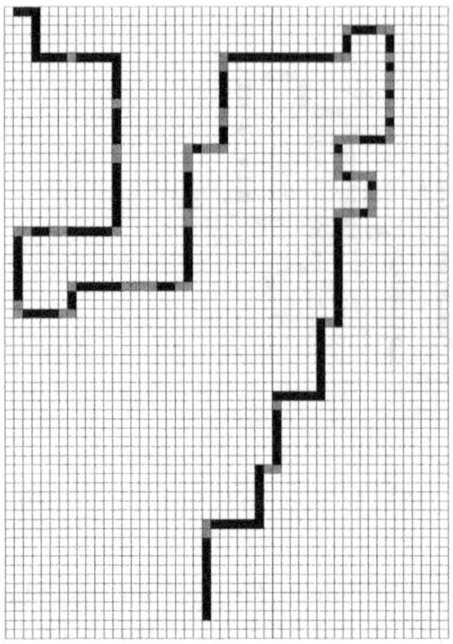

Figure 3: The Los Altos Hills trail

food is found, the macroaction stops and the machine goes to the next state corresponding to an input equal to 1. If the macroaction comes to an end, the next state is selected according to the value of the input at this time. The sequence of the actions corresponding to this macroaction is as follows: 3 3 1 1 1 2 3 3.

Action 5 This action is similar to the preceding action, but with an intermediate exploration: after a step ahead, the agent turns on itself "to observe" if at this stage there is not already a unit of food showing the way to be followed; if this is not the case, it still moves ahead a step, then turns on itself and finally returns to its initial position, but in the direction opposed to that which it had at its departure. The principle of connection and end of this action is the same one as that of action 4. The sequence of the actions carried out is as follows: 3 1 1 1 1 3 1 1 1 2 3 3.

The parameters of the algorithm used for this problem are given in the following table:

POP	SMAX	STEPS	TRIALS	PMUT
500	15	10'000	500	5%

The values of the learning parameters α and γ are still 0.6 and 0.9, respectively. The fitness is computed using the equation 2, where the weights w_i are set as follows: $w_1 = 10^7$, $w_2 = 10^5$ and $w_3 = 1$.

After less than 10 generations, and less than 100 learning iterations, the SOS+ algorithm finds an agent which collects all 157 units of food in 963 actions, by using 5 states out of the 15 available in the genome. Figure 4 shows one of the solutions obtained: it required only 17 learning iterations, and 8 generations.

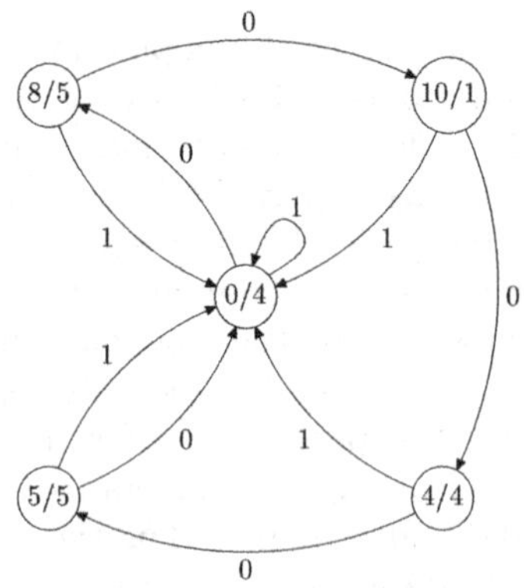

Figure 4: The best state diagram found by the SOS+ algorithm for Los Altos trail. Actions 4 and 5 are macroactions.

As expected, this solution is very similar to that of Santa Fe, with a more thorough exploration obtained thanks to the use of macroactions 4 and 5. If the number of states seems very small (5), it should not be forgotten that macroaction 4 breaks up in fact in 8 simple states and macroaction 5 in 12: indeed, at the lowest level of hierarchy, the number of states is equal to 41 (i.e., taking into account only the simple actions used in our first method).

Third Method: SOS++, Adaptive Rewards plus Evolution of Learning Parameters

Although the macroactions previously described make it possible to solve the problem of Los Altos Hills, this approach presents several disadvantages. First of all, the macroactions must be defined by the designer, who thus takes a very significant part in the resolution of the problem. Then, their presence in the solution can imply a significant increase in the number of basic states, and the understanding capability gained by their addition is obtained with the detriment of this number.

These disadvantages led us to more thoroughly analyze the failure of the first version of algorithm SOS, and therefore try to improve our method once more. A first reason to this failure comes from "over-learning": indeed, as more of the first half of Los Altos Hills problem is identical to the Santa Fe trail, our method quickly obtains an agent able to efficiently traverse this part by receiving a very great reward. It then becomes very difficult to make the agent change its strategy for the second part. The following subsection presents a solution to this problem.

Interpreting α

To control this "over-learning" problem, our first approach was to analyze the role played by the two learning parameters of the SOS algorithm, that of α more particularly.

Rewriting equation 1 as:

$$T(s, o, s') \leftarrow (1 - \alpha)\, T(s, o, s') + \alpha\, [T(s, o, s') + \delta]$$

allows us to note that the updated value of $T(s, o, s')$ is composed by the sum of two expressions. The first, $(1-\alpha)\, T(s, o, s')$, is the current value of the table for the transition (s, o, s'), weighted by a factor $(1 - \alpha)$. The second, $\alpha\, [T(s, o, s') + \delta]$, represents the value corrected by the learning for the same transition, weighted by a factor α. In other words, α indicates the percentage that the corrected value represents in the update of $T(s, o, s')$. Consequently, it becomes obvious that the value of α very strongly determines the learning quality and that it must be therefore adjusted according to the problem to solve. This is why it appeared necessary to us to include α and γ in the genome of an individual. The genome of an agent will be thus composed by a certain number of integer values (the actions associated with the states) and by two floating point values (the two parameters α and γ).

Island Evolution

Another modification was introduced in the algorithm in order to be able to process genomes of different size: the total population is now distributed in several islands, the inhabitants of each island having all the same size of genome, different from that of the other islands. Regularly, after a given number of generations, a given number of the best individuals of an island emigrate towards another island, thus exchanging their advantages. The sizes of the migrant genomes must adapt to that of the destination island: if it is smaller, the genomes are cut; in the other case, random genes are added. In all the cases, all the individuals of an island preserve the same size.

Adaptive Reward

In the first version of our SOS algorithm, the exploration of new solutions is limited by way of choosing the next state when several cases are possible, i.e. when all cases present the same maximum value of $T(s, o, s')$. In this case, one selects the state s' that presents the smallest index as the next state, and the other states will never be visited (unless the corresponding values change, of course).

In order to succeed with this limitation, we assign to each possible transition a uniform probability to be used: if there are n valid transitions, each one is assigned a probability of $\frac{1}{n}$. This probability will be employed to modify the reward granted to the agent after the choice of the next state. A negative reward (punishment) must be less significant if at the time of the choice of the transition there were several possibilities than if there was only one of them (i.e., a certainty should be punished more than a doubt, when it proves to be incorrect). In an equivalent way, a good choice of transition is rewarded more if there were several possibilities than if there was only one of them.

To quantify this uncertainty, we use the Shannon entropic measurement (Shannon 1948):

$$H = -\sum_{i=1}^{n} p_i \cdot \log(p_i)$$

where p_i is the probability of the ith choice.

As in our case the choices are equiprobable, one has $p_i = p = \frac{1}{n}$ where n is the number of choices. This leads to a simpler formula for the entropy:

$$H = -\log\left(\frac{1}{n}\right) = \log(n)$$

According to the assumptions formulated previously, the reward r must be proportionally weighted with the entropy if $r > 0$, and conversely if $r < 0$. To model this fact, we use weighting $\theta(n)$, defined by:

$$\theta(n) = \begin{cases} 1 + \log(n) & \text{if } r > 0 \\ 1 + \log(1 + n_{\max} - n) & \text{if } r < 0 \\ 0 & \text{otherwise} \end{cases} \qquad (3)$$

where $n_{\max}$ is the maximum number of possible choices, i.e. the maximum number of states.

The final version of the learning SOS algorithm, called SOS++, is now:

1. Initialize the table. $\forall s \forall o \forall s' : T(s, o, s') = c$ where c is a constant equal to the maximum possible reward (optimistic initialization).
2. Place the agent at the initial position: define $s = S_0$, $r = 0$ and observe the input o corresponding to the position.
3. Choose s' such that $T(s, o, s') = \max_{i \in [0,|S|[} T(s, o, S_i)$, where S is the set of states; if several states are possible, choose one of them randomly.
4. Calculate $\theta_1 = \theta(n)$ using equation 3, where n is the number of possible choices at the preceding stage.
5. Go to the state s', apply the action associated to this state (given by the genome) and recover the reward r.
6. Observe the input o' corresponding to the new position and choose s'' such that $T(s', o', s'') = \max_{i \in [0,|S|[} T(s', o', S_i)$; again, if several cases are possible, choose one of them randomly.
7. Calculate $\theta_2 = \theta(n)$ using equation 3, where n is the number of possible choices at the preceding stage.

8. Update the value $T(s,o,s')$ using the equation:

$$\delta = \theta_1 r + \gamma T(s',o',s'') - T(s,o,s')$$
$$T(s,o,s') \leftarrow T(s,o,s') + \alpha\,\delta$$

9. Let $s = s'$, $s' = s''$, $o = o'$, $\theta_1 = \theta_2$ and go to 5 as long as the end condition is not reached.

Los Altos Hills

Two tests were carried out on the problem of Los Altos Hills, using the islands model in both cases for the evolution and evolving the learning parameters. However, in the first test, the agent used our first SOS algorithm for learning, whereas in the second test, SOS algorithm with adaptive reward was used. For the two cases the agent has only the 4 basic actions: NOP (0), turn left (1), turn right (2) and move ahead of a step (3).

For the first test, the values of the parameters are as follows:

NISL	ISLPOP	NGBM	NEMIG
9	100	5	3

STEPS	TRIALS	PMUT	PREP
2000	1000	5%	75%

In the first table, NISL is the number of islands, ISLPOP is the number of individuals per island, NGBM is the number of generations before migration, and NEMIG is the number of emigrants. In the second table, STEPS, TRIALS and PMUT have the same meaning as before and PREP gives the percentage of individuals replaced at each generation.

For this test, the islands were populated with genomes of size 40, 50, 60, 70, 80, 90, 100, 30, and 20 (one size per island). The fitness of each individual is computed using the equation 2, where the weights w_i are set as follows: $w_1 = 10^7$, $w_2 = 10^4$ and $w_3 = 1$. The best solution was obtained on island number 6, after 6 generations. It uses only 12 of the 100 available states, making the course of the entire trail in 999 actions and using only 283 learning iterations of the 1000 available. The end values of the learning parameters for this solution were: $\alpha \approx 0.38$ and $\gamma \approx 0.98$. The state diagram obtained is given in figure 5.

An analysis of this graph enables us to understand the behavior of the agent. It begins with state 0 (move ahead of a step) and it remains there as long as it perceives an input 1; as soon as it is no longer the case, it enters in an exploration cycle starting at state 76. This cycle leads it to carry out the actions sequence 1 0 3 1 1 3 3 2 2 3 2, which corresponds to explore a cell on the left (1 0 3 1 1 3), then a cell on the right (3 2 2 3), then to return to the initial orientation (2). This behavior is very similar to the macroactions which we previously defined for the

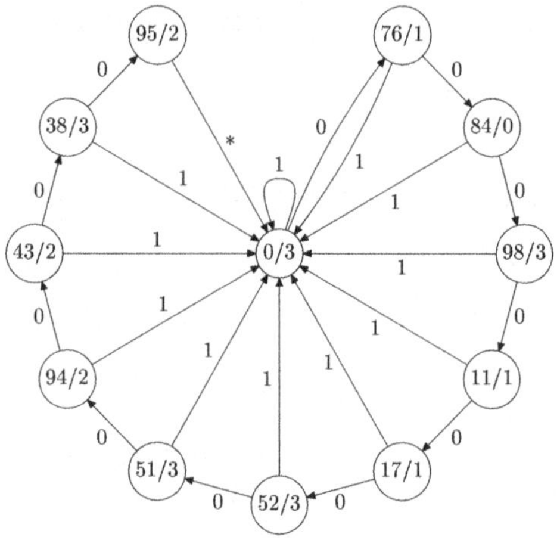

Figure 5: The best state diagram found by the SOS++ algorithm for Los Altos trail, without adaptive reward and with the NOP action.

same problem, except that here it is found by learning. If, during this cycle, the agent perceives an input 1, it returns to state 0 to move straight ahead, until next discontinuity. It is interesting to note the presence of an action NOP (even if this action has not been useful in our experiments, we left it to respect the original specification of the problem. Interestingly, it had always been eliminated by the learning and evolution algorithm). In fact, for learning, action NOP is as valid as the actions turn left or turn right, since all three generate a null reward; it is thus the evolution's responsibility to select better individuals, i.e. individuals not including in its genome the action NOP. However, an individual collecting all of the 157 units of food with only 12 states, as it is the case in our solution, has an enormous advantage over its colleagues. With such a large advantage, it is unlikely to be dethroned before many generations.

For the second test we removed the state NOP. The parameters used were the same as those of the first test, but with 10 islands populated of genomes of size 100, 90, 80, 70, 60, 50, 40, 30, 20, and 15 (one size per island). After only 3 generations, on island number 6, an individual was found able to traverse the trail in 679 actions, using only 10 states out of the 40 of its genome. This solution, which required 472 learning iterations, is given in figure 6.

In spite of the low number of states used, this solution remains nevertheless interpretable and presents a behavior quite surprising by its "intelligence". Indeed, the state diagram of figure 6 can be broken up into two sub-FSM; the first, composed of the states 0, 39, 8, 33, 2, 34, 7, and the second of the states 34, 7, 10, 12, 20, which corresponds to the two parts of the trail: that identical to the Santa Fe trail and that added later by Koza. Our method was thus able to differentiate between these two parts, finding a solution for each one and interconnect-

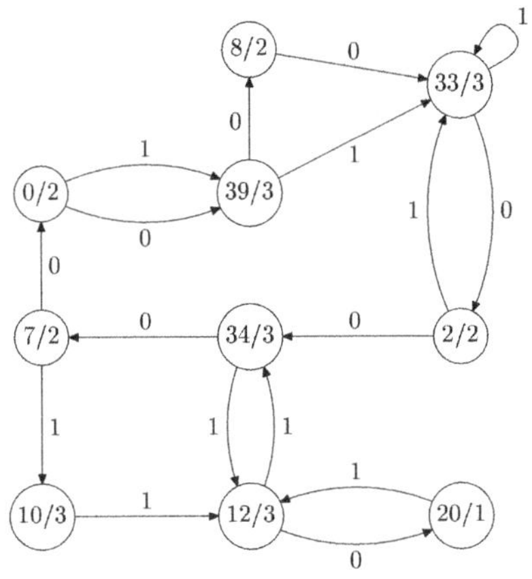

Figure 6: The best state diagram found by the full SOS++ algorithm for Los Altos trail, without the NOP action.

ing them. For the first part, the agent leaves state 2 and carries out the sequence of actions 2 3 2 2 3 (2) 3: when it is facing a discontinuity, it explores a cell to the right (2 3 2 2 3) and, if its still does not perceive anything (input 0), turns right (2) and moves straight ahead (3). This behavior makes it possible to navigate the complete Santa Fe trail. To change behavior, the agent must find the breaking point with Santa Fe, i.e. where the trail added by Koza starts. The strength of this method is shown when, in a surprising manner, this characteristic is actually found at the point of the first contour added by Koza. When it arrives there, the agent moves towards the south and is in state 33, with an input 0. This configuration leads it to turn right (state 2), then to move ahead (state 34). At this point, the agent is directed towards the west and perceives an input 1, which enables it to know that it engages in the second part of the trail (state 12). Here, it moves ahead, then turns left, so as to move towards the south, and oscillates between the states 12 and 34, which both make it move ahead. When the agent arrives at the following contour, it is at state 34 and perceives an input 0, turns right (state 7), then passes successively through states 10, 12 and 34 which make it move towards the next discontinuity. When it reaches that point, it is at state 34 with an input 0 and comes back to the first sub-FSM, which leads it to move backwards (actions 2 2 3), going back a cell (2 3) and turning to the west (2 3). At the end of this set of actions, the agent is at a cell below the discontinuity (on the gray cell). As input 0 is perceived on this site, this leads the agent to perform this set of actions for a second time, enabling it to find the trail, i.e. to have an input 1 when it is at state 2. A passage through state 33, then through state 2, enables it to be directed towards the south; then, the return to state 33 enables it to reach the next difficulty. The latter is passed in the same way as the preceding one, i.e. by exploring a cell on the right while going down, but this time the agent is at state 34 when it finds the trail. The final part of the trail is carried out thanks to the second sub-FSM. The last difficulty is then overcome by using the same exploratory behavior used in the previous discontinuity.

Wiering and Schmidhuber Maze

Reinforcement learning works particularly well for the trail problems because a reward is possible at almost all the steps of the problem. It is much more difficult to use this learning method if the reward is given only at the end, when the task is successfully accomplished. This is the case of the Wiering and Schmidhuber maze (Wiering & Schmidhuber 1997) (figure 7), a well-known problem in literature, for which traditional reinforcement learning does not give a solution.

Here, starting at the point S, the task of the agent is to arrive at the point G while following the shortest possible way. To accomplish this task, it can move in the four cardinal directions, with actions coded in the following way: 0 (west), 1 (north), 2 (east) and 3 (south). The knowledge of its environment comes to it from 4 sensors, placed in the 4 directions: the value of the input (observation) is thus the sum of the 4 sensors, weighted by 1 (west), 2 (north), 4 (east) and 8 (south). Thus, for example, walls in the west and the south of the agent generate an input $1 + 8 = 9$. In addition, the agent obtains a reward of -1 ($r = -1$) when it runs up against a wall, of 10 when it achieves the goal, and of 0 otherwise. In the evolution, the fitness rewards individuals reaching to the goal more than those using fewer operations to do so, and finally those using fewer states. Therefore, using the equation 2, we set the weights w_i as follows: $w_1 = 10^5$, $w_2 = 1$ and $w_3 = 10^2$.

The evolution and learning parameters used in our tests are as follows:

NISL	ISLPOP	NGBM	NEMIG
9	200	5	3

STEPS	TRIALS	PMUT	PREP
250	1000	5%	75%

The evolution uses nine islands, populated by genomes of size 20, 15, 10, 9, 8, 7, 6, 5, and 4 (one size per island). After 548 generations, our algorithm found an agent passing through the shortest way (28 actions) and using only 4 states among the 8 available in its genome, after 662 learning iterations, with $\alpha \approx 0.24$ and $\gamma \approx 0.93$. The state diagram corresponding to this solution is given in figure 7. It is interesting to note that although the optimal solution required 548 generations, other solutions are also obtained in the first generation, only by learning. These latter solutions generally use the shortest way, but none have less than 7 states. This result is

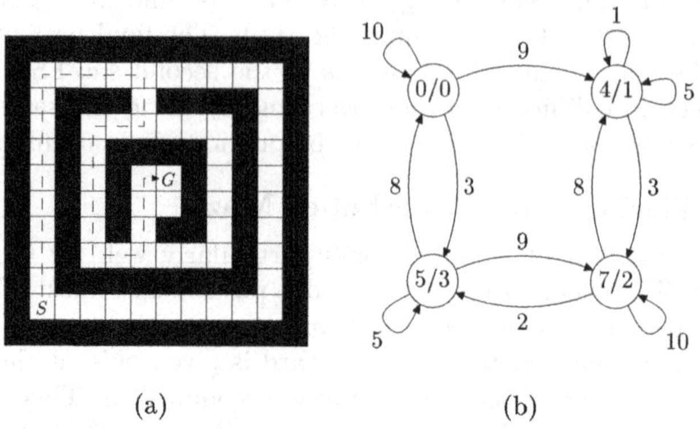

Figure 7: a) Wiering-Schmidhuber maze and b) the best state diagram found by the SOS++ algorithm. The numbers on the arrows indicate the input value computed as a function of its four sensors (e.g., 0: no obstacle, 1: obstacle to the right, 2: obstacle to the north, 6: obstacle to the north and to the west, etc.), the numbers on the circles indicate the state and the associated action (0: west, 1: north, 2: east, 3: south).

very significant since, as told previously, the traditional reinforcement learning never solves this problem.

Conclusions

The use of FSMs to realize the controller of autonomous agents is preferable to the use of neural networks, when planning to produce a hardware implementation: indeed, this method is the most commonly used when designing digital systems. Moreover, FSMs have the advantage of their "legibility": it is easier to understand a behavior if it is described in this form than as a neural network, for example.

Our method allows the automatic synthesis of the behaviors which an autonomous agent can perform with this type of controllers. These behaviors emerge by evolution and learning from the simple list of basic actions with which the agent was equipped at its "birth", and from the interactions between these actions and the environment. In addition, we can generalize the found solutions: the FSM produced by the solution of the Sante Fe problem, for example, can be used to correctly navigate through a whole family of other trails without additional learning (those where the trail discontinuities are always in straight lines with food and their end can be determined by a simple rotation of the ant).

Evolution, used in a traditional way, allows one to find good individuals who are able to achieve the expected behavior simply by learning. A very fast evolution is achieved thanks to the very small size of the genome, made up simply of a list of actions associated with the possible states of the FSM and two learning parameters.

Our learning method, derived from classical reinforcement learning, modified by the use of an evolution of its two learning parameters together with a reward adapted to the uncertainty of the prediction performed, proved very powerful. Indeed, learning can solve simple problems without evolution, finding a solution at the first generation. In addition, problems for which traditional reinforcement learning could not obtain any solution were solved.

The discrete character of the values used for the observations of the environment could be regarded as a disadvantage if one wants to use this method with real problems, such as the control of autonomous robots. However, it is possible to consider our basic actions as FSMs processing the lowest level of perception, and our method can deal in these cases with higher level behaviors. In fact, we are currently implementing the experiments described in this paper with a real Khepera robot: a film with these new results is viewable on the Web page of our Laboratory (`http://lslwww.epfl.ch`).

References

Brooks, R. A. 1999. *Cambrian Intelligence: The Early History of the New AI.* Cambridge, MA: MIT Press.

Koza, J. R. 1992. *Genetic Programming: On the Programming of Computers by Means of Natural Selection.* Cambridge, MA: MIT Press.

Michalewicz, Z. 1997 *Genetic Algorithms + Data Structures = Evolution Programs.* Springer-Verlag, Heidelberg, third edition.

Nolfi, S., and Floreano, D. 2000. *Evolutionary Robotics.* Cambridge, MA: MIT Press.

Sanchez, E. 1998. An Introduction to Digital Systems. In Mange, D., and Tomassini, M., eds., *Bio-Inspired Computing Machines: Toward Novel Computational Machines*, 13. Lausanne: Presses Polytechniques et Universitaires Romandes.

Sanchez, E., Perez-Uribe, A., and Mesot, B. 2001. Solving Partially Observable Problems by Evolution and Learning of Finite-State Machines. In Liu, Y., Tanaka, K., Iwata, M., Higuchi, T., and Yasunaga, M., eds., *Evolvable Systems: From Biology to Hardware, ICES 2001*, 267. Berlin: Springer-Verlag.

Shannon, C. E. 1948. A Mathematical Theory of Communication. *Bell Systems Technical Journal* 27:379.

Sutton, R. S., and Barto, A. G. 1998. *Reinforcement Learning: An Introduction.* Cambridge, MA: MIT Press.

Vose, M. D. 1999 *The Simple Genetic Algorithm.* MIT Press, Cambridge, MA.

Wiering, M., and Schmidhuber, J. 1997. HQ-Learning. *Adaptive Behavior* 6:2.

Temporally Adaptive Networks: Analysis of GasNet Robot Control Networks

Tom Smith *‡, **Phil Husbands** †, **Andy Philippides** * and **Michael O'Shea** *

Centre for Computational Neuroscience and Robotics (CCNR)
*School of Biological Sciences, †School of Cognitive and Computing Sciences
University of Sussex, Brighton, UK.
‡Email: `toms@cogs.susx.ac.uk`. Web: `http://www.cogs.susx.ac.uk/users/toms/`

Abstract

Identification of the fundamental properties necessary for the generation of adaptive behaviour is one of the primary goals for Artificial Life. In this paper, we address the related question of whether we can identify general useful properties of a given solution class. Such an approach provides a potentially scalable framework that may enable us to identify general properties of more complex adaptive systems. We develop a methodology based on analysis of successfully evolved solutions to an evolutionary robotics shape discrimination problem, allowing us to identify properties of solution classes that are potentially useful over a wider class of problems than the original task. We propose that the evolvability of the solution class is due to the fundamental property of *temporal adaptivity.*

Introduction

In a recent call to arms, Bedau et al. (2000) defined one of the primary goals for Artificial Life as identification of the minimal conditions for transition from specific to generic response systems. In other words, what are the fundamental properties necessary for a system to be adaptive?

Answering such a challenge is well beyond the scope of current understanding, however in this paper, we make some headway by investigating the solution classes underlying neural networks used as robot controllers. In particular, we address two questions. First, how can we evaluate the effectiveness of a given solution class on some problem? Second, can we evaluate how effective the solution class is likely to be on different problems? In other words, can we identify general useful properties of a solution class that may hold over a wider range of problems than simply the problem studied? Such an approach provides a potentially scalable framework that may enable us to identify general properties required for more complex adaptive systems.

We develop a methodology based on analysis of successfully evolved solutions to an evolutionary robotics shape discrimination problem, allowing us to identify properties of solution classes that are potentially useful over a wider class of problems than the original task. We go on to test these properties, through analysis of the evolved solutions in modified environments. We apply the techniques to a class of artificial neural network robot controllers inspired by work on diffusible neuromodulation, and argue that the evolvability of this biologically inspired GasNet solution class is due to the fundamental property of *temporal adaptivity.*

GasNet robot controllers

Artificial neural networks possess many useful properties for the generation of behaviour over time. However, the networks of simple units linked by weighted synapse connections typically used in ANN applications are extremely simplified abstractions of the real thing; nervous systems found in biology are far more complex, with a multitude of interacting processes operating over both space and time. The "GasNet" class of neural networks (Husbands et al., 1998) is explicitly inspired by the action of *diffusing gaseous neuromodulation* in real nervous systems, incorporating a mechanism based on the neuron-modulating properties of a diffusing signalling gas into a more standard sigmoid-unit neural network. In previous work the networks have been used in a variety of evolutionary robotics tasks, comparing the speeds of evolution for networks with and without (the "NoGas") the gas signalling mechanism active. In a variety of robotics tasks, GasNet controllers evolve significantly faster than networks without the gas signalling mechanism (see e.g. Husbands, 1998; Husbands *et al.*).

The GasNet and NoGas models

The GasNet is an arbitrarily recurrent ANN augmented with a gas concentration model, in which the instantaneous activation of a node is a function of both the inputs from connected nodes and the current concentration of gas(es) at the node. The basic network model consists of connected sigmoid transfer function nodes overlaid with a model of diffusing gaseous modulators; the gas does not alter the electrical activity in the network directly but rather acts by changing the gain of transfer function mapping between node input and output.

The network underlying the GasNet and NoGas models is a discrete time-step, recurrent neural network with a variable number of nodes. These nodes are connected by either excitatory (with a weight of +1) or inhibitory (with a weight of −1) links with the output O_i^t, of node i at time-step t determined by a continuous mapping from the sum of its inputs. This defines the basic NoGas class:

$$O_i^t = \tanh\left[K_i^t\left(\sum_{j\in C_i} w_{ji}O_j^{t-1} + I_i^t\right) + b_i\right] \quad (1)$$

where C_i is the set of nodes with connections to node i with connection weights w_{ji}, O_j^{t-1} the output of node j on the previous time-step, I_i^t the external (sensory) input to node i at time t, and b_i a genetically set bias. Each node has a genetically set default transfer function parameter K_i^0, and for the NoGas class this transfer parameter is fixed over the operation of the network: $K_i^t = K_i^0 \; \forall t$.

In the GasNet control system, in addition to this underlying network in which electrical signals flow between units, an abstract process loosely analogous to the gaseous diffusing modulators described above is at play. Some units can emit gases which diffuse and are capable of modulating the behaviour of other units through altering their transfer functions. As described below, this modulation changes the transfer parameter K_i^t as the network runs, thus the actual shape of the node's transfer function is altered via the gas modulation mechanism. This form of modulation allows a kind of plasticity in the network in which the intrinsic properties of units are changing during the operation of the network, that is during the robot controller lifetime. In the next sections we describe the gas diffusion and modulation mechanisms.

Gas diffusion in the networks

In order to incorporate the gas concentration model, the network is placed in a 2D plane, with node positions specified genetically. The GasNet diffusion model is controlled by two genetically specified parameters namely the radius of influence r around the emitting node, and the rate of build up and decay s. Spatially, the gas concentration varies as an inverse exponential of the distance from the emitting node with a spread governed by r, with the concentration set to zero for all distances greater than r (equation 2). The maximum concentration at the emitting node is one and the concentration builds up and decays from this value linearly as defined by equations (equation 3 and 4) at a rate determined by s. The governing equations are:

$$C(d,t) = \begin{cases} C_0 \, T(t) \, e^{-(d/r)^2} & d < r \\ 0 & \text{else} \end{cases} \tag{2}$$

$$T(t) = \begin{cases} H(\frac{t-t_e}{s}) & \text{emitting} \\ H(H(\frac{t_s-t_e}{s}) - H(\frac{t-t_s}{s})) & \text{not emitting} \end{cases} \tag{3}$$

$$H(x) = \begin{cases} 0 & x \leq 0 \\ x & 0 < x < 1 \\ 1 & \text{else} \end{cases} \tag{4}$$

where C(d,t) is the concentration at a distance d from the emitting node at time t. t_e is the time at which emission was last turned on, t_s is the time at which emission was last turned off, and s (controlling the slope of the function T) is genetically determined for each node. To summarise, within a radius of r from the node, gas builds up (and decays) linearly to a maximum of $e^{-2d/r}$ in s time-steps. The total concentration at a node is then determined by summing the concentrations from all other emitting nodes (nodes are not affected by their own concentration, to avoid runaway positive feedback).

Modulation by the gases

There are two virtual gases in the network, gas 1 and gas 2, which increase and decrease K_i^t (see equation 1) respectively in a concentration dependent fashion. Both the type of gas emitted by a node and the conditions under which it emits are specified genetically. Nodes emit either gas 1, gas 2 or no gas, and emission occurs when either the electrical activation at a node exceeds 0.5, or the concentration of gas in the vicinity of the node exceeds 0.1. The concentration-dependent modulation is described by equations 5 to 8, with transfer parameters updated on every time-step as the network runs. Thus we have:

$$K_i^t = \mathbf{P}[D_i^t] \tag{5}$$

$$\mathbf{P} = \{-4.0, -2.0, -1.0, -0.5, -0.25, -0.125, 0.0, 0.125, 0.25, 0.5, 1.0, 2.0, 4.0\} \tag{6}$$

$$D_i^t = f\left(D_i^0 + \frac{C_1^t}{C_0 K}(N - D_i^0) - \frac{C_2^t}{C_0 K} D_i^0\right) \tag{7}$$

$$f(x) = \begin{cases} 0 & x \leq 0 \\ \lfloor x \rfloor & 0 < x < N \\ N-1 & \text{else} \end{cases} \tag{8}$$

where $\mathbf{P}[i]$ refers to the ith element of set $\mathbf{P}$, D_i^t is node i's index into the set $\mathbf{P}$ of possible discrete values K_i^t can assume, N is the number of elements in $\mathbf{P}$, D_i^0 is the genetically set default value for D_i, C_1^t is the concentration of gas 1 at node i on time-step t and C_2^t is the concentration of gas 2 at node i on time-step t. Both gas concentrations lie in the range $[0, 1]$.

Thus, the concentration of each gas is directly proportional to any change in D_i^t, with a corresponding change in K_i^t. Although the change in K_i^t is non-linear these values represent a smooth change in the slope of the transfer function. Since the transfer functions can change throughout the lifetime of the network, this system provides a form of network plasticity not seen in most other ANNs.

Visual shape discrimination

The evolutionary task at hand is a visual shape discrimination task; starting from an arbitrary position and orientation in a black-walled arena, the robot must navigate to one shape (a white triangle) while ignoring the second shape (a white square), under the extremely variable lighting conditions produced by an array of spotlights flashing on and off at random time intervals. Both the robot control network, an arbitrarily recurrent ANN, and the robot sensor input morphology, i.e. the position of

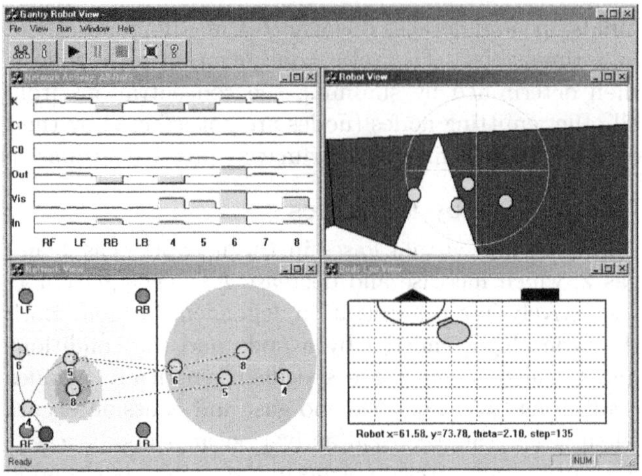

Figure 1: Screen shot of the simulated arena and robot. The bottom-right view shows the robot position in the arena with the triangle and square. Fitness is evaluated on how close the robot approaches the triangle. The top-right view shows what the robot 'sees', along with the pixel positions selected by evolution for visual input. The top-left view shows the current activity of all nodes in the neural network. The bottom-left view shows the robot control neural network.

the input pixels on the visual array, were under evolutionary control. Fitness over a single trial was taken as the fraction of the starting distance moved towards the triangle by the end of the trial period, and the evaluated fitness was returned as the average over 16 trials of the controller from different initial conditions. Success in the task was taken as an evaluated fitness of 1.0 over thirty successive generations of the evolutionary algorithm. In the work reported here, fitness evaluations are carried out in a verified *minimal simulation* (Jakobi, 1998), see figure 1 for screen-shot of a fitness evaluation in simulation. A large number of controllers evolved in simulation have been tested on the real robot, with all controllers displaying similar robot trajectories and fitnesses to the simulated fitness evaluations (Husbands et al., 1998).

A distributed asynchronous updating evolutionary algorithm was used, with a *PopSize* of 100 arranged on a 10×10 grid. Parents were chosen through rank-based roulette-wheel selection on the mating pool consisting of the 8 nearest neighbours to a randomly chosen grid-point. The child solution was a mutated copy of the parent (the mutation operator applied a $\mu = 4\%$ mutation probability per bit, and the same probability per genome of adding or deleting a network node. No crossover was used.) and placed back in the mating pool using inverse rank-based roulette-wheel selection. One generation was specified as *PopSize* such breeding events.

Speed of evolution results

Over a large sample of evolutionary runs with GasNet and NoGas conditions, GasNet networks allowed to use the gaseous signalling mechanism reached success significantly faster than the NoGas networks. This speed difference was seen in several different evolutionary robotics scenarios (Husbands, 1998; Husbands et al., 1998, e.g.) and over several different mutation rates, e.g. see figure 2.

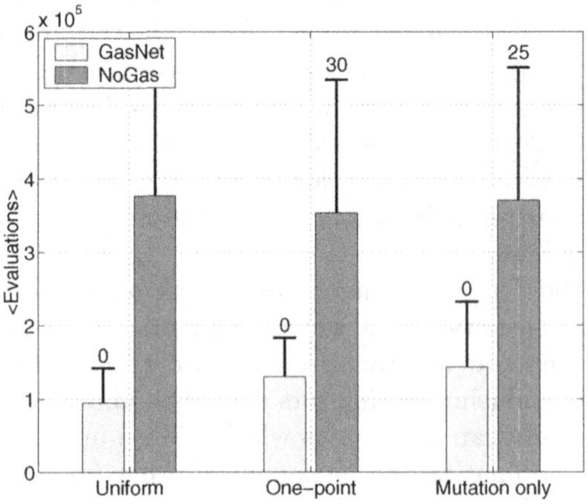

(a) Uniform, one-point, and no recombination

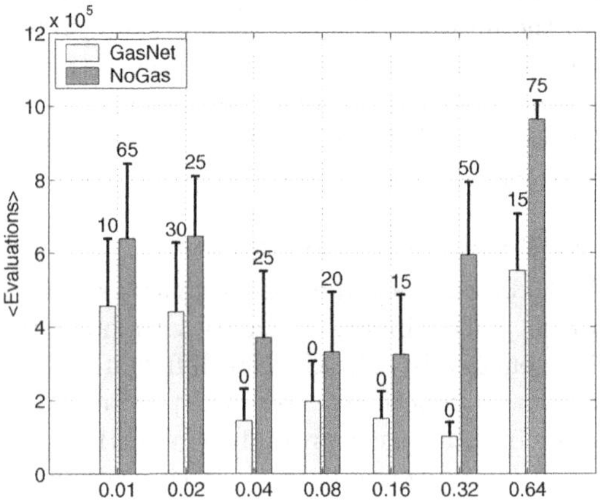

(b) No recombination, varying mutation rate μ

Figure 2: The mean number of evaluations required for **(a)** Uniform, one-point and no recombination, and **(b)** No recombination, varying mutation rate $\mu \in \{0.01, 0.02, 0.04, 0.08, 0.16, 0.32, 0.64\}$. Data averaged over twenty runs of the distributed evolutionary algorithm. The error bars represent 95% confidence limits for the mean, the number above the bar gives the percentage of runs failing to finish in $1,000,000$ evaluations.

Analysis of evolved solutions

A number of studies have carried out analysis of evolved solutions to robot control problems, notably the work by Beer and colleagues (Beer and Gallagher, 1992; Beer et al., 1999; Chiel et al., 1999, e.g). However, the emphasis has typically been on developing methods for analysis, or characterising the type of solutions generated by evolution. The literature is not well developed in terms of analysing evolved solutions *in order to test the suitability of the underlying solution class.* That is the approach we use in this paper.

Pattern generation

In a number of evolved robotic controllers, rhythmic pattern generation output was seen to occur, with one or more nodes locked into some limit cycle behaviour (Smith, 2002). Figure 3 shows the behaviour of a two-node subnetwork for a GasNet class solution, with output activity Y, transfer parameters K and gas concentrations C_0, C_1 plotted over 100 time-steps of a sample evaluation. Note the 'spiking' behaviour shown in the node activity Y_2 graph; once every eight time-steps this right-back motor node comes on. This spiking behaviour is crucial to the final fitness of the solution — with both motors on, the robot will move straight-forwards. However, the right-back motor node turning on once in every eight time steps produces a slow clockwise turn in the robot, which in evaluation results in the robot arcing towards the triangle.

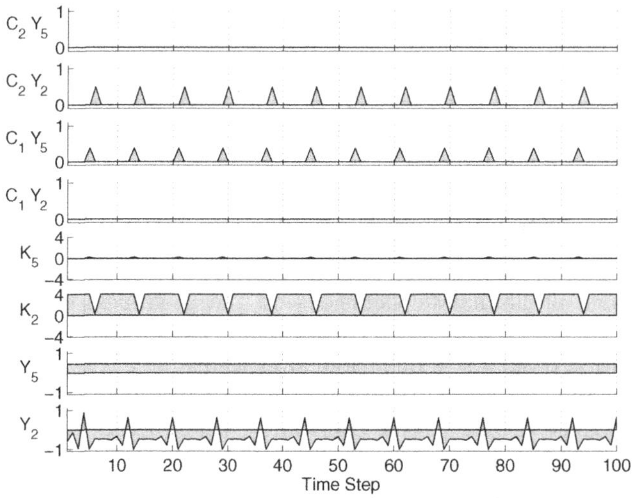

Figure 3: For nodes 2 (the right-back motor node) and 5, involved in the 'spiking' subnetwork, the figure shows data over a run of 100 time-steps for node output $Y \in [-1, 1]$, node transfer parameter $K \in [-4, 4]$, positive and negative gas concentrations $C_1, C_2 \in [0, 1]$ at the node site. Area between the output and time axis is shaded for clarity.

Detailed analysis (Smith, 2002) provides an explanation for this (and other) pattern generation, through the interaction between the gas and electrical mechanisms in the network. High electrical output activity of the right-back motor node stimulates gas emission from the second node in the network, which in turn inhibits the motor node, in turn stopping the emission of gas which in turn finally allows the motor node to return to high electrical activity, and the pattern repeats. In a number of other successfully evolved GasNet controllers we have observed similar subnetworks; it appears that the properties of the GasNet class lend themselves readily to pattern generation.

Functionally equivalent controllers

Many evolved solutions were found to use functionally equivalent mechanisms for shape discrimination. Figure 4 shows two functionally equivalent subnetworks, one GasNet class controller and one NoGas class controller. Both controllers time the duration over which bright input is received from visual inputs in the upper half of the visual field. A second visual input mechanism (not shown) acts simply as a bright finding detector. This mechanism is 'later' in the visual field than the timing mechanism, i.e. the position of visual input to this mechanism is such that it will 'see' things after the timing mechanism due to the direction of robot rotation, and is inhibited if the duration of bright input reception is sufficiently long. This inhibition will occur in the situation of scanning across the square but not when scanning across the triangle, so the controllers approach only the triangle. In the next sections we describe the methods by which the GasNet and NoGas classes produce such a timing mechanism.

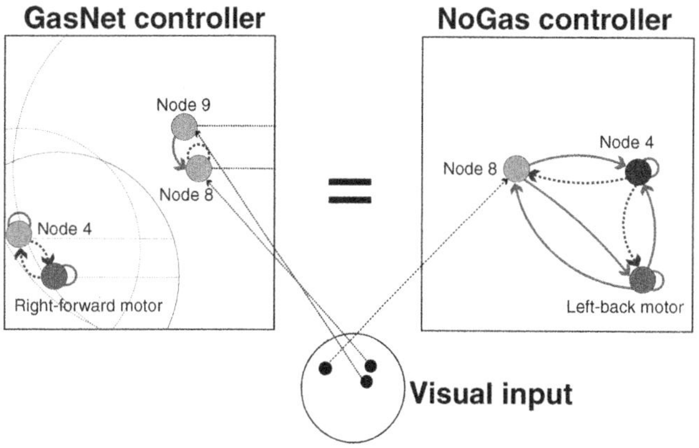

Figure 4: The two functionally equivalent subnetworks. Both employ the same strategy for triangle-square discrimination; timing the duration of receiving bright input in the upper half of the visual field. Due to triangles being narrower than squares at the top, this allows the shapes to be successfully discriminated.

The GasNet and NoGas "timers" In the GasNet class, a timing mechanism that retains activity for some time after the initial input has been received, is simple to produce. A single node receiving visual input, and with the property that gas emission occurs when the node output activity is high, will start emitting gas when bright input is received. The gas concentration built-up during emission will take some time to decay once bright input is no longer received. Recall from the section on diffusion that gas concentration decays exponentially with distance from the emitting node, but increases linearly over time during emission, and decreases linearly over time once emission stops. Figure 46.5(a) shows the gas concentration at the motor node over time when square wave visual input is received at nodes 8 and 9.

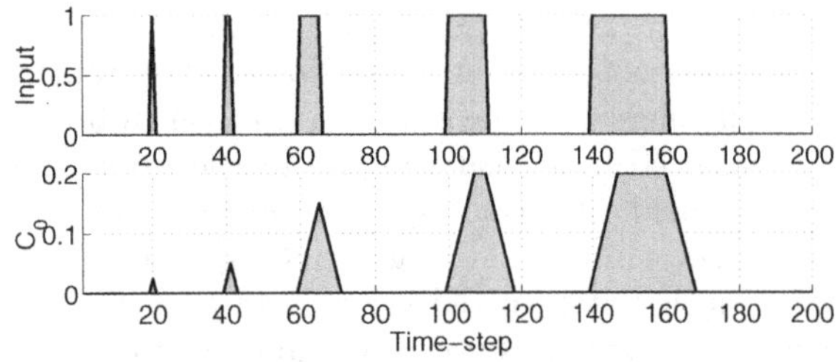

(a) GasNet timing mechanism

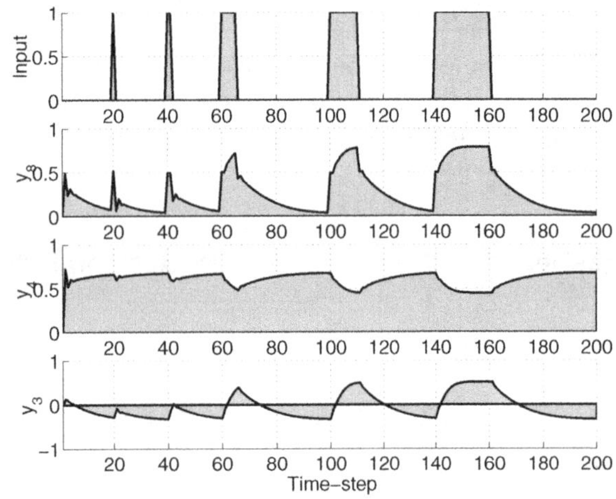

(b) NoGas timing mechanism

Figure 5: The GasNet and NoGas timing mechanisms. A square wave external visual input of increasing width is applied as input, to illustrate the differences between the output seen for the triangle and for the square. **(a)** Gas concentration C_0 over 200 time-steps. **(b)** Node output data (ranging from ± 1) for nodes 3, 4 and 8. Area between the output and time axis is shaded for clarity.

For this timing mechanism to affect the controller operation, we require the built-up gas concentration to affect the motor node activity. Again, this is relatively simple to effect, as the gas concentration can modulate either the motor node, or as in the controller analysed here, another visual input node which has an output connection to the motor node.

The mechanism underlying the NoGas timer is more complex, and as seen in the re-evolution analysis is harder to tune. Analysis of the fully connected three-node subnetwork (see the right-hand side of figure 4) shows a single stable equilibrium point for the system when visual input is below the input threshold, and a different single stable equilibrium when visual input is above threshold. The key to the timing mechanism is how the system moves between these fixed points when the visual input changes. With no bright input to node 8, the system settles into the first stable fixed point described above, while with bright input the system settles into the second stable point above. Once bright input is no longer received, the system slowly decays back to the first stable fixed point.

The feedback between the nodes ensures the decay between stable states is fairly slow, producing an effect which can build-up and decay over time, in a similar fashion to that of gas concentration. The longer that bright input is received for, the nearer the high visual input stable state the system reaches, and the longer it takes to decay back to the low visual input stable state. Figure 46.5(b) shows the outputs for the three nodes in the system when a square wave visual input is applied to node 8, and clearly shows the slow change from one state to another when visual input changes from dark to bright, or vice versa. It takes roughly ten time-steps for node 3 to reach the bright input stable state, and roughly thirty steps to decay back to the dark visual input regime. The motor node activity Y_3 is the crucial value; as this goes from negative to positive, the left motor is inhibited, and the robot does not approach the bright object. Only when sufficient bright input has been received will this occur, i.e. when the square has been scanned across.

So why are GasNets evolvable?

From our analysis of evolved controllers, we can frame some preliminary conclusions on the usefulness of the mechanisms utilised in GasNet controllers for the generation of adaptive behaviour over time.

First, tunable pattern generation is extremely easy to produce using GasNet controllers. In general, pattern generation is based on limit cycle behaviour, with the system cycling through some set of states (Beer et al., 1999; Chiel et al., 1999). The spiking subnetwork (figure 3) operated in exactly such a fashion; the high fitness of the controller was due to this subnetwork slowly turning the robot back towards the triangle. This leads to our first hypothesis for why the GasNet class is more evolvable than the NoGas class; the GasNets are more amenable to being 'tuned' to the specific characteristics of the environment. The pattern produced in which the right-back motor node spiked once in every eight time-steps was perfectly tuned to the speed and size of the robot wheels, the size of the triangle, and the size of the arena in which the robot operated. A different pattern would not have produced such high fitness in this environment, and the same pattern would not have produced such high fitness in a different environment. We hypoth-

	Double speed		Quarter speed	
	GasNet	NoGas	GasNet	NoGas
Number of cases	20	20	20	20
Mean evaluated fitness (σ)	0.17 (0.074)	0.15 (0.066)	0.36* (0.10)	0.21 (0.016)
Mean re-evolution generations (σ)	10 (5)**	409 (336)	30 (31)**	591 (346)
Median re-evolution generations	10**	360	19**	608

Table 1: Data for the two functionally equivalent networks shown in figure 4, re-evolved in two modified environments. The robot motors are set to double-speed and quarter-speed respectively, and the two controllers evaluated 100 times for fitness, then seeded back in to the evolutionary algorithm until 100% fitness was reached (20 runs were performed for each controller on each condition). The evaluated fitnesses, and mean, standard deviation σ and median generations of re-evolution required to reach 100% are shown. Significant differences between the GasNet and NoGas controllers are highlighted (both parametric T-tests and non-parametric Mann-Whitney U tests performed $^{*}p < 0.05, ^{**}p < 0.01$).

esise that the same kind of environmental tuning is more difficult with the NoGas class.

The tuning of generated patterns is closely related to our second hypotheses regarding useful properties in the GasNet class for adaptive behaviour; the ability to switch between stable states, in other words a discontinuous change of behaviour determined by external input, and the ability to mediate such switching. This is clearly possible to achieve without gas modulation, but the features of the gas diffusion mechanism allow such a switch to take place over several time-steps, through the build-up of gas concentration levels. This was seen in the functionally equivalent mechanisms, where the switch from rotation to straight-forwards motion was inhibited by bright input, *only when such bright input was received over several time-steps*. Thus the switching can be based on input patterns received over time, not just at a single time-point.

Finally, the ability to filter out noisy input is straightforward to produce when using the GasNet controller class, also through requiring that input be consistent over several time-steps. This was seen in a number of GasNet controllers, where build-up of gas concentration was used for filtering sensory input. Thus bright flashes and other noisy environment effects were efficiently excluded by the GasNet solutions.

We propose that the crucial property of the GasNet class is *temporal adaptivity*; the ability to be tuned to the specific temporal characteristics of the environment. In the next section we test this through re-evolving solutions in modified environments.

Re-evolution of controllers

Functionally equivalent controllers

The hypothesis that the functionally equivalent GasNet timing mechanism is easier to tune than the functionally equivalent NoGas mechanism can be investigated through the behaviour of the controllers in environments with modified properties. In this section, we analyse the controllers when evaluated in two separate environments, where the robot motor speeds are respectively set to double and quarter the usual motor speeds. This has the effect of making the robot move at a different speed in the arena, in particular spinning past the two shapes at very different rates to the speeds encountered during the original evolutionary phase. Note that the environments could similarly be modified through altering the size and properties of the shapes, and/or the size of the arena. Other modifications could also investigate the effect of re-evolving from lesioned or similarly modified control networks. However, in this work we focus on modification of the robot motor speeds.

We would expect the timing mechanisms to be affected by such speed change, with the time spent spinning past the triangle and square much shorter in the double speed environment, and much longer in the quarter speed environment. However, the hypothesis that the GasNet mechanism is in some sense easier to tune to the particular properties of the environment can be tested through seeding the controllers back into the evolutionary process, with fitness based on evaluation in the modified environments. We can then re-run the evolutionary process from the controller seeds, assessing how long before controllers of 100% fitness are again achieved. In this re-evolution, we allow only the parts of the genotype involved in the timing mechanism to be affected by the evolutionary process; we are assessing how easy it is to modify the actual mechanism itself, not the rest of the network.

Results for re-evolution studies of the two controllers are given in table 1. In the double speed environment, both controllers drop in fitness to well under 20%, but there is no significant difference between the two controllers in this environment. However, there is massive difference in the number of generations required to re-evolve controllers of 100% fitness; the GasNet controller is much easier to tune to the modified properties of the environment (10 generations on average compared with 409). In the quarter speed environment, the GasNet controller achieves significantly higher fitness than the NoGas controller, but the difference in the number of generations required to reach 100% fitness controllers is much larger than predicted by this fitness difference (the

	Double speed		Quarter speed	
	GasNet	NoGas	GasNet	NoGas
Number of cases	200	200	200	200
Mean evaluated fitness (σ)	0.27 (0.13)	0.26 (0.18)	0.35 (0.27)	0.29 (0.19)
Mean re-evolution generations (σ)	107 (190)**	240 (363)	108 (229)	116 (252)
Median re-evolution generations	36*	49	13**	21

Table 2: Data for samples of twenty GasNet and twenty NoGas controllers, re-evolved in two modified environments. See table 1 for details.

generations of re-evolution required for the NoGas controller to reach the fitness level of the GasNet controller does not affect the results). So in both modified environments, the GasNet controllers are much easier to evolve successful controllers than would be predicted from their fitnesses.

Sample of controllers

It may be argued that the two functionally equivalent controllers investigated are based on a mechanism which is in principle easier to produce using the GasNet control class. Thus re-evolving the timing mechanism in modified environments will unfairly favour the GasNet controller. By contrast other mechanisms may favour NoGas classes; here we counter this argument through extending the re-evolution analysis to a random sample of forty previously evolved GasNet and NoGas controllers of 100% fitness.

The forty controllers were used as initial seeds for the evolutionary algorithm, which was run until controllers once more showed 100% fitness, with fitness evaluated in the same double- and quarter-speed environments described in the previous section. Table 2 shows the results for the two conditions, averaged over ten evolutionary runs of each of the forty controllers. The results are not as striking as those from the functionally equivalent controllers, lending weight to the hypothesis that the previous analysis unfairly favoured the GasNet mechanism. However, the GasNet controllers still showed significantly faster re-evolution than the NoGas controllers. In the double speed environment, both samples of controllers fell to average fitnesses of 0.26, but the GasNet controllers on average re-evolved in 107 generations compared with 240 generations for the NoGas controllers. In the quarter speed environment, the differences are much smaller, with comparable mean numbers of generations for re-evolution, although there is some evidence of faster evolution from the median numbers of generations. Thus from our sample of GasNet controllers, we also see evidence of significantly faster re-evolution to modified environments; the GasNets are more tunable.

Summary

The detailed analysis of a number of GasNet and NoGas controllers allowed us to frame two hypotheses regarding the suitability of the GasNet class to robot control.

First, the ability to both produce and modify central pattern generation output was seen to be central to a number of evolved control solutions. This seems surprising. We are not investigating such behaviours as walking and swimming gaits, or rhythmic feeding, where behaviour is often based on central pattern generation. Our visual shape discrimination task might not at first sight appear to be related to such pattern generation. However, a number of GasNet controllers were seen to use pattern generation subnetworks in the final evolved behaviour.

Second, the ability to switch between dynamical states dependent on external input, and the ability to mediate this switch over a number of time-steps was seen to be extremely useful both in behaviour generation and filtering environmental noise. From analysis of the functionally equivalent GasNet and NoGas controllers, we argued that the kinds of active perception timing strategies able to mediate such behaviour switching and noise filtration were much easier to evolve using the GasNet class. To develop and tune the NoGas timing mechanism required the construction of a complex fully-connected circuit, while the corresponding GasNet timing mechanism was based on the build-up and decay of gas.

The twin hypotheses that GasNet classes were more amenable to both the development and tuning of pattern generation and the development and tuning of switching mechanisms were supported by the re-evolution studies. We saw that the functionally equivalent GasNet controller was much easier to tune to a modified environment than the corresponding NoGas controller. To a lesser extent, although still significant, this same re-evolution tunability was seen over a large sample of previously evolved controllers.

So can we draw any conclusions from this work on what makes an evolvable network class for the visual discrimination problem? The simple answer is yes. The key feature of the GasNets seen to be useful on this task is the ability to smoothly adapt to the temporal characteristics of the environment. This encompasses the initial development and subsequent tuning of the controllers to the detailed properties of the robot and environment in which it finds itself. Included in this ability to smoothly adapt to the temporal characteristics of the environment, is the ability to generate a rich variety of temporal patterns, through the interaction of the gas diffusion mechanism and the electrical synaptic mechanism. The different time courses over which these two mechanisms operate was seen to be crucial to this pattern generation.

Temporally adaptive networks

In the GasNets investigated in this paper, evolved controllers used the modulation of neuron transfer functions as a process operating over a different time course to that of the underlying network synaptic activity. The particular plasticity mechanism used, concentration-dependent neuronal modulation, allowed the GasNet controllers to easily generate and tune temporal patterns, and tune behaviour to the particular temporal characteristics of the environment. And this was seen to have a direct effect on the evolvability of the GasNet class.

By showing that the evolvability of the GasNets is due to this principle of temporal adaptivity, we have provided some support for the intuition of many evolutionary robotics practitioners, namely that robot controllers operating in the real world must incorporate temporal structure, and that the evolutionary process must be able to easily adapt that structure. For example, Harvey (1993) makes the point that "... in environments where physical events have natural time-scales, the dimension of time is not an optional extra, but fundamental." Similarly, Gallagher and Beer (1999) state that "... nontrivial behavior requires the integration of experiences across time and the ability to initiate actions independent of an agent's immediate circumstances."

On this fundamental principle of temporal adaptivity, the GasNet neural network class falls squarely into a larger class that is likely to contain other networks with temporally modifiable properties, such as continuous time recurrent networks (Beer and Gallagher, 1992), pulsed neural networks (Maass and Bishop, 1999), and networks with time-lagged synaptic activity (Harvey, 1993). However, we argue that simple recurrent networks such as the NoGas are not members of this class; although activity is retained over time and the connection architecture may be arbitrarily modified, it is not straightforward for the evolutionary process to temporally modify the activity of the network. For example, as seen in the NoGas timer, it is not easy to setup an effect that lasts for some given period of time. Similarly, generating and tuning patterns is more difficult with simple recurrent networks (Smith, 2002). It seems plausible that if we are to further develop evolvable artificial neural network classes for generating adaptive behaviour over time, the starting point must be from within the class of temporally adaptive networks.

Finally, we come back to the general direction in which this paper has aimed; identification of the fundamental properties necessary for adaptive behaviour. We have shown how analysis of successful solutions on one task can identify more general properties of the solution class that are potentially useful over a wider range of problems. It is of course necessary to apply the methodology developed here to both a number of robot control tasks and a number of solution classes, in order to fully support the temporally adaptive hypothesis presented in this paper. However, further analysis may also shed light on other fundamental properties necessary for the generation of adaptive behaviour over time. Such analysis of more complex adaptive systems can, in principle, similarly illuminate the general conditions necessary to make the transition from specific to generic response systems.

Acknowledgements

The authors would like to thank the members of the CCNR (http://www.cogs.susx.ac.uk/ccnr/) for constructive discussion. We would also like to thank the Sussex High Performance Computing Initiative (http://www.hpc.sussex.ac.uk/) for computing support. TS is funded by a BTexaCT Future Technologies Group sponsored CASE studentship (http://www.btexact.com/projects/ftg/).

References

Bedau, M. A., McCaskill, J. S., Packard, N. H., Rasmussen, S., Adami, C., Green, D. G., Ikegami, T., Kaneko, K., and Ray, T. S. (2000). Open problems in Artificial Life. *Artificial Life*, 6:363–376.

Beer, R., Chiel, H., and Gallagher, J. (1999). Evolution and analysis of model CPGs for walking II. general principles and individual variability. *Journal of Computational Neuroscience*, 7(2):119–147.

Beer, R. D. and Gallagher, J. C. (1992). Evolving dynamical neural networks for adaptive behaviour. *Adaptive Behaviour*, 1:94–110.

Chiel, H., Beer, R., and Gallagher, J. (1999). Evolution and analysis of model CPGs for walking I. Dynamical Modules. *Journal of Computational Neuroscience*, 7(2):99–118.

Gallagher, J. C. and Beer, R. D. (1999). Evolution and analysis of dynamical neural networks for agents integrating vision, locomotion, and short-term memory. In Banzhaf, W. and Smith, R. E., editors, *Proceedings of the Genetic and Evolutionary Computation Conference (GECCO'99)*. Morgan Kaufmann, San Mateo, California.

Harvey, I. (1993). *The Artificial Evolution of Adaptive Behaviour*. PhD thesis, School of Cognitive and Computing Sciences, University of Sussex, UK.

Husbands, P. (1998). Evolving robot behaviours with diffusing gas networks. In Husbands, P. and Meyer,

J.-A., editors, *Evolutionary Robotics: First European Workshop, EvoRobot98*, pages 71–86. Springer, Berlin.

Husbands, P., Smith, T., Jakobi, N., and O'Shea, M. (1998). Better living through chemistry: Evolving GasNets for robot control. *Connection Science*, 10(3-4):185–210.

Jakobi, N. (1998). Evolutionary robotics and the radical envelope of noise hypothesis. *Adaptive Behaviour*, 6:325–368.

Maass, W. and Bishop, C., editors (1999). *Pulsed Neural Networks*. MIT Press, Cambridge, Massachusetts.

Smith, T. M. C. (2002). *The Evolvability of Artificial Neural Networks for Robot Control*. PhD thesis, School of Biological Sciences, University of Sussex, UK.

Steps Towards a Systematic Investigation of Possible Evolutionary Trajectories from Reactive to Deliberative Control Systems

Matthias Scheutz and **Paul Schermerhorn**
University of Notre Dame, Notre Dame, IN 46556, USA

Abstract

Although they are vastly outnumbered by simpler control systems, complex, "deliberative" control systems have evolved on our planet. Hence, agents with deliberative capabilities must have adaptive advantages over agents with simpler control systems in some environments. This paper examines the tradeoffs between the costs of control systems and the benefits they offer in a variety of environments and discusses the implications of these tradeoffs on evolutionary trajectories from "reactive" control systems, through somewhat more complex "affective" systems, to genuine deliberative systems.

Introduction

Most of the Earth's biomass consists of simple organisms (like bacteria, insects, etc.), and the vast majority of evolved species have simple control systems. This seems to indicate that such organisms are very good survivors and must be well adapted to their environments. Furthermore, it suggests that most evolutionary trajectories lead to such simple organisms (at least starting from the Earth's initial conditions) in that there may be many niches in "niche space" (Sloman 2000) that can be occupied by simple creatures. Yet, not *all* evolutionary trajectories stop there. Complex organisms with complex control systems have evolved as well. The natural question then is: under what circumstances did these complex organisms evolve?

A complete answer to this question will obviously have to involve multifaceted arguments comprising considerations of physical, physiological, and control tradeoffs. There are several dimensions along which such tradeoffs can be studied: genotype vs. phenotype, nature vs. nurture, body size vs. brain size, r-selection vs. K-selection,indexK-selection altricious vs. precocious development, innate vs. acquired strategies, reactive control vs. deliberative control, etc. In particular, the argument will have to show how the transition from simple, expendable, fast-growing, etc. organisms with many offspring to complex, inexpendable, slow growing, etc. organisms with few offspring could work.

In this paper we will focus on tradeoffs at the level of architectures of agent control systems. This is not the level of brain and neural organization *per se*, but rather a higher level, implemented in neural brain tissue, at which we can study control systems consisting of functional components and their interconnections.

The architectural level allows us to study functional components and their effects on an agent's behavior, and *a fortiori* its chances of survival. We will compare different kinds of control systems (as defined by their architectures) under different environmental conditions in order to assess their advantages and disadvantages. Components in a control system will have a cost associated with them, reflecting the energy expenditure to build and maintain them in an operational state. By varying the associated cost under identical environmental conditions we can derive empirically a cost function, which points to the tradeoffs between the functionality (and the behavioral consequences) a particular component may add to the control mechanism of an agent, on one hand, and the increase in energy expenditure caused by adding and using the respective component, on the other. Systematic experiments with various agent architectures allow us to study possible trajectories from low-level reactive to high-level deliberative control architectures (two notions to be defined below), which we hope will contribute to some of the open questions in artificial life research (in particular, questions (5), (6), (7), (10), and (11) in (Bedau *et al.* 2000)).

In this paper, we do not attempt to answer the question of how deliberative agent architectures evolved directly (for the problem is by far too complex to be tackled at once). Rather, we approach the set of possible trajectories from reactive to deliberative systems by ruling out a large class of initial conditions under which deliberative systems would most likely not have evolved, because their cost outweighs their benefits.

The paper is organized as follows: first, we define what we mean by "reactive", "affective", and "deliberative" control architectures. Then, we introduce the employed agents, sketch their control architectures and briefly discuss the resultant behavioral dispositions. After pointing to previous experimental findings regarding the relation of reactive, affective, and deliberative agents with respect to their relative fitness [1] in different kinds of environments, we present our experimental setup and report new findings regarding the relative cost of affective and deliberative extensions of reactive agent architectures. Finally, we analyze the experimental outcome and discuss its significance in the light of evolutionary trajectories from reactive to affective, to deliberative control systems.

---

[1] 'Fitness' is here defined as the agent's ability to survive to reproductive age. It is measured indirectly by counting the number of survivors at the end of an experimental run; agents that generally fail to survive to reproductive age will be poorly represented in the population, whereas agents what generally succeed in surviving to reproductive age will be well represented.

Reactive, Affective, and Deliberative Architectures

Agent architectures play an important role in the understanding of natural and development of artificial systems (Sloman & Scheutz 2002). They can be thought of as blueprints of control systems, where different functional components and their interconnections are depicted (e.g., see (Russell & Norvig 1995) for a more detailed definition of "agent architecture"). Since we would like to understand (1) what kinds of components (and arrangements thereof) are required to produce particular kinds of behaviors, and (2) what the relative tradeoffs of different control systems (and their implementations) are, we first need to define what we mean by "reactive", "affective", and "deliberative" control, or more to the point, what "reactive", "affective", and "deliberative architectures" are.

Reactive Architectures

Unfortunately, there seems to be a wide range of definitions of "reactive" that differ in substance (e.g., "reactive" as "stateless" versus "reactive" as "tight sensor-motor coupling"). Hence, it seems that "reactive" is best defined in opposition to "deliberative", i.e., as "not deliberative", which puts the burden on a definition of "deliberative". Since we are interested in demarcating an intellectually interesting difference, rather than trying to say what "deliberative" *really means*, we will construe "deliberative" as "being able to produce and use representations of hypothetical past or future states or as yet unexecuted actions (or sequences of such actions)". Note that according to this (negative) definition of "reactive", reactive architectures may make use of simple representations of the state of the world and/or the agent. But these representations will not explicitly encode goals, hypothetical states of the world or sequences of possible actions. And while we may be able to ascribe intentional states such as beliefs and desires to a reactive agent, the agent architecture contains no explicit representation of these states. For example, an agent which exhibits a behavior that could be described as "avoiding obstacles" can be said to have a goal of "avoiding collisions", even though this goal is not explicitly represented in the agent's control system.

Deliberative Architectures

As mentioned before, a *deliberative* architecture is one in which there is some consideration of alternative courses of action before an action is taken. Hence, there is need for the capacity to represent counterfactual states referring to hypothetical past or future states or as yet unexecuted actions (or sequences of such actions), in which at least some of the basic operations of the architecture is to produce/read/write such counterfactual states. Such states include goals (descriptions of states to be achieved), plans (sequences of unexecuted actions), states describing the imagined consequences of performing an action in the current state or some hypothetical state, partial solutions generated during planning or problem solving, the hypothetical states of the agent's beliefs generated during belief revision and many others. We further require that such states should be influential in the production of actions, in the counterfactual sense that, had the (counterfactual) state not been generated, the agent would have chosen a different action to execute.[2]

To represent counterfactual states, a deliberative agent requires a reusable working memory for the construction and comparison of hypothetical states and some means of deriving the consequences of actions performed in these states. At its simplest, this might be a set of memories of the consequences of performing the action in similar states in the past. The use of a common working memory limits the number of alternative courses of action that can be considered in parallel, and hence the degree of parallelism possible within a deliberative architecture.

All other things being equal, a deliberative architecture must be slower and require more resources than a reactive architecture which encodes a solution to any specific goal solvable by the deliberative architecture, since the generation of alternatives will take time. However, a deliberative architecture will typically be more space efficient than an equivalent reactive architecture, even though it will often require more space than a reactive solution to any given problem instance, since it can solve a *class* of problems in a fixed amount of space, whereas a reactive architecture requires space proportional to the number of problems. We can view this as an example of the standard space-time tradeoff, though in this case there is also the time required to code or evolve all the reactive solutions.

Affective Architectures

An *affective* architecture is one in which there are explicit representations of affective control states such as preferences, desires or emotions (Scheutz & Sloman 2001). Such states are directly encoded within the overall state of an agent and implemented in components of the architecture (e.g., in a connectionist unit, a real-valued variable in a C program, etc.) rather than being *supervenient* on the architecture (as in the case of purely

[2] Note that this definition implies no commitments as to whether the states and operations are fine grained, e.g., dealing with partial plans or alternative solutions and their generation and comparison, or whether the states and operations are "coarse grained", e.g., a single "plan" operator which takes a goal and a description of the current state and returns a plan with the rest of the fine-grained states and operators buried in the implementation of the architecture and invisible to the agent program and the agent state. Both cases have at least one counterfactual state and one operator that takes a non-counterfactual state and returns a counterfactual state.

reactive agent). Note that this does not mean that *all* affective states that could be *ascribed* to the agent or *emerge* from interactions of various components of the architecture are directly represented in the architecture, only that some are.

Affective architectures are orthogonal to the reactive-deliberative distinction in that they can be combined with both (i.e., both reactive and deliberative architectures can be affective in the sense specified). The fact that some affective states are explicitly represented within the architecture (and do not merely supervene on it) means that the architecture could be extended to monitor the achievement or non-achievement of such states. Hence, affective architectures allow affective states to take a role in learning, deliberation, the modification of reactive behaviors, etc. In other words, the difference between reactive and affective architecture may not so much lie in the actual behavioral dispositions of agents instantiating the architectures, but rather in the counterfactual modifications (e.g., extensions) of the architectures. A deliberative mechanism could monitor an affective control state like hunger to create a representation of the agent's need for food. Such an extension may be easy to achieve (e.g., using evolutionary methods of duplication and specialization (Maynard Smith & Szathmáry 1999)) if the state is already *represented* in the architecture, while it will typically be more difficult (and require more additions) if no such representation is present.

Agents: Architectures and Behavioral Dispositions

In the experiments reported in this paper, we employ three different kinds of agents, *reactive*, *affective*, and *deliberative* agents, where affective and deliberative agents are extensions of reactive agents in that their architectures extend the architecture of reactive agents in different ways, leading to different behavioral dispositions and, hence, different behavior.

All agents are standardly equipped with exteroceptive "sonar", "smell", and "touch" sensors. *Sonar* is used to detect obstacles and other agents, *smell* to detect food and water sources, and *touch* to detect (1) impending collisions with agents or obstacles, and (2) consumable food and water sources that are within reach for digestion. In addition, the touch sensor is connected to a global alarm system (Scheutz, Sloman, & Logan 2000), which triggers an automatic reflex-like action pattern, which the agent cannot suppress, to move it away from other agents and obstacles. These movements are somewhat erratic and will slightly reorient the agent (thus helping it to get out of "local minima"). Furthermore, agents have two proprioceptive sensors to measure their energy and water levels, respectively. These sensors are also connected to alarm mechanisms, which will make agents (1) reduce their speed to the lowest possible level (to minimize the energy and water expenditure) and (2) pursue food or water sources exclusively depending on which level drops below a predetermined critical level first.

On the effector side, they have motors for locomotion (forward and backward), motors for turning (left and right in degrees) and a mechanism for consuming food and water (which can only be activated when the agent is not moving). When agents come to a halt on top of a food or water source, their ingestion mechanism suppresses the motors for locomotion until the item is consumed, which will take a time proportional to the amount of energy or water stored in the food or water source (depending on the maximum amount of food or water an agent can take in at any given time).

While different agents may have different short-term goals at any given time (e.g., getting around obstacles, consuming food, reaching a water source faster than another agent, or having offspring), there are two long-term goals that are common to all of them: (1) *survival* (i.e., to get enough food and/or water to maintain all bodily functions, and to avoid running into obstacles or other agents), and (2) *procreation* (i.e., to live long enough to have offspring). In the following, we will briefly describe the architectures and behavioral dispositions of each agent kind.

The Reactive Agents

All agents process sensory information and produce behavioral responses using a motor schema-based approach (Arkin 1989). Let $Ent_k = \{f, w, o, k, \overline{k}\}$ be an index set of the five types of objects *food*, *water*, *obstacle*, *agents of kind k* and *agents of a kind different from k* relative to a given agent kind k–all subscript variables will range over this set unless stated otherwise. For each object type in Ent_k, a force vector $F_{i,k}$ is computed, which is the sum, scaled by $1/|v|^2$, of all vectors v from the agent to the objects of type i within the respective sensory range, where '$|v|$' is the length of vector v. These five *perceptual schemas* are mapped into motor space by the transformation function

$$T_k(x) = \sum_{i \in Ent_k} g_{i,k} \cdot F_{i,k}(x) \tag{1}$$

where the $g_{i,k}$ are the respective gain values of the perceptual schemes. The gain values simply scale the effect of sensory input, providing a means by which to prioritize certain inputs (e.g., if food is especially important, its gain value could be higher than the other gain values, so that sensing food has a greater impact on the direction chosen than sensing other entities). These gain values are initialized to values determined to be reasonable via a series of experiments, and are kept constant throughout the life of a reactive agent.

Reactive agents always behave in the same way, given that their gain values are *constants*: their positive $g_{f,k} = g_{w,k}$ make them employ a "consume nearest" strategy (Spier & McFarland 1998), whereas their negative $g_{o,k} = g_{k,k} = g_{\overline{k},k}$ values make them avoid obstacles and other agents. Consequently, the behavior of reactive agents is completely determined by their input–hence their name–and can be described as "greedy".

The Affective Agents

Affective agents have in addition to architectural components of reactive agents a three-layer *interactive activation and competition* (IAC) neural network with five input units *in*, five hidden units *hid*, and five output units *out* (Rumelhart & McClelland 1986).[3]

The input units receive their activations (via appropriate scaling functions) from the internal water (in_w) and energy level sensors (in_f) as well as the global alarm mechanisms (which send impulses to in_o, in_k or $in_{\overline{k}}$ units depending on whether the alarm was triggered by an impending collision with an obstacle or an agent of the same or of a different kind).

The output units are connected to the gain values in the motor scheme via individual scaling functions $f_i(x) = x \cdot c_i + b_i$ (where b_i is the *base gain value* and c_i the scaling factor for the activation of out_i).

The activation value $act_i(t)$ of an IAC unit i at time t is defined by

$$act_i(t) = \begin{cases} (max - act_i(t-1)) \cdot net_i(t) - decay, & net_i(t) \geq 0 \\ (act_i(t-1) - min) \cdot net_i(t) - decay, & net_i(t) < 0 \end{cases}$$

where *min* and *max* are the minimum and maximum activation level, respectively, *decay* is a decay factor defined by $d \cdot (act_i(t) - rest)$ (where d is a constant), *rest* the rest level, and $net_i(t)$ the weighted sum of all inputs to unit i at time t.

The choice of IAC units over standard perceptrons is based on their update rule, which is particularly suited to implement important temporal features of affective states in that it (1) takes into account the *previous activation* (hence, can be used to implement "inner states"), and (2) incorporates a *decay term* to raise or lower the activation to a predetermined *base level* (both features that seem to be typical of the temporal development of certain affective states, e.g., basic emotional states).

[3]Note that neural networks employed in other simulations to control the behavior of agents (Menczer & Belew 1966; Seth 2000) usually compute the mapping from sensors to effectors, while the neural network here is intended to implement the affective system, thus adding another layer on top of the input-output mapping of reactive agents (which is accomplished in a schema-based manner; of course, this mapping, in turn, could have been implemented as neural network as well).

Although fully connected IAC networks are possible, we will focus on a subset of networks to reduce complexity, where weights between in_i and hid_i are always non-zero and some (possibly all) of the weights between hid_i and out_i, call them "gain weights" ow_i, are non-zero, all other weights being zero.

Foraging in affective agents, then, is not solely determined by their sensory inputs, but also by their "inner states" as defined by the activation of the hidden units in the neural network. These states can implement primitive motivational and emotional states like "hunger", "thirst", "fear", and "aggression" as argued in (Scheutz 2001). Hence, affective agents forage based on their perceptions and needs: they may avoid food if not "hungry", or ignore food if very "thirsty", or skip food if "afraid" of obstacles, etc. By modifying the gain values of the motor schema depending on their internal states, affective agents can influence the combination of the sensory vector fields in the motor schema to their advantage. Note that the integration of this affective system in the reactive system is *conservative* in the sense that no modification of the reactive system is necessary; the affective components are simply "added" to the existing components, which could be relevant for the evolution of force-field based control systems in nature (as adding components without the need to change the existing structure seems to be favorable over additions that require modifications, thereby raising the chances that a previously functional organization may become distorted in the extension process).

The Deliberative Agents

Deliberative agents extend reactive agents in various ways. First, they have an additional perceptual mechanism that allows them to extract objects in the environment and to represent their type, distances, and directions relative to an agent-centric polar coordinate system. This "vision facility" allows deliberative agents to single out and represent an individual entity (e.g., a food or water item) and store it in memory for later use (in planning, for example). It is first and foremost this ability of being able to represent items in the environment that opens up further possibilities such as storing and retrieving representations, using them in planning and plan execution, etc. None of these possibilities are available to reactive agents, which have access to sensed objects only in a holistic manner (via an agglomerated force vectors).

Second, they have memory components that allow them to store information about food and water items and obstacles. A "comparator" component constantly checks whether a perceived item is present in memory, and if it is not found there, causes it to be stored. In addition to the memory components, they have a mechanism that will update the relative positions of the object stored in memory depending on the agent's movements.

Furthermore, a coherence mechanism constantly checks whether a stored item within sensory range is actually perceived and removes an item from memory if it does not seem to exist any more in the environment.

Third, deliberative agents have a simple route planning mechanism which allows them to find a route to the nearest food or water item, avoiding obstacles. The planner is given a list of obstacles, food and water items known to the agent (i.e., stored in the agent's memory), and returns a *plan*, which is a list of headings and distances, of how to get to the nearest reachable item of a given type. The plan is then passed to a *plan execution mechanism*, which ensures that plan steps are executed by overriding the headings generated by the reactive mechanisms in a manner similar to subsumption-style architectures (Brooks 1986).

The planner is based on a simplified version of the A_ϵ^* algorithm (Pearl 1982). A_ϵ^* is a variant of A^* in which the cost of the solution returned is guaranteed to be no greater than $(1 + \epsilon)\times$ (the cost of the optimum solution). A_ϵ^* is a good choice for a route planning agent, as all that is needed are "good" rather than optimal plans. The cost of a plan is the distance the agent has to travel to reach the goal, with a penalty for routes which pass through the collision region around an obstacle (any reasonable cost function must be such that no route through a collision region is ever cheaper than a route around the region).

Planning (or "re-planning") can be triggered in various ways: (1) by the obstacle alarm mechanism, (2) by the completion of an existing plan, (3) by the disappearance of the goal item, and (4) by the appearance of a closer item of the same kind as the goal item within sensory range (for details of the planner and a description of some of the difficulties of integrating a discrete planner with the continuous control of a reactive system, see (Scheutz & Logan 2001)).

Decisions about the goal object for the planner (i.e., food or water) are made by explicitly comparing representations of energy and water levels; whichever is needed more (relative to the maximum capacity) will be selected as a goal. If, however, no goal item of the chosen kind can be sensed in the environment or retrieved from memory, deliberative agents will attempt to go for the other kind. If the other kind is not available either, agents will engage in an "search behavior" that makes them sample their environment (without moving) until they sense a food or water item.

Previous Findings

Various previous experiments have confirmed that affective control mechanisms can and will evolve under different environmental conditions. For example, we found that agents with primitive motivational states (i.e., "hunger" and "thirst" drives) can be evolved from reactive agents if reactive agents are allowed to mutate into affective agents, which in turn can mutate their ow_f and ow_w weights (Scheutz & Sloman 2001). Such "motivational agents" are likely to evolve from reactive agents independent of many environmental conditions such as the frequency of appearance of new food and water sources, or the numbers and initial distributions of food and water sources, obstacles and agents. Some of them can also be learned during the lifetime of an agent (using associative learning) if the corresponding weights have the right sign (i.e., lead to attractive or repulsive behavioral disposition depending on the affective state to be implemented (Scheutz 2000)). Furthermore, we found that starting with *motivational agents*, different kinds of agents with different combinations of primitive emotional state like "fear" or "anger" will evolve, if the ow_o and ow_a weights are mutated (Scheutz 2001). Such primitive "emotional" agents will also evolve directly from reactive agents (Scheutz 2002). In all of the above cases, we argued in detail that the evolved mechanisms (i.e., positive or negative "gain weights") indeed implement affective processes, based on (1) the functional characterizations of the involved affective processes, (2) the observable behavior of the agents in the environment, and (3) the evolved architectural components (i.e., connection weights).

In other previous experiments we compared the performance of particular kinds of reactive, affective, and deliberative agents in one-resource tasks (i.e., food foraging) and found that in certain environments affective agents perform better than certain kinds of deliberative agents (Scheutz, Sloman, & Logan 2000; Scheutz & Logan 2001).

Common to all these findings is that various kinds of affective agents seemed to perform better than merely reactive or even certain kinds of deliberative agents (in certain environments). However, none of the previous experiments attempted to assess the additional structural and processing costs of the added components in the employed affective or deliberative architectures (relative to the components in the basic reactive architectures). Hence, it was not clear to what extent affective or deliberative control would pay off relative to the energy expenditure required by the additional components. Such tradeoffs, however, are crucial to an understanding of possible evolutionary trajectories from simple to complex creatures, for if the gain in fitness is disproportional to the cost of the added mechanism, it is unlikely that it would have evolved as part of an agent control system in a multi-agent, multi-species environment.

In the following, we will remedy this lack by investigating the relative fitness of affective and deliberative agents with respect to different costs associated with their architectural features.

Experiments

The Agent-Based Alife Simulation Environment SIMWORLD

SIMWORLD is an agent-based artificial life simulation built on top of the SIMAGENT toolkit developed by Aaron Sloman and colleagues at the University of Birmingham, England.[4] It consists of a continuous, potentially unlimited two-dimensional surface populated with various kinds of spatially extended objects, in particular, different kinds of agents, static and moving obstacles of varying size, and food and water sources.

Static and moving obstacles are typically generated once at the beginning of a simulation run and either remain in place or move in a predetermined direction at a predetermined speed throughout the run of the simulation.

Food and water sources, on the other hand, pop up at random locations within predefined areas of the simulation environment, at predefined frequencies, and stay for a predefined period of time, after which they disappear unless consumed by agents. They contain a fixed amount of energy and water that can be consumed by agents at their maximum intake capacity per simulation update cycle.

Agents are in constant need of food and water. Every simulation cycle they will spend a certain amount of their stored energy and water to maintain the functionality of their bodies and their control systems (typically at least one unit of each). Moving agents consume even more energy and water as measured in terms of some function (typically quadratic) of their speed. When the energy or water level of an agent drops below a certain threshold ω, agents "die" and are removed from the simulation. They also die and are removed if they run into other agents or obstacles.

After a certain age α (measured in terms of simulation cycles), agents reach maturity and can procreate asexually, if their energy and water levels are above the minimum necessary for procreation.[5] The energy and water necessary for creating the offspring are subtracted from the parent, and a new agent will pop up in the vicinity of the parent in the subsequent simulation cycle. After giving birth, parents cannot have offspring for a predetermined time, which is due to a built-in mechanism that is intended to prevent them from depleting themselves too much (which typically results in their death).[6]

Experimental Setup and Results

We conducted various experiments to study the benefit of the added components in affective and deliberative agents with respect to their potential for survival (i.e., the increase in fitness) relative to the added cost imposed by these components. For all of the following experiments, we limited the world to a squared area of 800 by 800 units, where water and food appear equally distributed in the centered subregion of 720 and 720. The probability of a new food source appearing at any update cycle is 0.25, that for water 0.2.

To determine the effect of introducing additional cost on architecture extensions (i.e., "relative cost" to a given base architecture), we conducted various experiments in which two agent kinds had to compete for survival in various environments with different numbers of static obstacles. Each experiment started with 10 agents of each type, 10 food and 10 water sources, and a varying number of obstacles, and proceeded for 10,000 cycles; each generation (i.e., the average time between the birth of parents and that of their offspring) is slightly longer than ω, so 10,000 cycles allows roughly 35 generations. The performance measure used (and depicted in the tables below) is the average number of surviving agents of a particular kind at the end of an individual experimental run averaged over 20 runs with different initial positions of agents, obstacles, food and water sources. Over a series of experiments, the number of static objects in the environment was varied (from 30 to 50), as was the relative cost of the architecture of one agent kind compared to the cost of other (i.e., the cost of the first was set equal to the cost of the second multiplied by C, where C ranged from 1.0 to 5.0). Cost was assessed as a reduction in energy reserves derived from the consumption of food.

Table 1 gives the results for reactive and deliberative agents. When the relative cost of deliberation is 1.0 (i.e., the same as the cost of reactive agents), deliberative agents enjoy a clear advantage across all obstacle environments. Especially high numbers of obstacles make foraging a very difficult (if not impossible) task for reactive agents, for one because being repelled by the proximity of high density obstacle regions causes them to ignore safe routes through these regions to food and water, which deliberative agents are able to exploit. As the cost of deliberation increases (up to five times the cost of reactive agents), however, the reactive agents begin

[4]SIMWORLD is freely available and can be downloaded from http://www.nd.edu/~airolab/simworld. The SIMAGENT toolkit can be downloaded from http://www.cs.bham.ac.uk/research/poplog/newkit.tar.gz

[5]Note that both parameters, α and ω, can be used to specify whether the simulation is used as an exogenous or as an endogenous fitness model.

[6]SIMWORLD also features a complex mutation mechanism that can modify the architectural parameters of agents. If *mutation* is turned on, a predefined set of architectural components can be modified with a predefined probability μ, again according to predefined mutation operations. For example, a connection weight in a neural network could be increased or decreased with a certain probability, or a condition-action rule added to the ruleset of an agent. Hence, some offspring will start out with the modified parameters instead of being exact copies of the parent. Furthermore, it is possible to mutate agents of one kind into agents of another kind. In the experiments described below, mutation is not used; agents with predefined parameters are compared.

Cost	30 static obstacles				40 static obstacles				50 static obstacles			
	Reactive		Deliberative		Reactive		Deliberative		Reactive		Deliberative	
mult.	Av.	Std.	Av.	Std.	Av.	Std.	Av.	Std.	Av.	Std.	Av.	Std.
1.0	0.3	1.34	24.65	4.0	0.0	0.0	21.25	4.0	0.0	0.0	18.55	5.34
1.4	0.95	3.27	20.6	7.1	0.0	0.0	19.8	2.78	0.0	0.0	16.75	4.88
1.8	0.6	2.26	21.8	4.34	0.0	0.0	15.7	3.61	0.0	0.0	14.35	5.25
2.2	1.7	3.57	15.6	5.13	0.0	0.0	15.05	4.32	0.3	1.34	11.35	5.74
2.3	6.5	9.05	10.4	6.92	0.0	0.0	14.75	5.87	0.3	1.34	12.2	5.27
2.4	8.95	9.75	6.7	7.34	1.4	3.57	12.85	6.2	0.0	0.0	11.2	3.37
2.5	7.4	9.88	8.9	8.94	0.7	2.9	11.7	4.22	0.3	1.34	8.0	6.33
2.6	9.35	9.07	6.1	6.52	3.55	5.6	7.6	6.06	0.35	1.35	9.0	4.81
3.0	9.15	8.5	4.7	6.26	3.05	5.24	8.0	6.97	2.05	3.9	8.15	5.44
3.4	11.35	7.92	2.25	4.7	2.95	5.84	6.6	4.5	1.78	3.74	5.9	5.45
3.8	11.75	6.84	2.2	4.54	2.9	4.42	4.52	4.63	2.0	4.34	4.7	5.79
4.2	12.53	6.71	1.45	3.77	5.6	4.67	3.25	5.5	2.95	4.82	2.8	3.81
4.6	14.05	4.71	0.2	0.89	7.35	5.88	1.85	3.45	2.45	3.91	1.65	3.12
5.0	13.45	6.51	0.3	1.34	8.05	7.85	1.0	2.58	4.9	5.59	0.7	1.98

Table 1: Deliberative agent performance relative to reactive agents

to make inroads, as expected. Still, deliberative agents proved better able to navigate the environment as obstacle count increase (relative to reactive agents).

Comparing affective and deliberative agents, we find that affective agents fare better than their reactive counterparts against deliberative agents (Table 2). However, the same trend appears with regard to the obstacle environment, albeit less pronounced: deliberative agents are better suited for survival in cluttered environments.

Finally, comparing reactive to affective (in Table 3), we notice that the advantages of affective agents over reactive agents are sufficient to overcome only minor increases in the cost function of the affective agents. Reactive agents begin to perform better even before the cost of being affective is double the cost of reactive agents over all obstacle environments examined here.

Analysis

The above results point to a general fitness ordering among the examined agent kinds: deliberative agents are generally better at surviving than affective agents, which, in turn, are better than reactive agents. Moreover, the relative differences in fitness levels increase as the obstacle environment becomes more dense, which is not surprising, since the added deliberative mechanisms will only develop their fullest potential (relative to the other foraging mechanisms) in very cluttered environments, where the planner can detect routes that are not open to force field-based control systems. In fact, experiments using environments without any or with only very few obstacles show that deliberative agents are at a disadvantage against both reactive and affective agents, even without taking cost into account (which is largely due to the fact that they do not pick up items on the way to their goal location if these items are of a different kind than the goal item–a behavior that is a natural consequence of the force field-based control favored by many simple species).

Deliberative agents are able to maintain their advantage over both affective and reactive agents through more dramatic increases in relative cost, especially in more dense obstacle environments. However, further increase will eventually lead to an inversion of this ordering. By the time the cost of being deliberative reaches five times the cost of the competing agents, deliberative agents perform very poorly in comparison.

Comparing the relative cost of the added architectural mechanisms (i.e., memory to hold locations of items in the environment, updating mechanisms, coherency mechanisms for new perceptions, etc.) in terms of actual memory (at least 100 times) and actual computation time (at least 10 times) to the cost of the break-even point in the above experiments (between 3 and 5 if estimated conservatively), it is easy to see that deliberation would not pay off in the scenarios we investigated. Note that the problem here is not simply one of finding a trajectory from reactive/affective agents to deliberative agents composed of adaptations with costs small enough for deliberative agents to compete effectively; the "finished product", i.e., agents with fully developed memory capacity and planning mechanisms, fail to perform well enough even at very modest relative cost levels.

Affective control, on the other hand, despite its modest increase in fitness might well pay off given that the actual additional cost (again measured in terms of computation time and memory) of affective systems is only a fraction of that of the reactive system. Hence, while it seems unlikely that a deliberative control system (with similar capacities to the ones used here) would have evolved, affective control does have a "competitive edge" over mere reactive control within the given cost framework.

Discussion

Agents possessing deliberative capacities do exist in nature. The difficulty is to understand what ecological

Cost	30 static obstacles				40 static obstacles				50 static obstacles			
	Affective		Deliberative		Affective		Deliberative		Affective		Deliberative	
mult.	Av.	Std.	Av.	Std.	Av.	Std.	Av.	Std.	Av.	Std.	Av.	Std.
1.0	0.85	3.68	22.97	5.72	0.0	0.0	23.1	3.78	0.0	0.0	18.0	4.69
1.4	4.4	8.04	15.75	9.33	0.15	0.67	19.1	3.32	0.85	3.57	16.2	5.63
1.8	6.5	7.61	12.65	8.15	1.4	4.17	14.25	6.32	0.35	1.57	13.9	6.42
2.2	7.55	8.25	8.75	7.38	2.3	4.99	11.45	6.06	1.8	5.03	9.45	5.39
2.3	13.8	10.36	6.0	7.81	3.0	5.52	9.75	7.06	1.4	2.93	10.1	6.69
2.4	9.6	7.84	6.8	8.04	5.55	6.78	8.2	7.74	2.15	4.12	9.35	6.21
2.5	11.2	10.47	5.55	6.96	7.25	8.34	6.1	6.72	2.7	6.41	9.05	6.32
2.6	14.05	8.5	2.95	5.98	9.1	9.01	5.9	6.92	3.32	4.97	8.28	5.79
3.0	19.25	5.07	0.05	0.22	7.9	7.45	4.4	5.67	4.2	6.01	5.8	5.05
3.4	15.55	5.86	0.55	2.46	8.3	7.1	4.35	5.69	3.65	5.53	3.25	4.94
3.8	19.5	4.48	0.0	0.0	12.1	5.88	0.55	1.76	5.55	6.07	3.35	4.82
4.2	19.8	5.08	0.0	0.0	11.9	7.31	0.75	2.31	6.6	5.53	1.85	3.45
4.6	17.9	5.78	0.0	0.0	12.4	5.73	0.45	1.15	9.15	5.43	0.35	1.57
5.0	19.35	5.39	0.0	0.0	13.4	4.16	0.25	1.12	7.27	6.0	0.53	2.08

Table 2: Deliberative agent performance relative to affective agents

Cost	30 static obstacles				40 static obstacles				50 static obstacles			
	Reactive		Affective		Reactive		Affective		Reactive		Affective	
mult.	Av.	Std.	Av.	Std.	Av.	Std.	Av.	Std.	Av.	Std.	Av.	Std.
1.0	6.85	9.58	11.05	10.04	1.45	4.49	12.6	6.84	2.3	4.51	4.4	5.45
1.1	3.5	7.56	14.25	8.5	3.9	4.89	9.3	8.88	0.9	2.36	5.8	5.55
1.2	6.9	8.78	9.25	9.08	2.45	4.65	8.45	7.93	2.05	4.19	3.5	4.58
1.3	7.23	8.96	9.15	9.07	5.2	6.66	5.4	6.24	1.5	3.32	2.9	3.58
1.4	8.75	8.17	4.65	7.26	6.4	6.55	4.35	5.89	2.45	3.05	1.65	3.12
1.8	9.6	9.28	3.45	5.74	5.0	6.11	3.95	6.08	2.7	4.55	1.15	2.46
2.2	14.2	6.74	0.0	0.0	7.8	6.18	0.95	2.46	3.25	4.71	0.0	0.0
2.6	13.15	6.88	0.45	2.01	8.95	6.14	0.0	0.0	3.9	4.0	0.0	0.0
3.0	14.1	7.24	0.25	1.12	9.2	6.86	0.2	0.89	6.5	6.28	0.0	0.0
3.4	14.2	6.81	0.0	0.0	9.75	4.79	0.0	0.0	4.33	5.16	0.0	0.0
3.8	12.1	6.49	0.0	0.0	9.9	5.39	0.0	0.0	3.5	4.68	0.0	0.0
4.2	11.6	4.45	0.0	0.0	10.0	7.03	0.0	0.0	2.35	3.39	0.0	0.0
4.6	16.55	5.06	0.0	0.0	10.35	6.27	0.0	0.0	3.6	4.63	0.0	0.0
5.0	14.1	7.17	0.0	0.0	11.65	5.78	0.0	0.0	3.25	5.02	0.0	0.0

Table 3: Affective agent performance relative to reactive agents

niche might enable deliberative agents to perform better than reactive or affective agents despite the significant increase in cost caused by deliberative extensions of reactive or affective architectures.

For one, it seems that the more regular and predictable an environment is, while at the same time being dangerous and difficult to explore for agents with simple control systems, the more deliberation will pay off. In the above experiments, this can be seen from the fact that environments with more static obstacles become more predictable (as more items in the environment become predictable) and more dangerous (as there are more chances for agents to accidentally crash into an obstacle).

The defining properties of such "stable" environments, where change occurs only infrequently and essential resources are by and large predictable, square well with deliberative mechanisms. These properties ensure that information regarding the location of a resource will normally be accurate, hence representational capacities enabling information to be stored in memory and used in planning or reasoning are advantageous.

Conversely, in environments where resources are not predictable, the benefits of deliberative mechanisms are likely not sufficient to outweigh the increased cost of those mechanisms. In these "unstable" environments, affective agents will typically perform better than deliberative agents, and memory and planning may be of little use.

Conclusion and Future Work

We conjecture that most evolutionary trajectories of control systems starting with only reactive mechanisms reach a fitness maximum in some of their affective extensions. What is still unclear is exactly under what environmental conditions this fitness peak of affective control systems can be overcome by adding deliberative extensions. Predictability and stability of resources seem to be part of the requirement. This may either involve the prediction of locations where to find food, or in the case of a predator, the ability to predict its prey's behavior when confronted, chased, etc. Social factors (such as tracking mental states of other group members) will certainly play an important role, although they do not seem to be necessary for the development of deliberative control systems. Most importantly, perhaps, the co-evolution of control system and body may figure in the search for the need of more complex control systems (e.g., energy, size, and other constraints may make mere "reactive" extensions impossible).

Although deliberative extensions might not pay off right away, they need to add some initial benefit to the control system's function, otherwise they will not evolve in competitive multi-species environments (as their bearers will likely not survive in the long run). Based on preliminary evolutionary experiments with agent architectures, we predict that, when there is interspecies competition for resources, it will be difficult to find neighborhoods in design space of architectures where even primitive deliberative extensions are viable (relative to their cost). The main theoretical, explanatory difficulties are not so much connected to a full-fledged, fully functional deliberative system, which already has enormous adaptive advantage over affective control systems (e.g., in highly structured, regular environments). Rather, they are connected to explanations of the intermediary stages, where *some* deliberative capacities have evolved and are combined with affective control. What complicates the pictures is the fact that not all combinations of affective and deliberative control are beneficial, even if both the affective and deliberative subsystems may show satisfactory performance in isolation (e.g., see (Scheutz & Logan 2001)).

It almost seems that individual deliberative subcomponents in natural evolutionary trajectories must have had a sufficient benefit of their own, i.e., independent of other deliberative subcomponents, before they became part of a larger, even more beneficial deliberative system. We are currently investigating this hypothesis by adding various deliberative subcomponents (e.g., memory, "perceptual coherency mechanisms", etc.) to affective agents to see whether they are beneficial in certain environments (e.g., where food and water still appear at random, but are confined to certain subareas in the environment).

We are also working on a more detailed analysis of the notion of "cost of a component in an agent architecture", which will allow us to get a finer-grained break-down of the net benefit of different functional components with respect to the overall agent behavior, and hence on the likelihood that they will evolve in certain environments.

Finally, we see the need for many more experiments with different reactive and affective control systems in different environments to map out the space of possible control mechanisms. It is their relative fitness with which deliberative control systems will have to compete.

Only if we understand the potential and limitations of reactive and affective control, we believe, will we be able to understand the circumstances under which deliberative systems, and consequently minds, have evolved.

References

Arkin, R. C. 1989. Motor schema-based mobile robot navigation. *International Journal of Robotic Research* 8(4):92–112.

Bedau, M. A.; McCaskill, J. S.; Packard, N. H.; Rasmussen, S.; Adami, C.; Green, D. G.; Ikegami, T.; Kaneko, K.; and Ray, T. S. 2000. Open problems in artificial life. *Artificial Life.*

Brooks, R. A. 1986. A robust layered control system for a mobile robot. *IEEE Journal of Robotics and Automation* 2(1):14–23.

Maynard Smith, J., and Szathmáry, E. 1999. *The Origins of Life: From the Birth of Life to the Origin of Language.* Oxford: Oxford University Press.

Menczer, F., and Belew, R. 1966. From complex environments to complex behaviors. *Adaptive Behavior* 4(3/4):317–363.

Pearl, J. 1982. A_ϵ^*—an algorithm using search effort estimates. In *IEEE Transactions on Pattern Analysis and Machine Intelligence*, volume 4, 392–399.

Rumelhart, D., and McClelland, J. 1986. *Parallel distributed processing: Explorations in the microstructure of cognition.* Cambridge, MA: MIT Press.

Russell, S., and Norvig, P. 1995. *Artificial Intelligence, A Modern Approach.* Prentice Hall.

Scheutz, M., and Logan, B. 2001. Affective versus deliberative agent control. In Colton, S., ed., *Proceedings of the AISB'01 Symposium on Emotion, Cognition and Affective Computing*, 1–10. York: Society for the Study of Artificial Intelligence and the Simulation of Behaviour.

Scheutz, M., and Sloman, A. 2001. Affect and agent control: Experiments with simple affective states. In Zhong, N.; Liu, J.; Ohsuga, S.; and Bradshaw, J., eds., *Intelligent Agent Technology: Research and Development.* New Jersey: World Scientific Publisher. 200–209.

Scheutz, M.; Sloman, A.; and Logan, B. 2000. Emotional states and realistic agent behaviour. In Geril, P., ed., *Proceedings of GameOn 2000, Imperial College London*, 81–88. Delft: Society for Computer Simulation.

Scheutz, M. 2000. Surviving in a hostile multiagent environment: How simple affective states can aid in the competition for resources. In Hamilton,

H. J., ed., *Advances in Artificial Intelligence, 13th Biennial Conference of the Canadian Society for Computational Studies of Intelligence, AI 2000, Montréal, Quebec, Canada, May 14-17, 2000, Proceedings*, volume 1822 of *Lecture Notes in Computer Science*, 389–399. Springer.

Scheutz, M. 2001. The evolution of simple affective states in multi-agent environments. In Cañamero, D., ed., *Proceedings of AAAI Fall Symposium*, 123–128. Falmouth, MA: AAAI Press.

Scheutz, M. 2002. The evolution of affective states and social control. In Hemelrijk, C. K., ed., *Proceedings of International Workshop on Self-Organisation and Evolution of Social Behaviour.*

Seth, A. 2000. *On the Relations between Behaviour, Mechanism, and Environment: Explorations in Artificial Evolution.* Ph.D. Dissertation, University of Sussex, UK.

Sloman, A., and Scheutz, M. 2002. A framework for comparing agent architectures. In *UK Workshop on Computational Intelligence.* forthcoming.

Sloman, A. 2000. Interacting trajectories in design space and niche space: A philosopher speculates about evolution. In et al., M., ed., *Parallel Problem Solving from Nature - PPSN VI*, Lecture Notes in Computer Science, No 1917, 3–16. Berlin: Springer-Verlag.

Spier, E., and McFarland, D. 1998. Possibly optimal decision making under self-sufficiency and autonomy. *Journal of Theoretical Biology* 189(317–331).

Fast and Loose: Biologically Inspired Couplings

Andy Philippides [1], **Phil Husbands** [2], **Tom Smith** [1], and **Michael O'Shea** [1]
Centre for Computational Neuroscience and Robotics (CCNR)
[1]School of Biological Sciences, [2]School of Cognitive and Computing Sciences
University of Sussex, Brighton, UK
(andrewop|philh|toms)@cogs.susx.ac.uk M.O-Shea@sussex.ac.uk

Abstract

Recent years have seen the discovery of gaseous transmitters in biological nervous systems. An ANN inspired by such gaseous signalling, the GasNet, has previously been shown to be more evolvable than traditional ANNs. Here we present 2 new versions of the GasNet which take further inspiration from the properties of gaseous signalling. The plexus model is inspired by the cortical nNOS plexus and the properties of the NO signal it generates. The receptor model is inspired by the mediating action of neurotransmitter receptors. Both models are shown to significantly further improve evolvability. We describe preliminary results suggesting that the reasons for the increase in evolvability is the loose coupling of distinct signalling mechanisms. Issues surrounding the degree of coupling between these mechanisms, one 'chemical' and one 'electrical', are discussed.

Introduction

Beyond Connectionism

A connectionist model of neuron-to-neuron communication involving a tight coupling between electrical and chemical signalling has provided the basic biological inspiration for many forms of artificial neural networks (ANNs).This has lead to ANNs that have been successfully used in many applications, including as artificial nervous systems generating behaviour in autonomous robots. But the model represents an incomplete view of neuronal signalling which we know today operates over a very wide range of temporal and spatial scales. It might therefore be productive to augment standard ANNs to reflect this. But just how does the current view of neuronal signalling differ from the one that inspired conventional ANNs?

In the traditional model, neurons generate brief electrical signals (action potentials) which propagate along wire-like axons terminating at highly localised junctions (synapses) on other neurons where the release of a chemical signalling molecule or neurotransmitter is triggered. The neurotransmitter is confined to the region of the synapse and here the receiving neuron is equipped with receptors which directly translate the chemical signal into a brief electrical signal, either excitatory or inhibitory. Hence in standard ANNs based on this incomplete model, the notion of chemical signalling can be safely factored out leaving only the idea of electrical signals flowing between nodes in a network.

But some receptors do not directly activate electrical events in the receiving neuron at all. In this type of indirect chemical signalling, a released neurotransmitter initiates long-lasting changes in excitability, thereby modulating a neuron's subsequent response to other electrical signals. Thus while simple direct transmission between neurons certainly does exist, it operates in parallel with and sometimes conjointly with indirect chemical signalling systems that operate on an extended temporal scale (Changeux 1993).

In addition to this, the spatial scale over which neurons can communicate is extended by the recent discovery of non-synaptic chemical signalling (Snyder & Ferris 2000). The most important feature of this derives from the ability of some neurotransmitters, in particular small gaseous molecules, to diffuse away from their site of release and to occupy a volume of the nervous system perhaps containing many other neurons and synapses (Edelman & Gally 1992). To date three gaseous neurotransmitter molecules, NO, CO and H_2S have been identified, all of them curiously are highly poisonous. The most studied among them by far is NO, which is known to diffuse at above threshold concentrations many tens of microns away from a site of release (Philippides, Husbands, & O'Shea 2000). Diffusion takes time; so this is not a rapid signalling system. Furthermore the main receptor for NO is of the indirect type and can have long-term modulatory effects on neurons (Barañano, Ferris, & Snyder 2001; Snyder & Ferris 2000). So not only can NO operate over a large region, it can also mediate long-lasting changes in the chemical and electrical properties of neurons within that volume.

Transmission by gases is not and perhaps cannot be confined to the highly localised region of the synapse, as in classical point-to-point signalling, loosening the tight coupling between electrical and chemical signals. Thus the concept of volume signalling can now be added to the growing list of phenomena in the nervous system that might be a source of inspiration for new and perhaps improved styles of ANNs. This is probably especially true for ANNS intended for use as artificial nervous systems, an area where taking inspiration from biology is often particularly fruitful.

In our work we have attempted to incorporate into ANNs, in an abstracted form, some of the richness and complexity that characterises the temporal and spatial dynamics of real neuronal signalling, especially chemical signalling by gaseous transmitters. As these systems operate on different temporal and spatial scales to electrical signalling, it suggests that it might be useful to develop models in which electrical and indirect chemical signalling are controlled in ANNs by separate processes. Thus, we developed the GasNet, a standard ANN augmented by a diffusing gas which can modulate the response of other neurons. We have used the methods of evolutionary robotics to explore the suitability of this class of networks for generating a range of behaviours in a variety of autonomous robots (Husbands *et al.* 1998; 2001). Since as yet we have no deep formal theory for such systems, we have found the use of stochastic search methods (such as evolutionary algorithms) to be a very helpful tool in this exploration. Of course our ultimate aim is to gain a better understanding of autonomous behaviour generating mechanisms in real and artificial systems.

While the GasNet has been seen to be more evolvable (in terms of speed of evolution) on a number of robotics tasks (Smith, Husbands, & O'Shea 2002), it is a first version using a very abstract model of non-classical signalling. We therefore wanted to see if adding in more features of gaseous signalling could further improve the evolvability. To do this, however, one must first overcome a problem familiar to anyone attempting to simplify biological systems: which of the panoply of complex features of neuronal signalling seen does one take? Does one simply use intuition about what may be useful or are there perhaps some guiding principles that one should keep in mind? We decided to take inspiration from the type of gaseous signalling seen in the cerebral cortex and from receptor mechanisms to generate two new versions of the GasNet, the *plexus* and *receptor* models. We present the new models in the next section along with details of the original GasNet, and then go on to show that they significantly further improve the evolvability of the GasNet.

Coupling of signalling mechanisms

The question of why these particular new models worked while others failed, remains, and may have implications for the types of network we should be trying to develop in the future. One answer for this might be found in an analysis of the connectivity patterns of successfully evolved controllers. In the original GasNet model, the genotype to phenotype mapping meant that the coupling between 'electrical' and 'chemical' signalling was tighter than would be seen in the biological systems that inspired it. That is, if neurons were electrically linked to other neurons they tended to be chemically linked to those neurons as well. Here (section 4) we show that the two new models reduce this level of coupling significantly. Is this perhaps a guiding principle in generating future models, enabling us to reduce the vast space of features from which inspiration can be taken? When distinct processes involved in the functioning of the nervous system are loosely coupled it may be much easier for evolutionary mechanisms to effectively 'tune' one against the other without destructive interference (Gardner & Ashby 1970). This will help in satisfying the conflicting pressures of phenotypic stability and genetic instability needed for successful evolution (Conrad 1990). These issues are discussed further in the final section of the paper. In the next section we describe the GasNet, plexus and receptor models.

GasNets

The *GasNet* incorporates a mechanism based on the neuron-modulating properties of a diffusing signalling gas into a more standard sigmoid-unit neural network (Husbands *et al.* 1998). In previous work the networks have been used in a variety of evolutionary robotics tasks, comparing the speeds of evolution for networks with and without the gas signalling mechanism active, showing that GasNets are consistently faster to evolve than more standard networks (Husbands *et al.* 1998). A number of related studies have investigated the nature of the GasNet fitness landscapes (Smith, Husbands, & O'Shea 2001; 2002) in order to elucidate the reasons for the faster evolutionary search. Other authors have used abstract notions of chemical modulation in neural networks used for controlling agents (Kondo *et al.* 1999; Grand 1997) but on a more global level which does not involve the detailed spatiotemporal aspect we incorporate into our systems. In this section we introduce the basic GasNet model, and the two new variants (plexus and receptor) together with details of their biological inspiration.

The GasNet model

The 'electrical' network underlying the GasNet model is a discrete time step, recurrent neural network with a variable number of nodes. These nodes are connected by either excitatory (with a weight of +1) or inhibitory (with a weight of −1) links with the output O_i^n, of node i at time step n determined by a continuous mapping from the sum of its inputs, as described by the following equation:

$$O_i^n = \tanh\left[k_i^n\left(\sum_{j\in C_i} w_{ji}O_j^{n-1} + I_i^n\right) + b_i\right] \qquad (1)$$

where C_i is the set of nodes with connections to node i and $w_{ji} = \pm 1$ is a connection weight. I_i^n is the external (sensory) input to node i at time n, and b_i is a genetically set bias. Each node has a genetically set default transfer function parameter, k_i^0, which can be altered at each time-step according to the concentration of the diffusing 'gas' at node i to give k_i^n (as described later in the section on modulation).

Gas diffusion in the networks

In addition to this underlying network in which positive and negative 'signals' flow between units, an abstract process loosely analogous to the diffusion of gaseous modulators is at play. Some units can emit virtual 'gases' which diffuse and are capable of modulating the behaviour of other units by changing their transfer functions. The networks occupy a 2D space; the diffusion processes mean that the relative positioning of nodes is crucial to the functioning of the network. The original GasNet diffusion model is controlled by two genetically specified parameters, namely the radius of influence r and the rate of build up and decay s. Spatially, the gas concentration varies as an inverse exponential of the distance from the emitting node with a spread governed by r, with the concentration set to zero for all distances greater than r (equation 2 and figure 3). The maximum concentration at the emitting node is 1.0 and the concentration builds up and decays from this value linearly as defined by equations (equation 3 and 4) at a rate determined by s.

$$C(d,t) = \begin{cases} e^{-2d/r} \times T(t) & d < r \\ 0 & \text{else} \end{cases} \tag{2}$$

$$T(t) = \begin{cases} H\left(\frac{t-t_e}{s}\right) & \text{emitting} \\ H\left[H\left(\frac{t_s-t_e}{s}\right) - H\left(\frac{t-t_s}{s}\right)\right] & \text{not emitting} \end{cases} \tag{3}$$

$$H(x) = \begin{cases} 0 & x \leq 0 \\ x & 0 < x < 1 \\ 1 & \text{else} \end{cases} \tag{4}$$

where $C(d,t)$ is the concentration at a distance d from the emitting node at time t. t_e is the time at which emission was last turned on, t_s is the time at which emission was last turned off, and s (controlling the slope of the function T) is genetically determined for each node. The total concentration at a node is then determined by summing the contributions from all other emitting nodes (nodes are not affected by their own concentration, to avoid runaway positive feedback).

Modulation by the Gases

For mathematical convenience there are two 'gases', one whose modulatory effect is to increase the transfer function gain parameter and one whose effect is to decrease it. It is genetically determined whether or not any given node will emit one of these two gases (gas 1 and gas 2), and under what circumstances emission will occur (either when the 'electrical' activation of the node exceeds a threshold, or the concentration of a genetically determined gas in the vicinity of the node exceeds a threshold. Note these emission processes provide a coupling between the 'electrical' and 'chemical' mechanisms). The concentration-dependent modulation is described by equation 5, with transfer parameters updated on every time step as the network runs.

$$k_i^n = k_i^0 + \alpha C_1^n - \beta C_2^n \tag{5}$$

where k_i^0 is the genetically set default value for k_i, C_1^n and C_2^n are the concentrations of gas 1 and gas 2 respectively at node i on time step n, and α and β are constants. Both gas concentrations lie in the range $[0, 1]$. Thus the gas does not alter the electrical activity in the network directly but rather acts by continuously changing the mapping between input and output and can, for instance, change the output from being positive to being zero or negative even though the input remains constant.

Extensions to the basic GasNet I: The plexus model

Philippides (2001) introduces a number of variants to the original GasNet model, based on research into the diffusion of NO in real brains (Philippides, Husbands, & O'Shea 2000). In this section we investigate one such variant, the plexus model, directly inspired by the type of signalling seen in the mammalian cerebral cortex. Here activity in a neuron is translated via a plexus of exceedingly fine nNOS-expressing fibres into a volume signal in a different part of the network.

Nerve fibres constituting the nNOS plexus in the cerebral cortex have a maximum diameter of about 5m but the overwhelming majority are a fraction of a micron in diameter. They are therefore well below the critical size required for a volume signal, and cannot produce significant concentrations of NO unless many small sources effectively combine their production. An illustration of how such co-operation can occur is provided by figure 1 which shows the spatial extent of the NO signal generated by a single fibre of $2\mu m$ diameter and by arrays of four, nine and sixteen identical sources separated by $10\mu m$. The single fibre does not achieve an above threshold signal principally because the great speed of NO diffusion means that NO will spread rapidly over a large volume. So while NO does not reach threshold anywhere, the volume occupied by NO at a significant fraction of threshold is large relative to the source size. Thus NO derived from small and well-separated individual sources can summate to produce an effective NO cloud.

This method of signalling has several interesting implications for the spatio-temporal nature of the ensuing volume signal, making it very different to a signal generated by a single neuron of the same size (figure 2). The summation of NO from several separated fibres means that the concentration in and around them is, in a sense, averaged and hence smoothed. Thus due to the dynamics of diffusion one tends to get a relatively even concentration within the synthesising region with small peaks around the fibres themselves (figure 1 and figure 2 A), resulting in a much greater region being above threshold (figure 2 B). In conjunction with the use of a threshold concentration, this means that there will come a point when the concentration in a region around the fibres is just sub-threshold and a small increase in the general level of NO will result in large areas rising above thresh-

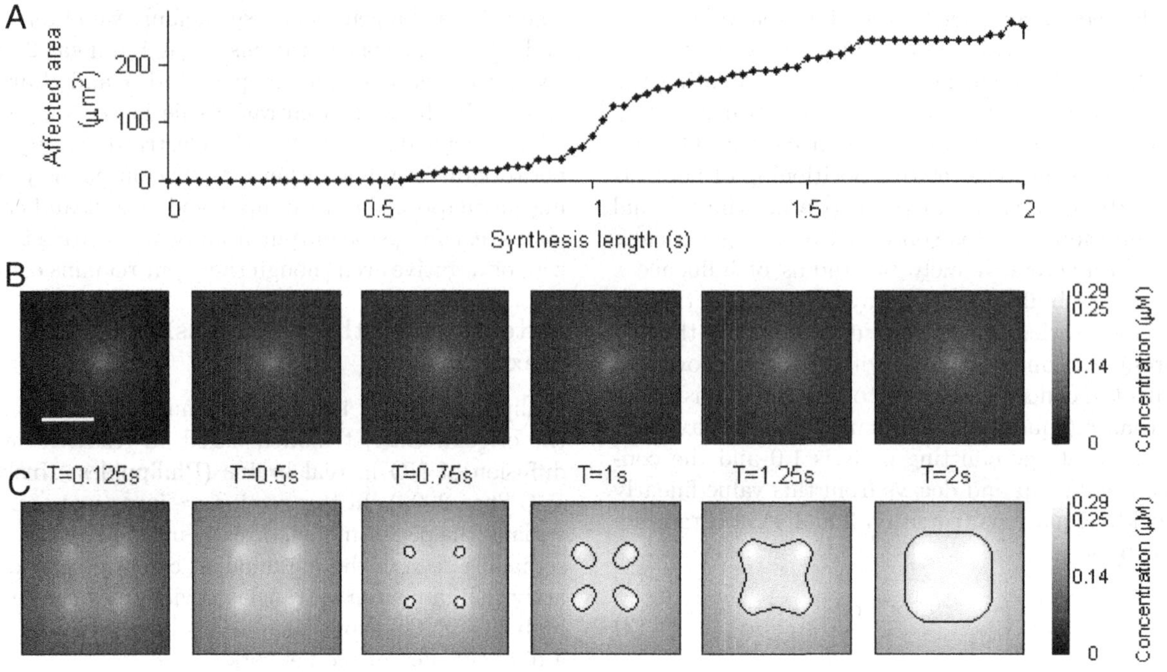

Figure 1: A. Volume of tissue above threshold per unit length of fibre for 4 fibres of diameter $2\mu m$ spaced $10\mu m$ apart for NO synthesis of length $2s$ plotted against time after synthesis. The fibre dimensions and spacing have been chosen so as to approximate the arrangement of the nNOS-expressing fibres in the optic lobe of the locust. B-C. Graphical representations of the NO concentration (dark = low, light = high) due to 1 (B) and 4 (C) fibres at times $T = 0.125, 0.5, 0.75, 1, 1.25$ and $2s$ after synthesis showing the build up of NO over time. The black line on each of the plots shows the $0.25\mu M$ (the threshold concentration) contour and thus indicates which regions can be affected by NO. Scalebar = $10\mu m$. Here 4 fibres can achieve an effective volume signal over the whole synthesising region but the single fibre cannot. In addition, note that inside the synthesising region the concentration is relatively even.

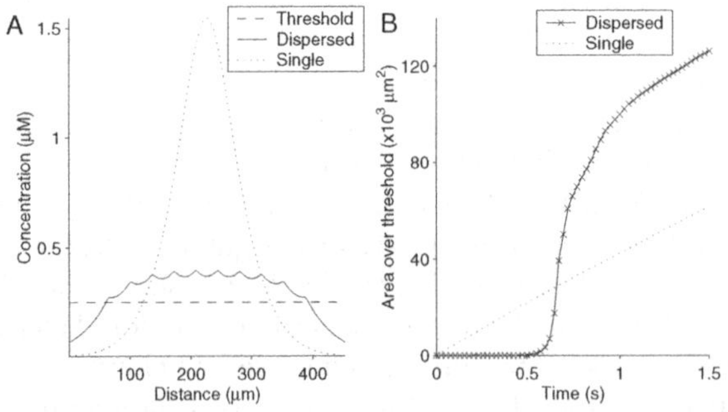

Figure 2: NO concentrations generated by a 10×10 ordered array of 100 NO synthesising fibres of diameter $2\mu m$ after $1s$ of NO synthesis. A. Concentration of NO due to 100 fibres separated by $36\mu m$ (solid line) and $0\mu m$, i.e. arranged as one single source, (dotted line) plotted against distance from the centre of the array. The dashed line shows the threshold concentration. B. Area over threshold due to 100 fibres separated by $36\mu m$ (solid line) and $0\mu m$ (dotted line) plotted against time after synthesis.

old. Thus we see a delay before a steep rise in the volume affected which is characteristic of signalling by dispersed sources.

What, though, if anything, can these features do for evolutionary robotics? In an attempt to answer this question we developed the plexus model, a variant of the GasNet, whose diffusion properties are modified so as to produce an abstraction of the type of signal seen in the cortex. Firstly, we changed the spatial distribution of gas concentration. In the original GasNet this was modelled as an exponentially decaying function (equation 2) which is loosely based on the type of spatial distribution of NO one would see outside a single neuron (figure 3). For the plexus model this has been modified to a uniform distribution over the volume of effect,with a peak concentration half that of the original (illustrated in figure 3):

$$C(d,t) = \begin{cases} 0.5 \times T(t) & d < r \\ 0 & \text{else} \end{cases} \tag{6}$$

The second change is to allow the centre of this gas diffusion cloud to lie anywhere within the space, not just at the emitting node position. Note that this model requires two extra parameters for the gas diffusion centre (x, y) coordinates. Thus the plexus model produces constant concentration within the the area of effect, with this area centred anywhere in the space (figure 4). All other details of the models are identical to the original GasNet model, as described earlier.

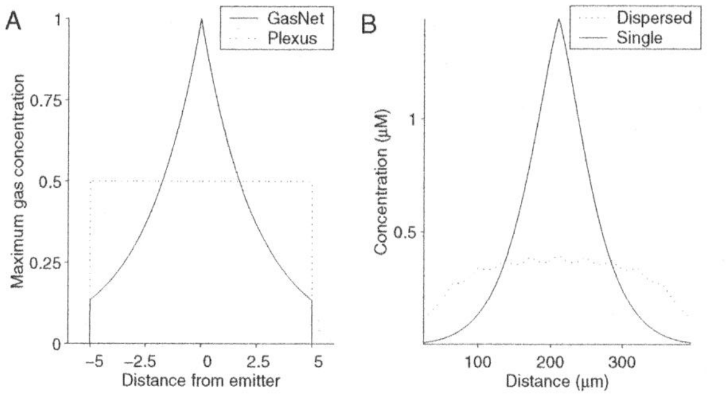

Figure 3: A. The spatial distributions of gas concentration for the different GasNet models. The solid line denotes the spatial distribution for the GasNet model, while the dotted line shows the spatial distribution for the plexus model. See text for further details. B. The spatial distributions of gas concentration outside the emitting (real) neuron for a single source (solid line) and dispersed sources (dotted line).

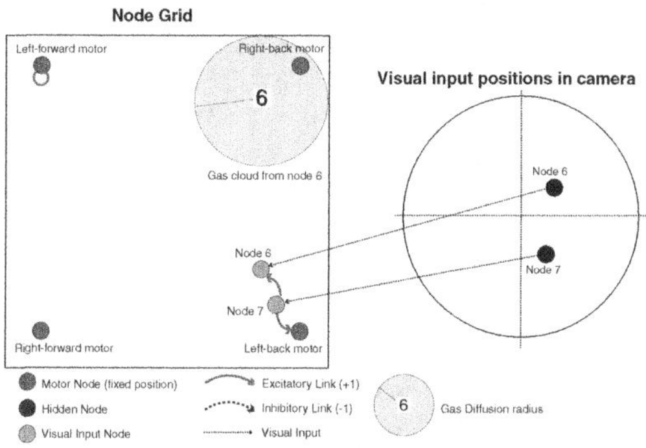

Figure 4: An example plexus architecture network. The node plane is shown on the left, with the positions and connections of the network nodes, while the camera on the right shows the position of the visual inputs. Node 6 has a dispersed gas cloud centre in the top-right of the network plane, with a uniform concentration over the area of effect, illustrating the effects of the plexus model. Thus node 6 can easily affect nodes which are far from its position in the node plane.

Extensions to the basic GasNet II: The receptor model

An aspect of biological neuronal networks that has no analog in the vast majority of ANNs is the role of receptor molecules. All neural signalling is mediated by a diverse group of proteins which act as receptors to which neurotransmitters bind.The act of binding triggers chemical processes which result in functional changes to the neuron involved (Changeux 1993; Purves 1997). In classical synaptic neurotransmission two basic classes of receptors have been identified: ionotropic and metabotropic. Ionotropic receptors are linked directly to ion channels in the postsynaptic membrane. These channels are opened or closed in response to transmitter binding, thus changing the postsynaptic membrane potential and hence mediating the postsynaptic electrical response. This type of receptor is generally involved in rapid timescale effects acting over milliseconds. Metabotropic receptors are not directly linked to ion channels but affect them by the activation of intermediate G-proteins (Purves 1997). G-proteins can interact directly with ion channels or with effector enzymes that give rise to intracellular second messengers that lead to complex biochemical signalling cascades, most of which are as yet poorly understood. Hence they can give rise to a wide range of modulatory effects that act over timescales ranging from seconds to hours or even months and years. The picture is significantly complicated by the fact that a single transmitter can activate both classes of receptors at a single site. As has already been stated, non-classical transmitters, such as NO, are not confined to act at localized synaptic sites, but diffuse freely. Accordingly, NO receptors are not membrane associated and can have a wide spatial distribution, been found anywhere in the nerve cell. NO triggers a variety of modulations through second messenger pathways that have the potential to interact in even more complex ways because of the spatially extended aspect of its action.

Although neuroscience is a long way from a full understanding of receptor mechanisms, especially those involved in indirect modulation by second messenger intracellular pathways, there are a number of powerful systems level ideas we can abstract and incorporate into our ANNs. This we have done with the second new GasNet variant: the receptor model, again taking inspiration directly from contemporary neuroscience .

Details are similar to the basic GasNet except there is now only one virtual gas and each node in the network can have one of three discrete quantities (zero,medium,maximum) of N possible receptors. Each diffusing neurotransmitter receptor pairing gives rise to a separate modulation to the properties of the node. The strength of a modulation at node i at time n, ΔM_j^n, is proportional to the product of the gas concentration at the node, $C_i^n$and the relevant receptor quantity, R_j as described by equation 7. Each modulation makes some change to one or more function parameters of the node. All the variables controlling the process are again set for each node by an evolutionary search algorithm.

$$\Delta M_j^n = \rho_i C_i^n R_j \qquad (7)$$

In the original GasNet any node that was in the path of a diffusing transmitter would be modulated in a fixed way. The receptor model allows site specific modulations, including no modulation (zero quantity of receptors) and multiple modulations at a single site. This provides a powerful context 'switching' mechanism that pulls the 'chemical' and 'electrical' processes further apart, allowing (but not forcing) looser coupling, while further increasing the potential for complex network dynamics. A number of different receptor linked modulations have been experimented with, including:

- Action of receptor1: increase gain of node transfer function as in original gasnet
- Action of receptor2: decrease gain of node transfer function as in original gasnet
- Action of receptor3: increase proportion of retained node activation from last time step
- Action of recetor4: if above a threshold switch transfer function of node for sustained period

Note the first two modulation are immediate and short-lived while the last two operate over a longer time-scale. Each possible subset of these receptors proved to be at least as evolvable as the original GasNet, while some were significantly better. A variant that proved particularly successful used receptor1 only. This is the model that will be referred to as the Receptor GasNet in the following sections on the comparative studies of the evolvability of different types of GasNet.

Comparative Experiments

Although most of the GasNet variants described in this paper have been successfully used in a number of robotic tasks, their evolvability and other properties were thoroughly *compared* on a robotic visual discrimination task. Starting from an arbitrary position and orientation in a black-walled arena, a robot equipped with a forward facing camera must navigate under extremely variable lighting conditions to one shape (a white triangle) while ignoring the second shape (a white square). Both the robot control network, one or other form of GasNet, and the robot sensor input morphology, i.e. the position of the input pixels on the visual array, were under evolutionary control. Fitness over a single trial was taken as the fraction of the starting distance moved towards the triangle by the end of the trial period, and the evaluated fitness was returned as the weighted sum of 16 trials of the controller from different initial conditions:

$$F = \frac{2}{N(N+1)} \sum_{i=1}^{i=N} i(1 - \frac{D_i^F}{D_i^S}) \qquad (8)$$

where D_i^F is the distance to the triangle at the end of the ith trial, and D_i^S the distance to the triangle at the start of the trial, and the N trials are sorted in descending order of $\frac{D^F}{D^S}$. Thus good trials, in which the controller moves some way towards the triangle, receive a smaller weighting than bad trials, encouraging robust behaviour on all 16 trials. Success in the task was taken as an evaluated fitness of 1.0 over thirty successive generations of the evolutionary algorithm. For further information on the task and robot see (Husbands *et al.* 1998).

The Evolutionary Search Algorithm

A geographically distributed asynchronous updating evolutionary algorithm was used, with a *PopSize* of 100 arranged on a 10×10 grid. Parents were chosen through rank-based roulette-wheel selection on the mating pool consisting of the 8 nearest neighbours to a randomly chosen grid-point. A mutated copy of the parent was placed back in the mating pool using inverse rank-based roulette-wheel selection. For full details see (Husbands *et al.* 1998).

The Solution Representation and Mutation Operators

The robot controllers were encoded as a variable length string of integers, with each integer allowed to lie in the range [0, 99]. Each node in the network was coded for by nineteen parameters (21 for the receptor and plexus models), controlling such properties as node positions, connectivity, sensor input, and all gas diffusion and modulation variables. Connections were formed as in figure 5, with each node connecting to nodes lying within one of two connection arcs.

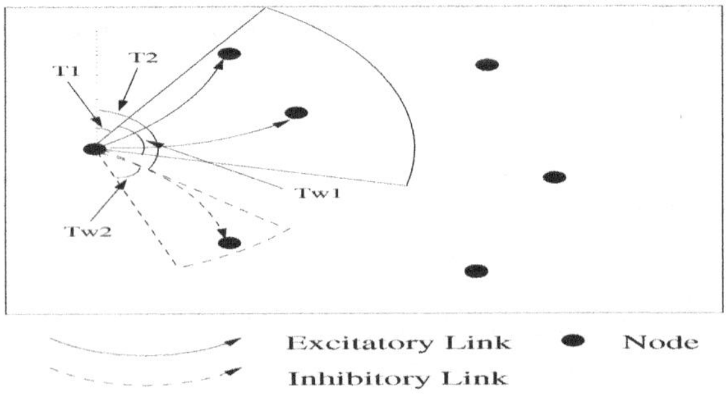

Figure 5: The connectivity of the network is defined by positive and negative arcs (T=θ, Tw=θ_{width}). Networks develop and function on a 2D plane. See text for further details.

Three mutation operators were applied to solutions during evolution. Each *integer* in the string had a probability (4%) of mutation in a Gaussian distribution around its current value. There was also an addition operator, with a 4% chance per *genotype* of adding one neuron to the network. Finally there was a deletion operator, with a 4% chance per *genotype* of deleting one randomly chosen neuron from the network. In the next section, we describe the speed of evolution results for the three models.

Speed of evolution results

Table 1 shows the speed of evolution results for the three GasNet variants. Forty runs were carried out with each model, with runs being terminated once controllers were evolved that achieved 100% fitness over thirty consecutive generations. Here we see that the plexus and receptor models evolve good solutions significantly faster (T-test analyses were carried out to confirm this) than the GasNet model. The receptor model gives particularly dramatic improvements. The question is therefore, what is it about the new features of these two models

	Original	Plexus	Receptor
Num Runs	40	40	40
Mean (S.D.)	3042 (3681)	1579 (2609)	260 (161)
Median	1201	512	158
Best	136	101	46
Worst	> 10000	> 10000	840

Table 1: Number of generations before consistent success is achieved, for the three models described earlier. Both plexus and receptor models results were significantly better than the original GasNet results. NB runs not achieving consistent success by generation 10000 were terminated.

that mediates this increase? In the remainder of the paper we will explore this question through an analysis of the coupling between the gas diffusion and electrical synaptic mechanisms in the networks.

Coupling

As described earlier, the plexus model allows network nodes to emit gas from anywhere in the grid. This partly separates the gas diffusion and the electrical synaptic activity mechanisms; synaptic connections are formed from the current node position, while gas diffusion connections are formed from the gas emission position. Thus gas connections in the grid can be changed through modifying the gas emission position, while synaptic connections can be altered through moving the node itself[1]. Similarly, the addition of receptors to mediate the modulatory affects of the virtual gas potentially allows even more independence between electrical and chemical signalling. This is because, as explained in section , the receptor GasNet used in the comparative experiments had only one type of receptor; its presence or absence at a node in the network essentially acts as a switching mechanism turning on and off modulation at the node.

There is no simple way of calculating the degree of coupling in the three forms of network; in principle one can measure the degree of ruggedness through correlation lengths or similar methods. However, Smith *et al.* (2001) shows that these types of measures do not discriminate between highly heterogenous problem spaces such as those found here. In this section, we introduce a very simple, and admittedly incomplete, description to measure the degree of coupling between the gas diffusion and electrical synapse mechanisms. We calculate the two connectivity matrices (electrical and chemical) for a given successful GasNet, and calculate the coupling as the number of overlapping connections, i.e the number of elements which are non-zero in both connectivity matrices.

Table 2 shows this coupling between the electrical and gas diffusion processes for the three models. The number of electrical synaptic connections and number of gas diffusion connections (averaged per neuron), and the percentage of overlapping connections, are shown for each of the successfully evolved controllers, over all models. Two points can be made. First, there are no significant differences between the numbers of electrical synaptic connections across the three models. Second, the percentages of overlapping connections in the GasNet are significantly higher than those in the receptor and plexus models; thus indicating that coupling between the electrical and diffusion processes is far stronger in the GasNet model than in the receptor and plexus models and may provide part of the reason for the faster evolutionary search. In the final section we discuss this hypothesis further.

[1]Note that the two mechanisms are not entirely separated: both act on the actual position of the destination nodes.

Discussion

There is some evidence from evolutionary theory that the degree of coupling between interacting and yet distinct processes might lie at the heart of some important principles for the development of complex systems. To evolve successfully, an organism must satisfy the conflicting pressures of *phenotypic stability* and *genetic instability*, i.e. that the organism be robust to phenotypic change (to not fall off the current adaptive peak), and amenable to genotypic change (to allow movement to a new adaptive peak). Conrad (1990) identifies genetic redundancy and multiple weak interaction as possible mechanisms by which these two conflicting pressures can be satisfied.

Such loosely coupled redundant systems contain the potential for genotypic change without phenotypic change; both multiple weak interactions and redundancy allow for gradual, or even neutral, transformation of function through genetic variation (Conrad 1990). In such systems, phenotypic fitness is likely to be highly correlated across the genotype landscape, either (or both) through significant levels of neutrality, and low levels of ruggedness. Such systems are also robust to phenotypic change; complex systems picked at random are more likely to be stable if the system is characterised by either multiply connected weakly interacting components, or sparsely connected strongly interacting components (Gardner & Ashby 1970; May 1972).

By contrast, strongly coupled non-redundant systems are far less amenable to variation; change in one component is more likely to affect the entire system, leading to

	Original	Plexus	Receptor
Num successful runs	33	37	40
Synaptic connections (S.D.)	1.89 (0.52)	1.72 (0.41)	1.61 (0.3)
Diffusion connections (S.D.)	2.27 (0.93)	2.78 (0.84)	2.1 (0.7)
Overlapping connection coupling (S.D.)	40.5% (13.2%)	10.8% (8.1%)	11.4 (5.5%)

Table 2: Coupling in the original GasNet and plexus models. For each of the successfully evolved controllers, the number of electrical synaptic connections and number of gas diffusion connections are shown (averaged per neuron). The percentage of connections which overlap, i.e. that connect the same neurons, are also shown. See text for further details.

phenotypic instability. We see this effect clearly in the theoretical NK fitness landscapes, where a higher degree of epistatic connection between the components leads to a less correlated fitness landscape (Kauffman 1993). In other words, even small changes in the genotype in a strongly coupled system lead to large changes in the phenotype. However, in tenably neutral versions of the NK landscapes, high degrees of redundancy compensate in some measure for the strong coupling, allowing genetic variation without massive phenotypic variation (Barnett 1998; Newman & Engelhardt 1998).

The results on degree of coupling and speed of evolution presented in this paper support our view that systems involving distinct yet coupled processes are highly evolvable when there is a bias towards a loose coupling between the processes; this allows the possibility of 'tuning' one against the other without destructive interference. The receptor model, in which the search process arguably has the most direct control over the degree of coupling, is seen to be by far the most evolvable. Indeed, preliminary experiments on extended versions of the shape discrimination task, involving more shapes and two stage discriminations, have proved highly successful with the receptor model.

This paper marks a first step in our attempts to gain deeper insights into the importance, or otherwise, of the coupling issue. As well as exploring the use of our artificial nervous systems for generating more complex behaviours, we are trying to build a formal framework to extend our theoretical understandings. In this we have some considerable distance to go. Although we have concentrated on changes (to plastic systems) over an evolutionary timescale, very similar issues are likely to be important at the timescale of the plastic changes themselves.

Acknowledgements: The authors would like to thank all the members of the CCNR (http://www.cogs.susx.ac.uk/ccnr/) for constructive discussion, as well as the anonymous referees. We would also like to thank the Sussex High Performance Computing Initiative (http://www.hpc.sussex.ac.uk/) for computing support. TS and AP are funded by BT Exact sponsored CASE studentships (http://innovate.bt.com/projects/ftg.htm).

References

Barañano, D.; Ferris, C.; and Snyder, S. 2001. Atypical neural messengers. *Trends in Neuroscience* 24(2):99–106.

Barnett, L. 1998. Ruggedness and neutrality: The NKp family of fitness landscapes. In Adami, C.; Belew, R.; Kitano, H.; and Taylor, C., eds., *Artificial Life VI: Proceedings of the Sixth International Conference on Artificial Life.* Cambridge, Massachusetts: MIT Press. 18–27.

Changeux, J.-P. 1993. Chemical signalling in the brain. *Sci. Am.* 269(5):58–62.

Conrad, M. 1990. The geometry of evolution. *BioSystems* 24:61–81.

Edelman, G., and Gally, J. 1992. Nitric oxide: Linking space and time in the brain. *Proceedings of the National Academy of Sciences, USA* 89:11651–11652.

Gardner, M., and Ashby, W. 1970. Connectance of large dynamic (cybernetic) systems: Critical values for stability. *Nature* 228:784.

Grand, S. 1997. Creatures: An exercise in creation. *IEEE Intelligent Systems Magazine* July.

Husbands, P.; Smith, T.; Jakobi, N.; and O'Shea, M. 1998. Better living through chemistry: Evolving GasNets for robot control. *Connection Science* 10(3-4):185–210.

Husbands, P.; Philippides, A.; Smith, T.; and O'Shea, M. 2001. Volume signalling in real and robot nervous systems. *Theory in Biosciences* 120:251–268.

Kauffman, S. 1993. *The Origins of Order: Self-Organization and Selection in Evolution.* Oxford, UK: Oxford University Press.

Kondo, T.; Ishiguro, A.; Uchikawa, Y.; and Eggenberger, P. 1999. Autonomous robot control by a neural network with dynamically-rearranging function. In *Fourth International Symposium on Artificial Life and Robotics: AROB99.*

May, R. 1972. Will a large complex system be stable? *Nature* 238:413–414.

Newman, M., and Engelhardt, R. 1998. Effects of selective neutrality on the evolution of molecular species. *Proceedings of the Royal Society of London, B* 265:1333–1338.

Philippides, A. O.; Husbands, P.; and O'Shea, M. 2000. Four-dimensional neuronal signaling by nitric oxide: A computational analysis. *J. Neurosci.* 20(3):1199–1207.

Philippides, A. 2001. *Modelling the Diffusion of Nitric Oxide in Brains.* Ph.D. Dissertation, U. Sussex.

Purves, D. 1997. *Neuroscience.* Sinauer.

Smith, T.; Husbands, P.; and O'Shea, M. 2001. Not measuring evolvability: Initial exploration of an evolutionary robotics search space. In *Proceedings of the 2001 Congress on Evolutionary Computation: CEC2001.* Piscataway, New Jersey: IEEE Press. 9–16.

Smith, T.; Husbands, P.; and O'Shea, M. 2002. Local evolvability, neutrality, and search difficulty in evolutionary robotics. *Biosystems.* In press.

Snyder, S., and Ferris, C. 2000. Novel neurotransmitters and their neuropsychiatric relevance. *American Journal of Psychiatry* 157:1738–1751.

Evolving Teamwork and Role-Allocation with Real Robots

Matt Quinn [1], **Lincoln Smith** [1], **Giles Mayley** [2] and **Phil Husbands** [1]
[1]Centre for Computational Neuroscience and Robotics, University of Sussex, Brighton, BN1 9QG, U.K.
[2] Mathematique Appliqué S.A. Brighton Innovation Centre, University of Sussex, Brighton, BN1 9QG, U.K.

Abstract

We report on recent work in which we employed artificial evolution to design neural network controllers for small, homogeneous teams of mobile autonomous robots. The robots are evolved to perform a formation movement task from random starting positions, equipped only with infrared sensors. The dual constraints of homogeneity and minimal sensors make this a non-trivial task. We describe the behaviour of a successful evolved team in which robots adopt and maintain functionally distinct roles in order to achieve the task. We believe this to be the first example of the use of artificial evolution to design coordinated, cooperative behaviour for real robots.

Introduction

In this paper we report on our recent work evolving controllers for robots which are required to work as a team. The word 'team' has been used in a variety of senses in both the multi-robot and the ethology literature, so it is appropriate to start the paper with a definition. We will adopt the definition given by Anderson and Franks (2001) in their recent review of team behaviour in animal societies. They identify three defining features of team behaviour. Firstly, individuals make different contributions to task success, i.e. they must perform different sub-tasks or roles (this does not preclude more than one individual adopting the same role; there may be more individuals than roles). Secondly, individual roles or sub-tasks are interdependent (or "interlocking") requiring structured cooperation; individuals operate concurrently, coordinating their different contributions in order to complete the task. Finally, a team's organisational structure persists over time, although its individuals may be substituted, or swap roles (Anderson & Franks 2001).

The designer of a multi-robot team faces a number of challenges. One of which arises because a team is a structured system. Robots must be designed to behave in such a way that the team will both become and remain appropriately organised. This requires ensuring that all the individual roles or sub-tasks are appropriately allocated. One way to address this problem is to design a team in which each individual's role is predetermined (Balch & Arkin 1998, e.g.). In addition to its organisational advantages, the pre-allocation of roles has the additional advantage of specialisation: Division of labour means that each robot's behavioural and morphological design can be tailored to its particular task. In natural systems, this type to team organisation is often found amongst eusocial insects, where roles may be caste-specific. (Detrain & Pasteels 1992, e.g). Despite the organisational advantages of system heterogeneity and the efficiency benefits of specialisation, we are interested in the design of homogeneous systems. In a homogeneous multi-robot system, each robot is built to the same design, and has an identical controller. Our interest in homogeneous robot teams stems from their potential for system-level robustness and graceful degradation due to the interchangeability of team members (although this is not an issue that we will be addressing in this paper). Since each robot is capable of performing any role or sub-task, homogeneous systems are potentially better than heterogeneous teams at coping with the loss of an individual member. Lack of role specialisation also has potential benefits for organisational flexibility (Stone & Veloso 1999). However, from the perspective of team organisation, the constraint of homogeneity makes the design task more difficult. In a homogeneous team there are no differences between robots' control systems or morphologies which can be exploited for the purposes of team organisation. Other mechanisms must be employed to facilitate the dynamic allocation and coordination of roles.

Dynamic role allocation and closely coordinated cooperation are two areas which have been addressed by a number of researchers in the field of multi-robot systems, resulting in successful implementations of such tasks such as cooperative transport (Chaimowicz *et al.* 2001), robot football (Stone & Veloso 1999), and coordinated group movement (Matarić 1995). Solutions have relied heavily on the use of essentially global information shared by radio communication. For example, in Matarić's (1995) implementation of coordinated movement with homogeneous robots, robots made use of a common coordinate system (through radio beacon triangulation) and exchanged positional information via radio communication in order to remain coordinated (Matarić 1995). Mechanisms for dynamic task or role allocation rely on communication protocols by which robots globally advertise or negotiate their current (or intended) roles (Chaimowicz *et al.* 2001; Matarić & Sukhatme 2001; Stone & Veloso 1999, e.g.).

Our work differs from that of these researchers. We wish to design teams in which system-level organisation arises, and is maintained, solely through local interactions between individuals which are constrained to utilise minimal and ambiguous local information. Systems capable of functioning under such constraints have some interesting potential engineering applications (see, for example, (Hobbs, Husbands, & Harvey 1996) for discussion of the need for minimal systems in the space industry). However, they are also interesting from an adaptive behaviour perspective, providing an example of a phenomenon often referred to as 'self-organising' or 'emergent' behaviour (Camazine *et al.* 2001).

Imposing the joint constraints of homogeneity and minimal sensors leaves us with a complex design task. One which cannot easily decomposed and addressed by conventional 'divide and conquer' design methodologies. Instead, it is a problem exhibiting significant interdependence of its constituent parts. For this reason, we have adopted an evolutionary robotics approach and employed artificial evolution to automate the design process, since such an approach is not constrained by the need for decomposition or modular design (Nolfi 1998).

We believe that the work reported in this paper is the first successful use of evolutionary robotics methodology to develop cooperative, coordinated behaviour for a real multi-robot system. To date, this research field has focussed almost exclusively on single robot systems. (See (Nolfi & Floreano 2000) and (Meyer, Husbands, & Harvey 1998) for a good surveys of evolutionary robotics research). Insofar as we are aware there are only two other published examples of the evolution of controllers instantiated on more than one physical robot. However, neither of these are co-operative systems. The first example is due to Floreano, Nolfi and Mondada. They evolved two populations of neural network controllers for Khepera mini-robots as part of a project investigating the dynamics of predator-prey co-evolution (Floreano, Nolfi, & Mondada 1998; Nolfi & Floreano 1998). One population were evolved to perform a 'predator' role, the other, a 'prey' role. Controllers were downloaded onto real robots and evaluated in pair-wise contests. The behaviour of the controllers that they evolved provides an interesting example of coordination, but in competitive system. The second example is due to Watson, Ficici and Pollack (1999). They evolved minimal neural network controllers for population of eight 'Tupperbot' mini-robots. The robots were evolved to perform photo-taxis—an individual task—and evolution was facilitated by local, probabilistic transfer of genetic material between robots via infrared communication. Their work is interesting as a proof-of-concept example of 'embodied evolution'. However, neither cooperative nor coordinated behaviours were required, nor evident in the behaviour which evolved.

The work which we will describe in this paper represents our first experiments in the evolutionary design of homogeneous multi-robot teams. We used three robots, each minimally equipped with four active infra-red sensors, and two motor-driven wheels. Robot controllers were evolved to perform a formation movement task, in an obstacle-free environment, starting from random initial positions. The robots and their task are introduced in more detail in next two sections. Robots were controlled by neural networks which were evolved in simulation, before being successfully transferred onto real robots. The networks, simulation and evolutionary machinery are covered in the fourth section. The penultimate section describes the successful behaviour of one of the evolved teams in some detail, showing that task success is dependent on the robots performing as team, in accordance with definition given at the beginning of this paper.

The Robots

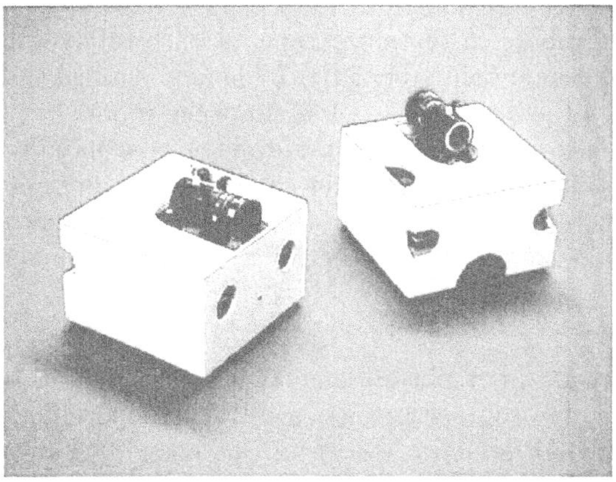

Figure 1: Two members of the three-robot team. The cameras shown are not used for the experiments described in this paper.

For these experiments, we used three robots, each been built to the same specification; two of the robots are shown in figure 1. Each robot's body is 16.75 cm wide by 16.75 cm long by 11 cm high (this excludes the additional height of its unused camera). Two motor-driven wheels, made of foam-rubber, are arranged one on either side of the robot and provide locomotion through differential drive; the robots have an average top speed of 6cm/s. An un-powered castor wheel, placed rear-centre, ensures stability. In the experiments described in this paper, a robot's *only* source of sensory input comes from its four active infrared sensors, each comprising a paired infrared emitter and receiver. Each robot has two infrared sensors at the front and two at rear, as illustrated in figure 2. Although each robots is also equipped with a 64 pixel linear CCD array camera (shown in the diagram), a 360 degree electronic compass, bump sensors, and wheel rotation sensors (i.e. shaft encoders), the controllers we evolved were prevented from making use of any of these devices.

The robots are controlled by a host computer, with each robot sending its sensor readings to and receiving its effector activations from this machine via a radio link. Each robot uses a 80C537-based micro-controller board for low-level control. The host computer is responsible for running the controller for each robot, updating each controller's inputs with the sensor readings from the appropriate robot, and transmitting the controller's output

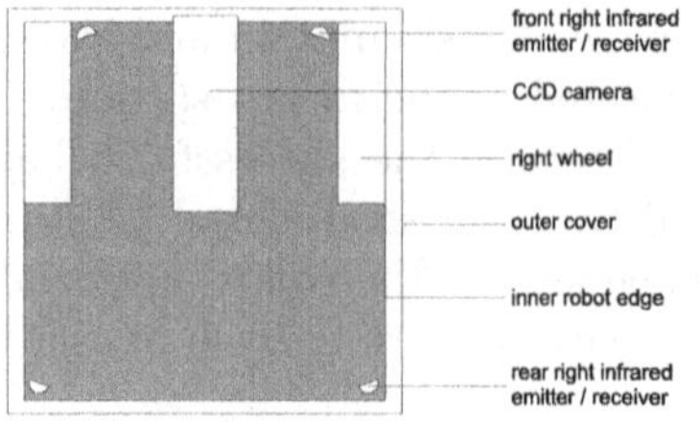

Figure 2: Plan view of a robot.

to the robot. In these experiments, each robot was updated at approximately 5 Hz. It should be noted that although the physical instantiation of the robots has been implemented as a host/slave system, conceptually the robots are to be considered as independent, autonomous agents by virtue of the logical division of control into distinct and self-contained controllers on the host machine.

Infrared Sensors

The reader may not be familiar with the limitations of active infrared sensors, especially those peculiar to a multi-robot scenario, so we will address them in some detail. An active infrared sensor comprises a paired infrared emitter and receiver. Its normal function is to emit an infrared beam and then measure the amount of infrared which reflects back from nearby objects. In this way our robots can use their sensors to detect other robots up to a maximum of about 18cm (i.e. just over one body length away). The dark grey beams in the left-hand panel of figure 3 approximately indicate the limited areas in which a robot can detect other robots in this manner. IR sensors are sometimes referred to as proximity sensors, however this is somewhat misleading. Whilst the sensor reading due to reflected IR is a non-linear, inverse function of the distance to the object detected, it is also a function of the angle at which the emitted beam strikes the surface of the object, and of the proportion of the beam which strikes that object. It is because an IR sensor reading combines these three factors into a single value that, even in normal function, sensor readings are ambiguous.

Figure 3: **Left:** The extent to which reflected IR can be sensed (dark grey area), and the extent to which IR beam is perceptible to other robots (light grey area). **Right:** The angles from which a robot can perceive the IR emissions of others

The ambiguity of IR sensors is significantly increased in a multi-robot scenario, because the robots' sensors interfere with one another. Since each robot is constantly emitting IR, a robot's IR emissions can also be directly sensed by other robots. The light grey beams in the left-hand panel of figure 3 indicates the approximate area in which a robot's infrared emissions may be directly detected by other robots. The maximum range at which emissions can be detected is approximately 30cm—almost twice the range at which a robot can detect an object by reflected IR. The right-hand panel of the same diagram illustrates the range of angles at which a robot can receive the IR emissions of other robots. The sensor value due to receiving another's IR emissions is also the combined function of a number of factors: It will depend on the distance between the robots, but also the angle at which the emitted beam strikes the other robot's receiver, and which portion of the beam strikes the receiver (IR is significantly more intense at the centre of the beam than at the edges). Readings due to direct IR are thus ambiguous for the same reasons as reflected IR. However, ambiguity is compounded by the fact that, to the robot, readings due to reflected IR are indistinguishable from those due to the reception of IR emissions of other robots. Moreover, a sensor reading may be the result of a combination of both reflected and direct IR and it may be due to one or both of the other robots.

The Task

The task with which we present the robots is an extension of that used in previous work which involved two simulated Khepera robots (Quinn 2001). Adapted for three robots, the task is as follows: Initially, the three robots are placed in an obstacle-free environment in some random configuration, such that each robot is within sensor range of the others. Thereafter, the robots are required to move, as a group, a certain distance away from their initial position. The robots are not required to adopt any particular formation, only to remaining within sensor range of one another, and to avoid collisions. During evolution, robots are evaluated on their ability to move the group centroid one metre within the space of three simulated minutes. However, our expectation was that a team capable of this would be able to sustain formation movement of much longer periods. The robots are not required to adopt any particular formation, only to remaining within sensor range of one another, and to avoid collisions. Since the robots start from initial random configurations, we anticipate that successful completion of the task will entail two phases. The first entailing the team organising itself into a formation, and the second entailing the team moving whilst maintaining that formation.

From the characterisation of the robots' sensors in the previous section, it should be clear that these impose significant constraints. They provide very little direct information about a robot's surroundings. Any given set of sensor input can be the result of any one of large number of significantly different circumstances. Furthermore, outside the limited range of their IR sensors, rbots have no indication of each other's position. Any robot straying more than two body-lengths from its teammates will cease to have any indication of their location. Of course, a robot controller may employ strategies to overcome some of the limitations of it sensors. For example, additional information can be gained by strategies which combine sensing and moving, and the integration of sensor input over time. However, it should be clear that the team's situation contrasts strongly with previous work in which robots utilised shared coordinate systems and global communication. It is worth noting that biological models of self-organising coordinated movement assume typically that agents are presented with significantly more information about their local environment than these robots have. For example, in models of flocking and shoaling, agents are typically assumed to have ideal sensors which provide the location, velocity and orientation of their nearest neighbours (see (Camazine *et al.* 2001) for an extensive review of such biological models; see also (Ward, Gobot, & Kendal 2001) for a recent evolutionary simulation model)

The team are also constrained by their homogeneity for the reasons discussed in the introduction. The team will move from their initial random configuration into the formation in which they will maintain whilst moving. In so doing it seems inevitable that different robots will be required to adopt different roles (for example, a leader and two followers). The robots must find some way of appropriately allocating and maintaining these roles despite the lack of any intrinsic differences between them. This is, of course, made all the more challenging by the poverty of the robots' sensory input.

Implementation

Evaluating Team Performance

A single genotype was used to generate a team by 'cloning' (i.e. decoding the genotype and then making copies of the resulting controller). Given that different starting positions will present different challenges, it was important that each team (i.e. each evolutionary individual) is evaluated under the same set of initial conditions. To this end, at each generation of the evolutionary algorithm, a set of 75 starting positions was randomly generated, as detailed in figure 4, and used for the evaluation of all the teams. Each evaluation involved multiple trials from the different starting positions. Fitness was measured as the average score over all the trials in the evaluation set.

Reflecting the task description, the evaluation function seeks to assess the ability of the team to increase its distance from its starting position, whilst avoiding collisions and staying within sensor range. It therefore consists of three main components. First, at each timestep of the trial, the group is rewarded for any gains in distance. Second, this reward is multiplied by a dispersal scalar, reducing the fitness increment when one or more robots are outside of IR sensor range. Third, at the end of a trial, the group's accumulated score is reduced in proportional to the number of collisions which have occurred during that trial. (The maximum number of allowed collisions per trial was 20, if this number was reached, the trial was ended). More specifically, a team's trial score, is:

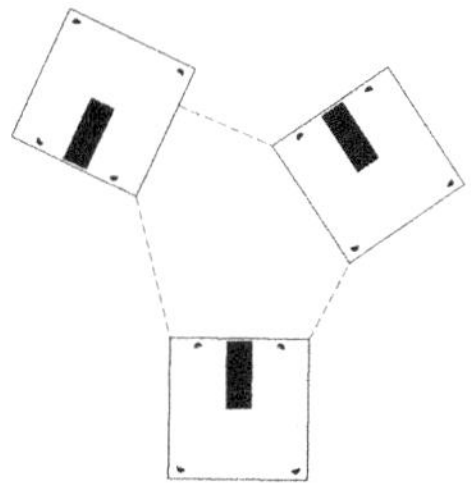

Figure 4: **An example starting positions:** Each robot's orientation is set randomly in the range $[0 : 2\pi]$, and the minimum distance between the edges of each robot and its nearest neighbour is set randomly in the range [10cm:22cm].

$$P.\Big(\sum_{t=1}^{T} \big[f(d_t, D_{t-1}).(1 + \tanh(s_t/20.0))\big]\Big)$$

Here P is a collision-penalty scalar in the range $[0.5 : 1]$, such that, if c is the number of collisions between robots, and $c_{\max}$ is the maximum number of collisions allowed, then $P = 1 - c/2c_{\max}$. The distance gain component is given by the function f. This measures any gain that the team have made on their previous best distance from their initial location. Here a team's location is taken to be the centre-point (or centroid) of the group. If d_t is the Euclidean distance between the group's location at time t and its location at time $t = 0$, D_{t-1} is the largest value that d_t has attained prior to time t, and $D_{\max}$ is the required distance (i.e. 100 c.m.), then the function f is defined as:

$$f(d_t, D_{t-1}) = \begin{cases} d_t - D_{t-1} & \text{if } D_{t-1} < d_t < D_{\max} \\ 0 & \text{otherwise} \end{cases}$$

The final component of a team's trial score, the scalar s_t, is a measure of the team's dispersal beyond sensor range at time t. If each robot is within sensor range of at least one other, then $s_t = 0$. Otherwise, the two shortest lines that can connect all three robots are found, and s_t is the distance by which the longest of these exceeds sensor range. In other words, the team is penalised for its most wayward member. Note that s_t used in combination with a **tanh** function, this ensures that as the robots begin to disperse, the team's score increment falls away sharply, the gradient of the tanh curve falls off as the distance between the robots increases, ensuring that increases in distance will still receive some minimal reward, even when the robots are far apart.

Simulation

Controllers were initially evolved in simulation, before being transferred to the real robots. A big problem with evolving in simulation is that robots may become adapted to inaccurate features of the simulation, not present in the real world (Brooks 1992). However, building completely accurate simulation model of the robots and their interactions would be an onerous, and potentially impossible task, moreover, it would be unlikely that such a simulation would have significant speed advantages over evolving in the real world (Matarić & Cliff 1996). To avoid this problem we employed Jakobi's minimal simulation methodology(Jakobi 1997; 1998b). This enabled us to build a relatively crude, fast-running simulation model of the robots and their interactions, based on a relatively small set of measurements. The parameters of this model were systematically varied, within certain ranges, between each evaluation of a team. Parameters included, for example, the orientation of each robots' sensors, the manner in which a robot's position was affected by motor output, and the effects of IR interference. Whilst it was generally either difficult or time-consuming to measure parameters needed for the simulation with great accuracy on the robots, it was relatively easy to specify a range within which each of the parameters lay, even if that range was wide. Varying parameters within these ranges meant that a robot of capable of adapting to the simulation would be adapted to a wide range of possible robot-environment dynamics, including those of the real world. In addition to compensating for inaccuracies in our measurements, variation was used in the same way to compensate for inaccuracies in our modelling, since we were able to estimate the error due to these inaccuracies and adjust parameter ranges to compensate. More importantly, this approach allowed us to sacrifice accuracy for speed and employ cheap, inaccurate modelling where more accurate modelling would have incurred significant computational costs. Space precludes a description of our implementation of this minimal simulation, but full details are available elsewhere (Quinn *et al.* 2002).

Neural Networks

The robots were controlled by artificial neural networks. Since it was unclear how the task would be solved, we could estimate little about the type of network architecture that would be needed to support the required behaviour. Thus we attempted to place as much of the design of the networks as possible under evolutionary control—specifically, the thresholds, weights and decay parameters, and the size and connectivity of the networks. Each neural network comprised 4 sensor input nodes, 4 motor output nodes, and some number of artificial neurons. These were connected together by some number of directional, excitatory and inhibitory weighted links. The network has no explicit layers, so any neuron may connect to any others, including itself; and may also connect to any of the sensory or motor nodes.

The neurons we use are loosely based on model spiking neurons (see Gerstner and Kistler, (2002) for a comprehensive review of such models). At any time-step, the output, O_t, a neuron is given by:

$$O_t = \begin{cases} 1 & \text{if } m_t \geq T \\ 0 & \text{if } m_t < T \end{cases}$$

where T is the neuron's threshold. Here m_t is analogous to membrane potential in a real neuron; it is a function of a neuron's weighted, summed input(s) integrated over time, such that:

$$m_t = \begin{cases} (\gamma_A)m_{t-1} + \sum_{n=0}^{N} w_n i_n & \text{if} \quad O_{t-1} = 0 \\ (\gamma_B)m_{t-1} + \sum_{n=0}^{N} w_n i_n & \text{if} \quad O_{t-1} = 1 \end{cases}$$

where γ_A and γ_B are decay constants, and w_n designates the weight of the connection from the nth input (i_n) that scales that input. γ_A and γ_B are constrained to the range [0:1], the values of weights and thresholds are unconstrained. For certain parameter settings this neuron will behave like a simple spiking neuron, accumulating membrane potential, firing and then discharging (i.e., with $\gamma_A > \gamma_B$ and $T > 0$). However, the neurons also exhibit a range of other interesting temporal dynamics under different settings.

Each sensor input node outputs a real value in the range [0.0:1.0], which is simple linear scaling of the reading taken from its associated sensor. Motor outputs consist of a 'forward' and a 'reverse' node for each motor. The output, M_{out}, of each motor nodes is a simple threshold function of its summed weighted inputs:

$$M_{\text{out}} = \begin{cases} 1 & \text{if} \sum_{n=0}^{N} w_n i_n > 0 \\ 0 & \text{if} \sum_{n=0}^{N} w_n i_n \leq 0 \end{cases}$$

The final output of the each of the two motors is attained by subtracting its reverse node output from its forward node output. This gives three possible values for each motor output: {-1,0,1}.

The network is encoded by a topological encoding scheme, described in (Quinn *et al.* 2002), which is designed to enable the size and connectivity of the network to be placed under evolutionary control with only minimal constraints on network structure. Through macro-mutation operators, described in following section, neurons and connections can be added to or removed from the network, and existing connections can become reconnected.

The Evolutionary Machinery

A simple, generational, evolutionary algorithm (EA) was employed for these experiments. An evolutionary population contained 50 genotypes. In the initial population,

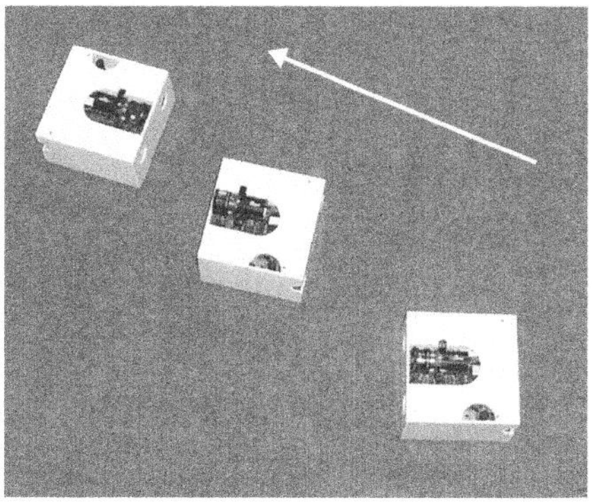

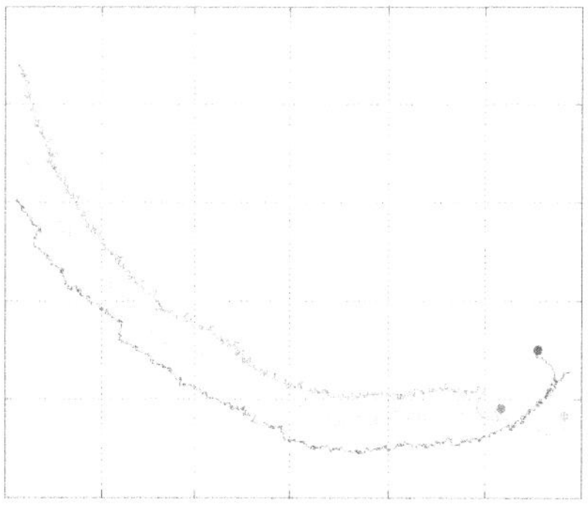

Figure 5: **Left:** Video still of the team travelling in formation. **Right** An example of team trajectory, tracing the position of each robot over a 5 minute period. Grid divisions are at 50cm intervals, robots' initial positions (bottom right) indicated by dots. Data generated in simulation.

each genotype encoded a randomly generated network with three neurons and an average of 6 connections per gene; weights and thresholds were initially set in the range [-5:5] but were thereafter not constrained. At the end of each generation (i.e. after all individuals had been evaluated), genotypes were ranked by score, the 10 lowest scoring individuals were discarded and the remainder used to generate a new population. The two highest scoring individuals ('the elite') were copied unchanged in the new population, thereafter, genotypes were selected randomly with a probability inversely proportional to their rank. 60% of new genotypes were produced by recombination, and mutation operators were applied to all genotypes except the elite.

Genotypes were subject to both macro-mutation (i.e. structural changes) and micro-mutation (i.e. perturbation of real-valued parameters). Micro-mutation entailed that a random Gaussian offset was applied, with a small probability, to all real-valued parameters encoded in the genotype, such that the expected number of micro-mutations per genotype was 2. The mean of the Gaussian was zero and its standard deviation was 0.33 of that parameter's range (in the case of decay parameters) or its initialisation range (in the case of weights and thresholds). Three types of macro-mutation were employed. Firstly, a new neuron could be added to, or a randomly chosen neuron deleted, from the encoded network. The probability of addition was 0.004, and of deletion was 0.01. Secondly a new connection could be added or a randomly chosen connection deleted with the respective probabilities of 0.02 and 0.04. Finally, a randomly chosen connection could be chosen and reconnected elsewhere, this occurred with a probability of with a probability of 0.04.

Evolved Behaviour

To date, we have undertaken a total of ten evolutionary runs. Four of these were terminated at early stage because they seemed unpromising. The remaining six runs produced teams capable of a consistently high standard of success after being left to evolve for between two and five thousand generations. There were significant behavioural differences between the successful teams, and we have chosen to focus on a single team rather than attempt to summarise them all. In describing the behaviour of the team, we wish primarily to achieve two objectives. The first is to demonstrate that the robots' behaviour is indeed that of a team, in the sense in which the term was introduced at the beginning of this paper. The second is to illustrate the process by which these roles become allocated in the absence of any intrinsic differences between the robots.

Paper really is too static a format to demonstrate how well the team transferred from simulation to reality, a problem which is lamented in more detail elsewhere (Jakobi 1998b). We can only report that the behaviour observed in simulation was qualitatively reproduced in reality. In simulation, averaged over 5000 trials, this team achieve a mean score 99.7 (out of a possible 100). We have not completed nearly so many trials with real robots, however, we have conducted a sequence of 100 consecutive trials (with random starting positions) with the real robots, the team successfully completed all of them.

Formation Movement

The team travel in a line formation, as can be seen from the video still in figure 5. The lead robot travels in reverse, whilst the middle and rear robot travel forwards. When travelling in formation, the team move at just over 1 cm/s, a relatively slow speed compared the 6 cm/s maximum speed that an individual robot is capable. The photograph fails to catch the dynamics of the team's movement which entails each robot swinging clockwise and counterclockwise whilst maintaining its position—watching the video footage sped up, team locomotion appears almost snakelike. The sequence of diagrams in figure 6 is an attempt to illustrates this aspect of the team's locomotion. Note from these diagrams, that the robots rely almost entirely on the direct perception of each other's IR beams (i.e. sensory interference) in order to coordinate their movement.

One illuminating way of illustrating relational movement patterns is changes in individual's orientation relative to the position of the individual with which it is interacting (see Moran *et al.* (1981), where this is used to

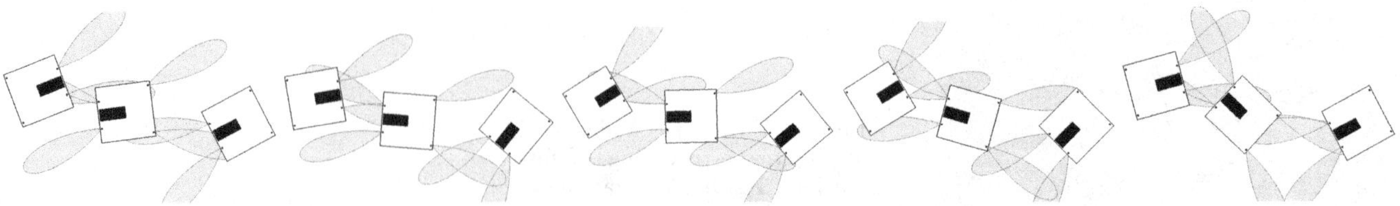

Figure 6: Time sequence illustrating relative positions during formation movement over a short (4 second) period. Robots maintain contact through direct sensing of each other's IR beams.

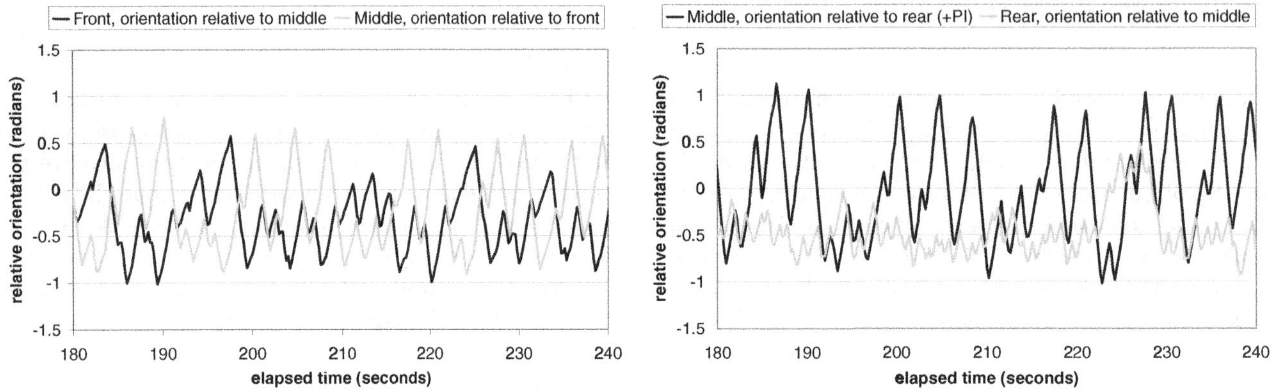

Figure 7: **Relative orientations of robots in formation over a 60 second period.** (Data taken from simulation.) *Left:* The movements of the front and middle robot are closely coordinated, with relative orientations predominantly in anti-phase. *Right:* The coordination of the middle and rear robot is much looser (For ease of presentation, the relative orientation of the middle robot has been offset by π) in the left-hand graph.

great effect in their analysis of social interaction between wolves). (Relative orientation is an egocentric measure; the orientation of A relative to the position B is the angle between A's orientation and the line AB). Figure 7 shows the orientation of each robot relative to its neighbours during a period of formation movement. It illustrates the high degree of coordination between the front and middle robot, each responding closely to the other's movements. It also illustrates the much lower degree of coordination between the middle and rear robots, and the difference, with respect to the frequency of angular oscillation, between the movement of the rear robot and the leading pair. Despite the oscillating angular displacement of the robots, their formation is extremely robust. The formation is maintained indefinitely, despite robots only having been evolved for their ability to move the group centroid one metre.

Roles

It should be clear from the above that robots perform the task we have set them. But are the robots actually operating as a team? In what follows we briefly show that each robot makes some necessary contribution to overall success and that these contributions are different and persist over time. To this end, we are interested in what each individual contributes to the maintenance of the formation and its continued movement. Perhaps the simplest way to assess individual contributions is simply by considering the effects of the removal of individual robot from the formation. To this end, we consider the effects of the removal of either the front or the rear robot (removal of middle robot is unilluminating, merely leaving the remaining two robots out of sensor range).

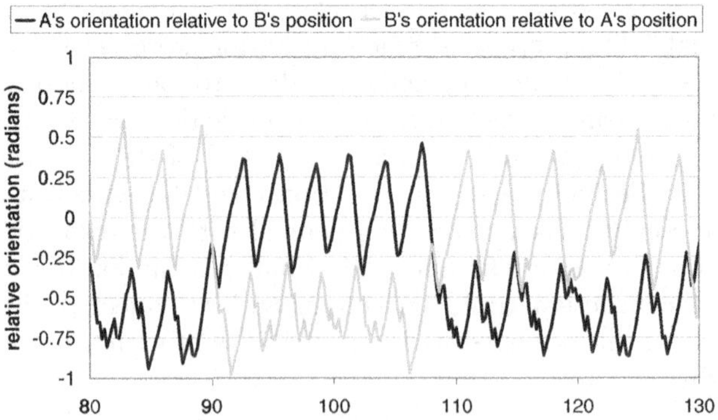

Figure 8: **Relative orientations of two robots, A and B, operating in the absence of a third robot.** Similarly to the front pair in a full formation, orientations are in anti-phase, although here the pattern is more regular. The configuration (and the pattern) is asymmetric, and maintained although robots periodically swapping positions within the configuration (seen at 90 and 110 seconds in the figure). Note that there is no significant displacement of the pairs' position.

If the rear robot is removed from the formation, the locomotion of the remaining pair ceases, there is no further significant displacement of their position. However, this is the only significant effect. The pair maintain the same configuration as when in full formation. Their cycle of angular oscillation relative to one another remains in anti-phase, although the pattern becomes more regular, as illustrated in figure 8. This is a dynamically stable configuration, tightly constrained by sensory feedback, which will persist indefinitely. If the rear robot is replaced, the group will move away once more. Now we consider the front robot. If this is removed from the full formation, the middle robot swings round toward the rear robot, and—after some interaction—the two robots form an opposed pair which maintain the same dynamically stable configuration as was just described.

From the above, we can say the following: Firstly, the rear robot has no significant effect on the other two robots' ability to maintain formation, but it is crucial to sustaining locomotion. Secondly, it is clear that the middle robot responds to the presence of the rear robot by moving forwards, since in the absence of the rear robot, the remaining pair cease to travel. For locomotion to continue, the configuration of the rear and middle robot must persist. That is, the middle robot must continue to sense the rear robot with its back sensors. Finally, in the absence of the front robot, the configuration adopted by the middle and rear robot in the formation is unstable.

This analysis is sufficient to show that these robots are working as team, concurrently performing separate but complementary roles which, in combination, result in coordinated formation movement. A more precise characterisation of each robot's contribution is difficult without presenting detailed analysis of the close sensorimotor coupling between the opposed front pair, and how this coupling is perturbed, but not completely disrupted, by the presence of the rear robot. Nevertheless, it is possible say something further about the team's organisation through investigating the effects of reorganising its formation. Firstly, when the middle robot is quickly picked up and rotated by 180 degrees, the formation is maintained and the team start to move in the opposite direction, with the robots which were previously front and rear adopting the roles appropriate to their new positions in the formation. Secondly, if the rear robot is removed from the formation and appropriately placed behind the front robot, formation again move off in the opposite direction, with each robot performing the role appropriate to its position. Thus, the fact that each robot remains in the same role within the formation is solely by virtue of the spatial organisation of the formation, rather than any long-term differences in internal state. This is not to say that the robots' behaviour is reactive. We know from analysis (not presented here) that the evolved networks rely heavily on temporal dynamics, such as short-term transient states. However, they do not rely on internal state to maintain their roles.

Role Allocation

How are the roles initially allocated within the team? This is essentially to ask how the robots achieve the formation position from random initial positions, since as has already been noted, that the maintenance of individual roles is a function of the spatial organisation of the team formation. Any discussion of the initial interactions of the robots will be difficult without at least some information about how the robots responds to sensory input, so we will start by giving a very simplified explanation. In the absence of any sensory input, the robots move in a small clockwise forwards circle (the motor output is a cyclic pattern of left motor forward for 3 time-steps, followed by one times-step of right motor forward). A robot is generally 'attracted' to any source of front sensor input. It will rotate anticlockwise in response to any front left input and clockwise in response to front right input. Activation of either (or both) of the rear sensors in the absence of significant front sensor input causes the robot to turn more tightly in a clockwise direction (i.e. the fourth step of the basic motor pattern is removed). This is an incomplete description, but should be sufficient for the purposes of our explanation.

From its initial position, a robot will begin to circle clockwise until its senses another robot. Recall that a robot can sense both IR reflected off the body of another robot and the IR beam of another robot, the latter being perceptible from twice the distance than the former. For this reason a robot will typically first encounter either the front or rear IR beams of another robot (direct IR), or one of its side panels (reflected IR). A robot 'attracted' to the side of another robot will simply be ignored as it cannot be sensed. A robot attracted to the rear IR beams of another robot will in turn activate that robot's rear sensors, causing it to turn sideways on. If however a robot becomes attracted to the front IR beams of another, it will in turn activate the front sensors of that robot as it approaches, both robots will turn to face each other—mutually attracted. The remaining robot will subsequently become attracted to rear sensors of one of the pair, bringing the formation into completion. Prior to the arrival of the third robot, the facing pair maintain the dynamic, stable configuration which was described in the previous section (illustrated in figure 8). In the present context, this serves as 'holding' pattern, in which the pair await arrival of the remaining team member.

The process of achieving formation is not always quite as simple as the above description might imply. The pairing process may have to be resolved between three robots (as for example, in panels ii and iii of figure 9) where one robot may disrupts the pair-forming of the other two. However, the explanation given above should be sufficient to inform the reader of the basic dynam-

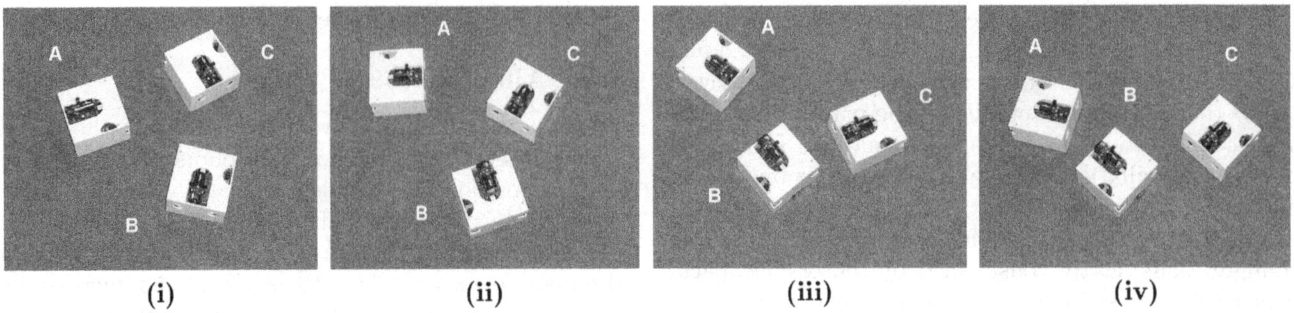

Figure 9: **An example of the team moving into the formation positions.** (i) The robot's initial positions. Initially, C is attracted B's rear sensors, causing B to turn tightly, A circles away, clockwise (ii) B and C begin to form a pair as A circles round towards them (iii) A disrupts the pair formation of B and C, subsequently pairing with B. (iv) C becomes attracted to B's rear sensors and begins to move into position. Shortly after this, the team achieve their final formation.

ics of the process of team formation. A process which can be seen as a one of progressive differentiation. The robots are initially undifferentiated with respect to their potential roles. The opposed pairing of two robots partially differentiates the team. The excluded robot's role is now determined—it will become the rear robot in the formation. Further differentiation occurs when the unpaired robot approaches the back sensors of one of the waiting pair, thereby determining the final two roles.

Conclusion

The structured cooperation required for the performance of a team task presents interesting problems for a distributed control system. This is particularly true when individuals are homogeneous, and constrained to make use of limited local information. We have suggested that artificial evolution is a useful tool for automating the design of such systems, and presented an example of an evolved homogeneous multi-robot team. We have shown that the evolved system is capable of organising itself into a team formation, and maintaining this organisation over time.

It is worth noting the novelty of this work within the field of evolutionary robotics. To date, this research field has focussed almost exclusively on single robot systems. Insofar as we are aware, the work reported in this paper represents the first published example of cooperative and coordinated behaviour for a real multi-robot system designed by artificial evolution. By virtue of involving multiple robots, it is also one of the few examples of evolutionary robots research in which controllers must engage with a non-static environment (single-robot exceptions include (Jakobi 1998a; Smith 1998)).

Finally, we suggest that such a system would be extremely difficult to design by hand, given the sensory constraints and the close coupling of the individual robots. Of course, this not an easy claim to prove. However, we will conclude with a quote from someone with a great deal of experience in hand-designing multi-robot systems. Discussing the need for more complex sensors in the design of a following behaviour, Matarić (1995) comments: "If using only IRs, the agents cannot distinguish between other agents heading toward and away from them, and thus are unable to select whom to follow".

Acknowledgements

We would like to thank Adrian Thompson for investing time and effort in robot modifications. Thanks also to Nick Jakobi and Kyran Dale for useful discussion. This work was funded by the B.N.S.C. Space Foresight project IMAR.

References

Anderson, C., and Franks, N. 2001. Teams in animal societies. *Behavioural Ecology* 12(5):534–540.

Balch, T., and Arkin, R. 1998. Behavior-based formation control for multiagent robot teams. *IEEE Transactions on Robotics and Automation* 14(6):926–939.

Brooks, R. 1992. Artificial life and real robots. In Varela, F., and Bourgine, P., eds., *Toward a Practice of Autonomous Systems*. MIT Press. 3–10.

Camazine, S.; Denouberg, J.-L.; Franks, N.; Sneyd, J.; Theraulaz, G.; and Bonabeau, E. 2001. *Self-Organization in Biological Systems*. Princeton University Press.

Chaimowicz, L.; Sugar, T.; Kumar, V.; and Campos, M. 2001. An architecture for tightly coupled multi-robot cooperation. In *Proc. IEEE Intl. Conf. Robotics and Automation*, 2292–2297. Seoul, South Korea: IEEE Press.

Detrain, C., and Pasteels, J. 1992. Caste polyethism and collective defense in the ant *pheidole pallidula*. *Behavioural Ecology and Sociobiology* 29:405–412.

Floreano, D.; Nolfi, S.; and Mondada, F. 1998. Competitive co-evolutionary robotics: From theory to practice. In Pfeifer, R.; Blumberg, B.; Meyer, J.-A.;

and Wilson, S., eds., *Proc. 4rd Intl. Conf. on Simulation of Adaptive Behavior*, 512–524. MIT Press.

Gerstner, W., and Kistler, W. 2002. *Spiking Neuron Models.* Cambridge University Press.

Hobbs, J.; Husbands, P.; and Harvey, I. 1996. Achieving improved mission robustness. In *Proc. 4th E.S.A. Workshop on Advanced Space Technologies for Robot Applications.*

Husbands, P., and Meyer, J.-A., eds. 1998. *Evolutionary Robotics: Proceedings of the First European Workshop, EvoRobot98.* Springer.

Jakobi, N. 1997. Half-baked, ad-hoc and noisy: Minimal simulation in evolutionary robotics. In Husbands, P., and Harvey, I., eds., *Fourth European Conference on Artificial Life*, 348–357. MIT Press/Bradford Books.

Jakobi, N. 1998a. Evolving motion-tracking behaviour for a panning camera head. In *Proc. 5th Intl Conf. Simulation of Adaptive Behaviour.* MIT Press.

Jakobi, N. 1998b. *Minimal Simulations for Evolutionary Robotics.* Ph.D. Dissertation, University of Sussex, U.K.

Matarić, M., and Cliff, D. 1996. Challenges in evolving controllers for physical robots. *Robots and Autonomous Systems* 19(1):67–83.

Matarić, M., and Sukhatme, S. 2001. Task-allocation and coordination of muliple robots for planetary exploration. In *Proc. 10th Intl Conf. Advanced Robotics.*

Matarić, M. 1995. Designing and understanding adaptive group behaviour. *Adaptive Behaviour* 4(1):51–80.

Meyer, J.-A.; Husbands, P.; and Harvey, I. 1998. Evolutionary robotics: A survey of applications and problems. In Husbands and Meyer (1998), 1–21.

Moran, G.; Fentress, J.; and Golani, I. 1981. A description of relational patterns of movemnet during 'ritualized fighting' in wolves. *Animal Behaviour* 29:1146–1165.

Nolfi, S., and Floreano, D. 1998. Co-evolving predator and prey robots: Do 'arm races' arise in artificial evolution? *Artificial Life* 4(4):311–335.

Nolfi, S., and Floreano, D. 2000. *Evolutionary Robotics: The Biology, Intelligence and Technology of Self-Organizing Machines.* MIT Press.

Nolfi, S. 1998. Evolutionary Robotics: Exploiting the full power of self-organization. *Connection Science* 10(3-4):167–183.

Quinn, M.; Smith, L.; Mayley, G.; and Husbands, P. 2002. Evolving formation movement for a homogeneous multi-robot system: Teamwork and role allocation with real robots. Cognitive Science Research Paper 515, University of Sussex, U.K.

Quinn, M. 2001. A comparison of approaches to the evolution of homogeneous multi-robot teams. In *Proc. Congr. Evolutionary Computation*, 128–135. Seoul, South Korea: IEEE Press.

Smith, T. 1998. Blurred vision: Simulation-reality transfer of a visually guided robot. In Husbands and Meyer (1998), 152–164.

Stone, P., and Veloso, M. 1999. Task decomposition, dynamic role assignment, and low-bandwidth communication for real-time strategic teamwork. *Artificial Intelligence* 110(2):241–273.

Ward, C.; Gobot, F.; and Kendal, G. 2001. Evolving collective behaviour in an artificial world. *Artificial Life* 7(2):191–210.

Watson, R. A.; Ficici, S. G.; and Pollack, J. B. 1999. Embodied evolution: Embodying an evolutionary algorithm in a population of robots. In *Proc. Congr. Evolutionary Computation*, 335–342. Washington D.C., U.S.A.: IEEE Press.

Multi-Objectivity for Brain-Behavior Evolution of a Physically-Embodied Organism

Jason Teo and **Hussein A. Abbass**
Artificial Life and Adaptive Robotics (A.L.A.R.) Lab,
School of Computer Science, University of New South Wales,
Australian Defence Force Academy Campus, Canberra, Australia.
{j.teo,h.abbass@adfa.edu.au}

Abstract

In this paper, we present a pareto multi–objective approach for evolving the behavior and brain (an artificial neural network (ANN)) of embodied artificial creatures. We will attempt to simultaneously minimize the network size while maximizing horizontal locomotion. A variety of network sizes and behaviors were generated by the pareto approach. The best networks exhibited a higher level of sensory-motor coordination and the creature was able to maintain the walking behavior under different environmental setups.

Introduction

Multi-objective optimization has been previously introduced for action selection in behavior-based robotics using conventional theory (Pirjanian 1998) and for the design of a robot arm using evolutionary theory (Coello Coello, Christiansen, & Aguirre 1998). In this paper, a multi-objective approach is investigated for evolving *artificial neural networks* (ANNs) that act as controllers for the legged locomotion of a 3-dimensional, artificial quadruped creature simulated in a physics-based environment. The Pareto-frontier Differential Evolution (PDE) algorithm is used to generate a pareto set of ANNs that trades-off between locomotion behavior and brain (*ie.* neural network) size. The concept of pareto defines a partial order dominance over the set of solutions. A solution X is said to be non–dominated (pareto) iff there is no other solution Y in the population where Y is better than X wrt all objectives.

The operational dynamics of the evolved creatures are analyzed to provide an insight into how a variety of controllers with different behaviors emerge from the evolution. A comparison between a set of pareto controllers showed that different brain sizes exhibit noticeably different locomotion behaviors. Although this may seem obvious, maintaining a variety of brain sizes and behaviors is mainly contributed by the optimization of conflicting objectives. We also found that a much higher level of sensory-motor coordination is present in the best evolved controller. Finally we investigated the effects of environmental, morphological and nervous system changes on the artificial creature's behavior. Similar to other studies, certain changes were found to be detrimental to the creature's walking-path. In contrast to other studies, however, the creature was able to maintain the walking behavior in a large majority of the experiments.

Situated and Embodied Evolution

The study of evolving physically situated and embodied artificial creatures has been a hotbed of research in recent years. The availability and maturation of commercial-off-the-shelf physics engines coupled with the dramatic increase of personal computing power have encouraged research into this intriguing field of artificial life (Taylor & Massey 2001). Since the pioneering work of Sims' (Sims 1994), there were notably few significant advancements in this field until very recently.

Research in this area generally falls into two categories: (1) the evolution of controllers for creatures with fixed (Arnold 1997; Bongard & Pfeifer 2002; Gritz & Hahn 1997; Harvey 1997; Ijspeert 2000; Reeve 1999) or parameterized morphologies (Lee, Hallam, & Lund 1996; Paul & Bongard 2001), and (2) the evolution of both the creatures' morphologies and controllers simultaneously (Bongard 2002; Hornby & Pollack 2001; Komosinski & Rotaru-Varga 2000; Lipson & Pollack 2000; Ray 2000; Sims 1994; Taylor & Massey 2001). Some work has also been carried out in evolving morphology alone (Eggenberger 1997) and evolving morphology with a fixed controller (Lichtensteiger & Eggenberger 1999). Related work using wheeled robots have also shown promising results in robustness and the ability to cope with changing environments by evolving plastic individuals that are able to adapt both through evolution and lifetime learning (Floreano & Urzelai 1998; 2000).

The emphasis of most of these studies have been on the role of genetic encodings and how different types of genotype-phenotype representations allow for greater evolvability (Bongard 2002; Hornby & Pollack 2001; Komosinski & Rotaru-Varga 2001). There have also been some investigations into the role of fitness functions and how they affect the direction of the evolutionary process (Floreano & Urzelai 2000; Komosinski & Rotaru-Varga 2000; Ray 2000). A very recent investigation explored how morphological complexity itself affects the emergence of more complex behavior in artificial creatures (Bongard & Pfeifer 2002). Considerably little has been said about the role of controllers in the artificial evolution of such creatures. It has been noted that the potential of designing more complex artificial systems through exploitation of sensory-motor coordination remains largely unexplored (Nolfi & Floreano 2002). As such, there is currently a lack of understanding of how the evolution of controllers affects the evolution of morphologies and behaviors in physically simulated creatures. It remains unclear what properties of an artificial creature's controller allow it to exhibit the desired behavior. A better understanding of controller complexity and the dynamics of evolving controllers should pave the way towards the emergence of more complex artificial creatures with more complex morphologies and behaviors.

Much work in evolutionary robotics have focused on evolving controllers for wheeled locomotion (Lee, Hallam, & Lund 1996; Floreano & Urzelai 1998; 2000; Nolfi & Floreano 1998). Less work have been conducted on evolving controllers for legged locomotion such as (Arnold 1997; Reeve 1999). Here we are attempting to evolve controllers that can generate walking behaviors for a four-legged creature.

Methods

The Physics Simulator

The simulation is carried out in a physically realistic environment which allows for rich dynamical interactions to occur between the creature and its environment. This in turn enables complex walking behaviors to emerge as the creature evolves the use of its sensors to control the actuators in its limbs through dynamical interactions with the environment. Furthermore, the accurate modelling of the simulation environment plays a crucial part in producing artificial creatures that move and behave realistically in 3D (Taylor & Massey 2001). A dynamic rather than kinematic approach is paramount in allowing for effective artificial evolution to occur. Physical properties such as forces, torques, inertia, friction, restitution and damping need to be incorporated into the artificial evolutionary system. To this end, the Vortex physics engine (Critical Mass Labs 2002) was employed to generate the physically realistic artificial creature (Figure 1) and its simulation environment.

Figure 1: Screen capture of quadruped in the simulation environment.

The artificial creature is a basic quadruped with 4 short legs. Each leg consists of an upper limb connected to a lower limb via a hinge (one degree-of-freedom) joint and is in turn connected to the torso via another hinge joint. The mass of the torso is 1 and each of the limbs is 0.5. The torso has dimensions of 4 x 1 x 4 and each of the limbs has dimensions of 1 x 1 x 1. The hinge joints are allowed to rotate between -1.57 to 0 radians for limbs that move counter-clockwise and 0 to 1.57 radians for limbs that move clockwise from their original starting positions. Each of the hinge joints are actuated by a motor that generates a torque producing rotation of the connected body parts about that hinge joint. The creature's overall central nervous system is illustrated in Figure 2.

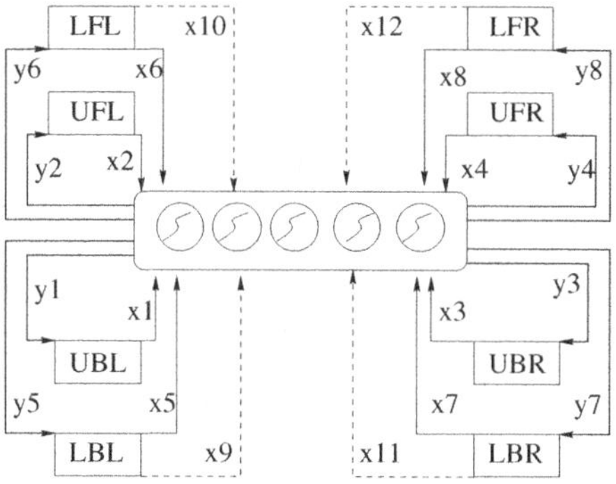

Figure 2: The quadruped's central nervous system.

Correspondingly, the artificial creature has 12 sensors and 8 actuators. The 12 sensors consist of 8 joint angle sensors $(x_1, x_2, x_3, x_4, x_5, x_6, x_7, x_8)$ corresponding to each of the hinge joints and 4 touch sensors $(x_9, x_{10}, x_{11}, x_{12})$ corresponding to each of the 4 lower limbs of each leg. The 8 actuators $(y_1, y_2, y_3, y_4, y_5, y_6, y_7, y_8)$ represent the motors that control each of the 8 articulated joints of the creature. These motors are controlled via outputs generated from the ANN controller which is then used to set the desired velocity of rotation of the connected body parts about that joint.

Controller Evolution Using PDE

Similar to (Abbass 2001; 2002), our chromosome is a class that contains one matrix Ω of real numbers representing the weights of the artificial neural network and one vector ρ of binary numbers (one value for each hidden unit) to indicate if a hidden unit exists in the network or not; that is, it works as a switch to turn a hidden unit on or off. The sum of all values in this vector represents the actual number of hidden units in a network. This representation allows simultaneous training of the weights in the network and selecting a subset of hidden units.

In the PDE algorithm for evolving ANNs, an entire set of controllers is generated in each evolutionary run without requiring any further modification of parameters by the user. The algorithm consists of the following steps:

1. Create a random initial population of potential solutions. The elements of the weight matrix Ω are assigned random values according to a Gaussian distribution $N(0, 1)$. The elements of the binary vector ρ are assigned the value 1

with probability 0.5 based on a randomly generated number according to a uniform distribution between [0, 1]; otherwise 0.

2. Repeat
   (a) Evaluate the individuals in the population and label those who are non-dominated.
   (b) If the number of non-dominated individuals is less than 3 repeat the following until the number of non-dominated individuals is greater than or equal to 3:
      i. Find a non-dominated solution among those who are not labelled.
      ii. Label the solution as non-dominated.
   (c) Delete all dominated solutions from the population.
   (d) Repeat
      i. Select at random an individual as the main parent α_1, and two individuals, α_2, α_3 as supporting parents.
      ii. **Crossover:** with some probability Uniform(0,1), do

$$\omega_{\text{ih}}^{\text{child}} \leftarrow \omega_{\text{ih}}^{\alpha 1} + N(0,1)(\omega_{\text{ih}}^{\alpha 2} - \omega_{\text{ih}}^{\alpha 3}) \quad (1)$$

$$\rho_{\text{h}}^{\text{child}} \leftarrow \begin{cases} 1 & \text{if } (\rho_{\text{h}}^{\alpha 1} + N(0,1)(\rho_{\text{h}}^{\alpha 2} - \rho_{\text{h}}^{\alpha 3})) \geq 0.5 \\ 0 & \text{otherwise} \end{cases} \quad (2)$$

otherwise

$$\omega_{\text{ih}}^{\text{child}} \leftarrow \omega_{\text{ih}}^{\alpha 1} \quad (3)$$

$$\rho_{\text{h}}^{\text{child}} \leftarrow \rho_{\text{h}}^{\alpha 1} \quad (4)$$

and with some probability Uniform(0,1), do

$$\omega_{\text{ho}}^{\text{child}} \leftarrow \omega_{\text{ho}}^{\alpha 1} + N(0,1)(\omega_{\text{ho}}^{\alpha 2} - \omega_{\text{ho}}^{\alpha 3}) \quad (5)$$

otherwise

$$\omega_{\text{ho}}^{\text{child}} \leftarrow \omega_{\text{ho}}^{\alpha 1} \quad (6)$$

where each weight ($\omega_{\text{ih}}, \omega_{\text{ho}}$), and hidden unit flag, ρ, in the main parent are perturbed by adding to them a ratio, $F \in N(0,1)$, of the difference between the two values of this variable in the two supporting parents. At least one variable must be changed.

      iii. **Mutation:** with some probability Uniform(0,1), do

$$\omega_{\text{ih}}^{\text{child}} \leftarrow \omega_{\text{ih}}^{\text{child}} + N(0, \text{mutation\_rate}) \quad (7)$$

$$\omega_{\text{ho}}^{\text{child}} \leftarrow \omega_{\text{ho}}^{\text{child}} + N(0, \text{mutation\_rate}) \quad (8)$$

$$\rho_{\text{h}}^{\text{child}} \leftarrow \begin{cases} 1 & \text{if } \rho_{\text{h}}^{\text{child}} = 0 \\ 0 & \text{otherwise} \end{cases} \quad (9)$$

   (e) Until the population size is M

3. Until maximum number of generations is reached.

Experiments

Experimental Setup

A total of 480 evolutionary runs were conducted with varying population sizes, crossover rates, and mutation rates while fixing the fitness evaluation window to 500 timesteps. The crossover rates used were 0, 0.1, 0.2, 0.5 and 1 and the mutation rates used were also 0, 0.1, 0.2, 0.5 and 1. The evolutionary setup with a crossover rate of 0 and a mutation rate of 0 was omitted since this setup does not generate any variability at all in the population. The maximum number of hidden units permitted in evolving the artificial neural network was fixed at 15 nodes. Each experimental setup was repeated using 10 different seeds to allow the artificial evolution to commence from different starting points in the search space. Two population sizes of 20 and 30 were used with the corresponding number of generations being 30 and 20 respectively. The use of a small population size and number of generations is a feature of PDE since genetic diversity is naturally maintained by the pareto selection mechanism. The total number of genotypes over the entire span of the evolutionary process was kept constant at 600 genotypes in both these setups. In the final set of experiments, the creature was subjected to environmental, morphological and nervous system changes to observe the resultant change in its behavior. The details of these changes are presented along with the results and discussions of these experiments.

Results and Discussion

Evolutionary Parameters First we analyzed the effect of population size on the evolved locomotion behaviors. Overall, there did not appear to be any obvious differences in the range and quality of the evolved controllers between population sizes of 20 and 30. Both produced a considerably similar quality of locomotion behaviors although a larger population size did seem to produce controllers that were slightly better in terms of average locomotion fitness. However, the difference was not significant to investigate larger populations.

Different combinations of crossover and mutation rates did appear to produce results that varied across two broad spectrums. With both population sizes of 20 and 30, two distinct groups of controllers were generated through the evolutionary process: (1) runs that produced high quality solutions but with a low spread of genotypes, and (2) runs that produced mediocre solutions with a high spread of genotypes. Again, the quality of solutions refers to the average locomotion fitness and the spread of genotypes refers to the number of ANNs with different sizes in terms of hidden units. The first group of pareto optimal solutions with high quality and low spread were observed when fairly low mutation rates of 0.1 and 0.2 were used in combination with a low to medium crossover rate of between 0.1 to 0.5. The second group of pareto optimal solutions with lower quality but with a much wider spread of controller sizes were observed when a high mutation rate of 1 was used.

Operational Dynamics In this section, we analyze five pareto optimal controllers resultant from a typical run. To conduct this analysis, the ANNs were used individually to control the quadruped and the simulation period was extended to 5000 timesteps. This enables analysis of not only the evolved behavior but also its behavior beyond the fitness evaluation window.

The correlation analysis of the best evolved controller with 4 hidden units has 6 strongly positive correlation coefficients (>0.7). This indicates that the creature has evolved an ANN that has learned how to coordinate the movement of 7 sets of its limbs in order to achieve the most successful locomotion behavior among the pareto optimal controllers. With a correlation of 0.98, there is almost perfect coordination between the upper front left (UFL) and lower front right (LFR) limbs. Another almost perfectly coordinated motion comes from the upper back left (UBL) and upper back right (UBR) limbs with a correlation of 0.95. There is also a high level of correlation between the upper front left (UFL) and upper front right (UFR), lower front left (LFL) and upper front left (UFL), lower front left (LFL) and upper front right (UFR), upper front right (UFR) and lower front right (LFR), and lower front right (LFR) and lower front left (LFL) limbs.

Figure 3 illustrates the correlation between the 8 limbs during motion over 5000 timesteps along with the number of times each leg makes contact with the ground. Negative and positive correlation coefficients are drawn in dashed and solid lines respectively.

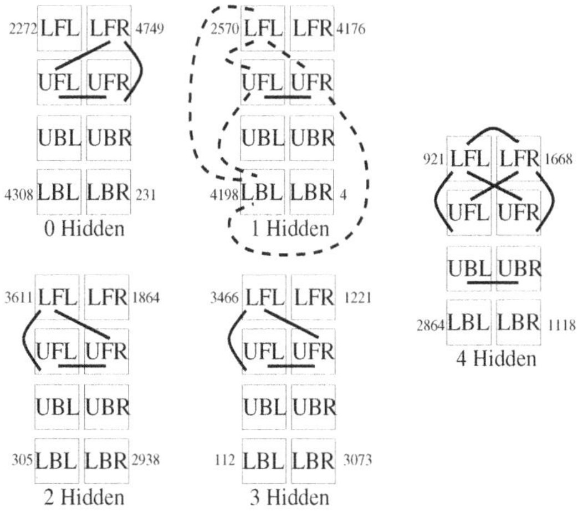

Figure 3: Illustration of correlation between limbs for pareto optimal controllers.

Analysis of the less successful pareto optimal networks reveals that there is far less coordination achieved by these controllers. At most 3 strongly correlated sets of limb movements were obtained using these controllers compared to 7 strongly correlated sets of limb movements using the best evolved controller. Furthermore, 5 strongly negative correlations (<-0.8) were detected in the controller with 1 hidden unit. These limbs are not only uncoordinated but are generating forces that act in direct opposition to each other, thereby further hindering the creature's ability to move.

Finally, we analyze the path of movement that was taken by the creature in attempting to maximize its horizontal distance covered during the extended simulation window of 5000 timesteps. Here we compared the paths of all networks on the pareto-frontier of the last generation of controller evolution.

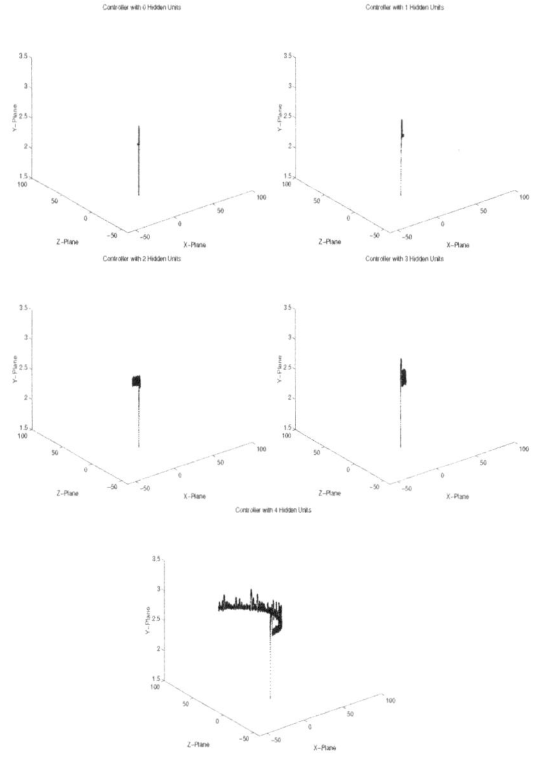

Figure 4: Path of movement using controller with 1. top left: 0; 2. top right: 1; 3. middle left: 2; 4. middle right: 3; and 5. bottom: 4; hidden units.

An interesting outcome from these multi-objective evolutions is that we get a range of controllers that vary in architectural complexity and locomotion capability. On the one hand, we have a totally random ANN with no hidden nodes (Figure 4.1) but which is still able to move the creature away from its origin, although the movement achieved within the stipulated 500 timesteps is extremely minimal (approximately 0.5m). In this random network, there is still an act of force on the creature permitting the small initial movement but it is unable to perform further locomotion due to the lack of synchronization ability. On the other hand, we have the best ANN that uses 4 hidden nodes (Figure 4.5) and is able to move almost 10m within the same time period. In addition, we have a further 3 ANNs (Figure 4.2,3,4) that utilize between 1 and 3 hidden nodes which again have differing locomotion capabilities. Thus, the multi-objective approach is able to provide the experimenter with a whole range of controllers within a single run that trades off between the individual optimization goals. This represents a significant advantage over single-objective evolutionary systems that need to be rerun multiple times in order to test the effect of other factors such as number of hidden units on the performance of artificial creatures (Bongard & Pfeifer 2002).

Effects of Friction In this section, we analyze the effects of changing some of the environmental parameters of the creature's world and observe the change in its behavior. Here, the same controller, which is the best evolved ANN with 4 hidden units, is used to control the creature across all different environmental conditions. The resultant behavior is again monitored over 5000 timesteps. First, we discuss the results obtained from changing the original frictional coefficient of 20 to lower values of 0, 5, 10 and 15. The purpose of this analysis was to investigate how the creature's ability to move would be affected by reduced amounts of grip with its locomotion surface.

The creature was not able to move horizontally at all with no ground friction. Its main movement here was mainly along the vertical direction as it attempted to stand up and repeatedly failed due to the lack of friction. With a very small friction of 5, the creature was able to move forwards although the overall distance travelled was less than in the original environment that had a significantly higher friction of 20. However, the path travelled in the environment with a friction of 5 was much straighter than in the original environment. This occurrence suggests that friction plays a larger role in making the creature turn compared to making it move forwards. From the next two environments which had increasingly higher frictions of 10 and 15, the overall trajectory of the paths begin to have more curvature as well as increasing overall distance travelled. Hence, it appears that varying locomotion surface conditions noticeably affect the creature's ability to walk both in terms of its trajectory as well as total distance travelled.

Effects of Gravity In this next section, we again change the environmental conditions but instead of surface condition, this time we change the world's gravitational field to approximately simulate conditions of that on the moon, Mars as well as Jupiter. The purpose of this set of experiments was again to see how the creature's behavior would be affected by environmental changes as well as exploring how hypothetical robots that are built under our planet's condition may be able to also function on numerous other planets that have significantly different gravities. Such robots may be desirable because firstly building them under normal terrestrial conditions will be significantly less complex than trying to simulate extra-terrestrial conditions. Secondly, if robots were able to perform reasonably independent of gravitational changes, then only a single group of similar robots need to be designed which would be able to explore multitudes of moons and planets with different surface gravities.

The creature was still able to function under the moon's much smaller gravity although the overall distance travelled was less than on Earth. There was also noticeably more vertical movement during the creature's locomotion as would be expected because of the smaller gravity. Under Mars' gravity, the creature's familiar U-shaped path becomes visible again although the overall distance travelled is again less than that achieved on Earth. The creature was significantly less successful under Jupiter's much higher gravity where after standing up, it was only able to move a small distance forward. From this analysis, it can be seen that the creature was still able to function under very different gravitational forces although it's locomotion was less successful than under Earth's normal gravity.

Effects of Morphological Changes Next, we analyze the change in the creature's behavior when there is a change in its morphology. Again the best evolved controller with 4 hidden units was used to control the creature and allowed to move for 5000 timesteps. In these experiments, we doubled the mass in certain parts of the creature's morphology.

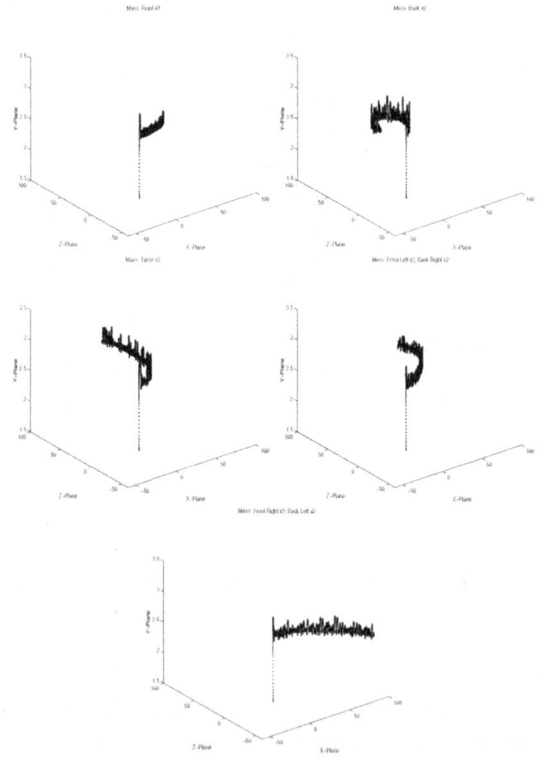

Figure 5: Path of movement with mass doubled in 1. top left: front legs; 2. top right: back legs; 3. middle left: torso; 4. middle right: front left and back right legs; 5. bottom: front right and back left legs.

Very pronounced changes were observed in the creature's locomotion behavior as a result of doubling the masses of all of its front limbs (Figure 5.1) and all of its back limbs (Figure 5.2). The doubling of mass in its front legs resulted in a locomotion path that had a straighter heading compared to the path observed with the original uniform mass distribution. Conversely, the doubling of mass in its back legs resulted in an even more pronounced curved locomotion trajectory than the original U-shaped path, where in this case the creature almost completed a full circle back to its original starting position. These phenomena may be explained by the fact that the creature achieved its locomotion from the coordinated movement of front limbs and back limbs respectively. As such, mass redistribution affecting entire front and back sections of the creature's body can be expected to result in significant changes to its locomotion behavior. The doubling of the creature's torso mass seemed to cause the creature's movement to head more directly towards the Z axis after making its initial left turn (Figure 5.3). The effect of doubling the mass of the front left and back right legs did not appear to alter the creature's path significantly except reducing the magnitude and turning effect of its horizontal movement (Figure 5.4). The most pronounced change in the creature's overall heading was observed when the front right and back left legs were doubled in mass (Figure 5.5). This set of morphological changes appeared to have altered the nature of the creature's locomotion path from a predominantly left-turning trajectory to a right-turning trajectory. This may suggest that the contribution to overall movement from different legs are very different depending on the relative position of the legs with respect to the creature's body and direction of motion.

Effects of Sensory-Motor Failure In this section, we were interested in observing what would happen to the creature's locomotion behavior if some sensory–motor failure occurred. This would be akin to partial paralysis in four-legged animals where there is loss of sense and movement in some of their limbs. Here we disabled the joint angle and touch sensor as well as the hinge motors in the creature's entire front right limbs in the first setup and the entire back left limbs in the second setup. The best evolved controller with 4 hidden units was again used to operate the original creature with uniform mass distributions over 5000 timesteps.

Disabling the creature's front right leg seemed to have a harmful effect on its locomotion behavior. It struggled in trying to stand up and upon visual inspection of the simulation, this was explained by the fact it could not maintain its balance. As a result, the creature could not perform any horizontal movement at all. On the other hand, disabling the back left leg did not seem to cause as much harm to the creature's ability to move although its overall distance travelled was still significantly less compared to the original creature which had no impairments. In fact, upon closer inspection, the distinctive U-shaped locomotion pattern could still be observed but on a smaller scale. These analyzes again seem to suggest that the contribution of different legs to the overall locomotion behavior appeared to differ quite significantly depending on the position of the legs relative to the orientation of the creature's body and direction of movement. Thus disabling particular legs in certain positions resulted in dramatically different behaviors.

Conclusion

We have demonstrated the use of a multi-objective evolutionary algorithm for evolving artificial neural networks that act as controllers for the legged locomotion of an embodied and physically situated quadruped. We have shown that multi-objectivity allows for the natural maintenance of genetic diversity. The pareto-frontier that resulted from each single evolutionary run produced a set of ANNs that maximized the locomotion capabilities of the creature and at the same time minimized the size of the controller. The correlation and path analyzes of the pareto optimal controllers in operation provided an insight into how the complex coordination between the quadruped's different limbs generated the emergent locomotion behavior. Finally, we also observed that certain environmental, morphological and nervous system changes markedly affected the creature's overall locomotion behavior and in some cases caused total failure of its horizontal locomotion capability.

References

Abbass, H. A. 2001. A memetic pareto evolutionary approach to artificial neural networks. In Stumptner, M.; Corbett, D.; and Brooks, M., eds., *Proceedings of the 14th Australian Joint Conference on Artificial Intelligence*, 1–12. Berlin: Springer-Verlag.

Abbass, H. A. 2002. An evolutionary artificial neural network approach for breast cancer diagnosis. *Accepted to appear in Artificial Intelligence in Medicine.*

Arnold, D. 1997. Evolution of legged locomotion. Unpublished masters thesis, School of Computing Science, Simon Fraser University, Burnaby, Canada.

Bongard, J. C., and Pfeifer, R. 2002. A method for isolating morphological effects on evolved behavior. In *Accepted to appear in Proceedings of the Seventh International Conference on the Simulation of Adaptive Behavior.*

Bongard, J. C. 2002. Evolving modular genetic regulatory networks. In *Accepted to appear in Proceedings of the 2002 Congress on Evolutionary Computation.*

Coello Coello, C. A.; Christiansen, A. D.; and Aguirre, A. H. 1998. Using a new GA-based multiobjective optimization technique for the design of robot arms. *Robotica* 16:401–414.

Critical Mass Labs. 2002. Vortex. http://www.cm-labs.com.

Eggenberger, P. 1997. Evolving morphologies of simulated 3D organisms based on differential gene expression. In Husbands, P., and Harvey, I., eds., *Proceedings of the 4th European Conference on Artificial Life*, 205–213. Cambridge, MA: MIT Press.

Floreano, D., and Urzelai, J. 1998. Evolution and learning in autonomous mobile robots. In Mange, D., and Tomassini, M., eds., *Bio-Inspired Computing Machines: Towards Novel Computational Architectures.* Lausanne, Switzerland: PPUR, 1st edition. chapter 12, 317–364.

Floreano, D., and Urzelai, J. 2000. Evolutionary robotics: The next generation. In Gomi, T., ed., *Proceedings of Evolutionary Robotics III*, 231–266. Ontario: AAI Books.

Gritz, L., and Hahn, J. K. 1997. Genetic programming evolution of controllers for 3-D character animation. In Koza, J. et al. eds., *Genetic Programming 1997: Proceedings of the 2nd Annual Conference*, 139–146. San Francisco: Morgan Kauffman.

Harvey, I. 1997. Artificial evolution and real robots. *Artificial Life and Robotics* 1(1):35–38.

Hornby, G. S., and Pollack, J. B. 2001. Body-brain coevolution using L-systems as a generative encoding. In Spector, L. et al. eds., *Proceedings of the Genetic and Evolutionary Computation Conference*, 868–875. San Francisco: Morgan Kauffman.

Ijspeert, A. J. 2000. A 3-D biomechanical model of the salamander. In Heudin, J.-C., ed., *Proceedings of the 2nd International Conference on Virtual Worlds*, 225–234. Berlin: Springer-Verlag.

Kauffman, S. A. 1993. *The Origins of Order.* New York: Oxford University Press.

Komosinski, M., and Rotaru-Varga, A. 2000. From directed to open-ended evolution in a complex simulation model. In Bedau, M.; McCaskill, J.; Packard, N.; and Rasmussen, S., eds., *Artificial Life VII: Proceedings of the Seventh International Conference on Artificial Life*, 293–299. Cambridge, MA: MIT Press.

Komosinski, M., and Rotaru-Varga, A. 2001. Comparison of different genotype encodings for simulated three-dimensional agents. *Artificial Life* 7(4):395–418.

Lee, W.-P.; Hallam, J.; and Lund, H. J. 1996. A hybrid GP/GA approach for co-evolving controllers and robot bodies to achieve fitness-specific tasks. In *Proceedings of the 3rd IEEE International Conference on Evolutionary Computation*, 384–389. Piscataway, NJ: IEEE Press.

Lichtensteiger, L., and Eggenberger, P. 1999. Evolving the morphology of a compound eye on a robot. In *Proceedings of the Third European Workshop on Advanced Mobile Robots*, 127–134. Piscataway, NJ: IEEE Press.

Lipson, H., and Pollack, J. B. 2000. Automatic design and manufacture of robotic lifeforms. *Nature* 406:974–978.

Nolfi, S., and Floreano, D. 1998. Learning and evolution. *Autonomous Robots* 7(1):89–113.

Nolfi, S., and Floreano, D. 2002. Synthesis of autonomous robots through evolution. *Trends in Cognitive Science* 6(1):31–36.

Paul, C., and Bongard, J. C. 2001. The road less travelled: Morphology in the optimization of biped robot locomotion. In *Proceedings of the IEEE/RSJ International Conference on Intelligent Robots and Systems*, volume 1, 226–232. Piscataway, NJ: IEEE Press.

Pirjanian, P. 1998. Multiple objective action selection in behavior-based control. In *Proceedings of the 6th Symposium for Intelligent Robotic Systems.* Edinburgh, UK.

Ray, T. S. 2000. Aesthetically evolved virtual pets. In Maley, C., and Boudreau, E., eds., *Artificial Life 7 Workshop Proceedings*, 158–161. http://www.hip.atr.co.jp/~ray/pubs/alife7a/.

Reeve, R. 1999. *Generating Walking Behaviors in Legged Robots.* Unpublished PhD thesis, University of Edinburgh, Scotland.

Sims, K. 1994. Evolving 3D morphology and behavior by competition. In Brooks, R., and Maes, P., eds., *Artificial Life IV: Proceedings of the Fourth International Workshop on the Synthesis and Simulation of Living Systems*, 28–39. Cambridge, MA: MIT Press.

Taylor, T., and Massey, C. 2001. Recent developments in the evolution of morphologies and controllers for physically simulated creatures. *Artificial Life* 7(1):77–87.

Simulating Turn-Taking Behaviours with Coupled Dynamical Recognizers

Hiroyuki Iizuka and **Takashi Ikegami**

Department of General Systems Sciences,
The Graduate School of Arts and Sciences, University of Tokyo,
3-8-1 Komaba, Tokyo 153-8902, Japan

Abstract

A coupled dynamical recognizer is proposed as a model for simulating turn-taking behaviour. An agent is modelled as a mobile robot with two wheels. A recurrent neural network is used to produce the motor outputs. By controlling this, agents compete to take turns on a two dimensional arena.

There are two novel aspects to the present study. First, a dynamical recognizer is not only used for producing motor outputs but also to predict the other agent's behaviour. Second, unlike a mere chasing game, turn-taking behaviour is established only when each agent automatically switches from chaser to evader and *vice versa*.

By using the genetic algorithm technique, we show that turn-taking behaviour is developed between two agents. It is worth noting that turn-taking is established only when an agent fails to predict the other agent's behaviour. In other words, the simultaneous generation of stable (predictable) and unstable (unpredictable) dynamics is inevitable to lead to successive turn-taking behaviour. A relationship between joint attention and prediction will be discussed from this and other related works.

Introduction

Imitation, prediction and theory of mind: these are thought of as mental functions/modules that are useful in explaining and synthesizing cognitive behaviours (J.L.Elman *et al.* 1996). Artificial cognitive behaviour is also synthesized with those modules (B.Scassellati 1999). However, it is also true that there are many cognitive behaviours that cannot be understood in terms of such modules.

One possible approach has been taken by Kerstin Dautenhahn with embodied intelligent agent experiments, in which functions of embodiment and of interactions between humans and robots are investigated (K.Dautenhahn 1999). In the present paper, we instead conduct computer experiments between two cognitive agents and simulate how one agent can, paradoxically, predict the other agent's behaviour but at the same time cannot predict it. This paradox leads to cooperative behaviours, such as successive turn-takings. In terms of dynamical systems, we stipulate that both stable and unstable (manifold) directions must be generated simultaneously to lead to cooperative behaviour patterns. The dynamical systems way of examining cognitive behaviours provides a different view from a mere module-type modelling approach. The main issue of dynamical systems modelling is not to propose an adequate combination of modules, but to study the dynamical rearrangements of modules. In other words, we have to destabilize the functionality of the module itself.

When taking turns for conversation between two persons, without setting any explicit cue to switch speakers people usually avoid overlapping or interrupting each other's speech. Some cues for this include eye contact and the detection of intonation changes. Here we generalize from this turn-taking behaviour to autonomous role-changing, such as games of tag among children, and investigate the generic underlying mechanisms using the dynamical systems method.

This paper is organized as follows. First, we describe the background motivation of the present study in terms of joint attention in Sect. 2. Then, the concept of dynamical recognizers as cognitive agents is introduced in Sect. 3. In Sect. 4, we explain a model in which the roles of agents are not pre-defined but are determined purely dynamically. In Sect. 5, an evolutionary design for neural nets is shown. The results of simulations are presented in Sect. 6 and Sect. 7 re-examines the results in terms of the internal dynamics of agents. Finally, our discussion and conclusions are presented in Sect. 8.

Interactivism

Even at a few months of age a baby can predict events and behaviour. Infants almost innately predict events as if they know simple physical laws (R.Baillargeon, E.S.Spelke, & S.Wasserman 1985). It has been argued that guessing what other people think from their behaviour and environment is also developed at an age of 3 to 4 years (S.Baron-Cohen, A.M.Leslie, & U.Frith 1985). The latter ability in particular is attributed to a psychological module called a theory of mind. It is also argued that autistic children may lack this theory of mind module and thus are deficient in their ability to predict other persons' behaviour.

On the other hand, joint attention, for example, has also been viewed as an important ability for cognitive development (e.g. see (R.P.Hobson 1993)). Joint attention is simply defined as a coordinated behaviour among more than two persons. A simple example is a child gesturing at its mother with the aim of getting something. This is not just important in its social context for three or more people, but it is also important for the initiation of interactions between two people. Unlike the ability given by the theory of mind, joint attention is important in introducing "novelty". To continue conversation or to continue play behaviour requires a kind of "novelty" which is defined as "partial" unpredictability. It is well known in developmental studies that infants watch new/surprising events longer. In other words, novelty inherently attracts infants to it and therefore an interaction is established between them and the event. We thus use novelty as a necessary factor to start and maintain interactions.

Novelty thus should be continuously generated to sustain interactions, but at the same time it is also true that novelty cannot be prepared beforehand: it is an ongoing property of the interaction. Joint attention can continuously introduce novelty into the interacting field. Certain types of interactions between "cognitive agents" can synthesize joint attention and thus create novelty.

Joint attention and prediction are two sides of the one coin. We have argued that they can only be treated as dynamical characteristics. This idea has been examined in several simulation examples, e.g., a language game (I.Igari & T.Ikegami 2001), the iterated prisoner's dilemma game (T.Ikegami & M.Taiji 1998) and some other game systems (T.Ikegami & M.Taiji 1999). In the following, we introduce a basic framework called coupled dynamical recognizers and showing how we can understand turn-taking behaviours with stable and unstable dynamics.

Coupled dynamical recognizers

We propose a dynamical systems way of studying interaction between two agents, where each agent predicts the other agent's future move and also determines its own action.

As Pollack first explicitly showed (J.B.Pollack 1991), a recurrent neural network can imitate the behaviour of some finite automaton. Therefore the reucurrent neural network is often called a dynamical recognizer(DR).

By coupling two DRs, we have simulated the iterated prisoner's dilemma game (T.Ikegami & M.Taiji 1998; M.Taiji & T.Ikegami 1999), Dubey's game (T.Ikegami & M.Taiji 1999) and some language games (I.Igari & T.Ikegami 2001). Those simulations show that i) DR can simulate the infinite state machine-like behaviour and ii)the instability of coupled DR enables mutual cooperation, temporal optimal behaviour and topic developments in discourse.

In the present study, we show how turn-taking behaviour is synthesized by the instability generated by the coupled DRs. Different from our previous works, the present model only deals with analogue input/output values so that it is easier to analyse the temporal behaviour from a dynamical systems point of view. Also, it should be remarked that an important part of turn-taking behaviour is "temporal role changing". This study therefore focuses on different perspectives from the fixed role-playing games (e.g. a pursuit-evasion game) (D.Cliff & G.F.Miller 1996).

Based on this and the previous related simulations, we discuss how cooperative behaviour such as joint attention is developed not by the nested predictions of agents but by the nature of the interaction itself. One of our main messages is that joint attention can be taken as a behaviour of sustaining uncertainty (i.e. autonomy) instead of removing it. This notion is somehow adequate to describe what we call 'play behaviour'.

The model

Turn-taking behaviour is observed when two people interact with each other such as during conversation or when playing a game of tag. One does not keep speaking all the time or one is not always a chaser. Temporal role-changing is performed spontaneously based on the history of interactions in such games. Here, we modelled playing tag in a physical space by extending the conventional pursuit-evasion game.

There have been some other studies in developing the controllers of agents' motions in physical spaces, based on the game of tag, where one plays a role of chaser and the other evader. In those models, the agents' roles are predefined and fixed all the time. The agents acquire controllers for their specified roles through learning or evolutionary processes (D.Cliff & G.F.Miller 1996). These conventional game models have mainly focussed on the histories of acquired strategies, designs of evolutionary mechanisms or the co-evolutionary algorithm itself.

In our game model, the role of chaser or evader is not given to agents in advance. The objective of the agents in the game is to get behind each other. Becuase the agents cannot get behind each other simultaneously, the objective is not achieved if both agents play chaser. Of course, if both agents play evader, mutual turn-taking cannot be achieved either. Therefore, it is necessary to have spontaneous symmetry break down so that one plays the role of chaser and the other plays the role of evader. But mere symmetry breaking is not sufficient: temporal role-changing is also required. By using the coupled DRs, we focus on how turn-taking dynamics self-organize.

There are also some game models in which the roles are not predefined (C.W.Reynolds 1995; E.A.DiPaolo 2000). Reynolds showed that the abilities of chasing and evading are also evolved simultaneously by Genetic Programming in a game of Tag, which is a symmetrical pursuit-evasion game. The variety of the behaviours of agents adapting to their environments is worth noting. In Reynolds' game, a switching between evader and chaser is predefined to happen when both agents come into physical contact. The difference between Reynolds' model and ours is the spontaneous emergence of behaviour. Whether an agent plays a role of a chaser or an evader will be dynamically determined in our model.

On the other hand, social coordination is studied with agents that interact acoustically in Di Paolo's model. In this, the objective of agents is not chasing or evading but approaching each other using only acoustic interactions. In this model, each agent can tell the others position from the signal the other is emitting, but their receiving and emitting signals interfere with each other. To avoid interference, their emission timings are entrained in an anti-phase state and the resulting behaviour resembles turn-taking process. There is a difference between Di Paolo's turn-taking and ours. It is similar in that turn-taking behaviour is established by the coordination of agents through a history of their interactions. However, Di Paolo's turn-taking is a result of anti-phase signals for avoiding signal interference. The advantage of our model for identifying the turn-taking event is that we can analyse it by predicting capability. By doing this, we can make connections between the present simulation and general cognitive behaviour: for example joint attention.

Game and Environment

Each agent here has a circular body of radius R, with two diametrically opposed motors (Fig. 1). The motors can take the agent backwards and forward in a 2-D unstructured and unlimited arena. Each agent's move is based on the following equation of motion:

$$M\ddot{x} + D_1\dot{x} + f_1 + f_2 = 0, \quad (1)$$

$$I\ddot{\theta} + D_2\dot{\theta} + \tau(f_1, f_2) = 0, \quad (2)$$

where f_1 and f_2 are the forward driving force given by two motors, θ denotes a rotational angle, and τ gives the torque. D_1 and D_2 denote the resistance coefficients of driving force and torque, respectively. M is the mass and I is the moment of inertia. In the simulation, we iterate the equations using the Runge-Kutta method.

We assume no collision between agents because we mainly focus on the internal dynamics of agents that generates turn-taking. What is important for agents is predicting the behaviour of a partner and acting cooperatively in taking turns.

Agents

An agent receives the other agent's position and the head orientation relative to the viewpoint forming their sensor inputs. They move freely in the arena by using two motors' outputs, which are computed at each game time-step. The agents compute the prediction of the other one's next relative position and relative orientation via five outputs from three inputs. We designed the agents with recurrent neural networks (Fig. 2)and evolved them by the genetic algorithm(GA). Recurrent neural networks have been applied for evolving relevant controllers of agents that determine their behaviour and motion pattern.

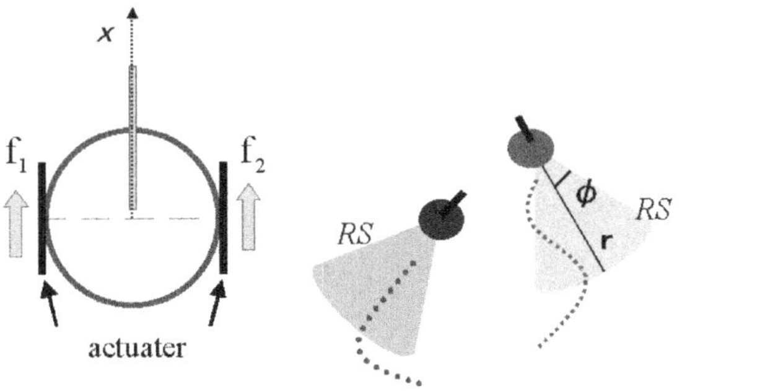

Figure 1: Left: a schematic view of the mobile robot with two wheels (actuators). It computes the forward force vector and the torque strength from the force vector (f_1, f_2) on each actuator. Right: Two mobile robots interact to perform turn-taking behaviour by sensing each other's position and direction of motion. It is called a robot A's turn when A enters B's rear side (RS) position. The shape of this RS is parameterized by r and θ.

One remarkable characteristic of using recurrent neural networks is that we can make internal models of the other one, so that the other agent's image is represented by complicated geometrical patterns in a context space. This characteristic is useful to clarify the relationship between the internal dynamics and turn-taking behaviour. The dynamics of the recurrent neural network are expressed by the following equations at the game time-step t,

$$h_j(t) = g(\sum_i w_{ij} y_i(t) + \sum_l w'_{lj} c_l(t-1)), \quad (3)$$

$$z_k(t) = g(\sum_j u_{jk} h_j(t)), \quad (4)$$

$$c_l(t) = g(\sum_l u'_{jl} h_j(t)), \quad (5)$$

$$g(x) = 1/(1 + e^{-x}), \quad (6)$$

where y_i, z_k, h_j and c_l represent input, output, hidden and context nodes, respectively. The respective number of nodes in these layers is set to $(I, K, J, L) = (3, 5, 10, 3)$ throughout this paper. The symbols w_{ij}, u_{jk}, w'_{lj} and u'_{jl} denote the weights from input to hidden, hidden to output, context to hidden and hidden to context, respectively.

Evolutionary design of neural architecture

Each agent with a recurrent neural network needs to change adaptively and to update the weights according to the behaviour of another agent. Therefore, GA is applied to evolve the structures of the neural networks. The weight set of the neural networks as phenotype is directly encoded by the genotype that is a vector representation of the real weight values in our GA design.

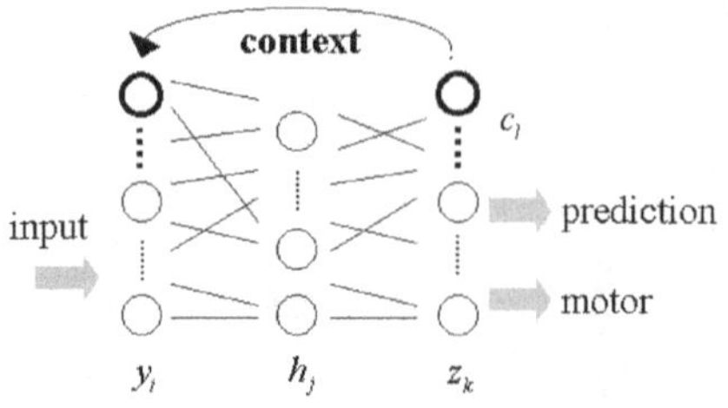

Figure 2: A recurrent neural network with three layers as a dynamical recognizer. Input nodes receive the other agent's relative position. The last layer consists of three kinds of nodes: context, prediction and motor. Context nodes feed back to the input layer. Prediction nodes predict the other's relative position in the future. Motor nodes provides the torque of an agent.

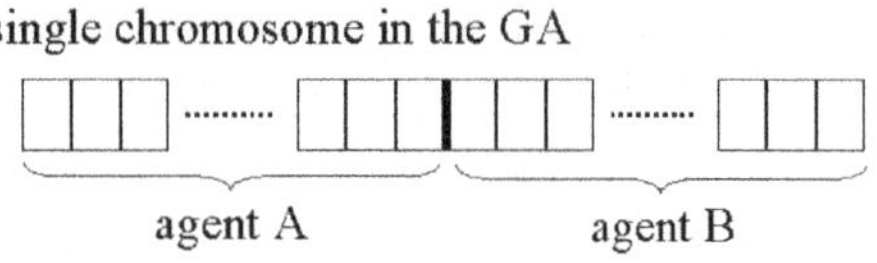

Figure 3: A chromosome used in the GA which is composed of two parts. Each encodes the real value of the weight set of one of the two agents.

We also designed each chromosome, which is composed of two parts, each encoding for the weights of one of the two agents (Fig. 3), because turn-taking patterns require a certain degree of behavioural coordination (E.A.DiPaolo 2000). The fitness of the chromosome is based on the performance of the two agents. In the case that a single genome is assigned to one agent, each agent's objective is individually optimized. This means that the fitness function becomes competitive. This situation can be interpreted as a non-cooperative game by game theory. It is difficult to acquire turn-taking behaviour by having independent agent coding under a competitive fitness function. Therefore, we introduced the coding of a single genome holding two weight sets. Although, this GA coding is relevant for our purpose to see what sort of dynamics can synthesize turn-taking, we cannot state how such dynamics are attained from scratch.

In our GA schema, a rank-based selection is used as a search technique with a fixed population, in which the phenotype of each individual represents a pair of agents. Our evolutionary process develops as follows. At first, the number P of individuals in the population is initialized with randomized weight values. Then, we calculate the fitness of each individual based on the results of the movements of agents in a match. Each match consists of (T=600) time steps. The fitness of turn-taking is a function of coordinated behaviour. Fitness takes the highest value when both agents take their turn alternately and the agents can predict each other's behaviour. A one-sided (i.e. role-fixed) behaviour is associated with the lower fitness values. Two agents play N matches with different initial values, while calculating the fitness by averaging over initial configurations. The fitness of gene i is calculated as follows:

$$\text{Fitness}_i = s_1 \times \text{Fitness}_i^{\text{turn}} + s_2 \times \text{Fitness}_i^{\text{predict}}, \tag{7}$$

$$\text{Fitness}_i^{\text{turn}} = \frac{1}{N}\sum^{N}\left(\sum_t F_{a_i}(t) \times \sum_t F_{b_i}(t)\right), \tag{8}$$

$$F_a(t) = \left\{ \begin{array}{ll} 1 & Pos_a(t) \in RS_b(t) \\ 0 & Pos_a(t) \notin RS_b(t) \end{array} \right\}, \tag{9}$$

$$\text{Fitness}_i^{\text{predict}} = -\frac{1}{N}\sum^{N}\left(\sum_t P_{a_i}(t) \times \sum_t P_{b_i}(t)\right), \tag{10}$$

$$P_a(t) = (Pos_b(t) - Pos_{a \to b}(t))^2, \tag{11}$$

where a_i and b_i are agents coded by the gene i. $Pos_{a_i}(t)$ represents the position of agent a_i, at time t in the match and RS indicates the space behind the other agent, which is specified by two parameters, r and ϕ (see Fig. 1). The agent in this scope is said to be in his turn and getting a point. $Pos_{a \to b}$ denotes a's prediction of b's relative position, which is used to calculate the precision of the prediction. According to the fitness function for turns, the fitness value becomes lower if only one agent takes turns in the match. To achieve the higher fitness, both agents need to take turns equally. This fitness function thus makes agents evolve so that the roles of pursuer and evader alternate in a match. After the calculation of fitness, crossover and mutation operations are performed using a rank-based selection. The generations proceed by repeating this process and the weights of the recurrent neural network are evolved.

Simulation results

Simulation is performed on GA with 20 individuals. Figure 4 shows the fitness against the generations in the GA. As is seen in the figure, the performance of two players at each GA generation fluctuates widely. We attribute this to the fact that good performance is found only in some narrow parameter ranges. As both players fine-tune to each other, a red queen-like co-evolution occurs here.

In the earlier GA stages, two agents can initially approach closely from any position. However, soon the symmetry of their dynamics and the associated roles break down. As is seen in Fig. 5, agent A moves around quickly, making small circles while agent B moves slowly with spiky carves. The role of the agent A becomes a chaser and that of the agent B becomes an evader. As a result, agent A is rewarded more than agent B because agent A takes more turns than agent B does. In the later GA stages, their rewards become more equal and coordinated behaviour is developed (see Fig. 6). Agent B cooperatively adjusts its speed and gets more rewards.

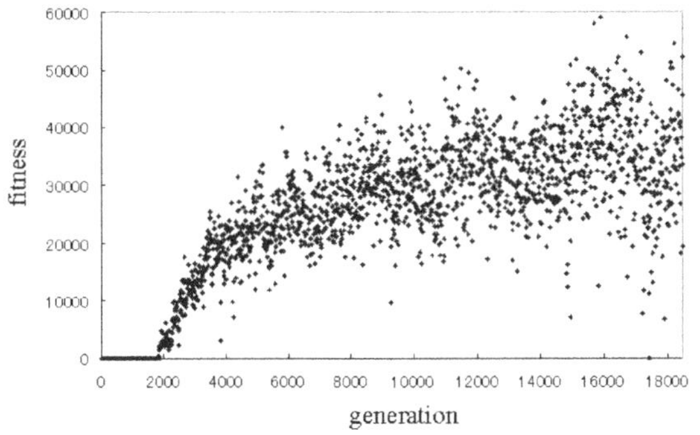

Figure 4: Fitness value of the best agent of each GA generation for a single run. Around 1800 generations, the fitness suddenly takes off and is saturated around 15000 generations. Dynamics of agents at 2500 generations and 18000 generations will be analysed in detail through this paper. The population size, mutation and crossover rates in the GA are set to 20, 0.9, and 0.1, respectively.

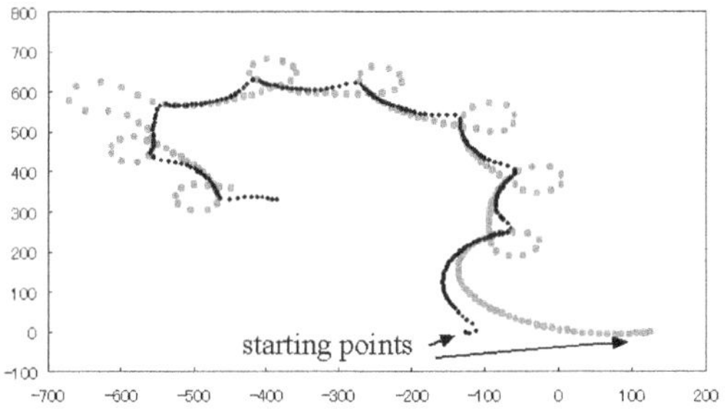

Figure 5: Spatial trails of two agents from generation 2500 in the GA are overlaid on a two dimensional arena. In the text we call one agent A and the other B. The dark coloured trail is agent B's and the light coloured is agent A's. Here agent A takes more turns than B.

In the earlier stages, their temporal behaviours can be described as follows: agent A chases agent B and at a certain point agent B abruptly escapes but soon A catches up with B; in the later stage, B gradually slows down to get its turn, while A holds the same local motion. This picture is also clear from Fig. 7 and 8. Fig. 8 shows that both A and B make turns as positive torques are generated synchronously. Therefore, evolution looks successful in the sense that rewards will be equally distributed as the GA time proceeds.

On the other hand, the dynamics which support equal rewards cannot become symmetric. This point will be discussed in the context space analysis.

This observation is now analysed by studying its prediction capability. Three outputs of the recurrent network simulate the other agent's future relative position and orientation. Those outputs are not recruited explicitly for doing anything in generating action sequences. However, because they depend on the common context neurons which determine the motion patterns, simulating each others behaviour and generating the motor outputs has indirect correlations. In Fig. 9, we show that the precision of predictions and the turn-associated sequences. In the earlier stages, B's prediction is almost always worse than A's, but in the later stages both predictions are improved but almost periodically break down when their turns are exchanged. The corresponding turns are displayed with piece-wise lines in the figure. It is worth noting that turn exchanges occur when predictions break down, while prediction holds for each turn holding phase. The spatio-temporal dynamics of the exchange phase look irregular, so that the space trails cannot form a circle. This reminds us of the heteroclinic cycles often observed in replicator dynamics (K.Hashimoto & T.Ikegami 2001). A system is attracted to a saddle point along the stable manifold most of the time course. However, in the neighbours of the saddle point, the system is repelled from the saddle along the unstable manifold, again being attracted to other saddle points. Therefore almost periodic motions are separated by chaotic transients. This generation of stable/unstable dynamics is inevitable to produce the equal turn-taking behaviours. To demonstrate this point more clearly, we show context space plots of recurrent nets in the next section.

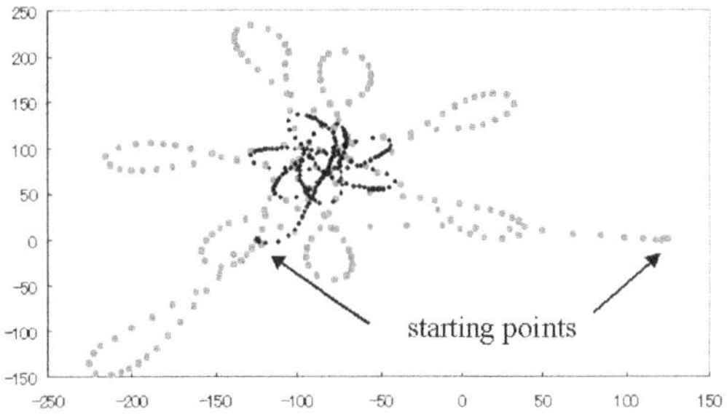

Figure 6: Spatial trails of two agents from generation 18000 in the GA are overlaid on a two dimensional arena. Here both agent A (light colour) and B (dark colour) can take turns equally.

Context Space Plots

To see how well a dynamical recognizer (DR) learned the given automaton, we examine geometrical patterns in the "context space", i.e., a plot of context neuron states against possible input states. If a DR can successfully imitate the given finite automaton, then the context space plotting will show finite islands of clusters. A clear correspondence is observed between each cluster and a node of the finite automaton. When the DR fails to imitate, or when the target function cannot be expressed

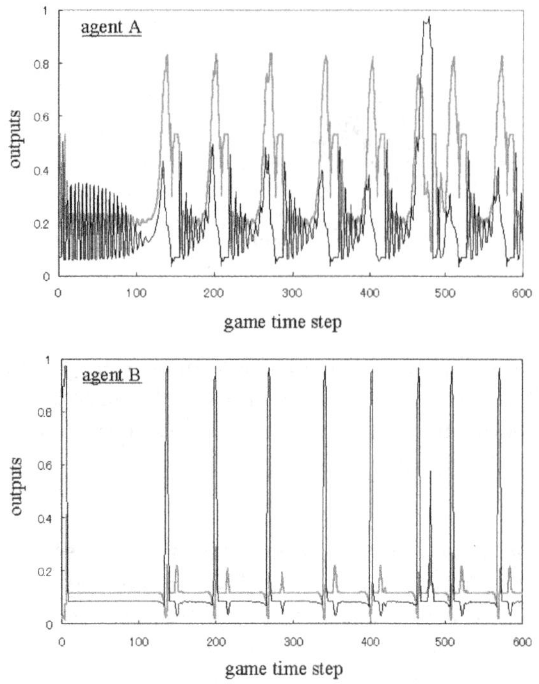

Figure 7: Dynamics of force amplitude on the left (light) and right (dark) actuators at generation 2500 in the GA. Agent A (the top graph) takes turns while agent B (the bottom graph) cannot. The spiky event corresponds to when A and B move apart in opposite directions. In between the successive spikes, A holds its turn.

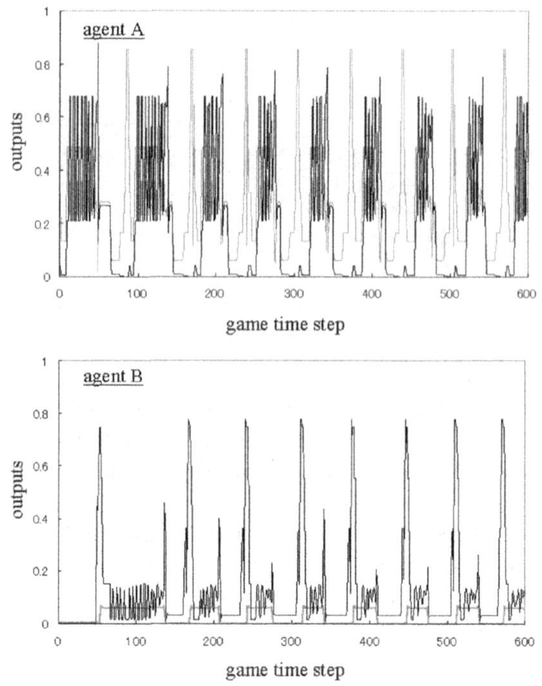

Figure 8: Dynamics of force amplitude on the left (light) and right (dark) actuators at generation 18000 in the GA. Both agent A (the top graph) and B (the bottom graph) can take turns equally. The spiky event now corresponds to switching turns from A to B and vice versa. A's turn corresponds to where both agents' forces oscillate, while in B's turn, the forces become constant. This asymmetry is reflected in the dynamics of prediction and the images in the context space plot.

as a finite automaton, the context space plotting shows a stretched and folded, fractal-like structure. Thus the context space plot characterizes the functional behaviour of a given recurrent neural network as a DR.

We present how the context space plots change in the earlier and later stages of the GA experiment (corresponding to Fig. 10 and 11). We notice that less clear patterns emerge in the context space in the earlier stages. In the context space of agent A, it is shown that there are clusters corresponding to the state of A's turns and those of B's turns. Those clusters are still distributed widely in Fig. 10. On the other hand, clusters are separated in the later stages. In particular, the context space of agent A has two symmetrical internal states corresponding to A's and B's turns. B's context space also separates its internal states but they do not look symmetric, as B's turn is corresponding to a point cluster. This asymmetry between A's and B's context space pattern reflects that A and B have different dynamics. Concerning Fig. 5 and 6, we see that agents A and B move in opposite directions to break A's turn in the earlier stages. On the other hand, both agents move in the same direction to sustain both turns in the later stages. The asymmetry in dynamics comes from the fact that the agent A always makes big circles and B makes small ones. Agent A just outruns B instead of exchanging turns in the earlier stages. However, agent B slows down when A is outrunning B, then A stays in the same direction to support B's turn in the latter stages. Therefore we argue that those are cooperative dynamics that sustains mutual turn-taking. The symmetrical separation of A's and B's turns in A's context space suggest that A can perceive both turns equally.

Here we only studied asymmetric solutions in that the two agents have different internal dynamics so that their spatio-temporal dynamics are not the same. However, we also found symmetric solutions with some different net architectures. In this case, two agents tend to move back and forth on the same circle. These results will be reported elsewhere (H.Iizuka & T.Ikegami).

Discussions

It is difficult to have temporal cooperative solution based on the traditional game theories. The present turn-taking behaviour can be taken as a temporal solution of a given game. The game called a battle of sex (J.Maynard-Smith 1982) cannot generate an apparent optimal solu-

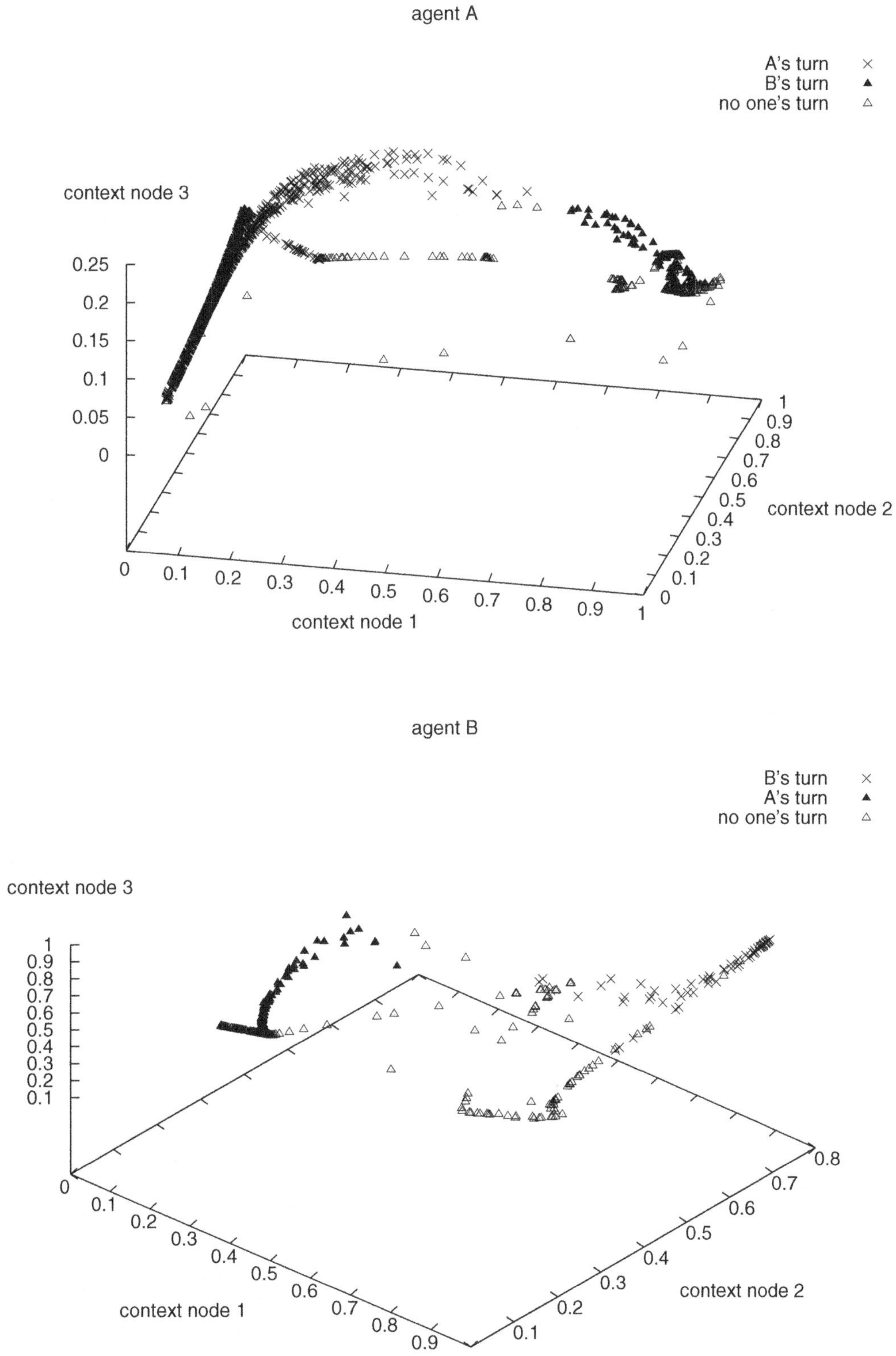

Figure 10: Context space plots for agents A (top) and B (bottom). These are the return maps of three context nodes obtained by plotting successive values of the context nodes for agents at generation 2500 in the GA. Points correspond to A's turn, B's turn or no one's turn.

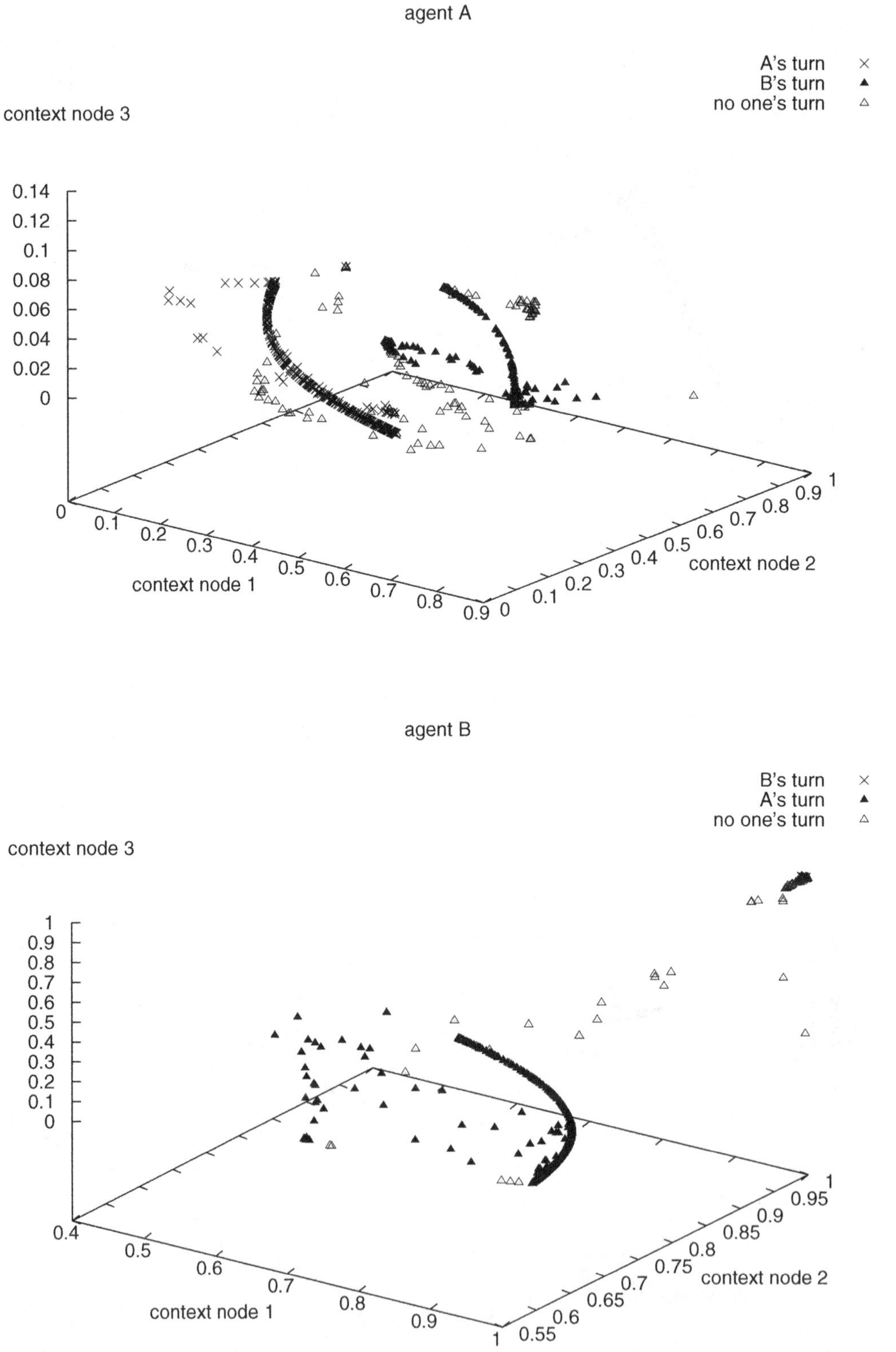

Figure 11: Context space plots for agents A (top) and B (bottom) at generation 18000 in the GA. Points of A's turn and B's turn are more structured than those at generation 2500 in the GA.

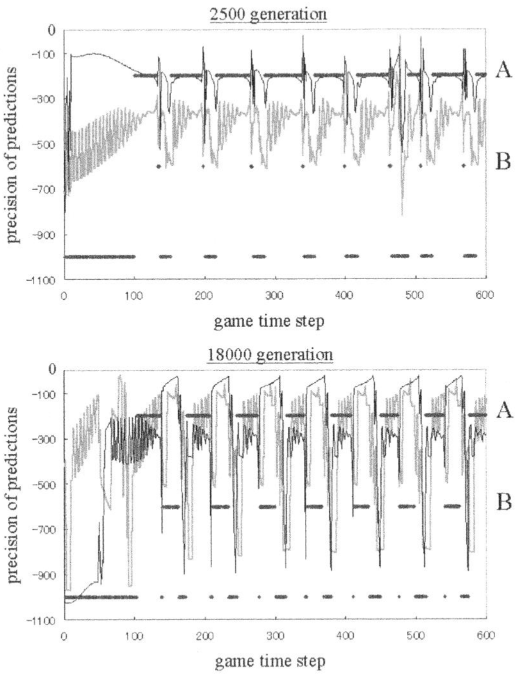

Figure 9: Dynamics of prediction precisions (light and dark) and turns (bold) are presented for generation 2500 in the GA (top) and generation 18000 in the GA (bottom). Prediction curves oscillate in time corresponding to Fig. 7 and 8. Turns are indicated in three discrete levels. The top level corresponds to A's turn, the middle to B's turn and the bottom to no one's turn. As is clearly seen from these graphs, predictions become worse when agents switch their turns from one to the other. In the top graph, B never takes its turn. In the bottom, B's turn is accompanied with predictions of relatively higher precisions, becuase the dynamics looks more regular in B's turn.

tion, i.e. period 2 behaviour. The three-person exclusion game also has period 3 optimal behaviour. In this case, Akiyama and Kaneko show that multiple periods of 3 appear through evolutionary dynamics (E.Akiyama & K.Kaneko 2000). The prisoner's dilemma game has a unique Nash solution, (defection, defection). But the iterated prisoner's dilemma (IPD) game can have mutual cooperation via a tit-for-tat strategy. In the IPD game, a periodic solution appears when we introduce mistakes. Dubey's space game has a unique Nash equilibrium with piece-wise linear pareto-optimal regions. Ikegami and Taiji show that the pareto-optimal solution can be realized via coupled dynamical recognizers (T.Ikegami & M.Taiji 1999). In the temporal solution, each agent's models of the other player temporally changes from a finite state machine-like to a strange ones.

In case of the real IPD game among humans, it is often reported that defection repeatedly takes place (T.Yamagishi 1995). We attribute this deviation from the requirements of the game theory to belief structures of players. A Turing machine cannot be a rational player if he can not decide whether the other player is rational or not, which was proved to be impossible by Anderlini (L.Anderlini 1990). A belief structure is an internally generated structure, with which we regulate interaction with other people. A simple notion of the belief structure is prediction action. The prediction load of dynamical recognizers in this model can be compared to the belief structure of players. Belief structure in general requires extension of an internal model to simulate what other players are going to play. Because any internal model cannot be complete, we expect to see the differences between the extension and the real. The difference thus perturbs belief structures. By allowing this perturbation, players can take and exchange their turns almost periodically.

In other words, the difficulty in satisfying both taking and losing turns provides an apparent paradox. Taking turns requires first to approach other player from its rear side. Therefore, prediction of the other one's dynamics will help taking turns and good prediction phases generate stable orbits. Losing turns, on the contrary, requires losing predictions. Dynamics becomes irregular so that prediction is difficult to hold; yet it is difficult to say whether losing prediction causes changing turns or vice versa. But at least this paradoxical situation makes the dynamics different from the usual chasing games.

Our main message here is that two complementary characteristics, predictability and uncertainty (i.e. unpredictability) are required to maintain interactions between cognitive agents. This notion sets out a new way of understanding cognitive functions between two people. Almost innately, infants seem to pay attention to the "novelty" of their surroundings. At the same time, infants start to interact with their carers and the interaction is usually sustained stably. A novelty in the carer, however, is not apparent nor prepared beforehand. It is constantly generated in the way of the interaction between an infant and a carer. What is the underlying mechanism of generating novelty and holding the interaction itself? The present turn-taking simulation partially answers this question. Further, based on our series of studies we can classify cognitive prediction and joint attention into two classes, respectively. Those are hot/cold prediction and tool/goal joint attention (R.Uno & T.Ikegami 2002). Prediction generally does not need other cognitive agents. Joint attention generally assumes that there are two or more agents. When we say cognitive agents, they have their own intentions and autonomous motions (i.e. autonomy). If prediction presumes autonomy in the other persons, we term the prediction "hot", otherwise "cold". Joint attention concerns how one can associate/synchronize one's intention with others. If a person uses joint attention as a tool to achieve a goal (e.g. establishing joint attention to let your dog pick up a ball), we call it "tool joint attention" But if a person takes joint attention itself as a goal, we call it "goal joint attention". For example, two people looking at the same sunset establish goal joint attention as it does not require further achievements.

Hot prediction and goal joint attention will not suppress the uncertainty found in the other one's autonomy. Instead they positively admire the existence of the autonomy. What is interesting with the goal joint attention is that the goal of the interaction is the interaction itself, to maintain the interaction under the uncertainty caused by the autonomy. In other words, joint attention is a product of interaction among agents. The present simulation suggests that unpredictability is a prerequisite to maintain joint attention (cooperative interaction), because the unpredictability causes turn exchanges. The selected agents do not evolve complete predictability to attain joint attention. As the result, they can continually interact with each other and perform successive turn-takings.

Acknowledgments: This work is partially supported by Grant-in aid (No. 09640454 and No. 13-10950) from the Ministry of Education, Science, Sports and Culture.

References

B.Scassellati. 1999. Imitation and mechanisms of joint attention: A developmental structure for building social skills on a humanoid robot. *Computation for Metaphors, Analogy and Agents, Vol. 1562 of Springer Lecture Notes in Artificial Intelligence, Springer-Verlag.*

C.W.Reynolds. 1995. Competition, co-evolution and the game of tag. *Artificial Life IV, Brooks & Maes (eds), MIT Press, pp.59–69.*

D.Cliff, and G.F.Miller. 1996. Co-evolution of pursuit and evasion ii: Simulation methods and results. *From Animals to Animats 4:Proceedings of the Fourth International Conference on Simulation of Adaptive Behavior (SAB96), MIT Press Bradford Books, pp.506–515.*

E.A.DiPaolo. 2000. Behavioral coordination, structural congruence and entrainment in a simulation of acoustically coupled agents. *Adaptive Behavior 8:1. pp25–46.*

E.Akiyama, and K.Kaneko. 2000. Dynamical systems game theory and dynamics of games. *Physica D 147 pp.221–258.*

H.Iizuka, and T.Ikegami. to be submitted to biosystems.

I.Igari, and T.Ikegami. 2001. Coevolution of mind and language. *(presented at the int'l conf. on Evolution of Language. (Paris, April, 2000) (unpublished). I.Igari, Ph.D. thesis (University of Tokyo).*

J.B.Pollack. 1991. The induction of dynamical recognizers. *Machine Learning, 7, pp.227–252.*

J.L.Elman; E.A.Bates; M.H.Johnson; A.Karmiloff-Smith; D.Parisi; and K.Plunkett. 1996. Rethinking innateness. *The MIT press.*

J.Maynard-Smith., ed. 1982. *Evolution and the theory of Games.* Cambridge univ. press.

K.Dautenhahn. 1999. Embodiment and interaction in socially intelligent life-like agents. *Springer Lecture Notes in Artificial Intelligence, Volume 1562, Springer, pp.102–142.*

K.Hashimoto, and T.Ikegami. 2001. Heteroclinic chaos, chaotic itinerancy and neutral attractors in symmetrical replicator equations with mutations. *j.Phys. Soc. Japan. 70, pp.349–352.*

L.Anderlini. 1990. Some notes on church's thesis and the theory of games. *Theory and Decision, 29, pp.19–52.*

M.Taiji, and T.Ikegami. 1999. Dynamics of internal models in game players. *Physica D, 134, pp.253–266.*

R.Baillargeon; E.S.Spelke; and S.Wasserman. 1985. Object permanence in five-month-old infants. *Cognition, 20, pp.191–208.*

R.P.Hobson. 1993. Understanding persons: the role of affect in understanding other minds:perspectives from autism. *Oxford Univ. press.*

R.Uno, and T.Ikegami. 2002. Joint attention, prediction and language. *in press Hitsuji-Books (Japanese).*

S.Baron-Cohen; A.M.Leslie; and U.Frith. 1985. Does the autistic child have a theory of mind? *Cognition, 21, pp.37–46.*

T.Ikegami, and M.Taiji. 1998. Structures of possible worlds in a game of players with internal models. *Acta Polytechnica Scandinavica Ma. 91, pp.283–292.*

T.Ikegami, and M.Taiji. 1999. Imitation and cooperation in coupled dynamical recognizers. *Advances in Artificial Life of Springer-Verlag, pp545–554.*

T.Yamagishi. 1995. Social dilemmas. *Sociological perspectives on social psychology, pp.311–335.*

breve: a 3D Environment for the Simulation of Decentralized Systems and Artificial Life

Jon Klein[1]

[1]Complex Systems Group
Department of Physical Resource Theory
Chalmers University of Technology and
Göteborg University
SE-412 96 Göteborg, Sweden

Abstract

BREVE is a 3D simulation environment designed for simulation of decentralized systems and artificial life. While breve is conceptually similar to existing packages such as Swarm and StarLogo, the implementation of BREVE–which simulates both continuous time and continuous 3D space–is quite different such that the environment is suited to a different class of simulations. BREVE includes an interpreted object oriented language; an OpenGL display engine; collision detection; as well as experimental support for articulated body physical simulation and collision resolution with static and dynamic friction. The ultimate goal of the system is to allow decentralized simulations to be implemented quickly and easily while providing a powerful framework to facilitate the construction of advanced artificial life simulations.

Introduction

The field of artificial life focuses on replicating lifelike behaviors in computer simulations. The goals of this research range from creating novel artificial life-forms to building models which will help researchers better understand biological life. Artificial life can also be seen as a necessary first step towards the goals promised by the field of artificial intelligence. Many artificial intelligence researchers have gradually shifted focus from huge monolithic artificial intelligence environments to studying intelligence as an emergent behavior of simple interactions.

The focus on emergent behaviors is a recurring theme in many artificial life and decentralized system simulations: carefully constructing the low-level interactions that dictate the laws of a virtual world can lead to the evolution of interesting high-level interactions and emergent behaviors.

The bulk of artificial life simulations to this point have focused on designing novel low-level rules in order to evolve novel life-like behaviors and observing life as it *could* be. These types of experiments often use discrete timesteps and agent states. Conway's famous Game of Life creates a life-like cellular automaton in which each cell picks a new state based on the states of its neighbors (Conway 1970). The Tierra system presented by Ray uses a virtual machine to evolve programs which compete for computational resources (Ray 1992). The low-level rules can even correspond to specific problems or games in order to evolve solutions or strategies. Lindgren used an agent's performance in the Iterated Prisoner's Dilemma as a fitness function in order to evolve strategies for the game (Lindgren & Nordahl 1994).

While most of these simulations use rules that are loose analogies of real life concepts of evolution and survival, other artificial life simulations have focused on the goal of implementing highly realistic environments in an attempt to evolve equally realistic simulated creatures. Sims used a realistic physics environment to evolve 3D creatures capable of walking, swimming and competing (Sims 1994). Lipson and Pollack (Lipson & Pollack 2000) took this technique a step further by evolving physically realistic mobile robots in simulation and then building real-world copies. The technique of building realistic simulations does not necessarily involve physical simulation, but can also involve low-level simulation of biological systems. Yaeger used artificial neural networks to evolve virtual creatures capable of developing realistic survival strategies (Yaeger 1993).

Despite the impressive artificial life simulations that have been presented through the years, they seem to be few and far between. The limiting factor of implementing many of these artificial life experiments is the amount of development required to simulate the virtual world. Many of the techniques associated with simulating realistic physics or biological processes are active fields of research without clear cut approaches to their implementations.

The BREVE simulation environment is presented which provides a simple programmable framework for artificial life in which creating realistic 3D simulations is as easy as defining the state of the environment and the behaviors of the agents. An agent's behavior, for example, may be to query the positions of other objects and adjust its velocity accordingly. The "guts" of the simulation–graphical display; physical simulation; acceleration, velocity and positions of agents; integration and object management–are all managed by the BREVE engine.

Background

Several existing environments provide frameworks for the simulation of decentralized systems, but do not provide the features required for realistic artificial life simulations. Many of the existing packages focus on more abstract types of simulations using discrete time-steps and agent states. Though these packages can be quite powerful, they are ultimately not suited to realistic artificial life simulations.

One of the most popular packages for simulation of decentralized systems is Swarm (Minar *et al.* 1996). While Swarm provides a sophisticated system for creating hierarchies of objects and triggering events, it does not provide frameworks for 3D simulations or visualization. The package is also somewhat complex–Swarm is a collection of libraries, and not a single application. Though the libraries can be accessed through many languages and interfaces, writing simulations in Swarm still involves a great deal of programming overhead.

Another popular package which makes writing simulations considerably easier is StarLogo (Resnick 1994). StarLogo provides a simple language and powerful environment of multi-agent systems. The simulations are based around a number of agents on a 2D landscape of "patches". While the environment is easy to use and powerful for more abstract discrete models such as cellular automata, simulating 3D models such as physical simulations is simply not possible.

Swarm and StarLogo are powerful simulation packages, but ultimately do not provide the features required for advanced artificial life simulations. BREVE is designed from the ground up to simulate 3D worlds with discrete time and discrete agent states, and to support real physical simulation. In addition to the simulation internals provided by BREVE, the package also aims to be easy to use for non-programmers, while simultaniously flexible enough for more experienced users to interface with their own external libraries and programs.

The "steve" Language

Simulations in BREVE are written using a simple interpreted object-oriented language called "steve". The steve language, specifically designed for implementation of 3D simulations, includes garbage collection, support for lists and 3D vectors as native types, as well as a set of included classes which interface with the simulation features of the BREVE engine. BREVE also offers a simple plugin architecture which allows users incorporate external libraries or languages and access them through steve.

steve is a declarative language and many of the features of the language should look familiar to users familiar with C. The most notable difference is the syntax of method calls which more closely resemble objective C. In steve, each argument of a method call is associated with a keyword. This means that arguments are not identified by their order, but instead by their keywords. In the following example, the method "move" takes a single vector argument with keyword "to":

```
self move to (1, 0, 0).
```

The order of the keyword/argument pair makes no difference to the interpretation of the simulation, but may affect the readability of the method call. The following two method calls are identical, but the first one reads more naturally:

```
self schedule method-call "print-status"
at-time 20.0.
self schedule at-time 20.0 method-call
"print-status".
```

steve provides a combination of dynamic and static type checking such that certain tasks involving type checking are delayed until run time. Types must be defined for all variables, but method calls are not bound to return a specific type–different types may be returned depending on the context of the call (if the programmer is daring enough). Likewise, objects are not bound to be of a specific class–looking up method calls is done at runtime.

The fact that steve is an interpreted language which delays several type checks and method lookups until runtime can cause speed concerns, but in practice, the bottleneck of BREVE simulations is most often the physical simulation and graphical rendering and not the execution of the language.

Included Class Hierarchy

Interacting with BREVE's built-in features is done using the included class hierarchy. The top level of the hierarchy is a class called Object which is the ancestor to all objects created in BREVE. The hierarchy is split in to Abstract classes and Real classes. Abstract classes are defined as classes which have no physical representation in the simulated world, while Real classes are associated with specific physical objects.

The Real class includes Mobile and Stationary objects. The functions of these classes are simple: Mobile objects represent agents which move around during the course of the simulation, while Stationary objects represent objects which are immobile over the course of the simulation such as a floor or obstacles in the world. The Mobile class is also the parent to the class MultiBody which is used to create articulated bodies made up of several links.

The most notable members of the Abstract hierarchy are the classes Control and Data. The class Control provides access to the BREVE engine such as camera and light settings, user interface and the actual integration of the world. A subclass of Control, PhysicalControl, provides special features required during physical simulations. The Data class is a special class that can be saved to disk or sent over a network. The class is limited in that it may only contain simple data types such as ints, floats or vectors. In order to save other instance types to disk or send them over the network, they need to be packaged into Data objects.

Events and Scheduling

Agent behaviors are written in steve as part of an object's definition. Each action an agent can take may be written as a separate method that gets called in response to certain events. There are several ways to trigger events within a BREVE simulation.

- Events called every iteration

Most instances in BREVE have actions that need to be performed at every iteration of the engine. These actions could include changing velocity or acceleration, examining their environment for certain cues or interacting with other objects in the simulation.

These types of actions are triggered simply by the existence of an ITERATE method in a class definition. All instances of classes which implement an ITERATE method will have the method automatically called at each time-step.

- Events scheduled for a specific time

Events can be scheduled to be triggered at a certain time using the method SCHEDULE:

```
self schedule method-call "<method>"
at-time <time>.
```

The scheduled method call takes no arguments.

- Events triggered by notifications

Because instances may appear and disappear over the course of a simulation, it can become difficult for instances to keep track of each other. In order to simplify the process of communicating with arbitrary instances, BREVE allows instances to post notifications about their current status using the method NOTIFY. These notifications then trigger actions for all instances that have registered themselves as observers using the method OBSERVE.

Using this technique, a new instance in the simulation can simply register itself with the key players in the simulation, instead of requiring the existing objects to keep track of objects which are created and destroyed over the course of a simulation.

This technique can be used not only for simple notifications in which one object announces a status change to the rest of the objects, but may also be used to set up complex notification hierarchies. Physical objects in the world can be grouped into separate "flocks" by encompassing them in an Abstract object for which the objects observe notifications. The objects containing the flocks can then in turn be grouped into more general categories, and so forth. The result is a notification hierarchy that can effectively be controlled using a single object.

- Events triggered by collisions

Events can be triggered whenever the collision detection algorithm detects a collision between two objects. This type of callback handles the behavioral changes that occur when two objects collide, such as one object destroying the other or an exchange of information. The simulation first registers to catch these collision events with a specific object type using the method HANDLE-COLLISIONS which is available to all Physical objects. When the physics engine detects a collision between two objects, the simulation is stepped forward to the precise time of impact before the collision callback is called.

- Events triggered through the user interface

Simulations can be set up to trigger events in response to user interaction. BREVE allows users to set up a global application menu, as well as contextual menus associated with each object in the simulation. This allows messages to be sent to a centralized controller object, or to specific objects in the simulation at any time. Additionally, a simulation callback is executed when the user clicks on objects in the simulation. The default behavior in this case is to select the object that the user clicks on, but this behavior can be overriden.

- INIT and DESTROY

If they are defined, the special methods INIT and DESTROY are automatically called for an instance when it is created and when it is freed, respectively. These methods allow the instance to handle initialization and deinitialization, if required.

Running Simulations

Every simulation is controlled by a single "controller" object–an instance of the built-in class Control (or one of its subclasses). The controller instance is defined in the simulation source code file and is the only instance which is automatically created when a simulation is run. Other instances may, in turn, be created by the controller instance in the INIT method. The controller instance also receives a number of callbacks associated user interaction, such as clicking on objects in the simulation or selecting menu items, so it is fair to think of the controller object as the main thread of the simulation.

Physical Simulation

The physical simulation engine takes the instantaneous state of the objects in the world, along with the internal forces (such as joint torque) and external forces (such as gravity) acting upon them and computes the state of the objects at the following time-step. The physical simulation engine in BREVE encompasses rigid body simulation, collision detection, collision response, as well as the general state of the simulated world and integration.

While the goal of the simulation engine is to provide realistic simulation, it does not aim to be a precise predictor of real-world behaviors. This distinction means that while the simulation must be "realistic", an emphasis is placed on performance rather than on accuracy. Collision impulses, for instance, are computed according to a fast algebraic algorithm rather than through a slower, but more accurate, simulation of the deformation of the colliding objects. In contrast to highly accurate systems which are expected to predict the motion of complex machinery or the results of a simulated car crash, it is acknowledged that small errors will find their way into the simulation. These errors are on the scale of variations due to imperfections in the ground, though conservation of energy is strictly enforced in order to prevent evolving agents from exploiting bugs in the physical simulation.

The physics engine currently implemented in BREVE is a work-in-progress and does have a number of limitations, but it is sufficient to simulate articulated creatures learning to walk on a flat plane such as those exhibited by Sims.

Integration

Integration is done using either a simple Runge-Kutta 4th order integrator or a Runge-Kutta-Fehlman integrator with adaptive step-size control. The initial integration step for physical simulations is generally between .005 and .01. In addition to integration step, the speed of a simulation depends on a large number of other factors. The most important of which are the number of bodies in the simulation and the number of joints in each body, as well as the number of collisions that must be resolved at each time-step. One of the demo simulations which features a single walking articulated body made up of 9 links can be run at more than 2x real-time on a 500 Mhz PowerPC Macintosh.

Articulated Body Simulation

The articulated body simulation algorithm computes the physics of a single body made up of several individual links. The articulated body simulation provided by BREVE was implemented specifically for the simulation of biologically inspired articulated bodies such as insects, animals or simple robots.

The articulated body simulation implemented in BREVE is the $O(n)$ algorithm presented by Featherstone (Featherstone 1983) and described in detail by Mirtich (Mirtich 1996). The algorithm takes as input the state of a rigid body and the forces acting upon it and gives as output the resulting acceleration of the body and its component joints. Integrating these values yields the velocity and, in turn, the positions of the simulated creatures at each time-step.

Collision Detection

The collision detection algorithm implemented here is based on the Lin-Canny closest feature algorithm (Lin 1993) with many of the improvements recommended by Mirtich (Mirtich 1998).

The algorithm works in two passes: the pruning pass which examines objects' bounding boxes to quickly determine which object pairs may be overlapping, followed by the more detailed collision detection pass of all candidate object pairs. The pruning pass works simply by projecting the bounding box vertices of all of the objects in the simulation onto each axis, and sorting the resulting lists. By inspecting the positions of the sorted minima and maxima, it is possible to determine whether two objects are overlapping on a given axis–those overlapping on all three axes are considered to be collision candidates. Although performing this check is in the worst case $O(n^2)$, in practice objects move very little from one time-step to the next, so the lists remain almost sorted at all times and this step of the simulation approaches $O(n)$.

Object pairs are examined using the second collision detection pass if and only if their bounding box vertices overlap on all three axes. The second pass works by locating the closest feature pair between two objects and calculating the distance between them. As with the bounding box phase, this stage exploits coherence, or the fact that object positions change very little from one time-step to the next such that the closest features for a given object pair are often already known from previous iterations.

Many simulations also require agents to query to position of other objects in the simulation before determining what kind of action to take. Although agents are often only interested in nearby objects, the task of determining which objects are "nearby" requires examining the position of every other object in the simulation. Performing this type of check quickly becomes the bottleneck of simulations with a large number of agents, even if the interactions between neighboring objects is relatively simple. This is especially relevant when dealing with flocking behaviors, swarms, or implementing senses such as smell or vision.

BREVE solves this problem by offering a feature called "neighbor detection" which uses a second pruning pass of the collision detection algorithm in order to find objects pairs which are not at risk of colliding with each other, but which are below a certain distance threshold that makes them "interesting". This simple technique means that many complex simulations that previously grew with complexity $O(n^2)$ can now be simulated in near $O(n)$ time, depending on the distribution of the objects in simulated space. In the worst case scenario in which all the objects are overlapping each others' neighbor spaces, all object pairs would be registered as neighbors and the simulation would still run with $O(n^2)$ complexity.

Collision Response

The collision response algorithm implemented by BREVE is the Chatterjee and Ruina (Chatterjee & Ruina 1998) collision impulse algorithm in which collision impulses are estimated mathematically according to the position and velocity of the colliding objects. The algorithm accounts for both static and dynamic friction.

At low speeds, contact "spring" forces are also applied in order to ensure that objects don't penetrate. These spring forces mean that fewer collisions need to be resolved and that larger integration steps can be taken in situations in which objects attain some sort of resting contact. In most physical simulation environments, spring forces are almost always avoided in favor of more accurate contact force algorithms, but due to the rather small number of situations that require any kind of contact force to be applied, the spring forces are adequate in the BREVE environment.

Examples

BREVE includes several demos which exhibit the power of the simulation engine and language. The demos implemented should be quite familiar to artificial life or decentralized systems researchers. The most notable difference is that in each case, the BREVE implementation requires only a few hundred lines of code. The more tedious steps of implementing these simulations, such as integration, physical simulation and graphical display are all handled automatically by the BREVE engine. The included demos also illustrate the diversity that BREVE is capable of. A few of the included demos are described below.

Flocking

The "Swarm" demo is more or less an implementation of Craig Reynolds classic "Boids" model. Using simple urges, such as matching velocity with and maintaining distance from neighboring birds, simulated birds exhibit realistic flocking behaviors. These urges are accumulated with certain weights in order to determine the bird's instantaneous acceleration.

The BREVE implementation is quite simple: each bird, in its iterate method, queries its neighbors for their velocities and locations, and adjusts its own acceleration accordingly. Users can dynamically adjust the weights placed on each urge in order to evoke different kinds of flocking behaviors.

Evolution of Walking Behaviors

In the "Walker" demo, a physically realistic simulated creature learns to walk using a genetic algorithm. The demo is inspired by Sims' creatures, but is ultimately a far more simple implementation. The most notable difference is that the body of the creature is hard-coded with four limbs, with each limb composed of two sections. Instead of using a neural network to control the motion of the joints, each joint is controlled by a sine-based function of time with a number of variables controlling the wavelength of the sine cycle, a phase shift and an amplitude shift. The values of these variables are evolved for each joint.

The implementation in BREVE involves a single creature which tries different walking strategies for 20 seconds at a time, noting how far it moved using a certain strategy. After every four tests, the best two individuals are bred together to replace the worst two. After a short period of time, the creature learns to coordinate its limbs in order to walk.

Diffusion Limited Aggregation

Diffusion limited aggregation is a simple decentralized model of fractal growth. The model begins with a single seed particle. Other particles then float in from an arbitrarily long distance one at a time. When the random particles touch any part of the growing mass, they freeze to become part of the structure themselves.

The BREVE implementation of this algorithm is incredibly simple. In order to simplify the simulation and improve performance, the mass is made up of stationary objects and the same random walking object is reused. The incoming particle is implemented as an object with two simple behaviors: the first behavior which changes velocity randomly is performed at every time-step and is implemented as the ITERATE method; the second behavior waits for collisions with the growing particle mass. When a collision occurs, a new particle is attached precisely at the point of collision and the random walking object is moved out to a new starting point away from the particle mass. After a short period of time the growing particle mass exhibits a fractal appearence.

Though the algorithm is normally presented in 2D, the BREVE implementation can be switched to a 3D simulation simply by changing a variable corresponding to the permitted velocities of the random walking object.

Future Work

Future work on the BREVE environment involves refining its use as an artificial life experiment platform. Work is already in progress to integrate advanced networking capabilities, recurrent and feed forward neural network simulations and more complex terrains. Another important goal is to parallelize the physical simulation engine such that real-time simulations can be run including perhaps hundreds of complex physically simulated creatures instead of just a few at a time.

Once these goals have been achieved, the focus will turn to creating realistic artificial life simulations in which creatures with evolved morphology and behaviors compete for resources in a physically simulated world.

Conclusion

The BREVE simulation environment is a unique simulation environment which is well suited for simulations of artificial life and other decentralized systems. A special emphasis is placed on the goal of implementing highly realistic low-level simulations in order to evolve highly realistic high-level behaviors. Features such as the ability to simulate and display 3D worlds, an easy to use object-oriented language, as well as physical simulation capabilities distinguish BREVE from existing simulation packages.

References

Chatterjee, A., and Ruina, A. 1998. A new algebraic rigid body collision law based on impulse space considerations. *Journal of Applied Mechanics* 65:939–951.

Conway, J. H. 1970. The game of life. *Scientific American* 223:120–123.

Featherstone, R. 1983. The calculation of robot dynamics using articulated-body inertias. *International Journal of Robotics Research* 2:13–30.

Lin, M. 1993. *Efficient Collision Detection for Animation and Robotics.* Ph.D. Dissertation, University of California, Berkeley.

Lindgren, K., and Nordahl, M. G. 1994. Evolutionary dynamics of spatial games. *Physica D* 75:292–309.

Lipson, H., and Pollack, J. B. 2000. Automatic design and manufacture of robotic lifeforms. *Nature* 406:974–978.

Minar, N.; Burkhart, R.; Langton, C.; and Askenazi, C. 1996. The Swarm simulation system: A toolkit for building multi-agent simulations. Technical report, Sante Fe Institute. working paper 96-06-042.

Mirtich, B. 1996. *Impulse-based Dynamic Simulation of Rigid Body Systems.* Ph.D. Dissertation, University of California, Berkeley.

Mirtich, B. 1998. V-Clip: Fast and robust polyhedral collision detection. *ACM Transactions on Graphics* 17:177–208.

Ray, T. S. 1992. Evolution, ecology and optimization of digital organisms. Technical report, Santa Fe Institute. working paper 92-08-042.

Resnick, M. 1994. *Turtles, Termites, and Traffic Jams: Explorations in Massively Parallel Microworlds.* Cambridge, MA: MIT Press.

Sims, K. 1994. Evolving 3D morphology and behavior by competition. In Brooks, R., and Maes, P., eds., *Artificial Life IV Proceedings.* Cambridge, MA: MIT Press.

Yaeger, L. 1993. Computational genetics, physiology, metabolism, neural systems, learning, vision, and behavior. In *Artificial Life III Proceedings.* Redwood City, CA: Addison Wesley Longman.

Evolutionary Bits'n'Spikes

Dario Floreano, Nicolas Schoeni, Gilles Caprari, Jesper Blynel
Autonomous Systems Laboratory (asl.epfl.ch), Institute of Systems Engineering
Swiss Federal Institute of Technology (EPFL), CH-1015, Lausanne, Switzerland

Abstract

We describe a model and implementation of evolutionary spiking neurons for embedded microcontrollers with few bytes of memory and very low power consumption. The approach is tested with an autonomous microrobot of less than 1 in^3 that evolves the ability to move in a small maze without human intervention and external computers. Considering the very large diffusion, small size, and low cost of embedded microcontrollers, the approach described here could find its way in several intelligent devices with sensors and/or actuators, as well as in smart credit cards.

Artificial Spiking Circuits

Most biological neurons communicate by sending pulses across connections to other neurons. The pulse is also known as "spike" to indicate its short and transient nature. Neurons are affected by incoming spikes and generate a spike when their membrane potential becomes larger than a threshold. Spike generation is followed by a short "refractory period" during which the neuron cannot generate another spike.

Computational models of spiking neurons are attracting increasing interest in engineering and computer science (Maas & Bishop 1999). On the one hand, computer simulations of spiking networks can help to address specific questions in neuroscience, such as how biological neurons communicate with each other (Koenig, Engel, & Singer 1996; Rieke *et al.* 1997). On the other hand, a better understanding of spiking neurons is leading to the development of new neuromorphic devices (Horiuchi 2001), some of which may replace lesioned fibers or sensory organs.

In addition, we argue that networks of spiking neurons represent suitable control systems for autonomous behavioral systems,[1] such as situated autonomous robots, because temporal patterns of sensory-motor events may be captured and exploited more efficiently (i.e., with fewer neurons or with higher probability) by the intrinsic time-dependent dynamics of spiking neurons than by other connectionist models (Rumelhart, McClelland, & PDP Group 1986).

Computational investigations of spiking neurons are often based on biophysical models that are significantly more complicated than models used in connectionism (McCulloch-Pitts, Perceptron, and Hopfield models, e.g.). These biophysical models are defined by coupled differential equations that attempt to capture the complex dynamics of membrane ion channels, generation and propagation of spikes, and synaptic conductances, among others. A representative sample of these models is presented in "road map" II.5 of the *Handbook of Brain Theory and Neural Networks* (Arbib 1998). Although such differential equations can be directly mapped into analog VLSI circuits exploiting the physics of sub-threshold transistors (Mead 1989; Indiveri & Douglas 2000), digital implementations of spiking networks often resort to complex simulations (Bower & Beeman 1994) and/or comparatively larger hardware resources (de Garis 1996).

Whatever choice of implementation, hand-design of spiking circuits that display a desired functionality is not a trivial task because of the highly non-linear dynamics. Furthermore, the learning algorithms developed so far for spiking circuits are often restricted to very simple and application-specific architectures (Maas & Bishop 1999). The most successful results in the field of robotics obtained so far focused on the first stages of sensory processing and on relatively simple motor control. For example, Indiveri *et al.* (2001) developed neuromorphic vision circuits that emulate interconnections among neurons in the early layers of the biological retina in order to extract motion information and implement a simple form of attentive selection. These vision circuits have been interfaced with a Koala robot and their output has been used to drive the wheels of the robot in order to follow lines using a hand-designed program (Indiveri & Verschure 1997). In another line of work, Lewis *et al.* (2000) developed an analog VLSI circuit with four spiking neurons capable of controlling a robotic leg and adapting the motor commands using sensory feedback. This neuromorphic circuit consumes less than 1 microwatt and takes less than 0.4 square millimeters of chip area.

In this paper, we take a different approach to the generation of functional spiking circuits in that *a)* we show that the architecture of functional spiking circuits can be evolved instead of hand-designed and *b)* we describe a software implementation of evolutionary spiking circuits in *digital* microcontrollers with size and power consumption competitive with analog VLSI chips mentioned above. Since the software operates at the level of *single bits* and uses few logic functions, both the neural circuit and evolutionary algorithm fit on the same chip in a few bytes of data memory. The method is tested with a 2-cm long microrobot that must develop navigation abilities without human intervention and external cables.

[1]They certainly showed to be excellent control systems for biological organisms!

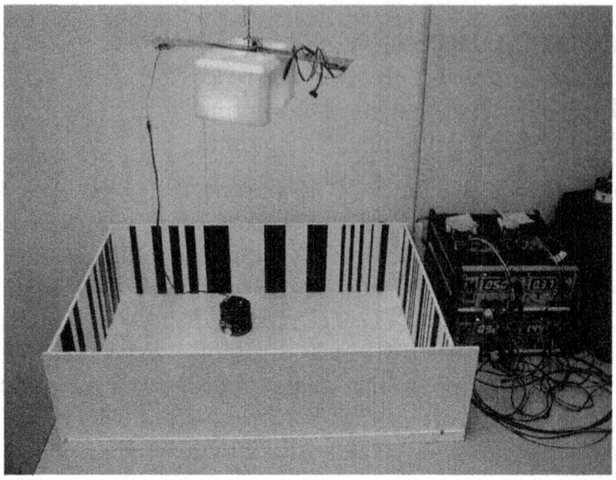

Figure 1: A Khepera robot equipped with a linear camera is positioned in an arena lit from above in order to let the evolutionary experiments continue at night. The robot is connected to a workstation through rotating contacts that provide serial data transmission and power supply. The spiking networks and genetic operators run on the workstation.

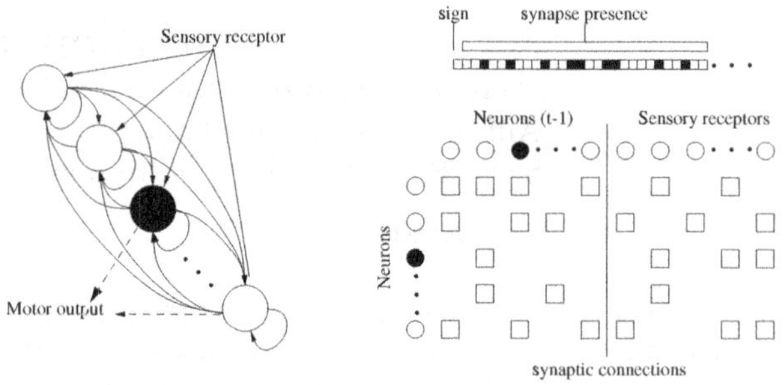

Figure 2: Network architecture (only a few neurons and connections are shown) and genetic representation for one neuron. *Left*: A conventional representation showing the network architecture. *Right*: The same network unfolded in time (neurons as circles, synaptic connections as squares). The neurons on the column receive signals from connected neurons and receptors shown on the top row. The first part of the row includes the same neurons at the previous time step to show the connections among neurons. Sensory neurons do not have interconnections. The signs of the neurons (white = excitatory, black = inhibitory) and their connectivity pattern is encoded in the genetic string and evolved.

Evolutionary Spiking Circuits for Robot Navigation

In previous work, some of us (Floreano & Mattiussi 2001) investigated the evolvability of spiking circuit architectures for vision-based navigation of a mobile robot. A Khepera robot with a linear camera was asked to navigate in a rectangular arena with textured walls (figure 1). The walls were filled with black and white vertical stripes of random size.[2] The fitness value was proportional to the amount of forward movement during 40 seconds of robot life. Therefore, robots that could move straight and avoid walls had higher probability of reproduction.

The architecture of a fully recurrent network of 10 spiking neurons connected to 16 spiking visual receptors was genetically encoded and evolved using a standard genetic algorithm (Goldberg 1989) with a population of 60 individuals sequentially evaluated on the same robot. The architecture is genetically represented by a binary string composed of blocks corresponding to each neuron. The first bit of a block encodes the sign of the corresponding neuron $\{1, -1\}$ and the remaining $n + s$ bits encode the presence/absence $\{1, 0\}$ of a connection from the n neurons and from the s receptors (figure 2). The synaptic strengths of all existing connections are set to 1. The spiking neuron model used in those experiments included the response profile of synaptic and neuron membranes to incoming spikes, time delays to account for axon length, and membrane recovery profile of the refractory period (Gerstner 1991). The parameter values for the equations were predefined and fixed for all networks. The neural network software, consisting of several hundred lines of C++ code in order to simulate the entire network activation and signal transmission, was run by an external workstation communicating with the robot every 100 ms through a serial connection that transmitted visual information and motor commands. The graph on the left of figure 3 displays population mean and population best fitness values averaged across six runs of evolutionary spiking networks. Fitness values between 0.15 and 0.2 already correspond to robots that can move forward and avoid walls. Further fitness gains correspond to faster and smoother trajectories. As a comparison, we performed another set of experiments with networks of sigmoid neurons using the same architecture, genetic encoding, and evolutionary parameters. The graph on the right of figure 3 shows the average fitness values measured across three runs of sigmoid networks. Despite allowing for an extra ten generations, none of the evolutionary runs could improve fitness values along generations. Occasional higher values are given by individuals that perform wide circles, independently of the sensory input, until they remain stuck against a wall.

Neural and behavioral analysis of evolved spiking controllers (figure 4) indicated that neurons exploit temporal correlation of spiking activity from sensory neurons as well as from internal neurons in order to avoid walls and maintain a smooth forward trajectory (Floreano &

[2]Random size was used to prevent development of trivial solutions whereby the neural network would use the size of the stripes to measure distance from walls and self-motion.

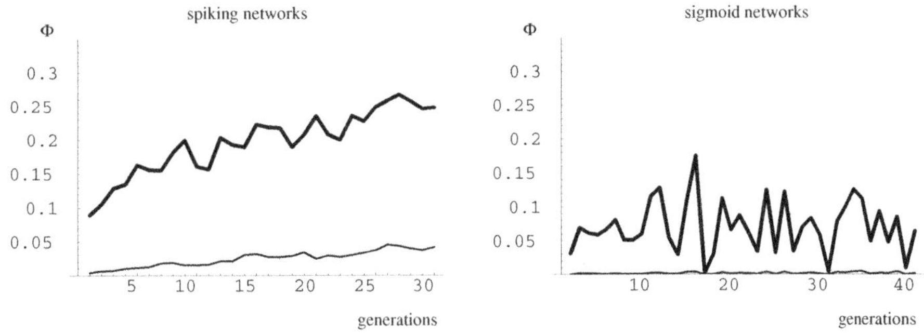

Figure 3: Fitness values obtained on the physical robot Khepera (best fitness = thick line; average fitness = thin line). Each data point is the average of several evolutionary runs with different random initializations. *Left*: Evolution of spiking networks (average over six runs). *Right*: Evolution of connectionist sigmoid networks where 10 additional generations per run were allowed to check for signs of improvement (average over three runs).

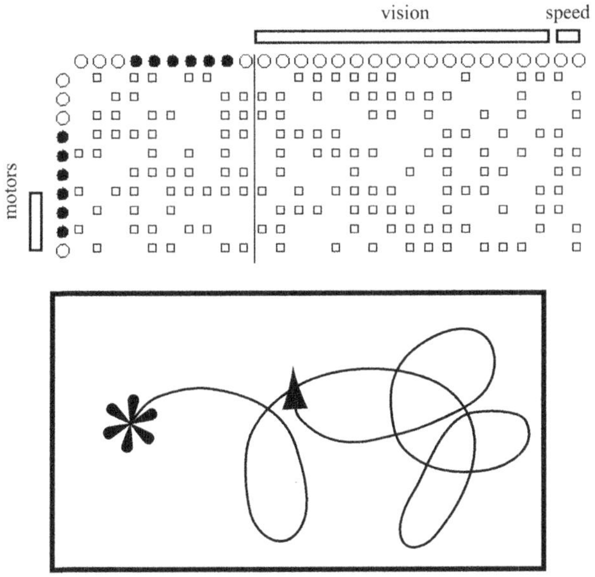

Figure 4: *Top*: Architecture of the best spiking controller after 30 generations. Black circles = inhibitory neurons, white circles = excitatory neurons. *Bottom*: Typical trajectory of robot displayed by this spiking controller. The asterisk indicates the starting point. The curvature of the trajectory depends on the pattern of stripes seen by the robot.

Mattiussi 2002).

Evolutionary Spiking Circuits in a Microcontroller[3]

A microcontroller is an integrated circuit composed of a microprocessor unit, memory, and input/output peripheral devices (figure 5). In other words, it is a full computer in a single chip capable of receiving, storing, processing, and transmitting signals to the external world. Microcontrollers are used for a wide range of smart devices, such as microwave ovens, telephones, washing machines, car odometers, and credit cards. More than 3.5 billion microprocessor units are sold each year for embedded control, exceeding by more than an order of magnitude the number of microprocessor units sold for computers (Katzen 2001).

Most applications using microcontrollers require very low power consumption, small size, robustness to hard operating conditions, and low price. These features come at the expense of the number of transistors and instructions per second, resulting in very low computing power compared to personal computers. Consequently, low-level languages, such as assembler, are often used to exploit efficiently every single bit of memory and complex functions are approximated by combination of simpler ones or represented as look-up tables of input-output numbers.

The core idea explored in this paper is that spiking circuits can be mapped quite easily into microcontrollers because spikes are essentially binary events and the nonlinear dynamics and precise coding of spiking circuits can be provided by spiking times, rather than by nonlinear, real-valued, activation functions used in connectionist neuron models. In other words, a few logic operations (such as AND and NOT) and instructions to move around single bits over time would be sufficient to build in tiny chips large circuits of spiking neurons that display complex abilities and behaviors.

The robotics experiment described in the previous section showed that artificial evolution can easily discover quite powerful spiking circuits by exploring only the space of neuron sign and connectivity. Both variables can be described by a single bit (1 = positive sign for neurons, connection enabled for synapses; 0 = negative

[3]© 2001, 2002 EPFL, Dario Floreano. The copyright applies to the software implementation of the neural circuit, of the evolutionary algorithm, and of their combination.

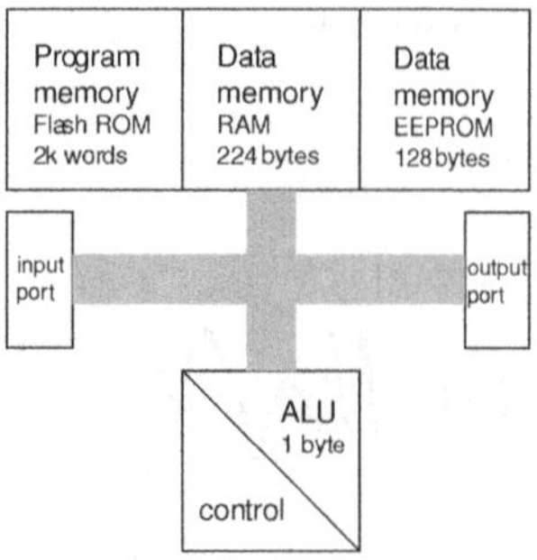

Figure 5: Components of a microcontroller with von Neumann architecture. The microprocessor unit is composed of an Arithmetic Logic Unit and of control devices to move data from/to memory banks and input/output ports. The memory banks are sometimes organized in physically separated locations. For example, a microcontroller may use ROM memory to store a program composed of a maximum of 2k instructions, each 14 bits long; a RAM memory to store 224 bytes of data; and an EEPROM memory to store 128 bytes of data. The input/output ports can be connected to sensors, keyboards, LEDs, motorized actuators, or any other peripheral. Gray lines represent the bus where one instruction or data item at a time is moved across components. The family of PIC microntrollers used in these experiments use the Harward architecture whereby the data memory and instruction memories can be accessed in parallel through two different buses.

sign, connection disabled) and therefore can be efficiently stored and easily manipulated in microcontrollers.

The next two subsections will describe the neuron and evolutionary model, respectively, as well as the implementation idea. The section that follows will describe an example of this implementation where a microrobot equipped with a microcontroller evolves without human intervention and external computers in less than two hours the ability to move around a maze.

The chips used in the experiments described here belong to the PIC (Peripheral Interface Controller) family of microcontrollers by Arizona Microchip Technology (www.microchip.com). However, the same implementation schema is applicable to any other type of microcontroller.

Neuron Model and Implementation

The neuron model used in the experiments with the Khepera robot described above is much too complex to be implemented in a microcontroller because it uses several non-linear functions, requires floating-point precision and relatively high computing speed. Therefore, the neuron model used here is a simple integrate-and-fire model with leakage and refractory period.

The neuron behavior (figure 6) is described by the following steps:

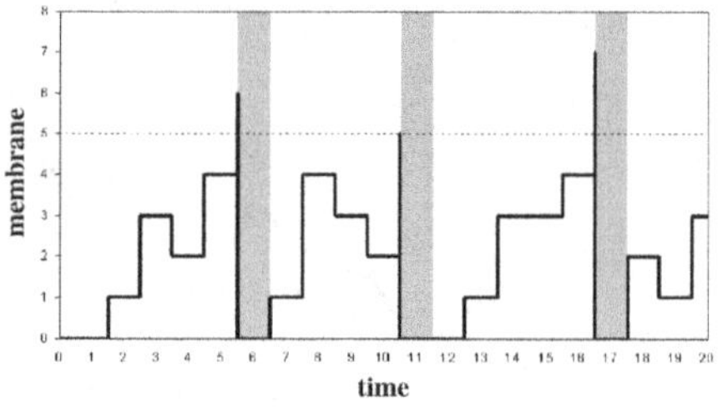

Figure 6: Behavior of a neuron with constant firing threshold. Values are those used in the experiments described in this paper.

1. *Refractory period.* If the neuron has emitted a spike within the previous Δt, do not update its membrane potential. In these experiments, $\Delta t = 1$.

2. Compute the *contribution of incoming spikes* e_i^t as the sum of spikes o_j^t at time t through existing connections w_{ij} weighted by the sign of emitting neurons s_j:

$$e_i^t = \sum_j^N o_j^t w_{ij} s_j \tag{1}$$

where $p_j^t \in \{0, 1\}$, $w_{ij} \in \{0, 1\}$, $s_j \in \{-1, 1\}$.

3. *Update membrane potential* v_i^t by adding the contribution of incoming spikes to the available potential, but do not go below a minimum level $v_i^{\min}$

$$v_i^t = \begin{cases} v_i^{t-1} + e_i^t & v_i^{t-1} + e_i^t \geq v_i^{\min} \\ v_i^{\min} & \text{otherwise} \end{cases} \tag{2}$$

where $v_i^{\min} = 0 \ \forall i$ in these experiments.

4. *Spike generation.* If the membrane potential is larger than, or equal to, a threshold $v_i^{\max}$, set the neuron output to 1 (spike) and the membrane potential to its minimum value $v_i^{\min}$; otherwise set the neuron output to 0 (no spike) and do not modify the membrane potential.

$$o_i^t = \begin{cases} 1 \text{ and } v_i^t = v_i^{\min} & : \ v_i^t > v_i^{\max} + r^t \\ 0 & : \ \text{otherwise} \end{cases} \tag{3}$$

where here the threshold $v_i^{\max} = 5 \ \forall i$ and r^t is a random integer in the range $[-2, 2]$ to prevent the emergence of locked oscillations in networks with feedback connections.

5. *Leakage.* Subtract a leaking constant k_i from the membrane potential, but do not go below the minimum level $v_i^{\min}$

$$v_i^t = \begin{cases} v_i^t - k_i & : \ v_i^t - k_i \geq v_i^{\min} \\ v_i^{\min} & : \ \text{otherwise} \end{cases} \tag{4}$$

Here $k_i = 1 \ \forall i$.

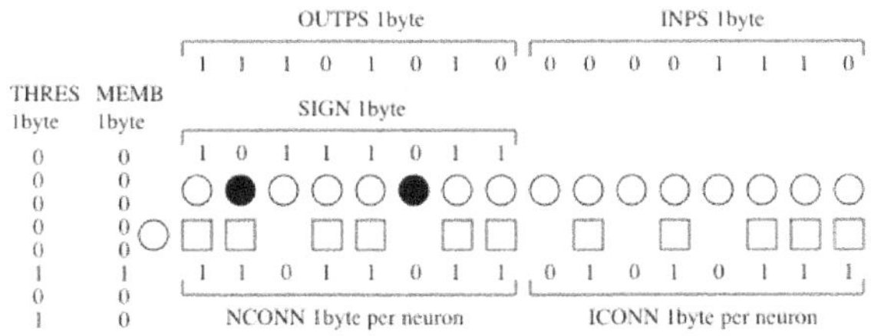

Figure 7: Digital representation of one neuron in the microcontroller.

The circuit architecture is similar to that used for the experiments on vision-based navigation described above. Each neuron can be connected to all neurons (including itself) and to all sensory neurons, as in figure 2. The sign of the neuron determines the effect of its spikes on other neurons (equation 2). The presence of a spike in the sensory neuron is determined by the activity of sensors, as explained later.

Since the Arithmetic Logic Unit (figure 5) of the microcontroller used in these experiments can operate on 8 bits in parallel, the circuit described here is composed of 8 interconnected neurons and 8 sensory neurons, which are stored in the RAM data memory (figure 7). The output (1 = spike; 0 = no spike) of the 8 neurons is stored in byte OUTPS (1 bit per neuron) and that of the 8 sensors in byte INPS (1 bit per sensor). The sign of the 8 neurons is stored in byte SIGN (1 = positive; 0 = negative). The connectivity pattern of one neuron is stored in one byte of block NCONN (connections from neurons) and in one byte of block ICONN (connections from sensors). NCONN and ICONN are blocks of 8 bytes each. The membrane potential of one neuron is stored in one byte of block MEMB, which is composed of 8 bytes too. The threshold is constant for all neurons and the stored in byte THRES; the minimum membrane potential is 0 for all neurons and thus does not require memory storage. The entire spiking circuit takes 20 bytes (INPS, OUTPS, SIGN, THRES, 8 x MEMB, 8 x NCONN, 8 x NCONN). Nine additional bytes are used to store random numbers, counters, and temporary variables (which are shared with the evolutionary algorithm described in the next section).

The steps of the neuron model described above are implemented as follows:

1. *Refractory period.* Check state of corresponding bit in OUTPS; if set to 1, go to step 3.

2. Compute *contribution of incoming spikes* and *membrane update.* Start with spikes from sensory neurons: increment MEMB variable by counting the number of active bits that result from the AND function of byte INPS and ICONN. Continue with spikes from positive neurons: increment MEMB variable by counting the number of active bits that result from the AND function of OUTPS and SIGN and NCONN. Finish with spikes from negative neurons: decrement MEMB variable by counting the number of active bits that result from the AND function of OUTPS and the complement of SIGN and NCONN. The decrement is stopped before MEMB goes below zero (which is readily signalled by a bit flag in a housekeeping byte of the microcontroller; the same byte can signal overflow, which does not occur here because there are few neurons in the network).

3. *Spike generation.* Compute random value for k_i and check whether MEMB is equal or larger to THRES incremented/decreased by k_i. If so (spike), set the corresponding bit in OUTPS to 1 and MEMB to zero. Otherwise (no spike), set corresponding bit in OUTPS to 0.

4. *Leakage.* If MEMB is greater or equal than the leaking constant (1), decrement it by the leaking constant.

The network is update synchronously, so that each neuron changes its state according to the state of all neurons computed at the previous cycle. Therefore, step 3 above updates only a temporary copy of OUTPS which is then moved into OUTPS once all neurons have been updated. Alternatively, one could update the network asynchronously by picking up a neuron at random and change directly OUTPS at step 3.

Once the entire network has been updated, the array of sensory spikes INPS is updated too. When run on a PIC16F628 using the embedded R/C oscillator running at 4MHz, the entire network is updated in approximately 2 ms. In some case, such as for the robotics experiment described here, the entire network can be updated faster than the time required by the physical sensors to collect information. Therefore, in between new sensory values, INPS is set to all 0's while the neurons continue to be updated using only internally generated spikes. Alternatively, one could decide to update INPS, or even the entire network, only when new sensory inputs are available.

Evolution Model and Implementation

The experiments on vision-based navigation described above suggested that functional spiking circuits can be evolved by genetically encoding only the sign of the neurons and the presence/absence of synaptic connections (see figure 2). The same genetic encoding has been used for the neuron model used here. Consequently, the genetic string of the spiking circuit described here consists of only 17 bytes: 1 byte for the sign of the neurons (SIGN), 8 bytes for its neural connections (NCONN), and 8 bytes for its sensory connections (ICONN).

The memory constraints of microcontrollers puts a severe limit on the number of genetic strings (individuals) maintained in the population. Therefore, a form of steady-state genetic algorithm, which experimentally showed to be suitable for small populations (Whitley & Kauth 1988; Syswerda 1989), has been chosen. The implementation used here, designed to maximize exploration while preserving the best solution obtained so far, works as follows:

1. Randomly generate a population of binary strings and initialize their fitness values to zero.
2. Pick an individual at random, mutate it, and measure its fitness.
3. If its fitness is equal or larger to the fitness of the worst individual in the population, write its genetic string over the old one, otherwise throw it away.
4. Go to step 2.

Mutated individuals are put back in the population even if they have the same fitness of the worst individual in order to allow for "neutral walks" (Kimura 1983) on the genetic landscape. This may be a useful property for evolution of small converged populations (Harvey & Thompson 1996).

In these experiments, each individual is mutated at three locations by toggling the value of a randomly selected bit. The first mutation takes place in the SIGN byte that defines the signs of the neurons. The second mutation occurs at a random location of the NCONN block that defines the connectivity among neurons. The third mutation occurs at a random location of the ICONN block that defines the connectivity from sensors. Mutations are performed by making an XOR operation between the byte to be mutated and a byte with a single 1 at a random location.

It is useful to store the population in the EEPROM because this type of memory can be read and written by the program just like the RAM memory, but in addition it holds its contents also when the microcontroller is not powered (at least 40 years for the microcontrollers used here). Each individual occupies a continuous block of bytes where the first byte is its fitness and the remaining bytes represent the genetic string. The very first byte of the EEPROM memory records the number of replacements made so far. Whenever the microcontroller is powered up, the main program reads the first byte of the EEPROM. If it is 0, the population is initialized (step 1 in the procedure described above), otherwise it is incrementally evolved (step 2). EEPROM memories can be written only a limited number of times (for example, the EEPROM of the microcontroller used here can be written/read approximately 10,000,000 times) and usage and temperature generate errors during reading/writing (bit values are toggled) that require error-checking routines.[4]

[4]These errors represent a free mutation operator during reading, if the corresponding error-checking routine is not used, and could substitute the XOR and random instructions mentioned above.

Figure 8: The mobile micro-robot Alice in the basic version.

Dimensions	21 × 21 × 22 mm
Weight	5 g
Max speed	40 mm/s
Power consumption	4 mW – 10 mW
System autonomy	up to 10 hours
Mechanical structure	plastic frame and PCB
Motors	2 bi-directional Swatch motors
Motion	2 wheels on the minute axis
CPU	PIC16F628 @ 4 MHz
Energy source	3 button batteries V377 (3 x 1.5V, 23 mAh)
Extra battery pack	rechargeable NiMH battery 3/V40H (3 x 1.2V, 40 mAh)
Sensors	4 infrared proximity sensors
Communication	tiny cables (debugging/analysis)

Table 1: Features and components of the Alice robot.

In the experiments described below, we have decided to keep a copy of the entire population in the free space of the RAM memory, use it for evolution, and copy it to the EEPROM at predefined large intervals.

The Alice Microrobot

The method described above has been tested on a simple evolutionary task for an autonomous micro-robot equipped with a PIC microcontroller. Alice (figure 8) is one of the smallest autonomous mobile robots in the world (Caprari *et al.* 1998). Its long energetic autonomy between 2 (regular batteries) and 10 hours (with an extra battery module) make it unique in its class. Alice is a programmable and modular robot. In its basic configuration it has 2 motors for locomotion, 4 active infrared sensors, a microcontroller and 3 button batteries. A number of modules can be added on its top, such as vision, radio, and an extra battery pack. Table details all the parts and characteristics of the version used for

Flash ROM	2 Kwords (14 bits)
RAM data	224 Bytes
EEPROM data	128 Bytes
Pins	18, (15 I/O)
Power consumption	< 2.0 mA @ 5.0 V, 4.0 MHz

Table 2: Data of the PIC16F628 microcontroller.

Figure 9: The mobile micro-robot Alice with the extra battery module providing up to 10 hour of energetic autonomy.

these experiments. Thanks to its programmability and interface with personal computers, Alice has been used in various research (Caprari, Arras, & Siegwart 2001; Siegwart *et al.* 1998) and educational projects (Caprari, Arras, & Siegwart 2000).

The microcontroller PIC16F628 from Microchip is the central part of the electronics and control of the robot. It directly drives the 2 low-power, step motors through 6 pins and serially reads the values of the analog-digital converter for sensor measurement. The PIC16F628 is a RISC (Reduced Instruction Set Computer) microcontroller whose entire package occupies approximately 2 mm^2 in the version used here. Most of the memory resources are taken by the management of the sensors and motors. The software core is composed of a very simple real time operating system which handles 5 different time-critical tasks (right and left motors, communication, sensor reading and switching) that have the priority on the spiking circuit update. The infrared sensors have a limited range of 2 to 3 cm, which is similar to the size of the robot itself. Since the sensor output is noisy, the last bit of a sensor activation that is read every 50 ms to re-initialize the pseudo-random number generator required to update the spiking circuit and run the evolutionary algorithm. For the repeated experiments described in this paper, a rechargeable battery-pack module (figure 9) has been developed instead of replacing every two-three hours the button batteries.

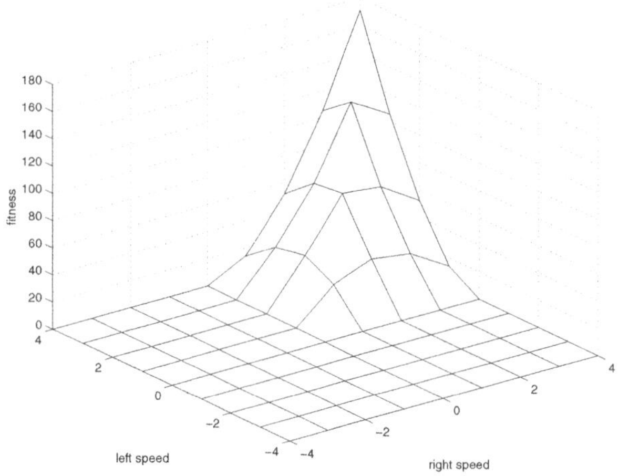

Figure 10: Fitness values shown as a function of wheel speeds (sensor activation $i = 0$). Positive values indicate forward rotation.

Evolutionary Experiments

The robot was positioned in a 25 by 18 cm arena with a wall in the middle and asked to move forward without hitting the walls. The fitness was computed and accumulated at each sensory-motor cycle using a truncated version of the often-used function to evolve straight navigation and obstacle avoidance (Floreano & Mondada 1994)

$$\Phi = V(1 - \Delta V)(1 - i)$$

where V is the sum of the speeds of the two wheels, ΔV is the absolute difference between the two wheel-speeds and i is the activity of the most active sensor. Since the Alice robot does not have wheel encoders to measure wheel rotation, the speed values used in the formula are taken from the output of the neural circuit. In addition, whenever one of the wheel speeds was in backward rotation, the entire fitness was set to 0. Finally, in order to use as few bytes of memory as possible to store the fitness value, each of the three terms were scaled so the maximal fitness value of each sensory-motor step multiplied by the total number of steps could fit in a single byte. Figure 10 plots the actual fitness values as a function of wheel speeds, provided that all infrared sensors are inactive.

The spiking circuit was composed of 8 neurons and 8 sensory units, as described above. Only the three frontal proximity sensors were used. To compensate for the steep drop-off response profile, the activation of each sensor is scaled in the range $[0, 7]$ and coded on three bits by setting active bits proportionally to the sensor activation, as shown in table . The network has a total of 8 sensor input bits. 3 bits are used for the front left and the front right sensor each and 2 bits for the center front sensor. In other words, the more active the sensors are, the more sensory units emit a spike. Furthermore,

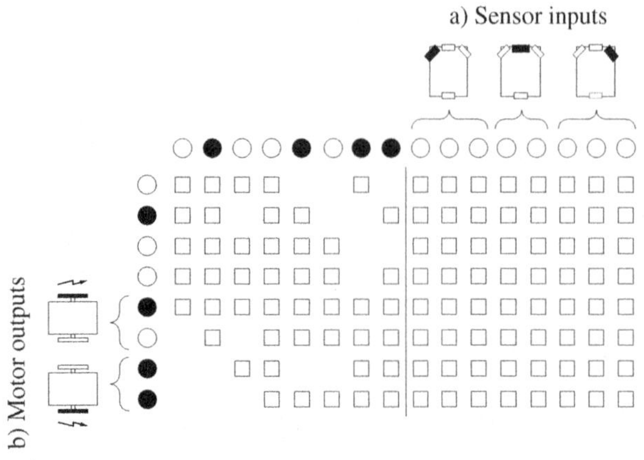

Figure 11: Architecture and connectivity of a randomly generated network. Squares indicate presence of a synaptic connections. Only the connections among neurons and neuron signs are genetically encoded and evolved. All neurons are always connected to all sensors (see text). The small drawings illustrate how the network is connected to the sensors (a) and motors (b) of the robot.

sensor value	bits set
0-1	000
2-3	001
4	011
5-7	111

Table 3: Coding of the sensory inputs for the three frontal sensors. The network has 8 sensory input bits. For the left and right frontal sensor all three bits are used while for the central front sensor the last bit is discarded.

given the simplicity of the navigation task considered here, we decided to genetically encode and evolve only the signs of the neurons and the connections among neurons, leaving all neurons fully connected to all sensors. That means that each neuron has the same sensory information and cannot tell where the walls are. Although this may slightly complicate the discovery of a good navigation stategy, it results in very short genetic encodings (1 byte for SIGN and 8 bytes for the NCONN block). The sensory input was computed anew every 28 ms during which the network was let free to update its entire state several times (once every 2ms for this microcontroller run at 4 MHz). At the end of the 28 ms, the velocities of the two wheels were set proportionally to the number of spikes emitted by the motor neurons in that interval. The speed of each wheel was the algebraic difference of the spike count of two motor neurons, one moving it forward and the other moving it backward. The result was scaled in the range $[-4, 4]$.

For each experiment, a population of 6 individuals was randomly initialized and evolved for 3 hours using on-

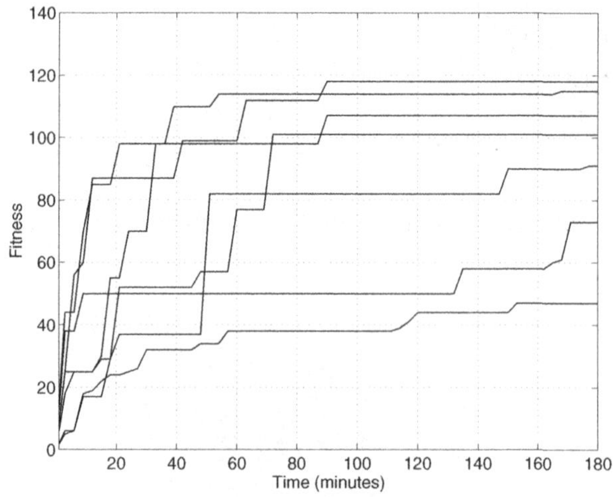

Figure 12: Fitness of the best individuals in 7 evolutionary runs. Data points are sampled every 3 minutes.

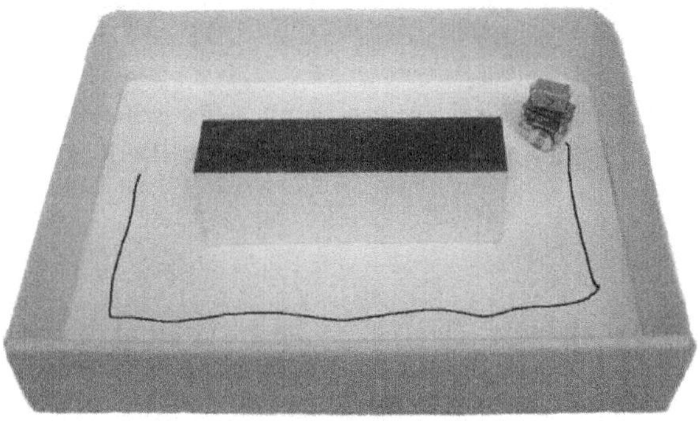

Figure 13: The robot in the environment used in the experiments. The environment is made out of white cardboard and has the dimensions 25×18 cm with an 12×3 cm obstacle in the middle. The path covered by an evolved robot in 10 seconds is over-layed from a video footage.

board batteries. Each individual was tested for 10 seconds while a random movement for 3 seconds was applied between individuals. Every three minutes the best fitness obtained so far was logged in a block of 60 bytes in the RAM and then downloaded to a computer at the end of the experiment. Figure 12 plots the fitness values of the best individuals for each of the 7 experiments with different random initializations of the population.

Figure 13 shows the path traced over 10 seconds by one of the best evolved robots with a fitness of approximately 120. Evolved robots go forward and whenever sensor activity becomes large they turn on the same side. The degree of rotation and speed depends on the sensory activity level and is quite tuned to the geometry of the environment. In best robots, this strategy corresponds to a careful wall following strategy. Small occasional jigs are most likely caused by the noise applied to the firing threshold. Robots with lower fitness values tend to rotate more frequently and thus remain in the same area of the maze, but always manage to move away from the walls.

Discussion

There is nowadays a consensus in Evolutionary Robotics (Harvey *et al.* 1997; Lipson & Pollack 2000; Nolfi & Floreano 2001) that it is necessary to search for the type of neural bricks that are most suitable for interface with the real world, recombination, and mutation. While most researchers use continuous-time recurrent neural networks, we believe that the spiking circuits described here represent a very promising alternative because not only they can display similarly complex non-linear time-dependent dynamics, but also are easily mapped into low level digital circuitery (which is more widely available and usable than analog VLSI). In addition, our preliminary experiments indicate that they may be more suitable for evolutionary systems in the real world.

The speed and reliability of the results obtained with the micro-robot Alice are also a promising indication of the efficacy of the models and methods suggested here to evolve circuits of spiking neurons in digital microcontrollers with a few bytes of memory. The experiments obtained with the vision-based Khepera robot let us think that the approach will scale up to more complex tasks and sensory inputs. Provided that enough data RAM is available, it is straightforward to implement circuits where the number of neurons and/or sensors is a multiple of 8. In addition, it is possible to build a network of several microcontrollers, each implementing a spiking module, and let them communicate spikes in parallel through input/output ports or using a time-stamp communication protocol, such as the Address-Event Representation (Lazzaro *et al.* 1993). Obviously, that would require a different type of genetic encoding, possibly one based on gene expression and module growth.

The approach described here could also find its way in a large set of intelligent devices with embedded microcontrollers. The microcontroller described here is an instance of a much larger variety of devices where the method can be adapted to meet different memory or energetic constraints. For example, to stay with the PIC family used here, the program could be easily modified to drastically improve occupation of instruction memory over data memory, or viceversa. Similarly, energy consumption could be significantly reduced by putting the microcontroller in standby mode (consumption drops to less than $1\mu A$) between sensory updates instead of continuously updating the neural network. For several applications, such as adaptive dishwashers and hairdryers, smart credit and identity cards, etc. the requirements for adaptation, non-linear dynamics, and input/output processing are likely to be less demanding than for autonomous mobile robots. In that case, much simpler spiking circuits could be evolved in less digital space.

Future work

Our current work is aimed at characterizing the dynamics and evolvability of the models described in this paper. We are also expanding the model to include vision inputs and distributed implementation across different microcontrollers within the same robot. The approach is being applied in both wheeled microrobots and flying robots where weight, size, and energetic constraints are a major issue.

In parallel, we are exploring new types of genetic encodings for evolution of adaptive and self-repairing circuits of spiking neurons implemented directly in reconfigurable digital hardware.

Acknowledgements

This work was partially supported by Swiss NSF grant No. 620-58049. Dario Floreano is grateful to Jean-Daniel Nicoud for providing the *PICgenial* board (distributed by Didel SA, www.didel.com) where the evolutionary spiking circuit was initially developed and tested.

Thanks also to Claudio Mattiussi and three anonymous reviewers for useful comments on the manuscript.

Dario Floreano conceived the model and experiments described here, implemented the evolutionary spiking network in assembler language, and wrote most of this paper. Nicolas Schoeni ported the software to the microrobot and ran the evolutionary experiments. Gilles Caprari developed the Alice microrobot, helped with the software interface and writing of this paper. Jesper Blynel helped with the experiments, logistics, and writing of this paper.

References

Arbib, M. A., ed. 1998. *The Handbook of Brain Theory and Neural Networks.* Cambridge, MA: MIT Press-Bradford Books.

Bower, J. M., and Beeman, D. 1994. *The Book of GENESIS: Exploring Realistic Neural Models with the GEneral NEural SImulation System.* New York: Springer Verlag.

Caprari, G.; Arras, K. O.; and Siegwart, R. 2000. The autonomous miniature robot alice: From prototypes to applications. In *Proceedings of the 2000 IEEE/RSJ International Conference on Intelligent Robots and Systems (IROS 2000).* IEEE Press. 793–798.

Caprari, G.; Arras, K. O.; and Siegwart, R. 2001. Robot navigation in centimeter range labyrinths. In Rückert, U.; Sitte, J.; and Witkowski, U., eds., *Proceedings of the 5th International Heinz Nixdorf Symposium: Autonomous Minirobots for Research and Edutainment, AMiRE 2001. Paderborn, Germany.* HNI-Verlagsschriftenreihe. 83–92.

Caprari, G.; Balmer, P.; Piguet, R.; and Siegwart, R. 1998. The autonomous micro robot alice: A platform for scientific and commercial application. In *Proceedings of the 9th International Symposium on Micromechatronics and Human Science.* 231–235.

de Garis, H. 1996. CAM-BRAIN. the evolutionary engineering of a billion neuron artificial brain by 2001 which grows/evolves at electronic speed inside a cellular automata machine (CAM). In Sanchez, E., and Tomassini, M., eds., *Towards Evolvable Hardware. The Evolutionary Engineering Approach.* Berlin: Springer Verlag. 76–98.

Floreano, D., and Mattiussi, C. 2001. Evolution of Spiking Neural Controllers for Autonomous Vision-Based Robots. In Gomi, T., ed., *Evolutionary Robotics. From Intelligent Robotics to Artificial Life.* Tokyo: Springer Verlag.

Floreano, D., and Mattiussi, C. 2002. Evolution and Analysis of Spiking Neural Circuits for Autonomous Robots. submitted.

Floreano, D., and Mondada, F. 1994. Automatic Creation of an Autonomous Agent: Genetic Evolution of a Neural-Network Driven Robot. In Cliff, D.; Husbands, P.; Meyer, J.; and Wilson, S. W., eds., *From Animals to Animats III: Proceedings of the Third International Conference on Simulation of Adaptive Behavior.* Cambridge, MA: MIT Press-Bradford Books. 402–410.

Gerstner, W. 1991. Associative memory in a network of biological neurons. In Lippmann, R. P.; Moody, J. E.; and Touretzky, D. S., eds., *Advances in Neural Information processing Systems 3.* San Mateo, CA: Morgan Kaufmann. 84–90.

Goldberg, D. E. 1989. *Genetic algorithms in search, optimization and machine learning.* Redwood City, CA: Addison-Wesley.

Harvey, I., and Thompson, A. 1996. Through the labyrinth, evolution finds a way: A silicon ridge. In Higuchi, T.; Iwata, M.; and Liu, W., eds., *Proceedings of the First International Conference on Evolvable Systems: From Biology to Hardware.* Tokyo: Springer Verlag.

Harvey, I.; Husbands, P.; Cliff, D.; Thompson, A.; and Jakobi, N. 1997. Evolutionary Robotics: The Sussex Approach. *Robotics and Autonomous Systems* 20:205–224.

Horiuchi, T. 2001. Neuromorphic VLSI links. Web page: www.enee.umd.edu/class/enee719t/links.html.

Indiveri, G., and Douglas, R. 2000. ROBOTIC VISION: Neuromorphic Vision Sensors. *Science* 288:1189–1190.

Indiveri, G., and Verschure, P. 1997. Autonomous vehicle guidance using analog VLSI neuromorphic sensors. In Gerstner, W.; Germond, A.; Hasler, M.; and Nicoud, J., eds., *Proceedings of the 7th International Conference on Neural Networks*, 811–816. Berlin: Springer Verlag.

Indiveri, G. 2001. A Neuromorphic VLSI device for implementing 2D selective attention systems. *IEEE Transactions on Neural Networks* in press.

Katzen, S. 2001. *The Quintessential PIC Microcontroller.* London: Springer Verlag.

Kimura, M. 1983. *The Neutral Theory of Molecular Evolution.* Cambridge, UK: Cambridge University Press.

Koenig, P.; Engel, A. K.; and Singer, W. 1996. Integrator or coincidence detector? The role of cortical neuron revisited. *Trends in Neuroscience* 19:130–137.

Lazzaro, J.; Wawrzynek, J.; Mahowald, M.; Sivilotti, M.; and Gillespie, D. 1993. Silicon auditory processors as computer peripherals. *IEEE Transactions On Neural Networks* 4(3):523–528.

Lewis, M. A.; Etienne-Cummings, R.; Cohen, A. H.; and Hartmann, M. 2000. Toward biomorphic control using custom aVLSI CPG chips. In *Proceedings of IEEE International Conference on Robotics and Automation.* IEEE Press.

Lipson, H., and Pollack, J. B. 2000. Automatic design and manufacture of robotic lifeforms. *Nature* 406:974–978.

Maas, W., and Bishop, C. M., eds. 1999. *Pulsed Neural Networks.* Cambridge, MA: MIT Press.

Mead, C. 1989. *Analog VLSI and Neural Systems.* Reading, MA: Addison-Wesley.

Nolfi, S., and Floreano, D. 2001. *Evolutionary Robotics: Biology, Intelligence, and Technology of Self-Organizing Machines.* Cambridge, MA: MIT Press. 2nd print.

Rieke, F.; Warland, D.; van Steveninck, R.; and Bialek, W. 1997. *Spikes. Exploring the neural code.* Cambridge, MA: MIT Press.

Rumelhart, D. E.; McClelland, J.; and PDP Group. 1986. *Parallel Distributed Processing: Explorations in the Microstructure of Cognition: Foundations.* Cambridge, MA: MIT Press-Bradford Books.

Siegwart, R.; Wannaz, C.; Garcia, P.; and Blank, R. 1998. Guiding mobile robots through the web. In *Workshop Proc. of IEEE/RSJ International Conference on Intelligent Robots and Systems, Victoria, Canada.*

Syswerda, G. 1989. Uniform crossover in genetic algorithms. In *Proc. of the Third International Conference on Genetic Algorithms.* San Mateo, CA: Morgan Kaufmann. 2–9.

Whitley, D., and Kauth, J. 1988. GENITOR: A different genetic algorithm. In *Proceedings of the Rocky Mountain Conference on Artificial Intelligence*, 118–130.

Meaningful Information, Sensor Evolution, and the Temporal Horizon of Embodied Organisms

Chrystopher L. Nehaniv [1,2], **Daniel Polani** [1,2], **Kerstin Dautenhahn** [1], **René te Boekhorst** [1], and **Lola Cañamero** [1]

[1]Adaptive Systems Research Group and [2]Algorithms Research Group

Faculty of Engineering & Information Sciences, University of Hertfordshire, Hatfield Herts AL10 9AB, U.K.

Abstract

We survey and outline how an *agent-centered, information-theoretic approach to meaningful information* extending classical Shannon information theory by means of utility measures relevant for the goals of particular agents can be applied to sensor evolution for real and constructed organisms. Furthermore, we discuss the relationship of this approach to the programme of freeing artificial life and robotic systems from reactivity, by describing useful types of *information with broader temporal horizon*, for signaling, communication, affective grounding, two-process learning, individual learning, imitation and social learning, and episodic experiential information (memories, narrative, and culturally transmitted information).

Meaningful Information & Sensor Evolution

This paper is a review and programmatic statement on the notion of meaningful information for organisms as temporally grounded entities. Our focus is information (in the sense of Shannon) as it is or might be employed by embodied organisms. We draw a circle from the level of reactively processed sensory information between organism and environment up through many different time-scales. The fact that an organism is able to perceive or be influenced by a given signal reveals the potential for that signal to be important to the agent. The fact that a biological agent has sensors that can detect any of a particular class of signal, such as eyes that respond to light in a certain range of wavelengths, is evidence that it is useful to do so. Similarly, effector channels, carrying information for acting on the world and for producing signals, have evolved. Sensoric and actuating channels are means for an organism to interact with and manipulate its world. Information can only be said to be *meaningful* with respect to a particular embodied organism; it then traverses such channels and is statistically helpful to the organism (Nehaniv & Dautenhahn 1998a; Nehaniv 1999a). It can be studied as such with tools of mathematical information theory (Nehaniv 1999a; Nehaniv, Dautenhahn, & Loomes 1999; Polani, Martinetz, & Kim 2001a; Tishby, Pereira, & Bialek 1999).

Organisms exist, live, act and reproduce in the field of time. Details of the fine temporal structure of an organism's behavior and enaction in the world, via its body, its sensing, and its acting, are crucial for an embodied artificial life perspective (Varela, Thompson, & Rosch 1991). The usefulness of such information to an organism may arise at various levels of increasing temporal scope: reactive, affective and/or learning, and episodic experiential information (Nehaniv, Dautenhahn, & Loomes 1999). See Table 1. As the *temporal horizon* of the relevant information that organisms use increases, this meaningful information may more profoundly affect the internal milieu, learning, the development and architecture of the organism. Acquisition of such information, increasingly temporally removed from the immediate present ('the *now*'), also requires the use of sensors and impacts on communication channels between organisms, and, in some organisms, possibly on social learning and cultural traditions. The maintenance and application of this information generally requires a corresponding internal elaboration of mechanisms, 'cognitive capacity' for learning, remembering, and representation of meaningul episodic information (whether symbolically, in internal dynamics, or encoded externally). One of the most impressive incarnations of the power of evolution is the adaptation of sensors. Information potentially useful to a biological (or artificial) organism in attaining its goals (e.g. homeostasis, survival, reproductive success, or maximizing a utility function) may play a crucial role in the *evolution of sensors* including the *channels* on which they focus; this holds as well for actuators by which the organism acts in the world, as well as for the internal architecture of the organism and how it exploits information (Nehaniv 1999a; Nehaniv, Dautenhahn, & Loomes 1999; Dautenhahn, Polani, & Uthmann 2001; Polani, Martinetz, & Kim 2001a; Liese, Polani, & Uthmann 2001). From chemical, olfactory, tactile, auditory to active (sonar), photoreceptive and general electrical and magnetic sensors, many sensoric channels are exploited to provide useful information to living agents.[1] Central to all these observations is the universality of exaptation in evolution in the sense that anatomical features and sensoric units are continually reused and reassigned for different sensoric tasks.[2] Equally important is also the observation that sensing is intimately connected with the appropriate processing of sensed information. Sensors are temporally immediate means providing access to meaningful information, but there exist other types of meaningful information of broader temporal scope (Table 1). The existence of channels of meaningful information is not given *a priori* as in the case of information theory. On the contrary, a formal approach to meaningful information allows one to address how such channels come into existence and evolve. By identifying sources and targets of information useful to agents, one has candidate endpoints of a channel of meaningful information. Over time, especially evolutionary time, channels of useful information need not remain static; however, sensory adaptation is limited by various trade-offs.[3]

---

[1]The development of photoreceptors ("eyes") shows a variety of approaches to solving different perceptual problems with 40–60 independent lines of descent and a variety of developmental levels (v. Salvini-Plawen & Mayr 1977; Liese, Polani, & Uthmann 2001). For example, the chameleon eye determines distances by active focusing (Ott & Schaeffel 1995), while pseudo-optical infrared sensors of pit vipers evolved from skin innervation common to most vertebrates (Noble & Schmidt 1937). There is a significant selection gradient towards complex eye structures (Nilsson & Pelger 1994).

[2]Some amphibians use their lungs to hear (Hetherington & Lindquist 1999). Among flies (which usually cannot hear) the parasitic fly *Ormia ochracea* uses sensory organs which originally served to determine the head position as auditory sensors by which it determines the direction of the chirping of its host (Lakes-Harlan & Heller 1992).

[3]Perhaps the most directly "Heisenbergian" one is that

An Information-Theoretic Notion of Relevant Information. An organism has to capture information from its environment via its sensors. The resources, information acquisition, as well as information processing of organisms are limited, in principle. It is therefore central to introduce an information measure that only relates to information *relevant* to the agent. The formalization of such a concept of relevant information is a central necessity to be able to develop an information-theoretical approach to understand the sensory processing of embodied organisms. In contrast to (Howard 1966)'s "information value", our notion is inherently information-theoretical and can be measured in *bits*; moreover, going further than standard practice in the field of animal communication, which also takes an information-theoretic approach, e.g. (Bradury & Vehrencamp 1998), we systematically relate *information* to *utility* for an organism. *Meaningful information* is defined here as *1) information in interaction games between an organism and its environment or between organisms mediated with respect to their own sensors and actuators and as 2)* useful *for satisfying homeostatic and other drives, needs, goals or intentions* (Nehaniv 1999a).[4] In particular, meaningful information need not be linguistically nor even symbolically mediated. It may or may not involve representations, but must arise in the dynamics realizing the agent's functioning and interaction in its environment (cf. the notion of 'structural coupling' of (Maturana & Varela 1992)), supporting adaptive or self-maintaining or reproductive behaviors, goals, or possibly plans.[5] Under evolution, sensor and actuator channels used in recurring types of interaction games will over generations to some degree be optimized in order to better achieve survival and reproduction, cf. (Adami, Ofria, & Collier 2000).

The simplest way to introduce usefulness to an agent is via a utility measure. Measuring the information-theoretic value of mutual information between the utility function and sensory information can guide behavior selection (Polani, Martinetz, & Kim 2001a). Moreover, it can provide feedback on the efficacy of the sensory information channel and thus guide the direction of modification, adaptation, or evolution of the channel itself (Nehaniv 1999a; Polani, Martinetz, & Kim 2001a). In the information bottleneck principle of (Tishby, Pereira, & Bialek 1999), relevance related to a random variable X (which one can interpret as the state of a system) is modeled by a *relevance indicator variable* Y, also a random variable, which is jointly distributed with X. Y can be seen as a (supervised) soft labeling of the states X. In this model, the relevance is completely modelled by Y. In other words, any feature in X is made relevant or irrelevant by being able to reflect the state of Y. (Tishby, Pereira, & Bialek 1999) therefore call the mutual information $I(X;Y) := H(X) - H(X|Y)$ (with $H(X)$ the entropy of X and $H(X|Y)$ the conditional entropy of X given Y) the *relevant information* in X. The information bottleneck principle now searches for a compressed random variable $\hat{X}$, obtained by a probabilistic mapping from X via a conditional mapping $p(\hat{x}|x)$. The mapping is chosen so that it compresses the information in X as far as possible (i.e. it minimizes $I(X;\hat{X})$) while keeping the relevant information in $\hat{X}$, i.e. $I(Y;\hat{X})$ at a constant level. Thus, it attempts to derive the most compact representation of relevant information (represented by Y) from the state X. If $I(Y;\hat{X}) = I(Y;X)$, compressing X into $\hat{X}$ does not lose any relevant information, and $\hat{X}$ is fully informative with respect to the relevance indicator variable Y.

In the information bottleneck model, Y is given externally, e.g. by manual labeling. How can we obtain a relevance indicator variable in the setting of agent modeling? For an organism, the choice of the right action is relevant. It is therefore natural to consider the choice of actions as relevance indicator variable (Polani, Martinetz, & Kim 2001b). Thus, for an agent model, Y is chosen as a random variable over the set of actions. To construct the probabilities for this random variable, one assumes a utility function $U(x, y)$ to be associated with an action y taken in a state x. From this utility, a joint conditional distribution $p(y|x)$ modeling the selection of an action y in a state x can be directly constructed by equiprobable selection of an optimal action in a given state (Polani, Martinetz, & Kim 2001a). Given an a priori distribution $p(x)$ for the states, one obtains a joint distribution for X and Y via $p(x,y) = p(y|x)p(x)$, from which e.g. the relevant information for an agent $I(X;Y)$ can be computed.[6] In the context of sensor evolution, X plays the role of the environment and $\hat{X}$ plays the role of the information transmitted by the sensors. The sensoric state $\hat{X}$ attempts to carry only *relevant* information and to discard the rest. This is – from a mathematical point of view – the principle that we believe underlies sensor evolution and governs its direction.[7]

between temporal and spatial resolution. For instance, flies have a higher temporal, but a lower spatial resolution than humans (Kortmann, Postma, & van den Herik 2001). Such trade-offs can arise due to aspects of light sensitivity, the necessity of depth perception, but interestingly also due to energetical causes. For example, information processing requires a certain degree of energy dissipation, of which the theoretical fundamental limit is given by thermodynamics on the quantum level (Bennett & Landauer 1985); in living systems the underlying "machinery" has a basal metabolic rate which determines the minimal rate of heat dissipation. (Kortmann, Postma, & van den Herik 2001) show that the necessity to dissipate excess heat created during the capture of visual information is a significant limiting factor.

[4]See (Nehaniv 1999a; Nehaniv, Dautenhahn, & Loomes 1999) for a discussion of the relationship of *interaction games* to *language games* (in the sense of Wittgenstein), and notions of *semiosis* (in the sense of Peirce) as a more appropriate model for an agent-based perspective on meaningful information than naive, "objectivist" notions of semantics.

[5]Similarly, these considerations apply to software agents, which might in a sense be considered embodied with respect to their particular environments as long as mutually perturbing channels exist between the agent and its environment (this ontology-independent definition of *embodiment* is due to (Quick *et al.* 1999)), with *degree of embodiment* measurable according to the complexity of the dynamics occurring between the two. The systematized, dynamic behavior of the system of agents and environment in such a case is referred to as an *interaction game*. Generalizing the ideas of Wittgenstein we say *meaning of the signals can be and can only be defined in terms of their usage in interaction games.*

[6]Unlike in the original information bottleneck principle, in the agent modeling view, the joint distribution of X and Y is not assumed a priori, but has to be constructed from the utility function.

[7]NB: Y models an action space. This space is usually much smaller than the typical sensor state space. In principle, with the present concept of relevant information, one would expect a much smaller sensor state space. However, the present version of the concept does not yet model temporal aspects of the perception-action cycle (but cf. the automata-theoretic approach of (Nehaniv 1999a; Nehaniv & Dautenhahn 1998b)). Such aspects will add complexity into the ac-

The Temporal Horizon of Organisms

The common feature of learning and memory is that they provide 'extrasensory' meaningful information by which an organism may modulate or guide its immediate or future behavior. With generally smaller temporal scope, this also occurs with moods and emotions. Remembering involves simple or complex episodic structure, and so communication of narrative (state-histories, memories, or stories) between agents can provide 'extrasensory' channels of meaningful information.[8] (See also Table 1). Martin Heidegger (Heidegger 1972) saw the state of man as being as situated in the Now, being here in the imminence of the Future in relation to the impinging Past. This *temporal horizon* seems extremely broad in humans compared to other animals, as is evidenced by our emotions such as hope and regret, concern with planning for future actions and story-telling about past or imagined events. Affect may combine with learning to provide further flexibility and widening of the temporal horizon. Extrasensory data from social learning and from narrative and historical temporal grounding help an organism escape from the present in its perception-action cycle.

Reactivity is the control of action based immediately on information from stimuli present in the surrounding environment with minimal use of internal state information. This works well for very simple behaviors such as obstacle avoidance. It even appears to be of primary importance in living systems. But for more complex behaviors a wider temporal scope in order to better contextualize actions is needed. The simplest behaviors are grounded in homeostasis, the property of biological systems to maintain key aspects of the internal milieu and interaction with the external environment within narrow ranges of important parameters. Here, *drives* realize internal informational signals (e.g. hormones), to modulate behavior. *Emotions* carry information that may be useful in behavior selection and *learning*, further freeing a biological agent from the lowest levels of blind reactivity. Information arising from experiences directly of the robot, animal or other agent itself are called "first person"; the experience of another is "second person" when this related to oneself; and "third person" information is information about objects and events from a completely external standpoint (Nehaniv 1999b). Attribution of intentions and extracting useful information from the behavior of a second person proceeds via some or all of: 0) recognition of the other as a potential interaction partner (rather than a non-agentive object); 1) the recognition of another agent as similar to the first person partner; 2) relating first person meaningful information in the present (current state) to the second person, which may make its actions, displays and signals (behavior) usefully interpretable; 3) relating first person past or temporally removed experience (narrative, stories, or history) to the second, attributing to the second person a historical groundedness and biography. Some cases of (2) are called *empathic resonance*, and are situated in the *now*, while some cases of (3) involve a wider temporal horizon – extending from the past toward the now and from the imminent future toward the now; these cases are called *biographic reconstruction* (Dautenhahn 1997; Nehaniv & Dautenhahn 1998a). Agents capable of dynamically reconstructing the biographies (histories) of the self and/or others during their life times are called *autobiographic agents* (Dautenhahn 1996; 1998). *Interaction* and *communication* between situated agents often carries second person information. *Social learning* and *imitation* can be used in the immediate temporal context to acquire behavioral competencies from others to be usefully applied later (see (Dautenhahn & Nehaniv 2002)). The *communication of experiential episodic information* (in whatever form) can be viewed as a generalization of "story-telling" or narrative intelligence, allowing organisms to benefit from one another's temporally removed experiences. In the intra-agent case this leads to a notion of *remembering* the agent's own useful experiences, and in the inter-agent case to story-telling and benefit from 'listening to' others' experiences.

Affect in Embodied Organisms. The reward or cost of experiencing reinforcing stimuli provide a uniform dimension along which an embodied organism may assess the result or desirability of action. Most attempts to introduce 'emotion-parameters' into AI systems can be seen as an attempt to solve the well-known contextualization problem in AI and robotics, i.e. to transcend simple reactivity by allowing the settings of parameters to modulate behavior, so as to respond appropriately to the given context. (Darwin 1872) realized the importance of emotions and their expression in animals, and his lead has been followed by recent builders of artificial systems.[9] The feeling of experience (*qualia*) is to be distinguished from operational notions of taxis/tropisms, drive, emotion: *Taxes* and *tropisms* are 'hard-wired' approach or avoidance behaviors in response to stimuli, e.g. turning toward light (in plants), or moving up a gradient of food (*E. coli*) or pheromone concentration. The behaviors are stereotyped and not instrumentally arbitrary, i.e. the agent does not employ and cannot even be trained to employ alternative strategies of behavior in response to the stimulus but reacts in a fixed manner. *Drives* are homeostatic and instinctual mechanisms of internal motivational change or modulators of behavior in response to internal aspects of state: hunger, thirst, sex drive, maintaining temperature and other variables within acceptable ranges while interacting to the environment. *Reinforcing stimuli* are those which an organism will work to obtain or continue (positive reinforcing stimuli), or will work to avoid or terminate (negative reinforcing stimuli). In experimental psychology, this constitutes an operational definition for the identification of stimuli as positively or negatively reinforcing. Some stimuli are reinforcing innately, i.e. by the design, nature, or default structuring of the agent, and are referred to as *primary reinforcers*. A neutral stimulus associated (by Hebbian learning) with a reinforcer becomes a *conditioned reinforcer* if the agent will either work to obtain or avoid it.

Emotion and Learning. *Emotions* for animals can be defined as changes in state in response to reinforcing stimuli (Gray 1975; Rolls 1999). Since the definition of reinforcer is operational, so is this definition of emotion. We observe that this formal definition also makes sense for artificial agents. Studies of emotion reveal that two dimensions are extremely relevant in what is understood to be required for emotion: first, emotions are *valenced*, they are either good or bad, pleasant or unpleasant; and second, they have *degree* (level of intensity). Since emotions are changes in state elicited by reinforcing stimuli, their valence and degree can serve as

tion and longer term behavior selection mechanisms, and require the consideration of memory and information of broader temporal scope in the calculation of relevant information (see below).

[8]We use the term "story" to refer to meaningful episodic information, although this substantially generalizes the usual (human-centric) notion.

[9]Emotion systems involved in feedback control of situated agents may serve to provide the grounding for embodied agents in the body/environment coupling (Cañamero 2001; Cañamero & Petta 2001).

measures of the [un]desirability of pursuing a course of action that leads to further stimuli. In particular, the course of action to take for obtaining or avoiding a reinforcing stimulus is not encoded in either the valence or degree of the emotion, yet the agent can take this valence and degree as a guide to suggest a course of action: to work (*by unspecified actions*) either to obtain or to avoid a stimulus. How the agent works to obtain a stimulus can be to choose to invoke more general strategies and behaviors generically applicable to large classes of situations: e.g. approach, grab, flee, hide. In this way, stimulus and response are de-coupled and the relations for behavior in response to a stimulus are modifiable, dynamically learnable and reconfigurable. The *common currency* of emotion can serve to modulate the control of the agent and to motivate or suppress certain responses in its interaction with the world. This provides a mechanism for a *two-process theory of learning* (Mowrer 1960; Gray 1975; Rolls 1999). A full implementation of two-process learning in constructed agents remains to be achieved. Emotions provide the utility information regarding different reinforcing stimuli and courses of action related to them, i.e. relevance information which might not be immediately accessible to sensors. Affective information is an analogue to sensory information but is pushed further "inside the body" and can have broader temporal scope for directing action and for learning than direct sensory experience.

Experiential Episodic Information. The problem of communicating episodic information can be approached by the passing of expressions (e.g., historical 'expanded' sequences of salient events). Such expressions ('histories') may refer to the agent's own experiences or the experiences of another agent. Passing such an expression corresponds to revealing part of one's autobiography or, more generally, to telling a story. Algebraic, but not yet information-theoretic, methods have been applied to communicating experiential episodic information (Nehaniv & Dautenhahn 1998b; 1998a). Such 'story-telling' is a basic element of remembering and re-construction of experiences of one agent, and is a central element in social communication of experience. Giving artificial social agents such a capacity could result in historically embedded artifacts and could help release them from the lowest levels of reactivity.

Worlds of experience have temporal horizons limited in various ways: 1) *reactive systems* – nearly completely limited to the *now*, respond quickly, with only minimal impact of internal state; 2) *affective systems* – systems whose drives, motivations, and emotions (as formally defined above) modulate their attainment of the goals (such as survival) and help contextualize behavior; 3) *learning / affective systems* – systems like those of type (2) which employ learning (e.g. two-process learning) – of course, learning without affect can and has been added to systems of type (1); 4) *post-reactive temporally grounded systems acting with respect to a broad temporal horizon*, story-telling and remembering systems, autobiographic agents, systems with various higher degrees of social and narrative intelligence. See Table 2. Post-reactive Artificial Life can be approached using encoded experiential episodic information to capture the temporal nature of being. Histories, memories, and shared stories must be grounded in the interaction games and channels of meaningful information for the particular agent. In a constructive biology of post-reactive systems, the sky over a broad temporal horizon opens for behavior arbitration to take better advantage of prior experience, anticipation, and future goals of the self and others, as well as demonstrated actions, or salient experience remembered, observed, or communicated.

References

Adami, C.; Ofria, C.; and Collier, T. C. 2000. Evolution of biological complexity. *Proc. Natl. Acad. Sci. USA* 97:4463–4468.

Bennett, C. H., and Landauer, R. 1985. The fundamental limits of computation. *Scientific American* 48–56.

Bradury, J. L., and Vehrencamp, S. 1998. *Principles of Animal Communication*. Sinauer.

Cañamero, L., and Petta, P., eds. 2001. *Cybernetics & Systems (special issue on Grounding Emotions in Adaptive Systems*, volume 32(5-6).

Cañamero, L. 2001. Building emotional artifacts in social worlds: Challenges and perspectives. In *Emotional and Intelligence II: The Tangled Knot of Social Cognition*, 22–30. AAAI.

Darwin, C. 1872. *The Expression of Emotion in Man and Animals*. London: Albemarle.

Dautenhahn, K., and Nehaniv, C. L., eds. 2002. *Imitation in Animals and Artifacts*. MIT Press / Bradford Books.

Dautenhahn, K.; Polani, D.; and Uthmann, T., eds. 2001. *Artifical Life (special issue on Sensor Evolution)*, volume 7(2). MIT Press.

Dautenhahn, K. 1996. Embodiment in animals and artifacts. In *AAAI'96 Symp. on Embodied Action and Cognition*. AAAI.

Dautenhahn, K. 1997. I could be you - the phenomenological dimension of social understanding. *Cybernetics and Systems Journal, Special Issue on Epistemological Aspects of Embodied AI* 28(5):417–453.

Dautenhahn, K. 1998. The art of designing socially intelligent agents - science, fiction, and the human in the loop. *Applied Artificial Intelligence, Special issue on Socially Intelligent Agents* 12(7-8).

Gray, J. A. 1975. *Elements of a Two-Process Theory of Learning*. Academic Press.

Heidegger, M. 1972. *On Time and Being*. Harper Torchlight Books.

Hetherington, T. E., and Lindquist, E. D. 1999. Lung-based hearing in an earless anuron amphibian. *Journal of Comparative Physiology* 184:395–401.

Howard, R. A. 1966. Information value theory. *IEEE Transactions on Systems Science and Cybernetics* SSC-2:22–26.

Kortmann, R.; Postma, E.; and van den Herik, J. 2001. Evolution of visual resolution constrained by a trade-off. *(Dautenhahn, Polani, & Uthmann 2001)*.

Lakes-Harlan, R., and Heller, K.-G. 1992. Ultrasound-sensitive ears in a parasitoid fly. *Naturwissenschaften* 79:224–226.

Liese, A.; Polani, D.; and Uthmann, T. 2001. Study of the simulated evolution of the spectral sensitivity of visual agent receptors. *Artificial Life (Special Issue on Sensor Evolution)* 7(2):99–124.

Maturana, H. R., and Varela, F. J. 1992. *The Tree of Knowledge: the Biological Roots of Human Understanding, revised edition*. Shambala Publications, Inc.

Mowrer, O. H. 1960. *Learning Theory and Behavior*. Wiley.

Nehaniv, C. L., and Dautenhahn, K. 1998a. Embodiment and memories — algebras of time and history for autobiographic agents. In Trappl, R., ed., *Cybernetics and Systems '98*, volume 2, 651–656. Austrian Society for Cybernetic Studies.

Nehaniv, C. L., and Dautenhahn, K. 1998b. Semigroup expansions for autobiographic agents. In Imaoka, T., and Nehaniv, C., eds., *Proc. First Symp. on Algebra, Languages, and Computation (Aizu, Japan – 30 October-1 November 1997)*, 77–84.

Nehaniv, C. L.; Dautenhahn, K.; and Loomes, M. J. 1999. Constructive biology and approaches to temporal grounding in post-reactive robotics. *Sensor Fusion and Decentralized Control in Robotics Systems II, Proceedings of SPIE* 3839:156–167.

	DISTANT PAST	OWN PAST	RECENT PAST	IMMEDIATE PAST	NOW	IMMINENT FUTURE	NEAR FUTURE	OWN FUTURE	FAR FUTURE
SELF		AUTOBIOGRAPHICAL REMEMBERING	MOODS & SHORT-TERM MEMORY	EMOTIONS & DRIVES	HOMEOSTASIS & AUTOPOIESIS	EMOTIONS & DRIVES	INDIVIDUAL LEARNING	INDIVIDUAL PLANS	
OTHERS	CULTURE & STORIES	BIOGRAPHICAL RECONSTRUCTION	EXPRESSION READING	EMOTIONS & DRIVES	COMMUNICATION & SIGNALING	EMOTIONS & DRIVES	INTENTION READING, IMITATION & SOCIAL LEARNING	GROUP PLANS	IDEOLOGIES
OBJECTS / GOALS		LONG-TERM MEMORY	TRACKING	EMOTIONS & DRIVES	SENSORS & EFFECTORS	EMOTIONS & DRIVES	PREDICTIVE ANTICIPATION	REASON	

Table 1. Possible Temporal Horizons for Information Useful to an Organism vs. Focus of Information.
Illustration of forms of information possibly useful for particular embodied organisms at various levels of temporal scope, directed towards self, others, or objects/goals.
Sensory and effector information in organismal pathways generally has small temporal scope, close to the '*now*'.
Affective information (emotions and drives) modulates behavioral control within a limited temporal scope.
Simple forms of *learning*, such as reinforcement learning, and immediate imitation appear to have a slightly broader temporal scope.
(However, some affective phenomena, related to learning and episodic information, may have extremely broad temporal scope.)
Episodic information may have still larger temporal scope, focusing on experiences of the self (memories, remembering, autobiographic information) or the experience of others (imitation, social learning, episodic memory, stories, narrative, culturally transmitted information); *plans* represent future-directed episodic information.

DISTANT PAST	OWN PAST	RECENT PAST	IMMEDIATE PAST	NOW	IMMINENT FUTURE	NEAR FUTURE	OWN FUTURE	FAR FUTURE
POST-REACTIVE	POST-REACTIVE	AFFECTIVE / LEARNING	AFFECTIVE	REACTIVE	AFFECTIVE	AFFECTIVE / LEARNING	POST-REACTIVE	POST-REACTIVE

Table 2. Possible Temporal Horizons for Organisms Employing Useful Information of Differing Scope.
Reactive Organisms: information in sensory and effector pathways generally has small temporal scope, yielding immediate responses.
Affective and Learning Organisms: emotions and drives modulate behavioral control within a small temporal scope, reinforcement learning, two-process learning (see text).
Post-reactive Organisms: Experiential episodic information with larger temporal scope, focusing on experiences (memories, remembering, auto-/biographic information, cultural knowledge, plans)

Misperception, Communication and Diversity

Jin Akaishi [1] and **Takaya Arita** [2]
Graduate School of Human Informatics
Nagoya University
Chikusa-ku, Nagoya, Aichi, 464-8601 Japan
[1]jin@create.human.nagoya-u.ac.jp, [2]ari@info.human.nagoya-u.ac.jp

Abstract

It is commonly agreed upon that misperception is detrimental. However, misperception might have a beneficial effect from a collective viewpoint when individuals mispercept incoming information that promotes a specific kind of behavior, which leads to an increase in diversity. First, this paper proposes our hypothesis regarding adaptive property of misperception based on the argument of the relationship between misperception and behavioral diversity, and the effects of communication on diversity. Then, a simple computational model is constructed for a resource-searching problem by using the multi-agent modeling method. We investigate both direct misperception, that are caused when obtaining information directly from surrounding environment, and indirect misperception, that are caused when obtaining information indirectly through communication by conducting simulation experiments. The experimental results have shown that misperception could increase diversity in behavior of agents, thus could be adaptive, while accurate communication could decrease a diversity of agent behavior, which might decrease fitness. This paper also discusses a correlative relationship between direct misperception and indirect misperception. We believe that the study on adaptive property of misperception based on an innovative frame of reference and a powerful methodology in the field of complex system or artificial life would shed light on fundamental issues in cognitive science, memetics and engineering.

Introduction

Diversity has been one of the central themes in various research fields. Especially, studies in complex systems or artificial life have directly or indirectly focused on diversity because these new study fields can provide an innovative frame of reference and a powerful methodology (Arita 2002). The "El Farol" bar problem is a typical economic problem devised by Arthur (1994), which focuses on diversity and self-organization of an inductive-reasoning system as a complex adaptive system. In his game, 100 agents decide at each step whether or not to go to the bar. However, space is limited and the evening is enjoyable (each agent receives a positive utility from attending the bar) if fewer than 60% of the possible 100 are present. Only information available is the numbers who came in past weeks. Each agent possesses and keeps track of an individualized set of predictors (e.g. the same as 2 weeks ago or an average of the last 4 weeks). In his experiment, agents modified the extent to which they rely on predictors, according to their accuracy in previous weeks. There is no deductively rational solution or no correct expectational model. Any commonalty of expectations gets broken up, because if all believe few will go, all will go, which would invalidate that belief. Therefore, diversity in the reasoning system will be forced to increase. The results of the experiment have shown that attendance at the bar fluctuates unpredictably around the optimal level of 60 based on an "ecology" of active predictors.

This problem can be seen as an instance of situations in which the fitness of an individual's behavior may depend upon how many others are also doing it. In general, this kind of dynamics can be generated by frequency-dependent fitness functions and has been studied especially in behavioral ecology and population genetics focusing on the equilibrium states or specific states under limited conditions. In negative frequency dependent selection, the fitness of a trait decreases as it becomes more common, in other words, less frequent traits have higher fitness than common ones. Game theory has proved that negative frequency-dependent selection favors increase in genetic diversity in populations (Maynard Smith 1982).

When we start from the El Farol bar problem and aim to explore the origin and evolution of diversity in various complex systems based on the frame of reference and a powerful methodology of the fields of complex systems or artificial life, it is very important to investigate the role of communication or languages. Suppose that there is information that promotes a rate of occurrence of a specific behavior, and that this behavior has a negative frequency-dependent property. Then, information sharing by communication would promote a rate of occurrence of a specific individual behavior and would reduce diversity in collective behavior, which could decrease collective fitness as a result.

There have been some studies that explicitly explore the origins and nature of linguistic diversity using micro-simulation models (Livingstone 2002). Arita and Koyama (1998) constructed a simple computational model for a communication system that is designed with regard to referential signaling in nonhuman animals. In their model, a conversation is realized when there are a signaler that utters a word and a listener that has the word in its vocabulary table where its meaning is equal to the meaning in the signaler's vocabulary table. However, for example, in the case of food call, some of the listeners that wish to obtain the food might nonetheless fail to do so, because of feeding competition. Therefore, a kind of negative frequency-dependent property exists in the communication system itself, and the diversity in the vocabulary table would become a subject of discussion. There is a tradeoff between the monopoly of the resources discovered by an agent itself and the sharing of the resources discovered by other agents (to be exact, sharing with risks of additional competition). The evolutionary dynamics of vocabulary sharing was analyzed based on computational experiments. The results imply that the communication system adapts to the growth of population size, mutation rate, or restriction on resources by increasing its linguistic diversity.

Origin and evolution of diversity in complex systems can be approached from different layers including reasoning systems conducted by Arthur and communication systems conducted by Arita and Koyama. We revisit the issue of the perception system as the fundamental part of the cognition system, and propose a significant aspect of it as an origin of diversity in information and behavior by constructing and running a simple computational model of misperception. We believe that this series of study on adaptive property of misperception would shed light on following challenging themes:

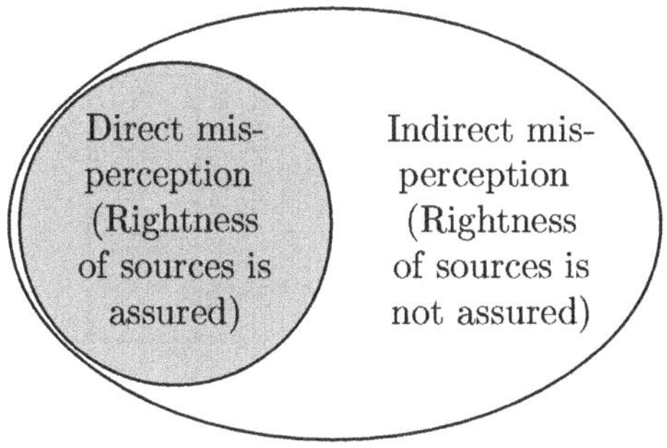

Figure 1: Classification of misperception

1. Human cognitive function — Can we comprehend imperfect human cognition or defective human discriminative organs based on evolutionary explanation?,

2. Memetics — Can we figure out the optimal mutation of the memes based on diversity in collective behavior driven by the memes in population?,

3. Engineering — May further improvements in sensors of robots lead to decrease in system performance caused by decrease in behavioral diversity of robots?

Very few computational studies have been conducted on adaptive property of misperception so far. Doran (1994, 1998) constructed a computational model in which the agents might have collective misbelief for studying ideologies in human societies. "Misbelief" is intended to mean a belief in a proposition that does not correspond to the actual state of affairs of the world (e.g. the belief in non-existing agents). He showed that collective misbelief could be beneficial to a population of agents by conducting a simulation, where adaptive property was not generated by diversity in behavior or information, and misperception never happened during communication.

Hypothesis

Misperception is defined as a process that produces a deviation between the actual state of affairs of the world and the perceived state when obtaining information about our surrounding world specifically through our senses. It is natural to suppose that collective misperception must be detrimental. However, misperception might have a beneficial effect from a collective viewpoint when individuals misidentify or mispercept incoming information which promotes a specific kind of behavior. Suppose that there is traffic information that traffic on a certain road is very light during rush hours and car drivers get the information in a moment. It is easy to imagine that cars would rush to the road and be forced to slow down after all. In this case, if a proportion of drivers would misperceive the information then the traffic jam might ease off.

Adaptive property of misperception is supposed to show itself typically as follows. First, individuals in a population share information that has a nature that promotes a specific behavior. This means that informational diversity decreases from a collective viewpoint. Then behavior of the population is homogenized and information sharing would be unadaptive as a result. On the other hand, if misperception occurs when obtaining information, the collective belief will be diversified and then collective behavior will be also diversified. In this context, misperception can be adaptive owing to diversification after all. Communication is a method of sharing information in general. In other words, communication tends to reduce the informational diversity and homogenize collective perception. Therefore, there is a possibility that misperception in communication is also considered to become adaptive.

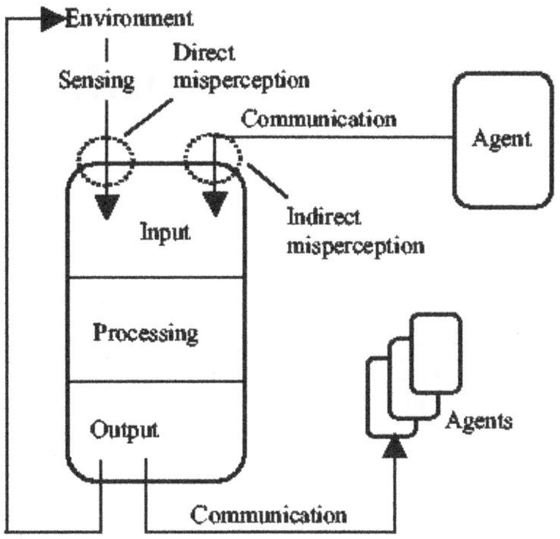

Figure 2: Information flow and occurance of misconception

Misperception can be classified into two categories depending on information sources (Figure 1). Misperception which occurs when each individual obtains firsthand information from passive and certified sources (e.g. environment) is termed *direct misperception*. On the other hand, misperception which occurs when each individual obtains indirect information from active and not-certified sources (e.g. other agents) is termed *indirect misperception*. Figure 2 shows the flow of information and occurrence of misperception. The rectangles express agents and the arrows indicate information flow.

Here, we summarize the hypothesis regarding adaptive property of misperception as follows.

1. Direct misperception of information promoting a rate of occurrence of a specific behavior increases diversity in behavior of a population, which can result in increase in collective fitness.

2. Information sharing by communication promotes a rate of occurrence of a specific individual behavior and reduces diversity in collective behavior, which could decrease collective fitness as a result.

3. Indirect misperception during communication could increase the collective fitness as is the case with 1).

4. The effects of adaptive property of misperception depend partly on specificity of the behavior accelerated by the information. If the information promotes all behaviors but one specific behavior (which means that the information prohibits a specific behavior), the effect will be minimized.

Model

Agents

Our hypothesis is tested adopting a foraging task on a two-dimensional field where autonomous mobile robots (agents)

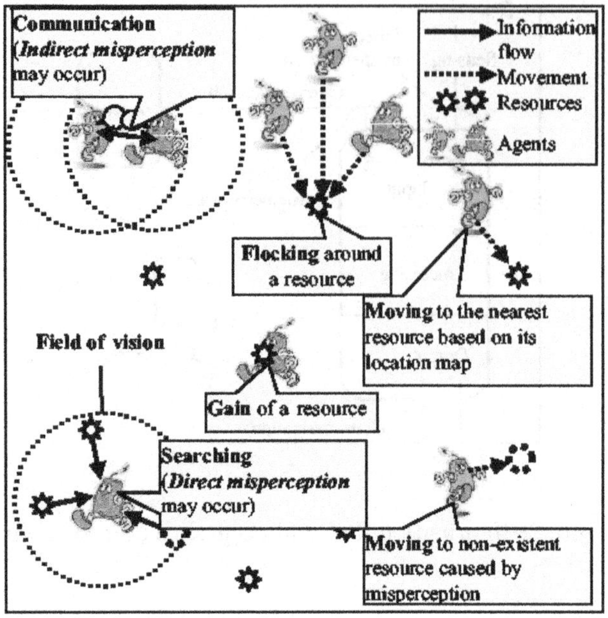

Figure 3: Model for a resource-searching problem in a virtual multi-agent world

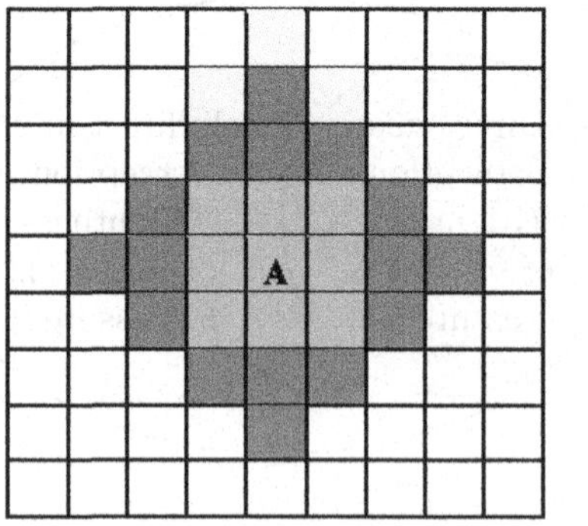

Figure 4: Field of sight (light gray cells) and movement range (light gray and dark gray cells).

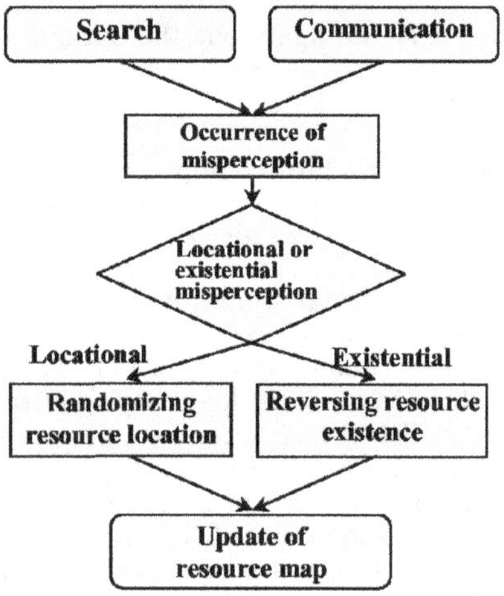

Figure 5: Information flow and occurrance of misperception.

wander in search of food resources (Figure 3) (Akaishi & Arita 2002). Resources are distributed uniformly when initializing the field. They have fixed locations during a run. When an agent gains a resource, the amount of the resource becomes zero. Then, after a turn has passed, the amount of the resource is increased at a rate of one unit per turn at the same place until the maximum value.

Agents are distributed randomly in the field at the start of each trial run. Each agent has a resource map with information about location and amount of resources. This information is obtained either by using their own visual sensors or by communicating with other agents. Each resource map is expressed by a memory area corresponding to the whole of the field, where each cell stores the information about whether resource exists or not, and the amount of the resource if it exists.

Each agent perceives both resources and the other agents in its field of sight that is represented as a square centering on the agent. The field of sight and the range of movement per turn are shown in Figure 4. "A" in this figure expresses an agent, light gray cells express the field of sight, and light gray cells and dark gray cells express the range of movement. Agents cannot move into a cell occupied by another agent. Movement speed of each agent per turn is expressed by the number of grids. Agents perceive existence/nonexistence of resources in their field of sight, and in case of existence, they obtain information of the location and the amount of them by using their own visual sensors. Recognized information is overwritten in their resource maps.

We have conducted simulation experiments under following two conditions:

1. Agents always have one-to-one communication with other agents if possible,
2. Agents never have communication with other agents.

They communicate the information of the location and the amount of the resources among them in the former case. The information of nonexistence is not communicated. Communicated information is overwritten in their resource maps even if new information conflicts with old information. For example, an agent recognizes a resource at location A by using communication. Later, if the agent itself recognizes nonexistence of the resource at location A, this new information is overwritten in its resource map. In the case that information that comes from visual sensors and information that comes from the other agents through communication are contradictory to each other, the former is given priority over the latter.

Each agent moves toward the nearest resource based only on the information of its own resource map, which does not depend on the amount of resources. A target resource is selected randomly if more than one resource are at equal distances. Agents will perform a random walk when their resource maps have no information of resource existence. When agents move to the cell where a resource exists, they get all of the resource.

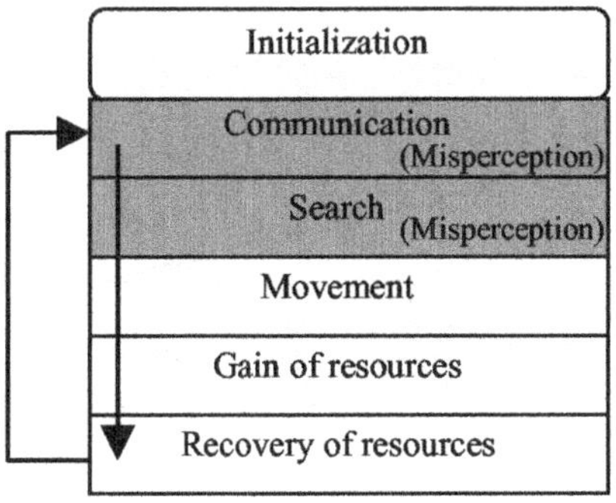

Figure 6: Flow of the process.

Occurrence of misperception

There is a possibility that misperception occurs when agents get information by their own visual sensors or through communication (Figure 5). Three kinds of information concerning the resources (location, existence/nonexistence, and amount) are communicated. We have conducted simulation experiments on the condition that misperception can change the information of location or existence/nonexistence. When misperception occurs, one of the following two types of information is selected randomly with equal probability as follows. In the case that misperception of location happens, random location concerning the communicated resource is stored in the resource map of the agent while the other information is communicated precisely. In the case that misperception of existence happens, existence-nonexistence is reversed concerning the communicated resource.

Algorithm

Simulation experiments are conducted as follows (Figure 6).

1. Resources and agents are distributed uniformly over the field.
2. Agents communicate with other agents within their sight.
3. Misperception might occur with a given probability ("indirect-misperception rate").
4. Agents might perceive resources. If so, misperception might occur with a given probability ("direct-misperception rate").
5. Each agent moves toward the nearest resource based on information of its own resource map. Agents with no resource in their resource maps move in a random direction at the specified speed.
6. Agents get the resources existing in their own cells. Resources will recover gradually in the same location.

The above cycle from 2) to 6) is termed "a turn" and will be conducted again and again.

Simulation experiments

Experimental setting

We conducted following five simulation experiments so as to examine the effects of misperception on the behavior of the population in relation to the effect of communication.

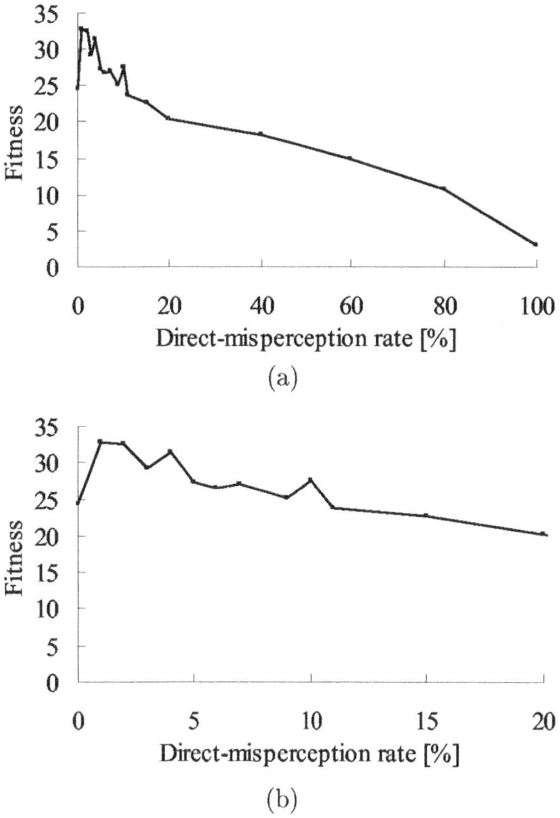

Figure 7: Flow of the process.

Experiment 1: Effects of direct misperception.

Experiment 2: Effects of communication.

Experiment 3: Effects of indirect misperception.

Experiment 4: Effects of indirect and direct misperception.

Experiment 5: Effects of behavioral specificity.

Experiments were conducted using following parameters:

Number of turns in a trial run:	10000
Field size:	50 × 50 (non torus)
Number of agents:	150
Sight:	3 × 3
Speed:	3 / turn
Resource density:	5 %
Maximum amount of each resource:	1
Number of trial run (Experiment 1, 2, 5):	6
Number of trial run (Experiment 3, 4):	60

The amount of the average obtained resource by all agents is evaluated as a fitness value of the population in all of the experiments in this paper, and some graphs have more sampling points than other graphs in order to search for peaks.

Effects of direct misperception

Agents searched for resources by using their own visual sensors, and didn't communicate with other agents. Thus, only

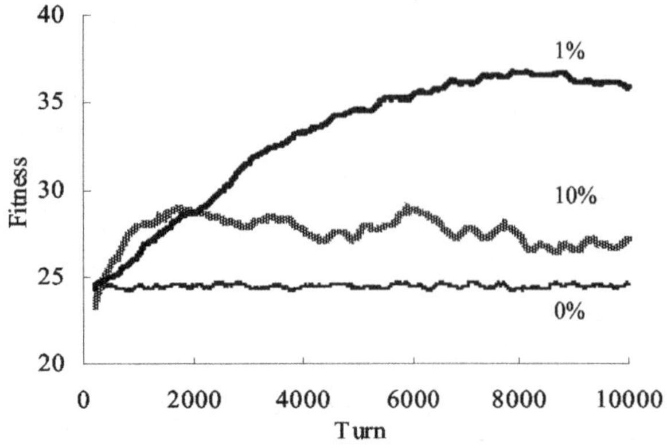

Figure 8: Flow of the process.

direct misperception could happen in this experiment. We changed direct-misperception rate from 0% (without misperception) to 100% (with misperception at all times), and investigated effects of direct misperception.

The results of the experiment are shown in Figure 7 and 8. Figure 7 shows the effect of direct misperception on fitness when varying direct-misperception rate. It is shown that the fitness has a peak when direct-misperception rate is around 1%. The fitness in the case that direct misperception is 1% is about 35% greater than the fitness in the case that no direct misperception happened (0%). The reason is supposed to be that the search range was enlarged because direct misperception diversified individual behavior. In this context, it is considered that misperception could contribute to adaptivity.

Figure 8 shows time transition of fitness by moving average, where each line corresponds to each value of direct-misperception rate. Before 2000 turns, fitness in the case that direct-misperception rate is 10% is larger than the one in the case with 1%. After that, fitness was stable at the value around 28. The cause of this result is that behavioral diversity made by direct misperception (10%) was larger than diversity in the case with 1%, which caused the search area to be wider. On the other hand, however, the fitness in the case with 10because agents could not surely gain resources because the misperception rate was too high. The reason of slight decrease after 8000 turns in the case with 1% is supposed to be that almost all locations of resources had been found by 8000 turns and thereafter the negative effect of misperception began to dominate the system to a certain extent.

Effects of communication

We introduced communication among agents in this experiment. Agents can obtain information by using their own visual sensors or by communicating with other agents. Misperception during communication was not investigated (indirect-misperception rate is 0%) in this experiment in order to grasp the effects of communication itself. We examined the influence of varying direct-misperception rate from 0% to 100%.

The results of the experiment are shown in Figure 9 and Figure 10, where they are compared with the result of the previous experiment. Figure 9 shows that the fitness was reduced by several percents by introducing communication among agents when direct-misperception rate is less than about 20%. The reason is supposed to be that the diversity of collective behavior was reduced owing to the share of the information concerning resources in the population. In this context, it is considered that communication can be unadaptive regardless of the truth of its content. It was also shown that introduction of accurate communication slightly increased the fitness when direct-misperception rate was 0%, though it is not easy to see from this figure.

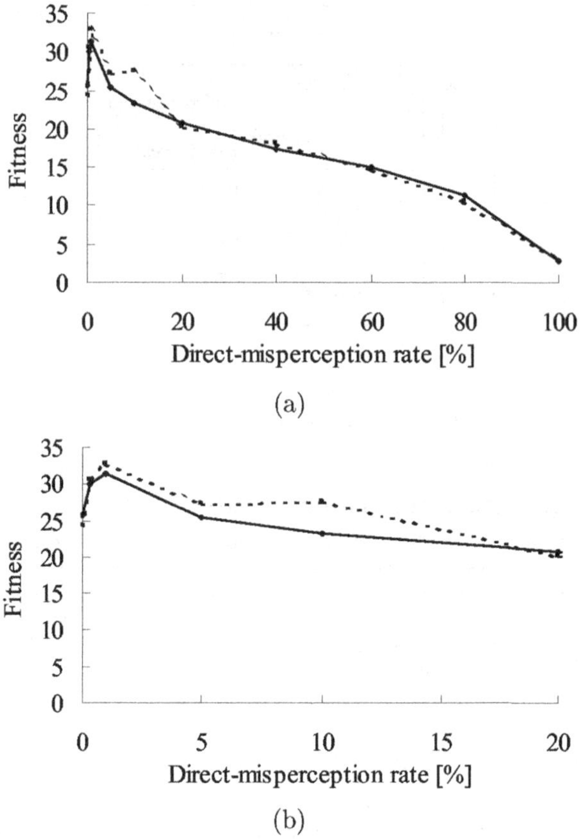

Figure 9: Flow of the process.

Figure 10 shows the transition of the fitness. We see from this figure that the fitness fell with progress of time when direct-misperception rate was 1% and 10%. This means that communication propagated the information and reduced adaptive diversity of collective behavior generated by direct misperception which was investigated in the previous experiment. The reason of small decrease after 7000 turns in the case with 1% is supposed to be that the negative effect of misperception was accelerated by communication in latter turns.

Effects of indirect misperception

We investigated the effects of indirect misperception on fitness under the condition that direct-misperception rate was fixed at 0% and indirect-misperception rate was varied between 0% (receivers receive exactly what senders have sent) and 100% (receivers always misperceive what senders have sent).

The results of the experiment are shown in Figure 11. The fitness was increased about 1.5% compared with the case of accurate communication when indirect-misperception rate was less than 40%. This means that indirect misperception can prevent communication from decreasing the diversity in collective behavior, and can make communication adaptive.

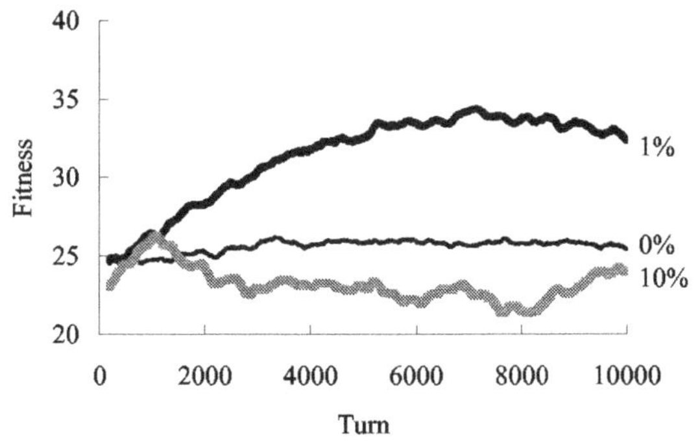

Figure 10: Flow of the process.

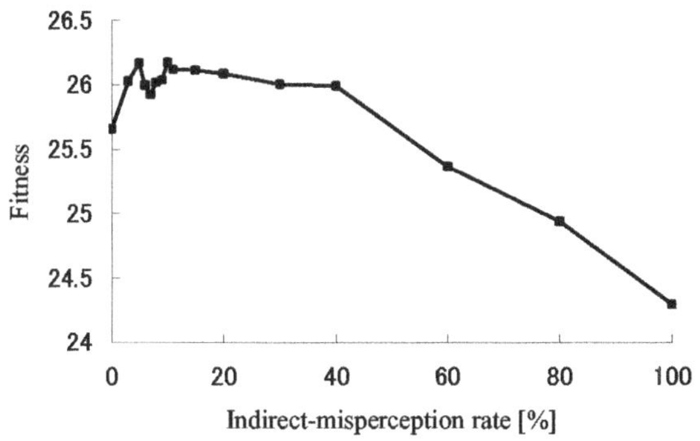

Figure 11: Flow of the process.

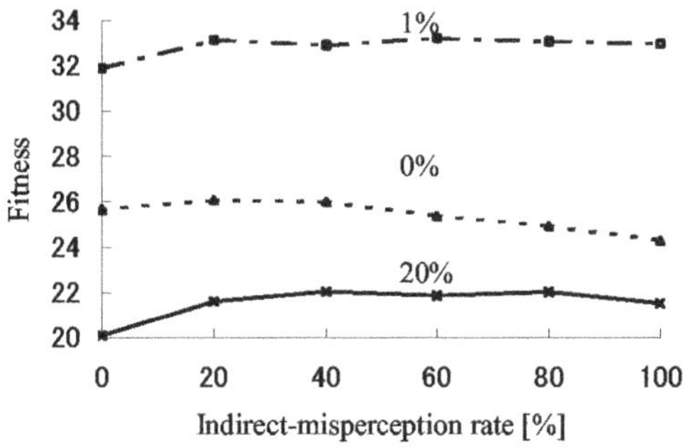

Figure 12: Flow of the process.

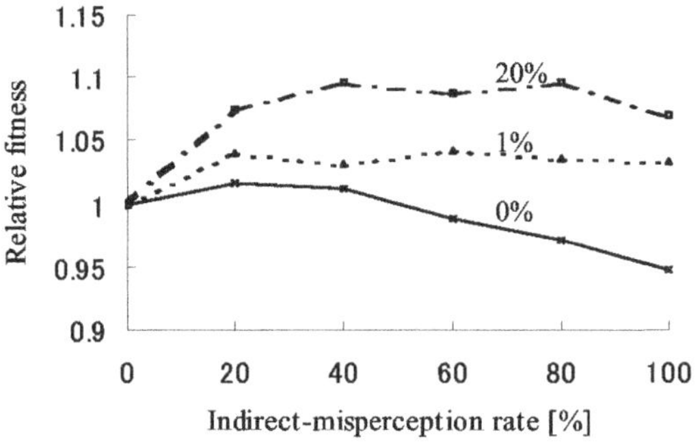

Figure 13: Flow of the process.

Correlative effects of direct and indirect misperception

We investigated the fitness when direct-misperception rate was varied from 0% to 20%, and at the same time indirect-misperception rate was varied from 0% to 100%. The result of the experiment which applied direct misperception and indirect misperception simultaneously is shown in Figure 12. The fitness when direct-misperception rate was 1% and indirect-misperception rate was 20% is approximately 1.5% greater than the fitness when direct-misperception rate was 1% and agents have no communication (this case is shown in Figure 7). In other words, the results of the case when both direct and indirect misperception were allowed could be better than the case when either of the misperception was allowed. This fact implies that both of the misperception has mutually complementary effects on fitness of collective behavior.

Next, we investigated relative fitness when indirect-misperception rate was varied compared with the case that it was fixed at 0%. To do this, Figure 12 was converted to Fig 13, in which the fitness when indirect-misperception rate was 0% was normalized to 1 in each case. Figure 13 shows the tendency that the more the direct-misperception rate is, the larger the effect of indirect misperception becomes. This figure also shows a tendency that the optimal indirect-misperception rate becomes larger as direct-misperception rate increases, which is contrary to what we expected. Our understanding is as follows. When direct-misperception rate is large, communication makes more false information be shared in population and thus the fitness of population becomes low. Therefore, larger rate of indirect misperception is necessary for being optimal because it prevents population from sharing false information.

Effects of behavioral specificity

We examined the effects of misperception of information that prohibits a specific behavior in this experiment. For this purpose, poisons were introduced into the model as the source of prohibiting information. The information about poisons was also stored in the resource maps of the agents. Misperception might occur when obtaining the information about a poison, as is the case with the information about resources and empty spaces. Each agent didn't move to the poison if the agent had its information in its resource map. When an agent went into a cell where a poison existed, the fitness of the agent was reduced by the amount of the poison and at the same time, the amount of the poison became 0. The value of the fitness could be negative in this experiment. The poison would recover gradually in the same cell.

Some of the parameters were modified in this experiment as follows.

Field size:	30×30
Number of agents:	50
Number of poisons:	45
Maximum amount of each poison:	1

First, we investigated relative fitness when direct-misperception rate was varied from 0% to 100% compared with the case that it was fixed at 0%. Agents searched for resources by using their own visual sensors, and didn't com-

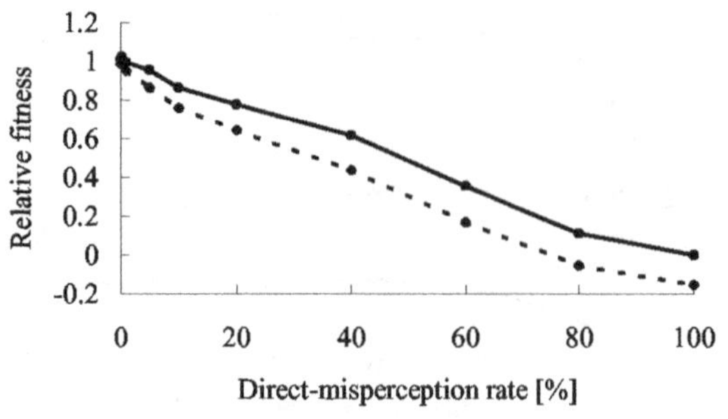

Figure 14: Flow of the process.

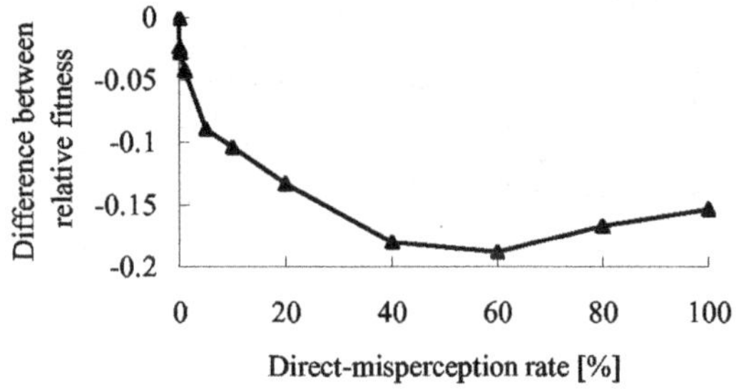

Figure 15: Flow of the process.

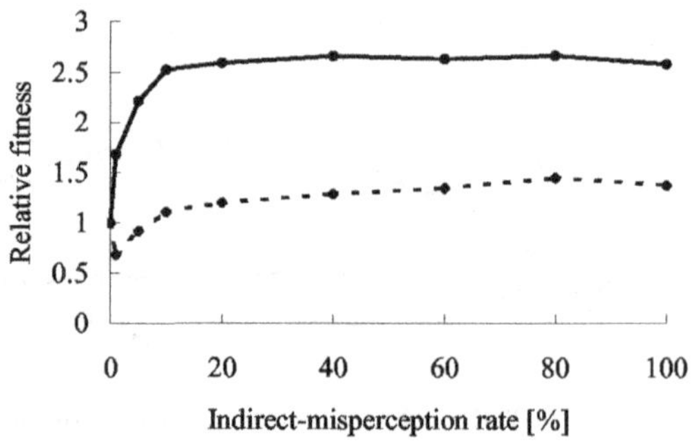

Figure 16: Flow of the process.

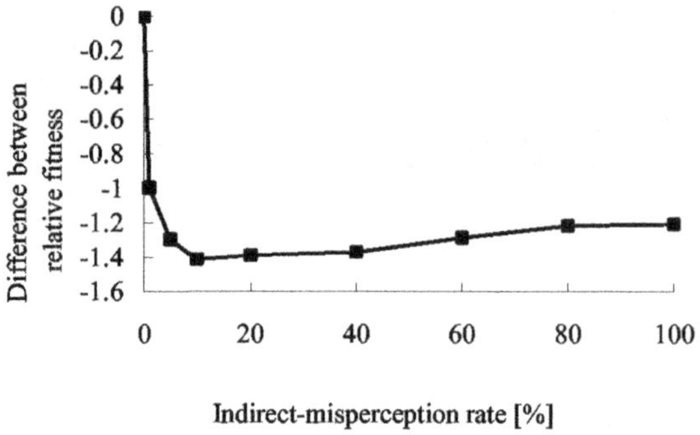

Figure 17: Flow of the process.

municate with other agents. Thus, only direct misperception could happen in this experiment. Figure 14 shows that introduction of poisons reduced the relative fitness to approximately 90%.

The fitness in the case without poisons has a peak when direct-misperception rate is around 0.2%, which shows the adaptive property of direct misperception though it is difficult to recognize it in this figure. On the other hand, the fitness in the case with poisons is the highest when indirect-misperception rate is 0%. In order to exclude the effect of the direct misperception regarding the resource, the former was subtracted from the latter. The result (Figure 15) is supposed to express approximately the effect of the direct misperception concerning the poisons. It has been shown that direct misperception has no adaptive property in the case that the objects were poisons.

Next, indirect misperception was examined. Figure 16 shows the difference between the case with poisons and the case without poisons when indirect misperception could occur. We see that the difference is larger than the one when direct misperception could occur. Figure 17 shows that direct misperception has also no adaptive property.

The difference between (food) resources and poisons is the specificity of the behaviors accelerated by the information about it. Possession of the information about a resource accelerates a specific behavior while possession of the information about a poison relatively accelerates broad range of behaviors except a specific behavior. Therefore, it can be said that this experiment supports the fourth property of the misperception in the hypothesis.

Conclusion

The role of random noise has been widely discussed in the field of complex systems and artificial life. For example, it is well known that introduction of noise improves the robustness of the cooperative relationships between players in the Iterated Prisoner's Dilemma game. This study focuses on the significant role of random noise at the level of perception system as the fundamental part of the cognition system.

In this paper, our hypothesis regarding the adaptive property of misperception was proposed, and simulation experiments were conducted so as to test it. The experimental results have shown quantitatively that misperception could increase diversity in behavior of agents, thus could be adaptive, or, to be more accurate, could contribute to adaptivity. (Hypothesis 1, 3). On the other hand, accurate communication could decrease a diversity of agent behavior, which might decrease fitness (Hypothesis 2). The paper has discussed a complex relationship between direct misperception and indirect misperception, besides detailed description of the simulation experiments. The last experiment has shown opposite results between the case with poison and the case without poison, which supports the hypothesis on behavioral specificity in adaptive property of misperception (Hypothesis 4).

The results of the experiments are deeply linked with the discussions in the field of memetics (Blackmore 1999). If we take meme-centered view, misperception originates in information itself (memes) while it has been assumed that the ability of the agents defines the misperception rate in our model. Dawkins argues that fidelity (replicate accurately), fecundity (easy to replicate), and longevity (last a long time) are the ways in which a meme is defined as successful (Dawkins 1976). The results of the experiments based on agent/gene-centered view in this paper are inconsistent with the first property (fidelity). It is a remarkable point that the inconsistency has been uncovered in the syntactic level and not in the semantic level (contents of the information) though there have been a variety of discussions over gene-meme competition (e.g. celibacy) (Bura 1994).

Also, in one sense, what the results of the experiments have shown is the antithesis of modern engineering. For example, the precision of sensors in robots has been improved without question. However, there is a possibility that improvement of sensors unexpectedly causes the decrement in total performance of distributed system of autonomous robots owing to the decrease in behavioral diversity in robots. At any rate, emergence of adaptive property of misperception in multi-robot systems depends on many factors including the sort of the task to be accomplished by robots and the ability of robots to communicate with other robots and to allocate jobs among robots. We are now developing a multi-robot system as a test bed for testing the hypothesis in the real world.

References

Akaishi, J., and Arita, T. 2002. Multi-agent simulation showing adaptive property of misperception. In *Proc. 2002 FIRA Robot World Congress*, 74–79.

Arita, T., and Koyama, Y. 1998. Evolution of linguistic diversity in a simple communication system. *Artificial Life* 4(1):109–124.

Arita, T. 2002. *Artificial Life: A Constructive Approach to the Origin/Evolution of Life, Society and Language.* IGAKU-SHUPPAN, 2nd edition. in Japanese.

Arthur, W. B. 1994. Inductive reasoning and bounded rationality. *American Economic Review* 84:406–411.

Blackmore, S. 1999. *The Meme Machine.* Oxford University Press.

Bura, S. 1994. MINIMEME: of life and death in the noosphere. In Cliff, D.; Husbands, P.; Meyer, J. A.; and Wilson, S. W., eds., *Animals to Animats 3 (Proc. the Third International Conference on Simulation of Adaptive Behavior.)*, 479–486. MIT Press.

Dawkins, R. 1976. *The Selfish Gene.* Oxford University Press.

Doran, J. 1994. Modeling collective belief and misbelief. In Keane, M.; Cunningham, P.; Brady, M.; and Byrne, R., eds., *Proc. AI and Cognitive Science*, 89–102. Dublin University Press.

Doran, J. 1998. Simulating collective misbelief. *Journal of Artificial Societies and Social Simulation* 1(1). http://www.soc.surrey.ac.uk/JASSS.

Livingstone, D. 2002. The evolution of dialect diversity. In Cangelosi, A., and Parisi, D., eds., *Simulating the Evolution of Language.* Springer Verlag. 99–118.

Maynard Smith, J. 1982. *Evolution and the Theory of Games.* Cambridge University Press.

ALife Investigation of Parental Investment in Reproductive Strategies

Steven Mascaro, **Kevin B. Korb** and **Ann E. Nicholson**
School of Computer Science and Software Engineering
Monash University, VIC 3800, Australia,
{stevenm,korb,annn}@csse.monash.edu.au

Abstract

Many organisms nourish and care for their offspring, boosting the offspring's reproductive potential. Trivers (1972) recognized that such parental investment, when made differentially across the sexes, could explain the existence of sexually dimorphic behaviour. However, parental investment in nature is difficult to measure, and explanations involving parental investment are hard to verify. Here we use an ALife simulation to investigate the effect of explicit, numerical parental investments on two reproductive strategies of interest — consensual mating and rape. With some preliminary empirical results, we demonstrate the potential of an ALife approach to evolutionary psychology.

Introduction

Organisms reproduce in many ways, raising the question of why organisms develop one form of reproduction over another. Parental investment theory can help answer such a question. Parental investment (PI) is defined by Trivers as any investment by a parent in an offspring that increases the offspring's chance of survival and reproduction, at the cost of investing in other offspring (Trivers 1972). For many species, members of the same sex typically invest in similar ways, while investments across the two sexes differ greatly. Trivers argues that these sex-based differences in PI are the ultimate causes of behavioural sexual dimorphism.

PI is hard to measure in the real world, complicating efforts to test PI theory. Also, most applications of the theory have focused on dimorphism in consensual mating (or just *mating* when the notion of consent does not apply). We apply PI theory to the reproductive strategies of consensual mating and rape and in the process demonstrate a new ALife method of investigation for studies in evolutionary psychology. To this end, we employ our simulation to explore how numerically-expressed PIs corresponding to various actions affect reproductive strategies.[1] We examine how varying the PI across the sexes produces sexual dimorphism with particular regard to consensual mating and rape.

Evolutionary psychology, particularly in the study of rape, is a contentious field. Along with most evolutionary psychologists, we take the view that behaviour is a product of many historical factors, with evolution being one. We suggest that the use of ALife simulations in evolutionary psychology give us the means to experiment with these factors. Such simulations could provide important insights not possible through traditional research or mathematical techniques. Our efforts here are primarily aimed at demonstrating the potential of ALife simulations in evolutionary psychology.

In the following section we review the relevant background on PI theory and evolutionary biology. We then detail briefly the ALife environment, before describing our ALife experiments and their results.

[1]The ALife environment is an extension of the one we have used in previous work investigating suicide as an evolutionarily stable strategy (Mascaro, Korb, & Nicholson 2001).

Background

PI theory began with Bateman (1948) and his experiments on Drosophila, but was formally described by Trivers (1972). Parental investment is "any investment by the parent in an individual offspring that increases the offspring's chance of surviving (and hence reproductive success) at the cost of the parent's ability to invest in other offspring."

Fundamental to PI theory has been the sexually distinct PIs evident in nature. There have been several suggestions as to why the sex-based differences in PIs might occur. Trivers speculated that the already large physiological PI made by the female in most species compels her to invest further, while the minimal PI made by the male in no way binds him to providing more. This idea was contested, however, by Dawkins & Carlisle (1976), who asserted that further PI must be assessed solely on the additional reproductive benefit that extra investment confers. Instead, they proposed another hypothesis: where one parent suffices to raise an offspring, the sex that can desert first, will. For instance, amongst teleost fish where females have the first opportunity to desert, paternal care is common, even though the female provides the initially larger investment. However, empirical results with other species do not support the desertion hypothesis (Krebs & Davies 1987). A popular alternative explanation for differential PI is that of Williams (1975): if one parent finds itself in the vicinity of the offspring, due to another preadaptation, the basis for further parental care is established.

Maynard Smith (1977) analyzes parental investment theory from a game-theoretic perspective, giving equations for conditions that would lead to desertion by either one or both parents. This gives mathematical form to the scope and consequences of parental investment theory.

Recently, a handful of researchers have studied human rape on an evolutionary basis (Shields & Shields 1983; Thornhill & Palmer 2000). They employ the concepts of female choice and male competition to explain the existence of rape, implicitly appealing to notions of PI. A problem common to all investigations of PI in nature, including these, is the difficulty of assessing the amount of investment made. How can one quantify the cost to parents of feeding and protecting their offspring and the benefit offspring derive? Game-theoretic models can provide greater detail to our analyses, however they deal with a form of PI very distant from that in nature. Simulation, however, can provide an alternative for testing our hypotheses in which parental investments are clear.[2]

The ALife Environment

The agents of our ALife simulation live on a 40×40 board. Only one entity (an agent or food) can inhabit a cell on this board at any given time. A certain amount of food is generated per cycle for the agents to eat. Agents have various numerical properties such as health, age and maximum age of death and nominal properties such as sex. Agents also have a genotype that specifies their behaviour probabilistically, from

[2]The epistemological problems posed by ALife simulation are important, impacting far more than our study. We will be exploring them in future.

	Female H.E.	Util	Male H.E.	Util
Mate				
With Birth	$-PI$	15	$-PI$	15
No Birth	−16	15	−16	15
Unsuccessful	−5	−5	−5	−5
Request Denied	0	0	0	0
Rape (Victim)				
With Birth	$-(2PI-10)$	−70	−10	−70
No Birth	−10	−70	−10	−70
Unsuccessful	−10	−10	−10	−10
Rape (Rapist)				
With Birth	$-(2PI-10)$	5	−10	5
No Birth	−10	5	−10	5
Unsuccessful	−60	−15	−60	−15

Table 1: The health effects and utilities associated with reproductive actions. *PI* stands for the value of the parental investment parameter for the current simulation.

a set of simple actions, based on their environment. Each action an agent takes has an effect on that agent's health (physical well-being) and utility (psychological reward — which feeds into health), while some actions also affect the health and utility of other agents. The specific effects of each action on health and utility are detailed further on.

The simulation uses a *cycle* as a convenient unit of time; in each cycle all agents currently alive are given (in random order) a chance to perform some action. An agent's age is measured in cycles since birth. Its maximum age is randomly selected (at birth) from the normal distribution $N(100, 100)$. A period of 5 cycles in the simulations is called an *epoch*; this unit of time is provided for statistics and used exclusively in the presentation of empirical results.

Agents are either male or female, sex being randomly determined at birth. Since there are no gametes, we define the male sex to be the one that invests least after mating, which is consistent with most species in nature.

Genotype. The decision of which action to perform in a cycle is determined by the agent's chromosome. Viewed functionally, the chromosome accepts a set of observations for the agent and returns its action. Structurally, the genotype is a set of production rules or condition-action pairs: each observable has a corresponding conditional. A condition has a fixed comparitor (e.g., *greater than*) and an evolvable value in [0,1]. An example might be '$x > 0.4$', where x is self-age (the agent's age) divided by the maximum age. There are seven production rules in each chromosome: two for self-sex (one rule that matches females and another that matches males) and five conditioning upon self-health, self-age, self-sex, local population density, local food density and whether a mating has been requested. At each cycle every rule's condition is checked for a match, in random order. Given a match, the rule's probability distribution is used to choose an action.

Recombination of the production rules is straightforward, using multi-point crossover of the two parent chromosomes at gene boundaries. Condition values and action probabilities are subject to Gaussian mutation after recombination.

Phenotype. There are six basic actions available to agents: eat, walk, turn, rest, consensual mate and rape. For brevity, consensual mating will be called 'mate'. A table of the health effects and utilities for reproductive actions can be seen in Table 1. These are not the only possible values that could be used, however we do suggest that they are plausible across a broad range of environments of interest. For all actions except rape, there is no difference between the sexes in the effect on health or utility. Agents choose neighboring entities for actions randomly. To ensure initial stability, generated genetic probabilities for eating and mating are initially high, but can freely evolve thereafter.

Parental Investments. The simulation model represents PI directly by health flows from parent to offspring. In these simulations, the PIs are fixed for each sex.

Mating. Mating is the basic reproductive action. To mate, an agent requests mating another agent, who can then accept or reject. If the agents are of opposite sex and have sufficient health, they produce an offspring. In these experiments, unless otherwise noted, both male and female provide the same PI after mating.

Rape. Rape forces the victim to copulate when an initiating agent chooses. The victim suffers a heavy utility penalty, while the perpetrator obtains a small positive utility. Victims and perpetrators can be either male or female. We allow attempted rapes to fail through the parameter, rape-completion probability (*rcp*). If the rapist and victim are of opposite sex, and the victim has sufficient health, the rape-completion probability is the chance that a rape results in conception.

Experiments

We investigated two factors affecting rape rates and sexual dimorphism: female PI and the *rcp*. All results show the average of 30 simulation runs, unless otherwise stated.[3]

Figure 1 shows the effect of these two parameters on the rape rate. Each graph represents an *rcp* of (a) 0.1 (b) 0.25 and (c) 0.5, while within each graph, along the x-axis, are the various female PI levels (the fixed male PI is 10 health units).[4] The combined PIs by both sexes after mating also increases to the same degree but with both sexes contributing equally. The graphs show the average rates for rape attempts for females and males over the last 400 epochs of a 2000 epoch run, after equilibrium has been achieved. We can see that at *rcp*=0.1, regardless of how large we set female PI, there is little discernible difference between the rape rates.

More detail about the differences in male and female behaviour can be seen in Table 2. This table shows average female rates for eating, mating and rape actions, together with the percentage changes to reach the male rate (in parenthesis), for each female PI level. As the female PI increases (i.e., as the combined male and female PI increases), the rates of eating go down, while the mate and rape rates go up. This can be explained by agents being born with more health, and so needing to eat less in general.

As we increase the *rcp* (*rcp* = 0.25 in Figure 1(b)) differences between male and female rape rates become apparent as the female PI levels increase. These statistically significant differences are again apparent across all actions as shown in the middle section of Table 2. The results for the *rcp*=0.5 (see Figure 1(c) and bottom section, Table 2) extend this trend. We can see that very strongly sexually dimorphic behaviour results, even with the lowest setting for female PI.

[3]A fuller description of our experiments can be found in (Mascaro, Korb, & Nicholson 2002).

[4]The PIs are in units of health. For context, the distribution of female health has roughly a mean of 800 and a s.d. of 500, while males have a similar s.d., but a mean health 100 units higher.

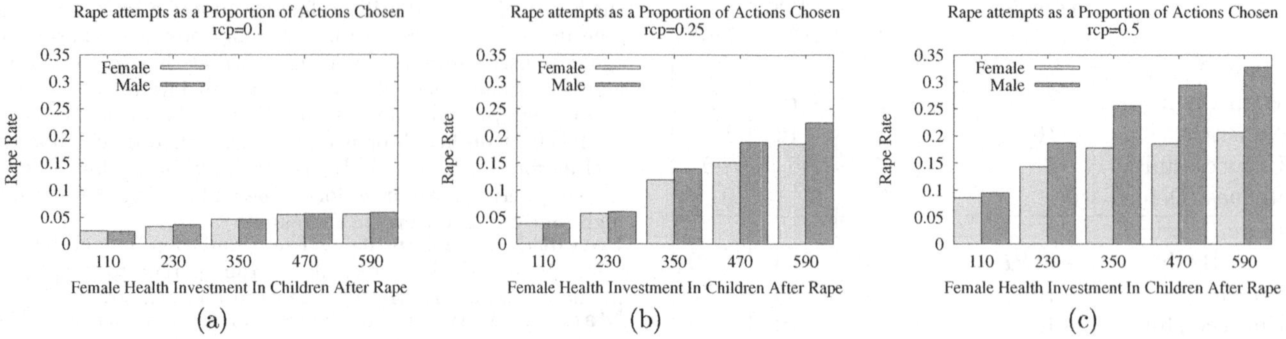

Figure 1: Rape rates for different levels of female PI (male PI = 10), for rcp = (a) 0.1 (b) 0.25 and (c) 0.5.

female PI	Eat	Mate	Rape
rcp=0.1			
110	0.547 (−1.0%)	0.266 (1.8%)	0.025 (−1.1%)
230	0.487 (−0.7%)	*0.311 (−0.3%)*	0.033 (1.8%)
350	0.422 (−1.9%)	0.362 (0.7%)	*0.046 (−0.6%)*
470	*0.377 (−0.2%)*	*0.384 (−0.2%)*	0.055 (1.0%)
590	0.361 (0.5%)	0.392 (0.7%)	0.056 (3.2%)
rcp=0.25			
110	0.562 (−2.2%)	*0.245 (0.7%)*	*0.038 (−0.3%)*
230	0.518 (−1.8%)	0.252 (4.7%)	0.057 (5.9%)
350	0.436 (−7.7%)	0.266 (1.1%)	0.119 (17.1%)
470	0.421 (−12.6%)	0.239 (8.6%)	0.151 (24.2%)
590	0.415 (−19.7%)	0.210 (15.0%)	0.185 (21.0%)
rcp=0.5			
110	0.590 (−2.9%)	*0.180 (0.6%)*	0.086 (9.9%)
230	0.597 (−10.3%)	0.108 (7.5%)	0.143 (30.9%)
350	0.596 (−18.3%)	0.071 (19.1%)	0.178 (43.4%)
470	0.568 (−21.3%)	0.085 (4.8%)	0.186 (57.9%)
590	0.549 (−28.2%)	0.074 (35.4%)	0.206 (58.8%)

Table 2: A table of the eating, mate and rape attempt rates for simulations with different (fixed) female PI and rcp (0.1, 0.25 and 0.5). Numbers show the frequencies with which **females** have attempted that action. Parenthetical numbers show the difference between male and female frequencies as a percentage of female frequencies. Italicized entries did not show statistically significant differences between males and females ($p < 0.001$).

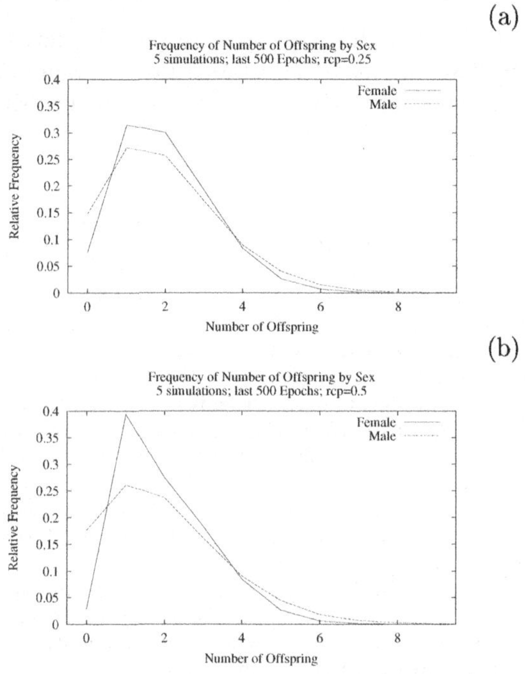

Figure 2: Frequency of number of offspring per agent with rcp equal to (a) 0.25 and (b) 0.5.

Rape also becomes the predominant reproductive method for both females and males, so the cost of rape appears to have been offset by the increased chance (due to the higher rcp) of producing an offspring.

We would also like to see if the dimorphism in rape behaviour has caused greater variability in the reproductive success of males than of females (something that is very difficult to assess in nature). Figure 2 shows the frequencies of numbers of offspring per agent when rcp=0.25 and 0.5. The frequency polygon of the male is flatter than the female's in both graphs (this difference is greatest when rcp=0.5), hence the male's reproductive success is indeed more variable.

We subsequently examined the agents' chromosomes to see which rules were causing the differences in rape behaviour. We found that the rules examining self-sex and self-health were the rules producing the sexually dimorphic behaviour. In particular, rules that triggered when the agent was male produced higher rape probabilities than when the agent was female. Furthermore, high health triggered rules with higher rape probabilities than low health. In all runs, males had higher average health than females, so this would have further contributed to the sexual dimorphism. We also ran several other simulation variations in order to test the robustness of our results. In one of these experiments we relaxed the assumption of symmetrical investments after mating. We found that, as expected, sexual differences in mating increase slightly with greater female investment, while the differences in rape rates are affected very little.

Conclusions and Further Work

We have demonstrated that ALife simulations can test the theories of evolutionary psychology. Our experiments, while preliminary, even offer support for some aspects of evolutionary psychology and, in particular, the story which PI theory tells of sexually dimorphic behaviour. We are currently extending our reproductive strategy experiments to abortion in order to see what conditions lead to the fatal termination of PI. In general, we intend to provide a fuller investigation of some of the issues central to PI theory, including an investigation of the evolution of differential parental investments.

Since the experimental or observational study of these matters in ethology and anthropology are difficult, we believe that our techniques offer an important supplement to such field research.

References

Bateman, A. J. 1948. Intra-sexual selection in drosophila. *Heredity* 2:349–368.

Dawkins, R., and Carlisle, T. 1976. Parental investment, mate desertion and a fallacy. *Nature* 262:131–3.

Krebs, J., and Davies, N. 1987. *An Introduction to Behavioral Ecology.* Boston: Blackwell.

Mascaro, S., Korb, K. B. and Nicholson, A. E. 2001. Suicide as an evolutionarily stable strategy. In *ECAL 2001*, 120–132. Springer-Verlag.

Mascaro, S., Korb, K. B., and Nicholson, A. E. 2002. Parental investment and reproductive strategies. TR 2002/112, CSSE, Monash.

Maynard Smith, J. 1977. Parental investment: A prospective analysis. *J. of Animal Behavior* 25:1–9.

Shields, W., and Shields, L. 1983. Forcible rape: an evolutionary perspective. *Ethology and Sociobiology* 4:115–136.

Thornhill, R., and Palmer, C. T. 2000. *A Natural History of Rape.* London: Cambridge, Mass.

Trivers, R. L. 1972. Parental investment and sexual selection. In Campbell, B., ed., *Sexual Selection and the Descent of Man.* London: Heinemann. 136–179.

Williams, G. 1975. *Sex and Evolution.* Princeton.

Better Group Behaviors in Complex Environments using Global Roadmaps

O. Burchan Bayazit, **Jyh-Ming Lien**, and **Nancy M. Amato**

Department of Computer Science, Texas A&M University, College Station, TX 77843-3112
{burchanb,neilien,amato}@cs.tamu.edu

Abstract

While many methods to simulate flocking behaviors have been proposed, these techniques usually only provide simplistic navigation and planning capabilities because each flock member's behavior depends only on its local environment. In this work, we investigate how the addition of global information in the form of a roadmap of the environment enables more sophisticated flocking behaviors and supports global navigation and planning. In this paper, we propose new techniques for four distinct group behaviors: homing, goal searching, traversing narrow areas and shepherding. Extending ideas from cognitive modeling, we embed behavior rules in individual flock members and in the roadmap. These embedded behaviors enable the creatures to modify their actions based on their current location and state. For example, the flock might move as an unordered group in open regions and in a follow-the-leader fashion through narrow passages. These behaviors exploit global knowledge of the environment and utilize information gathered by all flock members which is communicated by allowing individual flock members to dynamically update the shared roadmap to reflect (un)desirable routes or regions. We present experimental results showing how the judicious use of simple roadmaps of the environment enables complex behaviors to be obtained at minimal cost. Animations can be viewed at `http://parasol.tamu.edu`.

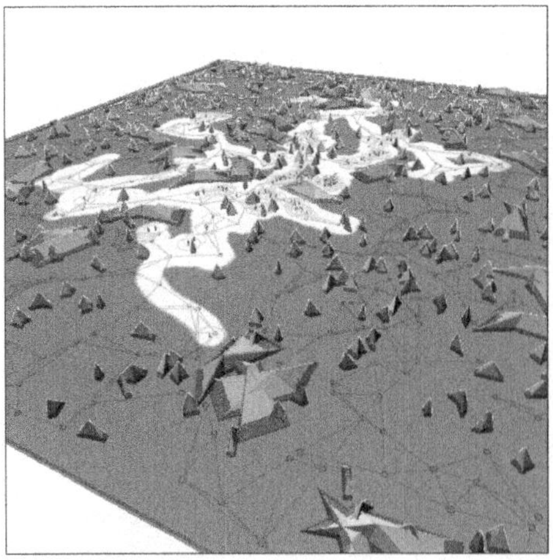

Figure 1: Complex behaviors, such as covering, can be improved using global information.

Introduction

The ability to simulate the coordinated movement of a group of creatures plays an important role in artificial life. For example, birds fly in flocks, fish swim in schools, and sheep move as a herd. An artificial representation of such creatures requires techniques for generating the motion of the individual entities within the flock and techniques for directing the global movement of the flock. While such methods have attracted much attention, most research has focused on techniques for modeling individual behavior within a flock, such as Reynolds' *boids* (Reynolds 1987). These techniques have been coupled with simple methods for guiding global flock movement, such as attractive potential fields centered at a goal location, to achieve realistic group movement in simple environments with few external obstacles, such as birds in the air or fish in the sea. Usually in this approach the flock shows homogeneous behavior. Tu and Terzopoulos extended Reynolds' flocking system to create more realistic, self-animating characters through biomechanical modeling with a behavioral finite state machine, the intention generator (Tu & Terzopoulos 1994). They also propose the idea of *cognitive modeling* (Funge, Tu, & Terzopoulos 1999), which controls how characters gather knowledge and how they act. Their *cognitive modeling language, CML*, eases an animator's task of specifying character behaviors. In brief, *cognitive modeling* provides an alternative to hard-coding for embedding behaviors into programs. It also enables heterogeneous flocks – different behaviors for different flock members. Unfortunately, these existing methods do not perform well if complex navigation is required, such as in cities, through crowded rooms, or over rough terrain. The ability to generate animations in complex environments is poor even if more elaborate behaviors are encoded in CML. This is due to, so-called, *emergent behavior* in which characters only react to immediate events.

In contrast, path planning algorithms developed in the robotics community are capable of navigation in complex environments (Latombe 1991). In particular we note the *roadmap methods* which can quickly answer many diverse path planning queries using a map, typically constructed during preprocessing, containing a network of representative feasible paths in the environment. In essence, these maps function similarly to driving maps in that one plans a route by first locating their initial and final positions and then selecting a route connecting them from the roads and highways shown on the map. While many good path planning algorithms exist, they have traditionally only been used to plan paths for a single moving object (the 'robot'). That is, roadmap methods have not been used to support group behavior.

Our Contribution

In this work, we explore the benefits of integrating roadmap-based path planning techniques with flocking techniques. We extend ideas from cognitive modeling (Funge, Tu, & Terzopoulos 1999), and embed behavior rules in individual flock members and in the nodes and edges of the roadmap. We find that the global information provided by our *rule-based roadmaps* improves the behavior of autonomous characters, and in particular, enables more sophisticated group behaviors than are possible using traditional (local) flocking methods. Key features of our approach include:

- The roadmap provides a convenient abstract representation of global information in complex environments.
- Adaptive roadmaps (e.g., modifying node and edge weights) enable communication between agents.
- Associating rules with roadmap nodes and edges enables local customization of behaviors.

We illustrate the power of our approach by proposing new approaches for four behaviors: homing, goal searching, traversing narrow passages and shepherding. Our new techniques can be applied to an entire flock, to individual flock members, or to an external agent that may influence the flock (e.g., a sheep dog).

To our knowledge, this is the first time global maps have been used to support group behavior. However, Parker's work supports our use of global information to enable sophisticated group behaviors (Parker 1993). In particular, she concluded that global knowledge should be used to provide general guidance for the longer-term actions of an agent, whereas local knowledge influences the more short-term, reactive actions. She also suggested that local information should be used to ground global knowledge in the current situation. This allows agents to remain focused on the overall goals of their group while reacting to the dynamics of their current situations.

Related Work

Reynolds' influential flocking simulation (Reynolds 1987) established the feasibility of modeling such a system. His work showed that flocking is a dramatic example of emergent behavior in which global behavior arises from the interaction of simple local rules. Each individual member of the flock (boid), has a simple rule set stating that it should move with its neighbors. This concept has been used successfully by researchers both in computer graphics and robotics. Tu and Terzopoulos (1994) used flocking behaviors with intention generators to simulate a school of fish in artificial life. Later, they implemented a search over possible situations expressed in formal logic (Funge, Tu, & Terzopoulos 1999). They also demonstrated shepherding behavior in which a T-Rex herds raptors out of its territory.

Nishimura and Ikegami (1997) used flocking dynamics to investigate collective strategies in a "prey-predator" game model. Ward et al. (2001) studied an evolving sensory controller for producing schooling behavior based on "boids". Brogan and Hodgins (1997) investigated group behavior with significant dynamics, such as human-like bicycle riders. Sun et al. (2001) achieve swarm behaviors based on a biological immune system. Balch and Hybinette (2000) propose a behavior-based solution to the robot formation-keeping problem. Fukuda et al. (1999) describe group behavior for a Micro Autonomous Robotics System. Mataric (1994) classifies a basic set of group behaviors which can be used to create more complex behaviors including flocking and herding. Saiwaki et al. (1997) use a chaos model to simulate a moving crowd. An interesting approach by Vaughan et al. (2000) used a robotic external agent to steer a flock of real geese.

Although there is little research on path planning for flocks, many methods have been proposed for planning for multiple robots. These methods can be characterized as centralized or decoupled. Centralized methods consider all robots as one entity, while decoupled methods first find a path for each robot independently and then resolve conflicts. In work from Li et al. (2001), each group of crowds is guided

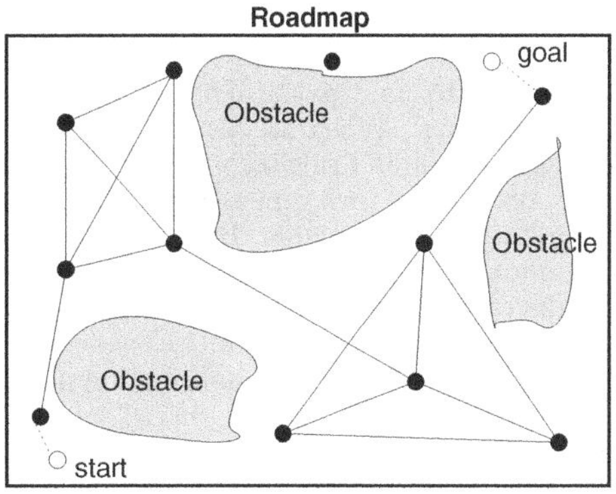

Figure 2: Querying a roadmap.

by a leader and the paths of the leaders are generated using a decoupled approach.

The observation of the behavior of ant colonies has inspired the ant colony optimization (ACO) meta-heuristic for discrete optimization. Dorigo et al. (1999) exploit this ant-like behavior to optimize solutions for several NP-Complete problems. In our work, the flock's ability to explore comes from using an ACO-like approach to adaptively adjust roadmap edge weights.

Rule-Based Roadmap Path Planning

Roadmap methods are among the most effective motion planning methods (Latombe 1991). These methods are based upon a map, usually computed during preprocessing, encoding representative feasible paths in the environment. Paths are planned by first locating their start and goal positions in the roadmap and then determining a route between them from the pathways in the roadmap. (See Figure 2.)

The roadmaps encode global navigation information, but they usually do not include 'local' information for influencing behavior differently in different regions. We propose providing such information in the form of pre-defined *behavior rules* which can be stored in the roadmap. When in the region of influence of a roadmap node (or edge), the group members' behavior is governed by the rule, if any, associated with that node. If no rule is specified, a default behavior will be followed. Rules may be as simple as

RULE: GO TO NEXT NODE IN YOUR PATH

or as complex as

RULE: WAIT FOR THE OTHERS, SELECT A LEADER, FOLLOW THE LEADER.

Rules are assigned to nodes automatically in our implementation. For example, narrow passage behaviors (rules) are assigned to nodes on path segments that have small clearance. This process can be done manually as well, enabling customization.

System Overview

The general components of our system are one or more AGENTS and an ENVIRONMENT. Environment-aware AGENT behavior is specified in RULES written in our custom script language.

System Components Each Agent is a flock member, and it has several attributes associated with it, such as `position`, `goal`, `role`, and `path`. These are stored in variables called `AgentVars`. When an Agent reaches a node, it starts executing that node's rule script. These rules might be executed only once, or at each time step that the Agent is in the region of influence of that node. In addition to pre-defined variables common to all Agents, recording properties such as position, Agents may also have dynamic (temporary) variables which are instantiated when rules are executed.

The Environment stores global information about the environment in the roadmap which is shared by all Agents. The roadmap nodes store Node attributes, such as node `position` and `edges` and functions to assist navigation (e.g., returning the minimum weight edge leaving the node) in `NodeVars`. The `NodeVars` and functions are shared by all Agents running the Node's script (when they are within the Node's influence area). In addition to the pre-defined `NodeVars`, a Node may also have dynamic `NodeVars` instantiated by the Node's script.

Rules describe Agent behavior. They are associated with regions of the Environment and are stored in roadmap Nodes. They can contain variables, assignments, control statements and loops. Triggers are special rules which are invoked to initialize and finalize variables governing behaviors. For example, in the narrow passage behavior, the first Agent to reach the passage is selected as the leader by the Trigger for that narrow passage. Triggers may be run only once, the first time an Agent reaches the associated Node, or they may run continuously until all Agents have left the region.

System Control Structure There is a main loop in the program which, at each time step, assigns Agents to Nodes, runs any necessary Triggers, and then calls individual agent rule scripts.

Rule scripts are stored with roadmap nodes, and are executed by Agents that are assigned to those nodes by the control loop (i.e., that are in the sphere of influence of those nodes). The structure of a rule script is as follows:

```
Definition of NodeVars
Definition of AgentVars
Definition of Triggers
Rules....
```

In our scripting language, the predefined variable `agent` refers to the Agent running the script. All Agents have `agent.position` and `agent.goal` attributes providing their current position and goal position, and an `agent.role` attribute defining their current role, which is *boid* by default. The Agent attribute `agent.path` has functions such `currentPosition, index, nextPosition, push, pop`, etc. The predefined variable `node` in the script represents the Node with which that script is associated. Each edge belongs to an `edge` structure made up of `start, end` and `weight` values. Agents can access the roadmap (or Environment) information through the predefined `node` variable or by calling functions which return information available in the `node` or `edge` structures, e.g., `node.edge(i)` which returns the *i*th edge.

Roadmap-Based Group Behaviors

In this section, we show how rule-based roadmap techniques can be used to achieve different behaviors. We consider four behaviors: *homing, goal searching, traversing narrow passages* and *shepherding*. The first two behaviors influence *where* the flock goes – reaching a pre-defined goal (homing) or searching for a goal (goal searching). The narrow passage behavior influences *how* the flock members position themselves relative to each other when they move through the passage. In the shepherding behavior an external agent influences the flock.

Homing Behavior

Homing behavior consists of two sub-models, one representing the individual behavior of flock members and the other influencing the global behavior of the flock. *"Boid"* dynamics (Reynolds 1987) sufficiently model individual behavior in most cases. In this model, individual members should: (i) avoid collision with neighboring flockmates, (ii) match velocity with them, and (iii) stay close to their neighbors. The neighborhood is defined by a distance, and an individual member of the flock is steered by angle and directional vectors satisfying the above criteria.

Global behavior is usually simulated using potential field methods by adding two directional vectors (Khatib 1986): one toward a goal and one away from nearby obstacles. However, this method may easily be trapped in a local minimum in an environment crowded with obstacles. A method commonly used in computer games requiring motion of a group of objects is a grid-based A^* search (Russell & Norvig 1994). In this approach, the environment is discretized to small grid cells and the search for the flock's path is based on expanding toward the most promising neighbor of already visited positions. Although A^* search finds shortest paths and it is usually fairly fast, it does have drawbacks. Of particular note here is the necessity of finding a completely new path for each new goal which reduces the efficiency of this approach and increases the computation time for complex environments.

In contrast, roadmap-based path planning methods have a global view and once the roadmap is generated, finding new paths is fast and efficient. In our approach, we use a *probabilistic roadmap method* (PRM) (Amato *et al.* 1998; Kavraki *et al.* 1996) motion planning method called MAPRM (Wilmarth, Amato, & Stiller 1999), to build the roadmap automatically and find a path for the flock. One of the advantages of MAPRM is that the paths we find tend to have large clearances from obstacles. Once a path is found, individual flock members follow the path. The path is discretized to subgoals based on an individual flock member's sensor range. Each member keeps track of subgoals and as soon as a subgoal comes within the sensory range the next subgoal becomes the steering direction for the global goal.

With other interacting forces from neighboring flock members and obstacles, steering toward the subgoal has the lowest priority, so individual members still move together while moving toward goal. This results in a flocking toward the goal and avoids getting trapped in local minima. The behavior is summarized in Algorithm I.

Algorithm I Homing

```
for (each individual flock member)
    if (goal is in view range)
        stay near goal
    else if (current subgoal is in view range)
        set next subgoal as the target
    else
        steer toward the target
```

```
    endif
endfor
```

The script to implement this behavior would be:

```
//Homing Script
agent.goal = agent.path.next();
stop; //don't run again at this node
```

Thus, as soon as an AGENT reaches a node within the path, the node's rule selects the next node in the AGENT's path as the goal.

Goal Searching Behavior

Goal searching is a type of exploring behavior. We assume the environment is known and the objective is to search for a goal and then move toward it. We achieve this behavior using a roadmap graph with adaptive edge weights. Each individual member behaves independently from its flock mates and uses the roadmap to wander around. Specifically, they follow roadmap edges and there are no predefined paths. If they reach a roadmap node with several roadmap edges, they probabilistically choose a roadmap edge to follow based on the weight of the edge. The edge weights represent any preferences for the current task, i.e., searching for and reaching the goal.

Our goal searching behavior is similar to *ant colony optimization (ACO)*. Although the individual flock members know the environment, they don't know the location of the goal. If an individual reaches a location where the goal is within sensor range, its location is communicated to the other members, perhaps indirectly, and they then attempt to reach the goal as well. We implemented this behavior using adaptive edge weights. The weight of an edge indicated how important it is believed to be, and edges leaving roadmap nodes are selected with some probability based on their weights. As an individual traverses a path in the roadmap, it remembers the route it has taken. Then, when it reaches a goal, it increases the weight of the edges on the route it took. If the individual reaches a roadmap node without any outgoing connections (i.e., with only one edge) or a node already contained in the current path (i.e., a cycle), the weight of the edges it followed will be decreased. See Figure 3.

The algorithm for this approach is summarized below.

Algorithm II GOAL SEARCHING

```
for (each flock member)
    if (goal found)
        increase edge weights on path to goal
    else if (dead end found)
        pop stack until a new branch is found
        decrease weight of edge corr. to popped node
    else
        select a neighboring node of the current node
        push this node onto the stack
    endif
endfor
```

This algorithm can be implemented using two different rule sets: one for all roadmap nodes except the node with the goal, and one for the roadmap node with the goal. The first rule set adds the visited nodes to the AGENT's path. The second set, which is only executed if the agent reaches the goal, will increase the weight of the edges the agent used to reach the goal. The script to implement the first set of rules is:

```
// Searching Script
AgentVar Node nextNode;
AgentVar Edge edge;
Trigger checkDeadEnd;
edge = node.probMaxOutEdge();
nextNode = edge.end;
agent.goal = nextNode.position;
agent.addPath(nextNode.position);
```

The first three lines define local variables and a trigger function. The fourth line calls a function of the predefined node variable which returns, with some probability, the maximum weight outgoing edge. Then, the AGENT's next goal is set to that edge's second endpoint and this information is added to path so that the AGENT can remember the route it has taken.

The goal searching behavior differs from the homing behaviors in that we need to monitor the AGENTS' path to deal with dead ends. We use special RULES called TRIGGERS for this purpose. TRIGGERS are instantiated when an AGENT reaches the associated NODE, and they may be run only once, or they may run *continuously* until some termination condition is met. For example, in this case, the TRIGGER function *checkDeadEnd* will run once for AGENTS in its influence range. It will check to see if the path so far contains a dead end, and if so, will remove the edges leading to it from the path and decrease their weights so other agents will be less likely to traverse them.

The following rule, which only resides in the node closest to the goal, will increase the weight of the edges on the path the AGENT took to the goal.

```
// Update the passed edges
agent.path.increaseEdgeWeights();
stop; //don't run again at this node
```

Narrow Passage Behavior

Sometimes the flock's behavior should depend on the surrounding environment. For example, different group formations may be used in relatively open areas than when passing through narrow regions.

A naive way to achieve narrow passage traversal by the flock is to use the homing behavior and to select two nodes as goals, first a node in front of the entrance to the passage and then a node outside the exit from the passage. One drawback of this approach is that flock members may bunch up and conflict with each other as they try to move through the passage.

A *follow-the-leader* strategy may avoid the congestion problems of the naive strategy. In this strategy, we first assemble the flock in front of the narrow passage, and then select the closest flock member to the entrance to the narrow passage as the leader. Then, the remaining flock members are arranged into a queue that follows the leader. Their position in the queue depends on their distance to the entrance of the narrow corridor. They can be kept from crowding each other by selecting appropriate values for the repulsive force from other flock members. This strategy provides more of a flow effect.

Note that different behaviors can be achieved by using a different criterion to select the next flock member in line 6 of Algorithm III. For example, instead of selecting the next closest flock member to the narrow passage, one might select

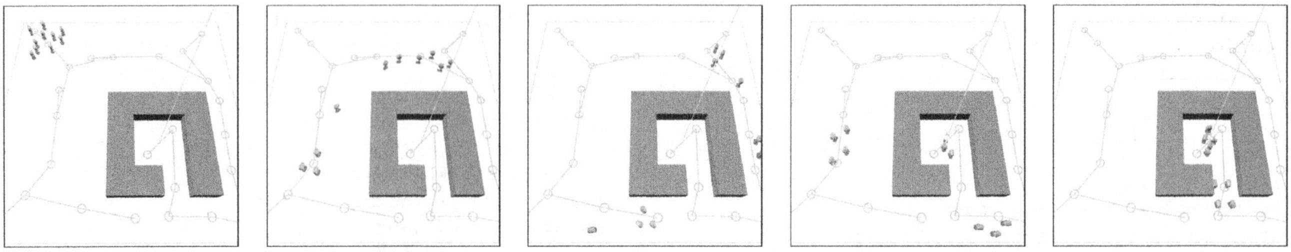

(a) (b) (c) (d) (e)

Figure 3: Ten flock members are searching for an unknown goal. (a) The flock faces a branch point. (b) Since both edges have the same weight, the flock splits into two groups. (c) After dead ends are encountered in the lower left and upper right, edge weights leading to them are decreased. (d) As some members find the goal, edge weights leading to it are increased. (e) The remaining members reach the goal.

the farthest, which would create a 'milling around' effect at the entrance to the passage.

Algorithm III NARROW PASSAGE

```
while NOT all flock members in gathering area
   set individual members' goal to gathering area
endwhile
set leader to NIL
while there are flock members outside passage
   select the closest unselected member as Current
   if Leader is NIL
      set Leader to Current
      set Leader's goal to next step in the path
   else
      set Current's goal to Previous
   endif
   set Previous to Current
   increase neighbor avoidance threshold
endwhile
```

A script for the NARROW PASSAGE behavior is given below. Initially, all agents are *boids*. After they all have gathered outside the passage, one of them is selected as the *leader* and the others become *followers*; these roles are maintained while traversing the passage.

```
NodeVar previous=-1; //define node vars
NodeVar closest;
NodeVar state=wait; //define initial state
Trigger continuous:  waitGathering;
Trigger continuous:  selectClosest;
  If (agent.role==boid && state==wait) { //wait
    agent.goal=node.position; //go to gathering area
  }
  Else If (agent.role==leader) { //if leader
    agent.goal=agent.path.next(); //follow path
    stop; //don't run again at this node
  }
  Else If (agent.role==follower) { //if follower
    agent.path.next(); //update path (not goal)
    stop; //don't run again at this node
  }
  Else { // agent is boid and state is not wait
    If(closest==agent.id) { //agent is closest
      If (previous==-1) { //no leader yet
        agent.role=leader;
        agent.goal=agent.path.next();//follow path
      }
      Else { //join queue - follow previous
        agent.role=follower;
        agent.goal=agent(previous);
        agent.path.next(); //update path
      }
      previous=agent.id; //update previous
      stop; //don't run again at this node
    }
  }
```

The *waitGathering* TRIGGER function continuously checks if all AGENTs have reached the gathering area. When they are there, it sets the NODEVAR state so that the follow behavior starts. The *selectClosest* TRIGGER function continuously runs. It can access and update variables applicable to all AGENTs within the region of the NODE (i.e., previous and closest) as well as private variables for each AGENT (i.e., role). At each iteration, it finds a new closest AGENT and sets the *closest* variable. Then, the AGENTs running the script compare themselves with the closest, if they are closest then they either follow their pre-assigned path (the leader) or follow the previous AGENT.

Shepherding Behavior

In the previous sections we have observed distinct flocking behaviors In the homing and narrow passage behaviors, the flock members were moving toward a goal together, i.e., as a flock. The motion was planned for the flock. In the goal searching behavior, the flock members were exploring and planning their motions individually. In a sense, the flock had control of the motion in the first case and individual flock members had control in the second case. In our last scenario, control is ceded to an outside agent who guides, or shepherds them. In the simulation snapshots shown in Figure 6, the external agent is a dog whose objective is to move the flock of sheep toward the goal. The only motion control for the flock is to move away from the dog. Vaughan et al. (2000) provide a similar implementation in which a robot was programmed to move geese toward a goal position. We would like to implement a similar algorithm where a subgoal will be a roadmap node found in the path (starting at the center of the flock). Until the subgoal is reached, the shepherd will move the flock toward that goal and then will choose the next roadmap node on the path as the next subgoal

To move the flock toward the subgoal, the dog steers the flock from the rear (see Figure 6, second and third columns, the robot is behind the flock's covering circle). If any subgroup separates from the flock, it is the dog's job to move the subgroup back to the flock (third column in Figure 6).

Algorithm IV SHEPHERDING (for dog)

```
Find a path on roadmap
while (goal not reached )
    Select the next node on the path as subgoal
    while (subgoal not reached)
        Move to rear of flock on the far side of subgoal
        if flock separates
            Move the subgroup that is farthest from
              subgoal toward other subgroups
        endif
    endwhile
endwhile
```

The script to implement shepherding behavior is shown below. Note that it should be applied everywhere in the environment, and hence every roadmap node should have this rule.

```
//Shepherding Script
AGENTVAR steeringLocation;
AGENTVARVAR dogAvoidance;
TRIGGER continuous:  findSteering;
TRIGGER continuous:  avoidDog;
  IF (agent.role==dog )
    agent.goal=steeringLocation;
  ELSE
    agent.externalForce=dogAvoidance;
```

The *findSteering* TRIGGER function continuously finds a steering location for the dog by checking the location of the sheep. The *avoidDog* trigger continuously computes an extra directional vector to avoid the dog (*dogAvoidance*). The internal variable *externalForce* is added to the boid rules.

Experimental Results

In this section we evaluate our roadmap-based techniques for the homing, exploring, narrow passage traversal and shepherding behaviors described previously. Movies illustrating these behaviors can be found on our webpage: (http://parasol.tamu.edu/).

Our experiments are designed to compare our roadmap-based techniques with more traditional approaches for simulating flocking behavior and to study the improvements possible by incorporating global information about the environment as encoded in a roadmap.

All of our experiments were run on a Linux system with Athlon 1.33 GHz processor and 256MB memory. While noting that our techniques could use any roadmap, our current implementation is based on the Medial-Axis Probablistic Roadmap Method, or MAPRM (Wilmarth, Amato, & Stiller 1999). MAPRM probabilistically generates a roadmap which is an approximation of the medial axis of the environment in two dimensional space.

Homing Behavior

For the homing behavior, our roadmap-based technique is compared with a basic flocking behavior using a potential field and a grid-based A^* search behavior.

The environment is a square with sides measuring 420 meters that contains six types of obstacles (see Figure 4(a)). A total of 301 obstacles are randomly placed in the environment. At any given time there is one goal, and when all flock members reach it, a new goal is randomly generated; this process continues until eight goals have been generated and reached. The experiment involves 40 flock members, which are initially placed according to a Gaussian distribution around the center of the square environment. The simulation is updated every 100 ms.

For the grid-based A^* behavior, a bitmap of the environment of 914×914 cells is constructed; the length of a side of each square cell is equal to the diameter of a flock member. Cells are classified as free cells and collision cells. Paths are found in this bitmap using A^* search. For the roadmap-based behavior, the roadmap is built using the MAPRM method to generate 400 roadmap nodes and we attempt to connect each node to its 4 nearest neighbors.

Homing behavior: Basic v.s. Roadmap

METHOD	#flockmate reaching the goal
Basic	10
grid-based A^*	40
Roadmap-based	40

Table 1: This table shows the number of the 40 flock members that reach their home within 30 seconds using the basic flocking behavior, the grid-based A^* behavior, and the roadmap-based behavior.

Table 1 shows that, without global information, only 25% of the flock members reach the goal and most of the others are trapped in local minima. On the other hand, when global navigation information is utilized, either with the grid-based A^* method or our roadmap-based method, all flock members reach the goal.

Homing behavior: Roadmap v.s. grid-based A^*

BEHAVIOR	init	find path	local minima	
METHOD	time	time	#	escape (s)
roadmap-based	0.88	0.652	255	22.99
grid-based A^*	6.02	5.757	2005	1035.43

Table 2: This table shows the time for initialization, the average time to find a path, and the total time spent by all flockmates escaping local minima.

In Table 2 we show the time spent searching for paths, the number of local minima encountered along all paths, and the total time spent escaping from local minima. Note that our roadmap-based method is faster than the grid-based A^* method, mainly because it spends less time escaping from local minima.

Goal Searching Behavior

In this experiment, the rule-based roadmap behavior is compared with simple flocking behavior that has only local information about the environment and no knowledge of the goal position and with an ideal variant of the roadmap-based

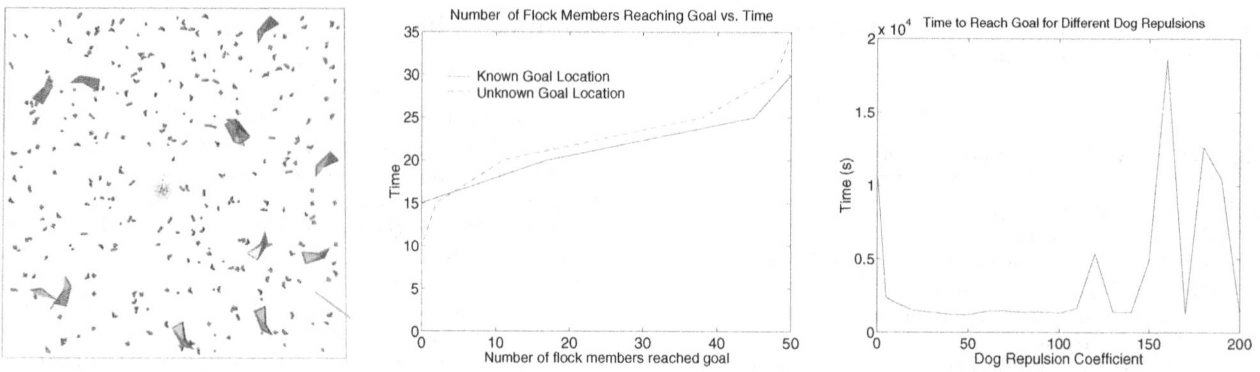

(a) Homing (b) Goal searching (c) Shepherding

Figure 4: (a) Environment for homing experiments. (b) Goal Searching: the number of flock members reaching the goal area in terms of time. (c) Shephering: The time to reach the goal with different dog repulsion coefficients.

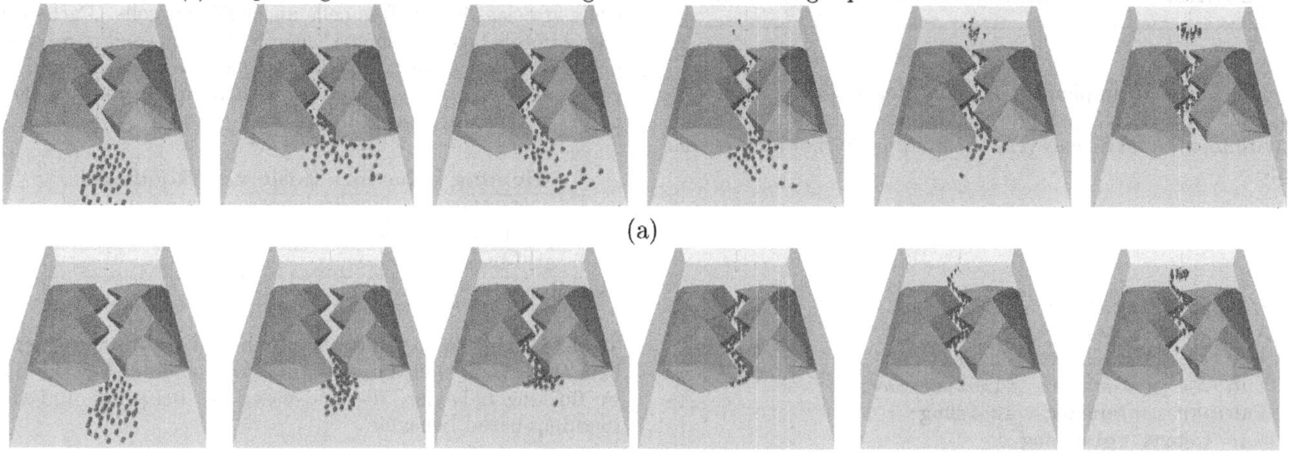

(a)

(b)

Figure 5: Passing through a narrow passage using (a) the follow-the-leader behavior, and (b) the naive strategy (homing to the exit node of the passage).

behavior that has *a priori* knowledge of the position of the goal.

The environment (80×100) is populated with 16 obstacles (6 types of obstacles) and in total 24% of the environment is occupied by obstacles. 50 flock members are simulated and states are updated every 100ms. We set the radius of the sensory circle at 5m. For the roadmap, 120 nodes are sampled and connections are attempted to each node's 4 nearest neighbors. We are interested in the number of flock members that reach the goal and how fast they get there. As mentioned before, the behavior with complete knowledge is used to establish a best case (lower bound) for the simulation efficiency, and the basic behavior using only local information is used to illustrate the importance of global knowledge.

The results of some experiments are shown in Figure 4(b). Flocks using the basic behavior did not discover any goals within 35 seconds, and hence this behavior is not shown in the plot. Overall, the roadmap-based behavior is competitive with the ideal roadmap-based behavior – only taking 5 seconds longer than the method in which the position of the goal is known *a priori*. In addition, it is surprising to note that two of the flock members in the roadmap-based method reach the goal earlier than any of their flockmates in the ideal roadmap-based behavior. While we expect the roadmap-based method to continue to perform well in more complex environments, we expect its efficiency relative to the ideal method to decline somewhat.

Narrow Passage Behavior

The narrow passage environment shown in Figure 5 contains 50 flock members and two mountain-like obstacles. Agents are asked to reach the goal on the other side of environment. The only way to reach their destination is to pass through the narrow passage between these two obstacles. As before, the roadmap is generated using MAPRM which attempts to generate high clearance nodes on the medial axis of the free space. We consider the naive and the follow-the-leader strategies described earlier.

In the follow-the-leader strategy, a node is automatically assigned the narrow passage rule if its clearance is below some threshold. All other nodes are assigned homing rules with the goal set as a node outside the exit of the narrow passage. The homing rule script also sets `agent.role = boid`, so that all AGENTs are boids when they gather outside the entrance to the narrow passage. Snapshots of the agent movement are shown in Figure 5(a). Note how the agents maintain clearance from each other as they move through the passage. The amount of clearance is adjusted by modifying the repulsive force between agents, which can be set in the rule scripts stored in narrow passage nodes.

In the naive strategy, homing rules are assigned to all nodes, with the goal of the homing rules set to the node at the exit of the narrow passage. Snapshots of the agent movement are shown in Figure 5(b). Note how the agents clump together and interfere with each other as they move through the passage.

Shepherding Behavior

In shepherding, we try to compare the roadmap-based method with the grid-based A^* search and we investigate how the magnitude of the dog's repulsive force affects the simulation. We conducted two sets of experiments.

In the first set of experiments, the flock consists of 30 sheep and the sheep dog is an external agent. The experiment starts the flock in a random location and the objective is to move it to a randomly selected goal. When the sheep reach the goal, the experiment is repeated again by selecting a new starting position and goal position at random.

We compare our method to a grid-based A^* method. The basic method using local information was not considered due to its observed inadequacies in the previous experiments. The environment is the same and the experiments are similar as for the homing experiments (Figure 4(a)). In our grid-based A^* implementation, the search for the path to the goal and the dog's path to the steering position use A^* search on a bitmap with 914 × 914 cells. The roadmap method used the MAPRM method with 400 roadmap nodes, with each node connected to its 4 nearest neighbors.

Shepherding behavior: Roadmap v.s. A^*

METHOD	init (s)	#steps	#local min.
Roadmap-based	0.88	2348.17	7.8
A^*-based	6.02	10612.08	32.2

Table 3: Shepherding behavior. This table shows time for initialization, the average number of simulation steps required to reach the goal, and the average number of local minima encountered.

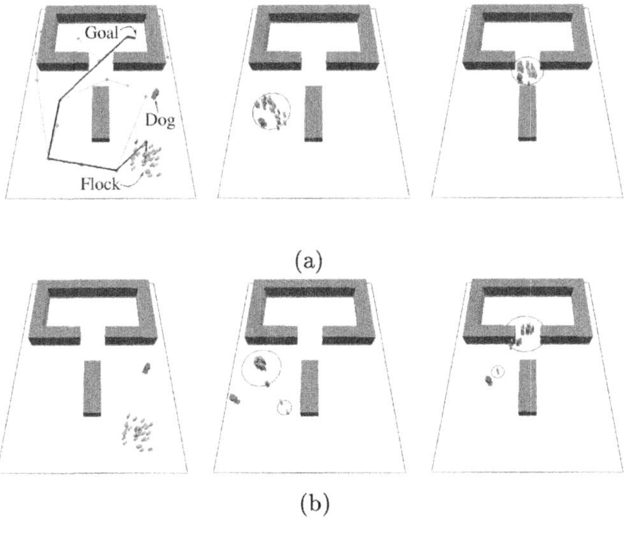

Figure 6: Shepherding behavior snapshots where the dog's repulsive force is (a) lower or (b) higher. Note that as the repulsive force increases, the flock may separate and become harder to herd.

Our results, shown in Table 3, include initialization times, the number of simulation steps required to reach the goal, and the number of local minima encountered. All values reported are averages over 40 experiments. We see that fewer local minima are encountered here than in the previous behaviors. This is influenced by the fact that MAPRM tries to generate paths that have high clearance from obstacles and because as the dog moves to the steering position it influences the individual members and increases the entropy of the system, resulting in relatively more randomness. Thus, even though some members are stuck in local minima, the dog would come and retrieve them. The table shows that the roadmap-based shepherding behavior performed better than the grid-based A^* search.

In the second set of experiments, we have varied the repulsive force coefficient of the dog between 0.1 and 200. The coefficient represents the degree to which the sheep will be repulsed from the dog. Note that, although the greater the coefficient the more repulsion occurs, it does not mean that the total force on the sheep is proportional to the coefficient since there are other forces on the individual sheep (to represent boid behavior). Snapshots of this experiment in a simplified version of the environment can be seen in Figure 6, and Figure 4(c) shows the relation between the magnitude of the dog's repulsive force and the time needed to herd the flock to the goal. If the repulsive force is very low, it takes longer for the dog to push the sheep to the goal. As the repulsive force increases, the dog controls the sheep better. However, after some point, the system becomes chaotic. This behavior can be explained by the fact that as the sheep become more repulsed, it becomes difficult for the dog to collect them into the herd. This can be seen in the second and third columns of Figure 6(b) where some group members are separated from the flock.

Conclusion

In this paper, we have shown that complex group behaviors can be generated using a roadmap providing global environment information. The information the roadmap contains, such as topological information and adaptive edge weights, enables the flock to achieve behaviors that cannot be modeled with local information alone. Moreover, since in many cases global knowledge involves high communication costs between individuals, indirect communication though dynamic updates of the roadmap's edge weights provides a less expensive means of obtaining global information.

The behavior rules embedded in our roadmaps and agents enable the agents to modify their actions based on thier current location and state. For example, the flock can move as an unordered group in open regions and in a follow-the-leader fashion through narrow passages. Our simulation results for the four types of behaviors studied show that the performance of the rule-based roadmap behaviors is very close to ideal behaviors that have complete knowledge.

In summary, we believe the techniques presented in this paper can be applied easily and efficiently to many diverse domains and have the potential to improve upon existing approaches.

Acknowledgments

This research supported in part by NSF CAREER Award CCR-9624315, NSF Grants IIS-9619850, ACI-9872126, EIA-9975018, EIA-0103742, EIA-9805823, ACI-0113971, CCR-0113974, EIA-9810937, EIA-0079874, and by the Texas Higher Education Coordinating Board grant ARP-036327-

017. Bayazit is supported in part by the Turkish Ministry of Education.

References

Amato, N. M.; Bayazit, O. B.; Dale, L. K.; Jones, C. V.; and Vallejo, D. 1998. OBPRM: An obstacle-based PRM for 3D workspaces. In *Proc. Int. Workshop on Algorithmic Foundations of Robotics (WAFR)*, 155–168.

Balch, T., and Hybinette, M. 2000. Social potentials for scalable multirobot formations. In *Proc. IEEE Int. Conf. Robot. Autom. (ICRA)*, 73–80.

Brogan, D. C., and Hodgins, J. K. 1997. Group behaviors for systems with significant dynamics. In *Autonomous Robots*, 137–153.

Dorigo, M.; Caro, G. D.; and Gambardella, L. M. 1999. Ant algorithms for discrete optimization. *Artificial Life*, 5:137–172.

Fukuda, T.; Mizoguchi, H.; Sekiyama, K.; and Arai, F. 1999. Group behavior control for MARS (micro autonomous robotic system). In *Proc. IEEE Int. Conf. Robot. Autom. (ICRA)*, 1550–1555.

Funge, J.; Tu, X.; and Terzopoulos, D. 1999. Cognitive modeling: Knowledge, reasoning and planning for interlligent characters. In *Computer Graphics*, 29–38.

Kavraki, L.; Svestka, P.; Latombe, J. C.; and Overmars, M. 1996. Probabilistic roadmaps for path planning in high-dimensional configuration spaces. *IEEE Trans. Robot. Automat.* 12(4):566–580.

Khatib, O. 1986. Real–time obstacle avoidance for manipulators and mobile robots. *Int. J. Robot. Res.* 5(1):90–98.

Latombe, J. C. 1991. *Robot Motion Planning.* Boston, MA: Kluwer Academic Publishers.

Li, T. Y.; Jeng, Y. J.; and Chang, S. I. 2001. Simulating virtual human crowds with a leader-follower model. In *Proceedings of 2001 Computer Animation Conference.*

Mataric, M. J. 1994. *Interaction and Intelligent Behavior.* Ph.D. Dissertation, MIT EECS.

Nishimura, S., and Ikegami, T. 1997. Emergence of collective strategies in prey-predator game model. *Artif. Life* 3:243–260.

Parker, L. E. 1993. Designing control laws for cooperative agent teams. In *IEEE International Conference on Robotics and Automation*, 582–587.

Reynolds, C. W. 1987. Flocks, herds, and schools: A distributed behaviroal model. In *Computer Graphics*, 25–34.

Russell, S., and Norvig, P. 1994. *Artificial Intelligence: A Modern Approach.* Prentice Hall, 1th edition.

Saiwaki, N.; Komatsu, T.; Yoshida, T.; and Nishida, S. 1997. Automatic generation of moving crowd using chaos model. In *IEEE Int. Conference on System, Man and Cybernetics*, 3715–3721.

Sun, S.-J., and Sim, D.-W. L. K.-B. 2001. Artificial immune-based swarm behaviors of distributed autonomous robotic systems. In *Proc. IEEE Int. Conf. Robot. Autom. (ICRA)*, 3993–3998.

Tu, X., and Terzopoulos, D. 1994. Artificial fishes: Physics, locomotion, perception, behavior. In *Computer Graphics*, 24–29.

Vaughan, R. T.; Sumpter, N.; Henderson, J.; Frost, A.; and Cameron, S. 2000. Experiments in automatic flock control. *J. Robot. and Autonom. Sys.* 31:109–117.

Ward, C.; Gobet, F.; and Kendall, G. 2001. Evolving collective behavior in an artificial ecology. *Artif. Life* 7:191–209.

Wilmarth, S. A.; Amato, N. M.; and Stiller, P. F. 1999. MAPRM: A probabilistic roadmap planner with sampling on the medial axis of the free space. In *Proc. IEEE Int. Conf. Robot. Autom. (ICRA)*, 1024–1031.

Programming with Stigmergy: Using Swarms for Construction

Zachary Mason
zmason4@attbi.com
Brandeis University, Waltham, MA 92154

Abstract

Social insects build extremely complex structures despite their limited perception and the absence of a global control system. Many of the structures built by termites can be construed as emergent phenomena driven by each worker's reaction to local pheremone levels. This work extrapolates from termite building to a system for specifying swarm activity. In the system, swarms are homogeneous and composed of simple, memory-less that perceive only their immediate environment. The swarm's activity is coordinated by virtual pheremone concentrations. The rules governing the agents' reactions can be designed to produce swarms that build complex, composable structures.

Introduction

Termite nests are large and complex. A nest may be as much as 10^4 or 10^5 times as large as an individual termite (Boneabeau *et al.* 1997) — a ratio unparalleled in the animal kingdom. The nests of the African termite sub-family Macrotermitinae are composed of many sub-structures, such as protective bulwarks, pillared brood chambers, spiral cooling vents, galleries of fungus gardens and royal chambers. For all the architectural sophistication of termite nests, termites themselves are blind, weak and apparently not responsive to a coordinating authority. This work attempts to borrow and generalize the termite construction-algorithm, permitting artificial, decentralized swarms to be programmed to build complex, composable structures.

How do small, blind termites manage to build (relatively) huge, intricate nests? Work on this question includes a simple, decentralized building model (Grasse 1959) (Grasse 1984), an empirical study of termite building behavior (Bruinsma 1979), a mathematical model of the synthesis of pillars in termite nests (Deneubourg 1977), and a model explaining how modest environmental variation can cause the same termite behaviors to generate qualitatively different structures (Boneabeau *et al.* 1997). Most relevant to this work is (Bruinsma 1979), which records three feedback mechanisms governing termite behavior. In the first, a termite picks up a soil pellet, masticates it into a paste and injects a termite-attracting pheremone into it. When the pellet is deposited, the pheremone stimulates nearby termites to pellet-gathering behavior and makes them more likely to deposit their pellets nearby. Second, small obstacles in the terrain stimulate pellet deposits and can seed pillars. Finally, a trail pheremone allows more workers to be drawn to a construction site.

Termites and many social insects interact stigmergically — that is, communication is mediated through changes in the environment rather than direct signal transmission. Computer simulations have used stigmergy to reproduce termite's pillar-making behavior and ant's foraging and the spontaneous cemetery building. These applications rely of qualitative stigmergy — individual agents react to a continuous variations in the environment. An example of quantitative stigmergy is (G. Theraulaz 1995), a simulation of wasp nest building. Wasps build nests by depositing cells on a lattice. Whether an empty cell is filled depends on the adjacent cells. Because all wasps have the same deposit-triggers, multiple wasps are able to simultaneously work on a single nest without without ruining each others work. A set of deposit-triggers is coherent if each no stage in the building process can be confused with an earlier stage by making only local observations, thus obviating the need for centralized control.

The goal of this work is to generalize the construction methodologies of the social insects and create a language for stigmergically assembling complex structures. Such a language permit swarms of agents to erect interesting architectures without benefit of a central controller or explicit inter-agent communication. The primary advantage of this approach is that stigmergically controlled swarms have minimal communication and no coordination overhead. Also, very little processing is demanded of agents, and the swarm can tolerate a degree of agent error. On a more abstract plane, this work is an example of *designing emergent behavior*.

There has been some work on using biomimetic robots inspired by social insects for construction — (Bowyer 2000) describes preliminary work. In the projected work, small mobile robots build structures by exuding polymerized diphenylmethane 4,4'-diisocyanate foam, a harmless, stable substance widely used as a commercial filler. The foam can be stored in a compressed liquid form which expands, hardens and sets when sprayed out. The solidified foam is strong (a small arch made of it can support a person), but easy to puncture, which makes it a good climbing surface for sharp-clawed robots.

Stigmergic programming

In this work, swarms are composed of agents moving randomly over a two dimensional lattice. The agents are identical and stateless. They build structures by moving (initially randomly scattered) bricks, coordinating their activities through pheremone plumes, which, unphysically, do not attenuate over time.

Agents' reactions are determined by rules — if an agent detects levels of certain pheremones within certain ranges, it takes a given action. Since these agents can only perceive pheremone concentrations at the point they occupy in the lattice, they are incapable of behaviors like chemotaxis and trail following. The pre-condition of a rule consists of a conjunction of acceptable bands of pheremone intensity. Pheremones can be enablers or suppressors of a rule. A rule's action is one or both of releasing a pheremone and, if a brick is carried, dropping it.

Deposited pheremones symmetrically through the grid according to an inverse power law. A rule triggered by a band of intensity of a particular pheremone will, given a single deposit of that pheremone, will be triggered in a ring centered on that deposit. Adding a second deposit breaks radial symmetry and creates an ellipse-shaped activation potential. By stringing together ellipses, directed chains of deposits can be formed. It is possible to build two pheremone chains parallel and at a fixed distance from each other — this produces pheremone gradients which can be used to distinguish left from right.

Rules that use local pheremone intensities to estimate the distance to the nearest deposit are inherently vulnerable to interference from other, unexpected deposits. Since interference diminishes with distance, this problem can be worked around by building rule-sets that keep deposits of each pheremone widely separated. An exception is "stabilizer pheremone", which tells passing agents that a brick has been

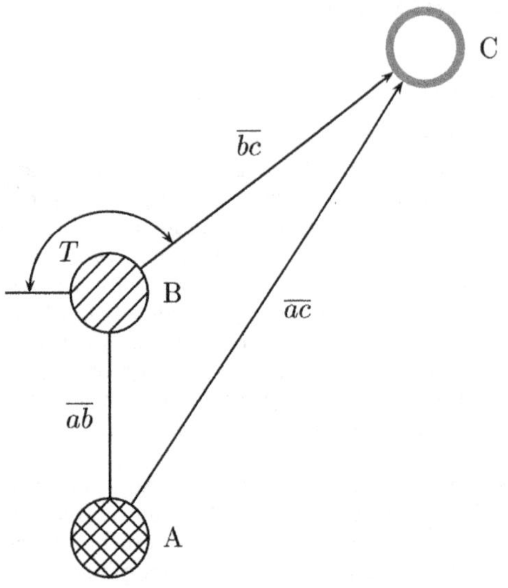

Figure 1: Schematic for a specifying the site of a potential C on the basis of two pheremone deposits A and B. When coding for a chain of pheremones it is convenient to specify the distances $\overline{ab}$ and $\overline{bc}$ and the angle T, but only $\overline{ac}$ and $\overline{bc}$ are perceptible, so solve for $\overline{ab}$ using $\overline{ac}^2 = \overline{bc}^2 + \overline{ab}^2 + 2\overline{bc} \times \overline{ba} \times \sin T$

dropped purposefully, and that they should therefore not pick it up. Pheremone-driven rules implement a kind of continuous cellular automaton, defined by changing reaction potentials, on top of a discrete one, defined by the motions of the agent swarm.

The mechanics of pheremone reactions lend themselves to composable actions. The most elementary kind of action is a two-point rule, in which an activation potential is defined by relative position to two precursor points, as shown in figure 1. This kind of rule can be used to add elements to a chain or to cap two converging chains.

Table 1 gives the rules used by a swarm that generates a left-curving arc of bricks. The swarm builds two parallel, left-curving chains. The left-hand chain is composed of links between A and B deposits, and the right-hand of links between deposits of C and D. Each rule will deposit a pheremone at a point *new* that is an estimated distance *near_new_distance*from the deposit *near_source*, where *near_source*is a distance *far_near_source*from the deposit of *far_source.* The angle between the first vector and the perpendicular of the second must make an angle *angle_from_perpendicular* , as illustrated in Figure 1.

Rules can code for the construction of invisible pheremone super-structures or for actually building structure by placing bricks. Structural rules generally create small activation potentials in order to precisely place future pheremone deposits. Brick-placement rules on which no other components of the intended architecture depend may have broader, less precise activation potentials.

The arc-building swarm is seeded with two with two pheremone deposits at a fixed distance. Figure shows an intermediate stage of arc formation. The super-structure of the

	1	2	3	4	5
far_source	C	A	D	B	
near_source	A	C	B	D	
far_near_distance	7	7	7	7	
near_new_distance	17.1	15	17.1	15	
angle_from_perpendicular	-20°	20°	-20°	20°	
suppressors	B	D	A	C	
suppressor_radii	26	26	26	26	
deposit	B	D	A	C	
drop triggers					A, B
total radii					15

Table 1: Arc Builder Rules

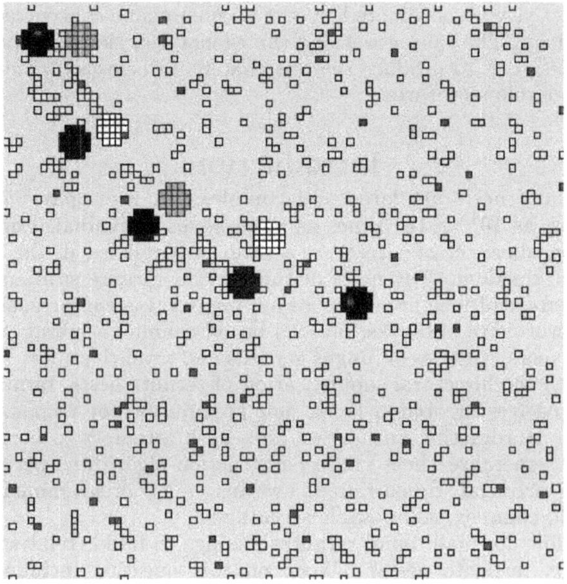

Figure 2: intermediate state of the arc builder. The circles are regions of high pheremone concentration.

arc has extended four links from the seeds, but the walls connecting pheremone deposits have not been built. In Figure the arc super-structure has been completed and almost every brick on the lattice has been incorporated into walls.

The swarm (partially) defined in 2 illustrates the composition of rule-sets by building a chain along which star shapes are regularly distributed. The rules for this swarm are composed of two subsets — the first encodes the stars, the second the chains along which the stars are positioned. The latter is encoded by means of four pheremones which are deposited in alternation to form a line. The former is encoded by positioning five deposits at angles of 18°, 90°, 162°, 234° and 306° from the line between two of the pheremones used to build the chain. shows the potential activations in an incomplete star-chain and shows the final product. Notice that there are few bricks (yellow pixels) left near the stars that have not been incorporated into them.

Conclusion

A decentralized, stigmergic control system can be used to program swarms. The swarms achieve fine-grained control by implementing a semi-deterministic cellular automata in

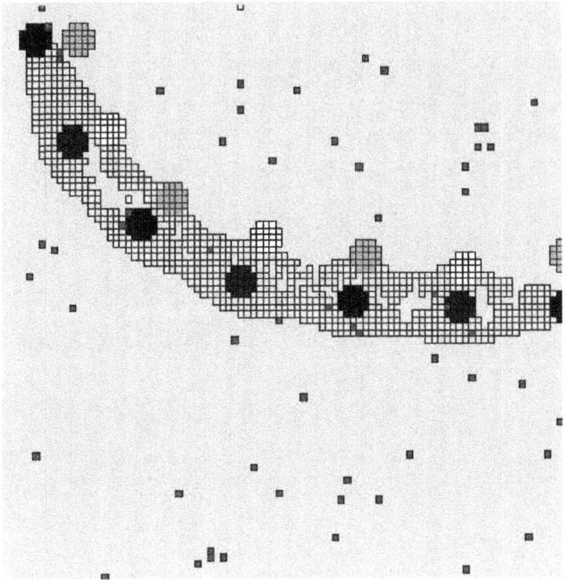

Figure 3: final state of the arc builder. Regions of intense pheremone activity are also shown.

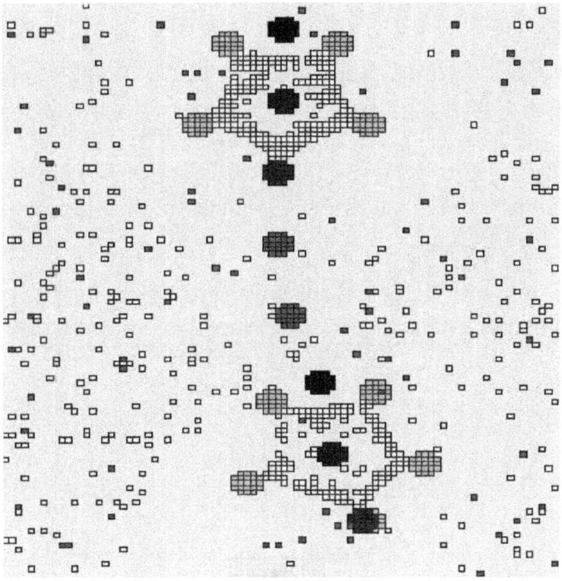

Figure 4: final state of the star-chain builder.

	1	2	3	4	5
far_source	A	A	A	A	A
near_source	B	B	B	B	B
far_near_distance	15	15	15	15	15
near_new_distance	15	15	15	15	15
angle_from_perpendicular	18	90	162	234	306
suppressors	C	C	C	C	C
suppressor_radii	6.5	6.5	6.5	6.5	6.5
deposit	C	C	C	C	C

Table 2: Star-chain Builder Rules. Rules 1-5 encode the star shapes while rules 6-10 encode the chain on which the stars are built.

which communication is mediated through virtual pheremone plumes. The swarms consist of identical agents which, based on only the pheremone concentrations in their immediate environment, follow a simple set of rules that can interact to allow the creation of complex structures. Thematically, this is a generalization of the building algorithms of termites. This kind of decentralized control is useful in cases where it is more practical to have many simple agents than a few complex ones and where direct communication and coordination are difficult.

In future work the system system will be extended to three dimensions. This will require modeling the stability of structures in gravity and refining the control of agent motion so that agents only walk where they are adequately supported. Other future work includes programming construction swarms by specifying the target structure directly, letting a compiler infer the corresponding rule-set (if one exists.) On the theory that simpler agents are better, it would be useful to be find the minimal set of pheremones capable of generating a particular target object, and of quantifying the trade-offs between pheremone number and various building metrics, such as accuracy and probability of failure. Also, the simulator could be more physically realistic — for instance, by introducing pheremone attenuation or variations in pheremone diffusion due to changes in the air or surrounding structures. The software for this system is available at

`http://www.cs.brandeis.edu/~zmason/stigmergy.html`

References

Boneabeau; Theraulaz; Deneubourg; Franks; Rafelsberger; Joly; and Blaco. 1997. A model for the emergence of pillars, walls and royal chambers in termite nests. *Phil. Trans. R. Soc. London* 353:1561–1576.

Bowyer, A. 2000. Automated construction using cooperating biomimetic robots. Technical Report 11/00, University of Bath Department of Mechanical Engineering.

Bruinsma, O. H. 1979. *An analysis of building behaviour of the termite Macrotermes subhyalinus* . Ph.D. Dissertation, Landbouwhogeschool.

Deneubourg, J. L. 1977. Applications de l'ordre par fluctuations a la description de certaines etapes de la construction du nid chez les termites. *Insectes Soc.* 25:117–130.

G. Theraulaz, E. Bonabeau, J. 1995. Modeling the collective building of complex architectures in social insects with lattice swarm. *J. Theor. Biol.* 177:381.

Grasse, P. 1959. La reconstruction du nid et les coordinations inter-individuelles chez *bellicostitermes natalensis* et *cubitermes* . sp. la theorie de la stigmergie: essai d'interpretation du comportement des termites constructeurs. *Insectes Soc.* 61:41–81.

Grasse, P. 1984. *Termitologia, Tome II - Fondation des societies construction.* Paris: Masson.

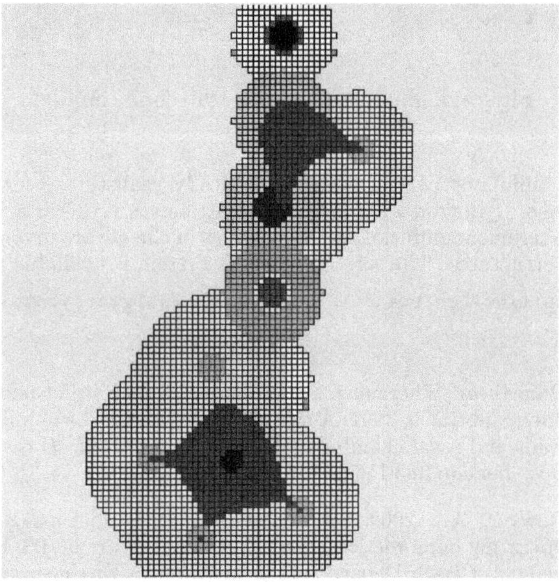

Figure 5: pheremone distribution in an intermediate state of the star-chain builder.

The Effect of Agreements in a Game with Multiple Strategies for Cooperation

Pedro Mariano and **Luís Correia**

{plm,lc}@di.fct.unl.pt, Informatics Department, New University of Lisbon
Quinta da Torre, 2829 - 516 CAPARICA, Portugal

Abstract

We present a model suited not only for the study of evolution of cooperation but also to study behaviours such as treason and exploitation. This game has multiple Pareto Optimal solutions, which causes shifts in the agent strategies that we can interpret as either treason or exploitation. This requires some form of coordination between agents to avoid penalising behaviours. We present results of our game with and without an agreement model. We show that our game provides rich evolutionary dynamics.

Introduction

The Iterated Prisoner's Dilemma has been used throughout the literature as a model of cooperation (Brembs 1996; Beaufils, Delahaye, & Mathieu 1997; Nowak, Bonhoeffer, & May 1994; Yamaguchi, Maruyama, & Hoshino 2000). In our view, treason, manipulation, and exploitation are not well modelled. Same authors have made extensions to the game in order to cope with player selection (Stanley, Ashlock, & Smucker 1995). Others have used emotions toward other players as a way to permit defection in the game to help partners (Bazzan, Bordini, & Campbell 1998). Manipulation is not well addressed in this game, while some authors engineer communication protocols for societies that clarify any information sent by lying agents (Sandholm 1999).

The game model we present has multiple Pareto Optimal strategies to choose from (where an agent cannot improve its outcome without impairing its opponent. This requires some coordination or a treaty (either explicitly or as a consolidated behaviour) among agents playing the game. The game also has the same characteristics of IPD, namely a set of play moves that are beneficial for both players (thus deemed cooperative) and another that is detrimental and used to penalise players. Multiple strategies with equal outcomes are well suited to study exploitation and treason. The coordination aspect was treated in (Mariano & Correia 2002). In this paper, we report the results related to treason.

Game Description

This game has been introduced in (Mariano & Correia 2002). Here we will only present the essential definitions to grasp the results we present. The game is inspired in resource sharing. In our case, there are two agents and one resource. Only one agent can have the resource in a single time unit. The agent with the resource can perform either the $none_g$ or *give* action. The agent without the resource can perform either the $none_t$ or *take* action. The *give* action has a bonus associated to it, b_g. The *take* action incurs losses in both the performer and the subject, c_{pt} and c_{st}. Possession or not of the resource is characterised by the parameters w_g and w_l.

In a single iteration, the wealth gain matrix for the player with resource is:

$$\begin{bmatrix} w_g & -w_l - c_{st} \\ -w_l + b_g & -w_l + b_g - c_{st} \end{bmatrix} \tag{1}$$

and for the player without the resource is:

$$\begin{bmatrix} -w_l & w_g - c_{pt} \\ w_g & w_g - c_{pt} \end{bmatrix} \tag{2}$$

When the game is played only once, the Nash equilibrium of the game is as follows: the agent with resource should play the *give* action; the agent without the resource should play the *take* action. This result was achieved using minmax analysis.

When the game is played several times (t time units), three cases are important in this game.

- The agent with the resource does not give it, and the other agent does not take it. Their wealth outcomes are the following:

$$t \times w_g \qquad \text{with resource} \tag{3}$$

$$-t \times w_l \qquad \text{without resource} \tag{4}$$

- When both agents give away the resource after t_{pg} time units (with $t \gg t_{pg}$), their wealth outcome is approximately:

$$\frac{t}{2}\left(w_g - w_l + \frac{b_g}{t_{pg}}\right) \tag{5}$$

- When both agents take the resource after t_{pt} time units without it (again $t \gg t_{pt}$), their wealth outcome is:

$$\frac{t}{2}\left(w_g - w_l - \frac{c_{pt} + c_{st}}{t_{pt}}\right) \tag{6}$$

When b_g is zero, expression 3 is greater than 5 which is greater than 6. These cases are extreme ones but we have presented them to show that: an agent is better of if it does not share the resource; however, if the opponent agent takes the resource, they get the worst result. Moreover, when b_g is zero there are multiple strategies with the same wealth outcome. Both agents can choose any t_{pg} value. We consider them as Pareto Optimal. This suggests some agreement between agents should be met. Consequently, it permits the study of treason and exploitation.

Contribution We expect that at this point, the analysis performed could shed some light on the game that we are proposing. Although some resemblance with IPD and the lumberjack dilemma, this game requires coordination in order to both agents collecting equal wealth gains. While in IPD agents must play cooperate to get equal benefits, in our game agents need to coordinate their actions because there are multiple Pareto Optimal strategies. In IPD any play of defect other than cooperate leads to wealth differences. In our game, a deviation from a balanced combination of actions, can lead to punishment if agents do wish so, or to a new combination of actions that guarantees equal wealth gains (a new Pareto Optimal strategy).

As in the lumberjack dilemma, agents share a resource from where they collect wealth. In lumberjack dilemma and other tragedy of the commons games, the resource is a distinct object with a dynamic of its own (it grows or evolves, its value changes in response to agent actions). In our game, the resource is an object that agents must possess and, at a single time only one agent can collect wealth from it. In order to other agents being able to collect wealth, some action must be performed to change the owner of the resource. It can change due to an altruistic action (*give*) or through a punitive and costly action (*take*).

The simulation

We will now describe how we implemented the game introduced in the previous section. The topics are: what is the agent strategy, the agreement model used, the evolutionary framework used, the parameter values, and the lattice type environment used.

Since this game has multiple Pareto Optimal strategies, we introduce an agreement model that allows two agents playing the game to select one Pareto Optimal strategy. The goal of the simulations reported here is to compare the evolutionary dynamics between populations of agents that are able to establish an agreement from those that are not capable.

Agent strategy The agent strategy uses a probabilistic mechanism to perform the actions. For each action, the agent waits a number of ticks until it performs the action with some probability. Therefore, we can describe a single strategy by tuple (p_g, p_t, t_g, t_t), in which p_g is the probability of an agent doing the *give* action after it holds the resource t_g ticks, and conversely, p_t is the probability of an agent doing the *take* action after it stayed t_t ticks without the resource – two probabilities and two time intervals.

Agreement model Each agent has a preferred period to hold the resource, t_h^A. When two such agents meet to play the game, they must first negotiate the period they are going to hold the resource. There are two other parameters: one describes how much an agent will exploit the agreement, t_e^A, that is, after this time has elapsed it will definitely give away the resource; the other describes how much time an agent tolerates that it has not received the resource, t_t^A, that is, after this time has elapsed it will definitely take the resource. In the intervals $[t_h^A, t_h^A + t_e^A]$ and $[t_h^A, t_h^A + t_t^A]$ the agent actions are determined by its underlying strategy. This agreement model allows us to use the probabilistic strategy described previously, or another strategy such as an finite state automata.

When two agents meet to play the game, they have to decide the period to hold the resource. Two agents must negotiate between their parameters t_{h1}^A and t_{h2}^A. In the results reported here, we use a simple rule: agents select the minimum value among them. We could use another rule, or some bargaining protocol. However, when the *give* bonus is zero, the multiple Pareto Optimal strategies are equivalent, since they all yield the same wealth outcome. Therefore, a simple rule suffices to reach an agreement.

Our model does not make any assumption about the truthfulness of the agent. An agent may announce some period to hold the resource, and during the course of the game use a completely different value. In this case, the agent is subject to its partner's tolerance time interval, t_t^A. The results we present are from simulations with truthful agents.

In our model agents always reach an agreement. We could for instance add another parameter that defines the probability of an agent making an agreement. If there were no agreement, agents would simply revert to their underlying strategy. Notice that, with agreement, this strategy is only applied in the exploitation and tolerance intervals.

Evolutionary Algorithm The agent chromosome is composed of the 4 strategy parameters and 3 agreement model parameters. The initial population parameters are taken from a random uniform distribution: probability parameters ranging from 0 to 1 and time parameters from 0 to 15. Only the mutation operator was used: gaussian noise addition. A population of size 100 is distributed in a square lattice. At every generation, agents choose N opponents from their 4-neighbour to play a match. Each match consists of 3 games. Game length varies uniformly between 100 and 130 time units. Since an agent chooses and may be chosen, every agent plays in average $N \times 3 \times 2$ games. Agent selection probability is proportional to agent's wealth (roulette wheel). Each simulation run took 1000 generations.

The choice of the game length values and of the time parameters values must comply with the fact that $t \gg t_{pg}$ and $t \gg t_{pt}$. The lowest value of the game length should be much greater than the highest value for the time parameter so that the approximations of expressions 5 and 6 are valid and there is sufficient time for the resource to be shared equally between the agents.

Parameter Values Some of the game parameters and evolutionary parameters were varied. For each parameter set, 10 simulation runs were performed. Table 1 shows the different parameters values.

parameter	value
w_g	5
w_l	0, 1, 2
c_{pg}	0
c_{sg}	0
c_{pt}	2, 4, 6, 8
c_{st}	10, 20, 30
N	1, 2, 3, 4
p_{mut}	0.05

Table 1: Parameters values used in the simulations.

Results

Two main setups were prepared: one with the agreement model and the other without it. The goal is to study the effect of the agreement on what kind of evolutionary dynamics we obtain. The results without agreement model were taken from a previous work (Mariano & Correia 2002). In order to compare results, we measured the number of actions performed and the wealth accumulated for each main setup.

Agreement

In the simulations without the agreement model we obtain different strategies. There are populations where the *give* action is performed very often, and others where the *take* action is not. Typically, the higher the *take* action costs, the higher is the average number of *give* actions performed. The agreement model favours the decrease of *take* action performed. There are two cases for $c_{st} = 30$, with $c_{pt} = 2$ and $c_{pt} = 4$ where instead an increase was observed, as can be seen in table 2.

c_{pt}	c_{st} 10	20	30
2	20.9	4.5	2.6
4	19.1	5.5	2.0
6	16.7	6.1	2.1
8	14.8	6.8	2.6

(a) Without the agreement model.

c_{pt}	c_{st} 10	20	30
2	4.8	4.5	4.5
4	4.8	3.0	2.1
6	5.2	2.9	1.6
8	5.4	2.8	1.3

(b) With the agreement model.

Table 2: Average *take* action percentage obtained in simulations.

c_{pt}	c_{st} 10	20	30
2	−4.9	9.8	11.2
4	−6.5	6.5	12.8
6	−6.4	3.9	12.2
8	−6.5	1.0	9.9

(a) Without the agreement model.

c_{pt}	c_{st} 10	20	30
2	13.8	9.7	5.5
4	12.8	12.4	12.4
6	11.3	12.0	13.8
8	9.9	11.8	14.7

(b) With the agreement model.

Table 3: Average wealth obtained in simulations.

Average wealth outcome improves with the agreement model. Without it, when c_{st} is low, average wealth is negative. A high value favours the appearance of agent strategies based on the *give* action, and as a consequence, the average wealth increases (see table 3). The agreement model improves the average wealth specially when the c_{st} is lower. There are two cases for $c_{st} = 30$, with $c_{pt} = 2$ and $c_{pt} = 4$ where we obtained a poorer result. We also noticed that results are quite independent of parameter variations as can be seen in table 3.

Evolutionary dynamics

The simulations obtained without the agreement model provided more complex evolutionary dynamics. Different probability strategies appear. When the c_{pt} parameter is high, the population is composed of an agent strategy with the following characteristics: high probability to give and take the resource; the time to perform the *give* action is lower than the one to perform the *take* action. This strategy is cooperative as the agents give the resource frequently. In addition, it prevents exploitation since there is a small time window before an agent takes the resource. When the *take* action costs are lower, the agent strategy most common is characterised by: low probability to give the resource; long time interval to give the resource; short time interval before taking the resource.

The simulations with the agreement model showed some examples of treason behaviour. They are characterised by high values for the t_e^A parameter. The lower is the c_{st}, (cost of the subject of the *take* action), the higher is the tendency to treason. However, tolerance to this behaviour depends on the c_{pt} parameter. The costlier it is to penalise a traitor, the higher is the tolerance level (t_t^A parameter).

In both simulation setups, the population goes through phases of cooperation, switching between Pareto Optimal strategies, and phases characterised by negative wealth outcome.

In other simulation results (Mariano & Correia 2002) we varied the *give* action costs. In this case we verified that when there is a bonus to give the resource, there is a cooperative agent strategy with the previous characteristics. We observed that in this case the time to perform the *give* action is generally 1 to 2 time units.

Conclusions and future work

We have presented a game model that exhibits multiple Pareto Optimal strategies. In order to agents be able to obtain above average wealth outcome, they have to cooperate. However, multiple Pareto Optimal strategies require some coordination or an agreement between agents. Even in the absence of such agreement, we obtained such cooperative strategies. This is mainly due to the parameter values that favoured this outcome. When we added an agreement model, results improved, since the average wealth did not show a strong relationship to game parameters.

The agreement model favoured the appearance of cooperative strategies. However, treason behaviour and its counter measures were observed. Their rate depended on the *take* action costs. The possibility not to enter an agreement should be assessed, as we have interactions between agents that do not establish any agreement, and others that make agreements.

The existence of multiple Pareto Optimal solutions leads to changes in the agent population. These changes are caused by new strategies that exploit or break the agreement. The population can stabilise into a new Pareto strategy. On the other hand, it can go through a phase of penalising strategies. Despite the evolutionary dynamics presented here, further research into the population diversity should be conducted.

The agreement model negotiation may be kept simple. A simple solution suffices to establish the agreement terms.

References

Bazzan, A.; Bordini, R.; and Campbell, J. 1998. Moral sentiments in multi-agent systems. In Müller, J. P.; Singh, M. P.; and Rao, A. S., eds., *Intelligent Agents V: Agent Theories, Architectures, and Languages*, volume 1555 of *Lecture Notes in Computer Science*, 113–132. Springer-Verlag.

Beaufils, B.; Delahaye, J.-P.; and Mathieu, P. 1997. Our meeting with gradual: A good strategy for the iterated prisoner's dilemma. In Langton, C. G., and Shimohara, K., eds., *Artificial Live V: Proceedins of the Fifth International Workshop on the Synthesis and Simulation of Living Systems*, 202–209. MIT Press.

Bedau, M. A.; McCaskill, J. S.; Packard, N. H.; and Rasmussen, S., eds. 2000. *Artificial Live VII: Proceedings of the Seventh International Conference on Artificial Life*. MIT Press.

Brembs, B. 1996. Chaos, cheating and cooperation: potential solutions to the prisoner's dilemma. *Oikos* 76(1):14–24.

Mariano, P., and Correia, L. 2002. A game to study coordination and cooperation. In *5th Workshop on Deception, Fraud and Trust in Agent Societies*, 101–112.

Nowak, M. A.; Bonhoeffer, S.; and May, R. M. 1994. Spatial games and the maintenance of cooperation. *Proceedings of the National Academy of Sciences* 91:4877–4881.

Sandholm, T. W. 1999. Distributed rational decision making. In Weiss, G., ed., *Multiagent systems: a modern approach to distributed artificial intelligence*. MIT Press. chapter 5, 201–258.

Stanley, E. A.; Ashlock, D.; and Smucker, M. D. 1995. Iterated prisioner's dilemma with choice and refusal of partners: Evolutionary results. In Morán, F.; Moreno, A.; Merelo, J. J.; and Chacón, P., eds., *Advances in Artificial Life*, volume 929 of *Lecture Notes in Computer Science*, 490–502. Springer-Verlag.

Yamaguchi, Y.; Maruyama, T.; and Hoshino, T. 2000. A co-evolution model of scores and strategies in IPD games: toward the understanding of the emergence of the social morals. In Bedau et al. (2000), 362–366.

Social Learning Mechanisms Compared in a Simple Environment

Jason Noble and **Daniel W. Franks**
School of Computing, University of Leeds
[jasonn|dwfranks]@comp.leeds.ac.uk

Abstract

Social learning can be adaptive, but little is known about the underlying mechanisms. Many researchers have focused on imitation but this may have led to simpler mechanisms being underestimated. We demonstrate in simulation that imitative learning is not always the best strategy for a group-living animal, and that the effectiveness of any such strategy will depend on details of the environment and the animal's lifestyle. We show that observations of behavioural convergence or "traditions" might suggest effective social learning, but are meaningless considered alone.

GETTING by in the world is all about doing the right thing at the right time: eat the fallen fruit, avoid the poisonous mushroom, run from the approaching predator. But how does an animal produce the best response, or at least a satisfactory response, in each of the many possible situations it may face? We can distinguish two main sources of information used in this constant action-selection task. First, there is genetically inherited information, such as instinctive drives or tendencies. You run from the approaching predator because you were born with a brain that was wired up that way. Second, there is information based on experience, i.e., the results of learning. You avoid the mushroom because you've learned that it will make you sick.

Learning sometimes involves an individual finding out through trial and error about what to do in different situations. However, in a social species, there is often valuable information to be gleaned from the behaviour of others: for example, why risk poisoning by sampling potential foodstuffs at random when you could simply eat the same things your conspecifics are eating? In this paper we are concerned with this idea of *social learning*, and will compare the performance of different social learning mechanisms in a simulated environment.

Researchers in animal behaviour are increasingly in agreement that social learning is an important element in the overall adaptive strategy of many species (see Heyes & Galef, 1996, for a general review, or Box & Gibson, 1999, for case studies on social learning in mammals). From lion cubs learning about how to bring down prey, to rats learning through smell about which foods are safe to eat, it is clear that animals use the behaviour of their more experienced peers as a source of valuable information. However, in reviewing the literature on social learning, we often find that although investigators believe social learning to be occurring in a particular species, there is very little known about the specific mechanisms that underlie it. For example, in Box and Gibson's edited collection, many contributors discuss the ecology of their chosen species in order to illustrate the likely roles that social learning may play, but can only speculate about exactly *how* the animals in question actually learn through the observation of another's behaviour.

Another curious fact about the social learning literature is the emphasis on imitation as a potential mechanism. Imitation — or "imitative learning" (Tomasello 1996, p. 324) — is a cognitively complex process that requires not only perceiving and reproducing the bodily movements of another, but understanding the changes in the environment caused by the other's behaviour, and finally being able to grasp the "intentional relations" between these, i.e., knowing how and why the behaviour is supposed to bring about the goal. This emphasis on imitation is particularly strong in the case of work on primates (Whiten 1998, e.g.). A focus on imitation is not surprising: it is likely to be implicated in the explosive cultural evolution of our own species, and so we have a natural curiosity about the extent to which other animals in general, and our primate cousins in particular, might share this ability. Nevertheless, looking at imitation alone may blind us to the potential of much simpler mechanisms through which the behaviour of one animal can influence the learning experience of another.

Although we often do not understand *how* social learning occurs, there is a body of work on *why* it might occur, i.e., on the conditions under which it would offer a selective advantage. Models of cultural transmission (Boyd & Richerson 1985) and related phenomena such as "highly horizontal transmission" (Laland, Richerson, & Boyd 1996) help to delineate the conditions under which it will be advantageous for individuals to learn from others rather than finding things out for themselves. However, these models tend to result in rather general conclusions. For example, Laland *et al.* (1996) summarize work on cultural transmission by relating it to rates of change in the environment: in static environments, genetic transmission of behaviour patterns can do the job, and in rapidly changing environments, only individual learning can keep up, whereas at intermediate rates of change, social learning will offer an advantage. Results like these are useful, but to get a complete picture of social learning we also need to understand the mechanisms involved.

Individual-based simulations, as used in artificial life research, represent an excellent way of instantiating a hypothesized social learning mechanism and thereby testing its plausibility. ALife models of this type have certainly been explored in related domains such as communication, dominance and territorial behaviour, and flocking or schooling. There are also a significant number of robotics researchers who share the primatologists' interest in imitation and see it as a way of improving human–robot or robot–robot communication (for a review of this work see Schall, 1999).

However, as yet relatively few ALife models have looked at social learning using mechanisms simpler than imitation. One example is the work of Toquenaga *et al.* (1995) who constructed a simulation of foraging and nesting behaviour in egrets. They used their model to demonstrate that learning socially about the location of food, through simply approaching other birds, is more likely to evolve when food resources are patchy rather than evenly distributed. Toquenaga, Kajitani, & Hoshino suggest that flock foraging and colonial roosting may be based on this principle. In the same vein, Noble *et al.* (2001) considered the selective pressures affecting social learning about food in Norway rats. They found that a surprisingly simple strategy, which involved ignoring signs of food poisoning in others, was favoured as long as toxins were very dangerous. This finding was used to explain apparently paradoxical aspects of rat behaviour.

Noble and Todd (in press) have previously argued that a focus on imitation has led to the power of simpler social learning processes being underestimated; they describe a number of candidate simple mechanisms, and encourage the use of simulation models as a way of demonstrating the potential of such mechanisms. The purpose of the current paper is to follow up on this work by instantiating some of the mechanisms discussed by Noble and Todd, in a simple environment that reflects the learning challenges faced by a hypothetical animal. The aim is to show that simple mechanisms can perform well under the right environmental circumstances, and hopefully to demonstrate that imitative learning has received a disproportionate amount of attention. We must stress that even though our simulated agents are inspired by several different primates, our goal is not to model learning in any particular species, but to set up a specific, controlled environment in which the performance of different social learning strategies can be compared.

In looking at the data that is output by our simulation, we want to adopt the perspective of an ethologist who is observing behaviour in the field and trying to come up with conclusions about the underlying mechanisms. Noble and Todd (in press) make the point, following Braitenberg (1984), that human observers of animal and robot behaviour have a propensity to invoke mechanisms that are more complex than those strictly needed to explain that behaviour. For example, the presence of a distinctive behaviour pattern across all members of a group could be taken as evidence for sophisticated social learning, but might result simply from similar individual learning experiences. We hope to show that much of the data a field observer might plausibly collect about a population could easily lead them astray in theorizing about what the animals were really doing.

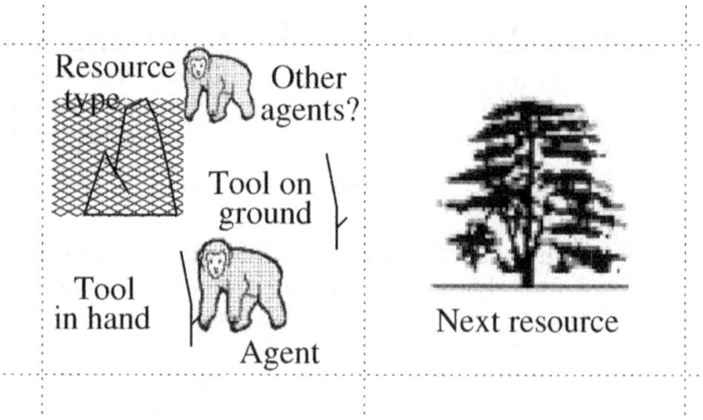

Figure 1: Aspects of the environment that can be perceived by each agent: the focal agent is in the left-hand grid square, and can perceive its local resource type — in this case a termite nest — the fact that it is grasping a stick, the presence of another stick on the ground, the presence of a second agent, and the proximity of a tree in the next grid square. If the agent chose the *travel* action, it would move to the tree.

The simulation

The environment consists of a 10 × 10 toroidal grid world, in which each square is either empty (20%) or contains a resource (80%). In addition, a grid square may contain a tool that agents are free to pick up and take away; agents may also drop tools. Agents occupy one square at a time, and more than one agent can occupy the same square. At each time step an agent chooses one of 12 distinct actions, and performing an action may lead to positive or negative payoffs depending on the context. An agent's choice of action is based on feeding its perceptual state into a reinforcement learning algorithm and choosing the action with the highest expected payoff (with a 20% chance of choosing a random action, in order to encourage exploration). Agents can perceive their local resource and the available tools — one on the ground and one in their grasp — as well as the presence of other agents (see Figure 1). They can also perceive the resource type in a randomly selected square drawn from the eight-square neighbourhood around their current location. If they choose to move, they will travel to this square.

The enviroment is deliberately simple, even playful: it is certainly not meant to be realistic. The guiding principles were, first, not to include an excessive number of distinct states, as this would make things difficult for the agents' reinforcement learning algorithm, and second, to ensure that some potential rewards were easily discovered and that others were harder to find (although possibly made easier with the right kind of social learning).

Generally, different resources are associated with distinct payoffs, and require the right action or sequence of actions to obtain them. The different resource types are listed below. Actions and tools are shown in italics, means and standard deviations for payoffs are shown as μ and σ respectively, P denotes the prevalence of that resource in the environment, and n refers to the number of times the resource can be used before it is exhausted. An exhausted resource reverts to empty, and a replacement appears in a randomly chosen empty square elsewhere in the environment.

Tree: being in the shade of a tree is pleasant, with a small constant reward ($\mu = 1$, $\sigma = 0$) regardless of the chosen action. $P =$ 10%, $n = \infty$.

Berries: an easy resource to figure out, berries are assumed to be automatically eaten ($\mu = 10$, $\sigma = 5$) regardless of action. If the agent *shakes* the berry bush, twice the payoff is obtained ($\mu = 20$, $\sigma = 5$). $P =$ 10%, $n = 20$.

Nettles: normally cause a nasty sting ($\mu = -10$, $\sigma = 5$) regardless of action but if an agent *folds* the nettle leaves, they can be safely eaten ($\mu = 30$, $\sigma = 5$). $P = 10\%$, $n = 20$.

Termite nest: the best way to get a meal of termites is to *poke* the nest with a *peeled stick* ($\mu = 100$, $\sigma = 20$) — the termites swarm on the stick and the agent can lick it clean. Also a reward for *poking* with a *stick* ($\mu = 50$, $\sigma = 10$) or without any tool ($\mu = 20$, $\sigma = 5$). *Bashing* the nest with a *stone* or a *big stone* will get some termites ($\mu = 35$, $\sigma = 10$). $P = 10\%$, $n = 10$.

Coconuts: need to be *bashed* to have a chance of opening them and getting the milk ($\mu = 150$, $\sigma = 20$). $P = 10\%$, $n = 5$. Chance of successfully opening a coconut depends on whether *stones* or *big stones* are available in hand and on the ground.

	On ground		
	Nothing	Stone	Big stone
Holding			
None	0.01	0.01	0.01
Stone	0.2	0.6	1.0
Big stone	0.4	0.6	0.8

Monkeys: can be caught and eaten ($\mu = 200$, $\sigma = 20$) if an agent *chases* them, but only if a second agent is present to block their escape route. Alternatively an agent can *throw* *stone* for a 10% chance of success, or *throw* a *stick*, a *peeled stick*, or a *big stone* for a 2% chance of success. $P = 10\%$, $n = 2$.

Thorns: are painful ($\mu = -20$, $\sigma = 5$) regardless of action. $P = 10\%$, $n = \infty$.

Beehive: there is a 20% chance that the bees will fly out and sting the agent ($\mu = -200$, $\sigma = 50$) regardless of action. $P = 5\%$, $n = \infty$. If the agent *shakes*, *pokes*, or *bashes* the hive the chance of stinging is 100%. The hardest trick to learn is getting honey from the hive ($\mu = 500$, $\sigma = 50$, $n = 1$): the agent must either *bash* the nest with a *stone* or a *big stone* for a 50% chance of success (and a 100% chance of getting stung) or smoke the bees out by starting a fire, i.e., *rubbing* two *sticks* of either type together (one on the ground and one in the hand).

Wasp nest: the same negative properties as the beehive but with no chance of reward. $P = 5\%$, $n = \infty$.

An important action not covered above is *scratching*, which leads to a modest reward ($\mu = 1$, $\sigma = 0$; $\mu = 2$ if the agent is carrying either kind of *stick*) regardless of the local resource. Scratching provides a kind of local optimum, in that it is easy for an agent to get locked into pursuing the modest rewards of this activity, perhaps under a tree, rather than moving around looking for more profitable resources.

Other actions include *peeling*, which converts a *stick* in the agent's hand into a *peeled stick*; *swapping*, which exchanges the tool on the ground, if any, for the one in the agent's hand, if any; and *travelling*, which moves the agent to the nearby resource they have most recently seen. Note that when an agent attempts an irrelevant action, such as bashing a tree, the payoff is always zero.

Tools are distributed generously, with 40 sticks, 20 stones, and 20 large stones present in the environment. Peeled sticks only appear if an agent peels a stick. Stones do not wear out, but sticks and peeled sticks break after 1000 or 500 time steps respectively; a replacement stick appears at a random location.

Reinforcement learning agents

The agent population is 25, but initially agents enter the world one at a time. Every 400 timesteps a new agent is born. When 25 agents are present, the oldest agent is always killed off to make room for the youngest; an agent's lifespan is therefore 10,000 timesteps. The middle-aged agent born 12 places ahead of a newborn is nominally regarded as its parent, and the new agent appears in the same square. The simulation is run for 100,000 time steps, or 10 agent lifetimes. Even though the simulation has "generations" of a sort, there is no genetic aspect to agent behaviour: each individual comes into the world as a blank slate and must learn for itself how to maximize payoffs.

Each agent makes its decisions on the basis of a history of reinforcement: it has learned to associate some states and actions with a reward and others with punishment. The different social learning mechanisms implemented all assume this underlying capacity for reinforcement learning. The specific learning algorithm used was Q-learning (Watkins & Dayan 1992) which allows an agent to take into account not just immediate but also delayed payoffs. This would be important, for example, in realizing that a higher long-term payoff could be gained by picking up and peeling a stick rather than just poking the termite nest immediately. The learning rate was 0.1, the temporal discounting factor was 0.5, and the proportion of random actions was 0.2.

Q-learning in its simplest form does not include any generalization: if an agent learns that it is good to shake a berry bush when there is a stone on the ground, it will not automatically transfer that knowledge to the case where there is no stone on the ground. Given 60,000 state-action pairs[1] and a lifetime of only 10,000 timesteps it is clear that an agent could not exhaustively sample its space of perceived situations. We therefore included some basic generalization: after updating a state-action pair through Q-learning, all other state-action pairs that differed only in terms of the tools available, the presence of others, and the resource seen in the distance (exception: the resource being left behind for the travel action) also had their expected returns updated by a small amount in the same direction.

Implementing social learning

To find baseline levels for payoffs in this environment, we looked at the performance of agents with completely random behaviour, and at that of agents capable only of individual learning. We then implemented three of the simple mechanisms described by Noble and Todd (in press): following or stimulus enhancement, contagious behaviour, and emulation. In addition, we implemented a version of imitative learning. Finally, we looked at the performance obtained when following was combined with each of the other mechanisms.

Following: (otherwise known as stimulus enhancement) is implemented simply by having each agent occupy the same square as its parent for the first 25% of its lifetime. Beyond that, agents learn for themselves.

Contagious behaviour: if another agent is present, there is a 10% probability that the first agent will do whatever the second just did. An instinctive behavioural contagion is assumed, as when one person's yawning stimulates another to yawn; actions are equally likely to be copied regardless of their payoff.

Emulation: if another agent is present and obtains a non-zero payoff, the first agent adjusts its estimated return for *all* state-action pairs related to its current state. The idea is that the agent has become aware of an affordance in

[1]10 resources × 5 tool-on-ground options × 5 tool-in-hand options × 2 others-present options × 10 next-resource options × 12 actions = 60,000.

the local environment, but has no idea about what specific action is needed to exploit it.

Imitation: if another agent is present and obtains a non-zero payoff, the first agent is able to take the perspective of the second. The first agent notes the perceptual state of the other, as well as the action the other chose, and updates its own relevant state-action pair accordingly. The advance on emulation is that the first agent not only knows which action achieved the reward, but also can perceive the other agent's state as opposed to its own (e.g., it might be holding a stick).

Data collection

How can we collect data from this simulation that parallels the data ethologists would collect when observing a real species? We assumed that observers watched the population for the final 1000 timesteps; i.e., they had a snapshot of the group's behaviour rather than being able to observe the rise and fall of socially transmitted behaviours in the long term. We then looked at the average payoff per agent during these 1000 timesteps. We can imagine that the ethologists are observing distinct groups in similar environments and comparing the average energy intake across groups. It is natural to assume that a population equipped with a richer social learning ability will be able to extract more energy from its environment.

We also wanted to measure behavioural convergence, i.e., the degree to which the various members of the population tend to choose the same action when faced with the same situation. This was done by compiling a list of 1000 states perceived by members of the population (the state of a randomly chosen individual was noted at each timestep). Then all 25 members of the population were faced with each of the 1000 states in turn, and the proportion of individuals who chose the modal response for each state was recorded and averaged. We can imagine that the ethologists have an outstanding ability to set up naturalistic experiments in the field, and are able to engineer things so that each member of the population can be placed into the same series of states and allowed to choose an action.

We looked at behavioural convergence because uniformity of behaviour within a population, especially when combined with behavioural variation *across* populations, is usually taken as a sign that social learning is going on. For example, if one group is observed to hunt monkeys by chasing them down, while another group tends to throw stones at them, then it seems to follow that each animal is not arriving at its own solution to the problem, but rather is being influenced by its fellow group members.

Finally, we looked at simple counts of the occurrence of various behaviours: the performance of more complex and hard-to-learn behaviours would probably be taken as a sign of sophisticated social learning. So, for example, if one species has mastered the trick of peeling sticks before poking them into termite nests, and another related species has not, one might assume that the former species has a better social learning faculty.

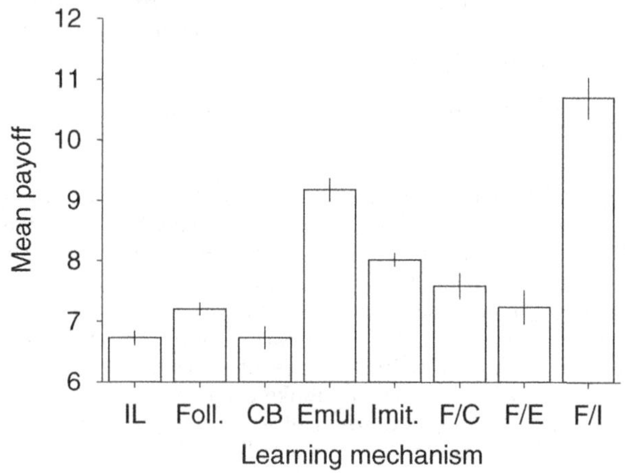

Figure 2: Mean payoff per agent per timestep across the different learning conditions: individual learning, following, contagious behaviour, emulation, imitation, following with contagious behaviour, following with emulation, and following with imitation. Each data point is averaged across 10 runs, and is shown ± 1 standard error.

Results and discussion

All of the learning mechanisms, both individual and social, ensured that the agents did far better than they would by choosing a random action. Figure 2 shows that the mean payoff per agent per timestep was at least 6 units; the mean payoff for random behaviour was -8.997 units. Behaviours such as scratching, eating berries, folding nettle leaves, and poking termite nests (although not often with tools) were all quite common and allowed the agents to extract a good return from the environment.

Omitting for a moment the cases in which following is combined with another mechanism, we have the surprising result that the best mean payoff is for emulation, not imitative learning. Why does this occur? Emulation means that an agent increases its estimated return for *all* state-action pairs associated with any state in which it witnesses another agent receiving a positive payoff. Effectively this means that emulation encourages exploration around beneficial resources, and results in more inquisitive agents who are persistent enough to crack a tricky resource like nettle leaves. Imitators, on the other hand, are quite conservative. Imitative learning is sophisticated enough to allow an agent to pick up any clever trick it might witness, but imitators appear to be caught in a vicious circle in which the only role models they observe are other conservative imitators (see the behavioural profiles in Figure 4).

Figure 2 also shows that the simple matter of following your parent around for the first quarter of your life is enough to increase your mean payoff significantly. This is more impressive than it seems, as the imposition of following behaviour threatens to *decrease* payoffs by increasing feeding competition: a resource will run out twice as fast if it is being consumed by both parent and child. Contagious behaviour, on the other hand, did not do any better than individual learning. It may be that occasional instinctive copying is unhelpful because agents already try random actions 20% of the time and will thus reach the same result in the end.

When following behaviour is combined with other mechanisms, the story becomes more complex. It is obviously not the case that following and the other three mechanisms mesh together in a simple additive fashion: the efficiency of imitation and contagious behaviour is increased, but the efficiency of emulation is decreased. Clearly it is important to imitate or emulate the right people: an experienced parent in one case, and a random cross-section of society in the other.

Behavioural convergence (Figure 3) was 0.55 even in the individual learning case. The convergence score for random behaviour was inevitably much lower at 0.18, and thus we are reminded that similar behaviour may be brought about by similar learning experiences rather than any form of social learning. Convergence was highest in the two imitation conditions, which makes sense. However, the low convergence for emulation belies the fact that these agents were doing well in terms of mean payoff, and convergence rates are the same across the two imitation conditions, despite the fact that it is only in the following / imitation condition that high payoffs are achieved. An observation of high or low behavioural convergence, which might lead one to suspect the presence or absence of effective social learning, is meaningless considered alone.

Figure 4 shows frequency counts for several behaviours across the different conditions. It shows that different learning mechanisms lead to quite different behavioural profiles, e.g., emulators spend a lot of time folding nettle leaves, whereas imitators have mastered the art of shaking berry bushes. It is not simply the case that the more "advanced" the social learning mechanism, the more behaviours are added to the repertoire.

Another surprising finding is that some behaviours that would seem to suit imitative learning, such as learning to peel a stick and then poke it into a termite nest, are in fact more often performed by agents with simpler mechanisms (Figure 4, bottom). Agents who follow their parents are the ones who do this most often. Even so, it seems that this behaviour was largely too hard: note the low frequency counts overall. Imitators could certainly have picked up this trick, but again it seems they did not have access to the right role models.

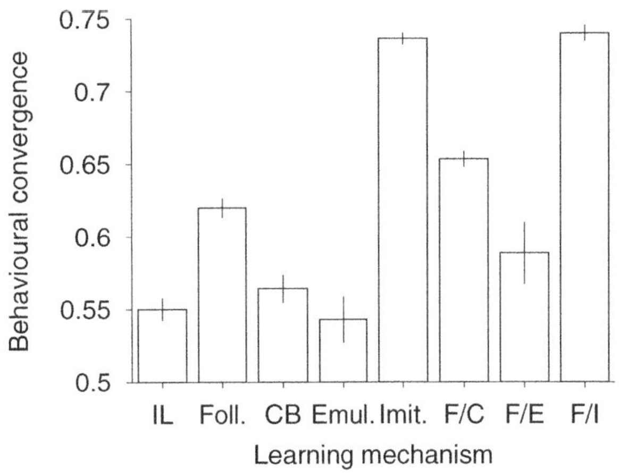

Figure 3: Behavioural convergence across the different learning conditions. Each data point is averaged across 10 runs, and is shown ± 1 standard error.

Conclusions

We hope to have demonstrated that imitative learning is not always going to be the best strategy for a group-living animal, and that the effectiveness of any social learning strategy will depend on details of the environment and additional facts about the animal's lifestyle. We readily admit that the impressive performance of emulation in our model, for example, is not likely to be a general result, but is tied to the particulars of the simulated environment and the underlying reinforcement learning system. But that is exactly the point.

The argument which inspired this paper (Noble and Todd, in press) had two aspects: first, simpler social learning mechanisms are inherently more likely to evolve; one reason for this is that complex mechanisms such as imitation will involve significant costs. It follows that we should look for simple mechanisms in nature. Second, in cases of doubt about which mechanism is at work, from an epistemological point of view it is good practice to start by proposing simpler mechanisms. The current simulation results show that an even stronger argument is possible: even if imitation was available via a cost-free, one-step mutation, it sill might not be the best learning mechanism for a given species.

A focus on imitation as the only kind of social learning worth having is misplaced. Researchers interested in imitation as a potential tool for instructing robots or software agents, for example, might do well to consider giving their creations more spartan mechanisms, which have the additional benefit of being far easier to program. If the agent is equipped with a reinforcement learning system, it would be a good start to simply have it follow a more experienced agent (e.g., a person).

We believe our model also shows that ethologists comparing how well two different groups of animals get on in

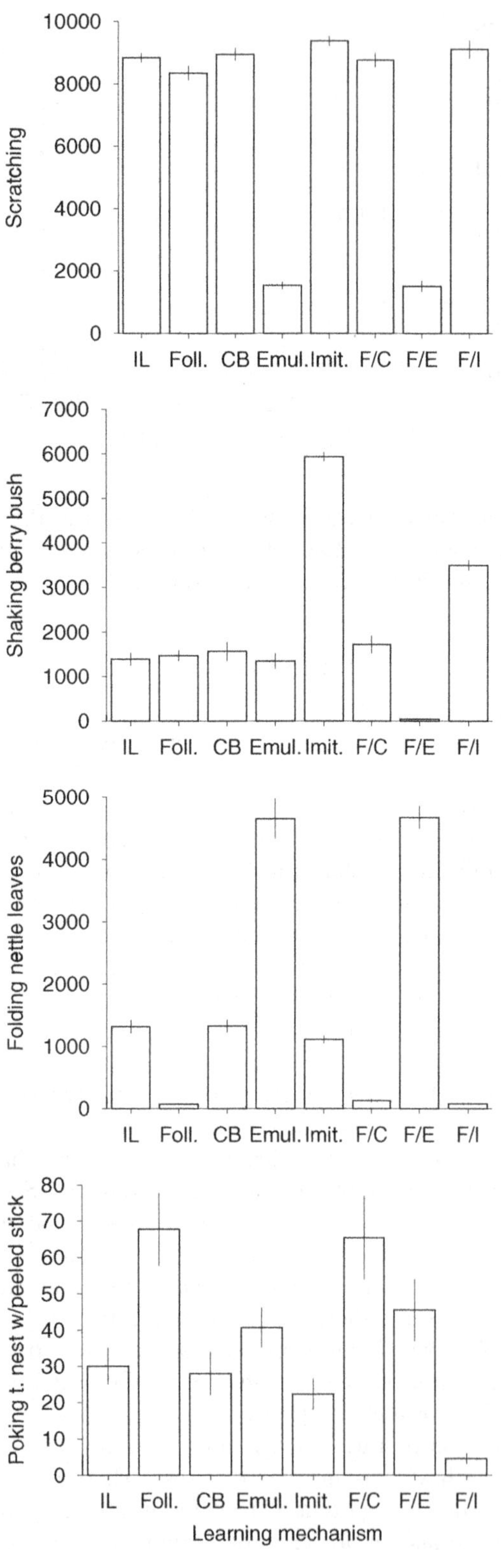

Figure 4: Frequencies with which various behaviours were observed across the different learning conditions: from top to bottom, scratching, shaking berry bushes, folding nettle leaves, and poking termite nests with peeled sticks. Each data point is averaged across 10 runs, and is shown ±1 standard error.

similar environments, or looking at data on "traditions" or "proto-cultural behaviour" (i.e., behavioural convergence) may find that data to be quite misleading as to the underlying social learning mechanisms at work. It is not the case, for example, that low behavioural convergence necessarily means an absence of social learning. One has to be careful in looking at exactly how behaviours are transmitted from one individual to another. Theories about the adaptive value of social learning, such as Laland *et al.*(1996), are useful, but ideally we want to move beyond such theories and look at hypotheses about the utility of a particular mechanism in a particular environment.

We deliberately omitted an evolutionary dimension from the current model as we wanted to look at the effects of learning alone. However, future work could incorporate an evolutionary aspect, in which different social learning mechanisms were selected for over generational time. The mean payoff results certainly suggest that this would not be a straightforward story of hill-climbing with imitation at the peak. Let us assume that a single-step mutation F controls following behaviour, and a two-step mutation leads from individual learning to emulation (S_1) and thence to imitative learning (S_2). This latter assumption is reasonable as imitative learning can be seen as a "sharpened" version of emulation. For an evolving population of individual learners, the final strategy will be emulation if S_1 occurs first, as F and S_2 will both be associated with a loss in fitness. On the other hand, if F occurs first, both S_1 and then S_2 will mean increases in fitness, and the population will end up as follower / imitators.

It would be useful to move away from our simplistic lookup-table implementation of Q-learning and use a neural network as a more natural way of generalizing across perceptual states. We are also interested in investigating whether infinite negative payoffs, i.e., actions that result in the death of the agent, push an evolving population towards imitative strategies. Finally, we would like to use the same basic technique described here to produce a high-fidelity model of social learning in a particular species, e.g., chimpanzees, and thereby comment on which mechanisms are plausibly being used by that species, much as Noble *et al.*(2001) do for Norway rats.

References

Box, H. O., and Gibson, K. R. 1999. *Mammalian Social Learning: Comparative and Ecological Perspectives*, volume 72 of *Symposia of the Zoological Society of London.* Cambridge: Cambridge University Press.

Boyd, R., and Richerson, P. J. 1985. *Culture and the Evolutionary Process.* Chicago: The University of Chicago Press.

Braitenberg, V. 1984. *Vehicles: Experiments in Synthetic Psychology.* Cambridge, MA: MIT Press.

Heyes, C. M., and Galef, Jr., B. G., eds. 1996. *Social Learning in Animals: The Roots of Culture.* San Diego, CA: Academic Press.

Laland, K. N.; Richerson, P. J.; and Boyd, R. 1996. Developing a theory of animal social learning. In Heyes and Galef (1996). 129–154.

Noble, J., and Todd, P. M. 2002. Imitation or something simpler? Modelling simple mechanisms for social information processing. In Dautenhahn, K., and Nehaniv, C., eds., *Imitation in Animals and Artifacts.* MIT Press.

Noble, J.; Todd, P. M.; and Tuci, E. 2001. Explaining social learning of food preferences without aversions: An evolutionary simulation model of Norway rats. *Proceedings of the Royal Society of London: Biological Sciences* 268(1463):141–149.

Schaal, S. 1999. Is imitation learning the route to humanoid robots? *Trends in Cognitive Sciences* 3(6):233–242.

Tomasello, M. 1996. Do apes ape? In Heyes and Galef (1996). 319–346.

Toquenaga, Y.; Kajitani, I.; and Hoshino, T. 1995. Egrets of a feather flock together. *Artificial Life* 1(4):391–411.

Watkins, C. J. C. H., and Dayan, P. 1992. Q-learning. *Machine Learning* 8:279–292.

Whiten, A. 1998. mitation of the sequential structure of actions by chimpanzees Pan troglodytes. *Journal of Comparative Psychology* 112(3):270–281.

Collective or Scattering: Evolving Schooling Behaviors to Escape from Predator

Tamon Oboshi, **Shohei Kato**, **Atsuko Mutoh** and **Hidenori Itoh**

Department of Intelligence and Computer Science,
Nagoya Institute of Technology.
Gokiso-cho, Showa-ku, Nagoya 466-8555, Japan.
{b-star, shohey, atsuko, itoh}@ics.nitech.ac.jp

Abstract

In this paper, we consider an artificial life, model of the fish behavior, and discuss the mechanism of fish school behavior by making it acquire the school behavior by evolutionary computation. An artificial ecology where fishes and a predator coexist is considered and we enhance one of the models for fish schooling with the ability to sense a predator's approach. This paper proposes an evolutionary method for the acquisition of evading behavior against predator. This paper also shows our computer simulation of the prey-predator system, and reports well simulated prey behaviors, especially evading behaviors of the predator with advantage of schooling.

Introduction

Most animals in groups maintain the group without a supervisor leading or external stimuli. Fish, one of the typical species which gather in aggregates, have been studied by many researchers, so as to elucidate the mechanism of the school behavior (Reynolds 1987; Huth & Wissel 1994; Aoki 1982; Gunji & Kusunoki 1997, for instance).

Some behavior models of fish on the basis of interaction underlying schooling are proposed from an observational standpoint (Aoki 1982; Gunji & Kusunoki 1997, for instance). The behavioral rules on the models are simplified to the two components of movement: speed and direction, and the components are independent or, at most, related to the location and heading of the neighbors. Schooling phenomenon is well simulated by the models. They, however, do not consider the coexistence of prey and predator. An ecological model for coexistence of prey and predator has been reported by Ward (2001). The model is based on BOID by Reynolds (1987), and coevolution is well performed. The aim of this research is not to perform coevolution, but to investigate the advantages of grouping: for example, dilution, confusion and so on, with respect to protection from predator. Our model is, thus, based on a biological model concept, which is based on the observational and empirical investigation of fish behavior.

In this paper, we consider an ecology of predator and prey fish, and then enhance one of the models for fish schooling with the ability to sense the predator's approach. We, after that, propose an evolutionary method for the acquisition of evading behavior against predator which is recognized as an evolved schooling behavior. This paper also shows our computer simulation of prey-predator system, and reports well simulated prey behaviors, especially evading behaviors against predator with advantage of schooling.

Behavioral Models

In this research, we adopt a biological model concept by Aoki (Aoki 1982), which is based on the observational and empirical investigation of interaction of fish behavior with its neighbors in the schooling phenomenon. Many behavioral models stand on Aoki's model (Huth & Wissel 1992; 1994; Inada 2001, for example). Aoki's model is, thus, considered to be a proper base for our research.

The concept of Aoki's model, however, does not consider the existence of a predator: i.e. no interaction between prey and predator. In this section, as the first step of this research, we enhance the model so as to examine the evading behavior of prey against predator. This paper, and then, provides an evolutionary approach by GA, as one solution for the discussion.

The basic behavior model for fish schooling

Firstly, suppose a *fundamental assumption* (Aoki 1982) for all of our models. In our models, a 2-D world is assumed. The movement of individuals is represented by two components: speed and direction, and interaction between individuals are restricted to the directional component. In addition, water depth, flow, and temperature and external stimuli are not considered.

On the basic model, movement of an individual has four basic behavior patterns: *repulsion* behavior, move with a high *parallel orientation*, biosocial *attraction*, and *searching* behavior. An individual selects one from these behaviors based on the distance between i and its neighbors. Each of the basic behaviors has a range, and the behavior is selected by reason that a neighbor appears in the range. Figure 1 shows the ranges of the basic behavior patterns for a individual (black one in the figure). Let us suppose that no individual can see the outside of attraction area, that is, the *sensory field* of individual is composed of repulsion, parallel, and attraction areas.

Decision of the movement (normal mode). Let i and j be individuals, and suppose that j lies in the neighborhood of i, and i reacts to j (j is called *reference individual* for i). As mentioned above, the movement of i is composed of direction and speed, and let $d_i(t)$ be the

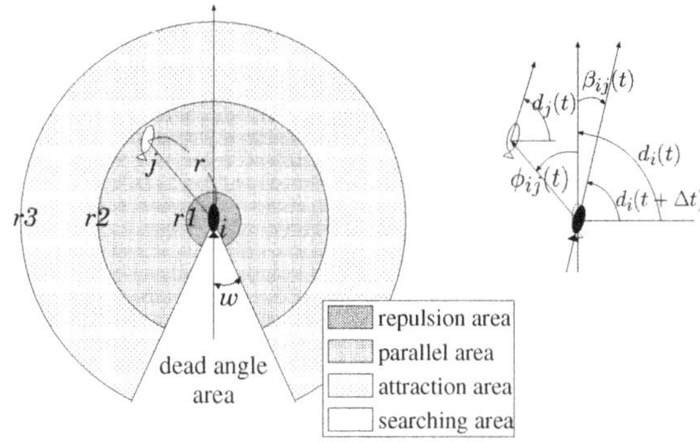

Figure 1: Ranges of the basic behavior patterns.

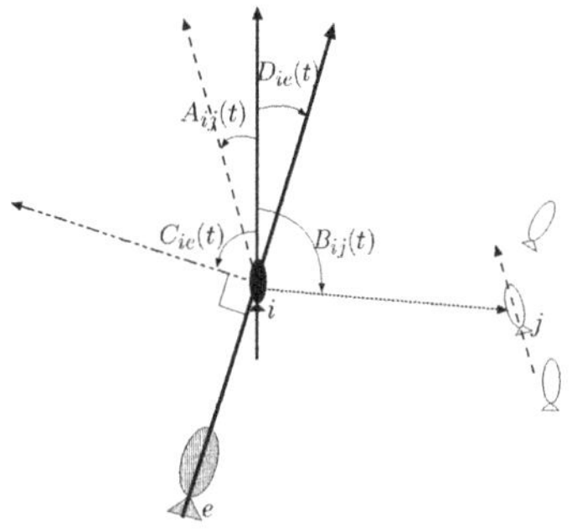

Figure 2: Turning Angles for Behavior in Urgent Mode.

direction of i at time t. On the basic model, $d_i(t+\Delta t)$, is defined as follows:

$$d_i(t+\Delta t) = d_i(t) + \beta_{ij}(t) + \beta_0, \quad (1)$$

where $\beta_{ij}(t)$, *distinct turning angle* of i for j, is determined by any of the following equations according to which area of i j appears in (see Figure 1):

repulsion area ($r \leq r1$):

$$\beta_{ij}(t) = \min(\phi_{ij}(t) \pm 90°), \quad (2)$$

parallel area ($r1 < r \leq r2$):

$$\beta_{ij}(t) = d_j(t) - d_i(t)), \quad (3)$$

attraction area ($r2 < r \leq r3$):

$$\beta_{ij}(t) = \phi_{ij}(t), \quad (4)$$

searching area ($r > r3$ or dead angle area):

$$\beta_{ij}(t) = \text{an angle } [-180°, +180°) \text{ chosen with uniform probability}, \quad (5)$$

where β_0 means wobble about each decision of the direction, and it has Normal distribution $Normal(0, \theta^2)$, and where $\min(a, b)$ returns the minimum value of a or b, by comparison between $|a|$ and $|b|$. In this model, reference individual j for i is selected with greater probability of nearer neighbor to i.

The velocity of an individual at any time is determined independently of other individuals. The velocity is a stochastic variable. It is described by a Gamma-distribution.

The enhanced model considering predator's existence

The section describes the urgent behavior of an individual when it senses a predator approaching.

Decision of the movement (urgent mode). Individuals shift to *urgent mode*, when a predator appears in the sensory field of the individual. Let i be an individual, and e be a predator which is sensed by i. In urgent mode, the direction $d_i^e(t+\Delta t)$ of i at time $t+\Delta t$, is defined as follows:

$$d_i^e(t+\Delta t) = d_i^e(t) + \beta_{ie}^e(t) + \beta_0, \quad (6)$$

where $\beta_{ij}^e(t)$, *distinct turning angle* of i for j against e, is determined by the following equation whichever areas in the sensory field e appears in:

$$\beta_{ie}^e(t) = \frac{\alpha A_{ij}(t) + \beta B_{ij}(t) + \gamma C_{ie}(t) + \delta D_{ie}(t)}{\alpha + \beta + \gamma + \delta}, \quad (7)$$

where $A_{ij}(t)$, $B_{ij}(t)$, $C_{ie}(t)$, and $D_{ie}(t)$ are turning angles for *parallel with* j, *attracted to* j, *averting from* e, and *away from* e, respectively (see Figure 2). In Equation (7), α, β, γ, and δ are weights on the turning angles: *parallel*, *attracted*, *averting*, and *away from* respectively. These weights determine the strategy of the individual for evasion of predator. The velocity of an individual in urgent mode is determined by the same manner as normal mode.

Predator's behavior

The section gives a brief description of behavior of the predator. Let e be a predator and i be an individual, and suppose that i lies within the sensory field of e. In this model, preying target i for e is selected from individuals in the sensory field of e, with greater probability of nearer neighbor to e. Predator e then chases i or changes the direction randomly, if no individual is in the sensory field of e. It should be noticed that the sensory field and speed of the predator are superior than the prey's; predator's sensory field is κ times larger, and the distribution of predator's speed is η times faster than individuals. The predator e preys on i, and i disappears when e approaches i to quarter of e's length.

Ecology and Evolution

The section fixes an environment for individuals and a predator, and describes an evolutionary method for individual's orientational configuration for evasion of predator.

The artificial ecology

We consider a $40BL$ by $40BL$ toroidal environment, where BL means the mean of the *body length* of individuals. We take N prey individuals (small fishes) and a predator (predatory fish) in the ecology.At each evolution, the ecology create the shortfall of individuals to the next generations, if there exists less than N individual.

Genetic algorithm

All of individuals have the parameters for orientational configuration for predator: α, β, γ, and δ (see Equation (7)). Chromosomes of individuals are composed of these parameters, that is, four sections, and each of the parameters is encoded in 10 bit-strings. We consider, as the quality of the solution, how many time steps the individual can survive with its evading behavior based on the orientational configuration the chromosome represents. We apply one point crossover for each section of chromosome (totally four points) to two parents, and assign 5% to probability of mutation for each bit of chromosome after crossover. An individual's chance of being chosen as a parent is proportional to its fitness.

Experiments

Method

In one of the experiments, we took 100 individuals (small fish) and a predator (predatory fish) in the ecology. Parameters for the basic behavioral model for small fishes, where $r1 = 0.5BL$, $r2 = 2.0BL$, $r3 = 5.0BL$, and $w = 30°$ for the ranges of their behavior patterns, and $\theta = 15.0$ for wobble on the decision of individual's orientation. Parameters for predator's superiority, where $\kappa = 4$ and $\eta = 1.2$. On the above conditions, we have run the system for 300 generations, with 1,000 moves in each, and total of 10 runs were made.

Results and discussion

Figure 3 shows the average proportions of parameters, α, β, γ, and δ, which determine orientation configuration of individuals for evading predators, with each generation. The result indicates that, as each generation, each of the parameters becomes more convergent; β becomes lower, δ becomes higher, and α becomes fairly higher. It is obvious that δ becomes larger so as to acquire the evading behavior. The increase in α should be noticed; this suggests that evolution takes schooling more into consideration of evading behavior.

We have, then, investigated the influence of predator's dominance on preys' behavior. Figure 4 shows the proportions of evolved parameter α, β, γ and δ when η, predator's dominance of speed, changes from 0.5 to 2.0 at 300-th generation. All parameters except η are the same with the above experiments. The result makes two remarks. One is that the proportion of α is moderately high, when η is lower (lower risk for prey). Another

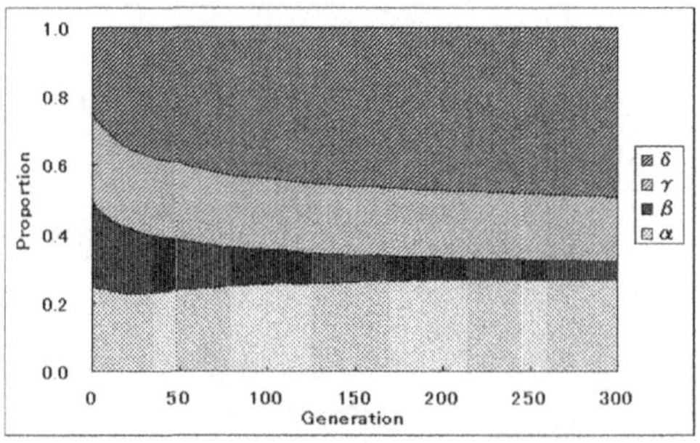

Figure 3: Average Proportions of α, β, γ, and δ in the Enhanced Behavioral Model.

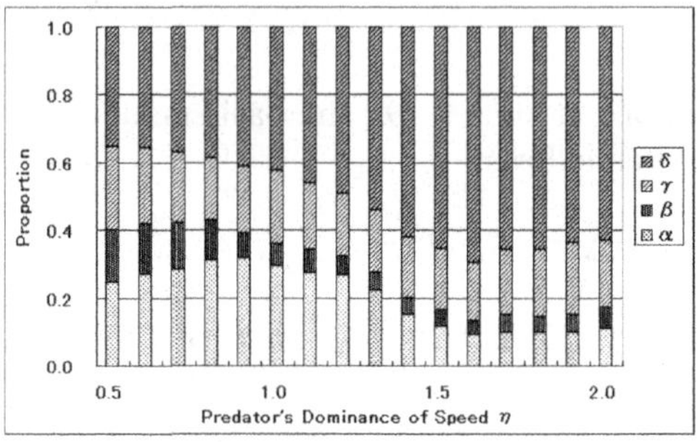

Figure 4: Average Proportions of α, β, γ, and δ Against Change η.

is that, as parameter η becomes higher (higher risk for prey), the proportion of δ increases; it has a maximum rate when $\eta = 1.6$, and afterwards, decreases gently. This suggests that the scattered evasion is a more effective behavior in the environment where there is higher risk of being eaten. If the predator's speed is excessively superior to individuals, individuals will be eaten no matter which evading behavior individuals have, that is, there is no strategy for evading the predator. We, thus, guess that the proportion of δ decreases if $\eta > 2.0$.

We have also made an observational investigation for our model by comparing real fish behavior with the simulation. Figure 5 shows snapshots of evading behaviors by sardines (as small fish) and bonitos (as predatory fish) in aquarium (the right frames), and by our simulation (the left frames). In the simulation, we prepared a situation similar to the observational result, with $\eta = 1.2$. The proportions of parameters α, β, γ, and δ are set by the values obtained from the above experiments (see Figure 4).

As one of the comparisons, we have measured the polarization of the fish school. The polarization ρ characterizes the intensity of parallel orientation in the school. The polarization is defined as the average of the angle deviation of each fish to the mean swimming direction of the school. For $\rho = 0°$ the school is optimally parallel, for $\rho = 90°$ the school is maximally confused. Figure 6 shows that transition of polarization ρ of fish behaviors shown in Figure 5. In the graph, (a),(b),(c) and (d) cor-

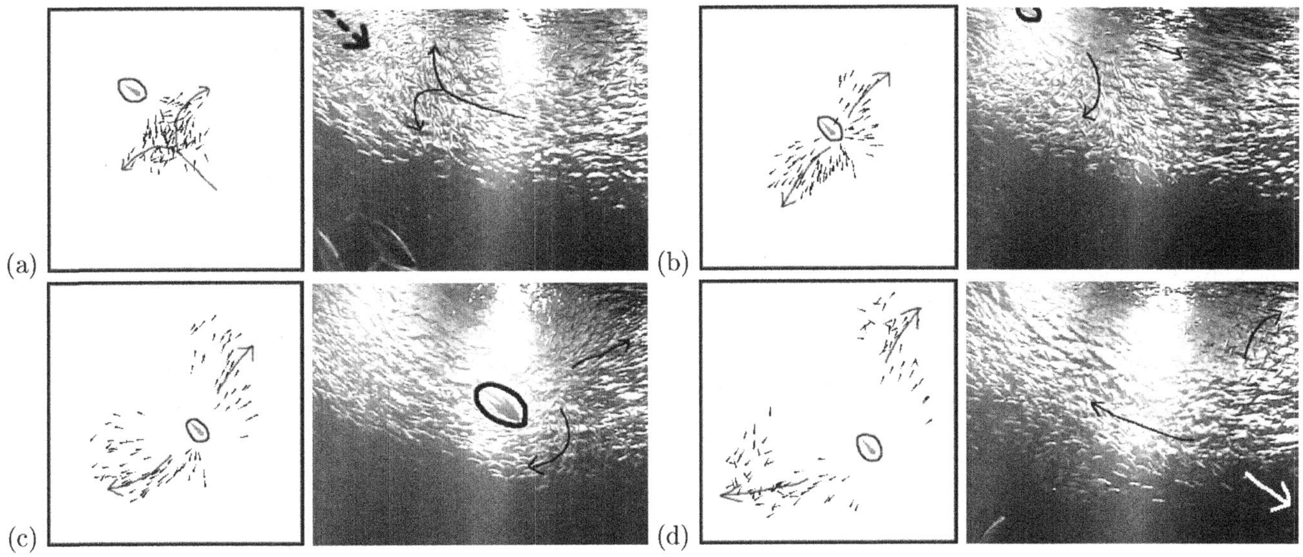

Figure 5: A Comparison of Fish Behaviors between the Real and the Simulation.

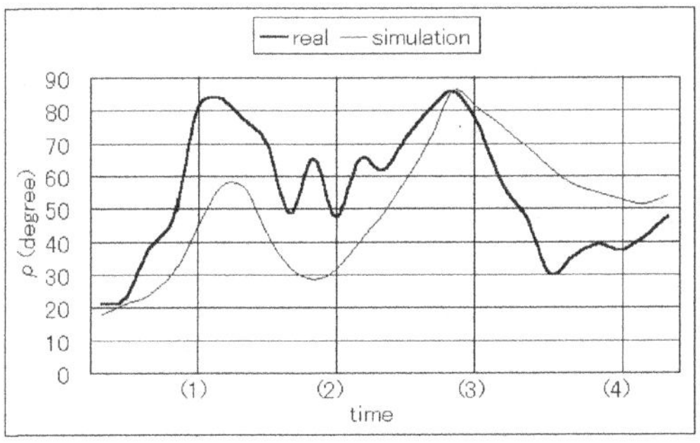

Figure 6: Transition for Polarization of Fishes.

respond to the labels in Figure 5. The graph shows that two transitions have fairly similar tendency each other. The results indicate that our model and evolutionary method can evolve evading behavior of individuals adaptively to their environment, and a collective strategy for evading predator emerges by our method.

Conclusion

In this paper, we considered an ecology where fish and a predator coexist, and then enhanced one of the models for fish schooling with an ability to sense for predator's approach. After that, we proposed an evolutionary method for the acquisition of evading behavior against predator. We also implemented simulation of a prey-predator system, and reported simulated prey behaviors, that agreed well with observations of real fish, especially evading behaviors against predator with advantage of schooling.

Acknowledgment

We are grateful to Mr. Watanabe and the Port of Nagoya Public Aquarium for observational support, advice and discussions. This work was supported in part by Ministry of Education, Science, Sports and Culture, Grant-in-Aid for Scientific Research under grant #11680387 and #14780307.

References

Aoki, I. 1982. A Simulation Study on the Schooling Mechanism in Fish. *Bulletin of the Japanese Society of Scientific Fisheries* Vol.48(8):1081–1088.

Gunji, Y. P., and Kusunoki, Y. 1997. A model of Incomplete Identification Illustrating Schooling Behavior. *Chaos, Solitons & Fractals* Vol.8(10):1623–1630.

Huth, A., and Wissel, C. 1992. The Simulation of the Movement of Fish Schools. *Journal of Theoretical Biology* 156:365–385.

Huth, A., and Wissel, C. 1994. The Simulation of Fish Schools in Comparison with Experimental Data. *Ecological Modelling* 75/76:135–145.

Inada, Y. 2001. Steering Mechanism of Fish Schools. *Complexity International* 8:1–9.

Reynolds, C. W. 1987. Flocks, Herds, and Schools, A Distributed Behavioral Model. *The Proceeding of SIGGRAPH'87* Vol.21(4):25–34.

Ward, C. R.; Gobet, F.; and Kendall, G. 2001. Evolving Collective Behavior in an Artificial Ecology. *Artificial Life* 7(2):191–209.

Emergent Behavior in Phonological Pattern Change

Mark Dras[1] and **K. David Harrison**[2]

[1] Department of Computing, Macquarie University, North Ryde 2109 Australia (madras@ics.mq.edu.au)

[2] Department of Linguistics, Swarthmore College, Swarthmore PA 19081 USA (dharris2@swarthmore.edu)

Abstract

Language change has recently come to be seen as a complex dynamical system, along the lines of evolutionary biology and economics, as opposed to previous conceptions as a linear or cyclical system. We model the change of a particular phenomenon, vowel harmony, and look at the conditions under which the trajectory of change matches theoretical and empirical predictions. Our experimental work shows that there are certain conditions under which the desired trajectories do not occur, implying that absence of these conditions is necessary for accurate modeling of language change.

Introduction

Language change has at various times been seen as linear—that is, languages are progressing or decaying monotonically—or cyclical—that is, languages pass through a life cycle of birth, maturity, death and rebirth. However, modeling language change in a formal way has led to a recognition that it is a complex dynamical system (Lass 1997): the interaction of individual speakers leads to emergent, global population characteristics of a language that are neither linear nor cyclical.

In all dynamical systems there is an observable pattern of change, and the object of a model is to describe the process such that the model output closely approximates the empirical data; e.g. in evolutionary biology, there is gene frequency change, the basic process of evolution. In language change, there is the replacement of one linguistic phenomenon by another, such as when historically English diverged from Germanic and lost the requirement that the verb come second in the sentence. Analogy with evolutionary biology (Bailey 1973) and empirical work (Chen & Wang 1975) have supported an S-shaped functional dependence on time as the fundamental trajectory of language change.

The focus of our research is vowel harmony in Turkic languages. These systems exhibit a great deal of change—instability, even—over the more than one millennium during which these languages have been recorded in writing. Most Turkic languages have two autonomous harmony systems, one based on tongue backness and one on lip rounding. The systems range from robust, nearly exceptionless harmony to highly variable or restricted harmony to no harmony at all. They thus provide rich material for constructing typologies of harmony and models of language change.

Changes at the level of the individual aggregate to give language-wide evolution in backness harmony systems. Agent-based simulation, where a community of computational agents interacts over time, is an appropriate way of modeling language-related complex systems, as language changes take place in a social context. In this paper we present some results on what sorts of simulation models can produce observed trajectories of language change, and which cannot.

	front	back
high	i y	ɯ u
non-high	e ø	a o

Table 1: Vowel inventory (IPA)

Vowel harmony

In most Turkic languages, backness harmony is apparent both as an ambient pattern of vowel co-occurrence within word roots, and as a productive pattern of vowel alternations (e.g., in suffixes). The condition imposed by harmony is that only vowels from the same class can co-occur in a particular context.

A typical Turkic vowel inventory includes four front and four back vowels, divisible into harmonic classes (Table 1). Under backness harmony, then, only back vowels can co-occur with other back vowels, and only front vowels with front vowels. As an example of the first manifestation of backness harmony, word roots can only contain all back or all front vowels; this is particularly apparent when words are adopted into a harmonic language from a nonharmonic one (loanwords), where these are mutated so that the localized word is harmonic. For example, the disharmonic word *araki* ('alcohol') in Mongolian, a non-Turkic language, was adopted into Tuvan, a Turkic language, as *araɣa*. Similarly, the French 'chauffeur' (phonetically *ʃofør*) has been adopted into some dialects of Turkish as *ʃøfør*. As a manifestation of the second type of vowel harmony, regarding suffixes, the suffix must match the vowel in the root it attaches to. For example, in Turkish *at* ('name') takes *-lar* to become the plural *atlar*, but *ev* ('house') takes *-ler* to become *evler*.

There are a number of hypotheses about how backness harmony may have emerged: that harmony arises from co-articulation, where the shape of the mouth from previous vowels predisposes the speaker towards uttering another with the same mouth shape; the structuralist notion that symmetry in vowel inventories provides an impetus to harmony; etc. (see Harrison and Dras (2001) for further references).

Historically, Turkic vowel harmony systems are constantly in flux. Old Turkic as attested in 8th–11th century runic inscriptions from Siberia had an eight vowel system and fully regular backness harmony. Modern

Turkic languages have from 5 to 10 vowels, and range from almost fully harmonic (Tuvan) to not harmonic at all (Uzbek). The Turkic family thus provides over one millennium of documented stages and scenarios in the evolution of harmony. These serve as data points showing harmony evolution along a definable trajectory.

But not all points on this trajectory are discernable in the historical record. There are stages we know must have taken place that were not recorded. For example, 8th century Old Turkic shows pervasive, almost exceptionless vowel harmony for backness. Prior stages in the emergence of this system were not documented, and the gap limits our empirical knowledge of how such systems originated. By contrast, the evolution of harmony systems in daughter languages of Old Turkic is quite well documented across a period of over 1,000 years, allowing us to precisely quantify stable or declining levels of harmony over time, up to the present day.

Related Work

Specifically on phonology, de Boer (2000) looks at how vowel systems can arise from nothing and how the vowels organise themselves in the vowel space of the population of speakers. He notes, however, that his aim is not to model historical evolution of vowel systems, because of its greater complexity; one such example of this type of complexity is the situation when there is structure (like harmony relations) within the vowel space.

We are interested in modeling the historical evolution of vowel systems; the work in this paper is one step towards understanding the sources of this extra complexity. Specifically, we look at the historical trajectory of vowel harmony evolution. Other work on simulation modeling looks almost exclusively at the binary question: Does the phenomenon emerge (or decay) at all? For example, Steels (1997) asks whether a shared vocabulary can emerge from agent interaction; Kirby & Hurford (2002) whether syntax can emerge in a simulation from initial randomness; Zuraw (2001) the more specific question of whether nasal coalescence in simulated Tagalog will replicate real life. In these situations there are effectively only two outputs to compare with observations: the start point (phenomenon not present) and the end point (phenomenon either present or not). Having such a small set for comparison does not allow one to determine with much confidence what the factors causing the phenomenon are: many possible factors could cause the same behavior. Modeling change as a trajectory constrains the simulation to a much greater degree, allowing us to rule out many possibilities. While it is of course possible to evaluate binary models by systematically modifying parameter settings, there is no corresponding empirical data to match it. That is, there is typically not a range of sets of linguistic data under minimally different conditions apart from changes over time. Wonnacott (2000) has also begun to look at how S-shaped curves as a trajectory of change arise, although in that work the factors that distinguish between full S-curves (slow–fast–slow change) and partial S-curves (an exponential fast–slow change) are not examined. In this paper we aim to tease out some such factors.

In building our simulation we adopted the full S-curve as a trajectory of evolutionary change. Several independent lines of research suggest that language change often proceeds along this trajectory. The rising curve shows the advancement of a new form at the expense of an old one. On the curve, change begins slowly, accelerates, then slows again, over a period of many generations. It was originally proposed for language change in Bailey (1973), as part of a "wave" model of linguistic change, with support coming from parallel behavior in population biology in the replacement of genetic alleles. As empirical support, Chen and Wang (1975) look at three case studies of historical data that demonstrate the S-shaped behavior of language change: the Chaozhou dialect of Chinese, where words have been shifting from one tone class to another, with the slow-fast-slow pattern in evidence; English diatones; and the Swedish optional final *-d*. The earliest work on quantitatively modeling language change (Kroch 1989), on the transition of Old English and Old French away from verb-second syntax, thus adopts the S-shaped curve, as has subsequent work, but in the model imposes it on the data. Kroch proposes:

> ... given the mathematical simplicity and widespread use of the logistic [a particular equation giving an S-curve], its use in the study of language change seems justified, even though, unlike in the population genetic case, no mechanism of change has yet been proposed from which the logistic form can be deduced. (Kroch 1989: 204)

Later work, including our own, is interested in how the S-shape observed in data can emerge from simple parameter interaction. The first of these are macro models that model the behavior of the whole speech community through mathematical recurrence relations (Niyogi & Berwick 1997). So, for example, the proportion of the population that is using the new variant at some time n, p_n, is a function of p_{n-1}, of the form $p_n = Ap_{n-1}^2 + Bp_{n-1} + C$, where A, B and C are coefficients determined by a model of language acquisition. However, these models have fundamental problems because they treat populations in the aggregate, and moreover non-stochastically (Briscoe 2000); Niyogi and Berwick's model in particular produces implausible equilibria under certain conditions. Incorporating stochastic behavior, and subdividing the aggregated population, leads logically to a computational agent-based simulation, as the mathematics otherwise becomes intractable.

In the case of Turkic harmony emergence, we are assuming an S-curve trajectory in the absence of historical data points. In the case of harmony breakdown, we also adopt an S-shaped curve, but we are guided here by a number of historical data points along the trajectory. We are not claiming that the S-curve is necessarily the right curve, merely that it is a plausible one for this type of change. For now, the S-curve is more or less in accord with the evolution we have been able to map out for Turkic harmony. It could be suggested that an S-curve will be the result of almost any model that is proposed. However, we demonstrate that that is not the case, and use it to rule out one class of possible models.

Basic Model

An important principle in building the simulation—in choosing which factors to include in the model, and in choosing how to realize them—is, following Occam's Razor, to start with as simple a model as possible. If this fails to model the data accurately, the model is made incrementally more complex until (hopefully) it properly fits the data. If we start with a complex model, it isn't possible to tell which factors are crucial for the outcome.

Globally in the simulation there is the language, consisting of 1000 disyllabic words based on a real Turkish lexicon. The proportion of harmonic words is a parameter, by default 50%—for disyllabic words, if front and back vowels are (overall) equally likely, this is the mean level of harmony that would occur just by chance. The words are represented by strings in the implementation, with vowel phonemes separate symbols with associated features (backness, height, roundedness).

An individual agent has a lexicon that is a subset of this language, and is capable of speaking, listening and reproducing. It is only aware of its own neighborhood, defined as the four adjacent spaces. Agents do not move. Throughout the simulation agents are distributed with medium density, so that on average an agent will have two neighbors.

An agent lives for between 20 and 50 turns[1]. It reproduces only once, so the population is stable. It begins with a starting lexicon of 6 words. For the initial population, this is taken from the global language; for others, it is taken randomly from the parent's lexicon. The lexicon also grows through conversation with a neighboring agent; a parameter controls the likelihood of a conversation taking place in a given turn.

A conversation consists of a single random word, one agent speaking and one listening. In the conversation, there is a uniform probability for all agents that the word will mutate either towards or away from harmony through the various factors above (co-articulation, misperception, hypercorrection); there are different probabilities for harmonizing and for disharmonizing. In a mutation, one vowel in the word is altered by changing the polarity of the backness feature.

[1]All random values are from a uniform distribution

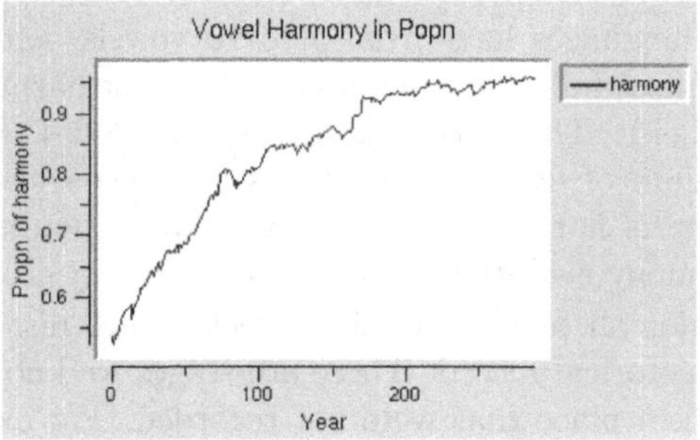

Figure 1: The basic model

This is so far very simple. We could, in principle, use a more complex mutation, for example, one that incorporates Bayesian probabilistic reasoning, as modeled in Zuraw (2001). However, it is not clear that this level of complexity is necessary—in fact, alternative models for Zuraw's results could be proposed using simple uniform probabilities that explain the data equally well. We show later with our own results that we can model the trajectory successfully without Bayesian probabilities.

We then plot a curve representing the proportion of harmony in the language. This is the average across all agents of the harmony of each agent's lexicon (that is, the proportion of words in the lexicon that are harmonic). This is not the only possible measure of language harmony, but it does reflect both the change in number of people adopting more extensive harmony, and the number of words that have become harmonized. Our first result is as in Figure 1. In this curve, the probability of harmonizing is 0.3 and of disharmonizing is 0 (in keeping with our native speaker informant's intuition that words are never deharmonized). The curve rises, and eventually plateaus at 1 (i.e. universal harmony), but too steeply: there is no period of slow change at the start. It is as if the agents were obeying a directive to "go forth and harmonize", rather than harmony evolving organically from social interactions: the result looks like a typical curve seen in machine learning. The same behavior occurs under all parameter settings tried where the probability of disharmonizing is 0; when this latter probability is non-zero, there is only random oscillation. Thus it is not the case that any type of model of interacting agents will produce a full S-shaped curve of some arbitrary phenomenon.

Variant Model

Systematically varying parameters never generated a real S-curve under the basic model. We therefore moved to a slightly more sophisticated definition for the probability of word change. Here we recognize that not all people in the real world will be equally likely to modify a word. For example, in adopting 'chauffeur' from French, a speaker from Istanbul is more likely to keep close to the original vowel sounds (*ʃoføɾ*), whereas a vil-

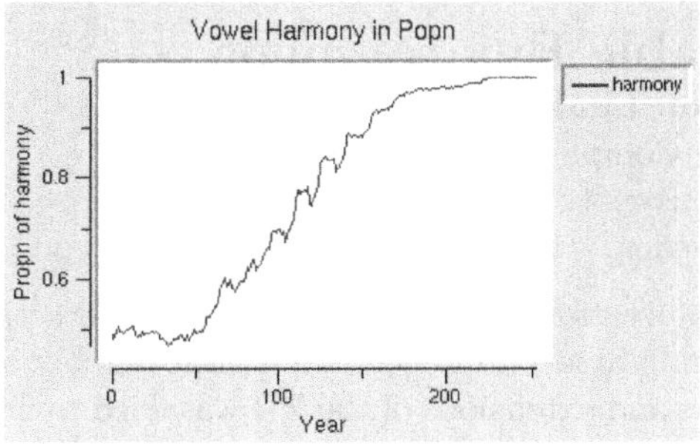

Figure 2: The extended model

lager from eastern Turkey whose lexicon contains many fewer disharmonic (foreign) words may harmonize it, to *ʃøfør* (in fact, both variants are attested in colloquial Turkish). That is, the likelihood of harmonizing a word is correlated with the strength of the pattern of harmony. We model this by making the probability of word change linearly proportional to the proportion of harmony in the lexicon. To do this, we replace the previous parameter representing the given probability of word mutation with a maximum probability of word mutation, and an agent's individual probability will be some fraction of this.

In addition, recognizing that a "pattern" that covers, say, 2% of the lexicon is unlikely to be pervasive enough to be really considered a pattern for an individual, we can set a threshold T below which a pattern is not recognized as significant. So for an agent x:

$$\begin{aligned} h(x) &= \text{proportion of } x\text{'s lexicon that is harmonic} \\ ph(x) &= \text{MPH} * h(x) \end{aligned}$$

where MPH is a parameter representing the probability that an agent with a fully harmonic lexicon would mutate a word. Then the probability of word mutation given the harmony of the lexicon, P, is

$$P = \begin{cases} ph(x) & \text{if } ph(x) > \text{T} \\ 0 & \text{otherwise} \end{cases}$$

In a sense, agents behave as if they assume that their neighbor's grammar resembles their own, even if they don't know exactly what it is.

In contrast to the basic model, this produces the first full S-curve, as in Figure 2. For this particular curve, MPH is 0.9 and T is 0.65. Smoother S-curves can be generated by lowering the threshold, with the middle section tending more towards linear the lower the threshold; at higher thresholds the curve is less clear, and could possibly be random drift followed by exponential change after passing a bifurcation threshold.

Conclusion

Our conclusion is that we have to some extent narrowed down how the S-shape in language change arises. Unlike earlier models, we are able to specify properties of individuals that lead, without explicit programming, to the emergent population behavior at least as described by its trajectory. In particular, we found that the most simplistic combinations of factors do not lead to the desired trajectory. However, if an agent does take into account its existing pattern of harmony in evaluating new words, effectively believing that its neighbors are similar to itself by projecting its own pattern onto other agents, it is possible to generate the S-curve of vowel harmony emergence. This incremental modification of the model, to one that produces the upward S-curve, gives us confidence that the model is a starting point for answering linguistic questions. Future work is to look at factors that could lead to a downward S-curve, such as homophony, and test against actual historical data.

References

Bailey, C.-J. 1973. *Variation and linguistic theory.* Washington DC: Center for Applied Linguistics.

Briscoe, T. 2000. Macro and micro models of linguistic evolution. In *Proceedings of the 3rd International Conference on Language and Evolution.*

Chen, M., and Wang, W. 1975. Sound change: actuation and implementation. *Language* 51(2):255–281.

de Boer, B. 2000. Self organization in vowel systems. *Journal of Phonetics* 28(4):441–465.

Harrison, D., and Dras, M. 2001. Agent-based modeling and microparametric variation: Modeling the evolution of vowel harmony. In *Proc. of NELS32.*

Kirby, S., and Hurford, J. 2002. The emergence of linguistic structure: An overview of the iterated learning model. In Cangelosi, A., and Parisi, D., eds., *Simulating the Evolution of Language.* Springer Verlag.

Kroch, A. 1989. Reflexes of grammar in patterns of language change. *Language Variation and Change* 1:199–244.

Lass, R. 1997. *Historical Linguistics and Language Change.* Cambridge University Press.

Niyogi, P., and Berwick, R. 1997. Evolutionary consequences of language learning. *Linguistics and Philosophy* 20:697–719.

Steels, L. 1997. The synthetic modeling of language origins. *Evolution of Communication* 1:1–34.

Wonnacott, E. 2000. Investigating the trajectory of language change. Master's thesis, University of Edinburgh.

Zuraw, K. 2001. The extension of semiproductive morphophonemic processes to novel forms: An optimality-theoretic model and simulation. In *Proc. of WCCFL XX.*

Cooperation in an Unpredictable Environment

Anders Eriksson and **Kristian Lindgren**
Department of Physical Resource Theory — Complex Systems Group
Chalmers and Göteborg University
SE-412 96 Göteborg, Sweden.

Abstract

A framework for studying the evolution of cooperative behaviour in a random environment, using evolution of finite state strategies, is presented. The interaction between agents is modelled by a repeated game with random observable payoffs. The agents are thus faced with a more complex situation, compared to the Prisoner's Dilemma that has been widely used for investigating the conditions for cooperation in evolving populations (Matsuo 1985; Axelrod 1987; Miller 1989; Lindgren 1992; Ikegami 1994; Lindgren & Nordahl 1994; Lindgren 1997). Still, there are robust cooperating strategies that usually evolve in a population of agents. In the cooperative mode, these strategies selects an action that allows for maximizing the payoff sum of both players in each round, regardless of the own payoff. Two such players maximize the expected total long-term payoff. If the opponent deviates from this scheme, the strategy invokes a punishment action, which aims to lower the opponent's score for the rest of the (possibly infinitely) repeated game. The introduction of mistakes to the game actually pushes evolution towards more cooperative strategies even though the game becomes more difficult.

Cooperation can be characterised as an interaction where agents refrain from taking short-term profit and instead act in a way that allows for a larger long-term gain. In this sense, cooperative behaviour may be seen at several levels in natural systems. As discussed by Maynard-Smith and Szathmáry (1995), cooperation may be one crucial factor for the major transitions that has occurred in the evolution of life on Earth — the creation of the more complex eukaryotic cell, the formation of multi-cellular organisms, the appearance of social animals, etc. In these transitions, previously separately reproducing components form a new self-reproducing entity, in which the different parts may have specialised roles.

In the field of Artificial Life, we have the opportunity to create models that allow for such major evolutionary transitions, but so far they seem to be missing in the models studied. One approach to get an increased knowledge about how such transitions may appear is to investigate under what circumstances cooperative behaviour may be advantageous for a replicating entity, and how cooperation may be achieved. During the past two decades there have been a large number of papers discussing the evolution of cooperation in the perspective of the Prisoner's Dilemma game. The work by Axelrod (1984) was a starting point for a series of papers putting an evolutionary perspective to how cooperation is established. The main conclusion from the initial work was that cooperation could be established if interactions between individuals are repeated. A large number of modifications and extensions of the PD was tried to firmly establish the fact that cooperation is possible under a wide variety of circumstances (Matsuo 1985; Molander 1985; Axelrod 1987; Boyd & Lorberbaum 1987; Boyd 1989; Miller 1989; Lindgren 1992; Nowak & May 1993; Stanley & Tesfatsion 1993; Ikegami 1994; Lindgren & Nordahl 1994; Nowak & El-Sedy 1995; Wu & Axelrod 1995; Lindgren 1997).

The possibility for a cooperative equilibrium to be established in a repeated game has long since been well known in game theory. The Folk Theorem states that in a repeated game, with sufficiently low probability for the game to end, any possible score above the min-max payoff can be supported at equilibrium by some strategy (Fudenberg & Tirole 1991; Binmore 1994). Such an equilibrium is kept by punishing those who deviate from the equilibrium strategy. One example of punishment is to minimise the possible score for the opponent in the present round.

One of the main limitations with the Prisoner's Dilemma game and many of the similar games studied is the static character of the interaction situation. Each time two individuals encounter each other, the situation is identical to the previous one, i.e., the payoff values for the different choices are unchanged. In a real situation, it may be much more common that they meet each other in different situations most of the time; some situations may be of the Prisoner's Dilemma type, other situations may be easy, so short-sighted profit maximisation coincides with the cooperative maximal payoff.

The advantage with the PD game is its simplicity, allowing for various extensions that investigate different characteristics of cooperative behaviour in simple models. Our aim with the current research is to keep the simplicity at the same time as the situation in which agents meet are less static. Therefore we generate a completely new random payoff matrix for each round in a repeated two-player game, but the players still have full information on the current payoff values for the different actions and players.

The questions are: How can cooperation emerge? What will it look like? Under what circumstances is it stable? In order to investigate possible answers to these questions, we have constructed an evolutionary model in which strategies replicate and mutate, with a replication rate depending on the score achieved in the game. Two types of dynamics are studied. First, in the mixed population, all interact with all and second, in the spatially extended model, interactions are restricted to the four nearest neighbours. We also study the effect of mistakes, as it is a complication for cooperation, and to what extent strategies may evolve to take care of this.

The random payoff game

The repeated random payoff game used in this study is a two-person game in which each round is characterized by two possible actions per player and a randomly generated but observable payoff matrix. The payoff matrix elements are random, independent, and uniformly distributed real numbers between zero and one. New payoffs are drawn every round of the game.

In the single round game a player performs a certain action that may depend on the observed payoffs. Therefore, the single round game can be characterised by its Nash equilibria (NE), i.e., a pair of actions such that if only one of the players switches action that player will reduce her payoff[1].

There are a number of simple single round (elementary) strategies that are of interest in characterising the possible types of behaviour. Assume first that there is exactly one NE, and that rational (single round) players play the corresponding actions. The payoff in this case is $\max(x, h)$, where x and h are independent uniformly distributed stochastic variables between zero and one, and this results in an expectation value of $2/3 \approx 0.667$.

Let us define a strategy "NashSeek" as follows. If there is only one NE in the current payoff matrix, one chooses the corresponding action. If there are two NE, one aim for the one that has the highest sum of the two players payoffs, while if there is no NE, one optimistically chooses the action that could possibly lead to the highest own payoff.

A second strategy, "MaxCoop", aims for the highest sum of both players' payoffs. If two such players meet, they score $\max(x_1+h_1, x_2+h_2, x_3+h_3, x_4+h_4)$ together, where x_i and h_i are independent uniformly distributed stochastic variables between zero and one, and this results in an expectation value of $s_C = 3589/5040 \approx 0.712$.

A third more optimistic and greedy strategy is "MaxMax", which selects the action that makes it possible to get the highest score provided that the opponent acts accordingly. Finally, we have also chosen to include a strategy that is punishing the opponent. The strategy Punish selects the action that minimizes the opponent's maximum payoff.

In an evolutionary model based on a round robin tournament for determining the fitness (based on the score of all pair-wise single round games) it is clear that NashSeek will take over sooner or later. If we extend the game, so that there is a high probability that players will encounter each other repeatedly in new situations (new random payoffs), other possibilities may appear. This requires, though, that the players may use composite strategies that in some way take into account what has happened before in the interaction with the same opponent.

A straightforward approach is to define composite strategies represented by deterministic finite state automata (FSA) (Miller 1989; Nowak & El-Sedy 1995; Lindgren 1997), in which a state corresponds to a certain elementary strategy as described above. From one round of the game to the next, a player may switch to a different internal state (and different type of behaviour) depending on what happened in the previous round. The opponent's action is classified in terms of the basic strategies, and it is checked whether the action is consistent with any of the elementary strategies. Different composite strategies will then react in different ways to the interpreted behaviour of the opponent. See Figure 1 for a sample strategy.

Mixed population dynamics

We consider a population of N agents, competing for the same resources. The population is at the limit of the carrying capacity level of the environment, so the number of agents N is fixed. In each generation, the agents play the repeated stochastic payoff game with the other agents, and reproduce to form the next generation. The population evolves according to the ordinary replicator dynamics (Taylor & Jonker 1978): the score for every composite strategy is compared to the average score of the population, and those above average will get more offspring, and thus a larger share in the next generation.

In the simulations of the model, in a few thousand generations, the average score of the population increases to a level corresponding to the single round Nash equilibrium. The evolution later on continues with a fast transition to the level of the MaxCoop score, indicating that a mechanism for avoiding the shortsighted single round Nash seeking behaviour has evolved. As is seen in Figure 2, showing a typical evolutionary pattern after the initial transient, the population does not seem to be able to stabilize on the cooperative level, but there are several sharp drops in the score when mutant strategies manage to take a more substantial part of the population. In some cases the score is brought down to the level of the Nash seeking strategy again.

When the population switches to the level of the MaxCoop score it is dominated by cooperating strategies that punish deviators like the Nash seekers. This results in the near extinction of the Nash seeking strategies, which means that the punishment mechanism is not needed any longer. Therefore, mutants that are cooperative but have lost the capability to punish may survive and may

[1] Since agents cannot randomise their actions, we only consider pure strategy Nash equilibria. Depending on the payoffs there are either zero, one, or two pure NEs in this game, appearing with probabilities 1/8, 3/4, and 1/8, respectively.

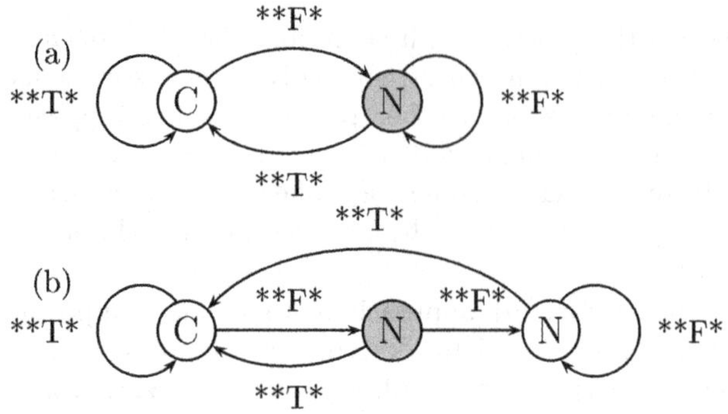

Figure 1: Mutation of a composite strategy into an equivalent strategy with an extra internal state is shown, from the parent (a) to the child (b). The letters in the nodes denote the elementary strategies MaxCoop (C) and NashSeek (N), and the black circle indicates the initial state. Depending on the interpretation of the opponent's previous action, the composite strategy may switch internal state. The transition **T* applies only when the opponent's action is consistent with MaxCoop (the third elementary strategy), but does not care about the other elementary strategies. The transition rule **F* is applied when the opponent does not follow the MaxCoop strategy. This composed strategy is similar to the Tit-for-tat strategy discussed in the context of the iterated Prisoner's Dilemma in that it cooperates by playing MaxCoop if the opponent played according to MaxCoop in the last round, otherwise it 'defects' by playing NashSeek. There are several different ways to change a strategy by mutations: by adding or removing states, changing the connectivity of the states, or by changing the actions in the states. Shown here is addition of a new state, by duplicating the grey node in such a way that the strategy's play is unchanged.

in some cases even have an advantage, since it may be costly to punish, depending on the exact mechanism. In Figure 2 it is clearly seen that the fraction of composite strategies that keep the punishment mechanism oscillates irregularly. If the fraction of punishers is too low the population becomes vulnerable to invasion by Nash seekers. If Nash seekers become common, cooperating strategies with punishment again has an advantage and the process repeats.

Under what circumstances could the cooperative level be stabilised? If the situation is changed so that mutants that have lost their punishment mechanism have a disadvantage, it should be possible to achieve a stable cooperating population. One situation in which this may happen is when noise in the form of mistakes is present in the repeated game.

We model mistakes as a probability ρ of taking the action opposite to the intended one. Since we consider infinite games, even a very small chance of mistakes has a huge impact on the overall payoffs and how the strategies evolve, even when the effect on the expected payoffs in the single round games are negligible (this effect is approximately proportional to ρ). Strategies that punish deviations from a mutual elementary strategy must now take the possibility of mistakes into account (Lindgren 1992). A pair of strategy like the one in Figure 1a, for example, will perform much worse since it will play NashSeek much more often. Especially when playing against itself, it will inevitably end up with long sequences of mutual "defects" when both players play NashSeek, and they will only get back on the cooperating track again (playing MaxCoop) if new mistakes occurs. It is thus essential that the players have some way of recovering from unintentional actions, from both parties. To this end, the players now monitor their own actions, as well as the actions of the opponents.

A player still cannot detect when the opponent makes a mistake, but by "apologising" after a mistake in some appropriate way (e.g. by playing MaxCoop) the long run cooperation might be preserved. This mechanism may leave the player open for greedy players to make use of it, though, so it is more complicated to find an appropriate mechanism.

It is clearly seen in Figure 3, that in the case of mistakes the population stabilises in the cooperative mode. Since cooperation now requires both a punishment mechanism to avoid exploiting strategies and a mechanism for restoring cooperation after a mistake, it takes a longer time before cooperation is achieved. It should be noted that there is no single simple mechanism present in the cooperative population, but the dominating strategies can be characterised as forgiving punishers. There is neither a synchronisation nor a handshaking mechanism involved, as has been previously observed in the case of the Prisoner's Dilemma game with mistakes (Lindgren 1992; 1997). It should be noted that the mistake probability is very low (10^{-4}), and if the level is increased cooperation is much harder to achieve, in the population dynamics. A more thorough investigation of the game with mistakes has been carried out and will be presented elsewhere.

Spatial population dynamics

In order to study the consequences of a small, local interaction neighbourhood on the evolution of strategies, we put each player on a site in a square lattice with periodic boundary conditions. The fitness of a player in a cell is given by the average of the expected payoffs from one by one games with its four neighbours. A cell is updated by replacing the player in the cell by the player with the highest fitness among the players in the cell and those in the neighbouring cells. In each generation, all cells are updated once, but the order is chosen randomly each time. In each generation, there is a probability of having mutations in the population, generated accord-

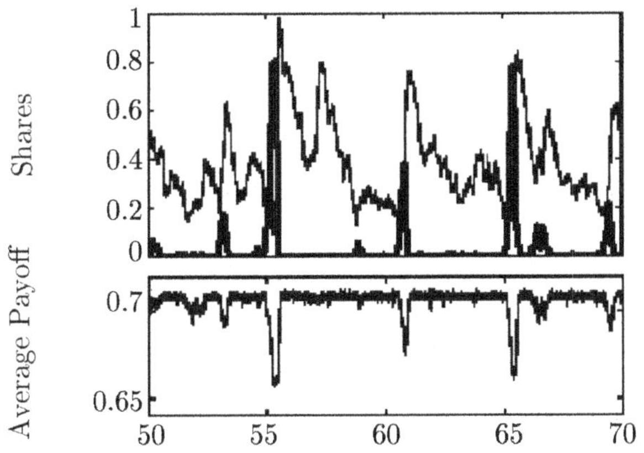

Figure 2: The figure shows a typical run of the model illustrating how non-punishing strategies take over from cooperating strategies with punishment, and the consequent collapses due to exploiting strategies. In the top is shown the share of players that play like MaxCoop when meeting others with the same behaviour but punish those that deviate from MaxCoop (thin line) and the share of exploiters (thick line). The bottom part shows the average payoff of the population. When the average payoff of the population is high, the share of strategies with a punishment mechanism decreases, due to an increase of mutant strategies without such a mechanism. Exploiting strategies are held back by the punishments. When the share of punishing strategies fall below a critical level, exploiters get payoffs above the population average and quickly come to dominate the population. This drastically lowers the population average payoff, which gives the cooperating-punishing strategies the edge, so that they can take over the population. This cycle then repeats.

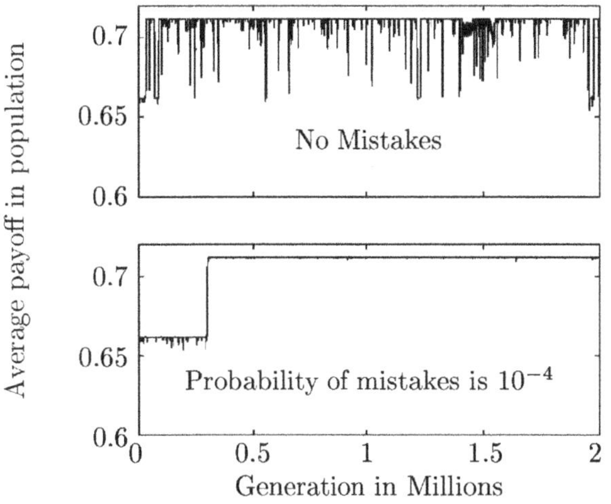

Figure 3: Typical runs without mistakes (top), and with mistakes (bottom). With mistakes, it is harder for the mutations to find a solution to the problem of cooperating by playing MaxCoop when possible, while evading exploiting strategies. The mutations of the resulting strategies are much less likely to be fit, and this imply that it is difficult for exploitable strategies to enter the population, as happens when there are no mistakes.

ing to a Poisson process with a mean of m events per generation.

A typical run is shown in figure 4, with a mistake rate $\rho = 0.01$. The world is 200 by 200 cells, and the mutation rate is 20 events per generation. The maximum number of strategies simultaneously in the population is 600 strategies. In the first few generations, the population converges to the NashSeek level. About a thousand generations later we see the first emergence of cooperation, with a short transition.

However, the cooperating strategies are easily exploited and we see a steady decline in the average payoff. The decline is roughly linear; the rate is limited by the mutation rate and the maximum number of strategies. During this period, the number of strategies rises very quickly. The mutants enter the square in small lumps, and do not tend to increase in size but do not die out either.

At some stage, and before the payoff reaches the NashSeek level, the trend turns and the payoff starts to rise again. As opposed to the initial, fast increase, this climb is gradual and consists of a constant replacement of strategies; there is typically no single strategy that takes over a large fraction of the population.

After a few ups and downs with much smaller magnitude than during the transient phase, the average payoff settles on a high level of cooperation. The payoff p_{CC} for the pure MaxCoop strategy is 0.7065 when the mistake rate is $\rho = 0.01$, and this corresponds to the maximum average payoff that can be stable. Note that the payoff is between 0.705 and 0.706, so it is quite close to the maximum level.

We have found that the populations evolve to high levels of cooperation, even for ρ up to and over 0.01. The level of cooperation is decreasing with increasing mistakes rate and discount rate, and the variation of this level between different runs is increasing with ρ. Also when ρ is zero, the level of cooperation is high and stable and we do not see the kind of fluctuations present in the simulations of the mixed population. This is consistent with results from the literature on spatial population dynamics in the Prisoner's Dilemma game (Lindgren & Nordahl 1994; Lindgren 1997).

Figure 5 shows a snapshot of the world at a given generation with different shades identifying different strategies. Figure 6 shows the fitness of the players encoded in a grey scale, given in the shaded bar to the right of

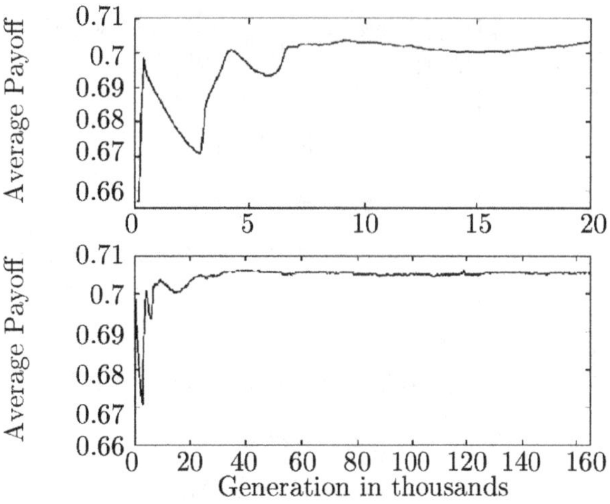

Figure 4: Time evolution of the average payoffs for a typical run. The top panel shows the initial transient, while the lower panel shows the convergence to a high, stable level of cooperation. The mistake rate is $\rho = 0.01$ and the mutation rate is 20 events per generation. Note that cooperation emerges readily on a level of mistakes where cooperation seems to be very hard to achieve in the mixed populations.

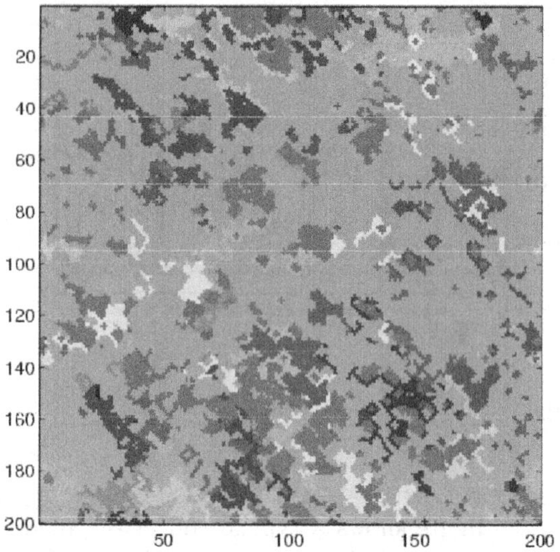

Figure 5: A snapshot of the distribution of strategies among the players at generation 162,000. The identity of the strategies are indicated by the different colours; there is no further significance to the choice of colours. Note the pattern of areas with the same strategy, interspersed by singlet mutations.

the image. Note that the mapping is non-linear; the intensity of cell i is calculated as $g_i = 1/(p_{\mathrm{NC}} - f_i)$, then scaled to so that all intensities fit into the interval [0,1].

Summary

In summary, in the case without mistakes we find that there are several strategies that play on equal terms with a MaxCoop strategy that punishes exploiting strategies. For example, strategies that by mutation lose their punishment mechanism may enter and increase their fraction of the population by genetic drift. This in turn leads to a population that is vulnerable to mutants exploiting the cooperative behaviour, for example by strategies playing NashSeek. Thus, the Nash equilibrium that characterises the population dominated by MaxCoop-punishment is not an evolutionarily stable one, as can be seen in the simulations. The effect is the same as the one in the iterated Prisoner's Dilemma that makes Tit-for-tat an evolutionarily non-stable strategy (Boyd & Lorberbaum 1987; Boyd 1989).

This genetic drift is prevented by the introduction of mistakes in the actions of the elementary strategies. The strategies cooperating at a high payoff level have evolved mechanisms that can simultaneously protect the players from greedy strategies, and lead the game back to cooperation when a mistake occurs.

The evolution of a population dominated by MaxCoop (with some punishment mechanism) is not unexpected. A population of players (using identical strategies) can always enforce a certain score s^*, if this score is larger than (or equal to) the smallest punishment score s_P and smaller than (or equal to) the maximum cooperation score s_C, $s_P \leq s^* \leq s_C$. This means that the population can punish a new strategy (mutant) that enters, unless it adopts the same strategy and plays so that the score s is reached in the long run. This argument follows the idea behind the Folk Theorem that appears in various forms in the game-theoretic literature (Fudenberg & Tirole 1991; Dutta 1995). As has been seen also in experimental economics, punishment seems to be a key mechanism for humans in order to force selfish individuals to behave in a more cooperative way (Fehr & Gächter 2000b; 2000a; 2002).

In the spatial setting, the players are distributed on a lattice. We find that the possibility to reach cooperation is greatly enhanced, compared to the mixed population dynamics. As the mistake rate and the discount rate increases, the average level of cooperation is decreasing, while the variation in this level is increasing. Still, cooperation at fairly high levels has been observed for mistakes rates of 0.01.

When the mistake rate is zero, the spatial model does not exhibit the type of fluctuation present in the mixed population — in the spatial model, a high level of cooperation can be maintained. This difference has been observed also in studies of the PD game (Nowak & May 1993; Lindgren & Nordahl 1994; Lindgren 1997). A common pattern that appears is islands or regions of cooperating behaviour with edges or borders of non-cooperating strategies. When a strategy is replaced it is more often by a strategy from the interior, i.e., by a cooperating

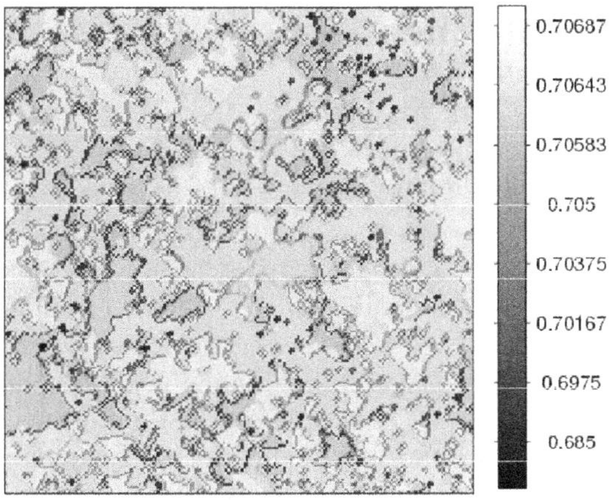

Figure 6: The fitness values of the players at generation 162,000, corresponding to figure 5. The fitness of the players is encoded in grey scale, given by the bar to the right of the image.

strategy.

The repeated game with stochastic observable payoffs offers a simple model world in which questions on the evolution of cooperation may be investigated. The model captures the uncertainty about the future situations we may find our opponents and ourselves in, and we think this may be a useful basis for further investigations of the circumstances under which cooperation may evolve.

References

Axelrod, R. 1984. *The Evolution of Cooperation.* New York: Basic Books.

Axelrod, R. 1987. The evolution of strategies in the iterated prisoner's dilemma. In *Genetic Algorithms and Simulated Annealing.* D. L. Los Altos, CA: Morgan Kaufmann. 32 – 41.

Binmore, K. 1994. *Playing Fair.* Cambridge, Mass.: MIT Press.

Boyd, R., and Lorberbaum, J. P. 1987. No pure strategy is evolutionarily stable in the repeated prisoner's dilemma game. *Nature* 327:58 – 59.

Boyd, R. 1989. Mistakes allow evolutionary stability in the repeated prisoner's dilemma game. *Journal of Theoretical Biology* 136:47 – 56.

Dutta, P. K. 1995. A folk theorem for stochastic games. *Journal of Economic Theory* 66:1 – 32.

Fehr, E., and Gächter, S. 2000a. airness and retaliation: The economics of reciprocity. *Journal of Economic Perspectives* 14:159 –181.

Fehr, E., and Gächter, S. 2000b. Cooperation and punishment in public goods experiments. *American Economic Review* 90:980 – 994.

Fehr, E., and Gächter, S. 2002. Altruistic punishment in humans. *Nature* 415:137 – 140.

Fudenberg, D., and Tirole, J. 1991. *Game Theory.* Cambridge, MA: MIT Press.

Ikegami, T. 1994. From genetic evolution to emergence of game strategies. *Physica D* 75:310 – 327.

Lindgren, K., and Nordahl, M. G. 1994. Evolutionary dynamics of spatial games. *Physica D* 75:292 – 309.

Lindgren, K. 1992. Evolutionary phenomena in simple dynamics. In Chris Lanton, e. a., ed., *proceedings Artificial Life II*, 295 – 311. Addison-Wesley.

Lindgren, K. 1997. Evolutionary dynamics in game-theoretic models. In B. Arthur, S. D., and Lane, D., eds., *The economy as an evolving complex system II*, 337 – 367. Addison-Wesley.

Matsuo, K. 1985. Ecological characteristics of strategic groups in 'dilemmatic world'. In *proceedings IEEE International Conference on Systems and Cybernetics.*

Maynard-Smith, J., and Szathmáry, E. 1995. *The Major Transitions in Evolution.* Oxford: Oxford University Press.

Miller, J. H. 1989. The coevolution of automata in the repeated iterated prisoner's dilemma. Technical Report 89-103, Santa Fe Institute.

Molander, P. 1985. The optimal level of generosity in a selfish, uncertain environment. *Journal of Conflict Resolution* 29:611 – 618.

Nowak, M. A., K. S., and El-Sedy, E. 1995. Automata, repeated games and noise. *Journal of Mathematical Biology* 33:703 – 722.

Nowak, M. A., and May, R. M. 1993. Evolutionary games and spatial chaos. *Nature* 359:826 – 829.

Stanley, E. A., D. A., and Tesfatsion, L. 1993. Iterated prisoner's dilemma with choice and refusal of partners. In Langton, C. G., ed., *proceedings Artificial Life III*, 131–175. Reading, MA: Addison-Wesley.

Taylor, P., and Jonker, L. 1978. Evolutionarily stable strategies and game dynamics. *Mathematical Biosciences* 16:7683.

Wu, J., and Axelrod, R. 1995. How to cope with noise in the iterated prisoner's dilemma. *Journal of Conflict Resolution* 39:183 –189.

The Creation of Novelty in Artificial Chemistries

Dominique Groß [1] and **Barry McMullin** [2]
[1]University of Bergen, Senter for Vitskapsteori, 5007 - Bergen, Norway
Dominique.Gross@svt.uib.no
[2]Dublin City University, School of Electronic Engineering, Dublin 9, Ireland
mcmullin@eeng.dcu.ie

Abstract

We observe that the world surrounding us perpetually creates novelty. The question we examine in this article is whether it is possible to build computer models that are similarly creative. The discussion focuses specifically on artificial chemistries.

Introduction

At a first glance the problem of novelty creation in computers actually does not appear to be a problem at all. Computer models are nothing but algorithms and as such unable to transcend the boundaries of their own world which has been created by the modeller. However, the general feeling is that we can simulate with arbitrary degree of precision the objects we find in nature; then, assuming that the latter is capable of creating novelty, we can ask: "Why should it not be possible to create novelty in computers if nature can do it?" One possible answer might be that novelty creation critically depends on the complexity of nature; this complexity, one might argue, cannot be mirrored in computer models because the time needed to implement and run such a complex model would exceed all limits of available human and financial resources—see (Gross & Jefferies 2001).

Although this answer might be valid for some types of problems, it potentially misses an important point. Nature might be complex on some levels, but is often assumed to be simple at the level of elementary particle physics and chemistry which are the most fundamental levels. This assumption of, and quest for, simplicity of the most fundamental laws of nature was introduced by Galilei. Free after Galilei, one might now look for artificial (= computer simulated) worlds which are both simple (in the sense that they function according to only a few comprehensive laws), but at the same time are able to create complexity of arbitrary degree. *Prima facie* then, there is no reason why this should not be possible using today's sophisticated technology and methodological tools.

The question of the creation of novelty in computer models is a central one for Artificial Life. If ever credible life-forms or evolutionary processes *in silico* are to be realised, then at least they have to have the capability to generate novelty. The question is also interesting on a more philosophical level: if we consider life as an essentially algorithmic process, then it should be possible to mimick its most important features in a computer-based model; we have only to figure out the "right" algorithm(s). On the other hand, it might also be that life is fundamentally non-algorithmic—see for example (Rosen 1991).

The concept of novelty we have in mind in this paper is clearly closely related to *complexity* in the informal sense formulated by John von Neumann (von Neumann 1949, p. 78); and the *creation* of novelty then corresponds to the (evolutionary?) *growth* of complexity (McMullin 2000). Nonetheless we deliberately choose the term "novelty" in this case, so that its natural vagueness and subjectivity may serve to emphasise the ill-defined nature of the problems under discussion.

Agent Based Models (ABMs)

Many ALife systems and simulations take the generic form of *Agent Based Models* or ABMs. At its most abstract, an ABM consists of a collection of primitive computational entities, called *agents*. We can, without loss of generality, assume that agents are implemented in the form of computational *objects*.[1] Thus an agent consists essentially of a package of *state variables* and *methods*. The methods are distinct computations which have been programmed for the agent, and which can be invoked by that agent or, indeed, other agents in the system.

Agents are organised into distinct *classes*, where a class is associated with a specific set of methods. A particular agent is then said to be an *instance* of its class. All agents of the same class share the same methods; but each individual instance has its own distinct state variables.

The computations realised by the agent methods may, in general, involve (pseudo-)stochastic elements; correspondingly, the entire system behaviour may be stochastic.

Agents generally have some "locality" of interaction. That is, a given agent can only ("instantaneously") interact with a subset of the other agents, thought of as those in its *neighborhood*.

Both the collection of agents, and the neighborhood relations between them, may be static. For example, a Cellular Automaton (CA) can be viewed as an ABM in this sense. However, more usually, the collection of agents, and the neighborhood relations between them, is *dynamic*; which is to say that agents can be *moved*, *created* and *destroyed*. These dynamics in the constitution

[1]That is, they are implemented in some *object oriented* programming environment such as *Java* or *C++* etc. Technically a single agent may consist of a number of distinct objects, but that will not affect the presentation here.

of, and relations between, agents are typically mediated through an encompassing "world"—which itself can be formally represented by one or more additional agents, albeit of particularly distinctive classes.

Conceptually, agents are normally regarded as *concurrent* computational units. However, ABMs are typically realised on serial computers such that, in fact, only one agent executes at a time. Some mechanism for scheduling CPU time, and providing for synchronisation, between the agents is therefore necessary; and the resulting system behaviours may be quite different depending on the details of how this is implemented. One simple approach is that an `update()` method is invoked, and allowed to execute to completion, on each agent in turn (in either a fixed or a stochastic sequence). Of course, in the course of executing its `update()` method a particular agent may invoke methods on other agents (within its neighborhood): so even with this apparently simple sequencing approach, agent activities may be interleaved in very complicated ways.

In all ABMs, each agent has a well defined instantaneous *agent state*, represented by the values of its state variables; and a dynamics, represented by its methods. By definition, the former can, and generally do, change during the execution of the model; whereas the latter cannot.[2]

Correspondingly, the entire system has an instantaneous system-wide state. This is, in effect, the array or vector of agent states (including any "world" or "environmental" agent states) for all agents instantiated at any given instant. Now the set of all possible states for any single agent (its phase space) is determined by its class specific set of state variables, and is thus fixed. However, in the general case where agents may be dynamically created or destroyed, the phase space of the system as a whole will be dynamic. We may say that it is of infinite (or, at least, indefinite) dimensionality; but that, at each time-step only a sub-space of dimensionality $\sum_{i=0}^{N} \mu_i^t d_i$ is occupied, where μ_i^t is the multiplicity of agents of class i at time-step t and d_i is the fixed dimensionality of agent of class i; altogether there are N different classes of agents.

At any given time then, the state of the system is uniquely identified by its position in the system phase space. We call this completely detailed system state the *micro-state*. The key feature is that the trajectory of the micro-states, including any changes in the dimensionality of the (micro-state) phase space, is completely entailed (whether deterministically or stocastically) by the micro-states themselves. In some sense, the micro-state *exhausts* the entailment of the model.

[2]Except in the degenerate sense of individual agent creation and destruction; but even then, the repertoire of available *classes*, and their associated methods, is taken to be static and immutable.

Now given such a model, with a particular repertoire of classes, scheduling and synchronization mechanisms etc..., this will give rise to a particular micro-state dynamics, or system behaviour, which must be examined and analysed. One possibility to do this is to look directly at the micro-state trajectory—but in general this is not useful. Instead, one is usually interested in the behaviours and interactions of agents at a coarser level of resolution. One might take averages over state variables of some or all agents, count associations between agents, or simply interpret some subjective *gestalt* patterns in graphical representation(s) derived from the micro-state.

In any case, the model is analysed at the level of some kind of user-defined description which (it is hoped) grasps the essential features of interest. At this level the history of the model is characterised by the succession of some *macroscopic* states, or macro-states, $\{F_{\theta=0}, F_{\theta=1}, \ldots, F_{\theta=m}\}$; these are determined by the micro-states together with some more or less arbitrary analysis rules which transform the micro-states into the macro-states. Even the timescale of the macro-states is not necessarily the same as that of the micro-states (reflected in the notation above by the letter θ as time index). Certainly, knowledge of macro-state alone is not generally sufficient to deduce the micro-state; thus the transition from the micro- to the macro-state generally (indeed, deliberately) involves some loss of information.

Note that we use both "micro-state" and "macro-state" here with senses that are derivative of, but still somewhat distinct from, the corresponding terms in statistical mechanics. Specifically, as we have noted, while the phase space of individual agents is fixed, the phase space of the whole system is not: its very dimensionality changes as agents are created or destroyed. Similarly, the macro-states of statistical mechanics are formally defined ensembles or equivalence classes of micro-states; whereas, in our case macro-states are rather informal, possibly even subjective, observables. They are not even necessarily features "of the system" (i.e., as a whole); this is a point we shall return to later.

On Novelty

In this section we would like to discuss the problem of novelty creation in computational systems in general and ABMs in particular.

The notion of novelty is a very difficult one. What is genuinely novel and what is just a different manifestation of something old is often hard to decide and the qualification depends largely on personal experience, insight and knowledge. To some degree, novelty is in the eye of the beholder, because something can only be novel relative *to* something or somebody. We shall not therefore pretend to be able to explicitly write down conditions under which we would accept a phenomenon (in the real or artificial worlds) as novel.

Of course, in a philosophical sense, it is sometimes contested whether there is "real" novelty at all in the world. But insofar as we are willing to stipulate that some interesting form of novelty does arise in nature, and continues to do so on an ongoing basis, and that this is exemplified in the phenomena of life itself, then it is reasonable to look for artificial or synthetic systems that can be at least *comparably* creative.

As a starting point, we might say that a "novel" state is reached whenever a system moves to a new (not previously occupied) point in its micro-state phase space. A slightly stronger form of novelty would be when the micro-state phase space itself changes—due to the creation or destruction of agents. However, given that, as we have already noted, each micro-state completely entails the next micro-state we can hardly identify anything expressed purely in these terms as "novel" in our sense.

Thus, for example, a trivial ABM might consist of a single agent whose only behaviour is to create new agents of the same class. This would result in a system with a constantly (indeed, exponentially) expanding—and thus "novel"—micro-state phase space; but we would clearly want to exclude this as an interesting or substantive example of the creation of novelty. Indeed, we might say that this is precisely the source for the intuition that computer models cannot, in general, exhibit novelty of any worthwhile kind.

Having said this, it seems that novelty should be looked for on some meso- or macro-scale. The attentive reader will already have noticed the somewhat paradoxical situation we find ourselves in. On the one hand, in some sense, the micro-state of the model contains **all** there is to know about the model's state; but on the other hand this undigested information is not adequate to judge whether something interestingly novel has happened in the system. In order to decide this we must first employ the selective analysis rule(s) which leads us to the macro-scale. It is clear that novelty at the micro-scale does not translate *necessarily* into a novel macro-state or macroscopic behaviour; depending on the rules which leads from micro-state to macro-state, the latter might even be completely unaffected by "novelty" of the former. To put it another way, in the absence of the rules that lead from micro-state to macro-state it is impossible to decide whether a certain novel micro-state is also macroscopically novel. Novelty creation on the macro-scale thus appears to depend as much on the micro/macro relationship as on the micro-state itself.

Another possible approach to the question of novelty focuses on the issue of *deterministic* versus *stochastic* dynamics. That is to say, the unsatisfying or uncreative nature of deterministic computational models is attributed precisely to the fact that the micro-state completely or *uniquely* determines the next (micro-)state (and thus, given the analysis rule, of the macro-state). Of course, the opposite extreme would be a "completely" stochastic dynamics—where there is no correlation between current state and next state at all. Such a model will then, at each time-step, take a completely random position in phase space. No doubt each microstate is then "novel", in the sense of "unpredictable"; but again, this is hardly an any more interesting form of novelty. Such a random state trajectory has—with overwhelming probability—no interesting intrinsic regularity; neither would there be a sensible analysis rules which could lead to interesting, (in the sense that it would not teach us anything interesting about the world) macro behaviour. We will therefore exclude this trivial kind of complete stochastic variation as an example of genuine novelty. But this still leaves us with the possibility of novelty generation in the intermediate case of deterministic dynamics leavened with some stochastic elements.

ABMs do often combine deterministic rules with stochastic elements; amongst other things, this allows the implementation of evolutionary models. Many will be intuitively inclined to regard some of those systems as novelty producing. However a closer look suggests that, if novelty is produced at all, it is rather strictly limited; see in this context, for example, (Bedau *et al.* 1997; Bedau & Brown 1997).

A first hint in this direction is the fact that repetitive runs of the system, with the same initial conditions, but different pseudo-random seeds typically lead to qualitatively similar behaviours.[3] For example in the `Tierra` system (Ray 1996), starting with the original ancestor organism, the phenomena of "parasites" and "hyperparasites" will essentially always emerge. Furthermore, very often the analogue is true for a variation of the initial conditions. This indicates already in those examples that it is not really the randomness that introduces the putatively novel phenomena into the system; the stochastic elements only change details of the occurrence of these phenomena. If the randomness really were the source of novelty, then a different seed of the pseudo-random number generator should presumably (nearly always) give rise to qualitatively different behaviour of the model.

Thus it seems that in most ALife systems the stochastic elements fulfil the function of perturbation from an otherwise deterministic attractor of the microscopic dynamics—potentially allowing ongoing transitions between these attractors, which would not be possible in a purely deterministic system. Transitions to (previously unobserved) attractors may then be identified with "novelty". But the randomness is not in itself the source of novelty. It is merely helping to make manifest the variety in the potential attractors of the underlying deterministic dynamics; which is to say, establishing a long term

[3] If this were not the case then the model might even be regarded as rather useless; see (Mitchell 2000).

probability distribution over the occupancy of these attractors. In Karl Popper's words, we must be inclined to conclude that "... indeterminism is not enough" (Popper 1973).

Of course, arguments for and against novelty-creation in existing ALife systems can go on forever. In order to avoid lengthy and unfruitful discussions, we may suggest an additional, albeit very informal, criterion: that novelty should be produced **perpetually**. In practice perpetual novelty creation does not need to mean *eternal* novelty creation, but only that the macroscopic behaviour does not quickly settle on one or a few attractors, but goes on exhibiting novelty for much longer than the typical simulation-time.

In the following sections we will look at the issue of novelty more concretely by considering two specific categories of ABM, featuring what we shall call *closed* versus *open* agents. There is not a sharp demarcation between these: but, roughly speaking, closed agents have a relatively small variety of *pre-conceived* (and pre-programmed) behaviours; whereas open agents can explore an indefinitely large variety of behaviours, which are not pre-conceived by the designer.

ABMs with Closed Agents

We will first investigate the potential for novelty creation in those "classical" ABMs having closed agents.

As already outlined, this might be typically implemented according to the scheme depicted in figure 1. Its basic underlying idea is clear: there is a central scheduler which invokes the `update()` method for each individual agent, according to some scheduling algorithm. In each case, the `update()` method invokes other appropriate methods (on the agent itself or on other agents in its neighborhood) in order to implement the agents' behavioural rules. Where the agents are thought of as modelling organisms then these behaviours may include such things as "movement", "feeding", "reproduction", "death" etc. The distinct "types" of agents correspond to different classes. The repertoire of classes is, however, fixed, and usually comparatively small.

By definition, a closed agent can only perform those tasks, or exhibit those behaviours, that are pre-coded in its methods. Consequently, any variations in agent behaviour in the course of model execution have to have been preconceived, at some level, by the programmer. The available classes (which is say the class methods) are not subject to variation.

Variability is firstly limited to varying populations of the particular set of implemented classes; and within the instances of a particular class, variability is limited to *state* variations—i.e., of the values of the state variables. However, it is common in ALife models to partition the state variables between some which can vary during the normal, somatic life-time of an agent; and others which

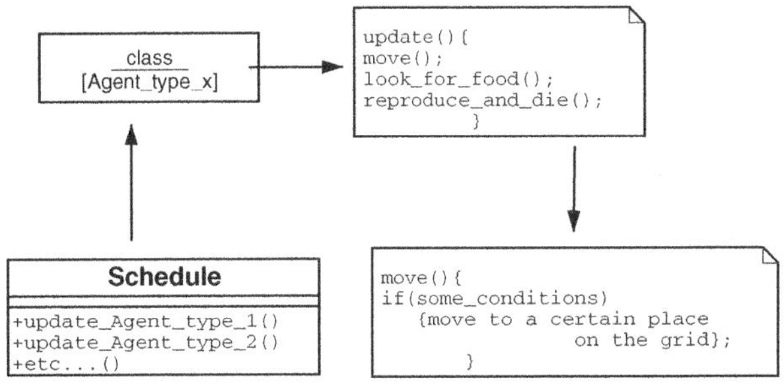

Figure 1: Schematic outline of a typical ABM with "closed" agents. The agents' `update()` methods are called according to a schedule. The update usually consist of a series of more basic actions to be taken, such as movement, uptake of food and reproduction and death. How exactly these actions are performed and under which conditions they are called may be variable—within some pre-defined limits—which enables evolutionary agent adaptation.

vary only when new agents are being created (i.e., at reproduction). The latter may be regarded as behavioural *parameters* or, in biological terms, represent agent *genotype*.

In this category of model then, the scope of evolution is either to select among the specific, pre-programmed, classes (if these come into darwinian competition) or to select among lineages within those classes created by parameter variation ("mutation").

This can, of course, provide useful and interesting tests of selectional conjectures; but insofar as the whole scheme boils down to the exploration of pre-determined variants of a small, fixed, set of agent classes, it seems it cannot qualify as generating novelty in our sense—*at least, not at the level of the individual agents.* It remains conceivable that genuinely novel phenomena may arise at some more macroscopic, collective, level, involving groups (colonies?) of agents. We shall see later (section *Novelty in Artificial Chemistries*) that this concept of novelty creation at the level of the collective behaviour of multiple agents—in the absence of novelty creation at the level of agents themselves—is a key motivation for a particular form of ABM known as an *Artificial Chemistry* (AC).

ABMs with Open Agents

First, however, we turn in rather a different direction—to consider systems where the *agent* level constraints assumed above are relaxed; that is, where the agents are *open.* By this we mean that the potential variability in agent behaviours is very large (if not infinite); but this variability is not merely parametric modulation of still fixed and stereotyped behaviours, but rather is of a scope which exceeds the capability of a designer to pre-conceive (never mind design) it.

At heart this means that among the methods (perhaps the only method) of an agent there is a *general purpose (Turing complete) computer*; and among the state variables (perhaps the only variable), there is a *programme*. On one level, the agents are still as rigid as ever—the available agent methods cannot be varied. Yet, on another level, there is literally unlimited scope for variation in agent behaviours. Indeed, this behavioural variation will even be formally *unpredictable* (in the sense of Turing halting).

Perhaps the best known example of this *genre* is `Tierra` (Ray 1996); beside this original there are a number of related ALife systems with a similar basic idea such as for example the `Avida` systems (Adami 1998). We will henceforth refer to those systems collectively as "`Tierra`-like systems".[4]

Whenever, as is the case in `Tierra`-like systems, the "code" which *essentially* defines the behaviour of the agents is created at run-time and not at compile time, then it seems clear that many of the restrictions which limited novelty creation in ABMs with closed agents should disappear. In particular, if the conditions exist for darwinian selection (the agents can reproduce, but with population growth limited by competition), and the embedded code in the agent state variables is subject to mutation, then it seems that there should be scope for continuing, open-ended ("perpetual") evolutionary creation of novelty. `Tierra`-like systems offer exactly this. The agents and their behaviours are not bound by the pre-conceiving imagination of the modeller/programmer, but can freely emerge from the evolutionary process.

There is no doubt that `Tierra` and similar systems do in fact show interesting evolutionary phenomena; but as already noted in the section *On Novelty*, it is also a well-known fact that the creativity of the evolution in those systems seems to be limited and cannot be sustained for a long period of time. Attempts to build `Tierra-like` systems with a more long-term evolution have largely failed.

The nature of these limitations is still very much an open question; however we can consider at least a few specific conjectures as to the explanation.

A first possible factor may be the rather small size of the artificial worlds which were initially studied. These allowed only a comparatively small number of creatures to exist simultaneously. This hypotheses is easily testable. The rapid increase in available computing power means that, even after a relatively short waiting time, the implementation of much larger experimental worlds has already become possible. However, at least for the case of `Tierra`, these larger worlds do not seem to have led to a significantly more interesting phenomenology.

A second possible explanation for the rather limited phenomenology of `Tierra` is that it is due to a lack of structure and complexity of the *environment* of the digital organisms. The environment as experienced by the agents may simply lack features to be adapted *to*. An interesting study of the dependence of adaptability on environmental complexity in ALife systems is provided by (Fletcher, Bedau, & Zwick 1997).

In the case of `Tierra`-like systems this points at a dilemma. The more complex their artificial worlds are designed, the more potential niches they offer to the agents. This should prolong the evolutionary process and increase the potential for the evolutionary development of interesting agent behaviours. On the other hand, the appeal and elegance of `Tierra`-like systems is exactly the simplicity of their initial world. To much designed and programmed complexity would to some degree defeat the purpose of those systems.

In the original `Tierra` the environment in which the agents live is quite deliberately minimalist. It essentially consists only of a "memory" space which the digital creatures inhabit; the "slicer" which allocates CPU time; and the "reaper" which kills off agents to ensure a continuing supply of free memory for further reproduction (and thus—hopefully—evolution).

It seems that we can therefore safely discount the emergence of, for example, predation in `Tierra`—that is, agents which kill other agents to exploit their resources. As `Tierra` is implemented, there is simply no mechanism for one organism to attack or kill another; and, in any case, the resources of a killed organism go back to a common pool and are immediately available for the next organism which attempts to reproduce—they would not be preferentially available to a (nascent) lineage of predators.

In order for predation to emerge, there would have to be generic mechanisms—presumably implemented by some "world" agent(s)—for redistribution of resources between agents. But the `Tierran` world agents (memory, slicer, reaper) are *closed*; they are *not* capable of evolving, but simply offer a fixed, stereotyped repertoire of interactions for the organism agents to engage with.

Of course, in a suitably enhanced and modified version of `Tierra` we may certainly observe more phenomena than in the original system. Specifically, one might add precisely the sorts of attack and resource redistribution capabilities that could underpin predation phenomena. Presumably one might then observe classical evolutionary arms races between predators and prey, with elaboration and refinement of more or less sophisticated strategies for both.

But of course, this all misses the point. Again, this world will ultimately be limited by the closed set of in-

[4] `Tierra` is not, in fact, implemented with the strict, object-oriented, ABM architecture we have presented in the section *Agent Based Models (ABMs)*; however, this is a technicality which does not affect the arguments we present.

teraction possibilities. So, to pursue the example even further, we could certainly ***still*** not expect to see organisms burying themselves in "sand" in order to avoid detection by predators—simply because there is nothing of the nature of "sand" in this world, nor any mechanism for it to spontaneously appear!

It should be clear that there are two, at least, conceptually distinct kinds of limitation being identified here:

- The fact that some (key) agents are still closed; worse, it is not at all apparent how one might even *conceive* of "opening up" these particular agents in an effective way.
- Even more fundamentally, there is the fixed nature of the agent *interfaces*. Although the agents may be *internally* capable of implementing arbitrary (Turing) computations, the evolutionary significance of this will be sharply limited if it can only impact on other agents in severly restricted, and fixed, ways. Or to put it another way, it is like imagining the evolution of organisms with general purpose, programmable, nervous systems—but imprisoned within completely immutable sensor and effector systems (Cariani 1991).

In summary then, the properties of the world in which the artificial organisms live is crucial to the evolutionary potential of the model-system; its "physics" and "chemistry", the ways in which organisms may be born, die and receive resources all constrain its evolutionary potential. Yet engineering a complex—but still fixed—world is no solution: it merely delays the still inevitable plateau of evolutionary exhaustion.

We conclude that, for our purposes at least, current ALife models with open agents (in the sense of evolutionarily programmable) turn out to be, at best, inadequate—and, at worst, a dead end. The challenge, of course, is to formulate a system where the world itself, including the very mechanisms or interfaces for agent interaction, is open and indefinitely mutable and creative. We see this as a major challenge ahead.

Novelty in Artificial Chemistries

We now turn our attention to a rather different kind of ABM: the *Artificial Chemistries* (ACs). For examples, see (Rasmussen *et al.* ; McMullin 1997a; 1997b; Fontana 1991; Dittrich, Ziegler, & Banzhaf 2001).

At first this will seem like a retrograde step, because ACs fall into the category of ABMs with *closed* agents. In fact, ACs do not normally even have the most limited evolutionary dynamics which we discussed in the section *ABMs with Closed Agents*. *Prima facie* then, the prospects for such systems to exhibit perpetual novelty seem extremely weak; but we will pursue the analysis nonetheless.

We must first characterize what we mean by ACs, and how they relate to the systems already described. As mentioned, ACs are ABMs with closed agents, and thus conform to the general framework shown in figure 1. However, the interpretation of the agents is now rather different. Instead of thinking of the agents as representing organisms, in ACs they are taken to denote *atoms* or (small) *molecules* (we will use the generic term "particles"). The agent classes now represent *elements* and/or *molecular species*. The interactions between agents are motivated as—usually highly abstract—models of chemical reactions. In simple cases, this can result in the replacement of the reacting agents with different agents representing the appropriate reaction products. In more complex cases, there will be at least one kind of agent interaction which attempts to explicitly model chemical *bonding*: the effect is to establish agents into more or less stable *aggregations*—corresponding to larger scale macromolecules or molecular complexes.

Now, in constrast to the situation of the previous section, where the emphasis was on novelty on the part of individual agents, in ACs the agents are actually *designed* to have entirely immutable behaviours (methods); and, further, to have only a small number of distinct varieties (classes, types of agents). However, the new prospect is of novelty on a higher, or more macroscopic level: the level of the macromolecules or agent-aggregates.

This deliberate limitation of artificial chemistries at the level of agent variety is of course an attempt to mimic fundamental processes in nature which seem to operate exactly this way. The variety of chemical elements is essentially static, and relatively tiny compared to the stunning variety of higher level aggregates (molecules, cells, organisms, colonies etc.) which they give rise to—in processes which therefore surely have to be regarded as novelty producing. An ultimate goal of research with artificial chemistries is therefore to exhibit similar higher order structures and novelty creating processes in computer based systems.

So what specific types of novel behaviour may we hope to produce in ACs? We will want the AC to have the potential to dynamically create new macromolecular species, with novel functions and properties. In a sense, of course, the concept here is a *generalisation* of the original motivation underlying `Tierra`: starting from a relatively simple "ur-chemistry," consisting of a few primitive agent classes (elements, primitive molecular species) only, we would hope that the complexity in such a system increases over time through the progressive emergence of new types of macromolecules, with new behaviours *and which can relate and interact in new ways.*

Note that while this "ur-chemistry" should ideally be maximally simple, some initial degree of complexity must presumably be supplied if certain functionalities are to emerge. For example, it is hard to imagine how enzymatic interactions could arise in a purely two dimensional chemistry.

In any case, it is clear that the implementation of *bonding* in an AC must be critical to the prospects for this open ended novelty at the macromolecular level. Let us therefore consider this in a little more detail.

A common, and conceptually simple, way to implement bonding in ACs is by specific and explicit state changes of the respective agents (McMullin 1997b). Thus, particle A registers in its state variables that it is now bonded with particle B, and particle B records a precisely complementary relationship in its state variables. Bonded particles are then not different from unbonded particles in any other respect than that they are "tagged" in this way as being bonded; but, of course, the methods for implementing particle motion are explicitly programmed in such a way as to respect this bonding (i.e., to maintain the spatial juxtaposition of the bonded particles within some specified constraints). Similarly, the exact conditions for bond formation and rupture are explicitly specified in advance, within the various particle methods.

However, we would like to suggest that this form of explicitly programmed bonding seems unlikely to support the sorts of emergent novelty which we are in search of. The "new" higher level particle formed as a result of this kind of bonding is little more than a collection of its primitive components plus a few motion constraints *which have been pre-conceived and explicitly pre-programmed.* In this sense bonds—their formation, behaviour, rupture—are completely pre-specified, *bottom-up* phenomena; they exclusively stem from the explicitly programmed properties of the bonded particles, rather than being emergent effects of the molecular configuration per se. This seems distinctly unlike the formation of new molecular species in nature and it also restricts the potential for novelty creation in the model.

It seems that bonding in ACs might be much more interesting (with respect to the creation of novelty) if it were emergent, or a product of constraints that are *top-down.* We mean by this that bonding would not stem from explicit, pre-programmed, properties of the particles, but rather from the macroscopic or collective properties of the particle configurations.This is also the way nature seems to work. Bonding between particles would then not simply amount to tagging the participating particles and invoking extra rules which implement the constraints of bonded particles. If the top-down philosophy is followed, then bonding becomes a phenomenon that emerges from the interaction of particles, not the other way round, i.e., bonding is possible because there are constraints on the single particles. The collective should restrict the behaviour of the constituents to such a degree that they form a new whole. If the kind of constraint the whole exerts on the parts is very sensitive to the configuration of the parts, then it seems that this may be a potential source of variety and novelty.

The question is now whether strictly agent-based ACs with this property can be constructed. The snake has to bite its own tail. Is it possible to generate top-down constraints in bottom-up models? Note that in real chemistry exactly these kinds of top-down constraints arise and are one of the sources of novelty. Proteins, for example, are only composed of a handful of different types of atoms, yet are very different from one another. Size and configuration matters in the real world, and is a genuine source of novelty. If we manage to implement a similar kind of mechanism in an AC, then we might also hope for similar creation of novelty.

In order to better illustrate the idea of top-down constraints we will schematically outline the description of a minimal AC which exhibits them. Note that this is an imaginary toy-model devised just to illustrate this particular point. We do not suppose that it would, in fact, demonstrate any continuing creation of novelty (not, at least in this minimal form).

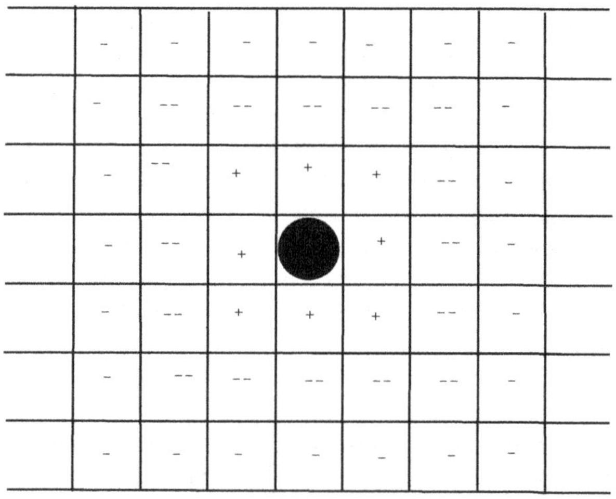

Figure 2: Potential field established by an isolated particle.

The AC is defined on a 2-dimensional square lattice and consists of only one type of particle (primitive agent). The particle exerts an attracting force in its immediate (Moore) neighbourhood, and a repelling force in the successive (Moore-like) neighbourhoods at distances 2 and 3. The corresponding potential field established by an isolated particle is indicated schematically in figure 2. The gradient of this field at any site would indicate the (vector) force imposed on a particle at that site. Potential fields from multiple particles are assumed to superpose linearly, as indicated in figure 3.

The underlying particle motion is imagined to be (approximately) newtonian—i.e., a conservative "billiard ball" mechanics.[5] Thus given the right amount of energy a particle may penetrate the "distant" potential barrier

[5]A number of technical implementation issues would arise

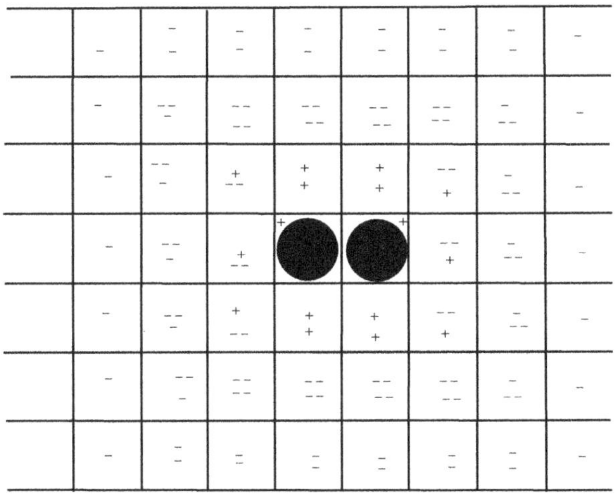

Figure 3: Overlapping potential fields superpose linearly.

of another particle, enter its "near" potential well, and the two particles will become "bonded". The configurations of figures 3 and 4 may represent such bonded particles (depending on the respective particle energies). If so, then this new (macro-)molecular configuration establishes a new collective potential field, quite different from that of either isolated particle. For example, it will offer distinctive, emergent, preferences for formation of further bonds.

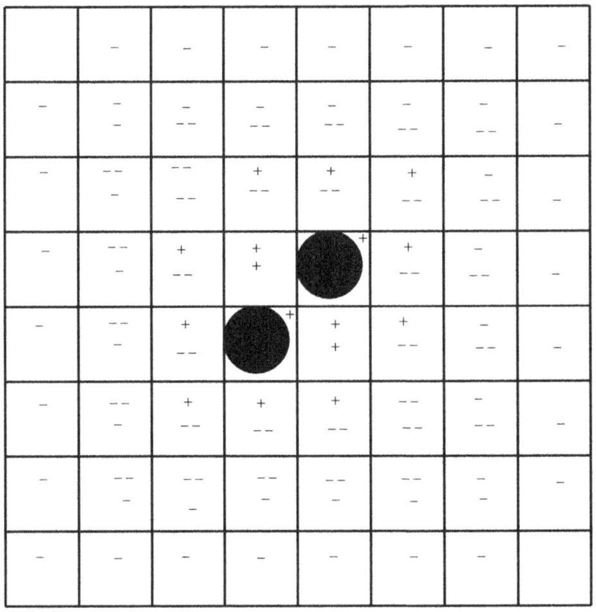

Figure 4: (Alternative) bond configuration.

This is already an example of a top-down constraint in our sense. Two or more particles which are trapped in each others potential wells become "bonded". Depending on the configuration, the (macro-)molecule might form further bonds with other particles or molecules. Which particles can bond with one another depends critically on the configuration of the whole. Likewise, the stability of the macromolecule will critically depend on how it is arranged, which itself increases the potentential for the emergence of novel higher-level particles (macromolecules). Note that the bonding rules, the allowed configurations or the conditions under which bonds break are nowhere explicitly defined, but are emergent properties of the underlying mechanics of the AC and the distinctive potential field of the particles. A macromolecule will thus have properties which are not, in effect, already pre-figured in programmed bonding properties of the constituent particles. Even in this toy version, it seems that a two particle molecule may be capable of forming a further bond with a third particle; such bonding may, in turn, alter the collective potential field, so that the bonding between all three particles is *stronger*.

We thus see that bonding—and consequently higher order "chemical" properties—in such a model will not be pre-conceived or pre-programmed in any substantial way at the agent level, but rather emerge in a highly dynamic way. Already in this toy model we may observe a significant variety of macromolecular configurations and behaviour. The richness of the phenomenology of the model would, of course, be enhanced by introducing different classes of particles with different fields; this might then be a viable way to introduce novelty on an ongoing basis, through the creation of new types of macromolecules.

In some respects, of course, the avenue suggested here is fundamentally close to that of (Rasmussen *et al.*); but it is also still different in its suggested degree of abstraction and in its purpose. We do not propose attempting to model any *particular* chemical species and the described toy-model explicitly renounces any realism; this shift of attention allows to explore the generative power of more generalised artificial chemistries, but still with emergent bond formation. The emphasis is thus mainly on methodological aspects: The question at this point is not how a specific phenomenon can be modelled, but more general, how ACs with high or even perpetual novelty creation might be constructed.

At this stage it is unclear whether these approaches will ever lead to a model which supports the perpetual creation of novelty (the toy model certainly would not), but the *ansatz* at least seems to merit investigation to show whether it is fruitful or not.

Summarising and Concluding Remarks

We have considered several different types of ABM models, relevant to ALife, from the perspective of *novelty*.

here, particularly due to the discrete nature of space and time. These will not be addressed in detail here; but see also, for example, (Rasmussen *et al.*).

The first type were generic ABMs with closed agents, but capable of exhibiting evolutionary dynamics. However, by the very definition of closed agents, these will have severely limited potential for novel behaviour—at the agent level. In essence, the programmer must prespecify and code the complete range of possible variations the agents can undergo. In spite of the limited potential for novelty creation, this type of model is often very powerful and can provide and has already provided a number of important insights into various theoretical and practical problems of selection and evolutionary dynamics. However, it is not fruitful with respect to its ability to create novelty.

This limitation can partly be overcome by a modification to the agent-based paradigm. If the agents are open—if they have embedded general purpose computing capability—then there is obviously a greater potential for spontaneous creation of novelty. Examples of existing artificial life systems which follow this principle are `Tierra` or `Avida`. However, these models seem ultimately to be disappointing; evolutionary development (of the agents) reaches a plateau and effectively ceases. How the phenomenology of these models can be substantially improved upon is an open research question of fundamental importance to the understanding of ALife modelling.

In real life, the emergence of new types of proteins with new functions is, in an evolutionary perspective, an example of a major source of perpetual novelty. The characteristic feature of real chemistries is that macromolecules and molecular complexes show fundamentally novel behaviours relative to the constituting particles; we say that the macromolecule constitutes a new entity which constrains its parts from the "top-down". We propose that similar mechanisms, implemented in ACs, may substantially enhance the creation of novelty in such models.

References

Adami, C. 1998. *Introduction to Artificial Life.* New York: Springer-Verlag.

Bedau, M., and Brown, T. 1997. Visualizing Evolutionary Activity of Genotypes. *Artificial Life.* To be published.

Bedau, M.; Snyder, E.; Brown, T.; and Packard, N. 1997. A Comparison of Evolutionary Activity and Artificial Evolving Systems in the Biosphere. In Husbands, P., and Harvey, I., eds., *Proceedings of the Fourth European Conference on Artificial Life.*

Burks, A. W., ed. 1966. *Theory of Self-Reproducing Automata [by] John von Neumann.* Urbana: University of Illinois Press.

Cariani, P. 1991. Emergence and artificial life. In Langton et al. (1991), 775–797.

Dittrich, P.; Ziegler, J.; and Banzhaf, W. 2001. Artificial Chemistries—A Review. *Artificial Life* 7:225–275.

Fletcher, J.; Bedau, M.; and Zwick, M. 1997. Dependence of Adaptability on Environmental Structure in a Simple Evolutionary Model. *Adaptive Behavior* 4(3):283–315.

Fontana, W. 1991. Algorithmic Chemistry. In Langton et al. (1991), 159–209.

Goldstein, J. 2001. Emergence, Radical Novelty, and the Philosophy of Mathematics. In Sulis, W., and Trofimova, I., eds., *Nonlinear Dynamics in the Life and Social Sciences*, NATO Science Series A: Life Sciences Vol. 320. Amsterdam: IOS Press. 133–153.

Gross, D., and Jefferies, D. 2001. Complexity Beyond Agent-Based Models. *Complexity International.* forthcoming.

Langton, C.; Taylor, C.; Farmer, J.; and Rasmussen, S., eds. 1991. *Artificial Life II*, volume X of *Santa Fe Institute Studies in the Sciences of Complexity.* Reading: Addison-Wesley.

McMullin, B. 1997a. Modelling autopoesis: Harder than it might seem! Dublin City University, School of Electronic Engineering, Technical Report: bmcm9704, URL: http://www.eeng.dcu.ie/ alife/bmcm9704/.

McMullin, B. 1997b. SCL: An artificial chemistry in Swarm. Dublin City University, School of Electronic Engineering, Technical Report: `bmcm9702` and Santa Fe Institute Working Paper: `97-01-002`.

McMullin, B. 2000. John von Neumann and the evolutionary growth of complexity: Looking backwards, looking forwards. *Artificial Life* 6(4):347–361.

Mitchell, M. 2000. Life and Evolution in Computers . Technical Report 00-01-001, Santa Fe Institute.

Popper, K. R. 1973. Indeterminism is not enough. *Encounter* 40(4):20–26. A revised version of this essay appears as *Addendum 1, pages 113–130, of:* (Popper 1988).

Popper, K. R. 1988. *The Open Universe: An Argument for Indeterminism.* London: Hutchinson. From the *Postscript to the Logic of Scientific Discovery*, edited by W.W. Bartley, III. First edition published 1982.

Rasmussen, S.; Baas, N.; Mayer, B.; Nilsson, M.; and Oleson, M. Ansatz for Dynamical Hierarchies. *Artificial Life* 7(4):329—354.

Ray, T. 1996. An Approach to the Syntheses of Life. In Boden, M., ed., *The Philosophy of Artificial Life*, Oxford Readings in Philosophy. Oxford: Oxford University Press. 111–145.

Rosen, R. 1991. *Life Itself.* New York: Columbia University Press.

von Neumann, J. 1949. Theory and organization of complicated automata. In Burks (1966). 29–87 (Part One). Based on transcripts of lectures delivered at the University of Illinois, in December 1949. Edited for publication by A.W. Burks.

SBEAT3: A Tool for Multi-part Music Composition by Simulated Breeding

Tatsuo Unemi
Soka University, Hachiōji, Tokyo, 192-8577 Japan

Abstract

This paper presents a design of support system for musical composition based on Simulated Breeding. In our system named SBEAT3, each individual in the population is a short musical section of sixteen beats including 23 parts, thirteen solos, two chords and eight percussions.The melody and rhythm are generated by a type of recursive algorithm from genetic information. By selecting favorite piece among scores displayed on the screen, the user listens to the sounds and decides which should be theparents to reproduce the offspring in the next generation. The genetic codes of children are generated through mutation and crossover. Iterating this process, the user obtains better pieces gradually. Embedding some domain specific functions, such as changing tempo and selecting tones, we can build a useful tool to make it easier for a beginner to compose his/her favorite musical pieces.

Introduction

This paper presents an application of *Simulated Breeding* (Unemi 2002b), a type of *Interactive Evolutionary Computing* (IEC) (Takagi 2001),that realize breeding the artifacts on the computer. The ordinary type of evolutionary computing consists of iteration of selection, crossover and mutation. Selection is done based on a fitness function that evaluate each individual. This framework works well if the human designer can drawan appropriate procedure to compute fitness values.However, we often suffer difficulty to figure it out explicitly bysome reasons, such as multi-objectivity, subjective criteria,dynamic environment, and so on. IEC is a promising technique to find better solutions in the domains for optimization by user's subjective criteria, of which root can be found in *Blind Watchmaker* by R. Dawkins (Dawkins 1986). Differently from ordinary methods of evolutionary computing,fitness values are not calculated automaticallyby the predefined evaluation function but are given by the userfor each individual in some manner.

Some researchers are calling this method as*Interactive Genetic Algorithm* (IGA) (Smith 1991),because it can be seen as a modified version of*Genetic Algorithm* (GA) (Goldberg 1989).Usually, the application systems have a methodfor the user to rate each individual, typically a graphical user interfaceusing a slider or a set of radio buttons.In the method named *Simulated Breeding*, the user directly picks uphis/her favorite individuals as parents for the next generation.This means the fitness values can take only one (selected) or zero (not selected).It disables stochastic selection, but has an advantage to reducethe number of user's operations to assign the fitness values.

Our project named SBEAT is to try to build a support tool for composing music. We started from a prototype of small system SBEAT1 (Unemi & Nakada 2001), of which individual includes sixteen beats of three parts, guitar, bass and drums. We extended it to eight parts by adding four more solos and percussion part (Unemi & Senda 2001). The current newest version SBEAT3 has ability to use full of sixteen channels of General MIDI (Mid 1995).

Some researches on a music application of IEC have already been tried in alternative methods. G. L. Nelson (1993) proposed some methods to generate music by emergent techniques, and built a system named Sonomorph to breed short musical scores in a similar style of Blind Watchmaker. J. A. Biles *et al* (1994) also proposed an alternative framework to breed improvisational phrases of Jazz music. His system named GenJam generates solo melody from each individual in the population in turn. The user pushes 'g' key for good and 'b' for bad to select appropriate individual. N. Tokui (2000) and M. Unehara (2001) are also independently challenging from their alternative points of view for rhythms and longer tune with a type of domain knowledge.

Our system resembles an extended version of Sonomorph (Nelson 1995), but has richer target domain and an improved graphical user interface toward more practical use as described later.

The following sections show our design of phenotype and genotype, describe the procedure to produce phenotype from genotype, present the graphical user interface to make the system more useful and practical, and then state concluding remarks.

Phenotype

An individual, the unit of breeding target, is a barof sixteen beats including 23 parts, thirteen solos, two chords and eight percussions. Figure 1 shows an example of field window of SBEAT3, quite same with SBEAT2. We named it *field* inspiring from a field of experimental farm for breeding agricultural products. Each of field window corresponds to a population and includes nine sub windows each of which corresponds to an individual in the population.

The score of each solos is a sequence of single notes. The score of a chord part is a sequence of combination of three notes. The score of a percussion part is a sequence of timbre. The timbre for each solos and chord parts are chosen by the user from more than 128 types of instruments programmed in MIDI.

Figure 1: A field window of SBEAT3.

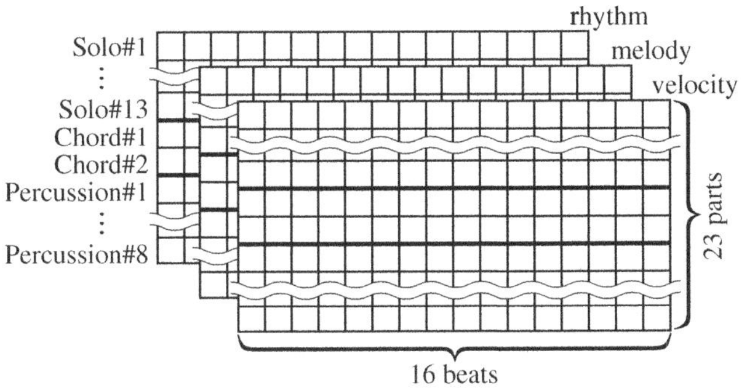

Figure 2: Structure of genotype.

Genotype

Figure 2 shows the structure of genotype, that consists of three types of chromosomes for melody, rhythm and velocity. Each chromosome is a two dimensional array of 16 by 23 elements, for beats and parts. The melody chromosome is for calculating pitches for each note by a development procedure described later. The values of each element for rhythm are interpreted in similar manner of GenJam as follows:

1. it continues the previous note or rest, if the most significant bit is one;
2. it rests, if the left most three bits are 011_2; and
3. it plays a new note, otherwise.

We employ mutation by bit flip in a constant possibility 5% for each bit in genotype. Relatively high mutation rate is useful when the population size is small. Crossover operation is done in a style of one point crossover, where it cuts a chromosome at randomly selected position of element boundary into two parts and exchanges them. Mutation is applied when the user selects only one individual as a parent to move to the next generation. Crossover is applied when more than one parents are selected.

Morphology

Morphology, the process to develop phenotype from genotype, plays an important role to generate feasible candidates in the initial population usually generated from random gene.

We employ the same type of recursive algorithm as SBEAT1 and 2 to guarantee some degree of similarity between parents and children in terms of human's feeling. Data in the chromosome for melody in the first chord part are used as parameter values for the algorithm. (See (Unemi & Senda 2001) for a detail.) Each integer for pitches is mapped onto a note in major or minor tonic scale in default, to generate a melody acceptable by a beginner. We call this melody line of sixteen beats *basic melody.*

In the chord parts, three notes, the note from basic melody, three steps above it, and three steps below it, are played in the same beat. The actual pitches for solo parts are calculated by adding a value from data in melody chromosome. The value can be −3, 0 or 3 steps to keep an acceptable harmony. The pitch data of the beats that the rhythm chromosome indicates rest or continuation are ignored.

User interface

Design of user interface is one of important features to make an IEC application successful.

Breeding in the fields

Unavoidable issue in any auditory domains is that it takes some length of duration for the user to certify the phenotype by listening to the sound of individual. It is easy to compare the features of twenty individuals in the domain of graphics art, such as (Unemi 2002a). However, in the case of music it is impossible to test more than one individuals at same time.

In our project, we restrict the individual to a short phrase, and make the population size simultaneously displayed on the screen to be only nine, as similarly to Sonomorph. As shown in Figure 1 before, each of field window has a button to play all of individuals in the population sequentially, and each sub window has a button to play only the individual repeatedly. Visualization in the popular style of music score is helpful to catch up the characteristic of phenotype before listing.

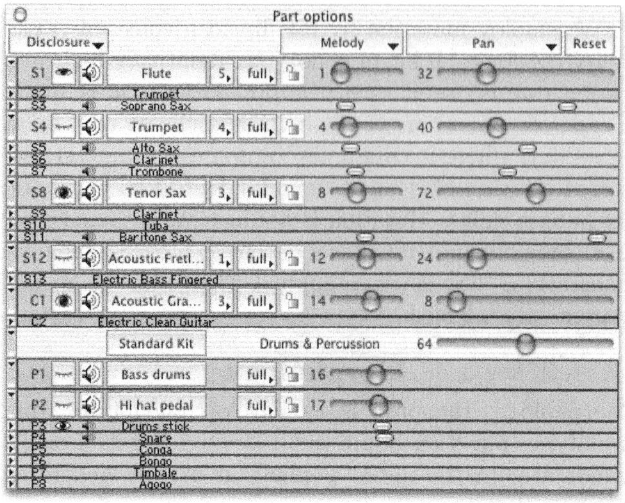

Figure 3: Part option dialog of SBEAT3.

Multi-field user interface

To improve the diversity of genotype, we employ a multi-field user interface (Unemi 1998). One of the issues in evolutionary computing is how it can avoid premature convergence to find a feasible solution. As know in breeding of living organisms, migration between populations separately evolved for several generations is often useful to obtain a new improved offspring. The fitness landscape of evolution of complex systems is usually multi modal, that is, there are a number of locally optimal peaks. A small size of population is easily trapped there because it has less diversity enough to find another peak.

By the reason described before, the population size of SBEAT is only nine. The operation of migration provides effective help for the user to cope with this drawback, by *copy & paste* and *drag & drop* operations for individuals between any different field windows.

Part options

Figure 3 shows dialog windows for setting parameters for each part by the user. As described before, the user can assign any instrument in General MIDI for solo and chord parts. For eight percussion parts, we prepared fourteen sets of timbre, bass drums, tom tom, snare, hi hat, ride cymbals, crash cymbals, conga, bongo, timbale, agogo, whistle, guillo, and others.

The sub window for individual includes only four parts to be displayed because of the restriction of screen space and human's ability of viewing. The user can select which parts are shown in the field. The user can also select which parts are played. We has been extended our system by increasing the number of parts, but of course it is not always need to use all of them.

The user is also allowed to set up some types of controls for each MIDI channel, such as pan, volume, reverb, chorus, and celeste. The range of pitches is also able to changed for each part by octaves.

Correspondence between parts in genotype and score can also be alternated. The parts sharing the same part in genotype of rhythm are played synchronously. The parts sharing the same part in genotype of both melody and rhythm are played in unison.

Player options

Another dialog window called *player option* is to set up the parameters applied to whole of parts. The user can indicate whether an individual is played at once or repeatedly, can set the tempo in the range from 20 to 180 quarter notes per minute, and can change the scale and key note. The key note is determined from the gene in default, but the user fix it by operating this dialog. In addition to the scales of eight notes in an octave, the user can select twelve pitches of half a step for one octave to add a flavor of avant-garde.

Protection of gene

Music has complex structure, but it is well organized, that is, any piece of ordinary music can be divided into smaller pieces and can be described by combination of common features such as rhythm, melody, expression, timbre and so on. By this reason, we sometimes want to fix some parts or some features of bred pieces and to try alternative candidates that varies the rest of parts or features. To realize it, the partoption dialog shown before includes a menu to choose the type of chromosome and of toggle buttons to indicate protection of each part. The protected parts of genotype are modified neither through mutation, crossover, nor reseting.

Integrating bars into longer score

To support music composition, it is necessary to be able to collect bred bars into longer sequence as the result tune. A score window is to integrate bars copied from any field window. As the same manner of migration, the user can copy any individual in a field window into any bar in a score window by *copy & paste* and *drag & drop* operation. The user can edit the sequence of bars by *cut, copy & paste* and *drag & drop* operation in a score window, and can modify the options for each bar using the part option dialog and the player option dialog.

Direct editing of genotype

Breeding is redundant when the user knows how the genotype should be modified to obtain his/her favorite phenotype. Figure 4 shows windows called genome editor that allows the user to directly edit genotype of an individual. It is possible to input a known melody using the genome editor. The current implementation does not allow to represent any type of melody in genotype, but this type of *reverse* morphology is useful to help user's task to make a variation of known tune.

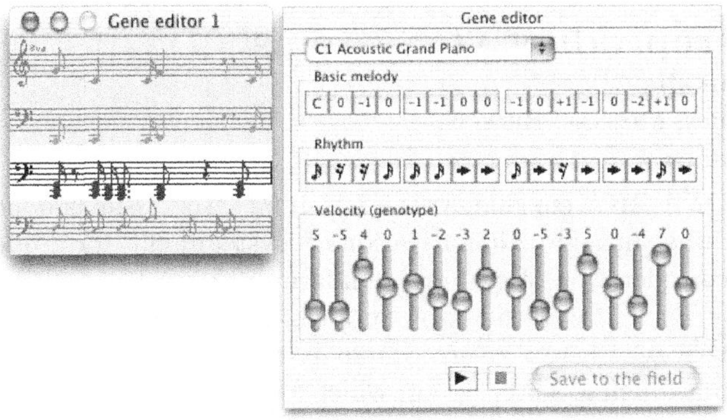

Figure 4: Genome editor of SBEAT3.

Conclusion

A design of tool for music composition using Simulated Breeding was described above. We have improved it in the aspect of the number of parts from three in SBEAT1, eight in SBEAT2, and then 23 in SBEAT3. These tools are useful for a beginner to compose his/her favorite and original music. And also it can be helpful for the user, who already has the knowledge of music, to get inspiration for a new melody.

Of course, there remains many works we should do in future, such as;

1. combination with breeding tools for another features, timbre, effects, chord progression, and so on,
2. more facilities to collaborate with other music tools,
3. facilities to use this tool as real time music performance, and so on.

SBEAT2 and 3 run on MacOS 9 and X. The executable binaries and some sample tunes in SMF and MP3 format can be downloaded from:
http://www.intlab.soka.ac.jp/~unemi/sbeat/ .
We hope many persons enjoy them.

Acknowledgment

The author thanks Eiichi Nakada and Manabu Senda who worked in the SBEAT project as students.

References

Biles, J. A. 1994. Genjam: A genetic algorithm for generating jazz solos. In *ICMC '94. International Computer Music Conference*, 131–137.

Dawkins, R. 1986. *Blind Watchmaker.* Essex, UK: Longman.

Goldberg, D. E. 1989. *Genetic algorithms in search, optimization and machine learning.* Addison-Wesley.

Midi Manufactures Association, La Habra, CA. 1995. *The Complete MIDI 1.0 Detailed Specification.*

Nelson, G. L. 1993. Sonomorphs: An application of genetic algorithms to growth and development of musical organisms. In *Proceedings of the Fourth Biennial Art & Technology Symposium*, 155–169.

Nelson, G. L. 1995. Further adventures of the sonomorphs. In *Proceedings of the Fifth Biennial Art & Technology Symposium*, 51–64.

Smith, J. R. 1991. Designing biomorphs with an interactive genetic algorithm. In *Proceedings of the Fourth International Conference on Genetic Algorithms*, 535–538.

Takagi, H. 2001. Interactive evolutionary computation: Fusion of the capacities of ec optimization and human evaluation. *Proceedings of the IEEE* 89(9):1275–1296.

Tokui, N., and Iba, H. 2000. Music composition with interactive evolutionary computation. In *GA2000. Proceedings of the thirrd International Conference on Generative Art.*

Unehara, M., and Onisawa, T. 2001. Composition of music using human evaluation. In *Proceedings of 2001 IEEE International Conference on Fuzzy Systems.*

Unemi, T., and Nakada, E. 2001. A tool for composing short music pieces by means of breeding. In *SMC '2001. Proceedings of the IEEE Conference on Systems, Man and Cybernetics*, 3458–3463.

Unemi, T., and Senda, M. 2001. A new musical tool for composition and play based on simulated breeding. In Dorin, A., ed., *Proceedings of Second Iteration*, 100–109.

Unemi, T. 1998. A design of multi-field user interface for simulated breeding. In *Proceedings of the third Asian Fuzzy Systems Symposium*, 489–494.

Unemi, T. 2002a. Sbart 2.4: An IEC tool for creating two-dimensional images, movies and collages. *Leonardo* 35(2):53, 71–73.

Unemi, T. 2002b. Simulated breeding – a framework of breeding artifacts on the computer. *Kybernetes* 31:(to appear).

Formal Definition of Self-reproductive Systems

Pavel O. Luksha
Higher School of Economics, Moscow, Russia
bowin@mail.ru

Abstract

Formal definition of self-reproduction may have importance the Alife research program, especially for application of its achievements outside the discipline. The paper examines two formal definitions of self-reproduction, suggested by McMullin and Löfgren. It is pointed out that these definitions form two major branches of self-reproduction analysis, described by ancestor-progeny and system-environment relationship. The ancestor-progeny definition allows to distinct between the exact / inexact reproduction. The system-environment definition brings in the original classification also allowing to differentiate between major classes of self-reproducers.

Introduction

A phenomenon of self-reproduction has an ultimate character, at least for our part of the Universe. Although presently studies focus around technical and biological applications, social systems are also an important case of self-reproducers (Luksha 2002).

Formalization of what is a self-reproducing system is substantially important for research programs in Alife (as set out by Langton (1989)), especially in a sense that such formalization provides basis for classification of self-reproducers. The latter is important for model design, since different types of self-reproducers may employ different techniques and strategies to reproduce themselves.

It should also be emphasized that artificial life models may well be transplanted back to natural and humanity sciences (by which they were first inspired) in order to understand better the phenomenon of self-reproduction, primarily self-reproduction of biological and social systems. Accordingly, formal definition may be important here as well.

Two main branches found in literature can be generalized as "progeny-ascendant relationship" and "system-environment relationship" definitions.

Progeny-ascendant relationship

A formal definition of a self-reproducing system, proposed by Barry McMullin (2000). Let $s \in \Psi$ be a system[1] s in system class Ψ, and $O(s) \subset \Psi$ is a set of systems that system s is capable of constructing (O as an offspring). System s is capable of producing another system, if $O(s) \neq \emptyset$. Then, if $s \in O(s)$, s is self-reproducing.

One may possibly find flaws in this definition (especially the fact that networks of interdependently producing systems are not covered by this definition, e.g. DNA-RNA-enzyme synthesis), in fact, this issue is done away through axiomatization of 'systemhood' (or crude consideration of system boundaries as given).

The more considerable problem is that in order to reveal whether a given system is a self-reproducer, one must define class Ψ for which this is determined. If Ψ is defined as any material object, the definition describes any repeated process: e.g. an oscillation in wave-like processes, even in mechanic waves, shall be "self-reproduction". To avoid problem of self-reproduction non-triviality (Langton 1984), there are two possible ways of varying the definition. Either one puts phenomenological restriction to Ψ: e.g. only objects of engineering (machines), biology (living organisms) and social sciences (societies and institutions) can be self-reproductive. Alternatively, one restricts the minimal level of complexity of objects in Ψ (but then the issue of complexity measure comes into view, which may exclude intuitively 'proper' objects or may include intuitively 'wrong' objects). In any case, a concealed requirement is that an observer must exist that shall determine the content of class Ψ. While this should not represent a problem for the purpose of Alife model transplantation into other sciences, it may somewhat undermine a theory's 'objectivity' (should Alife researchers be attached to observer-independent positivistic paradigm).

type of new system production	criterion	description
exact replication	$d(s_0, s_t) = 0$ (or $d(s_t, s_{t+1}) = 0$)	difference between each new copy and the original system must be minimal
near replication of an ancestor	$d(s_0, s_t) < D$	each new copy imitates the original system, with possible reversible mutations
near replication of a parent	$d(s_t, s_{t+1}) < D$	a new copy must have resemblance with its parent, but not necessary with all its ancestors (and thus this is a process of irreversible mutations)

Table 1: Types of self-reproduction

[1] While McMullin talks of *machines*, and his main issue is to find a definition for designable artificial life, I believe his definition is good enough to be generalized to a class of systems capable of producing other systems

The basis for classification of parent-progeny relationship is viewed as following. Some measure of qualitative difference, $d(l_i, l_j)$, can be introduced, so that:

- $d(l_i, l_i) = 0$ (a function has its minimum for an exact copy of a self-reproducer l_i).
- $d(l_i, l_j) \leq D$ if system is considered an imitation of a given one, where D is a level of acceptable variation (see Eigen *et al.*, (1981) for measures of this kind used in pre-life models).

The typology of ancestor-progeny relationship is analogue to Sipper distinction between self-replication and self-reproduction where copy being exact and inexact replica (Sipper *et al.* 1997). Three possible types of reproduction (exact replication, near replication of an ancestor, and near replication of a parent) are presented in Table 1, s_t being a system s produced in t-th generation. The case of near replication of a parent appears to be the most distributed naturally (and also initially studied by von Neumann (Aspray & Burks 1987)), although other cases may also exist[2].

A self-reproducing system, accordingly, is a system capable to produce its copies or imitations (which is, other self-reproducing systems with the equivalent, or similar, structure and functions), and it is a system created by another self-reproducing system with the equivalent, or similar, structure and functions.

System-environment relationship

All natural self-reproducers are purely material structures. Therefore, they must have matter and energy interactions with external environment, and they can only be reproduced through such interactions.

Following closely an approach proposed by Löfgren (1972), a refined definition can be suggested to describe a system reproduced in a given environment. A producing system S' urges its environment F to produce another system S'', by applying some "effort" (or targeted action) E to it:

$$(S' \xrightarrow{A} E) \rightarrow S'' \quad (1)$$

If S'' is such that S' and S'' have a substantial degree of similarity, then A is a process of self-reproduction. It is possible to say also that S' and S'' both belong to a system type S, and the definition can be written as

$$(S \xrightarrow{A} E) \rightarrow S \quad (2)$$

The action A transforms raw material of environment E into a target system S, also producing some non-usable by-product W. Then, it is possible to represent a process of self-reproduction in a from of an auto-catalytic reaction:

$$E + S \rightarrow 2S + W \quad (3)$$

S is self-reproducing in the environment of E, gradually "consuming" E in this process[3].

W denotes degraded matter and energy produced in the reaction which is not usable for further utilization by S. W may be usable for utilization by other self-reproducer types, or E may be renewable, so this process does not necessarily lead to the 'heat death'.

It obvious that various types of systems self-reproductive in their given environment have a completely different physical structure and also a different complexity of organization and functioning (compare e.g. a computer virus to a reproduction of multi-cellar organism); also a complexity of their environment can be different.

It is possible to distinguish between types of natural reproducers depending on a degree of complexity of self-reproducer S (of complexity $c(S)$) in relation to its environment E (of complexity $c(E)$), as presented in Table 2. One of appropriate measures to compare qualitatively different classes of self-reproducers with substantially discriminate environment is the measure of quantity and variety of elements and links in systems considered, and the quantity and variety of operation types for such systems (Edmonds 1999).

Comparative complexity is not the only issue in self-reproduction. For each of these types of self-reproductive structures, there obviously exists a lower limit of complexity that would allow them to operate purposefully and in particular to self-reproduce. There are clear evidences from cellular biology that such a limit exists for biological self-reproducers, such as prokaryotic cells. A minimum structure of a cell must have 15%-20% of components of *E.Coli* (Watson 1976).

Bacteria (such as *E. Coli*) are quite a complex structures capable of self-reproducing in a mixture of rather basic organic molecules. Yet, a computer virus is a comparatively simple program which requires quite a complicated hardware and software to get executed (i.e. to self-reproduce). This may imply that there exists a lower limit of complexity for "system and environment" aggregate structure, allowing a system to self-reproduce in a given environment.

Structuring of self-reproduction studies can further be achieved through the given definitions and classifications. It is evidential that many models claimed to be universal (e.g. von Neumann's automaton) actually

[2]A classification more specifically describing types of 'near replication of a parent' has been suggested by E. Szathmáry, classification based on hereditary potential and 'mode of synthesis' (Szathmáry 1995).

[3]Some self-reproducers, such as computer viruses or memes, can be thought of as reproduced at no cost, although a cost may be quite low so it can be neglected (energy required to reproduce a series of electronic signals is insignificant, especially when compared with amounts of energy required for hardware self-maintenance).

suit for a sub-class of self-reproductive systems (called "true self-reproducers" here). The distinction between various classes of self-reproducers may lead to models which on one hand suit the Alife research program being matter-independent (against what has been demanded in Emmeche (1992)) and yet become more specific by considering certain properties of the environment in which given systems reproduce themselves.

References

Aspray, W., and Burks, A., eds. 1987. *Papers of John von Neumann on Computing and Computer Theory.* MIT Press.

Edmonds, B. 1999. *Syntactic Measures of Complexity.* Ph.D. Dissertation, University of Manchester.

Eigen, M.; Gardiner, W.; Schuster, P.; and Winkler-Oswatitsch, R. 1981. The origin of genetic information. *Scientic American* 244:78–94.

Emmeche, C. 1992. Life as an abstract phenomenon: Is artificial life possible? In Varela, F., and Bourgine, P., eds., *Toward a practice of autonomous systems. Proceedings of the First European Conference on Artificial Life.* MIT Press.

Freitas, R., and Gilbreath, W., eds. 1980. *Advanced Automation for Space Missions.* Proceedings of the NASA/ASEE Study.

Langton, C. 1984. Self-reproduction in cellular automata. *Physica D* 10:135–144.

Langton, C., ed. 1989. *Artificial Life*, volume 6 of *SFI Studies in the Science of Complexity.* Addison-Wesley.

Löfgren, L. 1972. Relative explanations of systems. In Klir, G., ed., *Trends in General Systems Theory.* John Wiley & Sons.

Luksha, P. 2002. Society as a self-reproducing system. *Journal of Sociocybernetics* 2(2):13–36.

Maturana, H., and Varela, F. 1980. *Autopoiesis and Cognition.* Dordrecht.

McMullin, B. 2000. John von neumann and the evolutionary growth of complexity: Looking backwards, looking forwards. In *Proceedings of Artificial Life VII.*

Ray, T. S. 2001. Artificial life. In Dulbecco, R. e. a., ed., *The Origins of Life*, volume 1 of *Frontiers of Life.* Academic Press.

Sipper, M.; Sanchez, E.; Mange, D.; Tomassini, M.; Pérez-Uribe, A.; and Stauffer, A. 1997. A phylogenetic, ontogenetic, and epigenetic view of bio-inspired hardware systems. *IEEE Transactions on Evolutionary Computation* 1(1):83–97.

Szathmáry, E. 1995. A classification of replicators and lambda-calculus models of biological organization. *Proceedings of Royal Society, London, B* 260:279–286.

von Neumann, J., and Burks, A. 1966. *Theory of Self-Reproducing Automata.* Univ. of Illinois Press.

Watson, J. 1976. *Molecular Biology of the Gene.* London: W.B.Benjamin.

$c(E)$ to $c(S)$	type of self-reproduction	description	examples
>	quasi-self-reproducers	strictly dependent in reproduction on a system of higher complexity not produced as a part of its reproduction process	• viruses and genes; • memes; • computer viruses and computer "artificial life" (e.g. Tierra (Ray 2001))
≅	semi-self-reproducers	autonomous complex systems requiring another comparably complex system to self-reproduce	• organisms with sexual divergence; • (certain) organisms with parasitic reproduction
<	true self-reproducers	complex autonomous systems capable to self-reproduce in an environment of basic elements[a]	• prokaryotic / eukaryotic cells; • organisms with asexual reproduction; • self-reproducing society; • artificial self-reproducing plants (e.g. (Freitas & Gilbreath 1980))

[a]From theory point of view, it has been a type of system modeled by von Neumann (1966). For biological systems, this case of self-reproducers has been described by Maturana & Varela (1980), because complex structures must be produced inside such systems out of basic environment.

Table 2: Typology of natural self-reproducers

Organizing Relations and Emergence

Stephen Jones
387 Riley St, Surry Hills,
NSW, 2010, Australia
s_jones1@bigpond.com

Abstract

Emergence is largely used as an explanation: such and such an object — ranging from atoms through multi-cellular organisms to consciousness — is an emergent property of some ensemble of parts. But this leaves an inadequate level of understanding, making the term a representation of something almost mystical. For emergence to be useful an understanding of the mechanisms of emergence must be brought out. This paper proposes a system of orders of organizing relations that are the means by which complex objects "emerge" from the interactions of their constituent parts.

Introduction

The term emergence has a somewhat equivocal press. For some it is an explanation for the appearance of wholes or coherent objects in any system of things or understandings; while for others it is either meaningless or, conversely, an invocation of something mystical. The term is applied to the appearance of novel, coherent objects that are not predictable from the isolated properties of the system's parts, functioning as a shorthand for the development of new levels in a hierarchy of organization of complex and adaptive entities. Novelty and coherence are the primary properties of emergent objects. Two questions arise here:

1. How can a new thing come into being if it cannot be predicted by the properties of the stuff that constitutes it? and
2. What confers coherence on something made up of many kinds of parts so that it has obvious existence as a whole thing?

Ultimately the question of emergence is the problem of how any kind of organized system can come into being. How can a collection of things self-organize? Where does the ordered arrangement of the parts, the thing's organization, come from? How can it self-regulate or maintain that organization in the face of the entropy in its environs? These questions apply particularly to biological entities.

Most authors on emergence seem to want to set up an understanding of emergence such that a bottom-up, micro-physical-properties basis for its explanation cannot operate and that only a non-reductionist consideration of the behaviors of objects should obtain. I want to explore this issue here and propose a way in which the explanatory value of emergence can be made consistent with a micro-physical causality understanding of the world. Thus, I will argue that the proper study of emergence is in the study of the organizing relations that operate to link the parts of an ensemble. Artificial Life, then, is the study of the organizing relations that produce the emergence of coherent entities in computational situations.

Kinds of Emergence

For most philosophers there are two kinds of emergence: ontological and representational (Searle 1992). Ontological emergence covers explanations for how objects and organisms can exist in the world given thermodynamics and a causally closed microphysics. Representational emergence covers the development of theories about the things which we are able to observe in the world. Cariani (1991) includes computational emergence, in which "complex global forms can arise from local computational interactions" (p.776) thus modelling similar processes to those which, in material systems, might produce actual emergent objects. It appears, for example, in work on cellular automata and in Holland's work on complex adaptive systems (CAS). Not only can cellular automata replicate themselves, but they produce "gliders", or coherent groupings of cells that emerge from a few explicitly specified rules. Holland probes the properties of CAS and argues that aggregation and self-maintenance are specifically relevant to the study of emergence. Aggregation is a function of organizational hierarchy, and self-maintenance involves the continued coherence of an aggregation despite the flow of resources through it and the perpetual turnover of its constituent parts (Holland 1995).

Here I will consider the emergence of *physical* objects and systems from the *matter* of their constituents, and its simulation in computational emergence, rather than dwell on representational emergence. One of the reasons emergence is adopted as an explanation is that it seems that there are numerous physical ensembles which do not predict the behaviors that these systems, when suitably constituted, may demonstrate. Any climb up the levels of the biological orders produces novel emergent systems, *e.g.* many behaviors of a cell are not predicted by the isolated properties of any of its macromolecular components. In fact many of the behaviors of those macromolecules don't even come into operation until they are integrated into a cell.

There are two flavours of ontological emergence:

Weak emergence, where an object having emergent properties is physically determined by the properties of its lower level constituents, yet would not exist as such without those emergent properties. (Collier 1998).

Radical emergence, where the emergent properties of the whole are *metaphysically incompatible* with the properties and relations of its parts, perhaps involving the appearance of a totally new (e.g. mental) stuff.

In the view canvassed here, the kinds of things that radical emergence is used to "explain" are accounted for in the roles of the feedback relations discussed in the *Taxonomy* section.

Characteristics of Emergent Objects

Emergence is best represented as a jump in hierarchical level of organizational structure of the parts of some system such that they become coherently organized and might be characterized as being something with a new name. The problem of emergence becomes the problem of whether it is meaningful to talk about hierarchical levels of organization in systems, how one might describe the boundaries between levels and how a collection of constituents can actually become a new level. These issues concern every level of science from the jump from quarks and gluons to nucleons and atoms in microphysics, to the difference between collections of organic molecules and cells, to the organization of individual humans into societies. Emergence thus becomes the question of organization and I will proffer a taxonomy of relations by which organization might arise in a collection of parts giving it integrity, coherence and the status of a whole. But we must first cover some of the properties of organized wholes that persuade us that they are emergent.

Emergent systems can be characterised as dynamical processes showing:

a: novelty — Instances of the first time some thing appears in the universe, or the emergence of something new with every instance of a particular organization of constituents (Bickhard 2000).

b: unpredictability — The unpredictability of the properties of something is at the very basis of calling it emergent (Broad 1925).

c: coherence, integrity — Objects that are "held together by causal interactions that constitute their organic unity ... act[ing] coherently and resist[ing] internal and external fluctuations". (Collier 1998)

d: self-maintenance — Contingent stability with respect to variations in the environment. Self-maintenance is part of the cohesive nature of an emergent system (Collier 1998).

e: causal asymmetry — The emergence of "novel causal properties" is an essential criterion for emergence.

e:i) downward causation — Properties of the constituent sub-systems of an emergent system only revealed through its emergence.

e:ii) non-linearity — Step-functions, hysteresis and boundary development in far-from-equilibrium systems.

Suitable consideration of these integrative properties within levels of an organizational hierarchy, implies that al-though a full description of the processes involved in any particular emergence may be intractable, they are, in principle, precisely explainable in a reductionist procedure that acknowledges the organizational hierarchy of things. For example, in the deconstruction of vitalism as the principle that brought inanimate matter to life in biology, it was recognized that the organizing relations that had been attributed to some vitalistic (and radically non-reducible) principle were in fact the proper study of biology (Needham 1936). So by what mechanisms do these properties arise in making an ensemble of parts into an emergent whole?

Nature of Organizing Relations.

The organization of the constituents of a system is a result of the relations that operate in the physical world, or in the rules of procedure adopted for some computational simulation. Emergent objects depend on those *organizing relations* that can actually be operating in the physical world or in the rules of procedure adopted for some computational simulation. Explanations for emergences require description of the relations that link objects within some level of an integration and between hierarchical levels of order, but we need a definition of order. Von Foerster suggested that order allows us "to account for apparent relationships between elements of a set which would impose some constraints as to the possible arrangements of the elements of this system. As the organization of the system grows, more and more of these relations should become apparent". (von Foerster 1960, p.37). He then derives a relation between order and entropy such that for a system to be ordered it must carry less entropy than the maximum possible entropy of a set of the same elements not in any way so organized, i.e. a system wherein the elements are not in any relations (other than random spatial relations) with each other. So to produce order in a system it must possess relations among its elements which have the effect of *reducing the indistinguishability* of states of the system, thus organizing it. Whitehead defined relations as "abstractions from contrasts. A relation can be found in many contrasts; and when it is so found, it is said to relate the things contrasted". (Whitehead 1929, p.349) where a contrast is a difference between two perceptions such as the contrast between red and blue.

Now, if the system so organized becomes capable of some level of stability such that it develops constrained regions having boundaries and that for perturbations to its elements or its boundaries to be damaging they must be greater than a certain threshold, then that system can be said to be integrated (Ashby 1952). This integrity gives a system its emergent condition as a new order of object and we can then go on to describe various levels of order in which a set of integrated elements at one level become the parts which, in utilizing further kinds of organizing relations, constitute a new, higher level order. These organizing relations are complex networks of interactions among, for example, the physico-chemical and biochemical entities of biology or the neuro-anatomical structures of the brain or the individuals of a society.

Taxonomy of Organizing Relations

I offer here a taxonomy of the kinds of relations that could organize the parts of some ensemble into a coherent whole. The first and most prosaic are simple environmental relations which are the basic relations of arrangement or position such as shape, momentum, proximity (Searle 1992). They are not causal relations but the accidents of an object. They contribute to the emergence of an organized object through the opportunities they afford for other more interactive relations to operate.

Beyond environmental relations I want to draw out three orders of relations classified on the basis of their interactivity and thus on their organizational capacity.

First order: Feedforward relations: Where environmental relations have any emergent effect it will be through their enabling of local physical and chemical interactions. Feed-forward offers no situation in which the object takes into account the degree of impact of its relations with some other object affording it some kind of "information" by which it can regulate its action.

In ALife, rule-following is a feedforward process producing, *e.g.*, gliders in cellular automata. It includes sensing to find food, to gauge distance to neighbours, and other means of gathering environmental information. The rules in Reynolds' (1994) boids, each functioning in a feedforward only manner for each boid in a local region, allow a graded set of relationships throughout the larger global flock such that the autonomous behaviour of each boid produces an overall coherence in the flock.

The emission of signals may also be a feedforward only relation, but emission begs the question of to what end? Is it simply a marker, as with MacLennan's (1991) ants, or is it intentional behaviour leading to mutual interactions such as communication? Other feedforward relations include learning by repetition, or concentration gradient following in cellular development, but these may also be a function of third order mutualistic feedbacks.

Second order: circular causal Feedback relations: Feed-back is a function of sensing and enables an entity to regulate its behaviour. It arises when a signal emitted into the environment produces some impact back onto the originating entity and some aspect of that signal provides information to it about its ongoing presence in that environment. Feedback often involves learning when the individual modulates its own behaviour, by (1) emission of a signal for later reacquisition, or (2) alteration of a signal or marker by an individual for its own purposes. Relations between a system's internal self-regulation and its environment, afforded by feed-back, make the system possible, emerging from the soup as a distinct and distinguishable entity. All neural networks and classifier systems involve feedback learning via some path or another. The kind of feedback imposed by natural selection in a genetic algorithm (GA), is another example.

There are a number of different identifiable types of feed-back relations based either on the function of a comparison generating an error value (Wiener 1948) or on the re-entry of processed input (Edelman, 1989).

A: Feedback with error values:

1. Feedback in which a sample of the output is fed back into the input as a direct modulation of the input value. Negative feedback produces an inhibition of the system and helps a system survive perturbation. Positive feedback may cause a non-linearity, producing hysteresis in a system, and may also induce resonance. There are well understood conditions under which this resonance can occur (*e.g.* feedback oscillators and resonant filters in electronics) yet it is a perfectly good example of a weak emergence.
2. Feedback in which several processing stages operate in a system so that its output is filtered or otherwise modulated before it is returned to the input stage. These kind of feed-backs can provide emphasis of some particular aspect of the input and are probably involved in conscious attention in humans via the thalamo-cortical loop structure of the brain (Newman 1997).
3. Feedback with comparison to a norm or intended outcome, generating an error value which is returned to the input stage. This is the kind of control utilized in successive approximation processes like reaching for an object. Each stage of the articulation of the arm provides a fed back error value

narrowing the discrepancy between current and intended position.

B: Feedback without error values:

1. Unguided learning: This is feedback where the output behaviour of some system becomes part of its input stream, but without comparison. It occurs when a known goal state is not available and the system has to make its own way, categorizing as it proceeds. In a constructivist interpretation of the world, our categorization of input stimuli cannot have developed in comparison with pre-existing norms but must have been made according to a series of recurrences of events reinforcing certain particular ways of viewing the situation.
2. Memory is possibly the most important consequence of feedback networks, particularly in biological and neural systems. Something very similar to short-term memory occurs with the propagation delay and resonance effects that a neural system will thus contain. It is very likely that re-entrant feedback produces that slightly smeared experience of the present that we have as part of our consciousness.
3. Self-reflection: Our ability to reflect on what is occurring in comparison to things which have been experienced previously, categorized and learned as history is a function of re-entrant processing coupled with memory and the error-value generating processes that allow us to evaluate the effectiveness of some act.

Feedback systems and the kinds of relations that are sensing and probing in environments where there are other entities of adequate complexity, may lead to mutualistic (or third order) relations and bring about communication. Any of these processes will indicate some sort of primitive intentionality in the system.

Third order: mutualistic feedback relations. Different entities in an environment emitting signals and responding to each other in natural or ALife systems can lead to cooperative behaviour and co-evolution (Jones 2000). Interdependence of metabolic regulation produces multi-celled organisms from a soup of single cells. Human interactions: learning, teaching and influencing each other, competing or cooperating are the processes that bind individuals into a society.

Communication can lead to a likely increase in the fitness of both the signalling and the responding groups. By emission of a signal individuals can assist each other to survive. (Koza 1991) describes an ant foraging GA in which ants search for food by moving, sensing and depositing pheromones. In Co-evolution each of a pair of algorithms acts as the environment for the other. One program tries to adapt to the "environment" created by the other, by testing the performance of the one program relative to the other and then vice versa. This is essentially a "biological arms race" where each species develops defences and attacks against the other.

Organisms gain their integrity, boundaries and self-maintenance through open-system behaviors such as ingest-ion and sensing, processes that are active in all biological systems. When a complex system has adequate organization there will be a massive array of internal and external feed-back relations. A state of organization is maintained by the exchange of energy with the environment, which helps to maintain the chemical metabolism of the membrane bounded system, but it also produces potentially deleterious metabolic waste products. Excretion of these wastes through the membrane completes a circular relationship with the environment. These wastes may be the basis for the development of mutualistic relations (Jones 2000; Pachepsky, Taylor, & Jones 2002). In humans, perceptions and productions are the primary elements of exchange with the environment that keep us integrated as conscious beings capable of interaction with other entities and processes in the world of matter and ideas.

Conclusion

In a sense Cariani (1991) quite correctly dismisses emergence, but in so doing he throws the baby out with the bath-water. The value of emergence is that it alerts us to situations in which explanations must include causal processes that are not usually recognized from within the purview of micro-physics. Reductive explanation is, in principle, possible for those objects that we commonly think of as emergent. Nevertheless such reduction obscures the forest not simply by a description of the trees but by the demand for a description of the quantum processes that make the atoms and then the molecules and then the amino-acids and the proteins and then the cells and so on up to the ecology of the forest. Strict reductionist explanation is thus rather wasted, tedious if not intractably difficult and not very useful. To completely explain some complex thing we must carry out a *series* of explanations, each of which amounts to a reduction of one level into the level of its constituents and their organizing relations. In turn the constituents have to be explained from within their own level, working down to the ultimate micro-physical components in a series of steps.

Emergence, as explanation, is a shorthand. Useful explanations of a system need to actively account for the role of the organizing relations among the parts at each sub-level. This has the great value of opening up mechanistic explanation, rendering it relevant in understanding the dynamics of process. As Holland comments: "When we can formulate macrolaws that describe the behaviors of emergent phenomena (for instance, the laws of chemical bonding) we gain greatly in comprehension, whether of a model universe or a real one". (Holland 1998, p.189).

The dynamics of organizing relations enable emergence, affording the emergent object the means by which it can self-organize, self-regulate and, within the biological levels, be alive. In the simulations of computational emergence we need to find means by which emergent objects at one level may become the constituents of a further emergence, by generating their own organizing relations, thus climbing multiple levels in the hierarchy of organization.

References

Ashby, W. 1952. *Design for a Brain.* New York: Wiley.

Bickhard, M. 2000. Emergence. In Andersen, P. B.; Emmeche, C.; Finnemann, N. O.; and Christiansen, P. V., eds., *Downward Causation.* Aarhus, Denmark: University of Aarhus Press. 322–348.

Broad, C. 1925. *The Mind and its Place in Nature.* London: Routledge & Kegan Paul.

Cariani, P. 1991. Emergence and artificial life. In Langton et al. (1991), 775–797.

Collier, J. 1998. The dynamical basis of emergence in natural hierarchies. In Farre, G., and Oksala, T., eds., *Emergence, Complexity, Hierarchy and Organisation. Selected and Edited Papers from the ECHO III Conference, Acta Polytechnica Scandinavica, MA91.* Espoo: Finnish Academy of Technology.

Holland, J. 1995. *Hidden Order: How Adaptation Builds Complexity.* Helix Books.

Holland, J. 1998. *Emergence: From Chaos to Order.* Redwood City, California: Addison-Wesley.

Jones, S. 2000. Evolvability in the context of the biosphere. In Maley, C., and Boudreau, E., eds., *ALife VII Workshop Proceedings.*

Koza, J. 1991. Genetic evolution and co-evolution of computer programs. In Langton et al. (1991), 603–629.

Langton, C. G.; Taylor, C.; Farmer, J. D.; and Rasmussen, S., eds. 1991. *Artificial Life II.* Reading, Mass.: Addison-Wesley.

MacLennan, B. 1991. Synthetic ecology: An approach to the study of communication. In Langton et al. (1991), 631–658.

Needham, J. 1936. *Order and Life.* New Haven: Yale University Press.

Newman, J. 1997. Putting the puzzle together: Towards a general theory of the neural correlates of consciousness. *Journal of Consciousness Studies* 4(1 & 2).

Pachepsky, L.; Taylor, T.; and Jones, S. 2002. Mutualism promotes diversity and stability in a simple artificial ecosystem. *Artificial Life* .8(1).

Reynolds, C. 1994. An evolved, vision-based model of obstacle avoidance behaviour. In Langton, C. G., ed., *Artificial Life III.* Reading, Mass.: Addison-Wesley. 327-346.

Searle, J. 1992. *The Rediscovery of the Mind.* Cambridge, Mass.: MIT Press.

von Foerster, H. 1960. Environments of self-organizing systems. In Yovits, M., and Cameron, S., eds., *Self-Organizing Systems.* New York: Pergamon Press.

Whitehead, A. 1929. *Process and Reality: an Essay in Cosmology.* New York: Macmillan.

Wiener, N. 1948. *Cybernetics, or Control and Communication in the Animal and the Machine.* New York: Wiley.

Self-Assembling Dynamical Hierarchies

Alan Dorin and **Jon McCormack**
School of Computer Science and Software Engineering
Monash University, Clayton, Victoria 3800, Australia
{aland, jonmc}@csse.monash.edu.au

Abstract

This paper addresses the open problem of assembling multi-levelled hierarchical structure. It presents a model of an infinitely-levelled, self-assembling dynamical hierarchy that arises from the interaction of geometric primary elements with a fixed complexity. A formal description of the presented hierarchy is derived. This quantifies the relative compression achieved by describing the system in terms of components of different organization. The relationship between properties of representations and those of physical objects is then discussed to support the view that at each level in the hierarchy presented, the components exhibit emergent properties not possessed by those at the levels below. It is concluded that these new properties are trivial and that such infinitely-levelled structures may be constructed easily. However, since the definition of the problem in the literature admits such trivial possibilities, more specific definitions are required.

Introduction

Hierarchies are a useful way of understanding the organization of life (Nehaniv & Rhodes 2000; Baas 1994; Chaitin 1970; Simon 1962; Mirkin *et al.* 1996). Higher order biological organisms are constructed from atoms, molecules, organelles, cells and organs; hence, one aspect of relevance to constructing virtual organisms is the representation of this hierarchy. In software, a computer program specifies the primary components and their interactions. In contrast with the interactions of matter in the physical universe, computer programs deal exclusively with representations, the meaning of which is determined by observers. It is important to make this distinction, not only for the sake of clarity in discussions about virtual life, but also in defining hierarchies and their properties.

The notion that complex outcomes or behaviours may be arrived at through the interactions of simple building blocks is commonly held by artificial life researchers (Rasmussen *et al.* 2001a). Research has sought rules describing interactions between basic elements, in the hope that they will give rise to aggregates exhibiting new *emergent* properties not apparent in the primary elements themselves. These properties are understood to appear at, or even *define*, each level in the hierarchy — an idea discussed in more detail below.

Whilst *The Game of Life* (Berlekamp *et al.* 1982; Poundstone 1985) and other cellular automata may yet provide a basis for constructing hierarchies with emergent properties, producing a multi-level hierarchy through self-assembly of primary units remains an open problem (Bedau *et al.* 2000). For a given framework, Rasmussen et al. (2001a) propose that it may be impossible to extend the levels in a hierarchy, without adding to the complexity of the base units. This idea seems to run counter to the extreme view that it ought to be possible to derive complex global outcomes from simple local interactions.

Additional questions concerning hierarchies

The proposed relationship between the complexity of primary units and the number of hierarchical levels they may construct, raises a number of potentially interesting issues for artificial life. For example, how much complexity, if any, do the base units require to construct an extra level in the hierarchy (and how ought this be measured)? Is this amount independent of the order of the level being considered? Is there a threshold for the complexity of the basic building blocks, beyond which an infinitely levelled hierarchy may be achieved? Is the physical world limited in the number of hierarchical levels that are possible to arrange (and what is the evidence to support this)?

Representations, Hierarchies & Properties

Many systems in the artificial life literature are *computational/representational* rather than physical. The "building blocks" and "structures" discussed in these systems are commonly referred to as if they were material entities, even though they are only representations of those entities.[1] As authors of software, we must be certain our application of terms such as *hierarchy*, *complexity* and *property* are carefully considered. We propose in this paper, that one way to increase the rigour with which artificial life software is analyzed, is through the application of the principles of information theory (Chaitin 1987). Information theory is particularly applicable to the study of computational artificial life, as this field fundamentally concerns patterns in information.

In this paper we describe a hierarchical structure of unlimited order, which self-assembles from primary units of fixed complexity. Each level in the potentially infinite hierarchy is shown to possess properties arising from the interactions of its components, which the lower level components do not themselves possess.

The reason for presenting this hierarchy is not to demonstrate that *any* hierarchy may be assembled from

[1] Although the machine on which the representations are manipulated is obviously physical.

base units of fixed complexity, it is merely to show that hierarchies *do* exist that can be self-assembled in a manner which meets criteria specified in artificial life literature (Rasmussen *et al.* 2001a). The model illustrated is uncomplicated, and is not directly related to any specific biological system. This allows us to illustrate that the current definitions for *hierarchy* and *property* need to be formalized in the context of artificial life. Formalization will assist us to define more clearly the relationship of software models to real biological systems.

The following sections discuss aspects of the simulation presented here that satisfy previously proposed criteria for hierarchies. These sections also address criteria recently proposed for multi-levelled, dynamical hierarchies constructed from components of fixed complexity that exhibit new properties at each level.

Related work

This paper addresses issues raised in (Rasmussen *et al.* 2001a; 2001b; Gross & McMullin 2001) concerning self-assembly of hierarchical structures which model aspects of biology. The system below is a simple artificial physical/chemical system which bears resemblance to some of the more typical artificial chemistries documented in Dittrich, Ziegler, and Banzhaf (2001). However, the present system is more closely derived from cellular automata (Langton 1986), and systems that link the concepts of cellular automata and artificial chemistry in order to study self-assembly (Dorin 2000). Other related research is detailed in the individual sections below to which it is most relevant.

The self-assembling hierarchy

This section describes a self-assembling hierarchical system which exhibits new properties at each level and does not require added complexity at the base level to achieve any number of additional levels. The number of levels that may be assembled is limited only by the amount of basic building material available in the model and the memory constraints imposed by the machine. The basic elements of this system are equilateral triangles laid out on a planar, triangular grid (Figure 1). The entire system is updated simultaneously in discrete time steps. At each time step of the simulation each triangle may be shifted to a random, neighbouring, unoccupied location if one is available. The triangular lattice dictates the direction in which a triangle's vertices are oriented so that movement to a neighbouring cell includes a rotation by 180 degrees. This may also be viewed as a flip about a horizontal axis running through the triangle's centre. Triangles were selected for this model as they are the simplest regular polyhedra that can be used to tile a plane. Squares could equally well have been employed.

After the movement stage of each time step, all triangles are examined to see if they neighbour any others. If they do neighbour another triangle, the two triangles will bond to one another with a fixed probability, b, established at the start of the simulation. If two neighbouring triangles are already bonded together at this time step, they will dissociate with probability, d, determined similarly.

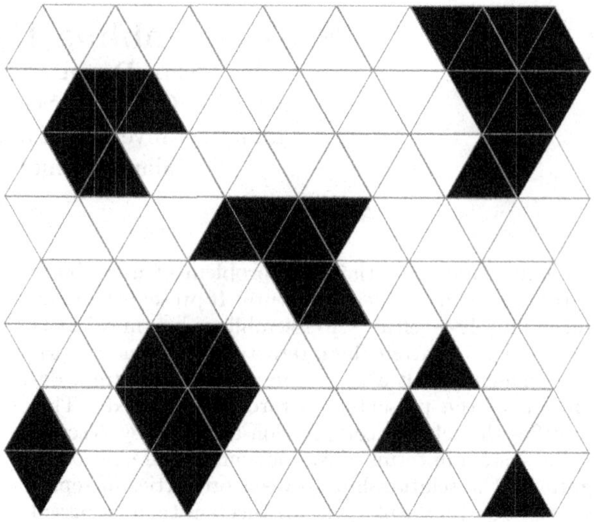

Figure 1: A section of the triangular grid

During the movement stage of each time step, if the upper and leftmost triangle in a bonded aggregate is selected to move into a neighbouring location, the movement of all triangles in the whole is constrained in this direction also. This ensures that the aggregate is treated as a rigid body. Any planned movement that would cause an intersection between a member of the aggregate and an occupied cell on the grid is cancelled and the aggregate remains stationary for this time step.

The next section describes possible behaviours of the system.

Operation of the model

The probabilities d (dissociate) and b (bond) dictate the tendency of the triangles to form larger aggregates and for these to break apart after having been constructed. As long as b is non-zero, the chance that at least a single bond will join two aggregates increases in proportion to the length of the edge. That is, if many potential bonding sites are presented, the chance that at least one of these will link the two aggregates increases. Conversely, if the value of d is not unity, aggregates with internal structures made of closely packed triangles, presenting many internal edges for redundant bonding, are much less likely to dissociate than aggregates with narrow cross-sections.

Overall then, large, broad structures with redundant internal bonds will tend to develop, whilst smaller or long narrow structures will tend to break down. The extent to which each of these phenomena occur depends

Figure 2: Sample shapes formed of primary elements

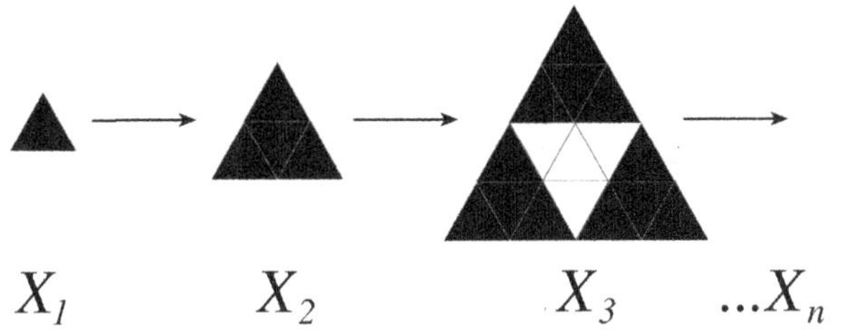

Figure 3: A hierarchical structure

on the values of b and d.

Some elementary structures that may appear from this system are illustrated in Figure 2. It is apparent from Figure 3 that triangles may form larger triangles (or other shapes), and these may be assembled into larger triangles (or shapes) still. Thus, here is a form that may assemble itself from primary elements into larger and larger structures — a nested hierarchy. It should be clear from the description above that no additional information needs to be given to the individual triangles to have them continue to build a hierarchy of multiple levels. A measure of this hierarchical organization is given in the discussion below. This will be followed by a discussion of the new properties that arise at each level in the hierarchy.

Identifying hierarchies

Hierarchies have been studied across a range of disciplines including Mathematics (Mirkin *et al.* 1996), General Systems Theory (Bertalanffy 1968, p.74), (Simon 1962), (Simon 1994, p.196), Information Theory (Boulton & Wallace 1970), in general biological terms (Polanyi 1968), and recently in Artificial Life (Nehaniv & Rhodes 2000). For the purposes of defining a hierarchy in this paper, we follow the description given by Baas (1994). Specifically, for a given set of elements X, X is a ***division hierarchy*** (referred to commonly as a ***nested-hierarchy***) if there is associated with it a system of levels $X_1, X_2, \ldots X_n$, such that $X_n = X$, with each X_i related by a series of mappings, $X_1 < X_2 < \ldots < X_n$. That is, nested hierarchies involve levels that consist of, and contain, lower levels.

In the present situation, we are dealing with representational systems and therefore an appropriate way of defining and comparing hierarchical organization in this context must be developed. The issue of concern here is the state of the variables being used to represent the properties of a system, and those of its components. This is fortunate as it allows us to find a measure of hierarchical structure or organization, which is difficult to find for real biological organisms or their artifacts (Chaitin 1970). Namely, we may specify the redundancy in a nested hierarchical structure, and thereby discover its levels and the collections of elements that are its components.

Information measure of the system

Let us take the triangular system X_3 illustrated in Figure 3 as an example to formally demonstrate the presence of a multi-level, nested hierarchy. A structure X of order n, written X_n, is composed of $4^{n-1}X_1$ primary elements (in this case simple triangles). If each primary element X_1 requires p bits to specify its position and orientation then, X_n requires $4^{n-1}p$ bits to specify as an aggregate of X_1's.

But, if X_n can be described in terms of the position and orientation of the 4 lower level elements X_{n-1} that compose it then, X_n requires $4p$ bits to specify in terms of X_{n-1}.

So, for n levels, X_n can be specified hierarchically in $4p(n-1)$ bits. Since $4p(n-1) < 4^{n-1}p$, for $n > 2$, the hierarchical description is clearly more efficient than that obtained in terms only of the primary elements. In accordance with Ockham's razor, which may be paraphrased, "if two theories explain the facts equally well then the simpler theory is to be preferred", the hierarchical scheme, because it requires less information (bits) to specify the aggregate's structure, is preferred (Wallace & Boulton 1968).

In practice, the triangles in the model must share edges to count as an aggregate. Even in continuous space the number of bits required to code a collection in terms of primary elements, is therefore substantially less than $4^{n-1}p$. This holds because once a primary element is fixed in space using p bits, the location of others in the aggregate may be specified relatively. For the purposes of this example therefore, $4^{n-1}p$ may be considered as an upper limit or worst case. Similar constraints reduce the number of bits required to specify all levels of the hierarchy. Furthermore, since the model proposed here actually constrains triangles to lie on a regular lattice, the number of bits required to represent an aggregate is substantially less than that required to do so in continuous space. The principles may be shown to hold equally in continuous or lattice space however.

There may be more than one way of viewing a compos-

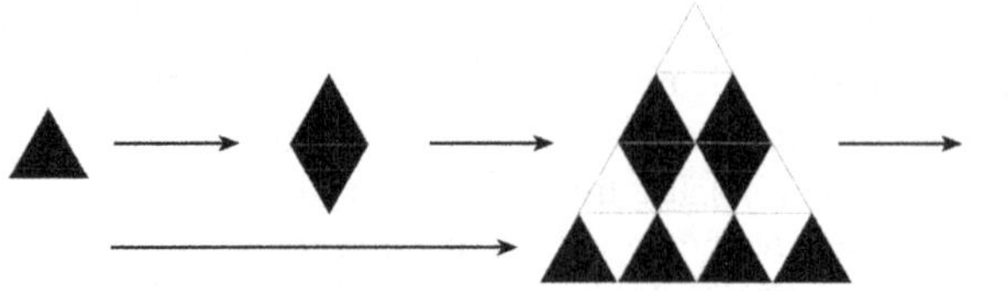

Figure 4: An alternative hierarchy to construct X_3

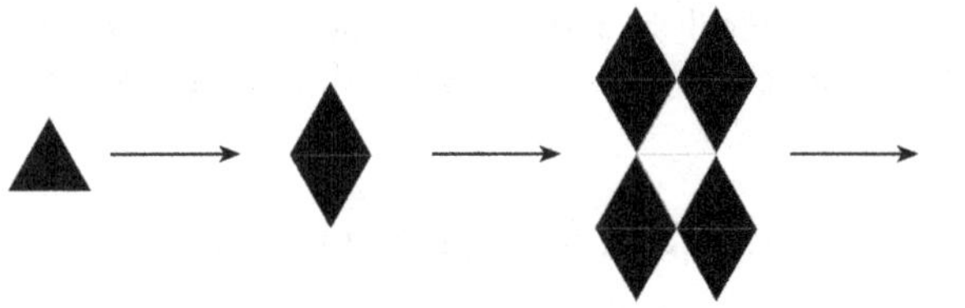

Figure 5: An alternative hierarchical structure

ite object as a hierarchy. For example, the structure X_3 in Figure 3 may also be seen in terms of components X_1 and Y_2 (Figure 4). We can obtain a measure of how succinctly this different way of viewing the system's components compresses the data using the procedure outlined above. If it results in a more concise description it is to be preferred over the decomposition given above.

Perhaps no compression is obtained in the hierarchy, for example, a trivial hierarchy in which an aggregate is made of two dissimilar components, X and Y, can also be specified in terms of these. There is no redundancy in the composition and hence no compression will be gained in the description. In this case there is no useful reason to view this aggregate as a nested hierarchy. One may as well accept that the aggregate is flat in its organization.

Whilst the example above is a hierarchy of triangles and larger triangles, of course it needn't be the case that the hierarchical structures formed by this model are perfectly regular, nor need it be the case that the same form be repeated at multiple scales. The form in Figure 5 serves as an example of a hierarchy with different shapes at each level. Of course there are a multitude of possible infinitely-levelled hierarchies. The development of specific structures in any given run of the model is currently left to chance. That the space supports the development of such structures however remains clear.

Now that it has been shown that the structures above may in fact be specified hierarchically, it remains to be shown that each level of the hierarchy exhibits new emergent properties not found in the lower levels. This is the subject of the following section.

Identifying properties

Seeing is a theory laden enterprise
— Hansen (1958)

In the physical world, a property is any observable aspect of an entity — an attribute, characteristic, feature, trait or aspect (Bealer 1999). For example, the wavelength of the light an object reflects is a property of that object, as are its length and mass.

In some artificial life literature, a property that arises through the interactions of many simple parts which do not themselves possess this property is labelled *emergent*. Hence, "A property that applies at a given level is emergent if it does not apply at any lower level" but with the proviso that "the specification of observable properties is somewhat arbitrary" (Rasmussen *et al.* 2001a).

Let us make a few remarks regarding properties. Firstly, properties are ***observed by people***. People overlook some things and are very good at detecting others. We deal with our environment by searching for certain kinds of pattern, ignoring, completely oblivious to, even incapable of grasping others (Dennett 1991; Tufte 1990). Technology may broaden the scope in which we search for patterns by mapping them from unobservable domains to those that we may examine.

We may well describe a particular system in terms of many properties. However, the properties which stand the test of time are those that aid our understanding or enhance our ability to predict the way the system behaves. These properties help us to form a model of the system under observation.

There is some (perhaps misleading) sense of objectivity when one "observes" a property of the physical world and measures it. In the world of representation, in this case software-based universes, what does it mean to "observe a property"? A property in the virtual world may be anything an observer wishes it to be, as long as it can be distinguished from other properties. Any symbol or bit may stand for a property. It may indicate the presence or absence of some object, concept or ability. It may represent colour, or even beauty, yet it does not necessarily offer any predictive power about the properties of real word objects. It is just a signifier.

The concept of a variable in a computer program running on a digital computer and the different values it may take on are fundamentally based on patterns in the underlying digital machinery. The statement "variable X has the value 2" about a computing system is a different pattern in memory to the state representing "variable X has the value 3". The observer defines the meaning of a symbol or pattern in the machine. If it has any relation to the real world, this too is assigned by an observer.

If we wish to distinguish between a property "2" and a property "3", whether they are represented as values of a variable in a digital computer or in some other way, we need two different signifiers, one for each property.

Hence, the number of properties which may be distinguished in a system of representations is limited by the number of discrete states it may enter. The properties of a collection of representations are determined by the kinds of relationships which those representations may be interpreted as participating in. The degree to which representations may interact of course depends on the number of ways in which they may be organized with respect to one another, which again, is determined by the number of states each may have.

To take a simple example, the "position" of a cell on a CA grid is simply a state of the data structure which represents it. If two cells are "neighbouring" this is *not* saying anything about their location in physical space, but is a comparison of their state variables which are used to *represent* position.

To say that an entity acquires a new property in the virtual/representational world (i.e. that a new property emerges) is to comment only on there being new relationships between the state variables used to represent the entity. The more state variables the entity has to describe it, the greater the number of properties it may be distinguished as having. To gain extra state variables therefore goes hand in hand with being able to distinguish new states, and therefore new properties.[2]

Let us return now to the hierarchy illustrated in Figure 3. As the number of triangles in an aggregate increases, the aggregate does in fact gain new properties through this increase. Specifically, consider the observed property of a single, un-bonded triangle, "I may move as a single triangle". A new property of a bonded set of 4 triangles is, "I may move as a body of 4 triangles", and surprisingly enough, a set of 16 triangles has the property, "I may move as a body of 16 triangles".

Discussion

Trivially then, larger structures have properties which none of their components may be observed to have. There are many possible ways a large aggregate may be internally bonded. In order for a primitive element to remain attached to an aggregate it only requires a bond across one edge, even if it presents three edges as potential bonding sites. The property of moving as a rigid body of a certain size then emerges from the (bonding) relationships between the components. This may not seem very interesting, the properties of the structures are trivial, but they are properties nevertheless.

Hence, this is a self-assembling, infinitely-levelled hierarchy, which exhibits emergent properties at each level. Additionally, the primary elements do not require extra complexity in order to extend the number of levels in the hierarchy.

[2]This is not the *only* way new properties may arise. For example, new relationships may also arise between *existing* state variables as they take on new values within the range of expressible values they already possess. However, this does not alter the fact that the addition of new state variables is equivalent to the addition of new properties.

Conclusions

The example presented here is trivial — the hierarchy is not "interesting" (but it is a hierarchy), the new properties are not "interesting" either (but they are new properties). Yet, by the description in Rasmussen et al. (2001a) our system meets all the criteria to disprove the proposed ansatz. We expect that the authors of the ansatz did not have such a trivial model in mind when they proposed it, and that our model would not interest biologists in the slightest. However, this has not been our aim in this paper.

We propose that what is needed is a more formal definition of the kinds of behaviours we wish to see in our representations at each level of the hierarchy. What is also needed is a more considered discussion about the kinds of properties and relations between components which we would like to arise at each level in the hierarchy. Specifically, a definition of emergence that enables us to measure a property and determine whether or not it is emergent would be of benefit.

One way to do this might be to consider the systems under investigation in terms of their information content. Since representations on a computer are created and manipulated using bits, information theory is an objective way of comparing different biological theories, especially where they relate to hierarchies and the emergence of new properties.

Acknowledgments

The authors would like to thank John Crossley for his suggestions on some of the concepts discussed in the paper. Alan would also like to thank Mark Bedau for a discussion that initiated some of the ideas presented here.

References

Baas, N. 1994. Emergence, hierarchies and hyperstructures. In *Proc. of Artificial Life III*, 515–537. Addison-Wesley.

Bealer, G. 1999. Property. In Audi., ed., *The Cambridge Dictionary of Philosophy*. Cambridge Univ. Press, 2nd edition. 751–752.

Bedau, M. A.; McCaskill, J. S.; Packard, N. H.; Rasmussen, S.; Adami, C.; Green, D. G.; Ikegami, T.; Kaneko, K.; and Ray, T. S. 2000. Open problems in artificial life. *Artificial Life* 6:363–376.

Berlekamp, E. R.; Conway, J. H.; and Guy, R. K. 1982. *Winning Ways for Your Mathematical Plays*. Academic Press.

Bertalanffy, L. v. 1968. *General Systems Theory, Foundations, Development, Applications.* George Braziller Inc.

Boulton, D., and Wallace, C. 1970. An information measure for hierarchic classification. *The Computer Journal* 16(3):254–261.

Chaitin, G. 1970. To a mathematical definition of 'life'. *ACM, SICACT News* 4:12–18.

Chaitin, G. 1987. *Information Randomness & Incompleteness, Papers on Algorithmic Information Theory.* World Scientific.

Dennett, D. 1991. Real patterns. *Journal of Philosophy* 88:27–51.

Dittrich, P.; Ziegler, J.; and Banzhaf, W. 2001. Artificial chemistries — a review. *Artificial Life* 7(3):225–275.

Dorin, A. 2000. Creating a physically-based, virtual metabolism with solid cellular automata. In Bedau, M. et al., ed., *Proc. Artificial Life VII*, 13–20. MIT Press.

Gardner, M. 1970. Mathematical games: The fantastic combinations of John Conway's new solitaire game 'Life'. *Scientific American* 223(4):120–123.

Gross, D., and McMullin, B. 2001. Is it the right ansatz? *Artificial Life* 7(4):355–366.

Hansen, N. 1958. *Patterns of Discovery.* Cambridge Univ. Press.

Langton, C. 1986. Studying artificial life with cellular automata. *Physica D* 22:120–149.

Mirkin, B.; McMorris, F. R.; Roberts, F. S.; and Rzhetsky, A., eds. 1996. *Mathematical Hierarchies and Biology*, volume 37 of *DIMACS Series in Discrete Mathematics and Theoretical Computer Science.* Am. Math. Soc.

Nehaniv, C., and Rhodes, J. 2000. The evolution and understanding of hierarchical complexity in biology from an algebraic perspective. *Artificial Life* 6(1):45–68.

Polanyi, M. 1968. Life's irreducible structure. *Science* 160(21):1308–1312.

Poundstone, W. 1985. *The Recursive Universe : Cosmic Complexity and the Limits of Scientific Knowledge.* Contemporary Books.

Rasmussen, S.; Baas, N.; Mayer, B.; Nilsson, M.; and Olesen, W. 2001a. Ansatz for dynamical hierarchies. *Artificial Life* 7(4):367–374.

Rasmussen, S.; Baas, N.; Mayer, B.; Nilsson, M.; and Olesen, W. 2001b. Defence of the ansatz for dynamical hierarchies. *Artificial Life* 7(4):367–374.

Simon, H. 1962. The architecture of complexity. *Proc. Am. Phil. Soc.* 106:467–482.

Simon, H. 1994. *The Sciences of the Artificial.* MIT Press, 2nd edition.

Tufte, E. 1990. *Envisioning Information.* Graphics Press.

Wallace, C., and Boulton, D. 1968. An information measure for classification. *The Computer Journal* 11(2):185–194.

Author Index

Concept Index

Made in the USA
Monee, IL
08 November 2026

68136724R00247